The Handbook of Linguistics

Blackwell Handbooks in Linguistics

This outstanding multi-volume series covers all the major subdisciplines within linguistics today and, when complete, will offer a comprehensive survey of linguistics as a whole.

Already published:

The Handbook of Child Language
Edited by Paul Fletcher and Brian MacWhinney

The Handbook of Phonological Theory
Edited by John A. Goldsmith

The Handbook of Contemporary Semantic Theory
Edited by Shalom Lappin

The Handbook of Sociolinguistics
Edited by Florian Coulmas

The Handbook of Phonetic Sciences
Edited by William J. Hardcastle and John Laver

The Handbook of Morphology
Edited by Andrew Spencer and Arnold Zwicky

The Handbook of Japanese Linguistics
Edited by Natsuko Tsujimura

The Handbook of Linguistics
Edited by Mark Aronoff and Janie Rees-Miller

The Handbook of Contemporary Syntactic Theory
Edited by Mark Baltin and Chris Collins

The Handbook of Discourse Analysis
Edited by Deborah Schiffrin, Deborah Tannen, and Heidi E. Hamilton

The Handbook of Language Variation and Change
Edited by J. K. Chambers, Peter Trudgill, and Natalie Schilling-Estes

The Handbook of Historical Linguistics
Edited by Brian D. Joseph and Richard D. Janda

The Handbook of Language and Gender
Edited by Janet Holmes and Miriam Meyerhoff

The Handbook of Second Language Acquisition
Edited by Catherine Doughty and Michael H. Long

The Handbook of Bilingualism
Edited by Tej K. Bhatia and William C. Ritchie

The Handbook of Pragmatics
Edited by Laurence R. Horn and Gregory Ward

The Handbook of Applied Linguistics
Edited by Alan Davies and Catherine Elder

The Handbook of Linguistics

Edited by

*Mark Aronoff and
Janie Rees-Miller*

Blackwell
Publishing

© 2001, 2003 by Blackwell Publishing Ltd

BLACKWELL PUBLISHING
350 Main Street, Malden, MA 02148-5020, USA
9600 Garsington Road, Oxford OX4 2DQ, UK
550 Swanston Street, Carlton, Victoria 3053, Australia

First published 2001 by Blackwell Publishing Ltd
First published in paperback 2003

Library of Congress Cataloging-in-Publication Data

The handbook of linguistics / edited by Mark Aronoff and Janie Rees-Miller.
     p. cm. — (Blackwell handbooks in linguistics)
    Includes bibliographical references and index.
    ISBN 0-631-20497-0 (hbk. alk. paper) — ISBN 1-4051-0252-7 (pbk. alk. paper)
    1. Linguistics—Handbooks, manuals, etc. I. Aronoff, Mark. II. Rees-Miller, Janie.
III. Series.

    P121 .H324 2000
    410—dc21   99-087401

ISBN-13: 978-0-631-20497-8 (hbk. alk. paper) — ISBN-13: 978-1-4051-0252-0 (pbk. alk. paper)

A catalogue record for this title is available from the British Library.

For further information on
Blackwell Publishing, visit our website:
www.blackwellpublishing.com

Contents

Contributors

Frank Anshen
State University of New York, Stony Brook

Mark C. Baker
Rutgers University

Lyle Campbell
University of Canterbury

David Caplan
Neuropsychology Laboratory, Massachusetts General Hospital

Bob Carpenter
Speech Works

Andrew Carstairs-McCarthy
University of Canterbury

Jennifer Chu-Carroll
Bell Laboratories

Abigail Cohn
Cornell University

Bernard Comrie
Max Planck Institute for Evolutionary Anthropology

Vivian Cook
University of Essex

Florian Coulmas
Gerhard Mercator University

William Croft
University of Manchester

D. A. Cruse
University of Manchester

David Crystal
University College of North Wales, Bangor

Peter T. Daniels
Independent scholar

Nigel Fabb
University of Strathclyde

James Paul Gee
University of Wisconsin at Madison

Christoph Gutknecht
University of Hamburg

Brian D. Joseph
The Ohio State University

Ruth Kempson
King's College, London

Shalom Lappin
King's College, London

John Laver
University of Edinburgh

Diane Lillo-Martin
University of Connecticut and Haskins Laboratories

Brian MacWhinney
Carnegie Mellon University

Pamela Munro
University of California, Los Angeles

Janie Rees-Miller
Marietta College

Suzanne Romaine
Merton College, University of Oxford

Christer Samuelsson
Xerox Research Center, Europe

Wendy Sandler
University of Haifa

Roger W. Shuy
Georgetown University

Andrew Spencer
University of Essex

Richard Sproat
AT&T Research

Rebecca Treiman
Wayne State University

Robert D. Van Valin, Jr
State University of New York at Buffalo

Thomas Wasow
Stanford University

Agnes Weiyun He
State University of New York, Stony Brook

Preface

For over a century, linguists have been trying to explain linguistics to other people who they believe should be interested in their subject matter. After all, everyone speaks at least one language and most people have fairly strong views about their own language. The most distinguished scholars in every generation have written general books about language and linguistics targeted at educated laypeople and at scholars in adjacent disciplines, and some of these books have become classics, at least among linguists. The first great American linguist, William Dwight Whitney, published *The Life and Growth of Language: An Outline of Linguistic Science*, in 1875. In the dozen years between 1921 and 1933, the three best known English-speaking linguists in the world (Edward Sapir in 1921, Otto Jespersen in 1922, and Leonard Bloomfield in 1933) all wrote books under the title *Language*. All were very successful and continued to be reprinted for many years. In our own time, Noam Chomsky, certainly the most famous of theoretical linguists, has tried to make his ideas on language more accessible in such less technical books as *Language and Mind* (1968) and *Reflections on Language* (1975). And more recently, Steven Pinker's *The Language Instinct* (1995) stayed on the best-seller list for many months.

Despite these efforts, linguistics has not made many inroads into educated public discourse. Although linguists in the last hundred years have uncovered a great deal about human language and how it is acquired and used, the advances and discoveries are still mostly unknown outside a small group of practitioners. Many reasons have been given for this gap between academic and public thinking about language, the most commonly cited reasons being: that people have strong and sometimes erroneous views about language and have little interest in being disabused of their false beliefs; or that people are too close to language to be able to see that it has interesting and complex properties. Whatever the reason, the gap remains and is getting larger the more we learn about language.

The Handbook of Linguistics is a general introductory volume designed to address this gap in knowledge about language. Presupposing no prior knowledge of linguistics, it is intended for people who would like to know what linguistics and its subdisciplines are about. The book was designed to be as nontechnical as possible, while at the same time serving as a repository for what is known about language as we enter the twenty-first century.

If *The Handbook of Linguistics* is to be regarded as authoritative, this will be in large part because of the identity of the authors of the chapters. We have recruited globally recognized leading figures to write each of the chapters. While the culture of academia is such that academic authors find it tremendously difficult to write anything for anyone other than their colleagues, our central editorial goal has been to avoid this pitfall. Our emphasis on the reader's perspective sets *The Handbook of Linguistics* apart from other similar projects.

The place of the field of linguistics in academia has been debated since its inception. When we look at universities, we may find a linguistics department in either the social sciences or the humanities. When we look at the American government agencies that fund university research, we find that the National Endowment for the Humanities, the National Science Foundation, and the National Institutes of Health all routinely award grants for research in linguistics. So where does linguistics belong? The answer is not in where linguistics is placed administratively, but rather in how linguists think. Here the answer is quite clear: linguists by and large view themselves as scientists and they view their field as a science, the scientific study of language. This has been true since the nineteenth century, when Max Mueller could entitle a book published in 1869 *The Science of Language* and the first chapter of that book "The science of language one of the physical sciences."

The fact that linguistics is today defined as the scientific study of language carries with it the implicit claim that a science of language is possible, and this alone takes many by surprise. For surely, they say, language, like all human activity, is beyond the scope of true science. Linguists believe that their field is a science because they share the goals of scientific inquiry, which is objective (or more properly intersubjectively accessible) understanding. Once we accept that general view of science as a kind of inquiry, then it should be possible to have a science of anything, so long as it is possible to achieve intersubjectively accessible understanding of that thing. There are, of course, those who deny the possibility of such scientific understanding of anything, but we will not broach that topic here.

We now know that the possibility of scientific understanding depends largely on the complexity and regularity of the object of study. Physics has been so successful because the physical world is, relatively speaking, highly regular and not terribly complex. Human sciences, by contrast, have been much less successful and much slower to produce results, largely because human behavior is so complex and not nearly so regular as is the physical or even the biological world. Language, though, contrasts with other aspects of human behavior precisely in its regularity, what has been called its rule-governed nature. It is precisely this property of language and language-related behavior that has allowed for fairly great progress in our understanding of this delimited area of human behavior. Furthermore, the fact that language is the defining property of humans, that it is shared across all human communities and is manifested in no other species, means that by learning about language we will inevitably also learn about human nature.

Each chapter in this book is designed to describe to the general reader the state of our knowledge at the beginning of the twenty-first century of one aspect of human language. The authors of each chapter have devoted most of their adult lives to the study of this one aspect of language. Together, we believe, these chapters provide a broad yet detailed picture of what is known about language as we move into the new millennium. The chapters are each meant to be free-standing. A reader who is interested in how children acquire language, for example, should be able to turn to chapter 19 and read it profitably without having to turn first to other chapters for assistance. But the physical nature of a book entails that there be an order of presentation. We begin with general overview chapters that consider the origins of language as species-specific behavior and describe the raw material with which linguists work (languages of the world and writing systems), frame the discipline within its historical context, and look at how linguists acquire new data from previously undescribed languages (field linguistics). The book then turns to the traditional subdisciplines of linguistics. Here we have followed most linguistics books in starting from the bottom, grounding language first in the physical world of sound (phonetics) and moving up through the organization of sound in language (phonology), to the combination of sounds into words (morphology), and the combination of words into sentences (syntax). Meaning (semantics) usually comes next, on the grounds that it operates on words and sentences. These areas are traditionally said to form the core of linguistics, because they deal with the most formally structured aspects of language. Within the last few decades, however, linguists have come to realize that we cannot understand the most formally structured aspects of language without also understanding the way language is used to convey information (pragmatics) in conversation (discourse) and in literature, and the way language interacts with other aspects of society (sociolinguistics).

Fifty years ago, many of our chapters would have been absent from a book of this sort for the simple but dramatic reason that these fields of inquiry did not exist: language acquisition, multilingualism, sign language, neurolinguistics, computational linguistics, and all of the areas of applied linguistics to which we have devoted separate chapters (the one area of applied linguistics that did exist fifty years ago was language teaching).

The chapters are of a uniform length, approximately 10,000 words each, or about 25 printed pages. This length is substantial enough for a major essay, while being short enough so as not to overwhelm the reader. Applied linguistics is divided into several distinct areas that would be of interest to students and others who want to know what practical applications linguistics has. Because each of the applied linguistics chapters covers a more specialized area, these chapters are somewhat shorter than the rest (approximately 4,000 words each, or about 10 printed pages).

We have tried not to emphasize ideology, but rather to divide things up by empirical criteria having to do with the sorts of phenomena that a given field of inquiry covers. We have thought long and hard about whether some of the major areas, especially syntax and phonology, should be broken down further, with a chapter each on distinct theoretical approaches. Our final decision was not to subdivide by theoretical approaches, based on a belief that the reader's perspective is paramount in books like this: readers of a companion do not want to know what the latest controversy is about or who disagrees with whom or who said what when. Rather, they want to have a reasonable idea of what linguistics or some subarea of linguistics can tell them. The authors have been able to do so without going into the latest controversies, though these controversies may occupy the linguists' everyday lives. The one area to which we have devoted more than one chapter is syntax, but this reflects the dominance of syntactic research in linguistics over the last half century.

We do not see this handbook as an introductory textbook, which would, for example, have questions or exercises at the end of each chapter. There are already enough introductory linguistics texts. We see it rather as an authoritative volume on what linguists know about language at the start of the twenty-first century. Each chapter covers the central questions and goals of a particular subdiscipline, what is generally accepted as known in that area, and how it relates to other areas.

When we embarked on this editorial enterprise, we expected to enjoy the interaction with many of our most distinguished colleagues that the preparation of this book would entail, which is so much easier now in the age of electronic correspondence. What we did not realize was how much we would learn from these colleagues about language and linguistics, simply from reading their work and discussing it with them. We thank all of the authors for this wonderful opportunity and we hope that the readers, too, will share in the same great pleasure.

ACKNOWLEDGMENT

The illustrations used in figures 22.2, 22.3, and 22.7 are reprinted with permission from *A Basic Course in American Sign Language, Second Edition*, 1994, T.J. Publishers, Inc., Silver Spring, MD 20910, USA.

1 Origins of Language

ANDREW CARSTAIRS-MCCARTHY

1 Introduction

Among the inhabitants of some African forests about eight million years ago were ape-like creatures including the common ancestors of chimpanzees and humans. Visualizing what these creatures were probably like is easy enough; one conjures up an image of something resembling a modern gorilla, living substantially in trees and walking on all four limbs when on the ground, and with a vocal communication system limited to perhaps twenty or thirty calls, like a chimpanzee's. But what about our ancestors' appearance and behavior two million years ago? By that stage they were a separate species from the ancestors of chimpanzees, but were not yet *homo sapiens*. How did these creatures live, and in particular what sort of language did they have? Visualizing these more recent creatures is harder. One feels that they must have been more like us, and in particular that their vocal communication system must have been more sophisticated than that of their ancestors six million years earlier. But how much more sophisticated? Which characteristics of modern human language did this communication system now possess, and which did it still lack?

There is something eerie and yet fascinating about these intermediate ancestors. This fascination underlies innumerable science fiction stories as well as the perennial interest in rumors that such creatures may still exist, in some remote Himalayan valley perhaps. To many nonlinguists, therefore, it seems self-evident that research on the linguistic abilities of such intermediate ancestors (that is, research on the origins and evolution of human language) should be a high priority in linguistics. Yet it is not. As a research topic, language evolution is only now beginning to regain respectability, after more than a century of neglect. In the remainder of this section I will say something about the reasons for this neglect before turning in sections 2–5 to the evidence recently brought to bear by anthropologists, geneticists, primatologists and neurobiologists, many of whom have for decades been more adventurous than linguists in this area. Then in section 6, I will discuss the kinds of contribution which some linguists also are now beginning to offer.

Many religions provide an account of the origin of language. According to the Judeo-Christian tradition, God gave to Adam in the Garden of Eden dominion over all the animals, and Adam's first exercise of this dominion consisted in naming them. The fact that there are now many languages rather than just one is explained in the story of the Tower of Babel: linguistic diversity is a punishment for human arrogance. So long as that sort of account was generally accepted, the origin of language was not a puzzle. But when secular explanations for natural phenomena began to be sought to supplement or replace religious ones, it was inevitable that a secular explanation was sought for the origin of language too.

The fact that the origin of language must predate recorded history did not inhibit eighteenth-century thinkers such as Rousseau, Condillac, and Herder, who were confident that simply by applying one's mind to the situation in which languageless humans would find themselves one could arrive at worthwhile conclusions about how language must have arisen. Unfortunately there was no consensus among these conclusions, and in the nineteenth century they came to seem increasingly feeble and speculative by contrast with the far-reaching yet convincing results attainable in historical and comparative linguistics (see chapter 5). At its foundation in 1866, therefore, the Linguistic Society of Paris chose to emphasize its seriousness as a scholarly body by including in its statutes a ban on the presentation of any papers concerning the origin of language. Most linguists still support this ban, in the sense that they believe that any inquiry into the origin of language must inevitably be so speculative as to be worthless.

Since the 1960s, the theory of grammar has come to be dominated by the ideas of Noam Chomsky, for whom the central question of linguistics is the nature of the innate biological endowment which enables humans to acquire a language so rapidly and efficiently in the first year of life (see chapter 19). From this viewpoint, it seems natural to regard the origin of language as a matter of evolutionary biology: how did this innate linguistic endowment evolve in humans, and what are its counterparts (if any) in other primates? But Chomsky has explicitly discouraged interest in language evolution, and has even suggested that language is so different from most other animal characteristics that it may be a product of physical or chemical processes rather than biological ones (1988: 167, 1991: 50). The paradoxical result is that, while Chomskyan linguists endeavor to explain characteristics of individual languages by reference to an innate linguistic endowment (or Universal Grammar), they are generally reluctant to pursue their inquiry one stage further, to the issue of how and why this innate endowment has acquired the particular characteristics that it has. To be sure, there are exceptions (e.g. Newmeyer 1991, Pinker and Bloom 1990, Pinker 1994). Nevertheless, Chomsky's influence means that linguists' reluctance to tackle this area is eroding only slowly.

In view of what has been said, it is not surprising that there is a shortage of introductory surveys of this topic from a linguistic point of view; but Aitchison (1996) can be recommended, as well as part II of W. Foley (1997). Hurford et al. (1998) is an up-to-date collection of contributions from a variety of disciplines.

2   Evidence from Anthropology and Archeology

Anthropology is concerned not only with human culture but also with humans as organisms in a biological sense, including their evolutionary development. (On human evolution in general, see e.g. R. Foley (1995) and Mithen (1996).) Language is both a cultural phenomenon and also the most salient distinguishing characteristic of modern *homo sapiens* as a species. The question of how and why humans acquired language therefore interests both cultural and biological anthropologists. So what light can anthropology shed on these questions?

The earliest direct evidence of language in the form of writing is no more than about 5,000 years old (see chapter 3). It is therefore much too recent to shed any light on the origin of spoken language, and we must resort to indirect evidence. Unfortunately the available evidence is doubly indirect. The vocal apparatus (tongue, lips, and larynx) of early humans would tell us much if we could examine it directly; but, being soft tissue, it does not survive, and for information about it we have to rely on what we can glean from bones, particularly skulls. Alongside such evidence we have tools and other artefacts, as well as traces of human habitation such as discarded animal bones; but, again, what is available to us is skewed by the fact that stone survives better than bone and much better than materials such as wood or hide. In view of this, the only relatively firm dates which anthropology can provide are two terminuses, one after which we can be sure that language in its fully modern form did exist and one before which we can be sure that it did not. For the long period in between, the anthropological evidence is tantalizing but frustratingly equivocal; there are no uncontroversial counterparts in the fossil record for specific stages in linguistic evolution.

We can be reasonably confident that modern-style spoken language evolved only once. This is not logically necessary. It is conceivable that something with the communicative and cognitive functions of language, and using speech as its medium, could have evolved independently more than once, just as the eye has evolved independently more than once in the animal kingdom. However, if that had happened we would expect to find evidence of it today, just as the eyes of octopuses, mammals, and insects reveal by their structure that they have no common ancestor. Yet no such evidence exists. For all their diversity, all existing languages display certain fundamental common properties of grammar, meaning, and sound, which is why Chomsky feels justified in claiming that, to a visitor from another planet, it might seem that there really is only one human language. Moreover, a child who is removed from her parents' speech community at a young age can acquire natively any language whatever, irrespective of what her parents speak; no child is born with a biological bias in favor of one language or type of language. This means that language of a fully modern kind must have evolved before any contemporary human group became geographically separated from the rest of the human race (separated, that is, until the invention of modern means of transport). The first such clearcut separation seems to have occurred with the earliest settlement of Australia by *homo sapiens*. Archeological evidence suggests that that event took place at least 40,000 years and perhaps as long as 60,000 or more years ago. We can therefore take this as a firm *terminus ante quem* for the evolution of a form of language which is fully modern in a biological sense.

As for a *terminus post quem*, it is clear that spoken language with more or less modern articulatory and acoustic characteristics presupposes something like a modern vocal tract. But how are we to interpret "more or less" and "something like"? One thing is clear: the acoustic properties of many human speech sounds, particularly vowels, depend on the characteristically human L-shaped vocal tract, with an oral cavity at right angles to the pharynx (see chapter 7) and with the larynx relatively low in the neck. This shape is characteristically human because in nearly all other mammals, and even in human babies during the first few months of life, the larynx is high enough for the epiglottis to engage with the soft palate so as to form a self-contained airway from the nose to the lungs, smoothly curved rather than L-shaped, and quite separate from the tube which leads from the mouth to the stomach. Having these two distinct tubes enables nearly all other mammals, as well as newborn human babies, to breathe while swallowing. The adult human characteristic of a pharynx through which both air and food must pass, on the other hand, is a vital contributor to the acoustic characteristics structure of speech sounds. So when did this L-shaped vocal tract develop?

Lieberman (1984, see Lieberman and Crelin 1971) has claimed that even in Neanderthals, who did not become extinct until about 35,000 years ago, the larynx was positioned so high in the neck as to prevent the production of the full modern range of vowel sounds. He suggests that this linguistic disadvantage may have been a factor in the Neanderthals' demise. But his argument rests on an interpretation of fossil cranial anatomy which has generally been rejected by anthropologists (Trinkaus and Shipman 1993, Aiello and Dean 1990). An alternative view is that the L-shaped vocal tract is a byproduct of bipedalism, which favored a reorientation of the head in relation to the spine and hence a shortening of the base of the skull, so that the larynx had to be squeezed downward into the neck (DuBrul 1958, Aiello 1996b). The question then arises: when did our ancestors become bipedal? The general consensus among anthropologists is: very early. Evidence includes fossil footprints at Laetoli in Tanzania, about 3.5 million years ago, and the skeleton of *australopithecus afarensis* nicknamed "Lucy," dating from over 3 million years ago. So, if bipedalism was the main factor contributing to the lowering of the larynx, the L-shaped vocal tract must have emerged relatively early too.

This conflicts with an opinion widespread among language origin researchers, namely that the lowering of the larynx (with its concomitant increased risk of choking) was a consequence of the evolution of more sophisticated language, not a precursor of it (a "preadaptation" for it, in Darwinian terminology). But this predominant opinion, it may be argued, is to some extent a hangover from the "brain-first" view of human evolution in general – the view that the superior intelligence of humans evolved in advance of substantial anatomical changes, broadly speaking. This view was popular when Piltdown Man, with its human-like skull and ape-like jaw, was still thought to be genuine, but is now generally rejected in the face of evidence for the small size of australopithecine and early human skulls.

Mention of skulls raises the possibility of drawing conclusions about language from hominid brains. (I use the term *hominid* to mean "(belonging to) a creature of the genus *australopithecus* or the genus *homo*.") Brain size tells us nothing specific (though we will revert to it in section 6). But what of brain structure? If it could be shown that an area of the modern human brain uniquely associated with language was present in the brains of hominids at a particular date, it would seem reasonable to conclude that those hominids possessed language. But this line of reasoning encounters three problems. First, since brains themselves do not fossilize, determining their structure depends on the interpretation of ridges and grooves on the inside of skulls, or rather of their counterparts on "endocasts" made from skulls. The region generally regarded as most closely associated with grammar and with speech articulation in modern humans is Broca's area; but identifying an area corresponding to Broca's area in hominid fossils has turned out to be highly controversial (Falk 1992). Second, no area of the human brain, even Broca's area, seems to be associated with language and nothing else. Third, Broca's area seems to have little or nothing to do with vocalization in monkeys, so even if it can be established that a counterpart of Broca's area exists in a certain hominid, its function in that hominid may not be linguistic. The implications of "brain-language coevolution," as Deacon (1997) calls it, are still frustratingly indeterminate.

Some scholars have connected language with the evolution of "handedness," which is much more strongly developed in humans than in other animals (Bradshaw and Rogers 1992, Corballis 1991). In most people the right hand is the dominant hand, controlled from the left side of the brain where the language areas are usually located. It is tempting to see this shared location as more than mere coincidence. If so, linguistic conclusions might perhaps be drawn from ingenious tests that have been carried out on fossil stone tools, to determine whether the people who made them were or were not predominantly right-handed. On the other hand, the correlation between language and handedness is far from exact: left-handedness neither entails nor is entailed by right-brain dominance for language. Also, even if evidence of a strong preponderance of right-handers in some group of hominids is taken as firm evidence of linguistic capacity, it furnishes no details about the nature of that linguistic capacity.

Let us turn from biology to culture. Common sense would suggest that a relatively sudden jump in the sophistication of human linguistic behavior, if it occurred, should leave immediate traces in the archeological record in the shape of a sudden jump in the sophistication of preserved artefacts (tools, ornaments, and artwork). So does any such jump in sophistication occur, and when? There is indeed a big increase in the variety and quality of tools found in Europe and Africa around 40,000 years ago, followed by the famous cave paintings of Lascaux and elsewhere from about 30,000 years ago. But this is inconveniently late as a date for the emergence of fully modern language, in that it is contemporary with or even more recent than the latest plausible date for the settlement of Australia. That has not discouraged some scholars from using this kind of evidence to argue that language evolved "late"; but on examination it generally turns out that what these scholars mean by "language" is not what linguists mean by it, but rather the self-conscious use of symbols (Noble and Davidson 1996). Moreover, there is scattered but intriguing evidence of "cultural" behavior thousands of years earlier, such as burial pits, incised bones and the use of red ochre pigment for body decoration. The implications of this for language are unclear, but it may be significant that some of the dates involved are not far removed from a milestone indicated by genetic evidence, to which we now turn.

3   Genetic Evidence

Since the late 1970s, molecular genetics has opened up entirely new techniques for assessing the relationship of humans to each other and to other primates. (It is genetic evidence which tells us that we are separated by only about five million years from the ancestor which we share with the chimpanzees.) Since the 1950s it has been known that the information which differentiates an individual genetically from all other individuals (except a possible identical twin) is carried by DNA (deoxyribonucleic acid) in chromosomes located in every cell in the body. Geneticists can now compare individuals and groups in terms of how much of their DNA is shared. Moreover, they can do this not only in respect of the DNA in the cell's nucleus, which is inherited from both parents, but also in respect of the DNA in the cell's mitochondria – some of the so-called "organelles" which the cell contains in addition to its nucleus. What is important about mitochondrial DNA is that it is inherited from the mother alone. It follows that the only reason that there can be for any difference between two people's mitochondrial DNA is inaccurate inheritance due to mutation; for, without this inaccuracy, both of them would have exactly the same mitochondrial DNA as their most recent shared ancestor in the female line. So, assuming that mutation in DNA occurs at a constant rate, the

extent of difference between two people's DNA is an indication of the number of generations which separate them from the most recent woman from
whom both are descended through her daughters, her daughters' daughters,
and so on.

Cann et al. (1987) used this technique to try to locate in time and space the
most recent woman from whom all living humans are descended in the female
line. With the help of elaborate statistical techniques, they argued that this
woman lived roughly 200,000 years ago in Africa, hence the nickname "African
Eve." Both the African location and the date corresponded quite closely to
the "out-of-Africa" scenario for early *homo sapiens* proposed on independent
grounds by some archeologists, so the two theories provided mutual support. The nickname "Eve" is convenient but unfortunate, because it suggests
that, apart from Eve's male partner or partners, none of her contemporaries
has any descendants alive today. That is a fallacy; all one can say is that anyone alive today who is descended from a female contemporary of Eve must
be linked to that woman through at least one male ancestor. However, the
argument of Cann and her colleagues does suggest that there was a population bottleneck relatively recently in human prehistory, such that most of the
humans alive around 200,000 years ago, scattered over large areas of Africa,
Europe, and Asia, have indeed left no surviving descendants. Why should
this be?

Many scholars have been tempted to suggest that what was special about
Eve's community – the characteristic which enabled their descendants to
outperform other humans and which discouraged interbreeding with them –
must have been superior linguistic abilities, presumably newly acquired. This
is only a guess, however. Cann herself has more recently mentioned one of
many alternative possibilities: infectious disease (Cann et al. 1994). But the
possible link with language evolution has been popularized by Cavalli-Sforza
and Cavalli-Sforza (1995) and by Ruhlen (1994), whose supposed reconstructions of Proto-World vocabulary might, if genuine, be roughly contemporary
with Eve. An equivocation on "mother tongue" underlies this view, however.
Even supposing it were possible to reconstruct the most recent language from
which all contemporary languages are descended, it would be a remarkable
coincidence if that ancestral language (the "mother tongue" in a historical
linguistic sense) were also the first linguistic variety with fully modern characteristics (the "mother tongue" in a biological sense). So, once again, we are
faced with evidence which, though tantalizing, does not point to any firm
conclusion.

4 Primatological Evidence

No living primate apart from man is equipped to speak. However, three
areas of current research on primates may shed light on language evolution.

These involve primate vocal call systems, primate cognitive abilities (particularly their knowledge of social relationships), and the results of experiments involving teaching sign language and artificial signaling systems to apes.

4.1   Vocal call systems

Until a few decades ago, it was generally thought that the calls uttered by all animals, including monkeys and apes, were exclusively reflections of physical or emotional states such as pain, fear, hunger, or lust. In this respect, the portion of the human vocal repertoire which primate call systems seemed to resemble most closely was the portion consisting of involuntary sounds such as cries of pain, laughter, or sobbing. No linguists have been reluctant to contemplate an evolutionary link between these cries and primate vocalizations. But primate "vocabularies" were thought to lack a central element of human vocabularies: referential calls identifiable with specific objects or classes of objects in the external world. Given that assumption, it was easy to dismiss animal calls systems as irrelevant to human language. However, students of animal behavior were becoming increasingly uncomfortable with this assumption, and Cheney and Seyfarth (1990) developed a particularly elegant and convincing way of testing it systematically. (On animal communication generally, see Hauser 1996; on the calls of chimpanzees in the wild, see Goodall 1986.)

In the 1970s and 1980s, Cheney and Seyfarth spent years investigating the behavior of vervet monkeys in their native habitat, the Amboseli National Park of Kenya. These small monkeys utter distinct warning calls for different types of predator, notably leopards, snakes, and eagles, for which different types of evasive action are appropriate: they run up trees to escape leopards, peer at the ground around them to avoid snakes, and hide in bushes to evade eagles. This kind of apparent referentiality had been noticed before, not just among vervets; but such awareness had not shaken the general conviction among both zoologists and linguists that animal cries were basically emotional or affective in content rather than referential. In crude terms, a vervet's eagle call would be interpreted as linked not to something in the outside world ("There's an eagle!") but rather to its internal state ("I am experiencing eagle-fear!" or "I feel an urge to hide in bushes!"). To be sure, if one vervet uttered the eagle call, others might take evasive action too; but this could only be because these others saw the eagle for themselves and hence experienced the same emotion (it was thought).

Cheney and Seyfarth showed this interpretation to be incorrect by a crucial experiment. They made recordings of predator warning calls and played them back from hidden loudspeakers in the absence of the relevant predators. If the traditional interpretation of the warning calls was correct, the vervets would be predicted to take no evasive action in response to these bogus calls. They might look around for the relevant predator but, failing to see one, they would not experience the relevant fear reaction and so would do nothing. However, what Cheney and Seyfarth found was that the vervets reacted to the bogus calls just as if they were genuine, by taking the appropriate evasive action. The call itself was the trigger to act, not the emotion or physical state engendered by the sight of a predator. Warning calls therefore really do contain referential information about the environment, on which vervets can act appropriately. To this admittedly limited extent, therefore, they resemble words of a human language.

A second respect in which human language differs from animal cries, it used to be thought, is that only human language can be unreliable. If an animal cry is an automatic response to an emotional or physical stimulus, its reliability is in some sense guaranteed. Humans, on the other hand, can tell lies or make mistakes. But Cheney and Seyfarth showed that in this respect too the gap between vervet monkeys' calls and human language is less than was once thought. Vervets' use of their warning calls is not entirely innately determined; for example, young vervets will often utter the eagle call even when they have seen something in the sky which is not an eagle or not even a bird at all, such as a falling leaf. And adult vervets react differently to young vervets' calls too. Instead of taking immediate evasive action, as they would if they had heard an adult call, they first check for themselves whether the relevant predator is present and, if not, ignore the call. It seems to be through observing when its calls are acted upon and when they are ignored that a young vervet refines its innate repertoire of vocal reactions into accurate warnings deployed according to the conventions of the adult community.

These observations show that, for vervets, calls have a content which is independent of their own physical or emotional state. Cheney and Seyfarth were also able to show that, in judging the reliability of a call that it hears, a vervet goes beyond merely identifying the caller. It is clear that vervets can distinguish individual "voices," because when a young vervet utters a cry of distress the adults in earshot will look towards that individual's mother, as if expecting her to respond. Cheney and Seyfarth compared reactions to recordings of different voices uttering a variety of calls. In the absence of a genuine eagle danger, hearers will become habituated to and hence ignore recorded eagle alarms in the voice of vervet A, but will still react to alarms in the voice of vervet B. But, even when so habituated to vervet A, they will not ignore a recording of vervet A uttering a call of a different kind (say one of the repertoire of calls relating to individual or group interactions). Vervets can evidently distinguish, in respect of another vervet, those topics on which it is a reliable witness from those on which it is unreliable.

To be sure, the vervet call system has no grammatical organization remotely resembling that of human language, and the same is true of all other primates' call systems. Nevertheless, the observations of Cheney, Seyfarth, and others tend to show that the differences between primate call systems and human language are not so great as was once thought, and hence weaken the case for denying any evolutionary connection between them.

4.2   *Cognitive abilities*

Long-term observations of primate groups in the wild, such as those of Goodall and Cheney and Seyfarth mentioned in section 4.1, show that primates know many more details about themselves, their conspecifics and their environment than was previously suspected. In particular, they can distinguish kin from nonkin, and by remembering who has done what to whom they can distinguish allies from enemies. This is relevant to language inasmuch as a fundamental characteristic of language is the ability to represent grammatically the roles of participants in a situation (Bickerton 1990, 1995). For example, the sentence *John gave Mary a banana* represents a situation in which John is the agent, Mary is the goal and the banana is the patient or "theme" in relation to an act of giving. In the terminology of semantics, such a set of relationships between participants in a situation is called a "thematic structure" or "argument structure" (see chapter 12). Higher primates do not produce sentences, but they certainly have mental representations of thematic structures of the kind which underlie sentences. To that extent they have evolved to a stage of cognitive readiness for language.

One of the Rubicons which have been claimed to separate humans from other animals is that, whereas other animals may possess "procedural" knowledge ("knowledge-how"), only humans have access to "propositional" knowledge ("knowledge-that"). (In similar vein, Donald (1991) distinguishes between "episodic," "mimetic," and "mythic" culture, among which only "episodic" culture is available to nonhumans.) If this is correct, it is tempting to see propositional knowledge as a prerequisite for language. In assessing whether it is correct, however, one immediately encounters a risk of circularity. If "propositional knowledge" means simply "knowledge of a kind which can only be represented in sentence form," then it is not surprising that propositional knowledge should be restricted to sentence-users, that is, to humans; but then to say that animals lack it is to say no more than that animals lack language. On the other hand, if "propositional knowledge" is defined so as to make it logically independent of language, such as in terms of thematic structure, it is by no means so clear that this Rubicon exists.

At least two further considerations support the idea that primates have access to "knowledge-that." One is the extent to which, in the admittedly artificial conditions of the laboratory, chimpanzees can acquire and display awareness of abstract concepts such as "same" and "different" and apply them by reference to a range of criteria such as color and size (Premack 1976). The other is the fact that primates can apparently indulge in deception, or display what has been called "Machiavellian intelligence" (Byrne and Whiten 1988, Sommer 1992). In interpreting "Machiavellian" behavior it is of course necessary to guard against overenthusiastic ascription of human personality traits to animals. Nevertheless, this behavior suggests that primates are capable of conceiving of situations which do not exist, that is to think in an abstract "propositional" fashion, and hence reinforces the worthwhileness of looking for precursors of language in other species.

Social relationships among primates are both more complex and less stereotyped than among other mammals, and it has been suggested that social factors may outweigh communicative ones in fostering language evolution. Dunbar (1996) and others have drawn attention to the relationship between group size, brain size, and social grooming in various primate species. Grooming is important in fostering group cohesion; on the other hand, time devoted to grooming increases exponentially as group sizes increase, thereby reducing the time available for other essential tasks such as food gathering. Dunbar suggests that language provided a way out of this dilemma: it is a form of vocal grooming, with the advantage that by means of language one can groom many other individuals at once. Traces of this original function can be observed in the extent to which, even today, language is used for gossip and for cementing social relationships rather than for the more abstract representational and information-conveying purposes which tend to interest grammatical theorists and philosophers.

4.3   Sign language experiments

Apes do not have vocal tracts fitted for speech, but their arms and hands are physically quite capable of forming the signs of deaf languages such as American Sign Language (ASL). In the 1970s great excitement was generated by experiments which purported to show that chimpanzees could learn ASL, so that language could no longer be regarded as a uniquely human attribute (Terrace 1979, Gardner et al. 1989). Linguists in general hotly denied that the sign sequences produced by chimpanzees such as Washoe and Nim could be regarded as genuine syntactic combinations or complex words, pointing to the fact that the chimpanzees' sign sequences never reached the variety and complexity of those of fluent human ASL signers. The chimpanzees' supporters, on the other hand, argued that the kinds of sign combination which chimpanzees produced were quite similar to the word combinations which human babies produce at the "two-word" or "telegraphic" stage of language acquisition, so that, if what the chimpanzees did was not a manifestation of language, one could not call babies' "telegraphic" speech a manifestation of language either. (We will return to this implication in section 6.) In the present context the issue is not whether the chimpanzees' and other apes' signing behavior can properly be called linguistic (which is in any case largely a sterile point of terminology), but whether this behavior sheds any light on language evolution.

One effect of the ape language experiments was to give new life to the old idea that language in humans may have originated in gesture, and only later been transferred to the vocal channel (Armstrong et al. 1995). Just as apes can sign without a human vocal tract, so could our australopithecine ancestors have communicated by sign before their vocal tracts had become capable of modern-style speech, perhaps. One of the attractions of this proposal has always been that it seems to provide a solution to the problem of how humans originally learned to handle the arbitrary relationship between words and meanings. The apparent solution lies in the fact that many signs in ASL and other sign languages are motivated ("iconic") rather than arbitrary ("symbolic"); that is, they resemble or recall in some way their referents in the outside world, while many other signs were once more clearly motivated than they are now. The proportion of sign language vocabularies which is iconic is far greater than the proportion of iconic (onomatopeic) words in spoken language vocabularies. These motivated manual signs could have constituted a scaffolding, so to speak, to assist the more difficult task of mastering arbitrary signs, whether manual or vocal. But the attraction of this reasoning disappears as soon as one recalls that vervet monkeys' call vocabulary is just as symbolic as most words of human language. Vervets' eagle, leopard, and snake calls do not in any way resemble or sound like eagles, leopards, or snakes. So, even if one regards the use of symbolic signs as a communicative Rubicon, it is a Rubicon which has been crossed by any nonhuman species with a clearly referential call vocabulary, and was almost certainly crossed by our primate ancestors long before the appearance of hominids.

More relevant to language evolution, perhaps, is what can be gleaned from observation of the bonobo (or pygmy chimpanzee) Kanzi (Savage-Rumbaugh et al. 1993, Savage-Rumbaugh and Lewin 1994). Savage-Rumbaugh set out to train Kanzi's mother in both sign language and the use of a keyboard of arbitrary wordsigns or "lexigrams," while the infant Kanzi was left to play and watch what was going on unmolested. The mother turned out to be an unpromising pupil; Kanzi, on the other hand, developed spontaneously a form of communication involving both manual signs and lexigrams, and also showed a surprising ability to understand spoken English – a somewhat more accurate understanding, in fact, than the two-year-old daughter of one of Savage-Rumbaugh's colleagues, at least within a deliberately limited range of syntactic constructions.

Savage-Rumbaugh argues that Kanzi shows evidence of rule-governed use of signs and lexigrams, and one may if one wishes call this set of rules a syntax. But it seems overhasty to conclude, as Savage-Rumbaugh does, that the difference between Kanzi's syntax and that of human languages is only in degree of complexity, not in kind. Of the two rules which Kanzi has invented rather than merely copied from human sign use, one ("lexigram precedes gesture") clearly has no human counterpart, while the other ("action precedes action, sign order corresponding to order of performance," as in *chase hide* or *tickle bite*) is interpretable as purely semantic or pragmatic rather than syntactic. Moreover, Kanzi's "utterances" are nearly all too short to permit clearcut identification of human-language-like phrases or clauses. A more conservative conclusion would be that Kanzi may indeed have invented a kind of rudimentary syntax, but it cannot be straightforwardly equated with the kind of syntax that human languages have. A task for the language evolution researcher, then, is to account for the differences between what the bonobo does and what humans do.

5 Neurobiological Evidence

To investigate systematically the relationship between language and the brain, one would need to carry out surgical experiments of an ethically unthinkable kind. Our knowledge has therefore to be gleaned in a relatively haphazard fashion, from the linguistic behavior of people suffering from brain damage due to accident or cerebral hemorrhage. This is less than ideal, because the extent of the damage is of course not subject to any experimental control and is determinable only indirectly, through methods such as magnetic resonance imaging (MRI), which is like an X-ray but much more detailed, and positron emission tomography (PET), which measures minute changes in bloodflow. With the patient's consent, it is also possible to test the linguistic effect of stimulating areas of brain tissue directly in the course of surgery for purposes such as the control of epilepsy (Calvin and Ojemann 1994). Not surprisingly, the literature on such research, though extensive, is somewhat confusing. However, it does suggest answers (though by no means conclusive ones) to two broad questions relevant to language evolution. The first question concerns the relative priority of the vocal and gestural channels for speech. The second concerns the extent to which syntax is an outgrowth of a general increase in the sophistication of hominids' mental representation of the world, including social relationships, and the extent to which it is an outgrowth of some more specialized development, such as better toolmaking, more accurate stone-throwing, or more fluent vocalization.

Before we consider these broad questions, it is worth emphasizing that the relationship between particular functions and particular brain locations is not clearcut and unchanging, either in the individual or in the species. Exercising one finger can increase the area of brain cortex devoted to controlling it, and in many blind people the cortex areas for finger control are larger than average. This functional plasticity is particularly evident in early infancy, so that a young child who suffers massive damage to the left brain hemisphere (where the control of language is generally located) may nevertheless acquire a considerable linguistic capacity, controlled from the right hemisphere. Indeed, without such plasticity and scope for functional overlapping it is hard to see how language could have evolved at all, because it must have involved a new role for parts of the brain which originally served other functions.

The brain region which seems most clearly implicated in regulating grammar is Broca's area, in the frontal lobe of the left hemisphere. In view of the scope for overlap in functions, it seems reasonable to predict that, if language was originally gestural, Broca's area would be relatively close to that part of the brain which controls movement of the hands; but it is not. Control of bodily movements resides on the so-called motor strip, just in front of the central sulcus or Rolandic fissure which separates the frontal lobe from the parietal lobe. Broca's area is indeed close to the motor strip; but it is closest to that part of the strip which controls not the hands but, rather, the tongue, jaw, and lips. Moreover, a similarly located Broca's area seems to be just as relevant to the grammar of sign language, even among people deaf from birth, as it is to the grammar of spoken language (Poizner et al. 1987).

Conceivably, the region for grammatical control could have migrated, so to speak, if the predominant channel for language switched from gesture to speech. However, since the present location of Broca's area does not prevent it from playing a role in sign language, a hypothetical language area located close to the manual section of the motor strip could presumably have retained its original control over grammar even while the vocal apparatus took over from the hands. So it seems more likely that the linguistic function exercised by Broca's area has not migrated, and its present brain location reflects the fact that human language has always been predominantly vocal.

Damage to Broca's area affects grammar and also the articulation of speech much more than vocabulary. Broca's aphasics can generally produce appropriate nouns, adjectives, and verbs for what they are trying to say; it is the task of stringing them together in well-formed sentences with appropriate grammatical words (determiners, auxiliaries, and so on) which causes them trouble. A complementary kind of aphasia, involving fluent grammar but inappropriate or nonsensical vocabulary, is associated with damage elsewhere in the left hemisphere, in a region of the temporal lobe and part of the parietal lobe known as Wernicke's area. In Wernicke's aphasics the grammatical equipment to talk about the world is intact, but access to the concepts for organizing their experience of the world (insofar as one can equate concepts with items of vocabulary) is disrupted. Wernicke's aphasia is therefore problematic for any suggestion that conceptual relationships such as thematic structures (mentioned earlier) were not merely a necessary condition for the evolution of syntax but, rather, the main trigger for it. On the basis of that suggestion, one would expect lexical and grammatical disruption regularly to go hand in hand, rather than to occur independently. So, in answer to our second question, the characteristics of Wernicke's aphasia suggest that, for syntax to evolve as it has, something more specialized than just general conceptual sophistication was necessary.

Various suggestions have been made concerning this more specialized ingredient. Some scholars have appealed to the hierarchical organization of relatively complex behaviors involving tools (e.g. Greenfield 1991). Calvin (1993) has pointed out the neurobiological advances necessary for muscular control in accurate throwing, and has suggested that the relevant neural structures may have been coopted for rapid, effortless syntactic organization of words in speech. Such approaches do not, however, account for the proximity of Broca's area to that part of the motor strip which controls the mouth in particular.

One suggestion which exploits that proximity will be discussed in the next section.

6   Linguistic Evidence

It may seem paradoxical that the section on linguistic evidence for the origins of language has been left until last. However, as explained in section 1, linguists have been relative latecomers to this field. Their contributions can be divided into those focussing on the relationship between language and "protolanguage" and a more recent and disparate group focussing on the evolutionary rationale for particular aspects of modern grammatical organization.

6.1   *Protolanguage and "true" language*

Students of language contact distinguish between pidgins, which are used as second languages in situations of regular contact between people with mutually unintelligible mother tongues, and creoles, which arise when children acquire pidgins natively. The creolization process involves faster spoken delivery and the rapid appearance of new grammatical features which may be expressed unsystematically or not at all in the parent pidgin. Study of creole formation, especially among children of workers on Hawaiian sugar plantations, led Bickerton (1981) to the controversial proposal that, in environments where creoles originate, the universal human linguistic "bioprogram" reveals its characteristics most plainly, because the local speech community lacks entrenched grammatical habits which might interfere with it.

Since proposing the bioprogram hypothesis, Bickerton has turned his attention to how the bioprogram may have evolved, and to what sort of linguistic capacity may have preceded it (1990, 1995). He has suggested that what preceded it is still present and in use among humans in certain situations: in "touristese," in the speech of people who are intoxicated or suffering from some kinds of brain damage, and especially in the "two-word" or "telegraphic" stage of infant speech already mentioned in section 4. This kind of language lacks any systematic grammar, so to understand it one must rely heavily on semantic and pragmatic cues. In particular, it lacks any systematic encoding of thematic structure of the kind which, in "true" language, allows us to distinguish reliably between agents, patients, beneficiaries, instruments, and so on (see section 4). In the English sentence *John killed a crocodile*, the identity of the agent and the patient is reliably indicated by word order, while in the Latin sentence *Johannes crocodilum interfecit* it is the endings -*s* and -*m* which serve this purpose; however, on hearing an English-based protolanguage utterance such as *John crocodile kill* one cannot know whether to mourn or rejoice without the help of contextual or background knowledge.

One striking fact about hominid evolution is that increase in brain size was not steady. Rather, there was a first burst of brain expansion between 2 and 1.5 million years ago, as *homo habilis* and *homo erectus* came to replace the earlier australopithecines, followed by a second burst within about the last 300,000 years, as *homo sapiens* came to replace *homo erectus* (Aiello 1996a). Various factors, such as diet and group size, have been invoked to explain this. Bickerton's approach to the problem is to ask why *homo erectus*, though capable of quite sophisticated toolmaking, failed to make any significant techno-logical or cultural advance for over a million years. His answer is that *homo erectus* was endowed not with "true" language but only with protolanguage. Those hominids were at least as aware of social relationships as present-day apes are, and could represent thematic structures (who did what to whom) mentally; but they had no reliable linguistic tool for talking about these rela-tionships or expressing these mentally represented structures. Linguistically, they were trapped throughout their lives at the two-word stage of the modern toddler.

Bickerton thus provides an intriguing, though speculative, answer to the question of what held *homo erectus* back for so long. But how did humans ever get beyond protolanguage? Bickerton's answer is that new neural connections in the brain allowed speech to be hooked up to thematic structure. This would have yielded a sudden and dramatic improvement in the reliability and versat-ility of language, and hence set the stage for the rapid advances of the last quarter of a million years. What is less clear is why the neural hookup should have occurred when it did, rather than earlier or later. Bickerton's scenario also supplies no particular reason why grammar should be more closely asso-ciated in the brain with control of the vocal tract than with the organization of vocabulary. But his proposals certainly suggest one way of reconciling the Chomskyan view of modern human language as qualitatively unique with the need to accommodate it somehow in an account of human evolution.

6.2   *Actual grammar versus conceivable grammars*

Is the sort of grammar that languages have the only kind that they could con-ceivably have, or does grammar-as-it-is represent only one of many directions which linguistic evolution might have taken? This is an ambitious question, and there is no guarantee that it can be answered; however, it is the sort of question which only linguists, among the various contributors to language evolution studies, are equipped to tackle.

If one says that the characteristics of grammar-as-it-is are inevitable, one is saying in effect that grammar is as it is for the same sort of reason that the cells in honeycomb are hexagonal rather than (say) square. It would be futile to look for a hexagonal-cell gene in the genetic endowment of bees. This is because, when numerous creatures are trying to build cells in a confined space, each exerting the same outward pressure in all directions, the outcome will inevitably be a hexagonal pattern for reasons not of biology but of physics and mathematics. That is the kind of possibility that Chomsky has in mind when he says that the ability to learn grammars "may well have arisen as a concomitant of structural properties of the brain that developed for other reasons" (quoted by Pinker 1994: 362). Chomsky has not looked for such structural properties of the brain himself, preferring to concentrate on Universal Grammar itself rather than on what may underlie it. But some researchers are now using computer simulation to explore what happens when a signaling system with certain initial characteristics is set up to be adaptable so as to fit better the needs of the system's "users" (Batali 1998, Berwick et al. 1998, Steels 1997). If common trends emerge from these experiments, and if these trends correspond to identifiable aspects of grammar and vocabulary, that may indicate that the aspects in question were bound to evolve as they have, irrespective of the fact that it is in the language of humans that they appear rather than in a "language" used by dolphins or Martians. Any firm findings in this line lie in the future, however.

What of aspects of grammar which are not inevitable in this sense? A central issue is whether or not all aspects of grammar are well-engineered responses to selection pressures to which humans are subject. Modern evolutionary theory by no means requires the answer yes. Many characteristics of organisms are mere byproducts of historical accident, and some characteristics are badly engineered for the purposes which they serve. An example is the mammalian eye, in which light has to pass through nerve fibres before it reaches light-sensitive tissue, and the optic nerve causes a blind spot at the point where it passes through the retina (Williams 1966, 1992). (Octopuses' eyes are more efficient from this point of view.) Natural selection can only tinker with what is genetically available, and perfect outcomes are often beyond its reach. So how much of grammar is well engineered, and how much of it is less than perfect owing to historical constraints?

Pinker and Bloom (1990) and Newmeyer (1991) are inclined to emphasize the positive aspects of grammatical engineering. That is understandable against the background of Chomsky's emphasis on neutral or even negative aspects. A different tack is taken by Carstairs-McCarthy (1998, 1999), who argues that the grammatical distinction between sentences and noun phrases, despite its familiarity and apparent inevitability, is in fact a piece of mediocre engineering, reflecting the cooption for syntactic purposes of neural mechanisms which evolved originally for the organization of the speech chain into syllables. He suggests that many of the syntactic habits of sentences, verbs, and noun phrases are reflections of the phonological habits of syllables, syllable nuclei (usually vowels), and syllable margins (consonants). This view is consistent with the proximity of Broca's area to the oral portion of the motor strip, as well as the frequent coincidence of grammatical and phonetic symptoms in Broca's aphasia. The invocation of imperfections in linguistic engineering as clues to the evolutionary origin of language is quite new, however, and it remains to be seen how fruitful it will be.

7   Conclusion

This tour of recent work on the origins of language has revealed few solid, uncontroversial conclusions. Nevertheless, the field is entering an exciting period. The long freeze in relations between linguists and other language origin researchers is at last beginning to thaw, just when discoveries in archeology, anthropology, primatology, and brain science are all helping to shed new light on the topic from a variety of directions. Will the evolution of language eventually come to be seen by linguistic theorists as not merely a quaint sideline but an essential source of evidence about why Universal Grammar is as it is? My guess is that it will, though the process may take a decade or more. Certainly, the justification for the Paris Linguistic Society's ban no longer exists.

2 Languages of the World

BERNARD COMRIE

1 Introduction

The aim of this chapter is to provide readers with an overview of current
views on the distribution of the languages of the world and on the genetic
relations among those languages. Needless to say, the mention of individual
languages will be on a selective basis, with emphasis on those languages that
are most widely spoken or that have played an important role in history,
although some departure from this principle will necessarily be made for parts
of the world, like the Americas, Australia, and New Guinea, where there are
few languages with large numbers of speakers.

The best currently available detailed account of the distribution of the world's
languages, with information on geographic location, number of speakers, and
genetic affiliation, is Grimes (1996a), which is accompanied by Grimes (1996b)
and Grimes and Grimes (1996). This work lists over 6,700 languages spoken
in the world today or having recently become extinct. While this figure is
towards the high end of estimates that would be given by linguists, it is nonetheless a reasonable estimate, based where possible on a linguists' definition
of "language" (as opposed to "dialect") as a speech variety that is not mutually intelligible with other speech varieties. This definition brings with it a
number of ancillary problems. For instance, testing mutual intelligibility is far
from straightforward (Casad 1974). There are, moreover, complicated cases,
like intelligibility that is greater in one direction than the other, i.e. speakers
of A understand B better than speakers of B understand A, and dialect chains,
i.e. a geographic chain of dialects A—B— . . . —N such that each dialect is
mutually intelligible with its neighbor(s), but the extremes of the chain, A
and N, are not mutually intelligible. Added to this is the fact that for many
speech varieties serious tests of mutual intelligibility have simply not been
carried out.

The question of the genetic affiliation among the languages of the world
is one that is currently fraught with controversy, in particular between those

who adopt a cautious stance, accepting that languages are genetically related only in the face of overwhelming evidence, and those who are more willing to accept genetic relatedness among languages on the basis of less compelling evidence. In this survey, I have in general included only language families that are universally or almost universally recognized by linguists, and I have specifically added notes of caution where I use terms that cover larger potential genetic groupings of languages. At the same time, this survey does have a duty to inform the reader about more speculative hypotheses that have gained the support of some reasonable set of linguists. I have therefore included notes on possible more widespread groupings, largely following Ruhlen (1994: 15–34). The other book dealing with the classification of the world's languages, Ruhlen (1987), likewise adopts in general an approach that includes both traditionally accepted and currently debated genetic groupings, though with an equally undisguised bias towards the latter; but the critical approach to less widely accepted groupings does not extend to its treatment of languages of the Americas.

In the space available, I have limited myself to geographic distribution and genetic affiliation, although there are a number of other questions that might have been touched on, such as the ways in which languages influence one another by contact, and more generally the historical processes that have given rise to the present-day distribution of the world's languages. Recent literature dealing with this latter problem includes Nichols (1992), Dixon (1997), and Nettle (1999).

Many of the references for individual language families are to volumes in the following series: Cambridge Language Surveys (Cambridge University Press, ongoing), Routledge Language Family Descriptions (Routledge, discontinued and effectively replaced by the following), Curzon Language Family Descriptions (Curzon, ongoing).

2   Languages of Europe and Northern Asia

2.1   Indo-European languages

The Indo-European language family (Ramat and Ramat 1998) covers most of Europe and spreads, with some breaks, across Iran and Central Asia down into South Asia. As a result of colonial expansion, it is now also dominant in the Americas and in Australia and New Zealand. In Europe itself, only a few peripheral areas are occupied by non-Indo-European languages, in particular areas where Basque and some Uralic languages are spoken and parts of the Caucasus. The Indo-European family subdivides into a number of well established branches.

The Germanic languages (König and van der Auwera 1994) are the dominant languages of northwestern Europe, extending into central Europe. This is the language family that includes English, and also Dutch, German, and the Scandinavian languages (including Danish, Norwegian, Swedish, and Icelandic); an offshoot of German with considerable admixture from Hebrew-Aramaic and Slavic is Yiddish, the traditional language of Ashkenazi Jews and a widely spoken language of eastern Europe before the Holocaust. The Scandinavian languages form North Germanic, while the other languages cited are West Germanic; a third subbranch of the family, East Germanic, is now extinct, the only substantially attested language being Gothic.

The Celtic languages (Ball 1993, MacAulay 1993) were once also dominant languages of western and central Europe, but with the expansion of Germanic and Romance languages in particular they have retreated to the western fringes of Europe, the living languages being Welsh in Wales, Irish on the west coast of Ireland, Breton in Brittany (France), and Scots Gaelic in northwestern Scotland.

The Romance languages (Harris and Vincent 1988, Posner 1996) occupy most of southwestern Europe, and are the descendants of Latin, the language of the Roman Empire. Strictly speaking, the branch of Indo-European is Italic, since it includes a number of languages other than Latin that died out by the early centuries of the Common Era as a result of Roman and Latin expansion, so that all living Italic languages are in fact Romance languages. The major living languages are French, Catalan, Spanish, Portuguese, Italian, and Romanian.

Turning to eastern Europe, the northernmost Indo-European branch is Baltic, now consisting of the two languages, Lithuanian and Latvian. The Baltic languages have a particularly close relation to the Slavic (Slavonic) languages (Comrie and Corbett 1993), now dominant in much of eastern and central Europe and including three subbranches. The East Slavic languages are Russian, Belarusian (Belorussian), and Ukrainian. The West Slavic languages include Polish, Czech, and Slovak. The South Slavic languages are Slovenian, Serbo-Croatian, Bulgarian, and Macedonian. As a result of ethnic differences, what linguists would, on grounds of mutual intelligibility, consider a single Serbo-Croatian language is now often divided into Serbian and Croatian, with Bosnian sometimes added as a third ethnic variety.

Two further branches of Indo-European, each consisting of a single language, are found in the Balkans. Albanian consists of two dialect groups, Gheg in the north and Tosk in the south, which might well be considered distinct languages on the basis of the mutual intelligibility test, although there is a standard language based on Tosk. Hellenic includes only Greek, although it is customary to give a different name to the branch, in part because it includes varieties of Greek over more than three millennia, from Mycenean through Classical Greek and Byzantine Greek to the modern language. Armenian, spoken primarily in Armenia though also in the Armenian diaspora originating in eastern Turkey, is another branch of Indo-European consisting of a single language, although the differences between Eastern Armenian (spoken mainly in Armenia) and Western Armenian (spoken originally mainly in Turkey) are considerable, and there are two written languages.

Finally, with respect to the living languages, the Indo-Iranian languages are spoken from the Caucasus to Bangladesh. Indo-Iranian divides into two sub-branches, Iranian and Indo-Aryan (Indic), the latter occupying an almost continuous area covering most of Pakistan, northern India, Nepal, and Bangladesh. The most widely spoken Iranian languages are Persian (Iran), with national variants Tajik (in Tajikistan) and Dari (in Afghanistan), Kurdish (mainly in the border area of Turkey, Iran, and Iraq), Pashto (in Afghanistan and Pakistan), and Balochi (in Pakistan).

The Indo-Aryan subbranch of Indo-Iranian (Masica 1991) includes Sanskrit, the classical language of Indian civilization; Pali, the sacred language of Buddhism; and a large number of modern languages, of which the most widely spoken are Hindi and Urdu, essentially different national forms of the same language, in India and Pakistan respectively; Sindhi and Western Panjabi (Lahnda) in Pakistan; Nepali in Nepal; and Kashmiri, Eastern Panjabi, Gujarati, Rajasthani, Marathi, Bhojpuri, Maithili, Assamese, and Oriya in India; Bengali in India and Bangladesh; and Sinhala, geographically separated from the other Indo-Aryan languages in Sri Lanka. It should also be noted that the various Romani languages, spoken by Rom (Gypsies), belong to the Indo-Aryan group of languages.

In addition, two branches of Indo-European consist of extinct but well attested languages. The best known of the Anatolian languages, spoken in what is now Turkey, is Hittite, language of a major ancient empire (seventeenth–twelfth centuries BCE). Tocharian is a family of two closely related languages, attested in texts from the latter half of the first millennium CE in what is now the Xinjiang region in northwestern China.

2.2   Uralic languages

The Uralic language family (Abondolo 1998) must once have been spoken over a continuous part of northeastern Europe and northwestern Asia, but inroads by other languages, primarily Indo-European and Turkic, have isolated many of the Uralic branches and languages from one another geographically. The family falls into two clear subgroups, Finno-Ugric and Samoyedic. The Samoyedic languages, all with small numbers of speakers, are spoken along the northern fringe of Eurasia, roughly from the Kanin peninsula to the Taymyr peninsula.

Finno-Ugric divides in turn into a number of branches: Balto-Finnic (around the Baltic Sea), Saamic (Lappish) (northern Scandinavia to the Kola peninsula), Volgaic (on the Volga, although the unity of this branch is now questioned), Permic (northeastern European Russia), and Ugric (western Siberia and Hungary, though the unity of Ugric is also questioned). The most widely spoken languages are two Balto-Finnic languages, Finnish and Estonian, and one of the Ugric languages, Hungarian. It should be noted that the present location of Hungarian is the result of a long series of migrations, so that Hungarian is now far distant in location from its closest relatives within Finno-Ugric.

2.3 Altaic families

Altaic is a proposed genetic grouping that would include minimally the Turkic, Tungusic, and Mongolic families, perhaps also Korean and Japanese. Each of these components is a well established language family, and Altaic lies perhaps at the dividing line that separates proponents of wide-ranging genetic groupings of languages from those that remain skeptical. Here the various families and the languages they contain will be noted without any commitment to the unity of the overall grouping.

The Turkic languages (Johanson and Csató 1998) are spoken, with interruptions, in a broad belt stretching from the Balkans in the west through the Caucasus and Central Asia and into Siberia. Classification of the Turkic languages has always been problematic, in part because most of the languages are very close to one another linguistically, in part because population movements and even, in recent times, language politics have tended to overlay new distinctions on old ones. It is recognized that two languages form separate branches of the family: Chuvash, spoken in the Chuvash Republic (Russia) on the Volga, and Khalaj, spoken by a small and dwindling population in the Central Province of Iran. Johanson and Csató (1998: 82–3) propose four other branches, listed here with representative languages. Southwestern (Oghuz) Turkic includes Turkish (Turkey), Azeri (Azerbaijani) (Azerbaijan, northwestern Iran), and Turkmen (Turkmenistan, also Iran and Afghanistan). Northwestern (Kipchak) Turkic includes Kumyk and Karachay-Balkar (both spoken in the Caucasus), Tatar and Bashkir (both spoken on the Volga), Kazakh (Kazakhstan and northwestern China), and Kirghiz (Kyrgyzstan). Southeastern (Uyghur) Turkic includes Uzbek (Uzbekistan) and Uyghur (mainly in northwestern China). Finally, Northeastern (Siberian) Turkic includes Tuvan and Altai (Oyrot) in southern Siberia and Yakut (Sakha) in the huge Sakha Republic in Russia.

The Tungusic languages have few speakers, scattered across the sparsely populated areas of central and eastern Siberia, including Sakhalin Island, and adjacent parts of northeastern China and Mongolia. One Tungusic language, Manchu, is well known in history as the language of the Manchu conquerors who established the Qing dynasty in China (1644–1911), but all but a few ethnic Manchu now speak Mandarin.

The Mongolic languages are spoken primarily in Mongolia and adjacent parts of Russia and China, although there is also one Mongolic language in Afghanistan while Kalmyk is spoken in Kalmykia (Russia) on the lower Volga. The most widely spoken Mongolic language is Mongolian (Mongolia, northern China), although both Buriat (to the south and east of Lake Baikal) and Kalmyk are languages of constituent republics of the Russian Federation.

The other two potential members of the Altaic family are Korean and Japanese. Korean (Sohn 1999) is a single language. Japanese (Shibatani 1990) is strictly speaking a small family, including not only Japanese but also the Ryukyuan languages, which are not mutually intelligible with Japanese or with each other; the family is sometimes called Japanese-Ryukyuan.

2.4   *Chukotko-Kamchatkan languages*

Chukotko-Kamchatkan is a small language family spoken on the Chukotka and Kamchatka peninsulas in the far northeast of Russia. All of the languages, which include Chukchi, are endangered.

2.5   *Caucasian families*

Some of the languages spoken in the Caucasus belong to language families already mentioned, in particular Indo-European (Armenian, Iranian) and Turkic. But there remain a large number of languages that do not belong to any of these families. These languages are referred to as Caucasian, but it is important to note that this is essentially a negative characterization. Indeed, it is currently believed that there are two or three families represented among the "Caucasian" languages.

The Kartvelian (South Caucasian) family is spoken in Georgia with some extension into Turkey, and the main language, the only one to be used as a written language, is Georgian, the official language of the Republic of Georgia.

The other two Caucasian families are Northwest Caucasian (West Caucasian, Abkhaz-Adyghe) and Northeast Caucasian (East Caucasian, Nakh-Daghestanian), although Nikolayev and Starostin (1994) present a detailed argument for considering them to constitute a single North Caucasian family; I will treat them separately here.

The Northwest Caucasian languages are spoken in Abkhazia, the northwestern part of the geographic territory of the Republic of Georgia, and in parts of Russia to the north of this. The main languages are Abkhaz (in Abkhazia) and the varieties of Circassian (Kabardian and Adyghe) spoken in Russia and by a sizeable diaspora in the Middle East.

The Northeast Caucasian languages are spoken primarily in the constituent republics of the Russian Federation of Chechnya, Ingushetia, and Daghestan, with some spillover into Azerbaijan. The languages with the largest numbers of speakers are Chechen (Chechnya) and Avar (Dagestan).

2.6   *Other languages of Europe and northern Eurasia*

A number of other languages or small language families are or were spoken in Europe or northern Asia but do not, at least unequivocally, belong to any of the above families. Basque is a language isolate spoken in the Pyrenees, divided by the Spain–France border. Etruscan was the language of Etruria in northern Italy before the spread of Latin; it is now known to be related to two less well attested languages, Rhaetian in the Alps and Lemnian on the island of Lemnos (Limnos) in the Aegean. Hurrian (sixteenth century BCE) and Urartean (ninth to seventh centuries BCE) are two related extinct languages once spoken in eastern Anatolia.

The Yeniseian family of languages has only one survivor, Ket, spoken on the Yenisei River in western Siberia, although other languages are known from historical records that became extinct from the eighteenth to the twentieth centuries. Yukaghir, spoken in the area of the Kolyma and Indigirka rivers in northeastern Russia, is sometimes treated as a language isolate, although many linguists believe that it is distantly related to Uralic. Nivkh (Gilyak) is a language isolate spoken at the mouth of the Amur River and on Sakhalin Island. Ainu (Shibatani 1990) is a virtually extinct language isolate spoken in northern Japan (Hokkaido Island). Some or all of the languages mentioned in this paragraph are often referred to collectively as Paleosiberian or Paleoasiatic, but this is essentially a negative characterization (they do not belong to any of the established language families), with no implication that they are related to one another.

2.7   Proposals for larger groupings

Two similar, but not identical, proposals have been made for grouping together a large number of the language families found in Europe and northern Asia. The Nostratic proposal, first worked out in detail by Illič-Svityč (1971–84), would include at least Indo-European, Uralic, Altaic, Afroasiatic (see section 4.1), Kartvelian, and Dravidian (see section 3.1). Eurasiatic, the subject of ongoing work by Joseph H. Greenberg, would include at least Indo-European, Uralic, Altaic, Chukotko-Kamchatkan, Eskimo-Aleut (see section 5.1), and possibly also Nivkh. For possibilities including some of the other languages, see section 3.10.

3   Languages of Southern, Eastern, and Southeastern Asia and Oceania

This section deals primarily with languages of southeast Asia and its island extensions into Oceania. There is unfortunately no up-to-date general survey of southeast Asia, or indeed of the individual language families, although James Matisoff is working on one for Cambridge University Press. Things are somewhat better for the islands, although this is an area where there is rapid ongoing work leading to frequent changes in accepted genetic classification.

3.1   Dravidian languages

The Dravidian languages (Steever 1998) are the dominant languages of southern India, with Tamil also spoken in northern Sri Lanka. The Dravidian family
is divided into four branches, Northern, Central, South-Central, and Southern,
although the four main, literary languages belong to the last two branches.
Telugu, the language of the Indian state of Andhra Pradesh, is a South-Central
Dravidian language, while the following are South Dravidian: Tamil (Tamil
Nadu state in India, northern Sri Lanka), Malayalam (Kerala state in India),
and Kannada (Karnataka state in India).

3.2   Austro-Asiatic languages

Austro-Asiatic languages are spoken from eastern India across to Vietnam
and down to the Nicobar Islands and peninsular Malaysia, although in most of
this region they are interspersed among other, more widely spoken, languages.
The family has two branches, Munda and Mon-Khmer. Munda languages
are spoken in eastern India and some neighboring regions. Most of the languages have small numbers of speakers, the main exceptions being Santali and
Mundari. Mon-Khmer languages start in eastern India, but their largest numbers are in Myanmar, Thailand, Malaysia, Cambodia, Laos, and Vietnam. While
most have few speakers, there are two notable exceptions. Khmer (Cambodian)
is the dominant language of Cambodia, while Vietnamese is the dominant
language of Vietnam. Another historically important Mon-Khmer language is
Mon, still spoken in the delta area to the east of Yankon (Rangoon), as the Mon
played an important role in the development of Burmese and Thai culture.
Vietnamese is typologically quite unlike the other Mon-Khmer languages and
has undergone considerable influence from Chinese, with the result that its
membership in Mon-Khmer was for a long time not recognized.

3.3   Sino-Tibetan

Sino-Tibetan is one of the world's largest language families in terms of numbers of speakers, and includes the language most widely spoken as a native
language, namely Mandarin Chinese. Sino-Tibetan languages are spoken primarily in China, the Himalayan region of India and Nepal, and Myanmar, with
excursions into some neighboring countries, in addition to a large Chinese
diaspora. (Ethnic Chinese make up, for instance, some three-quarters of the
population of Singapore.) Our understanding of Sino-Tibetan has been increased
considerably in recent years by the availability of descriptions of the less widely
spoken languages; a major impetus here has been the Sino-Tibetan Etymological
Dictionary and Thesaurus project (see http://www.linguistics.berkeley.edu/
lingdept/research/stedt/) at the University of California at Berkeley.

The usual classification splits the family into two branches, Sinitic (consisting essentially of the Chinese languages; Norman 1988) and Tibeto-Burman. Recently, van Driem (1997) has proposed, on the basis of the most recent reconstructions of the phonology of Old Chinese, that Sinitic may actually be a subbranch of Tibeto-Burman, grouped most closely with the Bodic languages – the family as a whole would thus more properly be called Tibeto-Burman. In what follows, I will retain the traditional classification, though emphasizing that this is more for convenience than through conviction.

Sinitic consists primarily of the various Chinese languages, which in terms of mutual intelligibility are clearly sufficiently different from one another to be considered distinct languages, even if all stand under the umbrella of a reasonably homogeneous written language. The major varieties are Mandarin, Wu (including Shanghai), Gan, Hakka, Xiang, Yue (Cantonese), Northern Min, and Southern Min (including Taiwanese).

The main groupings within (traditional) Tibeto-Burman are Baric, Bodic, Burmese-Lolo, Karen, Nung (Rung), and Qiang; proposals for subgrouping vary. The Baric languages include Meithei (Manipuri) in Manipur State, India. Bodic includes a number of languages spoken in the Himalayas, the most widely spoken and culturally important being Tibetan. The Burmese-Lolo languages are spoken mainly in Myanmar and southern China and include Burmese. The Karen languages are spoken in Myanmar and adjacent parts of Thailand, the most widely spoken being S'gaw Karen (White Karen). The Nung and Qiang languages are spoken in Myanmar and southern China.

3.4   Daic languages

Daic is one of a number of names (others including Tai-Kadai and Kam-Tai) for a family of languages with three branches, Kadai, Kam-Sui, and Tai. Kadai and Kam-Sui contain languages with small numbers of speakers spoken in southern China and parts of Vietnam. Tai, by contrast, includes two of the dominant languages of southeast Asia, namely Thai (Thailand) and the closely related Lao (Laos). Other Tai languages are spoken in these countries and in southern China, though with some excursions into Vietnam and Myanmar. The most widely spoken Tai language of China is Zhuang. It is now conventional to use the spelling Thai for the language, Tai for the branch, and Daic for the family.

3.5   Hmong-Mien (Miao-Yao) languages

The Hmong-Mien or Miao-Yao languages are spoken in parts of southern China and stretching into southeast Asia, especially Vietnam. Hmong and Mien are the indigenous ethnic names, while Miao and Yao are the Chinese equivalents. Hmong and Mien are the two branches of the family, and each consists of several languages. The most widely spoken variety is Hmong Njua (Western Hmong) in China and Vietnam.

3.6   *Austronesian languages*

Austronesian is one of the most extensive families, covering almost all the islands bounded by an area from Madagascar in the west via Taiwan and Hawaii to Easter Island in the east and down to New Zealand in the south, with the exception of most of New Guinea and all of Australia. Although predominantly an island language family, Austronesian languages are also dominant in peninsular Malaysia, while the Chamic languages are spoken in coastal areas of Vietnam and Cambodia as well as on Hainan Island, China. An overview of the Austronesian languages by Robert Blust is in preparation for Cambridge University Press.

Although the Austronesian languages of Taiwan are very much minority languages on an island where varieties of Chinese have become dominant, the internal diversity among the Austronesian languages of Taiwan, the so-called Formosan languages, is greater than that in all the rest of Austronesian put together, so there is a major genetic split within Austronesian between Formosan and the rest, the latter now usually called Malayo-Polynesian (although in some earlier work this term was used for the family as a whole). Indeed, the genetic diversity within Formosan is so great that it may well consist of several primary branches of the overall Austronesian family.

The basic internal classification of Malayo-Polynesian is reasonably well established. The primary branchings are into Western Malayo-Polynesian and Central-Eastern Malayo-Polynesian, with the dividing line running to the east of Sulawesi and through the Lesser Sunda islands. Western Malayo-Polynesian thus includes all the languages of the Philippines, the Asian mainland, western Indonesia, and Madagascar. It also includes all the Austronesian languages with large numbers of speakers, including Malay–Indonesian, the different national varieties of what is essentially the same standard written language, though with radically different local spoken varieties. Other widely spoken languages of Indonesia are Acehnese, Toba Batak, Lampung, and Minangkabau (all on Sumatra), Javanese, Madurese, and Sundanese (all on Java), Balinese (on Bali), and Buginese and Makassarese (on Sulawesi). Widely spoken languages of the Philippines include, in addition to the national language Tagalog, the following: Bikol, Hiligaynon, Ilocano, Pampangan, Pangasinan, and Waray-Waray. The other major Western Malayo-Polynesian language is Malagasy (Madagascar).

Central-Eastern Malayo-Polynesian further divides into Central Malayo-Polynesian and Eastern Malayo-Polynesian, the former comprising a number of languages spoken in parts of the Lesser Sunda islands and of southern and central Maluku. Eastern Malayo-Polynesian divides in turn into South Halmahera-West New Guinea and Oceanic, with the former including Austronesian languages of southern Halmahera and parts of northwest Irian Jaya. Oceanic includes all other Austronesian languages of Melanesia, Micronesia (except that Palauan and Chamorro are Western Malayo-Polynesian), and Polynesia. Oceanic thus includes the Polynesian languages, spoken in the triangle whose points are Hawaii in the north, Easter Island in the east, and New Zealand in the south. Polynesian languages include Hawaiian, Tahitian, Maori, Samoan, Tuvaluan, and Tongan. Genetically just outside Polynesian within Oceanic is Fijian. Kiribati (Gilbertese) is a Micronesian language, also within Oceanic but outside Polynesian.

3.7   *Papuan families*

The island of New Guinea and immediately surrounding areas form the linguistically most diverse area on earth, with over 1,000 languages spoken by a population of between six and seven million. While some of the coasts of New Guinea itself and most of the smaller islands of the New Guinea area are occupied by Austronesian languages, most of the interior, together with some coastal and island areas, are occupied by so-called Papuan languages. The term "Papuan" is basically defined negatively as those languages of the New Guinea area that are not Austronesian. Until recently, two radically different approaches to the internal classification of Papuan languages prevailed among specialists. On the one hand, Wurm (1982) divided the languages into five major "phyla" (i.e. large-scale families) and six minor phyla, plus seven or more language isolates. The most widespread of these large families is the Trans New Guinea phylum, containing most of the languages spoken across the highland backbone of the island but also extending southwest as far as Timor and neighboring islands. The other major phyla in this classification are: West Papuan (northern Halmahera and parts of the Bird's Head in Irian Jaya), Geelvink Bay (part of the north coast of Irian Jaya, to the east of the Bird's Head), Torricelli (western parts of the north coast of Papua New Guinea), Sepik-Ramu (large parts of northwestern Papua New Guinea), and East Papuan (on islands from New Britain eastwards to the Solomons). (Note that Geelvink Bay is now called Cenderawasih Bay; the Bird's Head was formerly called the Vogelkop.) Foley (1986), by contrast, maintains that work to date allows only the identification of about sixty genetic units, with internal diversification about as for Romance, among the Papuan languages, with higher-level relations among them remaining a task for future research.

Ongoing work, some of it published in Pawley (1999) and including contributions by Foley among others, suggests that there may well be a firm basis for using traditional comparative methods for a stripped-down version of the Trans New Guinea family, which would still include a substantial number of the smaller genetic units found along the backbone of the main island, although by no means all of Wurm's Trans New Guinea phylum finds justification in the ongoing work. But this does indicate that the time may be ripe or nearly ripe for a more systematic look at genetic relations among the Papuan languages.

As can be imagined from the low average ratio of speakers to languages, most Papuan languages have few speakers. The languages listed by Grimes (1996a) as having more than 100,000 speakers are Enga, Chimbu, and Medlpa in the highlands of Papua New Guinea, and Western Dani, Grand Valley Dani, and Ekari in the highlands of Irian Jaya. It is a general pattern that languages with more speakers tend to be found in the highlands, whose valleys are also the area of greatest population density.

3.8   *Australian families*

The classification of Australian languages is in something of a turmoil at present. Dixon (1980) proposed that all Australian languages form a single family, with the exception of Tiwi, spoken on islands off the north coast, and Djingili, in the Barkly Tableland. In a more recent work, Dixon (1997) takes a different stand, suggesting that the peculiar social history of Aboriginal Australia, with the absence of major power centers and continual contact among languages, may make the traditional comparative method unworkable for Australia. Many Australianists nonetheless retain the concept of language family, with about twenty language families in Australia, perhaps all or most being related as a single Australian language family. In particular, there is widespread accept-ance of a Pama-Nyungan family that would include the languages spoken in most of the island-continent except some of those in the far north, although Dixon (1997) explicitly rejects the genetic unity of Pama-Nyungan. A new syn-thesis of Australian languages, to replace Dixon (1980), is currently in pre-paration by Dixon and others. No Australian language has a large number of speakers, the most viable languages having at most a few thousand.

The records of the extinct Tasmanian languages are sparse, and Dixon (1980) concludes that they are insufficient to exclude the possibility that they may have been related to Australian languages, though equally they are insuffici-ent to establish such a relationship (or any other). Speakers of the Tasmanian languages must have been separated from the rest of humanity for about 12,000 years, from the time rising waters created the Bass Strait to the first visits by Europeans, making them the most isolated human group known to history; the genocide visited upon the Tasmanians in the nineteenth century is thus also a scientific tragedy of the first order.

3.9   *Other languages of southern, eastern, and*
southeastern Asia

A number of living languages spoken in this region have so far eluded genetic classification, in particular Burushaski spoken in northern Pakistan, and Nahali

(Nihali) in central India. Burushaski is reasonably well described, while Nahali is in urgent need of a detailed description. The Andamanese languages, spoken on the Andaman islands (politically part of India) also lack any widely accepted broader genetic affiliation.

In addition, reference may be made to two extinct languages. Elamite was the language of Elam, an important empire in what is now southwestern Iran around 1000 BCE; it is possible that it may be related to Dravidian (McAlpin 1981). Sumerian was the language of ancient Sumer, and is noteworthy as being probably the first language to have had a writing system; it was still used as a literary language in the Old Babylonian period, although before or during this period it was replaced as a spoken language by Akkadian (see section 4.1).

3.10 *Proposals for larger groupings*

For the suggestion that Dravidian might belong to the proposed Nostratic macro-family, see section 2.7.

Benedict (1975), building largely on his own earlier work, proposes an Austro-Tai macro-family that would include Austro-Asiatic, Daic, Hmong-Mien, and Austronesian. Ruhlen (1994: 24–8) reports on attempts to set up a Dene-Caucasian grouping that would include Na-Dene (see section 5.1), Yeniseian, Sino-Tibetan, Nahali, Sumerian, Burushaski, North Caucasian, and Basque (for some of these languages, see section 2.6).

Greenberg (1971) proposed an Indo-Pacific grouping that would include all Papuan languages plus the Andamanese and Tasmanian languages, but this proposal does not seem to have been taken up in detail by other linguists.

The possibility of a link between (some) Australian and (some) Papuan languages is mooted by Foley (1986).

4 Languages of Africa and Southwestern Asia

The starting point for recent discussions of the classification of African languages is Greenberg (1963), who proposes a fourway division into Afroasiatic, Niger-Congo (Niger-Kordofanian), Nilo-Saharan, and Khoisan families. Afroasiatic and Niger-Congo are now generally accepted, while more controversy has surrounded Nilo-Saharan and Khoisan.

4.1 *Afroasiatic languages*

The Afroasiatic (formerly Hamito-Semitic) family is the dominant language family of most of north Africa and large parts of southwestern Asia, and although individual languages have contracted or extended their geographical distribution, this distribution of the family as a whole goes back to antiquity. The family is generally considered to have six branches: Semitic in southwestern Asia, Eritrea, and much of Ethiopia, also of course now in most of North Africa as a result of the spread of Arabic; Egyptian in older times in Egypt; Berber across most of the rest of north Africa (though now in retreat before Arabic in most of this area); Chadic, in a belt centered on northern Nigeria and southern Niger; Cushitic in the Horn of Africa (Somalia, Djibouti, much of southern Ethiopia, and extending into Kenya and Tanzania to the east of Lake Victoria); and Omotic along the Omo River in southeastern Ethiopia. Omotic languages were formerly, and are still sometimes, considered a subbranch of Cushitic. There is need for an up-to-date survey of the family as a whole; in the meantime, reference may be made to Diakonoff (1988).

The Semitic languages are the best studied of the Afroasiatic branches, and Semitic languages can be traced back almost to the beginning of written history. The most recent survey is Hetzron (1997). The Semitic branch is divided into two subbranches, East Semitic and West Semitic. The East Semitic branch is extinct, although it contains Akkadian, the language of the Babylonian and Assyrian civilizations. West Semitic contains all the living Semitic languages as well as several historically important dead languages. The subdivision of West Semitic is more controversial, especially as regards the position of Arabic. The widely accepted current classification as given in Hetzron (1997) divides West Semitic into Central Semitic and South Semitic. Central Semitic subdivides into Arabic and Northwest Semitic. The older classification would put Arabic in South Semitic, and thus use Northwest Semitic for the other subbranch of West Semitic. The classification of Hetzron will be followed in the presentation here.

Arabic was, until the spread of Islam, the language of part of the Arabian peninsula, but as the language of Islam it has spread through much of southwestern Asia and north Africa, replacing the languages previously spoken across most of this area and becoming one of the modern world's major languages. The standard written language is still firmly rooted in the language of the Koran and medieval Arabic literature, but spoken varieties of Arabic are sufficiently different from one another that mutual intelligibility is not possible between extreme varieties. However, only one variety of Arabic has developed as a separate written language, namely Maltese.

Northwest Semitic includes the Canaanite languages and Aramaic. The best known of the Canaanite languages is Hebrew, used as the spoken and written language of the Jews until the early centuries CE, then as a written and liturgical language by Jews throughout the middle ages, to be revived as a spoken language starting in the late nineteenth century and reaching its culmination as an official language and the dominant spoken language of Israel. The other Canaanite languages are all extinct, the best known being Phoenician. Aramaic was a major lingua franca of the Near East from the eighth century BCE, but at present varieties of Aramaic are spoken in enclaves in Syria, Iraq, and Iran.

South Semitic includes the South Arabian languages spoken on the southern fringe of the Arabian peninsula. Most living South Semitic languages belong to the Ethiopian Semitic subgroup, and include Amharic, the dominant language of Ethiopia; Tigrinya, an important regional language of Ethiopia and Eritrea; and Tigré, another regional language of Eritrea. In addition, Ethiopian Semitic includes Ge'ez, the extinct language still used liturgically by the Ethiopian Church.

Egyptian, by which is meant here Ancient Egyptian, is a single language attested in various historical stages from the earliest writing in Egypt. The hieroglyphic writing system and its offshoots were used into the Common Era, but were soon replaced after Christianization by a Greek-based script, and this later variety of the language is called Coptic. Coptic survived as a spoken language to the late middle ages, when it was finally replaced completely by Arabic, although it continues in use as the liturgical language of the Coptic Church. A recent survey is Loprieno (1995).

The Berber languages are spoken in a scattered pattern across north Africa from just east of the Egypt–Libya border, though they are strongest in mountainous parts of Algeria and especially Morocco, and in the desert parts of Mali and Niger. Among the most widely spoken varieties are Kabyle (Algeria), Chaouia (Algeria), Tarifit (Northern Shilha) (Morocco, Algeria), Tachelhit (Central Shilha) (Morocco, Algeria), Tamazight (Southern Shilha) (Morocco, Algeria), Tamashek (the language of the Tuaregs, mainly in Mali and Niger).

Most of the Chadic languages have few speakers, but there is one significant exception, namely Hausa, the dominant indigenous language of northern Nigeria and southern Niger. Hausa is widely used as a lingua franca by speakers of other neighboring Chadic and non-Chadic languages.

The most widely spoken Cushitic languages are Somali (mainly in Somalia and Ethiopia), Sidamo (Ethiopia), Oromo (Galla) (Ethiopia), Afar (Ethiopia, Eritrea, Djibouti), and Bedawi (Beja) (Sudan). The most widely spoken Omotic language is Wolaytta (Ethiopia).

4.2   *Niger-Congo languages*

Niger-Congo languages cover most of Africa south of a line drawn from the mouth of the Senegal River in the west to where the equator cuts the coast of Africa in the east, with the major exception of the area in southwestern Africa occupied by the Khoisan languages. There are also considerable excursions of Niger-Congo to the north of this line, and less significant excursions of non-Niger-Congo languages to the south of this line, e.g. Cushitic and Nilotic languages spoken to the east of Lake Victoria. The internal structure of the Niger-Congo family was first worked out in detail in Greenberg (1963), although a number of changes have been proposed in more recent work, several of which are still the subject of debate. The most recent overview is Bendor-Samuel (1989), and the classification given there will be followed here.

One branch of Niger-Congo is spoken outside the area delimited above, namely Kordofanian, spoken in the Nuba mountains of Sudan, to the south of El-Obeid. While Greenberg considered Kordofanian genetically the most distant of the languages in the overall family, thus naming the family as a whole Niger-Kordofanian with two coordinate branches Kordofanian and Niger-Congo, the current view is rather that Kordofanian is at least no more distant genetically from the core of the family than are the Mande languages, and the name Niger-Congo is current for the family as a whole. It should be noted that one group of languages assigned tentatively by Greenberg to Kordofanian on the basis of fragmentary material, namely Kado or Kadu (formerly called Kadugli-Krongo), is now believed not to be Kordofanian or Niger-Congo, and perhaps Nilo-Saharan (Bender 1997: 25).

The Mande languages are spoken over most of west Africa to the west of 5°W and to the south of 15°N, although considerable parts of this territory, especially near the coasts, are occupied by other branches of Niger-Congo (Atlantic and Kru). Mende languages include Bambara, the major indigenous language of Mali, and some closely related languages such as Maninka; Jula, spoken in Côte d'Ivoire and Burkina Faso; Kpelle, the major indigenous language of Liberia; and Mende, the major indigenous language of Sierra Leone.

In Bendor-Samuel (1989: 21) the rest of Niger-Congo, once Kordofanian and Mende have been removed, is referred to as Atlantic-Congo, with Atlantic and Ijoid as the genetically next most divergent groups, the remainder being referred to as Volta-Congo. The remaining Niger-Congo groups, i.e. Bendor-Samuel's Atlantic-Congo, will be treated together in what follows.

Atlantic languages are spoken, predominantly in coastal areas, from the Senegal River in the north down into Liberia, although the most widely spoken Atlantic language, Fula (Fulfulde, Peul) has a different distribution. The Fulani, as the speakers of Fula are called, are pastoralists whose range is between the rain forest to the south and the desert to the north, with traditional seasonal moves along a north–south axis; the language is spoken in pockets from the Atlantic coast into Sudan and even Ethiopia, with concentrations in northern Nigeria and northern Cameroon. Another widely spoken Atlantic language is Wolof, the major indigenous language of Senegal.

The Kru languages are spoken in Liberia and southwestern Côte d'Ivoire, with relatively small numbers of speakers. Kru was included in Kwa (see below) by Greenberg (1963).

The Gur (Voltaic) group cover most of Burkina Faso, spreading also into northern parts of countries to the south. The Gur language with by far the largest number of speakers is Moore, the dominant indigenous language of Burkina Faso. One language sometimes considered to be Gur is Dogon, spoken around Bandiagara in Mali and adjacent parts of Burkina Faso, but current opinion questions this assignment and in Bendor-Samuel (1989) Dogon is considered at least provisionally a separate branch within Volta-Congo.

To the south of the Gur languages and continuing to the coast are the Kwa languages, stretching roughly from the Bandama River in the west to the

Benin–Nigeria border in the east. The precise extent of Kwa has shifted considerably since Greenberg (1963), and not all the innovations have been generally accepted. In Bendor-Samuel (1989), the term Kwa covers essentially Greenberg's Western Kwa, with his Eastern Kwa being mostly reassigned to Benue-Congo (see below). The least controversial part of these changes is the exclusion of Kru (see above) and Ijo (see below) from Kwa. In what follows, as in the geographical description given above, the restricted sense of Kwa as in Bendor-Samuel (1989) will be followed. Kwa languages, in this narrow sense, include Baule, an important regional language of southern Côte d'Ivoire; the Akan dialect cluster (Twi-Fante), the major indigenous language of Ghana; the Ga-Dangme dialect cluster, including Ga, the major indigenous language of the Ghanaian capital Accra; and the Gbe dialect cluster, including Ewe, a widely spoken indigenous language in Ghana and Togo, and Fongbe, the most widely spoken indigenous language of Benin.

Ijo, now usually considered a distinct branch of Niger-Congo, is spoken around the delta of the Niger River in Nigeria, and is the major indigenous language of Nigeria's Rivers State. Different varieties of Ijo are not all mutually intelligible, the most prestigious varieties being Kolokuma and Kalabari.

The Adamawa-Ubangi languages are spoken in a belt from eastern Nigeria into Sudan, with the main concentration in the Central African Republic. The languages of the Adamawa subgroup are spoken to the west, those of the Ubangi subgroup to the east. The most widely used Adamawa-Ubangi language is Sango, which is the national language of the Central African Republic; historically, it is a creole derived primarily from the Ubangi language Ngbandi.

The remaining branch of Niger-Congo, Benue-Congo, covers most of sub-Saharan Africa from the western border of Nigeria eastwards to the Indian Ocean and southwards to the Cape. Most of this area and population falls under Bantu, but from a historical linguistic viewpoint Bantu is a rather low-level subgroup within Benue-Congo and the present geographical distribution of Bantu is the result of an expansion from the Nigeria–Cameroon border area that took place for the most part within the last two millennia. The most widely spoken Benue-Congo languages outside Bantu are Yoruba, an official language in southwestern Nigeria; Edo, to the southeast of Yoruba; Nupe, to the northeast of Yoruba; Igbo, an official language in central southern Nigeria; Ibibio-Efik to the east of the Niger delta in Nigeria; and Tiv, a regionally important language of eastern Nigeria.

As already implied, the Bantu languages occupy most of Africa from the Nigeria–Cameroon border to the east and south, including several major indigenous languages. The most widely spoken Bantu language is Swahili, originally the language of Zanzibar and the adjacent coast, although it has now spread as a lingua franca and also, especially in Tanzania, as a first language across large parts of east Africa; it is the official language of Tanzania and an official language in Kenya. Comorian, the indigenous language of the Comoros, is closely related to Swahili. Several other widely spoken Bantu languages are here listed primarily by country: Fang (Equatorial Guinea, Gabon), Bangala

(Congo–Kinshasa), Kituba (Congo–Kinshasa), Lingala (Congo–Kinshasa), Kikongo (Congo–Kinshasa, Angola), Luba-Kasai (Congo–Kinshasa), Luba-Shaba (Congo–Kinshasa), Zande (Congo–Kinshasa and neighboring countries), Northern Mbundu (Angola), Southern Mbundu (Angola), Gikuyu (Kenya), Kamba (Kenya), Luyia (Kenya), Luganda (Uganda), Nyankore (Uganda), Soga (Uganda), Kirundi (Burundi), Kinyarwanda (Rwanda) – Kirundi and Kinyarwanda are essentially different national variants of the same language – Chagga (Tanzania), Haya (Tanzania), Makonde (Tanzania, Mozambique), Nyamwezi (Tanzania), Sukuma (Tanzania), Lomwe (Mozambique), Makua (Mozambique), Sena (Mozambique), Tsonga (Mozambique, South Africa), Nyanja (Malawi, Mozambique, Zambia), Tumbuka (Malawi, Zambia), Yao (Malawi, Tanzania), Nyakyusa-Ngonde (Malawi, Tanzania), Bemba (Zambia), Luvale (Zambia), Tonga (Zambia), Northern Ndebele (Zimbabwe), Shona (Zimbabwe, Zambia, Mozambique), Tswana (Botswana, South Africa), Southern Sotho (Lesotho, South Africa), Swati (Swaziland, South Africa), Northern Sotho (Pedi) (South Africa), Tsonga (South Africa), Venda (South Africa), Xhosa (South Africa), Zulu (South Africa).

4.3   Nilo-Saharan families

Nilo-Saharan, as proposed by Greenberg (1963), has proven to be more controversial than either Afroasiatic or Niger-Congo, although the most recent survey of the Nilo-Saharan languages (Bender 1997) is positive. The internal structure of Nilo-Saharan is also more controversial. In what follows I have therefore limited myself to citing some of the more widely spoken Nilo-Saharan languages and the branches of the family to which they belong.

Nilo-Saharan languages are not spoken in a continuous geographical area, and even in the areas mentioned below they are often interspersed with Afroasiatic (Chadic, Cushitic, also Arabic) and Niger-Congo languages. One Nilo-Saharan area is the middle course of the Niger River; another is Chad; a third is the Nile around the Egypt–Sudan border; while a fourth includes parts of southern Sudan, westernmost Ethiopia and Eritrea, northeastern Congo–Kinshasa, and parts of Kenya and Uganda to the north and east of Lake Victoria.

The westernmost language, or rather cluster of closely related languages, assigned to Nilo-Saharan is Songay, spoken along the Niger river in an area including the town of Timbuktu, although it is also the living language whose inclusion in Nilo-Saharan has proven most controversial (Bender 1997: 59). Another major western Nilo-Saharan language, assigned to the Saharan branch of the family, is Kanuri, the dominant indigenous language of Bornu State in northeastern Nigeria. Within the For(an) branch, mention should be made of For (Fur), spoken in the Darfur region in west-central Sudan.

Most of the more widely spoken Nilo-Saharan languages belong to the East Sudanic and Central Sudanic branches. East Sudanic includes the Nubian languages of the Egypt–Sudan border area, of which the most widely spoken is Nobiin. It also includes the Nilotic languages, a grouping which includes the Luo (Lwo) languages Acholi (Uganda), Lango (Uganda), Alur (Uganda, Congo–Kinshasa), and Luo (Dholuo) (Kenya); the Dinka-Nuer languages Jieng (Dinka) (Sudan) and Naadh (Nuer) (Sudan); the Eastern Nilotic languages Maasai (Kenya, Tanzania), Turkana (Kenya), Karamojong (Uganda), and Teso (Uganda, Kenya), and the Southern Nilotic language Kalenjin (Kenya). Central Sudanic includes Ngambay (Sara-Ngambay) (Chad), Lugbara (High Lugbara) (Congo–Kinshasa, Uganda), Mangbetu (Congo–Kinshasa), Ndo (Congo–Kinshasa), and Badha (Lendu) (Congo–Kinshasa).

It has been suggested that Meroitic, the extinct language of the Meroë civilization (ca. 2300–1600 BP), might be a Nilo-Saharan language, but Bender (1997: 32) considers the available data insufficient to resolve the issue. Finally, it should be noted that there are some as yet virtually undescribed languages spoken in the general Nilo-Saharan area that are as yet insufficiently known to establish whether or not they might be Nilo-Saharan. Many Nilo-Saharan and possible Nilo-Saharan languages are spoken in regions of current unrest (southern Sudan) or recent unrest (Ethiopia), which accounts in part for the rather poor state of our knowledge of such languages.

4.4   Khoisan families

The Khoisan languages are spoken predominantly in southwestern Africa. The area occupied by Khoisan languages has certainly contracted as a result of the spread of Bantu and, more recently, Indo-European languages, and all Khoisan languages have small numbers of speakers, with the largest, Nama (Khoekhoe), spoken in Namibia and South Africa, having an estimated 146,000 (Grimes 1996a: 323). Two otherwise unclassified languages of East Africa, namely Hadza and Sandawe of Tanzania, were proposed for inclusion in Khoisan by Greenberg (1963). However, even the genetic unity of Khoisan with the exclusion of Sandawe and Hadza is not accepted by all specialists, some of whom prefer to treat Northern Khoisan, Central Khoisan, and Southern Khoisan as distinct families. Sands (1998) is a recent treatment, concluding that there are striking parallels among the three nuclear branches of Khoisan plus Hadza and Sandawe, but that it is not clear to what extent this reflects common genetic origin versus contact.

4.5   Proposals for larger groupings

The proposal that Afroasiatic might form part of a larger Nostratic macro-family was discussed in section 2.7. Proposals that Niger-Congo and Nilo-Saharan might be distantly related are considered worth following up both in Bendor-Samuel (1989: 8–9) and by Bender (1997: 9).

5   Languages of the Americas

The internal and external genetic affiliations of the indigenous languages of the Americas have given rise to considerable debate in recent years, with proposals ranging from a total of three families (Greenberg 1987) to almost 200 (Campbell 1997). Since Campbell (1997) lists securely assured genetic units, but then also discusses proposals for broader genetic groupings, his account can serve as a survey that covers the range of proposals. In the space available, it would not make sense to list and discuss up to 200 genetic units, so in what follows a very selective choice will be made, concentration on larger families and languages with larger numbers of speakers.

5.1   *Languages of North America*

The languages of North America are surveyed in Mithun (1999).

The northern fringe of North America is home to the Eskimo-Aleut family. The family has two branches, Aleut, spoken on the Aleutian islands, and Eskimo. The latter starts in eastern Siberia and then stretches from Alaska to Greenland. Eskimo is properly a family of languages, with a major division between Yupik (Siberian and southern Alaskan varieties) and Inuit-Inupiak in northern Alaska, Canada, and Greenland. Greenlandic is the variety with most speakers, and is the national language of Greenland.

Another major family of North America is Na-Dene, although the precise extent of the family is controversial. Its core is Athabaskan, comprising most of the languages of the interior of Alaska, northwest Canada, with some languages (all extinct or moribund) in Oregon and northern California, and then a flowering in the geographically remote Apachean languages of the southwestern USA, including Navajo. It is established that the recently extinct Eyak language, spoken at the mouth of the Copper River in Alaska, is genetically related to Athabaskan, to give Athabaskan-Eyak. Less certain is whether Tlingit, (spoken on the Alaska panhandle) is related to these, which would justify the more inclusive term Na-Dene, and even more questionable whether Haida (spoken on Queen Charlotte Island) should be added.

Other language families of the Pacific Northwest include Wakashan (British Columbia and adjacent Washington state; the family includes Nootka) and Salishan (British Columbia, Washington state, with some excursion into Idaho and Montana). Other language families of California, sometimes extending to adjacent areas, are Miwok-Costanoan, Chumashan, and Yuman. The small Keresan family and the language isolate Zuni of New Mexico, though small in number of speakers (each in the thousands) are among the most vigorous indigenous languages of the USA, with high rates of acquisition by children.

The Siouan languages are a major language family of the North American Plains, stretching from north of the US–Canada border through the Dakotas,

Minnesota, and Wisconsin down to Arkansas, with outliers historically almost as far south as the Gulf and in Virginia. The Muskogean family, formerly concentrated in the southeastern USA, includes Choctaw, Chickasaw (these two arguably dialects of a single language), Alabama, and Seminole.

The Iroquoian languages are spoken around the Great Lakes, apart from Cherokee, originally spoken in Georgia; the family also includes Tuscarora, Huron (extinct), Seneca, and Mohawk. The Algic (Algonquian-Ritwan) family covers much of the northeast of North America, though also extending into western Canada and with two outliers on the Great Plains (Cheyenne and Arapaho). The family includes Blackfoot, the various forms of Cree spoken in Canada, and Ojibwa in Canada and the USA. These are all Algonquian languages. The two Ritwan languages, Wiyot (extinct) and Yurok (moribund), though indubitably related to Algonquian, are spoken in California.

Uto-Aztecan is one of the major language families of North America, spreading also into Meso-America. The Northern Uto-Aztecan languages include Shoshone, Comanche, Ute, and Hopi; while the Southern Uto-Aztecan languages include Pima-Papago (O'odham) in Arizona and Sonora; Cora and Huichol in Nayarit and Jalisco; and Nahuatl in central Mexico. Nahuatl was the language of the Aztec empire.

5.2   *Languages of Meso-America*

The languages of Meso-America are surveyed in Suárez (1983). The Uto-Aztecan family was discussed in section 5.1.

Other major language families of Meso-America are Otomanguean, Mixe-Zoquean, and Mayan. The Otomanguean languages are spoken mainly across the isthmus of Mexico, especially its southern part (Guerrero, Oaxaca, Puebla), including the Zapotecan languages and Mixtec, although some Otomanguean languages, such as Otomí, are spoken further north and separated from the mass of Otomanguean languages. Mixe-Zoquean languages are spoken in a number of geographically separated groups in the isthmus of Mexico; the Olmecs, the first of the great Meso-American civilizations, seem to have spoken a Mixe-Zoquean language. The Mayan languages cover or covered most of Mexico east of the isthmus and also Guatemala and Belize; individual languages include Yucatec, Chol, Kekchi, and K'iche' (Quiché); although Chol does not have one of the highest numbers of speakers among Mayan languages, it is important historically as the most direct descendant of the language of the Mayan hieroglyphic inscriptions.

For Chibchan languages of Meso-America, see section 5.3.

5.3   *Languages of South America*

For Amazonian languages, Dixon and Aikhenvald (1999) provide a survey; a comparable survey for Andean languages is in preparation by Willem Adelaar and Pieter Muysken for Cambridge University Press. Campbell's (1997) discussion of South American languages is based on Kaufman (1990).

The Chibchan language family includes a number of languages scattered from Costa Rica in the west through Panama to Colombia in the east. Cariban languages are scattered across northeastern South America, mostly to the north of the Amazon, although some languages are spoken as far west as Colombia and there is a geographically isolated group well to the south along the upper course of the Xingu River.

The precise extent of the Arawakan family is a matter of ongoing debate, although the group of languages that are clearly genetically related are sometimes referred to as Maipurean. They are scattered at great distances from one another across much of northern South America, from the Caribbean coast as far south as Paraguay, with Garífuna (also misleadingly known as Black Carib) spoken in Central America.

Tucanoan languages are spoken in northwestern South America (Colombia, Ecuador, Peru, adjacent parts of Brazil). Panoan languages are spoken in the Peru–Brazil border area, with some spillover into Bolivia, while the Tacanan languages, now believed to be related to Panoan in a Panoan-Tacanan family, are spoken in Bolivia with some spread into Peru. The Gê (Je) family is spoken in Brazil. Tupian languages are spoken both on the Amazon River and its tributaries and in an area that includes Paraguay and adjacent parts of Brazil, Bolivia, and Argentina. The most widely spoken Tupian language is Paraguayan Guaraní, spoken by 95 percent of the population of Paraguay and a national language of the country.

Quechumaran includes the Quechua and Aymara branches, although the nature of the relationship between Quechua and Aymara – genetic or contact – continues to be debated. Quechua is strictly speaking a language family rather than a single language, since different varieties are not mutually intelligible; in terms of numbers of speakers, it is the largest indigenous language family of the Americas. Quechua was the language of the Inca empire, and partly as a result of this empire and later use as a lingua franca by the Spanish administration it achieved a spread from Colombia in the north to Argentina in the south, although most speakers are in Peru. The most widely spoken Quechua languages are South Bolivian Quechua in Bolivia, Cuzco Quechua in Peru, and Chimborazo Quichua in Ecuador. Aymara is spoken predominantly in western Bolivia.

5.4   *Proposals for larger groupings*

For proposals that would group Eskimo-Aleut as part of Eurasiatic, see section 2.7. For proposals that would group Na-Dene with Sino-Tibetan and possibly other families, see section 3.10. Otherwise, the main proposal is that of Greenberg (1987) to group all the remaining indigenous languages of the Americas into a single Amerind family.

There are also more modest proposals for larger genetic units within the indigenous languages of the Americas, excluding Eskimo-Aleut and Na-Dene, of which Penutian and Hokan are perhaps the most engrained in the literature. Penutian would group together a number of languages and language families of the northern part of western North America, including at least: Maidu and Miwok-Costanoan (together California Penutian); Chinookan; Coos, Kalapuyan, and Yakonan (together Oregon Penutian); Klamath-Modoc and Sahaptin (together Plateau Penutian); and Tsimshian. Hokan would group together a number of languages and language families of the southern part of western North America and extending into Meso-America, including at least: Yuman; Karok-Shasta, Pomo, and Yana (Northern Hokan); Chumash, Salinan, and Seri; Tequistlatecan (Chontal of Oaxaca); and Washo.

6   Pidgin and Creole Languages

Since the main concern of this survey is the geographic distribution of languages as spoken by native speakers, pidgin languages (Holm 1989) will only be considered to the extent to which they are being creolized. Pidgin languages that are relevant in this way include the closely related Krio of Sierra Leone, Pidgin of Cameroon, and Pidgin of Nigeria, all of which are English-based pidgins undergoing creolization and widely used as lingua francas in the relevant countries. In addition, mention must be made of the closely related Tok Pisin of Papua New Guinea, Pijin of the Solomon Islands, and Bislama of Vanuatu, all likewise English-based pidgins undergoing creolization and widely used as lingua francas.

Otherwise, creole languages are particularly prevalent in the Caribbean and the islands of the Indian Ocean. They include English-based Sranan, the lingua franca of Suriname, and the French-based creoles of Haiti in the Caribbean and Mauritius, Réunion, and the Seychelles in the Indian Ocean. The case of Sango, in origin a creolized form of Ngbandi, was discussed in section 4.2.

7   Deaf Sign Languages

Most works on languages of the world deal exclusively with spoken languages, and this is certainly the emphasis of this survey. Recent work on deaf sign languages has shown, however, that deaf sign languages are languages in their own right, differing considerably in structure from the spoken languages used in the same territory (see chapter 22). Indeed, genetic relations among deaf sign languages often do not match those of the "corresponding" spoken languages, e.g. American Sign Language (ASL) is more closely related to French

Sign Language than it is to British Sign Language. Grimes and Grimes (1996) list 104 deaf sign languages, though without giving any internal genetic classification, and it is unfortunately true to say that our knowledge of all but a handful of deaf sign languages (such as ASL) is so poor that it is not at present possible to undertake such a task. This is clearly an area that merits further investigation.

3 Writing Systems

PETER T. DANIELS

Chapters on writing systems are very rare in surveys of linguistics – Trager (1974) and Mountford (1990) are the only ones that come to mind. For a century or so – since the realization that unwritten languages are as legitimate a field of study, and perhaps a more important one, than the world's handful of literary languages – writing systems were (rightly) seen as secondary to phonological systems and (wrongly) set aside as unworthy of study or at best irrelevant to spoken language. The one exception was I. J. Gelb's attempt (1952, reissued with additions and corrections 1963) to create a theory of writing informed by the linguistics of his time. Gelb said that what he wrote was meant to be the first word, not the last word, on the subject, but no successors appeared until after his death in 1985.[1] Although there have been few linguistic explorations of writing, a number of encyclopedic compilations have appeared, concerned largely with the historical development and diffusion of writing,[2] though various popularizations, both new and old, tend to be less than accurate (Daniels 2000). Daniels and Bright (1996; *The World's Writing Systems*: hereafter *WWS*) includes theoretical and historical materials but is primarily descriptive, providing for most contemporary and some earlier scripts information (not previously gathered together) on how they represent (the sounds of) the languages they record.

This chapter begins with a historical-descriptive survey of the world's writing systems, and elements of a theory of writing follow. Only one piece of theoretical machinery needs to be introduced in advance: the typology for categorizing the variety of scripts that have been used over the last five millennia or so. In the order they came into being, the six types of writing system are: *logosyllabary* (more precisely morphosyllabary), in which each character stands for a morpheme, and the characters can be used for the sound of the morpheme as well as for its meaning (in C. F. Hockett's formulation: "unit symbols represent syllables but with homophones distinguished" [1997: 381]) – there can be no purely logographic script; *syllabary*, in which each character stands for a syllable; *abjad* (the Semitic-type script), in which each character stands for a consonant; *alphabet* (the Greek-type script), in which each character stands for a consonant or a vowel; *abugida* (the Sanskrit-type script), in which each character stands for a consonant accompanied by a particular vowel, usually /a/, and the other vowels (or no vowel) are indicated by consistent additions to the consonant symbols; and *featural* script (the Korean type), in which the shapes of characters correlate with phonetic features of the segments they designate.

Writing was independently invented at least three times, in West Asia, in East Asia, and in Central America. Details and references for the information summarized below can generally be found in *WWS*.[3]

1   Writing and History

1.1   *Old world logosyllabaries and their relatives*

The first known writing system was Mesopotamian cuneiform. The first language to be written was Sumerian. The first writing surface-cum-material was clay, and the first writing implement was a reed stylus of triangular cross section: a scribe would shape a suitably sized patty of clay and smooth its surfaces, then touch a corner of the stylus to the surface, leaving shallow wedge-shaped impressions (hence the name, from Latin *cuneus* 'wedge'). From one to a dozen or so wedges make up a single cuneiform sign. A limited repertoire of wedge orientations combine in a limited range of patterns that recur in the individual "signs" (but there is no connection between the patterns and the sounds or meanings represented by the signs: see figure 3.1).

The first recognizable documents come from about 3200 BCE from the city of Uruk, and the script remained in use, recognizably the same, down to at least the third century CE (Geller 1997). Each Sumerian sign (and there were something over a thousand of them) originally stood for a Sumerian word, and was a picture of the object named by the word. (It took a very short time – measured in decades – for the recognizable pictures, which were hard to draw with a stylus on clay, to turn into the patterns of wedges.) Signs for objects could also be used for related verbs: a leg could represent "walk," for instance.

ᐃ	*xi*	"mix"	cf. ᐦ	*ša*	
ᐃ᛭	*'a*		cf. ᛭	*an*	"god"
᛭ᐃ	*mud*	"fear"	cf. ᛭	*ig*	"doorleaf"
᛭ᐃ᛬	*kun*	"tail"			
ᐃ᛫	*kam*	(number determinative)	cf. ᛫	*be*	"if"
᛬ᐃ	*gil*	"entangle"	cf. ᛬	*za*	

Figure 3.1   Parts of cuneiform signs do not reflect their sound or meaning

But also, since Sumerian words were mostly just one syllable long (consonant-or vowel-initial, open or closed), the signs that stood for those syllables could also be used for other similar words for items that could not be easily pictured; one of the earliest examples is the sign for *ti* "arrow" also being used for *ti* "life." (Such reuse is called the *rebus principle*.) As soon as signs came to be used in these transferred ways, they could also be used to record the wide variety of grammatical affixes of Sumerian. The reader could then know the writer's exact intent even when the content was not the stereotyped account-ing documents that were, as probably everywhere, the *raison d'être* of the writ-ing system in the first place – even if the writer was not present to explain the text – so that literary and religious compositions of various sorts were soon written down. (The number of such texts never came close to matching in quantity the mundane economic documents.) The vast majority of cuneiform documents record everyday transactions of the widest variety, and clay tablets are close to imperishable (if they have been baked, they are imperishable; if they have only been sun-dried, they can be damaged by water), so that Meso-potamian civilization emerges as the best documented until recent Europe.

The Sumerian language eventually went out of use, to be replaced by the Semitic language Akkadian, but Sumerian remained a language of liturgy and scholarship; and cuneiform writing was used for Akkadian. Akkadian cuneiform is more complicated than Sumerian, because any given sign could have sound value(s) based on its Akkadian meaning(s) as well as its Sumerian, and many syllables could be represented by several different signs, or could be spelled in different ways, and because the Akkadian sound system differs considerably from the Sumerian, and moreover signs could still be used for their mean-ings rather than their sounds without any indication of such use; in this lim-ited way, a logosyllabic writing system includes isolated instances of purely logographic writing. However, of the 600 or so signs in the Akkadian signlist, only about 200 would be used in any particular time period or area (a selection is shown in table 3.1; the Neo-Assyrian shapes are used in these illustrations). A device for clarifying the writing is the use of *determinatives*, signs (again taken from the normal repertoire) indicating the semantic sphere of the items they accompanied: personal names, wooden objects, cities, countries, plural nouns, etc.

Cuneiform was also used for many other languages of the ancient Near East, such as Elamite, Hurrian, and Urartian, and in these adaptations from Akkadian usage, the script was more syllabic than logographic. An exception is seen in Hittite, which incorporates both Sumerian and Akkadian spellings into texts that nonetheless were to be read in Hittite.

A language that was never written in cuneiform, because it had developed its own writing system, is ancient Egyptian. Rudimentary hieroglyphic writ-ing appears shortly after the beginnings of cuneiform, and it is speculated that the idea of writing somehow came from Sumer to Egypt; but from the very beginning there is no visual similarity and, more important, the sounds re-corded are not syllables, but consonants only. Egyptian hieroglyphs remained

Table 3.1 Inventory of basic cuneiform signs used in the pronunciation column of Syllabary A, the signlist studied by Mesopotamian scribal students[a]

	-a	-e	-i	-u	a-	e-	i-	u-
p b	⟨sign⟩ ⟨sign⟩	⟨sign⟩ 	 ⟨sign⟩	⟨sign⟩ 	⟨sign⟩ 	⟨sign⟩ 	 	⟨sign⟩
t d ṭ	⟨sign⟩ ⟨sign⟩ 	⟨sign⟩ 	⟨sign⟩ ⟨sign⟩	⟨sign⟩ ⟨sign⟩	 ⟨sign⟩	 ⟨sign⟩	 	 ⟨sign⟩
k g q	⟨sign⟩ ⟨sign⟩	⟨sign⟩ ⟨sign⟩	⟨sign⟩ ⟨sign⟩ ⟨sign⟩		 ⟨sign⟩		 ⟨sign⟩	 ⟨sign⟩
s z ṣ	⟨sign⟩ ⟨sign⟩ ⟨sign⟩	⟨sign⟩ ⟨sign⟩ ⟨sign⟩	⟨sign⟩ ⟨sign⟩ ⟨sign⟩	 ⟨sign⟩			 ⟨sign⟩	
š	⟨sign⟩ ⟨sign⟩	⟨sign⟩	⟨sign⟩	⟨sign⟩ ⟨sign⟩	⟨sign⟩	⟨sign⟩	⟨sign⟩	⟨sign⟩
m n	⟨sign⟩ ⟨sign⟩	⟨sign⟩ 	⟨sign⟩ ⟨sign⟩	⟨sign⟩ ⟨sign⟩	⟨sign⟩ ⟨sign⟩	 ⟨sign⟩	⟨sign⟩ ⟨sign⟩	⟨sign⟩ ⟨sign⟩
l r	⟨sign⟩ ⟨sign⟩	⟨sign⟩ ⟨sign⟩	⟨sign⟩ ⟨sign⟩	⟨sign⟩ ⟨sign⟩	⟨sign⟩ ⟨sign⟩ ⟨sign⟩	⟨sign⟩ 	⟨sign⟩ ⟨sign⟩	⟨sign⟩ ⟨sign⟩
w y	 ⟨sign⟩							
x ʾ	⟨sign⟩ ⟨sign⟩	⟨sign⟩	⟨sign⟩	⟨sign⟩			⟨sign⟩	
Ø	⟨sign⟩ ⟨sign⟩	⟨sign⟩	⟨sign⟩	⟨sign⟩ ⟨sign⟩				

[a] The following CVC signs are also used: *dim* ⟨sign⟩, *dím* ⟨sign⟩, *gír* ⟨sign⟩, *xar* ⟨sign⟩, *kal* ⟨sign⟩, *kil* ⟨sign⟩, *kin* ⟨sign⟩, *kul* ⟨sign⟩, *lag* ⟨sign⟩, *lam* ⟨sign⟩, *rig* ⟨sign⟩, *suk* ⟨sign⟩, *tan* ⟨sign⟩, *tin* ⟨sign⟩ (from WWS: 57).

recognizable pictures over the 3,500 years they were in use; but from quite early on, a cursive interpretation of them, known as hieratic, was used on papyrus. (*Cursive*: written with speed, character forms affected by the connection of strokes written separately in *formal* or *monumental* styles.) The demotic script emerged considerably later, in connection with a later form of the Egyptian language; there is a one-to-one relationship of hieratic and hieroglyphic signs, but demotic cannot be automatically transposed into the other two scripts.

Egyptian hieroglyphic signs represent one, two, or three consonants (table 3.2). (The monoconsonantal signs were never used as a discrete subsystem for writing Egyptian, so charts of an "Egyptian alphabet" are misleading.) Many signs also function logographically only. Determinatives are used much more

Table 3.2 All the phonetic Egyptian hieroglyphs beginning with labials

b		mḥ		p		wbn	
bꜣ		mỉ		pꜣ		wḏ	
bꜣs		mỉ		pds		wḥm	
bḥ		mn		pḥ		wn	
bỉꜣ		mnw		pr		wn	
bỉꜣ		mr		w		wp	
bỉt		mr		wꜣ		wr	
f		ms		wꜣḏ		wsr	
m		msn		wꜣḥ		wsx	
mꜣ		mt		wꜣs		wsx	
mꜣꜥ		mt		wꜥ		wšm	
mḏḥ		mw		wꜥr			

systematically than in cuneiform, as are *phonetic complements* – signs that give clues to the relevant reading of a logogram. (They are also found in cuneiform.)

Egyptian influence is assumed, but cannot be demonstrated, in the initial development of the writing systems that have spread to all the world except (until recently) East Asia. This development is first certainly seen in the handful of so-called "Proto-Canaanite" inscriptions from the second quarter of the second millennium BCE in the Levant. In the fourteenth century, a 27-letter abjad (with three supplemental letters) clearly standing in the main line of development is well attested at ancient Ugarit (it is written in wedges with a stylus on clay but has no other relation to Mesopotamian cuneiform). This large inventory continued to be used for inscriptions in the South Arabian languages and was taken across to Africa by Sabean colonists who passed it on to the Aksumite kingdom in present-day Ethiopia and Eritrea (by the fourth century CE).

By 1000 BCE or so, a 22-letter script similar to the Hebrew abjad was in wide use (the scattered examples that have been found vary sufficiently to suggest some lengthy period of separate developments; Naveh 1987). Over the next few centuries, indirect methods of indicating vowels developed in Aramaic and Hebrew (but not Phoenician) scribal traditions – to oversimplify, diphthongs (whose glide portions were written with the corresponding consonant letters) contracted into long vowels of related colors, and the consonant letters came to be used for other long vowels as well (*matres lectionis*: "mothers of reading" in Latin), albeit not obligatorily until well into the Common Era, and then only in Mandaic and Arabic. The Aramaic group of scripts tended to cursive developments, one of them surviving in Syriac (Estrangelo and Serto are the principal variants). Another is Nabatean, used by an Arab tribe to write Aramaic and from which a distinctive script for the Arabic language emerged (table 3.3). The Arabic language preserved the full panoply of Proto-Semitic

Table 3.3 West Semitic abjads[a]

Value[b]	Ugaritic	Sabean[c]	Phoenician	Hebrew	Mandaic	Estrangelo	Serto	Arabic	
ʾ (ʾa)								a	ا
b								b	ب
g								t	ت
(ḫ)								t	ث
d								j	ج
h {-î}								ḥ	ح
w								x	خ
z								d	د
ḥ {h}								d	ذ
ṭ								r	ر
y								z	ز
k								s	س
(š)								š	ش
l								ṣ	ص
m								ḍ	ض
(δ)								ṭ	ط
n								ẓ	ظ
ẓ								ʿ	ع
s								ġ	غ
ʿ								f	ف
p								q	ق
ṣ								k	ك
q								l	ل
r								m	م
ś								n	ن
š (θ)								h	ه
(γ)								w	و
t								y	ي
(ʾi)								lâ	لا
(ʾu)									
(ṡ)									
(ḍ)									
{dî}									

[a] Where two forms are shown, that on the right occurs at the end of a word.
[b] (Ugaritic and Sabean values); {Mandaic values}.
[c] Cf. table 3.11 for the ancient order of the Sabean abjad.

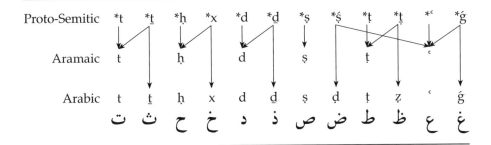

Figure 3.2 Sources of Arabic dotted letters

consonants, and the script includes diacritic dots to distinguish both letters whose shapes merged during its Nabatean prehistory and letters for sounds that had merged in Aramaic but not in Arabic (figure 3.2).

Two script traditions that ultimately left no issue are found at opposite ends of the ancient Near East (table 3.4). Several (logo)syllabic writing systems are found around the Aegean Sea – "Hittite" hieroglyphs (fifteenth to eighth centuries BCE) in western Anatolia, Linear B (sixteenth to thirteenth centuries BCE) in Crete, and Cypriote syllabary (eighth to third centuries BCE) in Cyprus (as well as some presumed antecedents of the latter two, including the still enigmatic Linear A) – for Luvian and two stages of Greek respectively. They are basically pictographic like Egyptian, but they record syllables, not consonants only, and representatives of earlier stages have not been found, so their origin is mysterious. To the east in Iran, a cuneiform script was devised for recording Old Persian (500 BCE). Some of its characters represent syllables, others consonants (probably combining features of the cuneiform and Aramaic scripts that were simultaneously in use in the Persian Empire), but oddly despite its wedge components, it was not used on clay.

A contemporary development in East Asia was the invention of writing for Chinese. While the earliest attested inscriptions (late Shang dynasty, ca. 1200 BCE) are "oracle bone" communications with the gods, most likely writing began there for the same mundane commercial reasons as elsewhere, but only perishable materials were used. The principles of writing Chinese have not changed over more than 3,000 years, though the esthetics and the shapes of the characters certainly have. Earliest written Chinese, like Sumerian, used primarily monosyllabic morphemes, but the combination of phonetic and semantic information was made explicit and obligatory in most "characters" so that the vast majority of characters comprise two parts (table 3.5), and there are considerably more characters in the repertoire. While the biggest dictionaries list upwards of 60,000, an inventory of 5,000 or so characters is adequate for most needs.

Chinese writing was tried for both Korean and Japanese, with unsatisfactory results in both cases. Japanese developed a pair of syllabaries (*kana*) from a selected group of characters that had been in use for their syllabic value.

Table 3.4   The Linear B,[a] Cypriote, and Old Persian[b] syllabaries

	LB	Cp	OP		LB	Cp		LB	Cp	OP		LB	Cp		LB	Cp	OP
a				e			i				o			u			
ba							bi							bu			
ča							či							ču			
ça							çi							çu			
da				de			di				do			du			
fa							fi							fu			
ga										?	gu						
ha							hi							hu			
ja				je			ji				jo			ju			?
ka				ke			ki			?	ko			ku			
la				le			li				lo			lu			
ma				me			mi				mo			mu			
na				ne			ni				no			nu			
pa				pe			pi				po			pu			
qa				qe			qi				qo						
ra				re			ri				ro			ru			
sa				se			si				so			su			
ša							ši							šu			
ta				te			ti				to			tu			
θa							θi							θu			
va							vi										?
wa				we			wi				wo						
xa				xe			xi				xo			xu			
ya							yi							yu			
za				ze			zi				zo			zu			

[a] An additional 16 characters represent variant sounds, and 11 more occur so rarely that they have not been identified. There are also a considerable number of ideograms, identifying commodities, which are not used as logograms in Mycenean Greek prose.

[b] Only the boxed Old Persian characters unambiguously identify the vowel of the syllable; a vowel character is required elsewhere (all -*a* signs used alone stand either for the bare consonant or for the consonant followed by short *a*).

Table 3.5 The construction of Chinese characters (after Gabelentz 1881: 50–1 and DeFrancis 1989: 107; compiled with the assistance of John DeFrancis)

Semantic	Phonetic			
	工 *gōng*	兼 *jiān*	堯 *yáo*	番 *fān*
人 "person"	仜 *hōng* "paunch"	傔 *qiàn* "servant"	僥 *jiǎo* "lucky"	僠 *bō* (a name)
手 "hand"	扛 *káng* "bear"	搛 *jiān* "drum"	撓 *náo* "scratch"	播 *bō* "strew"
水 "water"	江 *jiāng* "stream"	濂 *lián* (a river)	澆 *jiāo* "sprinkle"	潘 *pān* "ricewater"
系 "silk"	紅 *hóng* "red"	縑 *jiān* "silk cloth"	繞 *rào* "roll up"	繙 *fān* "translate"

Table 3.6 Japanese syllabaries[a]

Hiragana						Katakana				
	-a	-i	-u	-e	-o	-a	-i	-u	-e	-o
Ø	あ	い	う	え	お	ア	イ	ウ	エ	オ
k-	か	き	く	け	こ	カ	キ	ク	ケ	コ
g-	が	ぎ	ぐ	げ	ご	ガ	ギ	グ	ゲ	ゴ
s-	さ	し	す	せ	そ	サ	シ	ス	セ	ソ
z-	ざ	じ	ず	ぜ	ぞ	ザ	ジ	ズ	ゼ	ゾ
t-	た	ち	つ	て	と	タ	チ	ツ	テ	ト
d-	だ	ぢ	づ	で	ど	ダ	ヂ	ヅ	デ	ド
n-	な	に	ぬ	ね	の	ナ	ニ	ヌ	ネ	ノ
h-	は	ひ	ふ	へ	ほ	ハ	ヒ	フ	ヘ	ホ
b-	ば	び	ぶ	べ	ぼ	バ	ビ	ブ	ベ	ボ
p-	ぱ	ぴ	ぷ	ぺ	ぽ	パ	ピ	プ	ペ	ポ
m-	ま	み	む	め	も	マ	ミ	ム	メ	モ
y-	や	–	ゆ	–	よ	ヤ	–	ユ	–	ヨ
r-	ら	り	る	れ	ろ	ラ	リ	ル	レ	ロ
w-	わ	–	–	–	を	ワ	–	–	–	ヲ

[a] The syllabic nasal (hi. ん, ka. ン) comes at the end of the list.
Vowel length is indicated in kana by doubling, or more often with a following dash: ああ or あー is *aa*. Geminate consonants are written in kana with a preceding subscript hi. つ, ka. ツ *tu*; thus hi. あっか, ka. アッカ *akka*.

Hiragana are used for writing grammatical morphemes attached to Chinese characters (*kanji*) that are used for content words, and *katakana* are used for foreign words (table 3.6). Korean struggled with characters longer than Japanese and came up with a unique script described below.

Table 3.7   Brahmi-derived scripts of South and Southeast Asia[a]

	Kharoshthi	Brahmi	Devanagari	Gujarati	Gurmukhi	Bengali	Oriya	Sinhala	Kannada
a	𐨀	𑀅	अ	અ	ਅ	অ	ଅ	අ	ಅ
ā		𑀆	आ	આ	ਆ	আ	ଆ	ආ	ಆ
i	𐨁	𑀇	इ	ઇ	ਇ	ই	ଇ	ඉ	ಇ
ī		𑀈	ई	ઈ	ਈ	ঈ	ଈ	ඊ	ಈ
u	𐨂	𑀉	उ	ઉ	ਉ	উ	ଉ	උ	ಉ
ū		𑀊	ऊ	ઊ	ਊ	ঊ	ଊ	ඌ	ಊ
ṛ			ऋ	ઋ		ঋ	ଋ	ඍ	ಋ
ṝ			ॠ					ඎ	ೠ
e	𐨀	𑀏	ए	એ	ਏ	এ	ଏ	එ	ಎ
ē								ඒ	ಏ
ai		𑀐	ऐ	ઐ	ਐ	ঐ	ଐ	ඓ	ಐ
o	𐨆	𑀑	ओ	ઓ	ਓ	ও	ଓ	ඔ	ಒ
ō								ඕ	ಓ
au			औ	ઔ	ਔ	ঔ	ଔ	ඖ	ಔ
k	𐨐	𑀓	क	ક	ਕ	ক	କ	ක	ಕ
kh	𐨑	𑀔	ख	ખ	ਖ	খ	ଖ	ඛ	ಖ
g	𐨒	𑀕	ग	ગ	ਗ	গ	ଗ	ග	ಗ
gh	𐨓	𑀖	घ	ઘ	ਘ	ঘ	ଘ	ඝ	ಘ
ṅ		𑀗	ङ	ઙ	ਙ	ঙ	ଙ	ඞ	ಙ
c	𐨕	𑀘	च	ચ	ਚ	চ	ଚ	ච	ಚ
ch	𐨖	𑀙	छ	છ	ਛ	ছ	ଛ	ඡ	ಛ
j	𐨗	𑀚	ज	જ	ਜ	জ	ଜ	ජ	ಜ
jh	𐨘	𑀛	झ	ઝ	ਝ	ঝ	ଝ	ඣ	ಝ
ñ	𐨙	𑀜	ञ	ઞ	ਞ	ঞ	ଞ	ඤ	ಞ
ṭ	𐨚	𑀝	ट	ટ	ਟ	ট	ଟ	ට	ಟ
ṭh	𐨛	𑀞	ठ	ઠ	ਠ	ঠ	ଠ	ඨ	ಠ
ḍ	𐨜	𑀟	ड	ડ	ਡ	ড	ଡ	ඩ	ಡ
ḍh	𐨝	𑀠	ढ	ઢ	ਢ	ঢ	ଢ	ඪ	ಢ
ṇ	𐨞	𑀡	ण	ણ	ਣ	ণ	ଣ	ණ	ಣ
t	𐨟	𑀢	त	ત	ਤ	ত	ତ	ත	ತ
th	𐨠	𑀣	थ	થ	ਥ	থ	ଥ	ථ	ಥ
d	𐨡	𑀤	द	દ	ਦ	দ	ଦ	ද	ದ
dh	𐨢	𑀥	ध	ધ	ਧ	ধ	ଧ	ධ	ಧ
n	𐨣	𑀦	न	ન	ਨ	ন	ନ	න	ನ
p	𐨤	𑀧	प	પ	ਪ	প	ପ	ප	ಪ
ph	𐨥	𑀨	फ	ફ	ਫ	ফ	ଫ	ඵ	ಫ
b	𐨦	𑀩	ब	બ	ਬ	ব	ବ	බ	ಬ
bh	𐨧	𑀪	भ	ભ	ਭ	ভ	ଭ	භ	ಭ
m	𐨨	𑀫	म	મ	ਮ	ম	ମ	ම	ಮ
y	𐨩	𑀬	य	ય	ਯ	য	ଯ	ය	ಯ
r	𐨪	𑀭	र	ર	ਰ	র	ର	ර	ರ
l	𐨫	𑀮	ल	લ	ਲ	ল	ଲ	ල	ಲ
v	𐨬	𑀯	व	વ	ਵ	ব	ଵ	ව	ವ
ś	𐨭	𑀰	श	શ		শ	ଶ	ශ	ಶ
ṣ	𐨮	𑀱	ष	ષ		ষ	ଷ	ෂ	ಷ
s	𐨯	𑀲	स	સ	ਸ	স	ସ	ස	ಸ
h	𐨱	𑀳	ह	હ	ਹ	হ	ହ	හ	ಹ
ḷ			ळ	ળ				ළ	ಳ

Table 3.7 cont'd

	Telugu	Malayalam	Tamil	Tibetan	Burmese	Thai	Lao	Khmer	Javanese
a	అ	അ	அ		အ	อ	ອ	អ	ꦄ
ā	ఆ	ആ	ஆ		အာ	อ		អា	
i	ఇ	ഇ	இ					ឥ	ꦆ
ī	ఈ	ഈ	ஈ					ឦ	
u	ఉ	ഉ	உ					ឧ	ꦈ
ū	ఊ	ഊ	ஊ					ឩ	
ṛ	ౠ	ഋ							
ṝ	ౠ								
e	ఎ	എ	எ		ဧ				ꦌ
ē	ఏ	ഏ	ஏ					ឯ	
ai	ఐ	ഐ	ஐ					ឰ	
o	ఒ	ഒ	ஒ		ဩ			ឱ	ꦎ
ō	ఓ	ഓ	ஓ		ဪ				
au	ఔ	ഔ	ஔ						
k	క	ക	க		က	ก	ກ	ក	ꦏ
kh	ఖ	ഖ			ခ	ข ฃ	ຂ	ខ	
g	గ	ഗ			ဂ	ค ฅ	ຄ	គ	ꦒ
gh	ఘ	ഘ			ဃ	ฆ		ឃ	
ṅ		ങ	ங		င	ง	ງ	ង	ꦔ
c	చ	ച	ச		စ	จ	จ	ច	ꦕ
ch	ఛ	ഛ			ဆ	ฉ	(ຊ)	ឆ	
j	జ	ജ	ஜ		ဇ	ช ฌ	ຊ	ជ	ꦗ
jh	ఝ	ഝ			ဈ	ฌ		ឈ	ꦙ
ñ	ఞ	ഞ	ஞ		ည	ญ	ຍ	ញ	ꦚ
ṭ	ట	ട	ட		ဋ	ฏ ฎ		ដ	ꦛ
ṭh	ఠ	ഠ			ဌ	ฐ		ឋ	
ḍ	డ	ഡ			ဍ	ฑ		ឌ	ꦝ
ḍh	ఢ	ഢ			ဎ	ฒ		ឍ	
ṇ	ణ	ണ	ண		ဏ	ณ		ណ	ꦟ
t	త	ത	த		တ	ต	ຕ	ត	ꦠ
th	థ	ഥ			ထ	ถ	ຖ	ថ	
d	ద	ദ			ဒ	ท	ທ	ទ	ꦢ
dh	ధ	ധ			ဓ	ธ		ធ	
n	న	ന	ந		န	น	ນ	ន	ꦤ
p	ప	പ	ப		ပ	บ ป	ບ ປ	ប	ꦥ
ph	ఫ	ഫ			ဖ	ผ ฝ	ຜ ຝ	ផ	
b	బ	ബ			ဗ	พ ฟ	ພ ຟ	ព	ꦧ
bh	భ	ഭ			ဘ	ภ		ភ	
m	మ	മ	ம		မ	ม	ມ	ម	ꦩ
y	య	യ	ய		ယ	ย	ຍ	យ	ꦪ
r	ర	ര	ர		ရ	ร	ຣ ຮ	រ	ꦫ
l	ల	ല	ல		လ	ล	ລ	ល	ꦭ
v	వ	വ	வ		ဝ	ว	ວ	វ	ꦮ
ś	శ	ശ				ศ			
ṣ	ష	ഷ	ஷ			ษ			
s	స	സ	ஸ		သ	ส	ສ	ស	ꦱ
h	హ	ഹ	ஹ		ဟ	ห	ຫ	ហ	ꦲ
ḷ	ళ	ള	ள			ฬ		ឡ	ꦊ

[a] Some letters in only one or a few scripts, e.g. the Sinhala prenasalized series, are omitted. Phonetic values of letters may not be exact, especially in later (rightward in table) scripts.

1.2   From abjad to alphabet and abugida

Abjads seem well suited to Semitic languages, which are supposed to involve consonantal "roots" and vowel "patterns" (though this analysis is increasingly recognized as an artefact of the Arabic writing system as it was available to the Arab grammarians who devised it), but are less appropriate to Indo-European languages where vocalization is more unpredictable than in Semitic. Two different schemes for the obligatory recording of vowels emerged. The first, seen with the first attempts to write Greek with the Phoenician abjad, probably around 800 BCE, seems accidental and inevitable: Semitic has a larger repertoire of consonants than Greek, and (phonemic perception being what it is), the letters representing sounds, especially laryngeals, not found in Greek would be heard as indicating the succeeding vowels. Thus Phoenician ‹ʾ› was taken to represent /a/, ‹h› for /e/, ‹y› for /i/, ‹ʿ› for /o/, and ‹w› for /u/. And so the alphabet was born. The correspondences are seen in both the shapes of the letters and their positions in the respective alphabetical orders. Greek settlements used slightly varying inventories of letters; the most significant for the history of writing was in Italy, where the alphabet was passed on to the Etruscans and other local peoples, and in turn from the Etruscans to the Romans.

The second Indo-European adaptation of the Semitic abjad occurred in India (table 3.7), probably no earlier than the third century BCE (Falk 1993). Here the method was not separate letters for vowels, but appendages – left, right, above, or below – to the consonant letters to designate the vowels (short other than *a*, and long) and diphthongs of the Indic and Dravidian languages, using the type I call abugida (table 3.8). The first language written with the Kharoṣṭhi and Brahmi scripts was Prakrit (a colloquial variety that developed later than the Sanskrit "literary" language); it was several centuries before it became licit to write down the sacred Sanskrit texts that had been preserved orally for hundreds of years. Limited communication between the sundry regions and polities of India, as well as differences in writing materials, led to considerable diversity in appearance of the script, and Sanskrit texts as well as local languages would be written in each locality's distinctive hand, but the abugidic principle remained uniform. A consonant-final word had a mark to indicate that the final letter was pronounced vowelless, and immediately adjacent consonants (whether in the same syllable or not) were written by combining reduced forms of the consonant letters into a single symbol (figure 3.3). Today, ten standardized scripts serve the Indian subcontinent's literary Indo-Aryan and Dravidian languages.

The Indic style of writing was carried by Buddhist missionaries throughout Southeast Asia, where essentially the same principle remains at work in such diverse-looking scripts as the Thai and Lao, Burmese, Khmer (Cambodian), and Javanese, as well as a host of less standardized ones. The missionaries also brought writing to Tibet late in the first millennium CE (apparently from southern India, though the lineage of the Tibetan script is not entirely clear).

Table 3.8 Vowel indications in some scripts of South and Southeast Asia

		a	*ā*	*i*	*ī*	*u*	*ū*	*e*	*ai*	*o*	*au*
Brahmi	k	𑀓	𑀓𑀸	𑀓𑀺	𑀓𑀻	𑀓𑀼	𑀓𑀽	𑀓𑁂	𑀓𑁃	𑀓𑁄	𑀓𑁅
	g	𑀕	𑀕𑀸	𑀕𑀺	𑀕𑀻	𑀕𑀼	𑀕𑀽	𑀕𑁂	𑀕𑁃	𑀕𑁄	𑀕𑁅
Devanagari	k	क	का	कि	की	कु	कू	के	कै	को	कौ
	g	ग	गा	गि	गी	गु	गू	गे	गै	गो	गौ
Oriya	k	କ	କା	କି	କୀ	କୁ	କୂ	କେ	କୈ	କୋ	କୌ
	g	ଗ	ଗା	ଗି	ଗୀ	ଗୁ	ଗୂ	ଗେ	ଗୈ	ଗୋ	ଗୌ
Javanese	k	ꦏ		ꦏꦶ		ꦏꦸ		ꦏꦺ		ꦏꦺꦴ	
	g	ꦒ		ꦒꦶ		ꦒꦸ		ꦒꦺ		ꦒꦺꦴ	

Here, though, consonant clusters were not notated by combining symbols into a single character regardless of syllable division. Rather, the end of every syllable is marked with a dot, so that syllable-final consonants are kept separate from syllable-initial consonants, while vowels are still indicated by additions for *e, i, o* (above), and *u* (below).

Missionaries had been active in Europe as well. The Roman alphabet accompanied the Roman church with its Latin liturgy throughout western Europe, but in the Eastern church, where the liturgy was conducted in local languages, separate scripts were devised for a number of languages (table 3.9) – among them Coptic, Gothic, Armenian, and Georgian (fourth century), and, for Old Church Slavonic, Glagolitic and Cyrillic (ninth century). Coptic and Gothic are adaptations of the Greek alphabet; as is seen by the inherited letter order, the next two are inspired by it, though the shapes of the letters seem to be independent creations; the last two appear to be based on cursive and formal Greek writing respectively. All these alphabets except Gothic require considerably more letters than the Greek (Coptic's additions are taken from demotic Egyptian script). Northern and northwestern Europe saw local developments of runes

Brahmi	Devanagari	
𑀔 *kha* + 𑀬 *ya* = 𑀔𑁆𑀬 *khya*	क *ka* + ल *la* = क्ल *kla*	क *ka* + ष *ṣa* = क्ष *kṣa*
𑀧 *pa* + 𑀢 *ta* = 𑀧𑁆𑀢 *pta*	ह *ha* + न *na* = ह्न *hna*	क्ष *kṣa* + म *ma* = क्ष्म *kṣma*
Oriya	**Javanese**	
ଘ *gha* + ନ *na* = ଘ୍ନ *ghna*	ꦤ *na* + ꦭ *la* = ꦤ꧀ꦭ *nla*	ꦭ *la* + ꦲ *ha* = ꦭ꧀ꦲ *lha*
ସ *sa* + ଥ *tha* = ସ୍ଥ *stha*	ꦚ *ña* + ꦧ *ba* = ꦚ꧀ꦧ *ñba*	ꦢ *da* + ꦤ *na* = ꦢ꧀ꦤ *dna*
ଦ *da* + ଧ *dha* = ଦ୍ଧ *ddha*	ꦧ *ba* + ꦚ *ña* = ꦧ꧀ꦚ *bña*	

Figure 3.3 Some consonant clusters in South and Southeast Asian scripts

Table 3.9   Alphabets derived from Greek

(In the Armenian, Georgian and Glagolitic columns the transliteration value is given; the native letter-forms appear alongside in the original. The Coptic, Gothic and Old Cyrillic columns show letter-forms.)

Greek	Coptic	Gothic	Armenian	Georgian	Glagolitic	Old Cyrillic	Russian
Α α	ⲁ	𐌰	a	a	a	А	А а
Β β	ⲃ	𐌱	b	b	b	Б	Б б
Γ γ	ⲅ	𐌲	g	g	v	В	В в
Δ δ	ⲇ	𐌳	d	d	g	Г	Г г
Ε ε	ⲉ	𐌴	e	e	d	Д	Д д
Ϝ (6)		𐌵	z	v	e	Є	Е е
Ζ ζ	ⲍ	𐌶	ē	z	ž	Ж	Ж ж
Η η	ⲏ	𐌷	ə	ey	dz	Ѕ	З з
Θ θ	ⲑ	𐌸	t′	t	z	З	И и
Ι ι	ⲓ	𐌹	ž	i	i	И	Й й
Κ κ	ⲕ	𐌺	i	k	i	ï / I	
Λ λ	ⲗ	𐌻	l	l	ǵ	ħ	К к
Μ μ	ⲙ	𐌼	x	m	k	К	Л л
Ν ν	ⲛ	𐌽	c	n	l	Л	М м
Ξ ξ	ⲝ	𐌾	k	y	m	М	Н н
Ο ο	ⲟ	𐌿	h	o	n	Н	О о
Π π	ⲡ	𐍀	j	ṗ	o	О	П п
Ϙ (90)		𐍁	ł	ž	p	П	Р р
Ρ ρ	ⲣ	𐍂	č	r	r	Р	С с
Σ σ ς	ⲥ	𐍃	m	s	s	С	Т т
Τ τ	ⲧ	𐍄	y	ṭ	t	Т	У у
Υ υ	ⲩ	𐍅	n	wi	u	оу / 8	Ф ф
Φ φ	ⲫ	𐍆	š	u	f	ф	Х х
Χ χ	ⲭ	𐍇	o	p	x	х	Ц ц
Ψ ψ	ⲯ	𐍈	č′	k	o	ω / ꙍ	Ч ч
Ω ω	ⲱ	𐍉	p	ğ	c	Ц	Ш ш
ϡ (900)		𐍊	ǰ	q	č	Ч	Щ щ
	š ϣ		ṙ	š	š	Ш	Ъ ъ
	f ϥ		s	č	št	Щ	Ы ы
	h ϩ		v	c	″ / ъ	Ъ	Ь ь
	j ϫ		t	j	y	ы / ъи	Э э
	q ϭ		r	ç	′ / ь	Ь	Ю ю
	ti ϯ		c′	č	ě	Ѣ	Я я
			w	x	ju	Ю	
			p′	q	ja	Ꙗ	
			k′	ǰ	je	Ѥ	
			u	h	ę	Ѧ	
			ō	ow	ję	Ѩ	
			f		ǫ	Ѫ	
					jǫ	Ѭ	
					ks	Ѯ	
					ps	Ѱ	
					f	Ѳ	
					i / v	Ѵ	

a ‹Obsolete letters, no longer used in Georgian›.

Table 3.10 Runs, Ogham

		Runes				*Ogham*	
f	ᚠ	*fehu	"wealth"	b	ᚁ	Beithe	"birch"
u	ᚢ	*ūruz	"aurochs"	l	ᚂ	Luis	"blaze"
þ	ᚦ	*þurisaz	"giant"	f	ᚃ	Fern	"alder"
a	ᚨ	*ansuz	"god"	s	ᚄ	Sail	"willow"
r	ᚱ	*raiþō	"riding"	n	ᚅ	Nin	"fork"
		*kaunaz	"ulcer"	h	ᚆ	(h)Úath	"fear"(?)
k	< {	*kēnaz	"torch"	d	ᚇ	Dair	"oak"
		*kanō	"skiff"	t	ᚈ	Tinne	"metal rod"
g	ᚷ	*gebō	"gift"	c	ᚉ	Coll	"hazel"
w	ᚹ	*wunjō	"joy"	q	ᚊ	Queirt	"bush"
h	ᚺ	*hagalaz	"hail"	m	ᚋ	Muin	"neck"
n	ᚾ	*nauþiz	"need"	g	ᚌ	Gort	"field"
i	ᛁ	*isa-	"ice"	ng	ᚍ	(n)Gétal	"wounding"(?)
j	ᛃ	*jēra-	"year"	z	ᚎ	Straif	"sulfur"
ï	ᛇ	*eihwaz	"yew tree"	r	ᚏ	Ruis	"red(ness)"
p	ᛈ	*perþ-	?	a	ᚐ	Ailm	?
z	ᛉ	*algiz	"sedge" (?)	o	ᚑ	Onn	"ash-tree"
s	ᛋ	*sōwulō	"sun"	u	ᚒ	Úr	"earth"
t	ᛏ	*teiwaz	god Tyr	e	ᚓ	Edad	?
b	ᛒ	*berkana-	"birch twig"	i	ᚔ	Idad	?
e	ᛖ	*ehwaz	"horse"	ea	ᚕ	Ébad	?
m	ᛗ	*mannaz	"man"	oi	ᚖ	Ór	"gold"
l	ᛚ	*laguz	"water"	ui	ᚗ	Uilen	"elbow"
ng	ᛜ	*inguz	god Ing	ia	ᚘ	Pín	"pine"
d	ᛞ	*đagaz	"day"	ae	ᚙ	Emancholl	"double c"
o	ᛟ	*ōþila	"inherited land"				

for Germanic languages (first to ninth centuries) and Ogham for Irish (fifth to seventh centuries); both reveal the influence of the Latin alphabet (table 3.10).

Meanwhile, the Semitic scripts could not go forever with no means of explicitly indicating vowels. The first one to innovate such a device was the Ethiopic (table 3.11), which became an abugida suddenly at the same time as the country adopted Christianity (ca. 350); apparently some knowledge of Indic writing was involved, though the shapes of the vowel indicators are not similar in the two systems, and the basic consonants do not retain their shapes so rigorously as in India. Perhaps the ancient Christian communities of western India supplied personnel for the trading voyages that regularly crossed the Arabian Sea with the monsoons, and the idea, though not the details, of Indic writing went with them.

Table 3.11   The Ethiopic abugida (ancient Sabean order for comparison)

Value	-ä	-u	-i	-a	-e	-ə	-o	Sabean	
h	ሀ	ሁ	ሂ	ሃ	ሄ	ህ	ሆ	h	𐩠
l	ለ	ሉ	ሊ	ላ	ሌ	ል	ሎ	l	𐩡
ḥ	ሐ	ሑ	ሒ	ሓ	ሔ	ሕ	ሖ	ḥ	𐩢
m	መ	ሙ	ሚ	ማ	ሜ	ም	ሞ	m	𐩣
š	ሠ	ሡ	ሢ	ሣ	ሤ	ሥ	ሦ	q	𐩤
r	ረ	ሩ	ሪ	ራ	ሬ	ር	ሮ	w	𐩥
s	ሰ	ሱ	ሲ	ሳ	ሴ	ስ	ሶ	s²	𐩦
q	ቀ	ቁ	ቂ	ቃ	ቄ	ቅ	ቆ	r	𐩧
qʷ	ቈ		ቊ	ቋ	ቌ	ቍ		b	𐩨
b	በ	ቡ	ቢ	ባ	ቤ	ብ	ቦ	t	𐩩
t	ተ	ቱ	ቲ	ታ	ቴ	ት	ቶ	s¹	𐩪
x	ኀ	ኁ	ኂ	ኃ	ኄ	ኅ	ኆ	k	𐩫
xʷ	ኈ		ኊ	ኋ	ኌ	ኍ		n	𐩬
n	ነ	ኑ	ኒ	ና	ኔ	ን	ኖ	x	𐩭
ʾ	አ	ኡ	ኢ	ኣ	ኤ	እ	ኦ	ṣ	𐩮
k	ከ	ኩ	ኪ	ካ	ኬ	ክ	ኮ	s³	𐩯
kʷ	ኰ		ኲ	ኳ	ኴ	ኵ		f	𐩰
w	ወ	ዉ	ዊ	ዋ	ዌ	ው	ዎ	ʾ	𐩱
ʿ	ዐ	ዑ	ዒ	ዓ	ዔ	ዕ	ዖ	ʿ	𐩲
z	ዘ	ዙ	ዚ	ዛ	ዜ	ዝ	ዞ	ḍ	𐩳
y	የ	ዩ	ዪ	ያ	ዬ	ይ	ዮ	g	𐩴
d	ደ	ዱ	ዲ	ዳ	ዴ	ድ	ዶ	d	𐩵
g	ገ	ጉ	ጊ	ጋ	ጌ	ግ	ጎ	γ	𐩶
gʷ	ጐ		ጒ	ጓ	ጔ	ጕ		ṭ	𐩷
ṭ	ጠ	ጡ	ጢ	ጣ	ጤ	ጥ	ጦ	z	𐩸
ṗ	ጰ	ጱ	ጲ	ጳ	ጴ	ጵ	ጶ	δ	𐩹
ṣ	ጸ	ጹ	ጺ	ጻ	ጼ	ጽ	ጾ	y	𐩺
ḍ	ፀ	ፁ	ፂ	ፃ	ፄ	ፅ	ፆ	θ	𐩻
f	ፈ	ፉ	ፊ	ፋ	ፌ	ፍ	ፎ	ẓ	𐩼
p	ፐ	ፑ	ፒ	ፓ	ፔ	ፕ	ፖ		

Syriac was the first Semitic script to add optional symbols with the effect of denoting vowels: at first they were a single dot that marked a "fuller" vowel above the consonant it followed and a weaker vowel below; these developed into, on the one hand, markers of grammatical categories, and on the other, markers of vowel quality. This system has survived to the present in Eastern Syriac. In the western area, the optional symbols were Greek vowel letters, written small, that could be placed above or below their consonants. In Hebrew, several scholarly circles devised different sets of marks for indicating vowel quality, prosodic and syntactic characteristics of the text, and liturgical

Table 3.12 West Semitic vowel signs (shown with the consonant *b*)

	Hebrew	Syriac (Eastern)	Syriac (Western)	Arabic
i	־ְב	־ ܒ	־ ܒ, ܒ	־ ܝ (־ -in)
e	־ְ ב	־ ܒ		
ɛ	־ֱ ב	־ ܒ	־ ܒ, ܒ	
a	־ַ ב	־ ܒ	־ ܒ, ܒ	־ ܝ (־ -an)
ɔ	־ָ ב	־ ܒ (ā)		׀ (ʾā)
o	־ֹ ב	ܘ- ܒܘ	־ ܒ, ܒ	
u	־ְ ב, ־וּ-בוּ	ܘ- ܒܘ	־ ܒ, ܒ	־ ܝ (־ -un)
Ø	־ְ ב			־ ܝ
ə	־ְ ב			
ě	־ֱ ב			
ă	־ֲ ב			
ŏ	־ֳ ב			

melodies (the Tiberian system is the only one still in use). Arabic marks the three short vowels and a number of morphophonemic phenomena (with, as mentioned, all long vowels obligatorily notated within the line of consonantal letters). In all three languages (table 3.12), a major impetus for adding vowel (and accentual and musical) notation ("pointing") outside the consonantal text was the preexisting text of Scripture, which needed to be preserved in full detail; an explanation for the complications of Arabic is that the pointing seems to have been added by speakers of a different dialect from that used by the scribes who recorded the consonantal text of the Qurʾān (Versteegh 1997: 56).

While vowel notations were being devised for the major Semitic literary languages, the same was not happening for the Iranian languages that gradually adopted Aramaic writing, specifically the Manichean script: among others, in the west Parthian and Pahlavi, in the east Sogdian. Rather than a brusque adaptation, as described for Greek and Prakrit, the Iranian scribes apparently continued to keep their records in Aramaic, but as knowledge of Aramaic deteriorated, Iranian forms crept in. Eventually a system developed whereby many words that were pronounced as Iranian continued to be written with the Aramaic spellings – but with grammatical affixes spelled in proper Iranian. In effect, Pahlavi and so on were written logoconsonantally (Skjærvø 1997). (Moreover, a number of letters merged in shape, making these texts very difficult to read letter by letter, so the logogram gestalts are better than Iranian spellings would be.)

When it came time, however, to preserve in writing the oral tradition of the Zoroastrian scripture, the Avesta (which was in danger of being lost because the language was no longer clearly understood – the texts were preserved

Table 3.13   Manichean, Parthian, Pahlavi, Avestan, Sogdian[a]

Manichean < Aramaic	Parthian Inscrips	Pahlavi Psalter	Book Pahlavi	Avestan	Source of Avestan[b]	Sogdian
ʾ	a, ā		a, ā	a	Phl.	a, ā
				h	Av. *a*	
				x	Av. *h*	
				ā	Phl. *ay*	
				å, ā̊	Av. *āə*	
				ą, ą̇	?	
b	b, w		b, w	b	Phl.	b, β
g	g, γ	g, y	g, y	g, ġ	Phl.?	g, γ
d	d, δ	d, y	d, y	d	Ps.	d, δ
				δ	?	
h (ẖ)				ə, ə̄	Gk. ε	a, Ø
w	w, ŏ, ŭ	= ʿ, r	w, ŏ, ŭ	u, u	Phl.	w, ŏ, ŭ
z	z, ž	z	z	z	Phl.	z
ḥ (h)	h, x		h, x	xᵛ	Phl. *ḥw*	γ, x, h
				x́	Av. *xᵛ*	
ṭ						
y	y, ĕ, ī	y	y, ĕ, ī, ǰ	i, ī	Phl.	y, ĕ, ī
				e, ē	Phl. *ēw*	
k	k, g	k, g	k, g	k	Phl.	k
				γ	Ps. k	
l (δ)	l	l	l, r	r	Phl.	δ
				o	Phl. (ʾ)l [ō]	
				ō	Phl. ʾl [ō]	
m	m	m	m	m, m̨	Phl.	m
n	n	n	n	n	Phl.	n
				ń	Av. *n*	
				ŋ, ŋ́,	?	
				ŋᵛ, ṇ		
s	s	s	s, h	s	Phl.	s
				θ	Phl. s	
ʿ	= r	= w, r	Ø			Ø
p	p, b	p	p, b, f	p, f	Phl.	p
				β	Av. *p*	
ṣ (c)	č		č, ǰ, z	j	Ps.	č, ǰ
				c	Av. *j*	
				ž	Phl. ʾc	
q						
r	r = ʿ	= w, ʿ	r			r
š	š, ž		š	š, ś,	Phl.	š
				ẏ, ṣ̌		
t	t, d		t, d	t	Phl.	t, θ
				ṭ	Av. *t*	
				ẏ, v	?	

[a] Iranian fonts courtesy of P. Oktor Skjærvø, Harvard University.
[b] According to Hoffmann 1988, summarizing Hoffmann and Narten 1989.

Table 3.14 Uyghur, Mongolian, Manchu (after Coulmas 1996: 526, 344, 322)

Uyghur		Mongolian		Manchu			
ʾ	1	a		a		s	
β		e		e		dz	
γ		i		i		ts	
w		o u ụ		o		š	
z		ö ü ụ̈		u		ž	
x		n		ū		t	
y		ng (ŋ)		ã		ḍ	
k		q		n		t	
d(δ)		ġ γ		k		d	
m		b		g		tš	
n		p		χ		tšh	
s		s		ḱ		dž	
p		š		ǵ		džh	
č		t d		χ́		l	
r		l		ḱh		r	
š		m		ǵh		m	
t		č		χh		y	
l		j		b		v	
ž		y ï		p		f	
-m		k g ǵ					
q̈		r					
		v					
		h					

purely as long stretches of sound), a new Avestan alphabet was devised (fifth to sixth centuries CE) that used the shapes of the earlier Aramaic-based Iranian consonant letters, added new ones built on them, and thanks to familiarity with Greek, included letters for many vowels (table 3.13).

With the spread of Inner Asian polities, Altaic languages came into contact with Iranian ones: Turkic Uyghur, Mongolic Mongolian, and Tungusic Manchu in turn adopted (but scarcely adapted) Iranian writing, specifically Sogdian (turning it vertical to conform to the Chinese esthetic). This old Mongolian script is being revived in newly democratic Mongolia (table 3.14).

The Mongolian emperor Kubla Khan (thirteenth century), recognizing the inadequacy of Mongolian script for the variety of languages used within his realm, commissioned the Tibetan monk hPags pa to create a script to be used for Mongolian, Tibetan, Chinese, etc. (in the event, it was used primarily for Mongolian), and the script that bears hPags pa's name is modeled closely on Tibetan as to shape (though severely squared up) but is written in columns; it retains the abugidic principle, but places all the non-*a* vowel indicators after (i.e. below) the consonant they follow, and gives up indication of syllable boundaries (table 3.15).

Acquaintance with the hPags-pa script and deep familiarity with the Chinese grammatical tradition, as has been demonstrated by careful philological investigation (Kim-Renaud 1997), underlie the Korean alphabet, promulgated by King Sejong in 1443. It goes beyond both of these, however, in recognizing the separate existence of syllable-final consonants (as Chinese theory did not), identifying them with the initials that had been recognized by Chinese grammarians. Consonants and vowels receive very differently shaped symbols: the basic consonant signs are explicitly iconic representations of the vocal tract involved in producing each, and the basic vowel signs relate to the fundamental principles "heaven," "earth," and "man." Korean is thus a featural script (Kim 1980 [1988], Sampson 1985); and the consonants and vowel of each syllable are written within a square space, in imitation of Chinese characters, so that it is featural, alphabetic, and syllabic all at once (figure 3.4). Three of the scripts of western Eurasia have been adapted to write many languages during the last millennium or so: Roman-based alphabets and Arabic-based alphabets and abjads tend to account for new sounds by adding diacritics to existing letters, while Cyrillic-based ones tend to add new lettershapes.

1.3 Logosyllabaries of the New World and syllabaries of the modern world

Outside the two great old world families of writing systems, the Semitic-derived and the Chinese-derived, which converge in Korean writing, two further phenomena must be mentioned. First, in Meso-America, a large number of inscriptions are known, in upwards of a dozen different forms of writing or proto-writing. The interrelations of these systems are still being puzzled out, but the best understood one, the Maya hieroglyphs (perfected by the ninth century CE), has proven to be a logosyllabic script quite similar in structure to Sumerian (table 3.16).

Table 3.15 Tibetan, hPags pa, Korean

	Ti	hPp	Ko		Ti	hPp	Ko		Ti	hPp	Ko		Ti	hPp	Ko
k				kh				g				ñ			
				q				γ							
c				ch				j				ñ			
t				th				d				n			
p				ph				b				m			
ts				tsh				dz							
('a)				ž				z				l			
w				y				r							
u̯				i̯											
f				š				s				ss			
h				(a)											
i				u				e				o			
ey												wu			
ay												a			

Second, there are upwards of a dozen cases of scripts independently devised in modern times – invented by people who could not read or write in any language, but simply were aware of the existence of writing (usually that of Christian or Muslim missionaries). Earliest and most familiar is the Cherokee syllabary, devised in the 1820s by Sequoyah (table 3.17A). Over the next century or so, a number of syllabaries were invented in Africa, as well as some in North and South America and in Oceania.

This rapid survey of the world's writing systems closes with mention of scientifically created scripts, informed by phonetic science. Noteworthy is the Cree script of the Methodist missionary James Evans of the early 1840s (it and adaptations are used for several languages of Canada); it is featural-cum-abugida (table 3.17B). The two prominent shorthand systems, Pitman (1837) and Gregg (1888), are featural. So are some scripts devised by phoneticians for close recording of speech, but none of them remained in use; the International Phonetic Alphabet and similar systems used by various language specialists are in effect greatly extended alphabets, with featural diacritics available for additional subtlety (Pullum and Ladusaw 1996).

바 *pa* "rope"   밤 *pam* "night"
소 *so* "cow"   손 *so* "hand"
읽다 *ilkta* "read"   밟다 *palpta* "tread on"

Figure 3.4 Korean syllable formation

Table 3.16   The Maya syllabary (Coulmas 1996: 332–3)

	a	e	i	o	u
b					
ch					
ch'					
h					
c					
k					
l					
m					
n					
p					
s					
t					
tz					
dz					
u					
x					
y					

Table 3.17 The Cherokee and Cree syllabaries

A. Cherokee

-a				-e			-i			-o		-u		-v = [ə]	
a	D			e	R		i	T		o	Ꮈ	u	Ꮕ	v	i
ga	S	ka	Ꮷ	ge	Ᏻ		gi	y		go	A	gu	J	gv	Ᏼ
ha	Ᏺ			he	Ᏸ		hi	Ꮀ		ho	Ᏺ	hu	Ꭲ	hv	Ꮣ
la	W			le	Ꮣ		li	P		lo	G	lu	M	lv	Ꮧ
ma	Ꮉ			me	Ꮿ		mi	H		mo	Ꮂ	mu	y		
na	Ꮎ	hna	Ꮀ	nah G	ne	Ꮓ		ni	h		no	Z	nu	Ꮕ	nv	Ꮩ
qua	Ꮖ			que	Ꮖ		qui	Ꮙ		quo	Ꮢ	quu	Ꮗ	quv	Ɛ
s	Ꮘ	sa	Ꮪ	se	Ꮞ		si	b		so	Ꮢ	su	Ꮺ	sv	R
da	Ꮣ	ta	W	de	Ꮪ	te Ꮧ	di	Ꮪ	ti Ꮧ	do	V	du	S	dv	Ꮣ
dla	Ꮬ	tla	Ꮎ	tle	L		tli	C		tlo	Ꮣ	tlu	Ꮣ	tlv	P
tsa	G			tse	Ꮲ		tsi	Ꮯ		tso	K	tsu	Ꮬ	tsv	Ꮳ
wa	Ꮤ			we	Ꮻ		wi	Ꮝ		wo	Ꮼ	wu	Ꮽ	wv	Ꮾ
ya	Ꮿ			ye	Ᏼ		yi	Ꮿ		yo	Ꮶ	yu	Ꮹ	yv	Ᏼ

B. Cree[a]

-ê		-i		-o		-a		Final C	
ê	▽	i	△	o	▷	a	◁	-h	"
pê	∨	pi	∧	po	>	pa	<	-p	'
tê	∪	ti	∩	to	⊃	ta	⊂	-t	´
kê	ᑫ	ki	ᑭ	ko	ᑯ	ka	ᑲ	-k	`
cê	ᒉ	ci	ᒋ	co	ᒍ	ca	ᒐ	-c	‾
mê	ᒣ	mi	ᒥ	mo	ᒧ	ma	ᒪ	-m	ᑉ
nê	ᓀ	ni	ᓂ	no	ᓄ	na	ᓇ	-n	ᐣ
sê	ᓭ	si	ᓯ	so	ᓱ	sa	ᓴ	-s	^
šê	ᔐ	ši	ᔑ	šo	ᔓ	ša	ᔕ	-š	ˇ
yê	ᔦ	yi	ᔨ	yo	ᔪ	ya	ᔭ	-y	°/⁺
wê	·▽	wi	·△	wo	·▷	wa	·◁	-w	o
rê	ᕒ	ri	ᕆ	ro	?	ra	ᕒ	-r	ᙆ
lê	ᕓ	li	ᕄ	lo	ᓬ	la	ᓬ	-l	ᙆ

[a] A dot above the syllable (except for the *-ê* series) marks a long vowel.

2 Writing and Language

The theoretical aspects of writing systems presented here are grounded in a fundamental observation: writing is not like language, and it is not like language for biological reasons. The human language faculty evolved over some many generations, so that no human infant can avoid learning the language of the environment. No child, however, can learn to read or write simply by watching other people read or write: explicit instruction is required. For writing is so recent (anthropologically speaking) that no special capacity for it can have evolved – especially since literate populations have not reproduced in preference to nonliterate ones!

From this observation it follows that writing need not be structured or described in the same way as language, and in fact some language-derived analytical tools are not so well suited to writing. The linguistic terms phoneme, morpheme, and so on refer to an unconscious property of language (and other realms of human behavior). Each item in a class of "-eme"-designated things is an abstraction, its identity defined by its contrasts with all the other items in that class, and comprising a group of instantiations of the thing. Thus the English phoneme /t/ includes the conditioned allophones [tʰ] (in most circumstances), [t] (after /s/), and ['] (sometimes for some speakers); the English morpheme {past} includes the conditioned allomorphs /t/, /d/, and /ɪd/. Every language includes a fairly small inventory of phonemes, and every morpheme is realized with phonemes; every stretch of speech is made up entirely of morphemes, which are made up entirely of phonemes. Here the unconscious-ness is important: since writing is not an unconscious, built-in feature of a mind (as language is), it cannot a priori be assumed to be analyzable in a parallel way. Rather, all writing systems were at some point consciously devised (and, not infrequently, are deliberately modified). The phonemic organization of various phenomena was recognized only a century or so ago, so it is not surprising that the designed writing of language differs in several ways from the evolved speaking of language.

First, writing systems, unlike languages, do not all operate the same. Different writing systems relate to the sound systems they record in fundamentally different ways (in at least the six types identified above). These concern both the amount of speech each symbol represents, and the level of analysis the symbols embody.

Second, despite American structuralist attempts to approach writing as a subsystem of language, writing systems do not work like linguistic systems; there is no "emic" level, and the popular term *grapheme* is misleading. For instance, many alphabets use a pairing of symbols – capitals and lowercase, majuscule and minuscule – that has no equivalent in sound systems. Arguments can be made on both sides of the question as to whether ‹A› and ‹a› are members of the same grapheme (*allographs*). But more basically, no coherent definition of grapheme can be agreed on. Is it (like a phoneme) one of the set of elements comprising a writing system? (Then ‹A› and ‹a› might both be graphemes . . . but how is their relationship to be captured?) Is it (like a tagmeme) a correlation of sound and symbol? (Then ‹ea›, ‹ee›, and ‹e–e› might all be graphemes of English . . . but is ‹ough› then several different graphemes?) Is it (like a morpheme) a minimal extent of something? (Then the Mesopotamian cuneiform signs in figure 3.1 might all contain the same grapheme . . . though there is no phonetic or semantic similarity among these signs, and the recurring pattern by itself is *xi*.) The difficulty is that all these characterizations are reasonable for different writing systems, but no one characterization fits everything one might be tempted to call a grapheme. The upshot is that *grapheme* has become nothing more than a pretheoretic, fancy, scientific-sounding word for "letter" or "character" and ought not to be part of technical discourse. ("Allograph," however, remains useful for conditioned variants of lettershapes, as in the final variants in Greek and Hebrew, or the conjoined consonants in Indic scripts.)

Third, language is constantly changing, while writing generally obeys tradition and does not readily respond to changes. Simplification in some areas of language is accompanied by complication in other areas, as a language's overall "efficiency" tends to remain constant; but a script's efficiency – its "goodness of fit" to its language – is maximal when it is devised, and deteriorates thereafter.

Fourth, writing systems can be altered by fiat. Kemal Atatürk could not have ordered the minority peoples of Turkey to stop speaking their languages and use only Turkish, but he could decree that the Turkish language would be written with a Roman alphabet rather than an Arabic one beginning on November 3, 1928. Noah Webster could not successfully tell Americans to not split infinitives, say, but he could successfully recommend dropping the ‹u› from words like ‹colour›.

(Fifth, and in the wider picture probably most important, written language differs in significant ways from spoken language; the way most directly related to the physical existence of writing is the evanescence of speech versus the protracted availability of writing. Questions of literacy and society, of literacy and the individual are beyond the scope of this chapter [see Street and Besnier 1994].)

Writing systems, then, must be investigated on their own terms. Their changes in appearance over the centuries – their "outer form" – have attracted the most study and are well documented (see note 2), but most interesting to this author are questions of the origin of writing and the relation of the graphic shapes of script to the phonological shapes of language – their "inner form" (Coulmas 1996: 234).[4]

My approach to the origin of writing arose from dissatisfaction with the received view that there are three types of writing system – logography, syllabary, alphabet – and that the history of writing systems shows that all development has proceeded in that order and can only do so, with alphabets as the last and "best" type. This view is most closely associated with I. J. Gelb, and in order to make it work, he had to claim that what underlay the Greek alphabet was a syllabary. But since the Phoenician script does not explicitly denote syllables, Gelb had to claim that the characters of the Phoenician and other Northwest Semitic scripts in fact recorded syllables – but syllables with indeterminate vowel. As regards the Indic and Ethiopic scripts, which denote syllables but derive from alphabets, he simply threw up his hands (1963: 188).[5]

Two problems are immediately obvious. It is counterintuitive to call Northwest Semitic scripts syllabaries; and anyway, from only one example of the innovation of an alphabet, a general principle can hardly be drawn.

The solution is to recognize that the old tripartite typology is inadequate, and to replace it with the sexpartite one used above. Once abugidas are distinguished from syllabaries,[6] a different historical sequence can be identified, which no longer privileges the alphabet teleologically. Furthermore, this dichotomy also proves useful regarding the modern creation of scripts: scripts invented by persons who cannot read are syllabaries (not abugidas, not abjads, or alphabets). It can also be seen that it is not really the alphabet that represents the great intellectual achievement in linguistic analysis, but the abjad.

2.1   *Origin of writing*

The key to the history of writing is the primacy of the syllable. Psycholinguists find that people not literate in an alphabetic script are unable to manipulate portions of the speech stream at the level of the segment (Daniels 1988);[7] phonologists increasingly work with levels of analysis other than that of the segment or individual sound (but none seems to have broken entirely with the C's and V's of alphabet-based analysis). The inventions by untutored writing-inventors record syllables. Many nonliterate peoples keep graphic records that perhaps operate on the level of the word. These records do not turn into writing, however (the "reader" cannot determine exactly what sentences the delineator had in mind). Why did the pictographs used in Sumer, China, and Meso-America turn into writing systems? My view is that it is because the Sumerian, Chinese, and ancient Mayan languages were largely monosyllabic (meaning that most morphemes are just one syllable long). Thus each pictograph representing a word also represented a single syllable. It was thus easy, via the rebus principle, to record other similar-sounding words, words that did not lend themselves to pictography since they did not denote simple objects – as in the Sumerian example *ti* "arrow" for *ti* "life." Grammatical morphemes too were soon included in the script stream, and writing was accomplished.

Writing is thus defined as *a system of more or less permanent marks used to represent an utterance in such a way that the utterance can be recovered more or less exactly without the intervention of the utterer.* Implicit in this definition is the insistence that all writing is phonologically based, as stressed by John DeFrancis (1989); excluded are what Gelb calls "forerunners of writing" (DeFrancis shows that none of the "forerunners" actually "foreran" writing) and what Sampson calls "semasiographic systems." In Mesopotamia, what has been identified as an early accounting device, small clay objects ("tokens") that may have served as counters for commodities and were sometimes gathered inside a hollow ball of clay, sometimes after being impressed on the outside of the ball, might have prompted the notion of incising pictographs on lumps of clay and might underlie the shapes of early numerals in cuneiform (cf. Schmandt-Besserat

1992). The suggestion that the shapes of some tokens relate to early, abstract cuneiform signs is purely speculative, since there is no way to know what any particular token may have represented, nor whether there was any sort of uniformity in such representation across the vast extents of time and space from which they have been recovered.

Explanations for the fact that Egyptian hieroglyphics record only consonants are embryonic. But since Egyptian writing never become purely phonetic – logographs and determinatives remained fully in use to the very end of the tradition – we must turn to the abjad for the second great advance in writing, the first that can truly be called an invention. Evidence exists that Mesopotamian scholars recognized an affinity between signs for syllables beginning with the same consonant, and affinity between signs for syllables ending with the same consonant; but there is no evidence that affinity between (what we recognize as) the same consonants at the beginnings and ends of syllables was recognized. (In the Chinese grammatical tradition, syllables were identified according to their initial [consonant] and everything else [vowel + tone + final consonant].) So the greatest stroke of genius in the history of writing was the recognition that syllable-beginnings could be identified with syllable-endings, and the resulting unities could be represented by a single symbol wherever in a word they occurred. These symbols are the consonant letters. And, of course, many fewer consonant letters than syllable signs are needed for just about any language.

2.2   Script direction

I suspect, too, that the stroke of genius came from a left-handed individual. Most people are right-handed; most writing runs left-to-right ("dextrograde") or top-to-bottom. These are convenient directions for avoiding smeared ink (or clay) and for clear sight of the line of writing. But the direction of the earliest Northwest Semitic writing (and also the normal direction for Egyptian writing) is right-to-left ("sinistrograde"). This choice makes sense if it was initially made by a left-hander – a left-hander of great prestige, as would certainly befit the inventor of a writing system so much easier to learn than a syllabary or, especially, a logosyllabary (or logoconsonantary). Script direction proves to be a very tenacious attribute of a writing system: so long as the tradition remains unbroken, the direction does not change. Only with a "brusque" transition is an alteration found: this happened with the transfer to Greece: the earliest Greek inscriptions are boustrophedon (running in opposite directions in alternate lines), then the left-to-right order prevails. The transfer to Etruscan must have been early and "gentle," since the direction remained sinistrograde, but the Latin adaptation was less so, since early boustrophedon soon gave way to dextrograde.

Script direction depended on external factors. The Iranian languages all remained "gently" sinistrograde. Syriac scribes, however, would avoid the mechanical problems in such a script by rotating the page 90° counterclockwise and writing downward and left to right, turning the page back for reading in the traditional direction. (This accounts for the skewed orientation of the Greek-letter vocalizations.) Perhaps this practice was maintained for Sogdian and along with the dominant Chinese culture accounts for the columnar (and left-to-right) writing of the Uyghur, Mongolian, and Manchu traditions. hPags-pa, too, doubtless imitates this tradition. But another local script derived from Tibetan, the Lepcha of Sikkim, was written in columns from right to left – as if Tibetan was rotated clockwise to attain columns in imitation of Chinese.

2.3   Script transmission

Many "gentle" steps brought Aramaic script via Iranian and Altaic languages far to the east in Asia, as described above. But it is the "brusque" transfers that lead to the development of new script types. The accidental alphabet of (Indo-European) Greek has been mentioned. But at the other end of the ancient Near East, the Persian Empire impinged on the Indian world. The Persians brought the Aramaic abjad with them; and some bilingual inscriptions, in Aramaic and (Indo-European) Prakrit, were erected in the northern borderlands. But the Prakrit is not simply written in a variant of Aramaic script; as with Greek, vowel notation was added: not, though, with letters inserted among the consonants, but in abugida style. What lay behind this innovation? The rich grammatical tradition associated with the name of Pāṇini was already well developed by the time writing appeared in India, and it fully understood syllables, vowels, and consonants.

Tibet, too, supported a grammatical tradition. The Tibetan language is typologically quite different from the inflecting Semitic and Indo-European languages met so far: it is isolating, so it could be advantageous for a Tibetan script not to merge adjacent morpheme-final and -initial consonants as was done in the Indic scripts (see figure 3.3). Thus the syllable boundary marker was devised, while the basic abugidic principle of inherent basic vowel plus appendages for other vowels continued in use. Significantly, neither Iranian nor Mongolian culture supported a grammatical tradition, and the hPags-pa script gives up the Tibetan innovation; the morphological type differs yet again, and perhaps explicit syllable boundaries are less important for an agglutinative language like Mongolian. Lastly, as already mentioned, the Korean grammatical tradition played an important part in the design of the most sophisticated script yet devised. Every script reflects some degree of "native speaker analysis" (O'Connor 1983); the lesson of the Asian sequences of transmission is that real innovation in script transfer must be informed by grammatical understanding of the language that is to be written – metalinguistic knowledge of one's language: the result of deep study, not simple copying.

Ꭱ	Ꭰ	Ꮃ	Ꮵ	Ꮐ	Ꮽ	Ꮺ	Ꮅ	Ꮑ	Ꮌ	Ꭹ	Ᏹ	Ꮟ	Ꮲ	Ꭳ	Ꮇ	Ꮄ	Ꭽ
e	a	la	tsi	nah	wu	we	li	ne	mo	gi	yi	si	tlv	o	lu	le	ha
Ꮼ	Ꮰ	Ꮤ	Ᏼ	Ꮈ	Ꭿ	Ꮝ	Ᏺ	Ꮁ	Ꭺ	Ꮷ	Ꮍ	Ꮞ	Ꮠ	Ꮯ	Ꮘ	Ꮗ	Ꮜ
wo	tlo	ta	yv	lv	hi	s	yo	hu	go	tsu	mu	se	so	tli	qui	que	sa
Ꮖ	Ꮓ	Ꭷ	Ꮸ	Ꮢ	Ꮒ	Ꭶ	Ꮩ	Ꭸ	Ꮣ	Ꭼ	Ꮻ	Ꭲ	Ꭴ	Ᏸ	Ꮂ	Ꮫ	Ꭻ
qua	no	ka	tsv	sv	ni	ga	do	ge	da	gv	wi	i	u	ye	hv	dv	gu
Ꮶ	Ꮙ	Ꮔ	Ꮎ	Ꮆ	Ᏻ	Ꮴ	Ꮧ	Ꮾ	Ꮪ	Ꮥ	Ꮳ	Ꭵ	Ꮕ	Ꮦ	Ꮉ	Ꮡ	Ꮱ
tso	quo	nu	na	lo	yu	tse	di	wv	du	de	tsa	v	nv	te	ma	su	tlu
Ꭾ	Ꮀ	Ꮋ	Ꮭ	Ꮿ	Ꮹ	Ꮨ	Ꮮ	Ꮏ	Ꮚ	Ꮬ	Ꮊ	Ꮛ					
he	ho	mi	tla	ya	wa	ti	tle	na	quu	dla	me	quv					

Figure 3.5 Sequoyah's syllabary order (read left to right)

2.4 *Letter order*

A property possessed by many writing systems with a limited inventory of signs is a canonical order in which the signs are learned and which becomes an organizing principle for lists of words and for other things as well. Such orders may be arbitrary or motivated; and virtually the only motivated sign-order is phonetic.[8] The Indic scripts, following the native grammatical tradition, placed the vowels (in two groups) before the occlusives (back to front of mouth; within each place of articulation voiceless, voiced, and nasal; for each stop unaspirated and aspirated), which are followed by the continuants (see table 3.7). Modern syllabaries (including current usage for Japanese) are usually presented in a consonant versus vowel grid, with the consonants in some phonetically justified order (see table 3.6) – though the order for Cherokee used in textbooks follows the order of the corresponding consonants in English (see table 3.17A). Some of the syllabaries devised in recent centuries in fact have no standard order; others, including Cherokee, seem to be presented in nothing but the order in which the symbols were devised by the creator (figure 3.5).

This is the best we can say for the familiar order *a*, *b*, *c*, . . . as well. Despite centuries of conjecture – involving lettershape, phonetics, the names of the letters, and doubtless other considerations – no convincing account has ever been suggested. This order is found in the earliest abecedaries, from the fourteenth century BCE – and any speculation must take into account that five letters were dropped from the original 27 (seen in Ugaritic) to give the Hebrew-Aramaic sequence (see table 3.3). This sequence is modified in Arabic to bring together the letters that share a common basic shape and are distinguished only by dotting. Less familiar is the order recently discovered to have been used for the ancient South Arabian letters (and still more recently found at Ugarit), to which the standard Ethiopic order is similar (see table 3.11). The (North) Semitic order is also known in Ethiopia – since the Hebrew letter names appear as headings to the 22 parts of Psalm 119 (118) in the Septuagint[9] – where, labeled *abugidā*, it serves some liturgical functions. Similarly, when the ancestral order is referred to in Arabic, it is called *abjad^(un)*. (The vocalization of the Ethiopic word reflects the standard order for presenting the seven notated vowels.)

The ancestral Semitic order remains familiar to modern Arabic-speakers because of the "organizing principle" property mentioned above. The sequence of letters, being fixed, could label any sequence of things. This is equivalent to a sequence of ordinal numerals – and even after dedicated characters for numerals (as opposed to tallies: 1 stroke for 1, 2 strokes for 2, etc.) were introduced (first in India in the first half of the first millennium CE, then to the Islamic world around 800, including zero, thence to Europe around 1000), letters have continued to be used as numerals in limited contexts in Greek, Greek-derived, and Semitic scripts. Arabic's letters have been reordered with the additional ones inserted by shape within the inherited sequence, but the inherited numerical values are not altered; the new letters represent the values 500–1000.

Several alphabets have retained letters unneeded for any phonetic value because of already associated numerical values (such as Greek Digamma = 6). This phenomenon and the consistency of correlation of each nonad of letters with an order of numbers (Hebrew Alep–Ṭet = 1–9, Yod–Ṣade = 10–90, Qop–Taw = 100–400) leads Gamkrelidze (1994) to see this as a guiding principle in the creation of the Greek-based Eastern Christian alphabets, which do suspiciously contain multiples of nine letters. If this principle had been in operation from the beginning, however, one would expect five empty-letter numerals in Hebrew-Aramaic script, preserving the earlier total of 27.

Letters added to an abjad or alphabet are usually ordered at the end, as with the Greek "supplementals" after Tau, which corresponds to Taw, the last letter of the parent abjad – and, in fact, as with the last three Ugaritic letters. Sometimes letters are inserted according to graphic similarity (as in Arabic) and sometimes phonetic (as in Cyrillic). Armenian represents an exception, where the framework of the Greek order is discernible but no principle can be found for the placement of the additions.

2.5   *Letter names*

For letters to be learned in an order, they need to have names (table 3.18). Names of letters either are words in the language they record (Northwest Semitic), or they refer in arbitrary patterns to their sound (Greek; Latin). It is not clear which came first – what may be the earliest list of letter names

Table 3.18 Letter names (see also table 3.10)

Ugaritic?	Hebrew	Greek	Arabic	Ethiopic	Armenian	Old Slavic
a	ʾáleph	alpha	ʾalif	älf	ayb	azъ
be	bēth	bēta	bāʾ	bet	ben	buky
ga	gímel	gamma	ǰīm	gäml	gim	vědi/vědě
xa					da	glagoli
di	dáleth	delta	dāl	dänt	eč'	dobro
u	hē	e psilon	hāʾ	hoi	za	jestь/estъ
wa/i/u	wāw	u psilon	wāw	wäwe	ē	živěte
zi	záyin	zēta	zāy	zäi	ət'	(d)zělo
ku	ḥēth	ēta	ḥāʾ	ḥaut	t'o	zemlja
ṭi	ṭēth	thēta	ṭāʾ	ṭäit	žē	i, ižei
?	yōdh	iota	yāʾ	yämän	ini	iže
?	kāph	kappa	kāf	kaf	liwn	dervь
?	lámedh	la(m)bda	lām	läwə	xē	kako
?	mēm	mu	mīm	mai	ca	ljudije
?	nūn	nu	nūn	nähas	ken	myslite
?	sámekh	sigma	sīn	sat	ho	našь
?	ʿáyin	o micron	ʿayn	ʿäin	ja	onъ
pu	pē	pi	fāʾ	äf	łat	pokoj
ṣa	ṣādhē		ṣād	ṣädäi	čē	rьci
qu	qōph	(qoppa)	qāf	qaf	men	slovo
ra	rēš	rhō	rāʾ	rəʾəs	yi	tvrdo
śa	śīn/šīn	(san)	šīn	šäut	nu	ukъ/ikъ
xa					ša	frtь
tu	tāw	tau	tāʾ	täwə	o	cherь
			θāʾ		č'a	otъ
			xāʾ	xärm	pē	ci
			δāl		ǰē	črvь
			ḍād	ḍäppa	ṙa	ša
			ẓāʾ		sē	štja
			γayn		vew	jerь
				ṗäit	tiwn	jery
				psa	rē	jerь
i					c'o	ětь/jatь
u					hiwn	ju
zu					p'iwṙ	ja
					k'ē	(je)
					u	jusъ malyj
					fē	jusъ malyj jotirovannyj
						jusъ bolьšij
						jusъ bolьšij jotirovannyj
						ksi
						psi
						(thita)/fita
						ižica
						azъ

(incompletely preserved) gives a single syllabic Mesopotamian cuneiform sign opposite each Ugaritic letter. Many of these correspond to the beginnings of the names known much later for Hebrew and Aramaic, but some do not; and it is not easy to imagine why a scribe would not have recorded the letters' full names if they had existed. Most of the Hebrew/Aramaic names are words in Northwest Semitic, a few are not, and their earliest attestation is the aforementioned Septuagint passage. Interpretations of the "Proto-Sinaitic" inscriptions as Semitic based on reading their pictograms according to the initial letters of words for the objects depicted – the *acrophonic principle* – are thus unreliable. Some of the Ethiopic letter names, including the one that licensed the interpretation of the Proto-Sinaitic snake as *n*, are words only in Hebrew, not in Ethiopic, suggesting that the names (not used in Ethiopia) were first assigned by European scholars in the fifteenth or sixteenth century when Classical Ethiopic came to their notice.

The Greek letter names are meaningless in Greek: they are simply borrowed from the Semitic source; apparently the earliest complete list, though, is from ca. 200 CE (Athenaeus 453d), purportedly but dubiously reproducing a fifth-century BCE text. Some of the Arabic names preserve reminiscences of the earlier forms, but the Latin names, which prevail in Europe, are simply phonetic (including CV for stops, VC for continuants), as are those in Georgian and modern Russian, and in the Indic tradition. Words, chosen acrophonically, are used for letter names in Runes, Ogham, Armenian, and Old Slavic.

2.6 Writing materials

The shapes of characters can be influenced by the materials on which and with which they are written. We have already seen how cuneiform wedges result from the use of a stylus on clay – where the surface was not conducive to curving lines. Runes are angular because they were scratched into wood; Ogham is straight lines because it was carved on the edges of blocks of stone; and many scripts of India and Southeast Asia are curved because they were incised with a stylus on leaves.

Pigmented liquid (ink, paint) is probably the most common writing medium around the world, applied to surfaces with brushes made from vegetal fibers or hairs, or pens cut from hollow reeds or feathers or forged in steel. The surfaces can be any convenient wall (whether natural as of a cave or cliff, or built), or more portably a clay pot or a potsherd (inscribed sherds are called *ostraca*). The earliest known flexible writing surface is papyrus, prepared from the split pith of a reed native to the Nile valley. Animal skins appear subsequently: leather, prepared by tanning, found from the first millennium BCE, and parchment, somewhat later, prepared by liming. A reusable medium was wooden boards hinged together, their inner surfaces coated with wax, on which Mesopotamian scribes impressed wedges and Greek and Roman scribes scratched letters with a stylus (few of these fragile items have survived, so we cannot be certain how long they were in use). Paper, which is made from macerated, compacted vegetal fibers, was invented in China early in the Common Era and came west with Muslim contact, eventually superseding the other candidates.

Printing from movable type was devised in East Asia – probably Korea – early in the Common Era, and (perhaps not independently) by Johannes Gutenberg in Mainz in the 1450s. Gutenberg's techniques merged the skills of the goldsmith (for casting type), the vintner (for the press), and the chemist (for the ink). Quick, identical reproductions of texts made possible both religious reformation and the development of science (Eisenstein 1979), but widespread literacy awaited mechanical printing and typesetting in the nineteenth century.

Individual mechanical aids for writers followed: typewriters, cheap pencils, fountain pens, ballpoint and fibertip pens. A feared post-literate society of broadcast media seems now to have been forestalled by the worldwide network of personal computers, on which international communication is again achieved in writing.

3   Writing and Scholarship

Writing is indispensable for civilization – but entirely irrelevant for language. Most of the thousands of human languages were never written until recent years, and their speakers were none the worse for it. Their cultures were full and rich, lacking only accountancy and science. Everything else that is written need not be: poetry, narrative, law, and their apotheosis, scripture, are all part of every oral culture. Only in a city is the community so large that letters must be sent to communicate personal messages – and only when records of commerce can be kept can a city *be*. Cities are where production does not link directly with consumption: farmers and ranchers provide food, artisans provide goods, builders provide shelter, and administrators coordinate their exchange. Without writing, there is no administration.[10]

But cities characterize only a handful of human societies, and the vast majority of human languages never had written forms of their own. The discovery that languages other than the classical ones were every bit as rich as Greek, Sanskrit, and Chinese – a discovery due largely to the investigation of Native American languages by scholars originally trained as Indo-European philologists, on the whole – led linguists to concentrate on unwritten languages and then to devalue the study of written records in favor of fieldwork. Recently a reaction (associated with the "Toronto school" of literacy studies) to this view has set in, which in its most extreme form claims that there was no true literacy before the Greek alphabet, even in the ancient Near East: that the alphabet itself is necessary for elevated linguistic expression. What this attitude reveals is little more than ignorance of both the literary record of non-alphabetic societies (which is generally known to the partisans only through translation) and of the poetic accomplishments of nonliterate societies (represented most familiarly, of course, in the supposed foundational work of western literacy, the Homeric epics).

With that *parti pris*, we may turn to the branches of scholarship that have studied writing systems.

3.1   Philology, epigraphy, and paleography

Philology is the study of texts in the broadest sense. The preliminary task of philologists includes recovering and establishing the documents themselves, determining the orthography, grammar, and lexicon of their language, and reconstructing their history and context. Then their real work begins: interpreting the texts and the entire culture that underlies them. Among the sub-disciplines of philology are *epigraphy*, *paleography*, and *diplomatics* (the study of documents).

A distinction is often made between writing incised on solid surfaces and writing applied with a tool to flexible surfaces. The former is the province of epigraphy, the latter of paleography. A goal of both fields is tracing minute variations in *ductus* – the complex of features characteristic of a single scribal community – from generation to generation, from atelier to atelier, which might enable the dating of a text that has no explicit indication of when and where it was written, such as a colophon. This has largely been pursued as a purely descriptive study, with little attention to the physical processes of writing – movements of hand and fingers that always want to expend less effort, in competition with the cognitive need to keep characters recognizably distinct. In this tension lies legibility.

The appearance of a script is also closely connected to the prevailing esthetic of its society, as is familiarly seen in the affinity of spiky German hands to the pointed arches of Gothic architecture, and of curvaceous Italian hands to the rounded arches of Romanesque. Worldwide, artistic approaches to writing, calligraphy, mirror the arts of the society, sometimes even becoming the dominant decorative art, as in much of the Islamic world.

The more routine task of epigraphers and paleographers is the compilation of corpora of inscriptions and texts: the raw materials from which philologists extract descriptions of cultures, and linguists extract descriptions of languages and language change. Often, the preparation of a corpus of unreadable texts (Linear A, Indus Valley script) is all that can be done until some genius can discover the hint that makes it possible to read them.[11]

3.2   Decipherment

Ancient and mysterious scripts captured the imagination of adventurers whenever they came upon them, but not until the middle of the eighteenth century did anyone succeed in reading one whose interpretation had been forgotten with the culture that created it. The script that received this honor was not a specially worthy one; it was the Palmyrene variety of the cursive Aramaic group found throughout the Near East at the beginning of the Common Era. The rulers of Palmyra would place inscriptions in both Greek and Palmyrene Aramaic on the monumental columns that lined the public spaces, and in 1756, accurate copies of several such pairs were published in London and Paris as engravings. Virtually overnight, the abbé Jean-Jacques Barthélemy was able to interpret the Palmyrene. His method exemplified many of the principles that have been used many times since: identify a bilingual text; locate proper names; compare known scripts; guess what language is represented; determine from the number of different characters the likely type of script. (In short order, Barthélemy also deciphered Phoenician and Imperial Aramaic.)

Prior to all the steps in the actual decipherment, however, and so obvious that it is often overlooked, is the necessity of accurate reproductions of inscriptions in the unknown script. For a century and a half, photography has been available, but many important decipherments were accomplished in the century before that. Before Barthélemy, there had been publications of Palmyrene inscriptions going all the way back to 1616, none of them amenable to decipherment (yet no one who had not visited the inscriptions *in situ* could know that)! Fortunately, for both the best-known decipherment and also for arguably the most important one, the publications available to the decipherers were of the highest quality.

The most familiar deciphered script, of course, is Egyptian hieroglyphs. Napoleon invaded Egypt with an army of scholars as well as an army of soldiers. Over several years, the scholars prepared painstaking representations of the wondrous antiquities of the Nile, including scores of inscriptions on both monuments and papyri. Among the inscriptions was a large slab found in 1799 (and forthwith seized as booty when the British gained an advantage, so that the Rosetta Stone has been housed in the British Museum since 1802) inscribed in Greek and in demotic and hieroglyphic Egyptian (the hieroglyphic portion largely broken away). It was immediately seen that this could be the key to interpreting the Egyptian inscriptions that had fascinated Europeans since Classical antiquity – but the key could not be turned so long as the mental machinery was mired in the millennial mirage that the hieroglyphs were "ideograms" or mystical, occult symbols. An English dilettante (or polymath), Thomas Young, identified corresponding passages in the Greek and demotic texts but neglected the incomplete hieroglyphic version.

Meanwhile Jean-François Champollion, a young man from Grenoble, had resolved to understand ancient Egypt, and he believed the clue lay in the Coptic language, still used in the liturgy of the Christians of Egypt. Around 1820 he noticed that the pharaonic name "Ptolemy" occurred several times in the Greek in positions corresponding to cartouches (oval frames containing signs) in the hieroglyphs, confirming a long-ago suggestion of Barthélemy's that they would enclose royal names; but since that was the only royal name preserved in the hieroglyphic, he could not try assigning the phonetic values he suspected the Egyptians would have used to write foreign names (here, Greek). Fortunately, the name of Cleopatra appeared on an obelisk that had been in England since 1813 (Champollion may have known it from Young's publication), and there is sufficient overlap in the names that he could pair signs with sounds. Other names in Greek and Latin gave him several other phonetic values.

Champollion's true breakthrough came when he noticed a cartouche containing an obvious "sun" logogram followed by an unknown sign and two *s*'s. "Sun" in Coptic is *rē*, and the decipherer, against all expectations, guessed that the name was Ramses – showing that Egyptian names, too, could be written phonetically. This gave him the courage to search for Coptic words in the Rosetta prose, and soon he could read Egyptian.

The most important decipherment recovered Mesopotamian cuneiform. The basic materials here came from a brief span of ancient history, the Persian Empire. From the late sixth to the mid-fourth centuries BCE, kings Darius, Xerxes, and their successors inscribed on the walls of their constructions, their monuments, and on a cliff at Behistun, propagandistic annals and dedications in three cuneiform scripts. The most prominent was the simplest, comprising a few dozen different characters, the other two considerably more complicated. The prominence suggested to a junior faculty member in Göttingen, Georg Friedrich Grotefend, that the simplest script represented the rulers' own language, Persian. On the basis of Antoine Isaac Sylvestre de Sacy's recent decipherment of some Sassanian inscriptions (representing an Iranian empire a few centuries later), he expected to find introductory expressions along the lines of "X, great king, son of Y, great king." The names of the Persian kings were known, in Greek guise, from the Classical historians. Sure enough, Grotefend found the repetitious pattern, plausibly interpretable as "Xerxes, great king, son of Darius, great king, son of Hystaspes" – who was not a king. His discovery was announced in 1802, and over the next several years, scholars were able to clarify the characteristics of Old Persian.

Note that the initial breakthrough did not involve a bilingual; it was achieved through the insight that names known elsewhere could be expected in the unknown text. Such a correspondence can be called a *virtual bilingual*. The names in the Persian trilinguals did provide the initial clue to the other two languages, but they were soon superseded by a wealth of inscriptional material that became available during the first decades of the nineteenth century. Edward Hincks, an Irish clergyman, applied himself first to the trilinguals (coming up with an initial list of values for the signs of the second script in 1846), and then turned to annalistic materials coming from Babylonia; he used Semitic grammatical patterning to locate signs involving constant root consonants and affixes. His most useful source, though, proved to be a massive annalistic inscription in yet a fourth language, Urartian, where repetitious formulae provided spelling variants permitting the identification of the vowels of many syllables. By 1852, Hincks had succeeded in reading the third script, the language now called Akkadian, and moreover had identified the first of thousands of fragments of ancient dictionaries that made the study of Akkadian (and Sumerian) something other than decipherment. Meanwhile H. C. Rawlinson had, with great effort, made a copy of the huge, virtually inaccessible Behistun inscription of Darius. This accomplishment, plus his edition of parts of the Persian and Akkadian versions, have generally gotten him the credit for deciphering cuneiform, but he was kept abreast of Hincks's findings and incorporated them into his own work – and Behistun was not published until the decipherment was virtually completed, and had little or no impact.

A number of other decipherments have followed (and a few challenges remain); the most celebrated recent one was Michael Ventris's of Linear B, which proved to record an early form of Greek; here the virtual bilingual was the coincidence of the names of findspots of documents with what seemed to be placenames in the texts: sign values assigned on their basis and plugged into a C?V? grid established by Alice Kober and Ventris revealed familiar-looking inflections. Something similar played a part in the decipherment of Maya glyphs: after Yuri Knorosov interpreted a sixteenth-century Maya-Spanish "alphabet" as a syllabary, and saw in the images pictures that could be named with suitable modern Mayan words, Heinrich Berlin found that distinctive signs were associated with specific places. In both cases the attempt to fit a familiar language (Classical Greek, forms of modern Mayan) to the ancient writings provided the final, if surprising, success. The mysterious script most apt to be deciphered some day is the Indus Valley script used between about 2500 and 1900 BCE. This is likely to prove a fourth independent invention of writing, and the Dravidian family is the likeliest candidate to provide its language.

3.3 Writing, linguistics, and semiotics

Is the study of writing – *grammatology*, as Gelb dubbed it – to be seen as a part of linguistics? The study of written language certainly is. But the fundamental difference between language and writing suggests that perhaps writing is outside the scope of linguistics, especially when linguistics is seen as a part of psychology. Perhaps the study of writing truly belongs as a sister science under the umbrella of semiotics, the study of meaningful systems embracing but transcending language. Semiotic approaches to writing, however, have tended to slight philological concerns, to skip right over the details in favor of ungrounded theorizing. Perhaps when writing systems come back into the ken of linguists, the situation will improve.

The traditional arrangement of Japanese hiragana (each character is used once, to spell out the following poem, attributed to the Buddhist monk Kūkai):	いろはにほへとちりぬるを わかよたれそつねならむう ゐのおくやまけふこえてあ さきゆめみしゑひもせす *Iro wa nioedo chirinuru wo waga yo tare zo tsune naran ui no okuyama kyō koete asaki yume miji ei mo sezu*	"The colorful [flowers] are fragrant, but they must fall. Who in this world can live forever? Today cross over the deep mountains of life's illusions and there will be no more shallow dreaming, no more drunkenness."

The Javanese order: ꦲꦤ ꦕꦫꦏ ꦢꦠ ꦱꦮꦭ ꦥꦝ ꦗꦪꦚ ꦩꦒ ꦧꦛꦔ

Hana caraka, data sawala, padha jayanya, maga bathanga
"There were two emissaries, they began to fight, their valor was equal, they both fell dead."

Figure 3.6 "Motivated" canonical orders of scripts

NOTES

I am grateful for the comments and suggestions of the volume editors, and of Jerrold S. Cooper, John DeFrancis, Victor Mair, M. O'Connor, and P. Oktor Skjærvø. Space limitations preclude incorporating them all, which can only be to the detriment of the chapter.

1   Sampson 1985, Coulmas 1989, DeFrancis 1989.
2   Taylor 1883, Cohen 1958, Février 1948/ 59, Friedrich 1966, Diringer 1948/68, Jensen 1935/69, and Senner 1989. On a smaller scale, but useful, are Nakanishi 1980 and especially Woodard 1996.
3   A few recent items not included there are added in the references here.
4   Coulmas 1996 contains numerous insightful articles on societal aspects of writing. Unfortunately the work is arguably unreliable as to factual matters.
5   A more nuanced statement appears in the revision of this passage in Gelb 1974: 1038.
6   The name "abugida" (borrowed from Ethiopic languages) is used in preference to existing terms like "alphasyllabary," "neosyllabary,"

"pseudo-alphabet," and "syllabically organized alphabet" in order to stress the independence from both "syllabary" and "alphabet."
7   Prakash et al. 1993 find that even abugidic literacy does not suffice for segmental awareness.
8   The exceptions are Japanese, where the classical arrangement of the 50 characters of the syllabaries spells out a poem, and Javanese, where the 20 C*a* letters spell out a sentence summarizing an etiological tale (figure 3.6).
9   The Septuagint is the Greek translation of the Hebrew Bible, dating from ca. the second century BCE, which underlies all the ancient versions of the Old Testament.
10   The Inca quipu (elaborate knotted cords recording numerical information) fulfilled this function in Andean civilization; noteworthily, their Quechua language cannot be described as monosyllabic.
11   Pope 1975 is the best history of decipherments except cuneiform (for which see *WWS* 145–7 summarizing Daniels 1994).

4 The History of Linguistics

LYLE CAMPBELL

1 Introduction

Many "histories" of linguistics have been written over the last two hundred years, and since the 1970s linguistic historiography has become a specialized subfield, with conferences, professional organizations, and journals of its own. Works on the history of linguistics often had such goals as defending a particular school of thought, promoting nationalism in various countries, or focussing on a particular topic or subfield, for example on the history of phonetics. Histories of linguistics often copied from one another, uncritically repeating popular but inaccurate interpretations; they also tended to see the history of linguistics as continuous and cumulative, though more recently some scholars have stressed the discontinuities. Also, the history of linguistics has had to deal with the vastness of the subject matter. Early developments in linguistics were considered part of philosophy, rhetoric, logic, psychology, biology, pedagogy, poetics, and religion, making it difficult to separate the history of linguistics from intellectual history in general, and, as a consequence, work in the history of linguistics has contributed also to the general history of ideas. Still, scholars have often interpreted the past based on modern linguistic thought, distorting how matters were seen in their own time. It is not possible to understand developments in linguistics without taking into account their historical and cultural contexts. In this chapter I attempt to present an overview of the major developments in the history of linguistics, avoiding these difficulties as far as possible.

2 Grammatical Traditions

A number of linguistic traditions arose in antiquity, most as responses to linguistic change and religious concerns. For example, in the case of *the Old-Babylonian tradition*, when the first linguistic texts were composed, Sumerian, which was the language of religious and legal texts, was being replaced by Akkadian. This grammatical tradition emerged, by about 1900 BC and lasted 2,500 years, so that Sumerian could be learned and these texts could continue to be read. Most of the texts were administrative lists: inventories, receipts, and rosters. Some early texts for use in the scribal school were inventories (lists) of Sumerian nouns and their Akkadian equivalents. From this, grammatical analysis evolved in the sixth and fifth centuries BC; different forms of the same word, especially of verbs, were listed in a way that represented grammatical paradigms and matched them between the two languages (Gragg 1995, Hovdhaugen 1982).

Language change also stimulated the *Hindu tradition*. The Vedas, the oldest of the Sanskrit memorized religious texts, date from ca. 1200 BC. Sanskrit, the sacred language, was changing, but ritual required exact verbal performance. Rules of grammar were set out for learning and understanding the archaic language. Pāṇini's (ca. 500 BC) description (which contains also rules formulated by his predecessors, in a tradition from the tenth to the seventh centuries BC) originated in comparisons between versions called *padapāṭa* (word-for-word recitation) and *saṃhitapāṭa* (continuous recitation, of divine origin, unalterable) of the same Vedic texts. The grammatical rules were devised for this comparison and for checking textual accuracy, and technical methods of grammatical description were developed in connection with the formulation of these rules. In addition to Pāṇini, Kātyāyana's rules of interpretation (ca. 300 BC) and Patañjali's commentary (ca. 150 BC) are important in this tradition. Grammar was considered the most scientific of the sciences in India, and the scholars in other areas aspired to the ideal embodied in the Hindu grammatical tradition (Staal 1974).

The Greek grammatical tradition, which also owes its origin to language change, was developed originally by schoolmasters, though it is known only from later writings of philosophers. Homer's works (ca. 850 BC) were basic in early Greek education, but the Greek of the fifth to the third centuries BC had changed so much that explanations of Homer's language were important in the school curriculum. Observations taken from earlier school grammar are found in works of Plato, Aristotle, and the Stoics (Hovdhaugen 1982: 46). Themes important in the ancient Greek tradition have persisted throughout the history of linguistics, such as the origin of language, parts of speech (grammatical categories), and the relation between language and thought, to mention just a few. A persistent controversy was whether "nature" or "convention" accounted for the relationship between words and their meaning, and this had implications for the history of language and for the origin of words. Earlier opinions on the matter are contrasted in Plato's (427–347 BC) *Cratylus*. At issue was whether language originated in "nature" (*phúsis*), with the first words supposedly imitating the things that they name, or in "convention" (*nómos* or *thésis*), that is, in usage or naming, whether of human or divine invention, or in a synthesis of the two. Aristotle (384–322 BC) in *De interpretatione* favored convention over nature; the Stoics held that language originated in nature.

For the Greeks, morphology (word structure) was mostly a historical matter, about the creation of the structure of words (part of "etymology"). Syntax was not described directly, but aspects of syntax were treated in rhetoric and logic. With respect to parts of speech, we see in Plato's division of the sentence into *ónoma* ("name") and *rhêma* ("utterance") an example where the interpretation of the past has been based too much on present understanding. Plato's terms are at times equated with the modern categories "noun" and "verb," respectively, but they equally had shades of "subject" and "predicate," and "topic" and "comment," or even entity and relation. The parts of speech (grammatical categories) as understood in traditional grammar developed more fully with the Stoics and others (Hovdhaugen 1982: 41, 48).

Roman linguistics continued Greek themes. Aelius Donatus' (fourth century AD) *Ars minor* and *Ars major* and Priscian's (sixth century AD) *Institutiones grammaticae* (18 volumes) became exceedingly important in the middle ages. Except for Varro (116–27 BC) and Priscian, Roman grammarians also did not treat syntax (only parts of speech); rather, morphology dominated in an approach focussed on noun declensions and verb conjugations (Hovdhaugen 1982: 87).

The Arabic grammatical tradition had roots in the Greek grammatical traditions, especially following Aristotle. For Arabic grammarians, the Arabic language was sacred and immutable as enshrined in the Qur'ān, and they were concerned with explaining why Arabic was perfect. For example, the system of inflectional endings was believed to be proof of the symmetry and logicalness of the language. The major impetus for grammatical study came from linguistic change and the desire to preserve the integrity of the holy language of the Qur'ān. While no change was acknowledged in formal Arabic after the eighth century, the realization that the spoken Arabic of the eighth and ninth centuries was changing stimulated the development of Arabic grammatical study. Abū'l-Aswad ad-Du'alī (died ca. 688) is reputed to be the inventor of this grammatical tradition, which commenced seriously in the writings of al-Khalīl (died 791) and Sībawayhi (died 804) (a Persian) (Owens 1988).

The Hebrew linguistic tradition began with concern for establishing the correct Hebrew text of the Old Testament. Hebrew grammarians borrowed descriptive methods wholesale from the Arabic linguistic tradition and developed a system of analysis for the morphology (analysis of words into their meaningful parts). Between 900 and 1550, 91 authors composed 145 works on grammar that we know of. Saadya ben Joseph al-Fayyūmī (a.k.a. Saadya Gaon) (882–942) is generally held to be the first to produce a Hebrew grammar and dictionary (Téné 1995: 22). Ibn Janāḥ of Cordova's *Kitāb al-Luma'*, written in Judeo-Arabic, was the first complete description of Hebrew. For Ibn Janāḥ (born 980 AD), Hebrew, Arabic, and all other languages had three parts of speech: noun, verb, and particles (as in the Arabic tradition, inherited from Aristotle). The tradition reached its peak in David Qimḥi's (ca. 1235) grammar, *Sepher mikhlol*, whose main features were analysis of verbal forms with a set of affixes and roots. This kind of analysis came to have a strong impact on European linguistics. Johannes Reuchlin's (1506) comprehensive *De rudimentis Hebraicis* introduced the Hebrew method of morphological analysis in Europe, and Theodor Bibliander (1548) recommended this analysis of words into roots and affixes for the study of all languages. He thought languages described in the Hebrew manner would be "in conformity with nature" and could therefore be meaningfully compared (Percival 1986).

Early Christian writers returned to the philosophical themes of Aristotle and the Stoics. Classical Latin grammars, mainly Donatus' *Ars minor*, were adapted to church education. Teachings of Roman grammarians were mixed with folk views in a Christian frame. In the seventh and eighth centuries, Donatus predominated, though ca. 830 Priscian's *Institutiones* replaced Donatus as the basic grammar, resulting in a new tradition of commentaries, the first steps towards the shift of interest in the eleventh and twelfth centuries which gave rise to the theory-oriented speculative grammar of the thirteenth and fourteenth centuries. The origin of languages was also of natural interest to the multilingual early Christian world, with notions of Babel and of taking the "word" to the nations of the earth (Hovdhaugen 1982: 109). In this environment, the hypothesis that Hebrew was the original language from which all others sprang became predominant.

3   The Rise of Universal Grammar

Around AD 1000, a shift began in which logic came to dominate linguistic thought. Prior to 1100, most scholars adhered faithfully to Donatus and Priscian; from the twelfth century onwards there was a return to dialectics. The recovery through Arabic scholarship of Aristotle's lost writings was an important factor, and Arabic commentators were quoted amply. Grammarians followed Aristotle's view that scientific knowledge is universal or general and applies to all subject matter, including grammar, hence universal grammar. Semantic analysis (or logical theory) came to dominate Europe for the next four centuries. Pierre Abailard's (Abelard's) (1079–1142) *Dialectica* (ca. 1130) systematized logic as expressed through the structure of ordinary language, building on Aristotle and placing logic at the highest level of contemporary science. Robert Kilwardby (died 1279) insisted on the universal nature of grammar, a concept more fully developed by Roger Bacon (1214–1294), both Englishmen who taught in Paris. Bacon is famous for his statement that "grammar is substantially one and the same in all languages, although it may vary accidentally" (Bursill-Hall 1995: 131).

"*Speculative grammar*" developed, with concern for the notion of *modi significandi* "ways of signifying." Some 30 authors, called *Modistae*, most connected with the University of Paris, integrated Donatus and Priscian into scholastic philosophy (1200–1350), that is, the integration of Aristotelian philosophy into Catholic theology. According to the *Modistae*, the grammarian's job was to explain how the intellect had created a system of grammar; in language the grammarian expressed understanding of the world and its contents through the modes of signifying (Bursill-Hall 1995: 132). Such a grammatical system had to mirror reality as grasped by understanding; that is, grammar was ultimately underwritten by the very structure of the universe (Breva-Claramonte 1983: 47). The *Modistae* compiled lists of modes of signifying for Donatus' and Priscian's parts of speech, distinguishing essential modes (the same in all languages) from accidental ones. For example, "predication" (verb) was essential to communication, but "tense" was accidental, since its function could be signified by something else, for example by temporal adverbs. "Noun" was the most essential (echoing Aristotle).

In the fourteenth century, teaching grammars began to compete with the scholastic commentaries, and the Modistic approach faded; however, there was a revival of philosophical grammar in the sixteenth century, begun with Julius Caesar Scaliger's (l'Escale) (1484–1558) *De causis linguae latinae* (1540). For Scaliger, grammar was part of philosophy, including the causation or creation of language from nature (hence the *de causis* in his title) (Breva-Claramonte 1983: 62). Francisco Sánchez (Sanctius) de las Brozas (1523–1601) in *Minerva, seu de causis linguae latinae* (1587) attempted to reconcile Plato and Aristotle by explaining that the "convention" favored by Aristotle was "reasoned," and, since reasoning is universal, God-given, it comes from "nature," which is what Sanctius believed Plato to have favored. Thus Sanctius' philosophy of language was "a rational discovery of the underlying 'perfection' or logic of language from which actual speech is derived" (Breva-Claramonte 1983: 15). Sanctius' universal grammar, in turn, influenced Arnauld and Lancelot's *Grammaire générale et raisonnée de Port Royal* (1660), and James Harris's (1709–1780) *Hermes* (1751), seminal in universal grammar theory.

In medieval manuscripts, the inflectional paradigms of Latin were explicated or annotated with forms from the vernacular languages. This pedagogical practice was combined in the seventeenth century with the revival of scholastic logical grammar in the *Grammaire générale et raisonnée de Port Royal* (Arnauld and Lancelot 1660). Following René Descartes (1596–1650), with human understanding taken to be the same for all people, scholars held the basic forms of thought to be the basis of every grammar; the particular grammatical systems of existing languages were merely approximations of the universal ideal, partly corrupted by neglect in usage. The principal concern was with the manifestation of universal semantic concepts in individual languages. In the seventeenth century, language studies came to be based on new theories of cognition and the philosophy of language, in particular on John Locke's (1632–1704) *Essay Concerning Human Understanding* (1690).

4 The Rise of the Comparative Method

Through voyages, conquests, trading, and colonialization from the sixteenth century onward, Europe became acquainted with a wide variety of languages.

Information on languages from Africa, Asia, and America became available in the form of word lists, grammars, dictionaries, and religious texts, and attempts at classifying these languages followed. Historical linguistic interests had a background in the Greek tradition's nature-versus-convention debate about language origins and its interest in etymology, as well as in the biblically based notion of Hebrew as the original language (*Lingua Adamica, Lingua Paradisiaca*) from which all others were assumed to descend after the confounding of tongues at Babel. From the catalogue of languages and peoples in Genesis came the tradition of *Sprachlisten*, "inventories of known languages of the world successively fitted into the Biblical ('Mosaic') framework, usually placing Hebrew at the head, between the third and seventeenth centuries" (Robins 1990: 86, Borst 1959).

Large-scale word collections for language comparisons were a notable feature of the centuries after the Renaissance. Some landmarks were Konrad Gesner 1555, Gottfried Wilhem Leibniz 1717, Johan Christoph Adelung 1782, 1806, Lorenzo Hervás y Panduro 1784, 1800, Peter Simon Pallas 1786, among others. These played an important role in the development of comparative linguistics.

The development of comparative grammar is subject to interpretation, explaining why each of the following at one time or another has been considered the "father" of comparative linguistics: Giraldus Cambrensis 1194, Dante 1305, J. J. Scaliger 1610 [1599], Georg Stiernhielm 1671, Andreas Jäger 1686, Ludolf 1702, Adriaan Relander [Hadrianus Relandus] 1706, Edward Lhuyd 1707, Philip Johan Tabbert von Strahlenberg 1730, Johan Ihre 1769, Jo[h]annis [János] Sajnovics 1770, Sir William Jones 1798, Christian Kraus 1787, Sámuel Gyarmathi 1799, Franz Bopp 1816, 1833, Ramus Rask 1818, and Jacob Grimm 1818, among others. Hoenigswald's summary of the points upon which seventeenth- and eighteenth-century scholars agreed concerning criteria for establishing language families is telling:

> First, . . . there was "the concept of a no longer spoken parent language which in turn produced the major linguistic groups of Asia and Europe". Then there was . . . "a Scaliger concept of the development of languages into dialects and of dialects into new independent languages". Third came "certain minimum standards for determining what words are borrowed and what words are ancestral in a language", and, fourth, "an insistence that not a few random items, but a large number of words from the basic vocabulary should form the basis of comparison" . . . fifth, the doctrine that "grammar" is even more important than words; sixth, the idea that for an etymology to be valid the differences in sound – or in "letters" – must recur, under a principle sometimes referred to as "analogia". (1990: 119–20)

From the fifteenth century onward, etymology had been shifting away from its sense in classical antiquity of unfolding the true meaning of words toward a historical search for earlier stages in languages and the origin of words (Robins 1990: 86). Etymology thus became important in attempts to establish linguistic relationships. The *Dutch etymologists*, such as Scrieckius 1614, de Laet

1643, and ten Kate 1710, had a lasting impact. Their analysis of words into roots and affixes (prefixes and suffixes), which was inspired by the Hebrew grammatical tradition, became fundamental to the comparative method. They utilized three principal criteria for establishing family relationships which were to become standard: basic vocabulary, sound correspondences, and grammatical agreements.

4.1   The Scythian hypothesis and the notion of Indo-European

Eventually, comparative linguistics came to have Indo-European languages as its main concern. Early recognition of the family relationship among Indo-European languages is connected intimately with the "Scythian hypothesis." The *Scythae* of Classical writers (Herodotus, Strabo, Justin, etc.) were a nation on a sea in the north in extreme antiquity. Josephus and early Christian writers took them to be the descendants of Japheth (son of Noah), the assumed father of Europe (Droixhe 1984: 5), and the Scythian linguistic hypothesis emerged from these notions. Various proposals attempted to identify Scythians with different language groups of Europe and Asia, but proposed Indo-European associations came to dominate. With Johannes Goropius Becanus' (Jan van Gorp van Hilvarenbeek's) (1518–1572) (1569) emphasis on "Scythian," recognition of Indo-European as a language family began. Raphelengius (Ravlenghien) reported correspondences between Persian and Germanic languages. Marcus Zuerius Boxhorn(ius) (1602–1653) relied both on matches in words and on grammatical similarities to prove "that these people all learned their language from one same mother" (Muller 1986: 10). Others also advanced the Scythian hypothesis: Claudius Salmasius (Claude Saumaise) (1588–1653) (1643), Georg Stiernhielm (1598–1672) (1671), Andreas Jäger (1660–1730) (1686), Leibniz (1646–1716), and so on. So well known was the Scythian hypothesis that in 1733 Theodor Walter (1699–1741), a missionary in Malabar, "recognized similarities between Sanskrit, Greek, and Persian numerals and explained these with . . . Scythian theory" (Fellman 1975: 38).

4.2   Sir William Jones

The most repeated passage in linguistic history is Sir William Jones' (1746–1794) statement in 1786:

> The *Sanscrit* language, whatever be its antiquity, is of a wonderful structure; more perfect than the Greek, more copious than the Latin, and more exquisitely refined than either; yet bearing to both of them a stronger affinity, both in the roots of verbs and in the forms of grammar, than could possibly have been

produced by accident; so strong indeed, that no philologer could examine them all three without believing them to have sprung from *some common source*, which, perhaps, no longer exists. There is a similar reason, though not quite so forcible, for supposing that both the *Gothic* and *Celtick*, though blended with a very different idiom, had the same origin with the *Sanscrit*; and the old *Persian* might be added to the same family, if this were the place for discussing any question concerning the antiquities of *Persia*. (Jones 1798: 422–3)

Based on this, Jones is usually credited with founding comparative linguistics and discovering the relationship among Indo-European languages. However, this is a most unfortunate misreading of the history of linguistics. Jones neither initiated the comparative method nor discovered Indo-European, as a comparison of a remarkably similar quote from Andreas Jäger in 1686, one hundred years earlier, reveals:

An ancient language, once spoken in the distant past in the area of the Caucasus mountains and spreading by waves of migration throughout Europe and Asia, had itself ceased to be spoken and had left no linguistic monuments behind, but had as a "mother" generated a host of "daughter languages," many of which in turn had become "mothers" to further "daughters." (For a language tends to develop dialects, and these dialects in the course of time become independent, mutually unintelligible languages.) Descendants of the ancestral languages include Persian, Greek, Italic (whence Latin and in time the modern Romance tongues), the Slavonic languages, Celtic, and finally Gothic and the other Germanic tongues. (Andreas Jäger 1686, cited by Metcalf 1974: 233)

In fact, there were several notable predecessors to Jones (in addition to the supporters of the Scythian hypothesis mentioned above). For example, Edward Lhuyd (1707) compared several Indo-European languages (Celtic, Germanic, Slavic, Persian, etc.), presenting a long list of cognates, sound correspondences, and sound changes. He even discovered part of Grimm's law (which has to do with sound correspondences between Germanic and the other Indo-European languages), long before Rask and Grimm made it famous (see below). Johannis (János) Sajnovics (1770) demonstrated the relationship between Hungarian, Lapp, and Finnish. He used clear methods which were followed frequently in later work, and his work was very influential in the subsequent development of historical linguistics. For example, Rasmus Rask (1787–1832) (1993 [1818]: 283), famous early Danish historical linguist, felt confident of the evidence he presented for the kinship of Germanic with Greek and Latin because it compared favorably with Sajnovics' "proof that the Hungarian and Lappish languages are the same," which, Rask said, "no one has denied since his day." Some Africanists cite Abbé Lievin Bonaventure Proyart's *Histoire de Loango, Kakongo, et autres royaumes d'Afrique* from 1776 as a rival to Jones for its historical linguistic clarity. He pointed out that Kakongo and Laongo differ in many respects from Kikongo, but that "several similar articles [presumably prefixes], and a great number of common roots, seem, however, to indicate that these languages had a common origin" (quoted by Gregersen 1977: 97). Before Jones' famous pronouncement was published (in 1798), Jonathan Edwards, Jr (1745–1826) (1787) demonstrated the family relationship among the Algonquian languages; Edwards listed "some 60 vocabulary items, phrases, and grammatical features"; Jones, in contrast, presented no linguistic evidence.

Connections among Indo-European languages had been observed by many before Jones. Also, the relationship between Sanskrit and other Indo-European languages, which is generally attributed to Jones, also had already been observed by several others. For example, De Guignes (1770: 327) reported that "an infinity of travellers have already noticed that in the Indian languages and even in Sanskrit, the learned tongue of these peoples, there are many Latin and Greek words" – Jones cited de Guignes and also referred to the Scythian hypothesis.

In fact, Jones had little interest in linguistics. His plan was to write a history of peoples of Asia, and language was only one source of information, used together with information from philosophy and religion, remains of sculpture and architecture, and documents of sciences and arts (Jones 1798: 421). His interest in the history of the human "races" rather than in language was typical in eighteenth- and nineteenth-century scholarship, shared by Leibniz, Hervás y Panduro, Monboddo, Vater, Schlegel, Grimm, Humboldt, among others. Their linguistic comparisons were just part of a broader history of the nations and races of the world. This theme of language in concert with other sources of evidence to determine the history and classification of nations and races was to persist into the early twentieth century. In fact, with this orientation, Jones incorrectly classified many languages, both Indo-European and non-Indo-European ones. Nevertheless, Jones was famous before he went to India as a judge; he had written a famous Persian grammar and was renowned for his scholarship involving numerous oriental languages. People expected big things of him, and indeed through his translations of Hindu legal texts he made Sanskrit well-known in Europe. As a result, his contribution came to be interpreted too enthusiastically.

Rather than being the initiator of Indo-European and of methods of comparative linguistics, Jones reflected the thinking of his day. For example, Christian Jakob Kraus (1753–1807) (1787) reviewed the assumptions concerning the comparative study of languages at that time. He indicated that similarity of words alone may or may not be indicative of family relationship, but if the grammatical structures of compared languages contained far-reaching similarities, the conclusion was in favor of a genealogical relationship (Hoenigswald 1974: 348). Very influential, and much more sophisticated than Jones' work, was Sámuel Gyarmathi's (1751–1830) *Affinitas linguae Hungaricae cum linguis Fennicae originis grammatice demonstrata* (1799), which both reflected and led the intellectual concerns of the day, emphasizing grammatical comparisons. Holgar Pedersen (1867–1953) (1962 [1931]: 105), in his famous history of linguistics, considered Gyarmathi's comparative grammar "the principle which became the lodestar of incipient Indo-European linguistics," the key to "comparative grammar." Notably, Gyarmathi warned against arguing for a genetic relationship based on similarities due to universal grammar:

> it is beyond dispute that there are universal syntactic rules shared by most nations ... I believe that it is much more appropriate for my demonstration to bring up the kind of examples which are specifically found in Hungarian, Lapp and Finnish and which can hardly be expressed at all in Latin, German and other European languages. (Gyarmathi 1983 [1799]: 33)

With Friedrich von Schlegel [1772–1829] (1808), "comparative grammar" became a continuing focus of historical linguistic studies. Schlegel drew from biology and comparative anatomy, and employed the notion of a family tree. Grammatical structure was his main criterion of family relatedness; two languages were considered related only when their "inner structure" or "comparative grammar" presents distinct resemblances (Schlegel 1808: 6–7).

Rasmus Rask (1818) wove together the historical linguistic currents leading to his day and laid out explicitly "the principles one considers it most proper to follow" (1993 [1818]: 9). He stressed the importance of comparing grammatical structures according to Sajnovics' and Gyarmathi's methods, applying etymological principles to the genetic classification of languages (Rask 1993 [1818]: 11, Diderichsen 1974: 301). As Rask explained, "grammatical agreement is a much more certain sign of kinship or basic unity" (Rask 1993 [1818]: 33–4), but he also relied on sound correspondences and basic vocabulary as evidence (Rask 1993 [1818]: 34). Rask discovered the set of sound correspondences which later became known as Grimm's law (though Rask's version seems somewhat clumsy in hindsight; Rask 1993 [1818]: 161–2).

Grimm's law was a major milestone in the history of Indo-European and thus also in historical linguistics. Jakob Grimm [1785–1863], of Grimm Brothers' fairytale fame, is one of the largest luminaries in historical linguistics. In the second edition of his *Deutsche Grammatik* (1822) he included the section inspired by Rask's formulation of sound correspondences among Indo-European languages later called "Grimm's law." Grimm recognized the importance of sound correspondences as evidence of family relationships, saying his law had "important consequences for the history of the language and the validity of etymology" and that it "provided sufficient evidence for the kinship of the languages involved" (Davies 1992: 161). Grimm's law treats a series of changes in certain consonants from Proto-Indo-European to Proto-Germanic:

> p, t, k became f, θ [like "th" of *thing*], h, respectively
> b, d, g became p, t, k, respectively
> bh, dh, gh became b, d, g, respectively

(Not all the consonants involved are mentioned here.)

Some examples which illustrate Grimm's law are seen in figure 4.1, where the words in English (a Germanic language) show the results of the changes, whereas their cognates in French (not Germanic) did not undergo the change.

	French	*English*
*p > f	pied	foot
*t > θ:	trois	three
*k > h:	cœur	heart
*d > t:	dent	tooth (< tanθ)
*g > k:	grain	corn
*bh > b:	frère (from *bhráter)	brother

Figure 4.1 Examples illustrating Grimm's law

While Grimm's law accounts for the systematic correspondences between Germanic and non-Germanic languages, it had some exceptions. However, subsequent discoveries, in 1862, showed that these exceptions have satisfactory explanations, and this led to a major development in linguistics. In Sanskrit and Greek, as a result of Grassmann's law, two aspirated stops within a word regularly dissimilated so that the first lost its aspiration (bh, dh, gh became b, d, g, respectively), and as a consequence, some sound correspondences between Sanskrit and the Germanic languages do not match expectations from Grimm's law, as seen in figure 4.2.

Proto-Indo-European	Sanskrit	Gothic	
*bheudha-	bōdha	biudan	"to wake, become aware, bid"

Figure 4.2 Example illustrating Grassmann's law

In Sanskrit, the *bh* dissimilated to *b* due to the *dh* in this word (giving Sanskrit *b* though *bh* would have been expected). In the Gothic cognate, which means "to bid", by Grimm's law we expect the *b* of the Sanskrit word to correspond to *p* in Gothic, and we expect the Gothic *b* to correspond to Sanskrit *bh*. This exception to Grimm's law is explained by the fact that Grassmann's law deaspirated the first aspirated consonant in Sanskrit. In 1877 Karl Verner (1846–96) accounted for other exceptions to Grimm's law in a change known as Verner's law, illustrated in figure 4.3.

Proto-Indo-European	Sanskrit	Gothic	
*septém-	saptá	sibun	"seven"

Figure 4.3 Example illustrating Verner's law

By Grimm's law, we expect the *p* of Sanskrit to correspond to *f* in Gothic, not the *b* found in this Gothic word, and given the *b* of Gothic, we would expect Sanskrit to have *bh*. Verner's law explains this exception to Grimm's law. When the Proto-Indo-European accent followed the sound in question (and it was not the first sound in the word), as seen in Sanskrit *saptá* (*á* is accented), *p* became *b* in Germanic, as in the Gothic word; otherwise, Grimm's law applied.

4.3   *The Neogrammarians*

This success in accounting for what had originally appeared to be exceptions to Grimm's law spawned one of the most notable developments in linguistics. It led the Neogrammarians to the confidence that sound change was regular and exceptionless. The Neogrammarians, beginning in about 1876 in Germany, became extremely influential. They were a group of younger scholars who antagonized the leaders of the field by attacking older thinking and loudly proclaiming their own views. They were called *Junggrammatiker* "young grammarians" in German, where *jung-* "young" had the sense of "young Turk," originally intended as a humorous nickname for these rebellious and strident young scholars, although they adopted the name as their own. They included Karl Brugmann (1849–1919) (the most famous linguist of his time), Berthold Delbrück (1842–1922), August Leskien, Hermann Osthoff (1847–1909), Hermann Paul (1846–1921), and others. The Neogrammarian slogan, "sound laws suffer no exceptions," or, more precisely, "every sound change, in as much as it occurs mechanically, takes place according to laws that admit no exceptions," was declared virtually as doctrine in the so-called "Neogrammarian manifesto" of Hermann Osthoff and Karl Brugmann (1878), written mostly by Brugmann. This became an important cornerstone of reconstruction by the comparative method. By "sound laws" they meant merely "sound changes," but referred to them as "laws" because they linked linguistics with the rigorous sciences which dealt in laws and law-like statements.

Some scholars, many of them dialectologists, did not accept the Neogrammarian position that sound change is regular and exceptionless, but rather opposed this and the "family tree model" which represents languages related by virtue of descent from a common ancestor. The "family tree model" is often associated with August Schleicher (1821–1868), prominent pre-Neogrammarian figure in Indo-European linguistics (see Schleicher 1861–2). This model is typically linked in the literature with the development of the comparative method and eventually with the Neogrammarian notion of the regularity of sound change (though this connection is not necessary). The opponents' slogan was "each word has its own history." This slogan is often attributed to Jules Gilliéron (1854–1926), author of the *Atlas linguistique de la France* (1902–10), the dialect atlas of France, although it really comes from Hugo Schuchardt (1842–1927), a contemporary of the early Neogrammarians, of whose claims he was critical. The alternative to the family tree model which was put forward was the "wave theory," usually attributed to Johannes Schmidt (1872) though it, too, was actually developed earlier, in 1868 and 1870, by Hugo Schuchardt (Alvar 1967: 82–5). Interestingly, Schuchardt and Schmidt were both students of Schleicher, as were several of the leading Neogrammarians. The "wave theory" was intended to deal with changes due to contact among languages and dialects, where changes were said to emanate from a center as waves on a pond do when a stone is thrown into it, and waves from one center of dispersion (where the stone started the waves) can cross or intersect outward moving waves coming from other dispersion centers (started by other stones thrown into the water in other locations). Changes due to language contact (borrowing) were seen as analogous to successive waves crossing one another in different patterns. The dialectologists' slogan, that every word has its own history, reflects this thinking – a word's history might be the result of various influences from various directions, and these might be quite different from those involved in another word's history; hence each word has its own (potentially quite different) history.

Although some scholars have thought that dialectology naturally led to challenges to the Neogrammarian position, in fact the Neogrammarian founders gained support for their position in dialect study. They were impressed by Jost Winteler's (1876) study of the Kerenzen dialect of Swiss German in which he presented phonological statements as processes, modeled after Pāṇini's ancient rules for Sanskrit. This "regularity" which Winteler saw in the dialect's modern rules – for example that in Kerenzen every *n* became ŋ [like "ng" in English *sing*] before *k* and *g* – inspired them to have confidence in the exceptionlessness of sound changes (Weinreich et al. 1968: 115). Today it is recognized that both the family tree and the wave model are necessary to explain change and that they complement one another (Campbell 1998: 187–91).

5   Philosophical-Psychological (-Typological-Evolutionary) Approaches

While the Neogrammarian tradition has dominated the history of linguistics, there was another once influential orientation, a philosophical-psychological-typological-evolutionary outlook on the nature and evolution of language, now largely forgotten.

In the nineteenth century, there was a clash between views of linguistics as a *"Naturwissenschaft"* (physical science) and *"Geisteswissenschaft"* (humanities). Leading linguists attempted to place linguistics in the natural (physical) sciences, denying any value for the more humanistic, "sentimental" intellectual orientations. A close analogy of linguistics with biology had been insisted upon by Schlegel, Rask, and many others, a view associated especially with Schleicher (1861–2). Nevertheless, many in the past did not clearly separate language, race, nation, and culture. As seen above, Jones, Leibniz, Hervás y Panduro, Adelung, Rask, and others believed they were working out the history of races and nations in their linguistic works, rather than that of mere languages. Folk (or national) psychology, coupled with the assumed stage of social evolution attained by its speakers – often called "progress" – was thought to determine a language's typology and its history, the sort of gross linguistic history later eschewed by the mainstream as too psychological. In the eighteenth century, interest began to concentrate on the origin of differences in languages and cultures, and this led to the idea of the particular "genius" of each language and through this to a "typology" of languages. These types were often viewed as both descriptive and historical. Traditional etymology and theories of language relationship were merged with logical grammar in an evolutionary scheme. Languages were classified into types according to their morphological structure, the types taken as representing or being correlated with evolutionary stages. Structural change in a language was taken as nothing more than the result of social evolution. For many, following Wilhelm von Humboldt (1767–1835), the typological categories – isolating, agglutinative, flexional, and incorporating – were taken as reflecting the level of social evolution attained by the speakers of the language (a typical equation was: isolating = savagery, agglutinative = barbarianism, inflectional = civilization). For example, for Friedrich Müller (1834–1898), social evolution, racial type, and language type were correlated, so that hair shape and linguistic morphology (structure of words) could be associated with one another.

The notion of "inner structure" was persistent in this orientation. Johann Gottfried von Herder (1744–1803) (1772) had spoken of the "inner development of language," and the notion of "inner structure" was prominent in the work of Adelung, Schlegel, Bopp, Humboldt, Steinthal, and others.

Franz Bopp's (1791–1867) (1816, 1833) comparative grammar contributed significantly to growing interest in comparative grammar, but also incorporated aspects of the philosophical-psychological-typological-evolutionary outlook. Schleicher's (1861–2) *Compendium der vergleichenden Grammatik der indogermanischen Sprachen* is the acknowledged synthesis of nineteenth-century comparative linguistics for its time. Schleicher followed Humboldt's (1822) types, expounding the view that languages evolve, or "progress," from isolation to agglutination (with affixes arising from full words) and move onward to flexion, with gradual progress in the direction from simple to complex forms. Schleicher believed that "growth" (through agglutination) took place only in the prehistoric phase when languages were still young and capable of word-formation, during the period of *Sprachbildung* ("language formation"), whereas only changes of "decay" (by sound change and analogy) took place in the later historical period, after the growth process was assumed to have ceased entirely, during the period of *Sprachgeschichte* ("language history").

This view, that modern languages are but dim reflections of their more perfect progenitors, was called "glottogonic"; it characterizes the work of many early comparativists, but was severely criticized by Neogrammarians. They rejected Schleicher's and others' orientation as "glottogonic speculation." They denied its separation of stages, insisting that the same kinds of language changes apply to all phases of linguistic history; analogy and sound change operate throughout a language's history (Paul 1920 [1880]: 174, see Davies 1986: 154, Harris and Campbell 1995: 17–19).

Aspects of the philosophical-psychological-typological-evolutionary outlook endured into the twentieth century, although it was played down in the official histories written mostly by Neogrammarians, e.g. Pedersen (1962) [1931]; see Boas, Sapir, and Whorf, below; Campbell (1997: 27–9, 37–43, 55–66).

6   The Rise of Structuralism

Thinking which led to the replacement of the historical orientation in linguistics by emphasis on the study of living languages and their structure came from a number of quarters at roughly the same time. For example, incipient notions of the "phoneme" developed in several areas at about the same time, so that it is not possible to attribute it to any one person or school. The phoneme is a central concept of linguistics whose definition varies from school to school but which basically means the significant units of sound, the minimal unit of sound capable of changing the meaning of words. Some speculate that in the wake of World War I, linguists were happy to free themselves of the German domination represented by the Neogrammarian historicism which had been predominant until then, and indeed the new currents, partly convergent but also with individual characteristic differences, came not from Germany, but from Switzerland with de Saussure, Russia with Baudouin de Courtenay, and America with Boas.

6.1   *Ferdinand de Saussure (1857–1913)*

After early influential Neogrammarian work on the vowels of Indo-European in 1878, published when he was 21, and a doctoral dissertation in 1881 on the genitive in Sanskrit, Saussure published little else, nothing on the topics for which he is best known, and yet he became one of the most influential scholars in twentieth-century linguistics and modern intellectual history. The extremely influential *Cours de linguistique générale* (1916), published after his death in 1913, was compiled from his students' notes from his course in general linguistics (given three times between 1907 and 1911) at the University of Geneva. This book is credited with turning the tide of linguistic thought from the diachronic (historical) orientation which had dominated nineteenth-century linguistics to interest in the synchronic (non-historical) study of language. Defining linguistics was a main goal of the book.

Saussure emphasized the synchronic study of language structure and how linguistic elements are organized into the system of each language. His theory of signs has been very influential. His linguistic sign is a union of the *signifiant* ("signifier," the form, sound) and the *signifié* ("signified," the meaning, function); the particular form (sounds) and the particular meaning in individual signs are arbitrarily associated with one another; their connection is purely conventional; that is, the sound–meaning association in signs is not predictable from one language to the next. The thing signified, say the notion *tree*, is arbitrarily associated with the sounds (signifier) which signal it, for example with the sounds of *Baum* in German, *kwawitl* in Nahuatl, *rakau* in Maori, *tree* in English, and so on. In Saussure's view, linguistic entities were considered members of a system and were defined by their relations to one another within that system. He compared language to a game of chess, a highly organized "algebraic" system of relations, where it is not the actual physical attributes of the pieces which define the game, but rather the relation of each piece to the other pieces in the system which give it its definition, a system *où tout se tient* ("where everything holds together," where everything depends on everything else, that is, where everything is defined in terms of its relations to everything else), in the famous saying of Antoine Meillet (1866–1917) (student of Saussure).

Saussure, influenced by the social thinking of Emil Durkheim (1858–1917) (founding figure in sociology), held that language is primarily a "social fact" (rather than a mental or psychological one, as others had held), that is, that there is a "collective consciousness" which is both the possession of society at large but also defines society. ("Social fact" and "collective consciousness" are terms associated with Durkheim, which Saussure used.) Saussure's famous dichotomy, *langue* (language, as socially shared and as a system) versus *parole* (speech, the language of the individual), reflects the French social thinking of the day. The goal, naturally, was to describe *langue*, but, since the individual's speech would reflect and represent the language as possessed by society generally, the social (general) character of language could be approached through the study of the language of the individual.

Today, nearly all approaches to linguistics are "structuralist" in some sense and reflect Saussure's monumental influence. Saussure's structuralism has also had a strong impact on anthropology, literary criticism, history, psychology, and philosophy, promoted and modified by Jakobson, Lévi-Strauss, Foucault, Barthes, and Derrida, among others.

6.2   The Prague School and its antecedents

Jan [Ignacy Niecisław] Baudouin de Courtenay (1845–1929), born in Poland, was developing structuralist ideas at the University of Kazań in Russia at about the same time as Saussure was lecturing in Geneva. Saussure was familiar with Baudouin de Courtenay's thinking and parts of the *Cours* reflect this very directly; Saussure had said that Baudouin and his student Mikołaj Kruszewski (1851–1887) were the only European scholars who contributed to linguistic theory (Stankiewicz 1972: 4–5). Baudouin de Courtenay's thinking was instrumental in the development of the notion of the "phoneme," though the concept developed with influence also from several other directions at once. Baudouin and his students contributed the terms "morpheme," "grapheme," "distinctive feature," and "alternation," all basic terminology in modern linguistics. His thinking survived most vividly through linguists whom he influenced who became associated with the Linguistic Circle of Prague.

Serge Karcevskij (1884–1955), who had been in Geneva from 1906 to 1917, brought Saussure's thinking back to the Moscow Linguistic Circle, with its formalist movement. Roman Jakobson (1896–1982) and Prince Nicholai S. Trubetzkoy (1890–1938) recognized areas of convergent thinking with Saussure.

Later, Jakobson and Trubetzkoy (two Russians) became the best known representatives of the Prague School of linguistics. Jakobson, Trubetzkoy, and others of the Prague School developed aspects in structuralism which are important in current theories, for example "distinctive features," "markedness," "topic," and "comment," and the notion of "implicational universals," as well as "linguistic areas" (*Sprachbund*). Jakobson, who emigrated to the US in 1942, had a strong impact on the development of generative phonology both through his student, Morris Halle, and through his influence on Noam Chomsky (see below).

6.3   *Franz Boas (1858–1942)*

Franz Boas is considered the founder of American linguistics and American anthropology. A major concern for him was to obtain information on Native American languages and cultures before they disappeared, and indeed his is the last, sometimes the only, significant data on a number of now extinct languages, for example, Lower Chinook, Cathlamet, Chemakum, Pentlach, Pochutec, and Tsetsaut. He passed his sense of urgency for fieldwork on to his students, a dedication to getting accurate information while it was still possible. The methods Boas and his followers worked out for the description of such languages became the basis of American structuralism, a dominant force in twentieth-century linguistics.

   This approach reflects Boas' famous "linguistic relativity" and his emphasis on avoiding generalization. At that time, many erroneous claims were about, such as that certain South American Indians could not communicate in the dark, since, it was asserted, their language was so "primitive" they had to rely on gestures (which could not be seen in the dark) to convey concepts such as "here" and "there" or "yesterday" and "tomorrow" to make up for the assumed severe limitations of their vocabulary; that change in "primitive" languages could proceed so fast that grandparents could not understand their grandchildren; that the pronunciation of "primitive" languages could vary unpredictably and be so imprecise as to make learning such languages all but impossible; and so on. In particular, earlier descriptions of so-called "exotic" languages frequently attempted to force them into traditional European grammatical categories, missing or distorting many distinctions significant to these languages. The different categories available in human languages are far more extensive than had been supposed from the generalizations being made which were based on the more familiar European languages. In face of so many bad generalizations, Boas believed it important to avoid preconceptions and to describe each language and culture in its own terms – on the basis of information derived internally from an analysis of the language itself rather than imposed on it from outside. His students made this a matter of principle, an orientation to linguistics with emphasis on description and against generalizing, against theorizing about language. This orientation prevailed in American

Structuralism until Noam Chomsky's views reoriented the field towards universals, generalizing, and linguistic theory (see below).

The notion of "inner form" became the core of Boas' view of ethnology and linguistics. Boas used Humboldt's concept of "inner form" to deal with the diversity of American Indian languages, seeing languages as conditioning the world view of their speakers. He was strongly opposed to the evolutionism of philosophical-psychological-typological-evolutionary views of the past, but maintained a Humboldtian psychological orientation. Nevertheless, he succeeded in turning attention against the evolutionary determinism characteristic of this way of thinking. He showed that the traditional typological-evolutionary views of grammar were inaccurate and ethnocentric. His view is revealed in his conception of the *Handbook of North American Indian Languages* (Boas 1911) as a "morphological classification" of American Indian languages. The languages he selected for inclusion in the *Handbook* were chosen to represent as many psychologically distinct types of language as possible, with the goal to reveal their "morphological classification and psychological characterization" and to serve as "a uniform series of outlines of Indian languages to be published in synoptic form for use in comparative studies by the philologists [historical linguists] of the world." "His emphasis was on the diversity of linguistic structures and accompanying mental worlds to be found in North America" (Campbell 1997: 64). After Boas, with help from Sapir and Kroeber, the view of morphological types as representatives of stages of social evolution died out. The two most influential American linguists after Boas were Sapir and Bloomfield.

6.4   *Edward Sapir (1884–1939)*

Sapir (Boas' student) was highly admired during his life and is still something of a hero to many linguists. He published extensively in both linguistics and anthropology, did first-hand fieldwork on many American Indian languages, contributed to historical linguistics (in Indo-European, Semitic, and numerous Native American families; for example, he established once and for all the Uto-Aztecan family and proposed the once controversial but now established Ritwan-Algonquian family), and wrote theoretical works, for example on the phoneme, still read with profit today. His impact in these areas was monumental. At the same time, he was also no stranger to the psychological-typological current of thought. Trained in Germanic linguistics, he fully understood the Humboldtian psychological tradition. His 1921 book, *Language*, insightfully dealt with the broad morphological typologies of the past century, but without the evolutionism which characterized them in earlier views. His own typology rested on the tradition extending from the eighteenth and nineteenth centuries represented by Schlegel, Bopp, Humboldt, Schleicher, Müller, Steinthal, Wundt, and others. However, like Boas, he rejected the evolutionary prejudice that typified traditional typological studies: "all attempts to connect particular types of linguistic morphology with certain correlated stages of cultural development . . . are rubbish" (Sapir 1921: 219). He did not accept the notion of significant racial differences in the "fundamental conformation of thought," the belief that differences in linguistic forms (believed to be connected with the actual processes of thought) could be indexed to racial differences. However, he did uphold the psychological orientation of the earlier typological tradition and passed it along to his student Benjamin Whorf (1897–1941), in whose hands it was transformed into the Whorf (or Sapir–Whorf) hypothesis, which holds that a speaker's perception of the world is organized or constrained by the linguistic categories his or her language offers, that language structure determines thought, how one experiences and hence how one views the world. This became a lasting theme in linguistics, anthropology, psychology, and philosophy, though many are unaware of its pedigree from German Romanticism. In his descriptive work, Sapir maintained the mentalism and non-generalizing of Boas' approach.

6.5   *Leonard Bloomfield (1887–1949)*

Bloomfield is credited with giving American structuralism its fundamental form, making linguistics an autonomous field. His principal concern was to develop linguistics as a science. Bloomfield's (1933) *Language* is considered a milestone in linguistics, the foundation of American structuralist linguistic thinking. Of this book, Bloomfield reported that it showed Saussure's thinking on every page. Bloomfield was also heavily influenced by behaviorist psychology. He accepted the Boasian prohibition against generalizing but at the same time he denied the relevance of "mind"; that is, he opposed the mentalism that had characterized the American linguistics of Boas, Sapir, and their students. This left American structuralism (represented by Bernard Bloch, Zellig Harris, Charles Hockett, Henry Lee Smith, George Trager, and others – sometimes called the "Bloomfieldians") with essentially nothing more than method, the "discovery procedures" against which Chomsky later argued so effectively. With a mentalistic orientation but no theoretical assumptions (no generalization), followers of Boas and Sapir could hold their description of a given language up to some external measure to decide whether it was accurate or not, namely, by determining whether it reflected what native speakers knew of their language. However, Bloomfield and his followers were left with no means of validating a description – by denying generalizations (theory), they could not evaluate the description of a given language according to how well it conformed to an understanding of human language in general, and by denying "mind" (mentalism) they could not judge a description against the extent to which it matched what native speakers knew of the structure of their language. Thus, nothing remained except method, "discovery procedures," the search for contrast and complementary distribution in the data recorded by linguists. This is a particularly impoverished state for a "science" to find itself in – all method and no theory. Given this state of affairs, it is not surprising that Chomsky was able to bring about a revolution in linguistics.

7   Noam Chomsky and Linguistic Theory since 1957

The mainstream of linguistics since 1957, the year in which Chomsky's *Syntactic Structures* appeared, has been dominated by Noam Chomsky (1928–). It is difficult to overestimate Chomsky's impact on both linguistics and contemporary ideas in general: "Chomsky is currently among the ten most-cited writers in all of the humanities [and social sciences] (behind only Marx, Lenin, Shakespeare, the Bible, Aristotle, Plato, and Freud) and the only living member of the top ten" (Pinker 1994: 23). It is common to speak of "the Chomskian revolution," so radically distinct is Chomsky's program from that of his American structuralist predecessors. Unlike the Bloomfieldians, Chomsky brought back mentalism. For him, the goal of a grammar is to account for the native speaker's "competence," defined as what a native speaker knows, tacitly, of his or her language. Since speakers know, among other things, how to produce an infinite number of sentences, many of which are novel, never having been produced before (talked about as linguistic "creativity"), an account of "competence" would require the formal means to produce or generate these new sentences, hence a "generative grammar." A grammar was seen as a theory of a language, constrained and evaluated just as any other theory in the sciences. Unlike most of his predecessors, Chomsky focussed on syntax, and in so doing, laid the foundation for explaining this "creativity." The notation of generative grammar was invented to make explicit the notion of "competence"; a generative grammar is a formal system (of rules, later of principles and parameters) which makes explicit the finite mechanisms available to the brain to produce infinite sentences in ways that have empirical consequences and can be tested as in the natural sciences.

  Unlike the Boasians and the Bloomfieldians, Chomsky gave linguistics the goal of generalizing, of attempting to determine what languages hold in common and to establish a rich theory of human language. Chomsky's approach is often called "generative grammar" or "transformational-generative grammar." Transformations were essentially rules for relating one syntactic structure to another, for example, as in early versions where questions, such as *Is Pat here?*, were derived by transformation from the corresponding declarative, *Pat is here*. However, in later versions of the theory, transformations no longer play a significant role. In Chomsky's theorizing about language, universals hold a central place. He rejected the "discovery procedures" of his American structuralist predecessors, those inductive procedures for deriving the grammatical description of a language through the application of procedures sensitive essentially only to the distribution of elements in a corpus of data from the language. The primary task of the linguist, according to Chomsky, should not be to discover the structure of the language from a body of data; rather, the goals should be to describe and explain the knowledge of the structure of the language which the native speaker has. This shifted attention from actual behavior (or recorded data) to the system of knowledge that underlies the production and understanding of language, and, further, to the general theory of human language lying behind this knowledge. This was a radical reorientation of the field, rejecting the anti-mentalism of the Bloomfieldians and the anti-theorizing of the Boasians and Bloomfieldians.

Chomsky redirected the goal of linguistic theory towards attempting to provide a rigorous and formal characterization of the notion "possible human language," called "Universal Grammar." In his view, the aim of linguistics is to go beyond the study of individual languages to determine what the universal properties of human language in general are, and to establish the "universal grammar" that accounts for the range of differences among human languages. The theory of grammar relies on certain general principles which govern the form of the grammar and the nature of the categories with which it operates. These principles are conceived of as universal properties of language, properties that are biologically innate. The notion of innateness, developed by Eric H. Lenneberg (1960), was adopted by Chomsky and became central to his thinking. He argued that much of our knowledge about language is universal and innate, that is, in-born, genetically endowed, a language instinct, part of our biological birthright. Chomsky attacked a standard view at the time that children are born with minds that are essentially "blank slates" (the view of the behaviorist psychologists), that the human psyche is largely molded by the surrounding culture. Chomsky maintained that rather than being born blank slates, children have a genetic predisposition to acquire linguistic knowledge in a highly specific way. He posited innate principles that determine the form of acquired knowledge.

Chomsky's (1959) review of Skinner's *Verbal Behavior* became the basic refutation of behaviorist psychology (which had so influenced Bloomfield and his followers). B. F. Skinner (1904–1990) (1957) had claimed to be able to explain language as a set of habits gradually built up over the years – as in experiments with rats rewarded with pellets of food in their trial-and-error learning (*operant conditioning*), which Skinner assumed to be the mechanism by which the vast majority of human learning takes place, including language learning. Understand the "controlling variables" (stimuli) and responses, and you understood language learning, he claimed. Chomsky's criticism showed that rat behavior is irrelevant to human language learning and that Skinner had misunderstood the nature of language. Human utterances are not predictable in face of a particular stimulus; we might not say only "oh what a beautiful picture" when seeing a painting, but also, "it clashes with the wallpaper," "it's hanging too low," "it's hideous," etc. In caretaker–child interactions, says Chomsky, parents approve / reward statements which are true rather than those which are grammatically correct. A child's ungrammatical utterance, "Teddy sock on," is approved by the mother when the child shows her a teddy bear wearing a sock, but "Look, Teddy is wearing a sock" receives the mother's disapproval when the child shows the mother a bear without a sock. Perhaps some human activities, say learning to drive or to knit, may seem to be learned as the rats learned, but not language. Language structure is very complex, but children do not go through a prolonged trial-and-error phase. In Chomsky's words:

> A consideration of the character of the grammar that is acquired, the degenerate quality and narrowly limited extent of the available data, the striking uniformity of the resulting grammars, and their independence of intelligence, motivation, and emotional state, over wide ranges of variation, leave little hope that much of the structure of the language can be learned by an organism initially uninformed as to its general character. (Chomsky 1964: 58)

As evidence of innateness, the following have been offered. Language is extremely complex but children acquire it in a remarkably short period of time. The stimulus or experience children have with the language around them appears to be too poor to provide the basis for acquiring the mature linguistic capacities that they ultimately attain. The language around them that children experience consists partly of degenerate data which have little effect on the capacity which emerges; the speech children hear is full of unfinished sentences, mistakes, slips of the tongue (performance errors). It contains few or no example sentences to illustrate some of the complex structures that children "learn." Children's experience is finite (limited), but the capacity eventually attained includes the ability to produce an infinite number of grammatical sentences. This is often called "the poverty of stimulus argument." The acquisition of language is relatively independent of intelligence – the language learning ability of dim children is not noticeably inferior to that of bright children; all but those on the lowest rungs of mental deficiency learn language, and language emerges at about the same time in children all over the world, uniformly regardless of language environment, culture, or ethnicity. Skill or ability seem to have nothing to do with it; however, for most other learned tasks, like roller-skating, piano-playing, etc., there are enormous differences from child to child. Finally, the direct correction of children's language mistakes (as Skinner's model advocates) has been noted by numerous researchers to be pointless; children's production changes not with adult correction, but only as the grammar they acquire goes through the normal stages of language development in children.

Since this theory began, it has evolved through versions called "Standard Theory," "Extended Standard Theory" (and "The Lexicalist Hypothesis"), "Trace Theory," "Government and Binding" (later called "Principles and Parameters" approach), and finally "the Minimalist Program." It has also spawned a number of theories which compete in some ways but which nevertheless share most of the Chomskian goals of linguistics and many of the underlying assumptions, for example, "Case Grammar," "Generalized Phrase Structure Grammar," "Generative Semantics," "Head-Driven Phrase Structure Grammar," "Lexical-Functional Grammar," and "Relational Grammar."

8 Typology

An orientation to linguistics which contrasts with the "generativist" approach is that of the "typologists," sometimes called the "functional-typological" or "Greenbergian" approach. Typology, broadly speaking, is the classification of languages according to linguistic traits and the comparison of patterns (structures) across languages. The typological approach attempts to explain the patterns through appeal to language function in cross-linguistic comparison. Languages can be typologized according to almost any linguistic trait, and indeed classifications based on widely varied attributes have been proposed in the history of linguistics. For example, Wilhelm Wundt (1832–1920) (1990: 436) dealt with twelve oppositions or types, including prefixing versus suffixing languages, free versus fixed word-order languages, and languages with more extensive grammatical apparatus of verbs versus those with more elaborate treatment for nouns. Such typologies rest on a tradition extending from the eighteenth and nineteenth centuries represented by Schlegel, Bopp, Humboldt, Schleicher, and others. Typology throughout the nineteenth century was primarily morphological – the structure of the word (morphology) alone was held to determine a language's whole character.

Several concepts fundamental to modern approaches to typology come from the Prague School, for example, implicational universals – if a language has a trait *x*, then it is expected also to have a trait *y*; for example, the presence of nasalized vowels in a language implies that language will also have plain, non-nasalized vowels. Roman Jakobson (1958) brought implicational universals to broader attention and this marks the beginning of modern work on typology and universals. It inspired Joseph H. Greenberg's (1915–) classic article on word order (1963); Greenberg is generally considered the founder of modern typology. Typological study has contributed to the understanding of many concepts of grammar and of how they interact with one another, how they function, and how they are distributed in the world's languages. Typological research also incorporates many assumptions about how languages can change, and "grammaticalization" has become the subject of extensive discussion. Though notions of grammaticalization have a long earlier history in linguistics (Harris and Campbell 1995: 15–20, 45–7), Antoine Meillet (1912) introduced the term, which has come to mean primarily changes in which an independent word changes to become a grammatical marker, or where some less grammatical entity becomes more grammatical. A standard example is change from *will* with its original meaning of "want" to the grammatical "future tense" (Traugott and Heine 1991: 2).

9   Conclusions

In a brief survey of the history of linguistics such as this, much of significance goes unmentioned, though the major developments have been described here. Suffice it to say that linguistics is commonly held to be one of the most successful of the social sciences and as such has contributed both methods and models of rigor to other disciplines. As well as having its own robust history, linguistics has contributed richly to the general history of ideas and can be expected to continue to do so. Therefore to conclude, it may be appropriate to attempt to anticipate the future, what the continuing history of linguistics will bring. We may guess from the current "hottest" topics in linguistics what some future areas of high activity may be. Endangered languages will continue to be a major concern – languages are becoming extinct at an alarming rate; it is estimated that within the next 100 years, 50 percent to 85 percent of the world's 6,000 or so languages will become extinct or so near to extinction they cannot be revived. Human cognition and connections with formal grammar are a major focus of the discipline, and this is likely to grow rather than diminish. Interfaces between linguistics and computer science are growing and are likely to be of high interest to future linguists. Investigation into language universals and typology, within both formal and functionalist approaches, will no doubt persist, aimed at understanding language universals, the properties of universal grammar, and the function of language (and how function may help shape language structure). The extent to which these approaches will converge or diverge even further is anyone's guess. Reports in the non-linguistic media make the issue of remote language relationships appear to be one of the biggest concerns of present-day linguists. In fact, it is the concern of very few linguists; nevertheless, efforts to work out the history of human languages and their more distant family relationships will continue, though it is hoped that a more rigorous and careful methodology will be applied and that some progress will be made. Advances will be made in the explanation of how and why languages change. A favorite pastime of some linguists today is to speculate about what will happen to linguistics when Noam Chomsky retires and his personal influence no longer determines much of the central activity in linguistic theory. Here, speculations run rampantly in many directions. It will be fascinating to see what the future will bring.

5 Historical Linguistics

BRIAN D. JOSEPH

1 Introduction

One remarkably striking observation about language, seemingly trivial but actually quite important, is that languages change through time. It is at least conceivable that language could remain unchanged over time, as is the case with some other human institutions, e.g. various taboos or the rules to some games, and with some aspects of human communication systems, e.g. morse code or the value of a smile as a nonverbal signal,[1] but the facts tell us otherwise.

The mutability of languages can be demonstrated empirically through a comparison of a single language at different stages in its history. For instance, (1) below provides first lines of some great works from three periods of English: Old English as represented by Caedmon's hymn of the seventh century, Middle English as represented by Chaucer's Prologue to the *Canterbury Tales* from the late fourteenth century, and early Modern English as represented by Shakespeare's *Othello* from the early seventeenth century:

(1)   English at various stages in its history
    a.   **Nū wē sculon herian heofon-rīces Weard** (Caedmon, *Hymn*, ca. 660)
        "Now we ought to praise the guardian of the kingdom of heaven."
    b.   **Whan that Aprille** with its **shoures soote** (Chaucer, *Canterbury Tales*, ca. 1400)
        "When April with its sweet showers . . ."
    c.   **Tush**, never tell me! I take it much unkindly that **thou**, Iago, who **hast** had my purse as if the strings were **thine**, **shouldst** know of this. (Shakespeare, *Othello*, 1604)
        "Bah, never tell me! I take it much unkindly that you, Iago, who has had my purse as if the strings were yours, should know of this."

The boldface in (1) marks those features – pronunciations (as reflected in the spelling), words, sentence and phrasal constructions, and the like – which are not part of contemporary English usage. As the translations show, the differences are considerable and noticeable. For instance, the long monophthongal vowels of *nū* and *wē* in (1a) – assuming that such is the correct interpretation of the spelling – are pronounced as diphthongs in their modern counterparts *now* and *we*, respectively; *sculon* in (1a) shows a plural form absent in its modern counterpart *shall*; *whan that* in (1b) has two subordinating elements (a doubly-filled COMP(lementizer) node, in some interpretations) where the modern counterpart *when* has only one; and forms such as *tush, thou,* and *hast* of (1c), while marginally possible in present-day English, are certainly not at all usual. Significantly, examples like these, reflecting change in the language over a period of some 1,300 years, can be found in language after language for which records prior to the contemporary period exist; nor must the time-depth be great to reflect change – comparing Mark Twain's nineteenth-century usage *I am become* with twentieth-century *I have become* reveals a change in the selection of auxiliary verbs in the perfect tense of *become* within a span of approximately 100 years, and the current use of *be like* to introduce direct speech (e.g. *And I'm like "Oh my God!"*) seems to have arisen since the 1970s,[2] and is replacing the earlier colloquial use of *go* (e.g. *And I go "Oh my God!"*).

Moreover, it does not take a trained specialist to be aware of language change. Over the years, again and again, similar observations have been made by non-linguists, offering further support for recognizing the ubiquity of change in language. For instance, Socrates, as reported by Plato in the *Cratylus* (418C) commented on what he (incorrectly) analyzes as a conservative pronunciation on the part of women of his day compared to the pronunciation of others, which he mistakenly saw as innovative:[3]

> You know that our ancestors made good use of the sounds of iota [a vowel letter of the Greek alphabet / BDJ] and delta [a consonant letter], and that is especially true of the women, who are most addicted to preserving old forms of speech. But nowadays people change iota to eta or epsilon [two other vowels], and delta to zeta [another consonant], thinking they have a grander sound . . . For instance, in the earliest times they called day *himéra*, others said *heméra*, and now they say *hēméra*.

As Teodorsson (1979: 69) notes, all the evidence known now indicates that *hēméra* is the older pronunciation of "day" in Ancient Greek, so the proper interpretation of Socrates' observations is that "the i-pronunciation used by women was that of the innovative phonological system" and thus that this innovative pronunciation coexisted as part of a change in progress with the more conservative *heméra* and *hēméra*.

And, Chaucer himself remarked on the language of a thousand years before him in a famous passage from *Troilus and Creside* (II.22–8):[4]

> Ye knowe ek that in forme of speche is chaunge
> Withinne a thousand yeer, and wordes tho
> That hadden pris, now wonder nyce and straunge

Us thinketh hem, and yet thei spake hem so,
And spedde as wel in love as men now do;
Ek for to wynnen love in sondry ages,
In sondry londes, sondry ben usages.

You know also that there is change in the form of speech within a thousand years, and of words though, that had value, now wondrous foolish and strange to us they seem, and yet they spoke them thus, and they prospered as well in love as men now do; also for winning love in various times, in various lands, various were the usages.

All of these examples thus attest to change being a continuing force in language. Historical linguistics is the branch of linguistics that is concerned with language change in general and with specific changes in languages, and in particular with describing them, with cataloguing them, and ultimately, with explaining them. Thus in addition to looking at language change, historical linguistics is also interested in language history, i.e. in working out the details of how particular languages develop through time. Somewhat paradoxically, a concern for language history means that change is not the only focus of historical linguistics; in the course of time, while virtually all aspects of a language, excepting those that correspond to truly inviolable linguistic universals, can in principle change, some aspects of a language may remain stable and not change. In fact, for some linguists, unchanging elements in a language may provide important clues regarding its (pre)history (see below section 6).

To return to Socrates' linguistic comments in the *Cratylus*, he was really engaging in the observation of language change in the example cited above, since, under Teodorsson's interpretation, he was attending to variation evident synchronically around him in Greece of the fifth century BC. Chaucer, on the other hand, in his musings in *Troilus and Creside*, was engaging in an exercise in language history, by speculating on what earlier stages of English had been like. As should be clear, both types of pursuits have their place in historical linguistics. The study of synchronic variation, though associated with quantitative sociolinguistics (see chapter 23 by Florian Coulmas), is a window into change in progress, especially on the assumption that an innovation, whether internally caused or introduced through contact with speakers of other languages, starts in a restricted part of a speech community and then spreads (see below section 5); on the other hand, the study of language history is a window, perhaps a speculative one, into the past, and it is associated with reconstruction of earlier language states and with working out the relationships among languages that give clues to how they came to be as they are. Moreover, in order to understand the history of particular languages, one has to have some assumptions in place as to how languages can change, for otherwise there is no framework for analyzing observed or hypothesized changes, or the movement from one language state, whether attested or hypothesized (i.e. reconstructed), to another.

These two aspects of historical linguistics are linked also by the so-called "Uniformitarian Principle," which states (in the formulation of Hock 1991: 630): "The general processes and principles which can be noticed in observable history are applicable in all stages of language history." There may well be reason to believe that the bases for this principle are suspect,[5] in that, for instance, processes of change observable in modern urban settings need not be evident or have been operative in pastoral communities of millennia ago. Still, we do know that humans today and humans 4,000 or so years ago are not all that different physically, to judge from burial remains, and emotionally, to judge from themes in ancient literature, so that some parallelism in regard to language behavior would not be unexpected.[6] Moreover, with this principle, observing change in progress in the present day provides insights that can be used for unraveling aspects of language development in the past into which we often have no other basis for insight; that is, with the "Uniformitarian Principle," we are licensed to make educated guesses about the past generated by our study of the present.

2   Framing the Issues

To set the stage for the discussion to follow and by way of framing the various issues to be considered, we turn to five key questions concerning language change, the problems which Weinreich et al. 1968 say that "a theory of change must solve"; as restated and elaborated by Labov 1982, these problems are: the "constraints" problem, the "transition" problem, the "embedding" problem, the "evaluation" problem, and the "actuation" problem.

The "constraints" problem focusses on what general constraints on change, if any, there are that determine possible and impossible changes and directions of change. One side of this problem, as put in the restatement by Labov 1982, focusses on how a solution "would advance our understanding of the causes of change, since each constraint demands an explanation, and that explanation will usually bear on the cause of the change." There is also a purely descriptive side to this question in that knowing the inventory of changes that have occurred is the first step towards understanding what the range of possible changes is and thus what the impossible changes are. In this way, a third side to the "constraints" problem emerges, for it allows for an important connection to be made between diachronic linguistics, the examination of language through time, and synchronic linguistics, the analysis of a language at any given point in time.

One way of stating the goal of (synchronic) linguistic theory is that it aims to characterize the class of possible human languages, thereby ruling out those linguistic states which never occur and are "impossible" human languages. Moreover, the way most linguists have attempted to achieve that synchronic goal is to identify a set of linguistic universals. Now, in doing synchronic analysis we usually identify a "slice" of a language at a particular point in time, but clearly, the "point" in question is arbitrary and can be cut finely or broadly. Thus, while English of the twentieth century forms a synchronic "slice" that we can examine, so does Modern English, defined from Shakespeare's time in the late sixteenth century to the present, and so does English of the 1980s, etc. With this view of synchrony, diachrony can be defined as the transition through successive, finely cut synchronic states, and can be schematized as follows:

D	L1	Synchronic stage 1
I	L2	Synchronic stage 2
A	L3	Synchronic stage 3
C	L4	Synchronic stage 4
H	.	
R	.	.
O	.	.
N	Ln	Synchronic stage n
Y	Ln+1	Synchronic stage n + 1

Linguistic universals, assuming they can be determined, hold at each synchronic stage and define "possible" and "impossible" human languages at each stage. Presumably, also, they hold in the transition between synchronic stages, inasmuch as the division between these stages is arbitrary, and diachrony forms a continuum of synchronic stages. Under such a view, therefore, with an appropriate set of universals, the "constraints" problem of determining possible and impossible changes reduces to the synchronic question of determining possible and impossible human languages. In a sense, then, the two pursuits are the same, and this view of the relationship between synchrony and diachrony makes it clear just how similar they are.

The "transition" problem seeks to answer by what route language changes. The interest here is similar to the view in the above diagram, for a "dynamic perspective" is needed to allow for a seamless movement through successive synchronic states. As Labov 1982 notes, in essence, "solutions to the transition problem can be restated as solutions to the problem, 'How can language change from one state to another without interfering with communication among members of the speech community?'."

There is yet another direction in which this question can be taken, i.e., expressing an interest in the specific paths followed by a change: does a change from X to Z necessarily go through an intermediate stage Y? For example, in the transition from Old English [ē] (as in *wē* in (1a)) to Modern English diphthongal [ij] (as in *we*), must there have been an intermediate stage of [í] or [ej] or the like, or could [ē] become [ij] directly?

The "embedding" problem focusses on how a given language change is embedded in the surrounding system of linguistic and social relations. This issue on the one hand asks whether there are system-internal conditions that induce or inhibit change. For example, is the packing of several sounds into a

relatively small acoustic and articulatory space (as with Serbian voiceless affricates: dental [c], alveo-palatal [č], and palatal [ć]) likely to lead to a loss of
some of these distinctions?[7] On the other hand, since conditions external to the
linguistic system, e.g. social unrest, wars, forced migrations, etc., could also
conceivably contribute to or affect change in language,[8] this issue, together
with the evaluation problem, sets the study of language change squarely within
the social arena.

The "evaluation" problem asks how members of a speech community evaluate a given change, and what the effect of this evaluation is on the change.
Here the focus is preeminently sociolinguistic in nature, for any innovation in
a speaker's linguistic usage that is salient and perceptible – whether it is a new
turn of phrase or new lexical item, a new pronunciation, a new syntactic construction, a new meaning for an already-existing word – can evoke an evaluative response from the hearer: is this innovation one that I as a speaker like,
one that I might now choose to adopt in my own speech, or is it one I would
want to avoid? Language use in this view says something about each of us as
individuals and as members of a group, and this social dimension to language
use turns out to be crucial to understanding language change and especially
the spread of innovations.

Finally, there is the "actuation" problem of why a given linguistic change
occurred at the particular time and place it did. This problem seeks to find the
conditions that lead to a given change, and adds a further dimension to the
understanding of language change, for if we understand the causes of change
well enough and can pinpoint certain conditions present in a speech community and / or a linguistic system, we ought then to be able to "predict" (in
a retrospective way, so that perhaps "post-dict" or "retro-dict" would be more
appropriate) the direction of change. "Predict" here does not have its usual
sense of hypothesizing about what might happen in the future, and indeed,
scholars of language change, perhaps unnecessarily, generally avoid making
even educated guesses about future language states; rather, "predict" here
means giving an explanation for why a given element in a language – a sound,
a form, a construction, etc. – changed the way it did, rather than in some other
possible way. For example, why did Old English *ē* become in later English *ij*
rather than *e* or *a* or some other vowel?[9]

Several of these foundational questions are interconnected, as the discussion above makes clear, and lend themselves to the statement of other related
issues, such as the relation between synchrony and diachrony mentioned in
connection with the "constraints" problem. Moreover, other issues not overtly
stated by Weinreich, Herzog, and Labov can be mentioned. Particularly vexing
is the determination of "naturalness" in the direction of language change: can
change ever lead to an unnatural state? Are some changes more likely to occur
than others? Classification of changes and observation of the range of possible
changes are clearly of relevance here, but so too are an understanding of the
physiological bases for sound change, the psychological bases for morphological change, and the like.

In the sections that follow, we explore these various facets of historical linguistics as the study of both language change and language history; moreover, in so doing, we bring to light some of the methods used by historical linguists in their investigations.

3   Substance of Change: What Types Occur? How do They Spread?

It is stated above, almost as an axiom, that virtually all aspects of a language are subject to change, except for those that correspond to absolute linguistic universals that truly cannot be violated. Thus, the simple answer to what can change in a language is "(virtually) everything," though it is not the case that everything in a language at a given point must change – there can be diachronic stability as well as diachronic change. For example, except for the realization of the main accent, from high pitch to greater loudness, the Greek word *ánemos* "wind" has remained virtually unchanged for at least 2,500 years: in its segmental phonological composition, its morphological form, its syntactic behavior, and its meaning.

This simple answer about what can change makes it difficult to exemplify all types of change in a brief discussion, but an examination of any earlier stage of any language, and a comparison with a later stage, will reveal a certain number of changes. Examples are provided here from just two languages, but a similar exercise involving other languages would yield similar results.

Example (1a) from English of AD 660, as compared with Modern English, reveals changes in phonology, e.g. *nū* → *now*, *wē* → *we*; morphology, e.g. absence of plural marking on the verb *sculon*, which ultimately yielded *should*; and lexicon, e.g. the loss of the word *herian*, the addition of the word *praise*, which entered the language some six centuries later. The changes in the once-free word *ric-* "realm" straddle the boundary between morphology and the lexicon – it is now restricted to occurrence as a bound element, though possibly still recognizably segmentable as a morpheme, in *bishopric* "the diocese or office of a bishop" (segmentable due to the independent existence of *bishop*) but has no clearly recognizable morphemic status in *eldritch* "strange or unearthly." Moreover, Chaucer's subordinate clause with *whan that* as opposed to standard Modern English *when* by itself gives an example of a change in sentence structure (syntax).

Similarly, between Ancient Greek and Modern Greek, with regard to phonology and morphology, one finds changes in the realization of sounds, so that [ü, ü:, ē, oi, i, ī] all merged eventually to [i], aspirated voiceless stops [pʰ tʰ kʰ] became voiceless fricatives [f θ x], etc.; and in the form of grammatical endings, e.g. second person past tense imperfective aspect nonactive voice -*so* became -*sun*, matching the first person ending -*mun* in vocalism and final segment. Changes are also evident in the extent of word-formation processes, e.g. coordinative compounds of the type *maxero-píruna* "knife and fork; cut-lery" were rare in Ancient Greek but have become more numerous in Modern Greek and the type has been extended to verbs, as in *aniɣo-klíno* "I open and close." Further, Greek syntax has shifted drastically, as the infinitive of Ancient Greek has given way to finite-clause replacements, and constructions which once tolerated missing (understood) objects have yielded to ones with overt expression of the object, both illustrated in (2), among other changes:[10]

(2)   a.   ēn   ho trugētos hetoimos tou
           was/3SG the-harvest ready   COMP
           therizein   (1 Samuel 13.21 [second century BC])
           harvest/INF
           "The harvest was ready for harvesting."
           (NB: the object of the infinitive *therizein* is not overtly expressed)

      b.   ekhei   hetoimon ton daon na   ton
           has/3SG ready   the-torch COMP it/ACC
           eparei   (*Lybistros* 2663 [fourteenth century AD])
           take/3SG
           "She has the torch ready for him to take."
           (NB: literally, this is "... ready that he take it", with a finite comple-ment; the object of *eparei* is overtly expressed (*ton*))

Moreover, in keeping with the program suggested above whereby one can learn about language change from synchronic variation, an example from con-temporary American English can be cited. In Central Ohio, among younger speakers in the 1960s, the verb *bean* was used in baseball parlance to refer to being hit by a pitched ball on one's head, whereas for younger speakers 30 years later in the 1990s, it refers to being hit with a pitch anywhere on the body, thus with a broader meaning. The synchronic variation in the 1990s between younger speakers with the innovative broad meaning and (now) older speakers with the narrower meaning suggests a change that may ultimately spread across all age groups in the speech community as the now younger speakers age.

   From the point of view of the "evaluation" question discussed above, when these innovations, or any innovation, first entered the language, they must have provoked a certain reaction from those who heard them, perhaps even a negative one. Most readers will have had the experience of hearing some technology-oriented neologism for the first time, e.g. *access* as a verb (e.g. *You can access that information electronically*), *e-mail* as a count noun (e.g. *I received thirty e-mails this morning*), or *e-* as a prefix referring to electronic transmission (as in *e-mail, e-trade, e-commerce, e-talk*, etc.), of needing to decide whether to adopt such usages, and of finding that even if one winced on first hearing them, repeated use by others made it easy finally just to go along and join in the innovative usage.

   In a similar way, though surely with more complicated motivation on the part of adopting speakers, all innovations that ultimately are generalized over the (relevant) speech community must be positively evaluated by speakers and actively (though not necessarily consciously) adopted by them. Such innovations, once they have spread, can be called "real" changes, in that the behavior of the speech community at large has been affected. Significantly, as a corollary, it must be noted that not all innovations take hold and spread so as to become changes in a whole speech community; restricted spread of an innovation can lead to the formation of dialects within a larger speech community. Moreover, not all synchronic variation will result in a change in the long term, for there can be situations in which stable variation persists over long periods of time; for instance, the variable deletion of the past-tense marker *-t/-(e)d* (e.g. *kep'* for *kept*) in American English has been stable for several generations (Labov 1989). The dynamics of the spread of innovations and the resolution of competition between innovative and older variants largely constitute a sociological matter, but clearly, one with linguistic consequences (see also the end of section 4).

It is suggested above that at the simplest level, the mere repetition and recurrence of some innovative usages can inure a speaker to their novel nature and thus promote acceptance and eventual adoption and spread. Another dimension to the matter of recurrence of innovations is the fact that some changes are found to occur again and again, independently, in language after language, thus giving a basis for deeming such a change to be a natural one. Some examples of such recurring types of changes include the following:

(3)   a.   the change of [f] to [h] occurred in the ancient Italic language of Faliscan, in Spanish, and in some varieties of Chinese (and no doubt elsewhere)

b.   devoicing of word-final voiced stops occurred in Russian, Turkish, and German (e.g. earlier *rad* "wheel" has come to be pronounced [rat])

c.   reductions of clusters with concomitant lengthening of an adjacent vowel ("compensatory lengthening"), as in Late Latin *asnu* "ass" → French *âne* (pronounced [ān]), or Old English *thegn* → Modern English *thane*

d.   loss of unaccented vowels, especially word-medially (syncope), as in Middle English trisyllabic *chimenee* (accent on the initial syllable) becoming Modern English disyllabic *chimney*, with similar changes in Latin and Old Irish

e.   adjacent sounds coming to agree in certain features (assimilation), as in Old English *hænep* yielding (ultimately) Modern English *hemp*, with the nasal and stop consonants, adjacent after syncope of the unaccented *-e-*, agreeing in point of articulation (both labial, as opposed to dental versus labial earlier); similar changes occur in Greek, Latin, Sanskrit, Arabic, and virtually every other language known

f.   reanalysis of third person verb forms with a person-marking suffix as having no suffix (thus as base forms) occurred in Greek, Persian, and Sanskrit[11]

g.   in many languages, analogically innovated forms have taken over the primary function for a sign while the forms they replace, if they survive at all, take on a restricted function, as with English *brothers* ousting the older but now functionally quite limited *brethren*, among other cases[12]

h.   in many languages, words that were once free and independent have come to take on the status of bound affixes, as in Latin *mente*, the ablative case of "mind" coming to be the French adverbial suffix *-ment*, as in *clairement* "clearly" (and thus etymologically, "with a clear mind")[13]

i.   the broadening of referent seen in the above example of Central Ohio *bean* recurs in the development of Middle English *dogge* "hunting dog" → Modern English *dog*, referring to canines in general

Identifying such changes as "natural," and thus unsurprising when they occur is in keeping with Labov's "constraints" problem and the "actuation" problem, as discussed above.

Searching for parallels and deriving inferences about naturalness of developments is thus an important part of historical linguistics, but one has to be cautious about not going too far, in that "natural" need not mean "necessary" or "only in one direction." Thus many languages, including English, persist in having word-final voiced stops quite happily, and some have even undergone word-final voicing, as the evidence of the third person singular past ending *-d* in Old Latin, from Proto-Indo-European *-t shows, and cases of movement from bound affix to independent word (the reverse of the *mente* example) are known.[14] Moreover, in some domains, for instance, semantic change, the directions of changes are so tied to the real-world socio-cultural context that being able to label recurring results of changes, as with the cases of broadening mentioned above, does little to actually advance our understanding of why a change occurred. For instance, English *bead* changed in meaning from "prayer" to "small round glass object"; such an innovation in the referent associated with a particular form can make sense only in the context of the counting of prayers on rosaries, and so is one that no theory of semantic change could predict as "natural."

4   Mechanisms of Change: How Is Change Manifested in Language?

One way that language change is manifested, clearly, is through changes in the behavior of speakers, in that a word comes to be pronounced in a different way, used in a novel construction, extended in meaning, and so on. In such ways, language change is manifested as alterations in the actual form that language takes in the mouths (or hands)[15] of its users, what might in the terminology of recent decades be termed changes in the surface structure, i.e. in the output of the grammar.

However, for the most part, explicit synchronic accounts of a linguistic phenomenon are necessarily couched in a particular theoretical framework and the formalism associated with that framework. This enterprise is driven by the assumption made by (most) linguists that there is some correct linguistic theory that is operative – we may not yet have found the very best theory, but the exercise of positing analyses and testing them is part of the process that will lead ultimately to the discovery of that best theory. Moreover, given that, as the diagram in section 2 above indicates, diachrony is the progression through successive synchronic states, and further that the current conception of the "best" linguistic theory is the medium for describing and analyzing the grammars of each of those synchronic language states, it is natural to think that language change can be accounted for or at least best characterized in terms of change in these grammars.

Indeed, in the past forty years or so, there have been several attempts at devising an account of language change in just those terms: Halle 1962, for instance, equated sound change with the addition of a phonological rule to the end of a grammar; Kiparsky 1968 utilized changes in the form of phonological rules as well as in their order relative to one another as a means of accounting for phonological change; and Klima 1964, 1965 took a similar approach to syntactic change.[16] More recently, with a change in the dominant theoretical paradigm, in phonology in the United States at least, to Optimality Theory, a constraint-based approach to grammar, the view has been advanced that phonological change is the result of changes in the strengths of constraints relative to one another.[17]

This view treats (surface) language change as a function of changes in grammars, and thus a secondary side-effect, a derivative, of changes motivated by abstract properties of grammars; still, it is an attractive view, one that is easy to believe in. However, there is good reason to reject it as the right way to view the process and mechanisms of language change; at best, it would seem to provide a convenient description of the difference between two stages of a language. For one thing, as Andersen 1973 has observed, saying that sound change is the addition of a phonological rule to the grammar does not answer the question of where the rule comes from in the first place; he looks instead to the reinterpretation of ambiguous acoustic signals as a possible source of sound change (see also section 5) and sees rule addition as a construct that describes the diachronic correspondence between the grammar before the reinterpretation and the grammar afterward but does not give any insight into the process(es) that gave rise to the change.

Also, changes in phonological rule systems of the sort that motivated the treatment in Kiparsky 1968 were generally associated with changes in paradigms. For example, an early Latin rule of w → Ø that accounted for the relationship in the root between *par-os* "little / NOM.SG.MASC" and *parw-ī* "little / GEN.SG.MASC" is absent from later Latin, and that absence correlated with the appearance of a uniform paradigm in Classical Latin *parw-os / parw-ī* (spelled *paruus / parui*). However, that correlation is a complete accident if the motivation for change resides in abstract properties of a grammar, such as the number of rules a system has,[18] for the loss of a rule would not necessarily lead to a uniform paradigm. On the other hand, as Kiparsky 1971 recognized, one could instead place a positive value on aspects of the output of rules,[19] such as uniformity within a paradigm, and posit that the motivating force for changes in grammars resides in the nature of the output they generate. In that case, the loss of the Latin *w*-deletion rule would be a highly valued event, since the output of the resulting grammar without this rule has a uniform paradigm with *w* in all forms. If that is the case, though, one has to wonder why it is necessary to talk in terms of changes in rules and grammars at all! One could instead view the change in surface forms (e.g. *paros* → *parwos*) as the primary change (on the motivation for which, see section 5) and then view changes in the form of grammars as at best a description of the comparison of the grammar before the change with the grammar afterwards.

Looking at change as something that is manifested in and motivated by a rule system makes it hard to account for changes that have a restricted distribution, for the very notion of "rule" implies some generality over large sets of forms. For instance, as Hock (1991: 256) notes, at least some changes in form motivated by a (psychologically based or analogical) association do not lend themselves well to treatment in terms of rule change, since there are no rules at all involved in the change. He cites the example of so-called "contamination," as seen in the change of French *femelle* to *female* as it was borrowed into English, based on a perceived connection with the semantically close word *male*.[20] Similarly, the early Modern Greek weak third person subject pronoun, e.g. masculine singular *tos*, seems to have originated in a construction with the demonstrative *ná* "here is / are" and spread from there, but only to use with the locative question word *pún* "where is / are?"; thus while the use of this innovative form has expanded beyond its original locus, it has not done so to any great exent, so that speaking in terms of the extension of a rule here is not particularly insightful.[21]

As another case of a change that starts in a restricted linguistic environment and then spreads on a limited basis, consider the change by which a -*g*- has come to occur in the first person singular present indicative of certain verbs in Spanish, e.g. *salgo* "I depart." This -*g*- appears to have originated in a few verbs where it was the result of regular sound changes, and then to have spread to other verbs on a limited basis. Moreover, with verbs that acquired this -*g*-, it spread within the verbal paradigm in a very limited way, into all forms of the present subjunctive (e.g. *salgas* "you might depart") but nowhere else, not even other forms of the indicative.[22] It is difficult to see how a rule-based account would be explanatory here, since there is no obvious basis for deriving the subjunctive stem from the first person indicative stem; rather, the simple occurrence of a stem allomorph somewhere in the overall paradigm seems to have been basis enough for a spread into other, even distantly related, forms. The frequency of cases such as these – and examples could be multiplied – suggests that this might be the most accurate model of how change occurs and manifests itself in the grammar of a language and in the behavior (output) of speakers, with the widely seen apparently general changes simply representing the endpoint of a series of limited extensions of a change from its point of origination.

Another dimension to the issue of how change in language is manifested has to do with where change starts in a speech community and where it ends up, as suggested in section 3. Just as a change might start in a restricted part of the grammar, and be generalized from there, as with the Greek and Spanish examples just mentioned, it is also the case that most changes appear to start in a limited subset of the speech community and then spread from there (if they spread at all), largely driven by social factors such as the prestige (overt or covert) of the group originally identified with the innovative pronunciation, form, construction, turn of phrase, or whatever. This model for change was developed by William Labov, based on his observations of centralization of diphthongs in Martha's Vineyard in the early 1960s, and has been amplified upon in numerous studies since then.[23] Such a model for the spread of an innovation raises an important question that is not fully resolved to every linguist's satisfaction: when is a change said to have occurred, at the first point at which an innovation appears in the speech of some individual or only when the innovation has spread somewhat through at least some part of the speech community? Some linguists see the spread as a purely sociological phenomenon and thus concentrate on what permits the emergence of an innovation in the first place (system-internal factors, contact with other speakers, etc. – see section 5) while others say that individual perturbations in usage are insignificant unless others adopt them, so that "real" change is only at the level of the speech community, or some subset thereof. It needs to be noted as well that limited spread through a speech community is one basis upon which dialects are created, and if a sufficient number of innovations are shared by some subset of speakers to the exclusion of other parts of the speech community, a separate language can well result.

5   Explanation of Change: Why Does It Happen?

The preceding sections have shown that many different kinds of change in language as well as change at all levels are possible. Consequently, it may seem that change is inevitable, and in some sense it is, in that change is no surprise. Nonetheless, linguists tend to treat the lack of change, i.e. linguistic stability from generation to generation, as the unmarked situation, so that change, when it does occur, demands an explanation. It is useful therefore to consider the various factors that induce change, that is, to explore the underlying causation of language change.

There are four main kinds of factors that play a role in inducing language change: psychological factors, physiological factors, systemic factors, and social factors. These all make sense in that they correspond to different aspects of language: language as a psychological "entity" housed (somewhere) in the brains of speakers, language as the production of sounds and signs and forms through the physiology of the human body (e.g. the vocal tract), language as a system with regularities and interacting components, and finally language as a social "organism" that exists in the interactions between and among members of social groups. These various causal factors are briefly introduced in what follows.

Several of the examples discussed above can be explained by reference to psychological factors. Key among these is analogy, which can be described as the influence of one form or class of forms over another and is psychological in that it really reflects a mode of thinking in which a connection, a perception of sameness along some dimension (semantic, formal, phonic, etc.), is made between two linguistic units; changes caused by such influence are referred to as analogical changes and while a number of classificatory schemata are possible for the variety of attested analogical changes,[24] virtually all of these changes boil down to the same basic motivation, that of echoing the above-mentioned perception of sameness by the construction of a sameness in form. For instance, in the change of the Greek second person singular past ending, from -*so* to -*sun*, it appears that there was influence of (i.e., a perception of sameness with) the first person singular ending -*mun*, since in this case, there was no general change of *o* to *u* nor a general accretion of a word-final -*n* that could have altered the earlier -*so* to -*sun*. Moreover, the grammatical closeness of the endings in terms of what they mark on a verb makes an appeal to analogical influence particularly attractive here. Further, the change mentioned above of early Latin *paros* "small" to later *parwos*, the mismatch between a stem form *par*- in the early nominative singular and a stem form *parw*- in the genitive singular suggests that the change to both forms having *parw*- shows a similar motivation; a clear connection between the two – they are members of the same paradigm after all – can be taken as the basis for the influence of one form (here the genitive form) over another (here the nominative form) and the formal reshaping of the latter in accordance with this influence. The psychological link between the forms, here furnished by their grammatical sameness, provides the basis for the change. Even in the case of the generalization of meaning and semantic reinterpretations of the sort seen with *dogge* → *dog*, psychological factors play a role, since in a sense the changes represent reasonable guesses as to the connection between a word and the context it occurs in; that is, since even two animals of the same species are not point-for-point identical in all respects (trivially, they can differ in size and age), a speaker hearing *dogge* being used to refer to two separate canines, even ones ostensibly similar in some respects, could make the reasonable assumption that the word could be used in the case of *any* canine nonidentity – that is, such an assumption would be an instance of an abductive change, in the sense of Andersen 1973, motivated by a reasoning schema involving a "best guess" as to what the use of a particular word was focussing on. Finally, to the extent that universals of linguistic structure and use can be identified that have some reasonable cognitive basis, some changes can be attributed to such cognitive factors; the change in (2) above in which Greek came to require an object pronoun in a construction that previously did not require it may be a case in point, if a perceptually based universal constraint that favors finite clauses that are whole and intact, as opposed to the "streamlining" possible with reduced clauses such as infinitives, is responsible for the appearance of the object pronoun in the later Greek form of the construction (as suggested tentatively in Joseph 1980, though see Joseph 1990: 186–7, 197n.B, 201–2 for some counter-indications).

One way of telling that a psychological cause such as analogy is responsible for a change is that other causal factors can be ruled out. In particular, there is no reason to think that physiological factors, such as the constraints of the speech tract or the perceptual mechanism, a type of explanation pursued very compellingly by Ohala (see, e.g. Ohala 1993, 2000), were at work. Still, in most cases of pure sound change, physiology does play a leading role. The very common loss of unaccented, especially unstressed, vowels (see (3d)), can be attributed to the weak articulation of an unaccented vowel when the main accent involves heightened intensity (as it does in English), though the weak perceptual salience of such vowels plays a role too. Moreover, assimilation (see (3e)), surely the single most common type of sound change there is, is triggered mostly by the greater economy of articulator movements needed in the transition from one sound into the next when the sounds agree, e.g. in point of articulation (as in (3e)).

In a sense, both analogy and physiologically induced sound changes involve aspects of the language system as a system. Analogy, for instance, pertains in part to the mental storage of linguistic material or the cognitive side thereof, and has to do as well with the systems of relations among elements that speakers perceive and establish. Physiology, moreover, pertains to those parts of the system involved in the production or perception of speech. Still, there are other system-related factors that play a role in bringing on language change. Some of the shifts in long vowels seen in English, for instance, were not isolated events but, rather, were tied to other changes in the vowel system; thus, (roughly) not only did mid front *ē* become *ī* (as in *wē* to Modern *we*, discussed earlier) but low *ā* became *ē* (as in *name*) also. Such "chain shifts" seem to involve whole systems of sounds moving rather than there being a series of completely isolated and unrelated changes. Similarly, the crowding of phonetic space referred to above (section 2) concerning Serbian affricates would be a clear case of systemic pressures playing a role in a change in those dialects that have narrowed the original three-way contrast to a two-way one (see note 7). Finally, at the lexical level, one can observe the so-called "blocking effect" where the existence of a fixed expression in a language seems to be able to block the creation of synonymous expressions, so that the system of lexical(ized) expressions interacts with the productive mechanisms for spontaneous creation of lexical material; thus the presence of *yesterday* in English apparently blocks the phrase **the day before today*, whereas the absence of a word like **pre-yesterday* conversely seems to play a role in the acceptability of the phrase *the day before yesterday*.

Finally, there are social factors that play a role in causing language change. Some matters in language are directly sensitive to speakers' place in society and their relationship with other speakers, in particular terms of address and epithets; when there are changes in the social fabric, there can be correspond-ing changes in these linguistic aspects, usually involving lexical change. For instance, during the period around the French Revolution, changes took place in the form of second person address in French, in accordance with a general egalitarian ideology in which the reciprocal use of the ("familiar") second singular pronoun *tu* served as an expression of solidarity.[25] Similarly, changes in attitudes about various sorts of designated groups in American society have led to changes in their appellations, giving, for instance, *differently abled* instead of *handicapped*, *First* (or *Native*) *Americans* instead of *Indians*, etc.

There are, however, other, perhaps more important ways in which social factors play a role in change, for they provide the key mechanism for the spread of one of a set of competing forms throughout a speech community, largely through the attachment of prestige to one variant. As noted in section 2, both the "embedding" problem and the "evaluation" problem involve the recogni-tion of language as a quintessentially social phenomenon, and the evaluation problem is especially relevant to the matter of the spread of innovations. The use of language as a marker of social identity and group membership means that various aspects of language use can spread among members of a group, if – for whatever reason – these features are taken to be emblematic of indi-viduals identified as key or typical members of a group. This process can be seen, for instance, in the spread of slang expressions or jargon (i.e., occupation-ally related vocabulary), where one's "in-group" versus "out-group" status based on use of or knowledge of particular terms and phrases is often pain-fully evident, as any older speaker in the midst of a group of teenagers or a nonenthusiast amongst a group of "techno-philes" can readily attest to. Import-antly, the same mechanisms that foster the spread of such lexical innovations seem to be at work in more subtle kinds of change involving innovative pronunciations, constructions, and the like. Admittedly, though, it is still an unresolved issue among linguists as to when one can talk about a change – at the point at which an innovation arises, e.g. due to systemic or physiological factors, as outlined above, or at the point at which an innovation has spread, having been adopted by speakers beyond the point of origination.

The recognition of the role of social factors leads to one particular type of social situation involving speakers of a language, namely when they come into contact with speakers of a different language. Such language contact situations are in a sense no different in kind from the contact between speakers of dif-ferent dialects of the same language, though the degree of difference between the speech forms exhibited by each speaker is typically greater in the case of language contact. Language contact can be the source of innovations, most evidently in lexical matters. For example, new words or phrases can enter a language from models in another language, in the form of direct borrowings such as *praise*, borrowed into Middle English from early French and ultimately replacing earlier English *herian* (cf. (1a) above), and *coup d'état*, more recently borrowed, also from French, but also via so-called "loan translations" in which a foreign phrase is rendered into the borrowing language, as with the phrase *It goes without saying*, based almost literally on French *Ça va sans dire*. Sometimes, however, borrowings can directly or indirectly introduce structural innovations into a language. For example, the existence of plurals in English such as *schemata* or *criteria* or *bases* (from *basis*), all from Greek, has extended the range of plural formation possibilities, and has led to innovative forms such as *processes*,[26] pronounced with a final syllable [. . . sijz]), modeled analogically on *bases*; similarly, the active voice *-ing* form in *it goes without saying* is unusual from the English standpoint, where a passive form as in *it goes without being said* would be, strictly speaking, more "English-like."

Under intense conditions of sustained language contact, especially when there is some degree of bi- or multi-lingualism to be found among individuals in a speech community,[27] it is not unusual for languages to converge structurally. This has happened in the Balkans, where Albanian, Bulgarian, Greek, Macedonian, and Romanian, among other languages, have come to be syntactically quite parallel to each other, so much so that they have been spoken about as multiple lexicons with but a single grammar.[28] The social context in which contact takes place turns out to have a significant effect on the outcome of the linguistic contact, to the extent that the current thinking is that there are no linguistic constraints whatsoever on what may be transferred from one language into another in a contact situation – one finds all types of words and morphemes borrowed, sentence patterns passing between languages, meanings of words being affected, new sounds entering a language, and so on, all through contact.[29]

The effects of contact are so pervasive, especially when one considers that the spread of innovations within a language necessarily involves contact among speakers, in such a case though of the same language, as noted above, that it could be hypothesized that *all* change in language involves contact. Despite the potential for such a claim, the non-contact causes of change, outlined above, cannot be discounted, and it seems that the causes of language change are best understood by reference to both internal and external factors.

6   Some Dramatic Discoveries and Important Methods

This survey of historical linguistics would be incomplete without mention of two dramatic discoveries among the many that have emerged from this subfield:

language relatedness and regularity of sound change. These discoveries also have the benefit of allowing for a consideration of certain key methods that historical linguists have utilized over the years.

With regard to the former, we observe that scholars have long been intrigued by the mix of diversity and similarity that human languages show. Among the hypotheses that have been advanced to explain this mix, one of the most promising claims that at least some of the known languages show certain similarities because they represent later instantiations of a once-single speech community; that is, it has been hypothesized that a single speech community, through the accumulation of changes of the sort described in previous sections and perhaps aided by migrations, resettlement, and physical splits in the community, can over time divide and spawn numerous separate and ultimately distinct speech communities. In such a situation, the resulting distinct speech communities show some similarity by virtue of deriving from the same starting point, and more important, show various systematic correspondences of form for this same reason. These resulting languages are said to be *related* (actually, *genetically related*, where "genetic" has its etymological sense of "pertaining to origin," not the more modern, biological, sense), and the original speech community is referred to as a *proto-language* (or *parent language*) for its several offspring languages.

The recognition that languages could be viewed as related to one another, led, by extension, to the observation that some languages were more closely related to each other than to other languages. Such clusters of more closely related languages are said to form *subgroups* within a larger language family. With that recognition, therefore, grouping and subgrouping of languages became an important scholarly activity, and with the discovery of new languages, the question of how they fit into the emerging set of known language families was always asked.

Critical to the establishment of relatedness is the issue of methodology. Of paramount importance here is the Comparative Method, by which corresponding features (more usually sounds in corresponding words but also morphemes and even syntactic structures) are compared with an eye to determining a set of systematic relationships that hold among the languages being compared. Languages are generally held to be related when a sufficiently large set of such correspondences can be found, though there are controversies over just how large such a set needs to be to warrant a claim of relatedness, and whether the correspondences could instead be a matter of chance or perhaps due to contact between the languages in question. When such systematic correspondences can be found, then one can also draw inferences about the source from which the related languages arose, on the assumption that the comparable elements each derived through their own lineal descent from a common starting point. When the Comparative Method "works," therefore, it is possible to make hypotheses about the earlier states from which the related languages developed and thus to reconstruct (aspects of) ancestor languages that gave rise to the set of related languages in question. For example, the recurring correspondence set described below involving *p* in Greek, Latin, and Sanskrit matching *f* in Germanic (under certain conditions), has led most Indo-Europeanists to a reconstruction of *p* for the sound in the source language ("Proto-Indo-European") that gave rise to the corresponding elements in the offspring languages.

A side-benefit for the study of language change is the fact that the assumption of relatedness and the Comparative Method also provide another source of information about change. If an element A in one language can be systematically compared to a non-identical element B in another (putatively related) language, and the hypothesis is made that they derive from a reconstructed element C (usually affixed with a * to indicate that the reconstruction is a hypothesis not an attested form), then clearly at least one change has occurred – either A has changed and B reflects the reconstructed element faithfully, or B has changed and A has not, or both A and B have changed, in different directions. Thus if we reconstruct Proto-Indo-European *p for the set of Sanskrit (etc.) *p* = Germanic *f*, we are committing ourselves to the hypothesis that Germanic is innovative in this case; had we reconstructed something like an affricate *pf, then there would have been change in all the languages being compared.

As a result of all the research into language relatedness and grouping of languages into families, there are now numerous well-researched and well-established language groups. Among these, to name just a few, are *Indo-European* (covering many of the languages from India west into Europe, including English, French, Greek, Russian, among numerous others), *Finno-Ugric* (covering Hungarian and many languages in the Baltic area, including Estonian and Finnish), *Sino-Tibetan*, (including Tibetan, Burmese, and the numerous Chinese languages, Mandarin, Cantonese, etc.), *Semitic* (taking in languages of the Middle East, including Hebrew, Arabic, and ancient Akkadian), *Bantu* (covering numerous languages of Eastern and Southern Africa, such as Swahili, Setswana, and Zulu), *Algonquian* (including many native North American languages from the eastern seaboard across the Great Lakes area into the prairie provinces of Canada, such as Cree, Fox, Ojibwa, Micmac, Massachusett, Delaware, etc.), *Uto-Aztecan* (covering a huge number of languages of the western United States and Mexico, including Comanche, Southern Paiute, Hopi, Nahuatl, and others), *Athabaskan* (covering languages extending from Alaska into Mexico, including Chipewyan, Navajo, and Apache), and *Austronesian* (covering much of the South Pacific, including Tahitian, Samoan, Maori, Hawaiian, and Tagalog, but extending also into Madagascar where Malagasy is spoken). There are also several languages that have defied classification and so are called *language isolates*, e.g. Basque, spoken now in southern France and northern Spain; Burushaski, still spoken in the northern part of South Asia; and Sumerian, spoken in ancient times in Mesopotamia. Such languages have no known or demonstrable relatives, though it is conceivable, even likely, that they have relatives that are no longer spoken, i.e. that died out without a trace, or relatives that current methods simply are not able to link to the isolates with any degree of certainty (and see below).

Some of these groups are widely recognized to be themselves part of still larger, more all-encompassing groupings. For instance, Finno-Ugric is considered to be part of the Uralic family (covering various languages in Siberia, e.g. the Samoyed languages east of the Ural mountains), Semitic is held to be part of Afro-Asiatic (covering (Ancient) Egyptian, Berber, Hausa, and others), Bantu is seen to be part of Niger-Congo (covering West African languages such as Yoruba, Igbo, Twi, and others), Algonquian is taken to be related to two now extinct languages in California (Wiyot and Yurok) and thus to be part of a larger, so-called Algonquian-Ritwan or Algic, family, and so on.

These well-recognized larger groupings raise interesting questions, and ongoing controversies, regarding the extent to which all languages can be shown to fall into ever-larger groupings. Is Indo-European related to Uralic, as many believe, and to Semitic? Do these families cohere as part of an even larger so-called Nostratic family, covering as well other families such as Kartvelian (in the Caucasus), Altaic (in Central and Eastern Asia), etc.? Does Austronesian form a larger grouping with Sino-Tibetan? Do the numerous language families in North and South America show any further groupings, perhaps into as few as two or three mega-families? More generally, how far can such "lumping" of languages go? In particular, can a single proto-language be posited for all known languages?[30]

Armed with these hypotheses about relatedness, linguists in the nineteenth century, especially western European scholars investigating the Indo-European languages, were struck by the discovery of numerous systematic correspondences of sounds in various languages in Europe and Asia believed to be part of the IE family, and eventually also by their ability to formulate these correspondences in a precise way, so that apparent exceptions to the correspondences turned out to be systematic in their own right. For instance, the Danish scholar Rasmus Rask (1818) and the German polymath Jakob Grimm (1819) described various correspondences that held between stop consonants in Sanskrit, Greek, Latin, and Germanic, e.g. as noted above, Skt *p* = Grk *p* = Lat. *p* = Gmc *f*, but also *d* = *d* = *d* = *t*, with both correspondences seen in *pad-* = *pod-* (ποδ-) = *ped-* = *foot*. Moreover, many instances of these sets, and others like them involving other points of articulation, were brought to light. Exceptions to these sets were found too, though, yet they were soon explained; for instance, Skt *p* = Gmc *p* in Skt *spaś-* = Old High German *spehon* "see" or Lat. *p* = Gmc *p* in *spuo* = *spit*, were shown by Carl Lottner (1862) to occur only after *s*, and cases such as Skt *p* = Grk *p* = Lat. *p* = Gmc *v*, as in *saptá* = *heptá* (ἑπτά) = *septem* = *seven*, where Germanic showed a voiced fricative, were shown by Karl Verner (1877) to be conditioned by the original position of the word accent, since the p/p/p/f set occurs before the accent while the p/p/p/v set occurs after the accent, taking the Sanskrit and Greek accent to be indicative of its original placement.

Successes such as these, and others, meant that all of the exceptions to Grimm's observations could be accounted for in a systematic way. The result was that the sound correspondences could be said to be *regular*, in that they held for sounds meeting particular linguistic conditions, e.g. the nature of adjacent sounds, the position relative to accent, etc., conditions which really defined subregularities in their own right. The empirical claim that emerged from such observations was that sound change was regular, subject only to precisely formulable phonetic conditioning. The exceptionlessness of sound change became an important rallying point for historical linguists in the nineteenth century, and this hypothesis, often referred to now as the Neogrammarian view of sound change, after the scholars based mostly in Leipzig who advanced this notion most vigorously, put the field of linguistics on a scientific footing. Holding only phonetic factors responsible for sound change meant that sound change could be seen as triggered essentially only by physiological factors, of the sort discussed in section 5. The Neogrammarian assumptions about sound change have generally withstood the test of time and the challenges of careful examination of case after case of sound change from language after language and continue to have importance in linguistics today; for instance, it is not unreasonable to see the insistence in generative grammar on rule-governed aspects of language as an outgrowth of the discovery of the regularity of sound change.

7   For the Future: What Remains to Be Done?

It should be clear that much has been accomplished towards understanding what happens to languages through time, the basic subject matter of historical linguistics. But even with these impressive accomplishments, much still remains to be done.

First, for all that is known about the histories of numerous individual languages, there are still many languages whose history has not been investigated carefully. In some instances, such investigation is a matter of mining the available material, e.g. regarding Medieval Greek, or Albanian after the sixteenth century, while for others it involves working out or exploring further relations with other languages and using the comparative method and / or other methods to make inferences about the earlier stages of the language in question.

Even for well-researched languages, more cataloguing of changes, as well as the determination of a myriad of details of developments, is needed; many texts remain under-examined from all stages of even a language such as English and the same holds for Greek, French, Russian, Hindi, and so on. Here, what is needed also is information about the social setting for all these languages at all relevant stages, in keeping with the "embedding" problem referred to in section 2.

Besides filling the gaps in language history, such further research will help towards the development of a clear characterization of naturalness, and thus feed into the development of a general theory of language change, another desideratum that at present eludes us, as the discussion in section 2 of the "constraints" problem indicates.

With regard to relatedness among languages, it is fair to ponder whether we have hit a ceiling beyond which there is no further progress. The questions posed at the end of the discussion in the previous section are thus directions for future research, but are perhaps ultimately unanswerable. It is worth observing here that, as inherently interesting as these questions are, even if they could be answered, even if a "proto-world" language could be confidently posited, there would still be the question of how the diversity evident in the languages of the world arose. That is, remaining issues of relatedness are only part of what remains to be done in historical linguistics.

Moreover, what may be thought of as the ultimate historical linguistic question of the origin of language still awaits a definitive answer, and may never be resolved. See note 30, but especially the chapter on the origins of language by Andrew Carstairs-McCarthy (1) for some discussion.

Finally, putting together all the research on language change and historical linguistics leads one to wonder whether a general theory of change is possible. Here it must be recognized that such a theory would involve working out the parameters of change, essentially anwering the five key questions in section 2, but paying attention as well to diachronic stability, for it is not the case that everything in a language necessarily will undergo a change.[31]

8   Conclusion

Of necessity, this survey has not been able to provide detail on all matters that make up the subfield of historical linguistics, but one final important point is that in order to do historical linguistics properly, one needs above all else to be able to handle all sorts of subfields of linguistics correctly. A full understanding of the synchronic system of a language at (at least) two different stages is essential to understanding what has changed and what has not; sociolinguistics must be invoked in order to fully understand the context in which changes occur and especially spread; phonetics is relevant to understanding sound change; and so on. Thus while not in the center of the field of linguistics,[32] historical linguistics nonetheless draws on virtually all aspects of the field in ways that other subfields do not.[33]

NOTES

1   See Ohala 1980, 1994: 332–5 on the possible origins of smiling and thus its functional stability over the ages.

2   See Schourup 1982 / 1985 for an early discussion of this innovative use of *be*

like. Butters 1980 discusses the extent to which the narrative use of *go* was itself an innovation earlier in the twentieth century.

3   The translation is taken from Fowler 1977.

4 The translation here is based on the text and notes in Shoaf 1989.

5 See Janda 1999, and Janda and Joseph 2000 for discussion.

6 See Melchert 1991 for a particularly moving account of the universality of a Hittite king's fears when facing death; Joseph 1998 gives a classroom application of Melchert's insights.

7 As it happens, many Serbian speakers do not have this three-way distinction any more, so some mergers have occurred here. My thanks to Ronelle Alexander of the University of California, Berkeley, for clarification of this point.

8 Fodor 1965 has a very interesting, but ultimately inconclusive, discussion on this issue.

9 Note that ē → e and ē → a are changes that are attested in other languages (e.g. the former in Pontic Greek, the latter in Bulgarian (with a palatal on-glide), and are thus possible outcomes of change that one has to reckon with (though it is not clear if these are direct changes or the result of the accumulation of several changes). For a discussion of why vowels move along the paths they do, see Labov 1994, especially the appendix.

10 For instance, the use of the marker *tou* (originally a genitive case form of the definite article used as a nominalizer of verbs) as a generalized complementizer introducing the subordinated infinitive disappears from later Greek (compare the reduction in English from the double complementizer of Chaucerian *whan that* to the later single complementizer discussed above). Similarly, the status of the marker *na* has changed; it was most likely a fully fledged complementizer when it was first used as a generalized subordinator in Medieval Greek (it derives from the Ancient Greek final conjunction *hína* "so that")

but in Modern Greek it is arguably merely a grammatical marker of the subjunctive mood (see Philippaki-Warburton 1994).

11 This is the phenomenon known as Watkins' law (Watkins 1962), discussed with additional references in Collinge (1985: 239–40).

12 This is the observation embodied in Kurylowicz's fourth "law" of analogy (Kurylowicz 1947); see Hock (1991: 210–37) and Winters 1995 for discussion.

13 This phenomenon is referred to in the literature as "grammaticalization" (sometimes also "grammaticization" or even "grammatization"); see Hopper and Traugott 1993 and Heine 2000 for an introduction to the study of such phenomena, as well as Campbell 1999b, Janda 1999, Joseph 1999, Newmeyer 1998, and Norde 1999 for some critical reappraisals of some of the claims of so-called "grammaticalization theory."

14 See Janda 1999 for a summary of the rather considerable number of such cases that have been documented.

15 I say this to remind the reader that language is not exclusively a matter of the vocal channel, since manually based sign(ed) languages are fully fledged languages in all respects known to us. From a diachronic perspective, sign(ed) languages show many of the same types of change as vocally based languages do, and their users respond to the same types of social factors that affect change in all languages. See Frishberg 1975, 1976, and Hock and Joseph (1996: 129, 131, 170, 269) for some examples and discussion.

16 See King 1969 for a summary of these views in a (then-)definitive statement, and Jasanoff 1971 for a highly critical assessment of them.

17 See for instance, Nagy and Reynolds 1997.

18   Note that the view that grammar change is motivated by simplicity alone could use the number of rules as a metric for evaluating the simplicity of a grammar.

19   Compare also current versions of optimality theory where the constraints that are ranked are output-oriented.

20   Thus *male* "contaminated" *femelle* and a blended form *female* resulted.

21   See Joseph 1994, 1999, for more details on this development.

22   See Lloyd (1987: 162ff), and Penny (1991: 150ff) for some discussion. I am indebted to Rich Janda for bringing this example to my attention.

23   See Labov 1994 for an excellent and detailed survey of the results of this research program into the spread of change.

24   See the discussion and presentation of terminology in virtually any standard textbook on historical linguistics, e.g. Hock 1991 or Hock and Joseph 1996, among (many) others.

25   See Brown and Gilman 1960 for a discussion of these and other developments pertaining to second person address in various European languages.

26   The noun *process* is a borrowing ultimately from Latin, and thus a Greek-like plural would not be expected with it; once it enters English, of course, all bets are off, and the word is no longer bound by its heritage. Attaching the native English plural marker or a Greek-like marker or reanalyzing the word are all within the realm of possibility; note that *criteria* is quite commonly used as a singular by many speakers, and one can even occasionally hear *criterions*.

27   Recognizing the role of multilingualism in language change brings a seemingly "external" cause, namely language contact, into the "internal" – here psychological – domain, since

the "contact" is really in the mind of the bilingual speaker.

28   This quote is based on the observation of the Slovene linguist Kopitar who noted (1829: 86) concerning Albanian, Bulgarian, and Romanian that "nur eine Sprachform herrscht, aber mit dreierlei Sprachmaterie" ("only one grammar holds sway, but with three lexicons." I follow here the translation by Friedman 1999: 3, who has very interesting comments to make about the Balkan speech community.

29   See Thomason and Kaufman (1988: chapter 2) and Thomason 2000 for discussion of this point.

30   To some extent, therefore, such questions can lead into speculation about the ultimate origin of language (see Carstairs-McCarthy (chapter 1)) – if human language originated in a single place, then a "proto-world" might be conceivable, though most likely not reconstructible, but if language arose independently in various places around the world, then a "proto-world" could not be a coherent notion. Overlooked in much of the debate and speculation about a "proto-world" (though see the brief comments in Hock and Joseph 1996: 488, 496 and Salmons and Joseph 1998: 3n. 7) is the fact that numerous fully natural and complex sign(ed) languages have arisen spontaneously around the world in various communities with significant numbers of deaf people, so that at best, it would seem that "proto-world" is "proto-oral-world" and not a proto-language for *all* natural human languages.

31   See Nichols 2000 for a discussion of some aspects of language that show stability through time.

32   One might qualify this statement with the modifier "anymore," for in the nineteenth century, diachronic linguistics *was* linguistics, period.

33   The bibliography on historical linguistics is vast, and the works specifically referred to here do not even begin to cover the field. For reasonably good bibliographic coverage, relatively recent textbooks such as Campbell 1999a, Hock 1991, Hock and Joseph 1996, Trask 1996, among others, should be consulted; see also Janda and Joseph (eds.) 2000, for an up-to-date survey of the field at large.

6 Field Linguistics

PAMELA MUNRO

1 What is "Field Linguistics"?[1]

Unlike most of the other subfields of linguistics described in this book, field linguistics is not a theoretical discipline, and there is relatively little literature devoted to this area. Field linguistics, as I will use the term here, refers to the collection of primary linguistic data on the basic grammatical facts of a relatively little studied language in a relatively natural setting from ordinary speakers, and to the analysis and dissemination of such data. This type of data collection is usually called "fieldwork." Classic fieldwork is done in "the field," the area where speakers actually live (rather than in an artificial setting, such as a university classroom), or, even more classically, the area from which the speakers' ancestors originated.

Many types of linguistic endeavor share some of these features of field linguistics:

- armchair linguistics, where a native speaker linguist reflects on his or her own judgments (often confirmed by questioning other speakers) and analyzes these;
- psycholinguistics, where speakers produce responses to highly controlled stimuli;
- language acquisition studies, where children's language development is observed, often in a highly natural setting;
- sociolinguistics, where speakers' linguistic behavior is observed and correlated with facts about their backgrounds.

Most people would agree, however, that these domains are not really field linguistics.

Although field linguistics can be done anywhere, it is not normally based on introspection: linguists working on introspective data usually are not field linguists, even if their language is quite exotic. Thus, the languages on which field linguistics is done typically have few if any native speaker linguists, and one of the priorities of some field linguists is to train native speakers in the techniques of linguistic analysis.

A native speaker linguist might certainly use introspection to produce data to be analyzed for a basic description of his or her language, but introspective armchair linguistics is normally directed at puzzling out relatively obscure or at least higher-level problems in languages whose grammar is already fairly well understood. Similarly, psycholinguistic studies conducted in the laboratory, acquisition studies based on observation of children in their homes and elsewhere, and sociolinguistic studies conducted in a community generally do not have the goal of producing basic grammatical description.

Studies like these can succeed precisely because basic description already exists. The goal of field linguistics is to produce descriptions of languages – often the first such descriptions. For this reason, what I am calling field linguistics has also been called descriptive linguistics.

There are many techniques for collecting data and doing fieldwork (see section 2). But data collection is only the first step. The data collected must be analyzed (see section 4) and, very importantly, disseminated. (Data, even analyzed data, that remains in someone's notebook or computer or tapes is of little value to anyone.) Any circulated data must be written in a system that is analytically consistent and maximally useful to the widest range of users.

Although there is not much literature describing field linguistics as a field, the amount of linguistic literature that results from field linguistics is huge. The type of literature or other production that comes from the analysis of field data can vary considerably. Basic descriptions usually take the form of grammars (or articles on grammatical topics) or dictionaries. These works often serve as sources for reanalyzing the data, perhaps from a different theoretical viewpoint. Novel data from field linguistics has provided numerous vitally important insights to mainstream theoretical linguistics over the years, and may also be important for other scholarship (section 5). Many serious field linguists, however, feel a compulsion to make the results of their fieldwork available to the communities of speakers who use the language being analyzed (section 6). Because of these efforts, some field linguists may regard their work as having more social consciousness than many ivory tower enterprises, though possibly these feelings arise in part as a reaction against feelings that more theoretically oriented linguists hold those who collect primary data in low esteem.

Fieldwork is addictive, at least for some people. The reason I do field linguistics is that I feel energized and my spirits lift on days when I get to do fieldwork, and I cherish my relationships with the speakers I work with.

2   How is "Field" Data Gathered?

2.1   *Basic techniques of field linguistics*

Linguists gather data directly from native speakers of the languages under investigation. There are several ways in which this is done.

Most often, particularly in the early stages of fieldwork, a linguist uses an intermediary language in order to ask for translations of words, phrases, and sentences in the "target" language. This question and answer translation process is called "elicitation."

Some field linguists frown on the process of direct elicitation and prefer to work entirely from more natural "volunteered" data. Most often, this involves recording from the speaker an extended narrative of some sort (a "text"), such as a retelling of a traditional story or a personal reminiscence. The linguist then works carefully through the text with the speaker, obtaining not only a careful transcription and translation but following up on grammatical constructions and paradigms that arise in the text, in order to put together a full description of the grammar of the language in the text. A counterpart to such text analysis, where possible, is observing natural conversations between speakers. Even if the linguist cannot understand everything that is being said, he can take note of new words and grammatical structures that may appear only in discourse.

Both techniques have their pluses and minuses. Beginning the study of a completely unfamiliar language with simple words in isolation is a good way to become familiar with the language's sound system; hearing words only in complex context can make phonetic distinctions harder to hear than when those words are uttered in isolation.

But simple elicitation is never sufficient in itself. If the linguist makes up all utterances for translation or comments by the speaker, there is a significant possibility of creating unnatural or skewed data. For example, the speaker's translations may be influenced by the structure of the intermediary language, or, when the linguist grows confident enough to create new forms and sentences on his own, the speaker may be too polite to reject these. (Consequently, it is important for the linguist to ask a speaker to repeat back any sentence he makes up himself – if the speaker cannot repeat it, it is unlikely to be fully acceptable – and to carefully mark in notes any sentence that was not spontaneously produced by a speaker. If a construction never occurs in spontaneous speech, but is only accepted on the linguist's model, it is unlikely to be a standard feature of the language.)

Elicitation and textual analysis are important complements to each other. One cannot assume every grammatical structure will show up in a text, so it is important to elicit missing structures directly. On the other hand, texts and conversational data similarly may reveal words and structures that never appear in sentence elicitation.

Serendipitous events can produce spontaneous types of language that are hard to elicit and that may never appear in texts. I had studied the Muskogean language Chickasaw for eight years and hundreds of hours before I began bringing my new baby Alex to visit my Chickasaw teacher, Catherine Willmond. One day, she took him on her lap and patted with his hand on the table in front of them, telling him,

(1)   Pas pas pas aachi
       pas pas pas say

I had never heard this type of sentence before, but discovered that it was a type of "expressive" construction used to describe noises that speakers feel is particularly appropriate for illustration presented to children. (Catherine's remark could be translated either "He's going *pas pas pas* (making a slapping noise)," or as a command addressed to him, "Go *pas pas pas* (make a slapping noise)!" The sentence was especially striking because outside of words used in this construction, such as the expressive syllable *pas*, Chickasaw has no words ending in *s*; other expressive syllables exhibit similar phonological peculiarities (Munro 1998). I have also learned that the presence of a baby is helpful for stimulating a speaker to produce diminutive forms of verbs, which in a number of languages may be used to show that a verb has a small or dear subject (somewhat like honorific forms in many Asian languages) (Munro 1988). Of course I am not suggesting that all linguists should bring babies into the field as a standard prop. But it is important to follow the speaker's reactions and train of thought, and to pursue new lines of inquiry that are suggested by things that happen during the field session.

Up till now, I have not considered monolingual fieldwork, in which both the linguist and the speaker communicate only in the target language. Complete monolingual fieldwork is rather rare, since it requires enormous dedication by the linguist, if he is to really achieve a level of fluency such that he can discuss the speaker's subtle judgments entirely in the target language. However, many other forms of grammatical study can be conducted monolingually, or partly monolingually. One considerable benefit of any such work is that it increases the native speaker's respect for the linguist!

In what follows I will assume that field linguists will engage in some direct bilingual elicitation, but that this will be combined with other types of investigation.

2.2   Getting started with fieldwork

2.2.1   The field methods class

Many linguists' first experience with working with a native speaker comes in a field methods course in graduate school. In such a class the students meet with a speaker of an unfamiliar language and elicit forms, which they transcribe and analyze. Eventually, the students learn enough to have a fairly good understanding of the grammar of the languages.

Part of field methods class involves learning what might be called politeness or respect. In certain stages of a field methods class, occasional students sometimes become so excited by the data that they forget that it is being provided by a real person, with a real person's needs and feelings. (I've had students turn to me in the middle of a class elicitation session and say, "Why did he say that?", referring to the speaker in the third person, as if he would not understand or be interested in hearing himself discussed!) The respect that is due to the native speaker who assists with a field methods class necessitates finding a suitable word to refer to that speaker. Traditionally, the speakers who provide data for linguists are called "informants," a word that originally had at least a neutral sense. In the last few decades, however (at least since Watergate), the English word *informant* has become a euphemism for *informer*, and is has acquired all the negative connotations of that word in the minds of most non-academics.[2] I see no reason to apply such a loaded, unpleasant word to the wonderful people who introduce me and my students to the joys of their languages, so I don't use the word *informant*, and I don't allow my students to do so in my hearing. Having to think of a substitute term is positive, since it forces the linguist – or field methods student – to evaluate his or her own relationship with the speaker. The normal term I use is "consultant," but often (particularly when the speaker is older) "teacher" is more appropriate. Many of the native speakers who work with me are co-authors of books or papers about their languages; in this case, "collaborator" is probably the best term.

My own field methods classes follow a traditional model. The students are not told what the target language is until the first day of class, and after that they are asked not to read any literature on the language until they have figured out certain aspects of its grammar for themselves. I have them begin by eliciting nouns (since in most languages these can be pronounced in isolation more readily than other types of words); the class members discuss together first their initial phonetic transcriptions and then their first ideas about what the phonological system of the language is (what the phonemes or distinctive opposing speech sounds are, in other words). After the class members have worked out their own phonological analyses, we compare these to existing ones in the literature – if any exist – or attempt to work out a consensus, in the case of previously undescribed languages. (I discuss in section 4.2 below the question of how words in the language are to be spelled.)

I don't allow students to tape record early class sessions in field methods. The reason for this prohibition is that no one initially is very good at recording data from a new language, however hard they try: only practice and analysis develop this skill. But if they know that a tape recording is available, many students are less motivated to work hard on transcription. In theory, having a tape of the session would mean that the student could work diligently on improving his transcription later. But a tape is never as good as being there with the speaker, when you can listen again, ask for repetitions, ask for slower or faster versions, or look at the speaker from different angles, so I don't want students to adopt this crutch at the beginning. (We often do record a sample tape of interesting words after a few sessions, and students are welcome to tape sessions after they have learned to transcribe well, as long as they ask the speaker's permission. It is wrong to tape record anyone without asking permission.)

Words in isolation are fairly easy for anyone to elicit from a speaker, but problems can arise when moving on to simple sentences. If I ask someone, "How do you say, 'I'm going'?", that person may tell me the way to say "I'm going" in his language, but he may also say "You're going," responding not to

Table 6.1 Verbal agreement markers in Garifuna

	(P)	(I)	(T)	(D)	(R)	(S)	(N)
1sg.	n-	-na-	-tina	-dina	-dina	-na	-nina
2sg.	b-	-bu-	-tibu	-dibu	-dibu	-bu	-nibu
3m.	l-	-ni-	-ti	-li	-i	-i	-ni
3f.	t-	-nu-	-tu	-ru	-u	-u	-nu
1pl.	wa-	-wa-	-tiwa	-diwa	-diwa	-wa	-niwa
2pl.	h-	-nü-	-türü	-dürü	-dürü	-ürü	-nürü
3pl.	ha-	-ya-	-tiyan	-diyan	-yan	-yan	-niyan

Source: Munro 1997

the metalinguistic translation task but treating the request like a real-world event. Students learn early that context is very important, since if the speaker imagines a different context from the one they have in mind, the result may be unexpected or confusing. Similarly, speakers learn how to interpret the strange questions linguists ask, and generally become much more tolerant of funny sentences. After students acquire a small vocabulary and learn something about the grammar of the language, they make up their own words and sentences, asking the speaker to judge if they sound all right. (This is a difficult skill for both the student and the speaker. Speakers sometimes feel it would be impolite to criticize an understandable but ungrammatical utterance by the linguist, while linguists in love with their own theories may not listen hard enough to the way the speaker says, "Yes, you can say that.")

In the second major assignment, the students have to work out how subjects and objects of different persons and numbers are marked in different types of clauses with different types of verbs. This assignment can be quite easy for some languages, or quite difficult, for others.

In American Indian languages, which have been the subject of most of my own fieldwork, and which I try to use as the target language for every graduate field methods course I teach, it is very common to find both subject and object marked with affixes on the verb or verb phrase. Sometimes such marking is quite transparent, but often it is not.

Table 6.1 presents the different verbal agreement markers in the Arawakan language Garifuna (spoken in Belize, Honduras, and neighboring regions of Central America). Markers in the P column are prefixes; those in the I column are infixes; and the remaining markers are suffixes. Each set of markers is distinguished for seven person-number categories: first person singular, second person singular, third person singular masculine, third person singular feminine, first person plural, second person plural, and third person plural. Although there is a considerable amount of overlap among the sets, they are all distinct.[3]

The markers in the different sets of Garifuna person markers are used in different syntactic environments: a member of one of the seven sets is used to mark the subject and then, in certain constructions, a marker from a second set may be used to mark an object. Thus, for example, in a sentence like

(2)   N-áfaru ba-dibu   "I will hit you"
      1s-hit   aux-2s

two affixes are used: a P prefix *ba-* on the verb *áfaru* "hit" and a suffix *-dibu* on the future auxiliary *ba*. Speakers' usage is entirely consistent, but understanding it is a challenge for the analyst, and requires a fairly extensive amount of data, since both the particular syntactic construction and the semantics of the specific verb involved determine which markers will appear. Because of the partial overlap between sets, only full paradigms can determine which set of markers is used in a given construction. Thus, for example, in (2), the *-dibu* suffix could belong to either the D set or the R set of markers. Only with further data, such as

(3)   N-áfaru ba-yan   "I will hit them"
      1sP-hit aux-3pR

can we securely identify the suffixes in both (2) and (3) as belonging to the R set.

I have taught two field methods classes using Garifuna as a target language. Students have difficulty realizing the complexity of the pronominal agreement pattern (even taking into account the fact that they have not seen every marker in the data they are analyzing) – they are reluctant to believe that a system can be this complicated, and often prefer to assume that they may have misrecorded *-tibu* as *-dibu*, for instance, or to simply ignore troublesome pieces of data. The lesson here is to look for patterns and to accept that the data may be complex if that is the only consistent explanation.

An important class activity is analyzing a text from the speaker. After the text has been recorded on tape, students go through it individually, producing their own transcriptions of what they heard on the tape. Then we go through the text carefully with the speaker, as described earlier. Transcribing recorded texts like this in a language that one does not know well is extremely difficult. Although it is possible to produce a quick and dirty transcription of a recorded text by simply playing a bit of the text, asking the speaker to repeat what was on the tape, and writing this down, the effort of transcribing the text beforehand is worthwhile. Often speakers are mistaken about what was on the tape, or they may change an incomplete portion of the text to make it sound better out of context. Frequently, more than one version of the text is produced – a fully accurate transcription of the recording, containing pauses, hesitations, false starts, and so on, and the speaker's edited version, with everything said right. Each of these has different linguistic uses.

From collecting data, students move on to more extended grammatical description and analysis, choosing individual topics on which to write substantive papers based on individual elicitation with the speaker. Many students' field methods papers are later revised for publication, or may even be developed into masters' theses or dissertations.

Increased student facility with and access to computation has changed field methods. In my current class, we exchange copies of all notes via e-mail, and have improved tape transcription with a sound editor. Word processing makes paper writing smoother, and the collected data can be searched in many ways in various data bases (see section 3.1.3). Still, there is no substitute for just sitting and staring at the data, as all serious analysts know.

2.2.2   *Finding a speaker*

The field methods class teacher locates a speaker and makes all the arrangements for that speaker to show up for class and elicitation appointments: students just need to come to class and use their brains. (Of course, this is an ideal situation: field methods consultants are people, not data machines, and they may get sick or develop other conflicts in the middle of the term, posing logistical problems for the teacher.) But real fieldwork requires the linguist to find a speaker to work with, which may be easier said than done.

One might assume that one would choose a language first, then find a speaker, and this is, of course, what many people do. But many other linguists who want to do fieldwork – but who, perhaps, are located in places where few exotic languages are spoken – happily choose to study any language that they can find a speaker of.

There are many ways to find a speaker. Personal contacts and serendipity are often very important. Because I know that every couple of years I will be teaching field methods, I keep up my contacts in the Los Angeles American Indian community. Los Angeles has a very large Indian population (largely relocated from reservations by now discontinued federal programs), but increasingly fewer speakers of Indian languages, and it sometimes takes me 50 or more phone calls to find someone. All Indian languages of the United States are endangered, most critically, so I know that eventually there will come a time when UCLA linguists will not be able to find speakers of more than a few American Indian languages in the city. But as long as immigration from Latin America continues, there will be a steady stream of speakers of indigenous languages from Mexico and further south. Many of these languages have never been described.

Many linguists have a lot of trouble explaining their theoretical interests even to members of their families. Before you look for a speaker to work with, it's important to consider how you will tell that person about your work and goals. I normally tell a speaker that I am interested in learning his or her language, and in my case (since I'm such a terrific language junkie), this is completely true. Field methods class presents a problem, however. I usually try to explain to prospective consultants that students take the class because (in our department) it is a requirement, and that they want to learn the process of learning a language from a speaker rather than from a language class or from books or tapes. But this sounds a little cold, and it's not surprising that speakers have trouble believing that the students really may not be interested in their language for its own sake. I urge the students, therefore, to try to develop such an interest – to read more about the people and their culture than just about the language, and to work as hard as possible on their pronunciation. All of these help validate their interest to the speaker, and increase the speaker's trust. Doing these things, even if they start out as conscious behaviors designed to impress, increase the chances that the linguist will be successful, and really will learn a lot about the language.

3   What to Ask a Speaker, and What a Speaker Says

Some people begin fieldwork on a language with a definite question or agenda in mind. Perhaps they are researching a particular syntactic construction cross-linguistically, or maybe they are looking for data to compare with that in a related language they know better. Having too much of an agenda or coming to the work with too many assumptions, however, can produce unexpected results.

One linguist I know had an ambitious plan for a cross-linguistic study of the potential ambiguity of sentences with quantifiers, such as *Two men carried four boxes* (did they have a total of eight boxes, or only four boxes between them?). He had shown native speakers of a variety of languages cute pictures of various configurations of men and different types of boxes, with interesting results. When he asked the late Pollyanna Heath to describe the pictures in her language, Maricopa, however, he encountered problems. In Maricopa (as in many American Indian languages), verbs for various activities are selected based on the shape of affected objects. Since some of the boxes in the pictures were round and some were oblong, different verbs had to be used, and it was impossible to translate the sentences simply.

I was reminded that I didn't know everything about how to do fieldwork myself while I was studying Creek, a Muskogean language related to Chickasaw, which at the time I already knew very well. I was primarily eliciting Creek words to compare phonologically with those in other Muskogean languages, but also idly trying to learn a little about Creek grammar. After I had been working on Creek this way for about a year, I happened to ask my consultant, Betty Bland, for the translation of an English sentence containing a plural noun. I was chagrined to learn that Creek has noun plurals – I had never checked to find how these worked in Creek, because Chickasaw nouns have no plural form, and I wrongly assumed that Creek would share this feature.

For these reasons, it is good to begin work on a new language by doing a general survey of as many features of basic grammar as possible: verb and noun inflection, questions, negatives, existentials, passives (if they exist), causatives, reflexives, and so on. This procedure reduces the chance of embarrassing surprises and often pays dividends in the form of revealing areas where the grammar is particularly worth studying.

If the language has been studied already, it is certainly worthwhile to review existing descriptions. These can be used to help develop a plan for early elicitation sessions, and may speed analysis. Of course, earlier descriptions may not be correct, or may prove to be based on a different dialect from that of the current speaker, so important facts from such works should always be rechecked. (This is not the only thing that should be rechecked, of course. The linguist's own data, particularly old data, should be rechecked and added to regularly. It's horribly embarrassing to find that a crucial word or beloved sentence elicited only once and cited frequently since then in fact turns out not to be replicable!)

As in a field methods class, it is best to begin the study of any new language with simple words in isolation in order to develop a feeling for the phonetics. Nouns are usually more simply inflected than verbs, so they are often good to start with. If a full sentence is too difficult to hear all at once, one can ask the speaker to say parts of it on their own.

Certain types of phrases, however, are dangerous to elicit out of context. I find that speakers of many languages are uncomfortable translating complex noun phrases on their own, and often translate "the blue house" as "The house is blue." To see how to say "the blue house," then, it is usually best to find out how this phrase appears in a sentence like "My friend lives in the blue house." (Actually, the same comment can apply to certain types of sentences. A complete sentence that may seem very easy to understand to you may be interpreted completely differently by the speaker. It is often useful to ask when a particular utterance would be used.)

It is always wise to note many things about elicited data. Obviously, if a speaker says a sentence made up by the linguist is bad, that is worth noting, but it's also important for the linguist to make sure that a sentence he makes up that the speaker approves can actually be repeated. A sentence that the speaker says "sounds okay," but which he can't repeat back, is certainly not a perfect sentence. Similarly, a construction which the speaker agrees to and repeats willingly, but which he never volunteers himself either in translation or in other uses, is an odd construction, and it's worthwhile for the linguist to try to figure out why this pattern is avoided in natural speech. Similarly, if a given sentence is translated by the speaker only with great difficulty, that should be noted too.

I try to always write down any comments the speaker makes about data we discuss. Catherine Willmond, my Chickasaw teacher and collaborator, occasionally says, "That's the way white people say it." This is a surprising comment, since I am the only non-Indian I have ever encountered who can speak Chickasaw at all, and the sentences in question are often completely novel for me. But evidently such sentences share some (incorrect!) feature with the speech of non-fluent speakers. I haven't figured this out yet, but I diligently note this comment each time it's made, along with other cryptic remarks. The late Robert

Martin, my first Mojave teacher, would explain the difference between two synonymous sentences by saying that one meant "You're saying it" and the other meant "You're telling him." This is another one I haven't figured out yet. But maybe some day I will!

3.1   Working in the field

3.1.1   Fieldwork can be done anywhere

I have made many field trips away from home to study languages. I spend an average of a week or ten days in Oklahoma (studying Chickasaw and Choctaw, and occasionally Creek-Seminole) every year, and I have worked on Yavapai, Mojave, Chemehuevi, Hopi, and Apache in Arizona; Zapotec in Oaxaca; Kawaiisu in California; Choctaw in Mississippi; and Alabama and Koasati in Texas, in each case on one or more trips away from home. But all the hours on all these trips put together would constitute only a small percentage of my total hours spent doing fieldwork on days when I spent the night in my own bed. Most of my field data has been gathered from native speakers with whom I met during classes at UCLA, in my office, or in their homes a few hours' drive from Los Angeles.

Now, in a few cases the speakers in question were actually in their original ("aboriginal") locations, since I've studied a number of California Indian languages that are still spoken less than half a day's drive from where I live (such as Cahuilla, Tübatulabal, Luiseño, and Diegueño). Most of the speakers I've worked with in the Los Angeles area, however, are people who lived in Los Angeles, but who were born elsewhere. Most or all of my work with speakers of Zapotec (several languages, originally spoken in Oaxaca), Garifuna (originally spoken in Belize), Lakhota (originally spoken in South Dakota), Pima and Maricopa (originally spoken in Arizona), Navajo (originally spoken in Arizona and New Mexico), Cherokee (originally spoken in Oklahoma), Crow (originally spoken in Montana), and Yupik Eskimo (originally spoken in Alaska) was done in Los Angeles.

For the most part, linguistic data gathered away from speakers' traditional homelands can be just as valid as linguistic data gathered in those homelands. But of course there are tradeoffs.

An important worry for many linguists contemplating working with a displaced speaker is whether that person still commands his or her language as well as someone with the support of a whole community. This is a valid concern – anyone can forget his or her language with no practice or stimulation. But any minority language speakers – as almost all speakers of American Indian languages are these days – are in danger of not using their language enough. Displaced speakers often use their language more than people back on the reservation – it all depends on their personal situation and circumstances. It is certainly important to chat with prospective consultants about how and how much they use their language. And consultants may well bring different types of experience to different tasks. A field methods class, for instance, is primarily studying a single speaker's usage patterns – so it is not crucial that that speaker be a conservative follower of standard grammatical descriptions.

If the linguist contemplates writing the first description of the grammar of a language, it is important to work with more than one speaker, if possible, and to supplement work with displaced speakers with work in the homeland community. Even when the bulk of the work is done with a displaced speaker (such as Catherine Willmond, my Chickasaw collaborator, who has lived in Los Angeles since 1959), briefer exposure to other speakers can serve as a useful check on and addition to the data (for example, I have worked with over 40 other Chickasaw speakers in Oklahoma, some of them for over 20 years).

One really important and gratifying aspect of working with displaced speakers is that one can share the fieldwork experience with a much larger group of students and others than could ever come along on overnight excursions. I regularly bring Mrs Willmond and others to campus to introduce their languages to students who not only have never heard an American Indian language, but have never met an American Indian. Sure, we can tell such people about endangered languages – but meeting a speaker of such a language and experiencing first-hand the beautiful structures threatened with loss makes the point dramatically.

However, certain types of field linguistics can only be done where there are concentrations of speakers (as many as possible) located as near as possible to where their ancestors lived. Traditional dialect surveys are done only with the most conservative of speakers (never with those transplanted thousands of miles from home to a new multicultural environment); to be useful, these can only be done in the field. Other types of sociolinguistic data, particularly when relevant to a traditional cultural analysis, is also best gathered in a setting as nearly as possible approximating the ancestral one.

3.1.2   Linguistics in the field is more than linguistics

The main characteristic of actual fieldwork in the field – away from the ivory tower, specifically where the linguist does not get to sleep in his or her own bed – is that it's a 24-hour-a-day operation.

When I initially agreed to write this chapter, one of the editors of this volume opined that field linguistics must necessarily involve eating weird food and developing strange illnesses. Well, of course that is true. I have eaten grasshoppers (in Oaxaca) and squirrel (in Oklahoma); I have suffered from deeply embedded ticks that had to be surgically removed (in Oklahoma) and Montezuma's revenge (in Oaxaca)!

But weird food and illnesses are just part of the story, and not a very big part. What's different about fieldwork in the field is that the linguist participates in speakers' lives much more than when doing work with speakers in his or her own community.

A student of mine recently drafted a small grant proposal in which she estimated her daily mileage on a field trip at twice the distance between the motel she proposed to stay at and the location at which she hoped to meet with speakers. I suggested that this did not include the inevitable mileage spent driving around trying to meet speakers, or doing other things such as taking speakers without cars to forgotten doctors' appointments. Of course this isn't the fieldworker's job, but if you are there at someone's house with a car, won't you volunteer to take him or her to the clinic if there's no other way to go? Just as learning to be a good elicitor of data involves learning (or re-learning) basic politeness, learning to be a successful fieldworker means being willing to participate. It means not assuming that it's possible to make out a schedule of field sessions in advance (so many things intervene – especially, particularly when working with elderly consultants, funerals). And it means being ready to learn about other aspects of your consultants' culture. Being willing to give up your time to do this not only will prove to be personally rewarding, but will show speakers that you are really serious about learning their language. (An excellent memoir about linguistics in the field is R. M. W. Dixon's description of *Searching for Aboriginal Languages* in Australia (1984)).

3.1.3   Technology and the fieldworker

When I started doing fieldwork, there were no personal computers, and if I wanted to record a speaker I had to bring along a reel-to-reel tape recorder (and even the small portable models were bigger than a fat encyclopedia volume).

The first dictionary I did (a preliminary version of my Mojave dictionary) was compiled in three-inch by five-inch slips (some linguists, I know, prefer four-inch by six-inch slips!) – not cards (too thick!), but slips of ordinary paper, which were arranged alphabetically in a file box (one hundred slips take up only a little more than half an inch). Reluctantly, I have stopped introducing field methods classes to the joys of using file slips, which I still feel are unparalleled for their ability to be freely manipulated and arranged in different ways. But I don't use paper slips much myself any more, so it doesn't seem right to require students to make a slip file, as I once did.

Computers have changed fieldwork considerably, and they are now easily portable; with battery packs, they can be taken anywhere (and in fact solar chargers allow using them even where there is no electricity). With a portable computer, one can display and examine wave forms and pitch tracks, add to a growing database, and search for previous recordings and related data. There are now intricate programs for the construction of dictionaries and text analysis (though I still have found nothing that works as well for me as word processing programs).

Tape recorders have also improved exponentially in the last few decades. Even inexpensive portable tape recorders often produce excellent recordings, especially with a good microphone. The availability of high-quality digital recorders and microphones allows the recording of high-quality data, suitable for all types of laboratory analysis, under the most difficult field conditions. Video tape recorders also allow any fieldworker to record gestures and other non-verbal cues, stimulating types of analysis hitherto never attempted with exotic languages.

4   Analyzing the Data, and What to Do with It

4.1   Basic analysis

The most useful way to find out what you do not know is to try to describe what you do know. It is very important to keep writing – sections of a grammar (or dissertation), papers, anything – and to try to see how well the language can be described within the framework of what you already know about language and how it works.

Linguistic analysis of many sorts is covered in other chapters of this book. The main point for a field linguist to remember is that analysis must be ongoing. The notion (which one sometimes hears) that a graduate student can go off to the field and collect data for a year, and then come back to the university and begin writing a dissertation seems ridiculous to me. The only way to know for sure what you need to know next is to have tried your best to understand and analyze what you have already learned.

The minimum sort of ongoing analysis, which I recommend to all my students, is to type up reports of each field session (or, alternatively, to enter new data in some sort of data base), preferably with notes, comments, and preliminary analysis. Looking critically at the data in this way helps to reveal gaps in paradigms and new directions to take in the next session.

4.2   Writing the language

An early goal in any sustained fieldwork should be to arrive at an understanding of the language's basic phonology. This is obviously easier with some languages than with others (though almost all languages present some tricky analytical issues). But without knowing which sounds are contrastive and what sort of allophonic variation may occur in which environments, the linguist is apt to get bogged down in low-level phonetic transcription and to miss significant generalizations.

The particular phonetic transcription system adopted is not too important (I think), as long as it is used consistently. My own colleagues who work on American Indian languages mainly use the "Americanist" symbols rather than the International Phonetic Alphabet (IPA) (for instance, š instead of ʃ), but neither of these has any particular advantage over the other, as long as one clearly sets out what particular symbols mean for the particular language under study.

Once the phonology is analyzed, it is worthwhile to adopt a clear phonemic orthography. Using a phonemic orthography simplifies the presentation of data and makes it easier to present one's analysis in almost any forum, except for certain types of phonetic or phonological study. Failing to use a phonemic orthography (if you yourself understand the phonemic analysis) is insisting on obfuscation: you are depriving the more casual reader of knowledge you possess. (One of the classic descriptive grammars of all time is Edward Sapir's description of Southern Paiute (1930–1). But few of the people who have praised this careful and indeed beautifully complete fieldwork-based study[4] have spent much time with it, because it is exceptionally difficult for the casual reader, since it mixes at least three levels of transcription – very abstract phonemic, fairly superficial phonetic, and extremely detailed phonetic – and is often exasperatingly hard to work through.)

I strongly recommend that field linguists – and others working with languages that do not already have an established orthography – develop not just a phonemic orthography, but a practical orthography, one that can be written entirely on a standard keyboard (in other words, one that uses no special non-typeable phonetic symbols or diacritics). Using such an orthography means that one can enter data in any computer application (including e-mail!) without the use of special fonts, but it has a more important practical value. Ordinary people – native speakers and their relatives, scholars in other disciplines, and interested laypeople – can easily learn to read and use an orthography that doesn't make use of special symbols, but they are often mystified or even repulsed by an orthography that makes use of unfamiliar symbols. I have heard native speakers beg linguists to help them develop a way to write their languages without special symbols, but such pleas sometimes fall on deaf ears. This is odd, since the meanings of the symbols in a practical orthography can be explained just as clearly for the benefit of linguists (with a one-time use of IPA, perhaps) as other symbols can, so that everyone benefits.

Certainly, some languages are harder to devise orthographies for than others (particularly given the odd biases of current Euro-centered keyboards, which for example include *ã* and *õ*, but no comparable symbols for *e, i,* or *u*). But it is well worth it to put out the effort to develop such systems. (I discuss some of the problems of devising practical orthographies, and some clever solutions to these problems by a variety of field linguists, in Munro 1996, which incidentally presents an early orthography for San Lucas Quiaviní Zapotec, developed with my collaborator Felipe Lopez, that has now been modified several times!)

4.3   Describing the language

Some field linguists learn a lot about languages they work on, but never publish anything. This is a criminal shame, especially since the languages in question may not be spoken forever. I believe that any linguist who engages in extensive fieldwork has a duty to publish (or otherwise make available) as much of his or her analysis of the language as possible. Preferably, such material should be disseminated in the form of clear description that is accessible to as wide a range of readers as possible. This is particularly true of languages that are seriously endangered, for which it is (alas) relatively easy to foresee a time when today's linguistic description will be the only source of information on the language.

The late Mary R. Haas, who founded the Survey of California Indian Languages at the University of California, Berkeley, and trained several generations of field linguists, taught her students that the most important goal of the descriptive linguist should be to produce a grammar, a dictionary, and a collection of texts. Such material can serve as the basis for production of pedagogical materials for language revival, cultural enrichment materials, background research in many disciplines other than linguistics, and later comparative and theoretical linguistic research. My own teacher Margaret Langdon wrote, "Only after seriously confronting (if not completing) such a task can one call oneself a linguist. On the other hand, I am convinced that this task cannot be approached without some theoretical assumptions to guide the enterprise and to provide the questions to be answered" (quoted in Hinton and Munro 1998: 1).

There are, of course, bad and good descriptions.[5] A good description must be written with a solid understanding of the workings not just of the language being described, but also of language in general. For example, if someone making a dictionary has not worked out how many parts of speech the language has, with what morphological and syntactic characteristics, that dictionary will probably be incoherent.

It may come as a surprise to readers familiar only with European languages, but languages vary widely in just this regard. Although (I believe) all languages have verbs, nouns, and probably a few recalcitrant other types of words often called "particles,"[6] many languages have no words corresponding to articles, and quite a large number of languages have no adjectives or quantifiers as we understand those terms with regard to English. (In many languages, adjectival notions are expressed by a subclass of either verbs or nouns, and I know quite a few languages in which quantifiers clearly are verbs, taking all expected verbal inflection.) But to accurately list and define words in a dictionary, the linguist must understand what the significant syntactic and morphological oppositions in the language are, and endeavor to encode these as clearly and accurately as possible.[7]

It is perhaps because of the field linguist's inevitable preoccupation with the minutiae of describing everything, of letting no piece of data escape unrecorded, that basic description is often dismissed as "pretheoretical". This term is sometimes used by theoretical linguists to mean that a description contains nothing relevant to current theory – no new constraints, no new projections. The irony is that such description is very often used as input to new theoretical advances (as I discuss further below), but it could not (or should not) be so used if it were not rigorously presented.

5 Contributions of Field Linguistics to Linguistic Theory and Other Scholarly Work

Basic descriptive data and analysis by field linguists contributes to the development of linguistic theory in two principal ways.

First, good description advances the theory by "testing" it, examining the way in which new data can be presented within current models, and showing how those claims must be extended and modified to handle new facts. Perhaps the most important early example of the importance of novel field data for the development of theory is Sapir's seminal paper on "The psychological reality of phonemes" (1949 [1933]), which established the existence of native speakers' mental concept of the phoneme (in Southern Paiute, Sarcee, and Nootka), foreshadowing the development of generative grammar. The best example I know of of a linguist who in his own work and that of his students has been constantly concerned with the relationship of field data to theory is Kenneth Hale, practically all of whose works present new and interesting data within a highly relevant theoretical context. Among the most significant is Hale's work (based on languages of Australia and the Americas) on the notion of nonconfigurationality, which inspired extensive work on clause structure and pronominal and other arguments. Related work by Mark Baker, based in large part on fieldwork on Mohawk, resulted in important contributions to the theoretical treatment of incorporation (1988) and polysynthesis (1996), contributing to the development of the Minimalist program in syntax.[8]

Excellent contributions to linguistic theory based on solid fieldwork abound. Recent fieldwork-based dissertations by three of my students, for example, offered solutions to syntactic problems involving Binding in Choctaw (George A. Broadwell, 1990), Wh Movement in Western Apache (Brian C. Potter, 1997), and Antisymmetry in San Lucas Quiaviní Zapotec (Felicia A. Lee, 1999). Each of these works – like the best such descriptions – includes descriptive sections as well as theoretical argumentation.

Differences among languages provide valuable clues to how cognitive processes are related to speech, and the goal of much theoretical linguistics is to examine this relationship. But the theory can only be truly extended as it incorporates increasingly novel data-based observations. The relevance of these observations is not always immediately appreciated, so sometimes the most important contribution of a descriptive linguist will simply be to record facts about language that do not yet fit into any theoretical paradigm – but which will be relevant for future ones. Most typically, such pieces of data are noted by linguists without a theoretical axe to grind, whose whole purpose is to provide as complete a description as possible. Such people often note the existence of phenomena that are as yet irrelevant for current theory.

For instance, descriptive linguists have noted many ways in which pronominal agreement and case systems deviate from the Indo-European nominative-accusative norm. Since the 1970s, these have become an important subject for typological analysis – Anderson's (1976) and Dixon's (1979) important studies of ergativity would have been impossible without a vast body of primary "pure" descriptions. More recently ergativity has been a concern even in highly theoretical work (e.g. by Hale and Keyser 1993 and Laka 1992).

Many other aspects of typological research advance through the work of much earlier descriptive linguists. When I was in graduate school it was a commonplace truism that no language had a basic word order that began with the object. SVO, SOV, VSO were accepted basic word orders, VOS had been observed in a few languages, but OSV and OVS did not occur – of course prompting the development of typological theories to account for this observation. Even as I was being taught about this, however, field linguists associated with the Summer Institute of Linguistics were recording Amazonian languages with just this word order. They did not describe these languages with an eye toward upsetting typological claims that they may not even have been aware of; they simply wanted to describe the languages they worked on thoroughly and well. But their work led to the advancement of typological studies (Derbyshire and Pullum 1981).

The study of phonology traditionally draws on a wider linguistic data base than syntax. Although Chomsky and Halle's pioneering study of *The Sound Pattern of English* (1968) is now often viewed as the epitome of abstraction, this work set an important standard in terms of the number of languages that were cited in support of its claims (and, in particular, that went into the development of its feature system). In recent years, this trend has grown. Increasing numbers of phonetic studies have made possible sophisticated surveys of a very wide range of languages (e.g. Ladefoged and Maddieson 1996), which in turn provide input into theoretical studies of all aspects of phonology. Whole subfields of phonology, such as autosegmental phonology (1979), arose because of the realization that there were types of phonetic data that could not be handled easily within current theory.

Field linguists also contribute to other scholarly activity besides theoretical work in syntax, semantics, phonetics, and phonology. At the beginning of this chapter I mentioned several other areas of linguistics that rely on work with native speakers, such as acquisition studies and sociolinguistics. Such work cannot be done easily – or perhaps cannot be done at all – on languages for which no basic description exists, so providing basic descriptions lays the foundation for later linguistic analysis of almost any kind. Another field of linguistics for which basic description of as many languages as possible is vital is historical linguistics, and the related areas of classification and dialectology. Comparative and historical work must be based on basic field data.

Researchers in many other fields draw on primary linguistic description (and greatly appreciate it if it is as theoretically neutral and devoid of jargon as possible). Anthropologists, ethnologists, and historians make use of linguistic description for research both on contemporary populations and on historical records that may include material in minority languages. Scholars studying place names, ethnobotany, and many other aspects of culture make use of primary linguistic description, particularly in the form of dictionaries.

6   The Highest Contribution

One of the most important reasons to do primary description is to preserve languages that may otherwise pass away. Languages reflect much of their speakers' culture and experience. Much of a society's knowledge and unique expressions will inevitably be lost with the disappearance of language. Linguistic diversity is one of the most visible and important aspects of mankind's cultural diversity, and language loss diminishes this diversity. The passing of any language reduces the range of human expressive power, and may lessen our chance of figuring out how language is realized in the mind.

Some linguists do extensive fieldwork in graduate school, write a dissertation, and then go on to careers as professional academics, publishing only on theoretical issues. Others (like me) never recover from the bite of the fieldwork bug, and must always go on to study one more language, or to learn one more word to add to the current dictionary.

The best contribution this last group of field linguists can make is to produce descriptions like those I have described here, which can be used not only as the basis of linguistic and other scholarly research, but also by the communities of the native speakers who have helped us, for assistance in language revitalization and cultural awareness programs or to promote literacy. Dictionaries that can be used by ordinary people, written with clearly explained, easily understood orthographies, and grammars (especially teaching grammars) that can be used by intelligent, motivated laypeople, are among the descriptive linguist's most useful publications.

These can also, of course, be the most enduring of contributions. Check the circulation records of any large library. With virtually no exceptions, the linguistic books that are still being borrowed 30 or 50 years after they were written are basic descriptions, not theoretical tomes.

NOTES

1   I am grateful to a number of colleagues who sent me their answers to this question and others I consider here: Aaron Broadwell, Ken Hale, Jack B. Martin, Laura Martin, Russell Schuh, and Siri Tuttle. I have learned a lot about fieldwork from observing and talking to many other linguists over the years.

I must also thank all the wonderful native speakers without whom I could not call myself a fieldworker, especially those I mention here: Betty Bland, Felipe Lopez, the late Pollyanna Heath, Catherine Willmond, and the late Robert Martin. As always this is for Allen and JP, and dear Alex.

2   There are especially unfortunate potential parallels between a traditional police informer and a linguistic "informant": both are paid by an outsider in authority (surely a university professor is such a person) to reveal confidential information known only to the payee's intimate circle. I believe that there are many potential non-financial benefits to a native speaker who works with a linguist – the work is often intellectually stimulating, the native speaker usually winds up learning interesting things about his language, and he may receive the gratification of contributing to his language's preservation. Nonetheless, however, there are certainly groups who regard the teaching of their language to outsiders as a betrayal. Why should linguists use a term that invites this suggestion?

3   One might assume that the T set includes a morpheme -*ti* and the N set contains a morpheme -*ni*, which are added to the S set (with a rule deleting the first of two adjacent vowels), although it is difficult to suggest a meaning for these two morphemes. But this still leaves five separate sets!

4   Based for the most part, in fact, on data from a displaced speaker from Utah, Tony Tillohash, a student at Carlisle Indian School in Pennsylvania.

5   I could say a lot about bad description, but I won't. There are good grammars and bad grammars, and good dictionaries and bad dictionaries. Usually it's pretty easy to tell the difference just by inspection – inconsistencies and things that don't make sense are pretty easy to spot if you look for them. But sometimes one can't be sure one's dealing with a bad description until one actually studies the language being described. This is scary, given that some languages can no longer in fact be studied! But the only solution is for more people to try to do the best job with description that they can.

6   Perhaps it is true that there are indeed languages for which there really is no distinction between nouns and verbs, but I have no personal experience with such languages.

7   A colleague once said (seriously, I believe, at the time) that you don't even need to be a linguist to make a dictionary; all you have to do is write down words. This ignores the points just made in the text, as well as the need for a thorough phonological (and orthographic) analysis of the sort described earlier. I think that most likely this colleague no longer subscribes to this view, and perhaps spoke hastily even on this occasion. However, such remarks illustrate the relatively low standing of descriptive linguists in our field.

8   Polysynthetic languages are those that express many meanings within a single verb word. Baker's definition of polysynthesis is more restricted than the usual understanding of this term, consequently (from my point of view) making the term less useful and interesting. But his claims based on his notion of polysynthesis are provocative and important.

7 Linguistic Phonetics

JOHN LAVER

1 Introduction

Linguistics and phonetics are often characterized as *the linguistic sciences*, implying both similarities and differences. Both linguistics and phonetics are grounded in a basic interest in the nature of human communication. If the subject of *linguistics* is the scientific study of the nature, use, and variety of all aspects of language, the subject of *phonetics* is the scientific study of the nature, use, and variety of all aspects of speech. These are broad definitions of both subjects, and not all linguists and phoneticians would accept such a breadth of scope. But the two subjects have developed so widely in the second half of the twentieth century that a broad view probably better represents the modern diversity of both subjects. What is less controversial is that linguistics and phonetics share a common if partial domain in *phonology*, the study of communicative aspects of spoken language. (In the text below, the first significant mention of a technical term is printed in italics.)

The intersection of linguistics and phonetics in the study of spoken language is visible in the perspectives that each borrows from the other for phonological purposes. Linguistics contributes to phonetics its phonological understanding of the distinctive patterns that make up the coded, conventional aspects of speech which differentiate individual words and other units of spoken language. Phonetics contributes to linguistics its phonetic understanding of the production and perception of the detailed artefacts of speech that embody those significant phonological patterns. Each contribution is complemented by the other. To study formal patterns alone risks becoming over-abstract, and losing touch with the physical realities of spoken language. To study the artefacts of speech without due regard for their identity as conventionally coded signals risks losing sight of the communicative motive of spoken language. The name usually given to the study of spoken language from a phonetic perspective, following the example of Ladefoged (1971, 1997), is *linguistic phonetics*.

2   Linguistic Phonetics and General Phonetic Theory

The objective of linguistic phonetics, which most phoneticians would regard as the center of their professional domain, is to describe the phonetic correlates of phonological units of spoken language and their interactions. Another way of putting this is to say that the ultimate task of linguistic phonetics is to give a comprehensive account of speech patterns and their pronunciations in all languages and dialects of the world. To achieve this task, linguistic phonetics draws on *general phonetic theory*, which is the foundation for the phonetician's understanding of how speech is produced, transmitted, and perceived, against a background of a *general phonological theory* of spoken language. The aim of this chapter is to give a compact account of the shape and content of a model of linguistic phonetics within this framework of a general phonetic theory. Within the current volume, Cohn (chapter 8) presents a summary view of the shape and content of phonological theory, and the reader is referred to her chapter for definitions of basic phonological concepts used here, such as "phoneme," "allophone," "phonological feature," and "phonological syllable."

More extensive presentations of linguistic phonetics than is possible here are available in Abercrombie (1967), Catford (1977, 1988, 1994), Clark and Yallop (1995), Ladefoged (1993, 1997), Ladefoged and Maddieson (1996), and Laver (1994a). Hardcastle and Laver (1997) offer a comprehensive account of the phonetic sciences, including both linguistic and nonlinguistic aspects. A branch of phonetics with particular relevance to both linguistic phonetics and phonology is *acoustic phonetics*. Recommended publications in acoustic phonetics for readers interested in linguistic communication are Kent and Read (1992), Ladefoged (1971, 1993), and Stevens (1998). Laver (1994b) surveys nonlinguistic interests in phonetics, including *paralinguistic* interests in communication of attitudinal and emotional information through tone of voice, and *extralinguistic* interests in matters such as speaker-characterization. Coulmas (1993) provides a comprehensive account of phonetic and linguistic variation in different *sociolinguistic* speech communities. Goldsmith (1995) gives a wide-ranging review of many different approaches to phonological theory.

3   The Scope of Linguistic Phonetics

A comprehensive approach to linguistic phonetics might entail addressing at least four complementary objectives:

1   describing the phonetic basis for differentiating all contrastive (*phonemic*) and contextual (*allophonic*) patterns in speech which signal the identities of linguistic units in any given language;

2 describing the phonetic regularities which distinguish the speech-styles of a given sociolinguistic community from those of others within any given language;
3 describing the idiosyncratic but characteristic phonetic events which distinguish the speech of one member of any given sociolinguistic community from that of other members;
4 describing all recurrent aspects of speech that make one language sound different from others.

All four objectives could be thought relevant to capturing the full extent of the behavioral substance of spoken linguistic communication. Most linguistic phonetic accounts of languages, however, have almost entirely restricted themselves to the first objective. Research by a number of other specialisms has used this first objective as a foundation for pursuing one or more of the other objectives. Sociolinguists interested in the way that speech acts as an index of membership of different communities have investigated the second objective, usually in an urban context. Speech pathologists, and those interested in speaker characterization for other reasons, such as a focus on forensic phonetics, have addressed the third objective. Speech technology has successfully developed automatic systems for speech production, speaker recognition, and language identification (Laver 1994c); but the methods used mostly exploit automated machine learning about hidden statistical patterns in the acoustic waveforms of speech, which doesn't involve explicit "description" in the same sense. No language investigated so far has been comprehensively and explicitly described against all four objectives (though general phonetic theory could in principle be applied to each of these tasks).

Within the first objective, linguistic phonetic accounts also often limit themselves to specifying only the phonetic basis for distinguishing the patterns that contrastively identify one phonological unit from another, for example the consonant or vowel phonemes that discriminate minimally different words in English such as *call* and *tall*, or *seal* and *sill*. The contextual patterns associated with the incidence of contrastive linguistic units in different *structures* and in different *environments* are less often described in detail, rich in phonetic regularity though they are. These aspects of sound-patterning often ignored by linguistic phonetic accounts include the wide range of allophonic realizations of phonemes in different syllable structures and in different contextual environments within syllables.

The limiting of linguistic phonetic accounts of languages to a description chiefly of distinctive phonological contrasts is no doubt because it is seen as a means to a different end. An account of phonological contrasts is all that is normally felt by linguists to be needed for further discussion of linguistic behavior at higher levels than phonology, in morphology, lexis, syntax, and semantics. From the phonetician's perspective, however, once these contrastive patterns have been identified, it is in the phonetic detail of the contextual allophonic interaction of linguistic units that some of the most interesting and challenging phenomena in speech production and perception are to be found.

The presentation of a model of linguistic phonetics in this chapter will give priority to describing the phonetic basis for differentiating the contrastive and contextual patterns in speech which signal the identities of linguistic units in the different languages of the world, but will touch in passing on the other objectives as well. The phonetic symbols used in transcription, enclosed in square brackets [ ], will be those of the International Phonetic Alphabet (1993) of the International Phonetic Association (IPA), set out in what is usually called the IPA Chart. The chart is attached as an appendix to this chapter, for consultation about transcriptional symbols and their classificatory phonetic identification.

4 The Coverage of a Linguistic Phonetic Theory

When the full range of the vocal sound-making capabilities of the human species is considered, it becomes apparent that only a restricted subset of the range is used as the basis for contrastive and contextual patterns in spoken language. To offer a few examples, no language makes distinctive use of the percussive noise of the teeth colliding as the jaw is snapped shut. Nor is the noise of air being squeezed between the cheek wall and the outer surface of the teeth and gums used in language by normal speakers (though it is some-times used as a substitute for the voice by speakers who have had their larynx removed by surgery). The ability to simulate a snoring sound is not used con-trastively, nor is a falsetto voice used deliberately to contrast one sound against another, in any known language.

There is a further degree of constraint. Not only is the range of sounds that is used in language limited to a relatively small subset of those physiologically possible, but within that subset there is a core of frequently used sounds that turn up repeatedly in widely different language-families, within a broader range of less frequent sounds. As part of that core, most languages use [t], [n] and [s] as consonants, as in the pronunciations of English *tea*, *knee*, and *sea*. Relatively few, on the other hand, use consonants such as the initial sounds [f] in English *fin*, [θ] in *thin* or [ð] in *then*. A very large number use the vowels [i], [a], and [u], as in English *peel*, *pal*, and *pool*. But very few use the vowels [y], [ø] or [œ], as in French *lune* ("moon"), *yeux* ("eyes"), or *peur* ("fear") respect-ively. Only about one-third of all known languages use diphthongs, such as [aʊ], [eɪ] and [ɔɪ], in the word-final syllables of the English verbs *allow*, *allay*, and *alloy* (Lindau et al. 1990).

There seem to be five interactive principles that may explain this human tendency to use a somewhat restricted number of sound-types for purposes of linguistic communication (Lindblom 1983, 1986, Ohala 1989, Stevens 1972). These are:

1   perceptual stability;
2   adequate perceptual contrast;
3   ease and economy of articulatory performance;
4   ecological robustness;
5   ease of modifiability to the needs of the communicative situation.

Perceptual stability is achieved by languages tending to use sounds for which small articulatory adjustments make little auditory difference. Maintaining adequate perceptual contrast entails avoiding sound-differences close to the limits of human discrimination. Ease and economy of articulation are the outcome of choosing sound-types which do not unduly tax the capabilities of the speech production system. Ecological robustness reflects the ability of sounds to resist the perceptual masking effects of other sounds likely to be heard in the environment (especially speech from other speakers). Finally, given that the relative speed, loudness, and articulatory precision of the speech of a given speaker change frequently in response to variations in the social and physical circumstances of the conversation, it is helpful if parameters of speech control are used which can be appropriately modified without damaging intelligibility.

Different languages, and a given language at different times, reach differing solutions to the trading relationships between these five principles. That these solutions are not always optimal is one potential basis for the sound patterns of languages changing over time.

5   The Shape of a General Phonetic Theory

The obedience of spoken language to the five principles described above has an impact on the desirable shape of a general phonetic theory. A well-designed general phonetic theory is one whose posited features and organizational units cover the maximum range of data with the simplest descriptive constructs. If spoken languages in general tend most frequently to favor a core of speech sounds which are perceptually stable, adequately contrastive, relatively easy to articulate, ecologically robust, and intelligible in variable circumstances, then the basic constructs to be set up in general phonetic theory should be the ones whose nature and relationships give the simplest and most economical account of such sounds. The theory is then completed by adding a minimum set of more elaborate constructs, to cover the less frequent and usually more complex sounds.

6   Organic and Phonetic Aspects of Speech

Within the model of general phonetic theory to be offered here, it will be convenient first to distinguish *organic* versus *phonetic* factors in speech. *Organic factors* are those which are "to do with anatomical structure or morphology, and with the constraints which that structure imposes on the potential for physiological action" (Mackenzie Beck 1997: 256). *Phonetic factors* are those which arise from any learnable aspect of use of the vocal apparatus, with its acoustic and perceptual correlates (Laver 1994a: 28). The interplay between organic and phonetic factors in speech is one of the major sources of acoustic variation between different speakers. The recovery of relatively invariant properties in speech data from different speakers, to aid the decoding of linguistic messages (Perkell and Klatt 1986), can only be achieved by resolving the relative contributions of organic and phonetic factors.

Many theoretical and practical consequences arise from the fact that any two speakers of normal anatomy must be treated as capable of producing phonetically identical utterances, despite the often very substantial organic differences between them. The fact that the vocal organs of different speakers can be of very different sizes means that speech from two individuals can be acoustically very different, in absolute physical terms. Comparability of pronunciation therefore arises from considering not the absolute values of acoustic parameters, but their values relative to the individual speaker's own acoustic potential. So the intonational value of the pitch of a large adult male speaker's voice can be compared to that of a small female child by considering in each case whether the pitch should be counted as high (or mid, or low), in relation to the speaker's own pitch range (Ladd 1996). In absolute terms, the voice pitch ranges of these two speakers would be very unlikely to show any physical overlap at all. In relative terms, however, they can be brought into comparability, and when heard as the same in these terms they can be regarded as phonetically equivalent.

The same situation applies to comparisons of the phonetic quality of different speech sounds. Vowel-sounds, for example, are acoustically characterized by patterns of resonant frequencies of the vocal tract (Ladefoged 1993). The absolute values of the resonant frequencies depend on the overall length and shape of the tract. These frequencies change as the organs of the vocal tract manipulate it into different configurations, within organic limits set by individual anatomy. The configurations of two vocal tracts can be thought to be phonetically equivalent when the ratios of the lowest resonant frequency to higher resonant frequencies in each of the two cases are closely similar. In absolute terms, given that the resonant-frequency ranges for two such organically different speakers as the large man and the small girl would once again show virtually no overlap, it would not be feasible to say that these two speakers were producing comparable sounds. In relative terms, however, they can both be perceived as producing the same vowel [uː] in their pronunciations of the English word "boot" [buːt], for instance, when the resonant frequencies of each of them show appropriately similar ratios.

Phonetic equivalence is one end-point of a more general scale of *phonetic similarity*, which is a metric for comparing the phonetic characteristics of any two sounds. The concept of phonetic similarity is hence a necessary basis for the

whole of general phonetic theory. In addition, the view that organically different speakers can produce and perceive phonetically equivalent sounds has
profound implications for describing normal use by native speakers. Equally
profound are the implications for understanding the articulatory and perceptual processes of spoken language acquisition by infants, foreign-language
learning by non-native speakers, and pathological use in speech disorders.

The dimension of phonetic similarity is relevant, finally, not only to comparing speech sounds from all different speakers of normal anatomy, but also
to two further situations. The first is as the basis, within a single speaker, for
grouping phonetically similar allophonic variants into a single phoneme, as a
family of phonetically related sounds fulfilling the same contrastive phonological role. The second applies to decisions about the range of phonetic segment-
types that can be represented by a given character in alphabetically based
writing systems for whole language communities. The decision, for instance,
about what speech sounds in different languages are eligible to be written
with the letter "r" depends in part on the comparability of the phonetic and
perceptual qualities of the candidate sounds concerned.

7   Articulatory, Acoustic, and Perceptual Levels of Description of Speech

Emerging from the discussion in the section above is a second general distinction, between three different aspects of the phonetic description of speech.
These are related to the three links in the chain of speech, from the speaker's
generation of an utterance, to its transmission through the air, to its reception
by the listener. The first is the *articulatory* level of description, which accounts
for the changing configurations and other actions of the speaker's vocal apparatus. The second is the *acoustic* level, which consists of statements about the
physical consequences of articulatory actions in terms of vibratory patterns of
air molecules within the vocal apparatus and in the air between the speaker
and the listener. Finally, the third level of description concerns the *perceptual*
impressions of the listener receiving the acoustic information.

The rest of this chapter will focus on phonetic aspects of speech, and will be
concerned chiefly but not only with the articulatory level of description.

8   Linear and Non-linear Units of Speech Organization

The phonetic events that make up the time-course of speech tend to be continuous, with only relatively few steady states or sharply defined breaks that

could serve as the boundaries of natural, serial units of speech organization. Obvious natural breaks do occur, however, in two circumstances in the linear production of speech by a single speaker. One is at the beginning and end of a *speaking-turn* by one participant in a conversation. The other is at the beginning and end of an individual *utterance*, bounded by silence, within the individual speaking turn. Exhaustively dividing the rest of the stream of speech into a sequence of units smaller than the utterance involves appealing to a number of convenient assumptions. A key traditional assumption is that the continuum of speech can be appropriately handled, for analytic purposes, as if descriptive categories were discrete, not continuous. On this basis, it becomes reasonable to set up smaller-scale phonetic constructs such as the feature and the segment.

8.1   The relationship between phonetic segments and phonetic features as units of speech production

Phonetic features are collectively the ingredients of *phonetic segments*. In the minimum case, two segments may differ from each other by the presence or absence of just one phonetic feature. A feature exploited in every human language in this way is the phonetic feature of "voicing." Voicing is caused by vibration of the vocal folds in the larynx. Whether the vocal folds vibrate or not will be determined by the interaction of airflow from the lungs and the tension-states of relevant laryngeal muscles. The word-initial consonant-sounds in the two English words *zeal* /zil/ $\Rightarrow$ [ziːl] and *seal* /sil/ $\Rightarrow$ [siːl] differ in their voicing state, in that the vocal folds are being made to vibrate in the first case (making [z] a "voiced" segment) and not in the second (making [s] a "voiceless" segment). The transcriptional conventions in the example above are that slant brackets // show the phonemic status of the symbols; "$\Rightarrow$" means "is phonetically pronounced as"; square brackets [ ] show the phonetic status of the pronunciation of the words concerned; and [ː] after a segment means that the sound is produced "with relatively longer duration."

While segments can be thought of as linear units following one another sequentially in the chain of speech without interval, features are non-linear. They can overlap each other in time, and have start-points and end-points which do not necessarily align with those of the chain of segments. Phonetic segments, representing phonological vowels or consonants, are temporally anchored in the chain of speech by the cooccurrence and mutual timing of their constituent features.

8.2   Phonetic and phonological features

The constructs of a general phonetic theory should include a supposed *universal set of phonetic features*, whose comprehensive coverage of spoken language remains provisionally true until shown by further research to be inadequate. The general phonetic theory summarized here is based on these principles (Laver 1994a). It tries to include a set of phonetic features capable of describing the phonetic basis of all phonological contrasts, and of all the contextual patterns of their interaction, so far discovered in the spoken languages of the world. The set of phonetic features proposed in a general phonetic theory would nevertheless, in the ideal, always be larger than the set proposed to cover the languages of the world. This is because of the need to extend its coverage to the differentiation of sociolinguistic communities and the characterization of individual speakers.

It is important to appreciate the difference of technical status between descriptive phonetic features and distinctive phonological features. An example was quoted earlier of the phonetic feature of voicing providing the phonetic basis for a minimal contrast between two consonantal sounds in English, /z/ and /s/. Opportunities for conceptual confusion are rife at this point, in that the presence or absence of "voicing" can be seen in two quite different perspectives. Phonetically, the difference between [z] and [s] as physical speech sounds is described in terms of the presence or absence of vibration of the vocal folds, as mentioned briefly above and described in more detail in section 10.2 below. To expand on the phonetic example mentioned briefly earlier, /z/ and /s/ as consonants in English are phonologically differentiated by the distinctive presence or absence of a single *distinctive feature*, often represented as +VOICE versus −VOICE. (Capitalization of the name of the feature, with "+" and "−" indicating presence versus absence, is a useful way of distinguishing the status of phonological features from that of phonetic features, which often − potentially confusingly, as in this case − have the same or similar names.)

Viewed as a phonetic feature, "voicing" is part of the descriptive, objective vocabulary of phonetics. Viewed as a distinctive feature, VOICE is part of the formal vocabulary of phonology. The purpose of phonetic features is to describe the articulatory, acoustic, or auditory characteristics of speech sounds as events in the real, physical world, independently of the language concerned. The purpose of distinctive features is to focus on the role of the features as part of a conventional, semiotic code for identifying phonological units particular to a given language. The term "distinctive feature" is thus reserved for use as a contrastive phonological concept.

Part of a phonological interest in distinctive features is the exploration of the degree to which different phonological features fall into putatively *natural classes*, where the members of the class share some phonetic and / or distributional property that distinguishes that class from other classes. This often entails grouping classes into more abstract, superordinate classes, such as the phonological class of "sonorant." This superordinate class is normally taken to include the subordinate classes of English vowels, liquids (such as /r, l/), glides (/j, w/) and nasal stops (/m, n, ŋ/). For further discussion of distinctive features and natural classes, see the chapter on phonology in this volume by Cohn (8).

8.3   *The phonological syllable*

The *syllable* is not identified here as a unit of phonetic description. Many phoneticians have tried to develop a robust definition of the properties of a phonetic syllable, but no objective correlate that would link phonetic performance on a one-to-one basis to the phonological syllable has yet emerged (Laver 1994a: 113–15).

The term "syllable" is perhaps best reserved for use at the phonological level, where it is useful (though not itself unproblematic) for two purposes: for the location of word-identifying patterns of stress; and as an organizing concept for the mutual distribution of vowels and consonants. This organization is reflected in the traditional phonological view that *vowels* are nuclear in the syllable, with all syllables containing one and only one vowel.

Consonants are marginal in syllables, being either syllable-initial or syllable-final. Using "C" to mean "a consonant," and "V" to mean "a vowel," the structure of an English monosyllabic word like "strikes" /straɪks/ would be formulaically represented as CCCVCC. Languages differ in the syllable structures they allow. English allows both *open* and *closed* syllables (that is, syllables without and with, respectively, one or more final consonants), as in /aɪ/ "I" V, /saɪ/ "sigh" CV, /saɪd/ "sighed" CVC, and /saɪzd/ "sized" CVCC. Hawaiian allows only open syllables, as in the di-syllabic word /ola/ "life" V + CV.

9   The Componential Organization of Speech Production

The success of phonetics in developing an objective, replicable, internationally standard method of describing all speech sounds in all spoken languages lies in part in a componential approach to phonetic description. Each discriminable sound is regarded as the composite product of the action of a number of sub-processes of the speech production system. These are described in more detail in section 10 below. A schematic view of the *vocal organs* which make up the sub-processes, including the *lungs*, the *larynx*, the organs of the *mouth* and the *pharynx* in the vocal tract, and the soft palate (technically called the *velum*), is shown in figure 7.1.

This componential analysis underlies the conventions of phonetic transcription of the International Phonetic Association. As an illustration of this approach, and to inform the explanation offered below of descriptive phonetic categories, a typical (abbreviated) label for the sound represented in the phonetic transcription of the IPA's International Phonetic Alphabet (1993) as [b] would be "a voiced, labial, oral stop." The four elements of this label constitute individual phonetic features and identify independently controllable components of the production of the sound:

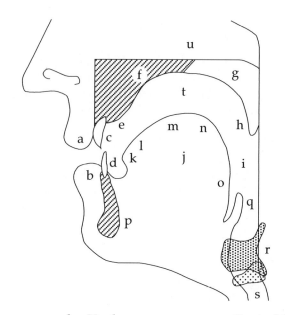

a. Upper lip
b. Lower lip
c. Upper teeth
d. Lower teeth
e. Alveolar ridge
f. Hard palate
g. Velum (soft palate)

h. Uvula
i.   Pharynx
j.   Body of the tongue
k. Tip of the tongue
l.   Blade of the tongue
m. Front of the tongue
n. Back of the tongue

o. Root of the tongue
p. Lower jaw
q. Epiglottis
r.   Cartilages of the larynx
s. Trachea (windpipe)
t.   Oral cavity
u. Nasal cavity

Figure 7.1 Schematic diagram of a cross-section of the vocal organs
Source: After Laver 1994a: 120

- *"voiced"*: the vocal folds in the larynx are vibrating (superimposing aerody-namic pulses on the moving column of air flowing out of the lungs);
- *"labial"*: the lips are involved as articulators;
- *"oral"*: the velum is in a raised position, sealing off the exit at the back of the mouth to the nasal cavity, causing any airflow to pass through the mouth alone;
- *"stop"*: the closure of the lips momentarily seals off the escape of the air in the mouth and pharynx to the outside atmosphere, causing a short-term rise in air-pressure in the vocal tract. As the lips open again, the compressed air is then released through them with a small, audible explosion.

An assumption in such abbreviated labeling is that the flow of air is gener-ated by the action of the lungs, with the flow being out of the body. (In a fuller label, this would add an explicit element "with pulmonic egressive airflow" – see section 10.1.) By identifying the activities of different sub-processes in this way, and with an underlying understanding of the activities thus represented, a componential labeling system in effect offers a set of instructions to informed readers about what to do phonetically with their own vocal apparatus to generate a phonetically equivalent or near-equivalent sound.

10   Speech Production Processes

There are only two basic ways in which a speaker can perceptibly differentiate one segmental speech-sound from another – by changing the *phonetic quality* of the sound, or its *duration*. Variation of pitch and loudness play their part at a suprasegmental level when speech is continuous, and may result in differences of meaning, but matters of the prosodic and metrical control of speech production will not be addressed in this chapter. For interested readers, these topics are discussed in Laver (1994a: 450–546), together with issues to do with continuity and rate of speech.

The control of phonetic quality and duration depends on the interaction of five major sub-processes in the production of speech:

1   initiation and direction of airflow;
2   phonation type;
3   articulation;
4   inter-segmental co-ordination;
5   temporal organization.

The remainder of this chapter is devoted to an explanation of the way that the activities of these different sub-processes in the control of speech can generate different sounds.

The traditional phonetic approach to the *segmental classification* of speech-sounds is said to be a classification by "place and manner of articulation." "Place" will be seen to be straightforward, but "manner" will turn out to be a complex of a range of different types of activity. Segmental classification by place and manner draws on all the factors in the list above, with their interaction producing segments of different phonetic quality and duration.

Description in the sections below will concentrate on the typology of phonetic features, rather than on exemplifying every cell of the resultant matrix of categories. For a comprehensive account of both segmental and suprasegmental categories of speech sounds, the reader is referred to Laver (1994a: 95–546). For the interpretation of specific phonetic symbols, the IPA Chart in the appendix to this chapter should be consulted.

10.1   Initiation and direction of airflow

There are three categories of *initiation of airflow* used for speech, and two of *direction of airflow*. The means of setting a column of air moving can be classified in terms of the initiating mechanism used. By far the most frequent initiator of airflow in speech is the pulmonic mechanism, setting lung air flowing in an egressive direction to the external atmosphere. This *pulmonic egressive airflow* is then modified in turn by the actions of the larynx, the vocal tract and the velum. Speech made on a *pulmonic ingressive* mechanism, on an inflowing breath, seems to be used only paralinguistically, for example in Scandinavian cultures to express sympathy or commiseration.

The second initiator of airflow used in speech is the larynx, in the *glottalic airstream mechanism*. As the name suggests, the *glottis* (the space between the vocal folds) is involved. With the glottis acting as a valve, and closing off the flow of air from the lungs, the larynx can be abruptly raised or lowered in the throat by muscular action, like a piston in a cylinder. The effect is to compress or rarefy the volume of air in the vocal tract, causing a sharp explosion (on release of a compressed *glottalic egressive* airstream) or an abrupt implosion (on the release of a rarefied *glottalic ingressive* airstream). Sounds made on a glottalic egressive airstream are called *ejectives*, and those on a glottalic ingressive mechanism *implosives*. In Zulu, the word [k'aːk'a] "surround" involves two ejectives, symbolized by the apostrophe ['] after the stop symbols.

If voicing is added to an implosive, by pulmonic egressive airflow making the vocal folds vibrate as the larynx descends during a glottalic ingressive initiation, a *voiced implosive* segment is the result. The contrastive difference between the two Hausa words [ɓaɓe] "estrangement' and [babe] "grasshopper" relies on the two stop segments in the first word being voiced labial implosive stops (hence involving two airstream mechanisms, glottalic ingressive and pulmonic egressive), and in the second on the two stop segments being voiced labial pulmonic egressive stops (involving only one airstream).

The third initiator of airflow used in speech is the tongue, in the *velaric airstream mechanism*. Because the tongue is involved, it is therefore also sometimes called the "lingual" mechanism. Velaric sounds are made by the body of the tongue trapping a volume of air between two closures in the mouth, one at the velum, and one further forward. The tongue then retracts the velar closure by sliding backward along the soft palate while maintaining the closed stricture, thus rarefying the air pressure enclosed in the expanded, sealed cavity. When the front closure is then released, the air implodes into the relative vacuum. Sounds made on this *velaric ingressive* airstream are called *clicks*. Since the velaric mechanism is confined to actions within the mouth, the rest of the vocal apparatus is free to add voicing and / or nasality to click sounds.

The languages that use click sounds contrastively are confined to southern and eastern Africa. Ladefoged and Maddieson (1996: 246–80) offer a comprehensive account of these sounds, with many examples from languages such as Nama, Zulu, and Xhosa. In English, clicks are used only paralinguistically, to indicate annoyance (usually written "tsk, tsk" in the English writing system), or to encourage horses to accelerate, or onomatopoeically to simulate the clopping-sound of their hooves.

10.2   Phonation type

The biological function of the larynx is chiefly to act as a protective and regulative valve for the airway to and from the lungs. The valving mechanism that has evolved is a delicate and complex muscular structure within a supporting framework of cartilages (Dickson and Maue-Dickson 1982, Laver 1980). The so-called *vocal folds* are two shelves of muscular tissue which run horizontally from front to back of the larynx, capable of separation at the back to leave a flat, triangular space with its apex at the front. This space was identified earlier as the glottis, and there are six modes of *phonation* used in spoken language to distinguish different segments, involving different adjustments of the glottis.

When pulmonic egressive air flows upwards from the lungs, a *voiceless* sound is produced if the triangular space of the glottis is left wide open, as if for breathing out. Examples of voiceless consonant-sounds widely used in languages are the word-initial sounds in English *see* [siː], *tea* [tiː], and *she* [ʃiː]. If the vocal folds are brought close enough together to make the continuous airflow through them turbulent, either through a gap left at the back or through a narrowed glottis, the result is called *whisper*.

Voicelessness can be heard in the pronunciation of some vowels in a number of languages. As an allophonic process before pauses, (described below as an outcome of the coordinatory process called "devoicing"), French vowels often lose their voicing. An example would be [wi̥ː] *oui* ("yes") at the end of an utterance, where [̥] below the symbol indicates voicelessness. Alternatively, this devoicing is often substituted by whisper, rather than strict voicelessness. English also exploits allophonic voicelessness, in optional pronunciations of unstressed vowels between two voiceless consonants, as in the first syllable of *potato*/pəteɪtəʊ/ ⇒ [p̥əteɪtəʊ] in Received Pronunciation of British English. Further examples of voicelessness or whisper on vowels in Amerindian, Sudanic, Sino-Tibetan and Australian languages are given in Ladefoged and Maddieson (1996: 315) and Laver (1994a: 295–7).

In the third type of phonation, vibration of the vocal folds is the basis for *voiced* sounds, as mentioned briefly in sections 8.1 and 9 above. Examples of voiced sounds widely used in languages are the word-medial consonant-sounds [z, d, g, m] in English *easy* [iːzɪ], *aiding* [eɪdɪŋ], *again* [əgeɪn], and *seeming* [siːmɪŋ], as well as the vowel-sounds in these words [iː, ɪ, eɪ, ə]. In voiced sounds, the vocal folds are brought lightly together by muscular action, blocking off the outflow of pulmonic air, and air pressure below the closed folds building until it is sufficient to blow the folds apart against the muscular tension holding them closed. Once airflow is re-established through the glottis, an aerodynamic effect is produced within the glottis, with the egressive pulmonic flow creating very local suction as it passes at high speed through the relatively small gap between the vocal folds. This local force sucks the vocal folds towards each other, and combines with the muscular tension to restore the closed position of the vocal folds. The abrupt restoration of closure sends a small shockwave traveling on the outflowing breath through the vocal tract, and acoustically excites it into resonance.

The cycle from closure of the vocal folds to separation and renewed closure typically happens very fast (in a range from 60 to 240 times per second in adult male voices in normal conversational English). The frequency of the vibration corresponds to the auditory *pitch* of the voice. The contour of pitch in the successive, intermittent voiced sounds of a whole utterance is in effect heard as a melody, and functions as the *intonation* of the utterance.

The fourth type of phonation used in spoken language is *creak* or *creaky voice* ("creak" is also sometimes called *vocal fry* or *glottal fry* in American publications). In this mode of phonation, the front part of the glottis vibrates, at a considerably lower frequency than in normal voicing, while the back part is pressed more tightly together. Pairs of Danish words can be distinguished by the presence of syllable-final creak (sometimes also called *laryngealization*) versus its absence, for instance in [dṵ] "tablecloth" versus [du] "you" (Laver 1994a: 330–3).

The fifth type of phonation is *whispery voice* (also sometimes called *breathy voice* or *murmur*). As in whisper, the vocal folds do not completely seal off the trans-glottal escape of the pulmonic airflow while vibrating, but leave a gap – either at the back of the glottal triangle, or along the length of the approximated but vibrating vocal folds. The result of the continuous leakage of air is to superimpose audible whisperiness on the pulsed voicing throughout the phonation. Whispery voice in English is used phonetically in English as an optional allophonic feature to replace the normal voicing of [h] when that consonant occurs in inter-vocalic position in some accents of British English, as a whispery voiced resonant [ɦ]. Examples are *ahead* /əhɛd/ ⇒ [əɦɛd] and *perhaps* /pəhaps/ ⇒ [pəɦaps], with phonetic voicing running right through these words, becoming momentarily whispery during the "h". Whispery voice of this sort is also used in English paralinguistically throughout an utterance to signal secrecy or confidentiality.

In a range of other languages, whispery voice is used contrastively to distinguish one consonant phoneme from another. An example is [bəla] "a snake" versus [bɦəla] "good" in Sindhi, using [ɦ] in association with the [b] symbol to indicate a whispery-voiced beginning to the syllable in the second word. Section 10.4 below classifies this as an inter-segmental coordinatory instance of "voiced aspiration" (Laver 1994a: 354).

Finally, closure of the vocal folds may itself constitute the medial phase of a stop segment, in which case it is called a *glottal stop* [ʔ]. Glottal stops are used only allophonically in English, for example as a phonetic realization of the final /t/ consonants in London Cockney *eat that pizza* /iːt ðat piːtsə/ ⇒ [əiʔ ðaʔ pʰəiʔsʌ].

10.3   Articulation

A key part of appreciating how descriptive phonetic classification works is understanding the relationship between segments and features. This section on articulation begins with a clarification of this relationship, and then discusses principles of classification by place of articulation, degree of stricture, multiple degrees of stricture and aspect of articulation. The technical vocabulary introduced in this section is then used in the discussion of intersegmental coordination.

10.3.1   *Featural phases of the structure of segments*

The complex relationship between segments and features can be clarified by appeal to the concept of three internal *phases* of a segment – the onset phase, the medial phase and the offset phase (Laver 1994a: 112–13). The configuration of the vocal tract during speech changes dynamically from moment to moment between variably greater and lesser degrees of local constriction of the airflow. These constrictions are created by a mobile, *active articulator* (such as the tongue, or lower lip) moving towards a fixed or less mobile, *passive articulator* (such as the hard palate, soft palate, or upper lip). The time occupied in maintaining the maximum degree of articulatory constriction (or degree of *stricture*) reached by the vocal tract during the production of an individual segment delimits the *medial phase* of the segment's performance.

During the *onset phase* of a segment the active articulator is approaching the maximum stricture, and in the *offset phase* is moving away from this towards the configuration for the medial phase of the next segment. One segment's offset phase overlaps with the onset phase of the next segment, in an *overlapping* phase.

The concept of the phasal structure of segments is important for two reasons to do with the temporal distribution of phonetic features. The first is that a given feature may start or finish within a particular segmental phase. For example, in English syllables anticipatory nasality begins relatively early within the medial phase of a vowel-segment before a nasal consonant-segment, as in *calm* /kam/ ⇒ [kʰɑ̃ːm]. (In the IPA transcription here, superscript [ʰ] means "aspiration," or "voice onset delay," [˜] means "is nasalized," with the soft palate open to allow airflow into the nasal cavity.)

A given feature may alternatively be co-terminous with the medial phase of the segment, as in the case of audible friction in [θ] in English *thin* /θɪn/ ⇒ [θɪ̃n]. Or the feature may run through the medial phases of two or more adjacent segments, as in the English word *soon*, /sun/ ⇒ [sʷũːn], where lip-rounding runs through the first two segments, relaxing to a neutral position towards the end of the word. (The vowel-segment [u] is inherently lip-rounded, and in the case of consonant-segments lip-rounding is phonetically symbolized by the attachment of the diacritic [ʷ] – see also section 10.3.4 below on multiple degrees of stricture.) A feature running through adjacent segments can be called a *setting* (Laver 1994a: 115, 391–427), and an analysis of features into settings is useful not only for linguistic phonetics, but also for *paralinguistic* analysis of affective or emotional communication through tone of voice, and *extralinguistic* analysis of speaker-characteristics (Laver 1980, Nolan 1983, Pittam 1994).

10.3.2   *Place of articulation*

Classification by *place of articulation* identifies the location of the articulatory zone in which the active articulator is closest to the passive articulator during the medial phase of a segment. An enabling concept for approaching this classification is to distinguish between neutral and displaced places of articulation. In its *neutral configuration*, the vocal tract is as nearly as anatomy allows in equal cross-section along its full length from lips to pharynx. (If a vowel-sound were to be produced in such a configuration, it would have the quality of the "neutral" vowel [ə] in the pronunciation of the first (unstressed) syllable of the English word *canoe* [kənu]; and acoustically the resonant frequencies would be such that the ratio of the higher frequencies were odd multiples of the lowest.)

In the neutral configuration, the potential active articulators (the lower lip and the tip, blade, front, back and root of the tongue) lie in their natural anatomical position opposite their passive counterparts along the longitudinal axis of the vocal tract. A segment whose place of articulation is neutral is made by an active articulator moving towards its neutral, passive counterpart. The neutral configuration of the vocal tract, and some labels for *neutral places of articulation*, are given in figure 7.2.

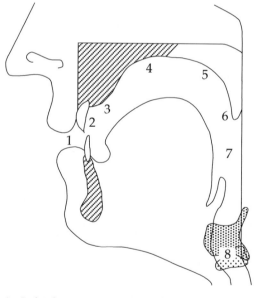

1. Labial
2. Dental
3. Alveolar
4. Palatal
5. Velar
6. Uvular
7. Pharyngeal
8. Glottal

Figure 7.2   Schematic diagram of some of the neutral places of articulation
Source: After Laver 1994a: 135

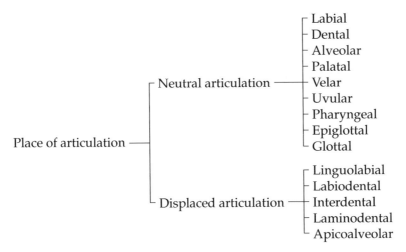

Figure 7.3   Labels for neutral and displaced articulations

Neutral places of articulation are thus involved when the bottom lip moves up against the top lip to create a *labial* articulatory narrowing or closure; when the tip of the tongue touches the inner surfaces of the central upper incisors to make a *dental* closure; when the blade of the tongue articulates against the alveolar ridge behind the teeth to make an *alveolar* closure; or when the back of the body of the tongue contacts the soft palate to create a *velar* closure.

When the bottom lip is retracted from its neutral place, however, to articulate instead against the central upper incisors, or the tip of the tongue is retracted to articulate against the alveolar ridge behind the teeth, the resulting *labiodental* and *apicoalveolar* strictures are classified as *displaced articulations*. Similarly, if the blade of the tongue is protruded between the lips, and makes a *linguolabial* closure against the upper lip, that too is a displaced articulation. The labels for neutral and displaced articulations are shown together in figure 7.3.

Examples of neutral articulations in English are all vowels (except those in some accents where the tongue-tip is curled upwards in anticipation of a following /r/), and the word-initial consonant-sounds in *pea* [piː] and *bee* [biː] (both labial); *theme* [θiːm] and *thee* [ðiː] (both dental); *teal* [tiːl] and *deal* [diːl] (both alveolar); *cash* [kaʃ] and *gash* [gaʃ] (both velar); and *he* [hiː] (glottal). Instances of displaced articulations in English are the word-initial consonant-sounds in *feel* [fiːl] and *veal* [viːl] (both labiodental).

Setting up the classificatory distinction between neutral and displaced articulations amounts to a claim about the relative frequency of incidence of different sounds in the languages of the world. The simpler, less elaborate concept of neutral articulations underpins a broadly sustainable assumption that neutral labial, dental, alveolar, palatal, velar, and glottal sounds are more frequently encountered, for instance, than the displaced linguolabial, labiodental, and apicoalveolar sounds. However, this claim becomes less successful when one considers the relative infrequency in the languages of the world of neutral uvular and pharyngeal sounds, for whose relative rarity more specific reasons would have to be advanced.

10.3.3   Degree of stricture

Classification by *degree of stricture* answers the question: "In the medial phase of the segment, to what degree is the gap between the active and passive articulators narrowed?" Languages exploit three types of segments defined by the criterion of degree of stricture – stops, fricatives, and resonants. In the medial phase of *stops*, the degree of stricture is one of *complete articulatory closure*. Examples from English are the word-initial consonant-segments [p, b, t, d, k, g] in *post, boast, toast, dosed, coast*, and *ghost* respectively.

In *fricatives*, the articulatory stricture in the medial phase is one of *close approximation*, with the airflow made turbulent by passing through a very narrow gap between the active and passive articulators, generating an audible hissing noise ("friction"). Examples of fricatives are the word-initial consonant-segments [f, v, θ, ð, s, z] of English *fan, van, thigh, thy, sink, zinc*, or the word-medial consonant-segments [ʃ, ʒ] in English *mesher* and *measure*.

In the medial phase of *resonants* (which can involve sounds representing both consonants and vowels), the stricture is one of *open approximation*. This is a stricture which is sufficiently open to allow the airflow to pass smoothly without turbulence. Open approximation is optimal for allowing the pulses of voiced vibration from the larynx to set the vocal tract into resonance as an acoustic tube.

Examples in an accent of British English of resonants which act as consonants are the word-initial segments representing /j, w, r, l/ in *yield* [jiːld], *wield* [wiːld], *raw* [ɹɔ] and *law* [lɔ]. Examples of resonants acting as vowels from the same accent are the word-final segments in *bee* [biː], *Shah* [ʃɑː], *paw* [pɔː] and *two* [tuː]. The IPA chart subclassifies the open-approximation degree of stricture of such resonants in terms of three further articulatory dimensions. The first two are divisions vertically and horizontally of the *vowel-space* in the mouth within which the highest point of the regularly curved tongue is located for the resonant in question. The vertical division is subdivided into *close, close-mid, open-mid*, and *open* resonants. The horizontal division is subdivided into *front, central*, and *back* resonants. The third classificatory dimension for resonants acting as vowels describes the lip-position of the segment, divided into *rounded* and *unrounded*. The resonant in *bee* [biː] is close, front, unrounded; in *Shah* [ʃɑː] is open, back, unrounded; in *paw* [pɔː] is open-mid, back, rounded; and in *two* [tuː] is close, back, rounded.

10.3.4   Aspect of articulation

The concept of *aspect of articulation* extends the concepts of "neutral." It is suggested that the majority of stops, fricatives, and resonants in the languages of the world will be performed with the tongue in a regularly curved shape (convex both longitudinally and laterally), with the velum closed, and with a stricture maintained more or less as a steady state throughout the medial phase in a single, neutral place of articulation. This set-up will be treated as a neutral reference against which three non-neutral groups of aspects of articulation can be described. These are the conformational, topographical, and transitional aspects (Laver 1994a: 140–7).

The *conformational aspects* deal with the routing of the airflow channel. There are three distinctions to be drawn. The first is between *oral* airflow versus *nasal airflow*. The second is between *central* versus *lateral airflow*. The third is between *single* versus *multiple strictures*.

As instances of differences between oral and nasal sounds, neutral voiced *oral stops* include [b, d, g], as in English *bib* [bɪb] (*oral labial stops*), *did* [dɪd] (*oral alveolar stops*) and *gig* [gɪg] (*oral velar stops*) respectively. Their non-neutral *nasal stop* counterparts are [m, n, ŋ], as in English *mum* [mʌm] (labial), *none* [nʌn] (alveolar) and *sung* [sʌŋ] (velar). An allophonic difference between an oral and a *nasal fricative* at the same place of articulation is in Igbo "to wedge in" [ɪfa] versus "to shriek" [ɪ̃fã] (Williamson 1969: 87), from Nigeria. Here both are non-neutral in a different respect, in that they share a displaced labiodental place of articulation. A phonemic difference between an oral and a *nasal resonant* can be found in Sioux "sun" [wi] versus "woman (abbreviated form)" [wĩ] (J. Harris, personal communication).

Stop articulations can show complex aspectual patterns of oral and nasal sequences within the medial phase of a stop. The place of articulation of the oral and nasal elements are *homorganic* – the oral stricture is at the same place of articulation. When the nasal element is minor compared with the duration of fully oral closure, and occurs at the beginning of the medial phase, the stop is said to be *pre-nasal*; when it is final with respect to the oral closure, it is called a *post-nasal stop*. The duration of such nasal elements is shorter than in full segmental sequence of nasal + oral stops, as in English *candor*, for instance. When the nasal element dominates the duration of the oral closure in the medial phase, it is said to be a *pre-occluded* or *post-occluded nasal stop*, depending on the initial or final location of oral closure. Examples of *complex oral / nasal stops* are found in a range of languages, including some in Africa, India, and South and Central America. An instance of pre-nasal stops comes from Kalam, a Papuan language of New Guinea, in "down valley" [ᵐbim] and "sinew" [kiⁿdɨl] (Pawley 1966). A fuller discussion of such complex oral / nasal stops is offered in Laver (1994a: 227–35).

For the sake of economy, sounds will from now on be assumed to be oral unless specific mention is made of their nasal status.

In the case of differences between central and lateral sounds, a neutral example would be the *voiceless alveolar central fricative* [s], as in English *sea* [siː]. A non-neutral instance would be a *voiceless alveolar lateral fricative* [ɬ], as in North Welsh "her ship" [iɬɔŋ], which is in phonemic contrast with a *voiced alveolar lateral resonant* "his ship" [ilɔŋ] (Albrow 1966: 2). In both lateral cases, the air flows through a gap at one or both sides of the tongue behind a central contact between the tip or blade of the tongue against the alveolar ridge.

The active articulators of the vocal tract are sufficiently flexible and versatile to be able to create articulatory strictures in two different places simultaneously (i.e. sharing the same medial phase). When two such strictures are of equal degree the conformational aspect of articulation shows (non-neutral) *double articulation*. Two examples from the West African language Yoruba are the words [k͡pe] "to call" and [g͡be] "to carry" (Bamgbose 1969: 164). The two simultaneous closures in these double stops [k͡p] and [g͡b] are made at the labial and velar places of articulation, and they are therefore called (voiceless and voiced) *labial velar stops*.

An example of a double articulation involving a consonant-sound in English is the initial segment in *well* [wɛl], in which the lips are in a rounded position, and the back of the tongue is raised to a position close to the soft palate, but in neither case close enough to create local friction. The result is a *labial velar resonant*.

When one stricture is of greater degree than the other during the shared medial phase, the narrower stricture is said to be the *primary articulation*, and the more open stricture is called the *secondary articulation*. The auditory effect of secondary articulations is usually to add a modifying "coloring" to the perceptual quality of the primary articulation. Examples include *labialization*, which adds lip-rounding to a segment; *palatalization*, in which the front of the tongue is raised towards the hard palate; *velarization*, in which the back of the tongue is raised towards the soft palate; *pharyngealization*, in which the root of the tongue is retracted towards the back wall of the pharynx; and *nasalization*, in which the soft palate is lowered, allowing air to flow through the nasal cavity and add nasal resonance to the oral resonance of the rest of the vocal tract.

The auditory effect of a neutral, single stricture without secondary articulation is sometimes referred to as "plain." The quality associated with palatalization is sometimes said impressionistically to be "clear," and that with velarization and pharyngealization "dark." In most accents of English, there is a structural allophonic difference between the pronunciations of /l/ in syllable-initial position and in syllable final position, in that both show secondary articulations, with the /l/ of *leaf* [lʲiːf], for instance, being a ("clear") *palatalized voiced alveolar lateral resonant* and that of *feel* [fiːɫ] a ("dark") *velarized voiced alveolar lateral resonant*. Another English example of secondary articulation is the *labialized palatoalveolar fricative* initial in *she* [ʃʷiː], where the primary articulation is the fricative stricture mid-way between the alveolar and palatal places of articulation (hence "palatoalveolar," symbolized by [ʃ]), and the secondary articulation is one of rounding of the lips, symbolized by the superscript diacritic [ʷ]). The use of secondary articulation is discussed further in the section on inter-segmental co-ordination below. Figure 7.4 summarizes the labels for double and secondary articulation.

The *topographical aspects* deal with the shape of the tongue as the active articulator both longitudinally and transversely. Laver (1994a: 141–2) discusses

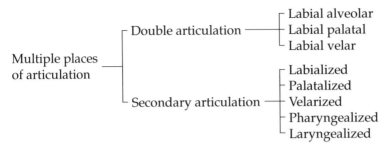

Figure 7.4   Labels for double and secondary articulations

longitudinal processes such as extending or withdrawing the tip of the tongue, and advancing or retracting the root of the tongue. But the most frequently found topographical aspect involving the long axis of the tongue is *retroflexion*, in which the tongue tip is curled up and backwards, sometimes to the extent of presenting the underside of the tip to the roof of the mouth. Margany, a language of South Queensland, shows a phonemic contrast between a (neutral) voiced alveolar stop and a *voiced postalveolar retroflex stop*, in "to cry" [badi] and "maybe" [baɖi] respectively (Breen 1981).

The major transverse aspect distinguishes a flat blade of the tongue from one in which the blade is *grooved*. In English, [s] is produced by most speakers with the air flowing through a very narrow channel in the tongue along the surface of the blade just opposite the alveolar ridge. *Flat alveolar fricatives* occur in Icelandic. In this case it is not clear which category should be treated as neutral, in that grooved alveolar fricatives are far more common than flat alveolar fricatives. It is possible that the higher "pitch" of the fricative noise made through a narrow groove is more audible, and hence ecologically more robust, than the lower pitch of a fricative made through a broader, flat gap. But the articulatory adjustment for creating a central groove is physiologically more complex than for a flat gap, and it may be that the concept of a neutral articulation as the more natural and more widespread sound breaks down at this point.

The *transitional aspects* handle the question of whether the active articulator is static during the medial phase of the articulation, or in dynamic movement. In performing a neutral stop articulation such as the voiced alveolar stop [d], the blade of the tongue rises at moderate pace up towards the alveolar ridge as the passive articulator, makes contact for an appreciable duration, then descends. A (non-neutral) *voiced alveolar tapped stop* is like the neutral version, but moves much faster into contact, makes a very brief closure with the alveolar ridge, and moves away fast. An example is found in many American English accents, as the pronunciation for "t" between two vowels, in a word like *city* [sɪɾɪ].

A tapped stop is sometimes likened to one tap of a trilled stop, another non-neutral example. A trilled stop is one where the active articulator, such as the tip of the tongue, is positioned close to the passive articulator and the airflow through the narrow gap (analogous to the aerodynamic situation in voiced vibration of the vocal folds) brings it repeatedly into full contact. The symbol for a *voiced oral alveolar trilled stop* is [r], and for one made at the uvular location is [ʀ]. A language that contrasts voiced alveolar tapped and trilled stops is Kurdish, as in the pair of words "wound (injury)" [bɾin] versus "cutting" [brin] (A. Ferhardi, personal communication). A contrast between an alveolar tapped stop and a uvular trilled stop is found in European Portuguese, in "dear" [karu] versus "car" [kaʀu] (Parkinson 1988: 138).

When a stop is *flapped*, it strikes the passive articulator in passing. A (non-neutral) *voiced oral alveolar retroflex flapped stop* [ɽ] starts with the tongue-tip curled upwards, and then in uncurling the tip strikes the alveolar ridge very briefly, making a sliding contact that is quickly broken. Westermann and Ward (1933: 76) cite the Sudanese language Gbaya as contrasting a trilled stop with a flapped stop, in "beans" [ere] versus "hen" [eɽe].

Transitional aspects of articulation affect resonants as well. A *monophthong* is phonetically a (neutral) resonant segment with a relatively steady-state articulatory position being maintained throughout its medial phase. A *diphthong* is a (non-neutral) resonant which changes its articulatory position from one position of open approximation towards another during the medial phase. A *triphthong* is a (non-neutral) resonant which changes articulatory position during the medial phase from one position of open approximation towards another and then another. English is unusual amongst the languages of the world in that resonants acting as vowels can show all three transitional aspects of articulation. In some accents of British English, the vowel in a syllable may be represented by either a monophthong (as in *awe* [ɔ]), a diphthong (as in *eye* [aɪ]) or a triphthong (as in *ire* [aɪə]).

10.4   Inter-segmental coordination

Segmental description in this chapter so far has been limited to events within the boundaries of a single segment. Some of the most phonetically interesting events occur in the overlapping phase between two adjacent segments, where the first segment's offset phase is co-terminous with the next segment's onset phase (Laver 1994a: 339–90). When a segment is next to utterance-marginal silence, the onset and offset phases involve transitions from and to the articulatory rest position. Also relevant is the effect of the characteristics of one segment's medial phase spreading, anticipatorily or perseveratively, into part or all of the medial phase of the adjacent segment. Significant phonetic events involving coordination of adjacent segments include the phenomena of devoicing, aspiration, release, affrication and co-articulation.

10.4.1   Aspiration

When a segment that in most contexts is fully voiced throughout its medial phase occurs next to a silent pause, say in utterance-initial position, the transition from silence may have the effect of delaying the beginning of voicing for that segment. In most accents of English, voicing for an utterance-initial voiced stop or fricative will start after beginning of the medial phase. Using [#] to indicate silence, and a subscript [͜] to mean "delay in the onset of voicing" the utterance-initial word "zeal" would be transcribed [# ̬zi:l]. Because [z] in most contexts is normally pronounced with full voicing through its medial phase, this delay is usually referred to as *initial devoicing* (though the phonological orientation of such a practice should be noted). Correspondingly, when such a segment is next to utterance-final silence, there may be an early offset of voicing, and the sound is said to be *finally devoiced*. Such utterance-final devoicing would be transcribed, in the English word "lees," as [li:z̥ #].

In both the initial and final cases, the devoicing is partial, in that not all of the medial phase is deprived of vibration of the vocal folds. When there is no voicing at all in the medial phase, the question is prompted of what differentiates a *fully devoiced segment* such as [z̥] from its voiceless counterpart [s]. Some phoneticians and phonologists make appeal to issues of differential muscular tension in the vocal apparatus, and set up the categories of *lax* and *tense* to describe hypothesized factors that continue to differentiate such devoiced and voiceless segments. It is probably more satisfactory, at a phonetic level of description, to accept the non-differentiability of fully devoiced and voiceless segments. Figures 7.5a and 7.5b characterize the timing relationships between the laryngeal and supralaryngeal events in the devoicing process, and relate them to the next category of coordination to be discussed, aspiration.

When a voiceless segment such as an oral stop is initial before a resonant in a stressed syllable in most accents of English, there is an audible delay in the onset of voicing after the end of the stricture of the medial phase, in the overlap phase between the stop and the resonant. This phenomenon is called *aspiration*. An instance is the English word "peat" [pʰiːt], where the aspiration is transcribed as a small superscript "h." The audible quality of the [ʰ] anticipates that of the oncoming resonant, for which the vocal tract is already assuming the relevant articulatory position. Aspiration is reasonably rare among the languages of the world. French, for example, does not aspirate syllable-initial stops in such circumstances, in words such as "paté" [pate]. Aspiration acts as an allophonic process in English, applying to all voiceless stops /p, t, k/, but is exploited phonemically in a number of languages, including Chengtu Szechuanese, in words such as "to cover" [kai] versus "to irrigate" [kʰai] (Fengtong 1989: 64).

Aspiration is perhaps best defined as "a delay in the onset of normal voicing," since a category of *voiced aspiration* is found in a number of languages of the Indian subcontinent and in central and southern Africa, as a relationship between voiced stops and following resonants. In this case, the phonatory quality of the transition from the stop to the following resonant is one of whispery voice, usually becoming normal (i.e. without audible glottal friction) before the end of the resonant. Examples of voiced aspiration, involving

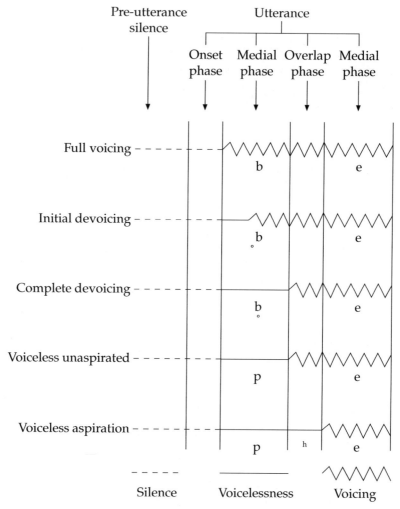

Figure 7.5a Timing relationships between laryngeal and supralaryngeal events in initial devoicing and aspiration
Source: After Laver 1994a: 340

both oral and nasal stops, are the Sindhi words "to speak ill of others" [gɪla] versus "wet" [gɦɪla], and "in" [mẽ] versus "a buffalo" [mɦẽ] (Nihalani 1975: 91).

Parallel to aspiration as a late onset of voicing in syllable-initial contexts is early offset of voicing in a resonant before a voiceless segment in syllable-final position, which is called *pre-aspiration*. This is a characteristic of many of the circumpolar languages. It can be voiceless, as in an example from Icelandic in "thank" [θahka] (Ewen 1982), or voiced, as in Hebridean Gaelic (of Lewis) in "bag" [pʰɔfɪk] (Shuken 1984: 127).

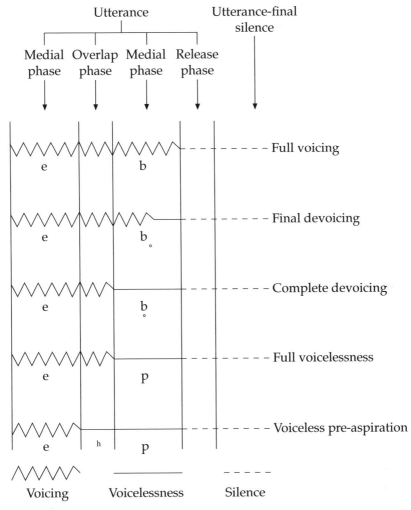

Figure 7.5b   Timing relationships between laryngeal and supralaryngeal events in final devoicing and pre-aspiration
Source: After Laver 1994a: 341

10.4.2   *Stop release*

The offset phase of any oral stop may release the compressed air built up during the medial phase in a variety of ways. Alternatively, the stop may be incomplete, and lack a final release. In this latter situation, the oral closure is sometimes reinforced by a simultaneous glottal stop, as a double articulation. Both modes are found in English, as optional variants. A syllable-final *unreleased stop* can be transcribed for an accent of British English as *top* [tɒpˀ] (and the glottally reinforced version as [tɒp͡ʔˀ]), with the released version as [tɒpʰ].

When the offset phase of a syllable-final stop is released, the channel for the release may be either oral or nasal, central or lateral. In English, the word *button* can be pronounced with *oral release* as [bʌtən], or *nasal release* as [bʌtn̩]. In the latter case, the diacritic below the [n̩] symbol indicates that the nasal segment is "syllabic," acting as the nucleus of the second syllable. The difference between central release and lateral release can be seen in the English word *little*, pronounced with *central release* as [lɪtəl], or with *lateral release* as [lɪtl̩].

10.4.3   Affrication

Affrication is also a characteristic of the offset, release phase of stops. The stop closure is released more slowly than in a non-affricated stop, so that a brief moment of audible friction is heard as the stricture passes momentarily from complete closure through close approximation. In English, the sounds at the beginning of the words *cheap* [t͡ʃiːp] and *Jeep* [d͡ʒiːp] are *affricated stops* (or "affricates"). The special relationship between the stop and the fricative element is symbolized by the use of the linker diacritic. The fricative element of an affricate is by definition homorganic with the stricture of the associated stop element, and affricates can be made at any place of articulation where stops can be formed. The fricative element may also be lateral or central, as in the first and second affricates respectively in the Nahuatl phrase "sit down please!" [ʃimot͡ɬalit͡sino] (Suárez 1983: 32).

10.4.4   Co-articulation and assimilation

It is not surprising, given the rate that segments follow each other in the stream of speech, that one segment may influence the articulatory characteristics of segments yet to be spoken, or be influenced by those that precede it. When such an influence crosses a word-boundary, it is said to result in assimilation; when it is restricted to word-internal action, it is said to show co-articulation.

An example of *perseverative assimilation* in an accent of British English is the continuing influence of voicelessness across the word boundary in *what's this?* pronounced as [wɒts ðɪs], where the underlying /z/ of *is* loses its voicing under the influence of the preceding [t]. An instance of *anticipatory assimilation* is *that boy* pronounced as [ðap bɒɪ], where the place of articulation of the underlying /t/ is made identical to that of the following [b].

Anticipating the structural requirements of oncoming segments in the stream of speech often results in secondary articulations. Labialized consonant-sounds are found in English before vowels which have rounded lip-positions, in words such as [pʷuːl] *pool*, [mʷɔː] *maw*, and [fʷʊl] *full*. A further example of a secondary articulation that characteristically anticipates future segmental requirements is nasalization. In *anticipatory nasalization*, when a vowel-sound precedes a nasal consonant, the soft palate opens during the medial phase of the resonant, anticipating the oncoming requirement for nasality. A language-differentiating facet of this process is that in these circumstances, the soft palate opens later in French than in English, presumably because of the need to protect the perceptual distinctiveness of French nasal vowel-sounds in phonemic opposition to their oral counterparts.

Co-articulatory *anticipations of place of articulation* also occur. In English, the stricture of velar stops such as [k] before a front resonant as in *keep* [kʰiːp] is made further towards the front of the mouth than [k] before a back resonant as in *calm* [kʰɑːm].

10.5   Temporal organization of speech

The discussion so far has concentrated on matters to do with the phonetic quality of speech sounds. The remaining variable is *duration*. Segments have certain inherent durational constraints which have physiological or perceptual explanations (Laver 1994a: 431–6). This section will concentrate, however, on the contrastive and contextual control of duration for phonological purposes. The terms "length," "long," and "short" will be reserved for use at a contrastive level, and greater or less "duration" for use at the phonetic level of description.

Phonemic distinctions of length in both vowels and consonants have been observed, with vowel-length distinctions predominating. Vowel-length distinctions abound in accents of English, though usually with associated differences of segment-quality. An example of a language using *contrastive vowel-length* (with length signaled by the diacritic [ː]) is Rarotongan Maori, in word-pairs such as "taro bed" [paʔi] and "ship" [paːʔi] (Buse 1966: 52).

Phonemic distinctions of consonant-length are much rarer, but are found occasionally, as in the Eskimo-Aleut languages of the Canadian Arctic. Inuktitut (Inuit) distinguishes short and long consonants in phrases such as "they arrive together" [tikiqɑtɑujutʰ] versus "they arrive frequently" [tikiqɑtːɑqtutʰ] (Esling 1991).

An instance of a language (unusually) contrasting both vowels and consonants is Finnish. An example of such a word-pair is "a crease" [rʏpːʏ] versus "a drink" [rʏːpːʏ] (T. Lauttamus, personal communication).

Allophonic adjustments of duration both to structural position and to phonetic environment are very common. In English, the duration of vowel-sounds is greatest in open syllables such as *bee*, and less in closed syllables such as *beat*. In syllables of comparable structure, the duration of a vowel-sound is greater before a voiced consonant-segment such as [d] in *bead*, and less before a voiceless consonant-segment such as [t] in *beat*.

11   Conclusion

The detailed resources of general phonetic theory that have only been able to be sketched in here are probably adequate for the task of describing the segmental make-up of almost all languages known today, though of course some problems of detail remain to be resolved. In the terms introduced at the beginning of this chapter, general phonetic theory is basically fit for the linguistic phonetic purpose of "describing the phonetic basis for differentiating all contrastive and contextual patterns in speech which signal the identities of linguistic units in any given language." Not so evident is whether it is yet fit for the three other purposes identified as relevant to a broader interest in linguistic phonetics – the description of phonetic regularities in the speech-styles of sociolinguistic communities, of the characteristic phonetic events that distinguish the speech patterns of individual members of those communities, and of the ways in which languages sound different from each other. Such questions raise large issues for the future about the nature and motivation of work in phonetics, and about the desirable and useful limits of resolution of the descriptive apparatus used.

APPENDIX 7

THE INTERNATIONAL PHONETIC ALPHABET (revised to 1993)

CONSONANTS (PULMONIC)

	Bilabial	Labiodental	Dental	Alveolar	Postalveolar	Retroflex	Palatal	Velar	Uvular	Pharyngeal	Glottal
Plosive	p b			t d		ʈ ɖ	c ɟ	k ɡ	q ɢ		ʔ
Nasal	m	ɱ		n		ɳ	ɲ	ŋ	N		
Trill	ʙ			r					R		
Tap or Flap				ɾ		ɽ					
Fricative	ɸ β	f v	θ ð	s z	ʃ ʒ	ʂ ʐ	ç ʝ	x ɣ	χ ʁ	ħ ʕ	h ɦ
Lateral fricative				ɬ ɮ							
Approximant		ʋ		ɹ		ɻ	j	ɰ			
Lateral approximant				l		ɭ	ʎ	L			

Where symbols appear in pairs, the one to the right represents a voiced consonant. Shaded areas denote articulations judged impossible.

CONSONANTS (NON-PULMONIC)

Clicks	Voiced implosives	Ejectives
ʘ Bilabial	ɓ Bilabial	ʼ as in:
ǀ Dental	ɗ Dental/alveolar	pʼ Bilabial
ǃ (Post)alveolar	ʄ Palatal	tʼ Dental/alveolar
ǂ Palatoalveolar	ɠ Velar	kʼ Velar
ǁ Alveolar lateral	ʛ Uvular	sʼ Alveolar fricative

SUPRASEGMENTALS

ˈ	Primary stress	ˌfoʊnəˈtɪʃən
ˌ	Secondary stress	
ː	Long	eː
ˑ	Half-long	eˑ
˘	Extra-short	ĕ
.	Syllable break	ɹi.ækt
|	Minor (foot) group	
‖	Major (intonation) group	
‿	Linking (absence of a break)	

TONES & WORD ACCENTS

LEVEL		CONTOUR	
e̋ or ˥	Extra high	ě or ↗	Rising
é ˦	High	ê ↘	Falling
ē ˧	Mid	e᷄ ˦↗	High rising
è ˩	Low	e᷅ ↘↗	Low rising
ȅ ˨	Extra low	ẽ	Rising-falling etc.
↓ Downstep		↗ Global rise	
↑ Upstep		↘ Global fall	

VOWELS

Where symbols appear in pairs, the one to the right represents a rounded vowel.

DIACRITICS   Diacritics may be placed above a symbol with a descender, e.g. ŋ̊

◌̥	Voiceless	n̥ d̥	◌̤	Breathy voiced	b̤ a̤	◌̪	Dental	t̪ d̪
◌̬	Voiced	s̬ t̬	◌̰	Creaky voiced	b̰ a̰	◌̺	Apical	t̺ d̺
ʰ	Aspirated	tʰ dʰ	◌̼	Linguolabial	t̼ d̼	◌̻	Laminal	t̻ d̻
◌̹	More rounded	ɔ̹	ʷ	Labialized	tʷ dʷ	◌̃	Nasalized	ẽ
◌̜	Less rounded	ɔ̜	ʲ	Palatalized	tʲ dʲ	ⁿ	Nasal release	dⁿ
◌̟	Advanced	u̟	ˠ	Velarized	tˠ dˠ	ˡ	Lateral release	dˡ
◌̠	Retracted	i̠	ˤ	Pharyngealized	tˤ dˤ	◌̚	No audible release	d̚
◌̈	Centralized	ë	◌̴	Velarized or pharyngealized	ɫ			
◌̽	Mid-centralized	ĕ	◌̝	Raised	e̝ (ɹ̝ = voiced alveolar fricative)			
◌̩	Syllabic	l̩	◌̞	Lowered	e̞ (β̞ = voiced bilabial approximant)			
◌̯	Non-syllabic	e̯	◌̘	Advanced Tongue Root	e̘			
◌˞	Rhoticity	ɚ	◌̙	Retracted Tongue Root	e̙			

OTHER SYMBOLS

ʍ Voiceless labial-velar fricative
w Voiced labial-velar approximant
ɥ Voiced labial-palatal approximant
ʜ Voiceless epiglottal fricative
ʢ Voiced epiglottal fricative
ʡ Epiglottal plosive

ɕ ʑ Alveolo-palatal fricatives
ɺ Alveolar lateral flap
ɧ Simultaneous ʃ and x

Affricates and double articulations can be represented by two symbols joined by a tie bar if necessary.
k͡p t͡s

8 Phonology

ABIGAIL COHN

1 Introduction

Consider the "words" shown in (1):

(1)

		I	II	III	
a.		xoda	poda	poda[z]	(cf. coda, codas)
		[x] as in			
		German **ch**.			
b.		rudih	hurid	hurid[z]	(cf. hoard, hoards)
		ngatus	matus	matus[ɪz]	(cf. mattress, mattresses)
		= [ŋ]			
c.		bnick	blick	blick[s]	(cf. block, blocks)

Fluent speakers of English would agree that none of these are actual words of English, yet most speakers would also agree that those in column I are not possible words, while those in column II are. In addition, most speakers would agree that the plurals of the would-be words in column II would be pronounced as indicated in column III. How do we know this? Our knowledge of the sound patterns of our native language(s) comes not through memorizing a list of words, but, rather, by internalizing information about the allowed and disallowed sound patterns of that language. As fluent speakers of English, we know which sounds, or segments, occur in our language and which don't. For example, in (1a), the [x] sound of German (written **ch** in borrowings from German, as in the German pronunciation of *Bach*) just doesn't occur in English. In addition, some sounds which are sounds of English are nevertheless restricted in the position where they occur within the word. For example, as shown in (1b), the sound represented by the spelling sequence **ng** [ŋ] can occur in the middle (si**ng**er) or end (si**ng**) of a word, but not the beginning, and **h** occurs at the beginning (**h**ot) or middle (a**h**ead), but not the end of a word. We also know which sounds can be combined into a sequence. Thus in

(1c), **bl** is an allowable sequence at the beginning of a word (**blue**), while **bn** is not. Finally, we also know how to manipulate alternating sound patterns. For example, in the regular formation of the plural in English, what is written as **s** or **es** is pronounced [s], [z], or [ɪz] depending on certain properties of the last sound of the word; as native speakers, we automatically produce the expected forms (block[s], hoard[z], mattress[ɪz]). It is this knowledge about sound structure – which sounds occur, what their distribution is, how they can be combined and how they might be realized differently in different positions in a word or phrase, that constitutes the study of *phonology*.

Central to the study of phonology is observing ways in which languages differ in terms of their sound structure, as well as what the full range of attested possibilities or options are within each facet of the phonology. In this chapter, we explore some of the central cross-linguistic generalizations about sounds, using some of the theories and tools that allow us to insightfully analyze these patterns. We will focus on three areas: sound inventories and contrasts (section 2), structure above the level of the sound unit or segment (section 3), and structure internal to the segment (section 4). Finally we conclude (section 5) with a brief discussion of phonology as a system.

2 Inventories and Contrasts

2.1 *Inventories*

All languages have consonants and vowels. Consonants are sounds with a constriction in the vocal tract, while vowels lack such a constriction. Vowels can serve as the core of a syllable (see below in section 3), while consonants generally cannot. Consonants must co-occur with vowels to produce forms which are pronounceable. Both consonants and vowels can be defined in terms of where in the mouth they are produced and how they are produced. For consonants, this is characterized in terms of *place* and *manner* of articulation. Place of articulation indicates where the obstruction occurs. The places relevant in English, as we'll see below, include the lips (labial), the tongue tip approaching the teeth (dental), the tongue tip approaching or contacting the ridge behind the teeth (alveolar), or a bit farther back (palato-alveolar), the body of the tongue approaching or contacting the hard palate (palatal) or the soft palate (velar), and finally the position of the vocal cords, or the glottis (glottal). The manner of articulation indicates the degree of constriction: complete closure (stops), noticeable obstruction (fricatives) or a combination of closure and obstruction (affricates), closure in the mouth with air escaping through the nose (nasals), or only slight approximation (liquids and glides). Vowels are generally characterized in terms of the height of the tongue or jaw (high, mid, low) and the relative backness of the tongue (front, central, back). In addition, other properties play a role, such as whether the vocal cords are close together and vibrating (voiced) or farther apart, allowing freer passage of air from the lungs.[1]

So far we have presented examples using English spelling, with some additional pronunciation information provided in [ ]'s. English spelling is sorely inadequate for describing the sounds of current American English accurately. The 26 symbols of the Roman alphabet are not sufficient to represent all of the consonant and vowel sounds of English (as we'll see below there are 39), and so in some cases two symbols are used to represent a single sound. But this isn't the only problem. In order to describe sounds reliably, we need a completely systematic relationship between sound and symbol, something which English spelling doesn't provide, since in the English spelling system there are far too many correspondences of sound to symbol. Take for example the sound [k], which can be represented by several different symbols or symbol combinations (as shown in (2a)) and the letter **c** which can represent various different sounds (in (2b)).

(2)   a.   symbols used to represent the sound [k]
         cat
         kite
         khan
         quite (**qu** = [kw])
         echo
         pack
         box (**x** = [ks])
      b.   sounds represented by the letter **c**
         (not including two-symbol combinations, such as **ch**)
         [k]   **cat**
         [s]   **cite**
         [tʃ]   **cello**

In addition we often need to be able to include more pronunciation detail. (The need for greater detail is true even of those languages which have much better spelling systems than English.) We need what is called *phonetic transcription*. The International Phonetic Alphabet (IPA) is a system of phonetic transcription which allows us to systematically represent the sounds of any language. This system, developed by the International Phonetic Association (founded in 1886) is periodically updated, to reflect changes in general thinking on transcription and to include new speech sounds which have been "discovered." In 1989, the International Phonetic Association had a congress to address such questions and fine-tune the system in a number of ways. The common systems of phonetic transcription used in the United States differ in a few small ways from the standard IPA, but still most such systems are quite close to the IPA.

A sound inventory is the selection of sounds occurring in a particular language. Looking across the inventories of the languages of the world, we find that the number of consonants and vowels, as well as the specific selection of sounds, varies enormously from one language to another. In his study of the sound inventories of 317 languages, Maddieson (1984) found that the number of consonants in a language ranged from 6 to 95, with a mean of 22.8; while the number of vowels ranged from 3 to 46 with a mean of 8.7; and 62.1 percent of the languages in his sample have between 5 and 9 vowels.

Considering this range of sound inventory size, let's see how the sound inventory of American English compares, shown in (3). For the consonants, the places of articulation are the column headings and the manners of articulation are the labels for the rows. When two sounds appear within a single cell in the table, the one on the left is voiceless (without vocal cord vibration) and the one on the right is voiced (with vocal cord vibration). For the vowels, in addition to tongue backness (marking the columns) and height (marking the rows), the adjacent pairs within a category differ in "tenseness" vs. "laxness." (C = consonant, V = vowel.)

(3) Sound inventory of English

C's	labial	dental	alveolar	palato-alv.	palatal	velar	glottal
stop	p b		t d			k g	
fricative	f v	θ ð	s z	ʃ ʒ			h
affricate				ʧ ʤ			
nasal	m		n			ŋ	
liquid			r l				
glide					j	w	

V's	front	central	back
high	i ɪ		ʊ u
mid	e ɛ	ɚ ʌ	ɔ o
low	æ	a	

Diphthongs: aj, aw, oj

There is some variation in the number of sounds argued to occur in English (for example should the affricates, [ʧ] (*church*) and [ʤ] (*judge*), be treated as single units or as sequences of sounds?); however, the characterization of American English in (3) with 24 consonants, 12 vowels and 3 diphthongs (vowel glide combinations that function as a single unit) is fairly common. Thus, English has an average-sized consonant inventory, though notable in its rich array of fricatives. There are whole classes of other consonants that English doesn't exemplify, such as clicks, found in some languages of Southern Africa. With 12 vowels, English has a relatively rich vowel inventory, especially considering that the distinctions are all made using only the two dimensions of tongue height and backness. (In the inventory above, we haven't included schwa [ə], which occurs only in unstressed position.) Some languages make additional, or different, vowel contrasts. For example, in English the front vowels have an unrounded lip position and the non-low back vowels have a rounded lip position, but in many other languages, there are both unrounded and rounded front and / or back vowels (e.g. French *riz* [ri] "rice," with a high front unrounded vowel, vs. *rue* [ry] "street," with a high front rounded vowel and *roux* [ru] "red" (of hair), with a high back rounded vowel).

Compare the English inventory with that found in Arabic (Modern Literary), as shown in (4):

(4)   Sound inventory of Arabic

C's	labial	dental	dental pharyngealized	alveolar	alveolar pharyngealized	palato-alveolar	palatal	velar	uvular	pharyngeal	glottal
stop	b bː	t d tː dː	tˤ dˤ tːˤ dːˤ					k g kː gː	q qː		ʔ ʔː
fricative	f fː	θ ð ðː	ðˤ ðːˤ	s sː z zː	sˤ sːˤ	ʃ ʃː		χ ʁ χː ʁː		ħ ʕ ħː ʕː	h hː
affricate						ʤ					
nasal	m mː			n nː							
liquid		l lː	lˤ lːˤ	r rː							
glide							j jː	w wː			

V's	front	central	back
high	i iː		u uː
low		a aː	

In Modern Literary Arabic, we find a very small vowel inventory, only three distinct vowel qualities (though length differences (indicated byː for a long vowel or consonant) also result in differences in meaning, e.g. [dur] "turn!" vs. [duːr] "houses"), but a very rich consonant inventory. Not only are most of the consonants seen in English found here, but there are additional places of articulation, notably at the back of the mouth (uvular – the back of the soft palate, and pharyngeal – the throat). In addition, there is a contrast between plain consonants and those with a superimposition of a back tongue position (pharyngealized) and finally consonants also contrast for length ([bara]

"sharpen" vs. [barːa] "acquit"). Including all these contrasting dimensions, there are 48 consonants in this dialect, though there is some variation in the consonant inventory of different dialects of Arabic.

While there is a tendency for languages with large consonant inventories to have correspondingly small vowel inventories and vice versa, this is not necessarily the case. Consider for example Rotokas, spoken in Papua New Guinea (following Maddieson 1984, the smallest inventory found in his database), with a very common 5 vowel inventory, but only 6 consonants for a total of only 11 segments.

(5)   Sound inventory of Rotokas

C's	labial	alveolar	velar
stops	p	t	k g
fricatives	β		
liquids		ɾ	

V's	front	central	back
high	i		u
mid	e		o
low		a	

While there is great variation in the segments that occur in particular languages – Maddieson identifies over 800 in his study – strong predictions can nevertheless be made about which sounds will occur. Some sounds and categories of sounds are just more common than others. For example, all languages have stops, but not all languages have fricatives. Beyond these basic observations, there are also many cases where the presence of one property implies the presence of something else in the same system; such generalizations are called implicational language universals. For example, if a language has the mid vowels [e, o] (as in English, *bait* [bet] and *boat* [bot]), it can be predicted that it will also have the high vowels [i, u] (English *beat* [bit] and *boot* [but] and the low vowel [a] (English *pot* [pat]); but the converse doesn't hold, as we've seen in Arabic which has [i, u, a], but lacks [e, o].

2.2   *Contrast*

When we characterize the inventory of sounds of a language, we need to draw an important distinction between those sounds that can be used to make meaningful contrasts in a language vs. those that occur, but are predictable in their distribution. The description of the inventories of English, Arabic, and Rotokas, provided above, present those sounds argued to be distinctive in the language (though, as we discuss below in section 4, the status of [ŋ] in English is debatable).

In order to determine the status of such sounds, we use a simple test to determine if two sounds are distinct by looking to see if there are *minimal pairs*. Minimal pairs (or sets) are words with distinct meanings differing only in one sound. Thus we can show that [m] and [n] (differing only in place of articulation) are distinct sounds in English, since the substitution of these sounds alone is enough to change the meaning of a word:

(6)   **meat** vs. **neat**
      simmer vs. **sinner**
      ram vs. **ran**

In (6) we see that the presence of [m] vs. [n] at the beginning, middle, or end of a word results in different words.

If a sound is used distinctively in a particular language, it is what we call a *phoneme* in that language (and is represented in / /'s). Phonemes are argued to be the level of representation at which segments are encoded in lexical entries (the forms in our mental dictionaries) and the level at which speakers judge "sameness" and "differentness." However, phonemes can vary in their actual realization or pronunciation, depending on the context of the neighboring sounds, the structure of the utterance, and so forth.

Two languages may have the same sounds or *phones* (the actual phonetic events, represented in [ ]'s), but their grouping into phonemes or contrastive units might be different. In English, for example, the sounds [b, p, pʰ] all occur (that is, voiced, voiceless unaspirated, and voiceless aspirated); while [pʰ] and [b] contrast, whether [p] or [pʰ] will appear is predictable from the context, as exemplified in (7). *Buy* [baj] contrasts with *pie* [pʰaj], but the realization of a voiceless stop as aspirated (*pie* [pʰaj]) or unaspirated (*spy* [spaj]) is predictable and there are no minimal pairs for [p] and [pʰ]. (We use an asterisk to indicate something non-occurring or "ungrammatical.") Thus these three phonetic categories are mapped to only two abstract phonological categories. Yet in Thai, all three sounds occur and can produce contrasts in meaning, as shown by the minimal set in (7).

(7)   *Thai*   *English*
                  phonemes   *phones*   *phonemes*
   [baa] "crazy"   /b/   —   **[b]**   —   /b/   buy [baj]
   [paa] "aunt"   /p/   —   **[p]**   ↗   /p/   pie [pʰaj]
   [pʰaa] "cloth"   /pʰ/   —   **[pʰ]**   spy [spaj]
                                              but no *[paj] or *[spʰaj].

To summarize, these three phones [b, p, pʰ] constitute three separate abstract sounds or phonemes in Thai, but only two in English.

In English [p, pʰ] are phones which stand in a special relationship to each other, since they are part of the same phoneme (usually taken to be /p/). Such sounds are called *allophones*. We can capture this relationship by describing the distribution, e.g. [pʰ] occurs at the beginning of words and [p] occurs after [s]. (There is a lot more to this pattern, but we won't pursue it here.) Or we can go a step further and argue that the phoneme /p/ occurs at an abstract or *underlying* level and account for the observed surface distribution with a rule (typically of the form a → b / c__d, which says that "a becomes b in the environment following c and preceding d"). This general approach is fundamental to the view of generative phonology (see Chomsky and Halle 1968, Kenstowicz and Kisseberth 1979) where the goal is to develop a theory which accurately models a speaker's knowledge of his or her language; we return to the issue of rules in section 4.

3 Structure above the Level of the Segment

The sound structure of a word (a unit which can be defined on several linguistic levels, including morphologically and phonologically) includes not only the sequence of sounds (made up in turn of bundles of distinctive features, as discussed in section 4), but also entails the hierarchical grouping of these sounds. Let's take the English word *information* as an example which we can use as a reference point:

(8)

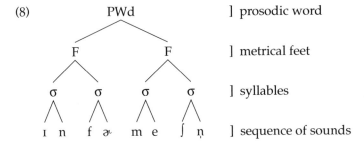

] prosodic word

] metrical feet

] syllables

] sequence of sounds

This word consists of a sequence of sounds ɪ-n-f-ɚ-m-e-ʃ-n̩. These sounds are grouped into sequences of consonants and vowels, known as syllables (σ). Most speakers of English would agree that this form consists of four syllables broken up as ɪn-fɚ-me-ʃn̩. Consonants and vowels are grouped into syllables in non-arbitrary ways, with a vowel forming the core or **nucleus** (such as [me], and consonant or consonants preceding (**onset**, such as [me]) or following (**coda**, such as [ɪn]). In the final syllable [ʃn̩], the nucleus is n̩, which is a syllabic nasal, serving the role of a vowel. These syllables are in turn organized into stress groupings (ìn-fɚ) (mé-ʃn̩). The third syllable is the most prominent (primary stress, indicated with a ´) and the first also has some prominence (secondary stress, indicated with a `). These patterns of prominence can be accounted for by grouping the syllables together into units known as metrical feet (F). Finally the feet are grouped together into the Prosodic Word (PWd).

The Prosodic Word often has the same shape as what we would define morphologically as a word, but not necessarily. There are, for example, grammatical words, which we take to be words morphologically, but which can't stand on their own phonologically, such as *a*, or *the*. The syllables, feet, and prosodic words are together the prosodic structure of a word. Words in turn can be grouped into higher levels of prosodic structure as well.

We can focus on the structure at the level of the segment and above, how segments are combined, how syllables, metrical feet, and prosodic words are constituted; and we can in turn examine the subsegmental structure, how distinctive properties of sounds are organized into segments. In the remainder of this section, we examine syllable structure as an example of the nature of structure above the segment and then turn to the question of subsegmental structure in section 4.

3.1   Syllable structure

Many processes result in the insertion or deletion of a segment. This is often due to the influence of syllable structure. Consider an example from Korean, shown in (9) where we observe that sometimes a cluster of consonants occurs and sometimes one of the members of the cluster is deleted. This is an example of what we call an *alternation* where the same morpheme varies in its realization, conditioned by some aspect of the sound system (in this case the allowable syllable structure). The result is an alternation between the presence of a consonant and zero in morphologically related forms. ([t'] represents a voiceless alveolar stop with a stronger articulation than a plain voiceless stop.)

(9)   Consonant ~ Zero alternations in Korean clusters

root	*+ vowel initial suffix*	*+ consonant initial suffix*
	-**a** nominalizing suffix	-**t'a** infinitive
/palp/ "tread on"	palp + a "treading on"	pap + t'a "to tread on"
/salm/ "boil"	salm + a "boiling"	sam + t'a "to boil"

The basic syllable structure in Korean is (C)V(C). The underlying clusters (/lp/ and /lm/) are allowed to surface before a vowel initial suffix, since the second member of the cluster can be syllabified as the onset of the second syllable, producing *palpa* and *salma*. But when the root occurs before a consonant initial suffix (verbs cannot occur without some kind of suffix), the first consonant of the cluster, in the cases illustrated here /l/, is deleted, producing *papt'a* and *samt'a*. (In other cases, it is the second consonant which is deleted.) The syllabification of forms with vowel initial and consonant initial suffixes respectively is shown in (10) for /palp/ (where < > indicates a segment not incorporated into the syllabic structure):

(10)

Here we can see that this deletion is directly driven by the allowable syllable structure.

As noted in section 1, restrictions also exist on possible sequences of sounds. For example in English, *[bn] can't occur at the beginning of a word (11a) or at the end of a word (11b), but it is not the case that the sequence [bn] is always bad in English.

(11)   a.   *bnick*
       b.   *kibn*
       c.   lab-network*
       d.   drabness*
       e.   Abner*

In (11c), this sequence is fine, but the word is a compound and we might argue that it consists of two prosodic words grouped together (into a structure such as [[lab]$_{pwd}$[network]$_{pwd}$]$_{pwd}$) and therefore it is not held to the same restrictions. The fact that (11d) is allowable might be attributed to the sounds belonging to different morphemes (*drab* and *-ness*). But in (11e) there aren't two words or two morphemes. So what is the difference between [bn] in (11a and 11b) and in (11d)? In the latter case, the [b] and [n] are in different syllables, while in the former they are in the same syllable.[2] The restriction holds of a sequence within a syllable and seems to be due to the fact that [b] and [n] are too similar in terms of *sonority*. Sonority can be defined loosely as the degree of constriction in the mouth during the production of a particular sound. Most important for our purposes here is the observation that there is a hierarchy of how *sonorous* sounds are. Vowels are more sonorous than consonants; and within the consonants, further divisions can be made. Stops, which have complete closure, and fricatives, which have enough of a constriction to create frication or noise (as well as affricates), together are known as *obstruents*, since there is a significant obstruction in each of these cases. These are less sonorous than the nasals, liquids, and glides, together known as *sonorants*. Thus we find the following strong cross-linguistic pattern:

(12)   Sonority hierarchy

more sonorous			*less sonorous*
vowels	>	sonorants >	obstruents

The sonority hierarchy characterizes the behavior of sounds in syllable structure and many other aspects of phonological patterning. Whether finer grained distinctions of the sonority hierarchy are required is a question open to much debate, though we will see some evidence for some additional distinctions below.

As mentioned above, syllables are organized around vowels, sometimes preceded and / or followed by consonants. All of the examples in (13) are well-formed English syllables (and in these cases independent words too).

(13)

coda:	Ø		C		CC		CCC	
onset: Ø	oh	[o]	ode	[od]	old	[old]		
					amp	[æmp]	amps	[æmps]
C	bow	[bo]	boat	[bot]	bolt	[bolt]	bolts	[bolts]
CC	blow	[blo]	bloat	[blot]				
			clam	[klæm]	clamp	[klæmp]	clamps	[klæmps]
CCC	spree	[spri]	split	[splɪt]	splint	[splɪnt]	splints	[splɪnts]

In English, anything from a single consonant to a complex structure of up to three consonants preceding and four following may constitute a well-formed syllable. (Four consonants following the vowel are not included in (13); an example is *texts* [tɛksts].) Many restrictions hold, however, on possible combinations of consonants preceding or following the vowel and only a small subset of the logically possible combinations occur. For example, in three-consonant clusters starting a syllable ($C_1C_2C_3$), the first sound (C_1) must be [s], followed by a voiceless stop ([p, t, k]), followed by a liquid ([r, l]) or glide ([j, w]). Many of the occurring patterns can be characterized with reference to the sonority hierarchy (12), though other factors also come into play. Thus in CCC clusters the pattern of C_2 and C_3 follows the sonority hierarchy, with the beginning of syllables showing a rise in sonority going from C_2 to C_3: stops followed by the more sonorous liquids and glides. Some evidence for the fact that a more fine-grained sonority hierarchy is required comes from the fact that stops (voiced or voiceless) followed by liquids or glides are well formed (e.g. **bl**oat, **cl**am), but stops followed by nasals are not (*bn, *kn). Yet nasals are also members of the class of sonorant consonants. This suggests that the sonorant consonants should be further divided into the oral sonorants (the liquids and glides) and the nasals, with the oral ones being more sonorous than the nasals. But the occurrence of [s] preceding such clusters is not predicted even with further modification of the sonority hierarchy, since [s] is not less sonorous than the stops, and therefore requires a distinct explanation.

Similarly in characterizing what coda clusters (the sequences of consonants following a vowel) can occur in English, sonority also plays an important role. In general, the first member of a two member coda cluster must be of the same or greater sonority than the second member (e.g. **lent**, **belt**, **lift**, **mist**, **apt**). In most monosyllabic words with more than two consonants following the vowel, these forms are morphologically complex, usually involving the [s] or [z] of the plural marker or third person singular or the [t] or [d] of the past tense (though there are some three consonants clusters which occur as codas in the same morpheme, such as [kst] in *text*). Such patterns can be characterized simply if we make reference to the syllable, but are much harder to characterize if we only refer to the string of segments.

Good evidence thus exists for making formal reference to the syllable as part of the hierarchical structure of the phonological system to account for observed alternations and also to be able to capture consonant sequencing restrictions. In addition, the syllable is often argued to be divided into subparts. Evidence for this comes from the fact that co-occurrence restrictions hold on the consonants preceding the core of a syllable, as well as following, but not generally across the subparts of the syllable. One general approach to the internal organization of the syllable is as shown in (14), where the substructure of *boat* and *clamp* are illustrated:

(14)

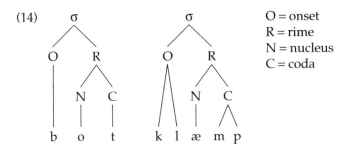

O = onset
R = rime
N = nucleus
C = coda

Based on a wide range of evidence, there is argued to be a major break in the syllable between the onset and the rime constituents. The division into onset and rime allows us to capture various consonant sequencing restrictions and is also relevant for other aspects of the phonology, as well as language games and poetry. The rime corresponds to the unit which rhymes, e.g. **oat**, **boat**, **bloat**; and the onset is the unit shared in poetic patterns of alliteration, e.g. **blue**, **blow**, **blithe**, **bloat**. The rime is then further divided into the nucleus, the core of the syllable which contains the vowel or vocalic elements(s), and the coda, which contains any following consonant(s). In English, the only required element of the syllable is the nucleus (e.g. **oh** [o], **I** [aj]), although in many languages the onset is also an obligatory part of the syllable.

How much explicit or formal internal structure to the syllable is warranted and how it should be encoded is a much debated question, which we won't pursue here, but reference to some degree of substructure of the syllable is useful in capturing insightful generalizations about allowable sequencing restrictions and other aspects of sound distribution. Indeed in English, we can capture the pattern presented in (11) by observing that the sequence [bn] cannot occur together as part of an onset or coda. In addition, reference to syllable subconstituency allows us to capture the broader distribution of sounds in many cases. For example, as noted in (1), the distribution of /h/ in English is limited: it can occur only in the onset of a syllable (and if it is not word-initial, only if the syllable is stressed, e.g. *vehicle* [véɪkl] vs. vehicular [vehíkjələ˞]).

While it is relatively straightforward to count the number of syllables in a word, it is often trickier to decide where to divide syllables in words of two or more syllables. Typically in the case of (C)VCV, the division is before the medial C, (C)V$CV (where $ is used to indicate a syllable break). In English, the situation is additionally complicated by the stress pattern. In words such as those in (15a), it is widely agreed that the syllable divisions are as shown, characteristic of the strong cross-linguistic tendency.

(15) a. attáck   [ə$tǽk]
          belów   [bə$ló]
      b. áttic   [ǽtɪk]
          béllow   [bélo]

However, many researchers have argued that in the cases such as (15b), the medial consonant either belongs to the first syllable or is shared by the two syllables in order to account for otherwise systematic observations about the relationship between syllable structure and stress in English. (Even though the middle consonants in the forms in (15), except for *below*, are written with a doubled consonant (tt, ll), they are just single consonants. The doubling of a consonant in English spelling usually indicates something about the pronunciation of the preceding vowel, not the pronunciation of the consonant itself (compare *tapper* [tæpə˞], *taper* [tepə˞]).

In the case of (C)VCCV(C), the syllabification depends on the specific sequence of consonants. In English, if the CC is an allowable word onset (and therefore an allowable syllable onset) the syllable division will be before both consonants (16a), but otherwise it will be between the two consonants (16b).

(16) a. apply   [ə$plaj]   cf. plea [pli]
          abrupt   [ə$brʌpt]   cf. brush [brʌʃ]
      b. Adler   [æd$lə˞]   *[dli]
          Abner   [æb$nə˞]   *[bni]
          ardent   [ar$dn̩t]   *[rdi]

Some other languages show much greater restrictions on syllable structure than English does. Consider some examples from Japanese in (17).

(17) Allowable syllables in Japanese: CV, V, CVN, CVC

      a. CV, V

              [ki]   "tree"
              [kokoro]   "heart"
              [mado]   "window"
              [tegami]   "letter"

      [ito]   "string"
      [origami]   "paper folding"

b. N\$C

      [tombo]   "dragonfly"
      [hantai]   "opposite"
      [neŋkin]   "pension"

c. C\$C

      [kitte]   "stamp"
      [onna]   "woman"
      [hakka]   "peppermint"
      [kaʃʃa]   "pulley"

As illustrated in (17), only (C)V and (C)VC occur in Japanese (as well as some limited cases of long vowels (C)VV(C)). CV syllables can occur in any position in the word (17a). But CVCs are allowed only if the coda consonant is a nasal (17b), or part of a geminate (long consonant) (17c), and in these cases usually followed by another syllable. Thus, [tom] is a well-formed syllable when followed by [bo], but it would not be an allowable syllable, if it occurred on its own or as the final syllable in a word. A final alveolar nasal (as in [neŋkin] above in (17b)) is well formed, but other nasals and other consonants in this position are not allowed.

Additional evidence for the allowable patterns can be seen by looking at the ways foreign words are modified when they are borrowed into Japanese. Let's consider what happens to some words borrowed from English, as shown in (18).

(18) Borrowings from English into Japanese:

	word	*English*	*Japanese*
a.	pin	[pɪn]	[pin]
	pie	[paj]	[paj]
	Chicago	[ʃɪkago]	[ʃikago]
b.	million	[mɪljən]	[mirion]
	avocado	[avəkado]	[abokado]
	rally	[ræli]	[rarii]

Some words are borrowed as is shown in (18a) (with slight modifications of vowel quality in some cases), or with modifications to any non-occurring segments, with these being substituted by a similar sound which does occur in Japanese (18b). (Some of the vowels of English (e.g. [i, e, o, u]) are perceived to be long in Japanese, indicated here with the doubling of the vowel symbol.)

Of particular interest are cases where non-allowable consonant clusters occur; in such cases, Japanese uses the strategy of adding extra vowels, as illustrated in (19):

194   *Abigail Cohn*

(19)   More borrowings from English into Japanese

	word	English	Japanese
a.	free	[fri]	[fUrii]
	spray	[spre]	[sUpUree]
b.	peak	[pik]	[piikU]
	kiss	[kɪs]	[kisU]
	Bill	[bɪl]	[birU]
	beat	[bit]	[biitO]
c.	speed	[spid]	[sUpiidO]
	cross	[krɔs]	[kUrosU]
	test	[tɛst]	[tesUtO]
	street	[strit]	[sUtOriitO]
	contrast	[kantræst]	[kontOrasUtO]
	baseball	[besbɔl]	[basUbarU]

Consider first cases with onset clusters as shown in (19a). The inserted vowels are indicated in upper case symbols. (The vowel which is inserted in these cases is usually [u] (U), except after alveolar stops, where an [o] (O) is inserted.) (19b) shows cases of either monosyllables or final syllables of the shape CVC. These too are modified, since a consonant can occur in coda position only if it is followed by an appropriate consonant in the next syllable in the same word. Finally cases with both onset clusters, final consonants and final clusters are shown in (19c). All of these clusters are broken up into many more syllables in Japanese than found in the original English source.

In the case of non-allowable clusters in borrowed words, other languages delete segments. Consider what happens to final consonant clusters in Indonesian in words borrowed from English or Dutch. In Indonesian, in general the allowable syllable structure is (C)V(C), so final clusters in borrowed words pose a problem. As shown in (20), the final clusters are simplified by deleting the final consonant (similar to the pattern seen for Korean above in (9), although for those examples, it was the first member of the cluster which was deleted).

(20)

word	English / Dutch	Indonesian
sport	[spɔrt]	spor
aqueduct	[ækwədəkt]	akuaduk
tolerant	[talɚrn̩t]	toleran
test	[tɛst]	tes

To account for such systematic syllable patterns, researchers have proposed various devices including rules, templates, and well-formedness conditions. A current approach, *Optimality Theory*, involves the idea of competing constraints, which can be ranked in importance with respect to each other. Due to such ranking, a less important constraint can sometimes be violated in order to obey a more important constraint (see Prince and Smolensky 1993, McCarthy and Prince 1993 inter alia). Languages differ in how they rank particular constraints. If we have correctly identified the relevant constraints (a major research agenda in itself), then the set of logically possible rankings of those constraints should match up with the range of sound patterns seen across languages. Optimality Theory offers an insightful account of syllable patterns and makes strong predictions about allowable syllable types cross-linguistically, and it also accounts for certain implicational universals such as the fact that if a language allows CVC syllables it will also allow CV syllables and if it allows V syllables, again it will also allow CV ones.

As discussed by a wide range of scholars, the ideal syllable is CV. Syllables minimally consist of a vowel; onsets are preferred; and codas are dispreferred. To account at the same time for the preference for CV syllables and the range of cross-linguistic variation observed in syllable structure, two general sorts of constraints interact. First there are markedness constraints – constraints which capture systematic cross-linguistic generalizations. In the case of the preference for CV syllables, this has been argued to emerge from three constraints, stated here informally:

(21)   Syllable structure markedness constraints:

	constraint	informal definition
a.	NUC	Syllables must have a nucleus
b.	ONSET	Syllables must have an onset
c.	NOCODA	Codas are not allowed

If this were all there were to the story, all languages would have only CV syllables, but this is clearly not the case. There are also constraints that mediate between the underlying representation or abstract form (the input to the constraints) and the actual realization of the form, or the output of the constraints. The two constraints relevant for our purposes, again stated informally, limit how different the input and output can be. (* = Don't)

(22)   Input / output constraints

	constraint	informal definition
a.	*ADD	Only the material of the input should appear in the output; don't add material to the input
b.	*DELETE	Underlying material should be incorporated in the output; don't delete material from the input

There are other constraints that can also affect syllable structure, but these five constraints are sufficient for our discussion here. To test constraint rankings, we compare the input of a form and a list of possible (expected) outputs (placed in the leftmost column in what is termed a "tableau") with respect to a particular ranking of the relevant constraints (placed in columns, going from higher to lower ranking as we go from left to right). No matter what the relative ranking of these five constraints in a particular language, if we have an input or underlying form of the shape CV(CV)(CV), then all of the above constraints, those affecting syllable structure and those affecting input / output relations, can be satisfied. This is true in both English and Japanese, as shown in (23a) for English *banana* and (23b) for Japanese [kokoro] "heart"; even though as we've seen above they have very different syllable patterns. In these tableaux, the constraints are all unranked, indicated by the dashed vertical lines, in contrast to solid vertical lines that we'll see in the tableaux below.

(23) a. English *banana*

/bənænə/	Nuc	Onset	NoCoda	*Add	*Delete
[bə$næ$nə]	√, √, √	√, √, √	√, √, √	√, √, √	√, √, √

   b. Japanese [kokoro] "heart"

/kokoro/	Nuc	Onset	NoCoda	*Add	*Delete
[kokoro]	√, √, √	√, √, √	√, √, √	√, √, √	√, √, √

Here a checkmark in the relevant cell indicates that the constraint is met; there are three checkmarks in each cell referring to each of the three syllables in these cases. It is the combination of Onset and NoCoda (no matter what their ranking) that ensures that an intervocalic consonant (VCV) will be syllabified with the consonant as the onset of the second syllable (V$CV).

Let's now consider some cases where the same input or underlying form results in different outputs in different languages. Consider the English word *test*, which as we saw above is realized as [tesuto] in Japanese and [tɛs] in Indonesian. I leave Nuc and Onset out of the following discussion, as they are met by all of the cases we are considering. This particular case doesn't provide evidence for the ranking of Onset, but the abundance of vowel initial forms in all three languages shows that Onset can be violated under certain circumstances. On the other hand, Nuc is very high ranking, and therefore unviolated, in each of the three languages.

In English, the input [tɛst] matches the output, even though it violates NoCoda twice. This provides evidence that NoCoda is lower ranked than both *Add and *Delete. In other words, meeting the requirements of the input / output constraints is more important in English than adhering to the markedness constraints.

(24) English *test* [tɛst]

/tɛst/		*Add	*Delete	*NoCoda
a. ☞	[tɛst]	√	√	**
b.	[tɛs]	√	*!	*
c.	[tɛ]	√	*!*	√
d.	[tɛstV]	*!	√	*
e.	[tɛsVtV]	*!*	√	√

The optimal or best formed candidate in this case is [tɛst], indicated by ☞. An ! indicates an insurmountable violation. This is followed by shading of the successive cells in the same row, indicating that the adherence to these lower ranked constraints isn't relevant to the outcome. (23a) is the optimal candidate in this case, even though this form violates NoCoda twice. This is still preferable to a violation of either *Add (24d and e) or *Delete (24b and c), providing evidence that both of these constraints outrank NoCoda (hence NoCoda is positioned to the right, separated by a solid vertical line). Since both *Add and *Delete have to be met, we don't have evidence for their relative ranking in English.

The pattern in Japanese is very different. In Japanese, priority is given to the markedness constraints over the input / output constraints. In order to meet the high ranking NoCoda constraint, vowels are inserted, providing evidence that *Delete outranks *Add, as shown in the tableau in (25):

(25) Japanese [tesuto] "test"

/tɛst/		NoCoda	*Delete	*Add
a.	[test]	*!*	√	√
b.	[tes]	*!	*	√
c.	[te]	√	*!*	√
d.	[testV]	*!	√	√
e. ☞	[tesVtV]	√	√	**

We see here that (25e) [tesuto], which respects both NoCoda and *Delete, is the optimal candidate. We use V to represent an inserted vowel and assume that it is a language-specific question what the actual quality of the inserted vowel will be. We also leave aside the additional question of the /ɛ/ being realized as [e]. As we saw above in (17b and c), some limited violations of NoCoda are tolerated. The intuition is that coda consonants cannot have their own place specification, rather, they must share it with the following onset consonant, either as part of a geminate or as part of a nasal-stop cluster agreeing in place of articulation.

Finally in Indonesian, we find a case where deletion is tolerated, indicated by the relatively low ranking of *Delete, though this is balanced with a violation of NoCoda, since the optimal form involves one violation of each NoCoda and *Delete (in contrast to English which violates NoCoda twice and Japanese which violates *Add twice).

(26) Indonesian [tɛs] "test"

/tɛst/		*Add	NoCoda	*Delete
a.	[test]	√	*!*	√
b. ☞	[tɛs]	√	*	*
c.	[tɛ]	√	√	*!*
d.	[testV]	*!	*	√
e.	[tesVtV]	*!*	√	√

The optimal candidate in Indonesian is (26b). Our analysis accounts for the fact that both (26d and e) are eliminated, but more needs to be said about why the optimal outcome is (26b) rather than (26a or c). An additional constraint must be involved; while I won't formalize it here, the intuition is that on one hand a single consonant in coda position is more acceptable than a cluster and on the other, there is a limit to how much deletion the system will tolerate. There is more to the story in Indonesian, since in the case of onset clusters, vowels are inserted rather than consonants being deleted, for example [sətasion] from Dutch *station*, but we leave aside these additional details in our current discussion.

There are clearly additional complexities, since all three languages allow vowel initial words (hence limited violations of ONSET) and more needs to be said about why, in Japanese, a final syllable such as [kin] is allowed but one such as [tom] is not. Finally, additional constraints are needed to account for the division of medial consonant clusters into codas and onsets, e.g. English *abrupt* [ə$brʌpt] vs. *Abner* [æb$nɚ]. In many languages, VCCV will surface as V$CCV if CC is an allowable onset (clearly additional constraints are required to define which consonant clusters are and are not allowable). If CC is not an allowable onset, the VC$CV syllabification would result in a minimal violation of NoCODA.

While I haven't provided a complete account of any of these three cases, we can see that the relative ranking of this limited set of constraints allows us to capture these different strategies of syllabification. Other languages are predicted to show different outputs. For example, the form [tɛstV] would result in a language that had some tolerance of single consonant codas (like Indonesian), but ranked *DELETE over *ADD.

In this section we have seen that reference to syllables as well as subsyllabic constituents offers a more insightful account than one where only reference to the segment can be made. In addition we have looked briefly at how a constraint-based approach, where minimal violation of constraints is tolerated, allows us to account for some of the cross-linguistic variation observed in syllable structure.

4   Subsegmental structure

4.1   *Features and segmenthood*

Up until this point in our discussion, we have focussed on segments (and larger units). Good evidence for the psychological reality of segments exists, including speaker intuition, alphabetical writing systems, speech errors, and the fact that phonological processes manipulate such units. But there is also good evidence that segments are made up of smaller units and that a more insightful discussion of sound patterning is possible, if we make reference to these smaller units. We have an intuition that [p, b] are more similar than [l, b]. This is because the former share more sound properties than the latter. These sound properties are called *distinctive features*. The notion of distinctive features grows out of the work of Trubetzkoy, Jakobson, and others (see Anderson 1985 for an excellent survey of the history of phonology). While numerous specific systems have been proposed, most current systems have evolved from that proposed by Chomsky and Halle (1968). Most approaches to phonology assume some kind of feature system and take the features to be the smallest building blocks of phonology. Segments thus consist of bundles of features, or feature matrices, as exemplified in (27):

(27) feature matrices

$$
\text{b} \quad
\begin{bmatrix}
+\text{consonantal} \\
-\text{continuant} \\
-\text{sonorant} \\
-\text{nasal} \\
\text{labial}
\end{bmatrix}
\quad
\text{ɪ} \quad
\begin{bmatrix}
-\text{consonantal} \\
+\text{high} \\
-\text{back} \\
-\text{tense}
\end{bmatrix}
\quad
\text{l} \quad
\begin{bmatrix}
+\text{consonantal} \\
-\text{continuant} \\
+\text{sonorant} \\
-\text{nasal} \\
\text{coronal} \\
\text{lateral}
\end{bmatrix}
$$

There are many interesting and important issues about the status of features. First there is much debate about an adequate specific set of features which can account for all the occurring sounds in the languages of the world. Additionally there are issues such as the number of values that characterize particular features. There are some features which clearly define two classes, for example [±sonorant], where [+sonorant] defines the class of sonorants and [−sonorant] defines the class of obstruents. Such features are appropriately characterized as two-valued or binary. In the case of other features, their presence or absence seems sufficient, that is, they are single-valued or privative; for example this is argued to be the case for [nasal]. Finally other parameters, such as vowel height or sonority seem to have multiple values. Such dimensions are often treated with two or more binary features (e.g. [±high] and [±low] to capture three vowel heights,

$$
[\text{i}] =
\begin{bmatrix}
+\text{high} \\
-\text{low}
\end{bmatrix},
\quad
[\text{e}] =
\begin{bmatrix}
-\text{high} \\
-\text{low}
\end{bmatrix},
\quad
[\text{æ}] =
\begin{bmatrix}
-\text{high} \\
+\text{low}
\end{bmatrix}),
$$

but some researchers argue that multivalued features should be incorporated directly into the system. While some have argued that place of articulation might also be multivalued, there is good evidence that the specific categories are grouped together into broader categories, e.g. those sounds involving contact with the front part of the tongue, the dentals, alveolars, and alveo-palatals sometimes pattern as a group and are referred to by the cover term *coronal*. I will not provide a systematic discussion of distinctive features, since a number of good overviews are available (see, for example, Keating 1987, Clements and Hume 1995) and I will refer somewhat informally to specific features here. Leaving aside finer differences between specific proposals, a striking result about the nature of most feature systems is that the features themselves are not arbitrary classificatory elements, but rather are closely linked to phonetic structure. Thus we find a convergence of phonetic events and the sounds that are found to pattern together in the phonologies of language after language.

Evidence for specific feature proposals comes from their adequacy in capturing the recurrent cross-linguistic grouping of sounds, referred to as *natural classes*. The same groupings of sounds are found in a wide range of phonological patterns. Take for example the feature [±sonorant]. [+sonorant] defines the class of sounds for which spontaneous vocal cord vibration (or voicing) is possible. This includes those sounds for which there is not a close obstruction of the vocal tract (nasals, liquids, glides, vowels). In the typical case the sonorants are voiced and do not show a contrast between voiced and voiceless. For the obstruents – the stops, fricatives, and affricates – on the other hand, which are [−sonorant], voicing involves certain articulatory adjustments to maintain air pressure and keep the vocal cords vibrating. For the obstruents, the least marked category is voiceless, but the obstruents often show a contrast between [+voice] and [−voice]. A strong implicational universal is that if there is a voicing contrast in the sonorants (as found, for example, in Burmese where there are both voiced and voiceless nasals and other sonorants), then there is also a voicing contrast in the obstruents. Additional examples of reference to the natural class defined by [±sonorant] include syllabic consonants in English (the nasals and liquids in the final syllable of such forms as *bottle* [l̩] and *button* [n̩]) and the division between the sonorants and obstruents crucial to the sonority hierarchy discussed earlier.

Sometimes the patterning of sounds is characterized in terms of the specific featural content of segments, but other times the presence or absence of segments themselves accounts for the observed pattern. Thus sometimes it is appropriate to refer to the segment as a unit independent of its featural content. To incorporate the notion of the segment as such, some approaches include so-called "timing units," and others propose an internal hierarchical grouping of features within the segment, including a "root node," which, in effect, identifies a bundle of features as a segment. Such approaches allow us to account for the changes in timing which are independent of segment content.

Sometimes a segment might be deleted without leaving any evidence behind (such as the Korean consonant deletion case illustrated above in (9)), but in other cases, the timing of a deleted segment "stays behind." This is the case of what is called *compensatory lengthening*. Consider the widely discussed case from Latin illustrated in (28).

(28) /kosmis/   [koːmis]   "courteous"
      /kasnus/   [kaːnus]   "gray"
      /fideslia/   [fideːlia]   "pot"

We see in (28) that an /s/ is deleted before another consonant. (The relevant consonants are labial and coronal nasals and /l/. Not all /s/'s disappear, as we can see by the fact that final /s/'s still surface.) But the /s/ doesn't completely disappear; rather, it leaves its timing unit (indicated here by an X) behind, resulting in a lengthening of the preceding vowel, hence the term compensatory lengthening. We can capture this change as follows (where I am informally representing the bundle of features which make up the content of relevant segments as **V** and **s**).

(29) X   X

    V   s

The feature bundle of /s/ is deleted but its timing unit is reassociated with the preceding vowel. Direct reference to the timing aspect of a segment allows us to capture this straightforwardly.

The facts of /s/ deletion in Latin are actually more complex, as there are cases where /s/ deletes, again before a nasal or /l/, but no compensatory lengthening occurs:

(30) /smereo:/   [merio:]   "deserve" (present)
      /snurus/   [nurus]   "daughter-in-law"

Once again syllable structure plays a role: the /s/ in these cases is in the onset of the syllable, while in the cases in (28) above it is in the coda. A strong cross-linguistic observation is that consonants deleted from coda position may result in compensatory lengthening, while those in onset position almost never do. (There are alternative proposals besides "timing units" which capture this asymmetry.)

4.2 *Alternations*

With these further refinements of the representation of phonological units – features organized into segments and timing units, in turn grouped into larger units – we are ready to consider one of the central observations in phonology. Often phonemes are realized in different ways in different contexts – position in the word, next to certain sounds, in stressed or unstressed position, and so forth. Such differences in the realization of a phoneme, and as a result alternations in the shape of a morpheme, are the clearest evidence of the effects of phonology. As already seen above, alternations can result from aspects of the higher level organization (as we saw, for example, in the consonant ~ zero alternations in Korean due to syllable structure). But effects are also found due to the quality of neighboring segments. To take a simple example from English, the prefix /ɪn-/ changes its shape depending on the following consonant:

(31) [ɪn]
inappropriate
intolerant
indecent

[ɪm]
impossible
imbalance

[ɪŋ]
incoherent
inglorious

Here the nasal is becoming more similar to the following consonant by sharing the place of articulation, with a coronal nasal [n] before coronals (and
also vowels), a bilabial nasal [m] before bilabial stops, and a velar nasal [ŋ]
before velars. The morpheme /-ɪn/ has three allomorphs: [ɪn-, ɪm-, ɪŋ-]. This
is an example of *assimilation*, whereby a sound becomes more similar to its
neighbor(s). While such patterns of nasal place assimilation are very common
cross-linguistically, this pattern is not as systematic in English as in some other
languages, since a nasal consonant doesn't always share the place of articulation of the following consonant. For example, in forms compounded with the
particle /ɪn-/, for some speakers, assimilation doesn't take place: cf. *input*,
[n-p] *income* [n-k]. (There are systematic explanations of these differences, but
considering these would take us beyond the scope of the present discussion.)
    It is also assimilation, in this case, of voicing, which accounts (in part) for
the alternation in the shape of the regular plural marker in English that we
saw above in (1). As we observed above, what is spelled as *s* or *es* is pronounced as [s], [z], or [ɪz]. The distribution of these three variant shapes or
allomorphs of the plural morpheme is not arbitrary. Rather, the distribution is
systematically determined by the voicing and place of articulation of the final
sound of the stem:

(32) a. [s]   b. [z]   c. [ɪz]
         cap   [p]   cab   [b]   match [ʧ]
         cat   [t]   fad   [d]   judge [ʤ]
         book [k]   dog   [g]   mess   [s]
                            can   [n]   buzz   [z]
                            file [l]   wish   [ʃ]
                            bow   [o]   garage [ʒ]

If the final sound of the stem is voiceless, as shown in (32a), then the shape of
the plural marker is [s]. (This holds systematically for the stops, but the situation with voiceless fricatives is more complicated: sometimes the voiceless
fricative itself becomes voiced and then takes the voiced allomorph [z], such

as *leaf* [f], *leaves* [vz], but sometimes the same pattern for the stops is found, *chef* [f] *chefs* [fs].) As shown in (32b), if the final sound of the stem, whether an obstruent, sonorant consonant, or vowel, is voiced, then the shape of the plural marker will be [z]. Thus the voicing of the final sounds in the stem conditions the shape of the plural marker, which agrees in voicing with that sound, another example of assimilation. But there is a systematic exception to the pattern seen in (32a and b), as illustrated in (32c). If the final sound is either an affricate [ʧ, ʤ], or an alveolar or palato-alveolar fricative [s, z, ʃ, ʒ], then the shape of the plural marker is [ɪz]. The intuition here is that [s] or [z] added to stems ending in these sounds would be too similar to be perceptually distinct and so a vowel is inserted to break up the cluster. While some limited exceptions exist, such as *mouse-mice*, *sheep-sheep*, *child-children*, there is good evidence for the fact that speakers intuitively know the rule that is responsible for the correct phonetic shape of the plural marker. Such evidence comes from the fact that both children acquiring English and adults when faced with new words added to the language apply these rules in forming the plural, for example *macs* [s] and *pentiums* [z] and some people even say *mouses* [ɪz].

We can see by comparing these two examples from English that assimilation can result from a preceding segment being affected by a following one as in the case of nasal place assimilation or vice versa as in the case of voicing assimilation of the plural marker.

Such patterns of assimilation are very common across the languages of the world. Again this is an area where we see a close parallel between phonology and phonetics. It is a common property of speech that neighboring sounds are coarticulated, that is, that the articulation of adjacent sounds overlaps. Such phonetic effects can become exaggerated and over time result in phonological assimilation. Let's consider another example, the case of vowel nasalization in Sundanese (a regional language of Indonesia).

(33) Sundanese vowel nasalization

a.	[atur]	"arrange"		[ŋãtur]	"arrange" (active)
	[obah]	"change"		[ŋõbah]	"change" (active)
	[parios]	"examine"		[mãrios]	"examine" (active)
b.	[tiis]	"relax in a cool place"		[nĩĩs]	"relax in a cool place" (active)
	[saur]	"say"		[ɲãũr]	"say" (active)

In Sundanese, an initial vowel or one following an oral consonant is oral, while one following a nasal consonant is nasalized. This alternation between nasalized and oral vowels can be seen in corresponding bare stems and active forms, since the active is formed by adding [ŋ] or [+nasal] to the initial consonant of the root, as shown in (33a). Not only is a single vowel following a nasal consonant affected, but a sequence of vowels will become nasalized, as shown in (33b). Such examples illustrate the importance of distinctive features for an adequate description of such alternations. If we couldn't make reference to a single feature (e.g. [voice] or [nasal]) or set of features (needed, for example, to account for nasal place assimilation), we would be missing a fundamental insight into what is going on in such cases. Within the generative framework, following the seminal work of Chomsky and Halle (1968), *The Sound Pattern of English* (SPE), such patterns are accounted for by rules of the following form:

(34)   a.   general rule schema: a → b / c__d
            "a becomes b in the environment following c and preceding d"

       b.   Sundanese Vowel Nasalization: V → [+nasal] / [+nasal] ____
            Condition: applies iteratively
            "A vowel becomes [+nasal] when it is in the environment following a sound which is [+nasal]"

       c.   Underlying representation   /tiis/   /[+nasal] + tiis/

            Vowel Nasalization   –   niis
               iterative   nĩĩs

            Surface representation   [tiis]   [nĩĩs]

The general rule schema offers a formalism for accounting for observed phonological alternations. Rather than just describing the distribution of the differing allophones (or allomorphs as the case may be), this rule formalism incorporates the fundamental idea that one of the variants is basic, or underlying, and that the other variant(s) are derived by rule. Such rules are an attempt to capture the knowledge that a speaker has about the sound patterns in his or her language. Following this approach, the pattern of nasalization in Sundanese can be represented as shown in (34b), with an example of the application of the rule or "derivation" in (34c).

Such formalism, central to the view that phonology is about capturing the speaker's knowledge about language, indeed offers an explicit account of phonological patterns. However there are also some serious limitations for which alternative proposals have been developed. First, this approach does not formally account for the fact that some kinds of assimilation are so common. For example, there is nothing in the notation itself that accounts for the fact that the [nasal] specification changes by its proximity to [+nasal] as opposed to some specification for a different feature. More recent work has suggested that a more accurate account follows from the idea of assimilation as "feature spreading," rather than the changing of feature values (see Goldsmith 1976). This is part of a more general approach termed *autosegmental phonology*, where specific features can function independently of segments. Following this approach, we could characterize vowel nasalization in Sundanese as follows:

(35)   a.   X   V   b.   n   i   i   s

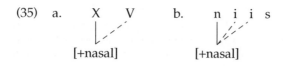

            [+nasal]   [+nasal]

The autosegmental rule in (35a) indicates that the [+nasal] feature specification spreads to the right to a following vowel, resulting in structures such as that illustrated in (35b). Here the pattern of assimilation is captured directly through the sharing of a single feature specification. This has the added advantage of allowing us a straightforward account of the iterative nature of this process.

We also saw an example of spreading in our characterization of compensatory lengthening above in (29), where the whole feature matrix specifying the vowel is shared between the vowel's timing unit and the following timing unit, freed up by the loss of the feature matrix of the /s/. Viewed in this way, this too can be seen as a sort of assimilation, in this case total assimilation. Within the formalism of SPE, such patterns of compensatory lengthening were represented as transformational rule as illustrated in (36).

(36)   compensatory lengthening

$$
\begin{array}{cccc}
V & s & \begin{bmatrix} +\text{sonorant} \\ -\text{anterior} \end{bmatrix} & \\
1 & 2 & 3 & \rightarrow \\
1 & 1 & 3 &
\end{array}
$$

"The string 1, 2, 3, where 2 = /s/ and 3 is $\begin{bmatrix} +\text{sonorant} \\ -\text{anterior} \end{bmatrix}$ is rewritten as 1, 1, 3 where 1 is the preceding vowel"

Use of transformational rules has generally been rejected now in both phonology and syntax due to their excessive power, since there are no predictions about what are allowable structures formally. There is also no insight resulting from such formalism as to why particularly these sorts of patterns occur in language after language.

In addition to assimilation of a single feature (e.g. vowel nasalization) and total assimilation (e.g. compensatory lengthening), there are cases where two or more features systematically pattern together, such as the case of nasal place assimilation, as exemplified above in English for the prefix /-ɪn/. In SPE notation, where place of articulation is represented with the two features [coronal] and [anterior], this would be represented as shown in (37).

(37) $\begin{bmatrix} -\text{continuant} \\ +\text{nasal} \end{bmatrix} \rightarrow \begin{bmatrix} \alpha \text{ anterior} \\ \beta \text{ coronal} \end{bmatrix} / \_\_\_ \begin{bmatrix} -\text{continuant} \\ -\text{sonorant} \\ \alpha \text{ anterior} \\ \beta \text{ coronal} \end{bmatrix}$

"A nasal consonant takes on the place specification (same values for [anterior] and [coronal]) as a following stop"

Here "alpha notation" is used to show that the resulting feature values are dependent on those elsewhere in the rule, in this case the values for both [anterior] and [coronal]. We see similar formal problems as in the case of single feature spreading and in addition, there is no explanation why certain features are seen to group together in language after language. In cases of nasal place assimilation, it is precisely the set of features that define place of articulation that pattern together.

Cases where a particular set of features pattern together in assimilation and other phonological processes provide strong evidence for the grouping of features (see McCarthy 1988 and Clements and Hume 1995 and work cited therein). This general approach, termed *feature geometry*, not only captures the notion of the segment as a unit independent from its featural content (represented by a *root node*), but it also offers an explicit proposal of hierarchical structure or subgrouping of features, making direct reference to elements such as the *place node*. An account of nasal place assimilation following this approach is schematized in (38).

(38)

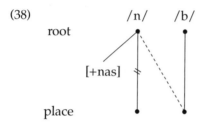

Most recently such patterns of feature "spreading" have also been characterized in Optimality Theory in terms of competing constraints.

Segments can influence each other in a wide variety of ways. There is a rich array of patterns of assimilation, including cases where the segments affecting each other are not adjacent, such as *vowel harmony* where vowels agree in a certain property (e.g. height or rounding) irrespective of the quality of the intervening consonants. We also find that segments can become less like each other; this is termed *dissimilation*. The contrast between segments might be lost in a particular environment. This is known as *neutralization*. Feature changes may be brought about due to the segmental context (that is, influence for neighboring segments), but it is also the case that the influence of prosodic structure can drive such effects. It is quite common that the range of contrasts which occurs in syllable onsets is reduced in syllable codas. One very common pattern of neutralization is what is known as Final Devoicing. Consider the following example from Polish:

(39)   Polish Final Devoicing
   a.   klup   "club" sg.   klubi   "club" pl.
        trut   "labor" sg.   trudi   "labor" pl.
   b.   trup   "corpse" sg.   trupi   "corpse" pl.
        kot   "cat" sg.   koti   "cat" pl.

We see the alternation in the voicing of the final consonant of the stem. Just looking at the forms in (39a), we might think that either the voiceless stops are underlying and become voiced in a particular environment (between vowels) or that the voiced stops are underlying and become voiceless in a particular environment (at the end of the word, though additional data suggest that it is actually syllable-final position more generally). But looking at the data in (39b), we see that not all cases show the same alternation; in these cases a voiceless stop surfaces in both forms. This makes it clear that it must be the voiced stops becoming voiceless. We also note that this pattern seems to be applying not to a random set of sounds, but to a natural class of sounds, in this case the stop consonants. We would predict that if we found forms ending in velar consonants, similar alternations would be observed. As we see in (40a), this pattern actually applies not just to stops including velar ones, but also to fricatives, that is to the class of obstruents or [–sonorant]. We can capture this pattern by positing underlying forms as shown in (40a) and applying a rule of Final Devoicing. This rule can be characterized in SPE terms as shown in (40c). Or we can account for such patterns in an autosegmental notation with the delinking of the relevant feature specification, in this case [+voice] (40d). In either case, we can see that the rule works by looking at sample derivations in (40e).

(40) Polish Final Devoicing

    a. wuk   "lye" sg.   wugi "lye" pl.
        grus   "rubble" sg.   gruzi "rubble" pl.

    b. /klub/ "club"
        /trud/ "labor"
        /trup/ "corpse"
        /kot/   "cat"
        /wug/ "lye"
        /gruz/ "rubble"
        /-Ø/   singular
        /-i/   plural

    c. [–sonorant] → [–voice] / ____ # (# = word boundary)
        "A member of the class of [–sonorant] becomes voiceless in word final position."

    d. root   [–son] #

        laryngeal   [+voice]

    e. Underlying representation   /klub + Ø/   /klub + i/
        Final Devoicing   klup   –
        Surface representation   [klup]   [klubi]

Polish also provides a nice example of how one phonological process can interact with another. Consider the additional data presented in (41).

(41)   Polish Vowel Raising
     a. bur "forest" sg.   bori "forest" pl.
          sul "salt" sg.   soli "salt" pl.
          ʒur "soup" sg.   ʒuri "soup" pl.
     b. sok "juice" sg.   soki "juice" pl.
          nos "nose" sg.   nosi "nose" pl.
     c. ruk "horn" sg.   rogi "horn" pl.
          vus "cart" sg.   vozi "cart" pl.

In (41a), we see that before liquids (actually sonorants more generally), there is an alternation between [u] and [o]. We might think that /u/ becomes [o] in some environment or that /o/ becomes [u]. Since, as we see in the third pair of forms ("soup"), some [u]'s correspond to [u], it must be that /o/ → [u], what we might term Vowel Raising. Here the relevant environment seems to be before sonorants. An important question is whether this process of Vowel Raising happens more generally. Above in (39), in the form /kot/ "cat" there was no such alternation. There is also no alternation seen in the cases in (41b), but consider the cases in (41c), where the forms include a following underlying voiced obstruent. In these cases we also see the [o] ~ [u] alternation. This suggests that the environment for this rule is more general, not just [+sonorant], but rather [+voice], grouping the sonorants (which are voiced) together with the voiced obstruents, as stated in (42a) (expressed in SPE terminology for ease of exposition), with the additional underlying representations as shown in (42b).

(42) a. $\begin{bmatrix} +\text{syllabic} \\ +\text{back} \\ -\text{high} \end{bmatrix} \rightarrow [+\text{high}] \ / \ \underline{\hspace{1cm}} \ [+\text{voice}] \ \#$

        "A back non-high vowel becomes high in the environment before a voiced sound in word final position."
     b. /bor/   "forest"
          /sol/   "salt"
          /ʒur/   "soup"
          /sok/   "juice"
          /nos/   "nose"
          /rog/   "horn"
          /voz/   "cart"

Since part of the trigger of the Vowel Raising rule, the following voiced sound, is the target of the Final Devoicing rule, an obvious question is how these two rules interact. It could be that Final Devoicing applies first or that Vowel Raising applies first. Consider the two possible orderings shown in the derivations in (43):

(43) a. Underlying representation   /rog + Ø/   /rog + i/
         Final Devoicing   rok   –
         Vowel Raising   –   –
         Surface representation   *[rok]   [rogi]
      b. Underlying representation   /rog + Ø/   /rog + i/
         Vowel Raising   rug   –
         Final Devoicing   ruk   –
         Surface representation   [ruk]   [rogi]

It is clear comparing the two derivations that the Vowel Raising rule must apply before Final Devoicing, otherwise Final Devoicing would in effect rob relevant cases from Vowel Raising. Such cases show that the ordering of rules may be crucial. We have characterized these patterns of alternation following a rule-based approach. We could equally well pursue a constraint-based approach, but in either case, we need to be able to account for the ways in which phonological processes might interact with each other.

Before concluding this section, let's return to the question raised above about the status of [ŋ] in English. While we included [ŋ] in the chart of the sound inventory in English presented in (3) above, we also noted in (1) that [ŋ] has a defective distribution. One approach to this would be to say that /ŋ/ just has a defective distribution, period – parallel to /h/. Yet this would leave a number of distributional observations unaccounted for. Consider the distributions of the three nasals of English, [m, n, ŋ] in (44):

(44)

	initial	medial	final	N–Vstop	N+Vstop	N–Vstop	N+Vstop
m	map	dimmer	dim, bomb	camper	amber	camp	–
n	nap	sinner	sin	canter	candor	can't	land
ŋ	–	singer[3] [ŋ]	sing [ŋ]	canker [ŋk]	anger, finger [ŋg]	bank [ŋk]	–

[m, n] can occur in word-initial position, as well as medially and finally. They can also occur before an oral stop, either medially or finally (except that [mb] doesn't occur as a cluster within a syllable coda, hence *bomb* [bam], but *bombardment* [bəmbardmn̩t]). [ŋ], on the other hand, doesn't occur in word-initial position. Basically [ŋ] only occurs in the syllable coda, not in the onset. This generalization accounts for why it can't occur word initially and accounts for all the cases except *singer*. The important observation here is that *singer* consists of the root *sing* plus the suffix -*er* and so the [ŋ] is, in effect, in syllable-final position until the suffix is added (assumed to cause resyllabification). This generalization accounts for the distribution, but doesn't explain why it

should be so. As noted above, sometimes sounds are limited in their distribution, but cross-linguistically we find if a consonant is limited, the more restricted distribution occurs in the coda, not in the onset. In other words, neutralization (such as the case of Final Devoicing) tends to occur in codas, not onsets. If we take the spelling as a cue in the cases of [ŋ], a solution presents itself. We might argue that [ŋ] is not part of the underlying inventory of English, but rather that it is derived from /ng/ or /nk/ sequences. Very briefly the analysis would work as follows. The underlying nasal consonants in English are /m, n/. As noted above in our discussion of the prefix /-ɪn/, English has a rule of Nasal Place Assimilation whereby a nasal assimilates to a following stop (schematized above in (38)). Based on the evidence from the lack of word-final [mb] clusters we might also posit a rule of Voiced Stop Deletion which applies to non-coronals, whereby a voiced stop following a nasal consonant is deleted word finally (45a). Given the underlying representations presented in (45b), the rules of Nasal Place Assimilation and Voiced Stop Deletion together (as well as some understanding of the interaction of phonology and morphology for cases like *singer* which we won't develop here) account for the observed patterns, as shown in the derivations in (45c). As in the Polish case, these rules must be crucially ordered, otherwise the deletion of the voiced stop would have removed the information about place specification needed for the Nasal Place Assimilation rule.

(45) a. Voiced Stop Deletion

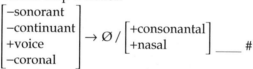

$$\begin{bmatrix} -\text{sonorant} \\ -\text{continuant} \\ +\text{voice} \\ -\text{coronal} \end{bmatrix} \rightarrow \varnothing / \begin{bmatrix} +\text{consonantal} \\ +\text{nasal} \end{bmatrix} \_\_\_ \#$$

"A voiced non-coronal stop is deleted word finally following a nasal consonant."

  b. /dɪm/
      /bamb/ or /banb/
      /bænk/
      /sɪng/
      /fɪngɚ/

  c. | Underlying representation | /banb/ | /bænk/ | /sɪng/ | /fɪngɚ/ |
      |---|---|---|---|---|
      | Nasal Place Assimilation | bamb | bæŋk | sɪŋg | fɪŋgɚ |
      | Voiced Stop Deletion | bam | – | sɪŋ | – |
      | Surface representation | [bam] | [bæŋk] | [sɪŋ] | [fɪŋgɚ] |

In the case of *bomb*, we might assume an underlying /n/ or /m/ or even a nasal consonant which is unspecified for place of articulation. /n/ when it occurs before a velar consonant assimilates in place of articulation and then in the case of a following voiced stop, this is deleted. The restricted distribution of [ŋ] in English follows directly from this approach without our having to posit an underlying phoneme with a defective distribution.

In this section we have seen a number of ways in which segments might affect each other and evidence for reference to distinctive features, as well as their grouping. We have also seen that the division we made between structure above the level of the segment and subsegmental structure is somewhat artificial, since syllable structure can affect feature specification and so forth.

5   Phonology as a System

In concluding this introduction to phonology, it is useful to step back and consider how all these aspects of phonology that we have discussed fit together.

Most basically a phonology consists of a set of representations – an inventory of sounds, in turn defined by distinctive features matrices – and a system of rules or constraints which act on the representations. Fundamental to the generative approach is the idea that the idiosyncratic and predictable information of the phonology are treated separately: the idiosyncratic information is part of the underlying representations and the predictable patterns arise through the systematic manipulation of these sounds through rules or constraints. Consider the following schematic figure:

(46)   underlying representations:

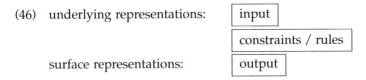

surface representations:

The underlying representation includes the abstract sounds or phonemes for each morpheme in the language and the surface representation incorporates the phonetic variations or allophones, seen in the systematic alternations of the language, introduced as a result of the applications of a system of rules or constraints. The phonological representation includes not only the sequence of sounds, made up of timing units and featural content, but also the hierarchical grouping of these sounds into syllables and higher level prosodic units.

A phonology of a language consists of the whole system taken together. A complete phonology consists of dozens and dozens of rules (or constraints) often with complex interactions. To illustrate both the nature of phonological patterns and the mechanisms involved in accounting for these patterns, we have considered a number of examples of phonological patterns, but only by studying the whole phonology of a language can we understand its full complexity.

NOTES

Thanks to Beverley Goodman, Lisa Lavoie, Ayako Tsuchida, and Draga Zec for providing helpful input on earlier drafts of this chapter.

1 The description of possible sounds used in language is part of the purview of (linguistic) phonetics and so I will not provide a full discussion here (for an introduction, see Ladefoged 1993, also chapter 7, in this handbook).

2 The situation is actually a bit more complex, since if we have a syllabic nasal, such as in *gibbon* [gɪbn̩], then the sequence is allowable, but here the [n] is functioning as a vowel and is in a different subconstituent of the syllable from the [b].

3 For some speakers, the author included, this is pronounced [sɪŋɡɚ], rhyming with *finger* [fɪŋɡɚ].

9 Morphology

ANDREW SPENCER

1 Introduction

Morphology is about the structure of words. All languages have words and in all languages some words, at least, have an internal structure, and consist of one or more *morphemes*. Thus, the form *cats* comprises the root morpheme "cat" to which is added the suffix morpheme "s" indicating plural. Now, for this characterization to mean anything we have to know what a word is. How do we know, for instance, that a string such as *the cat* is two separate words, and that *the* is not a prefix? Conversely, how do we know that the "s" of *cats* isn't a word in its own right. Here we need the help of syntax: *the cat* is a phrase which can be extended by addition of other phrases: *the very black cat*. The form *cats* can never be split up this way, the reason being that the "s" component is an element which can only exist as part of a word, specifically at the end of a noun. In other words, "s" is a suffix and hence a *bound morpheme*. The property of indivisibility exhibited by *cats* is *lexical integrity*. A single word such as *cats* contrasts rather neatly with the fully fledged (but synonymous) phrase *more than one cat*, in which it is clear that *more*, *than*, and *one* are all independent words and can all be separated by other words or phrases.

This chapter will examine the different structures words exhibit and the morphological relationships they bear to each other, and the nature of the morpheme. We begin by clarifying the notion "word" itself.

1.1 The lexeme concept

If we ask how many words are listed in (1) we can give at least two answers

(1) {cat, cats}

In one sense there are obviously two, but in another sense there is only one word, CAT, and only one entry will be found in a dictionary for it. The plural, *cats*, is formed by a completely general rule from the singular form *cat* and there is no need to record the plural form separately. In addition, we can describe *cat* as "the singular form of the word CAT" and *cats* as "the plural form of the word CAT." This gives us another interpretation for the term "word," as becomes clear when we look at the word "sheep." Here the singular form of the word SHEEP has exactly the same shape as the plural form, even though these are distinct linguistic entities. Given the vagaries of English orthography, this identity of shape can be true of the spoken form, the written form, or both (as with "sheep"). Thus, the written shape of the base form of the verb "read" (pronounced like "reed") is identical to that of the past tense, "read" (pronounced like "red") despite the difference in pronunciation, while *the taxes, the tax's* ("of the tax") and *the taxes'* ("of the taxes") differ solely in spelling.

It is rather useful to have different terms for these three different senses of the word "word." We will therefore say that there is a *lexeme* CAT which has two *word forms*, *cat* and *cats*. The names of lexemes are conventionally written in small capitals. The grammatical description "the singular / plural of CAT" is a *grammatical word*. Thus, *sheep* is one word form corresponding to one lexeme, but it is two grammatical words (the singular and the plural of SHEEP).

We can think of a lexeme as a complex representation linking a (single) meaning with a set of word forms, or more accurately, linking a meaning with a set of grammatical words, which are then associated with corresponding word forms. From the point of view of the dictionary (or lexicon), this is therefore a *lexical entry*. There is no demand here that the set of forms correspond to only one meaning, or that only one set of forms correspond to a given meaning. If several forms correspond to one meaning we have pure *synonymy*: e.g. {*boat, boats*}, {*ship, ships*}. If a single form corresponds to more than one completely unrelated meaning, as with {*write, right, rite*}, or {*bank, bank*} then we have *homophony* or *homonymy*. We then treat the homophones / homonyms as distinct lexemes which just happen to share the same shape (written and / or spoken). In some cases these meanings are felt as related to each other, and we have a case of *polysemy*. Thus, the word "head" means a body part, the person in charge of an organization, a technical term in linguistics, and so on, and these meanings are associated by some kind of metaphorical extension. In general, polysemy tends to be either ignored (where the meanings are close) or treated like homophony (but see below in section 3.2 on verbs like BREAK).

In linguistics a form-meaning pair is a *sign* and the lexeme is a prototypical example of a sign. The traditional definition of morpheme is "the smallest meaningful component of a word," and this entails that we consider all morphemes as signs. However, this turns out to be very controversial, for some types of morpheme, at least.

1.2 Inflection, derivation and compounding: preliminaries

In this section I briefly introduce certain important notions which will figure widely later: *inflection*, in which we create word forms of lexemes (such as the plural or past tense), *derivation*, in which we create new lexemes from old lexemes, and the *compound word*, a single word formed by combining two other words. We begin with compounds.

The most straightforward type of compound simply consists of two words concatenated together: *morphology + article = morphology article; house + boat = houseboat*. The right-hand member is the *head* of the compound, determining the syntactic category and meaning of the whole (a morphology article is a kind of article, a houseboat is a kind of boat, as compared with a boathouse, which is a kind of house). The left-hand member is the modifier. In transparent cases such as *morphology article* the meaning of the whole is derived from the meanings of the components (though the precise meaning is indeterminate and depends on the context of use).

There is an important distinction in many languages between compounds and phrases. In many cases the difference is obvious. In a hackneyed example such as *blackbird* as opposed to *black bird* the compound has stress on *black*, while the phrase is stressed on *bird* (in neutral contexts at least). Moreover, a black bird is necessarily black, while a blackbird is a particular species of bird whatever its colour (female blackbirds are brown, for instance). This means that the semantics of this compound is *non-compositional*, i.e. we can't determine the meaning of the whole just from the meanings of the parts. The semantics of phrases (idioms apart) is compositional. The difference can be illustrated syntactically as in (2, 3) (making very conservative assumptions about syntactic structure):

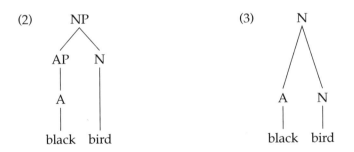

(2)   NP   (3)   N

     AP   N

     A

    black   bird   A   N

                                         black   bird

This is the standard story, though there are interesting subtleties. For instance, there is no way of determining the syntactic category of the modifier in *blackbird*, because it is fixed as part of the compound and can't be subjected to any of the morphological or syntactic manipulations that real adjectives can. Thus, compare (4) and (5):

(4) a. a very black bird
     b. a blacker bird
     c. a bird, black as coal, flew overhead

(5) a. *a very blackbird
     b. *a blackerbird
     c. *a black-as-coal-bird

Moreover, *black* doesn't mean "black" in *blackbird* (because a blackbird doesn't actually have to be black). Thus, the modifier *black* has neither category nor meaning; it just has a bare morphophonological shape. Therefore, (3) should be rewritten as (6):

(6)

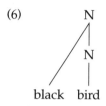

The point is that *blackbird* is a lexicalized compound whose internal structure is only of historical significance, unlike a non-lexicalized coinage such as *morphology article*. In time, with changes in pronunciation, even this historical structure becomes opaque. Thus, *husband* is derived etymologically from (modern) "house" and "bond," but it isn't recognized as a compound by anyone except students of Middle English.

Nonetheless, noun + noun compounding is a fully *productive* process in English. Simplifying somewhat, we can say that a process is productive if it applies freely in principle to all the lexemes of the language of the relevant type, allowing new forms to be created at will even if they have never been used before. Such processes therefore have to be semantically regular, without any lexicalized idiosyncrasy of meaning, otherwise, hearers would have no way of knowing what a new coining was supposed to mean (see Aronoff and Anshen 1998, for more detailed discussion). The meaning of such compounds is admittedly vague: a morphology article is an article which has some connection with morphology. On the other hand, adjective + noun compounds aren't productive and there are virtually no verb + noun compounds (there is a tiny handful of exceptions like *swearword* and *drawbridge*).

A variety of types of productive compounding are known in the languages of the world. A particularly interesting type, which has been the subject of some debate in recent years, is that known as noun incorporation (see Mithun 1984). In noun incorporation we see an alternation in which the direct object of a verb may form a compound with that verb. In (7) we see two examples from Chukchee (a member of a small language group spoken in northeast Siberia):

(7) a. Gəmnan tə   -piri -gʔen   pojgə-n
         I.ERG   1sgSUBJ-take-3sgOBJ   spear-ABS

b. Gəm tə   -pojgə-pere-gʔak
   I.ABS 1sgSUBJ-spear-take-1sgSUBJ
   "I took the spear"

In (7a) the subject pronoun is in the ergative case (the case used to mark the subject of a transitive sentence), while the object is in the absolutive case. Being transitive, the verb agrees with both the subject and the object. In (7b) the root of the object noun has formed a compound with the verb root. This renders the verb intransitive, so it agrees solely with the 1st person subject. The subject pronoun is now in the absolutive case, the case used for intransitive subjects. Finally, notice that the 1sg prefix comes to the left of the incorporated noun root and the vowels of the root have changed. This is due to vowel harmony, under which the "weak" vowel /i/ is changed to /e/ when there is a "strong" vowel elsewhere in the word (e.g. the /o/ of *pojgə*). Vowel harmony only operates within a word, and this helps us identify the incorporative complex as a single word form morphologically. Examples (7a, b) differ slightly in emphasis but are otherwise synonymous. Thus, it is clear that *pojgə* still realizes the "spear" lexeme even when it is compounded. Noun incorporation is completely productive in Chukchee, with very few restrictions.

Turning to derivation, the nouns *writer, painter, walker* are clearly related to the verbs *write, paint, walk*, meaning roughly "person who writes, paints, walks," by suffixation of *-er*. I shall call these *subject nominals*. It is customary to treat *write* and *writer* as distinct lexemes related by derivation, rather than word forms of a single lexeme. For instance, *writer* is a noun, while *write* is a verb. The morphological operations which realize derivation (such as *-er* affixation) may or may not be regular and productive. Thus, *apply* has a subject nominal *applic-ant*, with irregular suffix *-ant* added to an irregular form of the root, *applic-*. I discuss derivation in more detail in section 3.1.

As a verb lexeme, WRITE has its own set of grammatical words expressed by the forms *write, writes, writing, wrote, written*. Similarly, WRITER has its own set of forms: *writer, writers*. These grammatical words are the *inflected* forms of the lexeme and the process of constructing inflected forms is known as inflection ("inflectional morphology"). The meanings of the inflected form are predictable (plural of noun, past tense of verb, or whatever), while the shape of inflected forms is generally determined by affixation to the *stem* form of the lexeme. The stem consists of the root and any derivational affixes. In morphologically complex languages a given lexeme might have several stems for different types of inflection (for example, all verbs may have separate present tense and past tense stems). Irregularity, either in the stem or the affix, is not uncommon. Thus, *knife* has the irregular stem form *knive-* in the plural (*knives*), while *ox* has the irregular suffix *-en* (*oxen*). Irregularity of form can be complete as in *total suppletion*, when one inflected form bears no shape relation to the rest of the paradigm (e.g. *went* as the past tense of GO). Where there is still some overlap we talk of partial suppletion (as in *brought ~ bring*, where the first two consonants are identical). Even where the shapes are irregular, the past tense meaning is exactly the same as it is for any other verb, whether irregular (such as *write ~ wrote, bring ~ brought, go ~ went*) or regular (e.g. *scribble ~ scribbled*).

Inflections express grammatical or *functional categories*. The inflectional system organizes the forms of words into systematic groupings or *paradigms*. There are essentially two sorts of function subserved by inflection. Many inflections signal an aspect of meaning which is *grammaticalized*, such as number (singular vs. plural) or tense. This means that the words of a given class obligatorily signal the grammatical distinction: thus, all verbs in English have to have a past tense (even if these are not actually distinct forms, as in *put*). Booij (1994) refers to this as *inherent inflection*.

One typical inherent inflection for nouns is *case*, in which the grammatical or semantic role of a noun in a sentence is shown by its form. In Russian a noun generally has distinct forms for the subject, direct object or indirect object:

(8)   Len -a   dala Ir -e   knig -u
      Lena-NOMINATIVE gave Ira-DATIVE book-ACCUSATIVE
      "Lena gave Ira a book."

Lena, Ire, knigu in (8) are case-inflected forms of the lexemes LENA, IRA, KNIGA.

Verbs exhibit much greater variety in their inflectional systems. Two common inherent inflections are *tense* and *aspect*. Tense refers to anchoring in time, as with English *wrote* (past) as opposed to *writes* (non-past – present or future reference). A given language may distinguish a number of different tenses (such as recent vs. remote past) or no tense at all. Aspect refers to the manner in which an event unfolds over time. A very common aspectual distinction is that between completed (perfective) and non-completed (imperfective) events. In Slavonic languages most verbs have separate perfective and imperfective paradigms, e.g. *op'isat'* (perf.) ~ *op'isivat'* (impf.) "describe" (see also section 3.2). Many languages have very rich aspectual markings modifying the meaning of the base verb in very subtle ways. Below is just a small selection of the fifteen aspectual affixes described for Chukchee by Skorik (1977: 179–202):

(9)   -lʔet   prolonged continuous action:
      ʔəttʔe ninepiŋku-*lʔet*-qin . . . ottəlgən
      dog   jump-*ASP*-3/3   stick
      "The dog jumped over the stick *over and over again*."

(10) -cir   prolonged interrupted action:
      . . . ŋinqejmuri nʔejŋew-*cir*-muri jaralʔa
            us.children called-*ASP*-1plOBJ people.at.home
      "The people at home *kept* calling us children."

(11) -cit / -cet   alternating action:
      . . . natcə-*cet*-qenat . . .
            hide-*ASP*-3plSUBJ
      "They played at hide-and-seek"

(12) -skɘcet   accelerated action:
      qɘnwer ŋɘto-*sqɘcat*-gʔe gɘmnin tɘletumgin
      at last come.out-*ASP*-3sgSUBJ my companion
      "At last my companion sprang out"

More than one of these can be combined:

(13) mɘt-ra-tɘla-tenmawɘ-plɘtko-ŋŋo-gʔa
      1pl-FUT-GRADUALLY-prepare-FINISH-BEGIN-FUT
      "we will *begin to gradually finish* the preparations"

Other types of verb inflection include mood (whether a statement is presented as fact, possibility, hypothetical situation and so on) such as the subjunctive mood of Romance languages, the optative expressing a wish (e.g. Ancient Greek), imperative for issuing commands, and interrogative, a special set of verb forms used for asking questions (e.g. the Eskimo languages). Many language groups signal polarity (negation) inflectionally (Bantu, Turkic, Athapaskan, and others). It is very common for a given inflectional morpheme to signal a complex mixture of tense, aspect, mood, and polarity.

Any of the above functional categories can be expressed syntactically, by word order or by function words such as the English aspectual auxiliaries (*has been reading*). One purely morphological type of inherent inflection is *inflectional class*: *declensions* for nouns and adjectives and *conjugations* for verbs. Which noun or verb goes in which class is in general arbitrary. Russian nouns can be put into four main declensions depending on the inflections they take (though different descriptive traditions distinguish different numbers of declensions):

(14) Russian noun classes

	Class I inanimate "law"	Class I animate "boy"	Class II "room"	Class III "bone"	Class IV "place"
Singular					
Nominative	zakon	mal'čik	komnata	kost'	mesto
Accusative	zakon	mal'čika	komnatu	kost'	mesto
Genitive	zakona	mal'čika	komnati	kost'i	mesta
Dative	zakonu	mal'čiku	komnate	kost'i	mestu
Instrumental	zakonom	mal'čikom	komnatoj	kost'ju	mestom
Prepositional	zakone	mal'čike	komnate	kost'i	meste
Plural					
Nominative	zakoni	mal'čiki	komnati	kost'i	mesta
Accusative	zakoni	mal'čikov	komnati	kost'i	mesta
Genitive	zakonov	mal'čikov	komnat	kostej	mest
Dative	zakonam	mal'čikam	komnatam	kost'am	mestam
Instrumental	zakonam'i	mal'čikam'i	komnatam'i	kost'am'i	mestam'i
Prepositional	zakonax	mal'čikax	komnatax	kost'ax	mestax

(The symbol ′ represents palatalization. Consonants are always palatalized before /e/. The case names are traditional and represent a variety of syntactic functions.) I have given two subtypes of class I nouns, one animate the other inanimate. In the inanimates the accusative case is always the same as the nominative, while in the animates the accusative takes the form of the genitive. This type of situation, in which parts of a paradigm are systematically identical, is known as *syncretism*. There are other syncretisms here, too. For instance, the dative, instrumental and prepositional plural endings are the same for all classes, that is, the class feature is neutralized and there is effectively a single set of endings for the whole of the class "noun." On the other hand, the behavior of pairs such as "law" and "boy" require us to set up a covert category of animacy for Russian, which never has any direct expression (there is no form which has a suffix identifiable as the "animacy" suffix) but which is nonetheless part of the inflectional system. Note that it is the property "animacy" which is covert, not the accusative case. We know this because class II nouns have a separate accusative, in the singular at least (see Corbett and Fraser 1993, for more detailed discussion of the implications of these data).

Russian verbs inflect so as to indicate the person and number of their subject (see below on "agreement") as well as for tense and occur in two main conjugations (together with a plethora of minor variations on each of these classes):

(15)   Principal Russian verb classes

Class I verb *uznat′* "to recognize", class II verb *govor′it′* "to speak"

	Class I	Class II
Non-past tense		
1sg	uzn-aj-u	govor′-u
2sg	uzn-aj-o-š	govor′-i-š
3sg	uzn-aj-o-t	govor′-i-t
1pl	uzn-aj-o-m	govor′-i-m
2pl	uzn-aj-o-te	govor′-i-te
3pl	uzn-aj-ut	govor′-at

As can be seen, the endmost suffixes are common to both classes, except in 1sg, 3pl forms. Both types have a special stem forming suffix, *-aj-* and *-i-* respectively, and class I has in addition a "linking vowel" *-o-*. The *-aj/-i* formatives are found throughout the inflectional system of the verbs.

The other role of inflection is to realize the syntactic functions of *agreement* and *government*. This is what Booij (1994) calls *contextual inflection*, because it is determined by the syntactic context in which the lexeme is used. In many languages a verb must *agree with* its subject and / or object, by cross-referencing various of their properties. This occurs marginally in English for third person non-past verb forms: *Harriet writes* vs. *the girls write*. In Chukchee transitive verbs agree with both the subject and the object, in rather complex ways. The system for one of the six tense forms in the indicative mood is shown in

(16) (see Muravyova 1998; empty cells represent non-existent forms in which the subject and object would have the same person features):

(16) *pela-* "to leave (someone, something)" Simple past

Subj	Obj		Subj	Obj	
1sg	1sg	----------------	1pl	1sg	----------------
	2sg	tə-pela-gət		2sg	mət-pela-gət
	3sg	tə-pela-gʔan		3sg	mət-pela-gʔan
	1pl	----------------		1pl	----------------
	2pl	tə-pela-tək		2pl	mət-pela-tək
	3pl	tə-pela-nat		3pl	mət-pela-nat
2sg	1sg	ena-pela-gʔe	2pl	1sg	ena-pela-tək
	2sg	----------------		2sg	----------------
	3sg	pela-gʔan		3sg	pela-tkə
	1pl	pela-tko-gʔe		1pl	pela-tko-tək
	2pl	----------------		2pl	----------------
	3pl	pela-nat		3pl	pela-tkə
3sg	1sg	ena-pela-gʔe	3pl	1sg	na-pela-gəm
	2sg	na-pela-gət		2sg	na-pela-gət
	3sg	pela-nen		3sg	na-pela-gʔan
	1pl	na-pela-mək		1pl	na-pela-mək
	2pl	na-pela-tək		2pl	na-pela-tək
	3pl	pela-nenat		3pl	na-pela-nat

The verb references the person and number both of the subject and of the object, though there is no simple relationship between many of the affixes and their functions. Thus, although the prefixes *tə-* and *mət-* clearly meaning "1sg/1pl subject" respectively, the prefix *na-* seems to mean "3pl subject" or "3sg subject with 2nd person object or 1pl object" and the suffix *-nen* seems to mean "3sg object but only if the subject is 3sg." One consequence of this is that some forms correspond to more than one subject–object pairing, e.g. *napelagət*, which means either "3sg leaves 2sg (s/he leaves thee)" or "3pl leaves 2sg (they leave thee)." The system proves to be even more complex than this when the full set of tenses, moods, and voices is taken into account. Patterns such as this are typical of languages with rich agreement systems, and such data have been instrumental in changing the views of linguists about the nature of the morpheme.

Adjectives often agree with the nouns they modify. This is extremely marginal in English, only being found for *this* and *that* (*this / that cat* vs. *these / those cats*). In Russian, however, an adjective agrees with its noun in number and case:

(17) a. bol'šoj mal'čik   Masculine nominative singular
        big boy
   b. bol'šogo mal'čika   Masculine genitive singular
   c. bol'šim mal'čikam   Masculine dative plural

(18) a. bol'šaja devuška   Feminine nominative singular
        big girl
     b. bol'šoj devuški   Feminine genitive singular
     c. bol'šim devuškam   Feminine dative plural

It might be thought that the adjective agrees in declension, but this is wrong. All nouns in Russian have one of three *genders*, masculine, feminine, or neuter. Male and female humans are masculine and feminine respectively and for other nouns gender depends largely on declensional class. Members of class I are masculine, those of classes II, III are feminine and those of class IV are neuter. However, there are certain exceptions. Thus, the word *mužčina* "man" belongs to class II, yet it is masculine: *bol'šoj mužčina* "big man." As is stressed by Aronoff (1994), gender is an essentially syntactic property, which governs agreement. Declension class is a purely morphological property which the syntax has no direct access to. Aronoff points out that the existence of arbitrary inflectional classes is one of the prime motivations for treating morphology as an autonomous linguistic module.

We have seen that a direct object in Russian is in the accusative case. This can be thought of as an instance of *government*: a transitive verb *governs* the accusative. Likewise, prepositions in Russian have to take specific cases, as shown in (19):

(19) a. okolo dom-a
        near   house-GENITIVE
        "near the house"
     b. v dom
        in house.ACCUSATIVE
        "into the house"
     c. v dom-e
        in house-PREPOSITIONAL
        "in the house"

Notice how "motion towards" as opposed to "location at" is signaled solely by case choice in (19b, c), otherwise, it is an arbitrary matter which preposition governs which case.

One of the perennial theoretical problems in morphology is whether there is a clear-cut distinction between inflection and derivation and if so how to draw it. Inflection is often thought to be "of relevance to syntax," which is clearly true of contextual inflection, but not so obvious with inherent inflection. Yet we don't want to say that plurals or past tenses are derivational and hence create new lexemes. Booij's contextual / inherent distinction is designed to ameliorate this problem (though we are now left with the task of distinguishing inherent inflection from derivation). A typical borderline case is that of the aspectual forms of Chukchee given above. Chukchee has a set of six tense-aspect forms in which aspect (roughly perfective vs. imperfective) is grammaticalized and expressed as part of the obligatory conjugation system. However, the affixes illustrated in (9–13) are not like this. Rather, they are optional elements which are added to modify the overall meaning of the verb. Does this make them derivational, then? Do we wish to say that "to *verb* in a prolonged interrupted fashion" is a new lexeme related to *verb* (derivation) or a form of the word *verb* (inherent inflection)? Cases like this are quite common and promise to provide fertile ground for future research into the problem.

2   The Morpheme Concept and Agglutinating Morphology

2.1   *Item-and-arrangement morphology*

If we return to the example of *writer* we can easily segment it into two component forms or *morphs*, a verb base, *write*, and a derivational suffix -*er*. (I use "base" as a catch-all meaning anything to which an affix is added, whether derivational or inflectional). It is usually claimed that the suffix as well as the base has a meaning and that the meaning of the derived word is obtained by combining the meanings of the two component morphs as shown in (20):

(20)   [[WRITE] PERSON WHO]

On this basis both of the morphemes are a pairing of a pronunciation (or shape, the morph) and a meaning. They are thus signs and hence are both lexemes, making the combination essentially a compound, like *houseboat*. Admittedly, -*er* is a bound morpheme, but in many languages lexemes can be compounded in the form of a bound stem. Thus, the form *pojgə* in the Chukchee noun incorporation example (7b) is in fact a bound stem form (the word for "spear" itself always surfaces with a case suffix), and even in English one might argue that there are compounds consisting solely of bound roots, the so-called neoclassical compounds such as *gram-o-phone* (or *phon-o-gram*). The traditional account of plural morphology treats the plural suffix in the same way, a type of sign with a phonology and a semantics, as shown in (21):

(21)   -z   =   </z/, [plural]>

This way of looking at things immediately leads us to the conclusion that words have a hierarchical structure which can be represented as a tree diagram. A possible structure for *writers* is shown in (22):

(22)

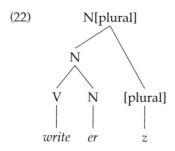

In (22) the grammatical property [plural] is said to *percolate* from the suffix to the top of the tree, ensuring that the entire word is interpreted as a plural form.

The set of assumptions underlying representations such as (22) derive from what is generally called the *item-and-arrangement* theory (IA for short): morphemes are "things" which are arranged in a particular way ("morphotactics") and which contribute their meaning to the meaning of the whole word. In an "ideal" morphological system each morpheme contributes one meaning and each meaning is associated with just one morpheme ("one form – one function"). Such a morphological ideal is often called *agglutination* (and morphologists still sometimes speak of "agglutinating" languages where this type of morphology predominates).

It should be obvious that this approach is at odds with the lexeme concept: the plural form *cats* would not, after all, be a word form belonging to an abstract lexeme, CAT, rather it would be a compound form, in which the meaning of the suffix (or perhaps we should say the head of the compound?), PLURAL, is grammaticalized. Where inflection is concerned this has proved impossible to maintain, for three main reasons. First, it is not always possible to identify a single segmentable morph for the putative morpheme; for instance, where is the plural morpheme in *men* (see section 2.2.2)? Second, there are significant deviations from the form-meaning pairing in affixation and these undermine the assumption that inflections are signs. Third, for such a theory to work we must be able to explain in a satisfactory way how complex words are constructed, and in particular how the morphemes get strung out in the right order. For complex inflectional systems this turns out to be very tricky.

2.2 *Deviations from agglutination*

The "ideal" type of morphology, then, is often seen as the addition of a semantically transparent affix to a base, so-called *concatenative* morphology. There are several ways in which morphological systems present deviations from the agglutinating ideal of one form – one function. The first of these is caused by the fact that a given morpheme may have more than one shape (allomorphy). Beyond this, we find that there are operations which can't easily be analyzed as the addition of a meaningful element but rather take the form of a phonological process, often called *non-concatenative* morphology. Languages abound in such operations and there have been a number of ingenious ways of dealing with them. I shall mention just three particularly salient cases here (introductory discussion of different types of operations can be found in Bauer 1988, Spencer 1991, 1998).

2.2.1   Allomorphy

The regular past tense ending appears as three different morphs depending on the final sound of the verb stem: *walk-ed* (/t/), *jogg-ed* (/d/), *trott-ed* (/əd/, where /ə/ is the schwa or reduced vowel). This variation is *allomorphy,* and we say that (/t, d, əd/) are the three *allomorphs* of the past tense morpheme. In this case the allomorphy is conditioned solely by the phonology of the stem: /əd/ after /t, d/, /t/ after a voiceless sound, /d/ elsewhere. Other cases of allomorphy may be irregular. For instance, while *mend* and *pen* have regular pasts, *mended, penned,* the verb *bend* takes an unexpected *-t* ending and adds this to an irregular stem form lacking the final *-d: ben-t.* Thus, both stem and suffix show irregular allomorphy. Where a given morpheme is realized by more than one allomorph we have a (mild) deviation from the agglutinative ideal.

2.2.2   Processual morphology

Certain types of irregular verb in English form their past tense by taking the basic root, *sing, run, drive, write* and changing its vowel: *sang, ran, drove, wrote.* This kind of process is called *ablaut* or *apophony.* In a number of languages, most famously Semitic languages such as Arabic and Hebrew, apophony is regular and widespread throughout the grammar. It is very difficult to represent this in terms of the addition of an affix to a base (though see McCarthy 1982, for the classic item-and-arrangement analysis of Semitic). Another well attested phenomenon is *reduplication,* illustrated by the Tagalog examples in (23):

(23)	a.	sulat	"writing"	su-sulat	"will write"
	b.	basa	"reading"		
		mambasa	infinitive	mam-ba-basa	nominalization
	c.	magpa-sulat	causative	magpa-pa-sulat	"will cause to write"

Here, morphological categories are signaled by a kind of prefix, which consists of a copy of certain of the segments of the stem. Any analysis of this phenomenon has to recognize that there is a process involved at some level (see McCarthy and Prince 1998, for a summary of some recent proposals).

A particularly drastic type of non-affixal morphology is so-called *subtractive* morphology in which a morphological category is signaled by loss of a portion of the base. Anderson (1992: 64–6) lists a number of inflectional processes which, apparently, have to be so analyzed, such as the example in (24) from the Muskogean group:

(24)   a.   balaa-ka "lie down (sg.)"   bal-ka "lie down (pl.)"   (Alabama)
       b.   bonot-li "roll up (sg. Obj.)"   bon-li "roll up (pl. Obj.)" (Choctaw)
       c.   atakaa-li "hang (sg.)"   atak-li "hang (pl.)"   (Koasati)

Here, the plural or plural object form of the verb is derived from the singular form by removing the rhyme of the final syllable of the stem: *bal<aa>, bon<ot>, atak<aa>*.

2.2.3   Form: meaning deviations

In this subsection we examine the idealization that one form corresponds to one meaning / function and vice versa. We already know of two types of deviation: synonymy (many forms – one meaning) and homonymy (one form – many meanings). However, four additional types of deviation can be distinguished when we look at the meanings or functions of morphemes within a single word.

2.2.3.1   One morph, two meanings

The Russian case system shown in (14) clearly has a grammatical category of "plural" but no single identifiable morpheme signaling number. Thus, *-am* means "dative" and "plural" simultaneously. Note that this is not homonymy, because the suffix simultaneously conveys both meanings within the same word form and these meanings are inseparable. We say that the morph shows *fusion* or *cumulation* of two separate meanings.

2.2.3.2   One meaning, two morphs

One and the same function can be signaled (redundantly) by different morphs in a given word. A simple example is found in Latin:

(25)   Latin verbs: *amo* "I love / I have loved"

P/N (sg.)	Present	Perfect
1st	am-o	am-a-v-i
2nd	am-a-s	am-a-v-isti
3rd	am-a-t	am-a-v-it

The *-v-* morph realizes perfect tense, and has no other function, so we can say that *-v-* is the *principal exponent* of (perfect) tense. However, the 1sg endings also differ with tense, and thus serve as secondary exponents of this category. This means that the meaning of "perfect tense" extends over both *-v-* and *-i* in *amavi*. This is often referred to as *extended exponence*.

2.2.3.3   One meaning, no morph: null morphemes

Notice that there is no ending in the genitive plural of Russian class II and IV nouns in (14). In a morpheme-based theory we must say that this property set, "genitive plural, class II/IV," is signaled (cumulatively) by a *null* or *zero* morpheme: *komnat-Ø*. Similarly, in derivation we often find cases of *conversion*, in which a word belonging basically to one category (such as the noun *chair* or the verb *run*) is used in another (the verb *to chair*, the noun *a run*). Given agglutination, this, again, would have to be handled by assuming a null morpheme.

2.2.3.4   *One morph, no meaning*

A traditional type of meaningless morpheme is the famous *cranberry morph*. Words such as *blueberry, blackberry, cloudberry, cranberry* etc. are clearly compounds of *berry* and refer to types of berry, but what does "cran" mean? More subtly, we saw that the *black* of *blackbird* doesn't have any meaning, strictly speaking. Aronoff (1976) argues in detail for English that there are cranberry morphs which have morphological properties (show allomorphy) and which therefore have to be regarded as morphemes. Thus, a verb such as *understand* is derived morphologically from the prefix *under-* (as in *underwrite, undertake, undermine,* . . .) and *stand* (as in *withstand*). This is clear because they have the same irregularity in the past tense as the base verb (*understood, withstood*). However, neither the prefix nor the base preserves its meaning, or any meaning. I return to such cases in section 3.2.

Cranberries are the examples of meaningless morphs most often cited, but the phenomenon is actually more widespread and more subtle. Thus, the adjectives in (26) illustrate a case in which a morpheme can be said to be meaningful only by stretching the meaning of "meaning" rather uncomfortably:

(26) | Noun | Adjective | |
|---|---|---|
| morphology | morphological | morphological theory |
| navy | naval | naval uniform |
| poetry | poetic | poetic license |
| nerve | nervous | nervous system |

These are different from normal adjectives ending in the same suffixes such as *topical, sympathetic,* or *adventurous* in that they don't express qualities or properties. Thus, we can say *very topical article, unsympathetic remark, highly adventurous project* but the adjectives in (26) can't be modified in this way: **very morphological theory*. The reason is that the adjectives in (26) are really no different from the basic nouns but used in the syntactic contexts where an adjective is needed, i.e. to modify a noun. Indeed, in a number of cases we can idiomatically replace such phrases with compounds: *morphology theory, navy uniform,* or marginally *nerve system*. Thus, the derivational morphology which creates the adjectives changes the syntactic category of the word but doesn't add any element of meaning and thus, strictly speaking, is a kind of cranberry suffix. This type of category-shifting morphology is often referred to as *transposition*.

2.3   *Morpheme order*

The order of morphemes in a word is usually strictly determined, even in languages with very free word order and linguistic theory has to have some set of mechanisms for guaranteeing this order. A simple example of polymorphemic inflection is provided by nouns in Finnish, a typical "agglutinative" language. It has number, case, and possessor inflection on nouns, with a separate formative for each function. Some examples of inflected forms of the word *talo* "house" are given in (27) (data from Karlsson 1987):

(27)   talo-ssa-ni   "in my house"
       talo-lle-mme   "onto our house"
       talo-i-sta-si   "out of thy house"
       talo-i-lta-nne   "off of your houses"

On a morphemic account a word form such as *taloissani* "in my houses" would have the form (28):

(28)

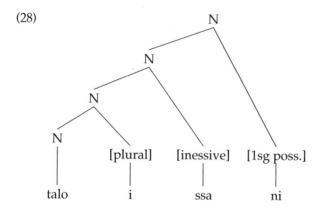

How do we ensure that the morphemes come in this order and not, say, *talossaini*, or *talonissai*?

Lieber (1992) argues that we can make use of the syntactician's notion of *subcategorization* or *selectional frame*. Each ending is given a frame in its lexical entry stating what kind of stem it can occur to the right / left of. For possessor suffixes the frame stipulates that they occur next to a stem marked for case, while case suffixes are marked to occur next to Number-marked stems. A possible entry for the inessive suffix *-ssa* is shown in (29):

(29)   <*ssa*, [CASE:Iness], . . . >:   [$_N$ [NUMBER:{Sg, Pl}]_____]

Notice that we have to allow for the Number specification to be either singular or plural. (An alternative would be to invent some notation meaning "any value of the feature NUMBER.")

Finnish, however, presents a problem for an approach of this sort. The point of the subcategorization approach is that the addition of a suffix is dependent on the structure of the stem as built up so far. The nominative case ending is zero in the singular and -*i* in the plural, so the nominative plural of *talo* should be *taloi. However, the real form is *talo-t*. The first problem is interpreting the meaning of the -*t* suffix: is it a plural marker found only in the nominative (30a) or a nominative marker found only in the plural (30b)?

(30)   root   NUMBER   CASE
   a.   talo t_{Pl} $\emptyset_{Nom}$
   b.   talo $\emptyset_{Pl}$ t_{Nom}

In analysis (30a) how does the grammar know that -*t* and not -*i* must be inserted after the stem? In analysis (30b) how does the grammar know that -$\emptyset$ and not -*i* must be inserted after the stem?

The only way around this problem is to reject the assumptions of agglutination and say that the -*t* formative appears next to the stem but cumulates case and number, as in (31):

(31) root   NUMBER / CASE

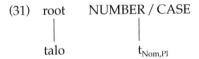

      talo $t_{Nom,Pl}$

However, this will lead to considerable complications because we will now have a stem marked for plural to which other case markers could attach. We must therefore impose some principle saying that once a form is marked for case it can't be marked again. Indeed, Lieber (1992) introduces essentially such a scheme by means of the "categorial signature," a significant departure from the item-and-arrangement model for inflection which makes it to all intents and purposes just a variant of the model to be discussed below.

2.4   *Rule function morphology*

The morpheme concept thus serves even agglutinative languages like Finnish rather badly. An alternative conception has been argued for by many morphologists (see Anderson 1992, Aronoff 1994, for examples and surveys of the literature), under which affixation is just one of a set of phonological operations which can be performed on a base, triggered by the inflectional properties of the whole word. This is a variant of the classical *item-and-process* approach to morphology but I shall refer to it as the *rule function* approach (since processes are stated as rules which are usually thought of as something like functions in the mathematical sense).

To handle Finnish nouns we would set up a battery of rules applying in three blocks, one essentially for number marking, one for case and one for possession. We start with a complete inflectional characterization of the word, say, {plural, inessive, 1sgpossessed}. This triggers three rules which take the current stem and add the appropriate suffixes:

(32) a. {Plural}(X)   = X + i
      b. {Inessive}(X)   = X + ssa
      c. {1sgpossessed}(X)   = X + ni

A rule such as {plural}(X) is intended to be read "the plural form of (the base form of) X is constructed by adding -*i* to X." Taking the base *talo* these build up the required form in the obvious way. Note that there is no need for subcategorization since morpheme order is reflected in the ordering of the rule functions. The "zero affixes" of the singular and the nominative are handled very naturally: there is no rule corresponding to these properties, therefore nothing is done to the base form. There is thus no need for dubious constructs such as strings of null morphemes.

The problem with nominative plural forms is handled by having a more specific (a) rule:

(33) a. (i)   {Plural, Nom}(X) = X + t
          (ii) {Plural}(X)   = X + i

The rules in (33) are regulated by a very general principle (often called the *elsewhere condition*): if two rules can apply to the same base, it is the more specific which wins out. Confronted with the need to construct the nominative plural form, rules (33a(i) and (ii)) are both applicable, but only (33a(i)) applies because it is the more specific. Rule (33a(ii)) is the rule which applies "everywhere else" or in the *default* case. The use of the notion of default in such systems has become extremely important in recent research and some form of it is even accepted by protagonists of a (very highly modified) type of item-and-arrangement theory (Halle and Marantz 1993, Wunderlich 1996).

The rules of (32) are affixations but could just as easily be any phonological process, such as vowel ablaut or reduplication. The rule function approach rejects the idea that affixes are lexemes compounded with base lexemes. Rule functions can also handle syncretisms very neatly. There can be a problem for morpheme-based theories because they are often defined over parts of the paradigm independently of the actual affixes. A simple example of this is the relationship between the perfect participle (*has cooked*) and the passive participle (*was cooked*). These are identical for all verbs despite variation in form (*has / was written, has / was sung,* etc.). It is hard to see how the generalization can be stated over such diverse "lexemes" as -*ed*, -*en, u*-ablaut and so on. This can be captured in the morphology by stating a *rule of referral* for constructing passive participles from perfect participles as in (34):

(34) {Passive participle}(X) = {Perfect participle}(X)

As Stump (1993) argues, (34) is just another type of rule function and can interact with other rule functions in a variety of ways. To achieve the same effect, morpheme-based theories have to undermine the morpheme concept fairly drastically, for example by reconstructing a rule of referral over the meaning content of morphemes independently of their form (as in the rules of impoverishment of Halle and Marantz 1993).

3 The Structure of the Lexeme

3.1 *Derivational morphology*

We saw in section 1.2 that compounds show varying degrees of semantic transparency: *morphology article, blackbird, husband.* Much the same can be said of derivational morphology. In (35) we see examples of fully transparent, compositional derivation:

(35) a. cat-like
      b. elephant-like
      c. lion-like
      d. ape-like

These all mean roughly "like a typical X" where X = {cat, elephant, lion, ape, . . . }, and we can call such forms *similitudinal adjectives.* This derivation is highly productive, in that "X" can be virtually anything: speakers can understand and use a coinage like *iguana-like* without ever having heard it before (though the exact force of *-like* is rather subtle, e.g. what is the precise semantics of *an iguana-like expression / skin / gait*?). This type of suffixation is so transparent that it resembles compounding – indeed, some might claim that *-like* adjectives are in fact compounds (though of a very rare type in English). Now contrast (35) with the examples in (36):

(36) a. cat   catty   cat + y
      b. elephant   elephantine   elephant + ine
      c. monster   monstrous   monst(e)r + ous

Although these may also be similitudinal adjectives, they are not compositionally derived from their bases. This means that the base has lost all meaning and functions much like the cranberry morpheme *stand* in *understand.*

Much derivational morphology is similar to that of (36), if not quite so dramatically so. For instance, *hopeless* means "without hope," but this isn't true for all uses. If we say "I wouldn't pick him for the job, he's hopeless" we

are saying that he is extremely bad and unsuitable. He himself is not necessarily without hope in the literal sense (he could be one of life's irrepressible
optimists). Such cases are the norm and it turns out that there is a cline of
transparency running from *cat-like* to *hopeless* to *catty* to *understand*.

3.2   Four types of lexical relatedness

Transparent derivational morphology defines a network of relatedness amongst
lexemes, but it is only one of four types of relatedness, one in which morphological relatedness goes hand in hand with semantic relatedness. The second
type of relatedness is that mediated solely through semantics, without any
morphological relatedness. For example, there are similitudinal adjectives which
mean "like *noun*" but which aren't morphologically derived from *noun* e.g.
infantile (= / = "like an infant"!), or *puerile* both meaning "child-like" (with
additional pejorative overtones). These could be said to end in an affix *-ile*. I
cited *writer* in section 2.1 as an example of a subject nominalization, and this
represents a very productive formation, but not all verbs permit it. The subject
nominal corresponding to the verb *fly*, as in "fly a plane (professionally)," is an
entirely different word, *pilot*. Admittedly, the form *flier* exists for other uses of
the verb, but we wouldn't say for instance **Tom was the flier of that Boeing 747*.
This is a kind of derivational suppletion.

The third type of relatedness is represented by *systematic polysemy*, that is,
where we have two different lexemes with the same form. A familiar example
is the alternation shown in (37) (referred to variously as *inchoative, causative,* or
anti-causative). Most linguists would probably say that there are two distinct,
though related, BREAK lexemes here:

(37)   a.   Tom broke the vase.
       b.   The vase broke.

In many languages such usages are conveyed morphologically (by what is
usually considered derivational morphology). Notice that the verb retains all
its purely morphological properties in both usages, so there is no conversion
or affixless derivation in the normal sense here. Rather, we seem to have two
closely related lexemes which share all the same word forms.

In section 2.2.3 I pointed out that both the prefix and base of *understand*
are cranberries. This is the fourth type of derivation in which there is clear
morphological relatedness but no semantic connection (*asemantic relatedness*).
In Russian this phenomenon is pervasive. Most Russian verbs are derived by
prefixation of a few hundred simplex verb roots. In some cases the prefix and
root contribute to the overall meaning compositionally, but in many cases it is
impossible to ascribe a clear meaning to either root or prefix, just as with
understand. Thus, from the verb *p'isat'* "write" we obtain *pr'i-p'isat'* "ascribe,"

o-p'isat' "describe," *pod-p'isat'* "sign," and so on. Each of the prefixes occurs in hundreds or thousands of verbs (sometimes with identifiable meaning). Moreover, each of these formations belongs to the same special subclass of class I that *p'isat'* belongs to (thus, the present tense stem is *p'iš-*, rather than the default stem form for class I, **p'isaj-*), and they all show the same pattern of stress shift as the base verb. Finally, they all behave like morphologically prefixed forms. We can see this because the base verb, *p'isat'*, is imperfective in aspect, but nearly all prefixed verbs in Russian are perfective and form a special secondary imperfective (usually by suffixation of *-iv-*). Sure enough, all the derived verbs from *p'isat'* are perfective and form their secondary imperfective in *-iv-*: *pr'i-p'is-iv-at'*, *o-p'is-iv-at'*, *pod-p'is-iv-at'* etc. Russian verbs thus present a much more convincing demonstration of Aronoff's original point because there can be no doubt that the verbs are prefixed, and because the base exists in nearly all cases as an independent verb with exactly the same morphological properties; the majority of the native verb lexemes in the language are like this (indeed, the majority of monomorphemic, non-prefixed verb stems are loans).

This property of the Russian lexicon is particularly damaging to the classical morpheme theory. Of the 28,500 or so verbs in Zaliznjak's *Grammatical Dictionary of Russian*, roughly 24,000 are prefixed. Of these a large proportion are highly regular aspectual or Aktionsart formations (which could be claimed to be more like inflections than lexeme forming derivations). Given this, I would estimate between a third and a half of these 24,000 are like the derivates of *p'isat'* discussed above. Thus, if we consider cases which are uncontroversially independent lexemes it turns out that the *majority* of Russian verbs consist of a cranberry prefix and a cranberry root. The significance of such cases has been significantly underplayed in the literature.

One might wish to claim that there is a fifth type of relatedness illustrated by denominal verbs in English formed by conversion (though deverbal nouns, such as *a bite* or *a broadcast* would do as well). Verbs such as *to saddle (a horse)*, *to shelve (books)*, *to skin (a rabbit)*, *to paper (a wall)*, and many others are clearly derived from nouns, but without any overt morphology. Presumably we would wish to say that this creates new lexemes (it seems far-fetched to regard *to saddle* as an inflected form of the base noun) and hence constitutes a derivational relation. However, this can either be regarded as a type of derivation which happens not to involve morphology (and hence a subtype of standard derivation) or a subtype of systematic polysemy.

In sum: lexemes can be related to each other by (1) morphology which induces a compositional meaning change; (2) systematic meaning relation which is not matched by any formal relatedness (*suppletive derivation*); (3) systematic meaning relation between different meanings associated with the same form (*systematic polysemy*); and (4) purely in terms of shape, *asemantic relatedness*. These extremes define a space within which word relatedness can vary, so that *catty* could be said to be an example of derivation with respect to the suffix but asemantic relatedness with respect to the base.

3.3   Mixed categories

We end this section by looking at a set of cases which occupy a borderline position in some sense, and which are currently the focus of a good deal of research effort. A very common form of verb-to-adjective transposition is illustrated by *participles*. These are adjectival forms associated with verb lexemes, often expressing verbal tenses, aspects or voices, but not adding any lexical meanings and hence usually considered inflectional forms. Examples in English would be the present and past / passive participles of *running water* or *a snatched / stolen kiss*. In many languages it is particularly obvious that the participles are adjectives; for instance, they not only modify nouns but also agree with them in number, gender or case (something verbs don't normally do).

Participles illustrate an intriguing problem, illustrated by the Russian examples in (38):

(38)   a.   Devuška čitaet gazetu
            girl.NOM reads newspaper.ACC
            "The girl is reading the newspaper"
       b.   devuška čitajuščaja   gazetu
            girl.NOM reading.FEM.NOM.SG newspaper.ACC
            "the girl reading the paper"

In (38a) we see that the transitive verb "read" takes a direct object in the accusative case. The participle in (38b) takes the same direct object marked in the same way but corresponding to the subject in (38a) is the noun modified by the participle, "girl," with which the participle agrees just like an adjective would (see (18)). This shows that the participle is not like a normal adjective because Russian adjectives do not take complements (especially not in the accusative case!). Participles, however, take exactly the same set of complements as their base verb, and mark them in exactly the same way as the verb. Forms with this Janus-like behavior are often referred to as *mixed categories*. Deverbal nominalizations provide further instances. Thus, in *Tom's writing the letter (would be surprising)* the nominal *writing* expresses an object in the manner of a verb (*Tom wrote the letter*) not a noun (cf. *Tom's writing of the letter*) but expresses its subject in the manner of a noun (cf. *Tom's letter*). This type of morphology, changing, so to speak, only half a category, raises a variety of theoretical questions and deverbal nominalizations in particular have been the subject of intense study in recent years by morphologists and syntacticians.

3.4   Complex predicates

We began the chapter with a discussion of lexical integrity and a good deal of recent research has been devoted to clarifying this notion, and hence the notion of word. Considerable research effort has been directed in recent years to cases in which there is a mismatch between the number of lexemes and the number of syntactically realized word forms. Such constructions are often referred to as *complex predicates*, a term which is used broadly of two types of phenomenon: (1) a single phonological, syntactic word form corresponds to two lexemes and (2) two phonological, syntactic word forms correspond to one lexeme. We saw one example of the type (1) complex predicate when we discussed noun incorporation (see examples (7), section 1.2). In this subsection I briefly mention two type (2) cases.

A simple example of a type (2) complex predicate is provided by an English phrasal verb such as *turn . . . off*. In *Tom turned the light off* we have a single verb lexeme *turn off* with the meaning "extinguish," but the two components can be separated by the verb's object. In the general case, we cannot predict the meaning of the phrasal verb from its components (compare for instance *Low temperatures will slow the process up / down* or *They ran a huge bill up*). A similar phenomenon is found in Hungarian, but with preposed particles ("preverbs"). Thus, *megérkez-* "arrive" has the preverb *meg-*. In (39) we see the preverb (PV) functioning as a prefix to the verb (the prefix receives the initial word stress, for instance; the accent in Hungarian orthography indicates vowel length, not stress):

(39) Meg-érkezett
      MEG-arrived
      "S/he arrived"

However, in certain morphosyntactic circumstances (negation, questions, focussing) it can appear separated to the right of the verb ((40), Szíj 1981: 209):

(40) Nem érkezett meg
      NEG arrived MEG
      "S/he didn't arrive"

In (41) we see forms of the verb *meg-néz-* "to watch, look at" as the comple-ment of the verb *akar-* "want," where it remains prefixed to the verb:

(41) Nem akarom meg-nézni ezt a   filmet
      NEG I.want MEG-watch this the film
      "I don't want to watch this film"

However, when the main clause is neither interrogative nor negative, as in (42) we find that the preverb appears to the left of the main verb:

(42) Meg akarom nézni ezt a   filmet
      MEG I.want watch this the film
      "I want to watch this film"

There is good reason to regard such phrasal verbs as single lexical items, i.e. lexemes: the meaning is often (though not always) idiosyncratic and, in Hungarian, processes which derive nouns or adjectives from verbs often apply equally well to the phrasal verbs. This is illustrated below where a simple verb (43) is compared with a particle verb (44) (Ackerman and LeSourd 1997: 89):

(43)   a.   old-ani
             "dissolve"
       b.   old-ás
             "(chemical) solution"
       c.   old-ható anyag
             "dissolvable substance"
       d.   old-hatatlan anyag
             "insoluble substance"

(44)   a.   meg-old-ani
             "solve"
       b.   meg-old-ás
             "solution (to problem)"
       c.   meg-old-ható feladat
             "solvable task"
       d.   meg-old-hatatlan feladat
             "unsolvable task"

Thus, in Hungarian, a single lexeme, *meg-oldani*, can be systematically realized as more than one word in the syntax. Ackerman and LeSourd argue that this calls for a more sophisticated concept of lexical integrity: word forms such as "meg," "oldani," "turn" and "off" are single indivisible words, they cannot be split up once they appear in sentences and thus they exhibit lexical integrity. However, a given lexeme may be realized by a combination of such words, (*meg = oldani, turn = off*) and these may be separated in the syntax, so that, as lexemes, they do not exhibit lexical integrity. In other words, lexical integrity is a property of word forms but not necessarily of lexemes.

4   Conclusions

The notion "word" covers several distinct linguistic concepts, including: lexeme, word form, grammatical word. Not all the properties of words can be explained in terms of syntax or phonology, in particular, the existence of arbitrary inflectional classes demonstrates the need to treat morphology as an autonomous component of grammar. The classical sign-based concept of the morpheme has been extremely influential in thinking about the internal structure of words, but this has been largely abandoned, at least for inflection, where morphologists increasingly appeal to the notion of rule functions and defaults to capture the structure of paradigms and the order of elements, and to account for deviations from the "ideal" of agglutinating morphology.

We surveyed four types of derivational relatedness, showing that words can be related to each other in four main ways: in terms solely of semantics, with no morphological relationship, in terms purely of morphology, with no semantic relationship, in terms of polysemy, in which there is a semantic relationship but the word forms remain the same, and, the standard case, in terms of a semantic relationship mediated by morphology. We also looked at important cases of mismatch between form and function, the mixed categories and complex predicates.

There are several important phenomena which I have had to pass over, in particular, the question of clitics, structural mismatches between word structure and syntactic or semantic structure, morphology and the semantic representations of words (especially verbs and argument structure) and questions of productivity and regularity and the storing of words in the mental lexicon. The reader should consult some of the references cited (for instance, the chapters of Spencer and Zwicky 1998) for overviews of these and other areas. However, enough has been said to illustrate that the structure of words, their organization into inflectional paradigms and their derivational relationships to each other is extremely rich and an important part of contemporary linguistic theory.

NOTE

Parts of this chapter are based on work conducted as part of research funded by the Economic and Social Research Council (Project Reference R000236115), to whom I express my gratitude. I am grateful to Mark Aronoff for helpful suggestions for improvement.

10 The Lexicon

D. A. CRUSE

1 Introduction

To take a simplistic view, the bare essentials for a language are, first, a set of basic units, and second, a set of rules for combining them into larger, more complex units like phrases and sentences. A list of the basic units constitutes the lexicon of the language; a specification of the combinatory rules constitutes the grammar.

The basic units must have both a form and a meaning (in the broadest sense); the entries in the lexicon must specify these, together with information necessary for the proper application of the grammatical rules. The combinatory rules will tell us not only what complex forms are allowed in the language, but also how their meanings are to be computed.

What are the units that are listed in the lexicon? The obvious answer is that they are words, and that is what we shall take them to be (although the matter is not quite so straightforward as it might at first seem). To the layperson, probably the most important thing about a word is what it means; this chapter has a similar bias, being chiefly about words and their meanings. We begin by looking at what sort of things words are, as a linguist sees them.

2 Words

It is notoriously difficult to frame a definition of a word which is satisfactory for all languages, and even for everything word-like in a particular language. We shall assume that, as in Wittgenstein's famous example of *game*, no succinct definition applicable to all cases is possible, and that the best approach is to look for features characteristic of central examples of the class.

2.1 *Lexical forms, lexical units and lexemes*

The word *word* is used in different senses, and it will be as well to clarify the most important of these right from the start. Suppose we are doing a cross-word puzzle. It is quite possible that, say, *walk* is the correct answer to a clue, but *walked* is not: from this perspective *walk* and *walked* are different words. Now imagine someone who encounters sentence (1):

(1)   I have disconfirmed the doctor's prognosis

and asks: "Is there such a word as *disconfirm* in English? Look it up in the dictionary." What does *word* mean here? Clearly not what it means in the crossword context, since the dubious sentence contained *disconfirmed*, but the question asks about *disconfirm*. Let us at this point make a terminological distinction between *word forms* and *lexemes*. We shall say that *walk* and *walked*, and *disconfirm* and *disconfirmed* are different word forms, but whereas *walk* and *disconfirm* represent different lexemes, *walk* and *walked* are different word forms belonging to the same lexeme.

What, then, is a lexeme? As a first step let us say that they are the units listed in a dictionary. A dictionary provides a list of the lexemes of a language, each indexed by one of its word forms. (Which word form a dictionary uses to indicate a lexeme is at least partly a matter of convention. For instance, in English, for verbs, we use the bare stem: *run, walk*; in French it is the infinitive: *courrir, marcher*; in Latin, the first person singular of the present indicative: *curro, ambulo*.)

A more technical characterization is that a lexeme is a set of related meanings associated with a set of related word forms. Sometimes meanings associated with a single word form are clearly unrelated, as in the case of *bank* (financial) and *bank* (river); these would therefore be assigned to different lexemes. In other cases a relationship can easily be intuited, as with *position* (location), *position* (opinion), and *position* (job), and these will be considered to belong to the same lexeme. Most dictionaries give separate main entries to distinct lexemes, even if they share the same forms, but group related meanings under a single main entry. What we shall call "a set of related word forms" is a set of forms which differ only in respect of inflectional affixes (such as the singular and plural forms of nouns, or the past, present, and future forms of verbs).

This is fine, but how do we then designate the three individual items *position*? It is usual to call the distinct meanings *senses*, but what is the sound-meaning complex? I shall call them *lexical units*. Actually, in many (perhaps most) contexts it is perfectly clear what *word* means: the expressions *word form*, *lexeme*, and *lexical unit* will therefore only be used when there is a danger of confusion.

2.2   Individuating word-forms: graphic and phonetic clues

Most modern writing systems (English is no exception) indicate word (here, obviously, "word form") boundaries by means of spaces. This makes reading a lot easier. However, there is usually no analog of written spaces in spoken language, although this usually comes as a surprise to the layperson, because spoken words are clearly demarcated perceptually. There may, nonetheless, be signals of other types which indicate the positions of the boundaries of spoken words. For instance, many languages have a regular stress pattern for words, as in Czech, where words are always stressed on the first syllable. Other signs may be more complex or subtle. For instance, to take a venerable example, English speakers can discern purely from the sound the different positions of the word boundaries in *night rate*, and *Nye trait*, and between *parks treat* and *Park Street*, at least when they are carefully pronounced, even though there is no silence between the words. This is because, for instance, the variety of /r/ which occurs at the beginning of a word is different from that which appears when it is preceded by /t/, and is different again if the /t/ is preceded by /s/.

2.3   Grammatical properties of words

Prototypically (we shall not explore the exceptions) the stretches of a sentence that constitute word(form)s can be recognized by the fact that they are the largest chunks of the sentence which cannot be interrupted by the insertion of new material. Take the sentence *The government is strongly opposed to denationalization*. The possibilities of inserting new material are as follows:

> The (present) government, (apparently), is (very) strongly (and implacably) opposed (not only) to (creeping) denationalization, but . . . etc.

It will be noticed that the insertions all respect word boundaries, and all sequences of two words can be interrupted.

The parts of a word also cannot be reordered (**ationizaldenation*), although, at least in languages with some freedom of word-order, the words themselves can be rearranged (obviously to varying degrees).

2.4   The semantic properties of words

There are several constraints on what a word can possibly mean. First, though, a non-constraint. It might be thought that there could not be a word meaning, for instance, "to eat corn flakes while standing facing south on a Sunday morning." However, a brief period of reflection should convince the reader that such a meaning is not really impossible, merely unlikely in our culture: in a society where corn flakes were ritually dedicated to the god of the south, it would not be at all surprising if such an action received a lexical label. We shall look at two more serious constraints on possible word meanings, conceptual unity and internal completeness.

Whatever attracts a lexical label must have some degree of conceptual coherence. Let us confine our attention to what can be referred to by a noun: in the broadest sense, these are "things." Prototypical things are characterized by spatial continuity and persistence through time. Non-prototypical things must have something which confers unity on them. In front of me as I write, I can see, among other things, a bottle of Buxton mineral water, a photograph of Commander Data from *Star Trek*, and a ball of string. Is there any chance that these could be designated collectively by a noun? In a sense, yes: they could constitute the whole of my worldly possessions, and there could be a name for this (on the lines of my "estate," when I die). But that would not be a name for that particular set of things. Alternatively, they could be the requisites for, say, the Klingon Ceremony of Nga (or whatever). But in the absence of some such extrinsic unifying factor, the items mentioned would not be (collectively) nameable.

What I am calling "internal completeness" is more easily illustrated than explained. Take the phrase *a very large man*. The notion that there should exist a word meaning "large man" is not at all exotic (think of *giant*); nor is the idea of a word meaning "very large" (e.g. *enormous*); there could well be a word meaning "very large man" (perhaps *colossus*), too. But what about a word meaning "very . . . man," i.e. a noun such that any adjective modifying it is automatically intensified? This, surely, offends against our deepest semantic intuitions: it is an impossible meaning for a word. The same would be true of a putative "word" *beve* meaning "drink chilled . . . ," such that *beve wine* would mean "drink chilled wine" (words meaning "drink wine" or "chilled wine," or even "drink chilled wine" could not be ruled out). The explanation seems to be on the following lines. We first need to distinguish *dependent* and *independent* components of a semantic combination. The independent component is the one which governs the external relations of the combination as a whole. So, for instance, in *very large*, it is *large* which governs the combinability of the phrase *very large* with other items. Thus the oddness of, say, *?very large air* is due to a clash between *large* and *air* – there is no clash between *very* and *air* (think of *very cold air*). By similar reasoning, the independent item in *chilled wine* is *wine*, and in *drink chilled wine* is *drink*. This process of reasoning allows us to establish chains of (semantic) dependencies (it does not matter whether the elements in a chain are expressed as different words, or are incorporated into the meaning of a single word). For instance, the chain for *very large man* is:

"very" → "large" → "man"

and that for *drink chilled wine* is:

"chilled" → "wine" → "drink"

The constraint that we are looking at says that the elements that constitute the meaning of a word must form a continuous dependency chain, with no gaps needing to be filled by elements from outside the word.

3   Lexical Semantics

The study of the meanings of words within linguistics is called *lexical semantics*. Under this banner a variety of spheres of interest, theoretical orientations and methods of study flourish.

3.1   *Theoretical approaches*

To a large extent, how one goes about the business of studying meaning depends on what picture one has of the sort of thing meaning is. Some grasp of the major options will be useful as a background to the more detailed discussions which follow. We shall concentrate on two issues, holism vs. localism, and the relation between linguistic meaning and concepts. Let us begin with the holism / localism debate. Essentially, a holist believes that the meaning of a word is fundamentally relational, that is to say, it is a matter of relations with other words in the language. A localist believes that a word's meaning is self-contained, and describable independently of the meanings of other words.

3.1.1   *The contextual / holistic approach*

Within linguistics, what philosophers of language call *holistic* theories of meaning are usually called *contextual* theories. These come in several varieties: two will be briefly illustrated here.

The first type falls under the heading of *structural semantics*. The basic notion of the interdependence of meanings can be illustrated as follows. Think of a child learning the names of the animals. The fact that a child can say *It's a dog* every time s/he is given a dog to identify, does not prove s/he has grasped what *dog* means; just as important, is that s/he should avoid saying *It's a dog* when faced with a cat, or fox, or whatever. In other words, the meaning of *dog* (or any other word) cannot be learnt in isolation. A structuralist such as Lyons (the seminal reference is Lyons (1963)) builds on this basic insight, and characterizes the meaning of a word as its position in a network of relationships. Let us consider what that would mean in the case of *dog*. First, *dog* belongs to a set of words with which it has an exclusion relationship, that is to say, *It's a dog* implies *It's not a cat / lion / camel / cow / squirrel / etc.*; furthermore, all these fall into the denotation of a more inclusive term *animal*. *Animal* (at least on one reading) also belongs to a set whose members are mutually exclusive (including *insect, fish, bird,* etc.); these in turn are included in *living thing,* and so on. But *dog* has many other relations, for instance, with *tail, paw, head*; with *pack*; with *bark, howl*; with *kennel,* which itself has relations with other structures such as *hut, cabin, house,* and so on. Ultimately, every word is linked directly or indirectly, by means of specific links such as "is a," "is not a," "has a," "is part of," "lives in a," etc., with virtually every other word in the lexicon: on the holist view, the meaning of a word is not fully comprehended until all these links are known (although, obviously, some links are more central than others).

An alternative version of a contextual theory takes its origin from Wittgenstein's dictum: *Don't ask for the meaning, ask for the use.* This is suggestive, but lacking in precision as a basis for a theory of meaning: what, precisely, do we mean by *use*? J. R. Firth (quoted in Mackin (1978)) gave the notion a useful twist when he said: *Words shall be known by the company they keep.* This line of thinking was developed into a holistic theory of meaning by W. Haas. (Haas's ideas are not readily accessible in published form; a summary can be found in Cruse (1986: ch. 1).) Haas started out from the idea that every grammatically well-formed sequence of words was either fully normal semantically, like *The dog barked,* or to some degree abnormal, like *?The cat barked* or *?The dog evaporated.* He then argued that if two words differ in meaning, this fact will inevitably be reflected in a difference of normality in some context or other. For instance, that there is a difference in meaning between *illness* and *disease* follows from the fact that *during my illness* is more normal than *?during my disease.* Haas went on to characterize the meaning of a word as its normality profile across all its grammatically well-formed contexts, actual or potential: absolute synonyms, on this view, are words which have the same normality in all contexts.

3.1.2 *The componential / localistic approach*

A localist believes that the meaning of a word is a self-sufficient entity which in principle is finitely describable. Whereas holists tend to see the meaning of a word as a set of relations, either with other words, or with possible contexts, a localist will typically say that these relations are a consequence of the word's meaning.

The most popular varieties of localism portray the meaning of a word as a finite assemblage of elementary bits of meaning, each of which accounts for some aspect of the semantic behavior of the whole. These "semantic atoms" (variously known as *semantic components, semantic features, semantic markers*) are drawn from a finite inventory, and in the strongest versions of the theory are psychologically real (in the sense that if we knew enough about the brain we would be able to identify a distinctive neuronal structure corresponding to each feature), and they are universal (in the sense that they form part of the language capacity that each human being is born with). It is impossible to give a satisfactory picture of any of the existing systems in a short space, but the following examples will give the flavor of such analyses:

filly   =   [HORSE] [FEMALE] [YOUNG]

boy   =   [HUMAN] [MALE] [YOUNG]

kill   =   [CAUSE] [BECOME] [NOT] [ALIVE]

chair   =   [OBJECT] [FURNITURE] [FOR SITTING] [FOR ONE PERSON] [WITH BACK]

3.1.3   The conceptual approach

Much debate centers on the relation, if any, (but surely there must be some) between linguistic meaning and concepts, or, as far as we are concerned in this chapter, between word meanings and concepts. Earlier semanticists (including Lyons and Haas) did not believe that anything solid was known about concepts; they therefore preferred to pursue their semantic studies without reference to such entities. The rise of cognitive psychology has made concepts more respectable, and few would now deny their significance. The debate now concerns whether, or to what extent, meaning can be identified with concepts: do words map directly onto concepts, or is there an intermediate level of semantic structure where word meaning is to be located, and the connection with concepts indirect? The present author's sympathies lie with the conceptual approach. A conceptual (or "cognitive") semanticist would argue that there is no theoretical work for an autonomous linguistic semantic level to do that cannot be performed at the conceptual level. He would also argue that the connection between words and the outside world is mediated through concepts, and that therefore examining world–word relations is not the most profitable approach to word meaning.

4   How Many Meanings? Contextual Variability of Word Meaning

Most words are capable of presenting different semantic faces in different contexts. Sometimes the differences are major and clear cut, as in:

(2)   The boat was moored to the bank.
(3)   She works in a bank.

At other times the difference is more subtle:

(4)   John's maths teacher is on maternity leave.
(5)   Bill's maths teacher is on paternity leave.

Here we can infer from the context that John's maths teacher is a woman whereas Bill's is a man.

It is important to be able to decide whether two interpretations of a word in different contexts represent one semantic unit or two. This is not a purely theoretical concern: for instance, a lexicographer will have to decide how many definitions to give for *bank* and *teacher*. We shall take the position that the basic unit of word meaning is the *sense*, and we shall say that a word has X senses if and only if it is X-ways ambiguous. We now need to be more explicit about what it means for a word to be ambiguous.

4.1   Ambiguity

Consider sentence (6):

(6)   We managed to get to the bank just in time.

In the absence of a biasing context, the two readings of *bank* are in competition with one another: like the two visual construals of a Necker cube, only one can be at the focus of attention at any given moment. In a particular context, a speaker will "intend" only one of the meanings and will expect the hearer to make the same selection. There is no general meaning of *bank* which subsumes the two alternatives, and the options of remaining uncommitted or of taking both meanings on board are not available (outside of deliberate word play). Contrast this with the following case:

(7)   We shall talk to Mary's teachers.

Of course, the individual teachers referred to in (7) must be either male or female, but (a) the speaker may not even know the sex of the teachers involved and will not expect the hearer to select a particular gender; (b) there is a general meaning of *teacher* which covers both possibilities; (c) the sex of the teachers can be left unspecified; furthermore, sentence (7) may well refer to a mixed group. By the criteria suggested, then, *teacher* is not ambiguous, and does not have two senses corresponding to "male teacher" and "female teacher"; a lexicographer would not need to give two definitions for *teacher*.

Ambiguous words typically pass the traditional *ambiguity tests*.

4.1.1   The identity test

In *John has changed his position; so has Mary*, the word *position* must be interpreted the same way in both halves of the sentence: if John has changed his mind on some political issue, then that's what Mary did, too; likewise if John has changed his location. This shows that *position* is ambiguous. In contrast, in

I spoke to a teacher; so did Mary, there is no pressure to interpret *teacher* in the same way (gender-wise) in each conjunct, hence *teacher* fails this test.

4.1.2   The independent truth-conditions test

It is easy to think of a situation where one could truthfully answer the following question both in the negative and the affirmative:

(8)   Have you had a drink in the last six hours?

This shows that the readings "take alcoholic beverage" and "imbibe liquid" are distinct senses. There is no comparable possibility for simultaneously true *Yes* and *No* answers to (9):

(9)   Have you spoken to a teacher?

4.1.3   The zeugma test

A context which activates more than one reading of an ambiguous word gives rise to a sense of punning:

(10)   The old man expired on the same day as his driving license.
(11)   When the chair became vacant, the University Appointments Committee sat on it for six months.

(The effect in (11) hinges on the ambiguity of both *chair* and *sat on*.)

4.2   Polysemy and homonymy

The alternative readings of an ambiguous word may be totally unrelated, as in the case of *bank*, or they may be related, as in the case of *position* (see below for some discussion of possible types of relatedness). An ambiguous word with unrelated readings is described as *homonymous*; if the readings are related, the word is said to be *polysemous*. Homonymous words are usually given two main entries in a dictionary; polysemous variants are normally listed under a single main heading.

5   Sense Relations

Sense relations are relations between word meanings. Of course, every word has a semantic relation of some kind with every other word, but not all such relations have any intrinsic interest. To be interesting, a relation must recur with significant frequency throughout the vocabulary, and must be capable of supporting significant generalizations. (A much fuller treatment of sense relations than can be accommodated here may be found in Cruse 1986.)

There are two major classes of sense relation, depending on the grammatical relation between the words bearing the senses, namely, *paradigmatic*, and *syntagmatic* relations. Paradigmatic sense relations are relations between the meanings of words which can occupy the same syntactic slot, and serve to unite the range of lexical meanings available at a particular point in a sentence into a more or less coherent structure. Take, for instance, the (incomplete) sentence: *John grows a number of ----- in his garden*. There is a structured set of choices of words to fill the gap. One may choose very general words like *trees, flowers*, or *vegetables*, or something more specific, falling under one of the general terms, for instance, *conifers, cabbages, carnations*. We shall look at the structuring in such a set in more detail in a moment, but it can already be appreciated that the words provide an articulation of the experienced world.

Syntagmatic sense relations hold between words in the same phrase or sentence. Intuitively, some words "go together" semantically, while others "clash": consider *drink wine* and *drink water*, compared with *drink rock* or *drink sound*. There is a relation of cohesiveness between *drink* and *wine* which is absent from *drink* and *rock*. Syntagmatic sense relations are thus involved with the semantic coherence of grammatical strings.

5.1   Paradigmatic sense relations

It is paradigmatic relations which have received the most attention from linguists. For convenience, they may be divided into two sorts, relations of identity and inclusion, and relations of opposition and exclusion.

5.1.1   Relations of inclusion and identity I: hyponymy

We begin with relations of inclusion. There are two basic types of these. In the first type, the inclusion is of one class in another, as in the case of *car* and *vehicle*, where cars constitute a subclass included in the larger class of vehicles; in the second type, the inclusion is observable at the level of individual entities, as in the case of *finger* and *hand*, where every individual hand includes a number of fingers as parts.

The class-inclusion relation, called *hyponymy*, is exemplified by *dog:animal*, *apple:fruit, tulip:flower, cathedral:building, beer:beverage, copper:metal, kitten:cat, mare:horse, actress:woman*, and so on; of the two related items the more specific is called the *hyponym* (e.g. *dog, apple*), and the more general is called the *superordinate* (less commonly, the *hyperonym*), e.g. *animal, fruit*. Notice that although *dog* is a hyponym of *animal*, it is a superordinate of, say, *spaniel*.

Hyponymy can be thought of as the "-- is a --" relation which guarantees the truth of general statements such as *An apple is a fruit* and *An actress is a woman.* For a lexical item X to be a hyponym of another item Y, the truth of *An X is a Y* must follow logically from the meanings of X and Y. An expectation that if something is an X, it is likely to be also a Y, is not enough. For instance, if someone talks about a cat, most people will assume that the cat in question is somebody's pet. However, this does not entitle us to say that *cat* is a hyponym of *pet*, because there are cats which are not pets, and so *Cats are pets* is not automatically true by virtue of its meaning.

5.1.2   Relations of identity and inclusion II: meronymy

The part–whole relation, in its lexical aspect, is called *meronymy* (sometimes *partonymy*); for instance, *finger* is a *meronym* of *hand*, and *hand* is the *immediate holonym* of *finger*. The notion of meronymy, like hyponymy, is relational rather than absolute: *hand*, for instance, is the holonym of *finger*, but it is at the same time a meronym of *arm*, which in turn is a meronym of *body*. The chain of relations stops at *body*, which may be termed the *global holonym*. Other examples of meronymy are as follows: *arm:body, petal:flower, engine:car, blade:knife*. Prototypical meronymous pairs (where X is a meronym of Y) are normal in frames such as: *X is a part of Y; A Y has an X; The parts of a Y are A, B, C . . . and so on.* Meronymy must be clearly distinguished from hyponymy, although both involve a species of inclusion. An easy way to highlight the difference is to note that a finger is not a kind of hand (meronymy), nor is a dog a part of an animal (hyponymy).

Not all portions of an object qualify as parts: a glass jug dropped on a stone floor does not break up into parts, but into pieces. The things we habitually call parts typically have a distinctive function or they are separated from sister parts by a formal discontinuity of some sort (or both). For instance, the wheels of a car have the function of allowing it to move smoothly over the ground, and transmit the motive power; the steering-wheel allows the direction of movement to be controlled; the door handles allow the doors to be opened and shut manually. Discontinuity manifests itself in a number of ways. For example, the wheels of a car are detachable and can move relative to the chassis; the fingers of a hand are not detachable, but have a certain freedom of movement; discontinuity may also be visual, like the cuff of a sleeve, or the iris of the eye.

Parts may be necessary or optional. The necessity in question is not a logical necessity, but a well-formedness condition: a hand with a finger missing is still a hand, but it is not a well-formed hand. In this sense, *finger* is a necessary (or *canonical*) part of *hand*, as is *prong* of *fork*. On the other hand, faces may be perfectly well-formed without beards, and doors without handles – here we are dealing with optional (or *facultative*) parts. Some parts are more tightly integrated into their wholes than others. An indication of less-than-full integration is the possibility of describing the part as "attached to" its whole; this is typically not normal with fully integrated parts. Contrast *The handle is attached to the door* (not fully integrated) and *?The handle is attached to the spoon* (fully integrated).

5.1.3   *Relations of identity and inclusion III: synonymy*

Dictionaries typically define synonyms on the lines of "words with the same or a similar meaning." This description undoubtedly applies to all words that we would intuitively call synonyms: *begin* and *commence, death* and *demise, wedding* and *marriage, motor* and *engine*. However, it is not restrictive enough, as it surely also applies to, for instance, *mare* and *stallion*, which both refer to horses, but which are not synonyms. It would seem useful, therefore, to examine more closely the notion of "same or similar meaning."

Synonym pairs or groups can be categorized according to how close the meanings of the words are. Three degrees of closeness can be recognized: *absolute synonymy, propositional synonymy,* and *near synonymy*.

The greatest possible resemblance between two senses is identity, in other words, absolute synonymy. A characterization of absolute synonyms based on Haas's contextual approach was offered earlier, namely, that they are equinormal in all (grammatically well-formed) contexts. This is based on the assumption that any difference of meaning will reveal itself as a difference in co-occurrence possibilities, hence the discovery of a context where one of the putative synonyms is more normal than the other rules out the pair as absolute synonyms. This is an extremely strict criterion, and a rigorous testing of candidate pairs leads rapidly to the conviction that absolute synonyms are hard to come by. From the semiotic point of view this should probably not be surprising: there is no obvious reason why a language should have two forms with absolutely identical meanings. Let us look at a few possible examples of absolute synonymy:

(i)   nearly / almost:

These are shown to be not absolute synonyms by the differences in normality between (15) and (16), and between (17) and (18):

(15)   We're very nearly home now.
(16)   ?We're very almost home now.

(17)   He looks almost Chinese.
(18)   ?He looks nearly Chinese.

(ii)   big / large:

The difference in normality between (19) and (20) is enough to disqualify these:

(19)   You're making a big mistake.
(20)   ?You're making a large mistake.

(iii)   begin / commence:

These, too, are disqualified:

(21)   Are you sitting comfortably, children? Then I'll begin.
(22)   ?Are you sitting comfortably, children? Then I'll commence.

Absolute synonymy presumably approximates to what those people have in mind who maintain that true synonyms do not occur in natural languages.

There is perhaps a case for saying that absolute identity of meaning can occur between forms belonging to different varieties, especially dialects, of a language. An obvious example would be *fall* and *autumn* in American and British English, respectively. These are no different in principle to translational equivalents in different languages. Notice, however, that these would not come out as absolute synonyms by the Haasian test, since *fall* would be less normal than *autumn* in a sentential context that was otherwise lexically marked as British English. Saying that *fall* and *autumn* are identical in meaning presupposes a non-Haasian notion of what meaning is.

Propositional synonymy is less strict than absolute synonymy, and examples of this variety are consequently more numerous. It can be defined in logical terms: propositional synonyms can be substituted in any declarative sentence *salva veritate*, that is, without changing its truth value. By this criterion, *begin* and *commence* are propositional synonyms, because if *The lecture began at nine o'clock* is true, then so is *The lecture commenced at nine o'clock*, and vice versa.

There are too few absolute and propositional synonyms in any language to justify the existence of a dictionary of synonyms; the majority of what lexicographers call synonyms are, in our terms, near synonyms. The following illustrate sets of near-synonyms:

(i)   kill, murder, execute, assassinate
(ii)   laugh, chuckle, giggle, guffaw, snigger, titter
(iii) walk, stroll, saunter, stride, amble
(iv)   anxious, nervous, worried, apprehensive, fearful
(v)   brave, courageous, plucky, bold, heroic
(vi)   calm, placid, tranquil, peaceful, serene

The words in these sets are not necessarily propositionally identical, so for at least some pairs it is not anomalous to assert one member and simultaneously deny the other:

(23)   He wasn't murdered, he was executed.
(24)   They didn't chuckle, they tittered.
(25)   He was plucky, but not heroic.

Near-synonyms often occur normally in the test-frame *X, or rather Y*, which signals first, that Y conveys propositional information not present in X, and second, that the difference is relatively minor. Thus, (26) is normal, but (27) is odd, because the difference in meaning is too great; (28) is odd because there is no propositional difference:

(26) He was murdered, or rather, executed.
(27) ?He was murdered, or rather, beaten up.
(28) ?He was killed, or rather, deprived of life.

Near-synonyms, then, are words which share a salient common core of meaning, but differ in relatively minor respects. There is at present no more precise characterization of "minor" in this context.

Synonyms (of all kinds) often occur in clusters, and it is common for the cluster to be centered round a neutral word which subsumes all the rest, and of which the others are a semantic elaboration. For instance, *kill, laugh, walk, anxious, brave*, and *calm* are the central items, respectively, in the sets detailed above.

5.1.4 Relations of opposition and exclusion I: incompatibility and co-meronymy

We have looked at relations of inclusion; equally important are relations of exclusion, especially those that hold between sister items under a common inclusive term. Just as there are two sorts of inclusion, there are also two corresponding sorts of exclusion, which receive the labels *incompatibility* and *co-meronymy*.

Incompatibility is the relation which holds between, for instance, *cat* and *dog, apple* and *banana, rose* and *tulip, man* and *woman, church* and *supermarket, bus* and *tractor*. The essence of this relation is mutual exclusion of classes: if something is a cat, then it follows ineluctably that it is not a dog, and vice versa – there is nothing that is simultaneously a cat and a dog. The same is true for the members of the other pairs mentioned. Note that this is not simple difference of meaning. Take the case of *novel* and *paperback*, which are both hyponyms of *book*. They clearly do not mean the same; on the other hand, they are not incompatibles, because something can be simultaneously a novel and a paperback. The same applies to *mother* and *doctor*, and *tall* and *blonde*.

A parallel relation of exclusion applies to sister meronyms of the same holonym, as in *nose, cheek, chin* of *face*, or *wheel, engine, chassis* of *car*, and so on. Here the exclusion is (at least prototypically) spatial: the sister parts of an individual whole do not have any material substance in common.

5.1.5 Relations of opposition and exclusion II: opposites

Oppositeness and synonymy are the only sense relations likely to be familiar to a layperson. Most languages have an everyday word for opposites; the relation is cognitively very basic and quite young children can grasp the notion. Opposites are incompatibles of a special type: they are inherently binary, that is to say, they belong together naturally and logically in pairs.

Opposites fall into a number of relatively clearly-defined types, the most important of which are *complementaries, antonyms, directional opposites* and *converses*.

Complementaries are probably the most basic sort. They can be distinguished from non-complementary incompatibles by the fact that negating either term logically implies the other. For instance, *Proposition P is not true* logically implies *Proposition P is false* and *Proposition P is not false* implies *Proposition P is true*; hence *true* and *false* are complementaries. They may be contrasted with ordinary incompatibles like *cat* and *dog*: *This is not a dog* does not imply *This is a cat*. Other complementary pairs are: *open:shut, dead:alive, stationary:moving, male:female*. A pair of complementaries bisects some conceptual domain, without allowing any "sitting on the fence"; whatever belongs in the domain must fall on one side of the divide or the other. (The negation test works only for items which belong in the domain presupposed by the test word: *This piece of chalk is not dead* does not imply *This piece of chalk is alive*, because chalk does not belong to the domain of things to which *dead* and *alive* properly apply.) The relation between complementaries can be portrayed as follows:

| true | false |

Antonyms (in the narrow sense – the term is also often used to refer to opposites in general) are gradable adjectives (i.e. ones which can be modified without oddness by intensifiers such as *very, rather, extremely, a little*, and so on). Typical examples are *long:short, fast:slow, heavy:light, difficult:easy, thick:thin, good:bad, hot:cold, clean:dirty*. They indicate degrees of some property such as speed, weight, or length, one term denoting a value on the scale above some implicit standard appropriate to the context, and the other term denoting a value lower than the standard. Unlike complementaries they do not exhaustively bisect their domain – there is a neutral area between them, which can be described as, for instance, *neither good nor bad, neither long nor short, neither hot nor cold*, etc. The relation between antonyms can be portrayed as follows:

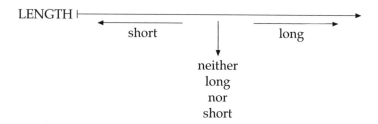

The comparative forms of antonyms vary according to whether they presuppose the positive forms or not. For instance, for something to be *hotter* than something else, it has to be already *hot*: *X is cold, but it's hotter than Y* is therefore odd. On the other hand, something that is *longer* than something else does not need to be *long*. *Hotter* is known as a *committed* comparative; *longer* is *impartial*. Committedness can be used to define three classes of antonyms: *polar, overlapping,* and *equipollent*.

Polar antonyms: both members of a pair are impartial in the comparative:

(29)   X is heavy, but it's lighter than Y.
(30)   X is light, but it's heavier than Y.

Other examples are: *long:short; high:low; wide:narrow; thick:thin; fast:slow; hard:soft.*
Polar antonyms indicate degrees of objective, usually measurable, properties.
   Overlapping antonyms: one member of a pair is committed in the comparative, the other is impartial:

(31)   ?X is good, but it's worse than Y.
(32)   X is bad, but it's better than Y.

Other examples are: *kind:cruel; clean:dirty; polite:rude.* The members of this class all have an evaluative polarity, one member being commendatory, the other derogatory.
   Equipollent antonyms: both members are committed in the comparative:

(33)   ?X is hot, but it's colder than Y.
(34)   ?X is cold, but it's hotter than Y.

Other examples are: *happy:sad; proud of:ashamed of.* The members of this group typically denote sensations or emotions.
   Membership of one of the groups described above correlates with other properties, of which the following are worth noting. One important feature of antonyms is the possibility of degree questions. There are two principal forms, (a) those using a noun related to the adjective, as in *What is the length / weight / thickness of X?*, and (b) *how*-questions, such as *How long / thick / heavy is it?* The characteristics of the degree questions in each group are as follows:

(i)   Polar antonyms: One antonym yields a neutral (impartial) *how*-question, the other (for most speakers) a somewhat abnormal question:

(35)   How long is the piece of wood?
        (normal and impartial)
(36)   How short is the piece of wood?
        (a bit odd, but if we have to interpret it, it is not impartial, but committed)

Polar antonyms also typically allow a *what*-question, but only with one of the terms of the opposition:

(37)   What is the length of the piece of wood? (impartial)
(38)   *What is the shortness of the piece of wood?

For both types of degree-question, the term which produces an impartial question is the one which indicates "more of" the gradable property (e.g. *long* = "more than average length," *thick* = "more than average thickness," and so on).

254 D. A. Cruse

254   *D. A. Cruse*

254   *D. A. Cruse*

254   *D. A. Cruse*

(ii)   Overlapping antonyms: One antonym yields a normal impartial *how*-question (e.g. *How good was the film?*) and its partner gives a normal, but committed *how*-question (e.g. *How bad were the exam results this year?*). In this case, it is the positively evaluative term which occurs in impartial questions, the other term being committed. Generally speaking, *what*-questions do not appear with antonyms from this group (*How clean was the room when you moved in? | ?What was the cleanness of the room when you moved in?; How polite was John when he came to see you? | ?What was John's politeness when he came to see you?*).

(iii)   Equipollent antonyms: Normal *how*-questions are possible with both terms, but both are committed: *How cold was it?; How hot was it?* A *what*-question is possible for *hot:cold* (*What is its temperature?*), but this pair seems unusual in this respect.

An interesting property of overlapping antonyms is the feature of *inherentness*. Take the case of *bad:good*. Of two bad things, it is always possible to describe one as *worse* than the other: *The exam results this year were bad, but they were worse last year; This year's famine was worse than last year's.* However, the use of *better* is curiously restricted: *The exam results were bad this year, but they were better last year; ?This year's famine was better than last year's.* The general principle is that only things that are contingently bad (i.e. where good examples are conceivable) can be described using *better*: inherently bad things can only be qualified as *worse* (and, incidentally, cannot be questioned using *How good ...?*: **How good was John's accident?*).

   Directional opposites: directional opposites are of two main types,

(i)   static directions, like *up:down, backwards:forwards, north:south*:
   west ◄————————————————————————► east

and

(ii)   dynamic directional opposites (usually called *reversives*) such as *rise:fall, advance:retreat, increase:decrease, lengthen:shorten, dress:undress, tie:untie, mount:dismount, enter:leave, damage:repair*, and so on.

We shall concentrate here on reversives. It will be noticed from the examples given that the notion of reversivity is extended from purely spatial domains to any sort of change of state. In general terms, a verb which is a member of a reversive pair denotes a change from an initial state (say S(1)) to a final state (S(2)); its partner will then denote a change from S(2) to S(1):

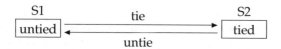

An important feature of such verbs is that the path of change is irrelevant. For instance, a train entering then leaving a station may well travel in only one direction: what is important for entering is to start out "not in" something, and to end up "in" it, and the reverse is the case for leaving. Or take the case of tying and untying one's shoes: a film of someone untying their shoes is not identical to one of someone tying them run backwards: the nature of the process of change is not specified by reversive verbs, only the initial and final states.

Reversive verbs have another curious property. Consider the following sentence: *Mary tied the knot, then untied it again five minutes later*. Assuming that *again* is unstressed, what is asserted to have been repeated, by the use of *again*? It is not, in fact, the act of untying – this may be the first time that Mary has ever untied a knot; what is said to recur is the state of being untied. This is presumably a further reflection of the importance of the initial and final states in the semantics of reversive verbs.

Converses: Converses are pairs like *above:below* and *parent:offspring*. Unlike most opposites, both terms can be used to describe the same state of affairs: for instance, *A is above B* means the same as *B is below A*, except in respect of which term serves as the reference point; similarly, *A is B's parent* designates the same relationship between A and B as *B is A's offspring*. For this reason, some linguists consider converses to be a variety of synonym.

Converses may be 2-, 3-, or 4-place relations, according to the number of arguments involved. *Above:below* are 2-place converses; *bequeath:inherit* are 3-place converses ("*John* bequeathed a *fortune* to *Mary*" designates the same event as "*Mary* inherited a *fortune* from *John*"); *buy:sell* are 4-place ("*John* bought *the car* for £1,000 from *Bill*" describes the same transaction as "*Bill* sold the *car* to *John* for £1,000").

5.2 Syntagmatic sense relations

We turn now to semantic relations between words which occur together in the same text. These can be roughly divided into two types. First, there are those which hold over relatively long stretches of text, between grammatically unrelated items, and which typically do not involve propositional meaning or directional properties. For instance, in *The Prime Minister attended the White House reception accompanied by his Dad*, there is a register clash between *Dad* and such formal items as *attended*, *reception* and *accompanied* (*Tony Blair went to the White House party with his Dad* sounds less weird); the clash would be resolved by replacing *Dad* with the propositionally synonymous *father*. Notice that in this case, the clashing items are some distance from one another, and are not directly related grammatically (*Dad* does not clash with *his*, nor *his Dad* with *by*). Second, there are relations which hold between closely related elements in the same grammatical construction and which do frequently involve propositional meaning and directional properties. For instance, the clashes in

?a male aunt, ?a highly strong man and *?John drank a filing cabinet* involve the second type of relation. Take the case of the latter example: there is no clash between *John* and *drank,* or *John* and *filing cabinet,* the clash involves specifically *drank* and its direct object *filing cabinet;* the clash involves propositional meaning, since it can only be resolved by substituting either *drank* or *filing cabinet* with something propositionally different (e.g. *bought* or *wine,* respectively); *drank* imposes semantic restrictions on its direct objects (e.g. they must be liquids).

There are three possible effects of putting words together in a grammatically well-formed construction: either the result is normal, as in *John drank the wine,* or there is a semantic clash, as in *John drank the filing cabinet* or *a highly strong man,* or the result is pleonastic (or redundant) as in *a female aunt.*

Generally speaking, for a combination of words to be semantically normal, two conditions must be satisfied. If two words are joined together in a construction, it is usually possible to identify a selector, which imposes semantic conditions on possible partners, and a selectee, which satisfies (or does not satisfy) the conditions; the first requirement for a normal combination is that these conditions must be satisfied. This will avoid semantic clash. In the case of an adjective-noun combination, it is the adjective which is the selector: compare the ease with which semantic conditions (usually called selectional restrictions), can be specified for normality in the following:

A ----- woman.

There is no semantic generalization which covers, for instance, *intelligent, tall, pregnant, kind, highly paid, left-handed,* all of which combine normally with *woman.*

A pregnant ----.

Here, the restriction is much easier to capture: *pregnant* requires a head noun which (a) denotes a mammal, and (b) is not specifically marked as "not female" (like, for instance, *bull*).

It is generally the case that in a modifier-head construction, such as adjective-noun or intensifier-adjective, the modifier is the selector; in a head-complement construction, such as *drinks beer* in *John drinks beer,* it is the head of the construction, i.e. the verb, which is the selector.

In *?a female aunt* there is no semantic clash, but the combination is still odd, which indicates that a further condition must be satisfied. This is that a grammatically dependent item (modifier or complement) must contribute semantic information not already present in the head. Clearly, the notion FEMALE is part of the meaning of *aunt,* so the word *female* adds nothing, and consequently *?a female aunt* is pleonastic, or redundant; *a lesbian aunt,* on the other hand, is semantically normal, because although *lesbian* incorporates the notion FEMALE, it also brings new information not predictable from *aunt* alone.

6   Meaning Extensions and Change

6.1   *Established readings and nonce readings*

Some of the alternative senses of a word are permanent and established features of the language, and we would expect them to be recorded in any dictionary worthy of the name. We may also assume that they are laid down in neural form in the mental lexicons of competent speakers of the language. This is the case with the two readings of *bank* discussed earlier. In a sentence like *Mary works in a bank*, we can say that the context "selects" a reading from among those that are permanently laid down, in the sense that only one of them yields a normal combination.

But take another case. Imagine a reception with a large number of guests who will later proceed to a dinner. There is no dining room large enough to accommodate all the guests, so they are divided into two groups. On arrival, each guest is presented with either a rose or a carnation. When it is time for dinner, the head waiter announces: *Will all roses proceed to Dining Room A, and carnations to Room B, please*. These uses of *rose* and *carnation* are perfectly comprehensible in context, but they are not an established part of the language, nor would we expect to find them in any dictionary, however complete. These are said to be nonce readings. How do they arise? Not by selection, but by coercion: if none of the established readings fits the context, then some process of sense-generation is triggered off, which produces a new reading.

A third possible effect of context is to enrich an existing reading, without producing a new sense. This is what happens to *teacher* in *John's maths teacher is on maternity leave*.

6.2   *Literal and non-literal readings*

A distinction is often made between literal and non-literal meanings of (polysemous) words, the assumption being that only one of the readings is literal. While at first sight this distinction seems intuitively clear, on closer examination it is not so straightforward. One thing is clear; a literal meaning must at least be an established one; the criteria for privileging one out of the set of established readings, however, are less clear. Dictionaries often order their entries in terms of chronological order of earliest attestation in the language. However, the earliest recorded meaning of a word does not necessarily strike speakers' intuitions as the literal meaning. There is no doubt, for instance, that the "die" meaning of *expire* predates the "cease to be valid" meaning, but (to my surprise) current British undergraduates, when asked to pick out the reading they intuitively feel to be the literal one, are virtually unanimous in selecting the "cease to be valid" reading. Another possible criterion is frequency in a language: one might reasonably expect the literal meaning to be the most frequent. Once again, however, this does not always accord with (strong) native speaker intuitions. For instance, few would dispute that the "have a visual experience" meaning of *see* is the literal meaning and "understand" an extended meaning, yet evidence from one very large corpus of English usage indicates that the latter is the more frequent. Two possibly more valid criteria are, first, the default meaning, that is, the one which comes first to mind when one is confronted by the word out of context, and, second, the reading from which the others can most plausibly be derived by standard semantic processes. The latter criterion is most reliable when there are more than two readings. Take the case of *position*, and three readings:

(i)   "location in space"
(ii)   "job in a large firm, etc."
(iii) "opinion"

Starting from (i), it is easy to see how (ii) and (iii) may have arisen by means of a process of metaphorical extension; but starting from either (ii) or (iii), there is no obvious way of deriving the other two.

6.3   Metaphor

There are a number of strategies for deriving one reading from another. Three will be illustrated here. The first of these is metaphor. Metaphor is essentially the projection of the conceptual structure appropriate to a familiar field onto a different and less familiar field, and depends for its effectiveness on a sufficient resemblance between the two fields for the projection to be intelligible. For instance, in the case of *expire*, projecting the notion of dying onto the life-cycle of, say, a credit card, allows an immediately intelligible parallel to be drawn between death and the end of the period of usability of the card.

6.4   Metonymy

The second strategy of meaning extension is metonymy, which is based not on resemblances or analogies between items in different conceptual domains, but associations within a single conceptual domain. Referring to people wearing roses as *roses* is intelligible, not because of any structural parallels between the concept of a rose and the people designated, but because of the close association between the latter and roses in a particular situation. This usage is unlikely to become established. An example of metonymy that is so well-established that we are hardly aware that it is non-literal is *The kettle's boiling*.

6.5 Specialization and generalization

A third process which produces new meanings from old ones is a change of inclusiveness, widening or narrowing down the meaning. The meaning "take alcoholic beverage" of *drink* is derived from the meaning "imbibe liquid" by specialization; *meat* has become specialized from meaning food of any kind to "animal flesh used as food"; *handsome* in Jane Austen seems to apply indifferently to men and women, but became specialized later to apply primarily to men, acquiring a particular nuance in its application to women; *interfere* in Jane Austen seems rather like current *intervene*, acquiring its disapproving connotations at a later date. The meaning of *cat* which includes lions, tigers, ocelots, and jaguars is derived by generalization from the meaning which includes only *felis domesticus*.

The loss of a whole sense may be considered a type of specialization: an example of this, again from Jane Austen, is *direction*, which has lost the reading "address" (as on a letter).

6.6 Amelioration and pejoration

Amelioration is when a neutral or pejorative term becomes commendatory, and *pejoration* is when the reverse movement occurs. The latter seems to be by far the more frequent, and is particularly prone to happen to words referring to women. Examples of words undergoing pejoration are: *madam, mistress, courtesan, wench, tart*, and so on. (The only two words referring to women that Jane Miller in *Womanwords* signals as having ameliorated are *jilt* which originally meant a prostitute, and *bat*, which "has lost its negative sexual connotations."

7 Larger Groupings of Words

7.1 Word fields

We have already seen that the vocabulary of a language is not just a collection of words scattered randomly through semantic space: it is at least partially structured by recurrent sense relations. In some areas of the vocabulary the sense relations unite groups of words into larger structures, known as *lexical fields* (or *word fields*). We shall look briefly at examples of one type of larger structure, namely, *lexical hierarchies*. Hierarchies may be *non-branching*, as in figure 10.1, or *branching*, as in figure 10.2:

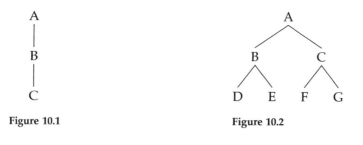

Figure 10.1   Figure 10.2

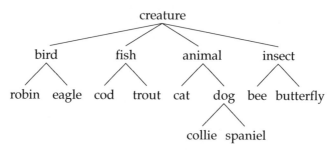

Figure 10.3
Note: A word of explanation is perhaps needed regarding the position of the word "animal" in the above hierarchy, which for some non-British speakers of English, who feel that "animal" and "creature" are synonyms, and that "animal" subsumes "bird," "fish," "insect," and so on, may seem anomalous. This is not so in British usage: the *Collins Handguide to the Wild Animals of Britain and Europe*, Ovenden et al. 1979, a field guide to identification, includes mammals, amphibians (such as frogs and newts), and reptiles (such as snakes and lizards), but no birds, fish or insects (which are covered by sister volumes). I am not aware of any other language which has a term with exactly this denotation.

If these are lexical hierarchies, then A, B, C, etc. represent word senses, and the lines joining them represent sense relations. The following are examples of non-branching hierarchies (turning them on their side for convenience):

(i)   general – colonel – major – captain – lieutenant – etc.
(ii) ocean – sea – lake – pond – puddle
(iii) scorching – hot – warm – lukewarm – cool – cold – etc.
(iv) tertiary (education) – secondary – primary – pre-school

A structural necessity for a branching hierarchy is that the branches must never converge. There are two main sorts of branching lexical hierarchy, which are called *taxonomies*, which are structured by hyponymy and incompatibility and *meronomies*, which are structured by meronymy and co-meronymy. Figure 10.3 illustrates a fragment of a taxonomy (valid for British English).

It will be appreciated that the hierarchy illustrated in figure 10.3 can be extended upwards, downwards, and sideways, ultimately producing a huge structure encompassing all living things. Most taxonomies are much more

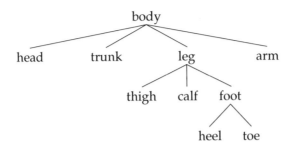

Figure 10.4

fragmentary than this, covering such areas as vehicles, buildings, clothes, and so on.

A taxonomy typically has well-defined levels: in figure 10.2, A is at Level 1, B and C are at Level 2, D, E, F, and G are at Level 3. One level of a taxonomy has a special status and is known as the *basic level*, as it seems that the structure is organized around this level. It is the level at which the "best" categories occur. This means that resemblance between fellow members and distinctiveness from members of sister categories are both maximized. Take the categories ANIMAL, DOG, and SPANIEL. Animals are distinct enough from non-animals, but their overall degree of mutual resemblance is relatively low; in the case of spaniels, they resemble one another highly, but differ in only minor ways from other types of dog; in the category DOG, on the other hand, mutual resemblance and distinctiveness are both high. Basic level items are also the default names for things, the names we use for simple, everyday reference. Suppose A hears a noise in the garden and asks B what it is. B looks out of the window and sees a spaniel. What does he say? Any of the following would be true:

(i)   Oh, it's just an animal.
(ii)   Oh, it's just a dog.
(iii) Oh, it's just a spaniel.

In the absence of special circumstances, (ii), which contains the basic level item, is by far the most likely.

Some examples (in capitals) of basic level items are as follows:

a.   vehicle – CAR – hatchback
b.   fruit – APPLE – Granny Smith
c.   living thing – creature – animal – CAT – Manx cat (British)
d.   object – implement – SPOON – teaspoon

The other main type of branching lexical hierarchy is the part–whole variety. (In figure 10.4, as in figure 10.3, only some of the branches are shown.) Part–whole hierarchies are just as numerous in the vocabularies of natural languages as are taxonomies. They differ from taxonomies in a number of respects, but perhaps the most significant difference concerns structural levels: meronomies tend to have no, or only weakly developed, levels, hence there is no equivalent to the basic level of a taxonomy.

7.2   Word families

Another type of grouping of associated words is the *word family*. Most complex lexemes are built up out of a *root* and one or more *derivational affixes*. For instance, the word *undress* is composed of the root *dress* and the prefix *un-*; the noun *re-entry* is composed of the root *ent(e)r*, the prefix *re-* and the suffix *-y*. A word family is composed of all the words derived from a given root. For instance, the following all belong to one word family:

nation	national (adj.)	national (n.)
nationally	nationalize	denationalize
nationality	nationalism	nationalist
international	transnational	nationhood
(etc.)		

As native speakers, we have a quite complex knowledge of which derivations are possible, and what they mean. We know, for instance, that although a *painter* is someone who paints, and a *painting* is the concrete end result of a painter's efforts, a *screwdriver* is not someone who inserts screws, but an appliance for doing this, and a *killing* is not the concrete end result of the process denoted by *kill* (i.e. a corpse), but an instance of the act itself. We also know that whereas a *diner* may be someone who is dining, it can also be a place where one dines, and we know that there is no parallel reading for *painter*.

7.3   Domain-specific vocabulary

Another type of word-grouping controlled by native speakers is the vocabulary appropriate to a particular situation, for instance, a race meeting:

1	2	3	4
horse	jockey	course	bet
favorite	owner	race	run
form	trainer	fence	win
odds	bookmaker	winner's enclosure	jump
colors	steward	starting-gate	take a fence
winner	stable-boy	heavy going	come up on the inside
handicap		reins	fall
yearling			disqualify
			scratch
			etc.

A broad grouping like this is composed of a number of nested sub-domains, such as weighing in, saddling, starting, running the race, laying bets, and so on.

7.4   Layers of vocabulary

We shall use the expression *layers of vocabulary* to refer to much larger groupings of words, each of which will incorporate many structures like those described, which are confined to certain areas of usage. For instance, there are technical vocabularies, such as those used by art historians, or doctors, when communicating with others of their kind. There are also collections of words which associate together at different levels of formality. These are effortlessly called up in appropriate contexts, and they must be somehow linked in storage.

7.5   The mental lexicon

Each of us has in our cognitive system some kind of inventory of all the words that we know, together with all the information – semantic, grammatical and phonetic / graphic – necessary for their correct use. Estimates of the number of words known by an average adult speaker vary from 150,000 to 250,000 (see, for instance, the discussion in Aitchison (1987: 5–7)). This represents a vast quantity of information.

The inventory is accessed via written or spoken forms every time we hear or read something in a language we know, and via some kind of semantic representation every time we produce language (recall that, because of widespread synonymy and polysemy, the mapping between forms and meanings is not one-to-one, but many-to-many). Although much is known, the details of representation and processes of use are still very imperfectly understood; nonetheless, the astonishing speed at which words are retrieved and identified – within about a fifth of a second from the start of the word, for spoken language – points to a highly efficient and organized storage system.

Every person's mental lexicon is different from everyone else's, yet by and large we manage to understand each other; this presumably indicates an adequate degree of overlap between individual lexicons.

7.6   Vocabularies

In addition to the mental lexicons of individual speakers of a language, it is possible to think of the total lexical stock of a language, which covers all its speakers, including those belonging to distinct speech communities, and including those who are now dead. Of course, the boundaries of such an entity are very vague, and will differ according to the purposes of the compilers and users (how far back in time do we go? how many dialect, or specialized technical forms do we include?, etc.). The natural home for such a vocabulary is the dictionary, and the natural way of drawing it up is by studying corpuses. The contents of a dictionary do not correspond to the contents of the mental lexicon of any single speaker, nor do they represent what is common to all speakers; yet every entry must be justified by some degree of common owner-ship in one or other of the sub-communities using the language.

8   Conclusion

We have now surveyed, at least in broad outline, the whole domain of words in language, from the detailed properties of individual words, through rela-tional properties along the major paradigmatic and syntagmatic axes, to com-munities of words, large and small, tightly or loosely structured.

It should be borne in mind, however, that many detailed aspects of the lexicon are still only imperfectly understood, and of these, a number are cur-rently the object of intense research activity. Two recent major stimuli to research on the lexicon are worth mentioning. The first has been the advent of powerful computers, and the attempt by computational linguists to develop programs capable of "understanding" natural language texts. The syntactic problems have proved relatively tractable; the big problem has turned out to be the lexicon – deciding what a computer must "know" about word meanings and how they are to be represented. The second major stimulus has been the develop-ment of large-scale corpuses of spoken and written language (together with tools for processing them), which allow an accurate picture to be gained of how words are actually used. This has, among other things, revolutionized lexico-graphy, and no doubt the full effects of both stimuli have yet to be seen.

11 Syntax

MARK C. BAKER

1 The Domain of Syntax

At its most basic level, syntax can be defined as the branch of linguistics that studies how the words of a language can be combined to make larger units, such as phrases, clauses, and sentences.

As such, syntax is deeply concerned with the relationship between the finite and the infinite. Most languages have a finite number of basic words, but those words can be put together to make an infinite number of sentences. Thus, one can buy a more or less complete dictionary of English, but it is unthinkable to buy a similar reference book that would list all the sentences of English. This is because there are rules and patterns that can be used in a dynamic way to create and understand new English sentences. Syntax is the study of these rules and patterns. For example, readers of this chapter will be aware of having encountered the English words *this, loves, elephant,* and *eggplant,* and they will find them listed in their dictionaries. However, they will not be aware of having encountered the English sentence in (1) before, and they will be unable to "look it up":

(1)   This elephant loves eggplant.

Nevertheless, they will have no hesitancies about recognizing it as English, or about being able to understand it and use it appropriately. Moreover, they will feel very differently about (2), even though it is made up of the same familiar elements:

(2)   *Loves elephant eggplant this.

In this arrangement, the words are not well-formed, but rather are *ungrammatical* (indicated by * symbol).

Syntax is primarily concerned with whether a sentence is "properly put together" rather than whether it is meaningful, or silly, or bizarre. Thus, it is concerned with the difference between (1) and (2), more than in the difference between (1) and the examples in (3) (Chomsky 1957: ch. 2).

(3)   a.   Those hippopotamuses hate asparagus.
      b.   #This eggplant loves elephants.

These sentences are all instances of the same basic pattern from a syntactic point of view, even though they mean different things ((3b) in particular being nonsensical, and unacceptable for that reason). What the new sentences formed by the patterns of syntax actually mean is the primary concern of semantics. However, aspects of how words are put together can influence how the sentence is interpreted; hence these issues can come into the domain of syntax as well. Indeed, there is a complex interaction between the disciplines of syntax and semantics, and it is controversial whether the topics can truly be distinguished.

The other branches of linguistics that are closely related to syntax are morphology and discourse analysis: morphology because it builds the words that are the starting point of syntax, and discourse analysis because it involves the construction of sentences into even larger entities, such as texts. Again, it is somewhat controversial to what extent syntax is a distinct topic from these others. It is conceivable that sentences are built in accordance with the same patterns and procedures as words or texts are. In that case, syntax would not be a separate topic from morphology or discourse analysis. Be that as it may, there is no doubt that some kind of syntax exists, and that it involves taking the finite building blocks made available by a given language and putting them together into an infinite number of representations, which in turn can express an infinite number of thoughts.

2   The Chomskyan Perspective

The study of syntax has flowered since 1950, having been given new impetus by the work of Noam Chomsky. One small but essential part of Chomsky's contribution has been to bring certain insights and perspectives from the study of formal languages in mathematics and computer science to bear on the fundamental problems of syntax. For example, the simple mathematical concept of a recursive function sheds crucial new light on how a finite number of words could be pieced together to make an infinite number of sentences (Chomsky 1975: chs 7, 8). In essence, a recursive function is one that is defined in terms of itself – a "circular" definition that succeeds in saying something substantive. For example, suppose that English contains the following rules:

(4)   a.   A sentence (S) consists of a Noun Phrase (NP) followed by a Verb Phrase (VP).
          (S → NP + VP)

    b. A VP consists of a verb (V), possibly followed by an NP and / or a clause (CP).

        (VP → V, or V + NP, or V + CP, or V + NP + CP)

    c. A CP consists of a S, possibly preceded by a complementizer (C)

        (CP → S or C + S)

English also includes the following words, which are members of the indicated lexical categories:

(5) Noun phrases: John, Mary, Bill
      Verbs: believes, likes
      Complementizer: that

This is a very small vocabulary, and a relatively short list of rules / patterns. However, the set of rules is *recursive* in the sense that a sentence contains a VP, and one of the things a VP can contain is a clause (CP), which always contains a new S. This S in turn contains its own VP, which can contain yet another S. And so on. Thus, with only these rules one can already make an infinite number of grammatical English sentences, depending on how many times one puts a new S inside the verb phrase:

(6) Mary likes Bill.
      John thinks that Mary likes Bill.
      Bill thinks that John thinks that Mary likes Bill.
      Mary thinks that Bill thinks that John thinks that Mary likes Bill.
      John thinks that Mary thinks that Bill thinks that John thinks that Mary likes Bill.

Note that each of these sentences expresses a distinct idea – one that is potentially useful in the complex world of high school courtship. Clearly there is much more to English than this, but it shows how the basic idea of recursion can elegantly address the apparent paradox of how people who have a finite amount of knowledge of English stored in their minds can produce and understand an infinite number of English sentences.

    Another foundational contribution from Chomsky and the cognitive science revolution of the 1950s and 1960s has more to do with the spirit of linguistic inquiry than its technical machinery. This is the ethos that when one is trying to discover the syntactic rules and patterns of a particular language, those rules should be stated explicitly and precisely, with (ideally) nothing being taken for granted or left to the imagination (Chomsky 1957: Preface). To see why this has proved important, consider the difference between telling a friend to do something and programming a computer to do something. Interacting with your friends is generally easier, because you automatically expect the friend to bring a great deal of common sense to bear on the request, filling in the details and interpreting the command in the light of circumstances. In contrast, computers have no inherent common sense; they do all and only what they are told in the most literal fashion. But while this can make working with computers exasperating, it can also make it educational, because trying to program a computer to do a task forces one to take stock of exactly what goes into that task, with no question-begging or step-skipping. This experience turns out to be highly relevant to the study of language. The syntax of English often seems deceptively simple, particularly in a monolingual situation. Since we all speak English (or another natural language), it is very easy to unconsciously fill in details without realizing it. If, however, one takes up the challenge of finding the patterns and principles of syntax to the point where one could (in principle) program a computer to judge sentences, manipulate them, and interpret them the way we do, one is forced to seriously investigate many issues that are otherwise easily overlooked. Sometimes this may seem obsessive to the outside observer: syntacticians sometimes seem to be telling needlessly complex stories when it is obvious that we say (1) and not (2) because "(1) sounds better" or "(1) makes more sense." But in fact linguists are at least as interested in exactly what goes into this "linguistic common sense" as they are about the salient and arbitrary rules of grammar that get most of people's attention (like "don't end a sentence with a preposition"). In fact, many important discoveries have been made by taking this perspective, some of which will be mentioned below.

The broadly Chomskyan approach to syntax is often called *formal* or *generative*: "formal" because it uses mathematical style formalisms and definitions in presenting its analysis, such as the recursive rules above; "generative" because it seeks to explicate how fluent speakers can generate new well-formed expressions of a language. Many current syntacticians still accept these labels for their work, while others have reacted against them and what they see as some deficiencies and excesses of this approach. However, it seems fair to say that even those that react most loudly against the Chomskyan approach have been positively influenced by its most basic ethos and by some of what has been learned from that perspective. For purposes of this chapter I will attempt to background these areas of disagreement, and foreground areas of relative agreement, simply noting in passing some areas where interpretations differ significantly.

3   Basic Lessons of Syntactic Research

What then are some of the substantive discoveries that have been made by adopting this perspective to syntax? Beyond the details of a vast number of particular discoveries, one can identify at least three broad themes: (1) that syntax is a vast topic; (2) that constraints are central to syntax; and (3) that there is a large component of syntax that is common to all human languages. I will discuss each of these themes in turn, using them as a context for presenting some more specific material by way of illustration.

3.1   *The vastness of syntax*

The first important lesson that comes from several decades of research on syntax is that there is much more to syntax than anyone ever imagined. Natural languages turn out to be enormously complicated, once one takes up the "take nothing for granted" attitude of the computer programmer. Prior to reflection, it is natural to think of an activity like playing chess as the epitome of a complex activity requiring great intelligence; in contrast, forming grammatical English sentences seems like a very ordinary, routine behavior. After all, playing chess requires conscious mental exertion and some people can do it much better than others, whereas English sentences are formed automatically, almost unconsciously by practically everyone. Indeed, the first blush of success over phrase structure rules could make one think that that is pretty much all there is to it. However, the actual experience of computer programming has shown vividly that the real complexity of the tasks is the reverse. Steady progress has been made in programming computers to play chess, to the point that they now beat even the best human players. In contrast, there is still no computer system that can match the ability to judge, generate, and interpret English sentences of an average ten-year-old child, in spite of the fact that enormous resources have been devoted to the problem. Indeed, the longest grammars of the best-studied languages are not close to complete descriptions, and new discoveries about languages like English and French are still made on a regular basis.

3.1.1   *Phrase Structure*

To see where some of the complexities come from, let us return to the notion of phrase structure. Rules like S → NP + VP and VP → V or V + NP express in a succinct way several facts (Chomsky 1965: ch. 2). First, they express the fact that all normal sentences must have at least a subject NP and a verb (except for imperatives, and certain elliptical expressions). If the subject is omitted, the sentence strikes native speakers of English as deviant.

(7) a. Mary likes the dress.
     b. *Likes the dress.

Second, these rules express the fact that the subject appears before the verb, and the object appears immediately after it. Thus, *The dress likes Mary* is a silly sentence with a completely different meaning from (7a); this is because it cannot be understood as having the object come before the verb and the subject after, but only as *the dress* being the subject and *Mary* being the object. The other logically possible rearrangements of the words are simply ungrammatical:

(8) a. *Mary the dress likes.
     b. *Likes Mary the dress.
     c. *Likes the dress Mary.
     d. (*)The dress Mary likes. (This is OK in context as a topicalization)

Third, the phrase structure rules as given also express the more subtle fact that the object and the verb together form a tighter unit in English, with the subject attached more loosely. Thus, in some special contexts one can put the verb and the object together at the front of the sentence, leaving the subject behind (see (9a)). In contrast, one can never put the subject and the verb at the front, leaving the object behind ((9b)).

(9)   I told you that John would like that dress, and indeed . . .
      a.   . . . Like that dress, John does.
      b.   *. . . John like, does that dress.

This unit that contains both the verb and the object but not the subject – the phrase that appears before the comma in (9a) – is called the Verb Phrase. Putting these pieces together, we can diagram the structure of a simple English sentence as follows:

(10)

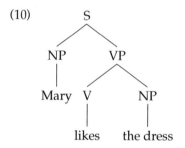

Similarly, the second sentence in (6) would have the phrase structure diagram in (11); note the recursion, where one S is embedded inside another.

(11)

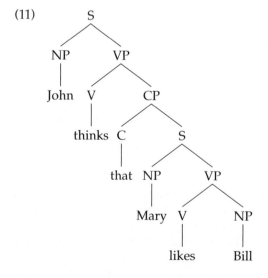

While these rules can be elaborated, refined, and added to, this gives some sense of how they are intended to work.

Already some complications arise. The phrase structure rules as given account for the ungrammaticality of (7a) compared to (7b), where the subject has been omitted. Now it is also ungrammatical to leave out the object of (7a):

(12) *John likes.

Indeed, (12) feels just as bad as (7b). However, unlike (7b), (12) can be generated by the phrase structure rules we have given. The difference is intentional. The reason is that (12) becomes grammatical when another verb is substituted for *likes*; for example, one can say *John smiles*. However, sentences like (7b) are impossible whatever verb is chosen (*Arrived the dress*, *Tore the dress*, etc.). Thus, it is a property of the particular English verb *like* that it needs to appear with an object, whereas it is a property of the English language as a whole that sentences need to have subjects. This difference between the status of subjects and objects is sometimes called the *(extended) projection principle* (Chomsky 1981). In contrast, the fact that objects must be present if and only if the particular verb of a clause specifically calls for one is sometimes called the *theta criterion* (Chomsky 1981).

3.1.2   *Transformational and interpretive rules*

Rich as they are, there seems to be more still to syntax than phrase structure rules. There are also certain systematic relationships between sentences that need to be captured, for which Chomsky originally proposed the formal device of the *transformational rule* (Chomsky 1957: ch. 7). These rules change one phrase structure into another. For example, consider the following English sentences:

(13) a. Mary will like the dress.
    b. *Mary will like what?
    c. What will Mary like?
    d. *What will Mary like the dress?
    e. *The dress will Mary like.

Like other languages, English has a special set of words that can take the place of a missing piece of information in order to form a question; these are often called *wh*-words after the letters that most of them begin with (*who, what, where, which . . .*). However, (13b) shows that it is not enough in English to simply put one of these words in place of the desired piece of information. Rather, the *wh*-word must appear at the beginning of the sentence, as in (13c). Moreover, (13c) is a striking exception to the generalization made above that the verb *like* must be immediately followed by an object. On the contrary, in this environment *like* must *not* have an object after it, as shown by (13d). One natural way to describe this network of facts is to say that the initial structure of (13c) is like that of (13a), with *what* substituted for *the dress*. However, the structure is "transformed" by a rule that can be stated something like this:

(14)   Move *wh*-words to before the first word of an S that contains them.

This rule applies to interrogative NPs, but not to other kinds of NPs; hence (13e) is not possible, even though it is perfectly parallel to (13c).

   Transformational relationships like these turn out to be relatively common. Indeed, (13) illustrates another one. Notice that the placement of the future auxiliary element *will* is different in declarative sentences like (13a) and interrogative ones like (13b). In declarative sentences, it always comes after the subject and before the main verb, whereas in interrogative sentences it comes between the *wh*-phrase and the subject. This change in word order is required (see (15a)) and one cannot have a second auxiliary of the same type in the usual position between the subject and the verb (15b).

(15)   a.   *What Mary will like?
        b.   *What will Mary will / may like?

Again, a movement transformation is a simple way to account for this fact:

(16)   Shift the auxiliary verb to the front of the subject NP in sentences that
        are interpreted as questions.

There may also be processes that apply to phrase structures that do not fall under the general category of movement. Suppose that we expand our miniature English dictionary to include NPs that are pronouns, such as *he, she,* and *it*. Then the phrase structure rules generate examples like (17):

(17)   John thinks that he likes Mary.

This sentence is ambiguous. Depending on context and expectations, it can easily be interpreted as meaning that John thinks that John himself likes Mary, or that John thinks that some other male we are discussing (say Bill) likes Mary. This is an essential feature of how competent English speakers understand and use sentences with pronouns. Now suppose that each distinct person referred to is associated with a unique number, written as a subscript to the Noun Phrase(s) that refer to it. Then the ambiguity in (17) can be captured by adding a rule like the following (Chomsky 1973; this rule is given for illustrative purposes; it is not now widely accepted, although the effect is genuine (Lasnik 1989: ch. 4)):

(18)   Copy the referential index of an NP onto a pronoun as its referential
        index.

This is called an interpretive rule, rather than a transformational rule. It is optional: one meaning of (17) comes from applying the rule, and the other meaning comes from choosing not to apply it.

(19) a.   John$_3$ thinks that he$_3$ likes Mary$_4$, *or*   (by (18))
      b.   John$_3$ thinks that he$_2$ likes Mary$_4$.

Just as the transformational rules apply only to a specific set of items (*wh*-words, auxiliary verbs), so (18) applies only to pronouns. Thus, if the man named John also happens to be a sentimental fool, one can in principle use either the NP *John* or *the sentimental fool* to refer to him. However, if one replaces the pronoun *he* in (17) with the NP *the sentimental fool*, the sentence can only have a meaning like (19b), where three distinct people are being discussed. This is because *the sentimental fool* is not a pronoun, and therefore rule (18) does not apply.

The existence of transformational rules like (14) and (16) and interpretive rules like (18) is more controversial than the existence of phrase structure. These elements of a linguistic analysis can be eliminated; one simply has to make up new phrase structure rules that will generate the desired sentences directly (Gazdar et al. 1985). Some syntacticians prefer this alternative approach, often for reasons of computational simplicity or formal elegance. However, there is no doubt that there needs to be *some* kind of general mechanism for expressing the relationships among the different parts of a syntactic structure – such as the relationship between the sentence initial question word in (13c) and the fact that the sentence has no NP in the object position of the verb phrase.

3.2   The centrality of constraints

This is far from exhausting the domain of syntax, however. Indeed, it merely sets the stage for what is perhaps the most interesting and significant discovery of all: the existence of *constraints*. When the various rules of syntax are stated in their simplest and most general form, they typically "over-generate," producing a number of ungrammatical sentences along with the grammatical ones. Therefore, syntacticians have proposed a system of constraints that prevent these rules from running wild.

As an example, let us return to the rule that moves *wh*-words to the front of sentences. This is a very general phenomenon, but it turns out to be far from exceptionless. Consider, for example, the following more complex examples:

(20) a.   John will think that Mary likes the dress
      b.   John will think Mary likes the dress.
      c.   What will John think Mary likes – ?
      d.   What will John think that Mary likes – ?

e.   Who will John think – likes the dress?
f.   *Who will John think that – likes the dress?

(20a) and (20b) are both simple sentences, formed by the phrase structure rules in (4). They differ only in whether the complementizer *that* is present or not: in (20a) the CP inside the VP containing *think* is expanded as C + S (where *that* is C); in (20b) the CP is expanded simply as S. Examples (20c) and (20d) are the result of generating *what* as the object of the embedded sentence and moving it to the front; both are grammatical, as expected. Examples (20e) and (20f) are the result of substituting *who* for the subject NP of the embedded sentence and moving it to the front. This time, we find something unanticipated: (20f) is ungrammatical for most speakers, even though our rules can construct this sentence just as easily as the others. There seems to be a special, additional constraint at work here, which can be phrased as follows (Chomsky and Lasnik 1977):

(21)   *Complementizer constraint*
       A sentence is ungrammatical if a complementizer comes immediately before a verb (in languages where subject phrases are generally obligatory).

Since only (20f) has the forbidden sequence of words ... *that – likes* ... it alone is ruled out by (21), as desired.

There are other constraints on *wh*-movement as well. We have seen that either a subject or an object can be replaced by a *wh*-word, which then moves to the front of the clause. However, a difference between subjects and objects arises when one tries to question only a part of the noun phrase. When a question word replaces part of an object noun phrase and moves to the front, the result is often perfectly acceptable, as in (22).

(22)   a.   You saw [a picture of *John*].
       b.   Who did you see [a picture of –]?

However, when a question word replaces a similar part of a subject noun phrase, the result is unacceptable:

(23)   a.   [A picture of *John*] disturbed you.
       b.   *Who did [a picture of –] disturb you?

There is no obvious reason why (23b) should not be as useful or meaningful a sentence as (22b); it just sounds awkward. To account for this, linguists have stated the following condition (Huang 1982):

(24)   *The condition on extraction domains* (CED):
       A phrase X can move out of a phrase Y only if Y is immediately contained in a Verb Phrase.

Since the object is inside the VP, as shown by the phrase structure diagram in (25), the movement in (22b) is possible:

(25)

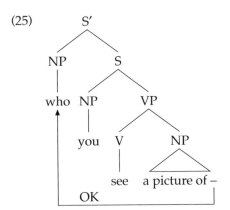

However, the subject NP is not inside the Verb Phrase; therefore question words cannot move out of the subject:

(26)

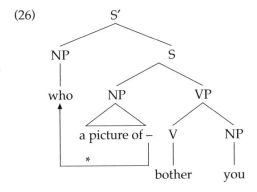

Thus, the condition on extraction domains correctly differentiates between sentences like (22) and (23).

There are also interesting constraints on the pronoun interpretation rule in (18). Suppose that the object of a sentence is a pronoun. That pronoun can easily be understood as referring to something contained in the subject noun phrase, as expected:

(27) *John's*$_2$ mother$_3$ loves *him*$_2$.

The situation is not symmetrical however. If we put a pronoun in the subject position, it cannot normally be understood as referring to something contained in the object. Thus, *he* cannot be John (or the mother) in sentences like (28), but must be some third person.

(28)   *He₂ loves John's₂ mother₃*

One might think that this is simply a matter of linear order – that a pronoun can never refer to a noun phrase that comes after it. However, this is not true. For example, in a sentence like (29), the pronoun *his* comes before *John*; nevertheless, *his* can be understood as referring to John, at least for most English speakers. (This interpretation is easier to get if one says the sentence with the main stress on the verb *loves*, rather than on *John*.)

(29)   (?)*His₂ mother₃ loves John₂.*

Thus, we need to add a condition to (18), which by itself implies that pronouns can always refer to any other NP in the same sentence (Lasnik 1989, Reinhart 1983). First, it helps to define the term *c-command*:

(30)   *C-command:*
       An element X *c-commands* another element Y if the first phrase which properly contains X also properly contains Y.

Given this, we can state the condition on pronouns as follows:

(31)   *Disjoint reference condition (DRC):*
       A pronoun X may not refer to the same thing as (have the same index as) a nonpronominal NP Y if X c-commands Y.

This explains the pattern of facts as follows. Consider (32), which is the structure of (27).

(32)

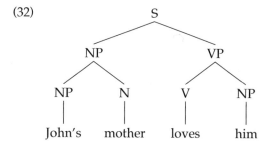

First we must check if the pronoun *him* c-commands the NP *John*. The first category that properly contains *him* is the VP, and *John* is outside this VP. Thus, the pronoun does not c-command *John* in this structure. Therefore, the DRC does not apply, and (18) can; thus, the pronoun may refer to the same thing as "John." However, (28) comes out differently:

(33)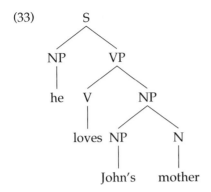

Here the first category that contains the pronoun *he* is S, the whole sentence, and S obviously contains the NP *John* as well. Therefore, the pronoun does c-command the noun phrase in this structure, so the pronoun cannot refer to the same thing as that noun phrase, by the DRC. Finally, (34) is the structure of (29):

(34)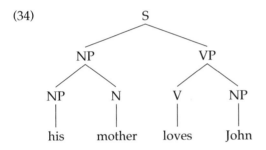

Here the pronoun *his* is not the whole subject, but only a part of the subject. Thus, the first phrase which properly contains *his* is the subject NP. This subject NP does not include the object *John*. Therefore, the pronoun does not c-command the NP in this example. Therefore, coreference is possible again. Thus, we see that a condition defined over the basic phrase structure of the sentence accounts for the usage of pronouns in English; indeed, it does so better than a simplistic rule that says that a pronoun must come after the Noun Phrase that it refers to.

Much of the beauty of these constraints comes from the fact that in many cases they regulate the operation of more than one transformational relationship (Ross 1967, Chomsky 1973, Chomsky 1977). For example, in addition to the transformations outlined above, English has a rule of relative clause formation that makes noun phrases out of sentence-like structures. A simple example is:

(35)   Mary likes the dress → The dress that Mary likes –

This is not the same process as question formation, but it is somewhat similar in that a noun phrase (here *the dress*) comes to appear at the beginning of the clause, and there is a gap inside the clause where a noun phrase normally has to be. Thus, this too can be thought of as a movement process. Now given the way the constraints are set up, we automatically expect relative clause formation to have the same limitations as question formation. This is correct. Like question movement, relative clause formation cannot create a configuration where the complementizer *that* comes immediately before the verb. The examples in (36) are exactly parallel to those in (20).

(36)   a.   The dress that John thinks Mary likes –
      b.   The dress that John thinks that Mary likes –
      c.   The woman that John thinks – likes the dress
      d.   *The woman that John thinks that – likes the dress

Similarly, relative clause formation obeys the CED, such that part of the object can be moved, but not part of the subject. (37) is parallel to (22b) and (23b).

(37)   a.   The man that you saw a picture of
      b.   *The man that a picture of disturbed you

This is an important finding, because it shows that the constraints should not be built into the individual transformations themselves; rather they are more general, and have a semi-separate existence. A priori, one could write the Complementizer Filter and the CED into the basic formulation of the question movement transformation. The result would be a rule that is rather complex and inelegant. Furthermore, the same complexities would have to be written into the relative clause transformation – and into a number of other transformations as well. Clearly, it is better to factor these out as separate conditions. This has led to the view that the constraints are really more fundamental than the transformations themselves, a shift from seeing language as fundamentally a list of construction rules to seeing it as a system of constraints that must be satisfied (Chomsky 1981).

Ongoing research has proceeded in the direction of uncovering constraints that are more and more general. A good illustration is the so-called "shortest move" constraint. Auxiliary inversion seems to be quite a different kind of process from both question movement and relative clause formation: it moves a very different kind of linguistic element (a verb, rather than a noun phrase) to a somewhat different position under partially different circumstances. As a result, constraints like the complementizer constraint and the CED do not seem relevant to this particular transformation. Nevertheless, there are similarities. Suppose that one tries to generate a sentence with two distinct *wh*-words, each substituting for a different piece of desired information, as in (38a). The *wh*-movement rule must apply exactly once to such a structure (in English), moving one of the *wh*-words to the beginning of the clause and leaving the other in place, as shown by the grammatical example in (38b). Strikingly, one does not have a choice as to which of the *wh*-words to move, as shown by (38c).

(38) a. John gave what to who.
      b. What did John give to who?
      c. *Who did John give what to?

Something very similar is found with *auxiliary inversion*. (39a) shows a structure that contains two distinct auxiliary verbs. Auxiliary inversion can apply once and only once to this structure to create the grammatical Yes / No question in (39b). Again, one does not have a choice of which auxiliary to move, as shown by the ungrammaticality of (39c).

(39) a. John will have eaten the sandwich by noon.
      b. Will John have eaten the sandwich by noon?
      c. *Have John will eaten the sandwich by noon?

There is a simple generalization here: in both cases it is the element that starts off closest to the front of the clause that must move. This has led linguists to propose the "shortest move" condition, which favors shorter movements to longer movements when there is a choice (Chomsky 1995). All the various kinds of movements arguably obey this very general condition. This condition can be looked at as a kind of *economy condition*, in the sense that it favors the smallest possible adjustment to the structure. One strain of current research explores the idea that all conditions can be reduced to a very small number of these "super-conditions," all of which have an economy flavor (Chomsky 1995).

3.3   *The similarity of all human language*

A third major lesson that emerges from contemporary syntactic research is that all natural languages are strikingly similar. This is certainly not one's first impression. There are some six thousand languages currently spoken in the world, many of which had relatively little contact with each other until recently. When speakers of an Indo-European language first start to learn a Native American language, or an Australian Aboriginal language, or an East Asian language they are usually more struck by difference than by similarity. However, the differences seem to be largely on the surface. We have already seen how once one starts to take nothing for granted one begins to discover many unsuspected intricacies of English grammar. It is not surprising that when one begins to study other languages from the same perspective, one finds unsuspected intricacies in those languages too. What is surprising is that the intricacies turn out to be largely the same, even across languages that are geographically separated and historically unrelated. Moreover, this seems to be more true the further one goes into the linguistic analysis. Thus, the phrase structures of languages are not necessarily the same; for example, verbs and prepositions come before their object noun phrases in English, but they come after their objects in Japanese, Hindi, and many other languages. Similarly, the transformational processes of a language may or may not be the same. For example, English has a rule that moves question words to the front of the clause, but languages like Chinese, Japanese, and Hindi do not. But at the level of syntactic constraints it is striking that constraints originally discovered for languages like English and French often show up in other languages – or at least it is possible to rephrase the constraint slightly so that it applies to all of the languages. Thus, the syntax of natural languages is not only vaster than we thought, but it is also more similar than we thought.

To get a flavor of how this kind of reasoning goes, consider the Edo language, spoken in Nigeria. This language had no contact with European languages until recent times, and has had no impact on the development of syntactic theory before now. Thus, it provides an interesting test case for the generality of that theory. In fact, it can be shown that Edo is strikingly like English in most of the syntactic features presented above. (The data in this section is from O. T. Stewart, personal communication.)

First of all, the same basic phrase structure rules that work in English work also in Edo. For example, the subject comes before the verb, and the object comes immediately after it:

(40)   Òzó guòghó àkhé.
       Ozo broke   pot.
       "Ozo broke the pot."

As in English, the subject noun phrase is obligatory in all clauses, but whether an object is needed or not depends on which verb is chosen:

(41)   a.   Òzó só.
            Ozo shouted
            "Ozo shouted."
       b.   *Guòghó àkhé.
            broke   pot
            ("Pot" must be the subject, not the object: Àkhé guòghó "the pot broke.")

While Edo does not have any process that fronts the VP that is directly comparable to the English one in (9a), it is possible to show that the object and verb ·form a relatively tight unit to the exclusion of the subject, as in English. Thus, the basic phrase structure patterns S → NP + VP and VP → V or V + NP (or V + CP) are equally valid for both languages.

There are also similarities between the two languages at the level of transformations. Edo, like English, has a rule that obligatorily moves question words to the front of the clause:

(42)   a.   *Òzó ghá guòghó dèmwìn?
            Ozo will break what

b. Dèmwìn nè òzó ghá gh<u>ó</u>'gh<u>ó</u>?
    what that Ozo will break
    "What will Ozo break?"

Edo also has the optional process of assigning a pronoun the same reference as a noun that appears elsewhere in the sentence. Thus, (43) is ambiguous in Edo, just as (17) is in English.

(43) Òzó hòó nè <u>ò</u> kpàá.
      Ozo wants that he leave. (he = Ozo, or he = the other guy under discussion)

However, Edo does not have the Auxiliary Inversion transformation. Thus, in (42b) the future tense auxiliary *ghá* does not shift to before the subject in Edo questions the way it does in English (**dèmwìn ghá òzó gu<u>ò</u>gh<u>ó</u>*). Instead a special functional word *nè* is inserted in this position. This kind of patterning gives syntacticians the impression that, while languages are certainly not identical, they seem to choose their syntactic structures from a limited set of options that are universally available.

Finally, consider the level of constraints. Recall that English puts limitations on when a *wh*-word can move to the front of the clause, such as the CED. The same constraint holds in Edo. (44a) shows a sentence in which a clause is in the object position with respect to the main verb *ta* "say." (44b) shows that one can generate a question word as the object of this embedded clause and then move it to the front of the sentence as a whole in the usual way.

(44) a. Úyì tá w<u>é</u>!<u>é</u> òzó d<u>é</u> ímótò.
          Uyi said that Ozo bought car.
          "Uyi said that Ozo bought a car."
      b. Dèmwìn nè Úyì tá w<u>é</u>!<u>é</u> òzó d<u>é</u> – ?
          what that Uyi said that Ozo bought.
          "What did Uyi say that Ozo bought?"

In contrast, in (45a) there is a clause that functions as the subject of the main verb *yee* "please." All things being equal, it should be possible to replace the object of this clause with a question word and then move that question word to the front, forming the question in (45b). But this is impossible.

(45) a. W<u>èé</u> òzó d<u>é</u> ím<u>ó</u>tò y<u>èé</u> Úyì.
          that Ozo bought car please Uyi.
          "That Ozo bought a car pleased Uyi."
      b. *Dèmwìn nè w<u>èé</u> Òzó d<u>é</u> – y<u>èé</u> Úyì?
          what that that Ozo bought please Uyi.
          "What did that Ozo bought please Uyi?"
          (i.e. "What did it please Uyi that Ozo bought?")

Note that exactly the same judgments hold true of the English translations. This confirms that the same constraint on question movement holds in both languages.

The DRC also applies in Edo, constraining how pronouns are interpreted. Consider the following range of examples:

(46) a. Wé̩é̩ né'né ékítà lèlé Ìsòkè̩n yè̩é̩ órè.
           That the dog followed Isoken pleased her (OK her = Isoken)
      b. Wé̩é̩ né'né ékítà lèlé érè yè̩é̩ Ìsòkè̩n.
           That the dog followed her pleased Isoken. (OK her = Isoken)
(47) a. Ìsòkè̩n hòó nè né'né ékítà lèlé é̩rè.
           Isoken wants that the dog follow her. (OK her = Isoken)
      b. Ò hòó né né'né ékítà lèlé Ìsòkè̩n.
           She wants that the dog follow Isoken. (Only OK if she ≠ Isoken)

The examples in (46) have an embedded clause that functions as the subject of the main verb *yè̩é̩* "please", and the speaker desires to express that the object of the embedded verb (the person who is followed) is the same person as the object of the main verb (the person who is pleased). This can be done by either putting a pronoun in the embedded clause and a name in the main clause, or vice versa. The examples in (47) are similar, except that this time the embedded clause is the object of the main verb *hòó* "want." Now if the speaker desires to express that the subject of wanting is the same person as the intended object of following, the options are restricted: the name must be used as the subject of the sentence as a whole, and a pronoun must be used as the object of the embedded clause, as in (47a). It is grammatical to use a pronoun as the subject and a name as the embedded object, as in (47b), but then the pronoun can only be interpreted as some third person, not Ìsòkè̩n. This is exactly what the DRC predicts. In (47b) the smallest phrase containing the pronoun is the sentence as a whole, which also contains Ìsòkè̩n. Therefore, the pronoun c-commands the name, and coreference is prohibited. However, the pronoun does not c-command the name in any of the other sentences in (46) or (47) (it is contained in the embedded VP in (46b) and (47a), and in the main VP in (46a); these phrases do not contain Ìsòkè̩n). Therefore, coreference is allowed. Again, the same judgments are valid for the English translations, confirming that the same constraint holds in both languages.

Sometimes even when languages look quite different, they are actually responding to a similar constraint in a different way. An interesting example comes from the complementizer constraint, stated in (21). The configuration of complementizer *wè̩é̩* followed by verb is also avoided in Edo:

(48) a. Dèmwìn nè Úyì tá wè̩é̩ òzó dé̩ –
           what that Uyi said that Ozo bought.
           "What did Uyi say that Ozo bought?"

b. *Dòmwàn nè Úyì tá wèé – dé ímótò.
who that Uyi said that buy car.
"Who did Uyi say that bought a car?"

However, English avoids the problematic configuration by omitting the complementizer; in contrast Edo avoids it by filling in the space left behind by the question word with a pronoun, as shown in (49) (see (Koopman 1982) for discussion of this pattern in Vata):

(49) a. *Dòmwàn nè Úyì tá dé ímótò.
who that Uyi said buy car.
"Who did Uyi say bought a car?"
    b. Dòmwàn nè Úyì tá wèé ó dé ímótò.
who that Uyi said that he buy car.
"Who did Uyi say bought a car?"

Moreover, this difference in the two languages is not an arbitrary one. Edo is different from English in that it normally requires embedded clauses to have a complementizer; in symbols, CP → C + S is the only option in Edo. Therefore, (49a) is ungrammatical in this language. On the other hand, there are other situations in which pronouns show up where question words once were in Edo. This then is a simple example of how even in areas where languages look somewhat different, important similarities can be discerned, particularly in the domain of constraints.

Over all, when one compares the syntax of different languages, they seem to be making different choices from a similar range of options: they have the same kinds of phrase structures, with possible differences in the order of the words; they have the same kinds of transformations; they have the same general constraints, although with different specific ways of satisfying them. This leads to the idea that much of human language is somewhat like a kit that you buy at a store: the basic pieces are prefabricated, although there is some variation in how you assemble them (and much freedom in how you decorate the final product).

Up to this point, there is reasonably broad agreement across a wide range of syntacticians, although significant differences in emphasis. Disagreement becomes more vigorous on the question of how to interpret this interplay of universal patterns and language-particular facts. Roughly three approaches are current. The first is the *principles and parameters* approach of Chomsky himself and his nearer followers. This takes the view that the principles of language are essentially universal, and they take the form of a certain number of stipulated abstract constraints. The set of these principles is often referred to as *Universal Grammar*. Language variation comes from fixing certain *parameters* – especially those that involve the idiosyncratic properties of the words of a language (Chomsky 1981). This has been called a "constitutional view." The second approach is more "architectural" (Bach 1988). It emphasizes the modes of composition of the words of languages (phrase structure rules or the equivalent) and tries to state those principles of combination in just such a way that constraints like the CED emerge as theorems of the system. This is roughly the view of more mathematically oriented theories like categorial grammar and generalized phrase structure grammar. Third, there are a variety of functionalist approaches. These see the universal constraints on language as functional in nature: they are design features that facilitate language's basic purpose of communication, a goal which is taken to be essentially the same across the species (see, for example, Croft 1995). On these views, language-specific idiosyncrasies are generally taken to have historical explanations, in which some communicative strategy that was originally a dynamic option gets entrenched as a habit, and thus becomes a "rule" of a particular language.

The CED facts surveyed above can provide an illustrative comparison of these perspectives. I stated the CED as an extrinsic constraint, in the style of the formal, "constitutional" approach: all movements are possible, *unless* they violate this "law." A functionalist approach, on the other hand, would investigate the communicative purpose of asking a question and the communicative purpose of expressing something as a direct object (rather than a subject or a modifier), looking for (in)compatibilities at that level. At first, it seems like it should be easy to determine which approach is correct by simple cross-linguistic comparison. The formal approach predicts that CED-type restrictions should appear when and only when there is a movement relation; the exact communicative purpose of the movement is not directly relevant. For example, (37) showed that the CED restricts the formation of relative clauses as well as questions, even though the communicative effects of the two are quite different. Conversely, I mentioned in passing that some languages form questions simply by replacing the unknown material with a suitable interrogative word, with no movement. On the formal view, it should be possible to ask a wider range of questions in these languages than in English, because the CED does not restrict this kind of question formation. For a number of languages, this seems correct. Thus, (50) is a grammatical question in Chinese, where the *wh*-phrase *shei* replaces an NP inside a clause that functions as the subject of the sentence as a whole (Huang 1982):

(50) [Lisi da-le   shei] shi   ni   hen bugaoxing? (Huang 1982: 496)
      Lisi hit-ASP who make you very unhappy.
      "Who did it make you very unhappy that Lisi hit?"

Strikingly, relative clause formation does involve movement of an NP in Chinese – although to the end of the clause, rather than to the beginning of the clause. Thus, the formal approach expects CED-style restrictions, and that is what one finds:

(51) ??Lisi da-le   – shi   wo hen bugaoxing de neige ren
      Lisi   hit-ASP – make I   very unhappy   DE that man
      "The man that it made me very unhappy that Lisi hit"

However, there is also evidence that points the other way. For example, Foley and Van Valin (1984: 22–4) mention that question words are not moved in the Native American language Lakhota; yet the kinds of sentences that violate the CED in English are also ungrammatical in Lakhota:

(52) #WiChaSa wã taku ophethũ ki he wãlaka he.
      man   a   what buy   the that you-see Q
      "What did you see the man who bought?"

They point out that the badness of (52) makes more sense from the functionalist perspective, assuming that there is some kind of basic incompatibility between the goal of asking a question and the goal of expressing an object modifier. This functional style of explanation can rule out sentences like (52) in the same way in Lakhota and English, irrespective of differences in how each particular language chooses to express questions. Much work remains to be done to sort out whether the formalist expectations or the functionalist expectations fit the facts better, or whether some kind of synthesis is called for. This is an area in which further research and debate can be expected.

4 Universal Grammar and Parameterization: A Concrete Example

So far, I have presented syntacticians' claims about Universal Grammar only by comparing English and Edo. While this is a fair test in as much as the languages developed quite independently of each other, it is clear that they are relatively similar typologically. In the rest of this chapter, I will illustrate the claims of syntax by way of a more radical comparison, between English and the Mohawk language. The analysis in this section, based on Baker (1991, 1996), is less a part of the standard canon than the material presented so far, and some features of it are controversial. However, its leading idea has wide acceptance, and it provides a good illustration of some characteristic features of contemporary syntactic research.

If one offered a prize for the language that looks the least like English, Mohawk would be a strong candidate. At first glance, one finds differences wherever one looks, starting with the most simple sentences. We saw that in English and Edo a transitive verb must appear with two NPs, a subject and an object. In Mohawk this is not so: either the subject or the object – or both – can be left out, and the result is still a complete and grammatical sentence:

(53) a. Sak ranuhwe's atya'tawi.
          Sak likes   dress
          "Sak likes the dress."
      b. Ranuhwe's atya'tawi.
          likes   dress
          "He likes the dress."

   c. Sak ranuhwe's.
      Sak likes
      "Sak likes it."
   d. Ranuhwe's.
      likes
      "He likes it."

In English and Edo, the subject must come before the verb and the object after; in Mohawk this is not so. Rather, the subject, the object and the verb can appear in any of the six orders that are logically possible for a three word sentence (see also (53a)):

(54) a. Ranuhwe's Sak atya'tawi.
        likes   Sak dress
        "Sak likes the dress."
     b. Sak atya'tawi ranuhwe's.
        Sak dress   likes
     c. Ranuhwe's atya'tawi ne Sak.
        like   dress   NE Sak
     d. Atya'tawi ranuhwe's ne Sak.
        dress   like   NE Sak
     e. Atya'tawi Sak ranuhwe's.
        dress   Sak like

In English, the object and the verb sometimes move together as a unit; in Mohawk this is never possible, as far as researchers have been able to determine. Thus the phrase structure rules of English do not seem applicable to Mohawk at all. Such languages are sometimes called *nonconfigurational* (Hale 1983).

    Moving on to the domains of transformations and constraints, recall that in English, a question word can move out of the direct object noun phrase to the beginning of the clause, but question words cannot move out of subject noun phrases (see (22) and (45)). One similarity between Mohawk and English is that question words must move to the front of the clause in Mohawk too:

(55) Uhka washakokv' ne Sak?
     who see   NE Sak
     "Who did Sak see?"

However, in Mohawk when one tries to move a question word out of some larger phrase that serves as the object, the result is just as ungrammatical as if the question word moves out of a subject phrase. Thus, there is no difference here between subjects and objects the way there is in English and Edo:

(56) a. *?Uhka wesatsituni'   ne akokara'?
        who   made-cry-you NE story
        "Who did the story of make you cry?"

b. *?Uhka senuhwe's ne akokara'?
who you-like NE story
"Who do you like the story of?"

In English, the DRC says that a pronoun subject cannot refer to an NP contained in the direct object, but a pronoun object can refer to an NP contained in the subject ((27) and (28)). In contrast, both kinds of coreference are possible in Mohawk.

(57) a. (Akauha) wa'akoya'takehnha' ne Uwari akona'tsu.
      her help NE Mary pot
      "Mary's pot helped her." (OK her = Mary)
    b. (Rauha) wahanohare' ne Sak rao'share.
      he wash NE Sak knife
      "He washed Sak's knife." (OK he = Sak)

Thus, our first impression is that the syntax of Mohawk is radically different from the syntax of English, and (except for question movement) virtually none of the rules and principles seem to carry over. Rather, it seems like, in order to analyze Mohawk insightfully, one must start from scratch, building a theory that accounts for Mohawk in its own terms.

There is another possibility, however. It could be that Mohawk is actually rather like English, but we are looking at it wrong. In fact, when one looks a little further, certain similarities begin to turn up. Consider once again the DRC. Before, I only used this to explicate differences between subjects and objects, but the condition is more general. For example, most English speakers find a difference between (58a) and (58b):

(58) a. I hired *him₂* [because *John₂* was a good worker].
    b. *I told *him₂* [that *John₂* was a good worker].

Superficially, these sentences look very similar, the main difference being the first verb. However, the pronoun *him* can be understood as referring to *John* in the first sentence, but not in the second. Why should this be? Part of the answer is that the embedded clauses in these two sentences are performing very different functions. In (58b), the clause is basically a special kind of object. As such, it can be replaced by a normal NP object:

(59) I told him [the news].

However, a similar replacement is not possible in (58a):

(60) *I hired him [the reason].

The embedded clause is not an object of the verb at all in (58a); rather, it is a *modifier* that helps put the main clause into context. As a result, the embedded clause is optional in (58a); if it is omitted, the sentence is still grammatical and complete. In contrast, (58b) sounds incomplete without the embedded clause. These differences translate into a difference in the phrase structure of the sentences. Since the clause of *tell* functions as a kind of direct object, it makes sense that this would be generated inside the VP, in the same kind of position as other direct objects:

(61)

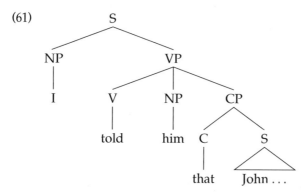

On the other hand, since the *because* clause is a modifier of the sentence as a whole, and only loosely attached to it, its phrase structure is as in (62):

(62)

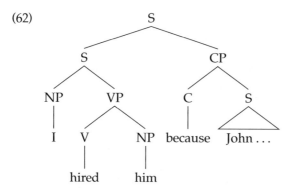

Now we can apply the DRC to these structures and we get the results we want. In (61) the object pronoun c-commands the NP *John* inside the embedded clause; therefore they cannot refer to the same thing. In (62), however, the object pronoun does not c-command the NP "John" inside the *because*-clause: the first phrase that properly contains the pronoun is VP, and this VP does not contain the modifier. Therefore, the pronoun can refer to the same thing as the NP, just as we observed.

Significantly, comparable sentences in Mohawk elicit the same pattern of judgments, as shown in (63).

(63) a. (Rauha) wahi'nha'ne' ne tsi   Sak rayo'tvhseriyo.
          him   I-hired   because Sak is-a-good-worker
          "I hired *him* because *Sak* is a good worker."   (OK him = Sak)

b. (Rauha) wahihrori' tsi   Sak rayo'tvhseriyo.
   him   I-told   that Sak is-a-good-worker
   "I told *him* that *Sak* is a good worker."   (Not OK: him = Sak)

Again, the pronoun object of the first verb can refer to an NP in the embedded clause when the verb means "tell," but not when it means "hire." Perhaps then the DRC applies in Mohawk after all.

Consider next the CED. Given the structures in (61) and (62), the CED predicts that *wh*-words should be able to move out of *that*-clauses but not *because*-clauses, because only *that*-clauses are immediately contained in VP. This is true in English:

(64)   You think [that Mary kicked *John.*]
       Who do you think [that Mary kicked –]?

(65)   You cried [because Mary kicked *John.*]
       *Who did you cry [because Mary kicked –]?

(In fact, this kind of contrast was part of the original motivation for the CED in Huang (1982).) Strikingly, the same contrast is found in Mohawk. Sentences like (66a) are perfectly grammatical, while sentences like (66b) are not:

(66)   Uhka ihsehre'   Uwari wahuwarasvtho'?
       Who you-think Mary kicked
       "Who do you think Mary kicked?"

(67)   *Uhka wa'tesahvrehte' ne tsi   Uwari wahuwarasvtho'?
       who   you-shouted   because Mary kicked
       "Who did you shout because Mary kicked?"

Thus, there is evidence that the CED applies in Mohawk too.

So far, we have something of a paradox. When we look at noun phrase objects and subjects, Mohawk and English seem completely different. However, when we look at embedded clauses, they seem very much the same. How can this conflicting evidence be reconciled?

In fact, there is a rather simple way of resolving the paradox. (Formal) syntactic analysis characteristically comes in two steps: first, one determines the basic structures of sentences in the language, and, second, one defines conditions over those structures. Given this, the fact that one gets different grammaticality patterns in Mohawk from English is not necessarily due to a difference in the conditions, but could be due to a difference in the basic structure that the conditions apply to. Let us then hypothesize that the conditions in Mohawk are indeed the same as those in English, based on the evidence from embedded clauses. Now, reconsider sentence (57b), repeated as (68).

(68)   (Rauha) wahanohare' ne Sak rao'share.
       he   wash   NE Sak knife
       "He washed Sak's knife."   (OK he = Sak)

Here the pronoun subject can be coreferent with the NP *Sak* inside the direct
object, unlike in English. If the DRC really holds in Mohawk, this can only mean
that the object NP is in some other position where it is not c-commanded by
the pronoun subject. In other words, it must be outside of the smallest phrase
that properly contains the subject. Is there such a position? The answer is yes:
we saw above that *because*-clauses can be attached loosely to the sentence as a
whole. This is only legitimate because the sentence is complete without the
because-clause. However, the same is true of object NPs in Mohawk; sentences
are complete without them (see (53c)). Thus, the structure of (68) is (69).

(69)

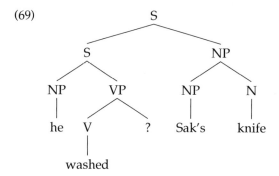

More generally, we can conjecture subject and object NPs are always loosely
attached to the clause in this way in Mohawk.

   This hypothesis about Mohawk sentence structure immediately solves some
other problems as well. Another difference between Mohawk and English was
that question words cannot move out of object NPs in Mohawk, as shown in
(56b). This now makes perfect sense. The NP that we are trying to move out of
is not a true object after all, but rather a loosely attached NP, in the same kind
of position as *because*-clauses:

(70)

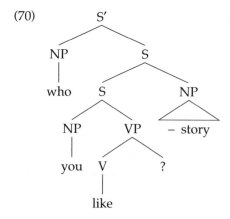

Since the loosely attached NP is not in the VP, it follows from the CED that a question word cannot move out of this NP. These sentences fall into place with no further adjustments.

The important thing to realize here is that the DRC and the CED both seem to go wrong in Mohawk – but *crucially they go wrong in the same way*. They both assume that object NPs are inside the VP. Once this assumption about basic structure is corrected, the conditions consistently give the correct results after all. Our first impression was that Mohawk was different from English in almost every imaginable way. We have now corrected that impression; in fact, Mohawk differs from English in only one way, as stated in (71) (see Jelinek 1984; the idea apparently has roots as far back as Humboldt's remarks on Nahuatl in the first half of the nineteenth century).

(71)   NPs are true subjects and objects in English, but are loosely attached to the sentence as a whole in Mohawk.

Since this affects the basic structure of the sentence, and many conditions are stated in terms of that structure, it causes ripples throughout the grammar of Mohawk. Nevertheless, most of the syntactic principles are the same.

In fact, there is reason to think that even (71) overstates the differences between Mohawk and English. Consider again the fact that the subject and object in Mohawk do not need to appear:

(72)   Ranuhwe's. (= (53d))
       likes
       "He likes it."

Why is such a sentence possible? The verb *nuhwe'* "like" is similar to its English translation in being a transitive verb; logically speaking, it is a two-place predicate. Thus, it should need to have two NPs, almost as a point of logical necessity. The reader may have noticed that when NPs are missing, the gaps are interpreted as pronouns – "he" and "it" in this case. Moreover, what pronoun to use is determined by agreement prefixes on the verb. Many languages such as Spanish use different verb forms for different subjects, depending on whether it is first person, or second person, or whatever:

(73)   a.   (el) habl*a* español.   "He speaks Spanish."
       b.   (tu) habl*as* español.   "You speak Spanish."
       c.   (yo) habl*o* español.   "I speak Spanish."

Moreover, languages that have enough of this kind of agreement typically allow one to omit the pronoun, because the information is already there on the verb; thus, it is normal to say simply *Hablo español*. Linguists often assume that there is still a pronoun present in the syntactic structure of such a sentence, but it is not pronounced. Now Mohawk is like Spanish in these respects, only more so: Mohawk verbs change form not only depending on the subject, but depending on the object as well. Thus, it is not surprising that Mohawks can leave out both subject and object pronouns unless they want to give them special emphasis.

With this in mind, we can reconsider Mohawk structures in (69) and (70). These structures are peculiar from the English perspective because there is no direct object (or the direct object is in the wrong place, depending on your terminology). However, given Mohawk's rich agreement system, it is reasonable to say that there is an object present, but it is simply one of the invisible pronouns just discussed. Then a more complete structure for (68) would be:

(74)

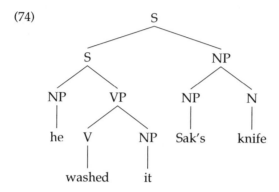

This structure does not look so unfamiliar. English too can have structures in which the true object is a pronoun, and some NP is attached to the sentence to clarify what that pronoun refers to, as shown in (75).

(75)   a.   That dress, he really likes it.
       b.   He really likes it, that dress.
       c.   That dress, he really likes it, John.

This phenomenon is called *dislocation*. It is colloquial and not particularly common in English, but it does exist. Thus, it is not really accurate to say that English and Mohawk have different structures; it is more accurate to say that Mohawk uses dislocation all the time, while English does not.

Finally, we can ask why NPs *must* be dislocated in Mohawk but not in English. Moreover, recall that embedded clauses do not need to be dislocated; rather they can appear inside the VP in Mohawk just as in English, as shown in (63)–(67). In fact, a similar contrast between NPs and clauses is found in English, although in a different part of the grammatical system. Some verbs like *believe* can have either an NP or a clause as their object:

(76)   a.   People generally believe [John]$_{NP}$.
       b.   People generally believe [that John is telling the truth]$_{CP}$.

However, when these verbs are put in the passive voice, the situation changes. The clause can still remain in its usual position after the verb, but the object NP cannot. Rather, it must be "dislocated" – in this case to the subject position:

(77) a. It is generally believed [that John is telling the truth]$_{CP}$.
      b. *It is generally believed [John]$_{NP}$.
          (Compare: [John]$_{NP}$ is generally believed –.)

Apparently putting the verb in the passive form disrupts its ability to take an NP object, but has no effect on clauses. This has led linguists to propose a principle which I state very informally as follows (a part of the case filter; Chomsky 1981):

(78) If an affix (of a certain type) is attached to a verb, it can no longer take an NP as a direct object.

Now we know that every transitive verb in Mohawk has affixes attached to it. In particular, it has an affix that agrees with the object in person, number, and gender. Suppose this agreement affix is in the same class as the passive voice affix. Then it follows that NPs will never be in the normal object position in Mohawk; they will always be dislocated. There will be no similar effect on clauses, however. If this is correct, then all of the many differences between Mohawk and English actually boil down to this:

(79) All Mohawk verbs have affixes that agree with their subject and object (but English verbs do not).

There is nothing mysterious or complex about (79); on the contrary, it is one of the first things one must face when learning Mohawk.

In closing, let us reconsider the basic question of whether Mohawk is like English. Crucially, the answer depends on what one means by the question. In one sense, Mohawk is obviously very different. In particular, the basic structure of most sentences in Mohawk is very different from that of comparable sentences in English. As a result, words can appear in any order, pronouns have different possibilities of interpretation, question words face different limitations, and so on. However, in another sense, the syntax of Mohawk and English is virtually identical. This comes out most clearly if one makes a list of the syntactic principles that hold in both languages and compares it to a list of the differences:

(80) a. *Common elements ("principles")*
          The disjoint reference condition
          The condition on extraction domains
          Question words become clause-initial
          Clauses must be "logically complete" (have the right number of NPs)
          NPs can be "dislocated" to the edge of a sentence
          The case filter, etc.
      b. *Differences ("parameters")*
          Verbs agree with both subject and object in Mohawk, not English

Almost all the principles are the same, and the one difference is a rather superficial one. However, that one difference just happens to be like a pebble that is in exactly the right position to start an avalanche: it has repercussions throughout the grammar.

Thus, this extended example should help to explicate what syntacticians mean when they speak of "Universal Grammar," and when they say that "all human languages are essentially the same." This claim makes sense, but only when one shifts from looking at languages as some kind of list of sentence structures to looking at them as a set of constraints in the minds of speakers that the sentences they form must satisfy. In other words, one must look not at particular Mohawk examples like (53) to (57), but rather at the abstract characterization of Mohawk in (80) that induces those examples. Chomsky (1986) refers to this as the shift from looking at "Externalized language" to looking at "Internalized language," a part of his emphasis on the importance of a psychological interpretation of syntactic theory. Hopefully, this example also illustrates something of the intellectual interest that surrounds the task of trying to tease out what is universal in human language and what is idiosyncratic and particular, which is a central focus of current syntactic research.

12 Generative Grammar

THOMAS WASOW

1 Introduction

1.1 "Grammar"

To most people, the word "grammar" suggests a normative enterprise, dictating what constitutes correct language use. For example, many educated English speakers would identify at least five supposed grammatical "errors" in the following sentence:

(1) Hopefully, we will be able to easily figure out who to talk to.

Yet native speakers of American English also certainly recognize that (1) would be an entirely acceptable and natural sounding sentence in ordinary discourse. Indeed, the supposedly "correct" alternative (2) would be an awkward and affected way of expressing the thought.

(2) I hope that we shall be able easily to figure out to whom to talk.

Modern linguistics has little use for this prescriptive conception of grammar. Linguists are more interested in the knowledge of English that allows native speakers to judge (1) as fully acceptable and (2) as somewhat less natural. The prescriptions of traditional grammar are attempts to impose the speech patterns of one region, class, ethnicity, or generation on speakers belonging to other groups. They may be of interest to sociologists, historians, and political scientists, but they tell us very little about the nature of language.

Language is a natural phenomenon, constituting an essential component of every human society. Linguistics is concerned with studying languages and language in general, much as biology studies living species and life in general. From this scientific perspective, the norms of prescriptive grammar are to linguistics as the American Kennel Club's breed standards are to biology: arbitrary evaluative standards of no relevance to objective description.

Linguists use the term "grammar," then, to refer to structural properties of language that have evolved naturally and that native speakers of the language have mastered without explicit instruction. These are largely properties of languages that are not even mentioned in traditional grammars, though some are addressed in foreign language instruction. They include facts about word order, for example, that *we*, *will*, and *be* in (1) must appear in that order, or else the sentence becomes unacceptable. They also include facts about the proper forms of words in particular contexts, for example, that replacing *figure* in (1) with *figured*, *figures*, or *figuring* makes the sentence unacceptable. Put in more technical jargon, "grammar" is taken by linguists to encompass syntax and morphosyntax. The term may also be construed more broadly to include principles relating linguistic forms to the meanings they express (semantics) and / or the sound patterns of languages (phonology).

1.2   *"Generative"*

The term "generative" is associated with the tradition of grammatical research initiated and inspired by the work of Noam Chomsky. This term is sometimes construed very narrowly to refer only to work directly derivative from Chomsky's. Here it will be used more broadly to refer to work generally within the Chomskyan tradition, irrespective of whether its formalism and terminology come directly from Chomsky.

Among Chomsky's most important insights is the observation (noted independently over a century earlier by the great German linguist Wilhelm von Humboldt) that there are infinitely many well-formed sentences in any natural language. This follows immediately from the fact that any limit one might impose on the length of sentences would be arbitrary: any supposedly longest English sentence S would be two words shorter than "I said S," which is surely well-formed if S is. On the other hand, a grammar, conceived of as a description of a language, should be finite.

How can we give a finite description of something infinite? Inspired by earlier work in mathematical logic and the foundations of computer science, Chomsky answered this question by proposing that we think of grammars as devices that put pieces of sentences together according to precise rules, thereby "generating" well-formed sentences. If some of the grammar rules can apply to their own outputs (in technical jargon, if some rules are "recursive"), then it is possible for finite grammars to generate infinite languages.

To illustrate this, consider the following very simple (nonlinguistic) example. The ordinary Arabic numeral system used to represent numbers has infinitely many well-formed expressions (one for each number) constructed out of ten symbols, namely, the digits "0" through "9." We can write a simple grammar for the numerals denoting positive integers with the following rules:

- Each of the digits 1, 2, 3, 4, 5, 6, 7, 8, and 9 is a numeral.
- If N is any numeral, then N0 is a numeral.
- If N is any numeral, then NN is a numeral.

One of many possible formalizations of this would be the following:

N→1	N→5	N→9
N→2	N→6	N→N0
N→3	N→7	N→NN
N→4	N→8	

Here N is the category of well-formed numerals, and the arrow can be interpreted to mean "may consist of." This little grammar generates the infinite "language" of numerals denoting positive integers, because it contains rules that are recursive (namely, the last two).

2   Tenets of Generative Grammar

Although the term "generative" orginally characterized a conception of grammars as such recursive rule systems, the term is now used somewhat more generally. In particular, what distinguishes work in generative grammar is the goal of describing languages systematically, as opposed to the more anecdotal approach of traditional grammars. While it is impossible to give a precise definition of generative grammar, there are several tenets shared by the vast majority of generative grammarians. These are summarized in the following subsections.

2.1   *Grammars should be descriptive, not prescriptive*

As discussed above, this proposition is generally accepted by modern linguists. Although it is not unique to generative grammarians, it is common to them.

2.2   *Grammars should characterize competence, not performance*

Despite its anti-prescriptivism, generative grammar is not an attempt to describe all or only the actual utterances of native speakers. This is implicit in the claim that languages are infinite: it would have been safe to assume that no sentence over one million words long will ever be uttered. But this upper bound exists because of limits on human memory and patience, not because of any linguistically interesting facts. Moreover, because of speech errors of various kinds, people frequently produce utterances that are not well-formed sentences, even by the judgments of the speakers. To distinguish between the idealized infinite languages that generative grammarians seek to describe and the far messier output of actual speakers, Chomsky introduced the terminology "competence" vs. "performance."

One common property of generative grammar in all its varieties is the focus on characterizing linguistic competence. Many generative grammarians would also like to develop models of linguistic performance, but most believe that a competence theory will be a necessary component of such a model. Put slightly differently, it is widely accepted that explaining how a language is actually used will require understanding speakers' knowledge of that language.

2.3   Grammars should be fully explicit

Traditional grammars presuppose some knowledge of the language under description and tend to focus on aspects of the language that are variable or have changed. Generative grammars are supposed to be precise rule systems that characterize the whole language, without relying on any prior knowledge of the language on the part of the reader. Many generative grammarians identify explicitness with formalization. Hence, the generative literature abounds with formalisms (though it is not always made clear how the formalisms are to be interpreted). Early work in generative grammar approached this goal of explicitness and formalization far more consistently than most recent work.

2.4   Linguistic analyses should be maximally general

If two grammars cover the same range of data, but one requires two distinct rules where the second has only one, generative grammarians take this as evidence for the superiority of the second grammar.

A famous example of this mode of reasoning is due to Postal (1964). He noted that what are called "tag questions" in English require a kind of matching between the tag and the initial portions of the main clause, as illustrated in (3). Following standard practice, asterisks are used to mark unacceptable strings.

(3)   a.   I have won, $\begin{bmatrix} \text{haven't} \\ \text{*won't} \\ \text{*aren't} \end{bmatrix} \begin{bmatrix} \text{I} \\ \text{*you} \\ \text{*we} \\ \text{*they} \end{bmatrix}$?

     b.   You will win, $\begin{bmatrix} \text{won't} \\ \text{*haven't} \\ \text{*aren't} \end{bmatrix} \begin{bmatrix} \text{you} \\ \text{*we} \\ \text{*they} \end{bmatrix}$?

Postal also observed that imperative sentences take only a restricted range of tags, though there is nothing overtly present in the initial portions of imperative sentences that the tags match.

$$(4) \quad \text{Close the door,} \begin{bmatrix} \text{won't} \\ \text{*haven't} \\ \text{*aren't} \end{bmatrix} \begin{Bmatrix} \text{you} \\ \text{*I} \\ \text{*we} \\ \text{*they} \end{Bmatrix} !$$

If we analyze imperative sentences as having an initial *you will* at some level of analysis, he reasoned, we could use a simple rule to generate tag questions on both declarative and imperative sentences. Such an analysis is said to "capture a generalization" – in this case, the generalization that tags on imperatives and declaratives are fundamentally alike. The desire to capture generalizations plays a very important role in the argumentation of generative grammar.

2.5 *The theory of grammar should make universal claims*

To the extent possible, facts about individual languages should be derived from general principles that apply to all languages. Information stipulated in the grammars of particular languages should be kept to a minimum. This is motivated in part simply by standard scientific methodological considerations: more general hypotheses are both more parsimonious and more interesting than less general ones. But it is also motivated in part by psychological concerns – specifically, by Chomsky's "argument from the poverty of the stimulus," which will be discussed in the next subsection.

The focus on the development of a general theory of grammar – "universal grammar" (UG), as Chomsky dubbed it – is perhaps the most distinctive characteristic of the generative tradition. Although other linguistic traditions involve extensive cross-linguistic comparisons resulting in important hypotheses about universal properties of language (see Croft, Chapter 14, this volume, for a sample of such work), generative grammar approaches these issues in a distinctive way. Specifically, the universals of generative grammar tend to be formulated as rather abstract principles of grammatical organization that are not directly observable in the linguistic data. Rather, their discovery and testing typically involve a complex combination of empirical observations, methodological assumptions, and inferential processes. This is in sharp contrast with more observationally transparent universals like those of Greenberg (1963), and much subsequent work on language typology. Some examples of linguistic universals in the generative style will be provided in section 4 below.

2.6 *Grammars should be psychologically relevant*

Generative grammarians characteristically (but not universally – see, for example, Katz and Postal 1991) take their theories to be relevant to psychological questions. Chomsky has been particularly outspoken on this issue, asserting that "a particular generative grammar" is "a theory concerned with the state of the mind / brain of the person who knows a particular language" (Chomsky 1986: 3).

More specifically, Chomsky has argued that a rich theory of universal grammar is necessary to account for the possibility of language acquisition. The most striking fact about human languages, he claims, is the gulf between knowledge and experience, observing that the following question, formulated by Bertrand Russell, is particularly applicable in the domain of language:

> How comes it that human beings, whose contacts with the world are brief and personal and limited, are nevertheless able to know as much as they do?

The fact that every normal human masters a language with little apparent effort or explicit instruction suggests that humans are genetically endowed with a "mental organ" specifically adapted to acquire languages of a particular kind. This is known as the "argument from the poverty of the stimulus."

While Chomsky has emphasized the issue of learnability, others have argued that work in generative grammar is relevant to psychology in other ways. For example, Bresnan (1978) argued that a generative grammar should be an integral component of a theory of language use – that is of the mental processes involved in speaking and comprehension.

3   Common Formal Elements

Since Chomsky's seminar work in the 1950s, many different theories of grammar have been articulated that fit the general characterization in the preceding sections. Almost all can be viewed as extensions of what is known as "context-free (phrase structure) grammar" (CFG).

3.1   Context-free grammar

CFG begins with the relatively uncontroversial assumption that words can be classified into categories, based on their morphological properties (that is, what changes in form they undergo through suffixation and the like), their distributional patterns (that is, what other words appear in their vicinity in sentences), and their meanings. The traditional categories of noun, verb, etc. (inherited from the grammatical studies of ancient Greece) are still quite generally employed, supplemented by a number of other categories, some of them idiosyncratic to particular theories.

A second generally accepted premise of CFG is that the words in sentences are grouped into phrases, which themselves are grouped together into larger phrases, and so on. It is common to represent the phrase structure of a sentence by means of a "tree diagram" like (5):

(5)

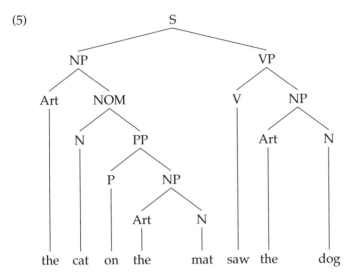

the cat on the mat saw the dog

Phrases are identified by their distributional patterns and usually function as semantic units as well. Like words, phrases are generally classified into categories; the most widely used phrasal category labels – e.g., noun phrase (NP), verb phrase (VP), prepositional phrase (PP) – derive from the categories of words that appear in canonical instances of those phrases. These words are called the "lexical heads" (or sometimes just the "heads") of the phrases.

A CFG has two parts:

- A lexicon, consisting of a list of words, with their associated grammatical categories (referred to as "lexical categories").
- A set of rules of the form A → Φ where A is a phrasal category, and "Φ" stands for any string of lexical and / or phrasal categories. The arrow is to be interpreted as meaning, roughly, "may consist of." These rules are called "phrase structure rules."

The left-hand side of each rule specifies a phrase type (including the sentence as a type of phrase), and the right-hand side gives a possible pattern for that type of phrase. Because phrasal categories can appear on the right-hand sides of rules, it is possible to have phrases embedded within other phrases. In fact, some types of phrases (such as NPs and PPs) can be embedded in other phrases of the same type, giving CFGs the recursive character needed to generate infinite languages.

A CFG normally has one or more phrasal categories that are designated as "initial symbols." These are the types of phrases that can stand alone as sentences in the language. Most simple CFGs have just one initial symbol, namely "S." Any string of words that can be derived from one of the initial symbols by means of a sequence of applications of the rules of the grammar is generated by the grammar. The language a grammar generates is simply the collection of all of the sentences it generates.

In the 1950s and early 1960s, Chomsky, Postal, and others argued that simple CFGs lacked the descriptive power to account for all of the syntactic regularities of natural languages. Although some of those arguments have since been called into question, the conclusion remains generally accepted (see Savitch, et al. 1987 for a collection of relevant articles).

3.2 *Transformational grammar*

Chomsky's earliest work suggests that the shortcomings of CFG could be remedied by associating with each sentence of a natural language, not just one tree but a sequence of trees. The initial tree in each sequence would be generated by a CFG (sometimes called the "base") and subsequent trees would be derived through a series of transformations – that is, rules that modified the trees in precisely specified ways.

This can be illustrated with the phenomena of tag questions and imperatives described above (see Baker's contribution to this volume for further illustrations). Space limitations require substantial simplifications: only non-negative sentences with pronouns as subjects and auxiliary verbs will be considered here. A simple transformational grammar for these phenomena might include the base grammar in (6) and the transformations in (7) and (8). Parentheses are used to indicate that an element is optional – for example, the fourth rule in (6) says a VP may consist of a verb, with or without a following NP. In (7) and (8), "⇒" means "may be transformed into."

(6)   A lexicon for English, plus:
        S→NP AUX VP
        NP→Pronoun
        NP→(Art) N
        VP→V (NP)

(7)   Tag formation transformation:

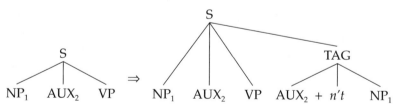

(8)   Imperative transformation:

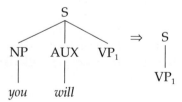

(7) takes as input trees for simple declarative sentences, and produces as outputs trees for the corresponding sentences with tags. It does this by copying the auxiliary verb, inserting a contracted negative, and copying the subject. (8) derives imperative sentences from declaratives starting with *you will* simply by deleting these two words (and the nodes right above them).

On this analysis, (4) is derived from the same base tree as *You will close the door*, by application of the two transformations, in the order given.

Early generative work was known as "transformational grammar," because the addition of transformations to CFG was seen as the crucial innovation. Throughout the history of generative grammar, transformational theories have had many advocates – always including Chomsky. Since the late 1970s, however, non-transformational alternatives have also been extensively developed.

3.3   Other enhancements to CFG

Several enhancements to simple CFG have been adopted in transformational and non-transformational generative theories alike. One of the earliest was the addition of a semantic component. It is evident that the acceptability of a sentence is influenced by what the intended meaning is, and it is often difficult to draw a sharp line between syntactic and semantic analyses. Consider, for example, the facts in (9).

(9)   a.   I excused $\begin{Bmatrix} \text{myself} \\ \text{*me} \end{Bmatrix}$.

      b.   He excused himself. [*He* and *himself* must refer to the same person]

      c.   He excused him. [*He* and *him* must refer to different people].

The facts in (9a) are manifestly about the distribution of the words *myself* and *me*. The contrast between (9b) and (9c) is evidently a semantic one. Yet there is clearly a single generalization covering both contrasts, namely, that in the configuration NP_1-V-NP_2, NP_2 can be a reflexive pronoun (that is, a form ending in -*self* or -*selves*) just in case it refers to the same individual as NP_1. This generalization will be developed in more detail below. For now, it can serve as an illustration of the role of semantics in grammar.

Another enhancement of CFG that has been generally adopted in generative grammar is the use of non-atomic category labels for words and phrases. For example, in the mini-grammar presented in (6), AUX and V are distinct categories, with no more in common than, say, N and V. But what this grammar calls AUX has traditionally been treated as a species of verb. This makes sense when one considers the word *have*. In a sentence like *We have won*, (6) would treat it as an AUX (consider *We have won, haven't we?*); in a sentence like *We will have fun*, (6) must treat *have* as an instance of V (consider *We will have fun, won't we?*).

There are many more arguments for allowing words and phrases to be treated as the same in some respects but different in others. This is accomplished formally by replacing atomic category labels with more complex information structures. In particular, almost all varieties of generative grammar employ "feature structures" as category labels. Feature structures consist of pairings of features with values. A feature is simply a name for something used in classifying words or phrases; features are associated with multiple values, corresponding to properties of the words or phrases in question. For example, nouns can be subclassified into proper and common nouns, and into singular and plural nouns. Representing this with features would involve positing two features, say COMMON and NUMBER, each of which has two values (in English, at least). Then the two features could be used in representing the categories of some representative words as follows:

$$(10)\quad child \begin{bmatrix} \text{COMMON} + \\ \text{NUMBER} \ \ \text{sing} \end{bmatrix} \qquad London \begin{bmatrix} \text{COMMON} - \\ \text{NUMBER} \ \ \text{sing} \end{bmatrix}$$

$$children \begin{bmatrix} \text{COMMON} + \\ \text{NUMBER} \ \ \text{pl} \end{bmatrix} \qquad Alps \begin{bmatrix} \text{COMMON} - \\ \text{NUMBER} \ \ \text{pl} \end{bmatrix}$$

All of the feature structures in (10) might also have something like [POS noun] (where "POS" is for "part of speech").

Treating categories as bundles of features makes it possible to represent large numbers of grammatical categories quite compactly, since every different combination of features and values is a different category. This allows grammarians to make fine distinctions, while still permitting reference to large classes of expressions. Some form of decomposition of categories into features has consequently been adopted in almost every variety of generative grammar. So long as there are only a finite number of features, each of which has only a finite number of possible values, this decomposition does not fundamentally alter the descriptive power of CFG. It does, however, make it possible to capture generalizations across categories of words and phrases, as well as characterizing categories at more or less fine-grained levels.

Some theories have taken this process one step further, however, allowing the values of features to be feature structures themselves. This constitutes a more fundamental enhancement of CFGs, allowing a great deal of information to be encoded into the representations of grammatical categories. As will become evident below, this increased descriptive power makes possible interesting alternatives to certain widely accepted transformational analyses.

One of the advantages of decomposing categories into features is that it permits efficient reference to classes of categories. For example, one can refer to all singular nouns with the feature specification

$$\begin{bmatrix} \text{POS} & \text{noun} \\ \text{NUMBER} & \text{sing} \end{bmatrix},$$

leaving other properties unspecified, including gender, case, and whether it is proper or common. This sort of "underspecification" is widely exploited in generative grammar.

One particularly influential case of underspecification is the suggestion by Chomsky (1970) that the phrase structure rules of languages could be reduced to a few very general schemas, with highly underspecified categories on both sides of the rules. This idea has been developed in many different ways, but has entered into most theories of generative grammar. In its simplest version, it holds that all phrases should be viewed as projections of lexical heads and that phrases uniformly have three levels: the lexical head, an intermediate level, and the full phrase. These are often designated as X, X', and X" (where X can stand for any combination of features). Then the principal phrase structure rules could be schematized as follows (where the superscripted asterisk is an abbreviation for zero or more occurrences of the immediately preceding symbol):

(11) $X'' \rightarrow (Y'') X'$ $X' \rightarrow X Y''^*$

These rule schemas embody the claim that all phrases have the same basic structure, consisting of a lexical head, possibly followed by some other phrases (known as "complements") and possibly preceded by a single phrase (known as the "specifier"). Variants of this idea go under the label "X-bar theory." Although there are many different versions of X-bar theory, schematizing the phrase structure rules through underspecification of the categories is common to many generative theories.

The rule schemas in (11), as stated, do not appear to be good candidates for universal grammar, because they stipulate particular orders of elements. But there are languages (such as Japanese) in which lexical heads consistently come at the ends of phrases, and others (such as Irish) in which lexical heads come at the beginnings of phrases. It has been proposed (e.g., by Gazdar and Pullum (1981)) that the information about hierarchical structure and the information about left-to-right ordering of elements should be decoupled. That way, the schemas in (11) could be regarded as universal, up to the ordering of elements on the right-hand sides. This is another idea that has emerged in a number of different generative theories.

4   Some Phenomena Studied by Generative Grammarians

The literature of generative grammar is full of detailed examinations of myriad syntactic phenomena in a wide variety of languages. Most analyses depend on assumptions that are controversial. Nevertheless, the field has made numerous genuine discoveries. Although different schools of thought employ disparate formalisms and terminology, we know far more about the structure of language than we did in the 1950s, thanks to research in generative grammar. This section provides an overview of two areas in which generative grammarians have made clear progress.

4.1   Binding principles

The examples in (9) above illustrate that English has two different types of pronouns, namely reflexives (*-self / -selves* forms) and non-reflexives. While *myself* and *me* both refer to the speaker (as does *I*), the environments in which they can be used differ. In particular, consider the following contrasts:

(12)   a.   *I support me.
       b.   I support myself.
       c.   They support me.
       d.   *They support myself.

(13)   a.   I don't expect them to support me.
       b.   *I don't expect them to support myself.
       c.   *They don't expect me to support me.
       d.   They don't expect me to support myself.

The following two generalizations (known as the "binding principles") roughly summarize the distributional difference between the two types of pronouns:

- A.   A reflexive pronoun must have a local antecedent.
- B.   A non-reflexive pronoun may not have a local antecedent.

For present purposes, "antecedent" can be taken to mean a preceding NP with the same reference. The term "local" is meant to convey the observation that the antecedent of a reflexive should not be too far away. However, giving a precise definition of "local" for these principles is not a trivial problem, as evidenced by examples like the following:

(14)   a.   The house has a fence around $\left\{ \begin{array}{l} \text{it} \\ \text{*itself} \end{array} \right\}$.

       b.   We wound the rope around $\left\{ \begin{array}{l} \text{it} \\ \text{itself} \end{array} \right\}$. [*it ≠ the rope*]

       c.   I wrapped the blanket around $\left\{ \begin{array}{l} \text{me} \\ \text{myself} \end{array} \right\}$.

These examples show that locality cannot be measured simply in terms of number of words or phrases intervening between the pronoun and its antecedent, for the three examples all have the same number of words and phrases.

There is a rich literature working out the details of the basic ideas in principles A and B above. These details need not concern us here. What is of interest is that English is by no means unique in having these two different kinds of pronouns. Indeed, a great many languages have parallel sets of pronouns that differ in just this way: one kind requires local antecedents and the other prohibits local antecedents. Just what counts as "local" (an issue we will return to) exhibits some cross-language variation, but the similarity is more striking than the difference. There is no a priori reason to expect languages to have more than one kind of pronoun, yet something like the principles above hold in language after language.

Notice, incidentally, that the binding principles interact in an interesting way with the analysis of imperatives suggested in section 3.2. Assuming that the principles are applied prior to the deletion of *you*, the principles correctly predict the following:

(15) a. Protect $\left\{ \begin{array}{l} \text{*myself} \\ \text{yourself} \\ \text{*himself} \end{array} \right\}$!

b. Protect $\left\{ \begin{array}{l} \text{me} \\ \text{*you} \\ \text{him} \end{array} \right\}$!

This provides further evidence that imperatives should be treated as having second-person subjects at some level of analysis.

4.2 Filler-gap dependencies

Context-free grammars provide a formal mechanism for expressing relationships between elements (words or phrases) that are close to one another in a sentence. But many languages have constructions involving dependencies between elements that may be far apart. An example of this in English is what are known as "*wh*-questions" – that is, questions requiring more than a yes-or-no answer, and hence containing one of the "*wh*-words" (*who, what, where*, etc.).

To illustrate this, consider the examples in (16).

(16) a. Pat relies $\left\{ \begin{array}{l} \text{on} \\ \text{upon} \\ \text{*of} \\ \text{*to} \end{array} \right\}$ a student.

b. $\left\{ \begin{array}{l} \text{On} \\ \text{Upon} \\ \text{*Of} \\ \text{*To} \end{array} \right\}$ which student does Pat rely?

c. $\left\{ \begin{array}{l} \text{On} \\ \text{Upon} \\ \text{*Of} \\ \text{*To} \end{array} \right\}$ which student does Kim say we think Pat relies?

(16a) shows that the verb *rely* requires a prepositional phrase complement beginning with *on* or *upon*; (16b) shows that, in a *wh*-question, although this phrase comes at the beginning of the sentence, rather than after the verb, the same restriction on the choice of prepositions is maintained; (16c) illustrates that this dependency between the verb and preposition holds even when lots of other material is inserted between them. In fact, there is no limit to the amount of additional text that can intervene.

Similarly, the dependency between verb form and the number (singular or plural) of its subject is preserved, even when the subject is a *wh*-phrase that is far away in the string of words.

(17) a.   The $\left\{\begin{matrix} \text{teacher} \\ \text{*teachers} \end{matrix}\right\}$ dislikes one student.

b.   The $\left\{\begin{matrix} \text{*teacher} \\ \text{teachers} \end{matrix}\right\}$ dislike one student.

c.   Which $\left\{\begin{matrix} \text{*teacher} \\ \text{teachers} \end{matrix}\right\}$ would the parents all claim dislike one student?

d.   Which $\left\{\begin{matrix} \text{teacher} \\ \text{*teachers} \end{matrix}\right\}$ would the parents all claim dislikes one student?

More generally, *wh*-phrases in such questions behave in some ways as though they were in a different position from where they actually occur. Dependencies like preposition selection or verb agreement, which are normally local, can hold between *wh*-phrases and elements far away in the sentence. This can be further demonstrated with the binding principles:

(18)   Which dog do you think we saw scratch $\left\{\begin{matrix} \text{*yourself} \\ \text{you} \\ \text{itself} \\ \text{it } [\textit{it} \neq \textit{which dog}] \end{matrix}\right\}$?

On the surface, *which dog* does not look like the required local antecedent for *itself*, because of the intervening material *do you think we saw*. Moreover, *you* cannot serve as the antecedent for a reflexive object of *scratch*, even though it is closer to the object position. The binding pattern here is just what principles A and B would predict if *which dog* were in the subject position of *scratch*.

A very natural way to account for such relationships in a transformational grammar is to posit a rule that moves *wh*-phrases to the front of the sentence. Then the *wh*-phrases in (16)–(18) can be generated initially in a position close to the relevant verb or reflexive, and the dependencies can be licensed locally, prior to movement.

With such a treatment of *wh*-questions and similar constructions, a question that naturally arises is whether the displaced elements (often referred to as "fillers") move from their initial positions (known as "gaps") to their final positions in one fell swoop or by means of a sequence of smaller movements. That is, in an example like (18), does the filler *which dog*, move from the gap position adjacent to *scratch* in one long movement, as in (19a), or in several smaller movements, as in (19b).

(19) a.

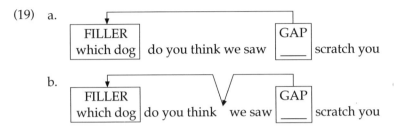

b.

The issue can be formulated in a more theory-neutral way by asking whether the relationship between a gap and its filler is a direct one, or is instead mediated by intervening material. This was a hotly debated topic within generative grammar in the 1970s (sometimes labeled the "swooping vs. looping" controversy). A real measure of progress in the field is that this debate has been definitively settled in favor of "looping." All generative grammarians now recognize that long-distance filler-gap dependencies are mediated by the intervening material.

The key evidence for this comes from languages which require some sort of marking of clauses that intervene between fillers and gaps. Quite a number of such cases have been discovered, from a wide range of language families (see Zaenen 1983 for presentation of a few). Exactly where in the intervening clauses the marking occurs, and what form it takes varies from language to language (though there seem to be some regularities).

A clear and relatively simple example is the relative clause construction[1] in Irish. Irish relative clauses, like those in English, immediately follow the noun they modify, and must contain a gap. The filler for the gap is the noun the clause modifies. Now consider the following examples (adapted from McCloskey 1979):

(20) a. Mheas   mé gur thuig   mé an t-úrscéal
          thought I   that understood I   the novel
          "I thought that I understood the novel."

      b. an t-úrscéal a   mheas mé a   thuig   mé
          the novel   that thought I   that understood I
          "the novel that I thought I understood"

      c. Shíl   mé go mbeadh sé ann
          thought I   that would-be he there
          "I thought that he would be there."

      d. an fear a   shíl   mé a   bheadh   ann
          the man that thought I   that would-be there
          "the man that I thought would be there"

e.   Dúirt mé gur shíl   mé go   mbeadh sé ann
     said I   that thought I   that would-be he there
     I said that I thought that he would be there."

f.   an fear <u>a</u>   <u>dúirt mé a</u>   <u>shíl</u>   <u>mé a</u>   <u>bheadh</u> ann
     the man that said I   that thought I   that would-be there
     "the man that I said that I thought would be there"

g.   an fear <u>a</u>   <u>shíl</u>   go mbeadh sé ann
     the man that thought that would-be he there
     "the man that thought he would be there"

h.   an fear <u>a</u>   <u>dúirt sé</u> <u>a</u>   <u>shíl</u>   go mbeadh sé ann
     the man that said he that thought that would-be he there
     "the man that said he thought he would be there"

i.   an fear <u>a</u>   <u>dúirt</u> gur shíl   sé go   mbeadh sé ann
     the man that said that thought he that would-be he there
     "the man that said he thought he would be there"

Underlining indicates the regions of these sentences that are between gaps and their fillers. That is, the word immediately preceding each underlined piece is a filler for a gap located immediately after the underlining. Now look at the words that have been translated as "that." Where there is no underlining, the Irish equivalent of "that" is either *go* or *gur* (the difference between them is not relevant to the present discussion). But wherever "that" translates an underlined word, the word it translates is *a*. These words are known as "complementizers" (see Baker, chapter 11, this volume, for more discussion of complementizers), because they introduce clausal complements to verbs like *mheas* ("thought"), *shíl* (also translated as "thought"), and *dúirt* ("said"). Examples like those in (20) indicate that Irish employs different complementizers in the region between a filler and a gap than elsewhere.

Modern transformational analyses of filler-gap relationships posit movement through a series of intermediate positions. This fits well with the Irish data, if the complementizer *a* serves as a special gateway through which long-distance movements must pass.

4.3   Island constraints

The notion of gateways for filler-gap dependencies has also been useful in discussions of another much-studied set of phenomena. Although there is no bound on the distance between fillers and gaps, there are a number of constraints on the relative positions in which fillers and their corresponding gaps may appear. These are known as "island constraints," following Ross (1967).

One such restriction on filler-gap dependencies is that the gap may not be in a relative clause if the filler is outside of it. Thus, for example, *wh*-phrases in

English questions cannot fill gaps inside of relative clauses, as illustrated in (21). The relative clauses are enclosed in square brackets, and the gap positions are marked "___".

(21) a. *Which dog did you criticize the person [who kicked ___]?
      b. *How many sources does the prosecutor have evidence [which was confirmed by ___]?
      c. *Who did everyone envy the writer [whose book claimed ___ was the real Deep Throat]?

If a *wh*-phrase has to pass through intervening complementizer positions on its way from its initial positions (the gap) to its surface (filler) position, then it seems natural to block examples like (21) on the grounds that the relative clauses already have *wh*-phrases (*who*, *which*, and *whose book*) in their complementizer positions. Such an analysis would also rule out gaps internal to embedded questions, as in (22).

(22) a. *Which dog did you ask [who had kicked ___]?
      b. *How many sources does the defense wonder [why the prosecutor asked for ___]?
      c. *Who did everyone inquire [whose book claimed ___ was the real Deep Throat]?

Not all island constraints are covered by this. For example, a gap cannot be in coordinate conjoined structures not containing its filler, unless all conjuncts have gaps filled by the same filler:

(23) a. *What did they [buy ___and forget their credit card at the store]?
      b. What did they [buy ___ and forget ___ at the store]?

A great deal of research has gone into island constraints: classifying them, checking their cross-linguistic variation, and, most extensively, seeking explanations for them. The question of explaining island constraints will be addressed again below.

5 Varieties of Generative Grammar

As noted earlier, generative grammar is not so much a theory as a family of theories, or a school of thought. The preceding sections have focussed on common elements: shared assumptions and goals, widely used formal devices, and generally accepted empirical results. (For convenience, the idiom of transformational grammar has been employed in the descriptions of tag questions, imperatives, and filler-gap dependencies, but the discussion in section 5.2 below shows that this was not essential.) This section explores some of the ways in which generative theories differ from one another. There are too many such theories to provide a comprehensive survey (see Sag and Wasow (1999: appendix B) for a brief overview of fourteen theories of grammar), but the following sections characterize some of the major divisions, beginning with a brief description of the historical development of transformational grammar.

5.1 Transformational theories

Transformational grammar has evolved considerably over the decades (see Newmeyer 1986). The earliest work (Chomsky 1957) was concerned largely with showing the inadequacy of context-free grammar for the analysis of natural languages, and with providing precise, explicit transformational descriptions of particular phenomena (largely from English). In the 1960s, transformational grammarians began paying more attention to the relationship between syntax and semantics, leading to heated debates over the best way to incorporate a semantic component into transformational theory. At the same time, the emphasis turned away from providing rule systems in careful detail to exploring the wider implications of transformational analyses. This was when questions about universal grammar and the relevance of linguistic theory to psychology came to the fore (Chomsky 1965). Since the early 1970s, the primary focus of transformationalists has been on developing a highly restrictive theory of grammar – that is, one that narrowly constrains what kinds of descriptions are possible (Chomsky 1981). The goal of this enterprise, as articulated by Chomsky, is to account for language learnability by making the theory so restrictive that a descriptively accurate grammar of any language can be inferred on the basis of the kind of data available to a young child.

As the goals and style of transformational grammar have evolved over the years, the technical details have changed, as well – many almost beyond recognition. Through all these changes, however, this line of research has maintained the idea that sentences are derived by means of a sequence of operations that modify tree structures in prescribed ways. Inherent in this conception is a directionality: derivations proceed from underlying structures to surface forms. This directionality found its way into analyses sketched in this chapter wherever one rule or principle was said to operate "before" another. Examples are the treatment of imperative tags, in which the tag formation transformation had to operate before the imperative rule, and in the account of island constraints in terms of one *wh*-phrase getting into the complementizer position before another one needed to move there.

Many linguists find this sort of talk troublesome. Grammars are supposed to be characterizations of linguistic competence – that is, the knowledge of language that underlies both speaking and understanding. Speaking involves articulating thoughts – going from meanings to sounds; understanding involves extracting meanings from sounds. So, in an intuitive sense, these processes operate in opposite directions. The knowledge of language that is common to both should be process-neutral and hence non-directional. It is possible to regard the talk of operations and directions as strictly metaphorical, a move that has sometimes been advocated. But translating from procedural formulations into more static ones is not always straightforward.

The problem is not just that readers tend improperly to read some psychological significance into the directionality inherent in transformational derivations (though this tendency certainly exists). But psycholinguists and computational linguists who have tried to use transformational grammars as components in models of language use have found that transformational derivations are typically not easily reversible. Precisely worked out systems to parse sentences – whether they are intended as models of human performance or as parts of computer systems for understanding languages – have almost never incorporated the transformational analyses proposed by theoretical linguists. These analyses do not lend themselves to being used in going from the surface form of a sentence to its meaning. Moreover, as noted by Fodor et al. (1974), psycholinguists have been largely unable to find behavioral evidence for the psychological reality of the intermediate stages of transformational derivations. While the nature of the intermediate stages posited by transformational grammarians has changed radically since Fodor et al. made that observation, the observation itself remains accurate.

5.2 Non-transformational analyses

A variety of alternatives to transformational grammar have been developed (see, e.g., Gazdar et al. 1985, Bresnan in press, Steedman 1996, Pollard and Sag 1994). Some grammatical theories have questioned the basic conception of phrase structure embodied in tree diagrams (e.g., Hudson 1984), but most are less radical departures. Instead, they build on context-free grammar, providing enhancements designed for the description of natural languages. This section offers a sample of what such descriptions are like by revisiting some of the phenomena discussed in earlier sections.

Consider first the imperative construction. Imperatives behave as though they had a second-person subject (i.e., *you*), based on evidence from tags and reflexives; but no subject appears in imperative sentences. The transformational analysis offered above posits two distinct trees for imperative sentences, one with a subject and one without. An alternative approach is to posit a single tree without an overt subject phrase, but with the information necessary to get the facts about tags and reflexives right.

Suppose that the category of a word is a complex feature structure (see section 3.3 above) that contains within it at least the following: (i) information about what other kinds of elements it can appear with; (ii) information about its semantics; and (iii) information about how the syntactic information in (i) is linked to the semantic information in (ii). For example, the lexical entry for the verb *protects* should indicate (i) that it requires a third-person singular

NP subject and an NP object; (ii) that it denotes the protection relation; and (iii) the roles played in that relation by the NPs' referents, namely, that the referent of the subject protects the referent of the object. One possible formalization of this information is the following:[2]

(24)
$$
\begin{bmatrix}
protects \\
\begin{array}{ll}
\text{POS} & \text{verb} \\
\text{FORM} & \text{present-tense} \\
\\
\text{SUBJ} & \begin{bmatrix} \text{NP}_1 \\ \text{PER} \quad \text{3rd} \\ \text{NUM} \quad \text{sing} \end{bmatrix} \\
\\
\text{OBJ} & \text{NP}_2 \\
\text{SEM} & \underline{protect} <\text{NP}_1, \text{NP}_2>
\end{array}
\end{bmatrix}
$$

In most cases, the arguments of the semantic relation (that is, the elements between the angle brackets) are linked one-to-one to the syntactic arguments, such as the subject and object. That is the case in (24). In imperatives and some other constructions, however, there may be a mismatch. So, for example, the lexical entry for the imperative use of the verb *protect* might be something like (25).

(25)
$$
\begin{bmatrix}
protect \\
\begin{array}{ll}
\text{POS} & \text{verb} \\
\text{FORM} & \text{imperative} \\
\\
\text{SUBJ} & \text{none} \\
\text{OBJ} & \text{NP}_2 \\
\\
\text{SEM} & \underline{protect} < \begin{bmatrix} \text{NP}_1 \\ \text{PER} \quad \text{2nd} \end{bmatrix}, \text{NP}_2>
\end{array}
\end{bmatrix}
$$

This representation incorporates both the information that imperative *protect* has a second-person argument and that it has no subject. Further, the second-person argument is the one that plays the protector role in the semantics.

Now, in order to get facts like (15) right, it is necessary to interpret the binding principles as making reference to semantic argument structures. That is, the term "local" in the binding principles, which was left undefined in the earlier discussion, can now be taken to mean "in the argument structure of the same predicate." Thus, principle A now says that a reflexive pronoun must have an antecedent that is an argument of the same predicate.

This characterization of locality makes an interesting new prediction: a reflexive pronoun in object position may not have an antecedent that is only part of the subject. That is, examples like (26) are correctly ruled out.

(26) a. *Your mother protects yourself.
    b. *A picture of them upset themselves.

A definition of "local" in terms of simple proximity (based on either word strings or trees) would very likely not cover (26).

Filler-gap dependencies can be handled in a way that is at least partially analogous. A feature – call it GAP – taking another feature structure as its value can encode what is displaced. That is, the value of GAP provides the information that there is a phrase missing in the environment, and specifies what properties the missing phrase should have. This information is represented on every node in the tree between the position of the gap and that of the filler. For example, in a sentence like *What would you like?* the category of *like* would include the information that it has no object, but that it has a GAP value that is linked to the second semantic argument of *like*, as in (27a). This GAP information would be shared by the VP and S nodes above *like* in the tree, as in (27b).

(27) a.
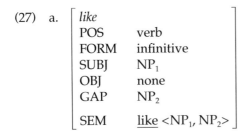

$$\begin{bmatrix} like \\ \text{POS} \quad verb \\ \text{FORM} \quad infinitive \\ \text{SUBJ} \quad NP_1 \\ \text{OBJ} \quad none \\ \text{GAP} \quad NP_2 \\ \\ \text{SEM} \quad \underline{like} <NP_1, NP_2> \end{bmatrix}$$

    b.
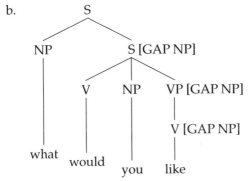

The phrase structure rule licensing the top part of this tree (where the gap is filled) must specify that the features on the NP must match those in the value of the GAP feature. The rule, then, is something like (28), where the identity of the subscripts is intended to indicate identity of all features.

(28) S → X″$_1$ S[GAP X″$_1$]

Informally, what (28) says is that a sentence containing a gap may be combined with a phrase of the appropriate type on its left to form a complete sentence (where the appropriate type of phrase is one that has the properties of the missing element that are encoded in the GAP value).

In addition, a principle is required that will guarantee that GAP values are shared between a node and the one immediately above it in a tree, except where rule (28) fills the gap. A GAP value on a node says that there is a gap somewhere within that phrase, and the filler for that gap is outside the phrase; the value of the GAP feature gives the syntactic details of the displaced element.

Many details have been left out of this account, but this minimal sketch is enough to address some of the phenomena discussed in sections 4.2 and 4.3. First of all, the fact that local requirements can be satisfied by a distant filler follows from the fact that the filler must share all its features with the GAP value. Any local requirements on the GAP value must therefore be met by the filler. Consider, for example, (18). If a reflexive pronoun appears as the object of *scratch*, then principle A requires an antecedent that is also an argument of the *scratch* relation. The feature structure for *scratch* in this sentence identifies the GAP value with the first argument of the *scratch* relation, and this GAP value must match the features of the filler, *which dog*. Hence, *which dog*, but not *you* can be the antecedent of a reflexive in (18), despite their positions in the sentence.

Turning now to the swooping vs. looping controversy, it is evident that no such issue arises in this non-transformational analysis. The information about gaps that must be available at the position of the filler is transmitted through the intervening structure. Hence, the presence of a gap in a phrase is necessarily encoded in the category of the phrase. Phenomena like the Irish data in (20) are easy to account for: the choice of complementizer differs depending on whether the clause introduced has a GAP value.

Similarly, island constraints can be straightforwardly formulated in terms of the GAP feature. In fact, if GAP is formulated as suggested above, the island constraints discussed here are almost automatic consequences. Relative clauses and embedded questions are constructions that involve filler-gap dependencies. As long as GAP can have only one value, this makes it impossible to introduce a second gap inside one of these constructions. For example, in an embedded question like *who had kicked that dog* in (29), rule (28) licenses the combination of the filler *who* with the S[GAP NP] *had kicked that dog*.

(29)   You asked who had kicked that dog.

If one tried to question the object of *kicked*, yielding (22a), the phrase *had kicked* would need to have two different GAP values.[3]

The facts illustrated in (23) – that filler-gap dependencies in coordinate constructions (i.e., phrases conjoined by *and* or *or*) are impossible unless they involve all conjuncts – are natural consequences of the analysis in terms of GAP. Coordinate conjuncts must share most syntactic features. For example, words with different parts of speech cannot usually be conjoined, and a VP whose FORM value is present-tense cannot be conjoined with one that is [FORM infinitive]. This is illustrated in (30).

(30) a. *Pat became famous and away.
     b. *Everyone wishes for comfort and happy.
     c. *Chris eats snails and drink wine.

If GAP is one of those features that must be identical across conjuncts, then facts like (23) are an immediate consequence. In a coordinate structure, either all conjuncts lack any GAP value, or they all have the same GAP value. That is, they either all are gap-free, or they all have a gap with the same filler.

6 The Future of Generative Grammar

Despite the variety of generative theories of grammar that have been put forward, the field has been dominated throughout its history by the work of one individual, Noam Chomsky. He was its founder; he has been its most prolific innovator; and the mainstream of generative research has always followed his lead. Even the proponents of alternative theories (such as the non-transformational approach sketched in the previous section) generally take work of Chomsky's as the point of departure for their proposals.

In the early years of generative grammar, the field was constituted largely by Chomsky and his students and collaborators. Over the decades, however, the number of generative grammarians has grown exponentially. Under these circumstances, it is remarkable that Chomsky has retained his dominant position. It seems likely that this will eventually change.

Given a saturated academic job market, increasing numbers of linguists are seeking employment in industry. This puts pressure on the field to give more attention to potential applications of its theories. The most obvious type of application for work in generative grammar would be in the development of natural language technologies – that is, computer programs that deal with human languages, e.g., doing machine translation, information retrieval from text files, summarization of texts, and the like. To the extent that such applications motivate theoretical work, considerations of computational tractability are likely to play an increasingly important role in theory construction. Likewise, such applications call for looking at how people actually use language, rather than focussing exclusively on what is grammatically possible. The investigation of real usage data is greatly facilitated by the availability of large on-line text files, which can be sampled and analyzed with computational tools that did not exist until quite recently. This is already having a noticeable effect on the sorts of data used by generative grammarians in their theoretical arguments.

These potential changes should not be worrisome. The history of generative grammar is one of numerous upheavals, as Chomsky has modified the foundations of the theory. These upheavals have been accompanied by vigorous debates and lively competition from alternative frameworks. The result has been – and promises to continue to be – a robust line of research that has greatly enriched our understanding of human linguistic abilities.

NOTES

1   Relative clauses are noun (or noun phrase) modifiers, such as the bracketed portion of the following:

    (i)   The student [that you rely on] isn't here yet.

2   This representation glosses over a great deal, including how the formalism is to be interpreted. Italics have been used in place of what should probably be a phonological representation, and underlining is used to designate a semantic relation, with the arguments in the relation listed immediately following, enclosed in angle brackets. The information in (24) also needs to be augmented by characterizations of subject and object in terms of tree configurations, but this is straightforward, at least for English.

3   Both this explanation for these island constraints and the transformational one based on the idea of a blocked gateway rely on the presence of a filler-gap dependency in the embedded structure to establish its status as an island. This seems plausible for English, since, overlapping filler-gap dependencies are not in general possible. Hence, in questions with multiple *wh*-words, only one can be a filler:

    (i)   What did Pat give to whom?
    (ii)   To whom did Pat give what?
    (iii) *What to whom did Pat give?
    (iv)   *To whom what did Pat give?

But there are other languages (e.g., Polish and Greek) that permit analogs to (iii) and (iv). In those languages, GAP would need to be allowed to take multiple values (or a value that is a list of feature structures). Unfortunately, the correlation between restrictions on overlapping filler-gap dependencies and island constraints is not perfect, so these matters remain issues of ongoing research.

13 Functional Linguistics

ROBERT D. VAN VALIN, JR

1 Introduction

If one were to take an informal survey among non-linguists regarding the primary function of human language, the overwhelmingly most common answer would be, "language is used for communication." This is the commonsense view of what language is for. It might, therefore, come as a surprise to many people that some of the most prominent linguists in the field reject this view and that many others hold that the fact that language may be used for communication is largely, if not completely, *irrelevant* to its study and analysis. Chomsky, for example, maintains that "human language is a system for free expression of thought, essentially independent of stimulus control, need-satisfaction or instrumental purpose" (1980: 239), and rejects as a "vulgar, instrumental" view of language the idea that communication is a necessary or even significant function of language (1975: 56–7, 1980: 229–30). Not all linguists share Chomsky's view, however, and many are strongly committed to a view of language which takes its role in communication as central to its study and analysis; they are a minority in the field at present. Such linguists are referred to as *functionalists*, and the general term applied to this approach is *functional linguistics*. Within contemporary linguistics there is an opposition between functionalists, on the one hand, and *formalists*, on the other, formalists being those linguists who are in substantial agreement with Chomsky's position. As we will see later, this distinction has evolved into a more subtle and complex opposition than it might seem at first glance.

The goal of this chapter is to introduce the reader to the basic ideas of functional linguistics and to give an account of how the ideas that today constitute functional linguistics arose. It will also be explained how the majority of professional linguists came to adopt a view of language which is so strikingly at odds with the view held by non-linguists.[1] In the next section, a number of terms and distinctions will be introduced that are relevant to elucidating functionalist and formalist approaches to the study of language. In the following section, a brief history of twentieth-century linguistics will be given and the development of the relevant ideas about language structure and function will be sketched. In the final sections, contemporary functional linguistics will be characterized and contrasted with formal linguistics, to see how genuine the opposition really is.

2   Communicative Functions of Language

What does the proposition "the primary function of language is communication" actually mean? What are the communicative functions of language? Many traditional accounts portray communication as being the conveying of propositions from the mind of one interlocutor to the mind of one or more other interlocutors, and the propositions are about some state of affairs, real or imagined. In the linguistic depiction of states of affairs, reference is made to entities in the states of affairs, and predications are made about actions involving the entities or relations among the entities in them. In this way speakers construct linguistic representations of situations, as in (1).

(1)   The boy ate the bread in the kitchen.

There are three referring elements and one predicating element in (1): *the boy* (referring to one participant in the event) *ate* (predicating an action of the boy) *the bread* (referring to the second participant) *in the kitchen* (referring to the location where the event took place). Hence reference and predication are often taken to be the fundamental communicative functions of language.

But language is used for much more than representing states of affairs. It is used in all kinds of verbal social interactions: asking questions, giving commands, making promises, expressing wishes, etc. These different uses are known as speech acts (Searle 1969). Foley and Van Valin (1984) emphasize the social nature of language use and stress that speaking is a kind of social activity:

> Communication is often construed in a narrow sense to mean "conveying propositional information from one person to another", and within such a view linguistic behavior consists primarily of referring and predicating about situations in the world, all other types of verbal behavior, e.g. asking questions or giving commands, being derivative of it. Silverstein (1976, 1977, [1987]) has cogently argued that such a view is fundamentally mistaken and that referring-and-predicating is only one of the many socially constituted functions of language and not a privileged one at that . . . Thus the assumption that language is a system of communication treats language as a crucial component of human social interaction and takes linguistic behavior, e.g. asserting, asking, promising, commanding, wishing and requesting, and the larger-scale speech activities which they constitute, to be social behavior. (p. 8)

It should be noted that the claim that the primary function of language is communication does not entail the view that all uses of language are necessarily communicative. Foley and Van Valin (1984) continue:

> There may well be instances of verbal behavior which are non-communicative, but this in no way undermines the fundamental functionalist tenet that an understanding of language structure requires an understanding of the functions language can serve ... This position is analogous to claiming that in order to understand the structure of hammers it is necessary to know that they are used primarily for driving nails, even though they may also be employed as doorstops or paperweights or for tapping the ashes out of a pipe. Indeed, it would be difficult to account for the fact that the head of a hammer is always heavy metal and the handle wood or plastic and never vice versa, if one ignores its primary function, since a hammer could easily be a doorstop, paperweight or pipetapper with a plastic head and metal handle. Languages are much more complex than hammers, both structurally and functionally, but in both cases one cannot understand form independent of function. (pp. 8–9)

Thus, the function of conveying propositional information, i.e. linguistic depictions of states of affairs, is but one of many communicative functions that language has.

All of these different functions may have structural ramifications in languages. As a simple example, let's look at how two different languages express assertions (statements), interrogatives (questions) and imperatives (commands). In English, each of these requires a different syntactic structure. This is illustrated in (2).

(2) a. The boy is eating the bread.   Statement
     b. Is the boy eating the bread?   Question
     c. Eat the bread!   Command

In a statement, the subject precedes the tensed verb, be it an auxiliary verb (*is*), as in (2a, b), or the main verb (*ate*), as in (1). In a question, on the other hand, the tensed verb precedes the subject, as in (2b). In a command, there is neither a subject nor tense; the bare verb begins the sentence, as in (2c). A combination of syntactic (word order) and morphological differences (presence or absence of tense inflection) signals declarative, interrogative and imperative sentence types. Contrast this with the situation in Lakhota, a Siouan language of North America.[2]

(3) a. Hokšíla ki agúyapi ki yúta-hą (yeló).   Statement
         boy   the bread   the eat-PROG DECL
         "The boy is eating the bread."
     b. Hokšíla ki agúyapi ki yúta-hą   he?   Question
         boy   the bread   the eat-PROG INT
         "Is the boy eating the bread?"

    c. Agúyapi ki   yúta ye!   Command
        bread   the eat   IMP
        "Eat the bread!"

Lakhota, unlike English, expresses these different types of sentences by simply adding particles at the end of the sentence; no change is made in their syntactic structure, except for the omission of the subject in the command in (3c). The direct object NP and the verb are in the same position in all three examples. The optional particle *yeló* in (3a) signals that the sentence is a declarative utterance, i.e. a statement; it also indicates that the speaker is male. The particle *he* in (3b) signals that the sentence is a question (it is neutral with respect to the sex of the speaker), while the particle *ye* in (3c) indicates that the sentence is a command and that the speaker is female. This way of expressing questions, statements, and commands is much more common across the world's languages than the English pattern in (2), and the contrast between the two illustrates how the same communicative functions can be carried out in very different ways in different languages.

    Functionalists normally focus on these linguistic functions from either of two perspectives. They will be referred to as the "pragmatics" perspective and the "discourse" perspective. The first perspective concentrates on the meaning of and the conditions on the appropriate use of different speech acts. The work is based on Searle's (1969, 1985) theory of speech acts and Grice's (1975, 1989) theory of the logic of conversation; Levinson (1983) provides an excellent overview. As an example of the kind of problem which this aspect of functional linguistics addresses, consider the following utterance.

(4)   Can you pass the salt?

Taken literally, this question is about the addressee's ability to give the speaker the salt; its literal meaning can be paraphrased as "Are you able to give me the salt?" This is not how it is normally interpreted, however; it is normally understood as a request, not a question, and if the addressee simply answered "yes" without handing the speaker the salt, such a response would be considered impertinent, rude, or smart-alecky. The theories of Grice and Searle make it possible for linguists (and philosophers of language) to explain how a sentence with one form (that of a question) and a clear-cut literal meaning can be interpreted in context as a different kind of speech act with a rather different meaning.

    The second perspective is concerned with the construction of discourse and how grammatical and other devices are employed to serve this end. As a simple example of this, consider the problem of keeping track of referents in discourse. When a speaker constructs a text about a number of states of affairs, each of which contains a number of participants, how does he or she code the referents so that the interlocutors can keep them apart but also keep track of the same referents that appear in more than one state of affairs? This problem is illustrated in the following English examples.

(5) a. Mary called Sam, and she talked to him for an hour. He scolded her
         for refusing to help her sister at the party, and she replied that she
         had been too busy.
     b. Mary called Sam, talked to him for an hour, was scolded by him for
         refusing to help her sister at the party, and replied that she had been
         too busy.

The two participants to be tracked are Mary and Sam, and in (5a) they are
unambiguously referred to by third-person pronouns that are differentiated in
terms of gender. Hence *she* or *her* always refers to Mary and *he* or *him* to Sam.[3]
The situation is somewhat different in (5b); there are nouns or pronouns referring to Mary only in the first (*Mary*), fourth (*her*) and fifth (*she*) sentences, and
yet she is clearly a participant in the state of affairs expressed by each clause.
In this sentence, Mary is being tracked by syntactic means: the NP *Mary* is the
subject of each clause, and it is omitted after the initial one. In this multiclause
construction, a missing subject must be interpreted as being the same as the
subject of the first clause in it; hence all of the clauses are construed as having
the NP referring to Mary as the subject. The other participant, Sam, is tracked
by means of a gender-marked pronoun, just as in (5a). This involves many of
the central mechanisms of English clause-internal grammar: the voice of the
verb (active vs. passive), grammatical relations (subject vs. non-subject), and
case marking (nominative [*he, she*] vs. accusative [*him, her*]). English thus has
two different ways of keeping track of referents in discourse: the gender-
marked pronoun system in both (5a) and (5b), and the syntactic system in (5b).
Why should it need the system in (5b), when the one in (5a) seems to work just
fine? Consider the slightly different examples in (6).

(6) a. Bill called Sam, and he talked to him for an hour. He scolded him for
         refusing to help his sister at the party, and he replied that he had been
         too busy.
     b. Bill called Sam, talked to him for an hour, was scolded by him for
         refusing to help his sister at the party, and replied that he had been
         too busy.

In these examples both participants are male, and therefore the pronouns *he*
and *him* are used to refer to both of them. The result in (6a) is serious ambiguity; who, for example, scolded whom? Either Bill or Sam could have done the
scolding. In (6b), on the other hand, there is much less ambiguity. The NP
referring to Bill must be interpreted as the subject of each of the clauses in the
construction, and therefore the pronoun *him* in non-subject position is interpreted as referring to Sam. The only real ambiguity is with respect to whose
sister it is; it could be either Bill's or Sam's. Thus in this case the syntactic
referent-tracking mechanism yields less ambiguity than the gender-marked
pronoun system. Different languages use different referent-tracking systems:
some use gender-marked pronouns primarily, some use syntactic mechanisms

primarily, and some use combinations of them (see Van Valin 1987, Comrie 1989, 1994, Kibrik 1991).

It was mentioned above that many of the basic mechanisms crucial to clause-internal grammar are involved in reference tracking, and this highlights an important aspect of functional analysis. Voice constructions like passive, or grammatical relations like subject and direct object are not treated as purely formal grammatical entities; rather, they are analyzed in terms of the functions they serve. With respect to voice constructions, in some languages they are part of a referent-tracking system, as in English, while in other languages they are not. If a language has a syntactic referent-tracking system, then grammatical relations like subject will be centrally involved in it; in languages which use a gender-marked pronoun system only, then neither voice nor grammatical relations will serve any role in referent-tracking. In functional linguistic analysis, forms are analyzed with respect to the communicative functions they serve, and functions are investigated with respect to the formal devices that are used to accomplish them. Both forms and functions are analyzed, not just functions. The interplay between form and function in language is very complex and is the prime focus of functional linguistics.

Even though examples from only two languages have been given so far, it should be clear that cross-linguistic comparison is a very significant feature of functional linguistics. As we will see in the next section, it is not a necessary part of this approach, as there are schools of functional linguistics which are not typologically oriented. In the United States in particular, the development of functional linguistics has gone hand in hand with the expansion of the study of language typology and universals. While there are typologists who are not functionalists, the combination of typology and functionalism is not just an accidental pairing of unrelated endeavors. Many of the major figures in the development of functional linguistics in the United States have worked on languages in which the grammatical marking of communicative functions is more obvious and direct than it is in English, the language on the basis of which most theorizing in linguistics in the US was done up through the end of the 1970s. For instance, since the mid-1950s linguists have recognized that the NP referring to the topic of the discourse (roughly, the participant the discourse is primarily about) is accorded special treatment in the grammatical systems of some languages (see Chao 1955, Hockett 1958, Lambrecht 1994). In the examples in (5) the sentences are about Mary, while in (6) it is Bill who is the topic. Two languages in which the notion of topic plays an important role are Mandarin Chinese and Japanese; in Mandarin, topic NPs may be given special syntactic treatment, and in Japanese they are marked by a special particle, *wa*.

(7) a.   Nèi   xie shù, shùshēn   dà.   Mandarin
          those CL tree tree.trunk big   (Li and Thompson 1976)
          "Those trees, the trunks are big."

b.   Nihon wa, Tokyo ga   sumi-yoi.   Japanese
     Japan TOP   SUBJ easy-live   (Kuno 1973)
     "As for Japan, Tokyo is easy to live in."

Linguists such as Kuno, Li, Thompson and others took the insights derived
from their study of Mandarin, Japanese, and other so-called "exotic" languages
and applied them to the analysis of English and other more familiar languages;
there they found functional motivations for grammatical phenomena, albeit
not always coded as directly as in these languages. Hence the investigation of
languages from Asia, Africa, Australia, and the Americas led to insights about
the interaction of form and function in language that led directly to the development of functional linguistics in the United States. Functional approaches
also arose in Soviet / Russian linguistics based on the study of the non-Slavic
languages of the former USSR (Kibrik 1979, 1985; Bondarko 1991); these were
undoubtedly influenced by the well-established Prague-based tradition of Slavic
functional linguistics, which will be discussed in the next section.

3   A Brief Look at the Development of Linguistic Theory in the Twentieth Century

At the beginning of the chapter it was noted that many linguists hold that the
fact that language is used for communication is largely irrelevant to its analysis. How did such a view arise? The answer lies in the theoretical development
of linguistics in the twentieth century. The primary concern of linguists such
as Franz Boas in the US and Ferdinand de Saussure in Europe at the start of
the twentieth century was to lay out the foundations for linguistic science and
thereby to define clearly and explicitly the object to be investigated in linguistic
inquiry. Culminating in Boas (1911) and Saussure (1917), this work defined
what came to be known as structural linguistics. Saussure drew a fundamental
contrast between language (*langue*) and speaking (*parole*): language is a system
of signs, whereas speaking is the use of the system on particular occasions. A
linguistic sign is the association of a sound (signifier) and a meaning (signified),
e.g. the Japanese signifier /inu/ has the signified "dog," while the English
signifier /əd/ (orthographic -*ed*) has the signified "past tense." Saussure argued
that the proper subject for linguistic investigation is the system of signs, not
the use of the system. Bloomfield (1933) proposed a similar distinction: grammar (the linguistic system) vs. meaning (the use of the system on particular
occasions). He too argued that linguistic analysis should concern itself only
with grammar.
     What is the nature of the linguistic system? Saussure proposed that there
are two fundamental relations among signs which define a structural system:
co-occurrence (syntagmatic) and substitution (paradigmatic). The English sign

-ed, for example, is in a syntagmatic relation with the verbs that it appears suffixed to, e.g. *load*, *pit*, and *include*, and it is in a paradigmatic relation with the other suffixes that can occur on these verbs, e.g. *-s* "present tense," *-en* "past participle," or *-ing* "present participle." Similarly, Lakhota *agúyapi* "bread" from (3) is in a syntagmatic relation with *ki* "the" and a paradigmatic relation with *hokšíla* "boy," since both *agúyapi* and *hokšíla* can co-occur with *ki* "the." In (3a, b), *hokšíla ki* "the boy" is syntagmatically related to both *agúyapi ki* "the bread" and *yúta* "eat," and it is paradigmatically related to other Lakhota NPs which can cooccur with these two other elements, e.g. *wičháša ki* "the man" or *wíya wa* "a woman," as shown in (8).

(8) a. Wičháša ki agúyapi ki yúta-ha   (yeló).
         man   the bread   the eat-PROG DECL
         "The man is eating the bread."
     b. Wíya   wa agúyapi ki yúta-ha   (yeló).
         woman a bread   the eat-PROG DECL
         "A woman is eating the bread."

Syntagmatic relations define the frame in which paradigmatic relations exist, and the elements in a paradigmatic relation to each other constitute classes which are in syntagmatic relation to each other. To continue the Lakhota example, "noun + article" constitute a syntagmatic frame, i.e. they co-occur with each other as a regular pattern in the language. Each of the constituents of this pattern, namely "noun" and "article," are themselves names for substitution classes; that is, in terms of the examples we have seen, *wičháša* "man," *wíya* "woman," *hokšíla* "boy," and *agúyapi* "bread" can be substituted for each other in the "noun" position in the frame, and *ki* "the" and *wa* "a" can be substituted for each other in the "article" position. Syntagmatic (co-occurrence) and paradigmatic (substitution) relations among signs constitute the structure of language, and it is this structure, and not the way signs are used in speaking, that is the proper domain of linguistic study, according to Saussure and Bloomfield.

Chomsky (1965) proposed a distinction analogous but not identical to Saussure's and Bloomfield's, namely competence vs. performance. Competence refers to a native speaker's knowledge of his or her native language, and performance is how a speaker puts that knowledge to use on particular occasions. Performance is very close to Saussure's *parole* and Bloomfield's meaning, but competence includes not only the linguistic system but also native speakers' knowledge of it. Hence it adds a cognitive dimension to linguistics that had been deemphasized by Saussure and denied by Bloomfield. For Chomsky, the proper domain of linguistic inquiry is competence only.

How do Saussure's, Bloomfield's and Chomsky's distinctions relate to the issue raised in the introduction, namely, the primary function of language? Since *parole* / meaning / performance concerns the use of language, and since one of these uses is surely for communication among humans, it is natural to associate the communicative function of language with *parole* / meaning /

performance. As we have seen, all three theorists maintain that linguistics is not concerned with the analysis of *parole* / meaning / performance but rather with the study of *langue* / grammar / competence. Hence it is but a short leap to the conclusion that the communicative functions of language are irrelevant to the analysis of language structure (*langue* / grammar / competence). Given that Saussure is generally acknowledged to have laid the foundations for the modern study of language, it is consequently not surprising that many linguists have adopted this view. Thus, a view of language that might seem puzzling to non-linguists arises rather naturally out of the way linguistic theory has developed in this century.

Does this mean that functional theories are theories of *parole* / meaning / performance? The answer is, for the most part, "no." Foley and Van Valin (1984) make this point explicitly.

> It must be emphasized that functional theories are *not* performance theories. That is, they seek to describe language in terms of the *types* of speech activities in which language is used as well as the *types* of constructions which are used in speech activities. They do not attempt to predict the actual *tokens* of speech events. In other words, the theories seek to describe the interaction of syntax, semantics and pragmatics in types of speech activities; they do not try to predict the occurrence of particular constructions in actual speech events. They are theories of systems, not of actual behavior. (p. 15 [emphasis in original])

How can the various communicative functions of language discussed in section 2 be incorporated into the study of language structure? The two fundamental relations defining a structural system are cooccurrence (syntagmatic) and substitution (paradigmatic), as mentioned above. The co-occurrence relations among substitution classes constitute a level of structure. If the elements in the substitution classes are phonemes, then the syntagmatic combinations of phonemes are morphemes. If the elements in the substitution classes are morphemes, the syntagmatic combinations are words. If the elements in the substitution classes are words, the syntagmatic combinations are sentences. This is the extent of the study of *langue* / grammar / competence as practiced by Saussure, Bloomfield, and Chomsky. But it is possible to extend the analysis further: if the elements in the substitution classes are sentences, then the syntagmatic combinations are discourses or kinds of speech events. In analyzing sentence types in terms of the kinds of speech events or discourse they can occur in, one is analyzing their communicative function. So, for example, the examples in (2)–(4) all occur in specific types of speech acts. The examples in (5) and (6), on the other hand, involve sentences with particular properties within a discourse context. Hence it is in fact possible to extend the study of *langue* / grammar / competence to take the communicative functions of linguistic forms into account. This is what Foley and Van Valin were getting at above: it is possible to analyze the potential contexts in which constructions appear, in order to uncover the contextual constraints on their distribution. We can take passive constructions to exemplify this point. In the active voice in

English, the doer of the action is the subject, while in the passive voice the NP referring to the participant affected by the action is the subject. In (5b) and (6b) passive is used in the third clause. The subject, which is the topic of the mini-discourse, is not the doer of the action of the verb in that clause. The construction in (5b) and (6b) requires that the topic be the subject of each sentence in it, and therefore passive must be used in the third sentence. This suggests that there is a connection between the topicality of participants and the occurrence of the passive construction, i.e., when the doer of the action is less topical than the other participant, a passive is favored, because it permits the more topical participant to appear as subject. Subjects in English and many other languages are typically topic-like, although there are instances of non-topic subjects. The overwhelming tendency in languages is for the NP referring to the topic to come first in a sentence, followed by elements introducing new information into the context. The following possible question–answer pairs illustrate this.

(9) a.   Who did Sally slap?
     b.   She slapped Pat.
     b'. Pat was slapped by Sally / her.

While the sentences in (9b) and (9b') are perfectly grammatical English sentences, they are not equally good as answers to the question in (9a); (9b) is much better than (9b'). (The most likely answer would be *Pat* by itself, but the whole sentence is included to help illustrate the point.) Part of the reason for this difference in appropriateness derives from discourse factors. The question in (9a) establishes Sally as the topic and also that slapping occurred; the new information requested is the identity of the person slapped. The sentence in (9b) presents the elements expressing established information first followed by the NP *Pat*, which is the answer to the question. The sentence in (9b'), on the other hand, presents the new information first followed by the established information, with the topic NP last in the sentence. Hence it is inappropriate in the context created by the question in (9a). This account is somewhat over-simplified, but it nevertheless illustrates how linguistic analysis can be extended to take communicative functions into account.

The idea of extending linguistic analysis to include communicative functions was first proposed by Czech linguists. Virtually all contemporary functional approaches trace their roots back to the work of the Czech linguist Mathesius in the 1920s as part of the Prague School (Mathesius 1928, 1929). He and his successors developed the theory of functional sentence perspective. They were the first to fully develop the observation that the elements expressing more established information (what was earlier called the "topic," what the Pragueans call the "theme") precede the elements expressing new information (what is often called the "focus" and what Pragueans call the "rheme"). This is a salient feature of Slavic languages, as the following examples from Russian (Comrie 1979) show. In the translations, the focus is in small caps, and the square brackets group the topical elements and focal elements together.

(10) a. Q: [Kto]   [zaščiščajet Viktor-a]?   "Who defends
               who.NOM defends   Victor-ACC   Victor?"
               Focus   Topic
          A: [Viktora   zaščiščajet] [Maksim-Ø].   "MAXIM defends
               Victor-ACC defends   Maksim-NOM   Victor."
               Topic   Focus

      b. Q: [Kogo]   [zaščiščajet Maksim-Ø]?   "Who(m) does
               who.ACC defends   Maksim-NOM   Maxim defend?"
               Focus   Topic
          A: [Maksim-Ø   zaščiščajet] [Viktor-a].   "Maxim defends
               Maksim-NOM defends   Victor-ACC   VICTOR."
               Topic   Focus

      c. Sp1: [Maksim-Ø] [ubivajet Aleksej-a].   "Maxim KILLS
               Maksim-NOM kills   Alexei-ACC   ALEXEI."
               Topic   Focus
          Sp2: [A Viktor-a]?   "And VICTOR?" [i.e.
               and Victor-ACC   "What is happening
               Focus   to Victor?"]
          Sp1: [Viktor-a   Maksim-Ø]   [zaščiščajet].   "Maxim DEFENDS
               Victor-ACC Maksim-NOM defends   Victor."
               Topic   Focus

Aside from the fact that question words like *kto* and *kogo* "who" occur at the beginning of the sentence, as they do in many languages, the ordering of elements is topic (theme) followed by focus (rheme). It was noted in section 2 that the study of so-called "exotic" languages by English-speaking linguists had led to insights about the functional motivation for grammatical phenomena, but here the crucial insight derives from the native language of the linguists. The theory of functional sentence perspective was developed primarily with respect to the analysis of Slavic languages, but its ideas have been applied by other linguists to a range of phenomena in many languages.[4] This theory was first brought to the attention of English-speaking linguists in Halliday (1967); Kuno (1972a, 1972b) and Chafe (1972) applied them to issues that were of concern to theoretical linguists in the US at that time. By the end of the 1970s, a number of functional approaches were emerging in both the US and western Europe.

4   Functional Approaches

There is a great diversity of views among those who label themselves as functionalists. One of the curious features of functionalism in linguistics is the apparent paucity of explicitly articulated, named theories. There are really just three: Functional Grammar (FG) (Dik 1978, 1989), Systemic Functional

Grammar (SFG) (Halliday 1967, 1994), and Role and Reference Grammar (RRG) (Foley and Van Valin 1984, Van Valin 1993, Van Valin and LaPolla 1997). Nichols (1984) presents a survey of functionalist approaches which usefully categorizes them as extreme, moderate, and conservative. Her descriptions of each are still valid and are given below.

> The conservative type merely acknowledges the inadequacy of strict formalism or structuralism, without proposing a new analysis of structure . . . The moderate type not only points out the inadequacy of a formalist or structuralist analysis, but goes on to propose a functionalist analysis of structure and hence to replace or change inherited formal or structural accounts of structure . . . Extreme functionalism denies, in one way or another, the reality of structure qua structure. It may claim that rules are based entirely on function and hence there are no purely syntactic constraints; that structure is only coded function, or the like. (1984: 102–3)

Conservative functionalism, as exemplified in the work of Kuno (e.g. 1972a, 1972b, 1975, 1987) and Prince (e.g. 1981a, 1981b), seeks to augment standard formal analyses with functional principles, thereby creating an additional functional "component" or "module" in the grammar. Kuno (1987) is very explicit on this point.

> Functional syntax is, in principle, independent of various past and current models of grammar . . . Each theory of grammar must have a place or places where various functional constraints on the well-formedness of sentences or sequences of sentences can be stated, and each can benefit from utilizing a functional perspective in the analysis of concrete syntactic phenomena. Therefore, in theory there is no conflict between functional syntax and say, the government and binding theory of generative grammar. (1987: 1)

These approaches assume the same basic notion of grammatical structure that formal theories do and propose constraints or rules that either supplement or in some cases even replace purely structure-oriented rules. They do not challenge the fundamental assumptions of formal theories, and therefore they represent an extension of them rather than an alternative to them.

Moderate functional theories do reject the assumptions of formal theories such as Chomsky's and are presented as alternatives to them. Two of the theories mentioned above, FG and RRG, are moderate functional theories. These theories reject the conceptions of grammatical structure that underlie formal theories, but each proposes a different replacement view of structure. However, they do not deny the validity of the notion of structure *per se* and do not claim that all grammatical structure is reducible to discourse structure or some other functional notion(s). Rather, they view grammatical structure as strongly influenced by semantics and pragmatics and undertake to explore the interaction of structure and function in language. The following are characterizations of moderate functionalist views of language. First, Dik (1991) characterizes the FG view of language as follows.

[A] language is considered in the first place as an instrument for communicative verbal interaction, and the basic assumption is that the various properties of natural languages should, wherever this is possible, be understood and explained in terms of the conditions imposed by their usage. The language system, therefore, is not considered as an autonomous set of rules and principles, the uses of which can only be considered in a secondary phase; rather it is assumed that the rules and principles composing the language system can only be adequately understood when they are analyzed in terms of conditions of use. In this sense the study of language use (pragmatics) precedes the study of the formal and semantic properties of linguistic expressions. (1991: 247)

Second, Van Valin (1993) lays out the basic assumptions of RRG as follows.

RRG takes language to be a system of communicative social action, and accordingly, analyzing the communicative functions of grammatical structures plays a vital role in grammatical description and theory from this perspective . . . Language is a system, and grammar is a system in the traditional structuralist sense; what distinguishes the RRG conception . . . is the conviction that grammatical structure can only be understood with reference to its semantic and communicative functions. Syntax is not autonomous. In terms of the abstract paradigmatic and syntagmatic relations that define a structural system, RRG is concerned not only with relations of cooccurrence and combination in strictly formal terms but also with semantic and pragmatic cooccurrence and combinatory relations. (1993: 2)

The rules and constraints proposed in FG and RRG bear little resemblance to those proposed in generative theories, and therefore these theories do not complement formal theories but, rather, are alternatives to them. Both of these theories are strongly typologically oriented. RRG, for example, grew out of attempts to answer the following questions: (1) what would linguistic theory look like if it were based on the analysis of Lakhota, Tagalog, and Dyirbal, rather than on the analysis of English?, and (2) how can the interaction of syntax, semantics, and pragmatics in different grammatical systems best be captured and explained? (Van Valin 1996: 281).[5]

Extreme functionalism, as manifested in the works of Hopper (1987) among others, rejects the validity of any notion of structure other than that of discourse structure and seeks a radical reduction of grammar to discourse. On this view, grammar is strongly motivated by discourse, and the emphasis on the primacy of discourse leads even to the rejection of semantics as a valid part of linguistic investigations, where "semantics" is understood as the study of the meaning of forms independent of their discourse function(s). Extreme functionalism abandons the basic Saussurean conception of language as a structural system, which underlies structural and generative linguistics, as well as conservative and moderate functionalism.

Falling somewhere between moderate and extreme functionalism is SFG, which takes a strongly discourse-oriented view of language, but which nevertheless does not deny either the reality of structure in language nor the Saussurean foundations of modern linguistics. SFG is a "top–down" analytic model which starts with discourse and works "down" to lower levels of grammatical structure. Halliday (1985) maintains that the ultimate explanations for linguistic phenomena are to be found in language use.

> Language has evolved to satisfy human needs; and the way it is organized is functional with respect to these needs – it is not arbitrary. A functional grammar is essentially a "natural" grammar, in the sense that everything in it can be explained, ultimately, by reference to how language is used. (1985: xiii) . . . The orientation is to language as a social rather than an individual phenomenon, and the origin and development of the theory have aligned it with the sociological rather than psychological modes of explanation. At the same time it has been used within a general cognitive framework. (1985: xxx)

SFG is less concerned with issues of sentence grammar than FG and RRG, and more with discourse structure. Hence it falls toward the more extreme end of the spectrum.

Among the three approaches, it could be argued that conceptually the biggest gap is between extreme functionalism and all the others, since it represents the greatest departure from the mainstream currents of twentieth-century linguistics. There is a context in which extreme and moderate functionalism fall together in opposition to conservative functionalism, however. This is the issue of the relationship between the functionalist and generative theoretical agendas. As the quote from Kuno makes clear, there is no inherent conflict between the goals of generative grammar and those of conservative functional syntax, but this is not the case with moderate and extreme functionalism. The extreme view rejects the generative enterprise and the questions it deals with altogether; for its adherents, the issues raised by generative researchers are pseudo-problems created by an invalid methodological approach to language. Moderate functionalists have a rather different perspective. Their agenda is broader than that of generative linguistics, since it is not limited to issues of sentence grammar but also includes discourse and other pragmatic issues, and therefore the moderate functionalist agenda *subsumes* the formalist agenda at the same time that it transforms it in terms of functional categories and relations. Thus in RRG, for example, research has focussed not only on discourse-related issues like reference tracking but also on formalist issues like constraints on *wh*-question formation and relative clause formation (Van Valin 1995).

One of the most salient features of Chomskyan (but not all formal) linguistics is the goal of describing a native speaker's grammatical competence and explaining the acquisition of language by children. Not surprisingly, functionalist approaches vary with respect to their stand on these issues. Since conservative functionalists basically follow general generativist doctrine, they too subscribe to this goal, and they follow the standard Chomskyan view regarding the existence of an autonomous language faculty. Moderate functionalist theories all adopt this goal, with the reinterpretation of grammatical competence as communicative or textual competence, and at least some (RRG) expressly reject the Chomskyan autonomy hypothesis. Van Valin (1991, 1994, 1998) and Van Valin and LaPolla (1997) present a model of the acquisition of syntax which does not assume an autonomous language acquisition device. Opinion among extreme functionalists varies on this issue; Hopper (1987) explicitly denies the validity of any psychological interpretation in linguistics, while Bates and MacWhinney (1982, 1987, 1989) develop what they call the "competition model" to account for language acquisition.

5   Formal vs. Functional Approaches to Language

This discussion began with contrasting views on the primary function of language, and a dichotomy was set up between those linguists who believe it to be communication and take the communicative functions of language to be important for its analysis (the functionalists) and those who at the very least consider the communicative functions of language to be irrelevant to its analysis, following Chomsky (the formalists). This contrast, as one might suspect, is rather oversimplified, and when one scans the topics that formalists and functionalists investigate, the distinctions become somewhat blurred. In the 1980s only functionalists talked about referent tracking, discourse and information structure (topic, focus), among other issues, but that has changed significantly. There are formal theories of discourse and information structure, e.g. Kamp and Reyle (1993) and Vallduví (1992), and analyses of the role of notions like topic in the syntax of different languages, e.g. É. Kiss (1987, 1994). Until the early 1980s the problems of so-called "exotic" languages were primarily the province of typologists and functionalists, but since then linguists of all theoretical persuasions have begun to investigate them. Whereas it was then possible to identify a formalist or a functionalist merely by the problems they investigated, this is no longer the case today.

What, then, distinguishes formalists from functionalists? There is one fundamental difference which sets functionalists of all persuasions off from formalists, and there is a second distinction which separates extreme functionalists from both formalists and conservative and moderate functionalists. This distinction concerns the type of explanatory criteria that the approach recognizes. Table 13.1 summarizes the relevant types of explanatory criteria.

The label "theory-internal" refers to the fact that within a particular domain, e.g. syntax, the criteria are applied to competing analyses within that domain; it does not mean that they are specific to any particular linguistic theory. They are explicated briefly in (11).

Table 13.1   Types of explanatory criteria

Domain to be explained	Theory-internal criteria	External criteria	
		Language-internal	*Language-external*
Syntax	Economy	Phonology	Reasoning
	Motivation	Semantics	Categorization
	Predictiveness	Pragmatics	Perception
		Processing	

Source: Van Valin and LaPolla 1997: 7.

(11)   Theory-internal explanatory criteria
  a.   Economy (also known as "Occam's razor"): is it the simplest account?
  b.   Motivation: are the main explanatory constructs independently motiv-
       ated or are they specific to the problem at hand?
  c.   Predictiveness: do the hypotheses predict phenomena beyond those
       for which they were formulated?

If an approach restricts itself to theory-internal criteria only, then syntactic
phenomena are explained in syntactic terms, semantic phenomena in semantic
terms, phonological phenomena in phonological terms, etc. This is often expressed in terms of the thesis of the autonomy of syntax, and it applies to
semantics and phonology as well; phenomena in each domain are to be
explained in terms of constructs, rules, or principles which involve elements
in that domain only. The external explanatory criteria involve factors outside
of the domain being studied, and they can be internal or external to language
itself. Invoking phonetics to account for some phonological phenomenon is
an example of permitting language-internal external criteria in explanation,
whereas invoking some feature of the human perceptual system to account
for some phonological phenomenon would be an instance of using language-
external external criteria in explanation.

As is evident from the citations earlier from Kuno, Dik, Van Valin, and
Halliday, functional approaches look to semantics and pragmatics as the basis
for explanations of syntactic phenomena. Formal approaches, on the other
hand, restrict themselves to theory-internal criteria in explanation, for the most
part. When formal and functional accounts of the same phenomena are compared, this contrast stands out clearly. For example, the explanation for the
difference in grammaticality in (12) is quite different in the two approaches.
These sentences involve sentence-internal pronominalization, and the issue is
whether a particular lexical noun and a particular pronoun can be interpreted
as coreferential (identical subscripts indicate intended coreference).

(12) a.   As for his$_i$ sister, Tom$_i$ hasn't talked to her in three weeks.
      a'.   *As for his$_i$ sister, she hasn't talked to Tom$_i$ in three weeks.
      b.   It is his$_i$ sister that Tom$_i$ hasn't talked to in three weeks.
      b'.   It is Tom's$_i$ sister that he$_i$ hasn't talked to in three weeks.

The fact to be explained here is why coreference between *his* and *Tom* is very difficult, if not impossible, to get in (12a') but possible in the other sentences. In standard formal accounts, e.g. Chomsky (1981), the explanation is stated in terms of the relative positions of the lexical noun and the pronoun in the syntactic phrase-structure tree representing the structure of the sentence. In functional accounts, e.g. Kuno (1975) and Bolinger (1979), the difference is attributed to the different information structures in the sentences, i.e. differences in which NP functions as topic and which as focus. Chomsky defines pronominalization as a syntactic phenomenon, and therefore only syntactic factors are relevant to its explanation; when competing syntactic accounts of pronominalization are evaluated, only the theory-internal criteria are employed. For functionalists like Kuno and Bolinger, on the other hand, semantics and pragmatics can be brought into the explanation, and competing accounts would be evaluated with both theory-internal and -external criteria. The centrality of external explanations for linguistic phenomena is a point that all functionalists agree on.

    The second feature which distinguishes extreme functionalists from the rest concerns the role of theory in linguistics. Virtually all formal linguists are strongly committed to working within a well-defined theoretical framework, but this is not the case with functionalists. Conservative functionalists, who view their work as augmenting formal grammars, fall in with formalists on this point. Many moderate functionalists are likewise theoretically oriented, as witnessed by the development of theories like RRG and FG, which employ technical metalanguages and explicit representations of the relevant syntactic, semantic and pragmatic phenomena they investigate. Extreme functionalists, on the other hand, deny the validity of functional theories and maintain that true functional theories are impossible. Givón (1989) argued that all theories are inherently formal, and therefore that a functional theory was a contradiction in terms. They also view the use of any kind of explicit notations or representations as inherently formalist and reject them as well. From an extreme functionalist perspective, RRG and FG do not even count as functional approaches, because of their commitment to theory development and use of explicit notation and representations.

6 Conclusion

The label "functional linguistics" is a cover term for a complex web of ideas and methodologies, many of which are more distant from each other than they are from many formalist ideas. Bates (1987) noted that functionalism is like Protestantism, a group of warring sects which agree only on the rejection of the authority of the Pope. Work by conservative functionalists has yielded important insights regarding the pragmatic nature of many syntactic constraints, but they do not address the crucial question of the nature of structure in language, particularly syntactic structure, since they assume a generative account of structure. Extreme functionalists have uncovered many important generalizations about discourse structure, information flow, and the discourse functions of grammatical forms, but by rejecting the notion of language as a structural system they have, like the conservative functionalists, avoided one of the central questions of linguistic theory, that of the nature of linguistic structure. Only moderate functionalists have attempted the difficult task of proposing alternative conceptions of linguistic structure and developing explanatory theories. While there has been some convergence between the work of conservative and moderate functionalists on the one hand, and many formalists on the other, they are nevertheless distinguished by their respective views on what counts as an explanation. All functionalists agree that language is a system of forms for conveying meaning in communication and therefore that in order to understand it, it is necessary to investigate the interaction of structure, meaning and communicative function.

NOTES

1   It is often asserted by advocates of Chomsky's view that science leads to results that defy common sense, the prime example being modern physics. However, the counterintuitive results of special relativity and quantum mechanics deal with phenomena outside the range of human experience, i.e. subatomic particles or objects moving at close to the speed of light. Linguistics does not deal with such phenomena; rather, it deals with what has long been considered the quintessential human phenomenon. Hence it is reasonable to question the denial of the relevance or the importance of the most obvious feature of the phenomenon to be described and explained.

2   Abbreviations used in glosses: CL "classifier," DECL "declarative," IMP "imperative," INT "interrogative," PROG "progressive," Sp "Speaker," SUBJ "subject," TOP "topic."

3   Strictly speaking, the pronouns could refer to other individuals of the appropriate gender. However, in this and all subsequent examples, we will limit our discussion to the universe of discourse defined by the first sentence in the construction.

4   For an overview of the Prague School, see Vachek (1964, 1983), and for more recent work by Prague School functional linguists, see Sgall et al. (1986) and Firbas (1964, 1992).

5   Tagalog, an Austronesian language, is the national language of the Philippines, and Dyirbal is an Australian Aboriginal language.

14 Typology

WILLIAM CROFT

1 The Diversity of Human Languages

There are approximately six thousand different languages spoken in the world today (see Comrie, chapter 2, this volume). Some of these languages are very closely related to each other; that is, the communities that spoke these languages became separated from each other relatively recently in time. Others have been spoken by communities that have been separated for millennia, and in some cases tens or perhaps hundreds of thousands of years (see Joseph, chapter 5, this volume). An obvious reflection of the differences among languages can be observed in vocabulary. An American moving to Britain will find a surprising number of different words for everyday things, but can largely understand and be understood. The same American visiting France or Germany will recognize a number of familiar words and perhaps even get the gist of signs or a newspaper headline. But the same American looking at something written in Yoruba (Niger-Kordofanian family, Nigeria), Tatar (Altaic, Russia), K'iche' (Mayan, Guatemala) or Nunggubuyu (Australian, Northern Territory) would be totally lost, even if the languages were written in the letters of the Roman script familiar to him or her. Although it may someday be proven that English is ultimately related to those distant languages, it would still be true that the vocabulary of the world's languages is incredibly diverse.

But even if our hypothetical English speaker could understand the meanings of words in these exotic languages, s/he would quickly realize that the grammar of these languages (not to mention their pronunciation) would be equally foreign to him or her. Looking at only the literal meanings of the words in a sentence or two of each of the aforementioned languages, our speaker would see something like this:

(1) *Yoruba:*

l'ákŏko tí ìwé yǐ ó bǎ fi tè̩ ó̩ l'ó̩wó̩
at'. time that letter this will meet take press you at'hand

o   ó   ti   kúrò l'ékŏ
you will come.from leave at.Lagos

(2) *K'iche':*

ch-oxib q'iij x-el bi   rii jun chicop ch-u-chii   rii mar
at-three sun it left away the an animal at-its-mouth the sea

pero naj-alaj   juyub   chik. aree k'u rii achi x-r-ilo
but distant-very mountains now. And   the man he it saw

chi algo   x-ok   apan   u-wach lee q'iij
that a.little it entered in.there its-face the sun

(3) *Tatar:*

jul   kərəj-ən-da mašina-da kil-üče-lär-ne kočag-ən-a
path edge-its-at vehicle-at going-those-of embrace-its-to

al-ərga
take-in.order.to

telä-gän-däj   botak-lar-ən ǯäj-ep   kart imän utər-a i-de
wished-having-as.if branches-of spreading.out old oak   sitting was

(4) *Nunggubuyu:*

ni = yayajarda-ɲi   ŋa   wu-ŋul-waj
he = pushed.to.bottom and.then the₁-groin-at

wiɲi-yaɽaŋi = lha-y   yiŋga wiɲi = ŋargiwi-'-ɲ
she.two-with.spear.shaft = stood nearly she.two = pulled-themselves-out

ŋa   girjag! aba ma-gu-ru ma = yaḷi-ɲ yamba
and.then no!   then it₂   it₂ = went-far because

niwaː-'ban = galhari-ɲ-jiɲuŋ ma = yama-ɲ-jiɲuŋ
he.it₃-ground = pierced-which it₂ = did.that-which

Although our speaker might figure out what these sentences mean (the translations are given below), the grammar of each of these is very different from
English, and moreover, all are very different from each other. The sentences in
(1–4), incidentally, illustrate what the typologist must do in examining the
grammar of languages s/he does not know: identify the parts of sentences and
of words in the original language, represented by the first line in the examples;
what their individual meanings are, represented in the line below the original
language; and what is the resulting meaning of the whole, represented by the
translations given below. (All non-English examples in this chapter will have
this three-line format. A list of abbreviations for grammatical terms occurring
in the second line of the examples is found at the end of the chapter.)

Yoruba: "By the time that this letter reaches you, you will have left Lagos."

K'iche': "On the third day the animal came out of the sea, but the mountains were very distant now. And the man saw that the sunlight was entering a little in there."

Tatar: "An old oak stood by the path, spreading out its branches as if it wished to take those traveling in the vehicle into its embrace."

Nunggubuyu: "He rammed it [a Y-shaped stick] deep below the surface of the ground. The fork ["groin"] of the spear shaft was almost through them [the women]. They tried to pull themselves out but they could not. It [the spear] which was jammed into the ground had gone in deeply."

The dramatic differences in grammar from one language to another – only a fraction of which are illustrated in the four short examples above – might strike one as rather surprising. It isn't so odd that vocabulary differs from one language to another. There is no a priori reason, after all, that a certain string of sounds should be associated with a particular concept. The pairing of sound and meaning, at least for individual words, is largely arbitrary.

Grammar should be another matter entirely, at first blush. One might think that there is one obvious way to group concepts into grammatical categories, or express combinations of concepts in sentences, based on the nature of concepts and their combination. Yet this does not appear to be the case. Languages can vary to a remarkable degree in what for English speakers, or even speakers of European languages, appears to be basic categories of grammar. For example, a plausible candidate for a pair of universal grammatical categories are the categories of *subject* and *object* of a verb:

(5)   The woman [S] didn't run.
      [S = "subject"]

(6)   The snake [A] bit the man [P].
      [A = "agent"] [P = "patient"]

The sentence in (5) has only a single phrase (*the woman*) referring to a participant in the event denoted by the verb (*run*). Such a sentence is called "intransitive" by grammarians, and *the woman* is the "subject"; we will refer to intransitive "subject" with the label S (mnemonic for "subject"). The transitive sentence in (6) on the other hand has two phrases referring to the two participants in the event (*bit*). It seems completely natural, indeed even necessary, that the first phrase, *the snake* (labeled A, mnemonic for "agent") should belong to the same grammatical category as *the woman* in (5). Both *the woman* and *the snake* occur before the verb. Substitution of a pronoun for *the woman* would require the (aptly-named) subject form *she*, not *her*. The grammatical category grouping S and A would be called "subject." The second phrase in (6), *the man* (labeled P, mnemonic for "patient") is grammatically different. It occurs after the verb, and substitution of a pronoun for *the man* in (6) would require the object form *him*, not *he*. The grammatical category consisting of P is generally called the "object."

But many languages do not categorize the phrases referring to the participants in events in the same way. Compare the translations of (5) and (6) in Yuwaalaraay, an Aboriginal language of Australia:

(7) waːl ṇama yinar   -Ø   banaga -ṇi
     not that woman -ABS run   -NONFUT
     "The woman [S] didn't run."

(8) ḍuyu -gu ṇama ḍayn -Ø   yiː -y
     snake -ERG that   man -ABS bite -NONFUT
     "The snake [A] bit the man [P]."

Yuwaalaraay does not have subject and object in the English sense. The grammar of participants is expressed by case suffixes on the noun. In an intransitive sentence like (7), the phrase labeled S has no suffix (notated here with the zero symbol -Ø). In a transitive sentence like (8) however, what an English speaker would call the "subject," A, has a case suffix -*gu*, which is called the *ergative* case (abbreviated ERG), and the "object" phrase P has no suffix, like the "subject" S in (7). In other words, whereas English categorizes both A and S together (as subject) and distinguishes P (as object), Yuwaalaraay categorizes P and S together (called the *absolutive*) and distinguishes A (as ergative). The difference between the categories of English and Yuwaalaraay can be illustrated in the following diagram:

(9) *English*:   subject   ⇒ | A   S | P | ⇐ object
     Yuwaalaraay: ergative ⇒ | A | S   P | ⇐ absolutive

This difference between English (and many other languages) on the one hand, and Yuwaalaraay (and many other languages) on the other, is very striking. It seems very unnatural to us to group together S and P against A – subject and object in the English sense seem to be such basic categories of grammar. This example suggests that the diversity of grammatical patterns in the world's languages is indeed far-reaching and pervasive.

The field of linguistic typology explores the diversity of human language in an effort to understand it. The basic principle behind typology is that one must look at as wide a range of languages as possible (given limitations of time and availability of information) in order to grasp both the diversity of language and to discover its limits. Typology uses a fundamentally empirical, comparative, and inductive method in the study of language. That is, typologists examine grammatical data from a wide variety of languages, and infer generalizations about language from that data. For this reason typology depends crucially on field linguistics (see Munro, chapter 6), and indeed many typologists have themselves done fieldwork on particular languages.

The basic discovery of typology is that there are in fact limits to linguistic diversity. Universals of grammatical structure describe constraints on how grammatical structures encode the meanings or functions they express. By comparing diverse languages and discovering universal grammatical patterns, one can attempt to disentangle what is universal about the grammars of English, K'iche' and other languages from what is peculiar to each individual language. Many explanations of typological universals take the form of interacting motivations that compete with each other and can be arbitrarily resolved in several different ways – this leads to the diversity of languages. The interacting motivations are generally explained in terms of language function – communication of meaning – or language processing – in the comprehension and production of utterances. More recently, diversity across languages has been integrated with variation and change within languages, offering a dynamic view of the forces shaping the grammatical structure of languages (and accounting for even more of the diversity of languages). The remainder of this chapter will elaborate these concepts and discoveries in describing the principal results of typological research since the emergence of the field around 1960.

2 The Nature of Language Universals: Word Order

One of the first areas of grammar where a cross-linguistic survey was undertaken and it was recognized that there are limits to grammatical diversity was the order of words. Word order is probably the most immediately salient difference in grammatical patterns from one language to the next, as can be seen in the four passages in section 1. For instance, while the word order in the Yoruba sentence is about the same as in English, the word order in the Tatar sentence is almost the mirror image of English. In particular, in Tatar the verb comes at the end of the sentence, after subject and object, while in English and Yoruba the verb comes after the subject and before the object. In K'iche' on the other hand, the verb or predicate comes before the subject in many cases ("it.left the animal" and "distant-very [the] mountains"); in Nunggubuyu there is no fixed word order of subject, object, and verb.

These observations illustrate the first steps in typological analysis. First, one must examine a sample of languages in order to infer the range of grammatical diversity and its limits. One cannot examine all of the world's languages: there are too many of them, very few of them are described and even those descriptions are often limited sketches. Hence various sampling techniques, taken from the social sciences, are used to give the highest likelihood of success. While sampling is a rather dry methodological issue, it is extremely important for assessing the validity of one's analysis (the issues are thoroughly explored in Bell 1978, Perkins 1989, Dryer 1989, and Rijkhoff et al. 1993). The two most important types of samples are a *variety sample*, intended to maximize the likelihood of capturing the full variety of grammatical patterns, and a *proportional sample*, which attempts to capture the relative proportions of different grammatical patterns. A variety sample collects as broad a range of languages as possible from different geographical areas and different genetic groupings. Its purpose is to ensure that all possible language types are identified. A proportional sample also aims for breadth but in addition preserves the proportions of numbers of languages from different geographical areas and genetic groups. Its purpose is to make more sophisticated probabilistic analyses of the occurrence of language types. Our minimal sample of languages in (1–4) of section 1 is a variety sample: four languages from different continents (Africa, the Americas, Eurasia, and Australia / Oceania), all from different genetic families.

Second, one must be able to identify phenomena from one language to the next as comparable. The basic problem here is the great variety of grammatical structures used in the world's languages. Grammatical patterns are essentially language-specific; this is one of the major insights of structuralism in linguistics at the beginning of the century (see Campbell, chapter 4). However, this fact poses a problem for comparability across languages. The solution to this problem is due to another insight of structuralism: the basic unit of the language is the sign, a form that conventionally expresses or encodes a meaning. The basis for cross-linguistic comparison is a particular linguistic meaning; once that is identified, we may examine the different structures used to encode that meaning (see Greenberg 1966, Keenan and Comrie 1977, Croft 1990: 11–18). Unfortunately, terminology does not always make this fact clear. For example, in discussing the word order of *noun* and *adjective* across languages, these apparently grammatical terms must be understood semantically, as "object being referred to" and "property used to describe an object referred to" respectively. Likewise, in comparing subject, verb, and object order across languages, *verb* must be understood as "action predicated of something," "subject" defined as the class of participant roles grouped together as A + S as in section 1, and "object" as the class of participant roles grouped under the label P. These semantic definitions may appear to have been chosen arbitrarily; but in fact there are good typological reasons for choosing these definitions.

Third, we must identify a range of grammatical patterns or types used to express the linguistic meaning being examined, and classify languages according to what type(s) is / are used in them. For instance, in describing word order of the sentence, the relative position of subject (S), object (O), and verb (V) are used to classify language types. This yields six possible orders: SVO, SOV, VSO, VOS, OVS, and OSV. English and Yoruba are SVO by this classification, while Tatar is SOV. The K'iche' example shows the subject sometimes preceding, sometimes following the verb. In fact, English also allows the subject to follow the verb in some utterances: *Down the alley ran the fox*. However, in both languages there are good reasons to identify one order as basic, and so K'iche' is classified as VOS. In other languages there is no basic order for the clause;

the order of subject, object, and verb is attributable to information status such as new information, focus of attention, and so on. Nunggubuyu is an example of a free or discourse-governed word order language. The classification of types that one chooses is not theory-independent: for example, Dryer 1997 argues persuasively that sentences should be classified in terms of the relative position of subject and verb (SV or VS) and of object and verb (VO or OV), leading to a four-way typological classification: SV/VO, VS/VO, SV/OV, VS/OV. But such refinements are made after the next step, the actual analysis of the cross-linguistic patterns.

The facts given in the preceding paragraph illustrate an important fact: languages vary considerably in their grammar. Objects may occur before or after the verb; so may subjects. The most widespread single pattern is for the subject to precede the object; but K'iche' and a number of other languages are VOS (there are also a very small number of OVS languages which also go against the most common pattern). The universals of language that can be inferred from these facts are more subtle, and can be seen when the order of other types of words in a language are taken into consideration.

Consider for example the relative orders of certain types of modifiers, in particular adjectives and numerals. In English both adjectives and numerals precede the noun:

(10) a. red book   b. three books
         Adj Noun   Num Noun

This pattern is found in many languages. In many other languages, both adjectives and numerals follow the noun:

(11) Kosraean (Austronesian, Caroline Islands)
      a. mwet kuh   b. mwet luo
          men strong   men two
          Noun Adj   Noun Num

A third group of languages has adjectives following the noun while numerals precede:

(12) Jamiltepec Mixtec (Mixtecan, Mexico)
      a. vēhē lúhlu   b. uvi vēhē
          house little   two house(s)
          Noun Adj   Num Noun

On the other hand, languages with the adjective preceding and numeral following are virtually unattested (although there are a few). The pattern of attested vs. unattested (or at least extremely rare) language types can be given in the four-cell table (table 14.1):

Table 14.1 Attested vs. unattested adjective and numeral word orders

	Noun-adjective order	*Adjective-noun order*
Numeral-noun order	Attested (Jamiltepec Mixtec)	Attested (English)
Noun-numeral order	Attested (Kosraean)	*Extremely rare*

The generalization can itself be described in terms of an *implicational universal*:

(13)   If a language has Adjective-Noun word order, then it (almost always) has Numeral-Noun word order.

The discovery of implicational universals of word order by Greenberg (1966) demonstrated that there could be universal properties of language that do not imply that all languages are identical in some respect. The implicational universal in (13) is not by itself a description of a fact about the grammar of a particular language. In fact, one could not even identify the implicational universal without looking across a set of languages. The implicational universal captures a contingent relationship between Adjective-Noun order and Numeral-Noun order. This contingent relationship must be a part of individual speakers' knowledge of language structure and meaning.

The model of speakers' knowledge most widely adopted in typology is that of *competing motivations* for determining grammatical structure. A competing motivation model posits two or more factors that determine language structure. However, the motivations typically do not determine a single grammatical pattern because they are often in conflict. In the case of conflict, there is no single optimal grammatical pattern that satisfies all of the competing motivations, and instead one finds cross-linguistic variation over several suboptimal patterns. In this way, universal properties of the human mind (the motivations) give rise to cross-linguistic diversity.

For example, Greenberg proposed two competing motivations for implicational universals of word order. The first, *dominance*, can be thought of as simply a default preference for one order over another. For example, noun-adjective order (NA) is dominant, as is numeral-noun order (NumN) and demonstrative-noun order (DemN). The second, *harmony*, can be thought of as a dependent relation of one word order upon another. For example, AN order is harmonic with both NumN order and DemN order.

Greenberg's two motivations compete with each other, and the result is described in the following principle:

(14)   A dominant order may occur at any time, but a recessive order occurs only when a harmonic order is also present.

The principle in (14) accounts for the distribution of languages in table 14.1. The upper left cell is the language type with both dominant orders (NA and NumN), which are not harmonic with each other. The other two attested types have one recessive order, but the harmonic order is also present. The extremely rare type would have both recessive orders (AN and NNum), neither of which is dominant. That is, the extremely rare type is not motivated by either dominance or harmony, which accounts for its rarity. Note that one cannot satisfy both motivations at once, since the dominant orders are not harmonic with each other.

Further explanations have been offered for the motivations of dominance and harmony. Dominance – the default order – appears to be explainable in terms of language processing in production and comprehension. The default or preferred pattern (other things being equal) is for smaller or shorter modifiers and complements to come first, while the longer or larger ones come last (see Hawkins 1983).

Two general explanations have been proposed for harmony. The first explanation is based on language processing. The harmonic orders (AN, DemN and NumN) are parallel: all involve a modifier preceding the head noun. It has been proposed that if parallel grammatical structures have parallel word order, they would be easier to comprehend and produce. The second explanation is basically a historical one. It has also been noticed that the constructions used for harmonic word orders are often the same across categories. For example, in the K'iche' example in (2), a genitive agrees with its head noun with a prefix:

(15)   **u**-wach lee q'iij   "sunlight [lit. the face of the sun]"
       its-face the sun
       AGR-Noun Genitive

And a preposition in K'iche' agrees with its complement with the same prefix set:

(16)   ch-**u**-chii rii mar   "at the edge of the sea"
       at-**its**-edge the sea
       . . . -AGR-Prep Noun

The fact that K'iche' has PrepN and NGen word orders is due to the fact that the preposition construction is historically derived from the genitive construction via a semantic change (from a noun meaning "mouth" to a prepositional term meaning "edge of"). The English translations also use the same construction, and indeed genitive constructions have given rise to prepositions (e.g. *in the side of* > *inside of* > *inside*).

These two types of explanation illustrate the general perspective of typology on the nature of language structure. Language structure is determined by factors of language use, such as processing. Language structure is also determined by historical relationships among grammatical patterns, which themselves are due to similarity in meaning. However, these factors do not uniquely determine a language structure, but compete with each other. Speech communities resolve the competing motivations in arbitrary, language-particular ways; this leads to the diversity of languages found in the world.

3   Language Universals and the Formal Encoding of Meaning

Word order universals appear to be motivated in part or perhaps entirely in terms of processing of linguistic structure in the act of producing and comprehending language. Word order is a fundamental grammatical property of sentences. Word order has generally been analyzed independently of the actual constructions used to encode the meaning of the sentence. An exception to this view is the historical explanation of word order harmony alluded to in section 2, where harmony is explained in terms of constructions shared across different categories. In this section I will describe language universals specifically pertaining to how concepts are encoded in word forms and constructions, and the model of linguistic knowledge these universals are taken to imply.

3.1   *Typological markedness and morphological representation*

Some of the earliest work in typology (also initiated by Greenberg) examined the coding of grammatical and lexical concepts in inflected word forms. The universals Greenberg and others discovered go under the name of (*typological*) *markedness*. This term was borrowed from the Prague school of linguistic analysis (Trubetzkoy 1939/1969), but the theory was substantially altered in the process. Typological markedness represents an asymmetric pattern of the expression of meaning in grammatical categories across languages.

   The category of number will serve to illustrate the general pattern. The simplest distinction that can be made in the category of number is between singular and plural. In many languages such as English and Tatar (see (17)), the singular form is expressed without any inflection (indicated by the zero symbol -Ø), while the plural is expressed by an overt inflection:

(17)   a.   imän-Ø   b.   botak-lar
            oak (SG)   branch-PL

Not all languages are the same as English and Tatar in the expression of singular and plural, however. Some languages express both singular and plural with overt inflection such as the Zulu (Bantu, South Africa) prefixes in (18):

(18) a. umu-ntu   b. aba-ntu
          SG-person   PL-person

Other languages, such as Lahu (Sino-Tibetan, Burma) in (19), make no distinction, or to put it another way, express both the concepts of singular and plural without any overt inflection:

(19) qhâʔ   "village / villages"

However, very few languages express the plural without an overt inflection and the singular with an overt inflection. (In the case of languages that do, the plural is designated a collective and the singular is a special singulative form, and indeed this pattern is typically associated with nouns for objects occurring in groups.) The typological pattern can again be described in terms of a table (table 14.2) and an implicational universal (see (20)).

Table 14.2 Attested and unattested singular and plural inflectional types

	Overt plural inflection	*No plural inflection*
No singular inflection	Attested (Tatar)	Attested (Lahu)
Overt singular inflection	Attested (Zulu)	*Extremely rare*

(20) If a language uses an overt inflection for the singular, then it also uses an overt inflection for the plural.

It is this cross-linguistic pattern which goes under the name of typological markedness. Typological markedness has two central characteristics. First, typological markedness is a property of *conceptual categories* – e.g. singular and plural – or more precisely, how those conceptual categories are expressed in the world's languages. For number, the singular is unmarked and the plural is marked. Second, unmarked status does not imply that the unmarked member is always left unexpressed and the marked member is always expressed by an overt morpheme. Calling the singular "unmarked" is like calling the order NA "dominant." It does not mean that the singular is always expressed without an inflection in every language, any more than all languages have NA order. It simply means that the singular is expressed by no more morphemes than the plural is, in any particular language. Languages such as Zulu and Lahu conform to the markedness universal just as much as English and Tatar do.

The presence / absence of an overt inflection encoding a conceptual category is only one symptom of markedness, namely *structural coding*. Typological markedness is found in another aspect of the coding of concepts in words and constructions. Most words in sentences express more than one conceptual category. Pronouns in English, for instance, can express gender as well as number:

(21)   *singular*   *plural*
   masculine   he   they
   feminine   she   they
   neuter   it   they

In English, neither the singular nor plural pronouns express number by a separate inflection; instead number is implicitly expressed by distinct forms such as *he* and *they*. However, the singular pronouns (in the third person) also express gender distinctions (*he* / *she* / *it*), while the plural does not (*they* is used no matter what gender the referents are). The grammatical coding of additional, cross-cutting, distinctions in the singular but not in the plural is an example of the second symptom of markedness, called *behavioral potential*. Behavioral potential is also represented by an implicational universal:

(22)   If the marked member of a category grammatically expresses a cross-cutting distinction, so does the unmarked member.

That is, alongside languages like English which express gender distinctions in only the singular, there are languages which express gender distinctions in both singular and plural, and languages which do not express gender distinctions in either the singular or plural. But the universal predicts that there are no languages that express gender distinctions in the plural but not in the singular.

A third property of typological markedness points to its underlying explanation. The unmarked member is more frequent than the marked member in language use, as revealed for example by text counts of singular vs. plural nouns. The form in which concepts are encoded is motivated by their frequency of use. Concepts that occur more frequently in language use (e.g. singular) will tend by default to be expressed by fewer morphemes than less frequently occurring concepts (e.g. plural). This explanation for how meaning is encoded in grammatical form is a processing explanation, called *economy* or *economic motivation*. Of course, we may also ask why people talk more about single objects or individuals than they talk about groups of objects or individuals. There are presumably deeper reasons for why this is true. But frequency in language use is the immediate cause of the asymmetric expression of meaning in form.

Likewise, more frequently used forms will introduce and maintain more cross-cutting distinctions than less frequently used forms. This latter explanation pertains as much to the storage of word forms and constructions in the mind as to their use in speaking and listening. Bybee (1985) has developed a model of the representation of grammatical knowledge in a speaker's mind, related to models of neural networks and connectionist networks in psychology, that accounts for typological markedness. Bybee's model also captures

Table 14.3 Analogical change from Old Church Slavonic to modern Polish

Old Church Slavonic		Polish	
jes-mǐ	"I am"	jest-em	"I am"
jes-i	"you are"	jest-eś	"you are"
jes-tŭ	"he / she / it is"	jest	"he / she is"
jes-mŭ	"we are"	jest-eśmy	"we are"
jes-te	"you (pl) are"	jest-eście	"you (pl) are"
sǫ-tŭ	"they are"	są	"they are"

other universals of the expression of meaning in form. A more frequent form is more firmly *entrenched* in the mind, independent of semantically closely related forms; while less frequent forms are less firmly entrenched, and in fact may be derived from (linked to) semantically nearby, entrenched forms. A more entrenched form can preserve cross-cutting distinctions more easily, while less entrenched forms can be derived by adding an inflection to a semantically nearby, more entrenched form.

Also, a more entrenched form can be irregular, in that it is independently stored in the mind, accounting for the fact that more frequent forms are more likely to be irregular than less frequent ones. Finally, a less frequent form may change to conform with a more frequent form in the same inflectional paradigm. For example, the third person singular is the most frequent form in a verbal paradigm: it is often the shortest, and is sometimes quite irregular. There are a number of cases in which the other forms of a verb change by being derived from the entrenched third singular form. An example of this is the Polish (Indo-European, Poland) inflection of the verb "be" compared to its Old Church Slavonic ancestor: all the Polish forms (except third person plural) have a *t*, based analogically on the third person singular *jest* (see table 14.3).

3.2 *Hierarchies and conceptual spaces*

In many languages, the plural inflection is found on only a subset of nouns and pronouns; other nouns or pronouns use the basic form to refer to either singular or plural number. It turns out that across languages, one finds only a small range of the possible subsets of nouns and pronouns to which the plural inflection is restricted. The attested subsets are given below:

- 1st / 2nd person pronouns (referring to speaker and hearer respectively) vs. 3rd person pronouns (referring to other people) and nouns: e.g. Guaraní (Carib, Paraguay) *né* "you [SG]" / *peẽ* "you [PL]" vs. *haʔé* "he / she / it / they."
- Pronouns vs. nouns: e.g. Mandarin Chinese *tā* "he / she / it" / *tāmen* "they" vs. *shū* "book / books."

- Pronouns and nouns referring to humans vs. nouns referring to nonhumans: e.g. Tiwi (Australian, Melville & Bathurst Islands) *wuɹalaka* "young girl" / *wawuɹalakawi* "young girls" vs. *waliwalini* "ant / ants."
- Pronouns and nouns referring to humans and animates vs. nouns referring to inanimates: e.g. Kharia (Austroasiatic, India) *biloi* "cat" / *biloiki* "cats" vs. *soreŋ* "stone / stones."

We can describe the cross-linguistic distribution of plural markings across classes of pronouns and nouns with a ranking, called the *animacy hierarchy*, given in (23):

(23)   1st/2nd person pronouns < 3rd person pronouns < human nouns < animate nouns < inanimate nouns.

The hierarchy is a succinct way to capture a chain of implicational universals: if inanimate nouns have a plural marking, then animate nouns do also; if animate nouns have a plural marking, so do human nouns; and so on. Another way of describing the generalization expressed by the hierarchy is that if any class of words has a plural, then all the classes to the left (or higher) on the hierarchy have a plural (conversely, if any class of words lacks a plural, then all classes to the right or lower on the hierarchy lack a plural).

The animacy hierarchy is manifested in many different parts of the grammar of languages. Agreement of the verb with a subject is often restricted to the upper portion of the animacy hierarchy, again, with different cutoff points in different languages. Direct objects in the upper portion of the animacy hierarchy often have a special object case inflection. Most striking of all, in a number of languages, if the object is higher on the animacy hierarchy than the subject, a special verbal inflectional form is used, the *inverse* form, in contrast to the *direct* form found when the (more common) opposite state of affairs holds. In many languages (including K'iche' for example), the passive voice cannot be used if the passive subject is lower in animacy than the agent; that is, in such languages a sentence equivalent to "The student was flunked by me" is ungrammatical.

Relatively recently, an explanation has been offered by typologists for what underlies grammatical hierarchies and related patterns. These patterns are defined over a *conceptual space*. The conceptual space describes a network of relationships among conceptual categories which is postulated to exist in the human mind and which constrains how conceptual categories are expressed in grammar. A hierarchy like the animacy hierarchy represents a simple one-dimensional conceptual space as shown in figure 14.1.

1st/2nd person – 3rd person – human noun – animate noun
– inanimate noun

Figure 14.1   One-dimensional conceptual space for animacy.

The conceptual space constrains possible grammatical groupings of words referring to various entities. Languages can group together only the conceptual categories that are linked by lines in figure 14.1. For example, the possible mappings of a plural inflection onto noun and pronoun categories are limited to the types illustrated in figure 14.2:

Guaraní: $\boxed{\text{1st/2nd prn}}$ – 3rd prn – human N – animate N – inanimate N

Mandarin: $\boxed{\text{1st/2nd prn – 3rd prn}}$ – human N – animate N – inanimate N

Tiwi: $\boxed{\text{1st/2nd prn – 3rd prn – human N}}$ – animate N – inanimate N

Kharia: $\boxed{\text{1st/2nd prn – 3rd prn – human N – animate N}}$ – inanimate N

English: $\boxed{\text{1st/2nd prn – 3rd prn – human N – animate N – inanimate N}}$

Figure 14.2   Map of plural inflection in various languages

In contrast, one does not find languages with a plural being used for classes of entities not linked together. For example, one does not find languages with a plural being used with 3rd person pronouns and animate nouns but not with human nouns.

The conceptual space model also make predictions about grammatical change: grammatical change must follow the links in conceptual space. For instance, a plural marking spreads from left to right in the animacy space (or retreats from right to left). Evidence from historical linguistics can be used to confirm the predictions of the conceptual space model. Sometimes the evidence is available in contemporary linguistic variation. For example, the plural in Mandarin Chinese, normally found only with pronouns, sometimes can be used for nouns referring to humans, indicating that it is spreading down the animacy hierarchy. Conceptual spaces are powerful explanatory tools for language universals: they specify what grammatical category groupings are found in, and how constructions spread (or retreat) over time in their application to grammatical categories.

Another important grammatical hierarchy is the *grammatical relations hierarchy*, given in 24 ("oblique" includes various relations indicated by prepositional phrases in English):

(24)   subject < direct object < oblique

If we compare absence vs. presence of *case marking* on nouns for the grammatical relations hierarchy, we find that absence of case marking occurs at he higher end of the hierarchy, and presence thereof at the lower end of the hierarchy, with the cutoff point between absence and presence varying from one language to another (see table 14.4).

Table 14.4   Distribution of absence vs. presence of subject, object and oblique case marking

	Subject	*Object*	*Oblique (dative)*	
Latvian	*ruden-s*	*ruden-i*	*ruden-im*	"autumn"
Hungarian	*ember-Ø*	*ember-t*	*ember-nek*	"man"
Big Nambas	*Ø dui*	*Ø dui*	*a dui*	"person"

(Latvian: Indo-European, Latvia; Hungarian: Uralic, Hungary; Big Nambas: Austronesian, Big Nambas Island.)
Source: Croft 1990: 104

The grammatical relations hierarchy also defines the distribution of *verb agreement* across languages. Languages vary as to how many noun phrases the verb agrees with: some have no agreement, others agree with one noun phrase, while still others agree with two or even three noun phrases in the clause. Verb agreement is associated with the higher end of the grammatical relations hierarchy – the ability to trigger verb agreement indicates the greater behavioral potential of the grammatical relation. As with case marking, the cutoff point for the presence or absence of agreement varies across languages:

(25)   *No agreement: Mandarin Chinese*

tā   néng shuō zhōngguó -huà
3SG can   speak China   -speech
"He can speak Chinese."

(26)   *Agreement with subject only: Spanish*

Los soldado -s   quebr **-aron**   las ventana -s
the soldier -PL break **-3PL.SBJ.PST** the window -PL
"The soldiers broke the windows."

(27)   *Agreement with subject and direct object: Kanuri (Nilo-Saharan, Nigeria)*

nzú-   rú **-kɔ́**   -nà
2SG.OBJ- see -1SG.SBJ -PERF
"I saw you."

The grammatical relations hierarchy as we have described it here does not apply to all languages, of course. In section 1, we saw that some languages have a distinct case marking for transitive subject (A), the ergative, while the transitive object (P) and intransitive subject (S) are encoded in the same way, the absolutive. However, the same kind of cross-linguistic pattern can be found as with subjects and objects. That is, we can formulate an alternative hierarchy of grammatical relations, given in (28):

(28)   absolutive < ergative < oblique

The alternative hierarchy in (28) makes the same predictions about case marking and verb agreement for the languages it applies to. Absence of case marking is associated with the upper end of this hierarchy (see table 14.5).

Table 14.5   Distribution of absence / presence of absolutive and ergative case marking

	Absolutive (S + P)	*Ergative (A)*	
Tongan	*'a he talavou*	*'e ha talavou*	"a young man"
Yup'ik	*nuna-Ø*	*nuna-m*	"land"
Tzutujil	*aachi-Ø*	*aachi-Ø*	"man"

(Tongan: Austronesian, Polynesia; Yup'ik: Eskimo-Aleut, Alaska; Tzutujil: Mayan, Guatemala.)
Source: Croft 1990: 105

And as with the ordinary grammatical relations hierarchy, the presence of verb agreement is associated with the upper end of the alternative grammatical relations hierarchy in the languages for which it is relevant (compare (29–31) with (25–7)):

(29)   *No agreement: Tongan:*

'E   'omi   'e   Sione 'a   e   siaine   kiate au
UNS bring ERG John ABS the banana to   me
"John will bring me some bananas."

(30)   *Agreement with absolutive only: Chechen-Ingush (North Caucasian, Chechnya):*

bier -Ø **d-** ielxa   [CM agrees with "child"]
child -ABS **CM-** cries
"The child is crying."

aːz   yz kiniška -Ø **d-** ieš   [CM agrees with "book"]
1SG.ERG this book   -ABS **CM-** read
"I'm reading this book."

(31)   *Agreement with absolutive and ergative: K'iche':*

k-   **at-**   **in-**   tzukuːj
PRES- **2SG.ABS-** **1SG.ERG-** look.for
"I look for you."

There is a single underlying explanation for this pattern: *token frequency*. The subject category occurs more frequently than the object category: subjects are found with both transitive and intransitive verbs, while objects are found with transitive verbs only. Hence the subject category is typologically less marked than the object category. The absolutive category occurs more frequently than the ergative category – for the same reason. Hence the absolutive category is less marked than the ergative category.

The two grammatical relations hierarchies illustrate an important point about typological universals. Typological universals do not presuppose the existence of any particular grammatical categories in all languages. Given a set of categories in a language, one can form generalizations about the expression of meaning in grammatical form based on the principles described in section 3.1.

The grammatical relations hierarchy, like the animacy hierarchy, is found in other parts of grammar as well. For example, one can classify relative clauses based on the grammatical relation of the head noun to the verb in the relative clause: *the book that fell* [S], *the man that stole my book* [A], *the book that I lost* [P]. Some languages form relative clauses for P (object) differently from A and S (subject), while other languages form relative clauses for A (ergative) differently from P and S (absolutive). For the former set of languages, subject is higher on the hierarchy than object, and for the latter set of languages, absolutive is higher on the hierarchy than ergative. The grammatical relations hierarchy also constrains the types of purpose clauses, such as *I went to town **to buy a sofa*** and coordinate sentences, such as *I went to town **and bought a sofa***, found in the world's languages (Kazenin 1994; lack of space prevents us from describing these patterns here). These facts demonstrate that the two grammatical relations hierarchies in fact reflect a deeper cross-linguistic universal pattern, found in many different parts of the grammar of languages.

What is universal, in fact, is the conceptual space underlying the two alternative hierarchies of grammatical relations. In the case of grammatical relations, the conceptual space is a bit more complex than for animacy. The relevant part for the examples given above consists of S, A, and P, each of which represents a cluster of semantic roles played by participants in events. (Similar systematic patterns of cross-linguistic variation are found with objects; the direct / indirect object distinction is no more universal than the subject / object distinction.) The conceptual space is given in figure 14.3.

Languages can group together grammatical relations linked by lines in the diagram. Hence S can be paired either with A (subject) or P (absolutive); the odd one out is the object (P) or ergative (A) respectively. Languages can use a single form (usually absence of case marking or agreement) to group all three together, or have distinct forms for all three; all these possibilities are attested (see figure 14.4).

The conceptual space in figure 14.3 however predicts that no language forms a grammatical category including A and P, with a distinct grammatical category consisting solely of S; this last type is extremely rare, if it exists at all (Comrie 1978).

Typological analysis has revealed complex and subtle patterns of grammatical variation across languages, and those patterns in turn allow typologists to

Figure 14.3   Conceptual space for semantic roles

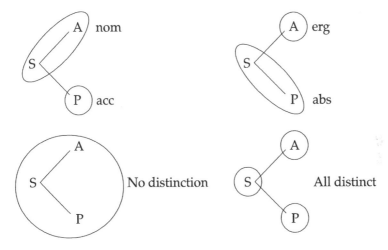

Figure 14.4   Map of attested systems of grammatical relations

construct hypotheses about the structure of conceptual space. Conceptual space is presumably a property of the human mind, and thus typology offers an important tool to uncover the structure of the mind.

3.3 *Economy and iconicity*

In section 3.1, we described typological markedness, which restricted the possibilities of presence vs. absence of grammatical expression of a conceptual category in languages. We introduced the concept of economic motivation: the more frequently used category is more likely to be reduced in expression or left unexpressed. However, one must still explain why languages such as Zulu, which express both singular and plural with inflections, and Mandarin Chinese, which express neither category, are also found. The Mandarin type demonstrates that some grammatical categories are simply not universal. The Zulu case demonstrates that another motivation is involved in the expression of meaning in form: *iconicity*. Iconic motivation is the preference for the structure of language to reflect the structure of concepts. In the Zulu example, each conceptual category, both singular and plural, are overtly encoded in the word form. In this section, we will discuss the ramifications of economic and iconic motivation more widely in the grammars of human languages.

We begin with a subtype of iconicity called *isomorphism*: the correspondence between forms and meanings in a language. There are two ways in which isomorphism between meaning and form occur in human languages. The first way is in the correspondence of forms and meanings found in the combination of words and inflections in a sentence. This sort of isomorphism is called *syntagmatic isomorphism*. Typological markedness is an example of syntagmatic isomorphism. We can illustrate syntagmatic isomorphism by observing the form–meaning correspondence in the English sentence *This car runs* in figure 14.5.

Figure 14.5   Form–meaning correspondence in "This car runs"

Economic and iconic motivation compete to produce the range of attested and unattested (or rare) correspondences between form and meaning. There are three predicted patterns (see table 14.2). Overt expression of each meaning by a single form, as with *car* and *run*, is iconically motivated: there is a one-to-one correspondence between meanings and forms. However, it is only moderately economically motivated: it is more economical than expressing a meaning with more than one word or morpheme, but less economical than not expressing the meaning at all. Non-expression of a particular meaning, such as the singular of English nouns like *car-Ø* (vs. plural *book-s*), is economically motivated but not iconically motivated: zero expression breaks the neat one-to-one correspondence between forms and meanings. The third possible option, zero marking of both singular and plural, corresponds to the absence of expression of the category, e.g. absence of the expression of number in Mandarin Chinese nouns. This option is economically motivated: either the meaning can be inferred from context, or it is not relevant to the communication.

There is another economically motivated pattern of expressing meaning in form that is commonly found in the world's languages, in particular in European languages: the combination or *fusion* of discrete meanings in a single form. For example, the suffix *-s* in English *run-s* indicates 3rd person subject, singular subject and present tense, all in a single suffix. In other languages, inflectional categories (when expressed) are found in separate suffixes, as in Turkish (Altaic, Turkey) *gel-e-sin-iz* (come-subjunctive-2nd-plural) "you may come." Another case of combination of meanings is found in *suppletion*, that is, the expression of root meaning and inflectional category in a single form: English *this* combines proximal (near speaker) demonstrative meaning and singular number (cf. *these*), in contrast to most English nouns which express (plural) number in a separate suffix. The Turkish forms are iconic, but not very economic. The English fused -*s* and suppletive *this* do not express a combination of meanings iconically, but they are economically motivated, packing multiple meanings in one form, either word or affix. As with zero expression, fusion and suppletion are found in the more frequent words or inflectional categories of languages, which suggests they all have the processing explanation given in section 3.1: more frequently occurring meanings are grammatically expressed in a more compact fashion.

The real test for an explanation based on competing motivations such as iconicity and economy is the rarity or absence of patterns that are not accounted for by either motivation. For example, a form that had no meaning associated with it would be neither iconic – it doesn't express any conceptual category – nor economic – it is superfluous. The same is true of a meaning expressed through two or more forms. Such forms, called *empty morphemes*, are in fact extremely rare, and when they occur, they are historically unstable. The most common example is double marking of category, with the loss of the second form. In the historical development of French, the negative was originally indicated by a particle *ne* before the verb: *jeo ne di* "I do not say." Later, *ne* was reinforced by particles after the verb. The particles used dwindled to one, *pas*, which lost its emphatic meaning, so that in Modern standard French, negation is expressed with two fixed forms, *ne* and *pas*: *Il ne parle pas* "he isn't speaking." In colloquial French, *ne* is analyzed as meaningless and dropped: *il parle pas*. An alternative fate for empty morphemes is fusion onto the root. In French, *de l'eau* means "water": *de* indicates a partitive meaning (the water is a subpart of the general mass of water) and *l'* indicates definiteness. In Haitian Creole, derived from French, partitive and definiteness are not part of the grammar any more; but instead of dropping *de* and *l'*, Haitian Creole speakers reanalyzed them as part of the word root: *dlo* "water."

The full range of logical possibilities for expressing meaning in form in syntagmatic isomorphism, and how they are (or aren't) motivated, is given in table 14.6.

Table 14.6   Possible form-meaning correspondences in syntagmatic isomorphism

Form(s)	Meaning(s)	Iconic	Economic	
1	1	Yes	No	Classic iconic structure
0	1	No	Yes	Zero expression of category
0	0	No	Yes	Absence of category
1	>1	No	Yes	Fusion / suppletion (inflectional / lexical)
1	0	No	No	Empty morphemes

The second type of isomorphism is the correspondence between form and meaning in the inventory of words stored in the mind; this is called *paradigmatic isomorphism*. Again, the possible means of expression of meanings in words are limited by economy and iconicity.

Here we will begin with the unmotivated possibility: the existence of more than one word with the same meaning, that is, *synonymy*. It is not iconically motivated – there isn't a one-to-one match between the inventory of words and the inventory of meanings – nor is it economically motivated – the synonymy is superfluous for communication. And in fact true synonyms are extremely rare, if they exist at all: there is almost always some subtle difference in denotation, connotation, stylistic register, dialect, etc. that distinguishes two words (see Cruse, chapter 10, this volume).

A one-to-one match between a word and a meaning is called *monosemy*. It is iconically motivated but not that economically motivated: we would need very many words to express each discrete meaning. Monosemy is probably most clearly found in specialized vocabulary dealing with technical topics. *Homonymy*, the grouping of several unrelated meanings under a single form, represents the converse pattern of motivation to monosemy. Homonymy is economically motivated (there is only one word with several meanings, such as English *bank* "financial institution; edge of a river" or *flour / flower*, pronounced the same), but it is not iconically motivated (many unrelated meanings are expressed by a single form). Homonymy is also common, especially among frequent word forms, as would be predicted.

By far the most common state of affairs in languages, however, is *polysemy*: the grouping of related meanings under a single form. For instance, in the K'iche' sentence in section 1, there are several examples of polysemy: *q'iij* means "day" and "sun," *chii* means "mouth" and "edge," and *wach* means "face" and "(sun) light," among other things. Polysemy is both economically and iconically motivated. It is economically motivated because it subsumes several meanings under a single form, as with homonymy. It is iconically motivated, unlike homonymy, because the meanings are related. The set of related meanings correspond to a contiguous region in conceptual space. The actual iconic correspondence between meaning and form is between a single form and a single region in conceptual space. Monosemy represents a correspondence between a form and a small region (a "point") in conceptual space. Polysemy represents a correspondence between a form and a larger region in conceptual space; the larger the region, the fewer total words necessary to cover the conceptual space, and the more economically motivated the form–meaning correspondence. The possibilities are summarized in table 14.7.

A higher degree of polysemy (i.e., a larger region in conceptual space) is found in more frequently occurring elements, in particular those expressing grammatical meanings and the most common lexical meanings; while monosemy is more likely to be found in less frequent, specialized vocabulary. Again, the economically motivated patterns (polysemy and homonymy) are found in higher-frequency forms.

Table 14.7   Possible form–meaning correspondences in paradigmatic isomorphism

Form(s)	Meaning(s)	Iconic	Economic	
>1	1	No	No	Synonymy
1	1	Yes	No	Monosemy
1	>1 (unrelated)	No	Yes	Homonymy
1	>1 (related)	Yes	Yes	Polysemy

Economy and iconicity play an important role in limiting cross-linguistic variation in the expression of individual meanings by individual forms. This is only the coarsest description of grammatical structure though. In the analysis of the grammatical structure of sentences, there is much more than just the division of the whole sentence into its parts (and the corresponding division of the meaning of the whole into its component meaningful parts). Words in sentences are organized hierarchically into phrases which themselves are put together into larger phrases and ultimately the sentence (see the chapter on syntax in this volume). Examination of the structure of phrases and sentences across languages indicates that these hierarchical structures are iconically motivated. The general principle can be formulated as the implicational universal in (32):

(32)   If a language has two near-synonymous constructions which differ structurally in linguistic distance, they will differ semantically in conceptual distance in parallel fashion (Croft 1990: 175, adapted from Haiman 1983, 1985).

Linguistic distance represents how tightly two forms are combined in a phrase, illustrated in (33) by grammatical constructions of increasing linguistic distance:

(33)   a.   book-s (X + Y)
       b.   red book (X # Y)
       c.   John-'s book (X + A # Y)
       d.   book *of* proverbs (X # A # Y)

The formulas next to the examples are abstract representations of linguistic distance. X and Y are the elements whose linguistic distance is being measured. Affixation (+) is linguistically closer than separate words (#) (cf. (33a–b)); and the presence of an additional affix or particle (A) grammatically linking X and Y indicates greater linguistic distance between X and Y than its absence (cf. (33c–d) vs. (33a–b)).

Conceptual distance is best illustrated by an example. The semantic relation of possession can be divided into two types. One type is called inalienable possession, roughly, those entities which are obligatorily possessed, such as one's hands or one's daughter. (Of course, a hand can be cut off from a person, and a daughter's parents may die before her, but the body part or person always originates as possessed by the person in question.) The other type is alienable possession, roughly, those entities which are not obligatorily possessed, such as artefacts and other physical possessions. Conceptually, inalienable possession represents a more intimate conceptual relationship between possessor and possessed than alienable possession does. Thus, there is less conceptual distance between possessor and possessed in inalienable possession than in alienable possession.

Many languages have two different syntactic constructions for possession, one for inalienable possession and the other for alienable possession. According to the implicational universal in (32), if a language distinguishes the two types of possession, using constructions of different syntactic structure, the linguistically closer construction is used for inalienable possession. This is indeed the case, as illustrated in table 14.8 (order of possessor and possessed does not matter here).

Table 14.8   Linguistic distance among expressions of possession

Language	Alienable possession	Inalienable possession
Mekeo (Austronesian)	eʔu ngaanga my canoe X # Y	aki-u brother-my X + Y
Warrgamay (Australian)	ŋulmburu-ŋu mindi woman-GEN dilly-bag X + A # Y	ŋulmburu bingany woman foot X # Y
Kpelle (Niger-Kordofanian)	ŋá pérɛi my house X # Y	ḿ-pôlu my-back X + Y
	`kâloŋ ŋɔ̀ pérɛi chief POSS house X # A # Y	`kâloŋ pôlu chief back X # Y

Source: Based on Croft 1990: 175

The Kpelle example is particularly interesting. One construction, the X # Y construction, is used for both alienable pronominal possession ("my house") and inalienable nominal possession ("the chief's back"). But what matters is the relative linguistic distance of the appropriate contrasting constructions:

"my back" uses a linguistically closer construction than "my house," while "the chief's house" uses a linguistically more distant construction than "the chief's back."

Linguistic distance has been shown to limit significantly the range of cross-linguistic variation found in a wide range of grammatical constructions, including possession, causative constructions (Haiman 1983), the different types of finite and nonfinite complements found with different verbs (Givón 1980), and the relative order of inflectional prefixes and suffixes on verbs (Bybee 1985). For example, the English sentence *He felled the tree* describes a more direct causal relation between agent and patient than *He made the tree fall*. The former sentence combines both "cause" and "fall" in a single word *fell*, while the latter sentence expresses "cause" and "fall" as separate words – greater linguistic distance corresponding to greater conceptual distance between agent and patient.

It has been suggested that iconic motivation accounts for the general grouping of words into phrases (*constituents*). For instance, the syntactic constituents in the following English sentence, indicated in brackets, belong together conceptually as well as linguistically:

(34)   [[A tall young man [with [a red beret]]] [came in]].

The adjective *red* describes the beret not the man, the adjectives *tall* and *young* describe the man not the beret, and the particle *in* describes the direction of motion of the action of coming, not a property of the man or the beret; and these facts are reflected in the syntactic positioning and grouping of these modifiers in the sentence.

This hypothesis, which has often been put forward (it is called Behaghel's law, after an early twentieth-century German linguist), has not been systematically investigated across languages. Supporting evidence for the hypothesis would be the existence of (constrained) variation where there are competing conceptual motivations for the grouping of words. One example is the expression of direction as in *Minnie walked into the room*. The directional word *into* is semantically associated with both the action (it indicates the direction of action) and the location (the room, since it acts as the reference point for the description of the path of movement). In fact, cross-linguistically there is variation as to whether the directional word (DIR) is associated with the verb (V) or the locational noun phrase (NP; Croft 1990: 182–3). The examples below are listed from closest association to the location NP to closest association with the verb:

(35)   *Hungarian (Uralic, Hungary)*

      Szabó úr   kiszáll a   vonat -ból
      Szabo Mr. get.out the train -out.of
                V   [NP + DIR]
      "Szabo got out of the train."

(36) *English:*

   "Minnie walked into the room."
         V   [DIR # NP]

(37) *Mandarin Chinese:*

   wǒ bǎ tā   tuī dǎo   zài shāfa shang
   I   OBJ her / him push down at sofa on
                    [V # DIR]   NP
   "I pushed her / him down onto the sofa."

(38) *Kinyarwanda (Niger-Kordofanian, Rwanda):*

   umugóre yooherejé -ho isóko   umubooyi
   woman   she.sent -to market cook
            [V   + DIR]   NP
   "The woman sent the cook to the market."

Economic and iconic motivation appear to be pervasive in determining many aspects of the expression of meanings and combinations of meanings in words and sentences. As in other areas of grammar, the universals defined by economic and iconic motivation constrain cross-linguistic variation without eliminating it. The existing variation is due to the competition between economy and iconicity, and between different iconically motivated pressures for the grouping and association of words in sentences.

4   The Dynamic Approach to Language Universals

English, Irish, and Hindi illustrate the most common word orders of sentences found in the world's languages – SVO, VSO, and SOV:

(39) *English:*

   Hannah doesn't speak English.
     S   V   O

(40) *Irish (Indo-European, Ireland):*

   labhrann Mícheál gaeilge le Cáit go minic
   speaks   Mícheál Irish   to Cáit often
     V   S   O
   "Mícheál often speaks Irish to Cáit."

(41) *Hindi (Indo-European, India):*

Raaman hindii boltaa hai
Raman Hindi speak AUX
  S   O   V
"Raman speaks Hindi."

However, all three languages belong to a single family, Indo-European. Hence, they are all descended from a single ancestral language (see Joseph, this volume). Yet the daughter languages all have different word orders. This simple fact implies that languages can change word order type. Thus, we may explore language change from a typological perspective: what are the range of possible language changes? How and why do languages change type?

In fact, *diachronic typology* – the typological study of language change – can explain many aspects of *synchronic typology* – the typological study of current language states. Current language states are the current stages in processes of language change. An explanation of the current language state will often refer to the forces that led to its establishment and its maintenance. Indeed we have already given a dynamic spin on the typological analyses presented above: competing motivations cause languages to change type, and language change follows the paths and topography of conceptual space. Of course, the establishment and maintenance of a grammatical feature of a language is a social phenomenon to a great extent: the innovation of a grammatical feature in language use is driven by the needs of communicative interaction, its propagation through the speech community by the prestige and social identification of its users, and its persistence in that community by conformity to social convention. But independent of these social factors are certain inherent properties of grammatical patterns that lend themselves to a higher likelihood of being innovated in the first place and a higher likelihood of resisting replacement. And these properties are revealed in the cross-linguistic distribution of the grammatical patterns.

For example, the verb-initial order of Irish is not very common in the world's languages; but where it is found, it tends to be found in most members of the language family (for example, most Celtic languages are verb-initial). This cross-linguistic distribution suggests that verb-initial order is *infrequent* – it arises rarely – but is fairly *stable* – it has survived into the daughter languages of Celtic and other language families. The word orders SVO and SOV are on the other hand very frequent and also stable: they occur everywhere in the world, and tend to conform to genetic groupings. There are also examples of grammatical features which arise quite frequently but are not very stable (definite articles), and features that are extremely rare and also unstable (object-initial word orders such as OVS). Cross-linguistic distribution alone, measured with a good proportional sample, tells us quite a bit about the dynamic aspects of grammatical features of languages.

Three working assumptions are made in the study of the typology of language change. First, the ancestral languages from which our contemporary

languages are descended are assumed to conform to the typological generalizations of contemporary languages: we do not expect ancestral languages to
be radically different from all contemporary ones. Historical records of ancient
languages such as Sanskrit, Ancient Egyptian, Sumerian, and Ancient Chinese
support this *uniformitarian* hypothesis. Second, it is assumed that any language
type can change into any other language type, albeit via intermediate stages in
many cases; this assumption is called *connectivity*. The fact that single language
families have a wide range of grammatical variation among their daughter
languages implies that all language types can be connected by processes of
change. Finally, it is assumed that all language change is *gradual* in one way
or another. This last hypothesis is supported by the wide range of variation
found in individual languages, which demonstrates the presence of a language
change in progress, and by direct historical evidence in the languages where
we have it.

One can use these working assumptions to take a synchronic typological
analysis and convert it into a hypothesis about universals of language change
that can be tested where historical data exist or where the history of a language can be reliably reconstructed. For example, it is well known that the
word order of a genitive modifier and noun is closely related to the word order
of an adposition (preposition or postposition) and noun. If a language has
prepositions, then it has noun-genitive order, as in Indonesian (Austronesian,
Indonesia): *dari kota* [to city] "to the city" and *rumah Tomo* [house Tomo] "Tomo's
house." If a language has postpositions, then it has genitive-noun order, as in
Amele (Papuan, Papua New Guinea): *Jelso dec* [Yelso from] "from Yelso" and
dana caub caja [man white woman] "white man's woman."

There are exceptions to this generalization. English is arguably one of those
exceptions: it has prepositions (*to the park*), but in addition to the noun-genitive
construction found in *the back of the chair*, it also has the genitive-noun construction *Nina's car*. However, it turns out that the exceptional languages all
have adjective-noun order that is harmonic with the genitive-noun order –
English has adjective-noun order (*black book*) in harmony with the anomalous
genitive noun order in *Nina's car*.

One can refine the cross-linguistic generalization to include adjective-noun
order in the pattern: "If a language has prepositions, then if it has genitive-
noun order, it will also have adjective-noun order." More interestingly, one can
then dynamicize this relationship and hypothesize that adjective-noun order
will change first, then genitive-noun order, and finally adposition order. To do
so we determine which language types are permitted by the implicational
universal, and then connect them so that only one word order changes at a
time:

  1 NA & NG & Prep
  2 **AN** & NG & Prep
  3 **AN** & **GN** & Prep
  4 **AN** & **GN** & **Postp**

This hypothetical universal of the sequence of word order changes in language presupposes the working assumptions given above. Uniformitarianism means one should not assume that ancestral languages belong to an unattested type. Connectivity means that one can connect the possible language types in a single network of changes. Gradualness means that one need only connect language types where only one word order changes at a time.

As a matter of fact, this sequence of changes has been discovered in Ethiopian Semitic, a subfamily of Semitic whose speakers migrated to Ethiopia from Arabia many centuries ago and who left written records of earlier stages of their languages (Greenberg 1980). The classical religious language Ge'ez has NA, NG, and Prep orders, although there are some instances of AN and a special genitive construction with a prefix on the genitive occurs in either NG or GN order. The next phase is found in modern Tigre, where AN and NA order are approximately equal in status. In Tigrinya, NA order is disappearing. In fourteenth-century Amharic, AN order is the only one found, and the old genitive construction with NG order only is lost. Also, postpositions are found in combination with prepositions, the latter sometimes reduced to a general particle ʔə or nothing at all. In modern Amharic, the newer genitive construction occurs in only GN order. Old Harari is essentially like modern Amharic, but modern Harari has only postpositions. A similar process took place in the Iranian language family.

The evolution of Ethiopian Semitic and Iranian not only confirms the dynamic interpretation of the word order universal. It also shows that there is a seamless connection between variation within a language and variation across languages. Most of the Ethiopian Semitic languages do not display a uniform word order for adjectives, genitives, and adpositions. Thus, technically, none of them belong to the types 1–4, and none totally conform to the word order universal. But the reason for this apparent problem with the word order universal is that languages are always in the middle of changes over time, and the contemporary grammar is often caught in the middle of the process. The process, however, is the true universal generalization: adjectives shift order first, then genitives, then adpositions. In this way, diachronic typology shifts the center of gravity away from language states and towards processes of language change, in explaining those very language states. Indeed, it may be that the languages which provide nagging exceptions to typological universals are merely unstable intermediate stages in universal processes of language change.

The example of Ethiopian Semitic describes only the demise of prepositions. It is hypothesized that the reverse process takes place as well: a language of type 4 in the table will change first its adjective order, then its genitive order, and finally its preposition order to return to type 1:

5   NA & **GN** & **Postp**
6   NA & NG & **Postp**
1   NA & NG & Prep

Each change is *unidirectional,* and the overall pattern constitutes a *cycle* of changes that returns to the original state. In this way, any language type can change to any other language type, gradually, even though language change is unidirectional. Unidirectionality is the final working hypothesis of diachronic typology. It is hypothesized that even when it appears that language type A changes to type B and vice versa, closer examination of the intermediate stages in the two processes (A > B and B > A) will demonstrate that there is in fact a cyclic pattern of unidirectional changes.

The most widespread (and best studied) set of unidirectional, cyclic changes found in languages are found in *grammaticalization.* Grammaticalization is the process by which grammar is created: grammar arises through the exploitation of ordinary words in constructions for grammatical expression. A simple English example is the use of the phrase *going to* for future tense. *Go to* originally referred to spatial motion towards a destination (and still does): *I'm going to the store.* It then came to be used to indicate motion to carry out a future action: *I'm going to buy a pizza.* Finally, it is now used to indicate a future action that does not necessarily involve motion: *I'm going to finish this letter by lunchtime.* In the process, the actual form of the verb plus *to* has been reduced and modified to *gonna.*

This process illustrates grammaticalization in a nutshell. Grammaticalization involves three synchronized processes of change: *phonological, grammatical,* and *functional.* In this example, the form of *go to* is reduced to *gonna* (phonological change); it is also reduced in status, from a main verb to a sort of auxiliary (grammatical change); and its meaning shifts from lexical content – motion towards – to a "grammatical" meaning – future tense (functional change). Moreover, the change of a verb of motion to a future tense marker is found in language after language; in one recent cross-linguistic survey, 20 out of 44 examples of future inflections are derived from "come" or "go" (Bybee et al. 1994). Hence, this change is a universal of language change, not just a quirk of the history of English.

The changes in linguistic form in grammaticalization – phonological and grammatical – represent a cycle (see Keller 1994, Lüdtke 1985). A new, periphrastic means to express a function such as future tense is chosen by speakers, possibly to express the concept more clearly or more precisely. The new means becomes conventionalized in its function and it becomes a fixed complex unit of expression. This unit is then ultimately reduced to a single unanalyzable form (*gonna* in the example). Ultimately, it may become affixed to the verb and disappear; but often by this time, the cycle is started again with a new construction. (After all, English *gonna* has not yet replaced the older future auxiliary *will.*)

The shift from lexical meaning to "grammatical" meaning is unidirectional, and represents a path in the relevant region of conceptual space (cf. section 3.2). The relevant part of conceptual space for the motion-to-future path of grammaticalization is shown in figure 14.6.

motion to a location – motion to a location then [future] action –
future action only

Figure 14.6 Conceptual space for grammaticalization path from motion to future action

A variety of explanations have been offered as to why forms spread in only one direction in grammaticalization. One hypothesis is that "grammatical" meanings are those that structure our conceptualization of the experience being expressed, so grammaticalization represents the shift from a word denoting the content of experience to a grammatical inflection structuring our experience. Another hypothesis is that "grammatical" meanings express the more situational or interactional aspects of the experience being expressed, so grammaticalization shifts words from a more "objective" to a more "subjective" meaning. Whatever the explanation, it is clear that most grammatical constructions arise from periphrastic expressions with ordinary words, and there are only a limited number of paths of grammaticalization for each grammatical category that are used by languages. An understanding of grammaticalization is a prerequisite for understanding the nature of grammar.

5 Conclusions

Typology, the exploration of the diversity of languages and the limits on that diversity, reveals new and important aspects of the nature of grammar and meaning. In order to compare the grammars of diverse languages, typologists have used equivalent functions to investigate variation in how meaning is expressed across languages. Typologists have also developed descriptions of grammatical form that can abstract away from the myriad language-specific categories and constructions, such as presence vs. absence of encoding of concepts, the presence vs. absence of cross-cutting distinctions, the mapping of meaning components into morphemes, and linguistic distance. The exploration of how grammatical form expresses communicated meaning across languages has led to the discovery of conceptual spaces which reflect commonalities in the structure of the human mind. The variation across languages reflects competing means of expressing form and competing forces in the production and comprehension of utterances. The grammar of a language at any given moment is a system balancing competing motivations as to how best to express communicative function in linguistic form. The balance is constantly shifting, giving rise to language changes, the most important of which are those processes that constantly renew the grammar of languages by the grammaticalization of new constructions.

APPENDIX 14   ABBREVIATIONS FOUND IN EXAMPLES

1, 2, 3: first person (I, we), second person (you), third person (he, she, it, they)

ABS: absolutive, a case marking used to indicate intransitive subjects (S) or transitive objects (P)

ACC: accusative, a case marking used to indicate transitive objects only (P)

AOR: aorist tense inflection

AUX: auxiliary verb

CM: noun class agreement marker

ERG: ergative, a case marking used to indicate transitive subjects (A)

GEN, POSS: genitive / possessive marker

IMPF: imperfective verbal aspect

NOM: nominative, a case marking used to indicate transitive subjects (A) and intransitive subjects (S)

NONFUT: nonfuture tense

OBJ: object (P)

PERF: perfective verbal aspect

PL: plural

PRES: present tense

SBJ: subject (A + S)

SG: singular

UNS: unspecified verbal tense-aspect-mood

15 An Introduction to Formal Semantics

SHALOM LAPPIN

1 Introduction

When people talk, they generally talk about things, events, and situations in the world. They are able to do this because they represent connections between the expressions of their language and extra-linguistic phenomena in a fully systematic way. The meaning of a sentence in a language is, to a large extent, dependent upon the ways in which the words and phrases from which it is constructed can be related to situations in the world. Speakers of a language are able to communicate effectively with each other because they have internalized the same rules for pairing the lexical items of the language with non-linguistic elements, and they use the same procedures for computing the meaning of a syntactically complex phrase from the meanings of its parts. Therefore, speakers will, in general, converge on the same sets of possible language–world connections which they assign to the sentences in their discourse. Formal semanticists seek to understand this aspect of linguistic meaning by constructing precise mathematical models of the principles that speakers use to define those relations between expressions in a natural language and the world which support meaningful discourse.[1]

Consider an example. Assume that two students in a class are discussing the class's progress on a term paper. One student asserts (1a) and the second responds with (1b).

(1) a. John has finished his paper.
    b. No one in the class has finished his / her paper.

For the second speaker to understand (1a), he / she must be able to pick out the person corresponding to *John*. He / She must also know what property *finished his paper* expresses and recognize that the first speaker is claiming that the person corresponding to *John* has this property. If (1b) is true, then it implies that (1a) is false by virtue of the fact that (1b) states that no person in

the class has the property of having finished his / her paper. Therefore, assuming that the second speaker understands both (1a) and (1b), then he / she
recognizes that asserting (1b) involves making a statement which is incompat-
ible with the one made by the first speaker.

To competent speakers of English all of this is thoroughly obvious. This is
because we have already internalized the semantics of English, which we rely
on in understanding the partial (and informal) description of the semantic
competence required to interpret the simple dialogue in (1). But consider what
is involved in developing a complete theory of this semantic competence which
renders formal and explicit our tacit knowledge of linguistic meaning rather
than presupposing it. Such a theory will specify what sort of properties verb
phrases (VPs) like *finished his paper* refer to, and it will model properties in
general as formal objects of a kind which can apply to the entities of the sort
identified by *John*. It will also capture the important semantic distinctions and
similarities between proper names like *John* and quantified noun phrases
(NPs) such as *no one*. Specifically, while *John* selects an individual, *no one* does
not. On the other hand, both kinds of expression can combine with the predicate *finished his paper* to yield a meaningful statement. It is also necessary to
explain the difference in the anaphoric relation which holds between the pronoun *his*(/ *her*) and the subject NP in (1a) and (1b).

A complete semantic theory will apply not only to the sentences in (1),
but to all syntactically well-formed sentences of the language. Specifically, it
must explain our capacity to assign interpretations to an unbounded number
of grammatical sentences. Given that we can only represent a finite number of
primitive semantic elements, this capacity requires the recursive application
of rules to the meanings of expressions in order to derive interpretations for
larger phrases.[2] There is, then, a direct formal analogy between the syntactic
component of the grammar, which employs recursive procedures to generate
a (potentially) infinite set of sentences from smaller lexical and phrasal units,
and the semantics, which combines the meanings of these units into the
interpretations of the sentences in which they are contained.

In the following sections I will look at some of the central questions which
arise in constructing a formal semantic theory for natural language, and I will
briefly indicate several of the major lines of research which formal semanticists
have pursued in their attempts to answer these questions.

2   Meanings and Denotations

Semanticists have traditionally focussed on theories of meaning which apply
to sentences that make statements, and are taken to be either true or false. The
assumption underlying this approach is that this type of sentence provides a
paradigm of the sort of relationship between linguistic expressions and the
world which is at the core of linguistic meaning. An additional assumption is

that if it is possible to construct a successful account of the meaning of declarative sentences used to make statements, then this account can be generalized to non-declarative sentences, like interrogatives that are employed for asking questions, and imperatives which communicate commands.[3]

It is possible to locate the beginnings of modern formal semantics in the work of the German logician, Frege, who created the foundations of first-order logic.[4] We have identified one of the key tasks of a semantic theory as the specification of a systematic correspondence between categories of expressions in a language and types of entities in the world. The main syntactic categories which Frege identifies in natural language correspond to the types of first-order logic. These types are (i) individual terms (names of individuals, and variables that occur in the same positions in sentences that names do), (ii) predicates (terms for properties and relations), (iii) connectives (*and, or, if ... then*, and *not*) for building composite sentences and negations out of component sentences, and (iv) quantifiers that are linked to variables (bind the variables). Proper names, like *John*, and definite descriptions like *the Prime Minister* are treated as individual terms that occupy the positions of arguments in predicate terms. VPs like *sings* and *introduced the bill* are one-place predicates in that they apply to single arguments to yield statements.

Frege claims that for each logical type an expression of that type can take a certain sort of entity as its *denotation* (the thing that it stands for). Individual terms denote individuals in the world (more precisely, in the domain of discourse shared by the speaker and his / her hearers). If one knows how a declarative sentence like (2a, b) stands in relation to the world, then one knows whether it is true or false.

(2)   a.   John sings.
      b.   The Prime Minister introduced the bill.

In this sense, the primary semantic value of a declarative sentence is its truth or falsity, and Frege takes declarative sentences to denote truth-values. One-place predicates denote functions from individuals to the truth-values true or false. Every function is a mapping from a set of arguments (its domain) to a set of values (its range). Therefore, the function f which a one-place predicate denotes can be represented as the set of objects in f's domain for which f yields the value true. The VP *sings*, for example, denotes the set of things in the domain of discourse of which *sings* is true. (2a) is true if and only if (iff) the individual which *John* denotes is an element of the set that *sings* denotes, and similarly for (2b).

This schema for category–type correspondence extends naturally to sentences formed with logical connectives like *and, or, if ... then*, and negation, as in (3).

(3)   a.   John sings and Mary dances.
      b.   John sings or Mary dances.
      c.   If John sings then Mary dances.
      d.   John doesn't sing.

Two-place connectives denote functions from pairs of truth-values to a truth-value. So *and* maps two true sentences into the value true, and every other combination of truth-values into false. (3a) is true iff both *John sings* and *Mary dances* are true. *Or* maps any two false sentences into the value false, and any other pair of values into true. (3b) is true iff at least one of the disjuncts connected by *or* is true. *If . . . then* is false if the antecedent (the sentence immediately following *if*) is true and the consequent is false, and true otherwise. It follows that (3c) is true iff either *John sings* is false or *Mary dances* is true. Finally, a negated sentence is true iff the sentence to which the negation applies is false. (3d) is true iff *John sings* is false.

What about quantified NPs like *nobody* in (1b), and the subjects of (4)?

(4)   a.   Someone sings.
     b.   Everyone dances.

Unlike individual terms, they do not denote individuals in the domain, but they do seem to occupy the same grammatical category as these terms. How, then, do we interpret them? Frege revolutionized logic by treating quantifiers as second-order functions, or, equivalently, second-order property (set) terms (see note 4 for the distinction between first- and second-order terms). On this view, (1b) and (4a, b) are not statements in which a predicate is applied to an argument, but quantified sentences in which a term that corresponds to a property of a set applies to a predicate (a term that denotes a set). (4a) is true iff the set of things that sing has at least one element, and (4b) is true iff everything in the domain of people dances. (1b) is equivalent to (5).

(5)   It is not the case that someone in the class has finished his / her paper.

This sentence is true iff the set of people in the class who have finished their respective papers is empty.

First-order logic has two basic quantifiers, *every* and *some*. Each of these quantifiers can be expressed as an operator that is prefixed to a sentence and associated with variables which appear in the argument positions of predicates in the sentence. The symbol commonly used for *some* is $\exists x$ (*for some x*), and for *every* it is $\forall x$ (*for every x*). The symbols frequently used for negation, conjunction, and implication are $\sim$ (*it is not the case that*), & (*and*), and $\rightarrow$ (*if . . . then*), respectively. Let's substitute *some student* for *someone* in (5) in order to give explicit expression to the restriction of the quantifier *some* to the set of students in the domain. Then we can represent (5) in first-order logic as (6a), which is equivalent to (6b).

(6)   a. $\sim\exists x(\text{student}(x) \ \& \ \text{finished } x\text{'s paper}(x))$
     b. $\forall x(\text{student}(x) \rightarrow \sim \text{finished } x\text{'s paper}(x))$

(6a) states that it is not the case that there is an object x in the domain which is both a student and finished its own (x's) paper. (6b) states that for every x in the domain, if x is a student, then it is not the case that x finished x's paper. Notice that each occurrence of the variable x is interpreted relative to the quantifier prefixed to the sentence where the variable appears. The quantifiers $\exists x$ and $\forall x$ *bind* the variable x in (6a) and (6b), respectively.

On Frege's view individual terms and variables, unlike quantifiers, are arguments of predicates. Therefore, (1a) is expressed in first-order logic by (7).

(7)   finished john's paper (john)

Notice that the anaphoric relation between the pronoun *his* and *John* in (1a) is captured by substituting the denotation of *John* for the pronoun in (7). By contrast, the anaphoric dependence of *his* (*her*) upon its quantified NP antecedent *no one* in (1b) is represented by using a bound variable for the pronoun in (6a, b).

Definite descriptions pose an interesting problem for a theory which attempts to explain the meaning of an expression in terms of its denotation. The definite descriptions *the former Governor of Arkansas* and *the President of the United States* denote the same object, Bill Clinton. Therefore, if we substitute one for the other as the argument of the predicate *plays the saxophone*, the truth-value of the resulting statement should not be affected. In fact, (8a) and (8b) do have the same truth values.

(8)   a.   The former Governor of Arkansas plays the saxophone.
      b.   The President of the United States plays the saxophone.

However, the two descriptions do not have the same meaning, and (8a) and (8b) assert different statements. *The former Governor of Arkansas* identifies the person who was the previous governor of Arkansas, but who no longer holds this position, and *the President of the United States* denotes the individual who is the current president at a particular point in time. The difference in meaning can be brought out clearly by evaluating (8a, b) relative to a particular point in time. During the 1992 American presidential election campaign, (8a) was true, as Clinton was the former Governor of Arkansas, but not yet the President. (8b), however, was false, because George Bush was the President.

The observation that the denotation of an expression does not exhaust its meaning led Frege to factor meaning into the two components of *denotation* and *sense*. He characterizes the sense of an expression as the principle for determining its denotation. Therefore, two terms with the same sense will always have identical denotations, but as (8) indicates, the converse does not hold. Frege does not give a precise description of the formal entities which correspond to senses. Carnap (1947) substitutes *extensions* for denotations and *intensions* for senses. Extensions correspond closely to Frege's denotations. We can take the extension of an expression E to be the entity which it denotes, where this entity is of the kind appropriate for E's logical type. The extension of a declarative sentence is its truth-value, of a name an individual object, and of a predicate a set of objects (or, in the case of a relation, a sequence of objects).

The intension of an expression E is essentially a rule for identifying E's extension in different situations. Carnap characterizes intensions as functions from possible worlds to denotations, where a possible world can be thought of as the result of specifying the properties and relations which hold for the objects of a domain in a way that defines a complete state of affairs for the entities of the domain. The actual world is one of many (in fact, an infinite number of) possible worlds. The intension of an expression takes a possible world as an argument and yields the extension of the expression in that world as its value. Therefore, the intensions of *the former Governor of Arkansas* and *the President of the United States* identify (i) the person who satisfies the property of being the previous governor of Arkansas and (ii) the person who is currently the President of the United States, respectively, in each world. These two denotations converge on the same individual in the actual world, but are distinct in other possible worlds (and times). Similarly, the intension of the VP *plays the saxophone* picks out the set of objects which play the saxophone for each world. The intension of a sentence assigns it a truth-value in each possible world. We obtained (8b) from (8a) by substituting one description for another with the same extension but a distinct intension. The substitution produced a sentence with the same extension (truth-value) in the actual world (at the present time), but a different intension (proposition).

We observed that one of the main tasks of semantic theory is to explain how speakers compute the meanings of complex phrases from the meanings of their parts. Frege adopts the principle of *compositionality* as a condition of adequacy on any account of meaning. Compositionality requires that the meaning of any well-formed phrase in a language be a function of the meanings of its syntactic components. This condition implies that, for any phrase P, given the meanings of the constituents of P, there is a function which maps these meanings into the meaning of P. This principle has enjoyed wide acceptance throughout the history of semantic theory. Clearly, if an account of meaning satisfies compositionality, it specifies the way in which the interpretations of complex structures are generated from their constituents. However, as we will see in section 5, it is possible to construct non-compositional semantic theories which also fulfill this task.

On the Frege–Carnap approach, the principle of compositionality yields two distinct sub-principles: (i) the extension of a phrase is a function of the extensions of its parts; (ii) the intension of a phrase is a function of the intensions of its parts; truth functional connectives produce complex sentences that satisfy (ii). So, for example, the truth-value of (3a) is a function of the truth-value of the two conjuncts of *and*.

(3) a. John sings and Mary dances.

However, verbs like *believe*, which map propositions into properties (sets) of individuals are problematic. Unlike truth functional connectives, *believe* is sensitive to the intension as well as the extension of the sentence which it takes as its grammatical complement. Substituting one complement sentence for another with the same truth-value but a different proposition can alter the extension, as well as the intension of the entire VP.

In addition to the Frege–Carnap view there is another approach, which dispenses with intensions and seeks to construct a theory of meaning solely in terms of the contributions which expressions make to the truth (i.e. extension) conditions of sentences. This approach is developed by Davidson, and it takes as its starting point Tarski's (1933) definition of truth for first-order languages.[5] Tarski constructs a recursive definition of the predicate *true-in-L* for a class of first-order languages similar to the first-order language characterized by Frege. The definition proceeds stepwise first to elementary sentences constructed from individual terms (constants or names, and variables) and predicates, next to compound sentences formed by applying truth functions to other sentences, and finally to quantified sentences. For each sentence S of type T in language L, it specifies the truth conditions for S in terms of the relations which must hold among the denotations of the constituents of S. As a result, Tarski's truth definition generates appropriate truth conditions for the full set of well-formed sentences of L.

Davidson regards Tarski's truth definition as the paradigm of a semantic theory.[6] If to know the meaning of a declarative sentence is to know its truth conditions, then Tarski's definition gives an explanation of sentence meaning in terms of a precise and fully systematic account of the connections between sentences and the world. It does this in a way which exhibits how the interpretations of sentences are built up from the interpretations of their constituents.[7] Davidson's general strategy is to associate the sentences of a natural language with first-order logical forms to which a Tarskian truth definition can apply.

Frege and Carnap on one hand, and Davidson on the other, share the assumption that the sentences of natural language are analyzed in terms of the types of first-order languages, specifically, individual terms, k-place predicates (predicates that take k number of arguments), truth-functional connectives, and first-order quantifiers like *every* and *some*. Montague (1974) discards this assumption, and establishes a far richer and more expressive type system for intensional semantics.[8]

The basic framework which Montague adopts for developing a formal syntax and semantics for natural language is categorial grammar.[9] In this system a small number of syntactic categories are taken as basic. All other categories are functions from input expressions of a certain category to output expressions of a given category. Assume, for example, that we take sentences and expressions which denote individuals (i.e. names) as basic, and that we indicate the former category by t (for truth-value) and the latter category by e (for entity). Categorial grammarians represent functional categories as slashed expressions in which the argument term appears to the right of the slash and the output term is to the left. A VP and a common noun are both a t/e (a function from names to sentences), a transitive verb is a (t/e) / e (a function from names to VPs), a verb like believe, which takes a sentential complement, is (t/e) / t (a function from sentences to VP's), an NP is a t / (t/e) (a function from VP's to sentences), and a determiner is a (t/(t/e)) / (t/e) (a function from common nouns to NPs. In each case, a slashed category expression combines with a term of the kind indicated to the right of the slash in order to produce a term of the sort which appears to the left of the slash.

Consider the sentences in (9a, b).

(9)   a.   Mary sings.
      b.   John likes Mary.

If we take *Mary* as name of category e, then *sings*, which is an intransitive verb of type e/t combines with the e term *Mary* on its left to produce a t term (sentence). Similarly, the transitive verb *likes* in (9b) is of category (t/e) / e. It combines with the e term object *John* on its left to yield an intransitive verb (VP) *likes John* of type e/t. This e/t term takes the e term *John* on its left to give a t term as its value.

Montague establishes a strict correspondence between the syntactic categories and semantic types (denotation types) of the grammar. The correspondence is expressed as a homomorphism, which is a mapping that assigns a single semantic type to each syntactic category. Sentences denote truth-values, and predicates (VPs and common nouns) denote functions from individuals to truth-values (equivalently, sets of individuals). For all other categories where *f* is a syntactic function of the form *a/b*, the semantic value (denotation) of *f* will be a function from the intension of *b* (*f*'s argument) to the extension of *a* (*f*'s value). So, for example, *believe* is an element of the category of functions from sentences to VPs, and it denotes a function from sentence intensions (propositions) to sets of individuals. This set contains the people who stand in the belief relation to the proposition expressed by the complement of *believe*. Montague grammar defines the category-type correspondence recursively for every expression of the language in a way which satisfies the principle of compositionality. Therefore, the meaning of every phrase in the language is a function of the meanings of its parts. Moreover, given the functional nature of syntactic categories and semantic types, it is possible to generate as many of each as one requires to accommodate complex syntactic structures in natural language. Each functional category will always map into a corresponding semantic type that specifies the set of possible denotations for the expression. Although there are, in principle, an unbounded number of functional categories and types, only a finite (and fairly small) number are used in the grammar of a language.

Two important differences between the Montague and Davidsonian approaches concern (a) the analysis of modification and (b) the treatment of NPs. Consider modifiers of common nouns, like the adjective *green* in *green house*, and modifiers of VPs, like the temporal adverb *on Thursday* in *arrived on Thursday*. On the Davidsonian view, modifiers are predicates which apply to individuals. A modified common noun is taken to be the conjunction of several predicates. (10a), for example, is analyzed as (10b), which states that there is an object x such that x is a house, x is green, and Mary has x.

(10) a. Mary has a green house.
       b. ∃x(house(x) & green(x), & has(mary, x)).

Adverbs are also taken as predicates, and they are applied to events, which are included in the domain of entities.[10] (11a) is interpreted as (11b), which asserts that there is an event e that has the property of John arriving in e, and e occurred on Thursday.

(11) a. John arrived on Thursday.
       b. ∃e(arrived(j,e) & on_Thursday(e)).

For Montague both common nouns and VPs are predicates. Syntactically, modifiers are functions from predicates to predicates, and semantically they are functions from predicate intensions to predicate extensions (sets). In (10a) *green* denotes a function which takes the intension of *house* as its argument and yields the set of green houses as its value. Similarly, in (11a) the function which *on Thursday* denotes applies to the intension of *arrived* to give the set of things that arrive on Thursday.

Davidson's account is attractively simple and straightforward. It reduces all modification to first-order predication. However, it encounters two problems. First, it assigns a semantic type to modifiers which is quite remote from their syntactic role. Syntactically modifiers are functions that apply to expressions to produce expressions of the same category. Adjectives and relative clauses apply to nouns to create modified nouns, and adverbs apply to VPs to create modified VPs. However, Davidson's analysis treats modifiers as semantic predicates that have the same kind of denotation as the predicates they modify. So, for example, in (10b) both the noun *house* and its modifier *green* are taken as one-place predicates. Similarly, in (11b) the verb *arrived* corresponds to a two-place predicate, and its adverb *on Thursday* is analyzed as a one-place predicate.

Second, the analysis does not extend to modifiers that produce expressions whose meanings cannot be taken as the conjunction of two predicate extensions. The adjective *toy* and the adverb *allegedly* in (12a, b), respectively, are examples of such non-extensional modifiers.

(12) a. John has a toy car.
       b. Mary allegedly submitted her paper.

(12a) cannot be paraphrased as there is an x such that x is a toy, x is a car, and John has x. The sentence means that John has an object which resembles a car in certain respects, but which is not a car. Similarly, (12b) cannot be taken to assert that there is an event e in which Mary submitted her paper, and e allegedly occurred. If (12b) is true, then there may have been no event of Mary submitting her paper. Non-extensional modifiers require a different kind of semantic representation. They cannot be analyzed as predicates that apply to objects and events. Therefore, Davidson's approach does not provide a unified treatment of modification.

Montague's account avoids both difficulties. The semantic type of a modifier is a function which works in strict parallelism with its syntactic function. Syntactically it is a function from predicates to predicates, and semantically it denotes a function from the intension of its syntactic argument to the extension of its syntactic value. An adjective denotes a function from the intension (property) of the noun to which it applies to the set of objects that the modified noun denotes. An adverb has as its denotation a function from the intension (property) of the VP which it modifies to the set of objects that provide the extension of the modified VP. This account covers non-extensional modifiers by virtue of the fact that the function that a modifier denotes applies to predicate intensions rather than extensions. In (12a) the denotation of *toy* applies to the intension of *car* rather than the set of cars (the extension of *car*) to give the set of toy cars (not the set of things which are both toys and cars). In (12b), the denotation of *allegedly* takes the intension of *submitted her paper*, not the set of submitted papers as its argument. It yields the set of (female) things which allegedly submitted their respective papers as the extension of the modified VP.

The disadvantage of Montague's treatment of modification is that it does not express the fact that when an extensional modifier applies to a predicate, it does produce a predicate whose interpretation is equivalent to the conjunction of two predicates. In order to capture this property of modification, it is necessary to add a set of rules to the semantic part of the grammar which insure that (10a) implies that Mary has a house, and it is green, and (11a) implies that John arrived and his arrival was on Thursday. Therefore, while Montague's approach offers a unified account of modification, it does so at the cost of a more complicated treatment of extensional modifiers.

Turning to the interpretation of NPs, we have already observed that Davidson follows Frege in taking proper names to be terms that denote individuals and appear as arguments of predicates, while analyzing quantified NPs as operators which bind variables in argument positions. Therefore, (13a) and (14a) are assigned the logical forms in (13b) and (14b), respectively.

(13)   a.   John sings
        b.   sings(john)

(14)   a.   Every student sings.
        b. $\forall x(student(x) \rightarrow sings(x))$

The advantage of this view is that it associates sentences like (13a) and (14a) with first-order formulas for which a Tarskian truth definition is available. The semantic interpetation of the sentence follows directly from its logical form. Notice, however, that while names and quantified NPs appear in the same syntactic roles (subject, object, indirect object, object of a preposition, etc.), they are mapped into distinct semantic types.

Because names and quantified NPs occupy the same syntactic roles (subject, object, object of a preposition, etc.), Montague treats them as members of a single syntactic category. He characterizes them as functions which take VPs as arguments to produce sentences (i.e. they are functions of the sort t / (e/t)). Recall that all elements of a given category receive the same semantic type in accordance with the general principle that specifies the category–type correspondence. It follows from this principle that all NPs denote functions from VP (predicate) intensions to truth-values. Predicate intensions are properties of individuals, and, as we have observed, a function from entities to truth-values is equivalent to the set of those entities to which it assigns the value true. Therefore, the function which an NP denotes can be represented by a set of properties (the set of properties for which it gives the value true). Recall that Frege treats quantifiers as second-order properties, i.e. as sets of sets. If we simplify Montague's account slightly by taking NPs as functions from predicate extensions (sets), rather than predicate intensions, to truth-values, then NPs denote sets of sets. For Montague, all NPs are, in effect, quantifiers. This semantic type is referred to as the class of *generalized quantifiers* (GQs), where a GQ is a set of sets of individuals.[11]

It is clear how an NP like *every student* can be interpreted as a generalized quantifier. It denotes the set of sets (or properties) each of which contains (at least) every student. (14a) is true iff the set of things that sings is an element of this set of sets. The set of singers is an element of the set of sets denoted by *every student* iff the set of singers contains the set of students as a subset, which is equivalent to the assertion that every thing which is a student sings. The truth conditions that Montague's GQ analysis assigns to (14a) are equivalent to those of the first-order sentence in (14b).

But it is not so obvious how proper names can be accommodated in this system. Montague's solution to this problem is to treat a name as denoting not an individual, but the set of sets containing an individual (the property set of an object). (13a) is true, then, iff the set of singers is an element of the set of sets containing John, which holds iff John is an element of the set of singers. As there is a one-to-one correspondence between the property set of an individual and the individual itself, these truth conditions reduce directly to those for (13b).

The GQ analysis sustains a uniform semantic representation of NPs. However, it does so at the price of certain complications. These become particularly clear in the case of NPs in non-subject position, like *Mary* in (15a) and *every paper* in (15b).

(15)   a.   John likes Mary.
       b.   Max read every paper.

The truth conditions of these sentences can be expressed by the first-order sentences in (16), where *likes* and *read* are naturally represented as denoting relations between individuals.

(16)   a.   likes(john, mary)
       b. $\forall x(\text{paper}(x) \rightarrow \text{read}(\text{max}, x))$

However, if *Mary* denotes a GQ, then *likes* denotes a function from GQs to sets.[12] This function must be characterized as applying to Mary's property set to yield the set of objects that like Mary as the denotation of *likes Mary*. Similarly, *read* in (15b) maps the GQ denoted by *every paper* into the set of objects which read every paper. Therefore, we are forced to adopt the counter-intuitive idea that transitive verbs stand for relations between individuals and sets of sets (GQs) rather than the more natural view that they denote relations between individuals.

An important advantage of the GQ approach is that it covers NPs like *most students*, which cannot be reduced to restricted first-order quantifiers like *every / some student*. To see this, consider what sort of logical form would correspond to (17).

(17)   Most students sing.

Assume that *most*(x) is a variable binding operator like $\exists x$ and $\forall x$, and that C is a truth-functional connective. Then the logical form for (17) will be an instance of the schema (18), with an appropriate connective substituted for C.

(18)   most(x)(student(x) C sings(x))

But there is no truth-functional connective which can be substituted for C to yield a first-order sentence with the correct truth conditions for (17). The reason for this is that *most*(x) quantifies over the entire domain of objects, while in (17) the natural language determiner *most* expresses a relation between the set of students and the set of singers which cannot be captured by a truth-functional connective. If we use & for C, then (18) states that most objects in the domain are both students and singers. Alternatively, if we take C to be $\rightarrow$, then (18) asserts that for most objects x, if x is a student, then x sings. (17) does not make either of these claims. It states that the majority of objects in the set of students are singers. In fact, there is no first-order sentence whose truth conditions give the intended interpretation of (17).[13]

Taken as a GQ *most students* denotes the set of sets which contain more than half the set of students. (17) is true iff the set of singers is in this set. This condition holds iff the the number of students who sing is greater than half the number of students. Clearly, these are the correct truth conditions for (17). The existence of quantified NPs like *most students* shows that the meanings of some expressions in our language cannot be fully expressed in terms of the

truth conditions of first-order sentences, and it is necessary to use more powerful systems, like GQ theory, to model the semantics of natural language.

3   Dynamic Semantics: beyond Static Sentence Meanings

Until now we have been concerned with the interpretation of sentences as static
and independent units of meaning. This perspective allows us to focus on the
way in which the meanings of a sentence's constituents contribute to its truth
conditions. But, in fact, we generally encounter a sentence as a part of a discourse, where we understand it on the basis of preceding contributions to the
conversation. When we situate sentence meanings in a discourse, they are no
longer static objects, but active devices that have the capacity to inherit semantic
content from previous sentences, modify it, and pass on the new information
to the next sentence in the sequence.

The simple two-sentence discourse in (19) illustrates this dynamic aspect of
meaning.

(19)   John came in. He sat down.

We understand *he* in the second sentence as referentially dependent upon *John*
in the first. We also impose an ordering relation on the events described by
these sentences, so that we take John to have sat down after he entered. The
interpretation of *He sat down* depends upon the information introduced by
John came in.

Now consider the discourse in (20).

(20)   A man came in. He sat down.

Although it resembles (19), there is an important difference. The proper name
John denotes an individual, but the indefinite NP *a man* does not. Notice, also
that because the pronoun occurs in a different main clause than the indefinite,
we cannot treat it as a variable bound by an existential quantifier. In general, pronouns can only be interpreted as bound by a quantifier in the same
clause. In (21a), *his* can be understood as a variable bound by the quantifier
corresponding to *every boy*, as in (21b).

(21)   a.   Every boy handed in his paper.
　　　 b. $\forall x(boy(x) \supset$ handed in x's paper(x))
　　　　　 (For every x, if x is a boy, then x handed in x's paper.)
　　　 c.   Every boy arrived. He had a good time.
　　　 d. $\forall x(boy(x) \supset arrived(x))$. had_a_good_time(x)
　　　　　 (For every x, if x is a boy, then x arrived. x had a good time.)

However, such an interpretation is not available for *he* in (21c). The quantifier in (21d) cannot bind the variable x in the following sentence, which is out of its scope. Therefore, x is free (unbound by the quantifier) in the second sentence of (21d). This sentence says that x had a good time without placing any restrictions on the values of x. We could have used y instead of x in the second sentence of (21d), which would give *had_a_good_time*(y), without changing the meaning of (21d).

The interpretation of *A man came in* in (20) makes available a possible referent which *he* can be used to identify in the next sentence. However, it is not clear precisely which part of the meanings of these two sentences creates this entity.

The cases in (22) provide examples of a similar but more complex anaphoric relation between a pronoun and an indefinite NP.[14]

(22)   a.   Every man who owns a donkey beats it.
       b.   If a man owns a donkey, he beats it.

As with the pronoun in (20), *it* is not within the scope of its antecedent, the indefinite NP *a donkey*, in either (22a) or (22b). This NP is contained either in a relative or subordinate clause rather than in the main clause where *it* appears. *He* is not within the scope of *a man* in (22b) for the same reason. However, both pronouns appear to function like variables bound by the universal quantifier *every*. On their most natural readings, (22a, b) assert that for every man x and every donkey y, if x owns y, then x beats y. The quantified NP subject in (22a) and the antecedent *if* clause in (22b) give rise to the representation of a set of ordered pairs <a, b> such that a is a man, b is a donkey, and a owns b. For each such pair, *he* in (22a) identifies a, and *it* in both sentences selects b. The problem is that because the pronoun *it* is anaphorically dependent upon the indefinite *a donkey* in (22a, b) it does not correspond to a variable bound by a universal quantifier. It is not obvious, then, how it is possible to interpret (22a, b) as equivalent in truth conditions to a sentence in which *it* is bound by a universal quantifier corresponding to *every donkey*.

There are three main approaches to dynamic anaphora, and I will briefly sketch each one in turn. The first is discourse representation theory (DRT).[15] In this framework an indefinite NP is treated not as a quantified NP, but as an expression which introduces a discourse referent that satisfies the content of the indefinite description. In (20) *a man* introduces an object u, which satisfies the predicate *man*, into the store of information available within the discourse. The sentence also applies the predicate *came in* to u. Therefore, the first sentence of (20) adds the conditions *man*(u) and *came in*(u) to the discourse information store. As u is now accessible at future points in the discourse, it is possible to use a suitable pronoun to refer to it. The second sentence of (20) contributes the condition *sat down*(u), which is obtained by taking u as the value of *he*. The conjunction of these conditions on u yields a discourse representation structure that holds iff there is a man who came in and that man sat down, which is the desired reading of the sequence.

Applying this approach to (22b), the two indefinite NPs in the antecedent clause introduce two distinct discourse referents u and v, and the conditions *man*(u), *donkey*(v), and *owns*(u,v). These referents and conditions are accessible to the consequent clause, where u and v are substituted for *he* and *it*, respectively, to produce the condition *beats*(u,v). However, the relation between the two clauses is not that of a simple sequential conjunction, as in (20), but a conditional connective. Therefore, it is necessary to interpret the combined discourse structure as asserting an *if . . . then* relation between the conditions of the antecedent and that of the consequent. On the preferred reading of (22b), the conditional sentence is within the scope of the implied adverb of universal quantification *in every case* (or *always*). Applying this quantifier to the conditional discourse structure gives a set of conditions that hold iff for every case, if there is a pair containing a man and a donkey which he owns, then the first element of the pair beats the second. This is the required interpretation for (22b). Assume that the universal quantifier *every* of *every man who owns a donkey* in (22a) sets up a universal conditional relation between the conditions imposed by the modified noun *man who owns a donkey* and those of the VP *beats it*, and that it also introduces a variable x into both sets of conditions. The antecedent of this conditional contains *man*(x), *donkey*(u), and *owns*(x,u), and the consequent adds *beats*(x,u). This discourse representation structure specifies the same interpretation as the one for (22b).

The second approach to dynamic anaphora is the dynamic binding account.[16] It retains the traditional view of indefinites as existentially quantified NPs. In addition to the classical logical connectives and quantifiers it introduces dynamic counterpart operators whose scopes can extend beyond single clauses. The dynamic existential quantifier $\exists^d x$ has the effect of introducing a discourse referent associated with the variable x which can be inherited by the informational state (discourse model) that serves as the input to a subsequent sentence. The dynamic conjunction $\&^d$ passes the referents in the information state produced by its first conjunct to the interpretation of the second. These dynamic operators are used to represent (20) as (23a), where the dynamic existential quantifier occurs in the first dynamic conjunct of the sentence. The interpretation assigned to this formula has the same truth conditions as (23b), in which a static (classical) existential quantifier has scope over all the conjuncts.

(23) a. $\exists^d x(man(x)$ & came_in (x)) $\&^d$ sat_down(x)
        (for some^{dynamic}x[x is a man and x came in] and^{dynamic} [x sat down])
    b. $\exists x(man(x)$ & came_in (x) & sat_down(x))
        (for some x[x is a man and x came in and x sat down])

The dynamic implication $\to^d$ holds between two sentences A and B for a given set R of discourse referents iff every information state which A produces for R gives rise to one which successfully interprets B. The connective $\to^d$ can be combined with the dynamic existential quantifiers $\exists^d x, \exists^d y$ to represent (22b) as (24a), where the dynamic quantifiers occur in the antecedent of the conditional sentence and dynamically bind the variables in the consequent. (24a) has the same truth conditions as (24b), in which the entire conditional is within the scope of two static universal quantifiers.

(24)   a. $\exists^d x \exists^d y(man(x) \ \& \ donkey(y) \ \& \ owns(x,y)) \rightarrow^d beats(x,y)$
           (for some^{dynamic}x and for some^{dynamic}y[if^{dynamic} x is a man and y is a donkey and x owns y], then^{dynamic} [x beats y])
       b. $\forall x \forall y((man(x) \ \& \ donkey(y) \ \& \ owns(x,y)) \rightarrow beats(x,y))$
           (for every x and for every y[[if x is a man and y is a donkey and x owns y], then [x beats y]])

(24a, b) are true iff for every pair <a,b> such that a is a man, b is a donkey, and a owns b, a beats b. However, 24a corresponds directly to (22b) in that it represents both indefinite NPs in (22b), *a man* and *a donkey*, as (dynamic) existentially quantified NPs rather than as universally quantified NPs as in (24b). Therefore, this analysis provides an explanation for the fact that, in sentences like (22b), pronouns which are anaphorically dependent upon indefinites behave like variables bound by universal quantifiers.

By defining a dynamic universal quantifier $\forall^d x$ and combining it with $\exists^d y$ and $\rightarrow^d$, it is possible to obtain (25) for (22a). (25) has the same truth conditions as (24a, b). In this formula, *every man* corresponds to a restricted dynamic universal quantifier and *a donkey* to a restricted dynamic existential quantifier.

(25) $\forall^d x((man(x) \ \& \ \exists^d y(donkey(y) \ \& \ owns(x,y))) \rightarrow^d beats(x,y))$
       (for every^{dynamic}x [[if ^{dynamic} x is a man and for some^{dynamic}y[y is a donkey and x owns y]], then^{dynamic} [x beats y]])

As in the case of (24a) and (22b), (25) corresponds directly to (22a) in that the indefinite *a donkey* is represented by a (dynamic) existential quantifier rather than a universal quantifier (as in (24b)). Therefore, the dynamic binding account of donkey anaphora also permits us to account for the fact the pronoun *it* in (22a) is understood as bound by a (classical) universal rather than a (classical) existential quantifier.

While DRT uses indefinites to introduce referents into a discourse and dynamic binding relies on dynamic operators to pass information concerning discourse referents from one sentence to another, the third approach locates the mechanism for dynamic anaphora in the interpretation of the pronoun which takes a quantified NP as its antecedent. This sort of pronoun, referred to as an E-type pronoun, effectively functions like a pointer to a description that refers back to an entity (or collection of entities) in the set that is determined by its quantified NP antecedent.[17] Taking *he* in (20) and (22b), and *it* in (22a) and (22b) as E-type pronouns gives interpretations of these sentences corresponding to (26a) and (26b).

(26) a.   A man came in. The man who came in sat down.
      b.   Every man who owns a donkey beats the donkeys he owns.
      c.   If a man owns a donkey, the man who owns a donkey beats the
           donkey he owns.

So in (20), for example, the E-type pronoun *he* is interpreted by the description
the man who came in, as in (26a).

Another way of understanding an E-type pronoun is to treat it as corresponding to a function which applies to objects in an appropriately specified
domain to give values in a set defined in terms of the denotation of its antecedent NP. The antecedent of *he* in (20) and (22b) is *a man*, which is not within the
scope of a quantified NP. Therefore, the E-type function associated with *he*
maps any object in the domain of discourse onto an element in the set of men
who own donkeys. In (22a, b) the antecedent of *it* is *a donkey*, which is in the
scope of *every man* and *a man*, respectively. It denotes an E-type function from
men who own donkeys to (collections of) the donkeys which they own.

The three approaches discussed here use different formal techniques for
modeling dynamic anaphora. However, common to all of them is the view
that a major part of understanding the meaning of a sentence is knowing its
possible influence on the informational structure of a discourse in which it
appears.

4   Meanings and Situations: beyond
Possible Worlds

In section 2 I described the intension of an expression as a function from a possible world to the extension of the expression. A world is the result of assigning the objects of a domain to properties and relations in such a way as to
produce a complete state of affairs containing these objects. There are at least
some cases where it seems to be necessary to use situations rather than worlds
to specify the interpretation of a sentence.[18] A situation is a smaller and more
fine-grained object than an entire world. It can be contained in larger situations, and it is, in effect, the specification of part of a world (equivalently, a
partial specification of a world).

To see the role of situations in representing meaning let's return to the
analysis of generalized quantifiers. In section 2 we characterized the denotation of an NP as a GQ (a set of sets). For quantified NPs, we can, equivalently,
take the determiner of the NP as denoting a relation between the set denoted
by the noun to which the determiner applies and the predicate set of the
VP. For example, the GQ corresponding to *every student* is the set of sets each
of which contains the set of students. Alternatively, *every* denotes the relation
that holds between any two sets A and B when A is contained in B. On both
conditions, (14a) is true iff the set of students is a subset of the set of singers.

(14)   a.   Every student sings.

Similarly, the determiner *the* denotes the relation that holds for two sets A and B when the unique element of A is a member of B. Therefore, (27) is true iff there is a single woman and she dances.

(27)   The woman dances.

If the intension of *the woman* takes the actual world (or any world which resembles it) as its argument, then it will yield the set containing the empty set as the extension of the NP. This is because it is not the case that the set of woman has only one element in the actual world. As the relation denoted by *the* does not hold between the set of women and the set of dancers, (27) is false in the actual world. It will only be true in a world containing a unique woman. But this is the wrong result. There are surely cases where an assertion of (27) is literally true in the actual world by virtue of the fact that the speaker is referring to a particular woman, despite the existence of other women in the world.

Instead of treating a property as applying to an object in a world, we can localize the relation to a situation within a world. This will give us statements of the form *Mary is a woman in s*. We can express this relation between a statement and a situation s by saying that s supports the information that Mary is a woman. If we identify a situation s containing a unique woman u and interpret *woman*, relative to s, as denoting the singleton set containing u, then (27) is true if u dances, even though u is not the only woman in the world. This s is the resource situation which we use to determine the GQ that *the woman* denotes.

Imagine a conversation in which I am telling you about two successive visits to the theater. On the first trip I saw a production of a musical with one female actor, and on the second I saw a comedy which also featured one female actor. Using each play as a resource situation I assert (28a) in describing the first production, and (28b) in my account of the second.

(28)   a.   The woman sang.
       b.   The woman did not sing.

Assume, also, that the same actress appears in both plays. It is still the case that both (28a) and (28b) are true. Although the two resource situations identify the same person, each situation supports one of the assertions.

Cooper (1996) uses resource situations to characterize the class of GQs denoted by NPs in natural language. He also points out that it is necessary to distinguish between the resource situation in which the restriction (common noun) set of a GQ is fixed and the situation in which the entire sentence containing the GQ expression is evaluated. (29) brings out the distinction clearly.

(29)   Everyone spoke to John.

The quantificational situation q which supports (29) includes John. Therefore, if we identify it with the resource situation r for setting the restriction set of the relation denoted by *every*, (29) implies that John spoke to himself. This consequence is avoided if r and q are distinct. We could, for example, take r to be properly contained in q, so that the restriction set is a subset of the set of people in q.

Cooper also argues that the quantificational situation must be distinguished from the individual situations i in which the property expressed by the VP applies to each of the elements of the restriction set. He invokes cases in which perception verbs, like *see*, take quantified complements to motivate this claim.

(30)   a.   John saw everyone leave the concert.
       b.   John saw each person leave the concert.

(30a) can be true in a situation in which John saw all of the people at a concert leave the hall, but he did not observe each person leave individually. By contrast, (30b) is true only if he saw each person leave. This difference in interpretation consists in the fact that the truth conditions for (30b) require the identification of q and i while those for (30a) do not.

Conditional donkey sentences in the scope of quantificational adverbs like *usually* provide another case in which situations play a central role in determining the meaning of quantifier terms. (31) allows at least two different interpretations.

(31)   Usually if a man owns a donkey, he beats it.

On one reading, (31) says that for most pairs <a,b> where a is a man, b is a donkey, and a owns b, a beats b. Given this interpretation, (31) is true in the following state of affairs. There are 10 donkey owners, 9 of whom each owns a single donkey, and one who owns 20. The 9 men who each own a donkey do not beat it, but the one donkey owner who has 20 beats all of them. There are 29 distinct pairs of men and donkeys they own. The man who owns 20 is the first element of 20 pairs, with each of his donkeys as the second element of one of these pairs. The 9 other owners and their donkeys contribute the remaining 9 pairs. The sentence is true because the first element beats the second in 20 out of 29 of these pairs. On the second reading, 31 claims that most men who own donkeys beat the donkeys they own. With this interpretation, the sentence is false in the situation described here, as it requires there to be more than 5 men who beat the donkeys they own.[19]

It is possible to account for these interpretations by treating adverbs like *usually* as quantifiers that denote relations between sets of situations.[20] *Usually* denotes a relation that holds between two sets of situations A and B iff most of the elements of A are also in B. The different readings are generated by varying the size of the situations in the restriction set that corresponds to the antecedent of the conditional sentence. If this set contains only minimal situations involving a donkey owner and a single donkey, then (31) asserts that most situations consisting of a man and a single donkey which he owns are situations in which he beats that donkey. This yields the first reading. When the restriction set contains maximal situations involving a man and all of the donkeys he owns, then (31) states that most situations in which a man owns donkeys are situations in which he beats the donkeys he owns. This provides the second reading. The first interpretation is symmetrical in that *usually* quantifies over situations defined by pairs of donkey owners and individual donkeys. The second is asymmetrical as *usually* effectively quantifies only over donkey owners.

By using situations to specify the extensions of predicates and quantificational expressions it is possible to represent aspects of interpretation which cannot be captured in classical intensional semantics.

5   Underspecified Representations: beyond Compositionality

As we observed in section 2, the condition of compositionality requires that the meaning of any expression P be computable by a function which, given the meanings of P's syntactic constituents as its arguments, yields P's meaning as its value. We have also seen that Montague grammar satisfies this condition by characterizing the relation between the set of syntactic categories and the set of semantic types as a homomorphism which maps each syntactic structure into a single denotational type.[21] In this framework the meaning of an expression is fully determined by (a) its syntactic structure and (b) the meanings of its constituents.

In order to sustain a homomorphism of this kind, the function which specifies the mapping from syntax to semantics must apply to expressions with fully specified syntactic representations and yield unique semantic values. Therefore, syntactic and semantic ambiguity are eliminated by the mapping which the function specifies. Ambiguous lexical items are divided into words which stand in a one-to-one correspondence with the distinct senses of the original term. The verb *run*, for example, becomes a set of verbs each of which is assigned a denotation corresponding to one of *run*'s meanings (move quickly, operate or administer something, flow, function, etc.).

(32) is ambiguous between two scope interpretations of the quantified NP *a painting* relative to the intensional verb *seek*.

(32)   John is seeking a painting.

If *a painting* receives narrow scope relative to *seeks*, then John wants there to be some painting or other which he finds. If it has wide scope, then there is a particular painting which he is looking for. Montague generates these readings from distinct syntactic structures. The narrow scope reading is obtained when *a painting* originates *in situ* as an argument of *seeking*. For the wide scope reading, *a painting* is generated outside of the sentence *John seeks it* and is substituted for the pronoun. The VP of the first structure denotes the set of things which stand in the seek relation to the intension of the GQ denoted by *a painting*. This set is the value that the function denoted by *seeks* assigns to the intension of *a painting*. On the second syntactic derivation, *a painting* is interpreted as a GQ which applies to the predicate set containing the objects that John is seeking. This derivation yields the interpretation that there is a painting x and John is seeking x.

In fact, it is possible to construct a semantic system that is non-compositional, but relates the meaning of an expression systematically and incrementally to the meanings of its parts.[22] This is achieved by allowing the mapping from syntax to semantics to be a relation which assigns more than one meaning to an expression under a single syntactic representation. In such a system the verb *run* could be paired with a disjunction of meanings corresponding to each of its senses. (33) would be represented as having one syntactic structure, with a VP headed by a single verb *run*, which is associated with at least two distinct semantic representations.

(33)   John ran the marathon.

On one, John was a runner in a race, and on the other he administered it. On this view, (33) would be represented by a single syntactic structure which is mapped to a set containing two interpretations, each providing a distinct set of truth conditions. To obtain a disambiguated reading of the sentence it is necessary to select one element of the set.

A more interesting case of non-compositional interpretation involves mapping a syntactic structure into a set of alternative scope readings. There are at least two ways of doing this. On one approach, quantified NPs can either be taken as GQs *in situ* (in the argument positions where they appear in the syntactic structure of the sentence) or interpreted through the device of quantifier storage.[23] When storage applies to an NP, a variable meaning is substituted for the argument position which it occupies, and the GQ is placed in a stored part of the meaning of the expression where the NP appears. The non-stored meaning of the expression, which includes the variable in the original argument position of the NP, is combined with the meanings of larger expressions until a point is reached where a predicate set is specified. The GQ can be released from storage at this point and applied to the predicate. As we have seen, if *a painting* in (32) is interpreted *in situ*, it is within the scope of the verb *seeks* and the narrow scope reading results. If it is placed in storage, the set of objects x such that John seeks x is computed as the interpretation of the open sentence (predicate) *John is seeking x*. The GQ denoted by *a painting* is released from storage and applied to this set to yield the wide scope reading of the sentence. Unlike Montague's analysis, this account assigns a single syntactic structure to

(32) where *a painting* is always in object position. The structure is associated with two distinct scope interpretations obtained by different procedures.

On the second approach, sentences containing scope-taking expressions are assigned schematic semantic representations in which the scopes of these terms are left unspecified.[24] In the representation for (32), for example, the scope relation between *a painting* and *is seeking* is undefined. Similarly, *a student* and *every program* are unordered for relative scope in the representation assigned to (34).

(34)   A student checked every program.

The second treatment of scope ambiguity is similar to the first in that it also associates a syntactic structure with a set of alternative scope interpretations. However, it implies a more far reaching revision of the compositional view of semantic interpretation. This approach takes the meaning of an expression to be a partial representation R defined in terms of a minimal set of conditions C on the interpretation of R. To obtain a more specified meaning one adds new constraints to C to restrict the set of interpretations with which R is compatible. A compositional semantics provides a homomorphism for mapping unambiguous syntactic structures into fully specified semantic values. An underspecified semantics, by contrast, establishes a relation between syntactic structures and partial semantic representations whose parameters characterize sets of possible values. These sets can be further restricted by adding constraints to the representation.

6   Conclusion

Initial attempts to construct a formal semantic theory for natural language used the syntax and truth definitions of first-order languages as a model. Therefore, they associate the categories of natural language with the semantic types of first-order logic. Montague introduced a richer type system which permits a direct mapping of complex functional categories into corresponding types. It also expresses the interpretation of higher-order expressions, such as non-first order generalized quantifiers. Dynamic semantics then moved beyond the static meaning of an individual sentence taken in isolation to representing semantic content in terms of the way in which a sentence transforms the information state inherited from previous sentences in a discourse. Situation semantics replaced the interpretation of expressions relative to a possible world with evaluation in a situation, where the latter is a more finely structured and partially specified entity than the former. Finally, underspecified semantics discards the condition of compositionality to construct a more flexible mapping between syntactic structure and semantic interpretation. This approach sustains a systematic connection between the meaning of a phrase and the meanings of its parts while using partially defined representations to capture ambiguity and under-determined interpretation.

It is important to recognize that as new paradigms of semantic representation have emerged, the leading ideas of the earlier programs have not disappeared. They have continued to survive in various formulations and to exert influence on successive generations of theorists, many of whom attempt to solve semantic problems by integrating the insights of earlier models into new frameworks.

In considering the recent history of semantic theory, it becomes clear that the past twenty-five years have seen considerable progress in the application of increasingly sophisticated formal techniques to the explanation of a wide range of semantic phenomena. This work has opened up new areas of investigation and yielded promising results which have turned formal semantics into a well-grounded and exciting domain of linguistic research.

NOTES

I am grateful to Ruth Kempson, Gabriel Segal, and the editors of this volume for helpful comments on earlier drafts of this paper. I am solely responsible for any shortcomings which remain.

1   There are numerous introductory texts on formal semantics, each highlighting different issues and tending to represent a particular theoretical paradigm. Chierchia and McConnell-Ginnet (1990), and Heim and Kratzer (1998) are two recent texts which offer interesting background and perspectives on the field. The papers in Lappin (1996a) provide introductions to current research in the major areas for formal semantics.

2   Rules are recursive if they can apply to their own output an unlimited number of times. By virtue of this property recursive rules can generate an infinite number of structures.

3   For a discussion of the relation between the semantics of declarative and non-declarative sentences see Lappin (1982). For analyses of the semantics of interrogatives see Karttunen (1977),

Hamblin (1973), Ginzburg (1996), Higginbotham (1996), and Groenendijk and Stokhof (1997).

4   See Frege (1879), (1891), and (1892). A logic is first-order when all of its predicates (property terms) apply only to individuals in the domain of discourse (the domain of the logic). A higher-order logic contains predicates which apply to properties or sets of individuals (and possibly other higher order entities). So, for example, "green" is a first-order predicate that applies to physical objects, while "partially ordered" is a higher-order predicate of sets.

5   See note 4 for the notion of first-order terms and first-order logic. A first-order language is a formal language all of whose predicates are first-order. We can say that a logic is a formal language which has additional principles that identify a set of sentences in that logic as true.

6   See Davidson (1967a) and the papers in Davidson (1984). For applications of Davidson's program within linguistic semantics see Higginbotham

(1985), May (1991), and Larson and Segal (1995). Sher (1991) and (1996) extends Tarskian semantics beyond first-order systems.

7　Interestingly, Tarski expressed skepticism about the prospects for developing formal truth definitions for natural languages. He claimed that their terms are often vague or ambiguous. Morever, they permit self-reference in a way which generates paradox, as in the famous liar paradox *This statement is false*, understood as referring to itself. Davidson, like most semanticists, attempts to get around these reservations by adopting an incremental program on which a formal truth definition is first constructed for a representative fragment of a natural language and then extended to progressively larger sets of sentence types.

8　Dowty et al. (1981) provides a very clear and detailed introduction to Montague grammar.

9　For recent introductions to Categorial Grammar see Moortgat (1988), Morrill (1994), and Jacobson (1996).

10　See Davidson (1967b) for this analysis of adverbs. Higginbotham (1985) proposes a Davidsonian treatment of modifiers within the framework of Chomsky's (1981) government and binding model of syntax.

11　For discussions of generalized quantifiers in natural language see Barwise and Cooper (1981), Keenan and Moss (1985), Keenan and Stavi (1986), van Benthem (1986), Westerståhl (1989), Keenan (1996), and Keenan and Westerstahl (1997). For a comparison of the Davidsonian and the GQ approaches to the semantics of NPs see Lappin (1996b) and (1998).

12　I am again simplifying the account by taking transitive verbs to denote functions on the extensions rather than the intensions of NPs. See Cooper (1983) for a treatment of transitive verbs as functions of this kind.

13　See Barwise and Cooper (1981) and Keenan (1996) for this result.

14　Geach (1962) introduced these sorts of cases into the modern semantics literature. The pronouns which are dependent upon indefinite NPs in (22) are generally referred to as *donkey pronouns*, and the anaphoric relation in these structures is described as *donkey anaphora*.

15　DRT was first proposed by Kamp (1981). An alternative version of this theory is presented in Heim (1982). For a recent model of DRT see Kamp and Reyle (1993).

16　The version of dynamic binding which I am summarizing here is essentially the one presented in Groenendijk and Stokhof (1990) and (1991). For an alternative account see Chierchia (1995). Groenendijk et al. (1996) propose a theory of update semantics based on dymamic binding. Kempson et al. (forthcoming) develop a deductive approach to dynamic semantics which has much in common with all three approaches discussed here.

17　Evans (1980) initially proposed the idea of an E-type pronoun. Cooper (1979), Lappin (1989), Heim (1990), Neale (1990), Chierchia (1992), and Lappin and Francez (1994) suggest different E-type accounts of donkey anaphora.

18　Barwise and Perry (1983) introduced a situation-based theory of meaning into formal semantics. For more recent work in situation semantics see Barwise (1989), Barwise et al. (1991), Cooper et al. (1990), Gawron and Peters (1990), Aczel et al. (1993), Cooper et al. (1994), and Cooper (1996). The treatment of generalized quantifiers in terms of situation theory discussed here is based on Cooper (1996).

19　Explaining these distinct readings for (31) is known as the *proportion problem* for conditional donkey sentences with quantificational adverbs of non-universal force. See Kadmon (1990), Heim (1990), Chierchia (1992), and Lappin and Francez (1994) for discussions of this problem.

20 Heim (1990), and Lappin and Francez (1994) pursue this approach. Lappin and Francez analyze quantificational adverbs as generalized quantifiers on sets of situations.

21 A homomorphism is a functional mapping from a domain A to a range B in which several elements of A can be associated with one object in B. Montague's category–type correspondence is a homomorphism because in some cases the same semantic type is assigned to more than one syntactic category. For example, both common nouns and predicates denote sets of individuals.

22 See Nerbonne (1996) for a non-compositional approach to semantics in a constraint-based framework. My discussion of compositionality in this section owes much to his treatment of the issue. Zadrozny (1994) shows that any mapping from syntax to semantic interpretation for a language can be formulated as a function, and so can be expressed compositionally. However, such functions may be non-systematic in the way in which they specify the dependence of a phrase's interpretation on the meanings of its constituents. Specifically, they may involve a case by case listing for subsets of the relevant ordered pairs of meanings for which the functional relation holds.

23 See Cooper (1983), Pereira (1990), Pereira and Pollack (1991), and Dalrymple et al. (1991) for accounts of quantifier storage. Lappin (1991) and (1996b) gives arguments for using storage rather than a syntactic operation of quantifier raising to capture wide scope readings of quantified NPs.

24 See Reyle (1993) and Copestake et al. (1997) for different versions of this view.

16   Pragmatics: Language and Communication

RUTH KEMPSON

1   The Puzzle of Language Use: How Do We Ever Understand Each Other?

How language is used may not seem to warrant a topic on its own. "When *I* use a word, it means just what I choose it to mean – neither more, nor less." This is the view of language expressed by Humpty-Dumpty in Lewis Carroll's *Alice through the Looking Glass*. It may seem mere commonsense that describing a person's knowledge of a language involves simply describing how they use the language. But this can't be *all* there is to say about the relation between our knowledge of language and the way we use it, for words invariably convey much more than they mean. The question is: What does this apparent gap between language use and meaning tell us about language? As Alice quite reasonably objected: "The question is whether you *can* make a word mean so many different things."

The starting point for looking at language use is to consider why Humpty Dumpty might have been right. Consider the conversation in (1):

(1)   A: Can you cook?
     B: I know how to put a kettle on.

Why are such conversations possible – why, for example, did B not just say "No"? After all, if B had understood the question, and knows what such a question "means," she should know that this type of question is a request for the answer *yes* or the answer *no*. So what did she "mean" by choosing that indirect mode of reply in apparent violation of this rule? In what sense could B have "meant" that she never did anything in the kitchen other than putting a kettle on, so the answer is that she cannot cook, or has no interest in cooking, etc.

Then there is the way we can describe things by using words in ways which only have a very indirect relation to what a dictionary would indicate is their meaning:[1]

(2)   You're a real race-horse.

How can the words *real race-horse* be predicated of a single individual, someone transparently not a horse? What could a speaker mean by saying something apparently blatantly far from the truth? One has sympathy with Humpty and yet also with Alice – What is it that we do with language that makes statements such as (2) meaningful and effective?

What these two examples show is that words can be used to convey both more than what they conventionally mean and also something quite different. But, if this is true, how do we manage to sort out which is which? How do we know when an expression is to be taken at its face value, when it is to be taken as conveying rather more than what it actually presents, and when it has to be interpreted in some other, metaphorical, way?

This is only the beginning of the problem of understanding meaning in language use, for even setting aside supposedly special rhetorical effects as in (2), expressions in language are notoriously prone to ambiguity. Yet, by and large, we have no difficulty in sorting out what the speaker is intending to say to us. How do we manage this? To take an extreme example (Sperber and Wilson 1982), consider (3):

(3)   A: How is your son?
      B: He's grown another foot.

Why is it that A is most unlikely to respond with horror, suggesting that it should be amputated? And, with a much less extreme case, how does the hearer decide whether the phrase "in March" describes the time of the exam, the time of discovering the results of the exam, or the time at which Sue made her report:

(4)   Sue reported to the Committee that Joan learnt that she had failed the exam in March.

Even in (1) itself, B's reply could have been intended as a deliberate understatement indicating her cooking talent, which she may be implying A ought to know about. How does A decide which B meant?

To put the problem in its most general form, when we probe the obvious truth that our knowledge of language is reflected in the way we use it, we seem to be faced with a perplexing mystery. How is it that using language is in general so effortless, when there seems to be no limit to what words can convey or what ambiguities they can give rise to? *Pragmatics* seeks to provide an answer to this question. Pragmatics is the study of communication – the study of how language is used. This study is based on the assumption of a division between knowledge of language and the way it is used;[2] and the goal of pragmatics is taken to be that of providing a set of principles which dictate how knowledge of language and general reasoning interact in the process of language understanding, to give rise to the various different kinds of effects which can be achieved in communication. In this chapter, we shall look at different approaches to pragmatics. We will look first at the question of the assumed interaction between language-particular (= linguistic) and general (= nonlinguistic) types of information; and I will argue in section 2 that what we need is a model which allows integration of linguistic and nonlinguistic forms of interpretation at all stages of the interpretation process. In section 3 we will take up the question of how the hearer chooses an appropriate interpretation, and I will introduce the two major alternative views of how interpretations are selected. In section 4, I will set out the view that all words should be defined in terms of procedures for building up structures representing interpretation in context (*propositional structure*). I will give one illustration to show how pragmatic processes can feed into linguistic processes, and the chapter ends with a discussion of the general significance of this "procedural" approach for establishing what it means to "know a language."

2   Pragmatics as the Application of Conversational Principles to Sentence Meanings

The starting point for studies in pragmatics[3] is the mismatch, often a big one, between what words "mean," which is encoded in rules of the language, and what speakers "mean" by using them, which may be much richer. In (1), the words in the sentence B utters convey the information that the speaker has the knowledge of how to put a kettle on. What speaker B means by using these words (on the interpretation indicated first) is that she cannot cook, opening up the possibility of further inferences such as that she has no interest in cooking. One way in which one might seek to generalize from this particular instance is to take (1) as evidence for the two aspects of language use being quite separate. There is the knowledge of language, on the one hand, which dictates the meanings of words and the ways in which they can combine to form sentence-meanings (to be studied under the label *semantics* as part of the grammar of a language). This is called the encoded meaning. On the other hand, there are general pragmatic principles (which I shall initially call "commonsense reasoning" principles) which enable a hearer to establish some rather different and richer interpretation – the nonencoded part of meaning. On this view, we would say that a hearer parsing B's utterance in (1) above first uses rules of the language to work out that B was conveying that she knew how to put a kettle on, and then, only subsequently, uses principles of commonsense reasoning to work out, say, that because B did not reply more directly, it must be that she is expecting A to access the knowledge that people who confess to knowing only how to put on a kettle are no good at cooking in order to work out the intended import of her answer – that she cannot cook. Once such general forms of reasoning are invoked, one might also anticipate that such indirect forms of answer convey more information than a simple negative answer would provide because they trigger such general reasoning processes – for example, communicating from B's implication that she has no interest in cooking the further suggestion that any attempt to extend the conversation with topics associated with food is likely to prove unsuccessful. This approach to pragmatics can be summed up as the view that a grammar of a language provides a characterization of meaning for each individual sentence as articulated in some semantic theory, and that pragmatic principles apply to the output of the grammar-internal characterization to yield its full import in context. This view has been justifiably influential (the Gricean view – Grice 1967, 1975, 1989). It keeps knowledge of language and general reasoning capacities quite separate – even in language use, the latter is seen as being brought into play only after the hearer has established a complete and use-independent characterization of sentence-meaning. It is particularly appropriate for a Chomskian view of linguistic knowledge as a body of knowledge which is encapsulated and independent of other cognitive capacities we humans display (see chapter 00). Moreover, given the full array of rhetorical effects such as metaphor, irony, etc., all of which are uses of expressions in context in some sense, the proposed approach maintains a natural separation between literal uses of words, which are reflected in sentence-meanings, and the various non-literal uses to which they may be put.

2.1   Knowledge of language: sentence-meanings as partial specifications of interpretation

There is however good reason to reject this simplistic separation of rules of semantics as part of grammar, and what I have so far called commonsense reasoning principles. The problem for this "clean" view is that we use commonsense reasoning, whatever this consists in, not merely in working out why a speaker has said something, but also in establishing what she has said in using the words chosen. Consider the conversation (5), remembering the event in the late summer of 1997 in which Diana Princess of Wales died in a car crash, vast crowds gathered in mourning outside Kensington Palace in Kensington Gardens where she had lived, quantities of flowers were left immediately outside the Palace gates which were reported to give off an intense aroma, all part of a series of events which led up to a funeral at which the singer Elton John sang the song "Candle in the Wind."

(5)   A: Elton John sang at Diana's funeral. Did you see it?
      B: I spent the whole day in Kensington Gardens. The smell was amazing.

The questions posed by this conversation are:

- how does B understand what A has referred to by using the word *it*?
- how does talking about Kensington Gardens answer A's question?
- why is *the whole day* taken to refer to the day of Princess Diana's funeral?
- how does A understand what the words *the smell* refer to?

The general problem we want to use this example to address is: how do language-internal principles interact with more general reasoning capacities? *It* presumably means the funeral service of Princess Diana. Since the funeral was televised, there were several means of seeing the funeral – either on television or by attending the event in person. B replies that she went to the area surrounding Kensington Palace for "the whole day." Since the funeral involved a procession from Kensington Palace to Westminster Abbey, as well as the service itself, B's reply is taken to imply that she was in the area in which the funeral took place at the time of the funeral, so her reply provides a positive answer to A's question – she was at the funeral, so indeed she saw it. B follows this reply up with the words *the smell*. She relies on A's being able to understand what these words mean by recovering information about the mass of flowers left in Kensington Gardens, and hence success in referring to the smell of these flowers. Almost none of this information is knowledge about the English language. There is nothing in the meaning of the word *funeral* which specifies a relation between this type of service and Kensington Gardens. There is nothing about the past tense in English which requires that the whole sequence of sentences should be taken to be about the same event.[4] And there is nothing in A's knowledge of the word *smell*, either, which specifies information about flowers left outside Kensington Palace in September 1997 – it is A's presumed knowledge of the objects so described which B relies on in choosing the words *the smell* as she does – just as it is A's presumed knowledge of the event which B relies on, in choosing to reply to A's question indirectly by referring to Kensington Gardens.

In this conversation, we see that the separation between knowledge of language and commonsense reasoning is much more blurred than in the conversation (1). There is no sense in which B can be said to have parsed the sentence *Did you see it* and worked out the meaning A intended to convey using language-internal principles alone – only subsequently bringing into play more general commonsense reasoning principles to work out some broader message. Similarly with A in processing B's reply. The different kinds of knowledge – one language-based, the other a much more general store of knowledge – have to be combined together in understanding what the word *it*, *the whole day*, and *the smell* mean in the particular context in which they are used. However, so the argument might go, there is certainly something separate about our knowledge of language and general reasoning capacities, because B has to parse the sentence first in order to establish that the word *it* has been uttered, she has to know that *it* is a pronoun which is the sort of word that is used to pick out some entity in the scene described in the conversation, that in the sentence A utters, the word *it* is presented as object of the verb *see*, and so on – all strictly English-internal information without which B will not retrieve the meaning A intends to get across. In reply, B uses the words *the whole day* relying on A's knowledge of English that an expression of this type can be taken to pick out a period of time relative to which the verb is understood. And, choosing the words *the smell*, equally, relies on A's being able to establish that *the smell* is intended as the subject being talked about, and *amazing* as the adjective predicated of it. Part of this language-specific knowledge is also the knowledge that *the* is the sort of word which leads to identifying some entity in the scenario being described; but, though words such as *it* and *the* trigger a process of identifying what is being talked about, they rely on a framework of structure constructed by parsing the sentence by language-internal rules. On evidence such as this, according to one current theory, the language system projects sentence-sized structures as sentence-meanings (*logical forms*), though these are incomplete. In the case of (5) the *logical forms* corresponding to A's question and B's reply will be along the lines indicated in (6) in which some parts of the interpretation are not filled in:

(6)   A: Question: Hearer saw X at time t_1.
       B: Speaker spent day-Y at Kensington-Gardens at time t_2. Smell-Z was amazing at time t_3.

X, Y, Z, Speaker, Hearer, t_1, t_2, t_3 are all parts that are missing and have to be filled in from context.[5] It is these missing parts which are transformed using general pragmatic principles of reasoning to create completed structures which more directly represent the thought that the speaker intended to convey. (Such structures are called *propositions* to distinguish them from the *sentence* that expresses them.)[6] Representations of the *propositions expressed* by A's question and B's answer might be given as follows:[7]

(7)   A: Question: B saw Princess Diana's funeral on Saturday.
       B: Spent Saturday at Kensington Gardens. The smell of flowers outside Kensington Palace on Saturday was amazing.

The pragmatic principles which dictate how these choices are made also have a much more general role to fulfill. For, on this view, it is these very same principles that determine the broad array of metaphorical, ironic, and other effects which a sentence can convey in context. The overall picture of interpretation is that grammar-internal principles articulate both syntactic and semantic structure for sentences, a semantic structure for a sentence being an incomplete specification of how it is understood. Pragmatic theory explains how

such incomplete specifications are enriched in context to yield the full communicative effect of an uttered sentence, whether metaphorical, ironical, and so
on. This view is the view adopted by relevance theory (Sperber and Wilson
1995); and it is this view and the Gricean view which constitute the two major
approaches to utterance interpretation.

2.2   Knowledge of language: a set of procedures for interpreting utterances

There is reason to think that the interaction of language-particular knowledge
and general commonsense reasoning is even more pervasive than is allowed
for by this modified separation of linguistic abilities and general commonsense reasoning principles. Consider a different way the conversation (5) might
have gone:

(8)   A: Elton John sang at Diana's funeral. Did you see it?
      B: I spent the whole day in Kensington Gardens. I felt I had to. The
           smell was amazing. Incredibly moving.

What is it that B has conveyed in uttering the words *I had to*: how is it that he
can rely on his hearer, A, to reconstruct from the word *to* a structure corresponding to "spend the whole day in Kensington Gardens"? In this case, the
speaker is giving a fragment which relies almost in its entirety on the ability of
the hearer, given the context in which the string is uttered, to reconstruct some
appropriate structure corresponding to the meaning of what in that context B
is trying to convey. It is not that B's words themselves project a full sentence-
structure with lexical meanings defined independent of context, on the basis of
which pragmatic principles provide some add-on means of identifying what is
being talked about. Here the words are mere triggers for a process of reasoning which has to reconstruct not only who is being talked about and why, but
also the process of building the structure which corresponds to the meaning
the speaker intended to convey. And all by the word *to* with nothing following
it. Similarly, in processing *incredibly moving*, the hearer has to use some form
of reasoning to establish what to take as the subject of the expression – is it
the flowers that are so moving, or the event in general? And what is the basis
on which B can rely on A to build the structure into which the expression
incredibly moving projects a predicate? There is no apparent subject to this
sentence, and no verb – so where does the structure come from? Is there a rule
internal to English which says that sentences with no subject and no verb are
well formed? If there is, it is certainly not one which any grammar book has
ever included. Evidence such as this suggests a third view. On this view, there
is still separation between the intrinsic content of individual words, which is
encoded (i.e. part of what an English speaker knows in virtue of knowing the
language), and the process of reasoning with them, which is not encoded.

Nevertheless, the process of building up the structure corresponding to some conveyed interpretation involves integrating one's knowledge of language with these general processes of reasoning at every step of the interpretation process. It is not that the rules of English syntax give rise to completed structures to which pragmatic principles fill in whatever open slots are left in the structure. Rather, we need to define a concept of structure internal to language which can be used both in building up meaning for complete sentences, and to process radically incomplete sentence "fragments" (cf. section 4.2 where the question of interpreting such fragments is taken up again).

3   The Process of Reasoning: How Do Hearers ever Manage to Choose the Right Interpretation?

I have so far sketched three possible perspectives on the nature of the interaction between what we might agree was knowledge of the individual language, and more general knowledge about the individuals being described. But we have not yet begun to look at the principles which form what is arguably the center of any pragmatic theory, which explain how a hearer selects the interpretation which the speaker intended – the so-called principles of commonsense reasoning (= inference). How is it that this inferential task for the hearer manages to be successful so much of the time, given that there are many possible ways of interpreting an utterance, direct, indirect, metaphorical, ironic, etc.? What is the criterion which enables people to choose the right interpretation?

3.1   Grice's cooperative principle and the conversational maxims

According to Grice who was the pioneer of the inferential approach to conversation (Grice 1975), there is a general assumption underpinning all utterance interpretation that the interpretation of utterances is a collaborative enterprise guided by a "co-operative principle" in which a speaker and hearer are engaged in some shared goal. This collaborative enterprise is structured by a number of maxims, which speakers are presumed to obey, amongst which Grice isolated:

- *The maxim of quality*: do not say that for which you lack evidence; do not say what you believe to be false.
- *The maxim of relevance*: be relevant.
- *The maxim of quantity*: make your contribution as informative as is required, but not more so.

- *The maxim of manner*: be perspicuous (avoid obscurity, avoid ambiguity, be brief, be orderly).

These are not rules that dictate behavior but, rather, maxims underpinning collaborative exchange of information. Take for example marking an exam, which in England involves two examiners. I suggest to you marks for each candidate, you disagree, and we then negotiate an agreed mark. Such collaborative endeavors are said to be directed by the cooperative principle and its maxims. Of course, it is not always the case that people do tell the truth, or are relevant. And I might get fed up with agreeing exam marks and walk away. But liars and people who refuse to cooperate are in some sense the exception that proves the rule; for in order for a lie to be successful, some presumption of the maxim of quality or its equivalent has to be in force, and people who refuse to cooperate are not engaged in any act of communication. More interestingly, the maxims are sometimes openly violated; and then they provide the trigger to a chain of reasoning which the hearer will use to reach an interpretation which the speaker intended to convey indirectly and which enables the cooperative principle to be seen to be reinstated. The conversation in (1) is an example of this. In (1), the manifestly irrelevant answer by B acts as a trigger for A to construct additional premises so that she will be led to see by indirect implication that B was trying to communicate something which is in accordance with the maxims. All such additional pieces of information, whether premise or conclusion, are said to be *conversational implicatures*. So B's answer in (1), which taken on its own is an answer that is either irrelevant or manifestly too little by way of answer, implicates that people who only know how to put a kettle on do not know how to cook, and that B does not know how to cook.

All such implicatures are derived by reasoning, and they are said to be acts of what is called nondemonstrative (i.e. nontrivial) reasoning in the face of some apparent clash with one or more of the maxims. Essential to the concept of implicature is that, unlike the intrinsic meaning of an expression, these implicatures can be "canceled" – hence their status as the result of reasoning, and not as the result of a linguistic rule. So there is nothing inconsistent with B's adding "Though I don't mean to imply that I can't cook. I can, I'm just not very interested in cooking." If, to the contrary, some aspect of interpretation cannot be consistently denied, then by definition it must be part of the meaning of the expression and not an implicature.[8]

It is this method of retrieving interpretation through a process of reasoning in the face of an apparent violation of the maxims which lies at the heart of the Gricean account of conversation (see Neale 1996). Take for example, the much-treasured compliment of being metaphorically described as a "real race-horse" in (2). This too is in blatant violation of the maxims of quality and relevance, and, in like manner, was taken by me in the situation in which it was uttered to implicate the assumptions that race-horses are extremely swift, and are exciting to watch, and that as something described as a race-horse, I was extremely swift, and exciting to watch and hence to be with. Notice that, said with a less admiring tone of voice, what was said could equally well have been taken, much less nicely, to mean that I was highly strung, bad tempered and easily upset. Like (1), (2) can be followed up by an explicit cancellation of at least some of these implicatures:

(9)   Though I don't mean to imply that you're bad tempered or anything like that – it's just that you're exciting to be with.

Such implicatures, which in the case of (2) gave rise to its interpretation as a compliment, are said to be derived through a process of reasoning which starts from the premise that the speaker is intending to obey the general tenor of the cooperative principle, but their utterance is in transparent violation of it.[9]
    The cases so far considered are clearly occasion specific; and it isn't any rule which licenses their interpretation. However, there are also cases which, though they can be construed as consequences of the maxims, are so regular that it is tempting to see their interpretation as the consequence of some kind of pragmatic rule, contrary to the general Gricean spirit. These are examples such as

(10)   Some people there were miserable

(10) would normally be taken to imply "Not everyone there was miserable," but it is cancelable as in (11):

(11)   Some people there were miserable. Indeed everyone was, though some were showing it less than others.

Since it is cancelable, according to the criterion defining an implicature, it is not an encoded principle of the grammar. Grice labeled implicatures such as these *generalized conversational implicatures*, but others since then have given them a rule-based characterization, suggesting that the concept of a grammar of a language might be extended by a pragmatic component which contains a set of default rules (see Gazdar 1979, Levinson 1983, 1987, 1996, forthcoming, and Lascarides and Asher 1993 for a concept of the *default inference rule*).
    One primary difficulty with these maxims of Grice's is that they are often not clear, and any single implicature can be reasoned to be a consequence of a number of maxims. Is for example, B's answer in (1) to be construed as a violation of the principle of relevance, or of quantity? Has B said too much, or not enough, or merely something irrelevant? Any one of these could be taken as triggers to the chain of reasoning that leads to the intended interpretation that B cannot cook. Then there is the problem of what it means for some utterance to be relevant, a question to which Grice provides no answer. The result is that, though suggestive, the content of the maxims remains extremely vague.
    A further problem is: What should the maxims be taken to explain? Grice articulated the maxims as a means of simplifying the overall account of the

relation between the use of language in logical arguments and the conversational use of language, arguing that recognition of maxims of conversational behavior could be used to explain a well-known problem – the apparent mismatch between how words such as *and, or, not, if-then* are used in logic and their use in ordinary language. In logic, which is the formal study of reasoning, the focus is on arguments that are valid in virtue of structure, for example that displayed in the English sequence:

(12)   If Bill is married to Mary and Mary is a Professor of English, then Bill is married to a Professor of English. Bill is married to Mary, but Mary isn't a Professor of English. Therefore Bill isn't married to a Professor of English.

Displaying the validity of argumentation in a sequence such as (12) involves defining *and* in such cases as combining two statements to yield a further statement of the form *P and Q* which is true if and only if the first statement and the second statement Q are both true. *And,* that is to say, has a purely cumulative effect. This use of the word *and* is unlike its characteristic use in conversational sequences, where it is often associated with sequencing in time. (13) for example does not merely imply that Bill was sick at some time in the past and that Bill went to bed some time in the past – it implies that he went to bed after he was sick, a sequence of events reversed in (14):

(13)   Bill was sick and went to bed.

(14)   Bill went to bed and was sick.

Examples such as these were used in the 1950s to 1970s (Strawson 1952, Cohen 1971, Walker 1975) to demonstrate the difference in content between natural language expressions and elements of logical languages, with the logical concepts being defined in terms of conditions necessary for the truth of a given element (e.g. *and* as in (12)). Grice however argued (1975) that the difference between *and* as in (12) and as in (13)–(14) was merely a difference in the implicatures that can arise as a result of the cooperative enterprise underlying the process of communication. This insight of Grice's was taken as a major advance, because it enabled natural language content to be defined in terms familiar from logic, and therefore taken to be better understood. Following this methodology, the meaning of sentences was defined in terms of truth-relations, the meaning of *It's raining* being said to be given by the set of conditions which have to hold in order for the sentence to be true. This gave rise (Gazdar 1979) to the slogan:

Pragmatics = meaning – truth conditions

Pragmatics was seen as the heterogeneous remainder left over once the account of descriptive content in the form of truth conditions is articulated as the basis of semantics – this left-over being explained in terms of maxims of behavior which provide the trigger for the "commonsense reasoning" process that adds to (or replaces) the stricter descriptive content of an uttered sentence. Notice how the slogan itself leaves open the question of whether these maxims should be characterized as constraining an inferential task (as Grice advocated – Grice 1975), or as default rules as some of his followers have assumed (see Levinson 1988, forthcoming).

As indicated earlier, the Gricean program is attractive to linguists as it buttresses the view that there is a clear separation between grammar-internal processes, which characterize sentence structures, and arguably also a specification of their meanings, and the interpretation of utterances (see Levinson 1988, Atlas 1989). It is attractive to semanticists also for the same reason: it allows concepts of truth-conditional semantics familiar from the study of logic to be extended to sentences, defining the domain of pragmatics as a form of explanation that takes as input such specification of sentence-meanings (Kamp 1979).

There are however serious difficulties with this view. The first is most obviously displayed by pronouns and other anaphoric expressions.[10] In order to establish the truth-conditional content expressed by a sentence containing a pronoun, some choice as to how the pronoun is to be interpreted has to be assumed; and these choices are not given as part of the grammar of a language in *any* sense – they depend on the interpretation of the sentence as understood in a context. The conditions under which (15) is true are, for example, quite different depending on whether the pronoun *she* is taken to refer to Princess Diana's body, or to each individual woman being talked about:

(15)   [*uttered in follow-up to (5)*]: Every woman cried as she went past the gates.

If *she* is construed as picking out Princess Diana's body, it picks out a fixed object: if *she* is construed as ranging over the same set of individuals as is picked out by *every woman*, it picks out a set of individuals, each one in turn. The two circumstances described are very different. Notice, too, the way the interpretation of the pronoun varies may be sensitive to details of the particular event described. The funeral procession that morning started from Kensington Palace, where the Princess had lived, and that morning no one came through the gates until the beginning of the procession. If the speaker and hearer can both presume on this sort of knowledge, then in (16), *she* will be construed as the Princess' body. However, in (17) *she* will be construed as each of the women being talked about, because it was bystanders who put flowers beside the gate (hardly the dead Princess!):

(16)   Every woman cried as she came through the gates.

(17)   Every woman cried as she put down her flowers.

The problem that truth-conditional content depends on specifics of a context is by no means restricted to anaphoric expressions such as pronouns. The women being talked about in an utterance of (17) as follow-up to (5) – who are assumed to be picked out by the speaker's utterance of the expression *every woman* – would be tightly restricted to the women described outside Kensington Palace as seen by B. It could not be every woman who went that day to put flowers down on some other grave elsewhere in the country, nor every woman at home watching the event on television. Even the predicate *put down* does not describe every event of putting down flowers that took place that day. Many people at the funeral event may have put down their flowers as they adjusted buttons on their coat, wiped a child's nose, etc. etc. – let alone women right around the world. But *put down* here refers only to the act of putting down flowers outside the gates of the Palace. Indeed the interpretation of *any* of the words may in part be due to the context in which the sentence is understood. From this we are driven to conclude that grammar-internal principles do not determine full specifications of truth-conditional content but much less complete specification; for "commonsense reasoning" principles are also dictating what is expressed by a sentence as uttered in a context. Grice himself did not see the construal of pronouns and other anaphoric expressions as a major problem, and, within the Gricean concept of utterance interpretation, this was not seen as controlled by the maxims (see Carston 1998 for discussion). However, as we shall see, the very same criterion that determines how indirect implicature effects are recovered by the hearer also determines how all such context-dependent aspects of interpretation are chosen.

Finally, as Grice himself pointed out (1975, 1989), there are some aspects of meaning projected by words that are signally left out of any program that defines the meaning of natural language expressions in terms of truth-conditions. These are aspects of meaning which do not have anything to do with properties of external objects that the word can be used to describe, but, rather, have to do with the mode of reasoning about such objects that the word triggers. Take the word *but*, used in the previous sentence. The word *but* is used to indicate some form of contrast, but this is not a contrast of content intrinsic to the entities described. We know that this is so, because of examples such as (18) and (19) where explicit identity of the predicate is asserted in the two clauses joined by *but*:

(18)   John is applying for the Liverpool job, but so am I; and I have more publications than he does.

(19)   John got 70 percent but so did his brother, so neither of them could boast about having done better.

The truth-conditions contributed by the use of *but* cannot be distinguished from that of *and*: a statement formed by joining together two statements by *but* is true if and only if the two statements are true, exactly as in the case of *and*. Any characterization of word meaning merely in these terms will miss the idiosyncratic contrastive flavor intrinsic to the meaning of *but* altogether. Yet the phenomenon is not a conversational implicature either, as it is an invariant aspect of sentences conjoined by *but* that some form of contrast is intended to be recovered. The Gricean program has to allow for special stipulations for aspects of meaning such as these which fall outside both the truth-conditional program, and the implicature form of explanation, as Grice himself pointed out (Grice 1975). He called these phenomena "conventional implicatures" to indicate that they were not regular implications of descriptive content but nonetheless part of the conventional meaning of the word in question; but this term was little more than a classificatory label.

3.2   Relevance theory

These various challenges to the Gricean program were taken up in Relevance Theory (Sperber and Wilson 1995). This theory claims to characterize pragmatic phenomena in terms of a single cognitive concept, that of relevance, replacing the social underpinnings of Grice's cooperative principle.

3.2.1   The principle of relevance

According to Sperber and Wilson, there is one overriding constraint on human cognition, the principle of relevance. All signals are said to be processed relative to an ever-evolving background context with the aim of retrieving more information from the signal than it itself presents; and optimal relevance is getting the right balance between size and type of context and amount of information derived for the task at hand. So in our Princess Diana example, we might say that the interpretation of the word *it* in (5) picks out the funeral because this has just been mentioned in the context and so costs no effort to recover, and that referring to Kensington Gardens and the smell of the flowers gives rise to a whole chain of impressions and so is highly informative in talking about the funeral. Hence the relevance of each succeeding sentence in the exchange in (5).

   This trade-off between cognitive effort and cognitive effect is at the heart of the concept of relevance itself. Humans are said to always subconsciously balance the amount of effort a task should have against the benefits to be gained from it – interpreting incoming signals to get as much information from them as is possible relative to putting in the minimum effort necessary to achieve that effect. This balancing of effort and inferential effect is the constraint of maximizing relevance. The more information some stimulus yields, the more relevant it is said to become, but the more effort the interpretation of that stimulus requires, the less relevant it will become. And to be minimally relevant a stimulus must lead to at least one non-trivial inference being derived.[11]

   To take in more detail a nonlinguistic example first, imagine yourself trying to write a letter in reply to some job advertisement which needs to be got off today if you are to have any hope of being treated as a serious candidate. Imagine also that it is raining. To you, the information that it is raining is not relevant because you are trying to work out how best to present yourself and your achievements. This can be characterized through considerations of amount of effort required for the inferential effects to be achieved. What you are currently focussing on – the context against the background of which you are constructing your application – are premises which concern this particular act of writing: "I must remember to mention my degree results" "I must remember not to use too many adjectives," "If I use the word *impressive* too often, they will think I am boasting." And so on. What the weather is like does not impinge on this activity, at least not just at the moment. The effort of retrieving and manipulating information about umbrellas, whether to go by train, car or bus, is not warranted relative to your current worries, for none of these premises will combine with premises about how best to communicate what an impressive individual you are. When, however, it comes time to go out of the house, then there will be decisions to be made, and these involve reasoning with premises about the weather and the nature of the journey to be made; and the information that it is raining will combine with these to yield appropriate inferential benefits (for example, if it were me I would be thinking things like "It's better to go by train and read, since the rain is likely to mean that going by car will be slow"). The cognitive effort of drawing such inferences at this later point in time is suitably rewarded, in the sense that noticing that it's raining combines with other things that are then on your mind anyway. According to this approach to understanding, the interpretation of a stimulus is defined as the manipulation of additional information relative to which a nontrivial set of inferential effects are achieved. Interpretation of signals of all sorts on this view invariably takes place relative to a context; because context is defined as the premises selected (the extra information) which ensure the relevance of a signal. There is no concept of a null context.

This example only involved one person, working away on their own, not being distracted by the rain. However interpretation of an act of communication involves two agents – the speaker and the hearer. The constraint of balancing cognitive effect (the drawing of nontrivial inferences) with cognitive effort will also apply to what the hearer does, but here the task of interpretation is more specific because the hearer has to try and recover what the speaker intended to convey. There are two aspects to the task:

1   Decoding the information intrinsically associated with an uttered expression – i.e. working out what words have been said and the information that they by definition carry.
2   Making choices which enrich that encoded information to establish what the speaker had intended to convey using those words.

To succeed in the first task, one has to know what the words of the language mean – what information they encode. This is the starting point from which the proposition expressed has to be recovered. To succeed in the second task means establishing (a) some proposition corresponding to the intended interpretation of the utterance, (b) additional propositions which establish the required inferential effect. These propositions are, however, not just those which happen to be maximally relevant to the hearer: they must at least include those which the speaker could have intended.

And this is where a somewhat different principle of relevance – the communicative principle of relevance – comes in. A presumption of optimal relevance, according to Sperber and Wilson, determines how the hearer succeeds in arriving not merely at some most informative interpretation, but at the interpretation which the speaker intended. The context against which these decisions are made is said to be the set of representations retrievable with least effort that establish requisite inferential effects (this is what corresponds to "optimal" relevance).[12] This set may be taken as containing just the immediately previously constructed proposition: and, indeed, direct answers to a question do combine with such a context, viz. the question itself, for which they provide an answer. However, the context selected could also be some extension of the minimal context, as long as the extra effort required is offset by additional inferential effects; and this is what is triggered in indirect replies to questions. For example in interpreting the uttered sentence *I went to Kensington Gardens* in response to *Did you see the funeral?* in (5), the proposition taken to be expressed will be "B went to Kensington Gardens." This indirect response, despite the increased effort required to process it, would have the advantage of triggering an extension of the context to include a premise such as "Kensington Gardens was the starting point for the procession preceding the funeral" from which A will deduce that "B saw the funeral procession by going to it" and probably also that she saw the service as well on the huge screens that were made available so that everyone outside the abbey could watch it. The benefit of the indirect answer here, according to relevance theory, is that for a minimal increase in effort of processing the given input, the hearer A is recovering extra information which she would not otherwise have got – here, the much richer stock of information that B did not see the funeral by watching it on tv, that B was part of a historic event, that B has much more information about some aspects of the event than she does, that B will not have seen other parts of the event, etc. Hence B's answer in (5), though indirect, and causing A more effort in parsing and constructing an interpretation, is optimal in guiding the hearer to the requisite range of inferential effects. The very indirectness of B's answer indeed is intentional, allowing an open-endedness in the interpretation since the choice of context is not fully determined.

3.2.2   Relevance and the recovery of what is "said"

One immediate advantage of the relevance-theoretic approach over the Gricean one is that the explanation of how implicatures intended by the speaker are worked out applies equally well in explaining how the proposition the speaker has expressed is arrived at. So, for example, (16)–(17) uttered in the context of (5) are predicted to give rise to different interpretations. Choice of *she* as the variable bound by *every woman* in processing (16) would not be possible because it would combine with the information that no woman went through the gates other than the dead woman in her coffin, giving rise to immediate inconsistency, and no further nontrivial inferences.[13] All such interpretations are therefore ruled out as not relevant. Hence *she* can only be used in that context to refer to the individual inside the coffin. Similarly, though to reverse effect in (17), *she* cannot be construed as Princess Diana since neither dead people nor their coffins can lay flowers. In both cases, the only available choice of representation is the one that is selected – a representation which meets the criterion of giving rise to a consistent set of inferential effects without undue cognitive effort. Exactly the same constraint dictates the construal of *put down* as "put down outside the gates of Kensington Palace," though this time for a different reason. It is perfectly possible that an individual can cry as she puts down her flowers to wipe a child's nose or do up her coat, but in this case, the type of premise required is one that combines with an assertion about every-one there. Information about women except in relation to events concerning the activities involved in the mourning at Kensington Palace has not been made salient and so is not easily recoverable. In contrast, the selection of *put down* as "put down beside the Kensington Palace Gates" in that same context naturally triggers such easily available premises as:

> Crying is an explicit gesture of mourning.
> Putting down flowers by Kensington Palace was an explicit act of mourning.

Such a choice of context would give rise to the inferential effect

> Every woman who put down flowers by Kensington Palace did at least two things as an explicit gesture of mourning.

Since such a set of premises is easily recoverable, the interpretation of *put down* as "put down by Kensington Palace" is the concept the speaker intended to convey.[14] Similar relevance considerations dictate that *every woman* picks out women standing by as mourners rather than, for example, women watching the same event at home on tv.[15]

So the principle of balancing cognitive effort and inferential effect can be seen to underpin both the deduction of so-called implicatures and the fixing of context-dependent aspects of the proposition expressed. It has the advant-age also of not requiring the explanation of additional pragmatic effects to be triggered only in the event of apparent violation of a conversational maxim, as does the Gricean account. Indeed it purports to explain why deduction of additional information is an unvarying consequence of interpreting an utterance, and not merely a feature of exceptional apparently anomalous conversational exchanges. Moreover it provides a natural distinction between implications which the hearer believes the speaker intended to convey (= *implicatures*), and those which she recovers from the utterance despite knowing that the speaker could not have intended to convey them (= *contextual implications*) (Sperber and Wilson 1995, Carston 1988). The implications the hearer believes the speaker intended to convey are those dictated by the criterion of optimal relevance (with minimal cognitive effort as the overriding factor). Those which the speaker need not have intended are the result of the less restrictive criterion of maximizing relevance. These will often add very considerably to the relevance of the overall utterance for the hearer, though they cannot be taken to be part of what the speaker has intended to convey. The fact that B went to the funeral for example will provide A with information about B, that B got completely caught up in the fervor that swept the country that weekend, that therefore she is probably a traditionalist, and so on – none of which B would have explicitly intended to convey in her reply. Such implications, by the way, would not be characterized by a Gricean system as part of the utterance interpretation process at all.

3.2.3   Relevance and speech acts

We have so far assumed that information retrieved from an utterance is solely about the object referred to by a speaker. However humans fluently reason at both the level of what is communicated, and at the level of how / why something is communicated. So A in our first conversation (1) will not only retrieve the information that B knows how to put a kettle on, but also that B wants A to believe that she only knows how to put a kettle on. Such higher level information is partly encoded – the differences between assertions, imperatives, and questions, in particular, rely on our ability to retrieve such higher level implications. An assertion implies that the speaker, if taken sincerely, believes the proposition his utterance expresses is true. An imperative is a request by the speaker that the hearer make some proposition true. A yes–no question is a request to the hearer to indicate to the speaker whether some proposition is believed by the hearer to be true. These higher level *explicatures* (as they are labeled in relevance theory (see Carston 1988) have been studied as part of semantics under speech act theory (initiated by the philosopher J. L. Austin in Austin 1962) and, following him, Searle and Bach and Harnish (Searle 1969, Bach and Harnish 1979). In this earlier theory (which predated Gricean pragmatics and relevance theory), language use was described in terms of a range of *speech acts* in terms of which the meaning of natural language expressions was explained.[16] There are many cases where we do much more with words than merely describing objects and activities around us. So, for example, when a minister holds a baby over a font, sprinkles a few drops onto his head, and says the appropriate words from the baptism service, he is not merely saying these words, he is carrying out the act of baptizing. And when I say "I promise you that I will send you a letter tomorrow," I am not merely saying those words – I am carrying out an act of promising. On the speech act view of language, language can best be understood in terms of acts such as these which speakers carry out in using language. The observation by speech act theorists that there is clearly more to language than just describing things is quite uncontentious – no one working in pragmatics doubts this. Nonetheless, in relevance theory, where the type of implications that can be drawn is quite unrestricted, there is no need of any special discrete categories for such different kinds of act. All these implications would fall under the category of *explicature*, and as part of the proposition expressed would come within the general umbrella of information retrievable from an utterance, for which the hearer's task is to recover those implications that the speaker intended to convey. Like all other implications, whether or not they are retrieved depends on their relevance to the participants. It may be relevant to construct the explicature that the speaker believes that P, for some arbitrary P, though in ironical utterances, this is contra-indicated. Questions normally require an answer, but so-called rhetorical questions signally do not. And, equally, it may be relevant that someone we speak to has specifically promised that P. Even in the highly conventionalized case of baptism, the implication that a child has been baptized through some specific act in a religious service is potentially relevant in just the same way as every other act of communication – it needs no special pragmatic category to explain its communicative effect – merely an explanation of the role of the priest within a given religious ritual, and the significance of baptism within a set of religious practices. I shall not have anything more to say about such "speech acts" in the remainder of this chapter, but they nonetheless have an integral role in establishing the relevance of an utterance, (see Wilson and Sperber 1988a, Carston 1988).

3.2.4   Procedural aspects of interpretation

The assumption that interpretation involves constructing both some distinguished proposition and some context set of propositions to combine with it provides a natural basis for explaining the conventional implicature phenomena problematic for Gricean approaches to meaning. Given the two-fold nature of the inferential task triggered by natural language input, it is entirely natural that the content of some words might be directed more towards constraining the context set of premises to be selected, rather than in establishing the proposition expressed (see Blakemore 1987, 1992). In this light, we can view connectives such as *but* as constraining the context relative to which the sentences it connects are to be construed, establishing both one form of context for the first conjunct, and a guaranteed modification of it in adding the second conjunct. Seen in these terms, *but* has to be defined as a procedure for context-construction, imposing a choice of context for the first conjunct which must lead to a conclusion, relative to which the context for the second conjunct (which will automatically contain the first conjunct) must yield a contradiction (Blakemore 1989).

4   The Interaction between Linguistic Processing and General Processing

This concept of procedures for interpretation has much more general application (see Wilson and Sperber 1993, Kempson 1996). In some sense words – all
of them – are the procedures we have to start the process of interpretation.
Consider first pronouns. Pronouns do not fix the way the hearer understands
them; they merely guide the utterance process. This guidance takes the form
of a constraint. Consider (20)–(21):

(20)   The Queen frightened her.

(21)   The Queen frightened herself.

(21) must mean that the Queen frightened herself, rather than anybody else.
(20) however cannot mean this – it must mean that it is someone other than
herself that the Queen frightened. More formally the pronoun provides a place-
holding device for which the hearer has to choose some representation, relative
to the constraint that the individual represented be female *plus* the constraint
that the representation the hearer selects must not be one that is already set
up within the propositional structure being constructed. It is for this reason
that (20) and (21) cannot be taken to mean the same. This "locality" restriction is
generally seen as a syntactic restriction defined over syntactic structure, separating some aspects of pronoun interpretation off from their use in discourse
as grammar-internal and subject to syntactic explication (see chapter 11, and
Chomsky 1981); but, looked at from a more procedural perspective, we can
see the pronoun as encoding a constraint on the building up of a propositional
structure (see Kempson 1988a, 1988b, Kempson et al. in preparation) – a procedure which guides the hearer but leaves open what it is that the pronoun
actually picks out on any occasion of use.

Notice how, with this concept of word meaning as a set of procedures for
interpretation, it is essential that interpretation be defined in terms of structured representations of content, and the progressive building up of such representations: locality conditions have to be defined over a level of representation,
and this can be construed as an encoded constraint on pragmatic interpretation *only* if the process of interpretation is also taken to be defined in terms
of structure. So far, however, the concept of structure over which anaphoric
interpretation is defined could be a structurally complete configuration of a
propositional structure, missing only some values to place-holding variables
(as presumed in relevance theory – see section 1). However, remember how
the interpretations of *the smell*, and *the whole day* in (5), *woman* and *put down* in
(17) also depended on context, displaying a similar gap between the characterization of the word independent of context and its particular interpretation in
a given utterance. This shows that it is not just pronouns whose interpretation

depends on context, but all words. The very generality of this phenomenon of context-dependence suggests that all specifications of words should be viewed as constraints, underspecifying interpretation, on the basis of which a hearer builds some propositional structure.[17]

4.1   *Metaphor as an enrichment process?*

There are two ways in which this concept of underspecification might be extended. On the one hand, current work on the construal of metaphor in relevance-theoretic terms is suggesting that an enrichment approach to interpretation should be extended to metaphorical uses of language, the word being but a trigger for the online construction of the concept specific to that interpretation (Carston 1998). There is an important background debate behind this suggestion. There has been disagreement within pragmatics to date over whether there should be any independent maxim of quality constraining people to tell the truth (Wilson 1995). The maxim of quality contains the heart of the social principle of cooperation intrinsic to Grice's theory of conversation. On the Gricean account, remember, the interpretation of metaphor involves transparent violation of the maxim of quality with the false proposition expressed by the sentence as its literal meaning having to be replaced by some quite different proposition (see Sperber and Wilson 1981 for a critical evaluation of the Gricean account). On the Sperber and Wilson account, which is *not* a social theory of communication, metaphorical interpretations involve a different relation between a proposition and the thought which the hearer recovers from the sentence as uttered in context. Just as drawings, such as cartoons, may "resemble" a person without depicting them at all accurately, so propositions can be used to resemble thoughts they convey, a use of language which is called "interpretive use." Metaphorical uses of language, like other rhetorical effects, are said to constitute an interpretive use, with the sentences being used to convey a relationship of resemblance between the proposition expressed by the utterance and the thought(s) it is intended to convey Sperber and Wilson (1995), Wilson and Sperber (1988b). On this view no maxim of quality is required – it is merely the criterion of presumed optimal relevance which, as elsewhere, constrains the interpretation process.

The view that all word meaning is but a set of procedures provides a new shift in this debate; for it suggests that any word is but the input to the construction of some novel "ad hoc" concept specific to that utterance. On this view interpretation of a sentence such as (22):

(22)   She cornered him.

involves constructing a concept on the basis of the presentation of the word *corner* in such a way as to yield extra information about the individuals picked out by the pronouns in that context, in ways which make the whole utterance relevant to the hearer. So *corner* has to be understood as a relation between individuals, something someone can do to someone else. The construction of the new concept is direct and not via a process of rejecting a literal interpretation. No maxim of quality needs to be invoked in this account of metaphor, but, equally, no indirect concept of resemblance is invoked either: it is, rather, that all that a word provides is a set of procedures relative to which a hearer establishes a relevant interpretation, constructing new concepts online from the presented word. The consequence is that it is not merely the pronouns whose encoded specification underdetermines their interpretation, but words that express concepts also.

4.2   Syntax as the building of propositional structure

The idea of expressing the content of a word as a procedure can apply in syntax too, for the projection of structure from the lexicon can also be defined as sets of procedures for building up propositional structure (Kempson 1996, Kempson and Gabbay 1998).[18] To take relatively straightforward cases first, names in a language can be defined as the projection of a representation uniquely picking out some individual. Intransitive verbs which involve the assertion of a property attributed to ("predicated of") some individual, can be defined as introducing a structure in which the property in question is represented at one node in a structure with another node also introduced to represent the subject of whom the property is predicated. Transitive verbs, such as *hit*, might be said to introduce a structure containing a position waiting to be filled by an object and a subject – notice how as soon as the hearer processes the word *hit*, she knows that there must be some object of the action of "hitting." Auxiliary verbs, such as *will*, *did*, can be defined as adding information about time to some propositional structure. And so on. In all cases, words can be seen not in terms of the structure of sentences in which the words occur as a string, but, rather, in terms of progressively building up a propositional structure (Kempson et al. forthcoming, Kempson et al. in preparation).

   Though highly unorthodox as a basis for describing syntactic properties, there is reason to think this is the right direction in which to go. First, there are elliptical constructions. These are radically incomplete strings, which have to be enriched in context by being assigned a structure corresponding to that of some antecedent structure:

(23)   A: Have you handed in your assignment yet?
       B: Nobody has asked me to.

The puzzle presented by examples such as (23) is that fragment reconstruction involves syntactic and discourse properties simultaneously.[19] Though the elliptical fragment is reconstructed as a process of interpretation, the output of such a building process displays structural properties exactly as does a sentence in which the structure of this interpretation is explicitly introduced. But, nevertheless, the structure that is reconstructed is not made up of the words of the previous sentence, despite the fact that it relies on them to provide the interpretation of the incomplete expression *to* in B's reply: what is reconstructed is the structure of the proposition expressed by the words; and in (23) this is a structure corresponding to "Has B handed in B's assignment yet?" (*you* / *your* are pronouns which serve to pick out the hearer). We know this because if the speaker B uses words to mimic the effect which the fragment has more economically expressed in (23), she must choose different words to reflect that content directly, and not the words actually in the previous sentence – hence the shift from *your* to *my* in (24):[20]

(24)   A: Have you handed in your assignment yet?
       B: Nobody has asked me to hand in my assignment yet.

By using a fragment, no such shift in the choice of words is necessary. In reconstructing interpretation as a structural process, the hearer will be building up a representation of the content expressed by the words (i.e. the proposition expressed), *not* a representation of structure defined over the sequence of words themselves. But this suggests that the syntax in terms of which this phenomenon has to be explained is the structure that underpins interpretation – not some structure displayed by the words themselves.

Second, it turns out that phenomena taken to be central to syntax can be revealingly characterized in terms of some rather weak starting point and its resolution in context, analogous to the way in which pronouns contribute to interpretation. Incompleteness of information is of course endemic to language processing, because, at least in speech, we process the input sequentially, progressively building up structure throughout the interpretation process.[21] Imagine now the parsing of (25) – what syntacticians call a *topicalization* structure:

(25)   John she admired.

Suppose we decide to represent the proposition expressed by a sentence as a tree structure (as in syntax – see chapter 11, Syntax), so that we can display the individual parts of the interpretation, and how they combine together. This means that the output structure of parsing this sentence, when it is finally established, will take the form shown in figure 16.1.

The first question in wondering how a string such as (25) is parsed to achieve this result is: What information has the hearer got when she has processed the word *John* in (25) on the assumption that she decides that this occurrence of *John* is not to be understood as the subject? We take it she knows which individual named *John* is being talked about – this is what the speaker assumes in using this name – but she doesn't yet know how to construct the resulting proposition the speaker is trying to convey. In particular, she doesn't know where John is to fit in any such resulting structure. All she will know at this

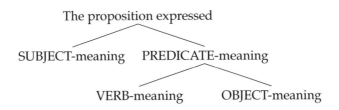

Figure 16.1

Figure 16.2

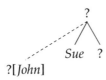

Figure 16.3

first stage is as in figure 16.2 (I put question marks above the parts of the structure which she knows must be there, but doesn't yet know how to fill out).

As the hearer then gets more information she is able to gradually build up
the structure, at the same time identifying any items (such as entities referred
to by pronouns). For example, in processing *she* (let us say identifying that it is
Sue that is being talked about), the hearer may add to her initial tree description, to establish the structure as in figure 16.3.

At this second stage she knows *she* is the subject picking out Sue and that
when she has established some property she can attribute to Sue she will have
a completed proposition about Sue. Hence the second node with a ?.

With the word *admired*, she gets yet further information that a two-place
relation of "admire" is asserted between Sue and some other individual, a
relation said to hold in the past. So she can add to the structure so far built up
and update it into the structure, figure 16.4.

With this as the full sequence of words, she can at last identify the position
in the propositional structure into which the representation of "John" should
fit – viz. as object of the relation "admire" asserted to hold between Sue and
John (figure 16.5). Each word has by this stage led to a concept being entered
at a fixed position in the tree: even the representation "John" has got its contribution in the propositional structure established.

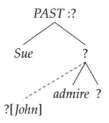

Figure 16.4

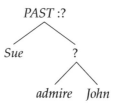

Figure 16.5

With the tree structure corresponding to the proposition expressed now completed, it follows that the hearer can establish what property it is that is asserted of Sue – it is "admire(John)." So now the hearer has established the full content of the proposition expressed, which represented as a tree structure, is figure 16.6:[22]

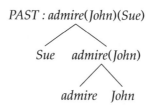

Figure 16.6

Notice what form the information presented by the words has to take in this step-by-step modeling of the interpretation process. What the hearer does is, simply, a progressive updating of an initially very partial tree description.[23] The words all provide sequences of actions, procedures, which enable the structure to be progressively built up. Structures like these, by the way – topicalization structures – have been the focus of much study as part of what linguists call syntax, where the metaphor, over many years, has been that the representation of *John* has moved from some original position to the position in the front of the string, leaving what is called a "gap" (see ch. 12). Looked at from a parsing perspective, the hearer, as we've just seen, does the reverse of this. She starts from very little information and gradually builds up a completed structure which this initial expression can be slotted into.

As confirmation of this processing perspective on syntax itself, we can now see that the way these partial trees are built up by a hearer may be affected by other processes of interpretation which we know to be pragmatic, an interaction which we would not expect if the projection of structure had to be characterized as quite separate from all pragmatic processes. The evidence comes from the interpretation of so-called relative clauses, and the way pronouns inside them can contribute to the building up of their structure.

First, by way of introduction, notice that languages have more than one kind of pronoun. There are not only the ordinary pronouns, *he, her, them* etc., but there are what traditional grammarians have called *relative pronouns* that introduce these relative clauses.[24] The function of these, rather crudely put, is to carry information from one piece of structure to another, enabling the hearer to build up two pieces of information at once. So in (26), through the use of the word *who*, the hearer is able to build up two pieces of information about *John* at the same time – that Sue says Tom admires him, and that he's likely to get the job:

(26) John, who Sue says Tom admires, is likely to get the job.

Specifically what *who* does within this structure is to shift the hearer temporarily away from the task of building up the first structure to start the building up of the second. With this shift, *who* also conveys the information that a second occurrence of the expression "John" is to play a part in building up this added structure. In this respect *who* is like a pronoun, for it is interpreted by information got from elsewhere in the context in which it is contained. However, there are two respects in which *who* is not like a pronoun. First, unlike pronouns, *who* cannot be understood freely; on the contrary, *who* in (26) has to be understood as picking out *John*: this is fixed by a rule of the language. Second, the word *who* has to come at the beginning of the structure in which it occurs, and, like in topicalization structures, it doesn't itself give any indication as to where in the tree this occurrence of "John" in the new structure should be placed.[25] In this respect, *who*, in this secondary structure, is behaving exactly like the word *John* in (25) – the hearer does not initially know where to fix it in the structure she is building up as interpretation, and the information where to slot it in comes later – after *admires*. In short, on the one hand, we have the word *who* in relatives behaving like a pronoun, and, on the other hand, we see that it behaves as though in a topicalization structure.

Now we are ready to see the interaction with what we know to be a pragmatic process – the process of establishing what a pronoun means in context. We need to focus specifically on the sequence of steps involved in the process of interpreting the remainder of the relative clause, but this time with a pronoun inside the relative clause itself:

(27) John, who Sue says she's *so* worried about him that she's taking him to the hospital, is begging her not to make such a fuss.

Sentences such as these occur on a daily basis, and we none of us have any difficulty processing them, though we may judge them less than perfect, because the pronoun isn't strictly necessary. Consider what happens in processing, as the hearer continues on from the point at which *who* is processed, this fixed as picking out "John." The task that lies ahead of her is how to decide what contribution this occurrence of "John" obtained from *who* makes in the interpretation of the relative. The question that arises is: can we assume that the pragmatic process of establishing an interpretation for a pronoun in such a context may feed into the process of working out how "John" is to contribute to the building up of this second structure? And the answer is "Yes, of course – what could possibly prevent it?" In (27), the pronoun occurs in a position where, *if* it is understood as picking out "John," it will establish how the representation of "John" is to be used in this second structure, which otherwise up to that point in the sequence of parsing actions the hearer can only identify as contributing somehow in the second structure, without knowing exactly how. Once the pronoun in the processing of (27) is construed as picking out John, then the hearer knows that John is the object of Sue's worry. But this result yields the pairing between the relative pronoun and the place in the structure to which it is to contribute which is definitive of topicalization structures.

This so-called resumptive use of the pronoun in (27) isn't strictly necessary in working out how *John* is to contribute to this second structure – after all (28) is just as acceptable, and its only difference from (27) is that it lacks this pronoun:

(28)   John, who Sue says she's so worried about that she's taking him to the hospital, is begging her not to make such a fuss.

In sentences such as (27), the speaker has slipped in a pronoun, presuming that the hearer will understand that it picks out the individual just described,[26] in so doing, providing the hearer an extra clue with which to work out how the relative is to be understood. In the case we've just seen, the use of the pronoun is optional, indeed possibly dispreferred (hence some linguists judge that such resumptive uses of pronouns are substandard, however widespread). But this is by no means always so. In (29), where the speaker is using the word *even* which forces her to emphasize the following word, the presence of this resumptive pronoun becomes obligatory:

(29)   My son, who sometimes even *he* gets fed up with me, is staying out tonight.

There is no other way to express this information within a relative clause like this, because you can't emphasize silence. Silence won't be said any louder. And without the pronoun, as in (30), the sentence means something quite different – it is the predicate "gets fed up with me" that is emphasized, not the expression "my son":[27]

(30) My son, who sometimes even gets fed up with me, is staying out tonight.

The significance of these data is that they provide us with cases where a pragmatic process – that of working out what a pronoun is picking out – can be seen to contribute towards establishing a perfectly regular grammar-internal relation – which is the pairing between a fronted expression and the position from which it contributes to the interpretation as a whole.

One could of course argue in rejoinder that this shows nothing more than that in language use, structural and pragmatic phenomena may reasonably interact; and that this doesn't show that the characterization of internal properties of the language needs to be in these dynamic use-directed terms. However, as we shall now see, it does indeed provide evidence of this stronger conclusion, for it is only by making this move that we retain a unitary account of the pronouns.

What these data unquestionably show is that the availability of pronouns in the processing of relative clauses presents the speaker with a choice: either to use a pronoun, or not. The choice that then confronts the analyst is what consequences this should have for the articulation of the underlying structural properties of language in the form of a grammar. The first option is to define two alternative rules of grammar for projecting relative clause interpretations, with a characterization of the extent to which they differ. On this alternative, there is some grammar-internal process that dictates the pairing between a fronted expression and a pronoun in relative-clause and topicalization structures, and this process is by definition quite distinct from the general pragmatic process of anaphora. The alternative, on the other hand, is to define a single process of relative clause construal, that of pairing an unfixed node with a fixed position in the structure; and allow that the pragmatic process of working out what a pronoun means may contribute to the process of establishing this pairing.

How should we decide which of these two approaches is correct? Evidence that would tend to favor adopting the second alternative would be evidence showing that some general principle of communication was sufficient to explain the interaction between the syntactic and pragmatic processes. And this is what we find. The puzzle is that, most of the time, these two processes are not freely available. When it is acceptable not to use a pronoun, it is generally much less acceptable to use it. For example, when the structure is less complex than in (27) it becomes quite unacceptable to use a pronoun resumptively:

(31) ??John, who Sue's worried about him, is begging her not to make a fuss.

And when a pronoun is used fully acceptably, then it's often because leaving it out would not convey the same information – as in (29)–(30).

The presumption of optimal relevance here explains this distribution very straightforwardly. If the speaker has two equivalent means of expressing what is characterized by a single grammar-internal process, then the presumption of optimal relevance should dictate that any choice available to the speaker which involves the hearer in processing additional lexical material for *no* additional inferential effect will always be less than optimal, unless this less economical strategy helped in what otherwise might be a potentially over-complex structure which risks causing the hearer undue processing difficulty. It is this processing account that explains the difference in acceptability between (27) and (31). (27) is, perhaps marginally, acceptable because the structure is somewhat complex: the pronoun helps in identifying the position from which the unfixed node is to be understood. The additional cost of processing the words is in this case just about offset by the contribution that this information makes to greater ease in retrieving the structure intended. In contrast, in (31), which is so much simpler, a pronoun cannot be used resumptively. Here there is no reason whatever to buttress the identification of the position into which the occurrence of "John" projected by the relative pronoun has to be fitted. Hence the unacceptability of the pronoun in this case – no speaker would judge the extra cost to the hearer warranted with such a simple example, no matter how little parsing effort would seem to be involved in processing just a pronoun.

Relevance theory can also explain the other type of case, where the resumptive use of a pronoun succeeds in conveying a particular kind of effect. For if the additional words in the more complex form of wording lead to a difference in pragmatic effect, then the additional effort for the hearer in processing the additional word(s) would be offset by the extra communicative effect achieved. And it is this property that explains why (29) is acceptable. In (29) the pronoun occurs with what is called a *focus* particle, *even*, which has a particular form of interpretation that demands the presence of the following pronoun – the interpretation is simply not derivable without the pronoun. Right across languages, indeed, resumptive pronouns are always acceptable where otherwise they would be debarred if the particular position is being emphasized by a word such as *even*, or even merely if the particular position is being stressed for some particular contrastive purpose (as in (32) drawing attention to the fact that the speaker believes that other people might well let her down):

(32)   John, who I'm certain *he* won't let me down, has said he'll come to my party.

This suggests that the correct conclusion to draw is that the grammar makes available a single principle underpinning such relative structures (shared with the process of topicalization), and that while the pragmatic process of anaphora itself remains free and controlled only pragmatically, it, nevertheless, feeds into the encoded process that drives the building up of interpretations for relative clauses. And though the system itself will freely allow use of the pronoun in such contexts, it will only be acceptable if either it leads to a reduction in processing costs or it enables additional communicative effects to be achieved. Now, the final step is that we can only characterize the problem in this way if the characterization of relative clauses has been defined in terms of the dynamics of how interpretation is built up. So these data do indeed provide evidence that pragmatic principles may contribute to establishing those structures which are characterized as part of our knowledge of language, hence as part of what we call the grammar of the language. The grammar on this view defines how structures may be developed in the parsing process, and, within this, the words define procedures that drive this process.

Of course, this one indication of the fruitfulness of looking at the way structures are processed is far from conclusive. At best, it cannot be more than a taste of results to be established in detail,[28] but it is indicative of how, if we take the dynamics of building up interpretation as integral to describing both natural language content *and* its structure, then not only can we model the interpretation process in an intuitive and natural way, but we have the bonus of providing a revealing perspective on structural properties of natural language.

5 Summary

In this chapter, we started by surveying the apparently acute problems facing any general account of communication. We set out the different types of separation that have been imposed on the distinction between linguistic knowledge and language use; and I argued that though there is a distinction between encoded and nonencoded information, nevertheless, there needs to be full integration of the two types of processing. I then sketched the two primary different sets of criteria for choosing the intended interpretation – the Gricean route through conformity to maxims governing conversational behavior, and the relevance theory route through a choice driven by balancing effort and effect. I then presented some of the evidence that words should be seen as procedures for interpretation, rather than having some fixed descriptive content. And finally, I sketched out one way in which the interpretation of topicalization structures and pronouns can both be explained in terms of the incremental building up of tree structure corresponding to interpretation.

On the view that is emerging from this much more dynamic, use-oriented perspective on linguistic description, all words provide a set of procedures relative to which a hearer progressively constructs a structure corresponding to the proposition expressed. The encoded specifications intrinsic to language are defined explicitly as the driving force in this incremental process of building up interpretations from a natural language sequence of words. Linguistic and nonlinguistic processes of interpretation, nevertheless, freely interact in determining what proposition or set of propositions is expressed by a given input. The only externally imposed restriction is that linguistic input, being an encoded set of instructions on structure building, cannot be set aside. The linguistic knowledge that we have as users of the language is the encoded input which the individual language provides to enable the structural dynamics of the interpretation process to take place. Pragmatic principles are the general cognitive principles that enable us to enrich information by general reasoning strategies, and to make choices between alternative structures as the interpretation is progressively established. This strongly suggests that modeling the process of communication itself provides a basis for explaining what it means to know a language (= competence – see chapter 12).

This view is a departure from the view that linguistic ability should be a body of knowledge which is quite independent of whatever principles determine how language is used (= performance). On this view, natural language ability is, rather, a capacity for natural language parsing. The current focus of debate in deciding on these views is barely begun, but at the center, as it always has been, is the status of our capacity for language. Is it a static store of knowledge relative to which pragmatic principles of use determine the apparently conflicting uses to which it can be put? Or is it the possession of a capacity for dynamically projecting structures which correspond to interpretation for a given piece of language uttered? At the present time, these remain questions over which researchers struggle to reach the most revealing answer; and much of what I have introduced in the last section of this chapter would be fiercely contested by many. One thing we can be sure of, however, is that study of the way people use language is a central preoccupation of linguistic study.[29]

NOTES

1 This was once said to me as a fervent (and much appreciated) compliment!
2 What a user of a language knows about her language is called a *grammar*. In a grammar there are facts about the sounds used to build words (*phonology*), facts about how words are arranged to form sentences (*syntax*), and facts about those aspects of the meaning of words / sentences that are integral properties of those words / sentences (*semantics*) (see chapter 8, Phonology; chapter 11, Syntax; chapter 15, Semantics).
3 A very useful collection which provides readings in all the major topics in pragmatics is Davis 1991.
4 Sentences in sequence are often used, contrarily, to imply events in sequence:

(i) I finished my Ph.D. I got it published. And I became pregnant.

5 It has long been recognized by both linguists and philosophers that pronouns such as *I* and *you* can only be interpreted relative to entities in the discourse context. In this connection, cf. the papers of Roman Jakobson writing in the 1950s, who referred to them as *shifters* (in Waugh and Halle (eds) 1984). In the philosophical literature, such pronouns are called *indexical pronouns*, cf. Perry 1979, 1993. However the recognition of the extent to which interpretation is dependent on context was not widely recognized until the early 1980s with the work of Kamp 1984, Barwise and Perry 1983, Sperber and Wilson 1986.

6 An important assumption here is that all cognitive activity involves the construction or manipulation of internal cognitive representations. We can, for example, only see that rose bush in the garden in virtue of setting up some internal representation of that rose bush (we don't have rose bushes in our heads – not even those of us who are obsessed with rose gardening). This view is known as representationalism and in its current form is largely due to Fodor, who has argued for a so-called language of thought (cf. Fodor 1975, 1981, 1983, 1998). What is controversial for linguistics is the relation of such representations to representations in linguistic description. There are substantial differences of opinion for example over whether any level of representation is required in modeling interpretation in language other than that articulated within syntax. This is a debate which has rumbled on in different forms for at least thirty years, cf. Katz 1972, Lewis 1972, Kamp 1984, Groenendijk and Stokhof 1991, Sperber and Wilson 1995, Kamp and Reyle 1993, Dekker 1996, Kamp 1996, Kempson et al. 1997, Carston 1998.

7 A proposition needs to be complete only to the extent that it is one for which inference can be defined. So for example, absolute precision as to time is generally not required (I would bet that anyone reading this chapter has forgotten the exact date of Princess Diana's funeral). Given the nature of the conversation, suggesting a recent event, I have recorded the time variable as being "Saturday." The date was in fact Saturday 6 September 1997.

8 Contrast (1) with:

    (i) I never cook anything but I make an omelette at the weekends.

9 The characterization of metaphor through the supposed violations of the maxim of quality is not entirely unproblematic. See Sperber and Wilson 1982 for a critique of Grice's theory of conversation and Wilson 1995 for a critique of the problems imposed by the maxim of quality characterization of metaphor. See also section 4.1.

10 An anaphoric expression is one which can only be understood by reference to some other representation made available during the interpretation process. Pronouns are the central type of case, but words as *the, this, that* are also anaphoric.

11 The qualification of "nontrivial" is important as from a purely formal perspective "P" implies "P and P," "P and P and P . . ."; P also implies "P or Q" for arbitrary Q, etc. A nontrivial inference is one which cannot be drawn from considerations of P alone.

12 The modification of maximal relevance to optimal relevance for the particular activity of utterance interpretation is because of the imposed task of recovering the speaker's intentions. Some utterance may be extremely relevant in terms of the hearer's own privately held assumptions but nonetheless not be the intended interpretation because the speaker couldn't possibly have had access to the assumptions that led to these implications. Paranoia is a good example of this, where one's private fears and anxieties are so easily retrievable that they constantly lead to inferential effects of one sort or another, but fortunately most of us, at least some of the time, realize that these private worries are not a reliable basis for recovering what speakers have intended to convey to us.

13 In logic, one is taught that from an inconsistency any proposition can be derived, so there is a trivial inference from "P and not-P" to Q for arbitrary

Q. As with the earlier trivial inferences, these have to be explicitly debarred.

14 There is no fixed choice of premises which must constitute the context, so any choice of premises will do as long as it licenses inferential effects associated with being at Princess Diana's funeral.

15 There are several alternative accounts of the way in which construal of language depends on the context in which it is uttered. In some of these, there is no commitment to any form of representation. Amongst these is Searle, who argues for a concept of *Background* relative to which language is interpreted, without any commitment to mental representations. Cf. Searle 1983, 1995.

16 The Speech Act theory of meaning, which was originally articulated as a theory of meaning for natural language under the slogan "Meaning is Use," played an important part in the development of pragmatic theory. Language was explained in terms of different kinds of actions that can be carried out by the use of language. Primary distinctions were made between *locutionary acts* (what the speaker said to the hearer), *illocutionary acts* (what a speaker does by performing such locutionary acts – e.g. baptizing, promising, threatening), and *perlocutionary acts* (the effect a speaker has on the hearer – e.g. persuading, frightening).

17 This view has been consistently championed by Atlas in connection with negation (cf. Atlas 1977, 1989).

18 The *lexicon* is the part of a grammar where all information about individual words is stored. Entries in the *lexicon* are generally referred to as *lexical items* but the simpler notion of *word* is sufficient for our present purposes.

19 The issue of ellipsis remains controversial. There are analyses of ellipsis which are purely syntactic (Fiengo and May 1994 and others), analyses which are purely semantic (Hardt 1993, Crouch 1995) or some mixture of the two (Kehler 1995, Lappin 1996). Cf. Kempson 1995, Kempson et al. 1999, for an account of ellipsis in terms of how interpretation is inferentially built up as a propositional structure. For a representative selection of views, cf. Lappin and Benmamoun 1999.

20 This type of example is problematic for purely syntactic accounts of ellipsis, requiring a concept of "vehicle change" (cf. Fiengo and May 1994, Lappin 1996).

21 Even in reading, the parsing process is broadly sequential, though some effects arising from effects of linearity are noticeably weaker in reading. For example, it is not possible to open a conversation with (i) and be confident that your hearer will interpret *his* as picking out the same individual as the following phrase *a friend of mine*:

(i) His mother attacked a friend of mine.

It's more likely to pick out, say, your partner, particularly if your hearer already knows you are worried about his mother's uncontrolled behavior. (Many people talk about people they live with through the use of pronouns without introducing them into the conversation by name first.) However a newspaper headline might well report this event in the form

(ii) His mother attacks young boy.

relying on the fact that short sentences can be visually processed with much less reliance on strict left-to-right processing.

22 The order of expressions in the propositional structure, with that projected by the object preceding that projected by the subject, is to reflect the way the interpretation is built

up, the two-place predicate "admire" applying first to "John," and then to "Sue." This is a standard notation in formal semantics. See Heim and Kratzer 1998, for discussion of the concept of functional application underlying this notation.

23 This is a very simple sketch, and to give it proper formal characterization we shall need a tree-description language, a matter which I shall here simply presume on (cf. Kempson et al. 1999b, in preparation).

24 See Jespersen 1927.

25 *Who* is no longer restricted to being construed as nominative and picking out subjects, as (i) indicates:

(i) I dislike the man who John is thinking of living with.

26 Notice that this is just what the presumption of optimal relevance would dictate – for the previous mention of "John" by using the name *John* is by far the most salient representation in this discourse context, hence recoverable with the least possible effort.

27 Indeed this is quite an awkward sentence, because it implies that it is somehow surprising or exceptional that my son should get fed up with me – contrary to most people's experience!

28 See Kempson et al. forthcoming, Kempson et al. in preparation.

29 I have been helped in the writing of this chapter by detailed comments on earlier drafts from David Swinburne, Johannes Flieger, and Lutz Marten, and the two editors Mark Aronoff and Janie Rees-Miller. Without their help, this chapter might have been even more partial in its coverage than it no doubt remains.

17 Discourse Analysis

AGNES WEIYUN HE

> [I]n the world of human beings, you won't find a language by itself – the Dutch language strolling the canals, or the English language having a nice cup of tea, or the German language racing madly along the autobahn. You only find discourse.
>
> Robert de Beaugrande (1997: 36)

To imagine a world without discourse is to imagine a world without language and therefore to imagine the unimaginable. We get through our day exchanging various oral and written language (or, talk and text). We live by *languaging* or *discoursing*, not in discrete audio or visual units but in connected sound waves and orthographic forms to which we assign meaning on the basis of our past experience with them and on the basis of the situations in which these waves and forms are used. Discourse analysis is concerned with the contexts in and the processes through which we use oral and written language to specific audiences, for specific purposes, in specific settings. Many years ago, the well-known linguist William Labov observed that the term "sociolinguistics" is redundant – to him language is inherently social and so should be linguistics, the study of language. Today, we might draw an analogy about discourse analysis: one cannot understand language fully without looking at language use.

1 What Is Discourse? A Preliminary Characterization

The term "discourse" is used by many in very different senses, some having little to do with language. For instance, the term "the discourse of racial discrimination" as used in the media and some of the social sciences often refers not to the language use of those who practice racial discrimination but to the ideologies and belief systems generated therein. In fact, studies of racial discriminatory discourse in political science or history for example may not pay any attention to language at all. To differentiate discourse studies which do not focus on language and those which do, some researchers have made the distinction between the big D which concerns general ways of viewing the world and general ways of behaving (including speaking) and the small d which concerns actual, specific language use. Here, we are concerned with discourse as situated language use, or the small d, if you will.

What makes discourse analysis stand out as a discipline independent from although intricately interwoven with other domains of linguistic inquiry is that, more than any other domains of linguistics, discourse analysis emphasizes that language is not merely a self-contained system of symbols but more importantly a mode of doing, being, and becoming. Comparing with other domains of linguistics which have a specific / definable scope of inquiry (e.g., phonology on sound systems, pragmatics on rules governing information processing in the mind), discourse analysis's concern may seem far broader and therefore more elusive: discourse analysis seeks to describe and explain linguistic phenomena in terms of the affective, cognitive, situational, and cultural contexts of their use and to identify linguistic resources through which we (re)construct our life (our identity, role, activity, community, emotion, stance, knowledge, belief, ideology, and so forth). Essentially, it asks why we use language the way we do and how we live lives linguistically.

To this end, discourse analysts insist on the use of naturally occurring language data (as opposed to invented data). However, in spite of the shared global aim, different discourse analysts may focus on vastly different aspects of communication, draw upon divergent analytical traditions, and resort to sometimes incommensurable theories and methodologies. The main purpose of this chapter is not to systematically trace the intellectual genesis or diversity of discourse analysis or to review all approaches and methods used in discourse analysis. Readers interested in these issues are referred to Schiffrin (1993), van Dijk (1997), Ochs et al. (1996). My objective here is to address in simple terms the following question: what is discourse analysis and what do discourse analysts do?

As mentioned before, discourse analysis focusses on language as not merely systems of acoustic and orthographic symbols and rules for sequencing words or inferring meaning, but, rather, on language use motivated by real communicative needs and language as a means through which we accomplish various actions and interactions. Broadly speaking, discourse research can be divided into two major types of inquiries: (1) why some but not other linguistic forms are used on given occasions and (2) what are the linguistic resources for accomplishing various social, affective, and cognitive actions and interactions. Below we will consider both emphases.

2   Communicative Motivations for the Selection of Linguistic Forms

One set of questions that discourse analysts are concerned with have to do with the communicative motivations for the selection of linguistic forms. Unlike formal linguists (or autonomist linguists) who believe that language is

a self-contained system, discourse linguists maintain that language is inseparable from other aspects of our life and that the selection of linguistic forms
should be explained in terms of authentic human communicative needs (i.e.,
social, interactional, cognitive, affective needs). This position is compatible
with and is inspired by insights from a number of different sources including
anthropology, cognitive science, functional linguistics, psycholinguistics, philosophy, and sociology.

The following is a transcript of the beginning of an actual face-to-face meeting between a university student Susan (S) and her academic advisor Neil (N).
The meeting was audio-recorded by myself as part of a project on institutional
discourse (He 1998). S intends to go to medical school and wishes to find out
which major will give her the best chance of being accepted by medical school.
Helen, mentioned in their talk, is another academic advisor. I will use this
segment and segments related to it to illustrate some of the main issues which
concern discourse analysts and some of the important analytical traditions
which have influenced the practice of discourse analysis.

(1) *":"* = prolonged syllable; *"="* = latching, i.e., when the
     current speaker barely finishes, the next speaker begins;
     "CAPS" = stressed syllable; *"(.)"* = untimed micropause; *"."*
     = falling intonation; *","* = rising intonation; *"(0.0)"* =
     silences roughly in seconds and tenths of seconds; *"( )"* =
     undecipherable hearing; *"["* = onset of overlap.
     001 N: So:.
     002 S: All right um so,=
     003 N: =RIGHT now you are a math major.
     004 S: I AM a math I mean I TRANSferred as a math major.
     005 N: Ok.
     006   (.)
     007 N: Oh (.) Probably PRE-math.
     008 S: Premath (.) that's right=
     009 N: =Ok,=
     010 S: =Lemme=
     011 N: =( ) look at your file.
     012 S: Trans- yeah I HAVE that.
     013   (.8)
     014 S: Ok I'll FIND it in a second,
     015 N: All right=
     016 S: =But um (.2) see (.) um I: would like to go to (.)
     017   med school,
     018 N: Uhuh,
     019 S: Ok, (.8) and uh when I (.2) when I was in the
     020   orientation, (.) Helen told me that (.2) it's a
     021   LOT better if I am a MATH major, (.) 'cause uh
     022   medical schools they prefer math major people.
     023   (.4) And I am not sure how that I mean I I
     024   believed her THEN but NOW I've been talking to

```
025       [people
026   N:  [And NOW you DON'T believe her.
027   S:  Yeah I am NOT sure if that is the (.2) the RIGHT
028       thing or no:t.
029   N:  I would say um (.) I'm not as much of an expert (.)
030       about what happens to math majors (.) as Helen is.
031       She's (.2) doing research with what WHAT (.) has
032       happened to CU math majors and where they GO.
033       (.3)
034   N:  Uh but I'd say that certainly (.) medical school
035       doesn't CARE what your major IS.
036       (.8)
037   N:  Y=
038   S:  =Yeah that's what I heard.
039   N:  What they do care is (.2) uh did you take the
040       appropriate classes, Do you have the: (.) the
041       grades for appropriate classes, Do you have the
042       overall GPA do you have letters of recommendation
043       and so on so on so on.
044       (.5)
```

Looking at this transcript, discourse analysts will consider a number of things, centered around the question why the speakers select the linguistic forms that they do on this particular moment. Below we discuss some of the concerns, not in any particular order.

2.1   *Context*

One of the first questions discourse analysts ask is what is happening in this stretch of talk, who the participants are, where they are, and why they are there. In other words, discourse analysts are quintessentially concerned with the *context* of language use. For discourse linguists believe that linguistic choices are not made arbitrarily but, rather, are systematically motivated by contextual factors. One influential model to describe context comes from a branch of linguistic anthropology known as ethnography of speaking or ethnolinguistics or ethnopragmatics (Duranti and Goodwin 1992). In this model, the range of parameters which need to be taken into consideration when characterizing context is summarized by the *SPEAKING* acronym (Hymes 1974), which stands for Situation (setting, scene), Participants (addressor and addressee), Ends (goals and outcomes), Act sequence (message form and message content), Key (tone, manner), Instrumentalities (channel, forms of speech), Norms (norms of inter-action and norms of interpretation), and Genres (text types). Context as so described helps us understand what type of *speech events* or *speech activity* – a set of interpersonal relationships and a set of interpretative frames in relation to some communicative goal – we are dealing with. Given that we have in front of us an academic counseling encounter and not a job interview, for example, we will have certain expectations about topical progression, turn-taking rules, and outcome of the interaction as well as constraints on context. In this case, the Situation is an academic advising meeting taking place in a university. Participants include the student and her advisor. The Ends are to help the student choose the optimal path while observing the university's rules and policies. The Act sequence entails problem presentation and problem solution. The Key is formal but friendly. The Instrumentality is spoken language. The Norms include the advisor withholding personal opinions and leaving decision making to the student. And the Genre is a face-to-face interview.

Another important tradition which has impacted the approach to context in discourse analysis is a school of functional linguistics called Systemic Functional Grammar (Halliday 1985, Hasan 1995). In this theory, the notion of context owes its origin to the notion of *context of situation* developed by the anthropologist Malinowski. In Malinowski's sense, the context of situation is indispensable for the understanding of utterances; in other words, a given utterance has no meaning unless it is accompanied by ethnographic analysis of situations within which interaction takes place. This notion was later elaborated and modified by Firth, a British linguist, who points out that a context of situation for linguistic work entails the following dimensions: (a) the relevant features of participants: persons, personalities, both verbal and nonverbal actions of the participants; (b) the relevant objects; and (c) the effect of the verbal action. When the idea is further developed by Halliday (1985), the leading figure in Systemic Functional Grammar, and his colleagues, context is represented as a complex of three dimensions: First, the *field* is the field of social action in which the discourse is embedded. Second, the *tenor* is the set of role relations among the relevant participants, including their statuses and roles and their permanent and temporary relationships. And third, the *mode* is the role of language in the interaction. In this view, language is a system of choices, choices made on the basis of a contextual configuration which accounts for field, tenor, and mode.

In our example, what is taking place (Field) is seeking and giving advice concerning academic matters in an American university setting. It is a routine activity for many undergraduate students in US universities and colleges and their on-campus academic advisors. The relationship between the student and the advisor (Tenor) is a complex one: on the one hand, the advisor represents the university institution and implements the university's various rules and policies; on the other hand, the advisor is also an advocate of the student's interests. Language in this instance constitutes the advising activity itself (Mode) – it is through talk that problems are identified and solutions formulated.

2.2   *Rhetorical goal*

On a more local level, some discourse analysts are concerned with the *rhetorical goal* of utterances. Consider lines 19–22 for instance:

```
019  S:  Ok,  (.8)  and  uh  when  I  (.2)  when  I  was  in  the
020      orientation,  (.)  Helen  told  me  that  (.2)  it's  a
021      LOT  better  if  I  am  a  MATH  major,  (.)  'cause  uh
022      medical  schools  they  prefer  math  major  people.
```

Is Susan's utterance here designed as a simple narration of a past event (that Helen told her something at some point) or is it a precursor to her counseling request (i.e. please tell me whether Helen is correct so that I can make up my mind about my major)? Does it function as an elaboration of what has been said before in line 16 "But I'd like to go to medical school" in which "but" already forecasts trouble? Or does it serve as a contrast to what has been said? These concerns fall within the domain of "rhetorical management" (Chafe 1980) or "rhetorical structures" (Mann and Thompson 1987) of information.

2.3   *Speech act*

Discourse analysts following a philosophical tradition called speech act theory will be asking what kind of *speech act* Susan's utterance is in these same lines and whether this act is accomplished through direct or indirect means. Speech act theory (Austin 1962, Searle 1969, 1979) says that language is used not only to describe things but to do things as well. For example, we use language to make requests (belonging to the class of directives), promises (commissives) or apologies (expressives). Utterances in instances like these (e.g., "But I would like to go to medical school") cannot be assessed in relation to truth and falsity; instead, they can only be assessed in relation to the necessary and sufficient conditions (known as "felicity conditions") for their accomplishment. Further, utterances act on three different levels: the literal level (locutionary act), the implied level (illocutionary act), and the consequence of the implied act (perlocutionary act). The locutionary meaning of what Susan says in lines 19–22 is thus what Helen told her. The illocutionary force is however subject to further determination: is it an indirect request for a second opinion? Or does it imply an invitation for Neil to ask further questions? Whichever the case, the perlocutionary upshot can be that Susan is taking advantage of the advisor–student relationship on this occasion to get Neil to do things without explicit requests. This line of inquiry leads to the analysis of language use by combining the analysis of the propositional content of utterances with their illocutionary force, which in turn permits us to draw inferences about the speaker's intentions and his / her inner world of beliefs, assumptions, desires, attitudes, stances, and so forth.

2.4   *Scripts / plans*

Psychologically oriented discourse analysts will also be interested in these lines, but more from the viewpoint of how this utterance will be processed in the head of the listener. What sorts of *scripts, plans,* and *macrostructure* (van Dijk and Kintsch 1983; Schanck and Abelson 1977) are relevant and necessary for Neil to understand Susan's utterance as it is intended? For instance, Neil would need to have a knowledge of what often takes place in an advice-seeking and advice-giving encounter so that any narration of past events may be assessed in terms of their problem-ridden nature. He would also need to properly position Susan's utterance in the context of her immediate and overall goals as well as in the context of the overall structure of meetings of this kind (which often begin with problem presentation, followed by problem solution, etc.). Script is a term used to describe the knowledge that we have of the structure of stereotypical event sequences such as seeking and giving academic advice in a university institutional setting. If such knowledge can be described in a formal way with explicit rules and conditions, then we may have a theory of how humans process natural language; furthermore, we may be able to program and test that knowledge on a computer.

2.5   *Referentiality*

Given the interest in the organization of information, discourse analysts have paid special attention to how entities are referred to in our utterances. Let us take a look at how Helen is referred to in the data segment. Below is the subsection containing reference to Helen.

```
019  S:  Ok, (.8) and uh when I (.2) when I was in the
020      orientation, (.) Helen told me that (.2) it's a
021      LOT better if I am a MATH major, (.) 'cause uh
022      medical schools they prefer math major people.
023      (.4) And I am not sure how that I mean I I
024      believed her THEN but NOW I've been talking to
025      [people
026  N:  [and NOW you DON'T believe her.
027  S:  Yeah I am NOT sure if that is the (.2) the RIGHT
028      thing or no:t.
029  N:  I would say um (.) I'm not as much of an expert (.)
030      about what happens to math majors (.) as Helen is.
031  N:  She's (.2) doing research with what WHAT (.) has
```

We see that when Helen is first mentioned in this spate of talk, she is referred to by her name (line 20). When she is mentioned again in the same speaking turn by Susan, she is referred to as "her" (line 24). She is referred to in the same way by Neil in line 26. The choice between a proper noun "Helen" and a pronoun "her" (and other possibilities such as "that lady," "this other advisor") partly has to do with whether and how Helen has been mentioned before in prior talk and whether the entity "Helen" is recoverable or accessible from previous discourse or from the listener's existing knowledge. In other words, it has to do with the *information status* of "Helen" – whether "Helen" is *given* information or *new* information (also known as old vs. new, or shared vs. new, or known vs. unknown) (Halliday 1967, Prince 1981, Givon 1983). In line 20, since Helen has not been mentioned before, the choice of "she / her" is out of the question. And presuming academic advisors know each other and often address each other on first name basis, it is appropriate and efficient for Susan to choose "Helen" among all possibilities. In line 24, since Helen has been introduced into the talk and since no other female person has been mentioned, "her" is the most efficient reference and cannot be mistaken for anyone else. In line 26, Neil shows that he really follows what Susan is saying by predicting what she will say next; "her" in this case then is intended and can only be interpreted to be coreferential with "her" in line 24. Some discourse analysts, sometimes known as text linguists (Halliday and Hasan 1976, de Beaugrande and Dressler 1981) are particularly interested in how referential forms make a stretch of discourse *cohesive* in form and *coherent* in meaning.

We may then ask why in line 30 Neil refers to Helen by her name again, since he has already previously referred to her with a pronoun "her." Well, besides old vs. new, other factors come into play. Note that between Neil's two speaking turns which respectively begin at line 26 and line 29, there is an intervening turn by Susan (lines 27–8). And that turn is about "I" (Susan) and says nothing about Helen. When Neil speaks again in line 29, he speaks of himself in comparison with Helen. In other words, lines 19–28 constitute a problem-presentation phase; beginning from line 29, Neil starts giving advice. These two sections are two different *episodes* (Fox 1987, van Dijk and Kintsch 1983). Discourse studies have shown that at the beginning of a new episode, references are likely to be made in ways similar to how they are made for the first time.

2.6 *Topicality and thematicity*

Another set of issues which concern how information is presented – what is an utterance about, what is the starting point of a message, what is the focus of a message – includes *topic* and *theme*. These are some of the most controversial concepts in discourse studies; until this day there remain substantial disagreements among discourse linguists as to whether these two notions are the same and what they entail.

Topic has been defined in terms of aboutness, i.e., the part of the utterance about which something is said. It has also been considered in terms of its grammatical and discourse functions. For example, in some languages such as Chinese, the element central to discourse is often placed initially preceding the utterance and assumes a certain grammatical role (e.g. "Xiaomei, wo zao jiu renshi ta le" (Xiaomei, I have known her for a long time) where "Xiaomei" specifies the topic). These languages are called topic-prominent languages (Li and Thompson 1976).

The notion of Theme was originally developed by a European linguistic tradition known as the Prague School (Danes 1974, Mathesius 1975). Working with Slavic languages whose word order is more flexible than languages such as English and depends crucially on degrees of knownness / givenness of information, Prague School linguists developed what is called the *functional sentence perspective* which says that word order has to do with how informative each element in the utterance is – *communicative dynamism,* or CD. A sentence begins with elements with the lowest CD and ends with those with the highest CD. Theme, in this framework, is the part of the utterance with the lowest degree of CD. Influenced by the Prague School approach, linguists working within systemic functional grammar take thematic information to be information from which the speaker proceeds and thematic organization to be a method of development of the text (Fries 1981, Hasan and Fries 1995).

Back to the interaction between Susan and Neil. We have seen that at the beginning of their meeting, Susan reported to Neil what Helen had told her about choices of major for medical school. At a later point, Neil comments as follows (presented clause-by-clause; indentation shows sub-clauses; initial elements up until the grammatical subject of the clause are in bold face):

```
(2) Neil2: 121-137
    N:  y' see there're there're two ways  (.2)
          you can read what she said.
        One way is (.)
      medical schools look at transcripts
            and look for major
        and they see math major
        and they circle with a red pen
        and they they add ten points to your your score or
          something
        and they let you in more often.
        (.3)
    N:  The other thing is
        they look at your transcript
          and look at your scores (.2)
        and (they look at) your MCAT
          and look at your letters of recommendation (.2)
        they admit people
        and when you look at the people they admit,
          there are more math majors than you expect.
        (1.0)
```

Here Neil outlines two ways of interpreting what Helen said with "One way" and "The other thing" at the beginning of his two main clauses. In each interpretation, he begins with "medical schools" or "they." A topical analysis says that, in this stretch of talk, "medical schools" is the entity about which something is said. A thematic analysis says that "medical schools" specifies the frame within which something is said. Hence Topic and Theme may (but do not necessarily) reside in the same elements, but they represent different meanings.

2.7 Sequential organization

The selection and interpretation of linguistic forms in a given utterance have a lot to do with the *sequential context* of the utterance (Couper-Kuhlen and Selting 1996, Ford 1993, Ochs et al. 1996, Schegloff 1979, 1996). For instance, where is the utterance positioned in interaction? Is this utterance opening a dialog? Or is it a response to some prior talk? Or is it a repair of some prior talk? Or is it part of a narrative episode? Discourse analysis in recent years has been profoundly influenced by a distinct approach to human interaction known as Conversation Analysis (Sacks et al. 1974, Sacks 1992, Atkinson and Heritage 1984). This analytical tradition has provided the most systematic and rigorous account of how we manage talk in interaction. Central to conversation analysis is the concept of *turn taking*, which can be described by a set of rules with ordered options that operate on a turn-by-turn basis as a locally, sequentially managed system. This system explains how speakers "earn" their right to speak, how speaking rights are negotiated and interactionally managed, how the next speaker is selected, how overlaps occur and how they are resolved, and how speakers fix problems in comprehension and miscommunication. A turn is constructed with turn-constructional-units, which refer to sentential, clausal, phrasal, lexical, intonational, or pragmatic units (Sacks et al. 1974, Ford and Thompson 1996). The rules of turn taking apply at the end of each turn-constructional-unit, which is called a transition-relevant-place.

I will introduce two more concepts from conversation analysis to prepare for the discussion of the following sample data segment. One of them is *adjacency pair* (Schegloff and Sacks 1973) – a sequence of two utterances adjacent to each other, produced by different speakers, ordered as a first part and second part, and typed, so that a first part requires a particular second part or range of second parts. A good example of an adjacency pair is a question–answer pair. The other concept is called *repair organization* (Schegloff et al. 1977). When trouble in conversation occurs, it is noticed and then corrected, either by the party whose turn contains the source of trouble or by some other party. This sequence of trouble + initiation-of-correction + correction is known as a *repair trajectory*. Repair occurs when one party corrects his or her own talk or that of another party and can be accomplished in a number of ways.

Now let's consider the following segments (3) and (4) from the same meeting between Susan and Neil. Here they are discussing specific courses Susan has taken and can take the next semester. I wish to show through these two segments how Neil and Susan define and modify the meanings of the modal verb "can" through interaction.

(3) *"italics"* = modal verbs
```
230  S:  No. Uh I'm going to (.2) well I have a Fortran,
231  N:  Uhuh,
232  S:  That Helen said we can just=
233  N:  =should should should accept that.
234  S:  Right.
```

(4)
```
283  N:  Ok. [you can swi- you can switch.
284  S:      [and I figured it's a lot harder.
285  S:  I can?=
286  N:  =Y'know you can take 8A 6B 6C if you want.
287      That's fine. [No problem.
288  S:               [Ok. Yeah.
289      (.)
```

In theory, *can* can mean a number of different things: it can index the speaker's knowledge or belief, it may imply necessity or logical possibility or probability, it may indicate interpersonal obligation, and so forth. In (3), Neil completes the turn that is initiated by Susan (lines 232–3). In the course of doing so, he replaces S's reported *can* (line 232) with *should* (233) and finishes S's turn, thereby interpreting S's report of what Helen said. S agrees with such an interpretation ("Right," line 234). Thus through Neil's completion and repair of Susan's turn and Susan's subsequent ratification, Neil and Susan jointly interpret *can* as used by Helen to mean "should."

(4) is a case involving S initiating repair (line 285) of N's turn (283), which results in N's repair in 286. The interpretation of *can* in 285 and 286 should not be made arbitrarily; it should be made in relation to *can* in the original turn of 283, as 285 is a repair initiation of 283 and 286 is a repair (a specification) of 283.

The above is not an exhaustive list of features to which discourse analysts attend. Neither is it an inventory list for anyone who does discourse analysis to follow. It only gives us an idea of some of the features which often draw the attention of discourse analysts. Depending upon their intellectual persuasion, different discourse analysts may focus on one or several of the above features. There is, however, no single study which considers all of them at the same time.

We have so far considered one set of questions which occupy discourse analysts: on given occasions, why do we select the linguistic form that we do? We have seen that the answer to this question is complex and multifaceted. Discourse analysts have sought to explain linguistic choices in terms of ethnographic contexts, knowledge structure, rhetorical organization, communicative intentions, textual organization, information management and sequential organization, among others. Next we turn to the other set of questions: how does language use contribute to our social, cultural, intellectual, emotional life?

3 Linguistic Resources for Doing and Being

As discussed previously, discourse linguists take a dialectical view of the relationship between language and other aspects of human life. On the one hand, the selection of linguistic forms is shaped by various contextual factors; on the other hand, the way in which we use language contributes to / constitutes other aspects of life. Thus our second set of questions are corollaries of the first set. In this section, I first sketch some of the topical areas of work along this line. I then illustrate how analysis may be performed by returning to the interaction between Susan, the university student and Neil, her academic advisor.

Some of the earlier work in discourse studies concerned how *ordinary, everyday activities* are accomplished linguistically. The tradition of Conversation Analysis, for instance, was developed in the late 1960s and 1970s and was motivated by a concern with the linguistic and interactional resources that we deploy in making sense of everyday life. Conversation, or talk-in-interaction, is considered the primordial means through which we conduct our social life and construct various social relationships. Discourse work from early sociolinguistics looked at, for example, how syntactic structures reconstructed life experience in narratives (Labov 1972).

Recently there has been a surge of research interest in how *institutional, professional activities* are carried out linguistically (e.g., Cazden 1988, Drew and Heritage 1992, Gunnarsson et al. 1997, He 1998, Lemke 1990, Young and He 1998). How do doctors talk to their patients, therapists to their clients, advisors to their advisees, business people to their counterparts, teachers to their students, prosecutors to their witnesses, interviewers to their interviewees, etc.? What kinds of speech exchange system (e.g., a particular turn-taking pattern; storytelling) are characteristic of the particular speech event? What are some of the salient lexico-grammatical forms (e.g., modal verbs such as *can* and *must*; generic uses of personal pronouns such as *you* or *they*) used in these events? How does the way in which the participants use language reenact, maintain, or alter their institutional roles and identities? How are institutional activities accomplished through verbal and nonverbal interaction?

Furthermore, discourse analysts have undertaken to examine how *identities* are reconstructed linguistically. Instead of treating the language user's identity as a collection of static attributes or as some mental construct existing prior to and independent of human actions, discourse analysts approach identity as something dynamic which is continually emerging and which identifies what a person becomes and achieves through on-going interactions with other persons and objects (Ochs 1993, Shotter 1993). Along this line, institutional identities (Sanders 1994), gender identities (Tannen 1990), ethnic / cultural identities (Scollon and Scollon 1981, Wierzbicka 1992) have been examined as they evolve together with language use.

In a similar vein, discourse analysts have pursued the role of language in the (re)construction of *ideology* (van Dijk 1991), *epistemology* (Whalen and Zimmerman 1990), *emotion* (Capps and Ochs 1995), *cognition* (Goodwin 1994), *expertise* (Jacoby and Gonzales 1991), *power* (Duranti 1995), among other facets of life.

Last but not least, research from a branch of linguistic anthropology, known as language socialization, has been dedicated to the scrutiny of the impact of language use on the *socialization* of values, norms, and other sociocultural knowledge. The focus is on the organization of communicative practices through which novices (e.g., children) learn to become competent members of their communities (e.g., Heath 1983, Ochs 1988, Schieffelin 1990). This body of research examines audio- / video-recorded, carefully transcribed, recurrent socialization activities involving experts (e.g., caregivers) and novices (e.g., children) and explores the impact of the verbal and non-verbal details of interaction on the construction of social and cultural ideologies that define a community.

Space does not permit me to include more topical areas of discourse work or to cite more studies for illustrative purposes. We can safely say that with our life and our world becoming increasingly rich and diverse, the possibility and potential for discourse analysis is unlimited. Let me next return to the data segment about Susan and her academic advisor Neil to illustrate how analysis of language data *vis-à-vis* some of the concerns sketched above may be carried out.

3.1   Roles and identities

The first order of business when the participants sit down in the counseling office is to establish who and what they are to each other *vis-à-vis* the counseling encounter. This may sound superfluous as clearly both participants already have pre-existing respective identities as "counselor" and "student" defined by the university. But these pre-existing titles do not specify what kind of counselor or student they are, nor do they provide concrete guidance as for example how one student's problem might be treated differently from another's or how one counselor's advice might be taken differently from another's. Despite their generic roles and identities, the participants still need to establish their attributes specific to their meeting – the student in terms of his / her academic conditions which occasioned his / her visit and the counselor in terms of his / her authority and expertise with respect to the student's conditions.

In the above data segment, how to categorize the student in terms of an academic major is the focus of talk in the initial minute. Is she a math major or a pre-math major? Is she a committed math major or a math major by virtue of the fact that she transferred to CU as a math major? How do the participants arrive at a shared understanding? Why do the participants choose academic major as an attribute relevant and important to the beginning of their encounter? How is this categorization to affect subsequent talk and subsequent counseling activities? Is the counselor a knowledgeable and competent one?

3.2 *Activities and tasks*

In addition to establishing occasion-specific identities, the participants also need to determine and agree upon the task and purpose of their meeting. What is the counseling problem? How is the problem presented, identified, and formulated? What role does each participant play in the identification and formulation of the counseling problem? When the student makes an appointment with the academic counseling office, he / she is asked what his / her needs are. The university representative who schedules the appointment summarizes the student's response on the basis of the former's understanding of what the problem is or could be. With that summary he / she (the representative) then fills in the slot "purpose of visit" on the appointment slip. Hence what is stated on the appointment slip as "purpose of visit" reflects how the person who schedules the appointment characterizes the problem, a characterization often inevitably too distilled to be informational and sometimes unfortunately too speculative to be accurate.

In the case of Susan, "choosing a major" was put down as purpose of visit on the appointment slip. This could mean a number of different things. It could be that the student has not declared a major and is in need of help with choosing a major. It could be that the student has not officially declared a major but has already made up her mind about which major to choose and is therefore in need of help with technical procedures to get into the major. It could be that the student already has a major but for one reason or another is contemplating changing into a different major. It could also be that the student has a number of concerns, the top one on the list being matters related to choosing a major. Each of the above scenarios presents a different set of tasks and activities – different forms to fill, different kinds of information to discuss, and different ways of talking and interacting. Although the student's record file can supply certain information (e.g., whether or not the student has officially declared a major), which scenario each specific case is can only be determined through the actual encounter between the student and the counselor.

It turns out that Susan already has a major. How do the counselor and student unpack the stated purpose of visit: "choosing a major"? Note that nowhere in the above segment can we find utterances such as "I am here because I would like to . . ." or "Tell me specifically what I can help you with." How then do the participants come to a shared orientation to re-considering majoring in mathematics as their task?

For ease of reference, let me reproduce the first 8 lines below:

```
001  N:  So:.
002  S:  All right um so,=
003  N:  =RIGHT now you are a math major.
004  S:  I AM a math I mean I TRANSferred as a math major.
005  N:  Ok.
006      (.)
```

```
007  N:  Oh  (.)  Probably  PRE-math.
008  S:  Premath  (.)  that's  right=
```

We see that in the very beginning Neil identifies Susan in terms of her major (line 3, "you are a math major") and displays his orientation to the service request; his "RIGHT now" (line 3) casts being math major as S's temporary identity and forecasts a change of major, which will be the focus of discussion. Subsequently, Susan corrects Neil's categorizing her as a math major through a self-repair of her own utterance (line 4, "I AM a math I mean I TRANSferred as a math major"). By changing from "I AM," indicating a present state of being, to "I TRANSferred," indicating a past action, Susan focusses on the process of how she became a math major. She also displays a lack of commitment to being a math major, and thereby converges with Neil's understanding (line 3) that their encounter is to be about a change of major. In what follows, Neil revises "math major" into "PRE-math" (line 7), an official university category which on this occasion also echoes and reinforces Susan's tentativeness displayed in her previous turn. Susan then acknowledges that Neil's categorization of her is accurate (line 8). Hence, before the first seven utterances are completed, a shared orientation to the student's identity and the institutional task at hand has been constituted.

Susan's identity, in this instance her academic major, is co-constructed in this case to scaffold the counseling problem (i.e., choosing a major); the selection of "math" or "pre-math" as an identificatory category is bound to what the participants collectively take this particular counseling encounter to be about. It can also be seen that the establishing of institutional identity is a reciprocal process; the establishment of the student's identity also establishes that of the counselor. Recall that Susan produces her initial correction of Neil as a self-repair of her own utterance ("I AM a math I mean I TRANSferred as a math major," line 4). With this self-correction, it appears that she is correcting herself and not the advisor, a strategy by which she collaborates in constituting the advisor's expert role. Though Neil mitigates his subsequent correction by using an adverb of uncertainty ("probably") in "probably PRE-math," this choice of modifier in fact enhances his expertise by invoking a large body of experience from which he can generalize. The advisor thus demonstrates his ability to make judgments on the probability of facts which are not explicit. By situating the identity of Susan's major within the specific counseling task at hand and in relation to the advisor's expert role, we are now able to view the identity of the student not only as embedded in the academic counseling context, but also actively contributing to the context.

3.3   Knowledge and stances

Equally important are the institutional knowledge the participants exhibit and the affective stances they project. How does Susan present her understanding that being a math major may pose a problem for her to later attend medical school? Does she appear to be certain or tentative? In either case, what does she do linguistically to help her construct that appearance? What is the function of quoting Helen, another advisor? What role does Neil play while the student is fleshing out her purpose of visit? How does Neil address her concern? Does he provide a straightforward answer? Is he assertive, direct, cautious, and / or empathetic?

In more general terms, how do the participants come to know what they know? How do they assign responsibility of what they say and what they experience? How do they position themselves in relation to each other and to the university institution? How does the counselor manage the dual role of being an institutional gatekeeper and an advocate of the student's interests?

Again, for ease of reference, here are lines 16–33:

```
016  S:  =But um (.2) see (.) um I: would like to go to (.)
017      med school,
018  N:  Uhuh,
019  S:  Ok, (.8) and uh when I (.2) when I was in the
020      orientation, (.) Helen told me that (.2) it's a
021      LOT better if I am a MATH major, (.) 'cause uh
022      medical schools they prefer math major people.
023      (.4) And I am not sure how that I mean I I
024      believed her THEN but NOW I've been talking to
025      [people
026  N:  [NOW you DON'T believe her.
027  S:  Yeah I am NOT sure if that is the (.2) the RIGHT
028      thing or no:t.
029  N:  I would say um (.) I'm not as much of an expert (.)
030      about what happens to math majors (.) as Helen is.
031      She's (.2) doing research with what WHAT (.) has
032      happened to CU math majors and where they GO.
033      (.3)
```

Here Susan reports that Helen has stated that medical schools accept a higher percentage of math majors. In the report, Susan carefully retains her own attitude separate from Helen's through her distinct temporal and modal choices. What Helen reportedly said is encoded with straightforward tense markers only (lines 19–22); whereas the student's own commentary is encoded with hedges ("not sure" in lines 23 and 27) which help construct a sense of doubt and uncertainty in contrast to the certainty and truthfulness of Helen's speech. Thus Susan portrays the account of the problem as certain and truthful and her own attitude as doubtful and uncertain, which in turn warrants Neil's attention, alignment, and subsequent advice. And Neil is not merely a passive recipient of Susan's report. Rather, he actively anticipates her account (line 18), sympathetically collaborates with her in her account (line 26), and cautiously provides his assessment of the situation without discrediting Helen, his colleague (line 29 and onward).

Hence we see the attitudes and dispositions of the advisor and the student interact closely with the task of seeking and giving advice as well as with the participants' role identities. Being a competent academic advisor means in part to be able to make clear to the students what is required, what is assumed, what is preferred and what is permitted by the university. Complementarily, part of being a competent student advisee entails being able to project others' as well as their own stances so as to effectively elicit the advisor's advice.

Put more generally, the above analysis views the university institution as not merely a represented entity but a lived one. Institutions such as a university academic advising center do not just exist in the form of physical structure, personnel, and various rule books such as the university catalog, written policies regarding course credits and so forth. They are lived by their members through seemingly routine actions, interactions, and activities. Knowledge and knowledgeability regarding institutional structures and constraints, institutional goals and institutional roles is produced and reproduced through the details of the participants' moment-by-moment conduct.

We have, to some extent, looked at the aspect of participants' conduct that is accomplished through language use. By language use, I have meant not only the use of vocabulary and grammar and but also the sequential organization of talk. These two jointly provide means through which institutions live and change. As academic counselors and student counselees talk to each other, as they ask and answer questions, as they tell and retell stories, as they quote others' speech, as they hedge or assert, they are actively engaged in reconstructing the institutional nature of their encounter.

4   Discourse Analysis, Linguistics, and More

By way of concluding this chapter, let me say a few things to re-situate our discussion both within and beyond linguistics. While it is correct to say that discourse analysis is a subfield of linguistics, it is also appropriate to say that discourse analysis goes beyond linguistics as it has been understood in the past. For as I have discussed above, discourse analysts research various aspects of language not as an end in itself, but as a means to explore ways in which language forms are shaped by and shape the contexts of their use. Further, discourse analysis draws upon (and is practiced by scholars in) not only linguistics (especially functional linguistics), but also anthropology, sociology, psychology, philosophy, cognitive science, and other disciplines in the humanities and social sciences concerned with human communication.

Discourse analysis is a wonderfully creative enterprise. It is also a disciplined enterprise. It is creative in the sense that one can, for instance, combine interests in conversation analysis, grammar, storytelling, institutional discourse and gender by investigating how gender is reflected and recreated through specific speech exchange systems and specific grammatical processes in conversational storytelling at workplaces. It is disciplined in the sense that not all approaches to discourse are equally defensible against all sources of doubt and that one needs to determine what constitutes the nature of the research question and to choose which set of theoretical and methodological constraints to abide by.

Discourse analysis promotes a view of language which says that language use is not only reflective of other aspects of our lives but is also constitutive of them. In this sense, it revitalizes, advances, and systematizes functional and anthropological oriented schools of linguistics, thus creating a healthy balance with autonomist linguistics. As it draws insights from various disciplines, it also contributes to interfacing linguistics with other domains of inquiries, such that for example we might now investigate the construction of culture through conversation or program computers to generate interactive texts based on our understanding of the rules and principles of human interaction. Finally, discourse analysis brings to linguistics and related disciplines a human dimension. It focusses on language as it is used by real people with real intentions, emotions, and purposes. It reminds us that "language has a heart" (Ochs and Schieffelin 1989) and that language users and linguists do too.

NOTE

The writing of this chapter was in part supported by a research grant from the Spencer Foundation. I am solely responsible for the statements made and the views expressed. I would also like to thank Peter Fries and the editors of this volume for their helpful comments. Remaining deficiencies are mine only.

18 Linguistics and Literature

NIGEL FABB

1 Introduction: Literary Linguistics

"Literary linguistics" is the application of linguistic theory to literature. In this chapter I consider ways in which two of the fundamental aims of linguistic theory relate to the special characteristics of literary texts. The first aim is to model the cognitive processes which shape verbal behavior. Literary linguistics adapts this aim to ask whether literature involves any specialized cognitive processes. The second aim is to explain how linguistic form can be used to communicate meaning. Literary linguistics adapts this aim by asking how the distinctive characteristics of literary communication can be understood in terms of a general theory of linguistic communication.[1]

1.1 Literary and linguistic cognition

Verbal behavior is regular: we can make generalizations and predictions about it. Regularities are "generated" by rules. Some rules are cognitive, in the sense that they represent the specialized cognitive systems which underlie behavior. Other rules are cultural or conventional in the sense that people acquire and use them as part of their general knowledge; these have no special cognitive status. In language, the rules of a generative grammar represent cognitive rules, while the rules of a traditional prescriptive grammar represent cultural or conventional rules.

Literary texts have regularities which are shared with verbal behavior in general, but they also have special regularities, which can be described by literary rules such as the rules of meter, of parallelism, of narrative form, of rhyme and alliteration, and so on. The interesting question about these rules is whether they are cognitive rules or cultural / conventional rules (or both at the same time). For a literary linguistics concerned with cognition, the fundamental question is whether any of the literary rules represent specialized cognitive processes. If this is the case, then we must ask what the relation is between these cognitive processes and general linguistic cognitive processes. On the one hand, are there general resemblances between the literary and linguistic rules; do metrical rules share cognitive subcomponents with phonological rules, for example? On the other hand, do the literary rules interact with the linguistic rules?

As an example of the issues involved, consider the ways in which Irish alliteration (a literary rule) operates, which suggest both that there is a specialized cognitive process in operation and that this process interacts with linguistic processes. The Irish words "white," "cow," and "great" have *bán, bó,* and *mór* as their respective forms at some underlying level but are pronounced as *mbán, βó,* and *mór* which are their forms at the surface level. (The underlying and surface forms are related by linguistic rules.) In Irish verse, alliteration is a relation between words which begin with the same consonant, and the first two words alliterate with one another while the third does not. This indicates that it is the underlying representations of the words which are taken into account by the alliteration rule, and not the surface representations (Malone 1988). The fact that alliteration governs a "hidden" aspect of linguistic form, apparently undoing the effect of phonological rules, suggests that the alliteration rules must themselves be cognitive rules since they are able to interact with cognitive rules.

1.2 *Literary and linguistic communication*

One of the fundamental problems for formal linguistics is to explain how form is related to meaning. Linguists recognize two distinct problems. The first problem is to relate phonological form to logical form. The logical form is the output of phonological and syntactic processing, and is a representation which is accessible to interpretive rules: thus, the logical form will identify the words which have been spoken, the phrases into which they fit, and their grammatical relationships (subject, predicate, object, etc.). The second problem is to explain how in communication a logical form is used to decide what the speaker's informative intentions are: that is, what does the speaker actually mean to tell us? The first problem is the domain of syntax (and a certain kind of semantics), and is almost certainly irrelevant in the study of literary texts, because literary texts are probably like any kind of text when it comes to the derivation of logical forms from phonological forms. The second problem is in the domain of pragmatics and is clearly relevant in the study of literary texts, because literary texts have unusual interpretive characteristics: in particular, they tend more than other kinds of texts to have interpretations which are indirect, multiple, and indeterminate. Thus metaphor and irony both involve quite indirect kinds of intepretation, and the ambiguity and unparaphrasability characteristic of many literary texts is an example of the multiplicity and indeterminacy of interpretations. Hence literary linguistics must ask this question about the interpretation of literary texts: do the distinctive interpretive characteristics of literary texts involve cognitive mechanisms which are different from the cognitive mechanisms involved in the interpretation of non-literary texts?

2   From the Perspective of Linguistics, What Is Special about a "Literary Text"?

A literary text is a place where we find certain kinds of rules operating – rules of meter, parallelism, narrative structure, and so on. In this sense, the fact that the texts which typically have these rules belong to a kind called "literature" is irrelevant, since we are interested in the rules and not the types of text where those rules occur.

However, there are reasons to be interested in the possibility that in any culture there is a distinct class of "literary texts" (also called "verbal art"). In an influential article published in 1960, Jakobson (1987) argued that one of the things which distinguishes literary texts from other utterances is that the literary text "focuses on the message" (by which he means the utterance and not its content), which we can restate by saying that a literary text communicates a description of its own form. The literary text does this by making form prominent; in verse this is achieved for example by meter or parallelism, where form becomes prominent because it is repeated. Hence attention is drawn to form; in effect the form of the text is communicated to the audience. Jakobson saw his approach as a way of understanding how literary rules exploited something fundamental about verbal behavior, with ultimately cognitive aims. His work has been adapted by Richard Bauman so that it it is part of a theory of language in use. Bauman (1984) adapts Jakobson's decontextualized approach to literary form and puts it into the context in which literary texts are presented to an audience, which is the context of performance. (Bauman focusses primarily on oral performance, but literary publication can be seen also as performance.) Bauman suggests that the communication of form is necessary because performance requires the performer (the author) to demonstrate to an audience that she is adhering to a set of rules, and expects the audience to evaluate her on this basis. Thus the rules must be prominent, as is achieved when the literary text communicates a description of its own form.

Jakobson and Bauman explore the possibility that literature is a special kind of verbal behavior, and hence of interest to linguists. A second source of interest relates to the possibility that our experience of literature has an "aesthetic" quality which is different from our experience of other kinds of text, giving rise to aesthetic experience. Aesthetic experience is a problem for psychology, with affective and physiological components as well as cognitive components. The key question for literary linguistics is whether the distinctive modes of exploitation of linguistic form in literature contribute to esthetic experience.

3 Metrical Structure and Phonological Structure

3.1 Meter

A metrical text is a text whose phonological form is governed by a set of metrical rules. Two aspects of phonological form are involved: phonological constituency, and (in rhythmic meters) phonological strength.

The smallest metrically relevant phonological constituent is the mora. A mora is a unit of phonological "weight," such that a short vowel is typically one mora, a long vowel typically two morae, with post-vowel consonants potentially adding additional weight. The meter which regulates the Japanese verse genre of haiku requires the complete text to contain 17 morae, which can be realized as 17 short vowels, or 13 short vowels and 2 long vowels, etc. The text must be divisible into 3 constituents which we can call "metrical lines," with lines ending after the 5 and 12th morae; one consequence of this is that a word cannot include both the 5th and the 6th morae (as it would be illegitimately split between lines). The following haiku (written 1686) by Matsuo Bashō illustrates the meter; it has 17 short vowels and hence 17 morae, with divisions (marked with a slash) after the 5th and 12th.

1 2 3 4 5	6 7 8 9 10 11 12	13 14 15 16 17
furu ike ya	/kawazu tobikomu	/mizu no oto
An ancient pond –	A frog leaps in.	The sound of water.

This haiku meter exemplifies two characteristics which all meters have: it divides the text into metrical lines, thus creating at least one basic level of metrical constituency, and it counts phonological constituents (here morae) into the metrical line. Meters can also count other kinds of phonological constituent; thus the French alexandrine is a meter which counts syllables (12 in the line), and it is possible that the Old English poem *Beowulf* is governed by a meter which counts phonological feet into the line (Russom 1987; a phonological foot is a group of syllables including one strongly stressed syllable).

These meters do not differentiate amongst the phonological constituents which they govern. However, meters are able to differentiate phonological constituents into two kinds, defined relative to one another as "strong" and "weak." Meters which have a pattern of strong and weak metrical constituents are experienced as "rhythmic." The notion of metrical strength correlates with some notion of phonological strength such that for example relatively stressed or relatively heavy syllables are more likely to be strong metrical constituents than are relatively unstressed or relatively light syllables, but there is not a perfect match between phonological and metrical strength – suggesting incidentally that metrical rules are not simply a variant kind of phonological rule (a point I return to later). Meters which differentiate constituents are usually sensitive either to relative stress among syllables (accentual meter) or relative weight among syllables (quantitative meters).

Syllables contain morae, and can be distinguished into heavy syllables (two morae) and light syllables (one mora); this difference is exploited by quantitative meters. Some quantitative meters stipulate long and complex patterns of heavy and light syllables; the meters of Classical Sanskrit are of this type. Other quantitative meters are periodic, which means that a relatively simple pattern is repeated throughout the line. The meter (dactylic hexameter) of Homer's verse is periodic: it stipulates a sequence of six subconstituents (called "feet"), each of which has the same basic internal pattern. The pattern consists of a heavy syllable followed by two morae, realized either by a heavy syllable or two light syllables. Each foot can be formulated as a single strong metrical constituent followed by a single weak metrical constituent.

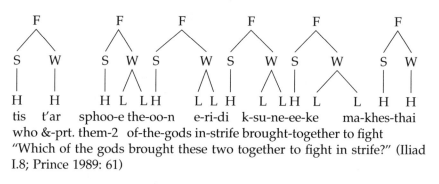

tis   t'ar   sphoo-e the-oo-n   e-ri-di k-su-ne-ee-ke   ma-khes-thai
who &-prt. them-2   of-the-gods in-strife brought-together to fight
"Which of the gods brought these two together to fight in strife?" (Iliad I.8; Prince 1989: 61)

The relative strength of the strong constituent is realized both by the fact that it contains a heavy syllable and is constrained in that it must contain this heavy syllable. In contrast the weak constituent is less constrained – one manifestation of its relative weakness – and can contain one heavy or two light syllables (see Prince 1989).

English iambic pentameter is an accentual meter, which is sensitive to stress. The basic metrical rules ensure that in each line there are ten syllables, and that stressed syllables in polysyllabic words are found only in even positions (positions 2, 4, 6, 8, and 10). While monosyllables are also constrained to some extent, the major constraint holds of polysyllables. Thus in the following line (from Shakespeare's sonnet 73), *ruined* is the only polysyllable and has its first-syllable stress in second position of the line (i.e. an even position); in contrast we might perform the verse with strong stress on the monosyllable *birds* but this is not in an even position even though it is stressed – and the meter does not require it to be because it is a monosyllable.

    1   2 3   4   5   6   7   8 9   10
    Bare *ru*ined choirs, where late the sweet birds sang.

Hanson and Kiparsky (1996) argue that this meter in fact governs stress indirectly, by actually controlling strong syllables. Stress is a source of strength, but strength is relative, which is why the meter controls only a stressed syllable in a polysyllable (where there are other less stressed syllables to compare it with). Because the meter does not control all the stresses in the line, but primarily the stresses in polysyllables, it is possible for a 14-line sonnet to have a different pattern of stresses in every line (so long as any polysyllables have their stresses in even positions).

A meter organizes phonological constituents into a metrical constituent, the line, and the line has interesting characteristics of its own. Metrical lines are the best examples of a phenomenon seen also in smaller metrical constituents, where the metrical rules constrain phonological form more strictly towards the end of the line (called the "cadence") than towards the beginning of the line (Hayes 1989). Thus for example the lines of the Sanskrit Rigveda are controlled by a quantitative meter, but this meter really only controls the second half of the line, with the first half of the line being strict in syllable-count but free in pattern of heavy and light syllables. Similarly, in iambic pentameter lines where the expectation is that stressed syllables in polysyllables will fill even positions, it is common to find an exception called "trochaic inversion" where a stressed syllable in a polysyllable is "misplaced" into the first position of the line, as in the following example from a sonnet by Shakespeare. Note that only the first polysyllable has its stress in an odd position; both *unseen* and *disgrace* have their stressed syllables in even positions as the meter predicts.

        1 2   3   4   5   6   7   8   9   10
    Stealing unseen to West with this disgrace

The ends of metrical lines also have distinctive characteristics, as though they have a particular status for metrical cognition: extra syllables are common here (in iambic pentameter for example, or in the Italian endecasillabo where the eleventh syllable can be seen as an expected line-final extra); light syllables can count as heavy; and phonological material can even perhaps be "borrowed" from line-endings and put elsewhere, as Hale (1984) argues for (Australian) Warlpiri verse.

3.2   Word-boundary rules

Many meters involve a constraint on the placement of larger phonological constituent boundaries, involving phonological constituents such as the lexical word, the clitic group, and the utterance. Constraints on the boundaries of the utterance typically include a requirement that a large phonological constituent must end at the end of a metrical line (in literary critical terms, "enjambment" will be ruled out by such a constraint). Constraints on word and clitic group boundaries can be formulated as "caesura" and "bridge" rules. A caesura rule forces a word boundary to appear at a certain place in the line, relative to the phonological constituent structure of the line; a bridge rule has the opposite effect, preventing a word boundary appearing at a certain place in the line. The "word boundary" involved can be a lexical word boundary or a clitic group boundary; in Greek drama, tragedies tend to constrain the former while comedies tend to constrain the latter (seen as a looser constraint); see Devine and Stephens (1984). In some meters, word-boundary rules take on a pervasive role in structuring the line. Thus in (Australian) Dyirbal "gama" songs, word boundaries are allowed at only three places within the 11-syllable line (and are obligatory in two of those three places); see Dixon and Koch (1996).

One of the interesting characteristics of caesura and bridge rules is that they sometimes seem "designed" to prevent a word boundary appearing at the boundary of a line-internal metrical constituent; thus in Homer's verse, a word boundary in the dactylic hexameter line may not fall exactly in the middle (between third and fourth feet) but usually falls within the third or fourth foot, as can be seen in the line cited above. It is not uncommon for different kinds of constituency (here metrical constituency and phonological word constituency) to mismatch in this manner, and it might potentially be a way of deriving an esthetic effect by causing complications for linguistic processing.

3.3   Methodological and conceptual problems for a metrical theory

Metrical theory faces a conceptual dilemma, relating to its object of study. Metrical verse is rarely fully regular, in the sense that it is impossible to formulate a rule system which correctly describes the relevant aspects of every line in a text or a genre. Two approaches can be taken to this problem. One, associated with generative metrics (Halle and Keyser 1971) is to say that lines which cannot be described are unmetrical (similar to ungrammatical sentences), and thus accidents of performance but not significant in the formulation of metrical rules. The second approach, associated with Russian theorists (Tarlinskaja 1989) is to treat the metrical rules as having some statistical relationship with actual metrical texts, such that we would expect a high degree of correlation.

There is also a significant methodological problem faced by metrical theory, particularly a metrical theory which looks for cross-linguistic validity. Because linguistic accounts take a sophisticated view of phonological form, they can offer reconsiderations of how some apparently well-understood meters actually work. This has proved true for most meters. Iambic pentameter appears to be a meter which controls stressed syllables, but Hanson and Kiparsky (1996) argue that it is actually a meter which controls phonological feet and only indirectly controls stressed syllables; the same arguments surround the meter of *Beowulf*. Even such apparently simple meters as the meter governing haiku may require reanalysis in other terms, as Poser (1990) suggests. In the case of archaic Celtic meters, lines appear at first sight to involve syllable counting, but it is possible that in actual performance stress was also involved, so that the meter might have been an accentual meter (Klar et al. 1984). Similar questions arise about the remarkable Classical Sanskrit meters, where we might wonder whether some hidden principle governs the shape of the rigidly but apparently randomly ordered sequences of heavy and light syllables. Chinese appears to have archaic meters which are sensitive to lexical tone (Chen 1979) but here too there is some question as to whether there is an underlying pattern of syllable weight to which tone itself is sensitive. As we will see, these methodological problems spill over into the problem of understanding the relationship between music and meter in songs (since many kinds of metrical verse are or were once sung).

A third problem which metrical theory faces is the presence of explicit metrical rules. In some – though not all – metrical traditions, there are explicitly formulated rules which poets know, and which they apparently follow in composing metrical verse. It is possible that these metrical rules are either good descriptions of cognitive rules, or that they are internalized as cognitive rules. But it is also possible that there is nothing of any particular cognitive interest occurring, and metrical composition is just another kind of behavior conforming to randomly formulated cultural conventions. Linguists argue against this position, and have several routes of attack. The most fruitful approach is to show that the explicit metrical rules do not in fact correctly describe actual metrical practice (this is true for iambic pentameter). This can demonstrate that explicit metrical rules are rather like the rules of a prescriptive grammar in describing what people think their verbal behavior is or ought to be, and not what it actually is.

3.4 Meter and cognition

If any literary rules are cognitive rules, metrical rules are the best candidate because of their complexity, their interconnection with the cognitive rules of phonology, their relative exceptionlessness and their inaccessibility to introspection. Metrical rules have some characteristics in common with phonological rules, such as the construction of constituents with strong and weak members, which is found both in accentual / quantitative meters and in the rhythmic aspects of the phonology. However, they also have characteristics which are quite unlike phonological (or other linguistic) rules. For example, meters can count constituents. Phonological rules (and other linguistic rules) can organize constituents into groups of two, and are sensitive to whether a constituent is first or second in a series; it is just possible that phonological rules can also count up to three. However, no phonological rule organizes phonological material into a five-member sequence (like iambic pentameter or the haiku meter), or a 19-member sequence (like one of the Classical Sanskrit meters). These distinct characteristics suggest that if metrical rules are rules of cognition, they are not some variety of phonological rule but involve some other capacity; it is possible for example that metrical cognition shares components with musical cognition.

If we think of metrical rules as cognitive rules, then two questions arise. First, is the cross-linguistic variation in meters a matter of parametric variation of basic cognitive principles (analogous to variation in language)? Hanson and Kiparsky (1996) present some relevant proposals. Second, might individual writers have their own idiosyncratic kinds of metrical rule (or their own variations on some common set of rules)? This has been a rich area for speculation, because it can often be demonstrated that different writers within the same tradition write metrical verse in different ways, which can be captured by slightly different rule systems.

If metrical rules are cognitive rules, what are the interconnections between metrical cognition and linguistic cognition? More specifically, do metrical rules have special access to underlying linguistic form (and similarly, are metrical rules blind to any aspects of surface linguistic form)? It seems, for example that when meters count syllables they are capable of counting syllables which exist in the underlying representations of words but are deleted in actual pronunciation; claims of this kind have been made by various linguists including Zeps (1963) for Latvian songs, and Kiparsky (1972) for the meters of Vedic Sanskrit. Thus the meter appears to have special access to phonological material which is not accessible to introspection; thus the metrical rules are interacting with (cognitive) linguistic rules.

4   Songs

It is common for literary texts to be set to music, which in many cases involves a relationship between phonological and musical form. When the text is metrical, a third kind of form exists, which requires us to consider the complex relations between musical, metrical, and phonological form. The work done in this area is primarily by ethnomusicologists (who are usually also linguists), but tends to focus on the specific problems of a specific tradition rather than considering the more general issues which arise. In this section I outline some of these more general issues (see also Fabb 1997: 98–106, Moyle 1986, Schuh 1989, Dixon and Koch 1996, Banti and Giannattasio 1996, for examples of linguistically sensitive musicological analysis).

When text and music are combined, a pre-existing text can be set to newly composed music, a newly composed text can be set to pre-existing music, or both can be composed together. In all three cases, the same question arises about the relation between musical form and linguistic form, namely which aspects of linguistic form constrain or are constrained by which aspects of musical form. As one example, in songs from the Polynesian island of Tokelau

(Hoem et al. 1992) a pitch rise within the melody is sensitive to the number of morae at the end of the line, with underlying morae (deleted in pronunciation) also taken into account. As another example, in Luganda songs from Uganda (Katamba and Cooke 1987) the musical form includes a recurring 36-beat constituent to which the text is matched with one mora to each beat. This might suggest that the text should be thought of as organized by a mora-counting meter, which in turn might derive from a patterning meter, derived from the musical form. More generally, it may be that metricists have underestimated the distribution of metrical systems (once claimed just to exist in Indo-European, Islamic, and Buddhist-influenced traditions) because they have paid insufficient attention to music and musical form as a source of metrical form.

Metrical texts can be set to music. In this case, what is the role of the meter in constraining the relation between musical form and phonological form? Does the meter control the phonological form completely independently of the matching of musical and phonological form, or does the meter mediate the matching of musical and phonological form? As an illustrative example, consider the iambic pentameter text "Go christall tears . . . ," set to music by John Dowland (published 1597). Dowland's music for this song is organized in four-beat constituents, with first and third beats strong and second and fourth weak. The meter is organized in two-beat constituents (five to a line), with first beat weak and second beat strong, controlling just the placement of polysyllabic stresses. In the setting of text to music, are polysyllables treated distinctively, and are lexically prominent monosyllables treated in an undifferentiated manner? (i.e. does the musical setting of the text reproduce characteristics of iambic pentameter?). In this particular instance, the answer to both questions is yes, suggesting that the meter does indeed mediate the mapping of phonological to musical structure. Thus while there are variable numbers of syllables in each bar, the stressed syllables in polysyllables always fall in first or third beat position; and the important lexical monosyllables seem unconstrained in where they fall. Thus while the musical performance of the text no longer sounds at all like an iambic pentameter line, it nevertheless preserves exactly the same abstract characteristics as iambic pentameter, at least in this particular song.

5 Rhyme and Alliteration

Rhyme and alliteration are repetitions of parts of the syllable. A syllable is a grouping of phonological segments (sounds) around a nucleus which is typically a long or short vowel. Its structure is as follows, with the onset and rime typically filled with consonants preceding and following the vowel which is the syllable nucleus.

```
                              syllable
                             /\
                            /   \
                           /     rime
                          /      /\
                         /      /   \
                      onset  nucleus  coda
        e.g. "brand"  [ b r     æ      n d ]
             "bridge" [ b r      ɪ      d ʒ ]
             "ridge"  [ r        ɪ      d ʒ ]
```

Rhyme is full or partial identity between two times (partial identity involves just the vowels being the same, or just the consonants being the same, two variants of rhyme). Thus *bridge* and *ridge* rhyme because they have identical codas. Alliteration is full or partial identity between two onsets; thus *brand* and *bridge* alliterate because they have identical onsets.

Sound patterning can be systematic or unsystematic (appearing unpredictably in a text). Systematic patterning is of most interest to linguists, since it is more clearly rule bound. Systematic rhyme is very common, not only in metrical verse but also in other kinds of text. Systematic alliteration is relatively rare. Most linguistic work on sound patterning has looked at the fact that the segments or segment-sequences which are repeated are not necessarily identical in all features, with particular "equivalence sets" allowed in particular traditions (e.g. a vowel-consonant sequence may count as the same if the vowel is identical and the consonant is any voiceless plosive). The question then arises as to what extent the segments count as "the same." Various proposals have been made about the sense in which the segments are "the same": in some cases it has been argued that the "sameness" can only be captured by looking at underlying phonological representations before the operation of late phonological rules (Malone 1982, 1988, Kiparsky 1970); in other cases it seems that the "sameness" more simply involves the sharing of features, perhaps involving underspecified underlying phonemes. In some cases, it may be that the "sameness" of distinct segmental sequences can reveal or confirm underlying form: for example, the fact that [sp], [sk], [st], and [s] do not alliterate in Germanic verse, where usually initial consonantal identity is sufficient, confirms an analysis which has support also from the phonology whereby [sp], [st], and [sk] each count as a single segment in some sense. There is, however, a methodological problem which confronts a linguistic explanation of why certain sounds are "counted as" the same in a poetic tradition: poets often have explicit knowledge of permitted combinations (e.g. it might be a prescriptive rule), and furthermore the permitted combinations are always restricted in number (e.g. they need not be generated by a general rule or principle but could just be learned individually). This does not undermine the linguistic study of segmental equivalences, but it does sound a cautionary note (see also Árnason 1991), as in other cases where explicit rules might seem to offer a non-cognitive explanation of regular verbal behavior.

Sound patterning offers other problems which are of linguistic interest. One problem involves the constituency of the material which is patterned. In most kinds of rhyme the repeated material is a well-formed constituent (e.g. the rime of the syllable; however, there are plenty of examples of sound-patterning where the repeated material is not a single well-formed constituent. Thus rhymes may include the final part of one syllable and the whole of the next as in the rhyme *pleasure / leisure / treasure* (used by Byron). Similarly, alliteration in Finnish involves not just the onset of the syllable but also (part of) the nucleus, illustrated by the line *Kalevalan kankahilta* from the *Kalevala*, where the alliteration is in [ka], which includes both the onset and the nucleus. The fact that non-constituents can be manipulated by sound-patterning rules is puzzling, and deserves further study. A second problem offered by sound-patterning relates to a difference between alliteration and rhyme. Two words which rhyme can be quite far apart (in all traditions), with intersecting rhyme patterns (ABAB) being common. In contrast, two words which alliterate must be very close – in adjacent feet, half-lines, or lines – and there may not be any intersecting ABAB alliteration systems (Fabb 1997: 121). This difference between rhyme and alliteration (reflected also in the cross-linguistic common-ness of systematic rhyme and the rarity of systematic alliteration) requires linguistic explanation.

6   Communication and the Sources of Interpretive Difficulty in Literary Texts

Literary texts often present difficulties for interpretation, including ambiguities, indirectness, indeterminacy, and obscurity. There are often functional explana-tions for these deliberate difficulties. Thus the special sacredness of prayers may require their lack of full interpretability, the deep indeterminacies of Romantic lyrics may realize the philosophical aims of the poets, and so on. There is general agreement that these difficulties arise not by the exploitation of a specialized semantics (or pragmatics) for literature, but instead are exploitations of general linguistic semantics and pragmatics. If this is true, then problems of specifically literary meaning may have no distinctive interest for linguistic theory, except to the extent that literary texts sometimes give particularly good illustrations of certain characteristics of general semantics. However, linguist-ics is able to offer ways of understanding how meaning arises in literary texts. In this section I consider three characteristic interpretive problems presented by literary texts, and look at how linguistics might come to the aid of literary studies: (a) how metaphor works, (b) how irony works, (c) how "point of view" is communicated. All three problems have been discussed within relevance theory (Sperber and Wilson 1995), a theory of communication and interpreta-tion, and it is the relevance theoretic approach which is the primary source for this section of the chapter. Most linguistic theories of interpretation would say that the utterance (including the literary text) provides partial evidence for interpretation and does not determine interpretation. In relevance theory, the communicator uses the utterance to provide partial evidence (but in the context, sufficient evidence) to enable a hearer or reader to determine the communicator's informative intention. Importantly, that informative intention can itself be vague or ambiguous; thus the interpretive difficulties of literary texts are built into the informative intention itself (see also Sperber 1975).

An utterance can be processed into a logical form which is a proposition. This proposition can in principle be taken as the intended meaning of the utterance; this is its "literal meaning." A metaphor arises where the logical form of an utterance must be rejected in favor of another proposition, derived by the use of bridging inferences which link the two propositions. Sperber and Wilson argue that metaphors are just instances of the kind of "loose talk" which is characteristic of all communication: literalness is not necessarily the most communicatively efficient way of saying something. They suggest that metaphors are ways of enabling a single utterance to communicate many thoughts (the range of interpretations licensed by the metaphor), and thus are an instance of the highly productive nature of literary language. In this account, metaphor is not specific to a literature but is a possibility in every kind of communication. Nevertheless, it may be that literature uses general characteristics of communication for particular experiential ends; Sperber and Wilson propose that the size and vagueness of the range of interpretations generated by a literary metaphor is a cognitive state which is experienced as "esthetic" (a "poetic effect" in their terms).

A different aspect of metaphors – the fact that they often have stereotyped meanings – has been explored by linguists interested in the cognitive organization of concepts (Lakoff and Johnson 1980, Lakoff and Turner 1989). Under this approach, the connections between logical forms and intended meanings are drawn from inventories of linkages, connecting concepts in the mental lexicon; thus for example there is a (possibly universal) link between life and a journey such that references to journeys, parts of journeys and so on can always be interpreted metaphorically as being about life. This approach takes the traditional literary study of topoi (conventionalized kinds of content), and makes it part of the study of cognition.

Irony arises where a speaker (or author) communicates a proposition while at the same time communicating her own lack of commitment to that proposition. As Sperber and Wilson show, irony is a possibility because it is not only propositions which are communicated, but propositional attitudes, consisting of propositions embedded under attitudes of belief, disbelief, doubt, certainty, and so on. Thus a communicated proposition is attributed to a source who has a particular attitude towards that proposition. The source is usually the communicator herself, and her communicated attitude is usually one of belief: however, it is equally possible that the proposition can be attached to another source; in this case, it is some third party's belief which is being reported and the communicator can signal her own lack of commitment to the proposition. Where the communicator communicates that a proposition is attached to a third party, and that it should be held in an attitude of doubt or disbelief, then irony arises. This is not specific to literature but a possibility in every communicative act.

Sperber and Wilson's account of irony is part of a more general account of the communication of "point of view." A reader's or hearer's interpretation of point of view (or "focalization") is her interpretation of which character (or narrator) is to be understood as experiencing a particular thought or experience in a narrative. Sometimes this is made explicit by the utterance as in the direct or indirect representation of speech or thought in a novel, where the speaker or thinker is explicitly mentioned and her relation to the speech, thought, or experience is explicitly expressed by a verb such as "said," "knew," "felt," etc. The use of hearsay particles (also called evidentials, meaning something like "they say that" or "it is said that") works to express attitude fairly directly, by indicating that the representations expressed by the narrative are known or experienced by (usually unspecified) third parties. And more generally, the modality of a sentence contributes explicitly to our knowing what commitment we should assume towards them. More generally, the possibility of "fiction" is enabled by the complex combinations of representations and attitudes allowed by linguistic communication: we can simultaneously both believe and not believe a set of propositions. Perhaps these modal contradictions of fiction are another kind of complexity which could be a source of esthetic experience.

These are all explicit ways of using linguistic form to tell us who the person is who entertains a proposition, their relation to that proposition, and our relation to that proposition. However, these kinds of meaning can arise also without explicit coding by the use of verbs of speaking or thinking, or hearsay particles. Thus it is possible to recognize shifts in point of view without any explicit coding of these shifts. For example, in the first few paragraphs of Jane Austen's novel *Emma*, we recognize a shift in point of view from narrator to character marked only by the italicization of a word and a sentence which (in its context) is unusually short. Here the text provides evidence for a shift in a point of view in an innovative (and hence not explicitly coded) manner; this exploits the general characteristic of communication which is that the text of an utterance provides only partial evidence for its interpretation, and hence that it is not only the propositional content which may be underdetermined by linguistic form but aspects of the propositional attitude more generally, including whose attitude it is. It is possible that all instances of what is sometimes called "free indirect speech and thought" are actually cases where the text provides partial evidence for a shift in point of view, without fully coding it (see also Fludernik 1993).

In conclusion, it appears that the various kinds of interpretive difficulty presented by literary texts involve the exploitation of general communicative possibilities, for particular functional ends.

7 Linguistic Form and the Interpretation of Narrative

Narrative form is not restricted to linguistic texts; narratives in many different media all exploit the same basic elements of narrative form. Nevertheless, there are two basic reasons why linguists are interested in narrative form. The first is that narratives are one of the most common types of verbal behavior, existing not just as literary texts but also in everyday interaction. Thus discourse analysis and sociolinguistics must include a study of narratives as a type of verbal behavior. The second reason is that linguistic form is clearly exploited in narratives, and has some relation to narrative form.

Linguistic form and narrative form are usually related in one of two ways. One possibility is that the linguistic form is evidence for narrative form, and falls under a theory of communication such as that outlined in the previous section; in this account, narrative form is a meta-description of the narrative which is communicated by elements of the linguistic form of the narrative (see Contini-Morava 1991). The other possibility is that linguistic form is functionally adapted to the demands of the narrative at any particular time, in just the same way that the choice of form serves expressive functions in all verbal behavior.

The "communicative" role of linguistic form in establishing narrative form is clearest when we consider the division of a narrative into episodes (see Hymes 1981, Woodbury 1987). A narrative episode is basically a unit of content within the narrative, characterized by internal stability in participants, place, and time, with these internal components changing between episodes. However, some traditions of verbal narrative appear to make a distinctive use of specific kinds of linguistic form at episode boundaries, in a manner which emphasizes the presence of those boundaries. Thus a North American Ojibwe narrative analyzed by Ghezzi (1993) typically begins a new episode with the connective *ninguting* ("and then . . .'); a Malay narrative analyzed by Cumming (1995) has marked word order at an episode boundary; a South American Apalai story analyzed by Koehn (1976) uses the historic past with greater frequency at episode boundaries; a Central American Tojolabal narrative analyzed by Brody (1986) has clausal repetition at episode boundaries, and so on. These uses of linguistic form have two important features. First, different languages use different kinds of linguistic form for essentially the same function. This is a fundamental characteristic of linguistic form in literature, that the same kind of form can serve many different kinds of function, and a single function can be served by many kinds of form. Second, the use of a specific linguistic form at episode boundaries is rarely fully consistent within a narrative. The second feature suggests that this is not a matter of linguistic form being generated by rules; instead the intermittent use of the linguistic form suggests that it is being used as evidence (combined with other evidence, including narrative content) of an episode boundary, and the linguistic form thus does not actually determine the division into episodes. This use of linguistic form communic- ates a description about the narrative (i.e. a meta-description), representing the narrative as divided into episodes. This possibly solves a problem about narrative form, which is its indeterminacy and inconsistency; if narrative form is not immanent in the narrative but instead is a self-description communic- ated by the narrative, we would expect narrative form to be like anything else which is communicated: that is, we would expect ambiguities of form, indeter- minacies of form, etc. Here, by offering a theory of communication, linguistics can suggest a solution to one of the central puzzles of literary form. However, it is still necessary to consider the other striking feature of boundary-markers, which is that different languages exploit (apparently in a consistent manner) different formal strategies. To some extent this arises because different languages offer different kinds of linguistic form which can be used for this purpose, but to some extent it also means that there must be some systematic coding of certain strategies as communicating the presence of an episode boundary.

The second kind of relation between linguistic form and narrative form can be seen as a variant of something that we find in any utterance, which is that formal options can be adapted to functional demands. Linguists often use the term "stylistic" to describe a difference between two sentences which give rise to similar logical forms. Thus constituents can be moved within a sentence without significantly affecting its propositional meaning (including stylistic movements such as topicalization, dative shift, etc.), and constituents can be omitted by passivization or nominalization without affecting crucial aspects of propositional meaning. These are options presented by linguistic form; dif- ferent languages offer different stylistic options, and they can be used in many kinds of verbal behavior (not just literature). The realization of syntactic valency (as active or passive, as verbal or nominal projection, etc.) communicates dif- ferent perspectives on an eventuality, and it is sometimes argued that these perspectives conspire to produce particular interpretations for a text; this is the basis of Halliday's analysis of Golding's novel *The Inheritors*, where he suggests that there is a consistent use of certain linguistic forms expressing transitivity which correlate with the novel's (literally) prehistoric human con- sciousness (Halliday 1981). A somewhat different sense of the "stylistic" use of transitivity options can be seen in the fact that "storyline" sentences in a nar- rative which contribute to the progression of the story are often formally dif- ferent from "non-storyline" sentences which provide contextual information. Storyline clauses tend to be more transitive than non-storyline clauses, in an extended sense of transitivity developed by Hopper and Thompson (1980); non-storyline clauses tend to be low in transitivity. It is less plausible here that the distinction communicates a meta-description of the narrative as consist- ing of storyline vs. non-storyline sentences; instead we should probably see the linguistic distinction as a reflex of the fact that we would expect storyline clauses to be high in transitivity because they typically describe actions with consequences, while the non-storyline clauses would be predictably low in transitivity because they typically describe states. An associated issue arises when we consider the fact that in languages with an option of expressing a proposition either in verb-medial or verb-peripheral sentences, there is a tendency for verb-peripheral sentences to be the storyline sentences. Again, this may possibly arise for functional reasons relating to the importance of the verb (and hence its need to be informationally prominent) in storyline clauses. Thus again the linguistic form may be functionally adapted to narrative form. A third example comes when we consider the use of strategies such as noun-incorporation (Velázquez-Castillo 1995) which make noun phrases more or less salient in the clause; in languages which have these as formal options, we find that the formal choice reflects narrative demands relating to how prominent a particular participant should be at any point in the narrative.

The same aspect of linguistic form can in some cases be seen both as evidence for narrative form and also as the consequence of narrative function. This appears to be the case for linguistic form which realizes what Labov (1972, 1997) calls the "evaluation" in a narrative. Narrators at least in some narrative genres evaluate narrative events in terms of what they might mean to the narrator and audience. Evaluation is thus a function of some part of the narrative, but as Labov shows, it is realized by typical kinds of linguistic form – for example by the use of modals, negatives, and so on, or by stylistic effects like repetition. Thus linguistic form is present in part to serve a narrative function. But at the same time, linguistic form provides partial evidence of narrative form, because as Labov and Waletzky (1967) showed, there is a major evaluative moment just before the narrative complication is resolved. Thus the linguistic form provides evidence for the structure of the narrative. Hence linguistic form both reflects narrative function and also communicates narrative form.

8   Parallelism

Parallelism is a relationship of partial identity between two sections of a text. When the partial identity involves the language of the text, it falls within the domain of literary linguistics. There are three major types of linguistic parallelism: syntactic, phonological, and lexical. In syntactic parallelism, the two sections of text share some or all aspects of their syntactic structure. Thus in the following pair of lines by William Blake, the second line has the same syntactic structure as the first, consisting of a verbal participle followed by a preposition phrase containing a noun phrase.

> Struggling in my father's hands
> Striving against my swadling bands

Note that the parallelism is not perfect: the two noun phrases look at first as though they have the same structure, but this is an illusion because the first has *my father's* as a possessor, and the second has *my* as a possessor and *swadling* as a modifier. This imperfection of the parallelism is typical; exact repetition appears to be often avoided, perhaps for reasons similar to the inherent variability within many meters, the use of equivalence sets in rhyme and alliteration, or the inconsistent coding of narrative structure; all may be designed to generate esthetic experience through complexity.

Lexical parallelism involves a pair of parallel words, one in each section of the text. "Struggling" and "striving" and "hands" and "bands" are instances of lexical parallelism in the above example, and it is common for syntactic parallelism to support lexical parallelism.

In phonological parallelism, the phonological structures of the two sections have some elements in common. For example, some eighteenth-century Gaelic songs are governed by a phonological parallelism such that all lines in a stanza have the same sequence of stressed vowels. Medieval Welsh poetry made extensive use of phonological parallelism, codified as specific patterns of possible *cynghanedd* (harmony). This is illustrated in the following line by the fifteenth-century poet Tudur Aled:

> serch a rois ar chwaer Esyllt
> s rch   r s r ch   r
> "he set his love to sister Isolde"

This is a type of parallelism called *cynghanedd groes o gysswllt* in which there is a parallel sequence of consonants within the line (i.e. s + r + ch + r). The line is divided by the meter into two halves, ending after *rois*, but in this kind of *cynghanedd* the division of the line by parallelism contradicts the division of the line by meter, thus generating the kind of complexity which I have suggested elsewhere might be a source of esthetic experience.

Parallelism is very widespread in the literatures of the world (see Fox 1977, 1988). In some literatures, genres of text can be found where parallelism is so pervasive in the text as to constitute a fundamental structuring principle (Jakobson called this "canonic parallelism"). In such texts, every second line might be parallel to the line which precedes it, a possibility realized for example in a funeral oration of the Indonesian Rindi (cited by Forth 1988). Where parallelism is a fundamental structuring principle it has some functional similarity to meter, and in fact meter superficially produces texts which have phonological parallelism. However, parallelism and meter are fundamentally different as structuring processes. In parallelism, the form of a line is directly influenced by the form of the preceding line; there need not be any overall consistency in form across the text as a whole. In meter, the form of a line is influenced by an external rule system, which ensures overall consistency; lines resemble each other only indirectly.

Parallelism in literature is of interest to linguists for two reasons. First, we might ask whether the processing of parallel texts involves some component of linguistic cognition which is specialized to deal with linguistic parallelism. Second, we might ask whether underlying linguistic form can ever be governed by parallelism, in a manner analogous to the metrical control of underlying form discussed earlier.

Jakobson, who pioneered the linguistic study of parallelism, believed that parallelism did indeed involve fundamental principles of linguistic cognition. He saw the flow of verbal behavior as a sequence of choices (at various levels of linguistic form). In ordinary verbal behavior, items which are equivalent (having some formal characteristic in common) belong together as a set of options which are presented at a point in the sequence: one option is chosen and the others are discarded. In verbal art, the set of equivalent items is retained and used again later in the text, with the result that equivalent items are put into sequence: hence, linguistic parallelism. Taking this perspective on verbal behavior, Jakobson argued that parallelism exploits the fundamental principles of verbal behavior to create verbal art (Jakobson 1987). While we may no longer see parallelism as involving a central aspect of linguistic cognition, we might, nevertheless, find parallelism operating as a principle in some part of linguistic cognition; thus Chomsky (1995: 125) refers to a "parallelism requirement" which holds at some level of linguistic cognition and gives rise to structures with partial parallelism (a process referred to by syntacticians as "gapping"). Another kind of example is presented by some cases of lexical parallelism. Traditions which have lexical parallelism sometimes group words into conventional sets, which then constitute an inventory for the production of verse, such that two words can be chosen from the same set to create a textual parallelism. For example, the Asmat of New Guinea have conventional sets of words which in their everyday meaning are somewhat related, and which are considered to be exact synonyms in poetry, and so used to produce parallel texts; the words *yow* "sun," *yesir* "morning star," and *piri* "moon" form such a set and in poetry are all interpreted as meaning specifically and only "sun" (Voorhoeve 1977). In some cases, the words in the set are independently close synonyms; in other cases, the words are clearly related but the grouping into the set reflects a fairly random convention. An interesting question to ask about conventional lexical sets is whether their construction involves access to the principles which organize the lexicon. For example, a linguistic mode of lexical organization is to put words into "classifier sets" of which linguistic gender is a relatively simple instance; words in classifier sets then correlate with particular morphologies (e.g. feminine and masculine nouns in French take different articles). It is worth asking whether the organization of words into sets for the purposes of parallelism draws on cognitive processes similar to the organization of words into classifier sets.

Do rules of parallelism have access to underlying linguistic form? A relevant example is presented by Efik tone riddles (Fabb 1997: 151, based on Simmons 1958). In these texts, the first and second lines have the same pattern of lexical tones, so that when they are spoken aloud the two lines have the same melody, the same sequence of rises and falls. However, while the shape of the melody is the same, its length is not; in one line there might be a sequence of a low vowel followed by three high vowels followed by a low vowel, which is parallel to a sequence of a low vowel followed by a single high vowel followed by a low vowel. Thus parallelism here is not between the tones on individual vowels, but on the (suprasegmental) tonal contour which lies above the utterance as a whole; here, it is possible that an aspect of underlying linguistic form is being governed by parallelism.

9   Conclusion

I began this chapter by suggesting that a cognitively oriented literary linguistics must ask two questions: are literary rules cognitive rules? and how does literature exploit the possibilities of linguistic communication?

We do not yet know the answer to the first question. There is intermittent evidence from the study of meter, of sound patterning, of the relation between music and text, and possibly from parallelism and narrative analysis, that literary rules are sometimes cognitive rules. These rules are constrained in specific ways, are not accessible to introspection, and interact with the rules of linguistic cognition. However, the evidence is fragmentary and what is lacking is some more global attempt to formulate universal principles, and examine exactly which manipulations of linguistic form are possible and which are not possible.

Turning to the second question, there is evidence that the special characteristics of literary communication (including indeterminacy, ambiguity, indirectness, and so on) are present in all kinds of verbal communication; literature just makes particularly extensive use of them. It seems possible also that some kinds of literary form (e.g. certain kinds of narrative form) are best reinterpreted as meta-descriptions of the text which the text itself communicates; thus some kinds of literary form resemble literary content more than they resemble linguistic form.

Both questions in turn lead to the question of esthetic experience. Our experience of literary texts is qualitatively different from our experience of other kinds of text, and we must ask whether this qualitative difference can in part be systematically related to the ways in which literary and linguistic rules operate and interact.

NOTE

1   This chapter is largely based on research reported in Fabb (1997). Historical snapshots of literary linguistics are provided by various anthologies and conference collections: Sebeok (1960), Freeman (1970, 1981), Fabb et al. (1987), Kiparsky and Youmans (1989). Bever (1986), Hobbs (1990), and Rubin (1995) offer accounts of linguistic cognition in the processing of literary texts. Preminger and Brogan (1993) offer an encyclopedic introduction to poetics (and literary linguistics).

19 First Language Acquisition

BRIAN MACWHINNEY

Nothing can make a parent prouder than a child's first word. Whether it be "Mama," "Papa," or even "kitty," we all recognize the first word as a major milestone in the child's development – a clear token of the child's entrance into a fuller membership in human society. We emphasize the child's first word, because of the enormous importance that we place on language as a way of communicating with other people After all, we reason, the only species that uses language is the human species. Moreover, it is through language that we come to understand the deepest secrets of other people and come to appreciate the extent to which we share a common humanity.

Fortunately, the ability to acquire language is present in almost every human child (Lenneberg 1967). Children who are born blind have few problems learning to speak, although they may occasionally be confused about words for colors or geographic locations. Children who are born deaf readily acquire a rich system of signs, as long as they are exposed to native sign language speakers. Even a child like Helen Keller, who has lost both hearing and sight, can still acquire language through symbols expressed in touch and motion. Children with neurological disorders, such as brain lesions or hydrocephalus, often acquire complete control over spoken language, despite a few months of early delay. Children with the most extreme forms of mental retardation are still able to acquire the basic units of human communication. Given the pervasiveness and inevitability of first language acquisition, we often tend to take the process of language learning for granted. But language is the most complex skill that a human being can master. The fact that nearly all of us succeed in this task indicates how remarkably well the structure of language adapts to our underlying abilities. Language is immensely complex, but its complexity is accessible to all of us.

To understand this remarkable achievement, we could adopt a variety of perspectives. First, we could view language learning from the viewpoint of linguistics. Linguists tend to think of language as having a universal core from which individual languages select out a particular configuration of features,

parameters, and settings. From this perspective, child language is an interesting slice of the universal pie. The shape of this slice is presumably limited both
by formal universal constraints and by the child's mental abilities or developmental status.

Psychologists view language learning from a very different perspective. To
the psychologist, language acquisition is a window on the operation of the
human mind. This window allows us to view the structure and functioning of
neural circuits in the brain. It also allows us to understand how these circuits
support processes such as reinforcement, generalization, imagination, and thinking. To better understand these processes, psychologists conduct controlled
experiments in which children learn new words, sounds, and rules. They may
measure these processes using neural imaging techniques, or they may simply
study the changes in the language of the child across time.

The study of child language development has been conducted chiefly from
the perspectives of professional psychologists and linguists, with parents and
educators playing the roles of interested bystanders. Important and engaging
though these various adult perspectives may be, the best way to appreciate the
dynamics of language development is to assume the perspective of the child.
By taking this perspective, we can understand the challenges the child faces
and the ways in which each are overcome.

Some say that language learning begins in the womb. However, in the womb,
the amniotic fluid muffles the sounds available to the fetus. If you have ever
tried to listen to people talk while you are underwater, you have a rough idea
of baby's initial perspective on human language. When the baby is born, all of
this changes suddenly. As the amniotic fluid drains out of the ears and the
child opens her eyes, she begins to hear sounds and see sights that were never
present before.

William James described the world of the newborn as a "booming, buzzing
confusion." It is certainly true that the change from the world of the womb to
the world outside the womb is radical and severe. But this does not mean that
the child is totally unable to structure this new perceptual world. On the one
hand, she places strict limits on how much information comes in at a given
moment. These limits apply to both visual and auditory perception. We know
that the brain provides powerful, flexible, and adaptable methods for detecting
shape, color, movement, texture, and depth in the visual world. These abilities
are supported by hard-wired structures in the incoming visual pathway, as
well as by dynamically configured structures in the visual cortex.

1   Auditory Processing and Memory

Auditory processing relies on extensive pre-processing of signals for pitch
and intensity in the cochlea and the auditory nerve. By the time the signal
reaches the auditory cortex, it is fairly well structured. In the 1970s, researchers

discovered that human infants were specifically adapted at birth to perceive contrasts such as that between /p/ and /b/, as in "pit" and "bit." However, subsequent research showed that even chinchillas are capable of making this distinction (Werker 1995). Thus, it appears that much of the basic structure of the auditory world can be attributed to fundamental processes in the mammalian ear.

Beyond this basic level of auditory processing, it appears that infants have a remarkable capacity to record and store sequences of auditory events. For example, if the six-month-old hears a sound pattern such as /badigudibaga-digudigagidu/ repeated many times, the parts that are repeated will stand out and affect later listening. In this example, the repeated string is /digudi/. If the infant is trained on these strings, she will grow tired of this sound and will come to prefer to listen to new sound strings to those that have the old /digudi/ string (Saffran et al. 1996). These habituation effects are strongest for stressed syllables and syllables immediately following stressed syllables. Recent studies of these effects in auditory memory suggest that we are born with an ability to store and recall the sounds of human language. During the first year, the child is exposed to several thousand hours of human language. By continually attending to the auditory patterns of her language, the child builds up a rich repertoire of expectations about the forms of words. However, during this early period, the child still has no idea about the link between sounds and meanings. From the infant's point of view, language is still nothing more than an entertaining, but rather superficial experience.

In addition to demonstrating early abilities to store sequences of sounds, babies also demonstrate preferences for the language that resembles the speech of their mothers. Thus, a French infant will prefer to listen to French, whereas a Polish infant will prefer to listen to Polish. In addition, babies demonstrate a preference for their own mother's voice, as opposed to that of other women. Together, these abilities and preferences suggest that, during the first eight months, the child is remarkably attentive to language. Although the child is not yet learning words, she is acquiring the basic auditory and intonational patterns of her native language. As she sharpens her ability to hear the contrasts of her native language, she begins to lose the ability to hear contrasts not represented in her native language. If the child is growing up in a bilingual world, full perceptual flexibility is maintained. However, if the child is growing up monolingual, flexibility in processing is gradually traded off for quickness and automaticity.

2   Early Articulation

Although we have good experimental evidence for a growing auditory awareness in the infant, the first directly observable evidence of language-like behaviors occurs when the child vocalizes. During the first three months, a baby's vocalizations are nothing more than cries and vegetative adaptations. However, around three months, at the time of the first social smile, babies begin to make the delightful little sounds that we call "cooing." These sounds have no particular linguistic structure, but their well-integrated intonation makes them sure parent pleasers. By six months, the baby is producing somewhat more structured vocalizations, including a larger diversity of nasals, vowel types, and syllables with the canonical consonant-vowel (CV) structure. The basic framework of early babbling seems to be constructed on top of patterns of noisy lip-smacking that are present in many primate species (MacNeilage 1998). These vocal gestures include some form of vocal closure followed by a release with vocalic resonance. Essentially, this is the CV syllable in which a consonant is followed by a vowel.

Until the sixth month, deaf infants continue to babble normally. However, by the age of nine months, deaf infants have lost their interest in babbling. This suggests that the babbling present at six months is sustained largely through proprioceptive and somaesthetic feedback, as the baby explores the various ways in which she can play with her mouth. After six months, babbling relies increasingly on auditory feedback. During this period, the infant tries to produce specific sounds to match up with specific auditory impressions. It is at this point that the deaf child no longer finds babbling entertaining, since she cannot obtain auditory feedback. These facts suggest that, from the infant's point of view, babbling is essentially a process of self-entertainment.

Between six and ten months, there seems to be a tight linkage between babbling and general motoric arousal. The child will move her arms, head, and legs while babbling, as if babbling is just another way of getting exercise while aroused. During the last months of the first year, the structure of babbling becomes clearer, more controlled, and more organized. Some children produce repetitive syllable strings, such as /badibadi badibadigu/; others seem to be playing around with intonation and the features of particular articulations.

In the heyday of behaviorism, researchers viewed the development of babbling in terms of reinforcement theory. They thought that the reinforcing qualities of language would lead a Chinese baby to babble the sounds of Chinese, whereas a Quechua baby would babble the sounds of Quechua. This was the theory of "babbling drift." However, closer observation of the babbling of eight-month-olds indicates that virtually no such drift occurs. By 12 months, there is some slight drift in the direction of the native language, as the infant begins to acquire the first words. Proponents of universal phonology have sometimes suggested that all children engage in babbling all the sounds of all the world's languages. Here, again, the claim seems to be overstated. Although it is certainly true that some English-learning infants will produce Bantu clicks and Quechua implosives, not all children produce all of these sounds.

3 The First Words

The child's ability to produce the first word is based on three earlier developments. The first, which we have already discussed, is the infant's growing ability to record the sounds of words. The second is the development of an ability to control vocal productions that occurs in the late stages of babbling. The third development is the general growth of the symbolic function, as represented in play, imitation, and object manipulation. Piaget characterized the infant's cognitive development in terms of the growth of representation or the "object concept." In the first six months of life, the child is unable to think about objects that are not physically present. However, as the infant learns more about objects, she becomes able to associate their properties with her own actions and other features of the context. In this way, subtle cues can be used to dredge up fuller representations from memory. For example, a child may see a dog's tail sticking out from behind a chair and realize that the rest of the dog is hiding behind the chair. This understanding of how parts relate to wholes supports the child's first major use of the symbolic function. When playing with toys, the 12-month-old will begin to produce sounds such as "vroom" or "bam-bam" that represent properties of these toys and actions. Often these phonologically consistent forms appear before the first real words. Because they have no clear conventional status, parents may tend to ignore these first symbolic attempts as nothing more than spurious productions or babbling.

If we look at early word learning from the viewpoint of the child, we realize the first steps toward learning words are taken in a fairly passive way. Even before the child has produced her first conventional word, she has already acquired an ability to comprehend as many as ten conventional forms. She learns these forms through frequent associations between actions, objects, and words. Parents often realize that the prelinguistic infant is beginning to understand what they say. However, they are hard-pressed to demonstrate this ability convincingly. Researchers deal with this problem by bringing infants into the laboratory, placing them into comfortable highchairs, and asking them to look at pictures, using the technique of visually reinforced preferential looking (Woodward et al. 1994). A name such as "dog" is produced across loudspeakers. Pictures of two objects are then displayed. In this case, a dog may be on the screen to the right of the baby and a car may be on the screen to the left. If the child looks at the picture that matches the word, a toy bunny pops up and does an amusing drum roll. This convinces the baby that they have chosen correctly and they then do the best they can to look at the correct picture on each trial. Some children get fussy after only a few trials, but others last for twenty trials or more at one sitting and provide reliable evidence that they have begun to understand a few basic words. Many children show this level of understanding by the tenth month – often two or three months before the child has produced a recognizable "first word."

This assessment may actually underestimate the time of the first auditory word. Even earlier, there is evidence that the child responds differentially to her own name. If two tapes are played to the right and left side of the six-month-old, the baby will tend to prefer to listen to the tape that includes her own name. Given the frequency with which the parent uses the child's name and the clarity with which it is typically presented, this is perhaps not too surprising. Although it is unclear whether the child actually realizes what this form means, she is clearly sensitive to its presence and responds when her name is produced.

Given the fact that the ten-month-old is already able to comprehend several words, why is the first recognizable conventional word not produced until several months later? No one has a sure answer to this question. Linguists have tended to emphasize the fact that some children go through a silent period between babbling and the first word, almost as if they are overtly reorganizing their conceptual and phonological systems in preparation for an attack on the adult target. However, many children do not go through this silent period. Instead, late babbling tends to coexist with the first words in most cases. Another account holds that the child's brain development has not yet succeeded in linking auditory cortex in the temporal lobe to motor cortex in the frontal lobe. The problem with this account is that it fails to recognize the linkage between audition and articulation that was established during babbling.

From the viewpoint of the infant, producing the first word is a bit like stepping out on stage. When she was babbling for her own entertainment, the only constraints the infant faced were ones arising from her own playfulness and interest. If she wanted to allow a sound to vary within certain limits, that was fine. Now, when faced with the task of producing word forms, the articulation has to be extremely accurate and within conventional limits. Why should a toddler be motivated to conform to these requirements? The answer is fairly simple. It is because she has something to say. Among the various things in the child's world, there are bound to be a few that are supremely important and interesting. They may be "kitty," "bottle," or even "bye-bye." These actions and objects are parts of what we could call the toddler's agenda. In the beginning, the learning of words is heavily driven by this agenda.

Undoubtedly, many of the child's first attempts to match an articulation with an auditory target fall on deaf ears. Many are so far away from the correct target that even the most supportive parent cannot divine the relation. Eventually, the child produces a clear articulation that makes some sense in context. The parent is amazed and smiles. The child is reinforced and the first word is officially christened. But all is still not smooth sailing. The child still has no systematic method for going from auditory forms for words she knows to the corresponding articulatory forms. Earlier experience with babbling provides some guide, but now the linkage requires increased precision and control over difficult articulators such as the tongue and the lips. The many simplifications that the one-year-old introduces to adult phonology are well known to students of phonological development (Menn and Stoel-Gammon 1995). Children tend to drop unstressed syllables, producing "hippopotamus" as "poma." They repeat consonants, producing "water" as "wawa." And they simplify and reduce consonant clusters, producing "tree" as "pee." All of these phonological processes echo similar processes found in the historical development and dialectal variation of adult languages. What is different in child language is the fact that so many simplifications occur at once, making so many words difficult to recognize.

4   Early Semantics

The salience of early articulatory limitations tends to mask other, more subtle challenges facing the toddler. With only a few words to her name, there is no great danger that one word will be confused with another. However, as the toddler's inventory of words or "lexicon" grows, the challenge of keeping words apart from each other increases. At the same time, the toddler also needs to figure out how broadly she can apply each new word.

The toddler is torn between two opposing strategies. On the one hand, children often try to be conservative in their first uses of words. For example, a child may use the word "dog" to refer only to the family dog and not to any other dog. Or a child may use the word "car" to refer only to cars parked outside a certain balcony in the house and not cars in any other context. This tendency toward undergeneralization can only be detected if one takes careful note of the contexts in which a child avoids using a word. The flip side of this coin is the strategy of overgeneralization. It is extremely easy to detect overgeneralizations. If the child calls a tiger a "kitty," this is clear evidence for overgeneralization. Of course, it is always possible that the child really meant to say something like, "That animal over there reminds me a lot of my kitty." However, if the child intended this, they would be operating with a rather strange set of ideas about how words are used.

At first, both undergeneralization and overgeneralization are applied in a relatively uncontrolled fashion. The child's first applications of undergeneralization are unreasonably rigid and she soon learns that words are meant to be generalized. At the same time, the child's first attempts at generalization are also often wildly overproductive. For example, a child may use the word "duck" first to refer to the duck, then to the picture of an eagle on the back of a coin, then to a lake where she once saw ducks, and finally to other bodies of water. These "pleonastic" extensions of forms across situations are fairly rare, but they provide interesting commentary regarding the thinking of the toddler when they do occur.

It would be fair to say that all children engage in both undergeneralization and overgeneralization of word meanings. At the same time, it is remarkable how accurate children are in their early guesses at the correct meanings of words. They quickly come to realize that words can be used across a variety of situations in addition to the original context in which they were used. This is fortunate, since reality never repeats itself. If a child thought that a word was limited to use in the original context, there would seldom be an opportunity to reuse a word. Instead, the child has to take each context and decide which aspects are likely to be generalizable for repeated uses of the word. But figuring out how to reuse words is not a trivial problem. In fact, scholars from Plato to Quine have considered the task of figuring out word meaning to be a core intellectual challenge. Quine (1960) illustrated the problem by imagining a scenario in which a hunter is out on safari with a native guide. Suddenly, the guide shouts "Gavagai!" and the hunter, who does not know the native language, has to quickly infer the meaning of the word. Does it mean "Shoot now!" or "There's a rhino" or perhaps even "It got away"? Without some additional cues regarding the likely meaning of the word, how can the hunter figure this out?

The problem facing the toddler is similar to that facing the hunter. Fortunately, the toddler has some good cues to rely on. Foremost among these cues is the parent's use of joint attention and shared eye-gaze to establish common reference for objects and actions. If the father says "hippo" while holding a hippopotamus in his hand, the child can use the manual, visual, verbal, and proxemic cues to infer that the word "hippo" refers to the hippopotamus. A similar strategy works for the learning of the names of easily produced actions such as falling, running, or eating. It also works for social activities such as "bath" or "bye-bye." The normal child probably understands the role of shared eye gaze even before learning the first words. At three months, children maintain constant shared eye gaze with their parents. In normal children, this contact maintains and deepens over time. For autistic children, contact is less stable and automatic. As a result, autistic children may be delayed in word learning and the general growth of communication.

The importance of shared reference is obvious to most parents. In fact, in the fanciful recollections in his *Confessions* (AD 405), St Augustine outlined an analysis not very different from the one presented here:

> This I remember; and have since observed how I learned to speak. It was not that my elders taught me words (as, soon after, other learning) in any set method; but I, longing by cries and broken accents and various motions of my limbs to express my thoughts, that so I might have my will, and yet unable to express all I willed or to whom I willed, did myself, by the understanding which Thou, my God, gavest me, practice the sounds in my memory. When they named anything, and as they spoke turned towards it, I saw and remembered that they called what they would point out by the name they uttered. And that they meant this thing, and no other, was plain from the motion of their body, the natural language, as it were, of all nations, expressed by the countenance, glances of the eye, gestures of the limbs, and tones of the voice, indicating the affections of the mind as it pursues, possesses, rejects, or shuns. And thus by constantly hearing words, as they occurred in various sentences, I collected gradually for what they stood; and, having broken in my mouth to these signs, I thereby gave utterance to my will. Thus I exchanged with those about me these current signs of our wills, and so launched deeper into the stormy intercourse of human life, yet depending on parental authority and the beck of elders.

Shared reference is not the only cue the toddler uses to delineate and pick out the reference of words. She also uses the form of utterances to derive the meanings of new words. For example, if the toddler hears "Here is a zav," she knows that "zav" is a common noun. However, if she hears "Here is Zav," then she knows that "Zav" is either a proper noun or perhaps the name of a quantity. If she hears "I want some zav," she knows that "zav" is a quantity and not a proper or common noun. Cues of this type can give a child a rough idea of the meaning of a new word. Other sentential frames can give an even more precise meaning. If the child hears, "This is not green, it is chartreuse," then it is clear that "chartreuse" is a color. If the child hears, "Please don't cover it, just sprinkle it lightly," then the child knows that "sprinkle" is a verb of the same general class of "cover." The use of cues of this type leads to a fast, but shallow, mapping of new words to new meanings.

5   Mutual Exclusivity and Competition

Even the fullest set of syntactic cues and the clearest shared attention cannot prevent occasional confusion regarding word meanings. Some of the most difficult conflicts between words involve the use of multiple words for the same object. For example, a child may know the word "hippo" and hear her hippo toy referred to as a "toy." Does this lead her to stop calling the toy a "hippo" and start calling it a "toy"? Probably, it does not. Some have suggested that children are prevented from making this type of error by the presence of a universal constraint called "mutual exclusivity." This constraint holds that each object can only have one name. If a child hears a second name for the old object, she can either reject the new name as wrong, or else find some distinction that disambiguates the new name from the old. If mutual exclusivity is an important constraint on word meaning, we would expect children to show a strong tendency toward the first solution – rejection. However, few children illustrate such a preference. The problem with the rejection solution is that objects almost always have more than one name. For example, a "fork" is also "silverware" and a "dog" is also an "animal." Linguistic structures expressing a wide variety of taxonomic and metonymic relations represent a fundamental and principled violation of the proposed mutual exclusivity constraint. The most consistent violations occur for bilingual children who learn that everything in their world must, by necessity, have at least two names. Mutual exclusivity is clearly not a basic property of natural language.

One reason why researchers have tended to devote so much attention to mutual exclusivity stems from the shape of the laboratory situation in which word learning is studied. The child is presented with a series of objects, some old and some new, given a word that is either old or new, and then asked to match up the word with an object. For example, the child may be given a teacup, a glass, and a demitasse. She already knows the words "cup" and "glass." The experimenter asks her to "give me the demitasse." She will then correctly infer that "demitasse" refers to the object for which she does not have a well-established name. In this context, it makes sense to use the new name as the label for some new object.

Instead of thinking in terms of mutual exclusivity, the child appears to be thinking in terms of competition between words, with each word vying for a particular semantic niche (Merriman 1999). The child also thinks in terms of the pragmatics of mutual cooperation. When two words are in head-on conflict and no additional disambiguating cues are provided, it makes sense for the child to assume that the adult is being reasonable and using the new name for the new object. The child assumes that, like a cooperative parent, the experimenter knows that the child has words for cups and glasses, so it only makes sense that the new word is for the new object.

In the real world, competition forces the child to move meanings around so that they occupy the correct semantic niche. When the parent calls the toy hippo a "toy," the child searches for something to disambiguate the two words. For example, the parent may say "Can you give me another toy?" or even "Please clean up your toys." In each case, "toy" refers not just to the hippo, but also potentially to many other toys. This allows the child to shift perspective and to understand the word toy in the framework of the shifted perspective. Consider the case of a rocking horse. This object may be called "toy," "horsie," or even "chair" depending on how it is being used at the moment. This flexible use of labeling is an important ingredient in language learning. By learning how to shift perspectives, children develop powerful tools for dealing with the competitions between words. In this way conflicts between meanings give rise to complex structures and cognitive flexibility.

6 Humpty-Dumpty and Whorf

In Lewis Carroll's *Through the Looking Glass*, Humpty-Dumpty chastises Alice for failing to take charge over the meanings of words. As he puts it, "When I use a word, it means just what I choose it to mean – neither more nor less." Undoubtedly, many children attempt to adopt this take-charge attitude toward language learning. The problem is that, without first understanding the conventional meanings of words, both children and Humpty-Dumpty could find themselves using words in ways that no one else would understand.

Children often have a rather fixed agenda of items to be expressed and would love to find simple ways of expressing each of those items. For example, many children want to learn words for finger, hand, ball, dog, bottle, Mommy, Daddy, and food. Most languages will oblige the child by providing words for these very basic concepts. However, once we leave the level of the first 20 words, all bets are off. Languages like Korean or Navajo require the child to learn verbs instead of nouns. Moreover, the verbs they learn focus more on position, shape, and containment than do verbs in English. For example, the verb "'ahééníshtiih" in Navajo refers to "carrying around in a circle any long straight object such as a gun." As learning progresses, the child's agenda becomes less important than the shape of the resources provided by the language. This is not to say that languages end up shaping core features of children's cognitions. However, the presence of obligatory grammatical markings in languages for concepts such as tense, aspect, number, gender, and definiteness can orient the child's thinking in certain paths at the expense of others. Benjamin Whorf suggested many years ago that the forms of language may end up shaping the structure of thought. Such effects are directly opposed to the Humpty-Dumpty agenda-based approach to language. Probably the truth lies somewhere between Whorf and Humpty-Dumpty. Important though language-specific effects may be, all children end up being able to express basic ideas equally well, no matter what language they learn.

7   The First Word Combinations

Throughout the second year, the child struggles with perfecting the sounds and meanings of the first words. For several months, the child produces isolated single words. With a cooperative parent, a child can go a long way at this level of language. For example, if a child is hungry, it is enough to simply say "cookie." There is no reason to say, "Would you please open the cupboard door and bring me down a cookie." In fact, most of the child's basic needs are met even without the intervention of language. Sometimes a child may be frustrated by the parent's failure to understand her intentions. This frustration can be a strong motivator toward acquiring fuller communication. However, it is unlikely that needs and frustrations are the roots of linguistic development. Nor is language learned simply for the sake of imitating adults. Instead, it seems that children learn to speak so that they can express a fuller shared view of the world.

Single words are not enough to articulate this fuller view. Instead, children need to be able to associate predicates such as "want," "more," or "go" with arguments such as "cookie" or "Mommy." The association of predicates to arguments is the first step in syntactic development. As in the other areas of language development, these first steps are taken in a very gradual fashion. Before producing a smooth combination of two words such as "my horsie," children will often string together a series of single word utterances that appear to be searching out some syntactic form. For example, a child might say "my, that, that, horsie" with pauses between each word. Later, the pauses will be gone and the child will say "that horsie, my horsie." This tentative combination of words involves groping on both intonational and semantic levels. On the one hand, the child has to figure out how to join words together smoothly in production. On the other hand, the child also has to figure out which words can meaningfully be combined with which others.

As was the case in the learning of single words, this learning is guided by earlier developments in comprehension. As in the case of studies of early word comprehension, we have to assess children's early syntactic comprehension by controlled experiments in the laboratory. Here, again, researchers have used the preferential looking paradigm. To the right of the child, there is a TV monitor with a movie of Big Bird tickling Cookie Monster. To the child's left, there is a TV monitor with a movie of Cookie Monster tickling Big Bird. The experimenter produces the sentence "Big Bird is tickling Cookie Monster." If the child looks at the matching TV monitor, she is reinforced and a correct look is scored. Using this technique, researchers have found that 17-month-olds already have a good idea about the correct word order for English sentences. This is about five or six months before they begin to use word order systematically in production.

The level of successive single word utterances is one that chimpanzees also reach when they learn signed language. Domesticated chimps like Sarah, Washoe, or Kanzi have succeeded in learning over a hundred conventional signs or tokens. They can then combine these words to produce meaningful communication. However, the combinations that chimpanzees produce never really get beyond the stage of successive single word utterances. Thus, it appears that children rely on some uniquely human ability for structuring combinations of predicates and arguments into tighter syntactic combinations. The exact neurophysiological basis of this ability is still unknown, although many researchers suspect that the growth of inferior frontal areas for motor control supports the ability to combine words into simple combinations.

The "grammar" of the child's first combinations is extremely basic. The child learns that each predicate should appear in a constant position *vis-à-vis* the arguments it requires. For example, in English, the word "more" appears before the noun it modifies and the verb "run" appears after the subject with which it combines. Slot-filler relations can control this basic type of grammatical combination. Each predicate specifies a slot for the argument. For example, "more" has a slot for a following noun. When a noun, such as "milk," is selected to appear with "more," that noun becomes a filler for the slot opened up by the word "more." The result is the combination "more milk." Later, the child can treat this whole unit as an argument to the verb "want" and the result is "want more milk." Finally, the child can express the second argument of the verb "want" and the result is "I want more milk." Thus, bit by bit, the child builds up longer sentences and a more complex grammar. This level of simple combinatorial grammar is based on individual words as the controlling structures. This type of word-based learning is present even in adults. In languages with strong morphological marking systems, word-based patterns specify the attachment of affixes, rather than just the linear position of words. In fact, most languages of the world make far more use of morphological marking than does English. In this regard, English is a rather exotic language.

8 Missing Glue

The child's first sentences are almost all incomplete and ungrammatical. Instead of saying, "This is Mommy's chair," the child produces only "Mommy chair" with the possessive suffix, the demonstrative, and the copula verb all deleted. Just as the first words are full of phonological deletions and simplifications, the first sentences include only the most important words, without any of the glue. In some cases, children simply have not yet learned the missing words and devices. In other cases, they may know the "glue words" but find it difficult to coordinate the production of so many words in the correct order.

These early omissions provide evidence for two major processes in language development. First, the child makes sure that the most important and substantive parts of the communication are not omitted. Unfortunately, the child makes this evaluation from her own, egocentric perspective. In an utterance like "Mommy chair" it is not clear whether the child means "This is Mommy's chair" or "Mommy is sitting in the chair," although the choice between these interpretations may be clear in context. The second factor that shapes early omissions is phrasal frequency. Children tend to preserve frequent word combinations, such as "like it" or "want some." These combinations are often treated as units, producing errors such as "I like it the ball" or "I want some a banana."

In English, omissions of auxiliaries are extremely common. For many months, children will produce questions without auxiliaries, as in "Why he go to the store?" for "Why does he go to the store?" or "Why not she come?" for "Why won't she come?" In languages with richer systems of morphological marking, the most common errors involve the use of the most frequent form of a noun or verb, even when some marked form is required. For example, in German child language, the infinitive is often used when a finite verb is required. These various errors can be traced to the fact that the child has limited resources to produce complex sentences and tends to settle for well-known forms in simple combinations.

9 Productivity

Productivity can be demonstrated in the laboratory by teaching children names for new objects. For example, we can show a child a picture of a funny looking creature and call it a "wug." As we noted before, the positioning of the word "wug" after the article "a" induces the child to treat the word as a common noun. The child can then move from this fact to infer that the noun "wug" can pluralize as "wugs," even if she has never heard the word "wugs." This type of productive generalization of linguistic patterns occurs from the earliest stages of language acquisition. For example, a German-speaking child can be taught the nonce name "der Gann" (nominative, masculine, singular) for a toy. The experimenter can then pick up the toy and ask the child what he is holding. Children as young as three-year-olds understand that they are supposed to place the noun "Gann" into the accusative case in their answer and they correctly produce the form "den Gann."

Three-year-olds also demonstrate some limited productive use of syntactic patterns for new verbs. However, children tend to be conservative and unsure about how to use verbs productively until about age five. After all, from the child's perspective these laboratory experiments with strange new toys and new words may tend to encourage a conservative approach. As they get older and braver, children start to show productive use of constructions such as the double object, the passive, or the causative. For example, an experimenter can introduce a new verb like "griff" in the frame "Tim griffed the ball to Frank" and the child will productively generalize to "Tim griffed Frank the ball."

The control of productivity is based on two complementary sets of cues: semantics and cooccurrence. When the child hears "a wug," she correctly infers that "wug" is a count noun. In fact, because she also sees a picture of a cute little animal, she infers that "wug" is a common, count, name for an animate creature. These semantic features allow her to generalize her knowledge by producing the form "wugs." However, we could also view this extension as based on cooccurrence learning. The child learns that words that take the indefinite article also form plurals. On the other hand, words that take the quantifier "some" do not form plurals. In this way, the child can use both semantic and cooccurrence information to build up knowledge about the parts of speech. This knowledge can then be fed into existing syntactic generalizations to produce new combinations and new forms of newly learned words. The bulk of grammatical acquisition relies on this process.

10   The Logical Problem of Language Acquisition

The problem with productivity is that it produces overgeneralization. For example, an English-speaking child will soon learn to form the past tense of a new verb by adding one of the variant forms of "-ed." This knowledge helps the child produce forms such as "jumped" or "wanted." Unfortunately, it may also lead the child to produce an error such as "*goed." When this occurs, we can say that the child has formulated an overly general grammar. One way of convincing the child to reject the overly general grammar in which "goed" occurs is to provide the child with negative feedback. This requires the parent to tell the child, "No, you can't say 'goed'." The problem here is that children seem to ignore parental feedback regarding the form of language. If the child calls a hamburger a "hot dog," the parent can tell her "No, it is a hamburger." The child will accept this type of semantic correction. But children are notoriously resistant to being corrected for formal grammatical features.

The fact that children tend to ignore formal correction has important consequences for language acquisition theory. In the 1970s, work in formal analysis convinced some linguists that the task of learning the grammar of a language was impossible, unless negative feedback was provided. Since negative feedback appeared to be unavailable or unused, this meant that language could not be learned without some additional innate constraints. This argument has led to many hundreds of research articles exploring the ways in which children's learning places constraints on the form of grammar. Referring back to Plato's *Republic* and the Allegory of the Cave, Chomsky, Gold, Baker, Pinker, and others have characterized the task of language learning as a logical problem. At its core, most of the search for innate constraints on language learning is grounded on the supposed impossibility of recovery from overgeneralization. To illustrate the ongoing importance of these issues for linguistic theory and language acquisition, consider this passage from Chomsky (1965):

> It is for the present, impossible to formulate an assumption about initial, innate structure rich enough to account for the fact that grammatical knowledge is attained on the basis of the evidence available to the learner. Consequently, the empiricist effort to show how the assumptions about a language acquisition device can be reduced to a conceptual minimum is quite misplaced. The real problem is that of developing a hypothesis about initial structure that is sufficiently rich to account for acquisition of language, yet not so rich as to be inconsistent with the known diversity of language.

In fact, the child has more resources available to her than Chomsky seems to suggest. Using these resources, the child can recover from overgeneralization without negative feedback. In the case of "goed," everyone agrees that recovery is easy. All the child has to do is to realize that there is only one way of producing the past tense of "go" and that is "went." In other words, the irregular form "went" comes to block production of the overregularized form "goed." Here, recovery from overgeneralization is based on the competition between the regular pattern and the irregular form. In such competitions, the irregular form must always win.

However, not all recovery from overgeneralization is so simple. Suppose that a child decides that the verb "recommend" patterns like the verb "give." After all, both verbs involve a beneficiary and an object being transferred. However, only "give" allows a double object construction, as in "John gave the library the book." Most people find "John recommended the library the book" ungrammatical. If the child makes this error, how does she recover? One solution to this error is to avoid making the error in the first place. If the child proceeds cautiously, learning each construction verb by verb, she will never attempt to use the verb "recommend" with the double object construction. Most children follow this course and never make the error. However, other children are less cautious. Do we want to assume that the cautious children have no need for innate constraints and that the less cautious children do? Fortunately there is a better way for even the incautious children to solve this "logical" problem.

The solution here is to record the strength of competing syntactic patterns. The correct way of saying "John recommended the library the book" is to say "John recommended the book to the library." This correct formulation should be strengthened whenever it is heard. As the strength of the frame for the verb "recommend" grows in comparison to the ungrammatical frame, the use of the competing frame is blocked. This solution assumes that the child realizes that the two frames are in competition. It may be that reaching this realization requires some attention to syntactic form. However, this solution does not require the child to pay attention to corrective feedback. Instead, she only needs to attend to correct sentences and to make sure that she understands that these are competing ways of saying roughly the same thing.

11   Lexical Groups

Most overgeneralizations can be controlled in a rote fashion. This involves strengthening single constructions for single verbs. However, there are some cases where stronger medicine may be necessary. Consider an error such as "*I poured the tub with water" or "*I filled water into the tub." The use of a goal construction vs. a direct object to express the entity being filled depends very much on the semantics of the verb. In effect, the child has to learn to break up the general class of "pouring" verbs into two subclasses, based on evidence from semantics and cooccurrence. Earlier, we discussed the role of lexical groups in supporting productivity. The problem here is the same one. However, the distinction is rather subtle, both semantically and syntactically. Verbs like "pour" do not emphasize the completion of the activity, but, rather, the ongoing process of transfer. These verbs use a goal construction. Verbs like "fill" tend to emphasize the completion of the activity and the change in state of the affected object. Most children learn to use these verbs conservatively and never produce these errors. However, once they are produced, the easiest way to correct them is to solidify the distinction between the two classes. Researchers (Li and MacWhinney 1996) have shown how the details of this learning process can be modeled formally using neural network models. Distinctions as subtle as this may not be acquired until the child produces some errors. Since errors of this type may not arise until about age six or later, the formation of lexical subclasses of this type is a rather late development.

Consider another example of how lexical classes help the child recover from overgeneralization. For example, a child might notice that both "cow" and "red" pattern together in forms such as "cow barn" and "red barn." This might induce the child to produce forms such as "I painted the barn cow" on analogy with "I painted the barn red." A conservative learner would stick close to facts about the verb "paint" and the arguments that it permits. If the child has heard a form like "I painted the barn white," it would make sense to extend this frame slightly to include the resultative predicate "red." However, an extension past the realm of colors and patterns would violate the basic principles of conservative learning. As a result, this type of category-leaping overgeneralization is extremely infrequent.

12   Errors That Never Occur

We have seen how children can recover from overgeneralization without rely-ing on innate constraints. However, there is another approach to language development that provides more convincing evidence for innate constraints. This approach focusses on errors that "never" occur. Consider this example:

(1) a.   The boy who is first in line will get the prize.
     b.   Will the boy who is first in line get the prize?
     c.   *Is the boy first in line will get the prize?

The claim here is that a simple surface analysis of the grammar would have led the child to produce (1c) instead of (1b). However, only (1b) is consist-ent with universal grammar, since auxiliaries are always derived from the main clause and not from some subordinate clause. Chomsky and others have claimed that children never hear sentences like (1b). It is certainly true that such sentences are not common, but it is not true that they never occur. Although the argument fails to go through in this case, the basic observation seems solid. Would a child ever even dream of producing something like (1b)? It seems unlikely. Moreover, it seems likely that, when the child learns to produce auxiliaries in questions, this learning is based not on surface word order, but on the underlying conceptual relations between words. Whether this learning amounts to evidence for innate constraints on grammar remains to be seen.

Similar analyses have been developed for a variety of other constructions. Examples (2) through (5) illustrate four additional patterns.

(2) a.   You put it on a hot plate.
     b.   You put it on a hot what?
     c.   *What did you put it on a hot?

(3) a.   Do you think a picture of Luke Skywalker should be on my cake?
     b.   Do you think a picture of who should be on my cake?
     c.   *Who do you think a picture of should be on my cake?

(4) a.   She chased the boy who stole her sandwich.
     b.   She chased the boy who stole her what?
     c.   *What did she chase the boy who stole?

(5) a. Luisa stood between the bookshelf and the fireplace.
    b. Luisa stood between the bookshelf and what?
    c. *What did Luisa stand between the bookshelf and?

In the case of (2c) and (3c), there is evidence that children actually produce the "non-occurring" error. In fact (2c) was produced by Bob Wilson's son Seth and (3c) was produced by Brian MacWhinney's son Mark. The corpora of child language data from which these examples were taken can be found in the CHILDES corpus on the web at http://childes.psy.cmu.edu.

Errors such as (4c) and (5c) have never been reported. Indeed, the constraints that block (4c) and (5c) are some of the most powerful constraints that have been identified in the linguistic literature. Both (4b) and (4c) seem to be possible ways of expressing these questions. However, they only make sense if we imagine conditions of noise that blocked out a single word. Not hearing well, we then echoed the sentence to try to recover the missing word. This suggests that neither (4c) nor (5c) is really well formed on semantic grounds.

13   Emergentist Accounts

Our overview of language learning has focussed on the challenges facing the child. We have also looked at language development from the viewpoint of universal grammar. Now we turn our attention to psychological views on language learning. Typically, psychologists see linguistic knowledge as emerging from regularities in the language heard by the child. To model the processes and mechanisms involved in this learning, many psychologists rely on the formalisms of neural network theory, which is also known as connectionism. This framework uses large numbers of units and the connections between these units to capture the patterns of language. This web-like architecture of nodes and connections is intended explicitly to resemble the structure of the human brain with neurons, synapses, and weights on synaptic connections.

Without burdening the reader with all the technical paraphernalia of neural network theory, let us take a brief look at how this type of analysis can be applied to a concrete problem in language acquisition. Let us take as an example the learning of German gender, as marked by the definite article (the word "the" in English). The task facing the German child is to combine each noun with one of the six different forms of the definite article. The article can take the form "der," "die," "das," "des," "dem," or "den." The choice of one of these six forms depends on three features of the noun: its gender (masculine, feminine, or neuter), its number (singular or plural), and its role within the sentence (subject, possessor, direct object, prepositional object, or indirect object). To make matters worse, assignment of nouns to gender categories is often quite nonintuitive. For example, the word for "fork" is feminine, the word for "spoon" is masculine, and the word for "knife" is neuter. Acquiring this system of arbitrary gender assignments is particularly difficult for adult second language learners. In his treatise on the "Aweful German Language," Mark Twain complained that German treats pretty young girls as neuter, the sun as feminine, and the moon as masculine. Twain was convinced that the choice of gender in German made no sense at all.

Although the cues governing German gender are indeed complex, it is possible to construct a connectionist network that learns the German system from the available cues (MacWhinney et al. 1989). To do this, the network is presented with a series of patterns across the "input units." Each pattern represents the phonological form of a given German noun. For example, a particular node may be used to code the fact that the first consonant in the third syllable is a voiceless consonant like /p/ or /t/. Using 168 of these feature units, it is possible to give a different input pattern for each of the 102 nouns that were used to train the network. For each noun, the input also includes features that determine the noun's case and number.

Processing begins when the input layer is given a particular German noun. For example, the input could be the phonological form of the masculine noun "Tisch" (table), along with information that the noun is in the accusative and is singular. These active input units then spread activation to the other units in the system and eventually the activation reaches the six possible output units – one for each of the six forms of the definite article. The output unit that receives the most activation is the one that is chosen for the noun on this trial. On the first pass through, the network will probably choose the wrong output. In this case, the output might be the article "die." This is wrong, since it treats the masculine noun "Tisch" as if it were feminine. When this occurs, the learning algorithm goes through all the connections in the network and adjusts them so that they are a bit closer to what would have been needed to activate the correct output item. This training continues for 50 cycles that repeat each of the nouns in the input corpus. At the end of this training period, the network is able to choose the correct article for 98 percent of the nouns in the original set.

To test its generalization abilities, we next present the network with old nouns in new case roles. If the network learned "Tisch" in the accusative, we now give it "Tisch" in the genitive and it should select the article "des." In these tests, the network chooses the correct article on 92 percent of trials. This type of cross-paradigm generalization provides evidence that the network went beyond rote memorization during the training phase. In fact, the network quickly succeeds in learning the whole of the basic formal paradigm for the marking of German case, number, and gender on the noun.

In addition, the network is able to generalize its internalized knowledge to solve the problem that had so perplexed Mark Twain – guessing at the gender of entirely novel nouns. The 48 most frequent nouns in German that had not been included in the original input set are then presented in a variety of sentence contexts. On this completely novel set, the network chooses the correct article from the six possibilities on 61 percent of trials, vs. 17 percent expected by chance. Thus, the system's learning mechanism, together with its representation of the noun's phonological and semantic properties and the context, produced a good guess about what article would accompany a given noun, even when the noun was entirely unfamiliar.

The network's learning parallels children's learning in a number of ways. Like real German-speaking children, the network tends to overuse the articles that accompany feminine nouns. The reason for this is that the feminine forms of the article have a high frequency, because they are used both for feminines and for plurals of all genders. The simulation also showed the same type of overgeneralization patterns that are often interpreted as reflecting rule use when they occur in children's language. For example, although the noun *Kleid* (which means clothing) is neuter, the simulation used the initial "kl" sound of the noun to conclude that it is masculine. Because of this, it chooses the form of the definite article that would accompany the noun if it were masculine. Interestingly, the same article-noun combinations that are the most difficult for children are also the most difficult for the network.

How is the network able to produce such a high level of generalization and such rule-like behavior without any specific rules? The basic learning mechanism involves adjusting connection strengths between input, hidden, and output units to reflect the frequency with which combinations of features of nouns were associated with each article. Although no single feature can predict which article would be used, various complex combinations of phonological, semantic, and contextual cues allow accurate prediction of which articles should be chosen. This is the sense in which language learning often seems to be based on the acquisition of cues, rather than rules.

14   A Fourth Perspective

Alongside the perspective of the linguist, the psychologist, and the child, we can also look at language learning from the viewpoint of the parent and the educator. Parents often worry about the fact that their child may be slow at learning to talk. When a child falls behind, the parent and the educator want to know how to help the child catch up. However, experience shows us that the overwhelming majority of late talkers end up with full control over language. Often children are simply insufficiently motivated to talk. A prime example of this type is Albert Einstein, who did not begin talking until age five. His case is a bit extreme, but certainly not unique. Even children who have lost portions of their cerebral cortex as a result of early brain injuries end up acquiring full control over language use, as long as they are raised in a normal, supportive family.

As much as 5 percent of the population suffers from some form of language impairment. In many cases, language impairment is an accompaniment to some other obvious cognitive or emotional impairment, such as Downs syndrome,

Williams syndrome, Fragile-X syndrome, or autism. Each of these genetically based syndromes has a wide variance of expression with some children achieving normal control of language and others less adequate language. Another, much larger group of children evidences some level of language impairment without any obvious genetic abnormality. These children can be further divided into about four major groups. In the first group, only the expressive use of language is impaired. Children with expressive impairments may find it difficult to articulate certain sounds or may stutter. These children typically have little impairment in language comprehension and no cognitive deficit. This deficit can be treated by articulatory speech therapy. A second group of children has deficits in low-level speech perception for sounds like /s/ and /f/. Careful training in the detection of auditory contrasts can help remediate this impairment. A third group of children shows some form of pragmatic impairment. These children have problems forming coherent discourse and connected narration. In some cases, this "deficit" may reflect stylistic effects related to dialect and social class. In other cases, it may reflect innate tendencies such as autism or difficulties with social perspective taking. Finally, there is a fourth group of children that have slight cognitive deficits that may be related to language impairments.

We are now just beginning to understand the neurological and genetic bases of these various impairments. Studies of familial genetic profiles have given us some clues regarding ways in which biology may determine language impairment. Recent advances in brain imaging methodology are now opening up the possibility of observing the actual neurophysiological bases of language processing as it occurs. Application of these new methods to the study of language impairments will help us better understand both normal and abnormal language development.

Not all parental concerns focus on language delay. Parents are also deeply interested in furthering normal progress and promoting genius. In some cases, the parent may find that the child has unusual interests in language and wants to help the child to develop these interests, whether they involve learning additional languages, growing up bilingual, or merely being introduced at an early age to great literature. Research on the roots of literacy has indicated the continuity between early literary practices such as reading books with children, reciting rhymes, or fantasy role-play, and later success in reading and literacy.

15   Conclusion

Language is a unique marker of humanity. It distinguishes the human species from the rest of creation, and it allows us to share our thoughts and feelings. Language is the most complex skill that any of us will ever master. Despite this complexity, nearly every human child succeeds in learning language. This suggests that language is optimally shaped to mesh with the abilities of the human mind and body. On the one hand, the universals of human language match up with our neurological, cognitive, and physical abilities. At the same time, parents provide rich contextual and emotional support to guide children through the process of language discovery. By studying language learning, we learn more about universals of human language, the shape of social inter-action, and the structure of the human mind.

20 Linguistics and Second Language Acquisition: One Person with Two Languages

VIVIAN COOK

Most linguistics concerns people who know, use, or learn a single language. Yet such monolinguals are probably in a minority in the world as a whole. Many people use several languages in the course of a day, whether in multilingual countries such as Pakistan or the Cameroon or in apparently monolingual countries such as England and Kuwait. This chapter looks at some of the questions raised by the fact that people know more than one language. General popular questions include: is learning a second language (L2) like learning a first (L1)? Are children better than adults at L2 learning? Can you speak a second language without an accent? Linguists are more concerned with questions such as: how does L2 learning relate to Universal Grammar? Does the language input the learner hears make a difference? How does one language affect the other? They are all fundamentally concerned with how one person can have two languages.

Any issue in linguistics can potentially be studied in the context of people who know more than one language. This chapter starts with some historical background and then discusses ten interrelated questions that have driven research into SLA (second language acquisition) within the overall context of one person with two or more languages. The aim is to put the reader in touch with some of the issues that have been investigated, touching on areas of linguistics such as phonology and vocabulary as well as syntax. The account represents one person's route through a large maze, trying not to stray down paths less connected with linguistics. Though a comparative newcomer, SLA research is a vast and expanding discipline with its own annual conferences such as EUROSLA (European Second Language Association). A survey by Ellis (1994) is 824 pages long despite barely touching on areas such as vocabulary or phonology.

1   Early Days: Links and Questions

A relationship between linguistics and SLA started to emerge with the influential distinction made by Weinreich (1953) between compound and coordinate bilinguals. A coordinate bilingual has two separate concepts for a word – two concepts, two words. The concept of "book" for example can be shown as 📖, expressed by *book* in the English of English / French bilinguals, or as 📖, expressed by *livre* in French. The two languages are separate in the mind; a coordinate bilingual may be unable to translate from one language to the other. Compound bilinguals on the other hand have a single concept 📖 expressed as two different words *book* and *livre*: the two languages are tied together in their minds via a common concept – one concept, two words. Though individuals were once thought to be either coordinate or compound bilinguals, more recently it is believed that both types of bilingualism are present to varying extents in the same person (de Groot 1993); that is to say, in a given individual, some aspects of the two languages may be linked, others may be separate.

The linguistic and behaviorist theories of learning of the 1950s also contributed the concept of transfer to SLA research. Transfer means carrying over the forms and meanings of one language to the other, resulting in interference – "instances of deviation from the norms of either language which occur in the speech of bilinguals as a result of their familiarity with more than one language" (Weinreich 1953: 1). French users of English fail to distinguish /iː/ and /ɪ/ in *keen* /kiːn/ and *kin* /kɪn/ because the distinction does not exist in French; Japanese learners of English produce spellings such as *adovocated*, *courese*, and *Engilish*, because Japanese consonants are always separated by a vowel. The concept of transfer led to the approach called Contrastive Analysis, which looked for differences between the two languages; these form the main areas of difficulty for learners and automatically lead to "negative" transfer from the L1 (Lado 1957). Though transfer remains an indispensable concept in SLA research, the Contrastive Analysis approach itself has mostly been subsumed within other traditions. One reason was that it was all too easy to carry out large-scale comparisons of languages to predict what learners might do, only to find the predicted errors do not occur but other errors do. It was more economical to start from the errors in actual L2 learners' speech and then to work back to their causes – a methodology that became known as Error Analysis (Corder 1971, James 1998). Bulgarian learners for instance produce sentences such as *The my car broke down* (Toncheva 1988); the probable cause is that possessives and articles can occur together in Bulgarian, i.e. their L1 transfer is established by the post hoc Error Analysis method rather than predicted in advance by Contrastive Analysis.

The overall issue emerging from these beginnings is how multiple languages relate to each other inside the mind of one person, both during the process of acquiring the L2 and while actually using it. This is reflected in the divergence of definitions for bilingualism itself. At one extreme are "maximal" definitions such as "native-like control of two languages" (Bloomfield 1933), renamed more transparently as "ambilingualism" by Halliday et al. (1964): bilinguals have as extensive control over their second language as over their first. At the other extreme are "minimal" definitions that bilingualism starts at "the point where a speaker can first produce complete meaningful utterances in the other language" (Haugen 1953): any real use of a second language counts as bilingualism, however minimal it may be. Hardly anybody meets the maximal definition since no one commands all the uses of both languages equally well; virtually everybody meets the second definition in that they are capable of using isolated L2 expressions such as *Goodbye*, *Bonjour* or *Konnichiwa* appropriately.

A strong early influence on SLA research came from the overall structuralist and behaviorist paradigm of linguistics laid down by Bloomfield (1933). When mainstream linguistics swung away from structuralist models, SLA research took on board certain Chomskyan tenets. The key concept was that children have independent grammars of their own that are not simply debased versions of the adult grammar. English L1 children who say *Him go shop* are not reproducing something that they have heard from an adult but have invented a rule of their own that *him* can be a subject. This led to the realization that L2 learners also build up grammars of their own that are not part of either the first language or the second but have an independent existence. L2 learners may say *I not get away* even though putting the negative *not* in front of the verb is found in neither their L2 (English) nor their L1 (German); they too have made up a rule. Several terms were coined for the idea that L2 learners had independent grammars with slightly different emphases, such as "approximative system" (Nemser 1971) and "transitional competence" (Corder 1967). The term that found favor was "interlanguage," derived from an eponymous paper by Selinker (1972).

The overall contributions of these early days of SLA research were that the two languages may be separate or closely linked in the mind, that the forms of one language may affect the other, and that L2 learners create a distinct interlanguage with its own rules and properties.

2   What Is the Sequence of L2 Acquisition?

The question that interested many of the first SLA researchers was the order in which people acquire an L2: is there a "natural" sequence through which all L2 learners progress or does it vary from one person to another, say, according to their L1? One research method was to score the presence of certain English "grammatical morphemes" such as continuous "-ing" *going* and plural "s" *books* in the speech of L2 learners. Spanish-speaking children learning English start with plural "s" and progress through continuous "-ing", copula "be" *is*, and so on (Dulay and Burt 1973). Fairly similar orders were found regardless of whether the learners were in a classroom (Lightbown 1987), whether they were in a country where the language was spoken or not (Makino 1993), and many other factors. Clearly L2 learners of English acquire these grammatical morphemes in a sequence of some kind. However, difficulties emerged with the methodology (was this really the order in which they learnt them or simply the order of difficulty?) and with the grammar (do these grammatical morphemes such as verbs "be," inflections "-s" and prepositions *to* really form a coherent group syntactically?) (Cook 1993).

More convincing sequences of L2 acquisition emerged from the ZISA project (Meisel et al. 1981). This studied the development of L2 German by migrant workers with various L1s over a period of time. It was mostly concerned with German word order, which differs from English in that the verb normally comes second in the sentence. Sometimes this yields a Subject Verb Object order, as in *Ich liebe dich* (I love you), but often it leads to an Adverb Verb Subject order, *Immer liebe ich dich* (Always love I you), and to other combinations in which the verb comes second. L2 learners of German start by putting subjects in front of verbs as in *Die Kinder essen Apfel* (The children eat apple) before they learnt how to get other verb second orders by moving elements around in the sentence, for example Adverb Verb *Da Kinder spielen* (There children play). The sequence of acquisition depends on first acquiring a typical word order and then learning how to move elements about. The essentials of this sequence were duplicated with L2 learners of English in Australia by Pienemann and Johnston (1987): the stage of Subject-Verb-Object *I like apples*, preceded the sentences with movement *Apples I like very much*. Learners differ from each other according to how much they simplify sentences, say, omitting items such as the copula verb *Ich Mädchen* (I girl) even if they are at the same developmental stage. This is called the "variation" dimension and complements the "development" dimension, leading to the name the Multidimensional Model, later known as Processability theory (Pienemann 1993).

The concept of sequence was taken further within the large-scale ESF (European Science Foundation) project, which looked at the learning of five L2s by young adult speakers of six L1s (Klein and Perdue 1992, 1997). It found that learners start with sentences without verbs, go on to use verbs without inflection *Its pinch some bread*, and finally have sentences with verbs with inflections *Man is coming in*. Regardless of which language they are learning, the learners arrive at a common basic L2 grammar, which has three main rules: a sentence may consist of:

1 a Noun Phrase followed by a verb followed by an optional Noun Phrase *Mädchen nehme Brot* (girl take bread);
2 a Noun Phrase followed by a Copula verb followed by a Noun Phrase, Adjective, or Prepositional Phrase *it's bread*;
3 a Verb followed by a Noun Phrase *pinching its*.

Progress beyond this basic grammar consists largely of fleshing out the different verbal forms. The stages of acquisition derive from communication and pragmatic principles: L2 learners "organise their utterances and texts according to elementary principles of their human language capacity" (Klein and Perdue 1997: 343).

The ESF project is thus a practical demonstration of the interlanguage hypothesis since it shows a common interlanguage independent of either L1 or L2. The project's aim was indeed to see "whether a learner variety is based on recognisable organisational principles, how these principles interact, and whether they also apply to fully-fledged languages" (Klein and Perdue 1992: 1).

Stages of development are not interesting unless they lead to insights into learning. The study of sequences of acquisition thus shades into explanation. For example Wieden and Nemser (1991) looked at phonological sequences in the acquisition of English by German-speaking children and found three distinct stages: pre-systemic (knowing the sounds only in individual words), transfer (systematically using the L1 categories in the L2) and approximative (restructuring the L2 sounds into a new system). Wolfe Quintero (1992) found that the stages of acquisition of English relative clauses by Japanese learners could be seen as an interaction of six learning strategies. Similarly Schwartz and Sprouse (1996) looked at the stages in which one Turkish learner acquired the verb position in German to determine whether the starting point is the Turkish SOV order.

The answer to the question is that there are indeed sequences of L2 acquisition common to learners in different areas of language and with different first languages. The stages through which L2 learners progress have much in common, thus reducing the role of L1 transfer.

3   What Are the Similarities between L2 Learning and L1 Acquisition?

A continuing theme has been whether people acquire a second language in the same way as a first. If the L2 stages outlined above are also followed by L1 children, both groups are probably using the same learning process. The L2 sequence for English grammatical morphemes was similar, though not identical, to that found in L1 acquisition by Brown (1972), the greatest differences being the irregular past tense (*broke*), articles (*the*), copula, and auxiliaries (Dulay et al. 1982). Other similar sequences of syntactic acquisition have been found in L1 and L2 learning. L2 learners, like L1 learners, start by believing that *John* is the subject of *please* in both *John is easy to please* and *John is eager to please* and only go on to discover it is the object in *John is easy to please* after some time (Cook 1973, d'Anglejan and Tucker 1975). L2 learners, like L1 children, at first put negative elements at the beginning of the sentence *No the sun shining* and then progress to negation within the sentence *That's no ready* (Wode 1981).

A sub-theme underlying several of the questions discussed here is that L1 acquisition is completely successful, L2 learning is not. Take two representative quotations: "Very few L2 learners appear to be fully successful in the way that native speakers are" (Towell and Hawkins 1994: 14); "Unfortunately, language mastery is not often the outcome of SLA" (Larsen-Freeman and Long 1991: 153). The evidence for this deficiency is held to be the lack of completeness of L2 grammars (Schachter 1988) or the fossilization in L2 learning where the learner cannot progress beyond some particular stage (Selinker 1992), both familiar "facts" in some sense. Part of the interest in SLA research is explaining why L2 learners are usually unsuccessful. However, this alleged failure depends upon how success is measured, as we shall see.

The answer to the question is far from settled. While there are many similarities between L1 and L2 learning, the variation in situation and other factors also produces many differences. One difficulty is filtering out differences that are accidental rather than inevitable. L1 children mostly acquire language in different settings with different exposure to language than L2 learners and they are at different stages of mental and social maturity (Cook 1969). It may be inherently impossible to compare equivalent L1 and L2 learners. A more precise version of this question asks whether adults still have access to Universal Grammar in the mind, to be discussed below.

4   Does Age Affect L2 Learning?

Following on from the last question, while everybody learns their first language with equal ease, there are vast differences between L2 learners, some acquiring a high level of fluency, others a few stumbling words. Such individual differences may reveal crucial aspects of L2 acquisition; the learners' motivation, their cognitive style, their personality and other individual factors may make a crucial difference. In general Lambert (1990) made a broad distinction between "additive" L2 learning which adds new skills and experiences to the L2 users' lives and "subtractive" L2 learning which detracts from their present state by, say, making them ashamed of their first language. More detailed investigations into differences between L2 learners belong more to psychology than linguistics and are covered in for example Skehan (1989) and Cook (1996).

The individual factor that has been thought to affect L2 learning most has, however, been the learner's age. There is a universal folk belief, shared by many linguists, that children are better at learning second languages. The starting point was Lenneberg's critical period hypothesis (CPH) which claimed language may be learnt only within a particular window of opportunity between 2 months and 13 years of age (Lenneberg 1967), though Lenneberg himself did not extend the CPH directly to L2 learning. A survey of the CPH can be found in Harley and Wang (1997). The classic case showing the failure of late L2 acquisition is Joseph Conrad, who wrote his novels in English though born in Poland (Lieberman 1984). Yet, according to Bertrand Russell, he spoke English with "a very strong foreign accent." There are, however, problems with this example: Conrad's level of writing in English is clearly exceptional; English was his third language and French, his second which he learnt after the age of 17, was spoken with "elegance" and "no trace of an accent" (Page 1986).

Some research has challenged the superiority of children. If all differences between children and adults are discounted other than age, adults often appear to do better than children. To take an example of a naturalistic learning situation, Snow and Hoefnagel-Höhle (1978) studied how English-speaking people of different ages developed Dutch during their first year in The Netherlands. Adults and 12–15-year-olds outshone younger children aged 3–10 during the first few months; by the end of the year the most successful learners were those between 8 and 10 and the least successful the 3–5-year-olds. Thus, while there seem some advantages for children, adults also have some short-lived assets. This appears also in the classroom situation. Asher and Price (1967) taught Russian through the total physical response method for six weeks to adults and children aged 8, 10, and 14; the adults learnt best, the youngest children worst. Yet there is also ample evidence that younger L2 immigrants achieve a higher level in a second language than adults on many tasks, whether accent (Oyama 1976) or communicative abilities (Patkowski 1980).

The accepted wisdom on age has become the view summarized in Krashen et al. (1982) and approved in the massive survey in Singleton (1989): adults acquire second languages better over the short term, children over the long term; adults are overtaken by the end of the first year. In other words, the eventual attainment of children is better even if they start off more slowly. Nevertheless there are problems with the methodology (Cook 1986). The learners are often drawn from a limited range of L1s acquiring English in the USA, untypical of the majority of L2 learners in the world. Age is usually defined in terms, not of when the person started learning the L2, but of when they immigrated to a country. One problem for example is that older immigrants tend to be better educated (Khanna et al. 1998).

The research has little to say directly about acquisition of second languages by children in countries where the second language is not spoken. That is to say, it contributes little to the perennial education debate on the best age to start *teaching* a second language. Ekstrand (1978) looked at two thousand L2 children learning Swedish in schools after their first year and found that the older children were better. Harley (1986) compared older and younger English-speaking children in immersion programs where over half the school day takes place in French; the older children had certain syntactic advantages with verb forms but were overall little different. But neither of these situations are typical of the secondary school teaching of modern languages in most of the world where the child learners are not immigrants and are not immersed in the L2. The early British experience suggested that teaching French in the primary school was not of great help in developing French in the secondary school (Burstall et al. 1974) but this may have more to do with the inability of secondary schools in England to handle children who have already studied French.

The controversy over age still continues. Johnson and Newport (1989) studied L2 learners who had gone to the USA aged between 3 and 39; given the same length of stay, the older the learners the better they were at grammaticality judgments. However, 7 to 9-year-olds did not have the expected advantage over 10 to 12-year-olds during the first three years after arrival (Slavoff and Johnson 1996). Possibly the more advanced structures that give older learners problems are encountered only after three years of acquisition.

The view that older L2 users cannot avoid a non-native accent has been progressively challenged. Neufeld (1977) showed controversially that the pronunciation of some adult L2 learners of Japanese could not be distinguished from natives after only eighteen hours of teaching. Bongaerts et al. (1995) elicited speech samples from adult native speakers of English and from two adult groups of Dutch L2 learners, one group of 10 people believed to be native-like, the other of 12 who were not. Judges put the top Dutch group within the range of the native speakers, with 4 Dutch people exceeding them. They argue that "there appear to be cases of 'late' second language learners who can pass for native speakers phonologically," contrary to the belief that a native accent is never attained. Bongaerts, van Summeren et al. (1995) redid the same experiment with tighter controls but still found a proportion of L2 users who were within the bounds of the native group. If an L2 user can pass as a native speaker for a brief period of time, there cannot be any difference between them, just as in the Turing test a computer that cannot be distinguished from a human being has to be credited with intelligence. This research covers accent rather than other aspects of language, or indeed any more rigorous view of phonology, and it is based on one highly gifted group of learners from a particular L1 learning a particular L2, whose behavior may be no more typical of L2 learners than Olympic runners are typical of human beings. But this line of research disproves the absolute claim that nobody learns a second language to native level when starting as an adult, at least so far as accent is concerned.

But accent is only a single aspect of language – does Conrad's foreign accent really outweigh his exceptional command of written English? Research has furthermore relied mostly on the comparison with the accent of the native speaker. In every language accent is used as a way of identifying speakers in terms of status, region, age, sex, and so on. Even L2 learners rapidly learn the appropriate pronunciations for their own gender, for instance that English-speaking men tend to pronounce the "-ing" ending of the continuous form *going* as /ɪn/ but women tend to use /ɪŋ/ (Adamson and Regan 1991). In a sense no one objects to people from Edinburgh sounding as if they come from Scotland but everyone believes that a Frenchman speaking English should not sound as if they come from Paris; native speakers may give away their origins but foreigners mustn't. Non-native speakers have every right to agree with a French wine-maker, "My English is not good but my French accent is perfect." Accent may be a misleading attribute for age effects. Vocabulary research that studied English learners of French older or younger than 12 for instance found no differences in the acquisition of vocabulary (Singleton 1995).

Again the main interest lies, not so much in the data, as in the explanations. Age manifests itself as change in the user or the user's environment in some way; the question is which of these changes affects L2 learning. Diverse explanations are offered ranging from changes in brain chemistry (Pulvermüller and Schumann 1994) to a shift in speech processing towards categorization at about the age of 7 (Flege 1992) to a lack of availability of Universal Grammar, to be discussed below. Age does seem to have effects on L2 learning but their exact nature is unclear and their causes are mostly speculative. If you care about having a good accent, start learning an L2 while still young; if you want to learn a basic ability quickly, start old.

5   Do L2 Learners Attain the Same Level of Language as Native Speakers?

The question of the end-point of L2 acquisition was already implicit in the question about age but has been raised more explicitly in recent years: what is the final state that L2 users can reach in the knowledge of a second language? Despite the interlanguage assumption that L2 learners have independent grammars, the final state of the L2 learner has frequently been seen in terms of whether L2 learners can achieve the same competence as a native, often called "ultimate attainment."

The starting point was a study by Coppieters (1987) who gave grammaticality judgments to near-native and native speakers of French on nine syntactic structures. Though the near-natives hardly deviated from the native speakers on some structures, on others they differed more, for example, tense contrasts. Even these advanced L2 users could therefore still be distinguished from native speakers. Their ultimate attainment differed from that of the native speaker.

Birdsong (1992) criticized the Coppieters research on a number of counts and essentially redid the experiment with near-native speakers of French with English as L1 and native speakers. He found that, while it was true that the near-natives differed from the natives as a group, when treated as individuals 15 of the 20 near-natives were within the native speaker range, while in the Coppieters study none were. That is to say, in effect five people should not have formed part of the near-native group. The L2 attainment of these speakers did not differ from that of native speakers.

White and Genesee (1996) continued this approach by comparing native speakers of English and L2 learners, divided into near-native and non-native groups, who were given a timed grammaticality judgments test of questions such as *Which one are you reading a book about?* and *Who did you meet Tom after you saw?* There were no differences between the natives and near-natives in accuracy and speed, with the exception of sentences such as *Which movies do the children want to rent?* The conclusion is that "Ultimate attainment in an L2 can indeed be native-like in the UG domain" (White and Genesee 1996: 258).

The balance of the research to date suggests that a small proportion of L2 learners can acquire the same knowledge of a language as native speakers, just as a small group seem able to acquire a native-like accent. But the question remains whether closeness to the native speaker is an appropriate yardstick to measure them by. Birdsong (1993: 717) construes "ultimate attainment in L2A [second language acquisition] in terms of whether non-natives can display evidence of possessing native linguistic norms." But bilinguals use languages for different purposes than monolinguals and have a total language system of far greater complexity in their minds; why should L2 users be measured against the knowledge of a person with only one language? As Sridhar and Sridhar (1986) point out, "Paradoxical as it may seem, Second Language Acquisition researchers seem to have neglected the fact that the goal of SLA is bilingualism." Indeed it is evident that L2 users can become more proficient than average L1 users, as we saw with Conrad's writing. L2 users for instance make fewer spelling mistakes in English than 15-year-old native children (Cook 1997d). Relating L2 ultimate state to native speakers may be convenient but does an injustice to the overwhelming majority of L2 users, who are thereby seen as failures for not achieving something which is, by definition, not an achievable target. The unique status of the two languages of the L2 user has been abandoned in favor of seeing whether the L2 is a defective version of the L1.

6 How Important Is Transfer to L2 Learning?

Transfer from the first to the second language involves both use and acquisition, i.e. it may affect both the processes of speaking in the short term and the processes of learning over a period of time. The influence of the first language on the second is obvious from our everyday experience; most native speakers of English can tell whether an L2 user comes from Japan, Germany, France, or Spain.

Some early research, however, attempted to minimize the role of L1 influence. Grammatical morphemes research, for example, suggested that people with different L1s had similar acquisition sequences (Dulay et al. 1982). Dulay and Burt (1974) tried to quantify transfer mistakes *vis-à-vis* developmental mistakes, claiming that only 24 out of 513 mistakes by Spanish learners of English could be ascribed to their L1.

In the days when linguists considered all languages varied from each other in arbitrary ways, each pair of languages had to be compared from scratch through contrastive analysis. Now that most linguists are concerned with overall relationships between languages, transfer can be seen to utilize overall systematic relationships between languages. Take the example of writing systems. These are mostly held to fall into two groups: meaning-based systems as in Chinese characters and sound-based systems as in the alphabetic system used for English (Paap et al. 1992). L1 transfer involves carrying the characteristics of the L1 writing system over to the L2. Chinese L1 speakers acquiring the Japanese syllabic writing system (kana) rely more on visual strategies, English users on phonological strategies (Chikamatsu 1996); Chinese L1 students have difficulty processing non-words in English, showing their phonological processing is under-developed (Holm and Dodd 1996). Speakers with meaning-based L1 writing systems are better at visual reading tasks in English than those with sound-based L1s (Brown and Haynes 1985). As in other areas, L1 transfer can be a help as well as a hindrance.

Other writing system research has looked at L1 transfer in spelling. Adult Spanish learners of English show characteristic Spanish transfer mistakes involving the double letters <rr> and <ll> and transpositions involving <l> or <r> (Bebout 1985). Some 38.5 percent of English spelling mistakes made by 10-year-old Welsh / English bilingual children can be attributed to interference from Welsh, whether from phonological interference in the L2 pronunciation, orthographic interference from Welsh sound / letter rules, or transfer of cognate words (James et al. 1993). Different L1s produce characteristic spelling mistakes in English; Japanese learners of English frequently confuse <l> and <r> as in *walmer, grobal* and *sarary* (Cook in press), perhaps because of their well-known pronunciation difficulties with the sounds /l/ and /r/, perhaps partly because of the way that English loan words are spelled in the kana syllabic system in Japanese.

Research into phonological transfer has also progressed from lists of phonemes to more general aspects. In the acquisition of English stress assignment by speakers of Polish and Hungarian, 95 percent of the mistakes consisted of transfer of L1 metrical settings (Archibald 1993). English syllables are made to conform to the structure of the L1 by adding epenthetic syllables – [filoor] (Egyptian *floor*), [piliz] (Hindi *please*), and [iskul] (Bengali *school*) (Broselow 1992). The role of transfer may change during L2 development. Major (1990, 1994) claims that phonological transfer decreases over time while developmental factors first increase, then decrease.

The transfer of pragmatic speech functions from L1 to L2 has mostly been seen negatively. German learners of English produce requests that are too direct (Kasper 1981); L2 learners of English thank people in ways that are more formal than native speakers, *Thank you very much* rather than *Thanks* (Cook 1985b). Again research has gone from unique features of languages to universal schemes. There is an overall pattern to apologizing in any language consisting of explicit apology, explanations, denial of responsibility, and so on varying in weight and emphasis from one language to another (Kasper 1996, Bergman and Kasper 1993). An inappropriate linguistic form may be transferred; a learner may use the conventional Japanese way of refusing by making a statement of principle *I never yield to temptations* (Beebe et al. 1990), with odd effects in English.

Transfer has been looked at within the Competition Model (MacWhinney 1987). This claims that all languages make use of four cues for the subject of the sentence – word order, agreement, case, and animacy – but these are weighted differently across languages. Thus German speakers should rely on the agreement between verb and subject *the horse hits the cow*; Italian speakers on the subject coming first THE LAMB *a dog pats*; and Japanese on the subject being animate *The eraser* THE COW *kisses*. L2 users indeed tend to carry over the weightings from the first language and only gradually lose them over time, whether Japanese animacy affecting English (Harrington 1987), or Dutch agreement affecting English (Kilborn and Cooreman 1987); Issidorides and Hulstijn (1992), however, showed that animacy may be an overriding factor with both English and Turkish learners of Dutch. Transfer here is carrying over the L1 weightings for processing the sentence to the L2.

The interpretation of transfer within the Universal Grammar (UG) theory has taken the most general point of view. If both L1 and L2 represent different choices from the same possibilities laid down by UG, the question of transfer is whether the L1 choices carry over into the L2 knowledge. The UG model has the great advantage of providing an overall descriptive syntactic model within which the two languages can be compared, even if UG theory changes constantly. It will be discussed in the next question.

In general, transfer has become a less overt concern in SLA research and has been subsumed within other issues concerned with the relationship between the two languages. Weinreich's original definition indeed allowed transfer to go in both directions: "Those instances of deviation from the norms of either language which occur in the speech of bilinguals as a result of their familiarity with more than one language" (Weinreich 1953). The L2 may also have an effect on the user's L1. In phonology this has been a popular subject of investigation. For example, Voice Onset Time (VOT) is the moment when the voicing of a stop consonant starts relative to the release of the consonant (Liberman et al. 1967). In the English /g/ in *got* the voicing starts before the tongue release, to be precise an average VOT of –50 milliseconds; in the /k/ of *cot* it starts after the release, a VOT of +80 milliseconds. Even though two languages seem to have the same phoneme, this may disguise differences in VOT. For example Spanish /g/ is –108 milliseconds, Spanish /k/ +29 milliseconds, both different from the typical values in English. L2 research has shown that French learners of English have a longer VOT for the voiceless /t/ sound in their L1 French than monolingual speakers (Flege 1987). Similarly L1 meanings for words may be influenced by the L2; a monolingual speaker of Korean uses *paran sekj* (blue) to mean something greener and less purple than a Korean who also knows English (Caskey-Sirmons and Hickerson 1977). Even language functions transfer from L2 to L1 (Kasper 1996); Locastro (1987) for example found English speakers of Japanese using *aizuchi* (nodding for agreement) when talking English.

Transfer in the sense of the relationship between the two languages in the same mind is at the heart of second language acquisition. If people simply acquired an L2 in the same way as their L1 there would be no need for a separate discipline of SLA research. A major factor in the different courses of L1 and L2 acquisition must be the developing links between the two languages.

In a sense any investigation of L2 learning or use that does not involve this relationship is not SLA research.

7   Do L2 Learners Have Access to Universal Grammar?

The Universal Grammar (UG) model of language acquisition developed in the 1980s, called principles and parameters theory, claims that the child's mind possesses universal principles that always apply to language and variable parameters that have different settings in different languages (Chomsky 1986). A sentence such as *Is Sam is the cat that black?* is not only impossible in English but is also forbidden in *any* human language because elements in the sentence can only be moved around to form questions according to the structure of the sentence not its linear order (Chomsky 1980); this principle of structure-dependency is built-in to the human mind so that a human language that breaks structure-dependency is literally inconceivable.

Sentences must have subjects in English. *He speaks* not *Speaks*, French *Il parle* and German *Er spricht*, but they are not compulsory in Italian *Parla*, Japanese *Hanasu* or Arabic *Yatakallamu*. This variation is called the pro-drop parameter: a language belongs either to the group of pro-drop languages that permit no subject or to the group of non-pro-drop languages that have compulsory subjects. L1 children do not need to learn the principles of UG because they are invariably true – no language could possibly break structure-dependency. But they do need to set the parameters appropriately for the language they are acquiring, say to pro-drop or non-pro-drop, which means hearing the right language input to set the parameters. And they also need to acquire a vast store of lexical information about how words behave within the structure of the sentence.

SLA research has reinterpreted several earlier questions within the principles and parameters model of UG. The correctness of the UG account of L1 acquisition is taken for granted, contentious as this may be in itself. The main question has been whether L2 learners have access to the UG built in to the human mind or have to manage without it; in other words, is L2 learning like L1 learning? This is often phrased as a choice between direct access to UG, indirect access, and no access (Cook 1985a), see figure 20.1. In direct access, the L2 learner applies the mental faculty of UG to the L2 input without hindrance and acquires a grammar consisting of the same principles, parameter settings and so on, as the L1 speaker: L2 learning is just like L1 acquisition. In indirect access, the L2 learner is able to access UG only via the L1 knowledge in the mind; those parts of UG that have been activated in the first language can be used again, but other parts are not available. In no-access, the L2 learner is effectively cut off from UG; everything has to be learnt using other aspects of the mind.

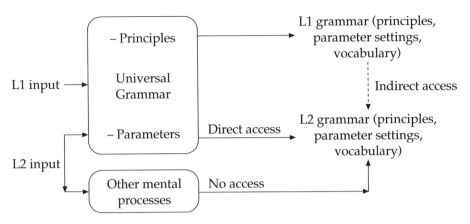

Figure 20.1 Models of access to Universal Grammar in SLA
Source: Cook 1994

The argument for direct access often recapitulates one used in L1 acquisition: if L2 learners know something they could not have learnt from L2 input or from their L1 knowledge, it could only come from the UG in their minds. In L1 acquisition, structure-dependency is part of UG because it could not be acquired from input (Chomsky 1988). However, languages which do not form questions etc. by movement do not need structure-dependency. If speakers of such L1s learn structure-dependency in an L2, this knowledge could derive neither from input nor from their L1 but must come directly from UG itself. Japanese (non-movement) learners of English indeed know structure-dependency according to Otsu and Naoi (1986); a range of L2 learners of English, including Japanese, Chinese, and Finnish L1s, all scored more than 86 percent on a test of structure-dependency (Cook and Newson 1996). So L2 learners clearly have direct access to UG, at least so far as this principle is concerned.

More controversy surrounds the principle of subjacency, which states that elements in the sentence must not be moved too far. A sentence like *What did Sam believe the claim that Mary had bought?* is ungrammatical because *what* has crossed too many barriers in moving to the front of the sentence from its original position at the end. Again some languages do not need subjacency because they have no movement, for example, Korean and Chinese. If L2 learners of such languages know subjacency in the L2, the source cannot be their L1. Korean and Japanese learners of English indeed do not know subjacency to the same extent as native speakers (Bley-Vroman et al. 1988) and older L2 learners are worse than younger learners (Johnson and Newport 1991). This research supports no access rather than direct access, at least for older learners.

The evidence for indirect access to UG is the effects of L1 parameter settings on the L2, i.e. a version of transfer. Japanese and Spanish learners for example

are influenced by the word order preferences of their first language in interpreting English sentences (Flynn 1987). The pro-drop parameter concerning
the compulsory presence of subjects in the sentence has been massively studied.
French learners of English, with the same non-pro-drop setting in L1 and L2,
were much better at saying that *In winter snows a lot in Canada* was ungrammatical than Spanish learners, who have a pro-drop setting in the L1 (White
1986); both English and French learners of Spanish had, however, no problems
with acquiring the Spanish pro-drop setting despite their different L1 settings
(Liceras 1989). Later research has linked the presence of subjects to verb inflections in the present tense, with confusing results (Lakshmanan 1991, Hilles
1991). Much research with parameters has tended to show effects from the L1;
that is to say L2 learners' access to UG is filtered indirectly through their first
language.

Recently the test for access has shifted to the presence or absence of verb
and noun inflections such as past tense "-ed" (*he likeD*) and agreement (*he
likeS*) in L2 learners' speech. L1 work has suggested that these are absent
from early child speech (Radford 1990); children's early sentences are strings of
lexical phrases without grammatical words or inflectional endings as in *Daddy
sleep*; the child's early grammars do not show all aspects of syntax from the
very beginning even if they are part of UG. In more technical terms, the child
does not initially have "functional phrases" built around grammatical forms,
inflections, determiners, etc., but only knows lexical phrases built round lexical
forms such as nouns and verbs. If L2 learners show a similar lack of functional
phrases at the outset, this could confirm the direct access position. Early SLA
research had already in a way made a similar point by demonstrating the
absence of grammatical morphemes in L2 learners. More recently, while Meisel
and Müller (1992) found these functional phrases in early L2 acquisition of
German and Grondin and White (1996) found them in the early ages of L2
acquisition of French, Vainikka and Young-Scholten (1991) suggest that the
sentences of early L2 learners of German include only the parts of the Verb
Phrase, that is to say they are not really functional phrases after all. They
suggest that, despite full access to UG, functional phrases have to develop
over time in response to the language input the child hears, as with parameter
setting in general. Epstein et al. (1996), however, argue for full access to functional categories in SLA, using evidence from Japanese adults and children
learning English. This is also in a sense supported by research with principles
in which English learners of Japanese show early use of the Empty Category
Principle (ECP) (Kanno 1996).

Finally the no-access position has largely based itself on two propositions.
One is that L2 learning could use other mental faculties than UG, such as
general problem-solving abilities; this might be plausible enough if concrete
suggestions were spelled out rather than simply mentioned. The other is that
L2 learners do not acquire the L2 as well as the native speaker (Schachter 1988,
Bley-Vroman 1989), summarized earlier. While L2 learners indeed score less
than natives on most UG-related syntax tests, they also score less on other tests

of cognitive functioning introduced via the L2, such as Working Memory (Brown and Hulme 1992) – the so-called L2 cognitive deficit (Cook 1997a). Such "deficiencies" may not be part of UG itself but reflect the overall working of their cognitive apparatus.

Deciding whether learners have access to UG is fraught with difficulties. Different research methods and different syntactic analyses come up with conflicting answers with no clear way of reconciling them; indeed the UG theory itself changes so rapidly that principles such as subjacency have a half-life of about five years. Access may not be a real question because it reifies UG as a separate object that learning has access to rather than as the changing state of the mind itself (Cook 1994). The relationship of L2 learning to L1 learning has been left as problematic as ever. There seem strong similarities, but there are also differences, perhaps due to the greater maturity of most L2 learners causing social or cognitive differences not directly part of language learning. The UG approach has often tested out the latest fashionable syntactic analysis on the access question rather than looked at a range of research questions: the question of access may have been a side-track away from investigating how one mind knows two grammars. The crucial question is whether the L2 learner's final state of language knowledge fits UG, not whether it fits native speaker grammars.

8   What Is the Role of Language Input?

Everyone would agree that people do not learn an L2 if they encounter no examples of it. Beyond this, there is little agreement over the role that language input plays, the amount that is necessary and the form that it should take. Perhaps the differences between L1 and L2 learning or between learners of different ages stem only from the different types of language they encounter. If certain types of input are more effective than others, this would have dramatic consequences for language teaching.

The starting point for research was the characteristics of language addressed to children. In many languages, adults use baby-talk to children, not only peculiar words such as *moomoo* in Japanese, *baâ* in Arabic and *moocow* in English (Cook 1997b), but also a higher frequency of commands and questions (Newport 1976). Is there an equivalent foreigner-talk to L2 users? Freed (1981) found that the types of sentence addressed to L2 users were more like that used to native adults than to children, reflecting the different topics adults talk about. Foreigners asking the way on the streets of Wellington, however, were not addressed differently from natives (Stocker-Edel 1977).

The issue then shifted, as it had done in L1 acquisition research, away from the grammatical features of the language input to the interaction between learner and non-learner. For example, while it is true that non-native speakers are addressed differently in places such as travel agencies, this is mostly due to the information they receive being more low-level, such as *It's a big jet* in response to *What kind of plane is it?* (Arthur et al. 1980). A survey by Long (1981) showed that interactional modification played more of a role than linguistic factors, for instance, by making the topic appear more transparent to the listener. Giving students opportunities to interact improved performance compared with editing or simplifying the language they heard (Pica et al. 1987).

The importance of input for learning came to the fore in the Input Hypothesis theory (Krashen 1985, 1994), perhaps the most widely known and controversial account of L2 acquisition. Its central claim is that language acquisition depends solely on "comprehensible input" – language which is slightly ahead of the learners' current stage but which they can comprehend through means such as situational clues; language is acquired through trying to understand what people are saying. The evidence for this claim comes from the adaptations in speech to language learners, from the initial "silent period" during which many L2 learners prefer not to speak, and from the success of immersion and bilingual classrooms (Krashen 1985). Fierce criticisms were made of Krashen's model (McLaughlin 1987, Cook 1993), in particular that learners need to speak as well as listen (Swain 1986). The model has gone into abeyance rather than being abandoned but it is still extremely attractive to many language teachers, and indeed to many linguistics students, because of the intuitive commonsense of comprehensible input, and because of its brave attempt at an overall model of L2 learning.

In the UG theory, some language input is necessary in acquisition in order to set the parameters and to acquire vocabulary. Everything L1 children need must either come from their minds or be present in the input as "positive evidence" – sentences that they hear – rather than "negative evidence" – parents' supplying corrections or pointing out forms that do not occur. Parameter-setting in L2 as in L1 requires responding to features of the input that the learner can make out. To set the pro-drop parameter for example, it may be necessary to hear all the forms of the present tense (Cook 1993).

A more radical view is that negative evidence is needed in L2 acquisition even if irrelevant to L1 acquisition. Possibly the L1 has put the learner into a position that is irretrievable from positive evidence alone – a highly restrictive version of indirect access. Negative evidence in an L2 context might be the teachers' corrections of students' speech or explanations that give the learners information about the facts of the language (Cook 1985a). French allows an adverb between a verb and a direct object *Jean embrasse souvent Marie* but English does not **John kisses often Mary*. White (1991) successfully taught English learners of French where to place adverbs in the sentence, thus using negative evidence to overcome their L1 parameter setting. Conversely Trahey and White (1993) exposed French-speaking children acquiring English to an input "flood" of English containing adverbs, leading to an increase in pre-verbal adverbs *Anna carefully drives her new car* but not to the decline of the ungrammatical post-verbal adverbs *Anna drives carefully her new car*. Thus negative evidence in the form of explanation can play an important role in L2 acquisition. Indeed it may be possible to enhance the L2 input to highlight specific points (Sharwood-Smith 1993), as is indeed claimed for phonological clues in speech addressed to L1 children (Morgan 1986).

So, in general, language input seems to play a similar role in L2 learning, apart perhaps from the need for some negative evidence. This may be useful to language teaching whose main influence on students is in a sense controlling their experience of the L2.

9   What Strategies and Processes Do L2 Learners Use?

The term "strategy" has been applied in L2 research to the mental processes, conscious or otherwise, used by L2 learners for learning and communication, often relying on theories from psychology such as the ACT model from Anderson (1983) or Levelt (1989). Much of it concentrates on compiling lists of strategies from observation rather than examining data from recordings or from experiments.

Early research into Good Language Learner strategies tried to isolate the processes used by successful L2 learners. Extensive research in Canada found that good learners tend to adopt the learning style that suits them, to involve themselves in the language learning process, and so on (Naiman et al. 1995), called by McDonough (1995) "wholesome attitudes" rather than strategies.

The research summarized in O'Malley and Chamot (1989) focussed more on learning, dividing strategies into "metacognitive strategies" for managing thinking, such as monitoring one's speech, "cognitive strategies" for thinking itself, such as note-taking, and "social strategies" which involve other people, such as asking for help. When O'Malley and Chamot (1989) asked students to report what they used, a cumulative list of 27 such strategies emerged. Most were non-linguistic in that they could apply equally to the learning of any subject rather than being unique to L2 learning. Such strategies say more about the characteristics of academic students in formal classrooms than about L2 acquisition itself.

A distinct branch of strategy research has concerned vocabulary. Cohen (1990) for instance showed that students remember vocabulary best when they make associations and learn cognates. Often this became linked to the idea of mnemonic strategies used since the ancient Greeks in which vocabulary items are associated with already memorized key words (Paivio and Desrochers 1979) or vivid images tie the new word into existing memories, summarized in Nation (1990). It can be disputed, however, whether vocabulary learnt in this fashion is readily used for everyday language purposes, as opposed to being produced in language tests or exercises of an artificial type.

The area of communication strategies had an easier task since the success of a communication strategy can be more readily gauged. In the L2 literature a communication strategy is needed only when things go wrong – a spare tire for when your car has a puncture rather than the steering wheel you use all the time. Lists of communication strategies were devised using categories such as "approximation" *animal* for *horse* (Tarone 1980) or "literal translation" *green things* for *vegetables* based on Danish (Faerch and Kasper 1983).

However the investigation of communication strategies in actual use by Poulisse (1990, 1996) showed not only that the majority of such strategies reflect a lack of vocabulary rather than of grammar, but also that they are used in the first language when speakers lack the vocabulary to express what they want to say. Hence they are better called "compensatory strategies" since they fill in gaps in vocabulary whether in the first or the second language. Thus the idea of communication strategy became part of normal language use rather than a specifically L2 phenomenon.

The underlying issue is whether strategies are born afresh in an L2 or are carried over from the speaker's existing knowledge. Strategies are a reminder that L2 learners bring more to L2 learning than L1 grammatical competence and that they need to communicate effectively in both languages by whatever means they can.

10   Can Two Languages Be Processed at Once?

To some extent we can ask whether L2 users comprehend and produce speech in similar or different ways compared to L1 users. The L2 user, however, possesses the unique process called codeswitching in which the speaker changes language in midstream, sometimes between sentences but often within the bounds of the same sentence, as in *Suami saya dulu slim and trim tapi sekarang plump like drum* (Before my husband was slim and trim but now he is plump like a drum) produced by a Bahasa Malaysia / English speaker. Grosjean (1989) sees L2 users as having two modes of language use: one is the monolingual mode in which one or other of the two languages is employed; the other is the bilingual mode in which both languages are used at once. Mostly codeswitching research has related to language use in advanced bilinguals, not to how learners codeswitch in the early stages or within the classroom.

Codeswitching within a single sentence can be investigated in terms of the points in the syntactic structure where a switch can take place. Poplack (1980) proposed two constraints. The "free morpheme constraint" is that the speaker may not switch language between a word and its inflection unless the word is pronounced as if it were in the language of the ending; hence it is possible to have an English / Spanish switch *flipeando* (English *flip* + Spanish *ando*), as *flip* is possible in Spanish, but not *runeando* as *run* is impossible. The "equivalence constraint" is that the switch-point must not violate the grammar of either language; so it is possible to have the English / French switch *J'ai acheté an American car* as it preserves the grammar of both languages but not to have *a car americaine* as this would violate English word order.

Other models of codeswitching have relied on deeper syntactic analysis. The "government" model of codeswitching proposed that the switch cannot come within a maximal phrase (DiSciullo et al. 1986), that is to say a lexical head of a phrase forces the rest of the phrase into the same language; for example, the head *see* governs the object Noun Phrase in *see the book* and so keeps the rest of the phrase *the book* in English. The alternative Matrix Language Framework Model holds that the sentence has a Matrix Language structure into which open class content morphemes are inserted from the Embedded Language (Myers-Scotton 1993); the Matrix Language dictates the grammatical words of the utterance. An example is the Alsatian / French switch *Noch schlimmer, wenne de client recalé wurd am permis weje de panne d'essence* (Even worse, when the learner is failed in the test because of the empty tank). Alsatian is the Matrix language and French is the Embedded Language, so the auxiliary *wurd* follows French Verb *recalé* in the Alsatian word order.

Exceptions have been found to all of these constraints. For example, the word *aunties* is found in Panjabi / English switches both with the English ending /aːntiːz/ and with the Panjabi ending /aːntijã/ (Gardner-Chloros 1995), despite the free morpheme constraint. Arabic to Dutch codeswitches take place between indirect and direct object *žib li-ya een glas water of zo* (Get for-me a glass of water or so) (Muysken 1995), despite being within the same verb phrase. The constraints seem to be probabilistic rather than determinative.

Codeswitching can be distinguished from other uses of L1 vocabulary in word borrowing or communication strategies by its functions. Overall, codeswitching is used by one speaker when the other participant knows both languages rather than resorted to out of ignorance of some aspect of the L2. It can be used for reasons such as the following (Romaine 1994):

- reported speech, Tok Pisin / English *Lapun man ia cam na tok* "*oh you poor pussiket*" (The old man came and said "you poor pussycat");
- appropriacy of topic, say "money", *La consulta èra eight dollars*;
- parenthetic remarks;
- directing speech at one of several people present;
- emphasizing the status of one language or the other.

Such lists are open-ended and do not reflect the switching conventions between two given languages in a particular situation. Again the fundamental issue is whether codeswitching involves two languages at once or fits some elements of one language within the framework of another. Investigating how a speaker can use two language systems at once reveals how the two languages relate in the same mind rather than how they work separately.

11   Do L2 Learners Have One Language or Two?

In a sense, the fundamental issue is still whether the knowledge of the two languages in one mind is separate or combined, back to the starting point of Weinreich (1953). The two languages coexist in the same mind: bilinguals do not have two heads. Yet clearly L2 users can separate the two languages, consciously choosing which language to use. At some level the two languages must be distinct.

This choice has often featured in the debate about whether bilingual children have one language system or two. A common talking-point is whether children mix the vocabulary of their two languages. Two children learning Italian and German had a single lexical system which separated at the next stage into two lexicons with one syntax (Taeschner 1983). Early sentences with unequal proportions from the vocabulary of the two languages have also been found such as *Quel couleur your poupée?* (Swain and Wesche 1975). A child learning English and Dutch used only 4.3 percent mixed sentences in speech addressed to Dutch speakers, 3.9 percent to English speakers, and 2.5 percent and 0.9 percent respectively that were balanced between the two languages ("Dutlish") (de Houwer 1990). Genesee et al. (1995) found five children under 26 months could differentiate the two languages, even if they code-mixed.

In terms of pronunciation, Leopold (1947) reported some confusion in the speech of his daughter between the sounds of the two languages and some carry-over of phonological processes from one language to the other; Fantini (1985) and Burling (1959) described children in whom the phonology of one language is dominant. Oksaar (1970), however, studied a child who kept the pronunciation of the two languages separate. Schnitzer and Krasinski (1997) found a bilingual Spanish / English child formed a single phonological system before separating the phonologies of the two languages. At best these pieces of research provide counter-instances to any absolute claim that *all* bilingual children necessarily have either merged or separate pronunciation systems.

In syntax, research into early bilingualism such as Burling (1959) found few signs of syntactic interference between the two languages. Dutch and English gender are kept distinct in the child studied by de Houwer (1990); bound morphemes such as the plural stay in one language; the child mostly uses the appropriate Object Verb word order in Dutch and Verb Object in English. Swain and Wesche (1975) find some interference between the two languages, such as the occurrence of French structures in English sentences, for example *They open, the windows?* Others have described a stage when children have two lexicons but a single syntactic system (Volterra and Taeschner 1978). Meisel (1990) concludes that "fusion is not necessarily a characteristic of bilingual language development, but mixing may occur until codeswitching is firmly established as a strategy of bilingual pragmatic competence." Paradis and Genesee (1996) found that bilingual children developed English and French functional categories at the same rate as monolingual children. The consensus seems to be that, after an initial semantically organized phase, children keep the systems of the two languages distinct. This does not of course mean that they are not part of the same system at some level: any native speaker uses a variety of styles and register for different purposes; the system I use for handwriting is quite different from the one I use for word-processing; there is no way in which I mix them; yet no one would claim that I speak two languages simply because I have two different ways of realizing written English. Indeed it is very hard to decide what would constitute codeswitching in young children, accepted as a normal feature of bilingualism, and what would be codemixing, apparently undesirable.

This recognition of two distinct systems in young children contrasts to a large extent with research into the phonology of adult L2 users. To go back to the VOT (Voice Onset Time) of stop consonants, bilinguals had about the same VOT whether they were speaking English or Spanish (Williams 1977); English learners of Portuguese lose their L1 VOTs the better they become in the L2 (Major 1990). L2 learners can have a VOT in between the values for the two languages, whichever language they are speaking. L2 users could be thought to have a single system for L1 and L2 phonology, or at least the two systems have influenced each other in both directions at some point in the past. Watson (1991: 44) comes to the conclusion that "the bilingual may have two systems but which differ in some way from those of monolinguals." In reading also, Greeks who know English read Greek differently in some respects, for example being affected by the order of presentation, while monolinguals are not (Chitiri and Willows 1997).

The evidence for one lexicon or two in adult L2 users is fairly mixed. One line of research has tended to show two separate lexicons: Kirsner (1986) claimed language-specific words had separate representations but not cognates. Another approach emphasizes the factors common to the two lexicons, Grosjean (1989) for instance arguing that the L1 cannot be switched off while processing the L2. A third possibility is that an independent semantic store connects two separate lexicons; Kroll (1993) found that similar meanings carry across languages, not similar forms. Overall the question of whether L2 users have one system or two is no more settled than the other questions despite fairly widespread discussion in early childhood bilingualism, phonology, and vocabulary. Only in syntax has the question hardly arisen, perhaps because, even in the UG model, it is taken for granted that the two grammars are distinct, even if they influence each other in processing or in development.

It is hard to see that much progress has been made in resolving this underlying question of SLA research since the days of Weinreich. There is still conflicting evidence about whether the L2 user has two systems or one and how these relate during development.

12   Conclusion

Doubtless many other questions and interpretations could be derived from this large and often contradictory area. The field potentially takes in all areas of linguistics and language acquisition, leading to a range of research techniques, described in Tarone et al. (1994). Many techniques are integral to some sub-field of linguistics, such as the phonologist's VOT used in Flege (1987) or the psychologist's task of counting the sounds in words used in Holm and Dodd (1996). Others are borrowed from the mainstream psychology tradition such as response time measures (White and Genesee 1996, Cook 1990), from descriptive linguistics such as analysis of corpora (Klein and Perdue 1992), or from techniques employed with L1 children such as elicited imitation in which learners repeat sentences (Cook 1973, Epstein et al. 1996). It is hardly surprising that there is a lack of comparability between results and a lack of agreement over conclusions, even when tackling a similar range of issues such as the ten questions seen here. A question such as age may be posed and answered in one way by specialists in phonology such as Flege (1992), in another by specialists in UG such as Bley-Vroman (1989), both of them legitimate in terms of their own fields of reference. One dangerous technique is the grammaticality judgements task (Birdsong 1989). People are asked to judge whether sentences such as *What did the teacher know the fact that Janet liked?* are grammatical. One problem is the difficulty in connecting such judgments with the speaker's normal language use. Another is that L2 users may not treat such tasks in the same way as monolinguals, for example translating the sentence back into their L1 (Goss et al. 1994), particularly because of their heightened awareness of language itself (Galambos and Goldin-Meadow 1990, Bialystok 1993).

Virtually all the techniques in the research mentioned here involve an overt or covert comparison of L2 learners with native speakers. The native speaker indeed provides a quick measure of comparison. Taken too seriously, however, this yardstick denies the interlanguage assumption by subordinating L2 users to native speakers (Cook 1997c). Useful as it may be to compare apples with pears, apples inevitably seem to make poor pears, just as it is persistently claimed that L2 learners make poor native speakers.

This account has looked at a selection of the areas where linguistics and SLA research cross paths and has not done justice to many others, for example the sociolinguistic approach described in Regan (1998). It has avowedly taken the prime goal of SLA research to be finding out how people learn and use second languages. Some researchers, however, see SLA research, not as a subject in its own right, but more as a test-bed for theories of linguistics and language acquisition (Cook 1981, Davies 1996, Epstein et al. 1996). While other disciplines may find it useful to have access to this rich source of data, as yet SLA research has hardly raised a ripple in the construction of linguistic theories, unlike L1 acquisition. One reason is the sheer recalcitrance of this complex field where no data collection is simple and no learner is tabula rasa; claims are too easily rebutted by other methods, other situations and other combinations of L1 and L2. A second reason is the rapid obsolescence of linguistic theory, particularly UG where the advent of the Minimalist Theory (Chomsky 1995) has undermined most of the prior UG-related SLA research. SLA researchers who attempt to contribute to UG theory seldom make stable discoveries about SLA because the theoretical ground has shifted under their feet before their research is out.

The uniqueness of SLA is indeed the relationship of the two languages in one person. Chomsky (1986) proposed that the first aim of linguistics is to answer the question "What constitutes knowledge of language?" Virtually all linguists have answered the question in terms of the knowledge of a monolingual. Is knowledge of a second language indeed a pale reflection of a first, or is it something in its own right – multi-competence (Cook 1991)? Borer (1996: 719) reminded the field that "The first question to be resolved is what is the steady state of L2 acquisition and whether given a constant L1 and a constant L2, this steady state is homogenous across speakers." The questions we have looked at here all circle around this issue and start to provide some inklings of what knowing and using two languages is actually like, something which after all is the everyday state of the majority of human beings.

NOTE

I am indebted to Phil Scholfield, Denise Chappell and the editors for comments on earlier drafts.

21   Multilingualism

SUZANNE ROMAINE

1   Introduction

Experts know that multilingualism is not the aberration or minority phenomenon many English speakers suppose it to be. It is, on the contrary, a normal
and unremarkable necessity for the majority of the world's population. Although there are no precise statistics on the number or distribution of speakers
of two or more languages, linguists estimate that there are roughly 5,000 languages in the world but only about 200 nation-states. This means that there are
approximately 25 times as many languages as there are countries. Grosjean
(1982: vii) estimates that probably about half the world's population is bilingual
and bilingualism is present in practically every country in the world.

It is thus monolingualism which represents a special case, despite the fact
that most linguists have paid more attention to it and have taken it to be the
norm in their theories of language. Chomsky (1965: 3), for instance, defined
the scope of reference for the study of language as follows: "Linguistic theory
is concerned primarily with an ideal speaker-listener, in a completely homogeneous speech-community, who knows its language perfectly." By contrast, in the
heterogeneous communities where multilinguals reside we find instead that
individuals are rarely equally fluent in the languages they know. Indeed, a
society which produced such individuals would soon cease to be multilingual
since no community uses two or more languages for the same set of functions
(see section 4).

In this chapter I will use the terms "bilingualism" and "multilingualism"
interchangeably to refer to the use of two or more languages. Because multilingualism exists within the cognitive systems of individuals, as well in as
families, communities, and countries, it is perhaps inevitable that the study of
different aspects of the phenomenon have been parceled out among various
subdisciplines of linguistics and related fields of research such as psychology,
sociology, and education, to name just a few. For instance, the acquisition of
proficiency in another language usually results in some degree of bilingualism,

yet its study is generally regarded as the province of a separate subdiscipline called second language acquisition (chapter 20).

Psychologists, for their part, have investigated the effects of bilingualism on mental processes, while sociologists have treated bilingualism as an element in culture conflict and have looked at some of the consequences of linguistic heterogeneity as a societal phenomenon. Educationists have been concerned with bilingualism in connection with public policy. Basic questions about the relationship between bilingualism and intelligence, whether certain types of bilingualism are good or bad, and the circumstances under which they arise, also impinge on education. Within the field of international studies, bilingualism is seen as an essential element in cross-cultural communication. In each of these disciplines, however, multilingualism is too often seen as incidental and has been treated as a special case or as a deviation from the norm.

Within the field of linguistics increasing attention has been given to the systematic study of language contact and the term "contact linguistics" is now used in a wide sense to refer to both the process and outcome of any situation in which two or more languages are in contact. A related field of research has focussed on particular types of languages called pidgins and creoles which have emerged in instances where the groups in contact do not learn each other's language or some other language of wider communication already in existence (see Romaine 1988). Linguists who study language contact often seek to describe changes at the level of linguistic systems in isolation and abstraction from speakers, thus losing sight of the fact that the bilingual individual is the ultimate locus of contact, as Weinreich (1968) pointed out many years ago. More than half of the nearly four hundred million people around the world who speak Spanish, for example, do so in situations of intensive contact with other languages (Silva-Corvalán 1995: 453).

A variety of textbooks now offer useful overviews of various aspects of the topic of multilingualism (see e.g. Appel and Muysken 1987, Baetens-Beardsmore 1986, Baker 1993, Edwards 1994, Grosjean 1982, Hakuta 1986, Hoffman 1991, Romaine 1995). Here I will confine my coverage to the following topics: 2 Origins of multilingualism: causes and consequences; 3 Individual vs. societal bilingualism; 4 Language choice; 5 Language shift and death. To conclude the chapter, I will say something about the changing character of multilingualism in the world today.

2   Origins of Multilingualism: Causes and Consequences

Multilingualism is a condition of life of considerable antiquity, possibly as old as the human species. With the rare exception of small isolated atoll communities, almost none of which are really isolated anymore, human communities were always in contact with other groups and connected to them either economically or socially through exchange of goods, knowledge, marriage partners, etc. Yet, the story from Genesis would have us believe that linguistic diversity is the curse of Babel. In a primordial time, people spoke the same language. God, however, decided to punish them for their presumptuousness in erecting the tower by making them speak different languages. Thus, multilingualism became regarded as an obstacle to further cooperation and placed limits on human worldly achievements.

Popular misinformed views on multilingualism are still commonplace. In 1994 media mogul Rupert Murdoch made a speech on Australian radio about the negative effects of multilingualism. His gist was that multilingualism was divisive, and monolingualism, cohesive. Multilingualism was in his view the cause of Indian disunity, and monolingualism the reason for the unity of the English-speaking world.

It takes but little reflection to find the many flaws in Murdoch's reasoning and to come up with cases where the sharing of a common language has not gone hand in hand with political or indeed any other kind of unity. Northern Ireland is one such example from the English-speaking world, which comes readily to mind, but there are many others from other parts of the globe. Certainly, the attempt at Russification of the former republics of the Soviet Union did not ensure unity in that part of the world either. Indeed, one of the first political acts undertaken by the newly independent Baltic states was to reassert their linguistic and cultural autonomy by reinstating their own national languages as official.

Humans have been managing or mismanaging multilingualism for centuries well before modern notions such as "language policy" or "language planning" came onto the scene. Thus, for example, Charles V decided in 1550 to impose Castilian on the Indians of South America. Long before Europeans came to the island of New Guinea the Motu people of the Papuan coast decided to use a simplified version of their language in their trade contacts with outsiders, and traders in Canton markets wrote numbers on slates to which buyer and seller pointed as they negotiated a price.

What is new, however, is the attempt to manage such linguistic and cultural contacts and potential conflicts resulting from them within the framework of agencies of the modern nation-state. The idea of "one nation–one language" is a European notion. In Europe, it has generally been the case that language differences have been associated with distinguishable territories, and later, the nation-states occupying those territories. Language and nation have thus tended to coincide. Because of the identification of national entities with linguistic integrity, heterogeneity has tended to be limited to the frontiers and was for that reason local and peripheral, e.g. the Basques in Spain and France, and the "Celtic fringe" in the British Isles and France. Thus, 25 out of 36 of the European countries are officially unilingual. In most of them, however, there are minorities (both indigenous and non-indigenous), whose languages do not have the same rights as those granted to the official languages. Many indigenous people today like the Welsh and Basque find themselves living in nations that they had no say in creating and are controlled by groups who do not represent their interests and in some cases, actively seek to exterminate them, as is the case with the Kurds in Iraq. The marginalization of the languages and cultures of minority peoples in the European states can be seen as a form of "internal colonialism."

In sixteenth-century France, for example, the possession of a common language was seen as the key to the egalitarian aims of the French Revolution. Speaking French meant being able to participate on equal terms in the newly established French nation-state. The idea of national unity was that France was to become bound together by common goals, administration, and culture. The French language was and still is symbolic of this unity. Since the revolution French nationalists have seen the persistence of non-French speaking groups and their cultures as threats to the stability and persistence of the union.

However, even by 1863 at least one-fifth of the population was still not French-speaking. As late as 1922 the General Inspector of Schools was to declare linguistic war on Bretons who persisted in speaking their own language: "It is of first order importance that Bretons understand and speak the national language: they will only truly be French on that condition . . . It is Frenchmen that are needed to Frenchify the Bretons, they will not Frenchify themselves by themselves" (cited in Kuter 1989: 77). A few years later the Minister of National Education said that "for the linguistic unity of France, the Breton language must disappear" (cited in Kuter 1989: 78). Even today some of the modest attempts to give Breton a limited place in the education system have been resisted by those who feel that any concessions to Bretons will inevitably lead to political separatism. While Mitterrand's socialist government issued a cautious recognition of France as a multicultural nation, it still advocated the fusion of cultures. Ironically, Mitterrand saw the resurgence of interest in regional language and culture as an effective force against the increasing influence of American popular culture (see section 6).

The boundaries of modern nation-states in Africa and in parts of the New World have been arbitrarily drawn, with many of them created by the political and economic interests of western colonial powers. With the formation of these new nation-states, the question of which language (or which version of a particular one) will become the official language arises and has often led to bitter controversy. Even countries with more than one official language, such as Canada (where French and English share co-official status), have not escaped attempts by various factions to gain political advantage by exploiting issues of language loyalty.

Some political scientists and linguists have used the term "Fourth World" to label indigenous dispossessed minority peoples who have been encapsulated within, and in some cases divided across, modern nation-states, e.g. the Sami and Inuit peoples of the Arctic region. They are people who do not have their own nation-state, but nevertheless regard themselves as ethnically and linguistically distinct from the majority population in the countries where they reside. Their struggle for the right to use their own languages continues too.

More than 80 percent of the conflicts in the world today are between nation-states and minority peoples (Clay 1990).

   Although multilingualism itself is often blamed for these conflicts, language is really a symbol of a much larger struggle for the recognition of minority rights. In 1951 Frisian language activists were involved in a street riot in the Dutch town of Leeuwarden protesting the inadmissibility of the Frisian language, spoken by many of the members of the major indigenous minority group, in Dutch courts.

3   Individual vs. Societal Multilingualism

Linguists usually draw a distinction between individual and societal multilingualism, although it is not always possible to maintain. Some countries such as Canada, are officially bilingual in English and French, although not all Canadians are bilingual. There are many more French-speaking Canadians who learn English as a second language than English-speaking Canadians who learn French. In other countries such as India, Singapore, and Papua New Guinea there is a high degree of individual bilingualism with the average person knowing at least two or more languages. In Singapore four languages, English, Mandarin, Tamil, and Malay share co-official status, and most people are bilingual in English and one of the other official languages.

   Some of the connections between individual and societal bilingualism become evident when we consider some of the reasons why certain individuals are or become bilingual. Usually the more powerful groups in any society are able to force their language upon the less powerful. If we take Finland as an example, we find that the Sami, Romanies, and Swedes have to learn Finnish, but Finns do not have to learn any of these languages. Similarly, in Britain, the child of English-speaking parents does not have to learn Panjabi or Welsh, but both these groups are expected to learn English. In Papua New Guinea few children know English before coming to school, yet most will still be educated in English because this language policy is a legacy of the country's colonial heritage. The middle-class anglophone parents in Canada who send their child to a French immersion school are, however, by contrast, under no obligation to do so. Many do so, however, as a means of enriching their children's development and because they believe knowledge of another language is an advantage. The co-official status that Singapore attaches to Tamil and Malay (also designated the national language) is not matched by supportive language policies that guarantee their transmission. School outcomes clearly reflect the advantages being given to the Chinese majority (Gupta 1994).

   Even in countries where minority languages are recognized for some purposes, what this means varies in practice. By "minority language" I mean one with a relatively small number of speakers living within the domain of a more widely spoken language, whose knowledge is usually necessary for full participation in society. Swedes in Finland probably have the best legal protection of any minority group in the world. The next strongest position is held by minority languages which have limited (often territorial) rights. This is the case in Canada, where certain provinces are officially declared bilingual, and others, like Ontario (where the national capital lies) are not.

It would be naive, however, to assume that bilingual countries were created to promote bilingualism, rather than to guarantee the legal right to more than one language in a society. We can distinguish between de facto ("by fact") and de jure ("by law") bilingualism. There are often fewer bilingual individuals in de jure multilingual or bilingual states than in those where de facto multilingualism or bilingualism occurs. A good example is Switzerland, where territorial unilingualism exists under federal multilingualism. Although Switzerland is widely cited as a successful example of multilingualism, only about 6 percent of Swiss citizens can be considered multilingual in the country's four official languages: German, French, Italian, and Romantsch. English is much preferred over the other official languages as a second language. Of the 26 cantons, 22 are officially monolingual. Economic and political power is more greatly concentrated among German speakers.

4 Language Choice in Multilingual Communities

In all multilingual communities speakers switch among languages or varieties just as monolinguals switch among styles. The fact that speakers select different languages or varieties for use in different situations shows that not all languages / varieties are equal or regarded as equally appropriate or adequate for use in all speech events. A foreigner who manages to learn a variety of Telegu sufficient to get by on the streets of Hyderabad will soon find out that this particular variety of Telegu cannot be used for all purposes which an English monolingual might use English for. The average educated person in Hyderabad may use Telegu at home, Sanskrit at the temple, English at the university, Urdu in business, etc. He or she may also know other varieties of Telegu, or Kannada, Tamil or Malayalam for reading, dealing with servants, or other specific purposes. Many south Asians have active control over what amounts to complex linguistic repertoires drawn from different languages and varieties. In societies such as these, multilingualism is not an incidental feature of language use, but a central factor and an organizing force in everyday life. In most parts of India, monolingualism would be problematic relative to the norms and expectations about the number of languages and varieties a person needs in order to manage the everyday things a normal person has to do.

Although language choice is not arbitrary, not all speech communities are organized in the same way. Through the selection of one language over another or one variety of the same language over another speakers display what may

be called "acts of identity," choosing the groups with whom they wish to identify (see Le Page and Tabouret-Keller 1985). There are, however, some common
motivations for such choices in different societies. The first step in understanding what choices are available to speakers is to gain some idea of what languages
and varieties are available to them in a particular social context. Context in
this case may be thought of in its widest sense as the varieties made available
either officially or unofficially within the boundaries of a nation-state such as
Canada, or in a very narrow sense, as the varieties available on a particular
occasion, e.g. shopping in an urban market in Kenya, or in a department store
in Strasbourg.

4.1   Domains of use

In research on the Puerto Rican community in New York City, a team of
sociolinguists arrived at a list of five "domains" in which either Spanish or
English was used consistently (Fishman et al. 1971). These were established
on the basis of observation and interviews and comprised: family, friendship,
religion, employment, and education. These domains served as anchor points
for distinct value systems embodied in the use of Spanish as opposed to English.
A domain is an abstraction which refers to a sphere of activity representing a
combination of specific times, settings, and role relationships. They conducted
further studies to support their claim that each of these domains carried different expectations for using Spanish or English.

They constructed hypothetical conversations that differed in terms of their
interlocutors, place, and topic. The way in which these variables were manipulated determined the extent to which the domain configuration was likely
to be perceived as congruent or incongruent. For example, a highly congruent
configuration would be a conversation with a priest, in church, about how to
be a good Christian. A highly incongruent one would be a discussion with
one's employer at the beach about how to be a good son or daughter.

People were asked to imagine themselves in hypothetical situations where
two of the three components of the conversational context were given. For
example, they might be asked to imagine they were talking to someone at
their place of work about how to do a job most efficiently. They were then
asked to whom they would most likely be talking and in what language. The
respondents tended to provide congruent answers for any given domain,
and their choice of language was consistent. The most likely place for Spanish
was the family domain, followed by friendship, religion, employment, and
education.

In each domain there may be pressures of various kinds, e.g. economic,
administrative, cultural, political, religious, etc., which influence the bilingual
towards use of one language rather than the other. Often knowledge and use
of one language is an economic necessity. Such is the case for many speakers
of a minority language, like Gujerati in Britain, or French in provinces of

Canada where Francophones are in a minority. The administrative policies of some countries may require civil servants to have knowledge of a second language. For example, in Ireland, knowledge of Irish is required. In some countries it is expected that educated persons will have knowledge of another language. This is probably true for most of the European countries, and was even more dramatically so earlier in countries like Russia, where French was the language of polite, cultured individuals. Languages like Greek and Latin have also had great prestige as second languages of the educated. As is the case with accent, the prestige of one language over another is a function of the perceived power of those who speak it. A bilingual may also learn one of the languages for religious reasons. Many minority Muslim children in Britain receive religious training in Arabic.

Due to competing pressures, it is not possible to predict with absolute certainty which language an individual will use in a particular situation. In trying to account for the choices made by Buang speakers in Papua New Guinea, a country with as many as 800 languages, we can take as one example Sankoff's (1980: 36) model which views the selections made by speakers in terms of social and situational variables in the speech event, e.g. formality, addressee, etc. Speakers have three languages to choose from: Buang, Yabem, and Tok Pisin. Tok Pisin is a variety of pidgin / creole English now widely used in the country, while Buang and Yabem are indigenous languages associated with different geographical regions. Knowledge of Yabem among the Buang is largely restricted to those who attended mission schools, where the language of instruction was Yabem, spread by Christian missionaries as a lingua franca. Figure 21.1 shows the main factors which serve to define certain types of situations in which particular choices are normally acceptable, appropriate, and likely.

4.2 Diglossia

The choices made by individuals may become institutionalized at the societal level in communities where bilingualism is widespread. Often each language or variety in a multilingual community serves a specialized function and is used for particular purposes. This situation is known as "diglossia." An example can be taken from Arabic-speaking countries such as Egypt in which the language used at home may be a local version of Arabic. The language that is recognized publicly, however, is modern standard Arabic, which takes many of its normative rules from the classical Arabic of the Qur'ān. The standard language is used for "high" functions such as giving a lecture, reading, writing, or broadcasting, while the home variety is reserved for "low" functions such as interacting with friends at home. The high (H) and low (L) varieties differ not only in grammar, phonology, and vocabulary, but also with respect to a number of social characteristics, namely, function, prestige, literary heritage, acquisition, standardization, and stability. L is typically acquired

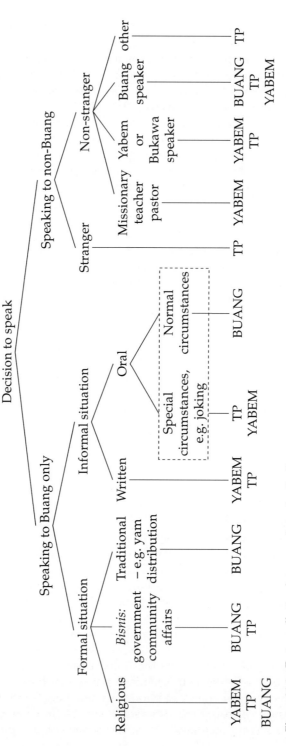

Figure 21.1 Factors affecting language choice for the Buang
Note: TP = Tok Pisin.

at home as a mother tongue and continues to be used throughout life. Its main uses are in familial and familiar interactions. H, on the other hand, is learned later through schooling and never at home. H is related to and supported by institutions outside the home. The separate domains in which H and L are acquired immediately provide them with separate institutional support systems.

Diglossic societies are marked not only by this compartmentalization of varieties, but also by restriction of access. Entry to formal institutions such as school and government requires knowledge of H. The extent to which these functions are compartmentalized can be illustrated in the importance attached by community members to using the right variety in the appropriate context. An outsider who learns to speak L and then uses it in a formal speech will be ridiculed. Speakers regard H as superior to L in a number of respects. In some cases H is regarded as the only "real" version of a particular language to the extent that speakers claim they do not speak L. Sometimes the alleged superiority is invoked for religious and / or literary reasons. For example, the fact that classical Arabic is the language of the Koran endows it with special significance. In other cases a long literary tradition backs the H variety, e.g. Sanskrit. There is also a strong tradition of formal grammatical study and standardization associated with H. The list shows a typical, though not universal, distribution for high and low varieties in diglossia.

Some situations for high and low varieties in Diglossia

	High	Low
Religious service	+	
Instructions to servants, waiters etc.		+
Personal letter	+	
Speech in parliament, political speech	+	
University lecture	+	
Conversation with family, friends, colleagues		+
News broadcast	+	
Radio soap opera		+
Newspaper editorial, news story	+	
Comedy		+
Poetry	+	
Folk literature		+

The analogy has been extended to other communities in which the varieties in diglossic distribution have the status of separate languages, such as Spanish and Guaraní (an Indian language totally unrelated to Spanish) in Paraguay. Spanish serves here as the high variety and is used for high functions. It is the official language of government and education, although 90 percent of the population speak Guaraní, which has the status of national language. Diglossia and bilingualism have been stable there and recent attempts to use Guaraní as a medium of education have met with resistance to extending Guaraní from intimate into public domains. The notion of diglossia is also sometimes expanded to include more than two varieties or languages which participate in such a functional relationship, e.g. in Tunisia, French, Classical, and Tunisian Arabic are in triglossic distribution, with French and Classical Arabic sharing H functions in relation to Tunisian Arabic, and French occupying the role of H in relation to the other two. The term "polyglossia" has also been used to refer to cases such as Singapore, where many varieties coexist in a functional relationship. English, Mandarin, Tamil, and Malay share co-official status, but each of these has local L variants. A child who speaks Hokkien at home may be schooled in Mandarin Chinese at school. English also functions as an H variety to the other three since it has more prestige.

The relationship between individual bilingualism and societal diglossia is not a necessary or causal one. Either phenomenon can occur without the other one (Fishman 1967). Both diglossia with and without bilingualism may be relatively stable, long-term arrangements, depending on the circumstances. As an example, we can take the Old Order Amish (also called the Pennsylvania Dutch) and Hasidic Jews in the United States. Both groups maintain stable diglossia with bilingualism. They control their own schools. The utilization of the non-group culture is restricted to economic pursuits, and even these are tightly regulated. For example, the Pennsylvania Dutch use electricity for pasteurization of milk, as required by law, but they are not allowed to have it in their homes for refrigeration or for use with farm machinery. The degree to which the outside world is engaged is justified only to the extent that it contributes to the maintenance of the group. By not accepting or implementing the other culture in its entirety, it is kept in strict complementary distribution with their own. English is specifically excluded from home and religious use. It encroaches only in a limited way in economic domains.

Stability, however, is a subjective notion. In some cases indigenous languages can be swamped by intrusive ones over a relatively short period of time (see section 5). There are many bilingual situations which do not last for more than three generations. Immigrant languages, for instance, have disappeared as their speakers have adopted the language of the new environment. This is true for many speakers of south Asian languages, like Gujerati and Bengali, in Britain. In cases such as these of bilingualism without diglossia, the two languages compete for use in the same domains. Speakers are unable to establish the compartmentalization necessary for survival of the L variety. In such instances language shift may be unavoidable (see section 5).

Many attempts to increase the domains of use for a low variety have had limited success, such as in Ireland, where there was no widespread knowledge of the classical written variety, and decreasing use of the spoken language. In Israel, however, the revival of Hebrew has been successful. There the task was to take a language which was widely known in its written form, and to add to it, vernacular use and a native-speaking community. Thus, in Ireland the problem was how to expand the language into H functions which had been taken over by English, and in Israel, how to add L functions to a high variety.

4.3   *Codeswitching*

Although the existence of bilingualism, diglossia, and codeswitching are all often cited as factors leading to language loss, in some cases codeswitching and diglossia are positive forces in maintaining bilingualism. Swiss German and Faroese may never emerge from diglossia, but are probably in no danger of death. In many communities frequent switching between languages serves important functions.

Many linguists have stressed the point that switching between languages is a communicative option available to a bilingual member of a speech community on much the same basis as switching between styles or dialects is an option for the monolingual speaker. Switching in both cases serves an expressive function and has meaning. The speech functions served by switching are presumably potentially available to all speakers, whether bilingual or monolingual, although it may not be possible to attribute only one meaning to a particular switch since switches may accomplish a number of functions at the same time. Moreover, the ways in which these functions are marked linguistically or the degree to which they are accomplished successfully will depend on the resources available in any particular case. In some cases the resources may come from more than one language, while in others they may come from within what is regarded as one language. This is why many linguists use the term "codeswitching"; the term "code," like "variety" is a neutral one and does not commit us to taking a decision as to whether the varieties or codes concerned constitute languages or dialects.

In an early study conducted by Blom and Gumperz (1972) in a rural Norwegian village called Hemnesberget, the concepts of "metaphorical" and "transactional" switching were introduced (sometimes referred to as "non-situational" vs. "situational codeswitching"). Transactional switching comes under the heading of the type of switching most commonly discussed as being controlled by components of the speech event like topic and participants as examined in the example from Papua New Guinea in the discussion of domains.

When residents in Hemnesberget step up to the counter at the post office, greetings and inquiries about family members tend to be exchanged in the local dialect, while the business part of the transaction, e.g. buying stamps, is carried out in standard Norwegian. This would be an example of transactional switching. Metaphorical codeswitching, however, concerns the various communicative effects the speaker intends to convey. For example, teachers deliver formal lectures in the official standard form of Norwegian, but lecturers shift to regional Norwegian dialect when they want to encourage discussion among the students. Thus, while the components of the speech event such as speaker, topic, listener, setting have not changed, the tone of the interaction has been altered by a switch in language.

There is a symbolic distinction between "we" vs. "they" embodied in the choice of varieties. Generally speaking, the tendency is for the minority language to be regarded as the "we," and the majority language as the "they" variety. The "we" variety typically signifies in-group, informal, personalized activities, while the "they" variety marks out-group, more formal relations. In this example from Panjabi / English switching in Britain, Panjabi serves to mark the in-group of Panjabi / English bilinguals and English, the out-group: *esi engrezi sikhi e te why can't they learn?* "We learn English, so why can't they learn [Asian languages]." Here the speaker makes the point that Panjabi speakers are expected to learn English, but that English people are not required to learn their language. The switch from Panjabi to English emphasizes the boundaries between "them" and "us."

A speaker may switch for a variety of reasons, e.g. to redefine the interaction as appropriate to a different social arena, or to avoid, through continual codeswitching, defining the interaction in terms of any social arena. The latter function of avoidance is an important one because it recognizes that codeswitching often serves as a strategy of neutrality or as a means to explore which code is most appropriate and acceptable in a particular situation. In many government offices in Canada, it is customary for bilingual employees to answer the telephone by saying "Bonjour, hello" in order to give the caller the option of choosing either language to continue the conversation.

In some multilingual exchanges the question of code choice is not resolved because the parties involved do not agree on definition of the domain. We can take an example from western Kenya where a brother and sister are conversing in the brother's store. These siblings are used to conversing on home territory as family members and not as store owner and customer. In such cases where code-choice has not been regularized, it must be negotiated on the spot. The sister wished to conduct the event on the basis of their solidarity as brother and sister because she wanted special treatment as a customer in her brother's store. Therefore, she chose their shared mother tongue, Lwidakho. The brother wanted to treat his sister as a customer and therefore used Swahili, which is an ethnically neutral choice in this speech community and the unmarked choice for service encounters of this type. The utterances in Lwidakho are in italic in this exchange. In some ways this conversation is like what happens in Hemnesberget, Norway, except that the sister does not switch to Swahili once the greetings are over, and the brother does not switch back to Lwidakho to accommodate his sister. The sister then goes away without everything she had hoped for (Myers-Scotton 1992: 144–5).

BROTHER: *Good morning, Sister.*
SISTER: *Good morning.*
BROTHER: *Are you alright?*
SISTER: *Yes, just a little.*
BROTHER: Sister, now today what do you need?
SISTER: *I want you to give me some salt.*
BROTHER: How much do you need?
SISTER: *Give me sixty cents worth.*

BROTHER: And what else?
SISTER: *I would like something else, but I've no money.*
BROTHER: Thank you, sister. Goodbye.
SISTER: *Thank you. Goodbye.*

The preference in market transactions in Jerusalem is for multilingualism, as this example shows, when four women soldiers walk up to look at bracelets outside a jewelry store (Spolsky and Cooper 1991: 108–9):

SHOPKEEPER 1:   You want bracelets?
SOLDIER 1:   How much?
SHOPKEEPER 1:   You want this one or this one?
SOLDIER 2 (*in Hebrew*):   Those aren't pretty.
SOLDIER 1 (*in Arabic*):   That's not pretty?
SHOPKEEPER 2 (*in Arabic, then Hebrew*):   Pretty. Like women soldiers.

The shopkeeper addresses the women first in English even though they are Israeli soldiers and obviously native speakers of Hebrew. Because Hebrew has a higher status than Arabic in Israel, for the Arab to use Hebrew would indicate a subordinate status. By choosing English, he downplays the nationalist dimensions of Hebrew, and opts for the even higher status associated with English. The first soldier accepts this choice of language, which permits the shopkeeper to continue in this more neutral language. The second soldier introduces Hebrew into the exchange to make a comment to her friend. This may be partly a bargaining ploy since she knows the shopkeeper will understand. The first soldier then switches to Arabic, making clear that she is not an English-speaking tourist or non-Arabic speaking shopper who can be taken advantage of. The shopkeeper replies in Arabic and then Hebrew, establishing his own ability to speak Hebrew and reciprocating the soldier's accommodation to his language.

Accommodation is possible here because all parties have the competence to carry on the activity multilingually. Speakers can exercise a choice only to the extent that they can speak a particular language well enough to choose it over some other in a particular domain. As noted in section 1, multilinguals rarely develop equal fluency in all the languages they know. There has been a tendency to regard bilingual competence as the sum of the acquisition of competence in each of the two languages rather than as a unitary system which allows the pooling of resources across both. If the proficiency of a bilingual is evaluated in circumstances where she / he is forced to stay within one code, e.g. in contacts with a monolingual community, then that person's communicative competence will seem less rich than it actually is. Greater proficiency in one language in a particular domain may prompt codeswitching to that language or result in interference from that language in the language less well known. The repertoires of multilingual speakers can be exploited fully in those multilingual settings where they can draw upon the resources from each of the available codes plus strategies for switching between them. Thus, this example from a Malay / English bilingual recorded by Ozog (1987) is totally unremarkable in the everyday life of the speaker concerned, as odd as it may appear to a monolingual:

> *This morning I hantar my baby tu dekat babysitter tu lah.*
> "This morning I took my baby to the babysitter."

It is difficult to say whether this utterance is basically English with some Malay words, or a Malay utterance with English words.

Popular attitudes towards some kinds of codeswitching, mixing and interference are, nevertheless, often negative, even among community members themselves who engage in this kind of multilingual behavior frequently. Indeed, in the Panjabi-speaking community in Britain many people label examples of the type cited above as *tuti-futi* ("broken up") Panjabi and do not consider it to be "real" Panjabi (Chana and Romaine 1984). In parts of French-speaking Canada the term "joual" has similar connotations. In communities like these there is almost an inherent conflict between the desire to adopt English loanwords as prestige markers and their condemnation as foreign elements destroying the purity of the borrowing language. Haugen (1977: 332) describes the ambiguity felt by Norwegian Americans who did not approve of people from their own group who tried to speak too bookishly, but at the same time they poked fun at those who adopted excessive numbers of English words, calling them "yankeefied." A visitor from Norway commented on hearing this variety of Norwegian that it was "no language whatever, but a gruesome mixture of Norwegian and English, and often one does not know whether to take it humorously or seriously" (Haugen 1977: 94).

A change in political consciousness, however, may lead to a change in attitudes with the result that codeswitching is taken very seriously. In parts of the southwestern USA and California, where codeswitching between Spanish and English is frequent among Mexican-Americans, terms such as "Tex-Mex," "pocho" and "caló" are used to refer to mixed varieties of Spanish / English used by Chicanos (Mexican-Americans). While the terms still have derogatory overtones in some quarters, these mixed codes have come to serve as positive ethnic markers of Chicano identity and are increasingly used in Chicano literature.

5   Language Shift and Death

Choices made by individuals on an everyday basis can also have an effect on the long-term relationships of the languages concerned. Language shift generally involves bilingualism (often with diglossia) as a stage on the way to eventual monolingualism in a new language. Typically a community which was once monolingual becomes bilingual as a result of contact with another (usually socially more powerful) group and becomes transitionally bilingual in the new language until their own language is given up altogether. In that case we can speak of language death. This is what has happened to the majority of the Aboriginal languages of Australia. For example, the Aboriginal population of Tasmania (ca. 3–4,000) was exterminated within 75 years of contact with Europeans. Some linguists predict that if nothing is done, almost all Aboriginal languages will be dead by the early decades of the twenty-first century (see section 6).

A number of researchers have commented on the extreme instability of bilingualism in the United States. Probably no other country has been host to more bilingual people. However, each new wave of immigrants has seen the decline of their language. Lieberson et al. (1975) report that in 1940, 53 percent of second generation white Americans reported English as their mother tongue. In the previous generation, however, only 25 percent had English as their mother tongue. Thus, this probably represents a substantial shift within one generation. Some groups, however, such as Spanish speakers, have shown an increase in numbers in recent years because they have renewed themselves via new immigration. The United States is now the fifth-largest Hispanic country in the world (see further in section 6).

In Australia the decline of non-English languages has been similarly dramatic. Only 4.2 percent of the Australian-born population regularly uses a language other than English. This figure includes Aboriginal languages too. Yet there are some major differences in the extent to which native languages are retained by the different ethnic groups. Greek-Australians display the greatest maintenance, and Dutch-Australians the least. Different languages are concentrated in different states, although there is no single minority language of equal significance to Spanish in the US (Romaine 1991).

There are many reasons for language shift and death (see the studies in Dorian 1989). In some cases shift occurs as a result of forced or voluntary immigration to a place where it is not possible to maintain one's native language, e.g. Italians in the United States, or as a result of conquest, e.g. the Gaels in Scotland and Ireland. The ultimate loss of a language is termed "language death." Among the many factors responsible for language shift and death are religious and educational background, settlement patterns, ties with the homeland (in the case of immigrant bilingualism), extent of exogamous marriage, attitudes of majority and minority language groups, government policies concerning language and education, etc. While each of these factors may be implicated in shift and death, they do not entirely determine the fate of a language.

Where large groups of immigrants concentrate in particular geographical areas, they are often better able to preserve their languages, e.g. third generation Chinese Americans who reside in China-towns have shifted less towards English than their age mates outside China-towns. Often a shift from rural to urban areas triggers a language shift. For example, in Papua New Guinea, where Tok Pisin is the language most used in the towns, many children grow up not speaking their parents' vernacular languages. When a language serves important religious functions, as German does among the Pennsylvania Dutch, it may stand a better chance of survival.

The inability of minorities to maintain the home as an intact domain for the use of their language has often been decisive for language shift. There is a high rate of loss in mixed marriages, e.g. in Wales, where if Welsh is not the language of the home, the onus for transmission is shifted to the school. Identification with a language and positive attitudes towards it cannot guarantee its maintenance. In Ireland the necessity of using English has overpowered antipathy towards English and English speakers. In some cases speakers may be forbidden to use their language altogether, e.g. the Kurds in Turkey. In a community whose language is under threat, it is difficult for children to acquire the language fully.

Languages undergoing shift often display characteristic types of changes such as simplification of complex grammatical structures. These changes are often the result of decreased use of the language in certain contexts which may lead to a loss of stylistic options. In some Native American Indian languages of the southwestern United States complex syntactic structures have become less frequent because the formal and poetic styles of language are no longer used. The degree of linguistic assimilation may serve as an index of social assimilation of a group. It depends on many factors such as receptiveness of the group to the other culture and language, possibility of acceptance by the dominant group, degree of similarity between the two groups, etc. Albanian speakers who emigrated to Greece have more readily given up their language and assimilated than have Albanian speakers in Italy, where attitudes towards diversity are more favorable.

There is no doubt that absence of schooling in one's own language can make maintenance difficult. In a study done of 46 linguistic minorities in 14 European countries, the clearest link to emerge between language and schooling is that a minority language which is not taught tends to decline (see Allardt 1979). Studies of language shift have shown time and time again that schools are a major agent of cultural and linguistic assimilation. Formal education is often the first point of contact children have with the world outside their own community.

English schools were destructive to Dyirbal-speaking children in Aboriginal Australia for several reasons. The very fact that Dyirbal has no presence in the school is a signal that it is seen as a useless language. Schools also provide a major context for the use of English and exposure to English-speaking children. By being immersed into a totally English environment, the Dyirbal child is denied the opportunity of learning in Dyirbal. An educational program of this type is called "submersion" because the child's native language is suppressed or ignored and the children have to sink or swim in a completely different language environment. The aim of such programs is cultural and linguistic assimilation.

In many parts of the world today children are not taught enough of their own language and culture to appreciate it. They become caught in a vicious circle. Because the school fails to support the home language, skills in it are often poor. The failure of the school to let children develop further in their own language is then used to legitimize further oppression of it. At the same time they do not progress in the majority language (often for reasons that have nothing to do with language, but which reflect the poorer socio-economic status of the minority in relation to the majority). The economic returns from schooling are greater for those who are advantaged to begin with.

As a European example, we can take the case of older Sami people in Finland who have been indoctrinated by the school system into believing that the speaking of Sami even at home weakens their children's knowledge of Finnish (Aikio 1984). Uninformed officials in school and health care continue to dispense such advice and are also likely to condemn language mixing and codeswitching as harmful to the child's development. The research evidence shows otherwise, but most of the so-called experts who offer such advice are monolinguals and think of bilingualism as a problem in need of remediation because they are unaware of the realities of normal bilingual development. Beliefs about bilingualism causing stuttering and delayed onset of language are also widespread, despite lack of evidence for them.

Results from so-called immersion programs which aim at enriching children's skills in another language without threat to the language they already know have been very positive in many parts of the world. In Hawaii, for instance, after 80 years of neglect and decline in the native Hawaiian-speaking population, a program of Hawaiian immersion preschools was set up in 1984 called Pu:nana Leo ("language nest"), modeled on a similar program for Maori immersion in New Zealand. This was the first indigenous language immersion program in the USA. At that time there were fewer than 1,000 Hawaiians in the state speaking the language. Fewer than 30 of those were under 18. Immersion education was subsequently extended vertically rather than horizontally in order not to lose any students. The program was introduced into two elementary schools in 1987.

An outside evaluation commissioned by the state's Department of Education concluded that the schools' instruction in Hawaiian had been successful on a number of grounds (Slaughter and Watson-Gegeo 1988). It had been conducted with no apparent loss to the children's English language skills. Parental support and involvement were also exceptionally high. The program has since been expanded to secondary education in 1995. Despite the lack of a library, science lab, and a range of course offerings in the new intermediate / high school program equivalent to what is found at the English-medium high school, each student scored above the statewide average on college admission tests.

However, school is only one and probably not the most important of all the societal institutions that contribute to and are responsible for language acquisition and maintenance. It would be wrong to leave the picture unduly rosy.

Provision of schooling in a minority language will not automatically safeguard its future. While it may seem a great opportunity for children to be schooled in their own language, such schools may attract adverse criticism if financed from tax funding of the majority's government, particularly under times of economic hardship. This is what we are seeing now in Hawaii, where immersion in Hawaiian is supported as part of the state's education budget. This is why Fishman (1991) argues that language maintenance efforts must begin in the community itself through voluntary efforts and be financed through community resources in the early stages. Nowhere have language movements succeeded if they expected the school or state to carry the primary burden of maintenance or revival.

That is not to absolve the state of responsibility, but financial aid comes at a price. Dependence on state resources undermines the minority's responsibility and right to control its own affairs. The greatest danger posed to Maori language revitalization in New Zealand is that in the name of equity and biculturalism the Maori language may be removed from control of the Maori people, and that proficient Maori speakers may be predominantly Pakeha (i.e. Europeans) in both ethnicity and ancestry. A similar phenomenon has affected the struggle for education in Sami in Finland. Even outsiders obtain qualifications in the language more easily than insiders and as a consequence Sami people are afraid of using their own language because only a few are deemed to be qualified (Aikio 1984).

In so far as a minority language represents an alternative point of view, which is potentially in conflict with that of the dominant culture, bilingual education may represent a threat to the powers that be. It is no accident that minority groups who have retained control over their schooling such as the old order Amish in Pennsylvania have shown greater language maintenance than those who have not.

6 The Changing Face of Multilingualism in the Modern World

Two patterns deserve comment in relation to the changing character of multilingualism in the world today. One is increasing bilingualism in a metropolitan language, particularly English. Many smaller languages are dying out due to the spread of a few world languages such as English, French, Spanish, Chinese, etc. It has been estimated that 11 languages are spoken by about 70 percent of the world's population. In this respect, the majority of the world's languages are minority languages. The second is increasing linguistic and cultural diversity in parts of Europe and the USA through continuing and new waves of immigration.

These two processes represent a struggle between increasing internationalization, cultural and linguistic homogenization (Coca Colonization, as it has sometimes been referred to) vs. diversification. There is a clash of values inherent in the struggle between the global and local, between uniformity and diversity. The language of McWorld is English: not to use it is to risk ostracization from the benefits of the global economy. It is for this reason that many developing countries opted to use the language of their former colonizers rather than try to develop their own language(s). Using English or French in Africa seems to be cheaper than multilingualism. Such utilitarian methods of accounting do not, of course, factor in the social cost of effectively disenfranchising the majority of citizens who do not know English or French in many Third World nations where these are the official languages. Such policies lead to cultural poverty when linguistic diversity is lost. When large portions of the population are denied forms of self-expression, the nation's political and social foundations are weakened. A nation that incorporates cultural and linguistic diversity is also richer than one which denies their existence. It can easily be shown that denying people the right to their own language and culture does not provide a workable solution either.

Ethnicity also grows stronger when actively denied, oppressed, or repressed. Throughout its 74 years of existence Yugoslavia was a powder keg of ethnic rivalries which go back centuries. The country that has been dissolving these past few years was an artificial creation of conflicting cultures held in check by a centralized Communist government until 1980. Once the old regime crumbled, historical tensions could surface leading to the unraveling of the country. The virtual collapse of the economies of the former Soviet bloc countries has shown the difficulties of centralized planning which rides roughshod over the regional and ethnic affiliations.

As far as the trend towards increasing diversity as a result of new immigration is concerned, in the European Union, for instance, 10 percent of the school age population already have a culture and language different from that of the majority of the country in which they reside. This figure naturally obscures wide variation among member states. In The Netherlands, for instance, Extra and Verhoeven (1993: 72) say that the influx of ethnic minority children in elementary schools in the four largest cities is presently about 40 percent and will increase to more than 50 percent in the early twenty-first century. As far as the future demography of the European Community as a whole is concerned, Extra and Verhoeven (forthcoming) state that by the early decades of the twenty-first century one-third of the urban population under the age of 35 will be composed of ethnic minorities.

Australia has also experienced a dramatic shift in its ethnic composition since World War II when its population was 99 percent white and almost entirely English-speaking. The population grew from seven million people of almost entirely British and Irish origin to eighteen million people, nearly a quarter of whom were born overseas and are non-English speaking. Some 75 to 100 immigrant languages are now spoken in Australia (see Romaine 1991).

In the US the projections for increasing diversity in the next century indicate that Hispanics alone may comprise over 30 percent of the total population. If we calculate the long-range social and economic cost of continuing the present pattern of undereducating these minority children in Europe and the US, the results are enormous. It is these children who will become the majority and upon whom the economic burden will fall of caring for the next generation of children and the previous generation soon to be retirees. At the same time the highly developed technological economies in Europe and the US will require an increasingly highly educated workforce. New member states in the European Union are almost certain to bring with them their own unresolved language problems and tensions between majority and minorities. Thus, conflicts will increase rather than decrease.

In most parts of the world there is little enthusiasm for the languages of immigrant minorities, even when the language concerned is a world language such as Spanish (as is the case in the US) or Arabic (as is the case in France and The Netherlands). This is due to status differences between the majority and minority populations. Distinctive food, dress, song, etc., are often accepted and allowed to be part of the mainstream, but language seldom is. Another irony in the resistance to providing support in the form of home language instruction to immigrant pupils is that opposition to it in the US has occurred side by side with increasing concern over the lack of competence in foreign languages. Thus, while foreign language instruction in the world's major languages in mainstream schools has been seen as valuable, both economically and culturally, bilingual education for minority students has been equated with poverty, and loyalties to non-mainstream culture which threaten the cohesiveness of the state.

7   Conclusions

Multilingualism is shaped in different ways depending on a variety of social and other factors which must be taken into account when trying to assess the skills of speakers and how speakers use the languages they know. It is possible for a bilingual to be fluent in both languages taken together without being able to function completely like a monolingual in either one on its own. The study of the behavior of multilingual individuals and societies thus requires us to go beyond many of the concepts and analytical techniques presently used within linguistic theory which are designed for the description of monolingual.

There is no evidence to indicate that multilingualism is an inherently problematic mode of organization, either for a society or for an individual. Because languages and dialects are often potent symbols of class, gender, ethnic, and other kinds of differentiation, it is easy to think that language underlies conflict in multilingual societies. Yet disputes involving language are really not about language, but instead about fundamental inequalities between groups who happen to speak different languages.

22 Natural Sign Languages

WENDY SANDLER and
DIANE LILLO-MARTIN

It has been some forty years since serious investigation of natural sign languages began to show that these languages are bona fide linguistic systems, with structures and rules and the full range of expressive power that characterize spoken languages. Researchers have spent most of that time demonstrating, with increasing rigor and formality, the sometimes surprising similarities between languages in the two modalities, spoken and signed. Concomitantly, scholars in the related disciplines of language acquisition and neurolinguistics have been discovering significant similarities between spoken and signed languages in these domains as well. It is safe to say that the academic world is now convinced that sign languages are real languages in every sense of the term.

If this were the whole story, however, there would be no need for a chapter on sign languages in this volume. Each sign language would be seen as a language like any other, English, Hungarian, Central Alaskan Yupik Eskimo, or Mandarin Chinese, each with its own contribution to make toward understanding the general language faculty of humans. But this is not the whole story. Rather, sign languages as a group are of special importance, crucial to our understanding of the essential nature of language, for two reasons. First, the study of natural languages in a different physical modality confirms in a novel way the hypothesis that all natural human languages are characterized by certain nontrivial and identifiable properties. And second, this study raises fundamental questions about the human language capacity, as well as challenges for language theory, that we would never have noticed were it not for the existence of sign languages.

Sign language research has already made a significant contribution to our understanding of human language – its structure; its acquisition by children; its representation in the brain; and its extension beyond communication, in poetry – all of which we survey in this chapter. But the survey would be incomplete without considering the *potential* contribution to be made by the investigation of sign languages in the future. Most importantly, we expect future studies to allow researchers to delve into the second issue we've mentioned above – questions and challenges for the theory of human language that sign languages bring to the fore. For example, it appears that, while the individual structural properties of sign languages are attested in spoken languages, no spoken language has the same *clustering* of properties that characterizes sign languages. Furthermore, despite the fact that vocabularies differ from sign language to sign language, their grammatical *structures* seem to be remarkably similar to each other. Recent neurological studies of the language-brain map indicate some differences in brain mediation of spoken and signed languages, posing another challenge. Developing an explanation for these observations will require language theorists to move well beyond the ideas generated by the study of spoken language alone.

The sign languages under discussion are the languages used by communities of deaf people all over the world. They are natural languages, in the sense that they are not consciously invented by anyone, but, rather, develop spontaneously wherever deaf people have an opportunity to congregate and communicate regularly with each other. Sign languages are not derived from spoken languages; they have their own independent vocabularies and their own grammatical structures. Although there do exist contrived sign systems that are based on spoken languages (such as Signed English, Signed Hebrew, etc.), such systems are not natural languages, and they are not the object of interest here. Rather, linguists and cognitive psychologists are most interested in the natural sign languages passed down without instruction from one deaf generation to the next, and used by deaf people in their own communities all over the world.

Sign languages exhibit the full range of expression that spoken languages afford their users. Different styles are adopted for different social contexts; storytelling has been heightened to an art in some deaf communities; deaf poets create artistic poetry in signs, marshaling the formational elements of the languages to convey images, emotions, and ideas. Sign language can "do" everything that spoken language can. We now turn to an examination of how it does so.[1]

1 Linguistic Structure of Sign Languages

We begin by offering a sketch of the evidence that sign languages have grammatical structures comparable to those of spoken languages.[2] First we examine the structure of the sentence (syntax), and then we move to the structure of the smaller units of language, those that may be compared to the meaningless but identifiable sounds of speech (phonology). We will end this section with a discussion of the structure of words (morphology).[3]

1.1 Sentence structure: Syntax

One of the fundamental properties of human language is that it can be used to create an unlimited number of utterances given a limited number of pieces. At the syntactic level, this property follows directly from a mathematical property of language called recursiveness. We're all familiar with recursiveness (even if not with the term). It is found in language, and computer programs, and even in children's stories, as in (1).

(1)   This is the farmer sowing the corn,
        That kept the cock that crowed in the morn,
        That waked the priest all shaven and shorn,
        That married the man all tattered and torn,
        That kissed the maiden all forlorn,
        That milked the cow with the crumpled horn,
        That tossed the dog,
        That worried the cat,
        That killed the rat,
        That ate the malt,
        That lay in the house that Jack built.

In (1), the process or rule that creates a relative clause (here, the clauses beginning with *that*) has applied repeatedly to the noun phrases inside other relative clauses. This repeated application of the same rule to create more and more complex sentences is an example of recursiveness. The children's story is amusing precisely because we all know that there is no theoretical limit to the application of this rule. Any speaker of English can add to the story by generating another relative clause at the beginning, as in (2).

(2)   This is the banker, his honor forsworn
        That foreclosed on the farmer sowing the corn . . .

The only limitations on the number of relative clauses are practical and not linguistic: the speaker may run out of things to say, or out of breath, or time, or memory. It is because the rules of syntax are allowed to apply recursively that language is non-finite: there is no limit to its expressive power. It is important that this recursiveness applies to create structures which are *embedded* inside other structures, to create subordinate clauses, such as the *that* relative clauses in (2). These embedded subordinate clauses involve more complex structure than coordinate clauses, which are illustrated in (3).

(3)   This is the dog, and the dog worried the cat, and the cat killed the rat, and the rat ate the malt, and the malt lay in the house and Jack built the house.

Embedding distinguishes subordinate clauses of the sort exemplified by *The House that Jack Built* from simple coordination. A simplified diagram of the structure of recursive subordinate versus coordinate clauses is given in figure 22.1. The rule that makes a relative clause – put a sentence inside a noun phrase

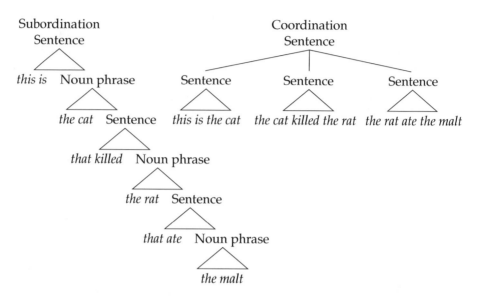

Figure 22.1 Simplified phrase structure diagrams of subordination and coordination

– produces a structure in which one sentence is inside another sentence. This is the key to recursion: by putting one phrase inside another of the same type, there is in principle no limit to the length of a sentence.

Human language is not limited to simple conjunction of one phrase after another (like that in (3)); it has both coordination and subordination. If someone found a human language that allowed only coordination, not subordination, this would shake our fundamental assumptions about what human language is. Thus, it should be rather surprising that exactly this was claimed about ASL in the early days of its study. Thompson (1977) attempted to discover the mechanisms for subordination in ASL, and, not finding what he considered to be evidence for it, decided that it was systematically missing. If this is correct, then either the character and structure of human language is not as has been commonly assumed, or signed languages are significantly different from spoken languages, missing recursivity, which is often taken to be a defining property of language.

Later research has made it unnecessary to choose between these two puzzling options. Liddell (1980) argued convincingly that Thompson's claim was incorrect, and Liddell's analysis has been substantiated by many researchers since.

Thompson had looked for several kinds of indications that ASL has subordination. For example, he looked for overt complementizers – an analog to English *that* in "I know that Susan will win" – and found none in ASL. He looked for relative clauses (like those in (1–2)) – and instead found sequences of signs as in (4).[4]

(4)   English Target: The girl Asa gave the dog to is pretty.
      ASL response: ASA GIVE DOG GIRL IND PRETTY IND
      [roughly: Asa gave the dog to the girl and she is pretty.]

He looked for clausal complements to adjectives like "happy" (cf. "He's happy that she passed.") and found instead unembedded sequences, as in (5).

(5)   English Target: I regret that Asa had to leave.
      ASL response: MUST ASA MUST GO / SORRY
      [roughly: Asa must go. I'm sorry.]

In some ways, these and other observations of Thompson's were correct. However, his conclusion that ASL had no grammatical means of embedding to create subordinate clauses was shown to be wrong. Liddell noticed that relative clauses are indeed grammatically marked in ASL, contrary to Thompson's claims – not by function words such as *that*, but by *non-manual* grammatical markers.

Liddell identified the non-manual marker of relative clauses as consisting of raised brows, a backward head tilt, and a tensed upper lip. This non-manual marker co-occurs with the material of the relative clause. In addition, Liddell argued that relative clauses in ASL are not like those of English. In particular, he showed that the noun that is modified by the relative clause occurs inside the clause in ASL, as in spoken languages like Diegueño, rather than outside it as in English. While in English the subordinating word *that* indicates a relative clause, in ASL the nonmanual markers that extend over the clause perform essentially the same role. A comparison of these aspects of relative clauses in ASL and English can be observed in (6).

(6)   a.   English relative clause: modified noun (underlined) outside the relative clause; relative marker *that*
           The dog that chased the cat came home.
      b.   ASL relative clause: modified noun (underlined) inside the relative clause; nonmanual relative marker, "rc."

$$\overline{\hspace{6cm}}^{\text{rc}}$$
RECENTLY $_a$DOG CHASE $_b$CAT $_a$COME HOME.

In the notation, the line marked "rc" indicates the scope of the relative clause non-manual marker. The lower case subscripts are indices for DOG and CAT. The "a" index on DOG and COME is expressed formationally in the language, indicating that it was the dog and not the cat that came home.

Clearly, the reason why Thompson thought ASL has no relative clauses was that he expected them to look more like English. However, once the characteristics of relative clauses in languages other than English are considered, it becomes clear that ASL does have relative clauses, formed by a rule of subordination that allows recursion.

Since Liddell's counterarguments to these and other claims of Thompson's appeared, other researchers have provided additional evidence for subordination in ASL (see especially chapter 3 in Padden 1988, which provides syntactic tests that differentiate embedded from main clauses), and all current work assumes it.

A controversy over word order properties in ASL was similarly resolved by more careful analysis, and by looking beyond English. Since basic word order is very flexible in ASL, some early researchers argued that only pragmatic considerations, such as emphasis of some part of the sentence, and not linguistic structure, dictate word order in ASL sentences – that there are no syntactic rules for ordering words. However, since then, many researchers have collected evidence to support the point of view that ASL – like Japanese, Russian, and other spoken languages which allow for relative flexibility in surface word order – has an underlying structure and word order (in the case of ASL, Subject-Verb-Object), which can be modified by rules of the grammar. Here too, most researchers now assume the basic order argued for in these works, and current work concentrates on the rules and principles which generate this order and its many variants.

Using the tools of linguistic analysis, it is possible to go much beyond the observation that ASL has recursion and subordination and a basic word order. Of crucial concern is whether or not ASL adheres to constraints hypothesized by proponents of the Universal Grammar hypothesis to characterize all languages. According to this hypothesis, the decisive constraints are those which are found to be operative across languages, but for which overt evidence in the linguistic environment does not seem to be available. If some knowledge which adults are shown to possess is not accessible to the language learner, it is hypothesized to be in some sense part of the innately determined universal human language capacity. For example, consider the paradigm in (7).

(7) a. Steve likes beer with pizza.
     b. What does Steve like beer with?
     c. Yoav likes wine and cheese.
     d. *What does Yoav like wine and?

Although the relationship between (7a) and (7b) is very similar to the relationship between (7c) and (7d), only the first pair are both grammatical. Making a question out of the noun phrase following a preposition is (usually) grammatical in (colloquial) English, but making a question out of a noun phrase which is coordinated with another noun phrase is not. In fact, the restriction on questions like (7d), which disallows extraction of material out of a coordinated structure, is virtually universal, and it has been proposed that a general universal constraint – the Coordinate Structure Constraint – prohibits it.

Whether or not one accepts the hypothesis that such constraints are innately specified, the fact that they are not easily deducible from the input but appear to be ubiquitous in spoken languages makes them key exemplars of the human language capacity. It is therefore important to determine whether or not they hold for sign languages as well. If so, we may conclude that the constraints are truly universal, and that sign languages have the same properties as any other natural language. In fact, several researchers have argued that this is the case.

The Coordinate Structure Constraint demonstrated in (7) provides the clearest example. Padden (1988) shows that coordinate structures are allowed in ASL, as illustrated in (8).

(8) $_i$INDEX $_i$GIVE$_1$ MONEY, $_j$INDEX $_j$GIVE$_1$ FLOWERS
     "He gave me money but she gave me flowers."

Furthermore, as expected, ASL, like English, clearly prohibits violations of the Coordinate Structure Constraint, as illustrated in (9). The "t" on the line over FLOWER in (9) indicates a nonmanual marker for topicalization, the process by which the topic, FLOWER, is extracted and moved out of the coordinated structure, to the beginning of the sentence.

$$\overline{\hspace{3.5cm}\text{t}}$$

(9) *FLOWER, $_2$GIVE$_1$ MONEY, $_j$GIVE$_1$
     "Flowers, he gave me money but she gave me."

In several domains of syntax, the constraints proposed to be universal (including the Coordinate Structure Constraint) can be demonstrated to apply to ASL as well as to spoken languages – and it is expected that other signed languages will also show adherence to these constraints.

1.2 The structure of sounds and their sign language equivalents: Phonology

In order to have sentences, one must have words, and words – at least in spoken language – are pronounced as a series of sounds. What about the sign of sign language? Does it have a level of substructure like the spoken word? Since spoken and signed languages are produced and perceived by different physical systems – oral / aural, and manual / visual – one might expect to find the least amount of similarity across the two modalities at this level of analysis. Yet, here, too, there is much common ground.

In 1960, William Stokoe published a monograph in which he demonstrated that the words of American Sign Language are not holistic gestures, but, rather, are analyzable as a combination of three meaningless yet linguistically significant categories: handshapes, locations, and movements. That is, by changing some feature of any one of those three categories, themselves meaningless, one could change the meaning of the sign. For example, by changing only the configuration of the hand, the signs DECIDE and PERSON are distinguished. In these two signs, the locations and movements are the same. Only the hand

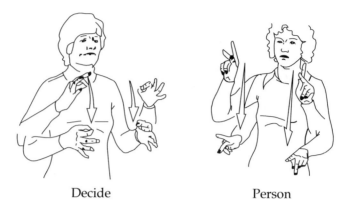

Decide   Person

Figure 22.2   ASL minimal pair
Source: Reprinted with permission from *A Basic Course in American Sign Language, Second Edition*, 1994, T. J. Publishers, Inc., Silver Spring, MD 20910, USA

configuration is different. Similar pairs exist that are distinguished only by their locations or only by their movements.

The example in figure 22.2 is analogous to the English pair, *pan, tan,* in which the first sound of each word – *p* and *t* – is different. The sounds are themselves meaningless, but they are linguistically significant because they make a difference in meaning when put in a word. In the sign language pair, DECIDE, PERSON, the hand configurations are also meaningless, yet they too make a difference in meaning. The other formational elements – locations and movements – can, like hand configurations, independently make a difference in meaning, though they are themselves meaningless.

This finding was of supreme importance. Ever since its discovery, it has no longer been possible to assume, as most people previously had, that signs are fundamentally different from spoken words, that they are simple iconic gestures with no substructure. Rather, Stokoe showed that ASL is characterized by a defining feature of language in general: duality of patterning. This duality is between the meaningful level (consisting of morphemes, words, phrases, sentences), and the meaningless level, which in spoken languages is the level of the sounds that make up the meaningful expressions. The meaningless elements of spoken language are linguistically significant (i.e., they independently make a difference in meaning); they obey constraints on their combination within morphemes and words; and they may be systematically altered in different contexts. This is the domain of phonology. The list of handshapes, locations, and movements are the formational elements of sign language phonology, comparable to the list of consonants and vowels in spoken language. We will now show that sign language phonology is also characterized by constraints on the combination of these elements, and by systematic changes in "pronunciation" according to context.

All languages have constraints on the cooccurrence of sounds in syllables and words. For example, English does not allow the sequences **sr* or **chl* at the

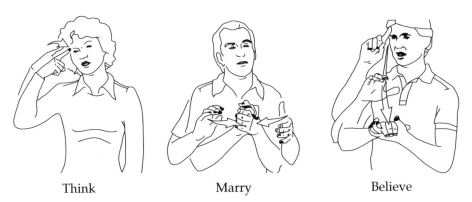

Think	Marry	Believe

Figure 22.3 ASL signs THINK and MARRY, and the compound BELIEVE with orientation assimilation
Source: Reprinted with permission from *A Basic Course in American Sign Language, Second Edition*, 1994, T. J. Publishers, Inc., Silver Spring, MD 20910, USA

beginning of a syllable or word (although other languages do permit such combinations). Sign languages as well have constraints on the combination of elements at this same level of structure. For example, only one group of fingers may characterize the handshape within any sign. While either the finger group 5 (all fingers) or the group V (index plus middle finger) may occur in a sign, a sequence of the two shapes, *5-V is prohibited in the native signs of ASL and other sign languages.

Similarly, all languages have assimilation processes, in which sounds borrow some or all aspects of neighboring sounds. For example, in the English compound words, *greenback* and *beanbag,* the sound [n] often borrows (assimilates) the place of articulation "lips" from the [b] that follows it: *gree[m]back, bea[m]bag*. In many common ASL compounds, part of the hand configuration may similarly assimilate from one part of the compound to the other. The example here (figure 22.3) is from the compound which means BELIEVE, made from the two words THINK and MARRY. Just as the [n] borrowed one of the features of [b] (the "lip" feature) in the English example above, in the ASL compound, the hand configuration of THINK borrows a feature from the following sign in the compound, MARRY. It borrows the orientation feature. That is, rather than being oriented toward the head as in the citation form of THINK, the dominant, signing hand in the compound BELIEVE is oriented toward the palm of the other hand, as in the sign, MARRY.[5]

The phonology of sign languages has been shown to be similar to that of spoken languages at even more surprising levels of analysis. For example, it has been demonstrated that the phonological elements of ASL words are not all simultaneously organized as Stokoe had claimed, but rather have significant sequential structure, just as spoken languages have one sound after another. A sign language equivalent of the syllable has even been argued for.[6]

An aspect of language structure that involves both phonology and syntax is prosody. Prosody involves rhythm, to separate the parts of a sentence;

Yes / no question   Shared information

Figure 22.4   ISL yes / no question and "shared information" facial expressions

prominence, to emphasize selected elements; and intonation, to communicate other important information, such as the discourse function of the sentence, e.g., whether an utterance is a plain declarative sentence or a question. Recent work argues that sign languages have the equivalent of prosody.[7] While spoken languages use the rise and fall of the pitch of the voice, volume, and pause to achieve these effects, sign languages employ facial expressions, body postures, and rhythmic devices in similar ways and for similar functions.[8] Examples are the Israeli Sign Language facial expressions for yes / no questions, and for information assumed to be shared by the signer and addressee,[9] shown in figure 22.4.

Sign language facial "intonation" is *different* from the facial expressions used by hearing people in their communication, which are affective and not mandatory or systematic. Rather, sign language facial expressions are like the intonational pitch patterns of spoken language. Both tonal melodies and facial melodies are *grammaticalized*, i.e., fixed and systematic. For example, the intonational melody used in spoken language to ask a question requiring an answer of "yes" or "no" is systematically different from the one used to make a declarative statement. The same is true of the facial intonations for these two types of sentences in sign language.

In the next subsection, what is perhaps the most central aspect of language is examined: the word.

1.3   Word structure: morphology

Most languages have both simple words, such as *teach*, and complex words, such as *teach+er*. Knowing English entails understanding the internal structure of its complex words, as well as the ability to create and understand new complex words that exploit those same kinds of internal structures. The study of the internal structure of words is called morphology.

For example, given a new verb *scaff*, as in *The purpose of this machine is to scaff computers against viruses*, we can also create or analyze the internal structure of the word *scaffer* and can deduce something about its meaning in the sentence, *The company purchased several expensive scaffers last year*. We would also immediately judge the nonce word **er+scaff* to be impossible in English. Speakers of English know the form and function of the meaningful word component-*er*, and they know that it is a suffix rather than a prefix. Although users of a language are usually not conscious of their linguistic knowledge, their use of language clearly reveals the existence of this underlying system.

Another type of complex word formation can be thought of as relating words to each other within a sentence. For example, the word *walk* has two different suffixes in the following sentences, *-s*, and *-ed*. The *-s* in sentence (10a) is an agreement marker; it shows that the subject of the sentence, *Hadar*, is third person singular ("he" or "she"). The *-ed* in sentence (10b) is a tense marker, showing that the event described by the sentence took place in the past.

(10)   a.   Hadar walks to school sometimes.
       b.   Stephanie walked to her friend's house.

The existence of complexity of structure within words is a typical property of spoken language, though many different kinds of word formation can be found in the languages of the world. Most languages have complex words, and many languages have far more complex morphology than English has.

What about sign languages? While one might expect any communication system to have syntax, one might not necessarily expect sign languages to have internal structure to their words. Rather, one might expect, as naive early descriptions of sign language used to claim, that signs are holistic gestures, each one representing a unitary concept. Concomitant with this view is the belief that the vocabulary of sign languages is purely iconic, that there is a one-to-one relationship between the form of a word or concept and its meaning. The ASL sign for AIRPLANE looks something like an airplane; the sign for GIVE looks something like the act of handing something to someone. If these sign words are iconic wholes, then adding grammatical complexity to them in a systematic way might seem counterintuitive.

Yet sign languages do have a great deal of morphological complexity. Such complexity is one of many sources of evidence that systematic grammatical structuring strongly dominates the presumably iconic origins of these languages. We will describe two kinds of word complexity here: verb agreement and verbs of motion and location.

We begin with verb agreement. In many spoken languages, verbs have some kind of marking on them that gives information about their subjects, objects,

"I look at you."   "You look at me."   "I look at you (plural)."

Figure 22.5   ISL verb agreement

or other nouns directly related to them in the sentence. Example (10a) above shows the only agreement marker that English has on main verbs, the -s which indicates third person and singular in the present tense. Other languages have far richer agreement systems. For example, Swahili has both subject and object agreement markers that indicate person ("I," "you," "s/he"), gender ("he" or "she"), and number (singular or plural):

(11)   Swahili
    a. `a –   ta –   ku –   penda
        he (subj) future you (obj) like
        atakupenda – "he will like you"
    b. u   –   ta –   m   –   penda
        you (subj) future him (obj) like
        utampenda "you will like him"

All sign languages investigated so far show a comparable kind of verb agreement. Consider for example the Israeli Sign Language verb LOOK-AT, shown in figure 22.5. To say "I look at you," the motion of the sign is from a point near the signer toward the addressee. To say "you look at me," the beginning and endpoints of the sign are just the opposite, beginning at a point near the addressee, and ending near the signer. The beginning and endpoints of the sign are markers for the subject and object of the verb it represents. To say, "I look at you (plural)," the hand moves in a horizontal arc in front of the signer.

In the first example, "I look at you," the first position of the hand corresponds to the prefix *a* in the Swahili example in (11) above: it marks agreement with the person of the verb's subject – third person ("he") in the Swahili example, and first person ("I") in the ISL example. The second position of the hand corresponds to the morpheme *ku* in the same Swahili example, agreeing with the person of the object of the verb – second person ("you") in Swahili, and second person also in ISL. The beginning and endpoints of the second example in figure 22.5 similarly mark agreement with subject and object – here, "you" and "me." To agree with the second person plural – "I look at you (plural)" – the shape of the movement is altered.

This kind of phenomenon can be described as subject-object agreement; in particular, sign language verbs agree for person and number of their subject and object. In this way, the verb agreement found in sign languages is similar to that in many spoken languages.

A characteristic of verb agreement systems in sign languages is that different categories of verbs participate in this system in different ways. For example, in addition to the subject-object agreement described earlier, some verbs, commonly called backwards verbs, have the opposite agreement pattern of the one shown above. In these verbs, the movement of the hand is from the object to the subject, instead of the usual direction from subject to object. This class includes verbs such as INVITE, TAKE, COPY, ADOPT, essentially the same list in ASL and ISL, and possibly in all sign languages. Other verbs agree with points in space denoting specific locations, rather than with the verb's subject and object. Still others do not agree at all. We will have more to say about the peculiarities of sign language agreement and possible implications for language theory in section 3.

A more complex type of morphology in sign languages is found in verbs of motion and location, first described by T. Supalla (e.g. 1986). In these constructions, handshapes that stand for classes of nouns combine with types of movements and with locations in space. As such, these complex forms differ from the morphologically simple signs of the language exemplified in the phonology subsection above.

As an aid to interpreting these forms, which have no analog in English, let us consider some words in the native American language, Navaho. This language incorporates into the stems of verbs of motion and location the shape and dimensionality of associated objects, as shown in the following examples.[10] The hyphens show that what are separate words in English are not independent words in these other languages. Rather they are morphemes, like -*er* in English, which combine with words or parts of words to form a new, complex word.

(12) Navaho
   a. beeso si-?a
       money be-located-of-round-entity
       "A coin is lying (there)."
   b. beeso si-ltsooz
       money be-located-of-flat-flexible-entity
       "A bill is lying (there)."
   c. beeso si-nil
       money be-located-of-collection
       "A pile of change is lying (there)."

In these constructions, *beeso* means "money" the prefix *si-* is a perfective marker, and the verb stems *?a*, *ltsooz*, and *nil* incorporate the shape and dimensionality of the entity involved.[11]

ASL (and other sign languages) has a comparable – if potentially more complex – system of verbs of motion and location. As in Navaho, each of the meaningful ASL morphemes is taken from a finite list that is determined by the lexicon and grammar of the language. In ASL, there is a list of noun "classifiers," that represent semantic classes such as "small animals," "humans," or "vehicles." Each of these classifiers is represented by a different handshape. Another type of classifier, also represented by different handshapes, specifies the size and shape of an object, such as "cylindrical objects," "flat objects," or "small round objects." These handshapes may combine, in compliance with constraints of the grammar, with one of a short list of motion morphemes (e.g., "straight," "pivot"), location morphemes, and manner of movement morphemes, each with a meaning of its own.

(13)   ASL
    a.   MONEY SMALL-ROUND-SHAPE-BE-LOCATED
         "A coin is lying there."
    b.   MONEY FLAT-WIDE-SHAPE-BE-LOCATED
         "A bill is lying there."
    c.   MONEY DOME-SHAPE-BE-LOCATED
         "A pile of change is lying there."

Figure 22.6 exemplifies just the first of these. The shape of the hand is the morpheme meaning "small round object." The short, downward motion means "be located," and the location refers to a particular reference point in the discourse.

"A coin is lying there."

Figure 22.6   ASL verb of motion and location

It is very important to note that these forms are linguistic entities, i.e., morphologically complex words. They are neither pantomime nor otherwise strictly analogic to real world things and activities. Furthermore, this type of morphology, which incorporates nouns, verbs, and other lexical categories into single words, is not uncommon in the world's spoken languages. As we have seen, there are even spoken languages such as Navaho that incorporate into verbs the shape and dimensionality of associated nouns, as sign languages do.

Constructions of this sort in ASL can become far more complex than the example in figure 22.6. For example, the two hands may each represent an independent classifier to create such forms as SMALL-ROUND-OBJECT-LYING-ON-FLAT-OBJECT ("A coin is lying on the table").[12] Manner of movement morphemes can add still more complexity, forming, for example, expressions meaning roughly, SMALL-ROUND-OBJECT-TRAVERSES-ARC-TO-ON-FLAT-OBJECT – "A coin flew in an arc shaped path, landing on the table." Such structures have the form of single words, though extremely complex ones.

All the ordinary words that make up the vocabulary of sign languages, words such as DECIDE and PERSON in figure 22.2 in the previous subsection, are thus different from the verbs of motion and location described here. To understand this, compare DECIDE, repeated in figure 22.7a. with "A coin is lying there," repeated in 22.7b. These two words are formationally very similar (except that DECIDE is two-handed), yet they are very different in their composition. Only 22.7b SMALL-ROUND-SHAPE-BE-LOCATED ("A coin is lying there") is decomposable: handshapes, locations, and movements each have meanings.

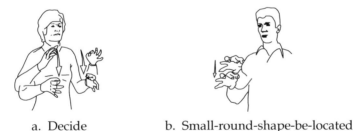

a. Decide   b. Small-round-shape-be-located

Figure 22.7 ASL monomorphemic and multimorphemic signs
Source: Reprinted with permission from *A Basic Course in American Sign Language, Second Edition*, 1994, T. J. Publishers, Inc., Silver Spring, MD 20910, USA

The properties we have described at each level of grammatical structure – syntax, phonology, and morphology – provide strong evidence that certain basic characteristics of language are indeed universal, belonging to language in either of the two natural modalities available to humans.

2 Language as an Art Form: Sign Language Poetry

Poetry takes language far beyond its primary task of everyday communication. By artfully manipulating the forms and meanings of language, the poet conveys a particular or heightened understanding of human experience. Devices such as meter, rhyme, and alliteration may filter the meaningful content of a poem, in order to create an impression or focus an image in the mind of the audience. A conventional meaning may be intentionally distorted in such a way as to enhance the perspective the poet wishes to present.

This union of language, culture, and art is found in some signing communities. We know of several accomplished deaf poets in the United States and Holland, and bring as an example of sign language poetry some work of Wim Emmerik from Amsterdam.[13]

Among the devices used by this poet are reiterative use of handshape, and a fluidity of style that results from the elimination of transitional movements. Entire poems may be characterized by one or two basic handshapes, such as the extended index finger handshape or the shape that extends all fingers. The esthetic effect is similar to that of rhyme or alliteration in spoken poetry. While the movements that are part of signs are retained or modulated in some way, lines of poetry are skillfully constructed so as to omit the movements that result from the transition between the end of one sign and the beginning of another, creating flowing verse.[14]

The explicitly poetic, somewhat paradoxical device of disrupting or distorting conventional meanings in order to enhance the intended meaning is also recruited by Emmerik. In his poem, "Member of Parliament," Emmerik presents a picture of the governmental representative as jaded and cut off from the occurrences and sensations of the real world. The closest that the member of parliament gets to events in his country is through reading the newspaper as he eats lunch. To convey the idea that the politician crudely ingests the news through his body, rather than experiencing events spiritually or intellectually, the poet portrays him *eating* the news. As he eats and reads, he alters the usual sign for *eat* (figure 22.8a) by changing its location to the eyes rather than the mouth (figure 22.8b). Intermittently, the member of parliament eats food and ingests news of the world.

The value of the work of Emmerik and other deaf poets is first and foremost artistic. But the fact that poetry arises in established deaf communities is instructive as well. It teaches us that the desire and ability to mold the formational elements of language into an artistic expression of its content is a hallmark of human culture. It also shows clearly that sound is unnecessary, not only for communicative use of language, but for artistic use of language as well.

a. "Eat."   b. "Eat with the eyes."

Figure 22.8 Sign language poetic form
Source: Wim Emmerik, videotape *Pöezie in Gabarentaal*

3   How Is Sign Language Acquired by Children?

Current linguistic theory which hypothesizes that humans are genetically endowed with the fundamental underpinnings of language is supported by the claim that languages are similar to each other in significant ways. This view gains further support from the sign language findings reported in the previous sections. As we mentioned earlier, current theories are also based on the related observation that children acquire language automatically, including aspects of the system that do not seem directly retrievable from the input they receive. This section reviews phases of the acquisition of sign language, to see whether this process has the hallmarks of automaticity and systematicity that are found in spoken language acquisition.

If sign languages represent the same cognitive system as spoken languages do, then they should be acquired in a similar way. If, on the other hand, the modality somehow prevents sign languages from belonging to the same cognitive system, then they may be acquired quite differently. Furthermore, if the acquisition of language represents the unfolding of a biological-cognitive program with innate components, then sign languages should be acquired at the same rate as spoken languages. Whether or not the underlying cognitive system is the same, the possibility exists that the modality – oral / aural or manual / visual – has an impact on the course of development. These issues form the context for sign language acquisition studies.

Numerous studies have examined the acquisition of sign languages by deaf children whose parents are deaf signers.[15] Although this population represents only 5 to 10 percent of deaf children, it is the relevant one to study because these children receive input in sign language from birth, just as hearing children receive input in their native language. In general, it has been found that deaf children who are exposed to sign language acquire it in very similar ways to the acquisition of spoken languages: they pass through the same milestones at the same rate.[16]

As one example, let us consider the child's first words or signs.[17] Research on the acquisition of spoken languages finds that on the average, children begin to use their first words at around 11 months of age. The age varies from child to child, but many studies across a variety of languages have converged on the same average age, so the acquisition of first words is often taken to be a milestone in language acquisition.

When do the first words of sign language appear? Some early studies claimed that deaf children begin to use their first signs around 6 to 8 months of age, much younger than the reported first words. Why would there be such a difference between first words and first signs? Two types of mutually compatible explanation have been proposed. One suggests that meaningful gestures are sometimes mistaken for signs, implying that there may not be a significant difference for all children, and the other assumes the difference is real, but offers a physiological explanation for the difference.

The first explanation points out that both deaf and hearing children make meaningful gestures during the time under consideration. If more stringent requirements are adopted for attributing "word / sign" status to some production of the child, the difference between the first spoken words and the first signed words shrinks to about one and a half months, or even disappears completely. Another possibility is that these first signs may be more easily recognizable by adult observers than first spoken words, due perhaps to iconic elements that stand out in communication contexts, or to the nature of visual perception. If this is correct, it would also point toward a smaller gap in the actual onset of first word production in the two modalities.

The second explanation considers the development of the articulatory mechanisms used for speech versus sign. Earlier maturation of the mechanisms for muscular coordination of the hands and arms over the vocal organs may make it easier for a child who is cognitively ready for first words / signs to produce a sign than a spoken word. Such explanations put the possible difference between the onset of signs and words in "peripheral" mechanisms rather than the biological timetable for language. In other words, it may not be the case that signing is more advanced than speech, but, rather, that speech is delayed *vis-à-vis* sign. That is, children are cognitively ready to produce words before the coordination of the speech production system allows them to do so. This possibility is supported by evidence that (hearing) children comprehend words before they are able to produce them. The apparent discrepancy between the onset of first words in spoken versus signed language thus focusses important research questions that never would have even arisen if we considered only spoken language.[18]

These explanations downplaying the apparent difference between sign and spoken language development are all the more reasonable when other areas of language acquisition are considered, where there does not appear to be a difference between sign and speech in the attainment of each milestone.

For example, another important milestone of language acquisition, the use of two-word(/ sign) combinations, seems to be attained at around 18 months for both signing and speaking children. Other later grammatical developments, such as the acquisition of verb agreement, also follow parallel time courses across the modalities.

Let us consider another area in which the modality might be expected to have an impact on language acquisition: iconicity – a direct correspondence between form and meaning. As should be clear from our discussion so far, signs have internal phonological and morphological structure, and are not merely "pictures" of their referents. However, it is fair to say that some signs are iconically based, in that there is a motivated (non-arbitrary) relationship between the sign and its denotation. Similarly, some aspects of the grammar may be thought of as iconic in origin. One might suppose that these iconic elements may aid in the acquisition of sign language, and in this way distinguish between the acquisition processes in signing and speaking children. What does the research show?

A clear example of non-arbitrary signed elements are the signs for "me" and "you": these signs are made with pointing gestures which are essentially identical to the gestures made by hearing people when referring to first and second person, i.e., an index finger directed at one's self or at the addressee. Since these indexic ASL signs are non-arbitrary, it might be expected that they would be particularly easy to learn, if the modality has an effect on language acquisition. However, it turns out that they are not.

For some hearing children learning a spoken language, it is found that for a short period in early language development, the terms "me" and "you" get mixed up: the child uses "me" to refer to "you," or "you" to refer to "me." We can see why they might do this, since the referent for "me" or "you" changes depending on who is doing the talking. The child has to learn this peculiarity of these terms, and some children go through a stage of mixing them up. For the deaf child, since the forms used for ME and YOU are so transparent, it might be expected that no such errors would ever occur. However, some deaf children learning ASL make the same kind of mistake that some hearing children make: they confuse the signs for "me" and "you," despite their iconicity (Petitto 1987).

Studies involving other seemingly iconic aspects of the grammar have revealed similar countericonic errors in acquisition. A study by Richard Meier describes a child signing GIVE erroneously, in a sentence meaning "give the plate to him." In the adult system, the verb agrees for the subject and the indirect object (i.e., the recipient), which is iconic with the real world activity of giving someone something. In the example, the child erroneously marks agreement with the direct object. He moves his hand toward the thing to be given, rather than the recipient – a gesture that seems iconically interpretable as "give something to the plate" (cited in Bellugi and Klima 1982). Here too, the child not only neglects to avail himself of iconic cues, he seems oblivious to them, focussing instead on the formal ingredients of the system – in this case, the reference points in the discourse. As in the acquisition of spoken language, the child acquiring sign language sometimes gets these formal elements mixed up.

So, although it would seem that the iconicity in the visual modality would have a helpful effect on the process of language acquisition, we find that children do not seem to be attuned to certain obviously iconic aspects of signs. They are treating signs as abstract words, and thus they are not facilitated by iconicity in cases where one might expect them to be. They are simply progressing according to the universal timetable for language acquisition.

Overall, studies of the acquisition of ASL in a number of deaf children have come to the conclusion that the natural acquisition of ASL is quite parallel to the natural acquisition of spoken language. In the end, it seems that the basics of ASL are acquired by deaf children by around the age of five years, just as in the acquisition of spoken language. This finding is quite important. For many years people thought that sound and sound patterning was a vital part of language, and that there could be no natural human language that did not rely on sound. The arguments for the linguistic status of American Sign Language are strongly supported by the finding that it is acquired naturally, taking a course that parallels that of spoken language.

The idea of a biological timetable for language is also compatible with the idea that biology has its limits. Since Lenneberg (1967), it has been observed that there may be a "critical period" during which exposure to language is required in order for the natural mechanisms used for its acquisition to be triggered. Learning language after this period seems to be qualitatively different from early language acquisition, in a way that is sometimes interpreted as loss of the brain's plasticity. Lenneberg used data about recovery after language loss due to traumatic or degenerative brain damage, and about second language learning, to argue that the critical period ends somewhere around puberty. Before that time, children can recover from aphasia or learn a second language much more easily than after this point.

His proposal was strengthened by the study of isolated children such as Genie, a girl who was discovered at the age of $13\frac{1}{2}$ after having been locked in a small room and not spoken to during her whole childhood. Genie was unable to learn many aspects of complex language even after her physical and mental condition were treated (Curtiss 1977). However, there are many questions about Genie's situation and those of other isolated children, and fortunately these cases are rare – so few conclusions can be drawn about the critical age hypothesis from the study of delayed first language acquisition in normally hearing children.

A unique opportunity for investigating the critical age hypothesis is presented by deaf children with hearing parents, however, because even in caring home environments, the age at which deaf children are exposed to sign language varies. Many deaf youngsters are not exposed to sign language at an early age, because their deafness is not diagnosed, or because their parents prefer to educate them in an oral-only manner, or simply because no one in the child's environment uses sign language. In most cases, these children have no natural input to serve as a model for acquiring a spoken language, and their acquisition of sign language may begin as late as at the age of five, when they enter school, or perhaps even later.[19] What, then, does sign language development in these children tell us about the critical period hypothesis? Here we may consider the gesture systems usually developed by young deaf children in the absence of a sign language model, often called "home sign"; the consequences of the late acquisition of conventional sign languages, where a model is only presented for the child in later childhood; and the birth of a new sign language in a new deaf community.

In a series of extensive studies of these systems, Goldin-Meadow and colleagues[20] have found that children systematically develop names for things, labels for actions, and ways to combine elements which are strikingly like those of real languages. The home sign systems are far from a fully developed language, but they share characteristics with language which tell us about its "resilience" (in Goldin-Meadow's terms). As far as we know, there is no "Home Talk" – the circumstances for its development do not exist. Only the study of sign systems allows us to observe the in-born drive for language which creates some kind of formal system even in the complete absence of experience.

Often, such children eventually are exposed to sign language and grow up to be adults who use it as their primary form of communication. How perfectly is the grammar of a sign language acquired when exposure to it begins after the critical period? In studies of adults who have used ASL for many years (e.g., Newport 1990) it has been found that the age at which exposure to language began is critical for the eventual acquisition of a complete grammar. Researchers find that even after 50 years of signing, people who were exposed to ASL only after the age of 13 systematically differ in their use of some of the complex mechanisms of ASL, as compared with similar-aged adults who acquired ASL from birth in signing homes. These later learners are fully expressive and use many of the same structures which the native learners use. However, their use of verbs of motion and location constructions as well as verb agreement, for example, is often very different. These results also support Lenneberg's proposal that there is a critical period for language acquisition, in a way which would not have been discovered if not for the study of sign languages.

The study of the development of a nascent sign language offers a unique perspective on the human language capacity and the critical age hypothesis. Research conducted by Judy Kegl, Ann Senghas, and their colleagues (e.g. Senghas 1995), has been charting the development of a new sign language in Nicaragua, where deaf people had been isolated from one another until 1979. At that time a school was established for deaf children, and a communication system of signs immediately began to develop spontaneously. The system that developed among the first group of signers is not fully conventionalized, and it is relatively simple in structure, much like spoken pidgins. The older children in Nicaragua had had no language model when they were at the critical age, so their communication remains pidgin-like. Over time, however, as children as young as four years old began to come to the school and take the pidgin system of the older children as a model, a more systematic and conventionalized language began to emerge in these younger signers. This language includes certain grammatical characteristics that have been found by linguists in established sign languages. This study shows that the human brain will create a communication system as soon as people congregate and have a need to communicate. Like creole studies in spoken language, it also shows that children have the capacity to further expand and regularize even relatively simple input and make it into a bona fide language.

4   Neural Control of Sign Languages

Neurolinguists attempt to gain insight into the nature of language by determining which areas of the brain control various components of the language system. One way in which this is done is by studying the performance of people who have incurred brain damage, such as the localized damage resulting from strokes. In hearing, speaking people, numerous studies have found that damage to certain areas of the left cerebral hemisphere typically results in some type of language dysfunction, called *aphasia*. There are different types of aphasia, in which damage to different areas of the brain results in different types of language deficits. It is assumed that if a given function y is lost after damage to a certain area A, then that area is involved in the control or processing of that function. In this realm of investigation as well, similarities between signed and spoken languages have been found.

Although damage to areas of the left hemisphere results in aphasia in hearing subjects, damage to areas of the right hemisphere typically does not. On the other hand, damage to the right hemisphere frequently results in the loss of various types of spatial functioning. For example, patients with damage to the right hemisphere may be unable to draw a complete picture of a clock (typically neglecting the left side), or they may get lost in places that were very familiar to them before the brain damage.

It was shown in section 1 that the use of space plays an important role in the grammar of sign languages. For example, verb agreement and verbs of motion and location forms described there both involve spatial representation and manipulation. This situation, in which spatial cognition operations are directly related to linguistic cognition, prompts basic questions about brain organization with respect to spatial and linguistic functions in deaf signers. Several studies of deaf signers who have suffered brain damage have revealed patterns of language breakdown which emphasize the similarity rather than the difference between signed and spoken language in the mapping of both linguistic and spatial abilities within the brain.[21]

Poizner et al. (1987) present case studies of six deaf patients with brain damage, and they show a striking difference between deaf patients with damage to the right vs. left hemispheres. Like hearing patients, deaf signers who have left hemisphere brain damage have aphasia – in this case, aphasia for sign language. Some patients have very slow, awkward signing, like the speech of a "Broca's aphasic" (named after the French physician who first associated the linguistic breakdown with damage to a particular area of the brain). Others have signing which is more fluent, but which doesn't make sense, like a "Wernicke's aphasic" (a syndrome which results from damage to a different area of the left hemisphere). However, these patients have generally intact spatial cognitive abilities, such as drawing, face recognition, or localization of objects.

In contrast, deaf signers who experience damage to the right hemisphere have severe spatial deficits. They show left neglect, get lost in the hospital, and lose the ability to draw or show spatial relations, just like hearing patients with right hemisphere damage. However, the most important point is this: their signing is not impaired. They sign fluently and meaningfully, even using the "spatial" grammatical devices, although they show some comprehension deficits, a point we will return to in section 5.2. This provides strong evidence that sign languages are controlled in the left hemisphere, where spoken language is controlled, rather than in the right hemisphere, where visuo-spatial abilities are controlled. These results imply that neural specialization for language is determined more by the type of cognitive operation involved – linguistic or spatial – than by the physical channel that mediates these operations.

The evidence for a human language capacity that transcends the physical channel for its expression is by now diverse and compelling. There is something about human cognition that converges on a complex and rich language system with particular formal and even neurological characteristics, even when the evolutionarily dominant channel for its transmission is not available.[22]

Yet this is still not the whole story. Some recent findings and new interpretations of existing results offer tough challenges to certain received views, and point the way toward important research in the future.

5 Recent Challenges

A context for the future investigation of the relationship between language and cognition is an existing fundamental dispute about the nature of the language faculty. At one extreme is the strong Chomskyan view that language is an "organ," innately specified, and both computationally and neurologically divorced from other aspects of cognition (e.g. Chomsky 1986). Other scholars argue that the experience of the child acquiring language plays a stronger role in determining language form. Jackendoff (1997) develops a theory according to which language is the outcome of a combination of factors, some specific to language (and possibly genetically specified), and others that tap more general concepts and knowledge about the world.

We now turn to certain outstanding questions about sign language that bear on this controversy. When they are seriously addressed, we believe the answers will lead us to a far deeper understanding of the language capacity than would have been possible without sign language research.

5.1   *Basic, unexplained similarities among sign languages*

We have argued that sign languages bear important similarities to spoken languages. But we have only hinted at how similar the grammatical structures of sign languages are to one another. As Elissa Newport stressed in an address to sign language researchers,[23] this important generalization needs to be explained.

Using various grammatical criteria, linguists sometimes find it instructive to group languages into categories or types. These criteria may be applied at any level of analysis – syntax, morphology, or phonology. For example, some languages have the Swahili type of morphology (see example 11); others have the Navaho type (see example 12); etc. In syntax, some languages have Subject-Verb-Object word order; others have Verb-Subject-Object, for example. Phonologically, some languages allow several consonants to occur together before a vowel appears; others allow only one consonant at the beginning of a syllable. The point is that spoken languages may fall into one of any of a number of categories at each level of description.

As we have hinted in section 1, in many ways, sign languages form a single language type, and one to which no spoken language belongs. If this is the case, then some essential questions arise, for both cognitive psychology and for linguistics. In the following paragraphs, we will demonstrate some of the typological traits of sign languages.[24]

Let us begin with the relationship between the elements of form and meaning. In figure 22.6 ("a coin is lying there"), we showed a complex sign, with three meaningful elements or morphemes. We pointed out that some spoken languages have equally complex forms, with substantively the same types of morphemes in them. But there are two important generalizations that we now wish to emphasize: (1) all sign languages that we know of have precisely this type of morphology (American Sign Language, Israeli Sign Language, British Sign Language, Danish Sign Language, Swedish Sign Language, Japanese Sign Language); and (2) despite the large number of meaning elements (morphemes) in signs of this type, they are all articulated essentially simultaneously, or within what may be viewed as a single syllable.

A moment's thought is enough to convince the reader that the first generalization is not true of spoken languages. Languages like English, for example, have nothing even remotely like this sort of word structure. As for the second, the spoken language equivalent would be a language like Navaho in example (12) above, but in which all the different meaning elements were pronounced within a single syllable. Such a spoken language analog – a language whose words contain many meaningful components within a single syllable – does not exist.

The sign language system is rule governed, grammatical, and violates no principles of universal grammar that we are aware of. It is also acquired by children at an age appropriate for a complex morphological system.[25] Yet the details of its form and use are particular to sign languages – all sign languages.

All sign languages also have the type of verb agreement we described in section 1. The literature on the subject includes American Sign Language, British Sign Language, Taiwan Sign Language, Swedish Sign Language, Japanese Sign Language, Italian Sign Language, Danish Sign Language, Sign Language of The Netherlands, Israeli Sign Language, and Australian Sign Language. In addition to formal similarity, all sign languages apparently also share the division into four classes of verbs which are arguably determined on the basis of meaning.

These similarities are so robust that they emerge spontaneously in the contact language used among signers whose native sign languages are not mutually intelligible. Supalla and Webb (1995) studied deaf lecturers at international conferences, communicating to an audience of signers of over twenty different sign languages. In a contact language called International Sign,[26] these lecturers use the same kind of verb agreement that we have been describing here, in addition to other grammatical structures. The authors say that this is because these devices exist in the native sign languages of the lecturers – whatever they may be. We add that the signers may expect such devices to be understood if they are (subconsciously) confident that they are sign language universal.

This contrasts sharply with the situation in spoken languages: not all spoken languages have agreement, and the agreement systems of those that do may have different properties from language to language. Where there are classes of verbs with different agreement markers within a spoken language, these classes are arbitrary, and they are not determined by meaning. Nevertheless, we emphasize that these sign language systems are grammatical and rule governed; they violate no known universal principle of grammar; and they are acquired by children at the same age that agreement is acquired in spoken languages.

In addition to these morphological similarities, sign languages all seem to share a particular type of phonological structure. For example, the constraint that only one finger group may characterize a sign applies to all sign languages we know of. Also, the fact that meaningful elements tend to be piled on simultaneously within single syllables, rather than linearly in a sequence, is a generalization about the phonological structure as well as the morphological structure of sign languages.

In short, sign languages form a language type. What makes this type different from the types posited for spoken languages is that the modality alone determines the type. No spoken language that we know of is of the sign language type, and, unlike sign languages, spoken languages fall into many different language types. These observations present us with a theoretical dilemma because they are not predicted by any explicit linguistic theory that we know of. The theory of universal grammar claims that certain generalizations can be made about the structure found in all languages, a claim that has been extended to include sign languages. However, this theory does not predict that a particular subset of these generalizations will characterize all sign languages. Future research must attempt to develop a paradigm for approaching this issue. Additional related challenges are posed by recent neurological findings.

5.2   Neurological differences

As reviewed in section 4, aphasia studies show clearly that both spoken and signed languages are controlled in the left hemisphere. Some recent brain research on normal subjects using modern techniques such as positron emission tomography and functional magnetic resonance imaging are suggestive of possible differences in brain organization related to sign language. In particular, recent results find right hemisphere involvement in sign language processing by deaf and hearing native signers.[27]

One research group used regional cerebral blood flow and positron emission tomography to examine sign and spoken language representation in hearing native signers (hearing people born to deaf parents who learned sign language as a first language). The two techniques showed bilateral activation (activation in both cerebral hemispheres) for both modalities. Another research group, using event related potentials, similarly found bilateral activation for both modalities, for both deaf and hearing native signers. Using functional magnetic resonance imaging, they also found bilateral activation for processing ASL by deaf and hearing native signers; however, they did not find bilateral representation for English.

In these studies, the classical left hemisphere regions have been implicated for processing sign language, but in addition, some areas of the right hemisphere have also shown activity. Recall that patients with right hemisphere lesions reported in section 4 also showed some comprehension deficits, indicating right hemisphere involvement in processing sign language. If it is true that the right hemisphere is involved in sign language processing, it will be important to consider why there might be such a difference between sign and oral languages (or between language users with and without early exposure to sign language). Certainly, the well-established fact that the right hemisphere is crucial for human visuo-spatial processing in general may play a role in explaining these findings. These possibilities overlap, but there are distinctions which are important for theoretical models of language (see Sandler 1993, Lillo-Martin 1997, and previous references in this section). Clearly, more research in this area is essential.

5.3 Putting the puzzle together

In an attempt to understand certain similarities across sign languages, some interesting suggestions have been made about the role of iconicity (transparent correspondence between form and meaning) in shaping sign language grammar. Such a possibility runs counter to the by now traditional view that grammatical structure and iconicity are mutually exclusive. This more traditional view assumed, with Saussure (1959), that the elements of language, to be language, must be arbitrary. Therefore, it was assumed to follow that whatever is iconic about sign language is not "linguistic." Nowadays, however, there is such an abundance of solid evidence that sign languages are real linguistic systems in every sense of the word, that it is possible to take a fresh look at the whole issue.

Allowing for the possibility that iconicity contributes to grammatical structure in sign language opens the door to the possibility that general cognitive concepts – such as spatial relations among referents in a discourse and physical characteristics of objects and their motion – interact directly with the grammatical system (Sandler 1993).[28] In this context it is reasonable, we believe, to develop research paradigms that examine the relationship between modality, iconicity, and grammatical structure. Only by studying the nature of language in the visual modality does this become possible. Attempts to create such paradigms will undoubtedly offer a much deeper understanding of language in general.

Another area meriting further exploration is the relation between home sign and developed sign languages. As sketched in section 3, Goldin-Meadow and her colleagues have discovered the kernels of a structured communication system in the home sign created by deaf children of hearing parents in the absence of a language model. In particular, it can be argued that the rudiments of both the verbs of motion and location system, and the verb agreement system, have been observed in these children. As we have explained, the communication system of these children is far simpler and less systematic than a developed language, and even what does exist differs from developed sign languages. Nevertheless, it seems significant that what these children develop without a model has characteristics that are not only language-like, but unmistakably sign language-like. In particular, the use of space in denoting the referents involved in verb-like signs (as in verb agreement), and the use of handshapes to iconically represent physical classes of objects (as in verbs of motion and location) are found.

As the study of the birth of a conventional sign language in Nicaragua reveals, the beginnings of the use of space for reference and handshape as a classifier in complex signs can become much more sophisticated and systematic in the space of one generation of signers. This rapid creolization of a home sign system to a sign language which has similar characteristics to other established sign languages reinforces our interest in accounting for the ubiquitous qualities of sign languages in an explanatory way.

A different line of inquiry that ought to be further pursued is the one begun by S. Supalla (e.g. 1990). He has observed deaf school children who have been exposed only to a contrived signing system in which signs are used to translate the words and morphemes of spoken English, and which involves none of the grammatical properties of sign language. In communication among themselves, these children add sign-language-like elements, such as moving verbs in space to refer to subject or object referents, although they have not been exposed to a sign language model. When fit together with future studies in the other areas mentioned here, this work will provide additional important pieces to the puzzle.

6   Conclusion

The study of sign language provides a natural laboratory for isolating certain fundamental properties of human language apart from the modality in which it is transmitted. Doing so has confirmed the existence of purported language universals, such as a systematic sub-word level of structure, syntactic embedding and recursion, and particular types of complex word formation. It has also strengthened the claim that the acquisition of language by children is a natural and automatic process with a set timetable, pointing to some degree of genetic predisposition for the development of just such a system.

Certain modality specific characteristics have also been found: a tendency for simultaneous layering of linguistic structure and particular types of grammatical constructions that are at once linguistic in the formal sense, and in some way iconic. The discovery of these sign language properties brings to light observations about spoken language that seem to be determined by the modality alone, such as the tendency to string linguistic information out linearly, and the generally arbitrary nature of the lexicon and grammar. Before research on sign language, such characteristics were thought to be properties of language universally. In the light of sign language research, we may suggest that these properties are artefacts of the oral–aural modality.

Our work is cut out for us. An important goal of future research must be to develop models of language that explain the clustering of characteristics found in sign languages, as well as the fact that they conform to more general linguistic universals. In developing such models, we are charged with an equally important task: explaining precisely what it is about the spoken language modality that makes it different from sign language. Only by examining these two natural language systems together can we reach a complete understanding of the human genius for language.

NOTES

Sandler's research was supported in part by Israel Science Foundation Grant no. 820/95 and Binational Science Foundation Grant no. 9500310/2; and Lillo-Martin's by National Institute on Deafness and Communication Disorders, National Institutes of Health, Grant no. R01 DC 00183, and the University of Connecticut Research Foundation. We would like to thank Mark Aronoff, Peter MacNeilage, Richard Meier, Irit Meir, and Yudit Rosenberg for their helpful comments.

1 This article is a distillation of the work of many researchers, whose work we often do not cite specifically. The references we include are of two types: (a) works that are accessible to a general audience, and (b), for linguists, survey articles or books with detailed bibliographies. For overviews see Klima and Bellugi (1979) and Emmorey (forthcoming).

2 Most but not all of our evidence comes from American Sign Language (ASL), since it is the most studied sign language to date. ASL is about 200 years old, and it is used by deaf people in the United States, much of Canada, and parts of Africa. For an interesting discussion of the history of ASL within the educational and political contexts of the time, see Lane 1984.

3 We have selected linguistic characteristics that are general and simple, to make our point. However, many other, more formal and more complex characteristics have been found to be common to languages in the two modalities as well. Sandler and Lillo-Martin (forthcoming) provides an overview of theoretical linguistic research on sign languages.

4 We follow the convention of using upper case English words to represent signs. "IND" stands for "index," a pointing gesture.

5 The nondominant hand is influenced as well, changing from a sideways to an upwards orientation.

6 See Corina and Sandler (1993), Sandler (1994) and Brentari (1995) for overviews of the field of sign language phonology, written for linguists.

7 See Sandler 1999, for an overview.

8 There is a significant body of literature on nonmanuals as syntactic markers in ASL – along the lines of Liddell's analysis of relative clauses shown in section 1.1, example 6b. In the interest of space, we only mention the prosodic treatments of such markers here.

9 Both yes / no questions and shared information are signaled by intonation in English as well.

10 An accessible description of this work, and the source of the examples of both ASL and Navaho in the present article, can be found in Newport (1981). The transcription shown here is simplified.

11 We thank Keren Rice for explaining the Navaho data to us. The transcription and explanation presented here are simplified for clarity.

12 The particular word signified by the classifier – *coin* and *table* in the example here – is introduced into the discourse by a sign prior to the signing of the classifier construction.

13 We thank Daphna Erdinast-Vulcan for lending her literary expertise to this interpretation of Wim Emmerik's poetry.

14 Both of these devices have been observed in American Sign Language poetry (Klima and Bellugi 1979).

15 See Newport and Meier (1985), Meier (1991), and Lillo-Martin (1999) for reviews.

16 The process of language acquisition for deaf children with hearing parents depends on their linguistic input,

which is quite varied. In some cases it might be a signed version of English, or in others, American Sign Language, or in many cases, spoken language input only (at least for the first several years of the child's life). Although there are many interesting properties of language acquisition in these differing sets of circumstances, we cannot go into them here.

17   See Meier and Newport (1990) for a thoughtful review of this research, on which this summary is based.

18   The purely motoric explanation may be oversimplified, however, since there is evidence that children's first spoken words are phonetically similar to their late babbling, and therefore do not represent a leap in coordination of the vocal apparatus. Other factors that make this issue difficult to evaluate are the small sizes of samples in some sign language studies. In any case, the research that has been conducted, partially summarized here, leads to interesting questions whose answers will be deeper and more accurate if both natural language modalities are taken into account.

19   Nowadays, many deaf youngsters in some countries are exposed to some form of signing at a relatively early age through school, community, or home programs which may begin when the child is little over a year old. However, even now many children are not exposed to sign language, or even any contrived sign system, until much later.

20   See Goldin-Meadow and Mylander (1990), for a review.

21   See Corina (1998) and Peperkamp and Mehler (1999) for overviews of the neural control of sign language.

22   Presumably, if evolution had selected both modalities, there would be hearing communities that just happen to use a sign language for their primary means of communication. Since no such communities are known, we may assume that the evolutionary

preference is for spoken language, whatever the reason. We thank Peter MacNeilage (p.c.) for bringing this reasoning to our attention.

23   Newport, Elissa L. (1996) Sign language research in the next millennium. Keynote address, conference on Theoretical Issues in Sign Language Research. Montreal.

24   In the discussion, we speak of "sign languages" or "all sign languages." What we mean by this is all sign languages about which we have relevant information, including some sign languages not known to have any historical relationship to each other. Since we have no counterexamples to the generalizations we are about to express, we take the strongest position by assuming they are true of all sign languages.

25   Lest the reader get the mistaken impression that this system is analogic to real world activity and not really grammatical, we point to a fascinating study by Newport and Supalla (see Newport 1981). They show that in the early stages of acquisition, children decompose the many elements of this system, and produce them sequentially rather than simultaneously, resulting in sign sequences that appear far *less* like the real world event than the grammatical, adult forms do.

26   International Sign is the form of communication used by deaf people with no common sign language, when they meet, for example, at international conferences. It is not a contrived language, but rather arose naturally out of a contact situation.

27   See Corina (1998), and Peperkamp and Mehler (1999), for overviews of research on sign language and the brain.

28   Some schools of spoken language research suggest that iconicity plays a nontrivial role in spoken language structuring as well, though somewhat differently and to a more limited degree.

23 Sociolinguistics

FLORIAN COULMAS

1 Introduction

Sociolinguistics is the empirical study of how language is used in society. Combining linguistic and sociological theories and methods, it is an inter-disciplinary field of research which attaches great significance both to the vari-ability of language and to the multiplicity of languages and language forms in a given society. Within this broad range of interest there are a number of specialities that investigate some aspect of the interaction of language and society, such as, how language relates to social categories of various kinds, e.g., social class, age, sex and gender, ethnicity, speech situation, network, etc. Some of these categories will be introduced in what follows. The present over-view also discusses such general questions as how the sociolinguistic notion of language differs from similar notions in other subfields of linguistics; what sociolinguistics contributes to the science of language; what aspects of language sociolinguistic theoretical models are designed to account for; and whether and how a sociolinguistic theory can be built.

2 Language as a Social Fact

Every language is a social product, and every society constitutes itself through language. To study the relationship between the two is a complex endeavor which can be expected to throw light on the foundations of both society and language. Sociolinguistics is concerned with "real-life" language issues in social context. While formal linguistics constructs a simplified language whose behavior can be predicted, sociolinguistics tries to cope with the messiness of language as a social phenomenon. It was Ferdinand de Saussure, the pioneer of structural linguistics as an autonomous science, who called language a social fact. Sociolinguistics can be understood as an attempt to take seriously

Saussure's characterization of language and to find ways of subjecting its social side to scientific inquiry. The concept of language upon which sociolinguistics is predicated differs in characteristic ways from that of formal linguistics. Rather than looking at language as a self-contained fixed structure, sociolinguistics puts language change and variation at the center of its deliberations.

Early on, when linguistics began to be conceived as a natural science, the historical dimension of language was conceptualized in terms of quasi-natural laws, the laws of sound change. For a long time, many linguists and historians of language held on to this approach which testified to a model of the social world where beneath history natural processes are assumed. Only those phenomena which could be reduced to natural processes were considered worthy of investigation. It was, accordingly, thought possible and desirable to study the history of language by focussing on language-internal motivations of change. However, as the body of historical linguistic knowledge grew, it became increasingly obvious that the twin questions of why and how languages change cannot find satisfactory answers in terms of linguistic structure alone. In many cases of observable sound-change it could not be demonstrated that the new form closed a gap in the sound system or was in a specifiable way better than the old one, or that the new state of the language was an improvement. In search of causes of change that lie outside language, scholars thus turned to society, looking at language as it is used and shaped, to some extent deliberately, by people in their social dealings with each other. Conceptually, language became a social fact in whose creation, perpetuation, and modification *homo loquens* had a part to play.

Sociolinguistics is a young discipline. Although social aspects of language have often caught linguists' attention, it was not before the mid-twentieth century that sociolinguistics emerged as a recognizable enterprise. A hybrid that draws on both linguistic and sociological scholarship, sociolinguistics combines an interest in linguistic structures with the recognition that examining the societal dimensions of language requires interpretive methods allowing us to understand how language is reflective of social processes and relationships and what it contributes to making society work as it does.

The formal modeling of logic which theoretical linguistics emulates is not germane to the study of language as a social fact. Nevertheless, sociolinguistics is one of the *language* sciences, and as such it is presented within the context of this handbook. At the same time, sociology lays claim to a number of research domains concerning the relations between language and society. However, the input of linguistics and sociology into the sociolinguistic endeavor has been uneven. Although several progenitors can be identified, historical linguistics and dialectology have contributed most to establishing sociolinguistics as a field of inquiry. Language has long been recognized to vary in both time and space. Historical linguistics and dialectology have demonstrated that such variation is systematic and patterned and could thus be the object of scientific inquiry. When it was found that language varied along yet another dimension which could not be reduced to geographical extension or historical depth, these two disciplines were quite naturally regarded as offering suitable models for dealing with the underlying dynamics of socially conditioned language diversity.

Traditional dialectology recognizes variability as an essential attribute of language, focussing on the regional distribution of variant speech forms. Identifying regional dialects and distinguishing neighboring dialects from one another are difficult tasks which require a large corpus of utterances by many speakers as a basis for description and involves quantitative analysis of linguistic features. While questionnaires have often been used, the preferred method of data collection is by means of face-to-face interviews with speakers of the varieties in question. In a pioneering study of French dialects Edmont interviewed speakers at some six hundred places throughout France, eliciting hundreds of speech items from a fixed list. The results of this survey were published in one of the first dialect atlases, a collection of maps which indicate the geographical distribution of speech forms (Gilliéron and Edmont 1902–13).

In many ways sociolinguistics remains indebted and closely linked to dialectology and historical linguistics. But it has also made its own innovative contributions to the study of language which put it at odds with established research paradigms. A dialect atlas is an absolute map in the sense that it consists of categorical dialect areas which are considered as having a center that is relatively stable. As an object of investigation a dialect thus appears much like a language, as an abstract, categorically distinct system. On the time axis, language is seen as evolving in one direction, one categorical language state following upon another. Any given utterance or piece of text is taken as exemplifying a particular dialect or language state. In contradistinction to these, admittedly simplified, conceptions of language diversity, sociolinguistics recognizes the fluidity of speech, refusing to accept the doctrine that linguistic data must be abstracted from the constraints and distortions of real life communication. It has, accordingly, replaced categoricity with frequency, that is, the frequency of occurrence of variant features of language use in a given speech community. Instead of categorizing a certain pronunciation or a certain construction as either belonging or not belonging to a language L, sociolinguistics would measure the frequencies with which such features and constructions occurred in variety X compared with variety Y. The fact that speech communities and individual speakers had a wide range of possible speech forms at their command was recognized as an essential rather than a haphazard condition of the social functioning of language. Discovering systematic patterns underlying the actual occurrences of variant speech forms and relating them to social characteristics of speakers and speech situations turned into the major challenge that sociolinguists set out to confront. Analyzing variable language data thus became the hallmark of sociolinguistic research, or, more correctly, of one influential strand of sociolinguistic research. Methods of gathering and analyzing such data were developed, giving rise to a notion of language which differs from that of formal linguistics in that it marries structure with inherent variability.

Tied to such a notion of language, the proposition that language is a social fact is now much more specific than it was in the garb of the general acknowledgment that language is a species-specific endowment and needs a community to be sustained. It is specific enough to turn the social dimension of language into an object of scientific investigation. Sociolinguistics is a data-driven empirical science. The researcher's intuition has a role to play for heuristic purposes, but not as the object of analysis. Data must come from speakers in their various social environments.

3   The Micro–Macro Distinction

Traditional scholarly division of labor assigns language and society to different fields of academic research. Sociolinguistics is essentially interdisciplinary in orientation. Crossing the boundaries of established disciplines, it is prone to become the target of criticism on either side of the frontier. In spite of this criticism, some of which will be discussed below, it is no longer contested that sociolinguistics has much to contribute to explaining the relationship between language and the social context in which it is used, and that its insights add to our understanding of the human condition. Its primary concern is to study correlations between language use and social structure. Attempting to establish causal links between language and society, it pursues the complementary questions of what language contributes to making community possible and how communities shape their languages by using them. Since sociolinguistics is a meeting ground for linguists and social scientists, some of whom seek to understand the social aspects of language while others are primarily concerned with linguistic aspects of society, it is not surprising that there are, as it were, two centers of gravity, known, respectively, as *micro-* and *macro-sociolinguistics* or alternatively *sociolinguistics in the narrow sense* and *sociology of language*. These represent different orientations and research agendas, micro-issues being more likely to be investigated by linguists, dialectologists, and others in language-centered fields, whereas macro-issues are more frequently taken up by sociologists and social psychologists. *Variation linguistics* has been used as yet another term for micro-sociolinguistics, and there have been attempts to confine sociolinguistics proper to the study of variation in language. However, sociolinguistic textbooks (for instance, Fasold 1984, 1990, Holmes 1992, Hudson 1990, Romaine 1994), journals (for instance, *Language in Society, Sociolinguistica, Current Issues in Language and Society, International Journal of the Sociology of Language, Multilingua*), anthologies and readers (for instance, Ammon et al. 1988, Coulmas 1997, Coupland, Jaworski 1997), and scholarly conferences treat a much wider range of issues. There is now general agreement that both perspectives, those of micro- and macro-sociolinguistics, are indispensable for a full understanding of language as a social phenomenon.

4 Micro-sociolinguistics

Stated in very general terms, micro-sociolinguistics investigates how social structure influences the way people talk and how language varieties and patterns of use correlate with social attributes such as class, sex, age, and ethnicity. It thus strives to correlate dependent linguistic variables with independent social variables. Speech is socially emblematic in the sense that speakers by their choice of words, manner of pronunciation, and other stylistic features identify with others with whom they share social characteristics, such as socioeconomic status, occupation, and education, but also place of residence, age, gender, and ethnicity. It is here that sociolinguistics relies most evidently on sociological theory. For, while it is intuitively clear that ways of speaking reveal social meaning, as immortalized in Bernard Shaw's famous play *Pygmalion*, it is much less obvious how individuals cluster into social groups, how social hierarchies are structured, and to what extent social hierarchies can be compared across speech communities, cultures, and polities.

5 Social Class

That social class has a bearing on speech behavior has been recognized for a long time. Among the first to address this issue were Fischer (1958), on the linguistic side, and Bernstein (1960), on the sociological side. The theoretical models of society which informed the early phase of sociolinguistic theory formation were based on notions of social class, as defined in Marxist or Weber-Parsonian terms. These were developed within the context, and for the analysis, of Western industrial societies. In Marxist social theory, class is defined in terms of possession of means of production whose unequal distribution is seen as the chief reason of social conflict (class struggle). The general model of society that is based on this notion is conflictual. According to Parsons' (1952) concept of a stratified social system, each individual is located on a continuum of hierarchically ordered class groupings. The general model of society that is based on this notion is consensual. Society is understood as a system which tends to maintain its equilibrium and, if disturbed, to re-establish it.

The suitability of both of these models for analyzing social systems outside the world of western industrialized countries cannot be taken for granted. Traditional social structures, such as the Indian caste system, remnants of a feudal system in Korea, or tribes and clans in rural African societies, to mention but a few examples, cannot be subjected easily to class analysis. What is more, class, especially as understood within a Weber-Parsonian framework (Parsons 1952), is a composite variable that is calculated by reference to a number of indicators. Income, profession, and educational level are most commonly used. They are more easily subjected to quantitative measurement than other indicators which, however, may be equally relevant, such as the availability of information. Whatever indicators are used, their relative weight is not necessarily the same for all societies. For instance, both the US and Japan are highly industrialized societies, but educational level is more predictive of social status in Japan than in the USA. Given that, it would be a reasonable and testable hypothesis that speech varieties that are indicative of the speakers' educational level correlate more strongly with social status in Japan than in the US. One of the most significant insights of sociolinguistics is that very minor speech differences are socially indicative, that is, that social speech systems are extremely fine grained.

In his study of English in New York City, Labov (1966) was able to demonstrate that the pronunciation of the initial consonant of words like *this* and *there* correlated with social class. The standard variant [ð] was more likely to be produced by middle-class speakers, while working-class speakers tended to use non-standard [d]. The class division used in the study corresponded roughly to the blue-collar / white-collar divide. Speakers were classified as socially upwardly mobile if their father's occupation was a lower-status or lower-income occupation than their own at the time of the survey. In Labov's sample upwardly mobile speakers were contrasted with speakers whose social class affiliation was stable. The incidence of [ð] in the speech of the upwardly mobile group suggests that speakers adjust their speech behavior to that of the target group of their social mobility. Upwardly mobile speakers were found to use fewer non-standard forms than speakers belonging to the stable group. Clearly, then, the [ð] / [d] distinction is socially meaningful. However, findings of this sort are open to different interpretations. Choice of the standard variant can be viewed as signalling desired class membership, or as the result of increased interaction with standard-pronunciation speakers, or both. In another study of class-indicative speech Trudgill (1974) found that vowel fronting was a class marker in the speech of Norwich, England. In words like *after* and *cart*, middle-class speakers use an unrounded [aː], whereas working-class speakers show a marked tendency to round [ɑː] or [äː] instead.

Many other studies (e.g. Macaulay 1976, Ammon 1979, Cheshire 1982, Habick 1991) have revealed correlations between language variation and social stratification, but social class, however defined, has rarely, if ever, been demonstrated to be the only independent variable which determines choice of speech forms. Labov's methodology builds on the difference between styles, ranging from casual to formal to reading. The variable here is the attention speakers pay to their own speech: There is little conscious monitoring in casual speech, whereas reading work lists directs speakers' attention to formal features of their speech, because the contents are clearly immaterial. It is assumed that speakers will conform more closely to the speech norms they have internalized the higher their attention level. On the basis of these assumptions style-shifting (toward more formal) was found to correspond to the effects of upward social mobility. This finding was interpreted as indicating that speech variation is systematically, though not necessarily consciously, used as a means of social class affiliation. Sex (Labov 1990, Chambers 1992) and ethnicity (Gal 1978, Laferriere 1979), to name but the most conspicuous variables, also interact in complex ways with social class in determining an individual's speech behavior, as do what Fishman et al. (1971) have called social domain (family, school, work, market, church). Speech variation feeds into the social construction of class differentiation, gender differences, and ethnic identities, but all attempts to find simple, constant correlations between these social categories and variation have been frustrated. Observable covariation of social and linguistic factors almost always allow for more than one interpretation. This testifies to the great complexity of the facts sociolinguists have to deal with and to some extent explains their inclination to try to couple positivist faith in objective methodology in gathering linguistic data with interpretations which are grounded in normative ideas about social structure. Owing to the complexity of the variables – speech forms and social class – it may be impossible to do more than make statistical generalizations about covariation. There are, hence, good reasons to look for alternative approaches to exploring the relationships between linguistic variation and social organization.

6 Social Networks

Relating linguistic variation to class is, of course, not the only possible way of analyzing language in society. Social network, a concept first introduced by Radcliffe-Brown (1940), has been proposed as an alternative social variable that is relevant to the study of the social dimensions of language. It is a notion which is focussed on the individual speaker. As a process that transforms the linguistic system, language change does not happen in the abstract. It is the result of speaker-activity in social situations. Some such activities exercise an influence on the speech of others and in this way effect change. Conversational speech is a social activity which can be studied in its own right without projecting a fixed social class model on to it. The nature of this activity itself may hold explanations about language change and variation. Speakers engage in a variety of conversations and entertain relationships with others. They can be described as participating in social networks. Family members, friends, colleagues, customers, neighbors, and other regular or occasional interlocutors can be viewed as points connected by lines (conversations) that form networks. The social networks of which individual speakers are a part vary in size and density and can, therefore, be expected to have an influence on their speech behavior. James and Lesley Milroy have developed a framework for the analysis of linguistic variation which is centered on the notion of social network (J. Milroy 1992, L. Milroy 1987). Networks display patterning, impinge upon speaker behavior, and thus provide a basis for analyzing social relations without assuming class stratification as the starting point. Rather than just being caused by and reflecting social change, linguistic change is understood, within the social network model, as being a composite part of social change.

Social networks have been demonstrated to function as norm-enforcing agents, for example, with regard to low-prestige varieties. In modern industrial societies use of a standard variety of speech is preferred in general education, most mass communication, and communication in formal settings. Under these conditions, speakers of substandard varieties not only come under pressure to adopt speech forms closer to the standard, but are also offered the possibility to do so. Yet, low-status varieties often persist, even though their speakers are aware of the social advantages – upward social mobility, prestige, power – associated with the standard. For example, the pronunciation as [ʌ] of the vowel in words such as *pull* is characteristic of the Belfast vernacular. Milroy discovered that this substandard variant is used markedly less by speakers with weak network ties. He interpreted this finding as indicating that "to the extent that ties are strong, linguistic change will be prevented or impeded" (Milroy 1992: 176). Social network analysis seems to be a more promising approach toward explicating social facts of this kind than an analysis which hinges on a stratificational class model of society. In accordance with many observations of the sort just cited, Milroy and Milroy (1992) have suggested that the relative density or strength of network ties is predictive of the persistence of speech varieties: strong and closely knit networks support the maintenance of varieties even if they are stigmatized. In L. Milroy's (1987: 175) words: "The closer an individual's network ties are with his local community, the closer his language approximates to localized vernacular norms." Since the strength of network ties, rather than being randomly distributed across a speech community, is a social variable and can hence be related to the wider organization of society, networks are indeed a meaningful construct to explicate the social motivation and significance of the coexistence of speech varieties associated with differential prestige values.

Close-knit networks are indicative of social solidarity. That language behavior can be expressive of social solidarity is a relatively old concept in sociolinguistics. However, as used by Milroy and Milroy, it offers a pivot for linking the social class and network models of sociolinguistics. As they point out (Milroy and Milroy 1997: 61), strong solidarity ties are characteristic of lower and higher social groups, while they tend to be weak in the middle sectors of society. "A high proportion of close-knit ties on the one hand, and of loose-knit ties on the other are consequent upon [different] life-modes which themselves are constitutive of distinct classes." The network model thus offers an approach to exploring language in the community and discovering in patterns of speech activity the socially meaningful aspects of language varieties which then can be correlated with social stratification. It is, in other words, not just speech forms which are socially indicative, but speech activities, too.

Whether the network approach will have a recognizable influence on the future development of quantitative variation studies time will have to show. So far the social class model of language variation as developed by Labov (1966) and many of his associates and disciples, which links language variation to variation in social class membership and social mobility, has been by far the most influential, although the notion of social class seems to be on the way out in sociology (Pahl 1989). The need to look for alternatives to social class in sociolinguistics has been acknowledged more than a decade ago by scholars working within the social class model (Rickford 1986). This would augur well for a more prominent place for network analysis. However, established research paradigms and schools of thought tend to be as persistent as low-prestige speech varieties, precisely because they rely on close-knit social networks.

To be sure, the social class approach has its merits and strengths. By accumulating a huge amount of empirical evidence that demonstrates how linguistic variation can be correlated to social parameters, it has added a significant dimension to our understanding of the obvious fact that language, whenever and wherever it is observed, is variable. However, it also has its weaknesses. Language use is found to be socially emblematic in all societies, but not all distinctions in language use are the result of social processes, nor can they be explained as manifesting social distinctions. And even where the distribution of linguistic varieties – dialects, specific expressions, the realization of certain phonemes – correlates with differences in social class membership, such correlations are not always very enlightening. For statistical correlations only state that a variable β, say, vowel tensing before nasals, tends to be present if another variable, α, say working-class membership in Philadelphia, is present. It does not say that vowel tensing before vowels is present *because* the speaker is a blue-collar Philadelphian. If the occurrence of β cannot be demonstrated to be caused by that of α, that is, if no causal connection can be established, the statistical probability of α and β to cooccur can be used to *describe* Philadelphia working-class speech, but has little for explaining its social significance.

So far, no definite set of social invariants that cause language variation has been identified. Rather, though certain generalizations, such as those about social networks and class membership, are possible, the divisions that are reflected in speech may exhibit patterns that are peculiar to one society or culture. Where particular ways of speaking are thought to be determined by social requirements and to reflect social stratification and group affiliation, the general problem is to identify meaningful social groups as independent variables. The problem is confounded by the fact that under certain circumstances individuals can move in and out of social groups, and that societies vary with respect to this kind of social mobility. Inequality in income and wealth is what most conspicuously marks social hierarchies, but while these distinctions are highly stable in some societies, more fluidity is characteristic of others. Social mobility is higher in the USA than in Indonesia, for example, and higher in urban than in rural settings. How this is reflected in language behavior and whether or how different degrees of social mobility affect the velocity and intensity of language change are questions which are as intriguing as they are difficult to handle. Reducing them to specific, testable hypotheses is one difficulty, and the general complexity of social and linguistic systems is another.

Communities that differ sufficiently in terms of social structure, but are comparable in terms of language behavior are hard to find. While this is yet another indication of how closely language and society are linked, it makes comparative research projects difficult to conceive and carry out. Most micro-sociolinguistic studies have, therefore, focussed on a single speech community and the social distinctions reflected in its members' speech. In its dealings with speech communities micro-sociolinguistics overlaps with macro-sociolinguistics.

7   Macro-sociolinguistics

"Speech community" is one of the basic notions of sociolinguistics, one which should not be used without an explicit definition. A common language distinguishes a social group in a sense, but the relationship between language and group affiliation is more complex than that. On one hand, where language is the only commonality, it does not really define a *social* group, and on the other, social groups may be defined in terms of language even though their members make use of more than one language. As Gumperz (1968: 220) was quick to point out, "regardless of the linguistic differences among them, the speech varieties employed within a speech community form a system because they are related to a shared set of social norms." Linguistic rules are like social norms in that their validity is guaranteed by social aggregates. An important lesson of sociolinguistics is that linguistic rules in this sense extend beyond the traditional areas of structural patterning, that is, phonology, syntax, and the lexicon. Choices speakers make of speech varieties including different languages are subject to shared expectations and are meaningful. That behavior is meaningful is another way of saying that it is social, since it can be meaningful only by virtue of being governed by rules, and rules presuppose a social frame of reference.

The speech community has also been defined as an attitudinal community. Stereotypes and values accorded different speech forms are viewed as determining membership (Labov 1972b). A more traditional definition reminiscent of dialect studies is that of a socio-geographical community whose members are assumed to exhibit a high degree of homogeneity in speech (Halliday 1978). Other definitions are based on shared repertoires affiliated with a common mother tongue (Kloss 1966), and speakers' claim to membership (Coulmas 1996). Most generally, speech communities can be defined in terms of shared expectations and rules. Whether or to what extent a set of social rules is shared by individual speakers must be determined by surveys. Specific surveys designed to gather data on language characteristics as well as censuses that include questions about language use and proficiency are an important instrument of macro-sociolinguistic research, that is, the sociology of language. Results of such surveys are used, along with other data, to describe the linguistic composition of speech communities, their delimitation and interaction with each other. Such descriptions are a precondition for analyzing what societies do with their languages, and for recognizing the attitudes and attachments that account for the functional distribution of speech forms in a society.

If sociology is concerned with explaining social life, social relationships, socially meaningful behavior, and group affiliations, language must occupy the sociologist's attention, if only because language is one of the social possessions which most obviously reflects the internal differentiation of human societies. It lends itself easily to being used as a symbol of signaling commonality and marking boundaries. This is, perhaps, most obvious in multilingual speech communities, but there is plenty of linguistic diversity in monolingual communities too, and its investigation by sociolinguists has demonstrated time and again that it is just as socially meaningful. This kind of variation not only manifests subdivisions within communities and "community loyalty" (Milroy and Margrain 1980: 26), it is also characteristic of the individual speaker's language skills. Speakers can and do make choices. In their normal communication behavior they choose to pronounce words such as *mad* as one syllable [mæd] or two [meːəd]; they say "thanks" or "thank you" or they choose some other expression of gratitude; they choose formal and less formal styles, dialectal or standard varieties. The inability to do so marks a speaker as socially incompetent. On the basis of the extensive research into language variation that has accumulated since the late 1960s, it is safe to say that social differentiation requires linguistic differentiation. If "requires" is understood here in a strict sense, it follows that explanations which can be derived from the relationship between language and society thus conceived will pertain, first and foremost, to language. "The social motivation of a sound change," the title of an early article by Labov (1963), is indicative of this perspective. In this article, Labov investigated vowel centralization on Martha's Vineyard, an island on the northeastern coast of the United States. He observed a generational change in the onset of the diphthongs in words such as *white, wide, house,* and *how* which he tried to correlate with social variables. In so doing he referred to social facts in order to explain linguistic phenomena, regarding social structure and stratification – in this case: occupational differences between farmers and fishers – as the cause of linguistic processes. However, attempts, such as Trudgill's (1978), to limit the sociolinguistic enterprise to establishing causal links in this direction only have not been successful, because language and society are so indissolubly connected with each other.

At any given time, the linguistic differentiation of social groups is a fact that can be observed. It not only reflects social structure, but is also part of the social fabric and as such determines how individuals and groups interact with each other. Language provides the stage on which many social conflicts are played out (Haugen 1966, Edwards 1985, Nelde 1989). People are appreciated and discriminated against for the way they speak (Fishman 1989, Honey 1989); their attitudes towards their own languages and those of others are emotional (Williams 1974), sometimes as strongly as religious beliefs. They have ideas about linguistic goodness and purity (Jernudd, Shapiro 1989, Thomas 1991), what does and what does not belong to their language, how language should be taught (Stubbs 1976), etc. Language is frequently used as a defining characteristic of nationhood (Wardhaugh 1983) and ethnicity (Fishman 1989b), and it is associated with stereotypes about these (Le Page, Tabouret-Keller 1985). Languages are acquired and defended in order to achieve social goals (Cummins 1986). They have economic utility and are a factor of the transaction costs of economic processes (Coulmas 1992). Accordingly, they are perceived as the key to empowerment and success (Tollefson 1993). These beliefs and attitudes, no matter whether or not they are borne out by reality, are social facts in their own right which interact with other social facts, which in turn may have an effect on how languages evolve. Not only does language reflect social order, it contributes to its perpetuation and / or change. Deliberately guided language change has been promoted as a means to advance modernization, eradicate or reduce racial and sexual discrimination, and create national cohesion (Cooper 1989, Weinstein 1983; see chapter 32). Policies designed to expand the geographical and / or social domains of a language – e.g., Swahili in post-colonial Tanzania – have created social facts (Calvet 1987, Pütz 1995). Dialects have broken away and been established as independent national languages for political reasons. For instance, Maltese, once a substandard Arabic trade jargon was accorded the status of Malta's national language (Hull 1994). Similarly, under German occupation during World War II, Luxembourgers reinforced the differences between Lëtzebuergesch and Standard German to turn their speech from a German dialect into a proper language (Kramer 1994).

Further, linguistic diversity, such as is characteristic of south Asia (Shapiro and Schiffman 1981) and many African societies (Herbert 1992), forces people to develop adaptive strategies such as creating and using a lingua franca (Calvet 1981). The multiplicity of languages is a social given for every member who is born into such a society. Here again language is a constituent of society rather than a mere reflection of its constitution. It interacts with other universals characteristic of human societies, i.e., technology (material culture), the organization of the social microcosm (kinship), the organization of the social macrocosm (politics) and the organization of the cosmos of beliefs (religion / ideology). The sociology of language explores these connections. Their relationships with micro-sociolinguistic issues are varied, some being more closely linked, others having a more distant connection. It has not proven feasible, however, to draw a sharp line between these two orientations.

Many questions can be investigated with equal justification within micro- or macro-sociolinguistics. For instance, Uriel Weinreich's (1968) concern with language contact focussed on the traces that can be detected in linguistic systems of the contact and interaction of neighboring speech communities through their bilingual members. However, the preconditions and consequences of language contact involve a range of interesting phenomena, social and linguistic, which have both micro- and macro-aspects. "Contact linguistics" is now recognized as a branch of sociolinguistics (Nelde et al. 1995). The following can all be viewed as consequences of language contact: Language generation, i.e., pidginization and creolization (Mühlhäusler 1986, Bickerton 1992); language degeneration, i.e., language displacement (Dorian 1989); and novel patterns of language use, i.e., codeswitching (Myers-Scotton 1993a, 1993b). These and some other matters such as diglossia and bilingualism are discussed at length in chapter 21 and, therefore, need not be dealt with here. It is worth noting, however, that it is quite impossible to say, without making arbitrary decisions, whether they should be treated properly in micro- or macro-sociolinguistics. The indissoluble connection between micro- and macro-issues has important repercussions for the question of a sociolinguistic theory.

8   Theories but No Theory

The double reliance on social and language sciences has sometimes been considered the major reason for what has been diagnosed as the theoretical deficit of sociolinguistics. Sociological theory has gone its own system-theoretic way, maintaining at best a very esoteric interest in language and more commonly ignoring the role of language in constructing society altogether. At the same time, the advent of the powerful generative paradigm in linguistics led mainstream linguists to turn their back on society and sociology. They acknowledge variation as an obvious fact which, however, is said to be of no interest to linguistic theory (Smith 1989: 180).

If it were true that there is nothing of theoretical importance in variation, then linguistics would fail to address a whole range of questions which many would ask who want to understand what language is and how it works. Some such questions are the following:

- How is it that language can fulfill the function of communication despite variation?
- What does it mean that most people in London and New York speak "English," even though it is evident that what is spoken in these two places differs in many significant ways?
- What part of the speech of Anglo-Canadians in Montreal is baffling to outsiders if only English is considered, but easily explained if we take notice of the fact that it coexists and, in the heads and conversations of bilinguals, interacts with French?
- Is the range of language units that are judged to be the same and treated as such by linguists defined by physical parameters or social conventions?
- Why do languages change, and what does it mean that they do; that is, what kind of an object is it that changes while in some sense preserving its identity?

By not admitting such questions to its agenda; by refusing to consider the possibility that social factors should play a role in linguistic analysis because language is essentially a socially constituted system; and by discounting variation as an imperfection rather than recognizing it as an inherent feature of human behavior and the working of the human mind, linguistics has constructed language as a highly abstract object about which statements can be made in the framework of a coherent theory. But what does this theory have to say about the nature of language? Linguistic theory hence is a theory about language without human beings. It is a formal model of structural relationships of which it is basically unknown how they relate to actual speech. Whatever the merits of this model, it is hardly the theory that will help unravel the structural foundations of society which linguistics was once expected to provide.

On the other hand, sociological theory generally pays minimal attention to language. Durkheim, Weber, and Parsons took little interest in language as a social fundamental. And even where language is assigned a role in explaining social facts, as in Schütz's (1965) concept of "intersubjectivity," the foundation of ethnomethodology, or in Habermas's (1985) "universal pragmatics," it is at a highly abstract level probing the (universal) conditions that make social interaction possible. Thus, sociological dealings with language have produced a theory of language use in social contexts no more than has linguistics.

Since all communities exhibit variation in their speech and the majority of all people use more than one language in their everyday lives, it would seem evident that these facts are something to be accounted for by a theory of language. The question is whether sociolinguistics can fill this gap or will ever be able to do so. To construct such a theory is seen by some as a vital task for putting what so far has been a mainly descriptive endeavor on a more solid foundation (Figueroa 1994). However, sociolinguists are divided amongst themselves as to the feasibility of such an undertaking. Fasold (1990: viiiff) has expressed pessimism about a unified theory of sociolinguistics on a par with that of "linguistics proper," whereas Romaine (1994: 221ff) thinks that such a theory is both desirable and feasible. It should, she argues, not only supplement linguistic theory with respect to phenomena which cannot be explained properly without reference to social factors, but indeed form the core of a "socially constituted" theory of language, i.e., an alternative paradigm for studying all aspects of language.

On the sociological side, Williams (1992) has criticized sociolinguistics for failing to produce a theory of its own while at the same time uncritically relying on Parsonian structural functionalism and the individualistic consensualist view of society associated with it. He calls for a conflict model of society to be regarded as the cornerstone of a sociolinguistic theory which takes into account power differentials within and across speech communities in analyzing the social forces governing speech behavior. The most promising approach to such a sociolinguistics, he argues, may be found in the work of French sociologists such as Bourdieu (1977) and Achard (1993). A theory about language in society will miss a crucial point if it fails to address power and social control. However, some of the difficulties that stand in the way of a sociolinguistic theory that does take issue with power differentials and means of social control stem from the fact that sociologists take language for granted rather than as an object of theorizing and at the same time fail to furnish a social theory to which a theory of language use can be easily linked.

It must also be noted that scientific fields differ considerably with respect to the importance that is accorded to theory formation. Sociology emphasizes abstract theories more than other social sciences, and sociologists have little patience with purely descriptive research. The same can be said of formal linguistics. The major purpose of empirical studies both in sociology and linguistics is to test theories. By contrast, sociolinguistics is preoccupied with descriptive research. Due to the complexity of the phenomena it has to deal with, methodological questions concerning the delimitation, collection, and processing of empirical data have been much more in the foreground than theory construction. Survey sampling, participant observation, questionnaire design, interview and elicitation techniques, multivariate analyses, probability theory and other methodological tools have been developed or adapted to fit language data. In contradistinction to the formal modeling along the lines of syntactic theory, logic, and computer science, sociolinguistic method is empirical and mostly quantitative, dealing as it does with observable speech behavior. This is not to say, however, that sociolinguistic research is atheoretical. Rather, there are numerous theories or sets of propositions of which it is expected that they will coalesce to form a theory about a particular aspect of the language–society nexus. The remainder of this chapter presents a brief overview of some of the theories and nascent theories that have grown out of sociolinguistic research. Space does not permit an in-depth discussion, and for theoretical notions pertaining to the study of multilingualism the reader is referred to chapter 21.

9   Language Change and Variation

As pointed out above, an important current of sociolinguistic research focusses on language change, and some of the most influential scholars in the field consider that the proper task of a sociolinguistic theory should be to explain and predict language change. Although based on assumptions that differ considerably in detail, this is the common position underlying three major works (Milroy 1992, Labov 1994, Chambers 1994). What are the causes and mechanisms of language change? Why are certain distinctions maintained, while others are lost? What are the forces that resist language change? What are the underlying principles that make predictions of changes in select communities possible? Such are the questions dealt with in this area of sociolinguistic scholarship.

Closely related to the pursuit of knowledge about language change is variation research (Romaine 1985). Indeed, both are often subsumed under the same heading, historical change being conceived as one kind of variation. Among the general questions addressed in this connection are the following: What

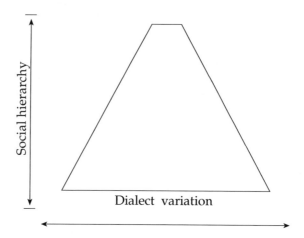

Figure 23.1   Regional and social variation

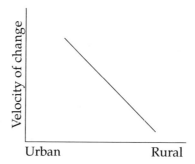

Figure 23.2   Velocity of linguistic change in urban and rural areas

is language variation and what does it imply for our conception of what (a) language is? What are the relevant social attributes that have a bearing on language variation? How do temporal, regional, and social variation interact, and how do they relate to age and gender? Interesting theoretical concepts have been developed which link regional and social variation. Various studies have demonstrated that in industrial societies adherence to a recognized standard increases with speakers' position in the social hierarchy, as indicated in figure 23.1 (adapted from Trudgill 1974).

Another generalization is about linguistic change in urban and rural areas, as portrayed in figure 23.2. Change tends to emanate from urban centers and spread to rural areas where speakers are less mobile and more conservative. However, at a time of rapid social transformations which affect economic conditions and social ties in both urban and rural areas, intervening variables have to be taken into account. In order to explain the retention of localized speech forms in specific settings, the above generalizations have to be supplemented by information about the socioeconomic conditions, social relations, ideology, and values of the community under investigation (Wolfram and Schilling-Estes 1995).

Since empirical data on the diffusion of linguistic innovation are available for few languages and with a relatively shallow real-time depth only, the investigation of change in progress makes use of the concept of "apparent time" (Labov 1994: 43ff), that is, the distribution of linguistic variables across age cohorts. If a significant correlation is discovered between age and a linguistic variable, then it has to be determined whether this correlation is a function of change in progress or of age differentiation of language use. In either case, the answer has to be theoretically founded.

10   Gender

Yet another dimension of linguistic variation is among sex and gender distinctions, where the former refers to biological and the latter to sociocultural differences (Eckert 1989). A vast research literature testifies to the great amount of interest that linguistic correlates of sex and gender have attracted in both sociolinguistics and gender studies (Miller and Swift 1976, Coates and Cameron 1988, Lorber and Farrell 1991). In most societies for which data are available, it has been demonstrated that women of all social strata are more sensitive toward prestige norms and deviate less from the prestige speech variety than men (Gordon 1997). The social significance of these differences clearly calls for explanation, and sociolinguistics has much to offer to the study of gender-based constraints in society.

11   Politeness

While most studies about gender and language deal with communities in North America and western Europe, there is also a growing body of literature about the speech of men and women in non-western societies (Chambers 1995: ch. 3). Many of these investigations border on another area of comparative research, politeness, that is, how language is used to define interpersonal relationships in terms of formality, intimacy, solidarity, and deference (Lakoff 1989, Watts et al. 1992). Many descriptions of politeness phenomena in various languages have been published in recent years and have stimulated theoretical discussions about such questions as whether politeness can be defined independently of a given language or speech community; whether it can be measured and how it can be compared across languages; and whether politeness should be construed as a notion belonging to the language system, language use, or both (Brown and Levinson 1978).

The nexus of politeness and gender differentiation in speech plays a significant role in discourse analysis (Schiffrin 1994, Tannen 1993), which has evolved
into an entire subdiscipline of sociolinguistics with its own analytic methods
and theoretical concepts (see chapter 17). Like variation studies, discourse
analysis uses tape recordings of real-life speech for analysis, but its method is
more interpretative. While variation studies insists on quantifiable generalizations, discourse analysis tends to draw conclusions on the basis of an in-depth
analysis of a small corpus of data. The view that gender-related language
variation corresponds to different views of the world and that misunderstand-
ings between men and women arise because the male and female worldviews
as encoded in language do not coincide has been articulated on the basis of
interpretative rather than quantitative findings (Tannen 1991).

12   Linguistic Relativism

The idea that worldviews are encoded in language has long played a role
in sociolinguistics. First advanced by Wilhelm von Humboldt in the early
nineteenth century, it came to be associated in the twentieth century with the
work of Edward Sapir and Benjamin L. Whorf. They focussed on Amerindian
languages in which the physical world was encoded in ways that differed
markedly from the more extensively studied languages of Indo-European stock.
Languages, they concluded from their observations, function as perceptual
and conceptual filters, a notion which subsequently became known as the
"linguistic relativity hypothesis." A rigid interpretation of this hypothesis sees
speakers' cognition strongly influenced, if not wholly determined, by the language they speak. While originally developed in the context of cross-linguistic
comparisions, this notion was also applied to intra-linguistic differences. When
Bernstein (1971) first introduced the notions of a "restricted" and "elaborated"
code, he drew on the linguistic relativity hypothesis, suggesting that habitual
use of restricted and elaborated codes implied differential cognitive abilities. Since Bernstein's restricted and elaborated codes were associated with
the working class–middle class division, his theory turned out to be politically
controversial. The question of whether or to what extent speech habits influence cognitive abilities was, therefore, by and large dropped from the agenda
of sociolinguistic research, and the concept of class-related deficient linguistic
abilities was replaced by that of differential codes which should each be
studied in their own right and not be judged against the "legitimate" norm.
Much discussed though it was when Bernstein published his first articles, his
theory of language, class, and cognition had little influence on the development of sociolinguistics outside Britain. The question whether the speech habits
of socially defined groups correlate with different cognitive abilities is not only
difficult to substantiate, but thought illegitimate by many, or at least undesi-
able to ask.

To what extent the structure of one's language shapes one's view of the world thus remains an unresolved issue. Yet, the idea that language exercises an influence on people's perception and concepts is still espoused by many (Lucy 1992) and often forms the underlying paradigm for describing the relation between language and society (Chaika 1989). The view that language and thought are related has informed sociolinguistics in many different ways. While few scholars these days support a strong variant of linguistic determinism, it is widely thought plausible that if the world is habitually talked about in certain ways, thinking can be influenced thereby. At the same time, it is generally acknowledged that all languages provide the means to express things differently and to express novel thoughts. How speech habits interact with ways of thinking, then, remains one of the many intricate questions into which empirical research is needed.

13 Conclusion

As this overview has demonstrated, sociolinguistics deals with an extremely wide range of observable phenomena that relate to language and society in ways that call for systematic explanations. So wide a range it is, indeed, that there is no room for an essentialist conclusion which would tell the reader in one paragraph what sociolinguistics is all about. We must settle for re-emphasizing the width and extraordinary complexity of the evidence that needs to be taken into account. Social variants have a bearing on language choices at virtually every conceivable level of patterning and use, while the linguistic resources of groups and individuals are at the same time basic to constituting social order. In many areas meaningful correlations, a system of regular connections, could be demonstrated to underlie seemingly disparate and multifarious facts. However, these various relations in both directions outreach the grasp of a single over-arching theory of language and society. At this time, sociolinguistics presents itself as a vast field into which many lines have been drawn. The result is not a unified pattern where everything falls into place, but, rather, a criss-cross of intersecting and overlapping figures. There is a huge number of descriptive studies on the basis of which many specific phenomena can be explained, in the strict sense of the term, although these particularistic explanations have resisted incorporation into a unified explanatory framework. This is not surprising or a reason for discontent. It simply attests to the fact that a single theoretical approach is insufficient to account for what is most essential to human existence, language as a means of conceiving and creating society.

24 Neurolinguistics

DAVID CAPLAN

The field of neurolinguistics has come to consist of two related areas of study: language disorders (which is sometimes called "aphasiology") and the relationship between language and the brain. Aphasiology has made important discoveries about what goes wrong with language after brain damage, some of which have implications for what language is and how it is processed. Aphasiology is closely linked to the study of the relationship between language and the brain. The combined study of patients' language deficits and neurological lesions provides evidence about the location and type of brain damage that affects language. This indirectly gives us information about how the brain is organized to process language normally. In fact, this traditional "deficit-lesion" or "clinico-pathological" correlational approach was the only way that we could learn about this subject for many years. This approach has been considerably refined as more detailed descriptions of language disorders have been produced that draw on linguistics and psychology and as advances in neuroimaging allow for much more precise and complete characterization of lesions than previously possible.

In recent years, the traditional deficit-lesion correlational approach to brain organization for language has been complemented by studies of brain function in normal subjects when they perform tasks that involve language. "Functional neuroimaging" uses positron emission tomography (PET) and functional magnetic resonance imaging (fMRI), which primarily measure regional cerebral blood flow (rCBF). Measurements can also be made on the scalp of electrophysiological potentials ("event related potentials" – ERPs) and small electromagnetic potentials (magnetoencephalography) to record neural activity that arises in relationship to language functions. In the late 1980s, most of these techniques were in their infancy, if they existed at all, and their evolution and application to the study of the relationship of language and the brain has made the present period one of the most exciting in the history of neurolinguistics. In this chapter, I shall present an introduction to this rapidly evolving field.

1   Aphasiology

1.1   *A very brief history of aphasiology*

Though it was known as far back as ancient Egypt that damage to the brain affected language, the scientific investigation of the relationship of the brain to language dates to the mid-nineteenth century. Speculative work by Brouillaud, Lordat, and others set the stage for the paper that started and defined both aphasiology and neurolinguistics – Paul Broca's presentation to the Anthropological Society of Paris of the now famous case of Lebourgne (Broca 1861). We shall review the "neurolinguistic" part of this paper below. The "aphasiological" part of the paper is fairly simple, but had profound effects on the field. Broca's case was a 57-year-old man who had come into the hospital 21 years earlier unable to speak. He could only utter the syllable "tan." He appeared able to understand what people said to him, and he could express his needs and emotions through gesture and by changing the tone of his voice. Over the years he developed a right sided weakness, and eventually became bedridden. He died of an infection that began in bed sores in his right leg, which had become ulcerated and infected as a result of having been lain on and improperly attended to. However, for the entire period of his hospitalization, his language capacities remained static – at least according to the information that Broca had and that he relayed to the Anthropological Society.

Broca's analysis of the language disorder in "Tan" was that he had lost the "faculty of articulate speech" while retaining the faculty for language comprehension and those for production and recognition of meaningful gestures. With this analysis, Broca defined the approach to aphasia that dominated medical and scientific thinking for decades – to think of language disorders as disorders of the ability to use language in the usual tasks of speaking, understanding, reading, and writing. This approach focussed attention on the common tasks by which linguistically based communication takes place. This is a domain of human linguistic functioning that, though complicated, is much more tractable and much better understood than domains such as verbally based reasoning and planning, self-expression, verbal creativity, etc. From the neurolinguistic point of view, these basic functions of speech, comprehension, reading, and writing are related to a relatively small part of the brain. Thus, this focus allowed researchers to make some headway into the question of how the brain is related to language functions. However, the division of language functions into these large areas also had its drawbacks as well. For decades it inhibited investigation of the components of these psycholinguistic tasks, which has had negative effects on aphasiology, neurolinguistics, and approaches to therapy. Fortunately, modern aphasiology has begun the task of taking apart tasks such as speaking, comprehending, etc., into their components and describing language disorders in terms of these components. Before turning to these modern studies, however, we should briefly review the "classic" clinically defined aphasic syndromes, since they still are commonly referred to by clinicians who diagnose and treat language disorders.

These "aphasic syndromes" are shown in table 24.1. "Broca's aphasia" is a severe expressive language disturbance reducing the fluency of speech without an equally severe disturbance of auditory comprehension. "Wernicke's aphasia" consists of the combination of fluent speech with erroneous choices of the sounds of words (phonemic paraphasias) and an auditory comprehension disturbance. "Pure word deafness" is the relatively pure case of an auditory receptive disorder in which the patient does not recognize spoken words, so spontaneous speech is normal but comprehension and repetition are disturbed. "Anarthria," "dysarthria" and "apraxia of speech" are output speech disorders in which both repetition and spontaneous speech are mis-articulated but comprehension is preserved. In "transcortical motor aphasia," spontaneous speech is reduced but repetition is intact; in "transcortical sensory aphasia," a comprehension disturbance exists without a disturbance of repetition. A disturbance in spontaneous speech and repetition without a disturbance in auditory comprehension is termed "conduction aphasia." All of these syndromes were claimed to have been discovered in relatively pure form by reseachers by 1885 (Lichtheim 1885). This classification was revived by Normal Geschwind in the 1960s (Geschwind 1965).

These syndromes reflect the relative ability of patients to perform language tasks (speaking, comprehension, etc.), not the integrity of specific components of the language processing system. For instance, the speech production problem seen in Broca's aphasia can consist of one or more of a large number of impairments – disorders affecting articulation such as dysarthria or apraxia of speech, disorders affecting sentence form such as agrammatism, etc. Patients with Wernicke's aphasia can have deficits affecting either the sounds of words or their meanings or both, as well as any number of other language processing deficits. There are at least two major deficits that underlie "conduction aphasia," one affecting word production and one affecting verbal short-term memory. At the same time as patients with the same syndrome can have different deficits, identical deficits occur in different syndromes. For instance, certain types of naming problems can occur in any aphasic syndrome. For these reasons, knowing that a patient has a particular aphasic syndrome does not tell us exactly what is wrong with his or her language. For that, one has to turn to more detailed studies.

1.2   *Modern aphasiology*

The contemporary approach to language disorders provides such studies. It sees human language as a code that links a set of linguistic forms to a number of aspects of meaning. These forms are activated in the usual tasks of language

Table 24.1   The classic aphasic syndromes

Syndrome	Clinical manifestations	Hypothetical deficit	Classical lesion location
Broca's aphasia	Major disturbance in speech production with sparse, halting speech, often misarticulated, frequently missing function words and bound morphemes	Disturbances in the speech planning and production mechanisms	Primarily posterior aspects of the third frontal convolution and adjacent inferior aspects of the precentral gyrus
Wernicke's aphasia	Major disturbance in auditory comprehension; fluent speech with disturbances of the sounds and structures of words (phonemic, morphological, and semantic paraphasias)	Disturbances of the permanent representations of the sound structures of words	Posterior half of the first temporal gyrus and possibly adjacent cortex
Anomic aphasia	Disturbance in the production of single words, most marked for common nouns with variable comprehension problems	Disturbances of the concepts and / or the sound patterns of words	Inferior parietal lobe or connections between parietal lobe and temporal lobe
Global aphasia	Major disturbance in all language functions	Disruption of all language processing components	Large portion of the perisylvian association cortex
Conduction aphasia	Disturbance of repetition and spontaneous speech (phonemic paraphasias)	Disconnection between the sound patterns of words and the speech production mechanism	Lesion in the arcuate fasciculus and / or corticocortical connections between temporal and frontal lobes
Transcortical aphasia	Disturbance of spontaneous speech similar to Broca's aphasia with relatively preserved repetition	Disconnection between conceptual representations of words and sentences and the motor speech production system	White matter tracts deep to Broca's area

Table 24.1   Cont'd

Syndrome	Clinical manifestations	Hypothetical deficit	Classical lesion location
Transcortical sensory aphasia	Disturbance in single word comprehension with relatively intact repetition	Disturbance in activation of word meanings despite normal recognition of auditorily presented words	White matter tracts connecting parietal lobe to temporal lobe or in portions of inferior parietal lobe
Isolation of the language zone	Disturbance of both spontaneous speech (similar to Broca's aphasia) and comprehension, with some preservation of repetition	Disconnection between concepts and both representations of word sounds and the speech production mechanism	Cortex just outside the perisylvian association cortex

use – speaking, auditory comprehension, reading, and writing – by different "components" of a "language processing system." For instance, a component of the language processing system might accept as input the semantic representation (meaning) activated by the presentation of a picture and produce as output a representation of the sound pattern of the word that corresponds to that meaning.

At least four levels of language representation are clearly identified in contemporary models of the language processing system: the *lexical level*, the *morphological level*, the *sentential level*, and the *discourse level*. Lexical items (simple words) designate concrete objects, abstract concepts, actions, properties, and logical connectives. The basic form of a simple lexical item consists of a phonological representation that specifies the sounds (phonemes) of the word and their organization into rhythmic structures (e.g., syllables). The morphological level of language allows the meaning associated with a simple lexical item to be used as a different syntactic category (e.g., the suffix -*tion* allows the semantic values associated with a verb to be used as a noun, as in the word *destruction* derived from *destroy*). This avoids the need for an enormous number of elementary lexical items in an individual's vocabulary. Morphology also signals grammatical information such as agreement (e.g., *I run*; *he runs*). The sentential level of language makes use of the syntactic categories to build syntactic structures (e.g., noun phrase, verb phrase, sentence, etc.) that define relationships between words relevant to the meaning of a sentence (its "propositional content"). Sentences convey information about who did what to whom (thematic roles), which adjectives go with which nouns (attribution or modification), the reference of pronouns and other referentially dependent categories, etc. They make statements that can be true or false, and that therefore can be used in logical and planning processes and serve as a means for updating an individual's knowledge of the world. Discourse conveys information about temporal order, causation, the number of entities involved in an event, which of these entities is in the current focus of attention, and other similar aspects of meaning. The structure of a discourse depends upon a complex interaction between linguistic forms (such as whether an entity in the discourse is referred to by a noun or a pronoun) and non-linguistic functions, such as what a person knows and infers. For more details regarding the structure of language, see chapters 11 and 16.

These levels of the language code are all activated in parallel in the acts of speaking, understanding, reading, and writing. Consider speaking, for instance. A speaker selects words to convey concepts on the basis of his / her knowledge of a subject and also as a function of what words s/he thinks the listener will understand. S/he selects the sounds of each word and their proper order. S/he puts the words into the grammatical structures needed to convey the relationships between their meanings and finds the right morphological form for each word in each grammatical position. S/he selects intonational contours that express whether a sentence is a statement, a question, a command, or has some other illocutionary force. Intonational contours and syntactic structures are also selected to express the focus of the discourse. The speaker sends commands to the muscles of the chest, the diaphragm, the larynx, and the oral and nasal tracts to integrate the movements of all these regions in a way that produces exactly the right sounds for each word with the right degree of stress. All these operations go on unconsciously, at a speed of about 120 words per minute, or 2 words per second, or roughly 1 sound (phoneme) every 100 milliseconds or so. A speaker is not only fast at doing these remarkable computations and retrieval operations; s/he is also accurate. Estimates of the number of errors that a speaker makes are in the range of one semantic mistake every million words and a comparable number of sound-based errors (see Levelt 1989, for an extensive review of these processes).

Speaking is a remarkable act, but no more so than understanding spoken speech (where the words, structure, and meaning of an utterance are extracted from the acoustic signal), or reading or writing. All these functions are the result of the integrated activity of dozens of highly specific operations acting in parallel and in critically ordered sequences. More detailed discussion of language processing can be found in chapter 16.

Modern aphasiology tries to understand disturbances of speaking, comprehension, reading and writing as disruptions of specific language processing components. It is impossible to present a review of all the disturbances that have been described that affect each of the components of the language processing system in each of the tasks of speaking, comprehending, reading, and writing. I shall instead sample from two areas of language – disorders affecting patients' abilities to understand the meanings of words and disorders affecting their abilities to understand sentences.

1.3   *Disturbances of word meanings*

Most recent research on disturbances of word meanings in brain damaged patients has focussed on words that refer to objects. The meanings of these words are thought to be stored in a specialized memory store, called "semantic memory" (Tulving 1972, 1983). Though semantic memory also is thought to house representations of entities other than objects (such as events, for instance), the concepts that correspond to objects have been the subject of the most extensive thought and investigation in philosophy and psychology. The representations of objects in semantic memory have traditionally been thought of as sets of features that list the properties that are necessary and sufficient for an item to fall into a given category, such as that for an entity to be a bird it has to have feathers and to fly. It is now appreciated that most concepts are not easily described in these terms, and that categorization must depend on probabilistic criteria (see Smith and Medin 1981, for discussion). For instance, penguins and ostriches are birds but do not fly. The concepts corresponding to concrete objects may be represented in both a "verbal" and a "visual" semantic memory system (Miller and Johnson-Laird 1976, Paivio 1971), though the evidence for this is controversial (Snodgrass 1984). The verbal semantic system may encode relations of one entity to another and functional properties of each item, such as the fact that some birds fly south in the winter. The visual semantic system may encode physical properties of an item that allow it to be recognized, such as the typical silhouette of a bird.

Disturbances of word meanings thus can be seen as problems affecting the ability of a patient to appreciate how an item is classified or what its necessary and typical features are. Such disturbances would be expected to affect a patient's ability to identify a word or a picture as an example of a specific concept, and therefore to cause poor performance on word-picture matching and naming tasks (Warrington 1975). The co-occurrence of deficits in word-picture matching and naming is not an adequate basis for diagnosing a problem affecting word meaning, however, because a patient may have separate disturbances that affect word recognition and production independently (Howard and Orchard-Lisle 1984). Co-occurring deficits in naming and word-picture matching are more likely to result from a disturbance affecting concepts when the patient makes many semantic errors in providing words to pictures and definitions, s/he has trouble with word picture matching with semantic but not phonological foils, s/he fails on categorization tasks with pictures, and when the same words are affected in production and comprehension tasks (Hillis et al. 1990).

It has been argued that brain damage may affect either the storage or the retrieval of word meanings. Shallice (1988a, 1988b), Warrington and Shallice (1979) and Warrington and McCarthy (1987) have suggested that there are five hallmarks of the loss of items in semantic memory – consistent production of semantic errors on particular items across different inputs (pictures, written words, spoken words), relative preservation of superordinate information as opposed to information about an item's features, relative preservation of information about higher frequency items, no improvement of performance by priming and cueing, and no effect of the rate at which a task is performed upon performance. These researchers have also suggested that disorders of *retrieval* of items from semantic memory is characterized by the opposite effects of these variables on performance. These authors have described patients with semantic impairments, whose impairments they say are of one or the other of these types. The criteria for distinguishing between storage and retrieval impairments remain controversial, however (Caramazza et al. 1990; see Caplan 1992: ch. 4, for discussion).

Disorders affecting processing of semantic representations for objects may be specific to certain types of inputs. Warrington (1975) first noted a discrepancy between comprehension of words and pictures in two dementing patients. Bub et al. (1988) have analyzed a patient, M. P., who showed very poor comprehension of written and spoken words but quite good comprehension of pictures. These impairments have been taken as reflections of disturbances of "verbal" and "visual" semantic systems, though this interpretation is debated (Riddoch and Humphreys 1987).

Semantic disturbances may also be category-specific. Several authors have reported a selective semantic impairment of concepts related to living things and foods compared to human-made objects (Sartori and Job 1988, Silveri and Gainotti 1988, Warrington and Shallice 1984). The opposite pattern has also been found (Warrington and McCarthy 1983, 1987). Selective preservation and disruption of abstract versus concrete concepts, and of nominal versus verbal concepts, have also been reported (Miceli et al. 1984; Schwartz et al. 1979, Warrington 1981a, 1981b, Zingeser and Berndt 1988).

A very interesting feature of many aphasic disorders is that they may affect conscious and unconscious processing differently. Though it is far from clear exactly what it is about certain types of processing that makes them "conscious," it is clear that there is a difference between the way we accomplish functions such as speech production and the way we do other types of tasks, such as long division. The operations involved in speech planning are unconscious; those in long division are controlled and conscious. Milberg and his colleagues (Milberg and Blumstein 1981; Blumstein 1982) have described patients who cannot match words to pictures or name objects, but who show evidence of understanding words unconsciously. The evidence that these patients process meaning unconsciously is that they show "semantic priming effects." These effects consist of responding more quickly to a word when it has been preceded by a semantically related word in a task that does not require the subject to process the word's meaning. For instance, if a subject is shown sequences of letters on a computer screen and asked to press a button to indicate whether a sequence is a word or not (a "lexical decision" task), s/he will respond faster to the letter string DOCTOR when it follows the string NURSE than when it follows the string TABLE. Milberg and his colleagues have found these priming effects in some patients who do not show evidence of understanding words when the task requires conscious processing of a word's meaning, suggesting that they are able to appreciate the meanings of words unconsciously but not process meaning in conscious, controlled tasks like word-picture matching. Conversely, Swinney et al. (1989) have shown that some patients who appear to understand words well may have abnormalities in tasks that examine unconscious processing of the meanings of words. These researchers reported that four aphasic patients who were good at word-picture matching performed abnormally in a priming task with ambiguous words (like *bank*). Unlike normals, who showed priming for both senses of an ambiguous word, the four patients studied by Swinney and his colleagues only showed priming for the most frequent sense of ambiguous words. This indicates that their unconscious processing of word meanings was abnormal, even if it did not affect their performance on untimed, controlled, conscious tasks such as word-picture matching.

1.4   Disorders of sentence comprehension

When a subject understands a sentence, s/he combines the meanings of the words into a propositional content in accordance with the syntactic structure of the sentence. There are many reasons why a patient might fail to carry out the operations that are needed to arrive at propositional content. Disturbances affecting comprehension of simple and morphologically complex words affect comprehension at the sentence level. In addition, there are disturbances affecting patients' abilities to understand aspects of propositional meaning despite good single word comprehension.

The largest amount of work in the area of disturbances of sentence comprehension has gone into the investigation of patients whose use of syntactic structures to assign meaning is not normal. Caramazza and Zurif (1976) were the first researchers to show that some patients have selective impairments of this ability. These researchers described patients who could match "semantically irreversible" sentences such as *"The apple the boy is eating is red"* to one of two pictures but not "semantically reversible" sentences such as *"The girl the boy is chasing is tall."* The difference between the two types of sentences resides in the fact that a listener can understand a sentence such as *"The apple the boy is eating is red"* because boys are animate and can eat, and apples are inanimate and can be eaten, whereas understanding *"The girl the boy is chasing is tall"* requires assigning the syntactic structure of the sentence since both boys and girls are capable of chasing one another. Caramazza and Zurif concluded that their patients could not assign or use syntactic structure for this purpose.

Disorders of syntactic comprehension have since been examined in considerable detail (Caplan and Futter 1986; Caplan and Hildebrandt 1988; Hildebrandt et al. 1987, Linebarger et al. 1983, Martin et al. 1989, Schwartz et al. 1980, Tyler 1985). Patients may have very selective disturbances affecting the use of particular syntactic structures or elements to determine the meaning of a sentence. For instance, two patients we studied showed a double dissociation in their abilities to understand sentences with reflexive elements (*himself*) and pronouns (*him*) (Caplan and Hildebrandt 1988). Some patients can understand very simple syntactic forms, such as active sentences (*The man hugged the woman*), but not more complex forms, such as passive sentences (*The woman was hugged by the man*) (Caplan et al. 1985). Many of these patients use strategies such as assigning the thematic role of agent to a noun immediately before a verb to understand semantically reversible sentences, leading to systematic errors in comprehension of sentences such as "*The boy who pushed the girl kissed the baby.*" Other patients have virtually no ability to use syntactic structure at all. Most of these patients appear to rely upon inferences based upon their knowledge of the real world and their ability to understand some words in a sentence, as seems to have been the case with the original patients described by Caramazza and Zurif (1976).

As with simple words, some patients can assign and interpret syntactic structures unconsciously but not use these structures in a conscious, controlled fashion. For instance, Tyler (1985) reported a patient whose online word-monitoring performances indicated that he was sensitive to certain syntactic anomalies, but who could not make judgments regarding these same anomalies at the end of a sentence. Linebarger and her colleagues (Linebarger et al. 1983; Linebarger 1990) have reported that some patients who have syntactic comprehension problems (who cannot match reversible sentences to pictures, for instance) can make judgments as to whether or not a sentence is grammatical. For instance, some patients can indicate that the utterance "*The woman was watched the man*" is ill-formed and the utterance "*The woman was watched by the man*" is acceptable, despite not being able to match sentences such as "*The woman was watched by the man*" to one of two pictures. These researchers have interpreted these results as an indication that some patients can construct syntactic structures but not use them to determine propositional meaning (a so-called "mapping" problem – Schwartz et al. 1985). As with other areas of language functioning, it appears that patients may retain unconscious, online sentence comprehension processes but lose the ability to use the products of these processes in a controlled, conscious fashion in some tasks.

Disturbance of short-term memory can produce sentence comprehension impairments, but the connection between the two disorders is more complex than one might suspect. Martin and Ramoni (1994) have related short-term memory impairments to difficulties in understanding parts of sentences that consist of lists of words, such as *big, noisy, and aggressive*, in the sentence *The neighbor's dog was big, noisy, and aggressive.* However, many case studies show that patients with short-term memory impairments can have excellent syntactic processing abilities (Caplan and Waters 1990, McCarthy and Warrington 1984, Butterworth et al. 1986, Waters et al. 1991). Short-term memory impairments may induce problems remembering the meaning of a sentence, not understanding that meaning in the first place (see Caplan and Waters 1998, for review).

1.5   Comments on modern aphasiology

This brief overview merely conveys some of the results of recent research into disorders affecting word meanings and sentence comprehension. Even this brief survey indicates that these disturbances are very complex, and vary in different patients. It shows that studies of brain damaged patients can suggest features of how language is structured, such as the suggestion that word meanings are organized into semantic categories, or that the assignment of syntactic structure is partially independent of the use of that structure to determine sentence meaning. The review indicates that modern aphasiology provides a list of representations and operations that ultimately need to be related to the brain – verbal semantic representations, visual semantic representations, category-specific semantic representations, specific syntactic operations, etc. Most of these representations and functions need to be better understood for us to be sure that what we are relating to the brain are the cognitive operations that are really those used by normal human beings. However, scientists have not waited for these cognitive functions to be completely understood before trying to see how the brain processes language; there are many studies of language–brain relationships that have been undertaken despite our current state of relative ignorance of the true nature of linguistic representations and psycholinguistic operations. Some of these studies will no doubt have to be revised as we discover that our models of language and language processing need changing, but others are quite solid. We now turn to this second aspect of neurolinguistics – the relationship of language to the brain.

2   Language and the Brain

2.1   The overall organization of the brain for language

The brain is perhaps the most highly differentiated organ in the body. It consists of a large number of regions, each of which contributes to sensation, motor function, thought, emotion, and other functions in special ways. Only a relatively small part of the brain is devoted to language (figure 24.1). This part

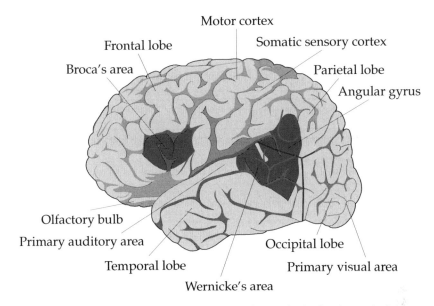

Figure 24.1 Depiction of the left lateral surface of the human brain showing perisylvian association cortex related to language
Source: Adapted from Carpenter 1983

lies in the cerebral cortex – a thin strip of neural cells and supporting tissue along the outermost edge of the brain – and consists of the association cortex in the region of the sylvian fissure (Luria 1970, Russell and Esper 1961, Basso et al. 1985, Weisenberg and McBride 1935, Brown 1972, Pick 1973). This region includes the pars triangularis and the pars opercularis of the third frontal convolution (Broca's area), the association cortex in the opercular area of the pre- and post-central gyri, the supramarginal and angular gyri of the parietal lobe, the first temporal gyrus from the supramarginal gyrus to a point lateral to Heschl's gyrus (Wernicke's area), and possibly a portion of the adjacent second temporal gyrus. On the basis of present knowledge, there is no other *cortical* area that can be confidently thought to subserve language functions. The supplementary motor area is the only other cortical structure that has been suggested to play a role in language processing. However, its primary function in language tasks appears to be to initiate vocalization, not to activate linguistic representations through subserving a component of the language processing system per se (Masdeu et al. 1978).

  The cortex does not exist or function alone; it is connected by large white matter tracts to subcortical nuclei in the basal ganglia, the thalamus, and the cerebellum. These structures are part of a "neural system" that processes language. Lesions of both the white matter tracts that connect the language cortex to these subcortical regions and of these regions themselves produce language impairments (Naeser et al. 1982, Cappa et al. 1983, Damasio et al. 1982, Mohr et al. 1975). However, the exact function of these structures is not completely understood. The white matter tracts presumably do not actually compute representations but only transfer the results of computations from one set of neurons to another. The basal ganglia, thalamus, and cerebellum may actually store and compute linguistic representations, and some researchers have suggested that these subcortical grey matter structures play roles in language processing (Damasio et al. 1982, Mohr et al. 1975, Crosson 1985). However, an alternative possibility is that the language disorders that follow subcortical lesions result from altered physiological activity in the overlying cortex, not disorders of the subcortical structures themselves.

The availability of patients with focal strokes that are visible only subcortically on CT or MR scans, in whom metabolic scanning is used to assess lesion site and size in both cortical and subcortical structures, provides an opportunity to investigate the role that both cortical and subcortical structures play in language. Across all the published cases of subcortical aphasia, there is a 1:1 correspondence between the presence or absence of cortical hypometabolism or hypoperfusion and the presence or absence of aphasic impairments in patients with strokes that are visible only subcortically on CT scans (Perani et al. 1987, Olsen et al. 1986). Moreover, studies correlating the degree of hypometabolism measured cortically and subcortically with the degree of language impairment indicate a much higher correlation of language impairments in aphasic patients with the indices of cortical hypometabolism (Metter et al. 1988, Metter et al. 1983, Kempler et al. 1988, Metter et al. 1987). There is not a single published case in which an aphasia has been documented in a patient in whom metablic scanning, blood flow studies, and physiological measures have all shown normally functioning perisylvian association cortex. The conclusion that is suggested by these results is that subcortical structures are not themselves responsible for language processing but serve only to activate the cortically based language processing system and to transfer the results of psycholinguistic computations from one part of the perisylvian association cortex to another. The simplest model consistent with available data is that language processing is carried out only in the perisylvian association cortex. However, nature does not always do things in the simplest possible way and this conclusion may be modified as more information accumulates.

A very important and well-attested feature of neural organization for language is lateralization – the fact that language processing relies upon one hemisphere more than another in most normal individuals. In about 98 per cent of strong right-handers from right-handed families, the left perisylvian association cortex accomplishes most, if not all, language processing functions (Luria 1970, Milner et al. 1964, Milner 1974). In individuals with other handedness profiles (Geschwind and Galaburda 1987, Geschwind and Galaburda 1985, Annett 1985), language functions are far more likely to involve the corresponding regions of the right hemisphere (Luria 1970, Russell and Esper 1961, Goodglass and Quadfasel 1954), with different likelihoods of right and left hemispheric involvement in language functions in different subgroups within this population (Subirana 1964). The data on differential lateralization as a function of sex are controversial (McGlone 1980).

A potentially important point is that many aphasic syndromes that follow either left or right hemisphere lesions in subjects who are not right-handed are often mild. Their occurrence suggests that many individual language processing components can be located in either hemisphere. Whether these language processing components are located in a given hemisphere in isolation from others can only be resolved by studies that establish whether the remaining intact language components are based in the intact portions of the lesioned hemisphere or in the undamaged hemisphere of patients with mild aphasias. In some cases (Kinsbourne 1971), intracarotid amytal injections (Wada studies) indicate that the latter appears to be the case. This would suggest separate control of lateralization for individual language processing components, but very few data are available on this point.

Though not as important in language functioning as the dominant hemisphere, the nondominant hemisphere is involved in many language operations. Evidence from the effects of lesions and split brain studies, as well as experiments using presentation of stimuli to one or the other hemisphere in normal subjects, indicate that the nondominant hemisphere understands many words, especially concrete nouns (Gazzaniga 1983, Chiarello et al. 1990), and suggest that it is involved in other aspects of language processing as well. For instance, our studies have shown effects of right hemisphere stroke upon syntactic processing, although these are much more mild than those found after left hemisphere strokes (Caplan et al. 1996), and this result has its counterpart in at least one study that showed minor but reliable increases in blood flow in the right hemisphere that were associated with syntactic processing (Just et al. 1996). Some language operations may be carried out primarily in the right hemisphere. The best candidates for these operations are ones that pertain to processing the discourse level of language, interpreting non-literal language such as metaphor, and appreciating the tone of a discourse as is manifest in, for instance, humor (Brownell and Gardner 1988, 1989, Joanette and Brownell 1990, Molloy et at. 1990, Roman et al. 1987). Some scientists have developed models of the sorts of processing that the right hemisphere carries out. For instance, Beeman (in press) has suggested that the right hemisphere codes information in a coarse way compared to the left. This and other suggestions provide the bases for ongoing research programs into the nature of language processing in the right hemisphere.

Overall, the gross organization of the brain for language is such that language processing takes place in a relatively small region of the cortex – the association cortex surrounding the sylvian fissure – with supporting connections to grey matter elsewhere in the brain. Much remains to be learned about the role that these subcortical grey matter structures play in actual psycholinguistic computations. There is specialization for language in one hemisphere, the details of which differ as a function of handedness. Much also remains to be learned about the details of what is lateralized and in whom. But at least the gross functional neuroanatomical facts are emerging. In comparison, the internal organization of the perisylvian cortex for language remains shrouded in mystery and steeped in controversy. To this, we now turn.

2.2   *The organization of the perisylvian association cortex for language*

Two general classes of theories of the relationship of portions of the perisylvian association cortex to components of the language processing system have been developed, one that maintains a distributed view of neural function (Jackson 1878, Freud 1891, Marie 1906, Head 1926, Mohr et al. 1978) and one that maintains a localizationist perspective (Luria 1970, Broca 1861, Wernicke 1974, Dejerine 1892, Lichtheim 1885, Henschen 1920, Neilson 1936, Geschwind 1965, Damasio and Damasio 1980, Luria 1973). Though theories within each of these two major groupings vary, there are a number of features common to theories within each class.

The basic tenet of distributed theories of the functional neuroanatomy for language is that linguistic representations and specific stages of linguistic processing are distributed widely across the perisylvian association cortex. Lashley (Lashley 1929, Lashley 1950) identified two functional features of distributed models that determine the effects of lesions upon performance – equipotentiality (every portion of a particular brain region can carry out a specific function in every individual) and mass action (the larger the neuronal pool that carries out a particular function, the more efficiently that function is accomplished). The features of equipotentiality and mass action jointly entail that lesions of similar sizes anywhere in a specified brain region have equivalent effects upon function, and that the magnitude of any functional deficit is directly proportional to the size of a lesion in this specified area. Computational models of lesions in "neural net" or "parallel distributed processing" (PDP) simulations of language and other cognitive functions have provided a mathematical basis for these properties of these systems (McClelland and Rumelhart 1986). Distributed models might also predict that activation studies in normal subjects would not find evidence for localized increases in blood flow or electrophysiological activity associated with particular psycholinguistic processes, although this prediction must be qualified by the consideration that some of these models suggest specializations within widely distributed neural nets, which may lead to such local increases in neural activity.

All of the traditional theories that postulate localization of components of the language processing system maintain the view that, discounting lateralization, the localization of components of the language processing system is invariant across the normal adult population. This is expected to result in localized increases in blood flow or electrophysiological activity associated with particular psycholinguistic processes, as well as to lesions in particular areas of the perisylvian association cortex interrupting the same language processing components in all individuals. Many localizationist theories also maintain that the specific localization of language processing components results from a computational advantage inherent in juxtaposing particular language processing components to each other or to cortex supporting arousal, sensory, and motor processes (Luria 1970, Geschwind 1965, Luria 1973).

Because of the large number of specific theories within each of these two general camps, it is impossible to critically review the empirical basis of all theories that have present-day adherents (for a partial review, see Caplan 1987). I shall focus on the most widely cited theories within each class, and then turn to what is known about the localization of the two functions considered above – semantic memory and syntactic comprehension.

2.3 *Distributed theories*

Several lines of inquiry provide evidence for distributed theories, and all distributed theories suffer from similar inadequacies in accounting for certain empirical findings.

The first line supporting distributed theories consists of the ubiquity of general factors in accounting for the performance of aphasic patients. For instance, a statistical analytic technique known as factor analyses has been applied to analyze the performances of groups of patients both on general aphasia tests and on tests of specific language abilities. These analyses have almost always resulted in first factors (usually accounting for more than half of the variance in performance) that are roughly equally weighted for most of the subtests used to test the population (for general aphasia batteries, see Goodglass and Kaplan 1982, and Schuell 1957; for examples within a specific domain, see Caplan et al. 1985, 1996). Such factors are usually taken to reflect disruption of a single function that affects performance on all measures, such as a limited amount of mental resources available for psycholinguistic computations. The existence of such factors would be the immediate consequence of a system in which such functions were disrupted by lesions in a variety of locations, and they have therefore been widely taken as evidence for a distributed basis for language functions.

A second finding supporting distributed theories is the frequent observation of so-called "graceful degradation" of performance within specific language domains after brain damage. An example of such degradation is the strong tendency of certain dyslexic patients to read irregularly spelled words according to a regularization strategy (e.g., *pint* is read with a short *i*), a tendency which is inversely proportional to the frequency of the word (Bub et al. 1985). Graceful degradation reflects the preservation of the simplest (in many cases, the most commonly occurring) aspects of language processing after brain damage. Modern work with neural net models indicates that such patterns of performance can arise following focal lesions in systems in which information is represented and processed in a distributed fashion (McClelland and Rumelhart 1986, Seidenberg and McClelland 1989).

A third source of empirical support for distributed theories comes from the finding of an effect of lesion size on the overall severity of functional impairments in several language spheres (Knopman et al. 1984, Knopman et al. 1983, Selnes et al. 1983, Selnes et al. 1984). This would follow from the principle of mass action (Lashley 1929). These results therefore are consistent with some form of distribution in the neural basis for linguistic representations and processes.

Against the complete adequacy of any distributed model is the finding that multiple individual language deficits arise in patients with small perisylvian lesions, often in complementary functional spheres. For instance, as noted above, in our studies of syntactic comprehension, we have documented patients who have trouble finding the referent of a reflexive form (e.g., *himself*) but perform normally on pronouns (e.g., *him*), and vice versa (Caplan and Hildebrandt 1988). The existence of these isolated complementary deficits in different single cases indicates that at least one abnormal performance cannot result from the relative complexity of processing required by one of these tasks. Double dissociations of this sort are common in the contemporary psycholinguistic aphasiological literature (see Shallice 1988). They indicate that the mode of organization of language in the brain must be one that allows focal lesions to disrupt specific aspects of psycholinguistic processing, not simply a mode of organization that produces complexity effects and degrades gracefully. Though some selective disruptions of function can occur when "lesions" are produced in simulated language processing systems that operate in parallel and distributed fashion (Wood 1982, Gordon 1982, Patterson et al. 1989), to date no mechanism of lesioning a distributed neural system has been shown to produce the range of specific patterns of language breakdown observed in patients.

Another major problem for distributed models is the finding that regional cerebral blood flow increases in specific parts of the perisylvian cortex when subjects do different types of language tasks (see discussion below). As noted above, this suggests at least some degree of cerebral specialization within any distributed system.

2.4   *Classical localizationist theories*

Though many localizationist models exist, the "connectionist" model of language representation and processing in the brain revived by Geschwind and his colleagues (Geschwind 1965) in the 1960s and 1970s probably remains the best-known localizationist model of the functional neuroanatomy of language, at least in medical circles in North America. This model is based upon the aphasic syndrome that we reviewed above, that was described over a century ago (Broca 1861, Wernicke 1974, Dejerine 1892, Lichtheim 1885).

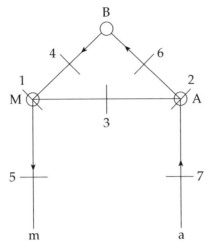

Figure 24.2   The classical connectionist model
Note: A represents the auditory center for word processing. M represents the motor center for speech planning. B represents the concept center. Information flow is indicated by arrows. Numbers indicate the location of lesions said to produce the classical clinical aphasic syndrome. For discussion, see text.
Source: From Moutier 1908, Lichtheim 1885

Figure 24.2 represents the basic "connectionist" model of auditory-oral language processing and its relation to areas within the dominant perisylvian cortex. This model postulates three basic "centers" for language processing, all in cerebral cortex. The first (A), located in Wernicke's area, stores the permanent representations for the sounds of words (what psycholinguists would now call a "phonological lexicon"). The second (M), located in Broca's area, houses the mechanisms responsible for planning and programming speech. The third (B), diffusely localized in cortex in the nineteenth-century models, stores the representations of concepts. A major innovation proposed by Geschwind is in the location of one aspect of the concept center (Geschwind 1970). Geschwind proposed that the inferior parietal lobule – the supra-marginal and angular gyri – are the location at which the fibers projecting from somesthetic, visual and auditory association cortices all converge, and that as a consequence of this convergence, associations between word sounds and the sensory properties of objects can be established in this area. Geschwind argued that these associations are critical aspects of the meanings of words and that their establishment is a prerequisite of the ability to name objects.

According to this model, language processing involves the activation of linguistic representations in these cortical centers and the transfer of these representations from one center to another, largely via white matter tracts. For instance, in auditory comprehension, the representations of the sound patterns of words are accessed in Wernicke's following auditory presentation of language stimuli. These auditory representations of the sounds of words in turn evoke the concepts associated with words in the "concept center." Accessing the phonological representation of words and the subsequent concepts associated with these representations constitutes the function of comprehension of auditory language. In spoken language production, concepts access the phonological representations of words in Wernicke's area, which are then transmitted to the motor programming areas for speech in Broca's area. In most versions of this model, the proper execution of the speech act also depends upon Broca's area receiving input directly from the concept center. Repetition, reading, and writing are modeled as involving similar sequences of activation of centers via connections.

The principal evidence in favor of this model is said to be the occurrence of specific syndromes of language disorders that can be accounted for by lesions of these centers and the connections between them, shown in table 24.1 above. A lesion in Broca's area said to be associated with Broca's aphasia; a lesion of Wernicke's area with Wernicke's aphasia; a lesion of the input pathway to Wernicke's area with pure word deafness; a lesion in the outflow pathway from Broca's area with dysarthria, apraxia of speech or another form of a motor speech disorder; a lesion between the concept center and Broca's area with transcortical motor aphasia; a lesion of the pathway between the concept center and Wernicke's area with transcortical sensory aphasia; and a lesion of the pathway connecting Wernicke's and Broca's area with conduction aphasia. All of these syndromes were claimed to have been discovered in relatively pure form by Lichtheim (Lichtheim 1885), and to have resulted from lesions in the appropriate cortical and subcortical areas of the brain. Recent studies using modern imaging technology have provided additional evidence of the correlation of these lesion sites with these aphasic syndromes (Basso et al. 1985, Damasio and Damasio 1980, Kertesz et al. 1982, Kertesz 1979, Naeser and Hayward 1978, Kertesz et al. 1979, Barat et al. 1978, Hayward et al. 1977, Mazzocchi and Vignolo 1980, Naeser and Hayward 1979, Naeser et al. 1981, Noel et al. 1977, Yarnell et al. 1976, Benson and Patten 1967).

Despite these data, there are many inadequacies in the database that supports this theory of the functional neuroanatomy of language. On the neurological side, problems exist with several aspects of the published data. Lesions have often been described in very general terms (Basso et al. 1985, Naeser and Hayward 1978). The techniques used to localize lesions are often imprecise and have at times been inconsistently applied to imaging data (Kertesz 1982). Ignoring these technical problems, the correlations between lesion sites and aphasic syndromes are far from perfect even in patients with stroke, and they become less reliable in other neurological diseases (Kertesz 1979). As early as 1908, François Moutier documented large numbers of stroke patients with lesions in Broca's area without Broca's aphasia and patients with the syndrome with lesions elsewhere (Moutier 1908, Lecours and Joanette 1984). Recent work has confirmed the failure of small Broca's area lesions to produce Broca's aphasia (Mohr et al. 1978), leading to various modifications of the simplest version of the connectionist localizationist model (Levine and Sweet 1982). The variability in lesions associated with Wernicke's aphasia has been well documented (Bogen and Bogen 1976).

From the psycholinguistic point of view, the principal problem with this correlational evidence for the classical localizationist theory is its dependence on the interpretation of the clinical aphasic syndromes. As we have seen, these syndromes reflect the relative ability of patients to perform language tasks (speaking, comprehension, etc.), not the integrity of specific components of the language processing system, and therefore they cross-classify patients with respect to their underlying functional deficits in language processing components and reflect disturbances of different language processing components in different patients (Schwartz 1984). Accordingly, knowing that a particular aphasic syndrome tends to be associated with a lesion in a particular part of the perisylvian cortex does not tell us what components of the language processing system are located in that area of cortex and does not guarantee that these same components are not also damaged by lesions in different cortical areas (that are associated with different syndromes).

Both lesion-deficit correlations in patients with more specific functional impairments and activation studies in normal subjects using functional neuroimaging and electrophysiological approaches have begun to provide data relevant to the localization of specific components of the language processing system within the perisylvian association cortex. I shall illustrate this work with a short review of some of studies in the areas of lexical semantics and syntactic comprehension.

2.5 *Localization of semantic memory*

Semantic memory is not easy to localize, since it consists of knowledge that we have about items, and such knowledge has many components. For all their localizing zeal, the nineteenth-century founders of aphasiology and neurolinguistics had no idea where the meanings of words were located in the brain. Broca (1861) did not deal with this issue at all and Wernicke (1974 [1872]) barely mentioned it; Lichtheim (1885), who thought he had codified all the aphasias, said of "the concept center" that it was located in an area of the brain above the temporal-to-frontal lobe system that was responsible for word recognition and word sound production. Some modern researchers have adopted theories that also deny a localization to semantic memory. For instance, Damasio (1989), like Geschwind (1965), has argued that the meanings of words consist of the characteristic features associated with the corresponding items – shape, color, texture, odor, taste, actions performed on the object, etc. Unlike Geschwind, who thought of the inferior parietal lobe as the place where these associations came together to produce meaning, Damasio maintains that the neural substrate for meaning consists of "retroactivation" of sensory and motor cortices in which these properties were encoded by sensory and motor experience. In Damasio's model, meaning changes as a function of context, so that the meaning of the word (or concept) "scissors" involves activation of stored motor representations to a greater degree if the word (or concept) is being activated in connection with the actual act of cutting than if the word is mentioned because someone is telling someone else that a piece of paper is lying under a pair of scissors. In this model, the location of meaning changes as a function of the mindset of the speaker or listener.

As opposed to these theories, which either ignore the location of meaning or explicitly deny that the meaning of a word or a concept can be localized for principled reasons, there are other researchers who have advanced hypotheses about the localization of the cortex involved in representing the meaning of words and concepts. For instance, as we have seen, Geschwind (1965) articulated a specific hypothesis regarding the location of word meanings within the inferior parietal lobe.

What does the evidence suggest? The best data from deficit-lesion correlational studies usually comes from patients with no neurological history who have a first stroke that is relatively small. These patients have normal brains up to the moment of injury, and the injury is circumscribed and maximal at its onset. The deficits that follow these strokes reflect disruptions of the functions that are supported by the area of the brain that is affected by the stroke. However, strokes do not usually produce isolated semantic impairments. It is often the case that patients with strokes cannot name objects or understand words, but the deficits seen in most of these cases usually involve disruptions to the mechanisms that activate word sounds and recognize words from the acoustic waveform or print. Patients with Wernicke's aphasia are typical in this respect – these patients almost certainly have semantic deficits, but their other problems make it hard to document these deficits clearly. Nonetheless, there are a few stroke patients in whom the deficits appear to affect meaning in isolation, and these few cases have by and large had lesions whose centers lie in the left temporal lobe (Warrington 1987). A temporal lobe location for the representations of the meanings of words is also suggested by the study of patients with herpes encephalitis, some of whom have been shown to have disorders of semantics without equally severe disruptions of the processes underlying word sound activation and word recognition (Warrington 1981b). In these cases, the brunt of the illness has been shown to affect the temporal lobes.

An important caveat about most of these cases relates to a feature of aphasia we reviewed above – the distinction between deficits that are seen in conscious, controlled tasks, and those that appear in tasks that do not require conscious controlled processing. As we noted above, Milberg, Blumstein and their colleagues have reported that some patients with Wernicke's aphasia show evidence of automatic, unconscious activation of meaning. Conversely, some patients with Broca's aphasia show some evidence of abnormalities in these automatic processes relating to manipulation of semantic information. However, there is too much variability in the performances of these patients and too little detailed study of their lesions to be able to draw any firm conclusions about the localization of deficits in either conscious or unconscious semantic processing from these studies.

Degenerative disease often presents a less clear picture than stroke because it is often diffuse. But this is not always the case. Diseases such as Parkinson's disease and Huntington's disease, which affect specific parts of the basal ganglia, have been very informative about the neural basis for motor control and, more recently, procedural memory. Recently, several researchers (Hodges et al. 1992) have described a degenerative disease that selectively affects semantic memory. The patients with this disease lose knowledge of the meanings of words but retain the ability to repeat and to recognize words. MR, SPECT, and PET studies of these patients have predominantly shown a left temporal lobe locus of atrophy and hypometabolism, though other parts of the brain – notably the left frontal lobe – have been implicated in some studies in some of these patients. It is unclear what the etiology of this degenerative condition is; Alzheimer's or Pick's disease are the leading possibilities (see Hodges et al. 1992, for discussion).

While the evidence from the effects of brain damage suggests a temporal lobe location for semantic knowledge about words, a group of researchers using functional neuroimaging have come to a different conclusion. Posner et al. (1988) reported a now-famous study in which they compared PET activity associated with subjects' generating a verb that conveyed the use to which a noun is put (e.g., "sweep" for "broom") with PET activity associated with subjects' repeating the noun. There was an increase in PET activity, representing increased regional cerebral blood flow (rCBF), in the left dorsolateral frontal cortex, just in front of Broca's area, when the repeat task was subtracted from the generate task. This result is very robust and has been replicated many times. The authors interpreted it as reflecting semantic processing associated with accessing the noun's meaning and generating an action associated with that meaning. Posner et al. (1987) reported a similar increase in rCBF in the same region in a task in which subjects listened to a list of animals and indicated which were dangerous (a semantic task) compared to their simply passively listening to the same list and making no response. These authors also found that, in the "ferocious animal detection task," there was no effect of the number of positive examples (fierce animals) in the list upon the presence of the rCBF increase in the left frontal region, suggesting that the increase in blood flow is a result of subjects' monitoring the meaning of each word, not confirming that an animal is fierce.

There are other interpretations of these PET and fMRI effects, however. One, which I favor, is that this increase in blood flow may represent subjects' switching from one category to another. Lesions in the dorsolateral region are well known to disturb the ability to switch one's mental set (Luria 1973). An argument against the view that the activation seen in Posner's studies is due to semantic processing is that patients with lesions in the dorsolateral frontal cortex do not have semantic deficits when tested on standard tests of word comprehension. Posner and his colleagues point to the fact that patients with lesions in this region have trouble producing lists of animals, which they consider a semantic task. These authors also point to the Milberg and Blumstein studies that document abnormal semantic priming in some Broca's aphasics as evidence for a role of left frontal cortex in semantic processing. But neither of these arguments is convincing. Deficits in semantic verbal fluency can be the result of many cognitive problems, including switching from one subset within a category to another. Normal subjects typically generate animals in subsets in this task (domestic animals, farm animals, fierce wild animals, reptiles, etc.). Difficulty switching from one of these subcategories to another may result in trouble generating lists of items within a broader category. As we have seen, the data on both semantic priming and lesion location in Broca's aphasia are too fragmentary and inconsistent to be interpreted as clearly showing that there is a semantic deficit in Broca's aphasia; moreover, the lesions in Broca's aphasia more often extend posteriorly from Broca's area, not anteriorly into the dorsolateral frontal cortex where rCBF increased in the Posner et al. (1988) studies.

There are also activation studies that do not find a frontal increase in rCBF associated with semantic processing. Murtha et al. (in press) reported the results of a task in which subjects had to say whether the animal designated by a presented word had hoofs, horns, or antlers – a task that requires visualization of features of the animal that are thought to be part of its semantic representation. When compared to passive listening to the same words, these authors found a left frontal increase in rCBF. However, the authors also used an interesting paradigm in which they subtracted out a dummy scan in which blood flow was measured while the subjects waited to begin the task. This was intended to subtract out the effects of anticipation and mental set associated with the semantic but not the baseline task. With this additional subtraction, the frontal activity disappeared and rCBF increased from the baseline to the experimental condition only in the left temporal lobe – exactly where the studies by Hodges and others suggest it should.

In summary, what evidence there is suggests that there are regions of the brain that increase their blood flow as a function of semantic processing and in which lesions disturb such processing. These regions do not seem to include the inferior parietal lobe, as Geschwind claimed, nor to depend upon the context within which an object is mentioned for a deficit to be observed, as Damasio's theory would suggest. The best candidate for the location of semantic memory for objects and concrete nouns is the cortex of the left temporal lobe, with the left dorsolateral frontal cortex also being in the running. But there is much more uncertainty than hard knowledge about this localization.

2.6   Localization of syntactic comprehension

The first studies of the neural basis for syntactic comprehension were deficit-lesion correlations. Caramazza and Zurif (1976), Heilman and Scholes (1976), and other researchers described disorders of syntactic comprehension in several groups of aphasic patients, including Broca's aphasics, "mixed anterior aphasics," and conduction aphasics. The theoretical emphasis in this literature was on the co-occurrence of an impairment in syntactic processing in comprehension with agrammatic speech in agrammatic Broca's aphasics. This co-occurrence led several researchers to suggest that the area that is usually affected in Broca's aphasia – Broca's area: pars triangularis and opercularis of the left third frontal convolution, Brodmann's areas 44 and 45 – play a special role in syntactic processing (Zurif 1982).

This area of research and theory development has been pursued along two lines: (1) more specific characterization of the syntactic structures that are affected in Broca's aphasics (Grodzinsky 1990, 1995, Hickok and Avrutin 1995, Hagiwara 1995), and (2) description of certain aspects of online syntactic processing in Broca's aphasics (Zurif et al. 1993, Swinney and Zurif 1995).

Grodzinsky, Hickok, Avrutin and others have argued that Broca's aphasics have selective disturbances affecting a restricted set of syntactic operations that can be characterized in terms provided by Chomsky's (1986, 1995) theory of syntactic structure. In this framework, the disturbances these patients are said to have affect the ability to "co-index traces." Traces are one of several sets of items that, according to this theory, are understood but physically unexpressed. The best examples of traces are found in sentences like *Who do you like [t]?*, and *John saw the man who the police were searching for [t]*. In both these sentences, the "*wh*-word" (*who*) is understood to be the object of the verb (*like, search for*). In Chomsky's theory, there is a trace (*t*) that is mentally but not physically present in these sentences after the verb, and the *wh*-word is co-indexed with it. Grodzinsky and his colleagues have documented disturbances on the part of Broca's aphasics in understanding sentences such as *Who do you like?* and *John saw the man who the police were searching for*, which they attribute to impaired abilities to accomplish the necessary co-indexation. (The exact characterization of the deficit varies somewhat in different reports, as does the description of normal syntactic structure, but this is the essence of these analyses.) Grodzinsky and his colleagues have argued that the brain region that is affected when these operations are impaired – Broca's area – is responsible for this aspect of syntactic processing in normals.

Zurif, Swinney and their colleagues investigated the online processing of these structures in Broca's and Wernicke's aphasics. They reported that Wernicke's aphasics – but not Broca's – showed priming to semantic associates of the antecedents of traces (*the man* in *John saw the man who the police were searching for*) at the point at which the trace occurred. They argued that this indicated that Broca's aphasics had a deficit in online processing of traces. This analysis is closely related to those of Grodzinsky, Hickok, and Avrutin in that it describes in processing terms a deficit that the previously cited authors describe in structural linguistic terms.

Some electrophysiological and metabolic data are consistent with this model. Researchers have identified several event related potentials (ERPs) that may reflect syntactic processing. The two leading candidates are the P600 or "syntactic positive shift (SPS)" in the central parietal region (Hagoort et al. 1993, McKinnon and Osterhout 1996, Neville et al. 1991, Osterhout and Holcomb 1992, 1993) and the "left anterior negativity (LAN)" that arises roughly over Broca's area (Kluender and Kutas 1993a, 1993b, Munte et al. 1993, Rosler et al. 1993). The more posterior wave (the P600, or SPS) appears to be elicited at the point at which violations of syntactic structure can be identified (McKinnon and Osterhout 1996, Osterhout and Holcomb 1992, 1993). The LAN appears to arise when subjects process sentences with traces that have moved over an intervening noun phrase (Kluender and Kutas 1993a, 1993b). The existence of this wave is broadly consistent with the localizationist model outlined above.

Recent work with PET has also provided evidence for localization of this same aspect of syntactic processing to Broca's area (Stromswold et al. 1996, Caplan et al. in press). In these studies, PET activity associated with making plausibility judgments about simpler object–subject sentences (e.g., *The award thrilled the actress that praised the producer*) was subtracted from that associated with making judgments about the same propositions phrased in syntactically more complex subject–object forms (e.g., *The actress that the award thrilled praised the producer*). The subtraction showed an increase in rCBF in the pars opercularis of Broca's area. The difference between the more and less complex sentences resides in the complexity of the trace coindexation operation; thus these studies are also consistent with the specific localizationist model discussed above.

However, there are contradictory data. Patients with aphasic syndromes other than agrammatic Broca's aphasia, whose lesions lie largely outside this region, often show impairments of syntactically based sentence comprehension that are indistinguishable from those seen in Broca's aphasics (Berndt et al. 1996, Caplan 1987, Caplan and Hildebrandt 1988, Caplan et al. 1985, 1996, 1997, Dronkers et al. 1994, Tramo et al. 1988). Conversely, patients with agrammatic Broca's aphasia often show good syntactic comprehension on sentence-picture matching tests (Berndt et al. 1996). Studies that have looked at lesion sites – rather than aphasic syndromes – have also found no relation between the presence of a lesion in particular parts of the perisylvian cortex and the presence of a disorder of syntactically based sentence comprehension (Caplan 1987, Caplan et al. 1985, 1996). In addition, the neuroimaging data that have been reported in these studies largely consist of CT, and some MR, images – often analyzed by quite subjective techniques – and the studies of patients with degenerative disease cited above (e.g. Hodges et al. 1992) show that areas of hypometabolism are important to consider when looking for the relationship of deficits with lesions.

Nor is the picture derived from functional neuroimaging studies perfect from the localizationist point of view. Using fMRI, Just et al. (1996) reported an increase in rCBF in both Broca's area and in Wernicke's area of the left hemisphere, and smaller but reliable increases in rCBF in the homologous regions of the right hemisphere, when subjects read and answered questions about sentences that were very similar to those used by Stromswold et al. (1996) and

Caplan et al. (1998). We have repeated our PET study with elderly subjects (between the ages of 70 and 80). We found a very specific increase in rCBF – but in the inferior parietal lobe, not Broca's area. Since the age of the patients in the studies by Swinney, Zurif, and their colleagues is much closer to that of our elderly than our young normal group, this finding makes the localization of this aspect of syntactic processing in Broca's area less secure. And we must remember that what is being proposed to be localized in Broca's area is only one particular syntactic operation related to an aspect of the structure and meaning of relative clauses. Detailed online studies of deficits in other operations and neuroimaging studies in normal subjects that highlight such operations are lacking.

3   Conclusion

Contemporary studies of language disorders and the relationship of language to the brain are beginning to deal with the hard problems: how do we represent linguistic information? what are the component processes that activate this information in the acts of speaking, listening, reading, and writing? What is the nature of disorders of these representations and processes? Where are these representations and processes localized in the brain? Research into these questions is now at a point where we can propose hypotheses and support (and attack) them empirically. This is a real advance over the level of description and modeling of language disorders and the neural basis for language of the late 1970s. I have outlined the types of studies that characterize this field, within a historical perspective, and illustrated some of the results of these studies. The reader will appreciate that these are new questions, being approached with new psycholinguistic paradigms and new technologies to describe the brain, and there are no sure answers at present to many of these basic questions. Nonetheless, however confusing parts of this field may at times appear to be, this research is clearly in the direction of a more detailed and accurate understanding of language disorders and the neural mechanisms that support normal language knowledge and use.

NOTE

This work was supported by a grant from the National Institute for Neurological Disease and Stroke (DC00942).

25 Computational Linguistics

RICHARD SPROAT, CHRISTER SAMUELSSON, JENNIFER CHU-CARROLL, and BOB CARPENTER

The field of computational linguistics is as diverse as linguistics itself, so giving a thorough overview of the entire field in the short space available for this chapter is essentially impossible. We have therefore chosen to focus on four relatively popular areas of inquiry:

- syntactic parsing;
- discourse analysis;
- computational morphology and phonology;
- corpus-based methods.

The order of presentation is motivated by historical considerations. Parsing and discourse analysis have had the longest continuous history of investigation, and are therefore presented first. Computational morphology and phonology only really began to grow as a separate discipline in the mid-1980s. Corpus-based approaches were, in fact, investigated as early as the 1960s (e.g., by Zellig Harris (1970)), but the field fell into disrepute until the late 1980s, since which time there has been a renaissance of work in this area.

1 Parsing

Parsing is the act of determining the "syntactic structure" of a sentence. Although syntactic theories differ on their notions of structure, the goal of such structure is typically to represent "who did what to whom" in the sentence. Any natural language processing system that needs to produce an interpretation from the utterance that is deeper than a bag of keywords thus involves some form of parsing (see section 1.5 for examples of existing practical applications of parsing).

Parsing typically involves tagging the words with an appropriate syntactic category and determining their relationships to each other. More often than not, words are grouped into phrase-like constituents, which are subsequently arranged into clauses and sentences.

1.1 Phrase structure grammars

For the purposes of this section, we will restrict our attention to the most widely studied form of grammars for computational purposes: *context-free phrase structure grammars*. We will assume familiarity with phrase structure grammars and the notion of phrase marker. Consider the following simple context-free grammar for verb phrases and noun phrases with prepositional modifiers:

VP	→	TV NP	TV	→	*saw, knows, liked, met*
VP	→	VP PP	NP	→	*Sandy, Chris*
NP	→	Det N	N	→	*kid, telescope, saw, field*
NP	→	NP PP	PP	→	*outside, somewhere*
PP	→	P NP	P	→	*in, on, near, with*
			Det	→	*the, a, every*

For any possible sequence of words, the grammar determines what, if any, valid *phrase structures* it has. For example, the expression *the kid* has exactly one analysis in this grammar, namely [NP [Det *the*] [N *kid*]]. According to this grammar, the expressions *kid the* and *the dog* are also ungrammatical; the former because there is no rule $C \rightarrow$ N Det (where C is any category) in the grammar, the latter because there is no lexical entry for *dog*. Some expressions have multiple analyses, such as the classic example *saw the kid with the telescope*, which has the two (abbreviated) structures [VP [VP *saw the kid*] [PP *with the telescope*]] and [VP *saw* [NP [NP *the kid*] [PP *with the telescope*]]]. This example contains a so-called *structural ambiguity* between the situation in which the prepositional phrase *with the telescope* modifies the noun phrase *the kid* and one in which it modifies the verb phrase *saw the kid*.

1.2 Parsing as search

Almost all parsers involve some notion of searching for possible analyses for a given sequence of words. *Top-down* parsers are goal driven, and begin their search from the answer (the top of a tree) and work down to the actual expression input to the parser. *Bottom-up* parsers are *data driven*, beginning from lexical categories from the input and combining them into larger phrases.

1.2.1 Bottom up: shift-reduce parsing

One standard approach to bottom-up parsing is the shift-reduce framework, which allows two operations: shifting lexical material (i.e., replacing words with their grammatical categories) and reducing sequences of categories based on rule applications. Parsing begins from the input sequence and the state of the parse during parsing is represented by two sequences: the sequence of words remaining to parse and the sequence of categories already found. For instance, the prepositional phrase *with the telescope* would invoke the following parser steps.

Words	Categories	Operation	Rule
with the telescope	found	initialize	
the telescope	P	shift	P → *with*
telescope	P Det	shift	Det → *the*
	P Det N	shift	N → *telescope*
	P NP	reduce	NP → Det N
	PP	reduce	PP → P NP

The parser is initialized with the string and allows two operations. First, the first word on the list of words can be replaced with one of its lexical entries through shifting, as in the first two steps after initialization above.

$$\frac{\mathbf{w}, u_1, \ldots, u_n \quad C_1, \ldots, C_m}{u_1, \ldots, u_n \quad C_1, \ldots, C_m, \mathbf{D}} \qquad [\mathbf{D} \to \mathbf{w} \text{ in lexicon}]$$

In general, our rules operate on sequences of words to parse and categories found, returning the same type of result. The first half of the input to the above rule is a sequence of words $\mathbf{w}, u_1, \ldots, u_n$, the first of which is the word $\mathbf{w}$ we are going to lexically rewrite. The second half of the input is the current set of categories found, $C_1, \ldots, C_n$. The result of the application of the rule is the sequence of categories $u_1, \ldots, u_n$ with the first element $\mathbf{w}$ from the input removed, along with the sequence of categories $C_1, \ldots, C_n, \mathbf{D}$ where the lexical entry category $\mathbf{D}$ has been added to the list of categories in the input.

The second operation allows the reduction of the rightmost sequence of categories by means of a rule, as in the last two steps in the derivation above.

$$\frac{w_1, \ldots, w_n \quad D_1, \ldots, D_m, \mathbf{C_1}, \ldots, \mathbf{C_k}}{w_1, \ldots, w_n \quad D_1, \ldots, D_m, \mathbf{C_0}} \qquad [\mathbf{C_0} \to \mathbf{C_1}, \ldots, \mathbf{C_k} \text{ in grammar}]$$

In this rule, the sequence of words $w_1, \ldots, w_n$ is unchanged. A final subsequence $C_1, \ldots, C_k$ of categories from the input sequence of previously derived categories $D_1, \ldots, D_m, \mathbf{C_1}, \ldots, \mathbf{C_k}$, is rewritten according to a grammar rule. Thus because $C_0 \to C_1, \ldots, C_k$ is a rule in the grammar, if we have found the categories $C_1, \ldots, C_k$ in the input, we can replace them with their mother category C_0 from the rule. Note that we can restrict our application of grammar rules to final subsequences without losing any parses.

In cases of ambiguity, there will be more than one alternative expansion at some point in the parsing process. For instance, consider the expression *saw Sandy outside*, which is a minimal length string displaying PP attachment ambiguity. Here are the two derivations.

saw Sandy outside		saw Sandy outside	
Sandy outside	TV	Sandy outside	TV
outside	TV NP	outside	TV NP
	TV NP PP	outside	VP
	TV NP		VP PP
	VP		VP

The critical decision here is made after the lexical categories for *saw* and *Sandy* have been shifted, when it must be decided whether to shift the preposition or complete the verb phrase. The parse trees can be straightforwardly reconstructed from the steps taken by the parser.

1.2.2 Top-down: recursive-descent parsing

A standard approach to top-down parsing is by means of *recursive descent*. This strategy involves recursively expanding categories until they match lexical material. This can be modeled procedurally in much the same way as bottom-up parsing, using a list of categories and of lexical material. The difference is that the list of categories are categories that have not been found yet, in contrast to the shift-reduce parser, where the categories list constituents which have already been found.

Words	Categories needed	Operation	Rule
with the telescope	PP	initialize	
with the telescope	P NP	expand	PP → P NP
the telescope	NP	lex	P → *with*
the telescope	Det N	expand	NP → Det N
telescope	N	lex	Det → *the*
		lex	N → *telescope*

With top-down parsing, initialization involves beginning with the category being sought, which in the case above, is PP. Although it may look the same, this is totally different from the representation in bottom-up parsing, because the categories involved in a step of top-down parsing have *not* been found.

Two rules then define the search. The first allows lexical matching of the first category being sought against the first of the remaining words.

$$\frac{\mathbf{w}, u_1, \ldots, u_n \quad \mathbf{D}, C_1, \ldots, C_m}{u_1, \ldots, u_n \qquad C_1, \ldots, C_m} \qquad [\mathbf{D} \to \mathbf{w} \text{ in lexicon}]$$

Thus if the first word we have on our list of words to be processed is **w** and the current category we are seeking is **D**, then if there is a lexical entry of category **D** for **w**, we can remove the word from the input sequence and the category from the sequence of categories being sought.

The second scheme allows a category being sought to be expanded according to a grammar rule.

$$\frac{w_1, \ldots, w_n \quad C_0, D_1, \ldots, D_m}{w_1, \ldots, w_n \quad C_1, \ldots, C_k, D_1, \ldots, D_m} \qquad [C_0 \to C_1, \ldots, C_k \text{ in grammar}]$$

This simply says that if there is a grammar rule $C_0 \to C_1, \ldots, C_k$ and the first category we are seeking is C_0, then we can remove the C_0 from the list of categories being sought and replace it with the sequence of categories $C_1, \ldots, C_k$. As with bottom-up parsing, we can restrict the position of the rule application without loss of generality. This time, we require the top-down rewriting to be applied to the first category on the sequence of categories being sought.

Consider the resolution of attachment ambiguity by means of the top-down processor.

saw Sandy outside	VP		*saw Sandy outside*	VP
saw Sandy outside	VP PP		*saw Sandy outside*	TV NP
saw Sandy outside	TV NP PP		*Sandy outside*	NP
Sandy outside	NP PP		*Sandy outside*	NP PP
outside	PP		*outside*	PP

The criticial decision here is made before the verb phrase is expanded; we must decide whether to expand it as a TV-NP sequence or as a VP-PP sequence, which decides the attachment.

1.2.3   Complexity of search-based parsing

In general, a search-based parser must explore the entire search space in order to find all parses (or to reject a string as ungrammatical). The problem with this is that the search space suffers a combinatorial explosion as the length of the string grows. Consider a string of k prepositional phrases each consisting of a preposition, determiner, and noun (for $k = 4$, an instance is *beside the dog near the radiator in the house by the street*). The problem is that there are more than $2^{(k-2)}$ valid structural analyses of a sequence k preposition, determiner, noun sequences. This means that both search-based parsing strategies will require at least $2^{(k-2)}$ steps to analyze a sequence of $3k$ words in the worst case. The actual growth in number of analyses follows the *Catalan Numbers*:

$$b_n = \frac{1}{n+1}\binom{2n}{n}$$

which give the number b_n of binary bracketings (or equivalently parse tree structures), for a string of length n.

Whether top-down or bottom-up parsers will be more efficient for a particular application depends on the grammar and input strings. Ambiguity in top-down parsing stems from having many rules with the same mother category, whereas ambiguity in bottom-up parsing arises from a high degree of lexical ambiguity or by having a high degree of ambiguity in the daughters of rules.

1.3   Parsing as dynamic programming

Dynamic programming is a standard computational technique for keeping track of subcomputations that have already been performed. In the context of parsing, it will amount to keeping track of all possible analyses for each subsequence of the input expression. The key insight is that we are dealing with context-free languages. That is, the possible categories that we can assign to a sequence of words does not depend on the context in which it is found. Thus no matter how many ways there are to analyze a sequence $(P\ Det\ N)^k$, the result is always a prepositional phrase and the internal structure will not influence how it can combine with other constituents in an analysis.

1.3.1   The Cocke–Kasami–Younger parser

The first and simplest parser involving dynamic programming is the Cocke–Kasami–Younger (CKY) parser (Younger 1967). The principle here is to iterate over ever-larger subsequences of the input, computing all possible analyses of the subsequence and recording them for future analysis. CKY parsing is only defined for grammars all of whose rules are binary branching, but there are other parsers based on dynamic programming which work over arbitrary grammars. For simplicity, we will restrict our attention to grammars all of whose rules are binary branching. A table representing all such analyses for the string *saw Sandy outside* is as follows, where the vertical axis represents starting positions and the horizontal axis represents ending positions.

	1	2	3
1	TV, NP	VP	VP
2		NP	NP
3			PP

For instance, the NP entry at (2, 3) indicates that there is a noun phrase spanning from the second to the third word, which is the string *Sandy outside*. Similarly, the PP entry from (3, 3), indicates that the substring *outside* can be analyzed as a prepositional phrase. The fact that there are two entries at (1, 1), indicates that the string *saw* is ambiguous between a TV and NP.

The method of constructing a matrix representation as above is to work from small spans outward. This ensures that when we come to analyze a longer sequence, all of the subsequences have been fully analyzed. We can work left to right, and fill out the entries in the table above in the order $(1, 1)$, $(2, 2)$, $(3, 3)$, $(1, 2)$, $(2, 3)$, $(1, 3)$. To fill in an entry (n, n) in the table, we simply fill in all possible lexical entries for the nth word in the input. To fill in an entry (n, m) for $m > n$, we inspect all break points k such that $m \leq k < n$. This enumerates all the ways a phrase spanning from n to m could be subdivided into two subphrases. For each such k, we consider all possible ways to combine the categories spanning the interval (m, k) with the categories spanning the interval $(k + 1, n)$ given the grammar rules. If there is a category C_1 spanning (m, k) and a C_2 spanning $(k + 1, n)$, and there is a grammar rule $C_0 \rightarrow C_1 C_2$, then there will be a category C_0 spanning (m, n). For instance, to fill in $(1, 3)$ above, we consider the break points 1 and 2. For $(1, 1)$ we have a TV and an NP, and for $(2, 3)$ we have an NP, and we can combine TV-NP to produce a VP, so VP is included in the categories in $(1, 3)$, but there is no way to combine an NP-NP sequence (in this grammar). The fact that we have an NP spanning $(1, 1)$ and an NP spanning $(2, 3)$ does not add any further analyses. The VP spanning $(1, 2)$ and the PP spanning $(3, 3)$ entails that we have a VP spanning $(1, 3)$. This represents the second way in which the string could be analyzed.

It is fairly easy to see that the amount of work carried out under the CKY approach is bounded by the number of boxes in the matrix and the amount of work that could be done for each box. For an input of length n there are n^2 possible boxes. For each box, we have to consider all possible split points of which there are at most n, which leads to n^3 points at which the grammar is consulted. The amount of work to do at each split point is bounded by the number of categories and rules in the grammar.

So what happens to our sequence of k prepositional phrases? Consider *in the box near the chair under the door*, for $k = 3$. In addition to lexical entries, we wind up with PP entries at $(1, 3)$, $(4, 6)$, $(7, 9)$, $(1, 6)$, $(4, 9)$, and $(1, 9)$, with NP entries at $(2, 3)$, $(5, 6)$, $(8, 9)$, $(2, 6)$, $(5, 9)$, and $(2, 9)$.

1.4 *Scaling up*

We now know that we can build a parser for context-free grammars that takes at most n^3 steps for an input sequence of length n. For wide coverage applications, this is still prohibitive. For instance, the Penn Treebank (Marcus et al. 1993), a corpus of one million words drawn from the *Wall Street Journal* and analyzed by hand, already involves an implicit grammar of roughly 8,000 rules and a lexicon of tens of thousands of words and is by no means complete. Sentences average just over 21 words each. These sentences, when fed back into the parser, result in hundreds of thousands and often millions of well-formed substrings. Current "large-scale" grammars for linguistic theories such as HPSG and LFG run to hundreds of pages of coding for the lexicon, lexical rules, and grammar.

1.5   Applications

Parsing has been successfully applied in a number of domains. State of the art machine translation systems employ parsing to derive representations of the input that are sufficient for transfer from the source to target language at either the syntactic or semantic level. Simple parsing has been used to detect phrasal boundaries for providing prosodic cues for use in speech synthesis. A great deal of attention is being applied currently to the application of syntactic parsing models for language modeling for automatic speech recognition. There have also been successful applications in information retrieval, where it is useful to know the syntactic form and arguments of phrases in retrieved documents in order to increase retrieval accuracy. Along similar lines, parsing has been used to generate database queries from natural language inputs. Finally, there is a great deal of activity in the cognitive psychology community aimed at explaining human sentence processing by modeling it as a parsing process.

1.6   The future

Of course, most linguists would feel rather constrained by the restriction to context-free grammars, and even more so by regular expressions. Unfortunately, there has been very little work in parsing that goes beyond the context-free grammar paradigm in a significant way. On the one hand, there has been work in parsing formalisms such as *lexical-functional grammar, generalized phrase structure grammar*, and *head-driven phrase structure grammar*, but these all depend on a context-free backbone driving a parser with a slightly generalized notion of category. Even approaches to *dependency grammar* parsing and transformational grammar parsing have wound up relying on conversions in large part to context-free representations. *Tree-adjoining* grammar parsers have been developed that use dynamic programming, indexing subanalyses by left and right external boundaries, as well as internal left and right boundaries for adjunction.

2   Discourse Analysis

The area of discourse analysis is concerned with inferring the intended meanings of utterances with respect to the world in which they were uttered, as well as with determining how utterances relate to one another to form a coherent structure. Discourse analysis is pertinent both to understanding monologue texts, as well as to correctly interpreting a conversational partner's utterances and subsequently providing an appropriate response in multi-party dialogues. For instance, consider the following exchange between a bank teller (T) and a customer (C):

(1) c: *I want to transfer some money from my checking account to my credit card account.*
(2) T: *What's your checking account number?*
(3) c: *It's 123 456 789.*
(4) T: *How much would you like to transfer?*
(5) c: *I'd like to pay off the balance on my credit card.*
(6) T: *Your credit card balance is $1,036.23, but you only have $962.14 in your checking account.*
(7) c: *Okay.*
(8) c: *I'd like to pay the balance due today then.*
(9) T: *Okay, I have transferred $792.02 from your checking account to your credit account.*

In order for the dialogue participants to successfully carry out a dialogue such as the above, they must be able to recognize the *intentions* of the other participant's utterances, and to produce their responses in such a way that will enable the other participant(s) to recognize their intentions. For instance, although utterance (5) does not directly provide an answer to the question in (4), C produced it with the intention of it being a sufficient answer to T's question based on the assumption that T, being a bank teller, will be able to look up the credit card balance. Furthermore, C must be able to recognize that T's utterance in (6), in addition to informing C of the balances in both accounts, is intended to convey to C the invalidity of the combined proposed action in (1) and (5). Finally, utterance (8) is intended as an alternative plan to satisfy a slight variation of C's original goal.

Discourse processing has been widely studied from a computational point of view since the late 1970s. Up until the last few years, the computational models developed for discourse analysis have, for the most part, taken a plan-based approach based on the speech act theory (Austin 1962, Searle 1975). Within this framework, the speaker is considered to have some goal he or she wishes to achieve, and the utterances in the discourse, whether they be part of a monologue or a dialogue, are actions that the speaker is carrying out in order to achieve the intended goal. Allen and Perrault 1980, and Cohen and Perrault 1979 pioneered this work in plan-based discourse processing in their efforts to formulate a part of Austin's (1962) speech act theory within a computational framework. Their work focussed on formulating simple speech acts such as *request* and *inform* within a plan-based computational framework, and on recognizing indirect speech acts within the simple domain of providing

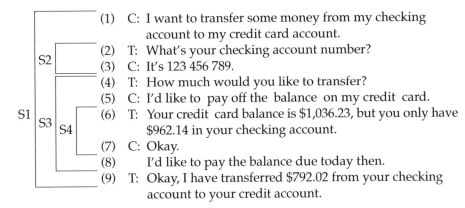

(1) C: I want to transfer some money from my checking account to my credit card account.

(2) T: What's your checking account number?

(3) C: It's 123 456 789.

(4) T: How much would you like to transfer?

(5) C: I'd like to pay off the balance on my credit card.

(6) T: Your credit card balance is $1,036.23, but you only have $962.14 in your checking account.

(7) C: Okay.

(8)   I'd like to pay the balance due today then.

(9) T: Okay, I have transferred $792.02 from your checking account to your credit account.

Figure 25.1   Sample dialogue and its discourse segments

users with information about either meeting or boarding a train. Since then, strategies have been developed to handle more complicated tasks and more sophisticated phenomena, such as incremental recognition of plans (Carberry 1990), and the recognition of ill-formed plans (Pollack 1990).

As discussed earlier, the goal of discourse processing is to understand utterances with respect to the context (and the world), and to relate utterances to one another. To illustrate this process, we further analyze the above dialogue segment, which is shown again in figure 25.1 with additional discourse segment information included. In order to understand the overall dialogue segment S1, we must recognize that the dialogue is carried out in order to achieve C's goal of transferring money from a checking account to a credit card account, expressed by C in utterance (1). Furthermore, we must recognize that dialogue segments S2 (comprising utterances (2) and (3)) and S3 (comprising utterances (4)–(8)) are subdialogues initiated by T in order to solicit missing information for carrying out C's intended action, in this case, C's checking account number and the amount to be transferred, for segments S2 and S3, respectively. Finally, we should recognize segment S4 (utterances (6) and (7)) as a subdialogue initiated by C to resolve a detected conflict between C and T with respect to the validity of the plan proposed by C. In this case, T chooses to resolve this conflict by providing evidence of why C's original proposal is invalid (utterance (6)) and then C subsequently proposes a valid alternative to satisfy a slightly different goal (utterance (8)). Based on this analysis, the structure of this dialogue segment may be represented by the tree structure shown in figure 25.2.

A plan-based discourse understanding system may be used to infer the structure of a discourse, such as that shown in figure 25.2, given utterances (1)–(9). The system infers the discourse structure in an incremental fashion, by modeling the current discourse structure and determining how the next utterance can best be incorporated into the current structure to form a coherent

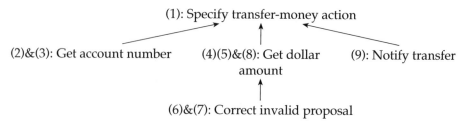

Figure 25.2   Dialogue structure for utterances (1)–(9)

piece of text or dialogue. For instance, given utterances (1)–(7), the discourse understanding system would infer the part of figure 25.2 that includes these utterances, i.e., the bulk of the left and center branches of the tree. Given utterance (8), the system must then determine how this utterance best fits in with the existing discourse structure, i.e., whether utterance (8) contributes to the top level action specified by utterance (1), to the "get dollar amount" action specified by utterances (4) and (5), to be "correct invalid proposal" action specified by utterances (6) and (7), or initiates a new topic that forms the root node of a separate discourse tree. A discourse understanding system capable of performing such a task typically contains three components: (1) a library of generic *recipes* (Pollack 1986), (2) the *plan inference* module, and (3) the system's private knowledge about the domain and about the world, and (optionally) its beliefs about the dialogue participants and their beliefs. Below we sketch the outline of the discourse understanding process.

A recipe is a generic template for performing a particular action. It typically consists of a *header* that specifies the action being described, a set of *preconditions* that specifies the conditions that must hold before the action is executed, the *body* of the action, which comprises the subactions that must be performed as part of performing the header action, and one or more *goals*, which are what the person intended to achieve by performing the action. A recipe for the top-level action in figure 25.2, *Transfer-Money*, is shown in figure 25.3. The header of this recipe shows that the *Transfer-Money* action takes five parameters: *?teller*, who is the agent performing the transfer action, *?customer*, the agent whose money is being transferred, *?from-acct-type*, the type of account from which money will be drawn, *?to-acct-type*, the type of account to which money will be deposited, and *?amount*, the amount of money to be transferred between the specified accounts. The preconditions indicate that before the body of the action can be executed, *?teller* must know both account numbers and that the balance in the "from account" must be greater than the amount to be transferred. The body of the action consists of two subactions, *Transfer*, which is the actual performance of the transfer request, and *Notify-Transfer*, in which *?teller* notifies *?customer* that the transfer request has been completed. Finally, the goal of performing the *Transfer-Money* action is to increase the balance in the "to account" by the amount transferred.

Header: Transfer-Money (?teller,?customer,?from-acct-type,?to-acct-
              type,?amount)
/* Gloss: ?teller transfers ?amount from ?customer's ?from-acct-type to ?to-acct-type */
Preconditions: knowref(?teller,?from-acct-num,account-number(?from-acct-
              type,?from-acct-num))
              knowref(?teller,?to-acct-num,account-number(?to-acct-type,?to-
              acct-num))
              greater-than(balance(?from-acct-num),?amount)
Body: Transfer(?teller,?from-acct-num,?to-acct-num,?amount)
              Notify-Transfer(?teller,?customer,?from-acct-type,?to-acct-
              type,?amount)
Goal: increase-balance(?to-acct-type,?amount)

Figure 25.3   Recipe for the "transfer-money" action

The recipe library contains a collection of generic recipes such as the above, and during discourse understanding, the plan inference module attempts to infer utterance intentions and relationships using information provided by this library. The plan inference process begins with the recognized semantic interpretation of the speaker's utterance, which is taken to be the observed action. First, plan inference rules are applied to the observed action to infer other higher level actions that may have resulted in the execution of the observed action. This process, called *forward chaining*, hypothesizes parent actions of observed or inferred actions, and results in a chain of hypothesized actions. A parent action (A_i) may be chained to an inferred or observed action (A_j) if one of two conditions holds. First, A_j may be in the body of the recipe for performing A_i; in other words, performing A_j *contributes* to performing A_i (Pollack 1986). In this case, we may hypothesize that A_j is performed as part of carrying out the higher-level action A_i. Second, the goal of A_j may match a precondition in A_i; in other words, performing A_j *enables* performing A_i (Pollack 1986). In this case, we may hypothesize that A_j is performed in order to make it possible to perform the higher-level action A_i.[1] Next, the plan inference process attempts to incorporate the chain of hypothesized actions (inferred from the new utterance) into existing discourse to form a coherent structure. The same basic inference process is again used to link the root node of the chain to some existing node in the discourse structure so that the root node of the chain either *contributes to* or *enables* an action in the existing discourse structure. When multiple interpretations are plausible, i.e., when the root node of the chain can be linked to more than one existing action, additional heuristics may be used to select from the possible interpretations. One such heuristic is the *focussing rule* (McKeown 1985, Grosz and Sidner 1986, Litman and Allen 1987), which prefers linking the chain to the node that is currently in focus in the discourse structure.

Throughout the discourse understanding process, knowledge about the application domain and about the world comes into play. For instance, knowledge

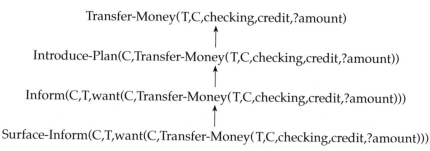

Transfer-Money(T,C,checking,credit,?amount)

↑

Introduce-Plan(C,Transfer-Money(T,C,checking,credit,?amount))

↑

Inform(C,T,want(C,Transfer-Money(T,C,checking,credit,?amount)))

↑

Surface-Inform(C,T,want(C,Transfer-Money(T,C,checking,credit,?amount)))

Figure 25.4   Existing discourse model after utterance (1)

Header: Request-ref(?speaker,?hearer,?var,?prop)
/* Gloss: *?speaker asks ?hearer the referent of ?var, which is a parameter in ?prop* */
Preconditions: knowref(?speaker,?var,?prop)
               believe(?speaker,knowref(?hearer,?var,?prop))
Body: Wh-Question(?speaker,?hearer,?var,?prop)
Goal: want(?hearer,Answer-Ref(?hearer,?speaker,?var,?prop))

Header: Obtain-info-ref(?speaker,?hearer,?var,?prop)
/* Gloss: *?speaker obtains from ?hearer the referent of ?var* */
Preconditions: knowref(?speaker,?var,?prop)
               believe(?speaker,knowref(?hearer,?var,?prop))
Body: Request-Ref(?speaker,?hearer,?var,?prop)
               Answer-Ref(?hearer,?speaker,?var,?prop)
Goal: knowref(?speaker,?var,?prop)

Figure 25.5   Additional recipes for recognizing utterances in figure 25.1

about the domain allows us to recognize that a list of accounts for a user can be easily obtained by a teller, and therefore satisfying one of the first two preconditions in figure 25.3 (obtaining either *?from-acct-num* or *?to-acct-num*) automatically satisfies the other. Furthermore, common sense knowledge allows us to understand what the *greater-than* predicate means in the last precondition and to know that all valid instantiation for the variable *?amount* must be either integers or fixed point numbers with one or two decimal places.

Given this brief overview of the discourse understanding process, we now illustrate how a portion of utterance (1)–(9) can be recognized to form part of the discourse structure in figure 25.2. We show how utterances (2) and (3) are interpreted with respect to utterance (1), which we assume to have already been interpreted and incorporated into the existing discourse model shown in figure 25.4. Utterance (2), based on its semantic representation, is recognized as a *Wh-Question*. Since *Wh-Question* is in the body of the *Request-Ref* action whose recipe is shown in figure 25.5, by forward chaining, the recognition system hypothesizes that utterance (2), intended as a *Wh-Question*, is performed

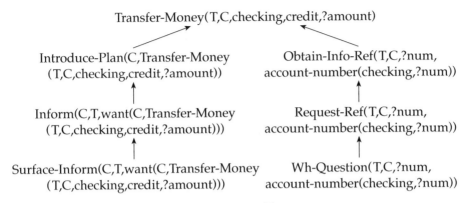

Figure 25.6 Existing discourse model after utterance (2)

in order to perform a *Request-Ref* action. Furthermore, since *Request-Ref* is one of the subactions in the body of *Obtain-Info-Ref* (figure 25.5), forward chaining again leads the recognition system to infer *Obtain-Info-Ref* as the parent action as *Request-Ref*. Since the goal of *Obtain-Info-Ref (?teller,?customer,?num, account-number (checking,?num))* is that *?teller* knows *?customer*'s checking account number, which matches the second precondition for the *Transfer-Money* action, this *Obtain-Info-Ref* action is inferred to have been performed in order to enable the *Transfer-Money* action in the existing discourse structure. Figure 25.6 shows the existing discourse structure after utterance (2).

Utterance (3), on the other hand, is recognized as a *Surface-Inform* action, which is again hypothesized to be an *Inform* action. The recognition component then attempts to incorporate this chain of actions into the existing discourse model by hypothesizing the antecedent actions of *Inform* and determining if each hypothesized chain of actions can be coherently linked to some action in the existing discourse model. One hypothesized parent action of *Inform* is *Answer-Ref*, which is the second subaction of *Obtain-Info-Ref*. As a result, utterance (3) is recognized as providing a response to the question in utterance (2). This analysis leads to the root node and the left branch of the dialogue structure shown in figure 25.2.

A closer analysis of the actions in the discourse model in figure 25.6 shows that our current representation of the discourse model conflates three different types of actions. First, there are *discourse actions* that describe the communicative actions being carried out by each dialogue participant, including actions such as *Inform* and *Request-Ref*. Second, there are *domain actions* (Litman and Allen 1987) that specify the domain-specific actions that the dialogue participants have chosen to satisfy their domain goal, such as *Transfer-Money*. Finally, there are *problem-solving actions* (Allen 1991, Lambert and Carberry 1991, Ramshaw 1991) which are meta-level actions describing how the dialogue participants are going about constructing their domain plan. Examples of problem-solving actions include *Introduce-Plan*, *Evaluate-Plan*, and *Instantiate-Parameter*.

For a decade, researchers have developed models for discourse analysis that distinguish between domain and discourse actions (Litman and Allen 1987), and more recently, models that further distinguish between domain and problem-solving actions (Lambert and Carberry 1991, Ramshaw 1991). By distinguishing among these three types of actions, these models are able to apply action-type-specific heuristics to the recognition process at each level while maintaining the overall uniform plan inference process across all levels. In addition, by distinguishing between domain-independent discourse (and problem-solving) actions and domain-specific actions, the models can be more easily ported to new domains.

Finally, although in this section we have focussed on plan-based discourse analysis, this is by no means the only method employed for computational discourse analysis. It had, however, been the most widely adopted method from the late 1970s until the early 1990s. Recently, with the success of applying statistical methods to other areas of natural language processing, such as part-of-speech tagging and parsing, researchers have started exploring applying such methods to problems in discourse processing, such as discourse segmentation, discourse act recognition, etc. However, such work is still in its infancy, and we expect much progress to be made with respect to statistical discourse analysis in the next few years.

3   Computational Morphology and Phonology

In many areas of computational linguistics it is commonplace to treat words as if they were atomic units with no internal analysis. A syntactic parser, for example, might consider the fact that *eats* is a third singular present verb form; but it would generally be of no interest to a parser that this word can be *morphologically* analyzed into two components, namely a verb stem *eat* and an affix +*s*, which marks form as being third singular present.

There are, nevertheless, applications of natural language technology where such considerations become more important. In text retrieval, for example, the problem is to search a large text database for a term or collection of terms, and to retrieve documents containing those terms. Frequently one is interested not only in finding the exact term, but also in finding morphological variants of that term: a search for *foxes* should retrieve documents containing the word *fox*, for instance.

As a second example, consider text-to-speech synthesis. In many languages, how one pronounces a string of letters depends in large part on what the morphological analysis of that string of letters is. It helps, for example, to know that the analysis of *misled* is *mis+led* in order to avoid pronouncing it as [mízəld] (*misle+d*).

This section will illustrate some basic approaches to word-form analysis. Roughly speaking, the topics that will be covered can be classified into *computational morphology*, which treats the analysis of word structure per se; and *computational phonology*, which (to a first approximation at least), deals with the changes in sound patterns that take place when words are put together. Since analysis of word structure invariably presumes that one can "untie" the effects of sound changes, we will start with computational phonology.

3.1   Computational phonology

As a straightforward example of phonological alternations within words, consider the formation of partitive nouns in Finnish. The partitive affix in Finnish has two forms, *-ta*, and *-tä*; the form chosen depends upon the final harmony-inducing vowel of the base. Bases whose final harmony-inducing vowel is back take *-ta*; those whose final harmony-inducing vowel is front take *-tä*. The vowels *i* and *e* are not harmony inducing; they are transparent to harmony. Thus in a stem like *puhelin* "telephone," the last harmony-inducing vowel is *u*, so the form of the partitive affix is *-ta*.

(1)
Nominative	*Partitive*	*Gloss*
taivas	taivas+ta	"sky"
puhelin	puhelin+ta	"telephone"
lakeus	lakeut+ta	"plain"
syy	syy+tä	"reason"
lyhyt	lyhyt+tä	"short"
ystävällinen	ystävällinen+tä	"friendly"

This alternation is part of a much more general *vowel harmony* process in Finnish, one which affects a large number of affixes. Within theoretical linguistics, there have been various approaches to dealing with phonological alternations such as the one exemplified in (1). For the purposes of this discussion we can assume a traditional string-based rewrite-rule analysis, rather than a more up-to-date prosodic declarative analysis: from the point of view of computational phonology, our choice here is largely irrelevant, since it is roughly equally straightforward to implement a modern analysis as it is a more traditional analysis. The latter is a little easier to understand, however.

A rewrite analysis – one that is an oversimplification of Finnish vowel harmony, but one that will do for current purposes – is given below:

(2)   a → ä / [ä, ö, y] C* ([i, e] C*)* ____

This rule simply states that an *a* is changed into *ä* when preceded by a vowel from the set *ä, ö, y*, with possible intervening *i, e* and consonants. This rule thus makes a particular assumption about the alternation in (2), namely that in a form like *-tä*, the vowel is underlyingly /a/, and that the underlying form of the partitive affix is therefore *-ta*, a form that surfaces only when preceded by back and neutral vowels.

A computational model that implements this alternation would seek to change /a/ into /ä/ in the appropriate environment; this is of course stated from the point of view of generating a surface form from an underlying sequence of morphemes. An equally legitimate (and actually much more widespread) interpretation is that one wishes to reconstruct the lexical form from the surface form: thus from *syytä* one wishes to reconstruct *syy+ta*. An ideal computational model would make these two interpretations, *generation* and *analysis*, equally easy to implement. One important property of *finite-state transducers* – the most widespread computational device that is used to implement phonological rules – is precisely this *reversibility*.

A finite-state transducer can be thought of as a variant on a *finite-state acceptor* (also often termed *finite-state automaton*), something familiar to anyone who has taken an introductory formal language theory course (see, e.g., Hopcroft and Ullman 1979). A finite-state acceptor, it will be recalled, is a device that has a finite number of *states* (hence its name), one of which (typically) is designated as a *start* state, and some subset of which are designated as *final* states. Transitions between states are termed *arcs* – there may be zero or more arcs going from any state s_i to any other state s_j – and each arc is *labeled* with a single element from a predesignated *alphabet*, or else it is labeled with the *empty string* element ε, in which case it is termed a *null arc*. A given *string* made up of elements from the alphabet is accepted by a given acceptor if and only if one can start at the start state of the acceptor, move from one state to the next matching the label of the arc against the next element of the input, and end up in a final state, having consumed *all* of the input. The set of strings accepted by an automaton is termed the *language* of that automaton, and the set of all languages accepted by all possible finite-state automata is the set of *regular languages*.

A finite-state transducer differs from a finite-state acceptor in having, not a single label on an arc, but rather a pair of labels, one being the *input label*, the other the *output label*. The machine works much as does an automaton, except that in addition to matching the input label against the symbol of the input, one also replaces it with the output label. Thus transducers transduce input strings into potentially different output strings. Note that either the input label or the output label might be ε: in the former case, one may transition an arc matching nothing on the input side (and thus consuming no input), but at the same time *inserting* a symbol on the output side; in the latter case, one must match the input label against the input, but the effect of transiting the arc is to *delete* the input symbol. Since transducers relate sets of pairs of (input and output) strings, they are said to compute *relations*: the set of relations computed by all possible finite-state transducers is termed the set of *regular relations*.

Returning now to phonology, it has been known for several decades (Johnson 1972, Kaplan and Kay 1994), that systems of standard phonological rewrite

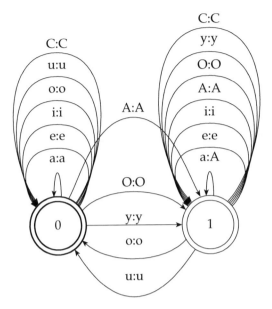

Figure 25.7 An FST implementation of the rule in (2)
Note: A represents *ä*, O represents *ö*, and C represents any consonant. The labels on the arcs represent the symbol-to-symbol transductions, with the input on the left and the output on the right of the colon.

rules, given certain restrictions, constitute regular relations: that is, the relation between the set of all possible lexical forms of a language, and the set of all possible surface forms is a regular relation. This means that phonological rule systems can be modeled as finite-state transducers, and there has to date been a large amount of work that develops this idea (e.g., Koskenniemi 1983, Karttunen 1983, Karttunen et al. 1992), and explicit methods for *compiling* transducers from phonological rewrite rule descriptions have been developed (e.g., Kaplan and Kay 1994, Mohri and Sproat 1996). The desired *reversibility*, discussed above, comes about quite simply. Suppose one has constructed a transducer that maps from lexical forms (as input) to surface forms (as output). One can produce a device that maps the other way by simply inverting the input and output labels on each arc.

It is time to give an example of a finite-state transducer, and for this we return to the alternation given in (1) and described by the rule in (2). A transducer that implements this rule is shown in figure 25.7. In this transducer, state 0 is the initial state, and both states 0 and 1 are final states. The machine stays in state 0, transducing *a* to itself, until it hits one of the front vowels in the input *ä, ö, y*, in which case it goes to state 1, where it will transduce input *a* to *ä*.

The approach to computational phonology outlined here is fairly traditional, and it presumes a model of phonology that is certainly not current. More up-to-date computational models include *declarative* approaches such as (Bird and Ellison 1994), as well as various implementations of *optimality theory*. In many cases, the computational devices used are formally rather similar to the transducers discussed here; in Bird and Ellison's case, for instance, finite-state acceptors are used. This is an interesting point to take note of, since while much has recently been made of the advantages of declarative, constraint-based approaches over traditional rule-based approaches, at the computational level, at least, the differences between models are often rather minimal.

3.2   Computational morphology

As with computational phonology, the most popular computational models of word structure have been finite-state ones (or ones that are mathematically equivalent to finite-state). This is by no means the only approach that has been taken, and indeed there are certainly limitations in finite-state methods, as has been discussed elsewhere (e.g., Sproat 1992). Nonetheless, a sufficiently rich array of morphological phenomena can be handled with finite-state devices that it will be reasonable to restrict our attention to finite-state approaches here.

As a concrete example of computational morphological modeling, let us consider a simple subset of Spanish verbal morphology, consisting of three verbs, *hablar* "speak," *cerrar* "close," and *cocer* "cook," conjugated in the present and preterite indicative forms; these are given in table 25.1. Note that these

Table 25.1   Some regular verbal forms in Spanish

Features	hablar	cerrar	cocer
ind pres 1sg	hablo	cierro	cuezo
ind pres 2sg	hablas	cierras	cueces
ind pres 3sg	habla	cierra	cuece
ind pres 1pl	hablamos	cerramos	cocemos
ind pres 2pl	habláis	cerráis	cocéis
ind pres 3pl	hablan	cierran	cuecen
ind pret 1sg	hablé	cerré	cocí
ind pret 2sg	hablaste	cerraste	cociste
ind pret 3sg	habló	cerró	coció
ind pret 1pl	hablamos	cerramos	cocimos
ind pret 2pl	hablasteis	cerrasteis	cocisteis
ind pret 3pl	hablaron	cerraron	cocieron

Table 25.2   An arclist model of Spanish verbal morphology

START	ar	habl	hablar **vb**
START	ar	cerr **diph**	cerrar **vb**
START	er	coc **diph c/z**	cocer **vb**
ar	WORD	+o#	+ind **pres 1sg**
ar	WORD	+as#	+ind **pres 2sg**
ar	WORD	+a#	+ind **pres 3sg**
ar	WORD	+amos#	+ind **pres 1pl**
ar	WORD	+'ais#	+ind **pres 2pl**
ar	WORD	+an#	+ind **pres 3pl**
ar	WORD	+'e#	+ind **pret 1sg**
ar	WORD	+aste#	+ind **pret 2sg**
ar	WORD	+'o#	+ind **pret 3sg**
ar	WORD	+amos#	+ind **pret 1pl**
ar	WORD	+asteis#	+ind **pret 2pl**
ar	WORD	+aron#	+ind **pret 3pl**
er	WORD	+o#	+ind **pres 1sg**
er	WORD	+es#	+ind **pres 2sg**
er	WORD	+e#	+ind **pres 3sg**
er	WORD	+emos#	+ind **pres 1pl**
er	WORD	+'eis#	+ind **pres 2pl**
er	WORD	+en#	+ind **pres 3pl**
er	WORD	+'i#	+ind **pret 1sg**
er	WORD	+iste#	+ind **pret 2sg**
er	WORD	+i'o#	+ind **pret 3sg**
er	WORD	+imos#	+ind **pret 1pl**
er	WORD	+isteis#	+ind **pret 2pl**
er	WORD	+ieron#	+ind **pret 3pl**
WORD			

three verbs come from two conjugations, namely the *-ar* conjugation (*hablar* and *cerrar*) and the *-er* conjugation (*cocer*). Also note the "spelling changes" in some of the stem forms, in particular the diphthongization of the stem vowel in certain positions in *cerrar* (*cierr-*) and *cocer* (*cuec-*), and the *c/z* alternation in the stem of *cocer*.

A simple finite-state model that allows one to recognize these verb forms is what we will term an *arclist* model, following (Tzoukermann and Liberman 1990), represented in table 25.2. Verb stems are represented as beginning in the initial state, and going to a state which records their paradigm affiliation, *-ar* or *-er*. From the paradigm states, one can get to the final WORD state by means of appropriate endings for that paradigm. The verb stems for *cerrar* and *cocer*

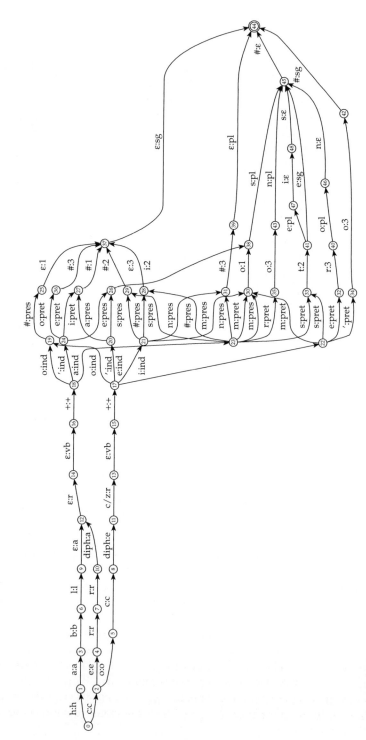

Figure 25.8 A transducer for a small fragment of Spanish verbal morphology

have lexical features **diph** and **c/z**, which trigger the application of spelling changes. This arclist can easily be represented as a finite-state transducer; see figure 25.8.

The spelling changes necessary for this fragment involve rules to diphthong-ize vowels, change *c* into *z*, and delete grammatical features and the morpheme boundary symbol. Thus the first of the following set of rules changes *e* into *ie* if it is followed by zero or more consonants (C*), zero or more lexical features (**feat***), the lexical feature **diph**, possible other features, and then a morpheme boundary followed by a vowel and an optional consonant sequence. The sec-ond rule similarly changes *o* into *ue*. The third rule changes *c* into *z* in stems marked with the **c/z** feature before [+back] vowels. Finally the last rule deletes lexical features and boundary symbols:

(3)   e → ie / __ C* **feat* diph feat*** + V C* #
      o → ue / __ C* **feat* diph feat*** + V C* #
      c → z / __ **feat* c/z** + [+back]
      (**feature** V **boundary**) → ε

(Note that it is *not* claimed that this is a correct set of rules for handling Spanish morphographemics in general: it is merely presented as a solution for the small fragment under discussion.) Following the discussion in section 3.1, we can represent this set of rules as a finite state transducer. One useful prop-erty of finite state transducers is that they are *closed under composition*: that is, if one has a finite state transducer T_1, that maps from set x to set y, and another transducer T_2 that maps from set y to set z, one can compose T_1 and T_2 together – notated as $T_1 \circ T_2$ – to obtain a third transducer T_3, that maps from x to z. Armed with this, we can produce a transducer that maps directly from lexical to surface forms, by simply composing the transducer representing the lexicon (figure 25.8) with the transducer representing the rules in (3). As we also noted in section 3.1, finite state transducers are invertible; hence one can simply invert this transducer to obtain one that maps from surface to lexical forms. This transducer is represented in figure 25.9.

Strictly finite-state models of morphology are in general only minor variants of the model just presented. For example, the original system of Koskenniemi (Koskenniemi 1983) modeled the lexicon as a set of letter tries, which can be thought of as a special kind of finite automaton. Morphological complex-ity was handled by *continuation patterns*, which were annotations at the end of morpheme entries indicating which set of tries to continue the search in. But, again, this mechanism merely simulates an ε-labeled arc in a finite-state machine. Spelling changes were handled by two-level rules implemented as parallel (virtually, if not actually, intersected) finite-state transducers. Search on the input string involved matching the input string with the input side of the two-level transducers, while simultaneously matching the lexical tries with the lexical side of the transducers, a process formally equivalent to the model we have presented here.

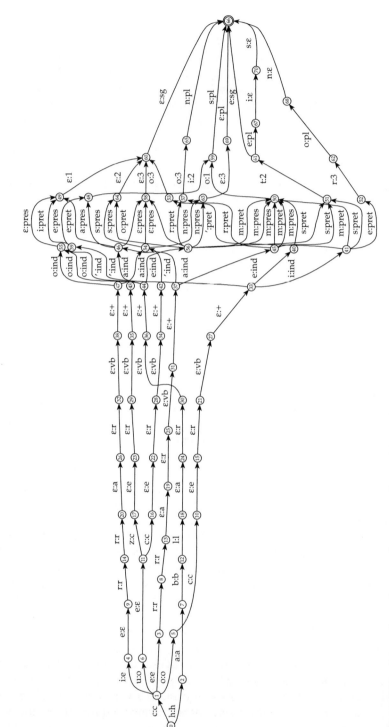

Figure 25.9 A transducer that maps between surface and lexical forms for a small fragment of Spanish verbal morphology

4   Corpus-based Methods

The word *corpus* is borrowed from Latin, in which it means "body." The word corpus is commonly used to refer to a body of writings of some sort, and in linguistics, this is typically a collection of texts. In the speech sciences, a collection of audio recordings, possibly transcribed and labeled, is also often referred to as a corpus. The corpus can consist simply of plain text, or it can be annotated using some set of special symbols. For example, it can be marked up according to an SGML scheme to convey information about the textual structure, which is to be interpreted by, say, a web browser. Or the corpus can be annotated to indicate structure according to some theory of linguistics. One example is assigning a part-of-speech (PoS) tag – a linguistically motivated label – to each word in the text; another example is assigning a parse tree – a hierarchical analysis using some grammar of rewrite rules – to each sentence in the text.

Corpora have been widely used by linguists to identify and analyze language phenomena, and to verify or refute claims about language. However, a corpus is normally considered to be more than the mere sum – or rather concatenation – of its parts, especially in the field of computational linguistics; it also reveals important quantitative information about the distribution of various language phenomena. This ranges from rather trivial observations such as "the most frequent word in almost any English text is the word *the*," to more sophisticated inferences in the vein of "there is a tendency to move long noun phrases towards the end of a clause."

The aspect of conveying quantitative information means that the corpus must in some sense be representative of the (sub)language from which it is drawn. Thus, a collection of "laboratory sentences," such as *That that Kim snores annoyed Sandy surprised Chris*, where each sentence has been included because it exhibits some interesting language phenomenon, does not quite qualify as a corpus. Such a collection of linguistically interesting examples is of course a very useful resource in itself for testing theories or developing language-processing systems, but it is usually referred to as a *test suite*, rather than a corpus. Indeed, much of the work in corpus-based computational linguistics has been concerned with extracting the quantitative information contained in a corpus and reformulating it in a more concise way, i.e., to extract a quantitative *language model* from the corpus. The purpose of the extracted language model is usually to study language as such, or to build language-processing devices. There are, however, other uses for such a compact description of language: speech recognition and text compression.

In text compression, the goal is to save storage space, and to this end, a language model can be very useful. And indeed, very similar work has progressed in parallel in the fields of language modeling and text compression. The scenario here is that you wish to encode a text as a sequence of binary digits. We can of course simply write down the seven-bit ASCII representation of each character in the text, and we are done. We could alternatively find some numbering of the words and instead write down the binary representation of the word number, most likely saving a lot of storage space. We could save even more space by having different lengths of the binary representations of the words, and encode more frequent words using shorter digit sequences. This is the basic idea behind coding schemes such as *Huffman coding* (see, e.g., Crochemore and Rytter 1994).

In speech recognition, we wish to try to predict the next word of an utterance, given the previous sequence of words in it, to constrain the search space of the speech recognizer. Also to this end, a language model can be very useful, and indeed, speech recognition has been a driving force in language modeling research. In particular, the word bigram model, to be discussed shortly, has proved crucial for much of the progress in the field of speech recognition.

Let us consider a very simple language model, namely a word-pair grammar. This grammar specifies what word can follow what other word. It might for example allow the word *computer,* but not the word *is,* to follow the word *the.* Such a model can easily be extracted from a plain-text corpus by simply observing what words follow each other in the corpus. This language model is best represented as a finite-state automaton (FSA). Each state of the automaton corresponds to a word, and a directed arc from one state to another indicates that the word of the second state can follow the word of the first state.

This model does not, however, capture any quantitative information. To remedy this, we add probabilities to the scheme; we now specify the probability of any word following any other word. For example, we might stipulate that the probability of the next word being *computer,* given that the current one is *the,* is 0.0042, while the probability of the next word being *is* is exactly zero. This is known as a *word bigram model,* and the probabilities are called *bigram probabilities.* This model is best represented as a probabilistic finite-state automaton. We now attribute a transition probability to each arc, which is the conditional probability of the next state given the current one, which in turn is just the bigram probability. We could in fact use this model to generate sentences: given the current state, i.e., the current word, we draw a next state at random, according to the transition probabilities, transit to it, and output the word corresponding to the state reached, etc. Such a model is known as a *generative language model,* which is the kind of language model used in, e.g., speech recognition.

The bigram probabilities can be estimated from a plain-text corpus by simply counting relative frequencies: if the word *the* occurred 10,000 times in the corpus, and the word *computer* followed it 42 times, we estimate the corresponding bigram probability to be $\dfrac{42}{10,000} = 0.0042$. If, on the other hand, we saw no instance of the word *is* following the word *the,* we assign this bigram probability the value zero. However, a little afterthought yields us the insight that these zero probability bigrams might not be all that desirable; just because we didn't see the word *small* following the word *the* doesn't mean that it cannot do so in new, hitherto unseen texts, which the zero probability would imply.

To remedy this, we resort to the black art of *smoothing* the probability estimates. This typically takes the form of a Robin Hood strategy, stealing probability mass from those who have, and giving it to those who have not. As a concrete example, to avoid the zero bigram probabilities, let us simply assign half a count to any word with zero observed count when doing the relative-frequency estimate. This means that the probability of the word *small* following the word *the* will be $\frac{\frac{1}{2}}{15,000} = 0.000033$.[2] Indeed, much research in language modeling for speech recognition has been on the theme of improving the smoothing techniques.

Let us now turn to linguistically annotated corpora. The perhaps simplest, and currently most popular approach is to assign to each word in the corpus a *part-of-speech (PoS) tag*, which is a linguistically motivated label. The set of possible PoS tags can consist of a small set of atomic labels – such as the basic word classes adjectives, adverbs, articles, conjunctions, nouns, numbers, prepositions, pronouns, and verbs, essentially introduced already by the ancient Greek Dionysius Thrax – or of a complex hierarchical tag set[3] such as the one used in the annotation of the Susanne corpus (Sampson 1995), which consists of over 400 different tags. The tags can even indicate the syntactic role of each word, such as subject, object, adverbial, etc.

Such a representation can be used for disambiguation, as in the case of the well-known, highly ambiguous, and very popular example sentence *Time flies like an arrow*. We can for example prescribe that *Time* is a noun, *flies* is a verb, *like* is a preposition (or adverb, according to taste), *an* is an article, and that *arrow* is a noun. We realize that words may be assigned different labels in different contexts, or in different readings; for example, if we instead prescribe that *flies* is a noun and *like* is a verb, we get another reading of the sentence. Thus, achieving the most appropriate reading of any given sentence can be done by finding the most likely assignment of tags to the words in it. There is an appropriate extension to the probabilistic finite-state automata encoding the word bigram models that is well suited for this task, namely *hidden Markov models (HMMs)*. This allows us to automatically make a preferred assignment of PoS tags to previously unseen text. Such a processing tool is known as an *HMM-based PoS tagger*.

To visualize a bigram tagger, consider the FSA representing the word bigram model, but replace the words with PoS tags. This gives us a tag bigram model, where the states correspond to tags. In the word bigram model, we could generate a sentence by moving around between states and outputting the word corresponding to the current state after each move. We will still move around between the states, but instead of outputting the corresponding tag, we will output a word. The word will be drawn at random according to a probability distribution associated with the current state, i.e., with the current tag. So if the current state corresponds to the tag noun, we expect the probability of the word *the* or the word *is* to be very low, if not zero, whereas when we transit to the state corresponding to the tag article, we expect the probability of the word

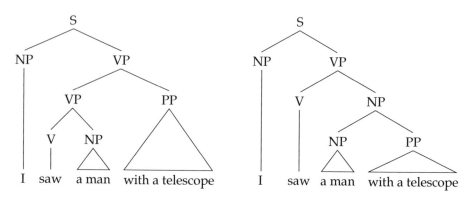

Figure 25.10   Two analyses of "I saw a man with a telescope"

the to rocket. The model is hidden in the sense that we cannot observe the state (tag) sequence, only the word sequence. The model has the *Markov property* since it is modeled by a probabilistic FSA, and the current state is the only memory of the previous history left to condition the transition and word probabilities on. The disambiguation task of finding the most likely tag assignment to the words of a given sentence, i.e., to guess the state sequence that generated the given word sequence, can be performed efficiently by a simple dynamic programming technique known as *Viterbi search*.

Some ambiguity is caused by the way the words relate to each other, rather by what PoS tag is assigned to them. In the case of the equally famous example sentence *I saw a man with a telescope*, the open question is: Who had the telescope, the man or I? We realize that in both cases, we have the same assignment of PoS tags; *I* is a pronoun (Pron), *saw* is a verb (V), *a* is an article (Art) twice, *with* is a preposition (Prep), and *man* and *telescope* are both nouns (N). The way linguists traditionally analyze this is to say that the prepositional phrase (PP) *with a telescope* modifies the word *saw* if I used the telescope to see the man, and modifies the word *man* if the man had the telescope. One way to distinguish between these two alternatives is to assign a parse tree to the sentence. The two parse trees corresponding to the two different analyses are shown in figure 25.10.

The idea here is that some *formal grammar* consisting of *rewrite rules* allows us to rewrite the top symbol[4] as a sequence of strings and the end result is the given sentence. The following simple grammar allows deriving the two different readings of *I saw a man with a telescope* from *S*:

$$
\begin{array}{ll}
S \rightarrow NP\ VP & Pron \rightarrow I \\
VP \rightarrow V\ NP & V \rightarrow saw \\
VP \rightarrow VP\ PP & Art \rightarrow a \\
PP \rightarrow Prep\ NP & Prep \rightarrow with \\
NP \rightarrow NP\ PP & N \rightarrow man \\
NP \rightarrow Pron & N \rightarrow telescope \\
NP \rightarrow Art\ N &
\end{array}
$$

Here is the derivation corresponding to the man having the telescope:

$S \Rightarrow NP\ VP \Rightarrow Pron\ VP \Rightarrow I\ VP \Rightarrow I\ V\ NP \Rightarrow I\ saw\ NP \Rightarrow I\ saw\ NP\ PP \Rightarrow$
I saw Art N PP $\Rightarrow$ *I saw a N PP* $\Rightarrow$ *I saw a man PP* $\Rightarrow$ *I saw a man Prep*
NP $\Rightarrow$ *I saw a man with NP* $\Rightarrow$ *I saw a man with Art N* $\Rightarrow$ *I saw a man with*
a N $\Rightarrow$ *I saw a man with a telescope*

Since any "grammatical" sentence can be derived from the top symbol *S*, this is also a generative language model.

A *parse tree* is a hierarchical representation[5] of a derivation. You may have noticed that in each derivation step, the leftmost possible grammar symbol was always rewritten. This is called a *leftmost derivation*, and is used to establish a one-to-one correspondence between derivations and parse trees; parse trees don't care in which order the various grammar symbols are rewritten, but derivations do. We realize that we can assign a parse tree to each sentence-level unit in our corpus to specify a particular reading of each one. Such an annotated corpus is usually referred to as a *tree bank* (e.g., Marcus et al. 1993).

We will finally look at a language model that we can extract from a tree bank that allows us to automatically assign preferred parse trees to previously unseen input text. We note that the only difference between the two parse trees, and between the two derivations, of the example sentence is that in one of them, we used the grammar rule $VP \rightarrow VP\ PP$, whereas in the other one, we used the grammar rule $NP \rightarrow NP\ PP$ to attach the prepositional phrase. Now, if we assign probabilities to every grammar rule, we can assign a probability to each parse tree, or derivation, by simply multiplying the probabilities of the rules used. This would allow us to select the parse tree with the highest probability when disambiguating. We recall that in a derivation, we must always rewrite the leftmost possible grammar symbol. This means that we really don't have any choice as to which grammar symbol to rewrite, and it makes sense to have the probabilities sum to one for each left-hand-side (LHS) grammar symbol separately. Such a grammar is called a *stochastic* (or *probabilistic*) *context-free grammar* (SCFG or PCFG).

The following is our previous grammar, now equipped with probabilities:

$S \rightarrow NP\ VP$	1.00		$Pron \rightarrow I$	1.00
$VP \rightarrow V\ NP$	0.65		$V \rightarrow saw$	1.00
$VP \rightarrow VP\ PP$	0.35		$Art \rightarrow a$	1.00
$PP \rightarrow Prep\ NP$	1.00		$Prep \rightarrow with$	1.00
$NP \rightarrow NP\ PP$	0.25		$N \rightarrow man$	0.58
$NP \rightarrow Pron$	0.30		$N \rightarrow telescope$	0.42
$NP \rightarrow Art\ N$	0.45			

This stochastic grammar tells us to prefer the reading where I had the telescope, since the probability of the rule $VP \rightarrow VP\ PP$, 0.35, is higher than the probability of rule $NP \rightarrow NP\ PP$, 0.25, and since the derivations differ only in the use of these two rules. In practice, we would estimate the rule probabilities from the relative frequencies of the rules in a tree bank, adding a measure of smoothing techniques for increased robustness.

We conclude by noting that the independence assumptions underlying the statistical model, namely that the only conditioning of the probabilities is on the LHS symbol of the grammar rule, exactly mirror the context-free assumption of the underlying context-free grammar. This means, amongst other things, that for any algorithm for parsing with a context-free grammar, there exists an equally efficient variant of it for finding the most probable parse tree of any given sentence, and for calculating the sentence probability, which is formally defined as the sum of all possible derivation probabilities, under a stochastic context-free grammar.

NOTES

1 In hypothesizing parent actions, in addition to satisfying either the *contribution* or *enablement* relationships, further constraints are placed by examining the preconditions in the recipes for the hypothesized parent actions. We will not provide the details in this chapter; interested readers should refer to Carberry 1990.

2 The denominator increased from 10,000 to 15,000, say, due to all the extra half counts, which in turn reduced the probability of the word *computer* from its previous value 0.0042 to $\frac{42}{15,000} = 0.0028$ – Robin Hood at work!

3 A hierarchical tag set is a set of labels with successively finer distinctions, e.g., N for noun, NS for singular noun, NSM for singular masculine noun, NSMN for singular masculine nominative noun, etc.

4 Typically *S*, for sentence.

5 Not to be confused with a hierarchical tag set.

FURTHER READING

A general introduction to natural language understanding, which includes a discussion of parsing and discourse analysis, is Allen 1995. An introductory text to computational morphology and phonology is Sproat 1992. A standard text for introductory formal language theory – a prerequisite to further study of several topics introduced in this chapter – is Hopcroft and Ullman 1979.

There are several papers that address issues in parsing of various particular syntactic theories: for LFG, see Kaplan and Bresnan 1982; for HPSG, Carpenter 1992; for GB, Stabler 1992. Finally for a discussion of some issues related to computational complexity and natural language, see Barton et al. 1987.

26 Applied Linguistics

JANIE REES-MILLER

What does a lawyer advise a client about the likelihood of success of a trademark infringement suit involving a similar sounding product name or slogan? What treatment is most appropriate for a child with a speech impairment? How should reading be taught to children, and what is the place of literature in the elementary school curriculum? What is the best way for a simultaneous interpreter to convey the joke made by a politician so that those who do not speak the same language can understand the humor? Should English be declared the official language of the United States? These are all questions for which an applied linguist might be consulted to offer problem-solving expertise that bridges the gap between theoretical linguistics and practical problems of language use in everyday life. The remaining chapters of this book illustrate in greater detail the multivariate field of applied linguistics.

Throughout its history, applied linguistics has stood at the interface between theory and practice, an uneasy position in which the applied linguist must decide whether s/he merely translates theory into practice or utilizes practice to build theory, and this uneasy position is illustrated here with reference to second language teaching. In fact, applied linguistics initially meant primarily solving the problem of second language teaching and only over time did applied linguists become involved in a plethora of other activities. The recent range of inquiry of applied linguistics covers more than can be described in a short overview chapter such as this one or even a series of chapters such as those in the remainder of the book; some of the areas briefly described here but not covered by specific chapters include second language teaching and cross-cultural linguistics, how discourse analysis has been applied to the description and solution of problems in language used in real contexts, and how a multidisciplinary approach to language use can aid efforts at language maintenance for minority or endangered languages and dialects.

1   History

The term applied linguistics dates back at least to the 1940s in the USA when linguists applied analytical methods to the practical problems of producing grammars and phrasebooks and developing language courses for the military especially in languages of the Pacific that were little known in the west. As a result of this history, the term applied linguistics first became associated with language teaching. In the 1940s, the University of Michigan established a program in applied linguistics for training language teachers and began publication of the journal *Language Learning: A Quarterly Journal of Applied Linguistics,* whose title and subtitle illustrate clearly the identification of applied linguistics with the teaching and learning of second and foreign languages. The 1950s saw the establishment of the University of Edinburgh's School of Applied Linguistics, which trained language teachers in applying the principles of linguistics to the practice of pedagogy. On the other side of the Atlantic, the Center for Applied Linguistics was founded in Washington, DC, with the goals of improving English language teaching, promoting the teaching of uncommonly taught languages, and conducting research into educational processes related to language use. In the next two decades, professional organizations devoted to applied linguistics were formed, such as the International Association of Applied Linguists (AILA) in 1973, and the American Association for Applied Linguistics (AAAL) in 1977. The establishment of journals devoted to applied linguistics, namely *Applied Linguistics* in 1980 and *Annual Review of Applied Linguistics* in 1981, put the field on a research footing, and articles published in these journals indicate that applied linguistics by the 1980s had moved into areas of inquiry beyond language teaching.

2   What Is Applied Linguistics?

As of 1980, broad agreement was achieved among the major practitioners in the field that applied linguistics: (1) was interdisciplinary, drawing on a multitude of disciplines including psychology, sociology, and pedagogy as well as theoretical linguistics; (2) was not limited to language teaching but included a broad range of fields including lexicography, stylistics, speech pathology, translation, language policy, and planning among others; (3) performed a mediating function between theory and practice (Buckingham and Eskey 1980: 2–3). To these three characteristics, we should add that applied linguistics is "problem-based" (Corder 1973: 10) and brings linguistic insight and analysis to bear on practical issues of language use "situated in time, place, society, and culture" (Sridhar 1993: 7). Unlike some branches of theoretical linguistics which are concerned with language as an abstract object, applied linguistics must take into consideration not only the nature of language but the nature of the particular world in which language is used, the beliefs, social institutions, and culture of its users, and how these influence language use.

Ideally, the job of an applied linguist is to diagnose a problem in real-world language use, bring the insights of linguistics to bear on the problem, and suggest solutions. An applied linguist, for example, might be called upon to recommend clinical treatment of a language impairment, design an educational program for immigrant children, or advise a school district on language policy. Because the questions addressed by applied linguistics deal with language use in the full richness of its context, applied linguists work closely with professionals in other disciplines such as psychology, sociology, anthropology, and education. An applied linguist who is a teacher trainer, for example, must draw not only on the field of linguistics, but also on the fields of education and psychology. An applied linguist working on language problems associated with immigrant and refugee concerns must perforce be familiar with social and political factors that will influence language use. Similarly, applied linguists working in institutional settings such as health care or law need working knowledge of the terminology, traditions, and practices of those institutions.

However, although applied linguistics is "problem-based," much work in applied linguistics has not reached a stage where specific solutions to problems can be suggested in particular settings. Rather, much research is conducted at the first stage, namely, accurately describing the use of language in particular settings or by particular participants. The goal of such research is to provide "the best possible explanations" which will highlight unexplained problems and lead to further questions that can in turn improve explanation, for this is the base for viable solutions to practical problems of language use in the real world (Brumfit 1997: 87).

Papers and colloquia at AAAL conferences in recent years illustrate the wide net cast by applied linguistics; the field now includes work in the general areas of cross-cultural pragmatics, psycholinguistics, language acquisition and socialization, language for specific purposes, literacy, language policy and planning, sociolinguistics, discourse analysis, rhetoric and stylistics, and translation and interpretation. These areas are in addition to the more traditional areas of concern: second language pedagogy, assessment, second language acquisition, bilingualism, and bilingual education. In other words, the questions that applied linguistics seeks to answer range over a multitude of disciplines and real-world settings.

3 Relation of Theory and Practice: the Case of Language Teaching

The applied linguist stands at the intersection of theory and practice, but it is not always clear how the applied linguist mediates between the two. Does theory lead to practice, or practice lead to theory, or is there a symbiotic relationship in which both theory and practice interact? S. Pit Corder (1973: 10) stated explicitly that applied linguistics "makes use of the findings of theoretical studies. The applied linguist is a consumer, or user, not a producer, of theories." This suggests a one-way street in which theory is at the starting point, and the applied linguist directs traffic from theory to practice. What does this mean in practice? Taking the traditional field of second language teaching as an illustrative example of this model, historically a particular theory of the nature of language and the nature of second language acquisition (see chapter 20, Linguistics and Second Language Acquisition) has formed the basis upon which applied linguists constructed language teaching curricula and recommended appropriate teaching techniques.

The audio-lingual method of language teaching in the 1940s to 1960s is a case in point. Influenced by structuralism in linguistics (see chapter 5, Historical Linguistics) and by behaviorism in psychology, applied linguists believed that language was a collection of discrete learnable structures, speaking was primary, and learning a language was a matter of correct habit formation. This theory was applied in the classroom by structuring language to be taught into carefully controlled increments with severely limited vocabulary to avoid the possibility of learner-produced errors. The presentation of skills was strictly prescribed, with listening first, followed by carefully controlled speaking practice (with no recourse to written forms), only much later followed by reading and writing. To inculcate correct habits, teachers drilled students incessantly in correct pronunciation and patterned practice of grammatical structures.

With new theories of the nature of language and the nature of language learning, we have moved beyond audiolingualism in language teaching; however, theoretical stance on the nature of language learning can still determine how errors are treated, for example, and the place of comprehension and production. Because the theory on which audiolingualism was based held that the nature of language learning is essentially habit formation, errors were avoided because they reinforced incorrect habits. Under the influence of the theoretical work of Noam Chomsky (see chapter 5, Historical Linguistics), applied linguists began to look at second language learners' errors in a new light. They saw language learning as a cognitive process of hypothesis testing, in which errors indicated the stage of the language learner's interlanguage (e.g. Corder 1967).

In terms of the emphasis placed on student production or comprehension, a theoretical stance that presumes second language acquisition mirrors first language acquisition will order the skills to reflect the order of first language acquisition (as in the natural approach [Krashen and Terrell 1988]). Students will be expected to undergo a silent period of listening to comprehensible input first, before they are required to speak. With such a theoretical underpinning, speaking follows listening; reading may be used with literate adult students after they have acquired basic speaking skills, and only later – if at all – will students be expected to begin writing. In contrast, if second language acquisition is held to be different from first language acquisition and if production is seen as critical to second language acquisition, then speaking and writing will be introduced from day one. In the most extreme applications of a production-based theory of second language acquisition, the teacher is virtually silent so that students become responsible for production of language. Even in less extreme examples, trainee teachers are advised to maximize student talking time and minimize teacher talking time.

A new theoretical model of the nature of language and language learning has given rise to the communicative method, which became the mainstream approach to language teaching in the last decades of the twentieth century. The theory of language underlying this teaching style focusses on the essential nature of language as communication (Brumfit and Johnson 1979). According to the theory, knowledge of a language is far more than knowledge of the grammar of individual sentences. Instead, knowing a language means knowing how to communicate in the language; it involves acquiring "communicative competence." When combined with speech act theory, the emphasis on communicative competence found application in the functional approach of the 1970s and 1980s in Europe. In this approach, communication was boiled down to discrete, teachable speech acts, and the syllabus was constructed around communicative functions such as requesting, asking permission, giving opinions, complaining, etc. Although the communicative approach has developed and expanded since the heyday of the functional method, the aim of learning a second language is still seen as being able to communicate in the language. The implications for syllabus design and teaching techniques are wide-ranging and have had a wide variety of applications. Instead of being presented with spoken texts created for the second language classroom and carefully controlled in structure and vocabulary (as was the case with audio-lingualism), students hear or read authentic texts by native speakers for native speakers. However, because native speaker-like pronunciation and absolute grammatical accuracy are unnecessary for efficient communication, gone are the pronunciation and grammar drills of the audiolingual method. The theory posits that language is learned through communication and a negotiation of meaning between interlocutors; therefore, the syllabus is organized to elicit student production of language for communicative purposes. Classroom activities may involve role-plays of situations that students might find themselves in, discussion of topics that students want to communicate about, or completion of tasks requiring students to share information and negotiate meaning.

The discussion of audiolingualism, treatment of error, comprehension-based or production-based approaches, and the communicative approach presupposes that theory is the starting point which is applied by the linguist to the problem of language teaching and put into practice by the classroom teacher. The problem, though, with this one-way street view is that the applied linguist directs traffic from theory to practice without taking account of whether the traffic actually arrives at the desired destination. In language teaching, this was certainly the case with contrastive analysis, which proposed that a careful comparison of similarities and differences between native language and target language would make predictions about what students would find difficult and easy to learn, with concomitant consequences for syllabus content and order. The problem was that the predictions made by the theory were not borne out in practice (see chapter 20, Linguistics and Second Language Acquisition). When the application of theory does not actually work in practice, the credibility of the applied linguist as mediator between theory and practice is undermined. Indeed, in the field of language pedagogy, many practicing teachers view new theoretical revelations with some degree of skepticism. As Crystal (1981: 20) noted, "the proof of the pudding is in the eating. If the aim of applied linguistics is to help solve a problem, then it must do just that – and moreover be judged by the pudding-eaters to have done so."

A richer model of the relationship among theory, practice, and applied linguistics sees it as a two-way street in which the applied linguist directs traffic from theory into practice and from practice into theory. In this view, "practical problems in which language is implicated are referred to theoretical ideas and, reciprocally, theoretical ideas are made relevant to the clarification of these problems" (Widdowson 1998: 138). The role of the applied linguist in this endeavor has been compared to that of an engineer who acts as an intermediary between the academic physicist and workers on site. As the engineer translates theory into practical applications of what can be done and how the work can be accomplished, so too does the applied linguist. However, this is not the end of the story since the engineer receives feedback from site workers about how well theory works in practice and can convey this information back to the academic (Bell 1981). Similarly in applied linguistics, practice provides a testing ground for theory, but it is more than that: real-world language use provides new questions and issues requiring new theories (Shuy 1987). Rather than practice being subservient to theory, "empirical research, theory-building, and practice go hand-in-hand" (Cumming 1998: 457). In fact, in the realm of language teaching, recent publications in second language pedagogy indicate a greater interest in the particular experiences of language teachers as reflective practitioners whose expertise in their field is of equal value to the expertise of the theoreticians; it is the job of the applied linguist to attend to both and to present not only the generalizability of research findings of theoreticians but also the "particularizability" of research findings for teachers (Clarke 1994). More generally, some have suggested that the very focus of applied linguistics on performance, on language variation in use, and on social context provides the base for its own theory to complement the more traditional emphasis on competence and context-free cognition in theoretical linguistics (e.g. Sridhar 1993).

4   Recent Range of Inquiry

In recent years, applied linguistics has been responsive to new developments in theory, in technology, and in the world in which language is used. Nevertheless, the central characteristics of applied linguistics remain: (1) focus on contextualized language use; (2) application of theory to practice and vice versa; (3) practical problem-based approach; (4) multidisciplinary perspective. Some of the areas to which applied linguists have turned their attention in recent years include second language teaching and cross-cultural linguistics, language use in specific contexts, and the maintenance of endangered languages and dialects.

4.1 Second language teaching and cross-cultural linguistics

In the field of second language pedagogy, new theoretical developments and changing circumstances in which language teaching takes place have led to new foci of research and directions of practice. Illustrative of these developments (but by no means an exhaustive overview of them) are reconsiderations of the place of grammar and lexicon respectively in the language teaching curriculum and new applications of the communicative and social uses of language.

Drawing on theory and research in psychology, applied linguists have revisited the explicit teaching of grammar in second language classrooms by investigating the facilitative role that noticing and conscious awareness play in enabling learners to acquire grammatical forms in a second language (Schmidt 1990). This research, known as Focus on Form (or FonF for short), has been applied to questions of how and when grammatical instruction can be implemented for most effective learning (e.g. Doughty and Williams 1998).

A different approach, initially associated with work in Great Britain, places lexicon at the center of second language learning and has explored ways and means of applying research to language teaching (e.g., McCarthy 1984). New technology has made possible the collection and analysis of large corpora of written and spoken language. Corpus-based applied linguistics (see chapter 25, Computational Linguistics) uses the corpora as resources of actual language use from which to write dictionaries for nonnative speakers, to revise understanding and teaching of English grammar, to design second language teaching curricula, to write materials, and to suggest teaching techniques (Biber et al. 1998, Lewis 1993).

The emphasis in applied linguistics on language in context has converged with the social fact of large numbers of nonnative speakers of English as students in North American schools and universities; as a result, an important trend in recent years in the USA and Canada is content-based instruction in which language lessons derive from academic course content (Brinton et al. 1989, Snow 1998).

Accurate description of language use with the ultimate goal of teaching has motivated research in cross-cultural discourse and pragmatics. Concentration on spoken language, combined with speech act theory among others, has engendered numerous research projects in applied linguistics investigating specific speech acts such as making requests and apologies in different languages and cultures (e.g. Blum-Kulka et al. 1989). Applied linguists have examined the development of pragmatic competence in second language learners and the possibilities for teaching pragmatics (e.g. Kasper 1996). Written language has not been ignored, however, and contrastive discourse has been applied to description and teaching implications for second language learners (e.g., Connor 1996).

4.2   *Language use in context: contributions of discourse analysis*

Outside the area of language pedagogy, the burgeoning of discourse analysis in the past two decades has provided a means whereby linguistic insight can be applied to numerous real-world situations, particularly of an institutional nature (see chapter 17, Discourse Analysis). Numerous colloquia and papers at AAAL conferences, for example, have presented research findings on how patients and health care professionals express power, solidarity, and politeness by use of various linguistic forms (e.g. Ainsworth-Vaughn and Saunders 1996). Special attention has been paid to Alzheimer's patients in particular and to the elderly in general. A long-term project investigating the language of ageing has described the language of disenfranchisement used in discourse between healthcare workers and elderly patients and is moving towards tentative recommendations for healthcare workers and society in general on anti-ageist language (Coupland 1997).

Other institutional and professional settings, too, have come under scrutiny from applied linguists using theoretical constructs to explain how language is used in real-world settings such as commerce, employment, and public services (DiPietro 1982). The attention of applied linguists has been turned to labor–management disputes and how power is expressed through subtle uses of language in conflict talk (O'Donnell 1990). The church, also, has received attention from applied linguists looking at how ministers use language to establish solidarity with their congregations even when they make requests, disagree, or admonish (Pearson 1988, Dzameshie 1995).

A field that has developed considerably in recent years in response to societal concerns is the investigation of language and gender. In both academic and popular work, for example, Deborah Tannen has noted the differing expectations that men and women bring to conversation, the language that reflects these differing perspectives, and the consequent miscommunication that can result (e.g. Tannen 1990). Recent empirical studies (e.g. Freed and Greenwood 1996) have enriched understanding of the interrelationship of language and gender and demonstrated that generalizations about male and female speech are unreliable when the particular communicative contexts in which the speech occurs have not been examined. Other work has examined gender and language cross-culturally and in specific institutional settings (Freed 1995).

4.3   *Language maintenance and endangered languages and dialects*

The work of applied linguists on endangered or minority languages and dialects brings together field linguistics (see chapter 6), anthropology, sociolinguistics and education. For example, a longitudinal study of language use and cultural context among young Inuit children in northern Quebec draws together socio-linguistic research into language use, research in language socialization, and second language acquisition research into educational discourse (Crago 1992). Similarly, work among Native Americans in Oklahoma that has been designed to maintain native languages has combined work with native speaker inform-ants to compile dictionaries and grammars with training of these same inform-ants as teachers of their ancestral languages in their communities (Yamamoto 1995). It is not only minority languages that are under threat, but also dialects. Work on the endangered dialect of Ocracoke Island off the coast of North Carolina has combined descriptive linguistics and dialectology with a program of education in the public school whereby children and the community are encouraged to document their distinctive dialect, cherish it, and – it is hoped – thereby preserve it (Wolfram and Schilling-Estes 1995).

5   The Chapters in This Section

While illustrative examples in this chapter have focussed on the traditional specialty of second language teaching, the previous section indicates that applied linguistics has expanded beyond this core area. The remaining chapters in this section of the book exemplify the work that applied linguists do outside the field of language teaching, the kinds of questions they seek to answer, the problems they seek to solve, and the processes by which theory and practice interact in applied linguistics.

James Gee's chapter on education (27) summarizes some of the many ways in which linguistics can inform educational practice. The chapter opens with a discussion of theories of language and how differing theories will produce dif-ferent results in curricula and classroom teaching. He also considers language use in academic versus informal texts and how the dialect and discourse con-ventions of the classroom may differ from those that children bring to school.

Rebecca Treiman's chapter on reading (28) demonstrates how theory and research can inform practice in teaching children to read. She applies the re-sults of psycholinguistic research on bottom-up and top-down processing and word recognition to teaching practice and demonstrates the contribution of linguistics to understanding the processes involved in learning to read and to spell. She considers the difficulties dyslexics have and closes with a discussion of the effects of literacy on cognition.

David Crystal's chapter on clinical linguistics (29) describes the contributions a linguist can make in accurately identifying symptoms of speech pathology. Crystal highlights the process by which the applied linguist clarifies, describes, diagnoses, and assesses the problem. By conducting a systematic survey, the clinical linguist can gain insight into the linguistic abilities of a patient and is thus able to suggest effective means of intervention.

Roger Shuy's chapter on forensic linguistics (30) considers ways in which applied linguistics can assist law and the legal profession. He describes some of the types of cases in which a linguist might be consulted such as trademark infringement, product liability, speaker identification, authorship of written documents, and criminal cases. Future work for forensic linguists includes analysis of the language of power used in the courtroom, interpretation of courtroom testimony and documents for non-native speakers of English, and analysis of speech acts in evidence presented in court.

Christoph Gutknecht's chapter on translation (31) places translation within a communicative framework. He points to the problem-solving nature of translation as it is related to the specific needs and goals of the translation. He discusses principles of translation and some of the difficulties caused by various types of false friends. He considers some of the factors that condition the act of translation and the function of these factors. Lastly, he considers the status of and outlook for machine and computer-assisted translation.

Frank Anshen's chapter on language planning (32) takes applied linguistics to the macro-level of national policies and planning with respect to language and demonstrates the multidisciplinary nature of applied linguistics. He describes examples of nations that have chosen monolingualism, equal multilingualism, and regional language systems and considers some of the factors affecting those choices and the consequences of language policies.

27 Educational Linguistics

JAMES PAUL GEE

1 Introduction

It would be impossible in the scope of a single short chapter to discuss all the educational issues to which linguistics is relevant or the many areas of education to which linguists are contributing. At the same time, linguistics has had much less impact on education, and teachers know much less about language and linguistics, than the current state of our knowledge about language in education, or the current dilemmas of our schools, would seem to merit. Thus, I concentrate on the importance of an overt focus on the structure of language, and the complex and varied relationships between language structure and communicative functions, for successful learning for all students, regardless of their cultural or socioeconomic backgrounds.

In section 2, I start my discussion with a consideration of the way in which different theories of language impact differently on educational debates. I take as my example the current debate over pedagogies like "whole language," which stress immersing children in language rich activities, but downplay overt instruction and an overt focus on language structure. In sections 3 and 4, I look at the different types or styles of language that are used in and out of school with explicit reference to the role an overt focus on language can play in helping children to acquire new forms of academic language and thinking. In section 5, I take up the issue of language and cultural diversity in classrooms and stress the need for teachers to understand the linguistic and cultural resources that all children, including minority and lower socioeconomic children, bring to their classrooms. Such culturally distinctive resources can serve as a base from which to build educational success for all children. In section 6, I discuss a related issue, the way in which a lack of understanding about the role of language in social interaction – for example, between teacher and student – especially as it intersects with cultural differences, can lead to assuming that "deficits" reside in children, rather than in the interaction itself. Finally, in section 7, I sum up some of the educational interventions that a focus on language and linguistics suggests are necessary for successful and socially just classroom teaching and learning.

2   Theories of Language

Different theories of language offer different perspectives on educational issues. I will discuss here one area where differing theories of language, based on different approaches to linguistic theory, are currently playing a crucial role in a major educational debate. The two differing linguistic theories I will discuss are "functional linguistics" versus "generativist linguistics." The educational debate I discuss is the one over "progressive pedagogies" (such as "whole language"), that is, pedagogies that immerse learners in language-rich activities, but downplay the role of overt instruction and any overt focus on language structure. Two differences among functional and generativist linguistic theories play a role in my discussion: first, these two perspectives view the relationship between form and function in language and language acquisition quite differently; second, they differ on whether or not they claim there is a significant biological basis for grammar and the acquisition of one's initial language.

Functional theories of language have informed a good deal of educational linguistics (Halliday 1994, Martin 1992, Thompson 1996). Such theories argue that there is in language a close "fit" between form (structure) and function (meaning). On this view, certain linguistic forms have evolved culturally and historically to serve (and are well designed to serve) certain communicative and interactional functions. Thus, understanding the functions a particular form is used to carry out is the key to acquiring and understanding that form. Functional theories tend to downplay the role of biology in language acquisition and to see language development of all sorts (e.g., first and second language acquisition, the development of literacy, the learning of "specialist languages" like those used in the sciences or the humanities) as similar processes of socialization or enculturation (Halliday 1993).

In contrast, generativist theories of language, such as Chomskian linguistics (Chomsky 1986, 1995), see no very close match between language form and language function, form being relatively autonomous from – and largely, but not completely, unpredictable – based on the communicative functions it happens to serve. For generativists, first language acquisition is heavily affected by a biological endowment for language and, thus, significantly different from the acquisition of literacy or later specialized forms of language for which there is no such biological endowment (see Gee 1994 for discussion).

I have pointed out that functionalist theories of language often draw an analogy between first language acquisition and other forms of later learning. This analogy, in fact, has been at the heart of many "progressive" pedagogies (Cazden 1972: 139–42). Progressive pedagogies stress immersing learners in "hands on" practice in meaningful environments where oral and written language are fully functional for the learners. Such pedagogies (which include movements like "whole language" and "process writing") downplay the role of overt instruction and rely more on learners inferring "rules" and patterns (generalizations) from the (often collaborative) practices in which they are engaged (Goodman 1986, 1993, see Edelsky 1996 for discussion).

Progressivists tend to make the following sort of analogical argument: Children acquire their native languages not by direct instruction (indeed, overt correction seems to have little impact on them), but by being immersed in rich, meaningful, and natural communicative settings. So, by analogy, it might be argued that in other areas, outside first language acquisition, humans learn best when their learning is self-motivated and self-directed in "natural" settings and not "imposed" on them by direct instruction.

This analogy has been attacked recently by a number of generative linguists (Melvold and Pesetsky 1995; 40 Massachusetts linguists signed a petition against the state's new whole language-inspired English standards in July 1996). These linguists have argued that, since biology plays a role in first language acquisition in a way it does not in later forms of language, literacy, and content learning, these later forms of learning are not properly analogous to first language acquisition. Thus, we ought not to draw educational implications from such an analogy.

Another way to state the generativist view on language acquisition is as follows: the child acquiring language is confronted with lots of "data" – the language she hears everywhere around her – though, of course, this data is always a very small subset of the infinite set of sentences in any language. There are always a great many hypotheses or patterns possible about what "rules" underlie the data (i.e., what generalizations there are in the data), especially granted the creativity of the human mind and the infinity of language. Therefore, *something* must "constrain" the child's "search space" such that the child does not "waste" exorbitant time considering fruitless or misleading hypotheses (see also Elman 1991). And, of course, generative linguists argue that this "something" is in the genes. For other sorts of learning – e.g., physics or literacy – evolution has not had enough time to build into human biology such a substantive and specific "head start," since things like writing and physics have simply not been around long enough in human history. Thus, in these cases, something else – not genes, but, let us say, teachers – must help the learner constrain the search space.

The generative linguists' argument addresses a very real problem. It demands that progressivists develop a coherent theory of instructional "guidance" in the case of literacy and school subjects that can play (replace) the focussing ("scaffolding") role that human biology plays in first language acquisition (Gee 1994). The argument implies that we cannot, at least for most learners, rely too strongly on "immersion in practice," no matter how rich the environment in which the learner is immersed. It, thus, helps us state a major goal of educational linguistics.

However, some people have taken the generativist argument further and claimed that it implies a return to a form of direct phonics instruction that stresses letters and letter combinations and the complex and multiple ways they map to sound. This, of course, does not logically follow from the generativist argument. All that follows is the need for some theory of "learning" or "teaching" that specifies *what* can make up for the role biology plays in the case of first language acquisition. Without further argument, we cannot necessarily conclude that this "what" is any particular form of "phonics," or anything else, for that matter.

Furthermore, the argument for the biological basis of language is an argument about *grammar* (and only part of grammar, at that), not everything else that goes under the rubric "language." To a generative linguist, "grammar" names the *structural* (phonological, morphological, lexical, syntactic, and logical) properties of *sentences*. Properties of meaning beyond the "logical form" of sentences and properties of "discourse" (both in terms of how language is put to use in actual contexts and in terms of how sentences are connected together to form "texts") do not (for the most part) fall under "grammatical theory" as generative linguists conceive it. But meaning and discourse are obviously crucial to later forms of language, content, and literacy learning (Gee 1996a). Furthermore, even if strongly functionalist theories were wrong for much of the grammar of our vernacular languages, they could, nonetheless, still be more nearly correct for the sorts of syntactic, rhetorical, and discourse systems connected with specialist uses of language (e.g., the language of physics, law, or medicine).

Educational linguistics alone cannot tell us what form of teaching needs to make up for biology and "constrain the learning space" for later learning. Educational linguistics must be supplemented here by studies in psycholinguistics and cognitive psychology about how the mind works and by studies in the social sciences about how teaching and learning work within and across different cultural and social groups.

For example, psycholinguists have convincingly argued that no one can learn to read unless he or she has some substantive degree of meta-awareness of the "phonological code" (see Adams 1990 for an overview). By the "phonological code" I mean conscious awareness of the phonemic units of the language and the ways these are characteristically sequenced into larger clusters (syllabic sub-units, syllables, and on up to the level of words). While such knowledge is unconsciously part of all native speakers' linguistic competence, gaining "conscious awareness of the phonemic structure of speech is among the most difficult and critical steps toward becoming a reader" (Adams 1990: 412).

Such knowledge comes from practices in which the formal structure of language is foregrounded. These practices may be oral or early literacy activities in which the growing awareness of graphemic principles facilitates meta-awareness of the phonemic structure of speech. Studies of different home cultures have shown that, in certain sorts of (typically, but not always, "middle-class") homes, children spend an enormous amount of time in language and literacy practices which lead to phonological awareness before they arrive at school (Adams 1990: 83–92). Such activities are supported by the guidance of adults and older peers, or they are supported by the structures built into materials (e.g., books) or media representations (e.g., *Sesame Street*).

According to psycholinguists, in addition to conscious knowledge of the phonological code, successful reading requires that the recognition of common letter patterns and common words has been rendered highly automatic (for an overview, see Perfetti 1997). This is so because only then can readers focus sufficient conscious attention on the higher-order aspects of reading (e.g., drawing inferences from the text, making connections across the text, figuring out the meanings of new words in context, etc.). Furthermore, both of these abilities – meta-awareness of the phonological code and automaticity of letter patterns and common words – appear to require a great deal of practice, practice that cannot simply be skipped or remedied through some "quick fix" in school.

It is important to note that much traditional phonics instruction focusses children on letters and the complex ways in which they map to sounds, parts of words, and words. Linguistic and psycholinguistic evidence suggests this is backwards (McGuinness 1997). Children need to be focussed (in contexts where they understand the point of what they are doing) on the sounds and the sound system of the language, on the basic ("unmarked") pairings of these sounds with letters, and, then, on the alternative graphic representations for given sounds.

Given what we have said about literacy, we run into an educational dilemma. For children who come to school without much meta-awareness of the phonological code and who have not rendered recognition of common letter patterns and words automatic, we have to worry about how we can supply (or replace) the large amounts of socially supported practice other children have already had (and will continue to have) at home.

We should keep in mind, as well, that sociocultural studies have argued that home immersion in school-related language and literacy practices connects such practices (and their concomitant values) in a deep way to children's emerging cultural identities (for an overview, see Gee 1996a, 1992). Such a connection (or lack of it) appears to be important for children's later literacy learning and for the ways in which they do or do not affiliate with schools. Many in-school practices do not seem to link to children's cultural identities, or create new ones, nearly as deeply as initial home-based socialization does. Nevertheless, it may well be true that unless children take on any given form of literacy as part of a valued cultural or social identity, it will not be fully mastered. Thus, we need to see what goes on in school as itself a form of enculturation that delivers any type of literacy (e.g., "the basics," literature, science, "critical thinking," and so forth) as part of a larger identity connected not only to ways of writing and reading, but to ways of talking, thinking, acting, interacting, believing, feeling, and valuing, as well.

In the end, linguistic and psycholinguistic research can help set the framework in which discussions of, and debates over, literacy pedagogy and curricula are carried out. Such research leads us to see that what is required in classrooms, for diverse learners, is more complex than simplistic debates over dichotomies like "immersion in practice" and "overt instruction" may imply. Children need to be overtly focussed on the structure of oral and written language (all the way from sound and morphology, through syntax and meaning, to discourse) and the way it relates to functions (and this relation is not transparent and differs across different styles of language and genre of texts). They need, as well, to engage in this focussing amidst a great deal of practice (up to the point of rendering "lower level" skills automatic and unconscious, thereby leaving cognitive energy for higher level skills and conscious reflection), practice that comes to constitute a form of socialization or enculturation.

3   Social Languages

Debates about education typically focus on language in the broad sense in which we talk about things like "English" and "Russian" as languages. But teaching and learning in classrooms, especially for native speakers of the language of instruction, is actually rarely about language at this broad level. Rather, it is about what I will call "social languages" (Gee 1996a – what I am calling a "social language" has sometimes been called a "register," though this is often a more restricted term). In fact, social languages become progressively more important as the child advances through school, since the acquisition of different "academic" social languages (in the broad sense of the word "academic") is one of the ultimate goals of the whole schooling process.

A given social language is composed of the lexical and grammatical resources (whether in speech or writing) that a recognizable group of people uses to carry out its characteristic social practices. Los Angeles street-gang members, laboratory physicists, medical doctors, successful middle-school science students, literary critics, and Los Angeles policemen all have characteristic linguistic resources they use to carry out their distinctive social practices. In addition, we all have a culturally distinctive vernacular social language that we picked up as part of our initial linguistic socialization (we might call this our "primary social language").

Social languages can be acquired in a variety of different ways. For example, Rogoff and Toma (1997) argue that in many middle-class families in the USA, caregivers use language with young children not just or primarily to carry out joint activity, which is usually dyadic, but also to focus on words themselves through such things as

> labeling objects or events for the sake of indicating their label (e.g., "here is his *hat*" or "Oh, you are putting on the *lid*") and test questions in which the questioner asks for information that they already know ("Where is your *belly button*?") and often evaluates the answer ("Very gooooood!"). (Rogoff and Toma 1997: 477)

This sort of practice facilitates early school success, since formal schooling demands an awareness of language as a semiotic object in its own right and not just as a device to refer to the world. And, of course, at school, specific social languages are acquired via yet more direct guidance and overt instruction.

On the other hand, Rogoff and Toma (1997: 477) argue that, in Mayan families in Guatemala, especially when caregivers have not been influenced a great deal by formal schooling, "caregivers usually used language with toddlers to suggest actions and to seek or provide information" as part and parcel of participation in ongoing activities of groups usually larger than simple dyads (see also Rogoff and Toma 1997: 478 and 481). Here there was less focus on language in and of itself and fewer provisions of "language lessons" amidst immersion in practice.

The Russian psychologist Lev Vygotsky (1987: ch. 6), though writing in the 1930s, developed a view of classroom learning that is deeply relevant to the sorts of debates over "immersion" vs. overt instruction with which we started this chapter. He argued that immersion in practice coupled with *a certain type* of overt guidance gives learners a degree of reflective awareness and conscious control over the relationship between form and meaning in a social language not typical of social languages acquired largely through immersion alone. The type of overt guidance that Vygotsky argued for was the sort that focusses the learner consciously on conceptual relationships, verbal links, and connections between form and meaning. He argued that this was the primary goal and effect of efficacious schooling.

Vygotsky further argued that the social languages we acquire with such a significant degree of reflective awareness and conscious control (e.g., the language of science) come to "reorganize," "formalize," or "regiment" (however we want to put the matter) social languages we have acquired earlier, often without much initial conscious awareness, (e.g., our "everyday" vernacular ways of talking about the natural world). We might say that such later social languages can come to serve as "meta-languages" for social languages we have acquired earlier. In fact, we have already seen above that early literacy serves as just such a meta-language for the child's early vernacular oral language: for instance, the graphemic system serves cognitively as a meta-level representation in terms of which the learner can think about the phonemic system of the oral language.

Vygotsky is, thus, arguing that making learners consciously reflect in conceptual and verbal relationships, that is, on the way form and function relate to each other in different types of social languages, leads to a new form of intelligence. It leads to a form of intelligence in which learners have gained a social language within which to think about their other social languages.

Let me give another and more complicated example of one social language serving as a meta-language for another one. This example is relevant, as well, to how children can move, in school, from "everyday" talk about science to progressively more complex forms of talk and thought in regard to science. Biologists, and other scientists, write differently in professional journals than they do in popular science magazines. Consider, for instance, the two extracts below, both written by the same biologist on the same topic (example from Myers 1990: 150):

1   *Heliconius* butterflies lay their eggs on *Passiflora* vines. In defense the vines seem to have evolved fake eggs that make it look to the butterflies as if eggs have already been laid on them. (Popular science)

2   Experiments show that *Heliconius* butterflies are less likely to oviposit on host plants that possess eggs or egg-like structures. These egg-mimics are an unambiguous example of a plant trait evolved in response to a host-restricted group of insect herbivores. (Professional journal)

The second extract, from a professional journal, names plants and animals in terms of the role they play in (and how they relate to each other within) a particular theory of natural selection, namely "coevolution" of predator and prey. Thus, consider "these egg mimics" (for parts of the leaf), "host plants" (for "vines"), or "a host-restricted group of insect herbivores" (for "butterflies"). Note, too, how the language of the professional passage generalizes over the sorts of things and events discussed in the language of the popular passage (the first extract), and formalizes them within a specific set of (in this case, experimental and theoretical) practices. It also uses linguistic structures that assume one has command over the sorts of linguistic structures used in the popular passage should one need to explicate the professional passage in more concrete terms. This is what I mean by saying that the language of the professional passage is a "meta-language" for the language of the popular passage.

We might add, as well, that the popular passage itself, as a form of "academic literacy" in its own right, represents a meta-language for, or a regimentation of, yet more "everyday" forms of language. For example, even the popular passage assumes the creation of technical terms that categorize things more "strictly" than we do in everyday language. It assumes, as well, a more specific and careful delineation of the grammar of argumentation than is typical of "everyday" language (e.g., note the chain: "In defense, . . . "seem to have" . . . "that make it look" . . . "as if" . . .).

In a case like the one we are discussing, we see that we have a chain of social languages something like this: everyday vernacular language → school-based sorts of oral and written language (e.g., early school science) → oral and written forms of "popular science" → oral and written forms of "professional science." Learning any social language in this chain with a substantive degree of reflective awareness and conscious control tends also to reorganize and give yet greater reflective awareness and conscious control to any of the languages lower in the hierarchy (just as graphemics does for phonemics), including one's vernacular language.

Of course, important ideological effects can happen here. As the language of science, for instance, regiments and reorganizes our everyday language about and understanding of the natural world, we can internalize beliefs and values some of which denigrate our everyday world or work against values we otherwise hold (Gee 1996b). Thus, it is important, too, that students come to a conscious and critical understanding of how specialist languages work, how they arise, compete with other social languages, and change. Such an understanding is sometimes called "critical literacy" (Martin 1991) or "critical discourse analysis" (Fairclough 1995).

This discussion of social languages suggests that having students pay much more overt attention than is typical of schools today to how language works in a variety of different sorts of texts in different social languages is important for efficacious classroom practice. In areas like science, struggling with language in texts, and not just test tubes in labs, is equally important for the acquisition of science in any form that constitutes deep understanding and not the superficial knowledge that is common in schools today, where even good students do not really understand the science they learn in any way that can actually be put to use (Gardner 1991, Perkins 1992).

4   Genre

Our discussion of the role of social languages in education, as well as Vygotsky's views on classroom instruction, leads naturally to a consideration of another current debate in education, namely over "genre approaches" to education. Linguists in a wide variety of countries have argued for an explicit focus on the features of language at a grammatical and discourse level that characterize a specific oral or written language "genre" (Christie 1990, Cope and Kalantzis 1993, Martin 1989, Swales 1990). By "genre" these linguists mean the forms of linguistic patterning in terms of which typical communicative tasks, like reports, explanations, descriptions, narratives, classifications, and so forth, are carried out within particular social languages.

The genre linguists have argued, as well, that teachers and students must have an explicit meta-language within which they can talk explicitly and clearly about form and function in language. Only on this basis can children achieve fluid mastery of specific school-based language practices, especially if they have not come from homes where they were immersed in early school-based literacy practices. Only on this basis, too, can all children achieve critical literacy, which requires one to be able to talk and think about how language and thinking work within and across diverse social languages. It should be apparent that the genre approach is related to the sort of approach I discussed in the last section, though the "social language approach" and the "genre approach" are not often explicitly related to each other, perhaps because one arose in the USA, influenced by Bakhtin (1986) and Vygotsky (1987), and the other in Australia, influenced by Halliday (1994).

The argument of both the social language and genre approaches is, then, that "grammar," in the broad sense of how language form relates to language function, is crucial for efficacious (and socially fair) education. It is such a focus on grammar, in the midst of immersion of communicative practices, that leads to reflective awareness and conscious control over different genres of spoken and written language within different social languages.

Consider, for example, the following short extract from a science textbook (taken from Martin 1990: 93):

> The destruction of a land surface by the combined effects of abrasion and re-moval of weathered material by transporting agents is called erosion . . . The pro-duction of rock waste by mechanical processes and chemical changes is called weathering. (Heading et al. 1967: 116)

A whole bevy of linguistic features mark these sentences as part of a distinct-ive academic social language. Some of these features are: "heavy subjects" (e.g., "the production of rock waste by mechanical processes and chemical changes"); processes and actions named by nouns or nominalizations, rather than verbs (e.g., "production"); passive main verbs ("is called") and passives inside nominalizations (e.g., "production by mechanical means"); modifiers which are more contentful than the nouns they modify (e.g., "transporting agents"); and complex embedding (e.g., "weathered material by transporting agents" is a nominalization embedded inside "the combined effects of . . ." and this more complex nominalization is embedded inside a yet larger nominaliza-tion, "the destruction of . . ."). No one grammatical feature marks the social language of this sentence. Rather, all these features, and others, form a dis-tinctive *configuration* (Gee, to appear).

This social language also incorporates a great many distinctive discourse markers, that is, linguistic features that characterize larger stretches of text and give them unity and coherence as a certain type of "genre." For example, the genre here is a type of explanatory definition and it is characterized by classificatory language of the form: "*Propositions densely packaged through nominalization* → are called → *Technical term*." Such language leads adept readers to form a classificatory scheme in their heads something like this: "There are two types of *change*, namely *erosion* and *weathering*; in turn, there are two types of *weathering*, namely *mechanical* and *chemical*," where each ital-icized word is rather like an icon on a computer desktop that can be clicked on to reveal more classificatory structure.

Of course, these explanatory definitions may well be embedded in a larger text and be part of a larger genre (e.g., a description, exposition, explanation, report, or what have you) with its own grammatical and discourse features. Genres are how social languages carry out their relatively routine, typical, or repeatable forms of work. While children from school-centered homes may pick up such forms of language through immersion in practices that use such forms of language, children to whom these and related forms of language are more foreign need, the genre linguists argue, a more overt focus on such forms and the work they do. This point returns us to the issue of children who have not had a lot of immersion in "school-based" literacy practices at home prior to and throughout their formal schooling, a topic I take up in the next section.

5   Language Differences in School

One of the most pressing issues in education today is the fact that many children from lower socioeconomic homes, many of them minority children, do poorly in school (Miller 1995). Such children have often had little practice at home with school-based forms of language and interaction. Because of this, it is often assumed that they come to school with "nothing" relevant in the way of language practices on which to base their initiation into schooling. However, in many cases, this is not true. Many of these children come to school well versed in language practices that, while not typical school-based literacy practices, are, nonetheless, rich verbal practices that can be leveraged to good effect by the school. Unfortunately, as I have said, the language practices of these children are often invisible to teachers and even, at times, denigrated. It should be a goal of schooling to allow such children to gain reflective awareness and conscious control over their own indigenous verbal practices as part of their acquisition of school-based social languages (in addition to their acquisition of "standard English").

For example, sociolinguists have known for years that African-American Vernacular English, spoken by many African-American children when they come to school, is a perfectly well designed and "logical" dialect, no better or worse, in grammatical terms, than any other English dialect (Baugh 1983, Labov 1972). Sociolinguists have also known for years that many African American children also bring to school richly intricate discourse practices, such as complex forms of storytelling (Smitherman 1977, Gee 1996a). For instance, consider the story below, told by a seven-year-old African-American girl ("Leona") at "sharing time" ("show and tell"). I have organized the story in terms of lines and stanzas that help to bring out its overall discourse organization (see Gee 1996a: 103–14, Hymes 1996):

Leona's story

FRAME
STANZA 1
1 Today
2 it's Friday the 13th
3 an' it's bad luck day
4 an' my grandmother's birthday is on bad luck day

PART 1: MAKING CAKES
STANZA 2
5 an' my mother's bakin' a cake
6 an' I went up my grandmother's house while my mother's bakin' a cake
7 an' my mother was bakin' a cheese cake
8 my grandmother was bakin' a whipped cream cupcakes

STANZA 3
9 an' we bof went over my mother's house
10 an' then my grandmother had made a chocolate cake
11 an' then we went over my aunt's house
12 an' she had make a cake

STANZA 4
13 an' everybody had made a cake for nana
14 so we came out with six cakes

PART 2: GRANDMOTHER EATS CAKES
STANZA 5
15 last night
16 my grandmother snuck out
17 an' she ate all the cake
18 an' we hadda make more

STANZA 6
(she knew we was makin' cakes)
19 an' we was sleepin'
20 an' she went in the room
21 an' gobbled em up
22 an' we hadda bake a whole bunch more

STANZA 7
23 she said mmmm
24 she had all chocolate on her face, cream, strawberries
25 she said mmmm
26 that was good

STANZA 8
27 an' then an' then all came out
28 an' my grandmother had ate all of it
29 she said "what's this cheese cake doin' here" – she didn't like cheese cakes
30 an' she told everybody that she didn't like cheese cakes

STANZA 9
31 an' we kept makin' cakes
32 an' she kept eatin' 'em
33 an' we finally got tired of makin' cakes
34 an' so we all ate 'em

PART 3: GRANDMOTHER GOES OUTSIDE THE HOME
NON-NARRATIVE SECTION (35–41)
STANZA 10
35 an' now
36 today's my grandmother's birthday

37 an' a lot o' people's makin' a cake again
38 but my grandmother is goin t'get her own cake at her bakery
39 an' she's gonna come out with a cake
40 that we didn't make
41 cause she likes chocolate cream

STANZA 11
42 an' I went t'the bakery with her
43 an' my grandmother ate cupcakes
44 an' an' she finally got sick on today
45 an' she was growling like a dog cause she ate so many cakes

FRAME
STANZA 12
46 an' I finally told her that it was
47 it was Friday the 13th bad luck day

It is common today, in movements such as "teacher-research," to encourage teachers to record children like Leona and to analyze their language as a way of gaining insight into the child's culturally specific "sense making capacity," as well as her culturally distinctive verbal resources. So, let's look briefly at Leona's story.

Leona's story is organized, through syntactic parallelism and lexical and syntactic repetition, in an intricately poetic way. Note, for example, that every line in stanza 2 ends on the word "cake" and that the stanza as a whole is organized by an aabb structure: ". . . bakin' a cake . . . bakin' a cake . . . bakin' a type of cake . . . bakin' a type of cake." Stanza 3 is organized in terms of an abab structure: "go over a house . . . make a cake . . . go over a house . . . bake a cake." Stanzas 5 and 6 are line by line stylistic variations of the same event, an event which stanza 7 "performs" or mimes. Such poetic structuring (including many sound and prosodic devices not transcribed above), typical of African-American oral storytelling, exists throughout the story.

The story also plays on a long-running theme in African-American culture, namely the nature of symbols or signification (see Jackson 1974, Smitherman 1977, Stuckey 1987). The grandmother – the matriarch of the home – eats lots of cakes, big and small, at home and never gets sick. However, when she eats little cakes (cupcakes) outside the home at the bakery, she does get sick and "growls like a dog" (loses her human status). What distinguishes humans from animals is their ability to see the symbolic value of things, to recognize, for example, that though they look alike, a cake made at home is a true symbol of kinship, while one made at a bakery is not. The grandmother's momentary failure to recognize the nature of "real" and "duplicitous" symbols (signs) is what causes her to get sick and "growl like a dog." Young African-American children often help listeners interpret their stories by giving crucial non-narrative, "evaluative" information (Labov 1972) right before the conclusion of the story (older storytellers spread such information throughout their stories).

Leona does this in stanza 10 where she stresses the importance of the fact that the grandmother is going to get a cake "that we [the family] didn't make."

Leona and other African-American children in her class were often told to sit down during their sharing time turns, because the teacher felt they were not "talking about one important thing" (Michaels 1981). The teacher heard such children as meandering among different topics, loosely associating ideas and themes, since she, like many teachers, had little knowledge about the grammatical and discourse features of African-American Vernacular English.

In school, children like Leona are often focussed only on standard English. However, there is evidence that such children (even at high school age) can be effectively introduced to the social languages of literature and literary criticism in ways that juxtapose their own discourse practices with these new social languages so as to allow these children to gain reflective awareness and conscious control over both the new social languages to which they are being exposed and their own dialect and discourse practices (Lee 1993). Such a juxtaposition, of course, requires a meta-language within which teachers and students can compare and contrast different genres and social languages. Students, thus, gain powerful knowledge about language, literature, forms of literacy, and rhetoric in a way that links integrally to their own cultural identity. After all, the sorts of poetic oral practices in which Leona is engaged, even as a seven-year-old, are historically at the roots of literature in the west and elsewhere (e.g., the oral tradition from Homer to Chaucer). They are also used and transformed in a wide variety of "high literature" written by African-American authors.

Again, we see the importance of consciously focussing children on how form and function work in social languages. We see here, too, the importance of teachers focussing on this same issue in regard to the children in the classrooms who are most different from themselves. In this way, they can build on, rather than ignore or unintentionally denigrate, the different sorts of verbal resources children bring with them to the classroom.

6   Social Interaction in Institutions

So far we have concentrated on language and not social interaction in classrooms. But many educational linguists focus on the ways in which language form and meaning, with concomitant consequences for empowering or disempowering people, are interactionally worked out moment by moment in specific educational contexts (Green and Dixon 1993, Gumperz 1982, Lemke 1995). There is not space here to go into details as this is a matter which would merit a full chapter of its own. Instead, I will simply give one example of how "minor" linguistic details can take on "major" importance in interaction and come to have important educational implications (Gee and Clinton, to appear).

Consider the following interaction between a white female researcher ("R") and a fourth-grade African-American girl ("S" for student) with whom the researcher is discussing light as part of a school science education project. In the transcript below, a comma indicates a short rise or fall in pitch that sounds as if there is more information to come. A question mark or a period indicates a longer rise or fall in pitch that sounds "final," as if a piece of information is "closed off" or "finished." A capitalized word indicates that that word was said emphatically. A colon after a vowel means that that vowel was drawn out. I have also indicated places where speakers paused briefly and where they lowered the pitch of their voice.

1 R: Where does the light come from, when it's outside?
2 S: Sun (low pitch).
3 R: From the sun (low pitch). (pause) hum
4 S: Cause the sun comes up, REALLY early.
5 R: um (pause) And that's when we get light (low pitch).
6 S: And that's how the the the me (pause) my (pause) me and my class, is talkin' about dinosau:rs, and how they die:d. And we found out, (pause) some things (pause) about how they die:d.
7 R: Oh really. Does that have to do with LIGHT?

After a long interaction from which this bit is taken, the researcher felt that the child often went off topic and was difficult to understand. However, it can be argued, from the above data, that the researcher "co-constructed" (contributed to) these topic changes and lack of understanding. And, indeed, there is evidence that this often happens when teachers interact with "non-mainstream" children without proper understanding of their language and culture (for an overview, see Cazden 1988).

Children in school are used to a distinctive school activity in which an adult asks them a question (to which the adult often knows the answer), the child answers, and the adult responds in some way that can be taken as evaluating whether the child's answer was "acceptable" or not (Mehan 1979). In the above interaction, the researcher starts with a question to which the student responds with the word "sun" said on a low pitch and with a final falling contour. This way of answering indicates (in many dialects of English) that the respondent takes the answer to be obvious (this already constitutes a problem with the question-answer-evaluation activity).

The researcher's response is said in exactly the same way as the child's (low pitch, final falling contour) – and in just the position in which a student is liable to expect an evaluation – indicating that she, too, takes the answer to be obvious. The student might well be mystified, then, as to why the question was asked.

In 4 the student adds a turn that has an emphatic "really" in it and which is said as a whole on a higher pitch (basically on her "normal" level) and with a falling contour. This way of saying her contribution indicates that the student takes this information to be new or significant. She may well have added this information in a search for some response that would render the initial question something other than a request for obvious information and in a search for some more energetic response from the researcher, one that would let the student know she was "on the right track" in the interaction.

However, the student once again gets a response from the researcher (low pitch, falling final contour) that indicates the researcher takes the student's contribution, again, to be obvious. The student, then, in 6, launches off on yet another contribution that is, once again, said in a way that indicates she is trying to state new or significant information that will draw a response of interest from the researcher. The student also here uses a technique that is common in the narratives of some African-American children (Gee 1985): she states background information first before stating her main topic (light), though her "found out, some things" clearly implies, in this context, that these things will have to do with light (which they, indeed, do – she has studied how a meteor blocked out sunlight and helped destroy the dinosaurs). The researcher, listening for a more foregrounded connection to light, stops the student and, with emphasis on "light," clearly indicates that she is skeptical that the student's contribution is going to be about light, a skepticism that is, from the student's perspective, not only unmerited, but actually surprising and a bit insulting (as subsequent interaction shows).

Here the "devil" is, indeed, in the details: aspects of the school-based "question–answer–evaluation" activity, different assumptions about how information is introduced and connected, as well as details of pitch and emphasis (and a good many other such details, too) all work together to lead to misunderstanding. This misunderstanding is quite consequential when the adult authority figure attributes the misunderstanding, not to details of language and diversity (most certainly including her own language and diversity), but to the student herself.

Examples like this one have led many educational linguists to argue that teachers need not only to be more sophisticated about grammar, discourse, and social languages, but need also to engage in their own research-like observations on their own interactional practices with their students. Such a demand amounts to a call for deep changes in how we train teachers and in the role language plays in that training and the subsequent teaching to which it gives rise.

7   Conclusion

I have ranged through a number of areas where knowledge about language and linguistics is relevant to current debates in education. My basic points have been as follows.

1 Children do not just pick up school-based social languages and literacy through the sorts of rich immersion in socialization that is characteristic of first language acquisition. Teachers need to supplement such immersion, which is necessary but not sufficient for learning in school, with more overt forms of focussing on the structure of language and its complex relationships to communicative functions within different styles of language and texts.

2 An overt focus on social languages and specific genres of spoken and written language leads to conscious control of and meta-awareness about language that is fundamental to real understanding and that reorganizes how students think about their earlier forms of language and ways of thinking about the world. This is, indeed, one of the ultimate goals of schooling, and is particularly important for those children who come to school from homes that have not immersed them in school-based forms of language and interaction.

3 Schools often ignore or miss the resources of children who come from "non-mainstream" homes – homes which may not have immersed their children in school-based forms of language and interaction, but which have, nonetheless, immersed them in complex and culturally distinctive linguistic and interactional practices. Schools can honor the resources these children bring with them to school and build on them. In fact, they can allow such children to focus on form and function in their own styles of language in juxtaposition to other styles, especially those used in school, as a way to appreciate variation in language, respect their own culturally distinctive forms of language, and gain meta-awareness of how form and function work across different social languages in and out of school.

4 And, finally, teachers often assume that when a child appears to make little sense, especially a child from a different social and cultural group than their own, that the problem resides inside the child as a "deficit" of some sort. However, such problems often reside in the very interactions in which the teacher is taking part and in the teacher's lack of knowledge about the culturally distinctive resources different children bring with them to school. This dilemma calls both for better training for teachers in regard to language and linguistics (training which, in the USA, is now virtually non-existent) and for teachers to engage in research on their own students and classrooms as a way to better understand the children they teach.

28 Linguistics and Reading

REBECCA TREIMAN

Linguists are primarily concerned with the structure and processing of spoken language. In this chapter, the focus changes to written language. The goal of the chapter is to review what is known about the processes involved in reading and in learning to read. Topics to be discussed include the controversies about the best way to teach children to read and the reasons why some apparently normal children have great difficulty mastering this skill. Another question is whether knowledge of written language changes people's basic intellectual or linguistic abilities. Researchers from a variety of disciplines, including cognitive psychology, developmental psychology, and education, have been active in research on reading. This mix reflects the fact that the study of reading is both theoretically interesting and practically important. Reading is a domain in which experimental psychologists study fundamental questions such as how knowledge and experience affect perception. Reading is also a domain in which research findings have implications for important social issues, such as the education of children. It is no wonder, then, that a large amount of research has been carried out on reading. The discussion of this research begins with a consideration of the cognitive processes that are involved in skilled reading.

1 Bottom-Up and Top-Down Processing in Reading

In the case of reading, as with other cognitive processes, psychologists have distinguished between two kinds of processing. *Bottom-up processes* are those that take in stimuli from the outside world – letters and words, for reading – and deal with that information with little recourse to higher-level knowledge. With *top-down* processes, on the other hand, the uptake of information is guided by an individual's prior knowledge and expectations. In most situations, bottom-up and top-down processes work together to ensure the accurate and rapid processing of information. However, theories about the cognitive processes involved in reading differ in the emphasis that they place on the two approaches. Theories that stress bottom-up processing focus on how readers extract information from the printed page, claiming that readers deal with letters and words in a relatively complete and systematic fashion (e.g., Gough 1972). Theories that stress top-down processing hold that readers form hypotheses about which words they will encounter and take in only just enough visual information to test their hypotheses (e.g., Goodman 1967, Smith 1971). In the words of Goodman, reading is a "psycholinguistic guessing game."

An example may help to clarify the distinction between theories that stress bottom-up processing and those that stress top-down processing. Suppose that a reader has just read, "Daylight savings time ends tomorrow, and so people should remember to change their . . ." According to the top-down view, the reader guesses that the next word in the sentence will be "clocks." The reader checks that the word begins with a "c" and, because the hypothesis has been supported, does not take in the remaining letters of the word. Theories of reading that stress bottom-up processing claim that the reader processes all of the letters in the last word of the sentence, regardless of its predictability.

Studies of readers' eye movements provide some insight into the roles of bottom-up and top-down processes in reading. Research has shown that the eye does not sweep across a line of text in a continuous fashion. Rather, the eye comes to rest for somewhere around a quarter of a second, in what is called a *fixation*, and then makes a rapid jump (a *saccade*) to the next fixation. It is during the fixation that visual stimulation is taken in; little or no useful information is extracted during a saccade. Researchers have found that skilled readers fixate at least once on the majority of words in a text. They do not skip a large number of words, as the top-down view predicts, but instead process the letters and words rather thoroughly. Readers do this, in part, because their span of useful vision is fairly small. For example, a reader who fixates on the "a" of "daylight" will be able to see all of the letters in this word. The reader may or may not be able to see enough to identify the next word, "savings," but will be unable to identify "time." Thus, the eye movement data portray reading as more of a bottom-up process than a top-down process. (See Rayner and Pollatsek 1989 for a review of the research.)

Comparisons of good and poor readers further support the claim that bottom-up processes play an important role in reading. If reading were a linguistically guided guessing game, as top-down theorists maintain, one would expect guessing ability to discriminate between good and poor readers. In this view, good readers are highly sensitive to context and use it to guide their uptake of print, whereas poor readers have trouble predicting the upcoming words in a sentence. However, research has shown that poor and unskilled readers use context at least as much as good readers (e.g., Perfetti et al. 1979). Skilled readers' perceptually based recognition skills are so accurate and automatic that they do not usually need to guess.

The statement that bottom-up processes play a central role in reading does not necessarily mean that top-down processes are completely unimportant. Studies have shown that words that are predictable from context are fixated for shorter periods of time and are skipped more often than words that are less predictable, although the effects are relatively modest (see Rayner and Pollatsek 1989). One interpretation of these results is that readers sometimes use their higher-order thinking skills to predict the upcoming words in a sentence. However, the results may alternatively reflect low-level associative processes within the *lexicon* (mental dictionary) itself. For example, readers may spend less time on "cake" in the sentence "The guests ate the wedding cake" than in the sentence "The guests ate the large cake" because the activation of "wedding" automatically sends some activation to "cake." Whatever the mechanism responsible for context effects, we must keep in mind that most words are not predictable or only minimally predictable from context. After "the," for example, almost any adjective or noun could occur. Therefore, bottom-up processing is often essential for reading.

2   Word Recognition

Many of the processes that are involved in understanding what we read are similar to the processes involved in comprehension of spoken language. In both cases, we must often use our knowledge of the world to make sense of and elaborate on the information. When reading about a wedding, for example, it is helpful to know about the kinds of activities that usually take place on such occasions. The grammatical knowledge that is necessary to understand a sentence is similar, too, whether the words are read or heard. What distinguishes reading from speech is the need to identify words by eye. Readers must recognize printed words accurately and automatically, linking them to representations stored in the mental lexicon. This process of *word recognition* has been a central focus of reading research.

To understand the processes that are involved in the recognition of words, one needs to consider the way in which printed words map onto speech. Although writing systems differ from one another in many ways, all full writing systems are based on speech (DeFrancis 1989, see also chapter 3, Writing Systems). For example, each syllable (roughly speaking) in spoken Japanese has its own symbol in the writing system called kana and so this system maps onto speech at the level of syllables. In alphabetic languages, in contrast, the link between print and speech is at the level of individual sounds or phonemes. Some alphabetic writing systems, such as Italian and Finnish, exemplify the alphabetic principle almost perfectly, with each letter representing one and only one phoneme. English is not a pure alphabetic writing system, which has led to widespread criticism of the system and many calls for spelling reform. Some English sounds have more than one possible spelling, as when /k/ is alternatively spelled as "c" ("cat"), "k" ("kit"), or "ck" ("pack"). Moreover, some letters have more than one possible pronunciation. For example, "c" can correspond to /k/ as in "cat" or /s/ as in "city." Although such complications make the English writing system more complex than some other writing systems, they do not negate the usefulness of the alphabetic principle. "Gove" could be pronounced to rhyme with "cove" or "love," for example, but skilled readers would never pronounce it as "mab." Certain deviations from the alphabetic principle are themselves principled, reflecting the tendency of English to spell morphemes (units of meaning) in a consistent fashion. For example, the past tense ending is variously pronounced as /t/ (as in "jumped"), /d/ (as in "hemmed") or /əd/ (as in "wanted"), but it is generally spelled as "ed." As another example, the "a" in "health," which makes the word an exception from an alphabetic standpoint, reveals the relationship in meaning to "heal."

Just as the printed forms of words reflect their linguistic forms, so the processing of printed words involves the recovery of the words' linguistic forms. In many cases, readers access the phonological (or sound) forms of words as part of the recognition process. This phonological activation is covert, for skilled readers who are reading silently, but psychologists have devised clever ways to detect it. In one technique, people are presented with a category name (e.g., "type of food") and must then rapidly decide whether various printed words belong to the category. College students sometimes misclassify words that sound like category members (e.g., "meet") as members of the category, even when they know the words' correct spellings. Participants make fewer errors on words that look equally like a member of the category but that do not sound like one (e.g., "melt") (Van Orden 1987). (See Frost 1998 for a review.)

There is some debate about exactly how readers derive the phonological forms of words from their spellings. Do skilled readers use explicit rules of the kind taught in phonics lessons ("b" corresponds to /b/, "m" to /m/, and so on), or do they rely on a network of implicit connections? Are the links between spellings and sounds based on individual graphemes, or letters and letter groups that correspond to single sounds (e.g., "b," "sh")? Alternatively, do readers sometimes rely on larger units, linking units such as "ead" and "ine" to their pronunciations? These units have been called *orthographic rimes*; they correspond to the *phonological rimes* (vowel + final consonant units) of spoken syllables (Bernstein and Treiman, in press). To investigate questions such as those described above, researchers are devising explicit models of the spelling-to-sound translation process and are testing the predictions of such models (Coltheart et al. 1993, Plaut et al. 1996, Seidenberg and McClelland 1989). These tests are no longer restricted to small-scale experiments but often involve assessing readers' performance on large samples of words (Spieler and Balota 1997, Treiman et al. 1995). Although areas of disagreement remain, it is widely believed that rapid, automatic word recognition is critical to reading success and that such recognition often involves activation of words' spoken forms.

3   Learning to Read

Much of the research on learning to read has focussed on the acquisition of alphabetic writing systems, especially English. In the United States and other English-speaking countries, there has been a debate between advocates of two different approaches to learning to read. (See Adams and Bruck 1995, Bergeron 1990, Liberman and Liberman 1992 for discussion.) The first of these, the *whole language* approach, is based on the idea that top-down processing plays an important role in reading. If fluent readers use context to predict the upcoming words in a sentence, only processing the print to the degree necessary to confirm their expectations, then children should do the same. Children should focus on the meaning of what they read rather than laboriously sounding out the individual words. Just as children will master spoken language if they are spoken to by others and given the opportunity to respond, so children will become literate if they are placed in an environment that is rich in print and are encouraged to explore it. Whole language teachers thus focus on the meaning and purpose of printed language rather than on individual letters and sounds. Activities may include reading stories to children and helping children use the pictures or the context to figure out the words. Sounding out an unknown word is typically considered a strategy of last resort, and children are given little guidance on how to do this. Whole language teachers also encourage the integration of reading and writing, expecting children to write independently from an early age and offering little or no instruction in conventional spelling.

The second class of approaches to literacy instruction, known as *phonics*, places primary stress on the bottom-up processing of letters and words. In this view, learning to read is quite different from learning to talk. Spoken language is deeply rooted in biological evolution and is as old as the human species itself. All normal members of the species learn to speak and understand without explicit tuition, provided only that they are exposed to a spoken language. However, the situation is quite different for written language. Writing is a cultural achievement dating back no more than 5,000 years; it is found among some groups of people but not others. Learning to read, phonics advocates claim, usually requires explicit instruction. Children must learn to convert the unfamiliar printed words into their familiar spoken forms by learning that "b" is pronounced as /b/, that "c" can be pronounced as /k/ or /s/, and so on. This sounding out process is slow and laborious at first, but becomes fast and automatic with practice. The phonics approach thus focusses on individual letters and sounds, repetition, and practice. Content and interest are not the only criteria for choosing reading materials; the words must also be easy to decode. For example, a story about a *bug* that can *fish* would be preferred to a story about a *worm* that can *talk*, as *o* does not have its typical pronunciation in *worm* and *a* and *l* do not have their typical pronunciations in *talk*.

In practice, many programs include a combination of whole language and phonics methods. For example, children who are receiving phonics instruction can learn about the meaning and function of print by reading (or being read) interesting stories and using written language for meaningful purposes. As another example, writing can be emphasized in phonics classrooms as well as in whole language classrooms. The central question is whether early reading instruction should include instruction in phonics. The answer to this question, most researchers now agree, is "yes." Across a large number of studies, programs that include explicit, intensive attention to phonics generally yield better results than programs that do not. (See Adams 1990 for a review.)

Still, dissatisfaction with conventional phonics remains. Part of the reason is that some children have trouble grasping phonics instruction and leave first grade able to read only a few words. Researchers have thus begun to examine the factors that make it difficult for some children to benefit from phonics instruction. One contributing factor appears to be a lack of *phonemic awareness*. Children's attention is normally on the meaning of what they hear and say, not on the individual words and sounds. In order to understand how the spellings of words map onto their spoken forms, children must begin to pay attention to smaller units of sound. For example, a child who is not aware that "bat" contains three units of sound, the first of which is the same as the first sound of "boy," will not understand why the printed form of "bat" contains three letters, the first of which is the same as the first letter of "boy." A number of tasks have been developed to tap phonemic awareness, ranging from counting phonemes (how many sounds do you hear in "bat?") to comparing phonemes (do "bat" and "boy" start with the same sound?) to deleting phonemes (what would you get if you took away the /b/ from "bat?"). Children's performance on such tests is an excellent predictor of their later reading success (see Adams 1990 for a review).

To teach phonemic awareness, one can take advantage of the fact that awareness of phonemes is the end-point of a long developmental process. The process begins with awareness of words and syllables and progresses to units that are smaller than syllables but larger than phonemes, including initial consonant clusters (e.g., the "bl" of "blast") and rimes (e.g., "ast"). Programs that use a gradual approach to teach phonemic awareness have been successful both in fostering phonemic awareness and improving later reading performance (see Adams 1990). Phonemic awareness instruction is particularly successful when it is closely integrated with reading instruction, allowing children to use their newly gained phonemic awareness skills in relating print to speech (e.g., Blachman 1987).

Another reason why children may have trouble benefiting from phonics instruction is that, when they first begin to learn to read, they believe that the links between printed words and spoken words are arbitrary and non-analytic (Byrne 1998, Frith 1985). For example, children may think that it is the color and shape of the McDonald's logo, not the letters it contains, that allow it to say "McDonald's." Young children are thought to be *logographic* readers, treating printed words as holistic symbols. Children must break away from the logographic hypothesis in order to learn that the parts of printed words (the graphemes) represent the parts of spoken words (the phonemes) in a systematic fashion.

Yet another stumbling block to conventional phonics instruction involves the teachers rather than the students. Many teachers have little or no opportunity to learn about linguistics and the structure of written language. As a result, they may not provide optimal instruction (Moats 1994). Because teachers are themselves good readers, they tend to think about language in terms of how it is spelled rather than how it is pronounced. They may find it hard to put themselves in the place of a child who does not yet know the conventional writing system. For example, a teacher may think that there is an /ɪ/ (or "short i") sound in "girl" because the spelling of this word contains an "i." However, the spoken word does not actually contain the same /ɪ/ vowel as "bit" and it would be misleading to suggest to a child that it does. As Moats (1994: 99) states, "lower level language mastery is as essential for the literacy teacher as anatomy is for the physician. It is our obligation to enable teachers to acquire it."

To summarize, reading instruction that includes explicit attention to phonics generally works better than instruction that does not. However, there is room for improvement in traditional phonics programs. Research suggests that improvement can occur by better preparing children to benefit from phonics instruction and by better preparing teachers to teach it.

4   Learning to Spell

One aspect of whole language programs that is attractive to many teachers and parents is the focus on writing. In many whole language classrooms, children write each day in personal journals. Correct spelling is not stressed, with children instead being encouraged to invent spellings for words they do not know. It is assumed that invented spellings like "bo" for "blow," "grl" for "girl," and "wet" for "went" will give way to conventional spellings as children learn to read, and that direct instruction in spelling is not necessary. However, research shows that children are less likely to learn words' spellings from the reading of meaningful, connected text than from the study of isolated words. Research further shows that the correlation between reading ability and spelling ability is far from perfect – that there are a number of people who are good readers but poor spellers. For most children, learning to spell requires something above and beyond immersion in a sea of print. The benefits of spelling instruction are not confined to spelling itself. Such instruction can also foster reading and phonemic awareness. For example, as children practice spelling consonant clusters like "bl" they learn to analyze these clusters into their component phonemes. Spelling instruction, like reading instruction, requires a teacher who is knowledgeable about children's errors and the linguistic reasons behind them. For example, a teacher who is aware that the middle part of "girl" is a syllabic /r/ sound rather than /ɪ/ followed by a separate /r/ will understand why young children frequently misspell this word as "grl." (See Read 1986 and Treiman 1993 for a discussion of children's common spelling errors and Treiman 1998 for a review of research on early spelling instruction.)

5 Dyslexia

Even with good instruction, some apparently normal children have great difficulty learning to read and spell. Such children are known as *dyslexics*. The popular view is that these children see letters and words backwards. As a result, they may misread "was" as "saw" or "day" as "bay." Similar errors occur in spelling, as when children write "bit" as "dit" or even "tid" (in what is known as *mirror writing*). However, research reveals that such mistakes do not constitute the majority of reading or spelling errors among dyslexics. Moreover, normal children make the same kinds of errors when they are first learning to read and write. Most researchers now believe that, in the great majority of cases, dyslexia is more a linguistic problem than a visual problem (Olson 1994, Vellutino 1987).

If dyslexia is a linguistic problem, what kind of linguistic problem is it? The most widely accepted hypothesis is that dyslexia reflects a weakness in the phonological component of language (Stanovich 1992, Olson 1994, Vellutino 1987). Dyslexics have difficulty becoming aware of the phonemic structure of spoken language and thus have trouble learning about the way in which spellings map onto sounds. Dyslexics' phonological problems also extend to remembering words and to producing them quickly and accurately. These problems are, in part, genetically based. For example, if one member of a pair of identical twins exhibits reading problems then the other member has an elevated chance of showing similar problems.

If dyslexia indeed stems from linguistic weaknesses, particularly weaknesses in the area of phonology, then teaching must attempt to remediate these problems. Instruction that centers on visual perception, such as exercises designed to improve eye tracking or binocular coordination, does not appear to be successful (Vellutino 1987). What is needed, instead, is an intensive reading program that includes a liberal dose of phonics. A successful program of this kind is provided at the Benchmark School (Gaskins 1998). Here, reading disabled children spend over four hours a day in literacy activities. These activities are designed to help the children become aware of the sounds in spoken words and how these sounds are represented with letters, as well as helping children use this knowledge in reading and writing connected text.

6   The Effects of Literacy

Does learning to read change people's basic cognitive or linguistic abilities? Some have suggested that literate individuals and societies differ greatly from non-literate ones, the former being more abstract, more rational, and more skeptical. Although research has not supported these grand claims, it has provided empirical evidence that literacy has certain cognitive consequences (see Stanovich 1993). For example, United States college students who read extensively have larger vocabularies and more knowledge about the world than their peers who do little reading in their free time. In our society, opportunities to learn new words arise more often while reading than while conversing or watching television.

Learning to read also appears to deepen and alter people's knowledge about language. Phonological awareness, and metalinguistic awareness in general, develop hand in hand with learning to read and write. Thus, preliterate children and illiterate adults tend to do poorly in tasks requiring access to the phonemic structure of language, although they do better on rhyming tasks and syllable-level tasks (Morais et al. 1986, Morais et al. 1979). Another effect of literacy is to color people's knowledge about the sounds of language. For example, seeing that words like "went" and "elephant" contain an "n" in their spellings, children may come to conceptualize /n/ after a vowel as a separate unit rather than as part of the vowel, as they did previously (Treiman et al. 1995). If people's ideas about spoken language are indeed influenced by their knowledge of written language, it may be difficult to study the structure or processing of spoken language without considering the written language (Derwing 1992).

7   Conclusions

Linguists have often assumed that speech is the primary form of language and that writing is secondary. This view implies that investigations of language and language processing should focus on spoken language and that there is little to be gained from studies of written language. This chapter has presented evidence, to the contrary, that the study of written language processing is interesting and informative in its own right. There are many questions to be answered about how people relate print to speech and about how children can best be taught to do so. This is an area in the study of language with important real-world applications. Moreover, it appears that written language takes on a life of its own once acquired, influencing the representation and processing of spoken language. The study of writing and written language processing can no longer be ignored within linguistics.

29 Clinical Linguistics

DAVID CRYSTAL

Clinical linguistics is the application of the linguistic sciences to the study of language disability in all its forms. The label "disability" should not be too narrowly interpreted. It relates to anyone whose ability to use language is sufficiently undeveloped or impaired as to require special treatment or teaching – whether or not they attend a "clinic" in a surgery or hospital. It is one of several which have been used to characterize the difficulties involved: others include *disorder, dysfunction, disturbance, disadvantage, deficit, deprivation,* and *handicap.* These labels differ in their nuances and expectations, and vary in their standing as terms with professional status; some, indeed, are emotionally loaded and politically sensitive. But from a clinical linguistic point of view, what is important is the way they indicate the existence of a domain of abnormal language use which, in its range and complexity, warrants specialist investigation. The aim of this chapter, accordingly, is to describe the kinds of difficulty typically encountered, and to illustrate the way in which clinical linguistics can provide insight into the nature of these conditions.

Language disability has a wide variety of causes, only some of which are demonstrably medical, and thus we are just as likely to encounter a person with a serious linguistic difficulty in a school classroom, a pre-school playgroup, a young adult training center, or a home for the aged. The professionals who are involved in the care and treatment of language-handicapped people also illustrate a wide range of backgrounds: they include speech and language pathologists / therapists, school-teachers, educational and clinical psychologists, pediatricians, and social workers. A six-year-old child with a language disability may attend a hospital clinic in the morning, receiving help from a speech and language clinician, then go to school in the afternoon and receive further help from a teacher. Although the settings are clinical and educational, respectively, it is the same child moving about, with the same problem – and clinical linguistics, as a branch of applied linguistics, was devised without reference to the social contexts in which diagnosis and intervention take place, being focussed specifically on the nature of the impaired linguistic system within the individual. Because there is no convenient term which subsumes both the medical and behavioral contexts of language disability; and as "educational" has already been appropriated for the study of language development in "normal" school settings, "clinical" has had to carry a heavier terminological responsibility than it is etymologically entitled to receive.

1   Identifying Linguistic Symptoms

The earliest references to difficulties with spoken or written language can be found in ancient texts: stuttering, loss of speech, and pronunciation disturbance are noticeable and dramatic effects, and have for centuries generated interpretations which have ranged from the medical to the demonic. If there is one generalization which can be made about the contribution of linguistics to this subject in recent decades, it is this: that attention has now come to be focussed on the less noticeable but often much more important symptoms of language disability, and to those aspects of the problem which have been ignored or misdiagnosed. "Less noticeable" here refers to any feature of speech production other than the audible qualities of pronunciation, the order and omission of surface grammatical elements, and the actual items which constitute vocabulary. These features exclude a great deal – in particular, most of the properties of phonological systems, the sense relations between lexical items, the constraints operating on discourse in interaction, and the many ramifications of underlying syntactic structure. All of these can and do play a major part in identifying the various kinds of language disability, but their importance has emerged only in the clinical linguistic era of study.

Here are two examples of the use of a linguistic perspective in these different areas.

- It is an easy matter to spot that a child is mispronouncing a sound, as in the various kinds of lisp; it is a much more difficult matter to determine what is wrong when a child is replacing sounds in an apparently random way, such as saying ['viwiː], ['wiwoː], or ['miviː] for "window." Establishing that there is an underlying pattern in such substitutions requires a phonological perspective. In this case, we would note the constant labial element in the consonant within the stressed syllable, and the influence which this syllable is exercising on the shape of the unstressed syllable – a kind of consonant harmony. We would also note that these kinds of substitutions are commonplace in normal child development during the second year. If, then, they were encountered in a much older child, they would support a diagnosis of delayed phonological development. ("Delayed" here is in contrast with "deviant," in which the phonological substitutions would be falling well outside the expected patterns – as when "window" might emerge as ['ʔaʔa], a typical early pronunciation from a child born with a cleft palate.)

- Similarly, in the field of grammar, it is easy to spot such morphological errors as *mouses* or *tooked*; far less easy to work out what is going on when there are problems with sentence structure. One six-year-old boy was able to say such sentences as *That car is red* and *My car is in the garage*, but could not be persuaded to say *That's a red car* or *My red car*. Asked "Is that a red car or a yellow car?" he would become non-fluent and produce such strings as *A car – a red*, losing control of the clause structure as a whole. The problem turned out to be a difficulty in simultaneously using a developed noun phrase within a clause: as long as the noun phrases consisted solely of a determiner + noun, there was no problem. But asked to insert an adjective (or any other extra element), and the whole sentence structure broke down. To appreciate the nature of this difficulty requires the analyst not only to make an appropriate syntactic analysis but also to appreciate the implications of a syntactic hierarchy for mental processing. Both syntactic and psycholinguistic perspectives are essential.

The use of a clinical linguistic frame of reference has also enabled people to make progress in identifying disorders of language *comprehension*, which are far more difficult to spot by comparison with language *production*. It is not difficult to hear from a taped sample of speech that a child has made an error in pronunciation or word order – a production error. It is much more difficult to establish that a child has failed to *perceive* a distinction between sounds or been unable to *understand* a grammatical structure or a particular choice of words. That requires careful testing and the controlling of variables. For example, one language-delayed four-year-old pointed to a picture of a bowl of mixed fruit, and said *apples*. The observation seemed acceptable, as there were indeed some apples in the bowl. It only emerged later that he was overextending the meaning of this word, using it to mean "fruit" as a whole. The point became apparent when the speech pathologist drew a series of pictures of different kinds of fruit, discovering in the process that, to the child, they were all "apples." Interestingly, precisely the same kind of problem has been observed in adults who have certain kinds of aphasia.

Disorders of a pragmatic kind, likewise, have often remained undiagnosed, or have been misdiagnosed as problems of a psychological or social behavioral type. A child who fails to follow conversational norms, perhaps by not responding to questions, or by showing bad behavior when asked to carry out a task, is often considered to be awkward or uncooperative. One child would persistently call everyone, adults as well as other children, by their surname. For those who did not understand the linguistic basis of his difficulty, this was unacceptably rude behavior. It is in fact only since the 1980s that people have begun to recognize the possibility that such behavior may ultimately be caused by an inability to cope with the pragmatic pressures of conversation – one of which, of course, is the ability to understand the rules governing the use of first names, second names, titles, and other conventional forms (such as "Sir" in classrooms).

It is partly because of these problems of missed and mistaken diagnosis that statistics vary so much about the number of people thought to be coping with a language disability. Very few statistics in this domain are reliable, because of the problem of deciding what counts as a language disability – given that disabilities have such a wide range of manifestations from "mild" through "moderate" to "severe," and that variations in methods of counting are so evident (Webster, 1988). If just the "noticeable" symptoms are taken into account, most estimates suggest that around 2 to 3 percent of the population are seriously affected by language disability; but if we include the "less noticeable" symptoms, that percentage will almost double; and if difficulties with reading and writing are added to those which affect speaking and listening, the figures will double again.

In many ways, the history of language pathology, and the identification of linguistic symptoms, has been a reflection of the history of ideas in linguistics. Impressionistic phonetic observations of the utterances of aphasic individuals were first made by neurologists in the late nineteenth century. By the mid-twentieth century these had been superseded by more systematic transcriptions, especially when a cadre of phonetically trained speech and language professionals came into being. By the 1950s phonetic descriptions were being routinely supplemented by some sort of phonological analysis (in phonemic terms). From the late 1950s, tests of language disability began to take into account basic (from the point of view of acquisition) morphological contrasts, such as singular vs. plural, or present vs. past tense; and in the 1960s the first serious attempts at sentence classification began to be made. Sophisticated syntactic accounts of disability emerged during the 1970s, and since then there have been sporadic yet insightful applications of notions from semantics and pragmatics – once again, reflecting the (also sporadically insightful) state of the art in those subjects.

There is another historical trend within linguistics which needs to be considered. The twentieth century has seen a slowly emerging *holistic* approach to language study. Its origins can be found in the integrated models of early theoreticians – such as Saussure's integration of synchronic and diachronic dimensions of inquiry, or the conception of the linguistic sign as a relationship between form and meaning. The emergence of interactional models of communication, both in communication theory and in the human sciences, brought a recognition of the complementary roles of production and reception in the communicative act (as in the influential model of the "speech chain" presented by Denes and Pinson 1973). The growth of semiotics, with its focus on patterned communication in all modes, whether in animals or humans, drew attention to the role of nonverbal communication (e.g. facial expression, bodily gesture), and thus helped to clarify exactly what was involved in the specifically linguistic dimension of communication (Sebeok et al. 1964). The influence of psychology brought a focus on the whole individual, whether as language-acquiring child or as language-using adult, and resulted in new developmental and clinical psycholinguistic perspectives (Clark and Clark 1977). And there was an increasing awareness of the need to bring language structure into connection with language use, with fresh perspectives deriving from sociolinguistics, ethnography, and pragmatics (Gumperz and Hymes 1972). All of this provides a theoretical background for the contemporary professional interest in holistic approaches, where the focus is on the patient or pupil as a "whole person," and in which a language disability is no longer seen solely as a problem of communication, but is viewed in relation to the whole range of cognitive and social factors which affect the ability of the individual to function in society (Crystal and Varley 1998).

Here is an example of this change of emphasis. A young man was concerned about his high-pitched voice, which he felt was impeding his ability to mix with other people and find a girlfriend. He complained he was often mistaken for a woman over the telephone. After a few sessions with a speech pathologist there was a significant lowering of pitch level – and, within a traditional therapeutic perspective, that would have been sufficient intervention. But the patient's social problems remained; and it was only when a holistic perspective was adopted that the real problem was uncovered. By observing the young man in his place of work, and seeing the way in which he behaved while interacting with other people, it emerged that he was someone who habitually invaded other people's personal space, standing too close to them while talking, and making them feel threatened and anxious. This, rather than his voice, was the true cause of his social difficulties. He perceived his voice to be a problem, but not his body-language. Further work on non-verbal (proxemic) communication skills was plainly necessary, and this in due course produced the desired result.

2 The Role of Clinical Linguistics

Seen within this historical perspective, the role of clinical linguistics, as an applied linguistic discipline, can be summarized under five headings.

2.1 Clarification

A long-standing aim for the subject has been to clarify areas of (especially terminological) confusion found in the traditional metalanguage and classification of disability. Over the past century there has been a proliferation of competing and overlapping terms for types and symptoms of disordered linguistic behavior. For example, what one author might describe as an *articulation error* others might describe as a *misarticulation, dyslalia, pronunciation defect*, or *phonetic handicap*. It would be naive to hope that systematic linguistic descriptions can resolve all such confusion – if for no other reason than that linguistics itself is by no means short of competing descriptions and terminology! – but a precise account, using explicit criteria, can at least clearly indicate the range of data to which a term relates, and thus contribute to better mutual comprehension.

2.2   Description

A major area of clinical linguistic research has been to provide ways of describing and analyzing the linguistic behavior of patients, and of the clinicians and others who interact with them. Until fairly recently, there were no published descriptive case studies of the language of individual patients, as encountered in a sample of their speech. There are still very few which look comprehensively at all linguistic levels; and even fewer which trace the progress of a patient longitudinally, over time, or sociolinguistically, over different social contexts. But the number of such studies is on the increase, as illustrated by the collection edited by Perkins and Howard (1995), and by the publishing policy of such journals as *Child Language Teaching and Therapy*, which strongly supports the need for case studies. The aim, as ever, is to establish system in what often seems to be randomness. For some disorders, such as cases of delay in child language acquisition, the systemicness is often easy to demonstrate, at least for the early years of acquisition, as there are normative models of language development which can be used as an orientation. For others, such as the various kinds of adult aphasia, the task is more problematic.

2.3   Diagnosis

An important aim of clinical linguistics is to provide a classification of patient linguistic behaviors, as part of the process of differential diagnosis. For decades, diagnosis of language disability was carried out on a solely medical basis, with the causes of a problem identified in terms of impaired anatomy, physiology, or neurology – aphasia, cleft palate speech, deafness, dyspraxia, dysphonia, and many other such "syndromes" were identified in this way. But, when an increasing number of people with language disability were encountered who did not have any medical reason for their problem (thought to be as many as 60 percent of all cases), it became evident that a purely medical model of investigation would not suffice. Most children suffering from language delay, for example, do not have a clear medical explanation for their condition. A linguistically informed classification, in which a language disability is characterized explicitly with reference to its use of phonetic, phonological, grammatical, semantic, pragmatic, and other variables, can provide an alternative diagnostic model, and one which is more able to provide insights about intervention in cases where there is no clear evidence of any medical condition.

2.4   *Assessment*

Clinical linguistics has also been much involved in devising more sophisticated assessments of abnormal linguistic behavior. The notion of *assessment* is
here being contrasted with *diagnosis*. A diagnosis tells us what is "wrong" with
a patient; an assessment tells us just how seriously the patient is "wrong." In
the case of children with language disability, assessment usually takes place
by locating a selection of the various features of the child's language on charts
(of phonology, grammar, etc.) which have been organized on developmental
lines, based on research in child language acquisition. Children can then be
seen to be so many months or years behind the norm, with respect to their use
of those features, or can be seen to be completely abnormal ("off the chart,"
deviant). For example, a seven-year-old child who was still using such forms
as *mouses* (typical of a four-year-old) would be seen to be three years delayed,
in respect of that feature. Similar procedures have been devised for use with
adult patients, though it has proved to be more difficult to keep control of the
larger number of variables involved in the adult language.

2.5   *Intervention*

The ultimate goal of clinical linguistics is to formulate hypotheses for the
remediation of abnormal linguistic behavior. Not all aspects of a patient's
problem are directly relevant to the need for linguistically based intervention,
of course – outside the linguist's purview are disorders of eating and swallowing, for example – but for those which are relevant, clinical linguistics can
help clinicians to make an informed judgment about "what to teach next," and
to monitor the outcome of an intervention hypothesis, as treatment proceeds.
To a large extent, this means moving well beyond the patient's language, to
include an investigation of the language used by the person(s) carrying out
the intervention, the kind of teaching materials used, and the setting in which
the interaction takes place.

   These five areas identify the scope of clinical linguistics, seen as a discipline
of applied linguistics. It should perhaps also be added that the subject also has
a potential theoretical linguistic relevance, in that its findings will doubtless
one day make a contribution to neuroscience and cognitive science. But that
goes beyond the remit of the present chapter (see further, Crystal, 1981/9: 6).

3   **Linguistic Insights**

We can summarize much of the preceding discussion by saying that the chief
aim of clinical linguistics is to provide the clinician with increasing levels of

insight and confidence in arriving at linguistic decisions. Basic insights are of course not difficult to achieve, as has been repeatedly shown since the 1960s through the analysis of short audio samples of clinical interactions: an influential early approach was Crystal et al. (1976) (see also Crystal 1982/92 and the collection of papers in Perkins and Howard 1995). A 15-minute sample is often enough to yield illuminating patterns of a phonological, grammatical, or semantic kind – patterns which would not otherwise be apparent to even an experienced listener. The problem lies not just in the listener's inability to distinguish the many variables which are being simultaneously used by the patient, but to notice the many variables which are *not* being used. To take an example from grammar, it is not difficult to spot that someone is using a pronoun wrongly or omitting an auxiliary verb (*him gone, she jumping*); it is a quite different matter to spot that certain features are completely lacking (e.g. no adverbs used at all, or no use of prepositional phrases). Only a systematic survey of all the potentially relevant features can guarantee that nothing of importance is being omitted, and such surveys invariably provide the clinician with insight into the linguistic abilities of the patient. They also, inevitably, generate clinical confidence – a sense that one is in control of the situation.

Rather more interesting are those cases where a linguistic analysis enables the clinical linguist to *explain* a general characteristic of a disability, or even of a class of disabilities. For example, research in child language acquisition has begun to show that, when children are making progress in one area of language, they may be making a loss in another (Camarata and Schwartz 1985, Panagos and Prelock 1982). A typical example is the observation that pronunciation deteriorates when children attempt more advanced syntactic constructions than those they have previously been producing satisfactorily. This kind of "trade-off" between phonology and syntax – and between other combinations of levels, and also between features within levels – has turned out to be an important effect in language disability, where it can be "manipulated" in a clinical intervention. For example, during a therapy session in which the six-year-old language-delayed boy referred to above was being taught to insert adjectives within noun phrases, the child's attempts at a noun phrase without the adjective were always pronounced with good phonology and fluency; whereas his attempts to say the noun phrase with the adjective in place resulted in erratic pausing, stuttering, and a deterioration in segmental phonological accuracy. This behavior could be "switched on and off" by the therapist, and provided clear evidence in support of the view that there are limitations on the amount of linguistic processing which may take place at any point in development (Crystal 1987). Once a phenomenon of this kind is noticed, of course, it can be put to use as a hypothesis in other contexts: if a normally fluent patient manifests non-fluency, it gives good reason for the clinician to suspect that a processing overload is taking place. Something may be being taught too quickly or in the wrong order.

This example illustrates the three pillars of any clinical linguistic approach: description – grading – intervention. Good description of an oral sample is at the heart of all clinical linguistic study – a principle which has its roots in classical linguistic anthropology – but in the context of language disability, such a description cannot stand alone. The information it contains needs to be graded in some way, so that the speaker's level of linguistic achievement can be assessed: such grading, as we have already seen, typically takes the form of a chart or scale on which stages of development are recognized – the stages deriving from a synthesis of the findings in child language acquisition research. Once the information contained in a sample is transferred onto such a chart, it is possible to make a tentative diagnosis, by establishing a pattern in the distribution of linguistic forms. Even if a diagnosis is not possible, it is at least possible to see the charted information as an assessment, which identifies the nature of the gap between where the patient is and where he or she ought to be. If the patient was five years old, but the distribution of linguistic forms was clustering around the two-year level, one would conclude that the patient was three years delayed – and of course it is possible that different degrees of delay might be found within different linguistic levels. A patient might be three years delayed in grammar, but only two years delayed in phonology (or not delayed at all). Similarly, a patient might be three years delayed in the acquisition of clause structure, but only two years in the acquisition of phrase structure. Plainly, there are innumerable possibilities, when all the variables in phonology, grammar, semantics, and pragmatics are taken into account. The expectation, however, is that certain patterns of delay will recur between patients, enabling us to group patients into a small number of linguistically defined diagnostic types (or syndromes). This is the long-term aim of a great deal of contemporary research. And a corresponding aim motivates much of the current work in adult language disability, too, though the extrapolation of grading procedures derived from child language research plainly has its limitations in such cases.

Once patients have been located on such a chart, and their linguistic age turns out to be below their chronological age, the targets of intervention are automatically set: the aim is to make them progress from where they are (on the chart) to where they ought to be. Because there are so many variables, a number of possible pathways suggest themselves. Clinical linguistics is not yet at the stage where it can provide principles enabling clinicians to decide which pathway will produce the best outcome. All that can be done, in the present state of knowledge, is to work systematically through some of the possibilities, slowly building up a more advanced linguistic system, and looking out for indications that the treatment is paying off (such as when a pattern is carried over to spontaneous use outside the clinic) or not (such as the appearance of unexpected non-fluency). All change needs to be regularly monitored, to demonstrate that progress is being made – this is the task of assessment. The keeping of comprehensive linguistic records is a further priority, without which the efficacy of intervention can never be demonstrated.

Clinical linguistics has been operating along these lines since the late 1960s, and a great deal of research has been carried out, especially in relation to the task of establishing reliable methodological procedures (e.g. how to stand-ardize samples) and practicable descriptive techniques. There are now several introductory books on the subject (Crystal 1981/9, Ball 1993, Grundy 1995), a growing number of case studies (Perkins and Howard 1995), and a major journal (*Clinical Linguistics and Phonetics*). However, although all areas of lin-guistic structure and use have received some investigation, certain areas are still much neglected. Semantics has received the least attention, judging by the record of published articles and textbooks. If we take, as an illustration, all the papers which have been published to date in *Clinical Linguistics and Phonetics* since its inception (1987–8), we find over 230 items. Excluding the 30 or so which deal with general issues of theory and method, we are left with 150 devoted to phonetics and phonology – illustrating the continuing importance attached to the most "traditional" areas of linguistic inquiry. The other levels of linguistic description are far less represented – grammar has some 20 items, prosody (including the rhythm problems found in stuttering) and pragmatics / discourse have some 15 each – but even these are well covered, by comparison with semantics. Semantic issues are indeed sometimes invoked as factors in studies of other topics, but there are only two items in the whole oeuvre deal-ing directly with "core" semantic issues, such as vocabulary (Herman 1990, Edwards 1992). There is one further item on the syndrome of "semantic-pragmatic disorder" (Snow 1996), but this largely deals – not untypically, it must be said – with the pragmatic factors involved in the syndrome (such as abnormalities of conversational interaction) rather than the semantic ones. A glance at other clinical journals suggests that this situation is by no means unique. Semantics, it seems, is a frontier which has still to be crossed in clinical linguistics.

30   Forensic Linguistics

ROGER W. SHUY

It's hard to imagine any area of life that linguistics does not touch. We usually think of language teaching or language learning but for decades now linguists have also extended their work to such areas as medical communication, advertising, and, even more recently, to the intersection of law and language. Law had received previous attention from anthropologists, psychologists, sociologists, and political scientists, but now linguists also have begun examining such matters as voice identification, authorship of written documents, unclear jury instructions, the asymmetry of power in courtroom exchanges, lawyer–client communication breakdown, the nature of perjury, problems in written legal discourse, defamation, trademark infringement, courtroom interpretation and translation difficulties, the adequacy of warning labels, and the nature of tape recorded conversation used as evidence (Levi 1994).

Although a good case could be made for simply calling this practice *applied linguistics*, the term, *forensic linguistics*, began to be used commonly in the 1980s and by now appears to be the established name for this area of study. By the 1990s, forensic linguistics had established its own academic organization, The International Association of Forensic Linguistics, its own journal, *Forensic Linguistics*, a growing number of books and articles, and an increasing number of linguists doing the work. Since *forensic* is commonly defined as dealing with the application of scientific knowledge to other areas, the term seems fitting enough.

1   Trademark Infringement

So what do forensic linguists do? Typically, they respond to requests of attorneys to help them with their law cases. For example, a lawyer may have a law suit involving a trademark dispute. One company may feel that another company's trade name is too much like its own. The more generic or descriptive the name, such as *Raisin Bran* or *Beer Nuts*, the less likely such a name can be protected against use by other companies. The more unique or fanciful the name, such as the coined words, *Kodak* or *Xerox*, the more likely such protection will be.

It's the names that fall between descriptive and fanciful that find their way to litigation. The law refers to such categories as "arbitrary" and "suggestive." Arbitrary trade names are non-fanciful words in common use but, when used with goods and services, neither suggest nor describe the ingredients, quality or character of those goods or services. The trade names, *V-8* (juice), *Ivory* (soap), and *Royal* (baking powder) are commonly used as examples of arbitrary trade names. Suggestive trade names are also usually words in common use, non-descriptive of the product's purpose or function, but suggesting some quality not indicated by the name itself. The trade names, *Camel* (cigarettes), *Shell* (gasoline), and *Arm and Hammer* (baking soda) are commonly used to illustrate suggestive trade names.

The burden of proof is on the allegedly offended party to show that the other party's name looks like, sounds like, and means the same as their own. To a linguist, "sounds like" obviously suggests phonology, "looks like" suggests graphology, and "means the same" suggests semantics. And this is why linguists are called upon to analyze and present their findings in trademark cases.

2   Product Liability

Forensic linguists are also being called in product liability law suits. It may seem surprising that linguistics has anything to do with a contention that a product has caused injury to a consumer. But suppose an attorney has a product liability law suit in which a person has suffered physical harm alleged to have been caused by inadequate package instructions or warning labels. A linguist is called upon to analyze the language of the warning label to determine whether or not the warnings follow the guidelines of the relevant regulatory agency and whether or not they are clear, unambiguous, and optimally effective. For example, does a manufacturer meet the US Food and Drug Administration's required warning to show that "tampons are associated with Toxic Shock Syndrome" when it labels its package insert warning with the words, "Important Information About Toxic Shock Syndrome (TSS)" (Shuy 1990). Does "Important Information About" meet the FDA requirement to be "associated with"? Does the fact that the warning finally makes this explicit association in the middle of the warning label satisfy the government regulation that this warning must appear "prominently" and in "terms understandable by the layperson?" Does the fact that the warning part of the insert averages 19 words per sentence while the "instructions for how to use" section averages 9.4 words per sentence suggest that the insert writer really knows how to write more readable sentences but chooses not to in the "warning" section?

The forensic linguist, of course, can get into the mind of neither the warning label writer nor the consumer who reads it. That is, the linguist cannot know the intentions of the writer or the actual comprehension of the reader. But the linguist, calling on knowledge of discourse analysis, semantics, and pragmatics, can determine the extent to which the message was clear and unambiguous and point out the possible meanings that the message presents. Once this is done, it is up to the attorney to determine whether or not to ask the linguist to testify at trial.

3   Speaker Identification

Linguists have been used by attorneys in matters of voice identification per-haps longer than in most other areas of legal dispute (Hollien 1990, Tosi 1979). For example, suppose a caller leaves a threatening message on an answering machine. The receiver of this message then takes the recording to an attorney or to a law enforcement agency. A linguist may be called upon to try to help identify the speaker, using only the characteristics of that voice in comparison with tape recordings of voices of various potential suspects. If the tapes are of sufficient quality, spectographic analysis is possible. If not, the linguist may rely on training and skills in phonetics to make the comparison (Baldwin and French 1990).

Several problems with such analysis have been posed. For one thing, spectographic analysis is not allowed in some courts. But even when it is allowed, it usually requires suspects to read the original phone message in order to produce exactly comparable words for analysis. Some argue that a reading voice is not the same as a talking voice. Others argue that the readers, having been alerted to their status as suspects, may try to alter their normal speech patterns. On the other hand, juries tend to be impressed with analysis based on electronic equipment rather than on an individual linguist's phonetic judgment, however expert that linguist might be.

In some voice identification cases, the linguist has used both spectographic and articulatory phonetic expertise to show that a suspect was not, indeed, the guilty party. For example, in one such case, the vowels of a suspect were shown to be characteristic of an entirely different dialect area than those of the person on the message machine tape, resulting in the suspect's acquittal. In this case, spectographic analysis was used to support the linguist's skills in auditory phonetics (Labov 1988).

4   Authorship of Written Documents

Written documents also serve as data for forensic linguistics. In many cases, for example, threats exist in written form. Law enforcement agencies process hundreds of these every year, often calling on the expertise of psychologists to provide what they call a "psychological profile" of the person who sent the message. In fact, the US Federal Bureau of Investigation has a profiling unit at its Quantico, Virginia, academy. It is only recently, however, that this agency has begun to call on linguists to add the dimension of linguistic profiling to their analyses. Such profiling has two parts. Calling on their knowledge of language indicators of such things as regional and social dialect, age, gender, education, and occupation, linguists analyze documents for broad clues to the identity of the writer. Linguists also provide stylistic analysis of such writings, usually by comparing the document's style with those of other documents written by possible suspects (McMenamin 1993). Stylistic analysis centers on a writer's habitual language features over which the writer has little or no conscious awareness, such as patterns of clause embedding, use of parallel structures, deletion of "that" in complementizer constructions, mechanical errors, punctuation, discourse features and organization, and print features such as underlining, bolding, or italicizing.

It should be pointed out that linguistic profiling has been most effectively used to narrow down a suspect list rather than to positively identify a suspect. This is not to say that such positive identification is impossible but, rather, that the potential for variability in language use is great and the texts offered for comparison are sometimes dissimilar in genre, register, and size.

When anonymous writers attempt to disguise their prose style, such effort usually involves the more conscious aspects of language use rather than the major features analyzed in the linguistic profile. For example, one set of threat notes recently analyzed linguistically contained expressions such as, "She will finally the seriousness of the problem recognize," "I will not give warning," "You can be transferred to better position," and "If I address it her." These and other expressions suggested the influence of Hindi-Urdu English interference. Such a speaker might be expected to place the verb at the end of the English sentence and omit articles and pronouns. Other language expressions, such as "I will take the proper course" and "she was in hospital at the time," pointed to a person educated under the influence of British English. These threat letters were written in several different handwriting styles, apparently in an effort to disguise the writer's identity. Nevertheless, some defining characteristics came through and were used by the law enforcement agency to identify the culprit.

5   Criminal Cases

The above are examples of how a forensic linguist is used in civil cases and in document analysis. But technological advances with recording equipment have opened the door also to criminal cases. Since the late 1970s, law enforcement agencies have used tape recorders to capture criminal activity in progress.

Suspects are either recorded with court authorized wire taps placed in such a way that none of the speakers is aware of being taped, or by using undercover agents who wear body microphones and engage suspects in conversation. Court authorization is not required for surreptitious body mike recording in the USA. American law regarding surreptitious telephone taping varies between jurisdictions, some requiring the consent of only one of the parties (obviously, the one doing the taping). Other jurisdictions prohibit the practice altogether unless both parties consent.

The linguist can be brought into a case either by the prosecution or the defense. If the law enforcement agency is concerned about the adequacy of the language evidence that they have gathered, they may call on a linguist to make (or correct already existing) transcripts of the conversations, analyze them and determine whether or not the agents' representations of illegality have been made clearly and unambiguously and whether or not the target has clearly suggested or agreed to the illegal act. If the defense attorney calls on the linguist, the same issues are central.

In transcript preparation, forensic linguists use the tools of their trade, depending on the specific task. The transcript task requires a good ear, access to good listening (and / or viewing) equipment, and knowledge of language variation, syntax, semantics, and phonology. It is amazing how difficult it is to produce an accurate, jury-ready transcript. In fact, major legal battles sometimes ensue about the differences between transcripts prepared by the prosecution and those made by the defense.

Once the tape recorded evidence is gathered and the suspect is indicted, copies of all tapes must be turned over to the defense as part of what is called "discovery." As soon as it is reasonably possible, the prosecution is then required to make written transcripts of the recordings and turn them over as well. In most cases, this turning over of evidence occurs well in advance of the trial, so that the defense can prepare for it.

The first step for the linguist is always to ensure that the transcript is accurate. The jury will indeed hear the tape but it is commonplace for the court to provide juries with a transcript in order to make their task easier. But people remember what they see much better than what they hear and transcripts become very important for this reason alone. In any case, surreptitious conversations recorded by body microphone are usually very difficult to hear. They are often taped in restaurants, bars, automobiles, and under conditions that do not promote easy hearing for later listeners. If the government transcript has a person saying "I'd wanna do it," for example, when the words are actually, "I don't wanna do it," serious jury misperception may occur.

It is not always clear just exactly how transcripts are produced but it appears that the government usually employs an office secretary or a court reporter to make it, then has the participating undercover agent review the transcript and correct perceived errors. When the defense makes a transcript, the same general procedure obtains, except that the reviewing and correcting is done by the defendant. The objectivity of such reviewing is, at best, suspect, since the schemas of participants sometimes cause them to think they hear something that is actually not on the tape at all. An outsider to the case, such as a linguist, does not (or should not) carry such schema or bias.

The tape recorded conversation itself points to the use of the other tools of the forensic linguist, including syntax, morphology, semantics, pragmatics, dialectology, and discourse analysis. The use of such analyses can give linguistic laypersons, such as juries, scientific reasons for their perceptions, opinions, or feelings that might otherwise be ungrounded. Likewise, such analyses can help laypersons see patterns of language use that are visible only through the help of forensic linguists. Just as medical experts are used to describe and define what is on an X-ray, so linguistic experts describe and define what is in a tape recorded conversation.

Grammatical referencing is often unclear in everyday language and unless the reference that the prosecution believes to be critical is actually clear, the prosecution's case may fail. In one criminal case in which a defendant was charged with agreeing to purchase narcotics for resale in order to make enough money to save his company from bankruptcy, the following utterance was considered central to the prosecution's case (Shuy 1993):

> UNDERCOVER AGENT: What do you think about investment?
> TARGET: I think investment would be a good thing.

The law enforcement officer thought that the target had thereby agreed to invest his remaining assets into the illegal drug scheme proposed by the agent. In thinking this, however, the agent overlooked the fact that six months of tape recording this target had clearly failed to elicit anything illegal. To that point, in fact, the agent had continuously offered the target two potential avenues of action. One was to help find the target some investors who might purchase stock in the target's company. The second was to get the target to pyramid his remaining assets by investing in a drug scheme, then selling the cocaine quickly for a large, quick profit. The target had said neither yes nor no, obviously not wanting to erase the potential of getting stock investors if he should say no to the drug scheme. In fact, the target was no clearer than the agent about what investment meant here. Neither had specified the defined referent to which "investment" could be associated.

In cases of ambiguity such as this, the prosecution's decision whether or not to indict is normally deferred until more unambiguous statements are elicited. In this particular case, the government's intelligence analysis was faulty. An indictment was made on the assumption that the target had actually agreed to invest in the drug scheme. At trial, the defendant was acquitted, thanks at least partially to the assistance of the forensic linguists in this case.

Discourse analysis is another important tool used by forensic linguists, especially in cases involving tape recorded conversations. The study of topic introduction and recycling, for example, provides a good clue to the agenda or intentions of a speaker. As noted earlier, the linguist cannot know for sure what the speakers' intentions really are, but a careful examination of the topics they bring up gives a useful snap-shot of what they are thinking about, what is foremost in their minds and, perhaps even more important, what is not on their minds. Likewise, a careful analysis of the responses that given persons make to the topics introduced by others offers a similar clue to their agendas and intentions. If persons either agree or disagree, the evidence is pretty clear. But if they change the subject or say nothing at all about it, they offer an indication that this topic was not to their liking, that they are not interested in it, or that they are politely side-stepping it. It is when the respondent offers only feedback markers such as "uh-huh" to another person's topics that law enforcement agencies become confused. Many times, the prosecution tends to consider "uh-huh" to be agreement or understanding when, in fact, it is only a feedback marker used to indicate that the listener is still listening but not necessarily agreeing, that he or she doesn't really understand the gist of the topic but will hear it out anyway, or that he or she is not really listening at all but is making polite social noises.

It is common for recorded conversation used as evidence in criminal cases to contain examples of feedback markers that the prosecution erroneously attributes to understanding and agreement. In one example, an undercover agent tried to elicit agreement from his boss that a commission paid to a consultant violated government regulations. The situation was complex, since this consultant was at the same time receiving perfectly legal commissions from another unrelated source. The portion of their conversation that the prosecution considered inculpatory was the following:

UNDERCOVER AGENT: Ari's calling me every day . . . He's worried, I guess, about his payment, his commission.
TARGET: Uh-huh.

The target's "uh-huh" can legitimately agree that Ari is worried about getting his commission but, since there is no specification about what this commission is for or who it is from, there is nothing here that would indicate that he agrees that this commission is from the target's company. Nor is there anything in the conversation to indicate that the target is even interested in Ari's problems about getting this commission, wherever it was from. Further complicating this exchange is the fact that the undercover agent has been a general nuisance by spending far too long updating his very busy boss with somewhat trivial information. It is even possible that the target's "uh-huh" was the polite noise making type that had nothing to do with his understanding or agreement.

Armed with the forensic linguist's analysis of this passage, the attorney presented it at trial himself. Perhaps the best help a forensic linguist can give an attorney is to make the analysis so clear that it does not need to be presented by an expert witness.

6   The Future of Forensic Linguistics

There are many other areas of forensic linguistics in addition to the ones cited above. For example, considerable work has been done on the problems of producing clear jury instructions (Charrow and Charrow 1979, Elwork et al. 1982). Before the jury retires to deliberate, the judge reads a list of instructions that are intended to guide them in arriving at their verdict. Linguists have found that such instructions are sometimes incomprehensible to the jurors. When the jury sends out a note requesting clarification, the same instructions are sometimes merely re-read. The field of law walks a fine line here, trying to translate the language of law into the language that laymen can comprehend without creating a reversible error that will lead to retrial. It is a classic case of a problem with the bureaucratic language of law. Such language may be appropriate and necessary within law but, like all specialized language, faces problems when trying to communicate outside its own province.

Likewise, some forensic linguists are concerned about the asymmetry of power in the courtroom (O'Barr 1982, Lakoff 1990). At trial, language power clearly resides with the court and the attorneys. The testimony of witnesses is controlled by a rigid question–answer format which enables the attorneys to structure the sequence and content of what is said. However useful or necessary this may be for trials, it runs counter to non-lawyers' natural, normal use of language. It prevents them from bringing up their own topics or telling their story in their own way. They run a serious risk of not getting out what they want to get out. They are vulnerable to being considered ineffective or even untruthful by their manner of speech, fettered as it is by courtroom constraints. One of the most frustrating experiences reported by lay witnesses is that they are forced to answer "yes" or "no" to questions for which neither answer is complete or adequate.

The attorneys' power of language and the witnesses' lack of power is the subject of much recent analysis, including the language used by judges (Phillips 1985, Solan 1993) and the language of the trial itself (Stygall 1994). It is also common that defendants, plaintiffs, or witnesses in court are not native speakers of English. This poses a serious problem for such people as well as for the attorneys and the court (Berk-Seligson 1990). In recent years, forensic linguists have begun to address this issue as well and some courts are now providing interpreters when it is deemed necessary. The US Federal Court Interpreters Act of 1978 (and its trickle down effect on state and municipal courts) was designed to avoid denying the constitutional rights of the non-English speaking and hearing impaired in the American court system. However worthwhile and necessary such action is, a multitude of problems remain. How do we best recruit and train such interpreters? How is it possible to provide such services for all possible languages for which there is need? How do we know the extent to which a non-English speaker has mastered enough English to go to trial in English only? Further complications come from the linguistic naiveté of some courts in these matters. For example, when under-cover tape recordings are made in Chinese or Spanish, the courts frequently hire a translator to provide an English translation of the conversations and then to present that translation as the evidence. What is missing here is the essential middle step, providing first a transcript of the conversations in the other language upon which the translation is based. The same errors in transcript preparation noted earlier can easily occur here as well. Without the intermediate transcript in the other language, dispute over accuracy of the translation is eliminated. Going straight to the translation without first providing a transcript may be time and cost efficient but it is linguistically naive, if not dangerous. Forensic linguists have recently been trying to make this point to the courts. Interpreting for the hearing impaired provides even further complications, since, for example, American Sign Language does not easily translate into neat English sentences.

In criminal cases, forensic linguists continue to apply their knowledge of speech acts to significant issues involving offers, promises, denials, and agreements found in tape recorded evidence. They also examine confessions elicited through police interrogation, in an effort to make clear what, if anything, was actually confessed and whether or not that alleged confession was tainted by the manner in which it was elicited. More and more law enforcement agencies are recording such confessions in order to guard against accusations of undue pressure or improper promises. Such tapes make it possible for forensic linguists to apply their skills for either the prosecution or the defense (Shuy 1998).

In summary, the future of forensic linguistics appears to be very promising indeed. In the United States, more and more courts permit forensic linguists to testify as experts at trial (Wallace 1986). In the few criminal cases in which judges have ruled that forensic linguists' testimony would not be permitted, the reason given was often based on an attorney's representations of what those linguists might say rather than on the reputation and respectability of the field of linguistics or the linguists themselves. But whether the linguist testifies or not, it is clear that more and more attorneys and government agencies are calling on forensic linguists to assist them in analyzing the spoken and written language that frames the evidence in both civil and criminal law suits. It is also the case that more and more universities are offering courses on topics of language and the law.

31 Translation

CHRISTOPH GUTKNECHT

1 Introduction

Communication between different individuals and nations is not always easy, especially when more than one language is involved. The job of the translator and / or interpreter is to try to bridge the gap between two foreign languages. This can also include translation problems arising from historical developments within one language. In this chapter, translating and interpreting will be characterized as a communicative device (section 2). After defining the modes of interpreting (section 3), the principles influencing the transfer of messages from one language to another will be outlined (section 4). In order to illustrate some of the lexical problems faced by the translator and / or interpreter, particular attention will be paid to the area known as "false friends" (section 5). As will be emphasized, each act of translation is conditioned by many factors (with various functions) which govern the choice of a target-language rendition of a given source-language text (section 6). In the final section, a brief survey of recent developments in machine translation will be presented (section 7).

2 Translation: a Communicative Device

Translation is undoubtedly a communicative device; moreover, as John Rupert Firth (1956: 135) put it, "The fact is, translation is a necessity on economic and on general human grounds." Some researchers postulate an autonomous status for translation studies, arguing that these studies bring together work in a wide variety of fields, including literary study, anthropology, psychology, and linguistics. Others claim that the domain of translation studies is an important sub-branch of applied linguistics. Proponents of both opinions would have to admit, however, that the field of translation studies has multidisciplinary dimensions and aspects.[1]

The term "translation" normally refers to written materials but is also an umbrella term used for all tasks where elements of a text of one language (the source language, SL) are molded into a text of another language (the target language, TL), whether the medium is written, spoken, or signed. There are specific professional contexts where a distinction is made between people who work with the spoken or signed language (interpreters), and those who work with the written language (translators). Although usually the two roles are seen as quite distinct, there are hybrid situations that blur this distinction. When, for instance, a court interpreter reads a legal document in one language while reciting it aloud in another s/he is said to be sight-translating. On the other hand, prosecuting authorities and law enforcement agencies often call on translators to transcribe and translate foreign language-conversations that were taped during investigations.

3   Modes of Interpreting: Consecutive and Simultaneous

There are two highly specialized modes of interpreting: *consecutive* and *simultaneous* interpreting.

One typically speaks of *consecutive interpreting* when the person requiring the interpreter participates in the communication directly. In such cases the interpreter waits for the person to finish speaking, or until the amount of information approaches the limit of the interpreter's retention capacity, and then the interpreter gives a translation. Interpreting skills include note-taking techniques, although the method and degree of reliance on note-taking as a memory aid varies from one interpreter to the other. Consecutive interpreting is usually bidirectional, i.e., from language X to Y and vice versa; it is commonly used for informal meetings, tours, business negotiations, etc.

The mode of *simultaneous interpreting* is typically used when the person who requires an interpreter is not participating in the communication directly. At international conferences with bilingual or multilingual audiences simultaneous interpreting is an effective method for helping to overcome language barriers; it allows presentations and discussion to proceed at the same pace as an ordinary unilingual conference. Simultaneous interpreting is usually performed using technical equipment to relay the sound to those delegates who do not speak the floor language. The interpreters work in soundproof booths, while the delegates listen to the language of their choice via headsets connected to multichannel wireless receivers. In such cases the translation is usually unidirectional, i.e., from language X to language Y but not vice versa.

Strictly speaking, however, the term "simultaneous interpreting" is misleading in that the word "simultaneous" suggests that the interpreter is interpreting a message at the same time as hearing it. In fact, there is a delay between the moment the interpreter hears a number of SL expressions and the moment s/he renders them into the TL, because it takes time to understand the SL message and turn it into the TL. Meanwhile, the speaker goes on to the next utterance, so the interpreter must generate the TL version of the first utterance while processing the second, and so on. This delay is known as *décalage*, from the French word for "time lag."

In simultaneous interpreting, the time factor is generally more crucial than in consecutive interpreting or in translation performed in the written mode. The decisive factor in simultaneous interpreting is how early the simultaneous interpreter can actually start speaking. Wilss (1978: 346) says, quoting Mattern (1974: 28) in order to specify that moment: "[T]he optimal moment of interpretation will differ depending on the subjective and objective factors involved; the objective or speech-language-linked factors being those which originate from the SL text and from relations of equivalence existing between SL and TL, and the subjective factors being those which depend on the interpreter himself."

In view of the time pressure under which the simultaneous interpreter has to work, one crucial subjective factor is the interpreter's memory. How long s/he is able to wait before s/he starts interpreting each sentence will depend upon the capacity to retain what was said by the SL speaker. S/he should be in a position to start interpreting as soon as possible to avoid being confronted with an information overload. But there are cases in which the simultaneous interpreter seems to be forced to wait for the conclusion of a long SL sentence before s/he can even start interpreting it. To evaluate this claim let us take a sentence from Wilss (1978: 348):

(1)   a.   *Namens meiner Fraktion darf ich den beiden Herren Berichterstattern für die Arbeit, die sie geleistet haben, sehr herzlich danken.*

It is true that, upon hearing the first three words, the German-English simultaneous interpreter can immediately start saying: "*On behalf of my political party.*" On hearing the next two words s/he might add: "*I may.*" Since the full verb follows the modal in English, the interpreter would have to wait until the very last German word of the complex sentence is uttered, i.e., the full verb *danken*. Such a late take-off or late continuation is "an extremely heavy stress on the short-term memory of the interpreter" (Wilss 1978: 347). Couldn't there be a solution providing a shortcut in this situation?

Mattern (1974: 3) suggests one such strategy, as reported by Wilss. If (1a) is uttered in an EU debate the experienced interpreter will know that "the German segment '*Namens meiner Fraktion darf ich (danken)*' is a standard phrase which is frequently used as an opening gambit in a follow-up speech statement . . . Once the simultaneous interpreter has heard '*Namens meiner Fraktion darf ich*,' he can legitimately infer from previous experience that some form of saying 'thank you' can be expected" (Wilss 1978: 348). This is why, having heard only the first five words, the interpreter can start or continue his TL rendition.

This form of "intelligent textual prediction," referred to by Wilss (1978: 348ff) as "syntactic anticipation," has yet another advantage. It saves the interpreter from mistakenly rendering the German *dürfen* by the English *may*, which would be appropriate in many other cases. Instead *would like to* has to be employed, as the following complete rendition of (1a) shows:

(1)   b.   *On behalf of my political group, I would like to thank the two spokesmen very cordially for their work.*

Even though *may* is in many cases the adequate rendition of *dürfen*, in the present case this principle has to be revised due to the modal's being part of the syntactic construction *"darf . . . danken"* which has to be considered as a whole. This construction may therefore be called a "revision factor" – the standard equivalence (English *may* = German *dürfen*) does not apply here but has to be revised. This shows that it is by no means invariably sufficient to go by a modal alone in order to render it; rather, there are different translation units which may be relevant to different SL texts.

Syntactic anticipation is but one of the interpreter's skills. Both interpreters and translators must be skilled in such generalized professional techniques, and they must also be intimately familiar with the material under discussion in a given text. This holds true for all types of interpretation and translation but is especially important in the areas of technology, medicine, and the law, where terminological accuracy is of paramount importance. Because of the rapid development of science and technology having resulted in a significant increase in the amount of knowledge being transferred across languages and cultures, it is imperative for any translator to have access to multilingual terminology databases.

For court interpreters, who have to deal with lawyers, court personnel, and the public, it is imperative that they have an understanding of the terminology and procedures used in court as well as an extensive vocabulary ranging from formal legal language to colloquialisms and slang expressions.

In the last few years there has been an increasing awareness of the importance of using trained professionals rather than well-intentioned amateurs for community interpreting. Many hospitals, courts, and other institutions in the USA (but fewer in Europe) now have staff positions for interpreters and translators to aid immigrants in communicating with and in gaining equal access to legal, health, and social services. It is especially for these positions that interpreters are required who are able to act as paranative speakers and biculturalists and are aware of the fact that "no language can impartially transmit information independently of particular forms of culture and knowledge . . . [and that] English therefore inevitably carries the biases and presuppositions of certain cultural traditions" (Hyland 1997: 20).

4   Translation Principles

Much valuable work has been carried out by translatologists on the methodical scrutiny of translation, establishing interesting but often contradictory translation principles. Savory's (1968: 54) collection includes the following:

- a translation must give the words of the original;
- a translation must give the ideas of the original;
- a translation should read like an original work;
- a translation should read like a translation;
- a translation may add to or omit from the original;
- a translation may never add to or omit from the original.

The idea underlying these statements is to postulate what is "right," but contradictory statements such as these can obviously not all be right at the same time. However, each of these postulates can be valid in its own right. To take an extreme interpretation of the first pair of principles as an example: The demand that "a translation must give the words of the original" preserving the successive units of the source text and arranging them in order of occurrence irrespective of the "normal" grammatical sequence of units in the TL (i.e., an *interlinear translation*) is justifiable *if* the aim is to carry out comparative linguistic research:

On the word level, Dutch *daarmee*, for instance, corresponds to English *therewith*, cf.

(2)   a.   *Daarmee   hebben we het gedaan, niet met de hamer.*
      b.   *Therewith have   we it   done,   not with the hammer.*

The English sentence gives "the words of the original." *If*, however, the main purpose of a translation is to describe to the hearer a certain state of affairs as closely as possible, then "a translation must give the ideas of the original." Along these lines, Hannay (1989: 224ff) points out that the standard translation of Dutch *daarmee* "is not the archaic *therewith* but *with it / with that / with them*, depending on the nature of the referent . . . :

(2)   c.   *'That's what we did it with, not the hammer.'* "

Note the two "ifs" used above: the statements just made are no longer as absolute and unconditional as those quoted by Savory; but rather, they are made relative to different target factors specifying the purpose of the translation. In this way the age-old question whether a translation should be literal ("word for word") or free ("sense for sense") is no longer a matter of controversy – it turns out to be not so much a question of arguments to be adduced for deciding which of the two principles is better or right per se; rather, opting for one or the other of the two principles – and, indeed, for any translation principle – is a matter of clear-cut requirements relative to a given purpose or target resulting from a specific commission. Or, to put it differently, the arguments in favor of each principle result from a set of factors that were previously defined. Taking these factors to constitute counterarguments against (an)other principle(s) is a futile endeavor since it is of no relevance to practical translation work.

Sándor Hervey et al. (1995: 43) recently referred to an extraordinary example of a translation where the sound of the source text was chosen to be the decisive factor "allowing the sense to remain at best a vague and suggested impression." Here is part of one of Catullus' (Latin) poems (3a), followed by Celia and Louis Zukovsky's "phonemic translation" (3b). They are attempting to replicate in their rendition the sound sequence of the source text:

(3) a. Ille mi par esse deo videtur,
          ille, si fas est, superare divos,
          qui sedens adversus, identidem te
          spectat et audit
          dulce ridentem, misero quod omnis
          eripit sensus mihi; . . . .
     b. He'll hie me, par *is* he? The God divide her,
          he'll hie, see fastest, superior deity,
          quiz – sitting adverse identity – mate, in-
          spect it and audit –
          you'll care ridden then, misery holds omens,
          air rip the senses from me; . . . .

What becomes obvious here is that this "translation" sets out to imitate as closely as possible the actual sound sequences of the original, while the content is only vaguely incorporated in the English rendition.

Be it such a phonemic translation, or a word-for-word translation, or a free translation – preferring one principle to another one is a matter of relevance to the target group as viewed by the client. Gutt (1991: 121) says that "the different 'translation principles' do reflect differences in what different readers consider to be relevant . . . Thus the contradictions can be resolved when each principle is not stated in absolute terms, but qualified by the condition: 'when required for consistency with the principle of relevance.'"

As we have just seen in the above example, the most important factor is not always required to be the original meaning of the text, but can be, for example, the original sound. This leads us to another important factor that involves sound – words that are identical or at least very similar in spelling and / or sound in two or more languages. I am referring, of course, to "false friends."

5   False Friends

You come across false friends more often than you would like to – not only in real life, but also in linguistics, especially when you happen to be doing a translation.

When someone refers to the so-called "translator's false friends," s/he means the English adaptation of *faux amis du traducteur*, a French expression that has been used since 1928, when Maxime Kœssler and Jules Derocquigny published a book in Paris with the title *Les Faux Amis ou les trahisons du vocabulaire anglais* ("False Friends or the treacherous pitfalls of the English vocabulary").

The fact that "false friends" sound alike often leads to the incorrect assumption that they have the same meaning; however, that is sometimes only partially the case, and often not at all.

We can safely say that these false friends are a serious linguistic problem which belongs to the field of *interference* (sometimes also called *negative transfer*). *Interference* is the phenomenon that we experience when linguistic structures that we have already learnt interfere with our learning new structures. Interference between two languages exists in all areas – for example, in pronunciation and spelling. Incidentally, interference exists not only between two languages, but also within one language. In semantics, one therefore refers to *intralingual* and *interlingual false friends*. Since a word may change its meaning in the course of time, this problem cannot be viewed only in the light of the current (i.e., *synchronic*) situation. Because the historical (i.e., *diachronic*) development must also be taken into consideration, there are altogether four types of false friends.

At this point it might be interesting to look at some illustrative examples of how the meanings of words can be confused because of misleading similarities in two languages. In the examples, the language pairs German-Italian, English-Italian, and English-French will be used.[2]

5.1   *Synchronic interlingual false friends*

Ronnie Ferguson, author of *Italian False Friends* (1994: ix), rightly emphasizes that "[a]ccurate translation . . . as well as the proper appreciation of advanced Italian texts, hinge on the confident handling of key words"; among other examples he mentions key words such as *attuale* (*present* / *topical*, never *actual*), and *eventuale* (not *eventual* but *possible*), which – like their German "true friends" (*aktuell*, and *eventuell*) – are false friends of the English words resembling them in form. Similarly, anyone who would translate the German *luxuriös* and the English *luxurious* with the Italian expression *lussurioso* would be committing a big *faux pas*. The correct translation would be *lussuoso* and not the Italian word *lussurioso*, which has the same meaning as the German word *lasziv* and the English *lascivious*.

5.2   Diachronic intralingual false friends

We can encounter *diachronic intralingual false friends* if we translate linguistic elements from one historical period into another period, when the process of shift in meaning has to be taken into account. A spectacular case in point is the word *nice*: In Old French, which gave the word to English in the thirteenth century, it meant "simple," "silly," and in turn was based on Latin *nescius*, which meant "ignorant." In the fourteenth century, *nice* in English acquired the meaning of "wanton," "loose-mannered," even "lascivious." This sense occurs, for instance, in line 1285 of Geoffrey Chaucer's "The Romaunt of the Rose" (1366): "Nyce she was, but she mente Noone harme ne slight in hir entente, But oonely lust & jolyte." So translating Chaucer's *nice* with the modern English *nice* (meaning "friendly, agreeable, pleasing") would be incorrect.

5.3   Diachronic interlingual false friends

Since language changes constantly, the meaning of expressions can broaden as well as narrow down, and can denote something "better" as well as something "worse." For this reason, words in two languages that were originally true friends can develop into false friends (and vice versa). Carlo Milan highlighted *diachronic interlingual false friends* in an essay in a 1989 volume of the journal *Sprachwissenschaft*, where he compared the German words *Artist* and *realisieren* with their Italian counterparts. He pointed out that the German word *Artist* was derived from the French expression *artiste*, meaning "artist" in the general sense of "somebody performing an art." However, the meaning of this expression was gradually narrowed down in German to *Artist* in the sense of "acrobat," and thus became a false friend because the Italian word *artista* has preserved its original meaning (and can even be modified, such as in *artista di circo* or *artista di varietà*); the correct modern German equivalent of the Italian word *artista* (denoting "somebody performing an art") is *Künstler*. We can see then that a gradual intralingual change in meaning leads to the creation of interlingual false friends.

As indicated above, words that are false friends at a certain point in time can later become true friends. One factor that plays a decisive role in this change is the increasing tendency to internationalize certain words which sound the same in two or more languages although they originally had (at least partially) different meanings. An interesting example is the German *realisieren* and the Italian *realizzare*, which were originally both used exclusively in the sense of "to realize profits, projects, hopes or dreams" or "to make." Both words were greatly influenced by the English *realize* in that their meanings today also include "to comprehend."

In their book *Faux Amis & Key Words: A Dictionary-Guide to French Language, Culture and Society through Lookalikes and Confusables*, Philip Thody and Howard

Evans pointed to a similar development. They commented on the English equivalents of the French verb *réaliser*, stressing that the verb originally meant "'to achieve (one's ambition),' 'to realize (one's assets),' but not – at least for the purists – 'to realize (become aware),' which is *se rendre compte que* or *de*, though most French people do, in conversation, use *réaliser* in the latter sense" (1985: 78). We can therefore conclude that the English verb *realize* is in the process of becoming truly international.

5.4 *Synchronic intralingual false friends*

Further problems for the translator are caused by *synchronic intralingual false friends*, even by native speakers. For instance, in German one has to distinguish between *fremdsprachiger Unterricht*, i.e., "teaching in a foreign (or target) language" and *fremdsprachlicher Unterricht*, i.e., "foreign-language teaching."

Many English words that appear to mean the same can also lead to confusion and make life very difficult for translators and interpreters. It would be extremely dangerous, for example, to assume that *inflammable* is the opposite of *flammable*; in fact, both words mean the same. The 1992 edition of the *BBC English Dictionary* defined the two words as follows: "An *inflammable* material or chemical 'burns easily.' – Something that is *flammable* 'catches fire easily.'"

Nevertheless, even in England *inflammable* is incorrectly used in the sense of "non-flammable" because many people believe that the *in-* at the beginning of the word gives it a negative meaning, similar to the *in-* at the beginning of *incomplete* and *indirect*. In an attempt to avoid any grave errors, the British Standards Institution issued the following warning in 1959: "It is the Institution's policy to encourage the use of the terms *flammable* and *non-flammable* rather than *inflammable* and *non-inflammable*."

The fact that even in England often the wrong meaning "non-flammable" was ascribed to the word *inflammable* shows that the word *inflammable* is both an intralingual and an interlingual false friend.

We have seen that there is a host of factors affecting the act of translation and that the translator should take them all into consideration when translating – in other words, s/he should "translate by factors."

6   Translating by Factors

Each act of translation is conditioned by a huge variety of factors – factors that can and must be identified for the act of translation to be taught, learnt, and practiced.[3]

A worthwhile endeavor of translation theory would be to do research into the ways and means of creating optimum TL renditions of (different kinds of) SL texts in the light of different factors which have to be taken into account.

As was pointed out in section 3 ("Modes of Interpreting: Consecutive and Simultaneous"), rendering the German modal verb *dürfen* by English *may* is adequate in many cases but inappropriate in the context where sentences (1a) and (1b) are uttered. In section 5 ("False Friends"), another "revision factor" was mentioned which comes into play when the translator wrongly believes in false friends, words which look or sound similar but do not have an identical meaning.

As was shown, translating by factors does not mean taking prescribed factors into account as such but bearing in mind the specific roles or functions these factors fulfill. Gutknecht and Rölle (1996: 5ff) list a number of basic functions of translation factors. Besides revision factors as exemplified above, every translator / interpreter is, for instance, faced with "blocking factors" on which the revision factors are based. These blocking factors make a specific TL rendition impossible. An example will make this point clear.

An indefinite number of English combinations of the form *adjective plus noun* can safely be translated into German:

red rose	*rote Rose*
interesting film	*interessanter Film*
beautiful house	*hübsches Haus*

In English, also the expression *simultaneous interpreter* may be added to the list, but in German the structurally corresponding construction *simultaner Dolmetscher* is not possible. The reason is that it would suggest that the interpreter himself is simultaneous. In German the rule is that for an adjective to premodify a noun it must denote a characteristic of the referent of that noun; otherwise the formation will be ungrammatical. So in the case of the SL expression *simultaneous interpreter* a semantic factor (viz., the information that *simultaneous* is no characteristic feature of *interpreter*) will act or function as a blocking factor to the TL rendition **simultaner Dolmetscher*: the correct German version would be *Simultandolmetscher*.

In addition to revision factors and blocking factors, there are, among others, "invariance factors," which make an SL feature reappear in the TL rendition (e.g., the English expression *This book is a must* can be rendered into German by *Dieses Buch ist ein Muss*). "Change factors" make an SL feature disappear or a new or additional feature appear in the TL rendition: in German *ein Muss* cannot be pluralized the way *a must* can, such as in *three important musts*. Change factors often become effective in everyday language and in specialized communication whenever concepts from different languages differ considerably in their characteristics, or when a concept exists in only one language. Lynne Bowker (1994: 184) has outlined "five strategies for handling such 'untranslatable concepts': use of footnotes, use of the closest corresponding TL equivalent, paraphrasing the SL term, use of loan words and loan translations, and creation of neologisms."

"Target factors" relate to the target or purpose of the translation as determined by the client, for instance, carrying out comparative linguistic research or describing to the hearer a certain state of affairs as closely as possible (see section 4, "Translation Principles"). It is the client who makes basic choices in each act of commissioning and who prescribes how to translate. For instance, the client is the one to decide how faithful or how free the translation is to be, whether the target is an interlinear translation, a phonemic translation (both exemplified above), or another kind of rendition.

7   Machine Translation and Computer-assisted Translation

Because factors are objectifiable, the factor approach is an ideal tool for machine translation. Machine-aided human translation (MAHT) is to be distinguished from fully automatic machine translation (FAMT). MAHT, also known as computer-assisted translation (CAT), involves some interaction between the translator and the computer. In contrast, FAMT, better known as machine translation (MT), is characterized by the absence of any human intervention during the translation process. Judith Klavans (in William O'Grady et al. 1997: 656) rightly emphasizes that "[t]he purpose of a machine translation system is the same as that of any translation system: taking text written or spoken in one language and writing or speaking it in another . . . Translation poses challenging problems both for the human translator and for the machine attempting to do what the human does."[4]

Tests conducted at the offices of many international organizations, for instance at the Pan American Health Organization, the WHO Regional Office for the Americas, have demonstrated that in its present stage of development, fully automatic translation technology is not considered cost-effective because its resulting output needs extensive revision work (post-editing). The machine-aided human translation approach, on the other hand, seems to be more suited to the needs of many organizations which have to handle the translation of documents. Computer-assisted translation systems are based on "translation memory." With such systems (that are sometimes combined with terminology databases), translators have immediate access to previous translations of portions of the text, which they can then accept, reject, or modify. By constantly archiving their final choice, translators will soon have access to an enriched "memory" of ready-made solutions for a wealth of translation problems. Other recent developments in computer technology also help the translators to perform their job. There is, for instance, a new and very effective productivity tool available for PC-based translators: automatic dictation software. At the present state of speech-recognition technology, however, to use dictation effectively the translator must master a new foreign language: "paused" speech that–the–computer–can–understand.

Regardless of the degree of usefulness of machine translation, there seems to be unanimous agreement that translators cannot be replaced, either now or in the foreseeable future. Only the human translator as an expert will be able to fully survey all the factors relevant to felicitous translation processes.

NOTES

1 Two useful collections of readings on general aspects of translating and interpreting are Owens (1996) and Sofer (1997); for a comprehensive overview of translation studies as an academic discipline, see Baker (1997).

2 From the mass of literature dealing with false friends, I select the following for additional mention:

- The *Cambridge International Dictionary of English* (CUP, 1995) is unique in that it uses special symbols to warn its consulters about false friends and contains lists of false friends for 16 languages (Czech, Danish, Dutch, French, German, Greek, Italian, Japanese, Korean, Norwegian, Polish, Portuguese, Russian, Spanish, Swedish, and Thai).
- For the English-speaking translator of German, Fred Bridgham (1996)

is especially interesting since his explanations are illustrated with examples from literature, the press and everyday life.

- Henri van Hoof (1989) offers most valuable hints for the English translator of French.

3 For an attempt to verify this statement, see Gutknecht and Rölle (1996: chapters 2–7).

4 For further reading on human and machine translation, consult the following translation periodicals: *Babel* (Amsterdam), *Interpreting* (Amsterdam), *Language International* (Amsterdam), *Lebende Sprachen* (Berlin), *Machine Translation* (Dordrecht / The Netherlands and Norwell, MA), *Meta* (Montreal), *Multilingua* (Berlin and New York), *Perspectives* (Copenhagen), *Target* (Amsterdam), and *The Translator* (Manchester).

32 Language Planning

FRANK ANSHEN

Every nation does, in fact, have a language policy regulating which languages are spoken in which situations. In many countries this policy is explicit, often a constitutional provision naming a number of languages and their respective roles. This is the situation in Indonesia, India, Ireland, and Canada among others. Other nations may specify the domains of languages by specific laws; this is what France has done. In still other nations such as the United States, language policy may be largely implicit. There is no law, for instance, stating that acts of the United States Congress shall be published in English, but this is and has been the invariant practice for over the 200 years that the nation has existed.[1]

Language policies can be classified into three major approaches: monolingualism, equal multilingualism, and national / regional language systems. France has followed the first since the seventeenth century, Belgium had adopted the second in the twentieth century, and India has moved to the third since independence. Of the three, only the first comes about implicitly, the other two are always established by legislation. Of course classification into one of these three schemes is not always easy. Spain's language policy, for example, officially constituted as a national / regional language situation very much resembles an equal bilingualism scheme, at least as far as the relationship that exists between Spanish and Catalan. Paraguay's constitution provides for equality between Spanish and Guaraní but, in fact the nation functions much as if Spanish were the sole national language.

There appear to be four major factors at work in the selection of a national language. These are: nationalism, ethnic self-interest, linguistic demographics, and the prestige of languages involved. Often there is a combination of the first two, with the second frequently masquerading as the first.

For a case where nationalism was dominant and ethnic self-interest nonexistent, consider Indonesia. The pertinent facts are that there are hundreds of languages spoken in Indonesia, of which Javanese is the native language of somewhere over half, and less than two-thirds[2] of Indonesians are native speakers of Javanese.

In 1928, during Dutch colonial rule, a Congress of National Youth in Indonesia committed itself to the slogan *Indonesia – satu bangsa, satu bahasa, satu tana* (Indonesia – one people, one language, one fatherland). The *satu bahasa* chosen, Malay, was renamed Bahasa Indonesia. It was primarily a trade language used widely in the archipelago but the native language of but a minute fraction of the population of Indonesia. Thus the Indonesian nationalist movement consciously chose a national language which was not that of the largest or most influential indigenous ethnic group but, rather, one which was neutral among the various ethnic groups of the country.[3] During World War II, Bahasa Indonesia was used as a language of administration by the Japanese occupation government. This necessitated an accelerated modernization of the language, as Japanese sponsored groups created needed vocabulary and began the process of standardization. At the end of the war, Bahasa Indonesia was in place as a national language of administration.[4] Upon independence, after World War II, Bahasa Indonesia was, indeed, chosen as the national language. The effect of this decision was to remove language almost entirely from the political arena except, as planned by the conferees, as an instrument of national unity. In addition, knowledge of Bahasa Indonesia has spread widely and it is increasingly becoming a first language of a sizeable portion of the population of Indonesia. It has also been a positive factor in increasing literacy in the nation. In 1945, at the end of the Japanese occupation, the literacy rate was 20.7 percent.[5] In 1986, it had reached 72 percent.

One negative factor is that with the great success of the language policy, Bahasa Indonesia is increasingly threatening the existence of many of the smaller languages of the nation and is even weakening the position of Javanese, a language with approximately 60 million native speakers.

A somewhat similar, although more extreme, situation exists in Israel. When Hebrew was chosen by the nationalist movement as the national language for the hoped-for independent state, it was spoken as a first language by nobody. It has become the first language of an overwhelming majority of Jews born in Israel since independence. Here too, communal first languages such as Yiddish and Jewish dialects of Arabic are dying out, although there are no signs of lesser use of Arabic among the substantial non-Jewish Arabic speaking population.

Compare the experience of Indonesia with that of India. Like Indonesia, India is linguistically heterogeneous with hundreds of languages spoken within the nation. However, unlike what happened in Indonesia, the Indian independence movement decided to adopt a major indigenous language as the national language. The choice, after much debate was Hindi. Hindi is the first language of over half, but less than two-thirds of the people of India, making its demographics resemble those of Javanese in Indonesia. This choice has been noticeably less successful than the adoption of Bahasa Indonesia. Speakers of other major languages of India, languages with millions of speakers and centuries of literary tradition, have seen the choice of Hindi as the national language both as a promotion of the interests of Hindi speakers at the cost of non-Hindi speakers and as an insult to their languages. Language policy has been a central and divisive element of Indian politics since. Violence has occurred in response to attempts to implement the constitutional provisions and the political map of India has been changed with the redrawing of state lines to reflect linguistic loyalties. The current compromise allows Indian states to choose their own language for state purposes, asserts Hindi as a national language and the language with which Indians are expected to relate to the nation, and provides for a special position for English, the former colonial language, in the realm of education and for intergroup communication.

The comparison of Indonesia with India suggests an interesting generalization: nations such as the US, Sweden, and Portugal have been reasonably successful with language policies which dictate that the nation will be officially or de facto monolingual in the language spoken as a first language by a large majority (call it more than 80 percent) of the population. Nations such as Indonesia, and many of the nations of subsaharan Africa have been successfully monolingual in a language which very few citizens speak as a first language. Clearly major benefits are bestowed upon native speakers of the national language: they will have an advantage to the extent that school and civil service tests are given in their language. These benefits will translate into improved educational and career paths. Where the language chosen as the national language is spoken natively by a large majority of a nation's population, speakers of other languages may agree that the choice is obvious. Where the language chosen as the national language is spoken natively by an infinitesimal proportion of the nation's population, all linguistic groups are equally handicapped and no group has reason to think itself the victim of linguistic discrimination.

An alternative approach to having a single official language is to have a small number of languages as co-official languages on the basis of constitutional equality. In American discussions of language policy for the United States, three nations which are officially bilingual, Belgium, Sri Lanka, and Canada, are often held up as horrible examples of the dangers of a multilingual policy.[6] All are officially bilingual. An examination of these nations' language policies, however, reveals that the lesson is the exact opposite of the one drawn by US English and similar groups advocating a policy of intolerance towards languages other than English in the US.

When Belgium[7] became an independent nation in 1831, the constitution provided that French would be the language of legislation, justice, secondary and higher education, and the armed forces. Notwithstanding this, individuals were guaranteed the right to use the language of their choice, although clearly a native speaker of Flemish[8] would have to speak French as well if (s)he wished an education or to take part in national life. Already by 1840 this enforced monolingualism was the object of a petition signed by 10,000 Flemish speakers asking that the courts and government to the provincial level in Flanders conduct their business in Flemish. This petition was not given serious consideration. The next century and a quarter were marked by continual efforts by Flemish speakers to establish the equality of Flemish to French within Belgium. In response to this assertion of linguistic nationalism by the Flemish, French speakers became increasingly protective of French in their part of the country.[9]

The situation was resolved in the 1960s when a linguistic dividing line was drawn, separating the country into Flemish and French speaking sections.[10] Along with constitutional reforms giving each section of the country significant areas of self-government, these actions seem to have created a modus vivendi under which the Belgian nation can continue as a single unit.

A similar conclusion can be drawn from the history of Sri Lanka since it attained independence in 1947. The population of Sri Lanka is composed principally of two ethnic groups, usually identified by their respective languages, Sinhala speakers and Tamil speakers, with the former holding an approximately two to one numerical advantage over the latter. Under British rule, the language of education and administration was English. With independence, the Sinhala portion of the population moved to transform its numerical preponderance into economic and cultural hegemony. In 1956 a law was passed declaring Sinhala the national language. Further laws in the next five years provided that Sinhalese be used in civil service exams, education, and administration in the predominately Tamil northern and eastern provinces and that legal decisions be in Sinhalese even in predominantly Tamil speaking areas. Although the violent reaction of the Tamil speakers to this move convinced the majority to write a new law in 1966 providing some protection for the status of the Tamil language in predominately Tamil areas, the damage had been done (and not wholly repaired). This attempt to impose the language of one ethnic group on the other, was one of the prime causes of the civil war on the island.

In an attempt to end communal strife based on linguistic rivalry, the draft constitution proposed by the current government provides that the official languages of the nation shall be Sinhala and Tamil while the national languages shall be Sinhala, Tamil, and English. Every citizen of the country is to be guaranteed the right to transact business with the government in any one of the national languages and to an education in Sinhala or Tamil, with English authorized where available. It is clear that Sri Lanka is an example of the divisive force of imposed monolingualism and that the tolerance and encouragement of language rights is seen by the government as contributing to the establishment of a peaceful, united nation.

A third example is the case of Canada. In 1763, by the Treaty of Paris, France ceded its rights in what is now Canada to the British. A provision of that treaty protected the cultural and linguistic rights of French inhabitants of the ceded territory. The Act of Union promulgated by Great Britain in 1867, granting dominion status to Canada preserved those rights, and they were part of the "unwritten constitution" of Canada until Canada adopted a written constitution, also incorporating the linguistic rights of its francophone population. At least since the 1960s there has been an active movement in Quebec advocating independence for the province, and in the 1995 referendum independence was defeated by only a few percentage points. Canada would seem to be a clear case illustrating the dangers to national unity of toleration of linguistic minorities.

However, the situation looks somewhat different if we compare the situation in Canada with that in the British Isles. Specifically, if we compare the approach of the Canadian government to the linguistic and cultural minority which they ruled, the French, with the approach of the British government to the linguistic and cultural minority which they ruled, the Irish. From the time of Cromwell, British governments had ruled Ireland in English and were either indifferent or hostile to Gaelic, the language of the vast majority of the Irish people at the beginning of this period. By the end of the nineteenth century, the Irish had overwhelmingly become first language speakers of English; by 1922 less than 5 percent of the population of the island spoke Gaelic.

The results of this Englishization were not what its advocates might have wished. The year 1922 was also when the Irish Free State was established, creating an Ireland independent of British rule. Not only had the imposition of a single language not contributed to unity of the British isles, but the nearly 100 percent successful effort to eradicate Gaelic was one of the major grievances used to rally people to the rebel cause. The fate of Gaelic loomed so large in the nationalist cause that the Irish constitution declared Gaelic to be the first national language and the government of Ireland has expended a great deal of energy and resources trying to revitalize the language.[11]

The end result of this experiment with two language policies is that the union of Ireland with England is severed with no prospect of reunion while the union of Quebec with the rest of Canada, while troubled, continues. Indeed, just as nationalists in Ireland regarded the fate of Gaelic as a major nationalist issue, the future of French was and is one of the major concerns of francophones in Canada. It is easy to see that a more aggressively anti-French policy on the part of the majority anglophones would make the continued adherence of Quebec to the Canadian union untenable.

Another possible answer to the linguistic problems of multilingual nations is to maintain a policy whereby a number of languages are authorized for official use in specific geographical areas of a nation, but one language has special status as the "national language" and is expected to be known by the entire nation's population and used for matters of national concern. Since the dissolution of the Soviet Union, India is probably the most prominent example of this approach.[12]

As mentioned above, the original plan, envisioned in the constitution, would have made Hindi the national language, spoken as a first or second language by all citizens of the country. Opposition, sometimes violent, from speakers of other languages to this empowerment of Hindi, has resulted in a modus vivendi known as the three language policy. Under this policy, every Indian is expected to know at least three languages, English and Hindi as the national languages plus their state language, where this is not Hindi. For residents of states in which Hindi is the state language, they are to learn another Indian language, preferably one from the south of India.[13] The object of this policy is to equalize the linguistic burdens between Hindi speakers and other Indians, and, at the same time, equip every Indian with languages to communicate with the national government.

In practice this policy, while providing a framework within which the nation can function, is implemented in a manner far from what was envisioned. Increasingly, the non-Hindi states, especially the Dravidian ones, are functioning monolingually in their state languages while minimizing the role of Hindi. This has the effect of creating a series of monolingual[14] entities, coexisting in one federal unit. In this, India might best be compared with the officially bilingual states that we looked at, Belgium and Canada, with the differences that there are considerably more languages in play in India and that the other two nations have a constitutional commitment to the equality of the regional languages while the Indian constitution asserts the primacy of Hindi.

Much the same situation has arisen in Spain, albeit with many fewer languages. On the death of Franco, a new constitution was adopted providing for regional language status for Basque and Catalan.[15] At least in Catalonia, this has meant that education and regional government have become increasingly monolingually Catalan and the use of Spanish is being narrowed.

Interestingly, many of the nations which are successful on the basis of legal equality for two or several languages such as Canada, Belgium, and Switzerland and the most successful of the national language / regional language countries such as India and Spain use a system of either de jure (Switzerland, Belgium, and Spain) or de facto (Canada and India) regionally defined monolingualism.

It is clear from the above that demographic factors are important in determining language policy. We have seen that monolingual policies work best when the language chosen is either the first language of a large majority of the speakers in a country or the first language of an insignificant portion of the population. Similarly, legal equality among two or more languages is associated with countries such as Canada where there are a small number of languages which together are spoken by the vast majority of the population. National language–regional language situations are harder to define. The most prominent of these, India and the former Soviet Union, seem to come about in countries with large numbers of languages spoken by significant portions of the population. However, Spain offers us an example in which only three languages are involved.

However, there is more to explain. At first glance, India and Nigeria are similar. Both are former British colonies with linguistically diverse populations. India has chosen a national language–regional language policy while Nigeria has gone to official monolingualism in a non-indigenous language: English. Further, neither country has seriously considered the language policy of the other. The differentiating factor would seem to be the prestige of the indigenous languages, some feeling of the speakers of the language that it is worthy of being the national language. This prestige is tied to a language having a written literary tradition. In India, all eleven languages which function as state languages have a written tradition of centuries, while, for example, none of the indigenous languages of Nigeria do.

The importance of the prestige factor is shown when we consider the situation in Senegal, Burundi, and Paraguay. What they have in common is that although in each case there is an indigenous language spoken by a large majority of the population, Wolof, Kirundi, and Guaraní, the countries are officially monolingual in languages spoken natively by a very small percentage of the population, French in the first two instances and Spanish in the third. None of the three majority languages, Wolof, Kirundi, or Guaraní, have a written tradition which predates colonization.

The factor of prestige is further emphasized when we observe that, notwithstanding the fact there are hundreds of languages spoken in the 53 independent nations of Africa, one of the four languages with long literary traditions: Arabic, English, French, or Portuguese, is a national language of every nation on the continent, despite the fact that the three European languages have virtually no native speakers in most of these countries. In most of these countries they are the sole national language. Clearly, it is not a coincidence that the three European languages are those of the major colonial powers in Africa; but more than colonial tradition is involved. The countries of North Africa, Morocco, Algeria, Tunisia, and Libya have forsaken the colonial languages, French in the first three cases and Italian in the last, for an indigenous language, Arabic. Arabic, of course, has tremendous prestige as the holy language of Islam as well as a long and important literary tradition.

Another factor helping to determine the prestige of a given linguistic variety is the extent to which speakers of various linguistic varieties regard them as separate languages or as dialects of one another. To a great extent, this is not a linguistic question. Varieties which are not mutually intelligible, such as Mandarin and Cantonese, are generally regarded as dialects of the same language, which is itself identified with Mandarin, while varieties which are virtually identical, such as Hindi and Urdu, are not. It is, indeed, possible for two varieties to be so distinct that they must be considered different languages, despite proximity and political unity. This becomes clear if we consider Basque and standard Spanish versus Sicilian and standard Italian. In both cases the former variety is spoken by an ethnic minority within a nation state. But Sicilian is generally considered a dialect of Italian while nobody has ever claimed Basque to be a dialect of Spanish. Clearly Basque is sufficiently distinct from Spanish both typologically and genetically as to make a claim of a language / dialect relationship foolish on the surface. On the other hand, although Sicilian and standard Italian are not mutually intelligible, they are closely related both typologically and genetically.

In terms of language policy there are serious consequences to the assignment of two varieties to a single language or distinct languages. Varieties that are regarded as distinct languages are often objects of nationalist sentiment while dialects are usually regarded simply as incorrect forms of the dominant linguistic variety. In China, for instance, the linguistic varieties that are genetically close to Mandarin are regarded as dialects of Chinese and have no constitutional protection. On the other hand, the constitution provides that the government should protect and encourage varieties such as Mongolian and Tibetan, which are considered distinct languages. The government thus publishes materials for the fewer than three million speakers of the Mongolian language in China, while providing no such accommodation for more than 77 million speakers of what is regarded as the Wu dialect of Chinese.[16] This neglect of the dialects seems to be accepted as the proper state of affairs both by speakers of Mandarin, the dominant variety, and speakers of the other varieties.

Similarly, in Italy, Lombard, Neapolitan, Piedmontese, and Sicilian are all distinct enough from standard Italian to be non-mutually intelligible, but they are all considered dialects of Italian and questions of their status are not prominent on the political agenda of Italy.[17]

The potential for what is regarded as a language to be a vehicle for nationalist aspirations has been recognized for centuries. As part of his plan to unify the French nation Richelieu established a government policy of imposing standard French upon the nation and reducing the other Romance varieties spoken in France to the status of dialects of French. It has been continued to this day. Similarly, the rulers of Spain attempted for centuries to establish a standard language–dialect relationship between the Spanish of Castile and the other genetically related language varieties in what is now Spain. As noted above, they have been less successful than the French government. Despite several centuries of official policy which has treated Catalan as a dialect of Spanish, the Catalan people maintained their belief that it is a separate language and have in recent years succeeded in having their view enshrined in the constitution.

One further example of the importance of a variety being classified as a language or dialect comes from the recent American controversy over African-American Vernacular English, also known as Ebonics. The Oakland School board fired the first shots in the Ebonics War by issuing a policy advocating that teachers in its predominately African-American schools should have some familiarity with the speech variety of many of their students. Their document also asserted that Ebonics was a language. Opponents of Ebonics were equally firm in their assertion that Ebonics was a dialect of English. Linguists who were questioned on the subject often found the first question to be "is Ebonics a language?" Examining the debate on the subject it is clear that an affirmative answer to this question was an assertion that Ebonics was a worthy subject of study and possible use. A negative answer suggested that Ebonics, being merely a dialect, was essentially a series of mistakes to be corrected.

In sum, then, national language policies can be based upon recognition of a single variety as the sole national language, recognition of two or more varieties on a legally equal basis, or recognition of a single major variety throughout the nation along with official status for other varieties in specified portions of the nation. Any of these policies may be accompanied with greater or lesser toleration of other languages within legal and educational spheres. A successful language policy will consider both the demographic facts of language distribution within the nation and the prestige afforded each of the competing linguistic varieties.

NOTES

1 This is not to deny that a number of laws have been proposed or passed in the last two centuries, nor that judicial opinions and bureaucratic regulations have been issued, but that, in the main, the United States has had little language law compared with many other countries.

2 I regret being vague, but language statistics are notoriously difficult to compile in the best of situations, and more so where there are lots of languages and many remote areas and peoples. I will use approximate numbers in this paper to avoid giving the reader a spurious sense of exactitude. Where, as with the number of Irish speakers in the Republic of Ireland, there are more reliable figures, I will use less approximate language.

3 Compare this with India and the Philippines: in India the nationalist movement chose Hindi, the largest indigenous language to be the national language after independence, with results which will be discussed later in this chapter, and in the Philippines the nationalist movement chose to base the national language on Tagalog, the language of the most influential indigenous ethnic group.

4 Interestingly, much the same process took place in the Philippines, where Pilipino, a standardized form of Tagalog, was used during the Japanese occupation and was thus shaped for use by the national government at the end of colonial rule.

5 This literacy rate accords with earlier figures and is not an aberration caused by the war.

6 Usually officially bi- or multilingual countries such as Switzerland, Finland, and Singapore which are not subject to high degrees of inter-ethnic stress are ignored in these discussions. It is too soon to judge the success of the constitutional provision in the Republic of South Africa which establishes 11 languages on a coequal status, but it is hard to be optimistic about the chances of a nation actually functioning with so many legally equal national languages. The problems are exacerbated by the relative lack of development of nine of the languages after years of neglect under the previous regime. It should be noted that the actual motivation of these groups, that of maintaining the position of English speakers *vis-à-vis* speakers of other languages is revealed not only in some explicit statements by present and past leaders of the movement, but also by the horror with which they view laws passed in Quebec to protect the position of the French language. Laws similar to those they advocate for the US if one would only substitute *English* for *French* in the laws' wording.

7 Most of the information on the history of the language struggle in Belgium is taken from Rita Moore-Robinson's chapter in Stephen B. Wickman, ed., *Belgium: A Country Study*, The American University, 1984.

8 Flemish is the variety of Dutch spoken in Belgium.

9 This is not to assert that linguistic issues were the only ones in the conflict between Flanders and Wallonia,

but, as in many cases, other issues were symbolized by linguistic ones, and the linguistic issues contributed to a general hardening of the lines.

10 Actually a German speaking section was also established to accommodate the approximately 3 percent of the population which is German speaking.

11 Unfortunately, this effort has not been crowned with success as the Irish people, having one usable language, English, have not felt a need to learn another. The number of Gaelic speakers at last count was approximately the same 5 percent that it was in 1922. Of course, given the decline in the number of speakers prior to that date, halting the decline may be counted as a partial victory.

12 India actually maintains two languages of wider communication, Hindi and English, alongside the languages used for official purposes on a regional basis.

13 The four major languages of the south of India are of the Dravidian language family, where the bulk of the languages of the north of India are Indo-European and genetically close to Hindi.

14 Ignoring here the role of English.

15 Galician, too, received some official status, but the area has lagged behind the others in promoting the use of the regional language.

16 Of course the nature of the Chinese writing system allows for texts to be written in Mandarin to be read with the lexicon of the various dialects, but the syntax of written material is Mandarin.

17 In the past few years, northern separatist groups have made some appeal for the recognition of Lombard as the language of their proposed new nation, but this does not seem to have been a major issue.

Bibliography

Abailard, Pierre (Peter Abelard). (1970) [ca. 1130]. In L. M. de Rijk (ed.), *Dialectica*, 2nd edn. Philosophical Texts and Studies, Assen, Holland: Van Gorcum.

Abercrombie, D. (1967). *Elements of General Phonetics*. Edinburgh: Edinburgh University Press.

Abondolo, D. (ed.) (1998). *The Uralic Languages*. London: Routledge.

Achard, P. (1993). *La sociologie du langage*. Paris: Presses Universitaires de France.

Ackerman, F. and Lesourd, P. (1997). Toward a lexical representation of phrasal predicates. In A. Alsina, J. Bresnan, and P. Sells (eds), *Complex Predicates* (pp. 67–106). Stanford: CSLI.

Aczel, P., Israel, D., Katagiri, Y., and Peters, S. (eds) (1993). *Situation Theory and Its Applications*, Vol. 3. Stanford: CSLI.

Adams, M. J. (1990). *Beginning to Read: Thinking and Learning about Print*. Cambridge, MA: MIT Press.

Adams, M. J. and Bruck, M. (1995). Resolving the "great debate." *American Educator*, 19:7, 10–20.

Adamson, H. and Regan, V. (1991). The acquisition of community norms by Asian immigrants learning English as a second language: a preliminary study. *Studies in Second Language Acquisition*, 13:1, 1–22.

Aiello, L. C. (1996a). Hominine preadaptations for language and cognition. In P. Mellars and K. Gibson (eds), *Modelling the Early Human Mind* (pp. 89–99). Cambridge: McDonald Institute Monographs.

Aiello, L. C. (1996b). Terrestriality, bipedalism and the origin of language. In W. G. Runciman, J. M. Smith, and R. I. M. Dunbar (eds), *Evolution of Social Behaviour Patterns in Primates and Man* (pp. 269–89). *Proceedings of the British Academy 88*. Oxford: Oxford University Press.

Aiello, L. C. and Dean, C. (1990). *An Introduction to Human Evolutionary Anatomy*. London: Academic Press.

Aikio, M. (1984). The position and use of the same language: historical, contemporary and future perspectives. *Journal of Multilingual and Multicultural Development*, 5, 277–91.

Ainsworth-Vaughn, N. and Saunders, P. (1996). Conversational practices in medical settings. Colloquium organized at the Annual Conference of the American Association for Applied Linguistics. Chicago, IL.

Aitchison, J. (1987). *Words in the Mind*. Oxford: Basil Blackwell.

Aitchison, J. (1996). *The Seeds of Speech: Language Origin and Evolution*. Cambridge: Cambridge University Press.

Albrow, K. H. (1966). Mutation in spoken north Welsh. In C. E. Bazell, J. C. Catford, M. A. K. Halliday, and R. H. Robins (eds), *In Memory of J. R. Firth*. London: Longmans Green.

Allardt, E. (1979). *Implications of the Ethnic Revival in Modern Industrialized Society: A Comparative Study of the Linguistic Minorities in Western Europe*. Helsinki: Societas Scientariarum Fennica.

Allen, J. (1991). Discourse structure in the TRAINS project. In P. Price (ed.), *Darpa Speech and Natural Language Workshop* (pp. 325–30). Pacific Grove, CA: Morgan Kauffman.

Allen, J. (1995). *Natural Language Understanding*, 2nd edn. Redwood City, CA: Benjamin Cummings.

Allen, J. F. and Perrault, C. R. (1980). Analyzing intention in utterances. *Artificial Intelligence*, 15, 143–78.

Alvar, M. (1967). *Linguistica Romanica* [originally by I. Iordan, reworked and heavily annotated by M. Alvar.] Madrid: Ediciones Alcala.

Ammon, U. (1979). Regionaldialekte und Einheitssprache in der Bundesrepublik Deutschland. *International Journal of the Sociology of Language*, 21, 25–40.

Ammon, U., Dittmar, N., and Mattheier, K. (eds) (1988). *Sociolinguistics. Soziolinguistik. Ein internationales Handbuch zur Wissenschaft von Sprache und Gesellschaft*. Berlin and New York: Gruyter.

Andersen, H. (1973). Abductive and deductive change. *Language*, 49, 765–93.

Anderson, J. (1983). *The Architecture of Cognition*. Cambridge, MA: Harvard University Press.

Anderson, S. (1976). On the notion of subject in ergative languages. In C. N. Li (ed.), *Subject and Topic* (pp. 1–24). New York: Academic Press.

Anderson, S. (1985). *Phonology in the Twentieth Century*. Chicago: University of Chicago Press.

Anderson, S. (1992). *A-morphous Morphology*. Cambridge: Cambridge University Press.

Annett, M. (1985). *Left, Right, Hand and Brain: The Right Shift Theory*. London: Erlbaum.

Appel, R. and Muysken, P. (1987). *Language Contact and Bilingualism*. London: Edward Arnold.

Archibald, J. (1993). *Language Learnability and L2 Phonology: The Acquisition of Metrical Parameters*. Dordrecht: Kluwer.

Armstrong, D. F., Stokoe, W. C., and Wilcox, S. E. (1995). *Gesture and the Nature of Language*. Cambridge: Cambridge University Press.

Arnason, K. (1991). *The Rhythms of Drottkvaett and Other Old Icelandic Metres*. Reykjavik: Institute of Linguistics, University of Iceland.

Arnauld, A. and Lancelot, C. (1660). *Grammaire générale et raisonnée de Port Royal*. Paris: Pierre le Petit. [English translation 1975: *General and Rational Grammar: The Port-Royal Grammar*, ed. and tr. J. Rieux and B. E. Rolling. Janua Linguarum, Series Minor, 208. The Hague: Mouton.]

Aronoff, M. (1976). *Word Formation in Generative Grammar*. Cambridge, MA: MIT Press.

Aronoff, M. (1994). *Morphology By Itself*. Cambridge, MA: MIT Press.

Aronoff, M. and Anshen, F. (1998). Morphology and the lexicon: lexicalization and productivity. In Spencer and Zwicky (eds), pp. 237–47.

Arthur, B., Weiner, M., Culver, J., Young, L., and Thomas, D. (1980). The register of impersonal discourse to foreigners: verbal adjustments to foreign accent. In D. Larsen

Freeman (ed.), *Discourse Analysis in Second Language Research* (pp. 111–24). Rowley, MA: Newbury House.

Asher, J. and Price, B. (1967). The learning strategy of total physical response: some age differences. *Child Development*, 38, 1219–27.

Asher, R. E. and Simpson, L. M. Y. (eds) (1993). *Encyclopedia of Language and Linguistics*, 10 vols. Oxford: Pergamon.

Atkinson, J. M. and Heritage, J. (eds) (1984). *Structures of Social Action: Studies in Conversation Analysis*. Cambridge: Cambridge University Press.

Atlas, J. D. (1977). Negation, ambiguity, and presupposition. *Linguistics and Philosophy*, 1, 321–36.

Atlas, J. D. (1989). *Philosophy without Ambiguity: A Logico-linguistic Essay*. Oxford: Clarendon Press.

Augustine, St (1943). *The Confessions of St Augustine*. Tr. F. J. Sheed. New York: Sheed and Ward.

Austin, J. L. (1962). *How To Do Things With Words*. Oxford: Oxford University Press.

Bach, E. (1988). Categorial grammars as theories of language. In R. Oehrle (ed.), *Categorial Grammars and Natural Language Structures* (pp. 17–34). Dordrecht: Reidel.

Bach, K. and Harnish, R. (1979). *Linguistic Communication and Speech Acts*. Cambridge, MA: MIT Press.

Baetens-Beardsmore, H. (1986). *Bilingualism: Basic Principles*, 2nd edn. Clevedon, Avon: Tieto.

Baker, C. (1993). *Foundations of Bilingual Education and Bilingualism*. Clevedon, Avon: Multilingual Matters.

Baker, M. (1988). *Incorporation: A Theory of Grammatical Function Changing*. Chicago: University of Chicago Press.

Baker, M. (1991). On some subject / object non-asymmetries in Mohawk. *Natural Language and Linguistic Theory*, 9, 537–76.

Baker, M. (1996). *The Polysynthesis Parameter*. New York: Oxford University Press.

Baker, M. (ed.) (1997). *Routledge Encyclopedia of Translation Studies*. London and New York: Routledge.

Bakhtin, M. M. (1986). *Speech Genres and Other Late Essays*. Tr. V. W. McGee, ed. C. Emerson and M. Holquist. Austin: University of Texas Press.

Baldwin, J. and French, P. (1990). *Forensic Phonetics*. London: Pinter.

Ball, M. (1993). *Phonetics for Speech Pathology*, 2nd edn. London: Whurr.

Ball, M. (ed.) (1993). *The Celtic Languages*. London: Routledge.

Bamgbose, A. (1969). Yoruba. In E. Dunstan (ed.), *Twelve Nigerian Languages: A Handbook on their Sound Systems for Teachers of English* (pp. 163–72). London: Longmans Green.

Banti, G. and Giannattasio, F. (1996). Music and metre in Somali poetry. In R. J. Hayward and I. M. Lewis (eds), *Voice And Power: The Culture of Language in North-East Africa* (pp. 83–128). London: School of Oriental and African Studies.

Barat, M., Constant, P. H., Mazaux, J. M., Caille, J. M., and Arne, L. (1978). Correlations anatomo-cliniques dans l'aphasie. Apport de la tomodensitometrie. *Revue Neurologique*, 134, 611–17.

Barton, G. E., Berwick, R., and Ristad, E. (1987). *Computational Complexity and Natural Language*. Cambridge, MA: MIT Press.

Barwise, J. (1989). *The Situation in Logic*. Stanford, CA: CSLI.

Barwise, J. and Cooper, R. (1981). Generalized quantifiers and natural language. *Linguistics and Philosophy*, 4, 159–219.

Barwise, J. and Perry, J. (1983). *Situations and Attitudes*. Cambridge, MA: MIT Press.

Barwise, J., Gawron, J. M., Plotkin, G., and Tutiya, S. (eds) (1991). *Situation Theory and Its Applications*, Vol. 2. Stanford: CSLI.

Basso, A., Lecours Roch, A., Moraschini, S., and Vanier, M. (1985). Anatomoclinical correlations of the aphasias as defined through computerized tomography: exceptions. *Brain and Language*, 26, 201–29.

Batali, J. (1998). Computational simulations of the emergence of grammar. In Hurford et al. (eds), pp. 405–26.

Bates, E. (1987). Language acquisition and language breakdown from a functionalist perspective. Presented at University of California Davis Conference on the Interaction of Form and Function in Language.

Bates, E. and MacWhinney, B. (1982). Functionalist approaches to grammar. In E. Wanner and L. Gleitman (eds), *Language Acquisition: The State of the Art* (pp. 173–218). Cambridge: Cambridge University Press.

Bates, E. and MacWhinney, B. (1987). Competition, variation, and language learning. In B. MacWhinney (ed.), *Mechanisms of Language Acquisition* (pp. 157–94). Hillsdale, NJ: Erlbaum.

Bates, E. and MacWhinney, B. (1989). Functionalism and the competition model. In B. MacWhinney and E. Bates (eds), *The Crosslinguistic Study of Sentence Processing* (pp. 3–76). Cambridge: Cambridge University Press.

Bauer, L. (1988). *Introducing Linguistic Morphology*. Edinburgh: Edinburgh University Press.

Baugh, J. (1983). *Black Street Speech: Its History, Structure and Survival*. Austin: University of Texas Press.

Bauman, R. (1984). *Verbal Art as Performance*. Prospect Heights, IL: Waveland Press.

BBC English Dictionary (1992). (Editor-in-chief, J. Sinclair). London: HarperCollins.

Bebout, L. (1985). An error analysis of misspellings made by learners of English as a first and as a second language. *Journal of Psycholinguistic Research*, 14:6, 569–93.

Beebe, L. M., Takahashi, T., and Uliss-Weltz, R. (1990). Pragmatic transfer in ESL, refusals. In R. Scarcella, E. Andersen, and S. Krashen (eds), *Developing Communicative Competence in a Second Language* (pp. 55–73). Rowley, MA: Newbury House.

Beeman, M. (in press). Coarse semantic coding and discourse comprehension. In M. Beeman and C. Chiarello (eds), *Getting It Right: The Cognitive Neuroscience of Right Hemisphere Language and Comprehension*. Hillsdale, NJ: Erlbaum.

Bell, A. (1978). Language samples. In J. H. Greenberg, C. A. Ferguson, and E. A. Moravcsik (eds), *Universals of Human Language*, Vol. 1. *Method and Theory* (pp. 123–56). Stanford, CA: Stanford University Press.

Bell, R. T. (1981). *An Introduction to Applied Linguistics: Approaches and Methods in Language Teaching*. New York: St Martin's.

Bellugi, U. and Klima, E. (1982). The acquisition of three morphological systems in American Sign Language. *Papers and Reports on Child Language Development*, 21, 1–35. Stanford, CA: Stanford University Press.

Bender, M. L. (1997). *The Nilo-Saharan Languages: A Comparative Essay*, 2nd edn. Munich: Lincom Europa.

Bendor-Samuel, J. (ed.) (1989). *The Niger-Congo Languages*. Lanham, MD: University Press of America.

Benedict, P. K. (1975). *Austro-Thai: Language and Culture*. New Haven, CT: HRAF Press.

Benson, D. F. and Patten, D. H. (1967). The use of radioactive isotopes in the localization of aphasia-producing lesions. *Cortex*, 3, 258–71.

Bergeron, B. S. (1990). What does the term whole language mean? Constructing a definition from the literature. *Journal of Reading Behavior*, 22, 301–29.

Bergman, M. L. and Kasper, G. (1993). Perception and performance in native and non-native apologizing. In G. Kasper and S. Blum-Kulka (eds), *Interlanguage Pragmatics* (pp. 82–107). New York: Oxford University Press.

Berk-Seligson, S. (1990). *The Bilingual Courtroom: Court Interpreters in the Judicial Process*. Chicago: University of Chicago Press.

Berndt, R., Mitchum, C., and Haendiges, A. (1996). Comprehension of reversible sentences in agrammatism: a meta-analysis. *Cognition*, 58, 289–308.

Bernstein, B. (1960). Language and social class. *British Journal of Sociology*, 11, 271–6.

Bernstein, B. (1971). *Class, Codes, and Control. Towards a Theory of Educational Transmission*. London: Routledge and Kegan Paul.

Bernstein, S. and Treiman, R. (in press). The special role of rimes in the processing of printed and spoken English. In R. Smyth (ed.), *Birdtracks in the Sand: A Festschrift for Bruce Derwing*. New York and Philadelphia: John Benjamins.

Berwick, R. C., Niyogi, P., and Jenkins, L. (1998). Language evolution and the minimalist program: the origins of syntax. In Hurford et al. (eds), pp. 320–40.

Bever, T. G. (1986). The aesthetic basis for cognitive structures. In M. Brand and R. Harnish (eds), *The Representation of Knowledge and Belief* (pp. 314–56). Tucson: University of Arizona Press.

Bialystok, E. (1993). Metalinguistic dimensions of bilingual language proficiency. In E. Bialystok (ed.), *Language Processing in Bilingual Children* (pp. 113–40). Cambridge: Cambridge University Press.

Biber, D., Conrad, S., and Reppen, R. (1998). *Corpus Linguistics: Investigating Language Structure and Use*. Cambridge: Cambridge University Press.

Bibliander (Buchmann), T. (1548). *De ratione communi omnium, linguarum et literarum commentarius*. Zurich: C. Froschauer.

Bickerton, D. (1981). *Roots of Language*. Ann Arbor, MI: Karoma.

Bickerton, D. (1990). *Language and Species*. Chicago: University of Chicago Press.

Bickerton, D. (1992). The sociohistorical matrix of creolization. *Journal of Pidgin and Creole Languages*, 7, 307–18.

Bickerton, D. (1995). *Language and Human Behavior*. Seattle: University of Washington Press.

Bird, S. and Ellison, T. M. (1994). One-level phonology: autosegmental representations and rules as finite automata. *Computational Linguistics*, 20:1, 55–90.

Birdsong, D. (1989). *Metalinguistic Performance and Interlanguage Competence*. New York: Springer.

Birdsong, D. (1992). Ultimate attainment in second language acquisition. *Language*, 68, 706–55.

Blachman, B. (1987). An alternative classroom reading program for learning disabled and other low-achieving children. In R. F. Bowler (ed.), *Intimacy with Language: A Forgotten Basic in Teacher Education* (pp. 49–55). Baltimore, MD: Orton Dyslexia Society.

Blakemore, D. (1987). *Semantic Constraints on Relevance*. Oxford: Blackwell.

Blakemore, D. (1989). Denial and contrast: a relevance theoretic analysis of *but*. *Linguistics and Philosophy*, 12, 15–38.

Blakemore, D. (1992). *Understanding Utterances*. Oxford: Blackwell.

Bley-Vroman, R. W. (1989). The logical problem of second language learning. In S. Gass and J. Schachter (eds), *Linguistic Perspectives on Second Language Acquisition* (pp. 41–68). Cambridge: Cambridge University Press.

Bley-Vroman, R. W., Felix, S., and Ioup, G. L. (1988). The accessibility of Universal Grammar in adult language learning. *Second Language Research*, 4:1, 1–32.

Blom, J. P. and Gumperz, J. J. (1972). Social meaning in linguistic structures: code-switching in Norway. In J. J. Gumperz and D. Hymes (eds), *Directions in Sociolinguistics* (pp. 407–35). New York: Holt, Rinehart, and Winston.

Bloomfield, L. (1933). *Language*. New York: Holt, Rinehart, and Winston.

Blum-Kulka, S., House, J., and Kasper, G. (eds) (1989). *Cross-cultural Pragmatics: Requests and Apologies*. Norwood, NJ: Ablex.

Blumstein, S. E., Milberg, W., and Shrier, R. (1982). Semantic processing in aphasia: evidence from an auditory lexical decision task. *Brain and Language*, 17, 301–15.

Boas, F. (1911). Introduction. In F. Boas (ed.), *Handbook of American Indian Languages*, Vol. 1. Washington: Bureau of American Ethnology.

Bogen, J. and Bogen, G. (1976). Wernicke's region: where is it? *Annals of the New York Academy of Sciences*, 280, 834–43.

Bolinger, D. (1979). Pronouns in discourse. In T. Givón (ed.), *Syntax and Semantics*, Vol. 10. *Discourse and Syntax* (pp. 289–310). New York: Academic Press.

Bondarko, A. V. (1991). *Functional Grammar: A Field Approach*. Amsterdam and Philadelphia: John Benjamins.

Bongaerts, T., Planken, B., and Schils, E. (1997). Age and ultimate attainment in the pronunciation of a foreign language. *Second Language Research*, 19, 447–65.

Bongaerts, T., Planken, B., van Summeren, C., and Schils, E. (1995). Can late starters attain a native accent in a foreign language? A test of the Critical Period Hypothesis. In D. Singleton and Z. Lengyel (eds), *The Age Factor in Second Language Acquisition* (pp. 30–50). Clevedon: Multilingual Matters.

Booij, G. (1994). Against split morphology. In G. Booij and J. van Marle (eds), *Yearbook of Morphology 1993* (pp. 27–49). Dordrecht: Kluwer.

Bopp, F. (1816). *Ueber das Conjugationssystem der Sanskritsprache in Vergleichung mit jenem der greichischen, lateinischen, persichen und germanischen Sprache, nebst Episoden des Ramajan und Mahabharat in genauen, metrischen bersetzungen aus dem Originaltexte und einigen Abschnitten aus den Veda's*. Frankfurt am Main: Andreische Buchhandlung.

Bopp, F. (1833–52). *Vergleichende Grammatik des Sanskrit, Zend, Armenischen, Griechischen, Lateinischen, Litauischen, Altslavischen, Cothischen und Deutschen*, 6 vols. Berlin: Ferdinand Dummler.

Borer, H. (1996). Access to UG: the real issues. *Behavioral and Brain Sciences*, 19, 718–20.

Borst, A. (1959). *Der Turmbau von Babel*. Stuttgart: Hiersemann.

Bourdieu, P. (1977). *Outline of a Theory of Practice*. Cambridge: Cambridge University Press.

Bourdieu, P. (1991). *Language and Symbolic Power*. London: Polity Press.

Bowker, L. (1994). Applied terminology: a state-of-the-art report. *Terminology*, 1:1, 181–92.

Bradshaw, J. and Rogers, L. (1992). *The Evolution of Lateral Asymmetries, Language, Tool Use, and Intellect*. San Diego: Academic Press.

Breen, J. G. (1981). Margany and Gunya. In R. M. W. Dixon and B. J. Blake (eds), *Handbook of Australian Languages*, Vol. 2 (pp. 274–393). *Wargamay, the Mpakwithi Dialect of Anguthimri, Watjarri, Margany and Gunya Tasmanian*. Canberra: Australian National University Press.

Brentari, D. (1995). Sign language phonology. In J. Goldsmith (ed.), *The Handbook of Phonological Theory* (pp. 615–39). Cambridge, MA: Blackwell.

Bresnan, J. (1978). A realistic transformational grammar. In M. Halle, J. Bresnan, and G. A. Miller (eds), *Linguistic Theory and Psychological Reality* (pp. 1–59). Cambridge, MA: MIT Press.

Bresnan, J. (in press). *Lexical Functional Syntax*. Oxford: Blackwell.

Breva-Claramonte, M. (1983). Sanctius' theory of language: a contribution to the history of renaissance linguistics. *Studies in the History of Linguistics*, 27. Amsterdam: John Benjamins.

Bridgham, F. (1996). *The Friendly German–English Dictionary. A Guide to German Language, Culture and Society through Faux Amis, Literary Illustration and Other Diversions*. London: Libris.

Brinton, D., Snow, M. A., and Wesche, M. B. (1989). *Content-based Second Language Instruction*. Boston: Heinle and Heinle.

Broadwell, G. A. (1990). *Extending the binding theory: a Muskogean case study*. Ph.D. dissertation, UCLA.

Broca, P. (1861). Remarques sur le siege de la faculté de la parole articulée, suives d'une observation d'aphemie (perte de parole). *Bulletin de la Société d'Anatomie*, 36, 330–57.

Brody, J. (1986). Repetition as a rhetorical and conversational device in Tojolabal (Mayan). *International Journal of American Linguistics*, 52, 255–74.

Broselow, E. (1992). Non-obvious transfer: on predicting epenthesis. In S. Gass and L. Selinker (eds), *Language Transfer in Language Learning* (pp. 71–86). Amsterdam: John Benjamins.

Brown, G. D. A. and Hulme, C. (1992). Cognitive processing and second language processing: the role of short term memory. In R. J. Harris (ed.), *Cognitive Processing in Bilinguals* (pp. 105–21). Amsterdam: Elsevier.

Brown, J. (1972). *Aphasia, Apraxia and Agnosia: Clinical and Theoretical Aspects*. Springfield, IL: Thomas.

Brown, P. and Levinson, S. (1978). Universals in language usage: politeness phenomena. In E. Goody (ed.), *Questions and Politeness. Strategies in Social Interaction* (pp. 56–289). Cambridge: Cambridge University Press.

Brown, R. (1972). *A First Language: The Early Stages*. Cambridge, MA: Harvard University Press.

Brown, R. and Gilman, A. (1960). The pronouns of power and solidarity (pp. 253–76). In T. Sebeok (ed.), *Style in Language*. New York: Wiley.

Brown, T. and Haynes, M. (1985). Literacy background and reading development in a second language. In T. H. Carr (ed.), *The Development of Reading Skills*. New York: Academic Press.

Brownell, H. H., Carroll, J., Rehak, A., et al. (1989). The effects of right hemisphere brain damage on the apprehension of linguistic and affective cues in conversations. *Academy of Aphasia*, October.

Brownell, H. H. and Gardner, H. (1988). Neuropsychological insights into humour. In J. Durent and J. Miller (eds), *Laughing Matters* (pp. 17–34). Essex: Longman Scientific.

Brownell, H. H., Potter, H. H., Bihrie, A. M., and Gardner, H. (1986). Inference deficits in right brain-damaged patients. *Brain and Language*, 27, 310–21.

Brumfit, C. (1997). How applied linguistics is the same as any other science. *International Journal of Applied Linguistics*, 7, 86–94.

Brumfit, C. and Johnson, K. (1979). *The Communicative Approach to Language Teaching*. Oxford: Oxford University Press.

Bub, D., Black, S., Hampson, E., and Kertesz, A. (1988). Semantic encoding of pictures and words: Some neuropsychological observations. *Cognitive Neuropsychology*, 5:1, 27–66.

Bub, D., Cancelliere, A., and Kertesz, A. (1985). Whole-word and analytic translation of spelling-to-sound in a non-semantic reader. In M. Coltheart, J. C. Marshall, and K. E. Patterson (eds), *Surface Dyslexia* (pp. 15–34). London: Erlbaum.

Buckingham, T. and Eskey, D. E. (1980). Toward a definition of applied linguistics. In R. Kaplan (ed.), *On the Scope of Applied Linguistics* (pp. 1–3). Rowley, MA: Newbury House.

Burling, R. (1959). Language development of a Garo and English speaking child. *Word*, 15, 45–68.

Bursill-Hall, G. L. (1995). Linguistics in the later middle ages. In E. F. K. Koerner and R. E. Asher (eds), *Concise History of the Language Sciences: From the Sumerians to the Cognitivists* (pp. 130–7). Oxford: Pergamon.

Burstall, G., Jamieson, M., Cohen, S., and Hargreaves, M. (1974). *Primary French in the Balance*. Windsor: NFER Publishing.

Buse, J. E. (1966). Number in Rarotongan Maori. In C. E. Bazell, J. C. Catford, M. A. K. Halliday, and R. H. Robins (eds), *In Memory of J. R. Firth*. London: Longmans Green.

Butters, R. (1980). Narrative *go* "say." *American Speech*, 55, 304–7.

Butterworth, B., Campbell, R., and Howard, D. (1986). The uses of short-term memory: a case study. *Quarterly Journal of Experimental Psychology*, 38, 705–37.

Bybee, J. L. (1985). *Morphology: A Study into the Relation between Meaning and Form*. Amsterdam: John Benjamins.

Bybee, J. L., Perkins, R. D., and Pagliuca, W. (1994). *The Evolution of Grammar: Tense, Aspect and Modality in the Languages of the World*. Chicago: University of Chicago Press.

Byrne, B. (1998). *The Foundation of Literacy: The Child's Acquisition of the Alphabetic Principle*. Hove: Psychology Press.

Byrne, R. W. and Whiten, A. (eds) (1988). *Machiavellian Intelligence*. Oxford: Clarendon Press.

Calvet, L.-J. (1981). *Les langues véhiculaires*. Paris: Presses Universitaires de France.

Calvet, L.-J. (1987). *La guerre des langues et les politiques linguistiques*. Paris: Payot.

Calvin, W. H. (1993). The unitary hypothesis: a common neural circuitry for novel manipulations, language, plan-ahead, and throwing? In K. R. Gibson and T. Ingold (eds), *Tools, Language and Cognition in Human Evolution* (pp. 230–50). Cambridge: Cambridge University Press.

Calvin, W. H. and Ojemann, G. A. (1994). *Conversations with Neil's Brain: The Neural Nature of Thought and Language*. Reading, MA: Addison-Wesley.

Camarata, S. and Schwartz, R. (1985). Production of action words and object words: evidence for a relationship between semantics and phonology. *Journal of Speech and Hearing Research*, 28, 323–30.

Cambridge International Dictionary of English (1995). (Editor-in-chief, P. Procter). Cambridge: Cambridge University Press.

Campbell, L. (1997). *American Indian Linguistics: The Linguistic History of Native America*. New York: Oxford University Press.

Campbell, L. (1998). *Historical Linguistics*. Edinburgh: Edinburgh University Press.

Campbell, L. (1999a). *Historical Linguistics: An Introduction*. Cambridge, MA: MIT Press.

Campbell, L. (1999b). What's wrong with grammaticalization? To appear in a special issue of *Language Sciences* (L. Campbell, ed.).

Cann, R. L., Rickards, O., and Koji Lum, J. (1994). Mitochondrial DNA and human evolution: our one lucky mother. In M. H. Nitecki and D. V. Nitecki (eds), *Origins of Anatomically Modern Humans* (pp. 135–48). New York: Plenum.

Cann, R. L., Stoneking, M., and Wilson, A. L. (1987). Mitochondrial DNA and human evolution. *Nature*, 325, 31–6.

Caplan, D. (1987). Discrimination of normal and aphasic subjects on a test of syntactic comprehension. *Neuropsychologia*, 25, 173–84.

Caplan, D. (1992). *Language: Structure, Processing, and Disorders*. Cambridge, MA: MIT Press.

Caplan, D. and Futter, C. (1986). Assignment of thematic roles to nouns in sentence comprehension by an agrammatic patient. *Brain and Language*, 27, 117–34.

Caplan, D. and Hildebrandt, N. (1988). *Disordered Syntactic Comprehension*. Cambridge, MA: MIT Press.

Caplan, D. and Waters, G. (1990). Short-term memory and language comprehension: a critical review of the neuropsychological literature. In T. Shallice and G. Vallar (eds), *The Neuropsychology of Short-term Memory* (pp. 337–89). Cambridge: Cambridge University Press.

Caplan, D., Alpert, N., and Waters, G. (1998). Effects of syntactic structure and propositional number on patterns of regional blood flow. *Cognitive Neuropsychology*, 10, 541–52.

Caplan, D., Baker, C., and Dehaut, F. (1985). Syntactic determinants of sentence comprehension in aphasia. *Cognition*, 21, 117–75.

Caplan, D., Hildebrandt, N., and Makris, N. (1996). Location of lesions in stroke patients with deficits in syntactic processing in sentence comprehension. *Brain*, 119, 933–49.

Caplan, D. and Waters, G. (in press). Verbal working memory and sentence comprehension. *Behavioral and Brain Sciences*, 69.

Caplan, D., Waters, G. S., and Hildebrandt, N. (1997). Syntactic determinants of sentence comprehension in aphasic patients in sentence-picture matching tests. *Journal of Speech and Hearing Research*, 40, 542–55.

Cappa, S., Cavalotti, G., Guidotti, N., Papagno, C., and Vignolo, L. (1983). Subcortical aphasia: two clinical CT scan correlation studies. *Cortex*, 19, 227–41.

Capps, L. and Ochs, E. (1995). *Constructing Panic: The Discourse of Agoraphobia*. Cambridge, MA: Harvard University Press.

Caramazza, A., Hillis, A. E., Rapp, B. C., and Romani, C. (1990). The multiple semantics hypothesis: multiple confusions? *Cognitive Neuropsychology*, 7:3, 161–89.

Caramazza, A. and Zurif, E. B. (1976). Dissociation of algorithmic and heuristic processes in language comprehension: evidence from aphasia. *Brain and Language*, 3, 572–82.

Carberry, S. (1990). *Plan Recognition in Natural Language Dialogue*. Cambridge, MA: MIT Press.

Carnap, R. (1947). *Meaning and Necessity*. Chicago: University of Chicago Press.

Carpenter, M. B. (1983). *Human Neuro-anatomy*. Baltimore: Williams and Williams.

Carpenter, R. (1992). *The Logic of Typed Feature Structures*. New York: Cambridge University Press.

Carstairs-McCarthy, A. (1998). Synonymy avoidance, phonology and the origin of syntax. In Hurford et al. (eds), pp. 279–96.

Carstairs-McCarthy, A. (1999). *The Origins of Complex Language: An Inquiry into the Evolutionary Beginnings of Sentences, Syllables and Truth*. Oxford: Oxford University Press.

Carston, R. (1988). Implicature, explicature and truth-theoretic semantics. In R. Kempson (ed.), *Mental Representation: The Interface between Language and Reality* (pp. 155–82). Cambridge: Cambridge University Press.

Carston, R. (1998). Pragmatics and the explicit implicit distinction. Ph.D. dissertation, University College London.

Casad, E. H. (1974). *Dialect Intelligibility Testing*. Norman, OK: Summer Institute of Linguistics.

Caskey-Sirmons, L. A. and Hickerson, N. (1977). Semantic shift and bilingualism: variation in the colour terms of five languages. *Anthropological Linguistics*, 19:8, 358–67.

Catford, J. C. (1977). *Fundamental Problems in Phonetics*. Bloomington: Edinburgh University Press and Indiana University Press.

Catford, J. C. (1988). *A Practical Introduction to Phonetics*. Oxford: Clarendon Press.

Catford, J. C. (1994). Articulatory phonetics. In R. E. Asher and J. M. Y. Simpson (eds), *The Encyclopedia of Language and Linguistics*, Vol. 6 (pp. 3058–70). Oxford: Pergamon Press.

Catullus (1969). *Gai Valeri Catulli Veronensis Liber*. Tr. C. and L. Zukovsky. London: Cape Goliard.

Cavalli-Sforza, L. L. and Cavalli-Sforza, F. (1995). *The Great Human Diasporas: The History of Diversity and Evolution*. Reading, MA: Addison-Wesley.

Cazden, C. (1988). *Classroom Discourse: The Language of Teaching and Learning*. Portsmouth, NH: Heinemann.

Cazden, C. B. (1972). *Child Language and Education*. New York: Holt, Rinehart, and Winston.

Chafe, W. (1972). *Meaning and the Structure of Language*. Chicago: University of Chicago Press.

Chafe, W. (ed.) (1980). *The Pear Stories: Cognitive, Cultural, and Linguistic Aspects of Narrative Production*. Norwood, NJ: Ablex.

Chaika, E. (1989). *Language: The Social Mirror*, 2nd edn. New York: HarperCollins.

Chambers, J. (1992). Linguistic correlates of gender and sex. *English World-Wide*, 13, 173–218.

Chambers, J. (1994). *Sociolinguistic Theory*. Oxford: Blackwell.

Chana, U. and Romaine, S. (1984). Evaluative reactions to Panjabi / English code-switching. *Journal of Multilingual and Multicultural Development*, 6, 447–73.

Chao, Y. R. (1955). Notes on Chinese grammar and logic. *Philosophy East and West*, 5, 13–31.

Charrow, V. R. and Charrow, R. P. (1979). Making legal language understandable: a psycholinguistic study of jury instructions. *Columbia Law Review*, 79, 1306–74.

Chen, M. Y. (1979). Metrical structure: evidence from Chinese poetry. *Linguistic Inquiry*, 10:3, 371–420.

Cheney, D. L. and Seyfarth, R. M. (1990). *How Monkeys See the World: Inside the Mind of Another Species*. Chicago: University of Chicago Press.

Cheshire, J. (1982). *Variation in an English Dialect: A Sociolinguistic Study*. Cambridge: Cambridge University Press.

Chiarello, C., Burgess, C., Richards, L., and Pollock, A. (1990). Semantic and associative priming in the cerebral hemispheres: some words do, some words don't . . . sometimes, some places. *Brain and Language*, 38, 75–104.

Chierchia, G. (1992). Anaphora and dynamic binding. *Linguistics and Philosophy*, 15, 111–83.

Chierchia, G. (1995). *Dynamics of Meaning*. Chicago: University of Chicago Press.

Chierchia, G. and McConnell-Ginet, S. (1990). *Meaning and Grammar*. Cambridge, MA: MIT Press.

Chikamatsu, N. (1996). The effects of L1 orthography on L2 word recognition. *Studies in Second Language Acquisition*, 18, 403–32.

Chitiri, H.-F. and Willows, D. M. (1997). Bilingual word recognition in English and Greek. *Applied Psycholinguistics*, 18, 139–56.

Chomsky, N. (1957). *Syntactic Structures*. The Hague: Mouton.

Chomsky, N. (1959). Review of *Verbal Behavior*, by B. F. Skinner. *Language*, 35, 25–37.

Chomsky, N. (1964). *Aspects of the Theory of Syntax*. Cambridge, MA: MIT Press.

Chomsky, N. (1970). Remarks on nominalization. In R. A. Jacobs and P. S. Rosenbaum (eds), *Readings in English Transformational Grammar* (pp. 184–221). Waltham, MA: Ginn-Blaisdell.

Chomsky, N. (1973). *Conditions on Transformations*. New York: Holt, Rinehart, and Winston.

Chomsky, N. (1975a). *Logical Structure of Linguistic Theory*. Chicago: University of Chicago Press.

Chomsky, N. (1975b). *Reflections on Language*. New York: Pantheon.

Chomsky, N. (1977). *On Wh-movement*. New York: Academic Press.

Chomsky, N. (1980a). On cognitive structures and their development. In M. Piattelli-Palmarini (ed.), *Language and Learning: The Debate between Jean Piaget and Noam Chomsky* (pp. 35–52). London: Routledge and Kegan Paul.

Chomsky, N. (1980b). *Rules and Representations*. New York: Columbia University Press.

Chomsky, N. (1981). *Lectures on Government and Binding*. Dordrecht: Foris.

Chomsky, N. (1988). *Language and Problems of Knowledge: The Managua Lectures*. Cambridge, MA: MIT Press.

Chomsky, N. (1991). Linguistics and cognitive science: problems and mysteries. In A. Kasher (ed.), *The Chomskyan Turn* (pp. 26–53). Oxford: Blackwell.

Chomsky, N. (1995a). *Barriers*. Cambridge, MA: MIT Press.

Chomsky, N. (1995b). *The Minimalist Program*. Cambridge, MA: MIT Press.

Chomsky, N. and Halle, M. (1968). *The Sound Pattern of English*. New York: Harper and Row.

Chomsky, N. and Lasnik, H. (1977). Filters and control. *Linguistic Inquiry*. 11, 1–46.

Christie, F. (ed.) (1990). *Literacy for a Changing World*. Melbourne: Australian Council for Educational Research.

Clark, H. H. and Clark, E. V. (1977). *Psychology and Language*. New York: Harcourt Brace Jovanovich.

Clark, J. and Yallop, C. (1995). *An Introduction to Phonetics and Phonology*, 2nd edn. Oxford: Blackwell.

Clarke, M. A. (1994). The dysfunctions of the theory / practice discourse. *TESOL Quarterly*, 28, 9–26.

Clay, J. W. (1990). Indigenous peoples: the miner's canary for the twentieth century. In S. Head and R. Heinzman (eds), *Lessons of the Rainforest* (ch. 8). San Francisco: Sierra Club.

Clements, G. N. and Hume, E. (1995). The internal organization of speech sounds. In J. Goldsmith (ed.), *The Handbook of Phonological Theory* (pp. 245–306). Oxford: Blackwell.

Coates, J. and Cameron, D. (eds) (1988). *Women in their Speech Communities: New Perspectives on Language and Sex*. London and New York: Longman.

Cohen, A. (1990). *Language Learning: Insights for Learners, Teachers, and Researchers*. New York: Newbury House / Harper and Row.

Cohen, L. J. (1971). The logical particles of natural language. In Y. Bar-Hillel (ed.), *Pragmatics of Natural Language* (pp. 50–68). Dordrecht: Reidel.

Cohen, M. (1958). *La grande invention de l'écriture et son evolution*, 3 vols. Paris: Imprimerie Nationale.

Cohen, P. R. and Perrault, C. R. (1979). Elements of a plan-based theory of speech acts. *Cognitive Science*, 3, 177–212.

Collinge, N. E. (1985). *The Laws of Indo-European*. Amsterdam: John Benjamins.

Coltheart, M., Curtis, B., Atkins, P., and Haller, M. (1993). Models of reading aloud: dual-route and parallel-distributed-processing approaches. *Psychological Review*, 100, 589–608.

Comrie, B. (1978). Ergativity. In W. Lehmann (ed.), *Syntactic Typology* (pp. 329–94). Austin, TX: University of Texas Press.

Comrie, B. (1979). Russian. In T. Shopen (ed.), *Languages and their Status* (pp. 91–150). Cambridge, MA: Winthrop.

Comrie, B. (1989). Some general properties of reference-tracking systems. In D. Arnold, M. Atkinson, J. Durand, C. Grover, and L. Sadler (eds), *Essays on Grammatical Theory and Universal Grammar* (pp. 37–51). Oxford: Clarendon.

Comrie, B. (1994). Towards a typology of reference-tracking devices. Paper presented to the International Symposium on Language Typology, University of Tsukuba, January.

Comrie, B. and Corbett, G. (eds) (1993). *The Slavonic Languages*. London: Routledge.

Connor, U. (1996). *Contrastive Rhetoric: Cross-Cultural Aspects of Second-Language Writing*. Cambridge: Cambridge University Press.

Contini-Morava, E. (1991). Deictic explicitness and event continuity in Swahili discourse. *Lingua*, 83, 277–318.

Cook, V. J. (1969). The analogy between first and second language learning. *IRAL*, 7:3, 207–16.

Cook, V. J. (1973). The comparison of language development in native children and foreign adults. *IRAL*, 11:1, 13–28.

Cook, V. J. (1981). Some uses for second language learning research. *Annals of the New York Academy of Sciences*, 379, 251–8.

Cook, V. J. (1985a). Chomsky's Universal Grammar and second language learning. *Applied Linguistics*, 6, 1–8.

Cook, V. J. (1985b). Language functions, social factors, and second language teaching. *IRAL*, 13:3, 177–96.

Cook, V. J. (1986). Experimental approaches applied to two areas of second language learning research: age and listening-based teaching methods. In V. J. Cook (ed.), *Experimental Approaches to Second Language Learning* (pp. 23–37). Oxford: Pergamon.

Cook, V. J. (1990). Timed comprehension of binding in advanced learners of English. *Language Learning*, 40:4, 557–99.

Cook, V. J. (1991). The poverty-of-the-stimulus argument and multi-competence. *Second Language Research*, 7:2, 103–17.

Cook, V. J. (1993). *Linguistics and Second Language Acquisition*. Basingstoke: Macmillan.

Cook, V. J. (1994). The metaphor of access to Universal Grammar. In N. Ellis (ed.), *Implicit Learning and Language* (pp. 477–502). London: Academic Press.

Cook, V. J. (1996). *Second Language Learning and Language Teaching*, 2nd edn. London: Edward Arnold.

Cook, V. J. (1997a). The consequences of bilingualism for cognitive processing. In de Groot and Kroll (eds), pp. 279–300.

Cook, V. J. (1997b). *Inside Language*. London: Edward Arnold.

Cook, V. J. (1997c). Monolingual bias in second language acquisition research. *Revista Canaria de Estudios Ingleses*, 34, 35–49.

Cook, V. J. (1997d). L2 learners and English spelling. *Journal of Multicultural and Multiracial Development*.

Cook, V. J. and Newson, M. (1996). *Chomsky's Universal Grammar: An Introduction*, 2nd edn. Oxford: Blackwell.

Cooper, R. (1979). The interpretation of pronouns. In F. Heny and H. Schnelle (eds), *Syntax and Semantics*, Vol. 10 (pp. 61–92). New York: Academic Press.

Cooper, R. (1983). *Quantification and Syntactic Theory*. Dordrecht: Reidel.

Cooper, R. (1989). *Language Planning and Social Change*. Cambridge: Cambridge University Press.

Cooper, R. (1996). The role of situations in generalized quantifiers. In Lappin (ed.), pp. 65–86.

Cooper, R., Mulai, K. and Perry, J. (eds) (1990). *Situation Theory and Its Applications*, Vol. 1. Stanford: CSLI.

Cooper, R., Crouch, R., Van Eijk, J., Fox, C., Van Genabith, J., Jaspers, J., Kamp, H., Pinkal, H., Poesio, M., Pulman, S., and Vestre, E. (1994). *The State of the Art in Computational Semantics: Evaluating the Descriptive Capabilities of Semantic Theories, FraCas Deliverable D9*. Edinburgh: Centre for Cognitive Science, University of Edinburgh.

Cope, B. and Kalantzis, M. (1993). *The Powers of Literacy: A Genre Approach to Teaching Writing*. Pittsburgh: University of Pittsburgh Press.

Copestake A., Flickinger, D., and Sag, I. (1997). Minimal recursion semantics: an introduction. MS, Stanford University.

Coppieters, R. (1987). Competence differences between native and near-native speakers. *Language*, 63:3, 545–73.

Corballis, M. (1991). *The Lopsided Ape*. New York: Oxford University Press.

Corbett, G. G. and Norman, F. (1993). Network morphology. *Journal of Linguistics*, 29, 113–42.

Corder, S. P. (1967). The significance of learners' errors. *IRAL*, 5:4, 161–70.

Corder, S. P. (1971). Idiosyncratic errors and error analysis. *IRAL*, 9:2, 147–59.

Corder, S. P. (1973). *Introducing Applied Linguistics*. Harmondsworth: Penguin.

Corina, D. (1998). Studies of neural processing in deaf signers: toward a neurocognitive model of language processing in the deaf. *Journal of Deaf Studies and Deaf Education*, 3:1.

Corina, D. and Sandler, W. (1993). Phonological structure in sign language. *Phonology*, 10:2, 165–208.

Coulmas, F. (1989). *The Writing Systems of the World*. Oxford: Blackwell.

Coulmas, F. (1992). *Language and Economy*. Oxford: Blackwell.

Coulmas, F. (1996a). *The Blackwell Encyclopedia of Writing Systems*. Oxford: Blackwell.

Coulmas, F. (1996b). *Gewählte Worte. Über Sprache als Wille und Bekenntnis*. Frankfurt and New York: Campus.

Coulmas, F. (ed.) (1997). *The Handbook of Sociolinguistics*. Oxford: Blackwell.

Couper-Kuhlen, E. and Selting, M. (eds) (1996). *Prosody in Conversation*. Cambridge: Cambridge University Press.

Coupland, N. (1997). Language, ageing, and ageism: a project for applied linguistics? *International Journal of Applied Linguistics*, 7, 26–48.

Coupland, N. and Jaworski, A. (eds) (1997). *Sociolinguistics: A Reader and Coursebook*. London: Macmillan.

Crago, M. B. (1992). Communicative interaction and second language acquisition: an Inuit example. *TESOL Quarterly*, 26, 487–505.

Crochemore, M. and Rytter, W. (1994). *Text Algorithms*. Oxford and New York: Oxford University Press.

Croft, W. (1990). *Typology and Universals*. Cambridge: Cambridge University Press.

Croft, W. (1995). Autonomy and functionalist linguistics. *Language*, 71, 490–532.

Crosson, B. (1985). Subcortical functions in language: a working model. *Brain and Language*, 25, 257–92.

Crouch, R. (1995). Ellipsis and quantification: a substitutional approach. *Proceedings of the Seventh European Chapter of the Association of Computational Linguistics* (pp. 223–6). Dublin.

Cruse, D. A. (1986). *Lexical Semantics*. Cambridge: Cambridge University Press.

Crystal, D. (1981). *Directions in Applied Linguistics*. London: Academic Press.

Crystal, D. (1981/9). *Clinical Linguistics*. Vienna: Springer-Verlag and London: Whurr.

Crystal, D. (1982/92). *Profiling Linguistic Disability*, 2nd edn. London: Edward Arnold and London: Whurr.

Crystal, D. (1987). Towards a "bucket" theory of language disability: taking account of interaction between linguistic levels. *Clinical Linguistics and Phonetics*, 1, 7–22.

Crystal, D. and Varley, R. (1998). *Introduction to Language Pathology*, 4th edn. London: Whurr.

Crystal, D., Fletcher, P., and Garman, M. (1976/89). *The Grammatical Analysis of Language Disability*, 2nd edn. London: Edward Arnold and London: Whurr.

Cumming, A. (1998). Issues and prospects: introduction to the 50th Jubilee Special Issue. *Language Learning*, 48, 453–63.

Cumming, S. (1995). Agent position in the Sejarah Melayu. In P. Downing and M. Noonan (eds), *Word Order in Discourse* (pp. 51–83). Amsterdam: John Benjamins.

Cummins, J. (1986). Empowering minority students: a framework for intervention. *Harvard Educational Review*, 56, 18–36.

Curtiss, S. (1977). *Genie: A Psycholinguistic Study of a Modern-day Wild Child*. New York: Academic Press.

Dalrymple, M., Shieber, S., and Pereira, F. (1991). Ellipsis and higher-order unification. *Linguistics and Philosophy*, 14, 399–452.

Damasio, A. (1989). Time-locked multiregional retroactivation: a systems-level proposal for the neural substrates of recall and recognition. *Cognition*, 33, 25–62.

Damasio, H. and Damasio, A. (1980). The anatomical basis of conduction aphasia. *Brain*, 103, 337–50.

Damasio, A., Damasio, H., Rizzo, M., Varney, N., and Gersch, F. (1982). Aphasia with nonhemorrhagic lesions in the basal ganglia and internal capsule. *Archives of Neurology*, 39, 15–20.

Danes, F. (1974). Functional sentence perspective and the organization of the text. In F. Danes (ed.), *Papers on Functional Sentence Perspective* (pp. 106–28). The Hague: Mouton.

d'Anglejan, A. and Tucker, G. R. (1975). The acquisition of complex English structures by adult learners. *Language Learning*, 15:2, 281–93.

Daniels, P. T. (1988). The syllabic origin of writing and the segmental origin of the alphabet. Paper presented at the Milwaukee Symposium on Linguistics and Literacy. In P. Downing, S. D. Lima, and M. Noonan (eds), *The Linguistics of Literacy: Typological Studies in Language*, Vol. 21 (pp. 83–110). Amsterdam: John Benjamins, 1992.

Daniels, P. T. (1994). Edward Hincks's decipherment of Mesopotamian cuneiform. In K. J. Cathcart (ed.), *The Edward Hincks Bicentenary Lectures* (pp. 30–57). Dublin: University College, Dept of Near Eastern Studies.

Daniels, P. T. (2000). Review article on popular books on writing. *Sino-Platonic Papers*, to appear.

Daniels, P. T. and Bright, W. (eds) (1996). *The World's Writing Systems*. New York: Oxford University Press.

Davidson, D. (1967a). The logical form of action sentences. In N. Rescher (ed.), *The Logic of Decision and Action* (pp. 81–120). Pittsburgh, PA: University of Pittsburgh Press.

Davidson, D. (1967b). Truth and meaning. *Synthese*, 17, 304–23.

Davidson, D. (1984). *Inquiries into Truth and Interpretation*. Oxford: Clarendon Press.

Davies, A. M. (1986). Karl Brugmann and late nineteenth-century linguistics. In T. Bynon and F. R. Palmer (eds), *Studies in the History of Western Linguistics, in Honour of R. H. Robins* (pp. 150–71). Cambridge: Cambridge University Press.

Davies, A. M. (1992). Comparative-historical linguistics. In W. Bright (ed.), *International Encyclopedia of Linguistics*, Vol. 2 (pp. 159–63). Oxford: Oxford University Press.

Davies, W. D. (1996). Morphological uniformity and the null subject parameter in adult SLA. *Studies in Second Language Acquisition*, 18, 475–93.

Davis, S. (ed.) (1991). *Pragmatics: A Reader*. Oxford: Oxford University Press.

de Beaugrande, R. (1997). The story of discourse analysis. In van Dijk (ed.), Vol. 1, pp. 35–62.

de Beaugrande, R. and Dressler, W. U. (1981). *Introduction to Text Linguistics*. London: Longman.

de Groot, A. (1993). Word type effects in bilingual processing tasks: support for a mixed representational system. In Schreuder and Weltens (eds), pp. 27–52.

de Groot, A. and Kroll, J. F. (eds) (1997). *Tutorials in Bilingualism: Psycholinguistic Perspectives*. Hillsdale: Erlbaum.

De Guignes, J. (1770). *Histoire de l'Academie des Inscriptions*. Paris.

de Houwer, A. (1990). *The Acquisition of Two Languages from Birth: A Case Study*. Cambridge: Cambridge University Press.

Deacon, T. W. (1997). *The Symbolic Species: The Coevolution of Language and the Brain*. New York: W. W. Norton.

DeFrancis, J. (1989). *Visible Speech: The Diverse Oneness of Writing Systems*. Honolulu: University of Hawaii Press.

Dejerine, J. (1892). Contribution a l'étude anatomoclinique et clinique des differentes variétés de cecite verbale. *Memoires de la Société de Biologie*, 4, 61–90.

Dekker, P. (1996). Reference and representation. MS, University of Amsterdam.

Delbruck, B. (1880). *Einleitung in das Sprachstudium: ein Beitrag zur Geschichte und Methodik der Vergleichenden Sprachforschung*. Leipzig: Breitkopf and Härtel.

Denes, P. B. and Pinson, E. N. (1973). *The Speech Chain*. New York: Anchor Books.

Derbyshire, D. C. and Pullum, G. K. (1981). Object initial languages. *International Journal of American Linguistics*, 47, 192–214.

Derwing, B. L. (1992). Orthographic aspects of linguistic competence. In P. Downing, S. D. Lima, and M. P. Noonan (eds), *The Linguistics of Literacy* (pp. 193–211). Amsterdam and Philadelphia: John Benjamins.

Devine, A. M. and Stephens, L. D. (1984). *Language and Metre: Resolution, Porson's Bridge, and their Prosodic Basis*. Chico: Scholar's Press.

Di Pietro, R. J. (ed.) (1982). *Linguistics and the Professions: Proceedings of the Second Annual Delaware Symposium on Language Studies*. Norwood, NJ: Ablex.

Diakonoff, I. M. (1988). *Afrasian Languages*. Moscow: Nauka.

Dickson, D. R. and Maue-Dickson, W. (1982). *Anatomical and Physiological Bases of Speech*. Boston, MA: Little, Brown.

Diderichsen, P. (1974). The foundation of comparative linguistics: revolution or continuation? In D. Hymes (ed.), *Studies in the History of Linguistics: Traditions and Paradigms* (pp. 277–306). Bloomington: Indiana University Press.

Dik, S. C. (1978). *Functional Grammar*. Amsterdam: North-Holland.

Dik, S. C. (1989). *The Theory of Functional Grammar*, Vol. 1. Dordrecht: Foris.

Dik, S. C. (1991). Functional grammar. In F. Droste and J. Joseph (eds), *Linguistic Theory and Grammatical Description* (pp. 247–74). Amsterdam and Philadelphia: John Benjamins.

Diringer, D. (1948). *The Alphabet: A Key to the History of Mankind*. New York: Philosophical Library. [3rd edn, 2 vols, New York: Funk and Wagnalls, 1968.]

DiSciuillo, A. M., Muysken, P., and Singh, R. (1986). Government and code-mixing. *Journal of Linguistics*, 22, 1–24.

Dixon, R. M. W. and Koch, G. (1996). *Dyirbal Song Poetry: The Oral Literature of an Australian Rainforest People*. St Lucia: University of Queensland Press.

Dixon, R. M. W. (1979). Ergativity. *Language*, 55, 59–138.

Dixon, R. M. W. (1980). *The Languages of Australia*. Cambridge: Cambridge University Press.

Dixon, R. M. W. (1984). *Searching for Aboriginal Languages: Memoirs of a Field Worker*. Chicago and London: University of Chicago Press.

Dixon, R. M. W. (1997). *The Rise and Fall of Languages*. Cambridge: Cambridge University Press.

Dixon, R. M. W. and Aikhenvald, A. (1999). *The Amazonian Languages*. Cambridge: Cambridge University Press.

Donald, M. (1991). *Origins of the Modern Mind*. Cambridge, MA: MIT Press.

Dorian, N. C. (ed.) (1989). *Investigating Obsolescence: Studies in Language Contraction and Death*. Cambridge: Cambridge University Press.

Doughty, C. (1991). Second language instruction does make a difference. *Studies in Second Language Acquisition*, 13, 431–69.

Doughty, C. and Williams, J. (1998). *Focus on Form in Classroom Second Language Acquisition*. Cambridge: Cambridge University Press.

Dowty, D., Wall, R., and Peters, S. (1981). *Introduction to Montague Semantics*. Dordrecht: Reidel.

Drew, P. and Heritage, J. (eds) (1992). *Talk at Work*. Cambridge: Cambridge University Press.

Droixhe, D. (1984). Avant-propos. In D. Droixhe (ed.), *Genèse du comparatisme indo-européen* (pp. 5–16). Histoire Épistémologie Langage, 6, 2.

Dronkers, N. F., Wilkins, D. P., Van Valin, R. D., Redfern, B. B., and Jaeger, J. J. (1994). A reconsideration of the brain areas involved in the disruption of morphosyntactic comprehension. *Brain and Language*, 47, 461–3.

Dryer, M. (1989). Large linguistic areas and language sampling. *Studies in Language*, 13, 257–92.

Dryer, M. (1997). On the six-way word order typology. *Studies in Language*, 21, 69–103.

DuBrul, E. L. (1958). *Evolution of the Speech Apparatus*. Springfield, IL: Charles C. Thomas.

Dulay, H. C. and Burt, M. K. (1973). Should we teach children syntax? *Language Learning*, 3, 245–57.

Dulay, H. C. and Burt, M. K. (1974). Errors and strategies in child second language acquisition. *TESOL Quarterly*, 8:2, 129–36.

Dulay, H. C., Burt, M. K., and Krashen, S. (1982). *Language Two*. Rowley, MA: Newbury House.

Dunbar, R. (1996). *Grooming, Gossip and the Evolution of Language*. London: Faber.

Duranti, A. (1995). *From Grammar to Politics*. Berkeley, CA: University of California Press.

Duranti, A. and Goodwin, C. (eds) (1992). *Rethinking Context: Language as an Interactive Phenomenon*. Cambridge: Cambridge University Press.

Dzameshie, A. K. (1995). Social motivations for politeness behavior in Christian sermonic discourse. *Anthropological Linguistics*, 37, 192–215.

É. Kiss, K. (1987). *Configurationality in Hungarian*. Dordrecht: Reidel.

É. Kiss, K. (ed.) (1994). *Discourse Configurational Languages*. Oxford: Oxford University Press.

Eckert, P. (1989). The whole woman: sex and gender differences in variation. *Language Variation and Change*, 1, 245–67.

Eckstrand, L. (1978). Age and length of residence as variables related to the adjustment of migrant children with special reference to second language learning. In G. Nickel (ed.), *Proceedings of the Fourth International Congress of Applied Linguistics* 3 (pp. 179–97). Stuttgart: Hochschulverlag.

Edelsky, C. (1996). *With Literacy and Justice for All*, 2nd edn. London: Taylor and Francis.

Edwards, J. (1985). *Language, Society and Identity*. Oxford: Blackwell.

Edwards, J. (1994). *Multilingualism*. London: Routledge.

Edwards, J., Jr (1787). Observations on the Language of the Muhhekaneew Indians. (Communicated to the Connecticut Society of Arts and Sciences, and published at the request of the Society.) New Haven: Josiah Meigs. [Repr. London: W. Justins, Shoemaker-Row, Blackfriars; 1788, also repr. with notes by John Pickering, in the Massachusetts Historical Society Collection, second series, 10:81–160, and Boston: Phelps and Farnham, 1823.]

Edwards, S. (1992). The single-word lexicon of a severely mentally handicapped child. *Clinical Linguistics and Phonetics*, 6, 87–100.

Eisenstein, E. L. (1979). *The Printing Press as Agent of Change: Communications and Cultural Transformations in Early-Modern Europe*, 2 vols. Cambridge: Cambridge University Press.

Ellis, R. (1994). *The Study of Second Language Acquisition*. Oxford: Oxford University Press.

Elman, J. (1991). Incremental learning, or the importance of starting small. *Technical Report 9101*. Center for Research in Language, University of California at San Diego.

Emmorey, K. (forthcoming) *Sign Language: A Window into Human Language, Cognition, and the Brain*. Mahwah, N. J.: Lawrence Erlbaum and Associates.

Epstein, S. D., Flynn, S., and Martohardjono, G. (1996). Second language acquisition: theoretical and experimental issues in contemporary research. *Behavioral and Brain Sciences*, 19, 677–758.

Esling, J. (1991). *Phonetic Database (Instruction Manual)*. Pine Brook, NJ: Kay Elemetrics Corporation and University of Victoria, British Columbia: Speech Technology Research.

Evan, G. (1980). Pronouns. *Linguistic Inquiry*, 11, 467–536.

Ewen, C. J. (1982). The internal structure of complex segments. In H. van der Hulst and N. Smith (eds), *The Structure of Phonological Representations*, Vol. 2 (pp. 26–67). Dordrecht: Foris.

Extra, G. and Verhoeven, L. (1993). A bilingual perspective on Turkish and Moroccan children and adults in the Netherlands. In G. Extra and L. Verhoeven (eds), *Immigrant Languages in Europe* (pp. 67–100). Clevedon, Avon: Multilingual Matters.

Extra, G. and Verhoeven, L. (forthcoming). Processes of language change in an immigration context. To appear in G. Extra and L. Verhoeven (eds), *Language Change in Immigration Contexts*.

Fabb, N. (1997). *Linguistics and Literature: Language in the Verbal Arts of the World*. Oxford: Blackwell.

Fabb, N., Attridge, D., Durant, A., and MacCabe, C. (eds) (1987). *The Linguistics of Writing*. Manchester: Manchester University Press.

Faerch, C. and Kasper, G. (1983). Plans and strategies in foreign language communication. In C. Faerch and G. Kasper (eds), *Strategies in Interlanguage Communication* (pp. 20–60). London: Longman.

Fairclough, N. (1995). *Critical Discourse Analysis: The Critical Study of Language*. London: Longman.

Falk, D. (1992). *Braindance*. New York: Holt.

Falk, H. (1993). Schrift im alten Indien: Ein Forschungsbericht mit Anmerkungen. *ScriptOralia*, 56. Tübingen: Narr.

Fantini, A. (1985). *Language Acquisition of a Bilingual Child: A Sociolinguistic Perspective*. San Diego: College Hill Press.

Fasold, R. (1990). *The Sociolinguistics of Society*. Oxford: Blackwell.

Fellman, J. (1975). On Sir William Jones and the Scythian language. *Language Science*, 34, 37–8.

Fengtong, Z. (1989). The initials of Chengdu speech. *Journal of the International Phonetic Association*, 15, 59–68.

Ferguson, C. A. (1959). Diglossia. *Word*, 15, 325–40.

Ferguson, R. (1994). *Italian False Friends*. Toronto: University of Toronto Press.

Fevrier, J.-G. (1948). *Histoire de l'écriture*. Paris: Payot. [2nd edn, 1959.]

Fiengo, R. and May, R. (1994). *Indices and Identity*. Cambridge, MA: MIT Press.

Figueroa, E. (1994). *Sociolinguistic Metatheory*. Oxford: Pergamon.

Firbas, J. (1964). On defining the theme in functional sentence perspective. *Travaux linguistiques de Prague*, 1, 267–80.

Firbas, J. (1992). *Functional Sentence Perspective in Written and Spoken Communication*. Cambridge: Cambridge University Press.

Firth, J. R. (1956). Linguistic analysis and translation. In M. Halle, H. G. Lunt, H. McLean, and C. H. van Schooneveld (eds), *For Roman Jakobson: Essays on the Occasion of his Sixtieth Birthday 11 October 1956* (pp. 133–9). The Hague: Mouton.

Fischer, J. L. (1958). Social influences on the choice of a linguistic variant. *Word*, 14, 47–56.

Fishman, J. A. (1967). Bilingualism with and without diglossia; diglossia with and without bilingualism. *Journal of Social Issues*, 23, 29–38.

Fishman, J. A. (1968). Some contrasts between linguistically homogeneous and heterogeneous polities. In J. A. Fishman, C. A. Ferguson, and J. DasGupta (eds), *Language Problems of Developing Nations* (pp. 53–68). New York: Wiley.

Fishman, J. A. (ed.) (1989a). *Language and Ethnic Identity: Before and after the "Ethnic Revival". Comparative Disciplinary and Regional Perspectives*. New York: Oxford University Press.

Fishman, J. A. (1989b). Language, ethnicity and racism. In J. A. Fishman, *Language and Ethnicity in Minority Sociolinguistic Perspective* (pp. 9–22). Clevedon and Philadelphia: Multilingual Matters.

Fishman, J. A. (1991). *Reversing Language Shift: Theoretical and Empirical Foundations of Assistance to Threatened Languages*. Clevedon: Multilingual Matters.

Fishman, J. A., Cooper, R. L., and Ma, R. (1971). *Bilingualism in the Barrios*. Bloomington: Indiana University Press.

Flege, J. E. (1987). The production of "new" and "similar" phones in a foreign language: evidence for the effect of equivalence classification. *Journal of Phonetics*, 15, 47–65.

Flege, J. E. (1992). Speech learning in a second language. In C. Ferguson, L. Menn, and C. Stoel-Gammon (eds), *Phonological Development: Models, Research, and Applications* (pp. 565–604). Parkton, MD: Rork Press.

Fludernik, M. (1993). *The Fictions of Language and the Languages of Fiction*. London: Routledge.

Flynn, S. (1987). *A Parameter-setting Model of L2 Acquisition*. Dordrecht: Reidel.

Fodor, I. (1965). *The Rate of Linguistic Change: Limits of the Application of Mathematical Methods in Linguistics*. Janua Linguarum, Series Minor, 43. The Hague: Mouton.

Fodor, J. A. (1975). *The Language of Thought*. New York: Crowell.

Fodor, J. A. (1981). *Representations*. Hassocks: Harvester Press.

Fodor, J. A. (1983). *The Modularity of Mind*. Cambridge, MA: MIT Press.

Fodor, J. A. (1998). *Concepts: Where Cognitive Science Went Wrong*. Oxford. Clarendon Press.

Fodor, J. A., Bever, T., and Garrett, M. (1974). *The Psychology of Language*. New York: McGraw-Hill.

Foley, R. (1995). *Humans before Humanity: An Evolutionary Perspective*. Oxford: Blackwell.

Foley, W. A. (1986). *The Papuan Languages of New Guinea*. Cambridge: Cambridge University Press.

Foley, W. A. (1997). *Anthropological Linguistics: An Introduction*. Oxford: Blackwell.

Foley, W. A. and Van Valin, Jr, R. (1984). *Functional Syntax and Universal Grammar*. Cambridge: Cambridge University Press.

Ford, C. (1993). *Grammar in Interaction*. Cambridge: Cambridge University Press.

Ford, C. and Thompson, S. (1996). Interactional units in conversation: syntactic, intonational, and pragmatic resources for the management of turns. In E. Ochs, E. A. Schegloff, and S. A. Thompson (eds), *Interaction and Grammar* (pp. 134–84). Cambridge: Cambridge University Press.

Forth, G. (1988). Fashioned speech, full communication: aspects of eastern Sumbanese ritual language. In Fox (ed.), pp. 129–60.

Fowler, H. N. (tr.) (1977). *Plato in Twelve Volumes*, Vol. 4: *Cratylus, Parmenides, Greater Hippias, Lesser Hippias*. Loeb Classical Library, 167. Cambridge, MA: Harvard University Press.

Fox, B. (1987). *Discourse Structure and Anaphora in Written and Conversational English*. Cambridge: Cambridge University Press.

Fox, J. J. (1977). Roman Jakobson and the comparative study of parallelism. In C. H. von Schooneveld and D. Armstrong (eds), *Roman Jakobson: Echoes of His Scholarship* (pp. 59–90). Lisse: Peter de Ridder Press.

Fox, J. J. (ed.) (1988). *To Speak in Pairs: Essays on the Ritual Languages of Eastern Indonesia*. Cambridge: Cambridge University Press.

Freed, A. F. (1995). Language and gender. *Annual Review of Applied Linguistics*, 15, 3–22.

Freed, A. F. and Greenwood, A. (1996). Women, men, and type of talk: what makes the difference? *Language in Society*, 25, 1–26.

Freed, B. (1981). Foreigner talk, baby talk, native talk. *International Journal of the Sociology of Language*, 28, 19–39.

Freeman, D. C. (ed.) (1970). *Linguistics and Literary Style*. New York: Holt, Rinehart, and Winston.

Freeman, D. C. (ed.) (1981). *Essays in Modern Stylistics*. London: Methuen.

Frege, G. (1879). Begriffsschrift. In Geach and Black (eds) (1970), pp. 1–20.

Frege, G. (1891). Function and concept. In Geach and Black (eds) (1970), pp. 21–41.

Frege, G. (1892). On sense and reference. In Geach and Black (eds) (1970), pp. 56–78.

Freud, S. (1891). *On Aphasia*. Liepzig: Deuticke.

Friedman, V. (1999). *Linguistic Emblems and Emblematic Languages: On Language as Flag in the Balkans*. K. E. Naylor Memorial Lecture Series in South Slavic Languages, ed. B. D. Joseph, Columbus, OH: Department of Slavic and East European Languages and Literatures, Ohio State University.

Friedrich, J. (1966). *Geschichte der Schrift unter besonderer Berücksichtigung ihrer geistigen Entwicklung*. Heidelberg: Winter.

Fries, P. H. (1981). On the status of theme: arguments from discourse. *Forum Linguisticum*, 6:l, 1–38.

Frishberg, N. J. (1975). Arbitrariness and iconicity: historical change in American Sign Language. *Language*, 51, 696–719.

Frishberg, N. J. (1976). Some aspects of the historical development of signs in American Sign Language. Ph.D. dissertation. University of California, San Diego.

Frith, U. (1985). Beneath the surface of developmental dyslexia. In K. E. Patterson, J. C. Marshall, and M. Coltheart (eds), *Surface Dyslexia: Neuropsychological and Cognitive Studies of Phonological Reading* (pp. 301–30). Hove: Erlbaum.

Frost, R. (1998). Toward a strong phonological theory of visual word recognition: true issues and false trails. *Psychological Bulletin*, 123, 71–99.

Gabelentz, G. von der (1881). *Chinesische Grammatik*. Leipzig: Weigel.

Gal, S. (1978). Peasant men can't find wives: language change and sex roles in a bilingual community. *Language in Society*, 7, 1–16.

Galambos, S. J. and Goldin-Meadow, S. (1990). The effects of learning two languages on metalinguistic awareness. *Cognition*, 34, 1–56.

Gamkrelidze, T. V. (1994). *Alphabetic Writing and the Old Georgian Script. A Typology and Provenience of Alphabetic Writing Systems*. Delmar, NY: Caravan Books.

Gardner, H. (1991). *The Unschooled Mind: How Children Think and How Schools Should Teach*. New York: Basic Books.

Gardner, R. A., Gardner, B. T., and Van Cantfort, T. E. (eds) (1989). *Teaching Sign Language to Chimpanzees*. Albany: State University of New York Press.

Gardner-Chloros, P. (1995). Codeswitching in community, regional and national repertoires: the myth of the discreteness of linguistic systems. In Milroy and Muysken (eds), pp. 68–89.

Gaskins, I. W. (1998). A beginning literacy program for at-risk and delayed readers. In J. Metsala and L. C. Ehri (eds), *Word Recognition in Beginning Literacy* (pp. 209–32). Hillsdale, NJ: Erlbaum.

Gawron, J. M. and Peters, S. (1990). *Quantification and Anaphora in Situation Semantics*. Stanford: CSLI.

Gazdar, G. (1979). *Pragmatics*. New York: Academic Press.

Gazdar, G. and Pullum, G. (1981). Subcategorization, constituent order, and the notion "head." In M. Moortgat, H. van der Hulst, and T. Hoekstra (eds), *The Scope of Lexical Rules* (pp. 107–23). Dordrecht: Foris.

Gazdar, G., Klein, E., Pullum, G., and Sag, I. A. (1985). *Generalized Phrase Structure Grammar*. Cambridge, MA: Harvard University Press and Oxford: Basil Blackwell.

Gazzaniga, M. S. (1983). Right hemisphere language following brain bisection: a 20-year perspective. *American Psychologist*, 38, 525–49.

Geach, P. (1962). *Reference and Generality*. Ithaca, NY: Cornell University Press.

Geach, P. and Black, M. (eds) (1970). *Translations from the Philosophical Writings of Gottlieb Frege*. Oxford: Blackwell.

Gee, J. P. (1985). The narrativization of experience in the oral style. *Journal of Education*, 167, 9–35.

Gee, J. P. (1992). *The Social Mind: Language, Ideology, and Social Practice*. New York: Bergin and Garvey.

Gee, J. P. (1994). First Language Acquisition as a guide for theories of learning and pedagogy. *Linguistics and Education*, 6, 331–54.

Gee, J. P. (1996a). *Social Linguistics and Literacies: Ideology in Discourses*, 2nd edn. London: Taylor and Francis.

Gee, J. P. (1996b). Vygotsky and current debates in education: some dilemmas as afterthoughts to Discourse, Learning, and Schooling. In D. Hicks (ed.), *Discourse, Learning, and Schooling* (pp. 269–82). Cambridge: Cambridge University Press.

Gee, J. P. (to appear). Progressivism, critique, and socially situated minds. In C. Edelsky (ed.), *Progressive Education: History and Critique*.

Gee, J. P. and Clinton, K. (to appear). An African–American child's "science talk": co-construction of meaning from the perspective of multiple discourses. In M. Gallego and S. Hollingsworth (eds), *Challenging a Single Standard: Multiple Perspectives on Literacy*. Hillsdale, NJ: Erlbaum.

Gelb, I. J. (1952). *A Study of Writing*. Chicago: University of Chicago Press. [2nd edn, 1963.]

Gelb, I. J. (1974). Writing, forms of. *Encyclopaedia Britannica*, 15th edn, *Macropaedia*, 19, 1033–45.

Geller, M. (1997). The last wedge. *Zeitschrift fur Assyriologie*, 87, 43–95.

Genesee, F., Nicoladis, E., and Paradis, J. (1995). Language differentiation in early bilingual development. *Journal of Child Language*, 22, 611–31.

Geschwind, N. (1965). Disconnection syndromes in animals and man. *Brain*, 88, 237–94, 585–644.

Geschwind, N. (1970). The organization of language and the brain. *Science*, 170, 940–9.

Geschwind, N. and Galaburda, A. (1985). Cerebral lateralization: biological mechanism, associations and pathology i–iii: a hypothesis and a program for research. *Archives of Neurology*, 42, 428–59, 421–52, 634–54.

Geschwind, N. and Galaburda, A. (1987). *Cerebral Lateralization: Biological Mechanisms. Associations and Pathology*. Cambridge, MA: MIT Press.

Ghezzi, R. W. (1993). Tradition and innovation in Ojibwe storytelling. Mrs Marie Syrette's "The orphans and Mashos." In A. Krupat (ed.), *New Voices in Native American Literary Criticism* (pp. 37–76). Washington: Smithsonian Institute Press.

Giacalone Ramat, A. and Ramat, P. (eds) (1998). *The Indo-European Languages*. London: Routledge.

Gillieron, J. and Edmont, E. (1902–13). *Atlas linguistique de la France*, 13 vols. Paris: Champion.

Ginzburg, J. (1996). Interrogatives: questions, facts, and dialogue. In Lappin (ed.), pp. 285–322.

Givón, T. (1980). The binding hierarchy and the typology of complements. *Studies in Language*, 4, 333–77.

Givón, T. (1983). *Topic Continuity in Discourse*. Amsterdam: John Benjamins.

Givón, T. (1989). *Mind, Code and Context: Essays in Pragmatics*. Hillsdale, NJ: Erlbaum.

Goldin-Meadow, S. and Mylander, C. (1990). Beyond the input given: the child's role in the acquisition of language. *Language*, 66:2, 323–55.

Goldsmith, J. (1979). *Autosegmental Phonology*. New York: Garland.

Goldsmith, J. A. (1995). *The Handbook of Phonological Theory*. Oxford: Blackwell.

Goodall, J. (1986). *The Chimpanzees of Gombe: Patterns of Behavior*. Cambridge, MA: Belknap Press.

Goodglass, H. and Quadfasel, F. A. (1954). Language laterality in left-handed aphasics. *Brain*, 77, 521–48.

Goodglass, H. and Kaplan, E. (1982). *The Assessment of Aphasia and Related Disorders*, 2nd edn. Philadelphia: Lea and Febiger.

Goodman, K. (1967). Reading: A psycholinguistic guessing game. *Journal of the Reading Specialist*, 6, 126–35.

Goodman, K. (1986). *What's Whole in Whole Language?* Portsmouth, NH: Heinemann.

Goodman, K. (1993). *Phonics Phacts*. Portsmouth, NH: Heinemann.

Goodwin, C. (1994). Professional vision. *American Anthropologist*, 96:3, 606–33.

Goodwin, C. and Duranti, A. (1992). Rethinking context: an introduction. In A. Duranti and C. Goodwin (eds), *Rethinking Context: Language as an Interactive Phenomenon* (pp. 1–42). Cambridge: Cambridge University Press.

Gordon, B. (1982). Confrontation naming: computational model and disconnection simulation. In D. Caplan, J. C. Marshall, and M. A. Arbib (eds), *Neural Models of Language Processes* (pp. 511–29). New York: Academic Press.

Gordon, E. (1997). Sex, speech, and stereotypes: why women use prestige forms more than men. *Language in Society*, 26:1, 47–63.

Goss, N., Ying-Hua, Z., and Lantolf, J. P. (1994). Two heads may be better than one: mental activity in second language grammaticality judgements. In Tarone, Gass, and Cohen (eds), pp. 263–86.

Gough, P. B. (1972). One second of reading. In J. F. Kavanagh and I. G. Mattingly (eds), *Language by Ear and by Eye* (pp. 331–58). Cambridge, MA: MIT Press.

Gragg, G. B. (1995). Babylonian grammatical texts. In E. F. K. Koerner and R. E. Asher (eds), *Concise History of the Language Sciences: From the Sumerians to the Cognitivists* (pp. 19–21). Oxford: Pergamon.

Green, J. and Dixon, C. (1993). Talking knowledge into being: discursive practices in classrooms. *Linguistics and Education*, 5: 231–9.

Greenberg, J. H. (1963a). *The Languages of Africa*. Bloomington, IN: Indiana University and The Hague: Mouton.

Greenberg, J. H. (1963b). Some universals of grammar with particular reference to the order of meaningful elements. In Greenberg (ed.), *Universals of Language*, pp. 73–113.

Greenberg, J. H. (ed.) (1963c). *Universals of Language*. Cambridge, MA: MIT Press.

Greenberg, J. H. (1971). The Indo-Pacific Hypothesis. In T. E. Sebeok (ed.), *Linguistics in Oceania: Current Trends in Linguistics*, Vol. 8 (pp. 807–71). The Hague: Mouton.

Greenberg, J. H. (1980). Circumfixes and typological change. In E. Traugott, R. Labrum, and S. Shepherd (eds), *Papers from the Fourth International Conference on Historical Linguistics* (pp. 233–41). Amsterdam: John Benjamins.

Greenberg, J. H. (1987). *Language in the Americas*. Stanford: Stanford University Press.

Greenfield, P. M. (1991). Language, tools and the brain: the ontogeny and phylogeny of hierarchically organized sequential behavior. *Behavioral and Brain Sciences*, 14, 531–51.

Gregersen, E. A. (1977). *Language in Africa: An Introductory Survey*. New York: Gordon and Breach.

Grice, H. P. (1975). Logic and conversation. In P. Cole and J. Morgan (eds), *Syntax and Semantics*, Vol. 3. *Speech Acts* (pp. 41–58). New York: Academic Press.

Grice, H. P. (1989). *Studies in the Ways of Words*. Cambridge, MA: Harvard University Press.

Grimes, B. F. (ed.) (1996a). *Ethnologue: Languages of the World*, 13th edn. Dallas: Summer Institute of Linguistics. Also available on-line at http://www.sil.org/ethnologue/.

Grimes, B. F. (ed.) (1996b). *Ethnologue: Languages Name. Index to the Thirteenth Edition of Ethnologue*. Dallas: Summer Institute of Linguistics.

Grimes, B. F. and Grimes, J. E. (1996). *Ethnologue: Language Family Index to the Thirteenth Edition of Ethnologue*. Dallas: Summer Institute of Linguistics.

Grimm, J. (1822) [1819]. *Deutsche Grammatik*. Erster Theil. Gottingen: Dieterich.

Grodzinsky, Y. (1990). *Theoretical Perspectives on Language Deficits*. Cambridge, MA: MIT Press.

Grodzinsky, Y. (1995). A restrictive theory of agrammatic comprehension. *Brain and Language*, 50, 27–51.

Groenendijk, J. and Stokhof, M. (1990). Dynamic Montague grammar. In L. Kalman and L. Polos (eds), *Papers from the Second Symposium on Logic and Grammar* (pp. 3–48). Akademiai Kiado, Budapest.

Groenendijk, J. and Stokhof, M. (1991). Dynamic predicate logic. *Linguistics and Philosophy*, 14, 39–100.

Groenendijk, J. and Stokhof, M. (1997). Questions. In Van Benethem and ter Meulen (eds), pp. 1055–124.

Groenendijk, J., Stokhof, M., and Veltman, F. (1996). Anaphora, discourse, and modality. In Lappin (ed.), pp. 179–213.

Grondin, N. and White, L. (1996). Functional categories in child L2 acquisition of French. *Language Acquisition*, 5, 1–34.

Grosjean, F. (1982). *Life with Two Languages: An Introduction to Bilingualism*. Cambridge, MA: Harvard University Press.

Grosjean, F. (1989). Neurolinguists, beware! The bilingual is not two monolinguals in one person. *Brain and Language*, 36, 3–15.

Grosz, B. J. and Sidner, C. L. (1986). Attention, intentions and the structure of discourse. *Computational Linguistics*, 12:3, 175–204.

Grundy, K. (ed.) (1995). *Linguistics in Clinical Practice*, 2nd edn. London: Whurr.

Gumperz, J. (1968). The speech community. *International Encyclopedia of Social Sciences* (pp. 381–6). London: Macmillan.

Gumperz, J. J. (1982). *Discourse Strategies*. Cambridge: Cambridge University Press.

Gumperz, J. J. and Hymes, D. (eds) (1972). *Directions in Sociolinguistics: The Ethnography of Communication*. New York: Holt, Rinehart, and Winston.

Gunnarsson, B. L., Linell, P., and Nordberg, B. (eds) (1997). *The Construction of Professional Discourse*. London and New York: Longman.

Gupta, A. F. (1994). *The Step-Tongue: Children's English in Singapore*. Clevedon: Multilingual Matters.

Gutknecht, C. and L. J. Rölle (1996). *Translating by Factors*. Albany, NY: State University of New York Press.

Gutt, E.-A. (1991). *Translation and Relevance: Cognition and Context*. Oxford: Basil Blackwell.

Gyarmathi, S. (1799). *Affinitas linguae Hungaricae cum linguis Fennicae originis grammatice demonstrata*. Gottingen: Johann Christian Dieterich. [English translation 1981: *Grammatical Proof of the Affinity of the Hungarian Language with Languages of Fennic Origin*, tr., annotated, and introduced by V. E. Hanzeli, Amsterdam: John Benjamins.]

Habermas, J. (1985). *The Theory of Communicative Action*. New York: Beacon Press.

Habick, T. (1991). Burnouts versus rednecks: effects of group membership on the phonemic system. In P. Eckert (ed.), *New Ways of Analyzing Sound Change* (pp. 185–212). San Diego: Academic Press.

Hagiwara, H. (1995). The breakdown of functional categories and the economy of derivation. *Brain and Language*, 50, 92–116.

Hagoort, P., Brown, C., and Groothusen, J. (1993). The syntactic positive shift (SPS) as an ERP measure of syntactic processing. *Language and Cognitive Processes*, 8:4, 485–532.

Haiman, J. (1983). Iconic and economic motivation. *Language*, 59, 781–819.

Haiman, J. (1985). *Natural Syntax*. Cambridge: Cambridge University Press.

Hakuta, K. (1986). *Mirror of Language: The Debate on Bilingualism*. New York: Basic Books.

Hale, K. (1983). Warlpiri and the grammar of nonconfigurational languages. *Natural Language and Linguistic Theory*, 1, 5–49.

Hale, K. (1984). Remarks on creativity in aboriginal verse. In J. C. Kassler and J. Stubington (eds), *Problems and Solutions: Occasional Essays in Musicology Presented to Alice M. Moyle* (pp. 254–62). Sydney: Hale and Iremonger.

Hale, K. and Keyser, S. J. (1993). On argument structure and the lexical expression of syntactic relations. In K. Hale and S. J. Keyser (eds), *The View from Building 20: Essays in Linguistics in Honor of Sylvain Bromberger* (pp. 53–108). Cambridge, MA: MIT.

Halle, M. (1962). Phonology in generative grammar. *Word*, 18, 54–72.

Halle, M. (1987). A Biblical pattern poem. In Fabb, Attridge, Durant, and MacCabe (eds), pp. 252–64.

Halle, M. and Keyser, S. J. (1971). *English Stress: Its Form, Its Growth, and Its Role in Verse*. New York: Harper and Row.

Halle, M. and Marantz, A. (1993). Distributed morphology and the pieces of inflection. In Hale and Keyser (eds), pp. 111–76.

Halliday, M. A. K. (1967). Notes on transitivity and theme in English. *Journal of Linguistics*, 3, 37–81(Pt 1), 199–244 (Pt 2).

Halliday, M. A. K. (1978). *Language as a Social Semiotic: The Social Interpretation of Language and Meaning*. London: Edward Arnold.

Halliday, M. A. K. (1981). Linguistic function and literary style: an inquiry into the language of William Golding's *The Inheritors*. In Freeman (ed.).

Halliday, M. A. K. (1985). *An Introduction to Functional Grammar*. Baltimore: University Park Press.

Halliday, M. A. K. (1993). Towards a language-based theory of learning. *Linguistics and Education*, 5, 93–116.

Halliday, M. A. K. (1994). *An Introduction to Functional Grammar*, 2nd edn. London: Edward Arnold.

Halliday, M. A. K. and Hasan, R. (1976). *Cohesion in English*. London: Longman.

Halliday, M. A. K., McIntosh, A., and Strevens, P. (1964). *The Linguistic Sciences and Language Teaching*. London: Longman.

Hamblin, C. L. (1973). Questions in Montague grammar. *Foundations of Language*, 10, 41–53.

Hannay, M. (1989). Translating structures: the role of contrastive syntax in translation dictionaries. In J. L. Mackenzie and R. Todd (eds), *In Other Words: Transcultural Studies in Philology, Translation and Lexicology Presented to Hans Heinrich Meier on the Occasion of his Sixty-fifth Birthday* (pp. 211–34). Dordrecht: Foris.

Hanson, K. and Kiparsky, P. (1996). A parametric theory of poetic meter. *Language*, 72:2, 287–335.

Hardcastle, W. J. and Laver, J. (eds) (1997). *The Handbook of Phonetic Sciences*. Oxford: Blackwell.

Hardcastle, W. J. and Marchal, A. (1990). *Speech Production and Speech Modelling*. Dordrecht: Kluwer.

Hardt, D. (1993). Verb phrase ellipsis: form, meaning and processing. Ph.D. dissertation, University of Pennsylvania.

Harley, B. (1986). *Age in Second Language Acquisition*. Clevedon, Avon: Multilingual Matters.

Harley, B. and Wang, W. (1997). The Critical Period Hypothesis: where are we now? In de Groot and Kroll (eds), pp. 19–52.

Harrington, M. (1987). Processing transfer: language specific processing strategies as a source of interlanguage variation. *Applied Psycholinguistics*, 8, 351–77.

Harris, A. C. and Campbell, L. (1995). *Historical Syntax in Cross-linguistic Perspective*. Cambridge: Cambridge University Press.

Harris, J. (1751). *Hermes, or a Philosophical Inquiry concerning Languages and Universal Grammar*. London: J. Nourse.

Harris, M. and Vincent, N. (eds) (1988). *The Romance Languages*. London: Routledge.

Harris, Z. (1970). *Papers in Structural and Transformational Linguistics*. Dordrecht: Reidel.

Hasan, R. (1995). The conception of context in text. In P. H. Fries and M. Gregory (eds), *Discourse and Meaning in Society: Functional Perspectives* (pp. 183–283). Norwood, NJ: Ablex.

Hasan, R. and Fries, P. H. (eds) (1995). *On Subject and Theme*. Amsterdam: John Benjamins.

Haugen, E. (1953). *The Norwegian Language in America*. Philadelphia: University of Pennsylvania Press.

Haugen, E. (1966). *Language Conflict and Language Planning: The Case of Modern Norwegian*. Cambridge, MA: Harvard University Press.

Haugen, E. (1977). Norm and deviation in bilingual communities. In P. A. Hornby (ed.), *Bilingualism: Psychological, Social and Educational Implications* (pp. 91–103). New York: Academic Press.

Hauser, M. D. (1996). *The Evolution of Communication*. Cambridge, MA: MIT Press.

Hawkins, J. A. (1983). *Word Order Universals*. New York: Academic Press.

Hayes, B. (1983). A grid-based theory of English meter. *Linguistic Inquiry*, 14, 357–94.

Hayes, B. (1989). The prosodic hierarchy in meter. In P. Kiparsky and G. Youmans (eds), *Phonetics and Phonology*, Vol. 1. *Rhythm and Meter* (pp. 201–60). San Diego: Academic Press.

Hayward, R., Naeser, M. A., and Zatz, L. M. (1977). Cranial computer tomography in aphasia. *Radiology*, 123, 653–60.

He, A. W. (1998). *Reconstructing Institutions: Language Use in Academic Counseling Encounters*. Greenwich, CT, and London: Ablex.

Head, H. (1926). *Aphasia and Kindred Disorders of Speech*. New York: Macmillan Press.

Heading, K. E. G., Provis, D. F., Scott, T. D., Smith, J. E., and Smith, R. T. (1967). *Science for Secondary Schools*, Vol. 2. Adelaide: Rigby.

Heath, S. B. (1983). *Ways with Words*. Cambridge: Cambridge University Press.

Heilman, K. M. and Scholes, R. J. (1976). The nature of comprehension errors in Broca's, conduction, and Wernicke's aphasics. *Cortex*, 12, 258–65.

Heim, I. (1982). The semantics of definite and indefinite noun phrases. Ph.D. dissertation, University of Massachusetts, Amherst, MA.

Heim, I. (1990). E-type pronouns and donkey anaphora. *Linguistics and Philosophy*, 13, 137–77.

Heim, I. and Kratzer, A. (1998). *Semantics in Generative Grammar*. Oxford: Blackwell.

Heine, B. (2000). Grammaticalization. In Joseph and Janda (eds).

Henschen, S. E. (1920). *Klinische und Anatomische Beitrage zur Pathologie des Gehirns*. Stockholm: Nordische Bokhandler.

Herbert, R. K. (ed.) (1992). *Language and Society in Africa*. Cape Town: Witwatersrand University Press.

Herder, J. G. (1772). *Abhandlung uber den Ursprung der Sprache*. Berlin: C. F. Voss.

Herman, R. (1990). How do deaf speakers talk about time? *Clinical Linguistics and Phonetics*, 4, 197–207.

Hervey, S., Higgins, I., and Loughridge, M. (1995). *Thinking German Translation: A Course in Translation Method: German to English*. London: Routledge.

Hetzron, R. (ed.) (1997). *The Semitic Languages*. London: Routledge.

Hickok, G. and Avrutin, S. (1995). Representation, referentiality and processing in agrammatic comprehension: two case studies. *Brain and Language*, 50, 10–26.

Higginbotham, J. (1985). On semantics. *Linguistic Inquiry*, 16, 547–94.

Higginbotham, J. (1996). The semantics of questions. In Lappin (ed.), pp. 361–83.

Hildebrandt, N., Caplan, D., and Evans, K. (1987). The man left without a trace: a case study of aphasic processing of empty categories. *Cognitive Neuropsychology*, 4:3, 257–302.

Hilles, S. (1991). Access to Universal Grammar in Second Language Acquisition. In L. Eubank (ed.), *Point Counterpoint: Universal Grammar in the Second Language* (pp. 305–38). Amsterdam: Benjamins.

Hillis, A., Rapp, B., Romani, C., and Caramazza, A. (1990). Selective impairment of semantics in lexical processing. *Cognitive Neuropsychology*, 7:3, 191–243.

Hinton, L. and Munro, P. (1998). Introduction. In Hinton and Munro (eds), pp. 1–4.

Hinton, L. and Munro, P. (eds) (1998). *Studies in American Indian Languages: Description and Theory*. University of California Publications in Linguistics 131.

Hobbs, J. (1990). *Literature and Cognition*. Stanford, CA: CSLI.

Hock, H. H. (1991). *Principles of Historical Linguistics*, 2nd edn. Berlin: Gruyter.

Hock, H. H. and Joseph, B. D. (1996). *Language History, Language Change, and Language Relationship: An Introduction to Historical and Comparative Linguistics*. Berlin: Gruyter.

Hockett, C. (1958). *A Course in Modern Linguistics*. New York: Macmillan.

Hockett, C. (1997). Review of Daniels and Bright 1996. *Language*, 73, 379–85.

Hodges, J., Patterson, K., Oxbury, S., and Funnell, E. (1992). Semantic dementia. Progressive fluent aphasia with temporal lobe atrophy. *Brain*, 115, 1783–1806.

Hoem, I., Hovdhaugen, E., and Vonen Kupi, A. M. (1992). *Mai Te Tutolu: Tokelau Oral Literature*. Oslo: Scandinavian University Press.

Hoenigswald, H. M. (1974). Fallacies in the history of linguistics: notes on the appraisal of the nineteenth century. In D. Hymes (ed.), *Studies in the History of Linguistics: Traditions and Paradigms* (pp. 346–58). Bloomington: Indiana University Press.

Hoenigswald, H. M. (1990). Descent, perfection and the comparative method since Leibniz. In T. de Mauro and L. Formigari (eds), *Leffiniz, Humboldt, and the Origins of Comparativism* (pp. 119–32). Amsterdam: John Benjamins.

Hoffman, C. (1991). *An Introduction to Bilingualism*. London: Longman.

Hoffmann, K. and Narten, J. (1989). *Der Sasanidische Archetypus: Untersuchungen zu Schreibung und Lautgestalt des Avestischen*. Wiesbaden: Reichert.

Hoffmann, K. (1988). Avestan language. *Encyclopaedia Iranica*, 3:1, 47–62.

Hollien, H. (1990). *The Acoustics of Crime*. New York: Plenum.

Holm, A. and Dodd, A. (1996). The effect of first written language on the acquisition of English literacy. *Cognition*, 59, 119–47.

Holm, J. A. (1989). *Pidgins and Creoles*, 2 vols. Cambridge: Cambridge University Press.

Holmes, J. (1992). *An Introduction to Sociolinguistics*. London: Longman.

Honey, J. (1989). *Does Accent Matter?* London and Boston: Faber.

Hoof, H. van. (1989). *Traduire: L'anglais: théorie et pratique*, 2nd edn. Paris: Editions Duculot.

Hopcroft, J. and Ullman, J. (1979). *Introduction to Automata Theory, Languages and Computation*. Reading, MA: Addison-Wesley.

Hopper, P. (1987). Emergent grammar. *Berkeley Linguistics Society Proceedings*, 13, 139–57. Berkeley, CA: University of California.

Hopper, P. J. and Thompson, S. A. (1980). Transitivity in grammar and discourse. *Language*, 56, 251–99.

Hopper, P. J. and Traugott, E. C. (1993). *Grammaticalization*. Cambridge: Cambridge University Press.

Hovdhaugen, E. (1982). *Foundations of Western Linguistics: From the Beginning to the End of the First Millennium AD*. Oslo: Universitetsforlaget.

Howard, D. and Orchard-Lisle, V. (1984). On the origin of semantic errors in naming: evidence from the case of a global aphasic. *Cognitive Neuropsychology*, 1, 163–90.

Huang, C.-T. J. (1982). *Logical Relations in Chinese and the Theory of Grammar*. Cambridge, MA: MIT Press.

Hudson, R. A. (1984). *Word Grammar*. Oxford: Basil Blackwell.

Hudson, R. A. (1990). *Sociolinguistics*, 2nd edn. Cambridge: Cambridge University Press.

Hull, G. (1994). Maltese: from Arabic dialect to European language. In I. Fodor and C. Hagege (eds), *Language Reform, History and Future*, Vol. 6 (pp. 331–46). Hamburg: Buske.

Humboldt, F. W. C. K. F. von (1822). *Ueber das Entstehen der grammatischen Formen, und ihren Einfluss auf die Ideenentwicklung*.

Humphries, T., Padden, C., and O'Rourke T. J. (1994). *A Basic Course in American Sign Language*, 2nd edn. Silver Spring, MD: T. J. Publishers.

Hurford, J. R., Studdert-Kennedy, M., and Knight, C. (eds) (1998). *Approaches to the Evolution of Language: Social and Cognitive Bases*. Cambridge: Cambridge University Press.

Hyland, K. (1997). Scientific claims and community values: articulating an academic culture. *Language and Communication*, 17, 19–31.

Hymes, D. (1974). *Foundations in Sociolinguistics: An Ethnographic Approach*. Philadelphia: University of Pennsylvania Press.

Hymes, D. (1981). *"In Vain I Tried to Tell You." Essays in Native American Ethnopoetics*. Philadelphia: University of Pennsylvania Press.

Hymes, D. (1996). *Ethnography, Linguistics, Narrative Inequality: Towards an Understanding of Voice*. London: Taylor and Francis.

Illic-Svityc, V. M. (1971–84). *Opyt sravnenija nostraticeskix jazykov*, 3 vols. Moscow: Nauka.

International Phonetic Association (1993). *International Phonetic Alphabet*, revised to 1993. Cambridge: Dept of Linguistics, University of Cambridge.

Issidorides, D. and Hulstijn, J. (1992). Comprehension of grammatically modified and non-modified sentences by second language learners. *Applied Psycholinguistics*, 13, 147–71.

Jackendoff, R. (1997). *The Architecture of the Language Faculty*. Cambridge, MA: MIT Press.

Jackson, B. (1974). *"Get Your Ass in the Water and Swim Like Me"*: Narrative Poetry from Black Oral Tradition. Cambridge, MA: Harvard University Press.

Jackson, J. H. (1878). On affections of speech from disease of the brain. *Brain*, 1:2, 304–30, 203–22, 323–56.

Jacobson, P. (1996). The syntax–semantics interface in categorial grammar. In Lappin (ed.), pp. 89–116.

Jacoby, S. and Gonzales, P. (1991). The constitution of expert–novice in scientific discourse. *Issues in Applied Linguistics*, 2:2, 149–82.

Jager, A. (1686). *De Lingua Vetustissima Europae, Scytho-Celtica et Gothica*. Wittenberg.

Jakobson, R. (1958). Typological studies and their contribution to historical comparative linguistics. In E. Sivertsen, C. J. Borgstom, A. Gallis, and A. Sommerfelt (eds), *Proceedings of the Eighth International Congress of Linguists* (pp. 17–25). Oslo: Oslo University Press.

Jakobson, R. (1987). Linguistics and poetics. In K. Pomorska and S. Rudy (eds), *Roman Jakobson: Language in Literature* (pp. 62–94). Cambridge, MA: Harvard University Press.

James, C., Scholfield, P., Garrett, P., and Griffiths, Y. (1993). Welsh bilinguals' spelling: an error analysis. *Journal of Multilingual and Multicultural Development*, 14:4, 287–306.

James, C. (1998). *Errors in Language Learning and Use: Exploring Error Analysis*. London: Longman.

Janda, R. D. (1999). Beyond "pathways" and "unidirectionality": on the discontinuity of language transmission and the counterability of grammaticalization? In a special issue of *Language Sciences*, ed. L. Campbell.

Janda, R. D. and Joseph, B. D. (2000). On language, change, and "language change." In Joseph and Janda (eds).

Jasanoff, J. (1971). Review of King 1969. *Romance Philology*, 25, 74–85.

Jelinek, E. (1984). Empty categories, case, and configurationality. *Natural Language and Linguistic Theory*, 2, 39–76.

Jensen, H. (1969). *Sign, Symbol and Script*, 3rd edn. Tr. George Unwin. London: George Allen and Unwin; New York: Putnam's. [Original German edn, 1935.]

Jenudd, B. H. and Shapiro, M. J. (eds) (1989). *The Politics of Language Purism*. Berlin: Gruyter.

Jespersen, O. (1927). *A Modern English Grammar on Historical Principles*, Vol. 3. London: George Allen and Unwin.

Joanette, Y. and Brownell, H. H. (1990). *Discourse Ability and Brain Damage: Theoretical and Empirical Perspectives*. New York: Springer-Verlag.

Johanson, L. and Csato, E. (eds) (1998). *The Turkic Languages*. London: Routledge.

Johnson, C. D. (1972). *Formal Aspects of Phonological Description*. The Hague: Mouton.

Johnson, J. S. and Newport, E. L. (1989). Critical period effects in second language learning: the influence of maturational state on the acquisition of ESL. *Cognitive Psychology*, 21, 60–99.

Johnson, J. S. and Newport, E. L. (1991). Critical period effects on universal properties of language: the status of subjacency in a second language. *Cognition*, 39, 215–68.

Jones, Sir W. (1798). Third anniversary discourse: on the Hindus (February 2, 1786). *Asiatick Researches*, 1, 415–31.

Joseph, B. D. (1980). Linguistic universals and syntactic change. *Language*, 56, 345–70.

Joseph, B. D. (1990). *Morphology and Universals in Syntactic Change: Evidence from Medieval and Modern Greek*. New York: Garland Publishing Inc. [Updated and augmented version of 1978 Harvard University Ph.D. dissertation.]

Joseph, B. D. (1994). On weak subjects and pro-drop in Greek. In I. Philippaki-Warburton, K. Nicolaidis, and M. Sifianou (eds), *Themes in Greek Linguistics* (pp. 21–32). Papers from the First International Conference on Greek Linguistics, Reading, September 1993. Amsterdam: John Benjamins.

Joseph, B. D. (1998). Linguistics for everystudent. *Studies in the Linguistic Sciences*, 28:2, 123–33.

Joseph, B. D. (1999). Is there such a thing as "grammaticalization"? To appear in a special issue of *Language Sciences*, ed. L. Campbell.

Joseph, B. D. and Janda, R. D. (eds) (2000). *Handbook of Historical Linguistics*. Oxford: Blackwell.

Just, M. A., Carpenter, P. A., Keller, T. A., Eddy, W. F., and Thulborn, K. R. (1996). Brain activation modulated by sentence comprehension. *Science*, 274, 114–16.

Kadmon, N. (1990). Uniqueness. *Linguistics and Philosophy*, 13, 273–324.

Kamp, H. (1979). Syntax vs. semantics. In Guenthner and Rohrer (eds).

Kamp, H. (1981). A theory of truth and semantic representation. In J. Groenendijk, T. Janssen, and M. Stokhof (eds), *Formal Methods in the Study of Language* (pp. 277–322). Amsterdam: Mathematical Center Tracts.

Kamp, H. (1984). A theory of truth and semantic interpretation. In J. Groenendijk et al. (eds), *Truth, Interpretation and Information* (pp. 1–43). Dordrecht: Foris.

Kamp, H. (1996). Discourse representation theory and dynamic semantics: representational and non-representational accounts of anaphora. MS, University of Stuttgart.

Kamp, H. and Reyle, U. (1993). *From Discourse to Logic*. Dordrecht: Kluwer.

Kanna, K. (1996). The status of a non-parametrized principle in the L2 initial state. *Language Acquisition*, 5:4, 317–34.

Kaplan, R. and Bresnan, J. (1982). Lexical-functional grammar: a formal system for grammatical representation. In J. Bresnan (ed.), *The Mental Representation of Grammatical Relations* (pp. 173–281). Cambridge, MA: MIT Press.

Kaplan, R. and Kay, M. (1994). Regular models of phonological rule systems. *Computational Linguistics*, 20, 331–78.

Karlsson, F. (1987). *Finnish Grammar*. Helsinki: Werner Sörderström Osakeyhtiö.

Karttunen, L. (1977). Syntax and semantics of questions. *Linguistics and Philosophy*, 1, 3–44.

Karttunen, L. (1983). KIMMO: a general morphological processor. In L. Karttunen (ed.), *Texas Linguistic Forum*, 22 (pp. 165–86). Austin, TX: University of Texas.

Karttunen, L., Kaplan, R., and Zaenen, A. (1992). Two-level morphology with composition. In COLING-92 (pp. 141–8). *International Conference on Computational Linguistics*.

Kasher, A. (ed.) (1991). *The Chomskyan Turn*. Oxford: Blackwell.

Kasper, G. (1981). *Pragmatische Aspekte in der Interimsprache*. Tübingen: Narr.

Kasper, G. (1996). The development of pragmatic competence. In E. Kellerman, B. Weltens, and T. Bongaerts (eds), *EUROSLA 6: A Selection of Papers, Toogepaste taaletenschap in Artikelen*, 55:2, 103–20.

Kasper, G. (ed.) (1996). *Studies in Second Language Acquisition*, 18.2. Special issue: *The Development of Pragmatic Competence*.

Katamba, F. and Cooke, P. (1987). Ssematimba ne Kikwabanga: the music and poetry of a Ganda historical song. *World of Music*, 29, 49–68.

Katz, J. (1972). *Semantic Theory*. New York: Harper and Row.

Katz, J. J. and Postal, P. (1991). Realism versus conceptualism in linguistics, *Linguistics and Philosophy*, 14: 515–54.

Kaufman, T. (1990). Language history in South America: what we know and how to know more. In D. L. Payne (ed.), *Amazonian Linguistics: Studies in Lowland South American Languages* (pp. 13–67). Austin: University of Texas Press.

Kazenin, K. I. (1994). Split syntactic ergativity: toward an implicational hierarchy. *Sprachtypologie und Universalienforschung*, 47, 78–98.

Keating, P. (1987). A survey of phonological features. *UCLA Working Papers in Phonetics*, 66, 124–50.

Keenan, E. (1996). The semantics of determiners. In Lappin (ed.), pp. 41–63.

Keenan, E. and Comrie, B. (1977). Noun phrase accessibility and universal grammar. *Linguistic Inquiry*, 8, 63–99.

Keenan, E. and Moss, L. (1984). Generalized quantifiers and the expressive power of natural language. In J. van Benthem and A. ter Meulen (eds), *Generalized Quantifiers* (pp. 73–124). Dordrecht: Foris.

Keenan, E. and Stavi, J. (1986). A semantic characterization of natural language determiners. *Linguistics and Philosophy*, 9, 253–326.

Keenan, E. and Westerstahl, D. (1997). Generalized quantifiers in linguistics and logic. In van Benthem and ter Meulen (eds), pp. 838–93.

Kehler, A. (1995). Interpreting cohesive forms in the context of discourse inference. Ph.D. dissertation, Harvard University.

Keller, R. (1994). *On Language Change: The Invisible Hand in Language*. London: Routledge. [Translation and expansion of Sprachwandel 1990.]

Kempler, D., Metter, E., Jackson, C., Hanson, W., Riege, W., Mazziotta, J., and Phelps, M. (1988). Disconnection and cerebral metabolism: the case of conduction aphasia. *Archives of Neurology*, 45, 275–9.

Kempson, R. (1988a). The relation between language, mind and reality. In R. Kempson (ed.), *Mental Representations: The Interface between Language and Reality* (pp. 3–25). Cambridge: Cambridge University Press.

Kempson, R. (1988b). Logical form: the grammar–cognition interface. *Journal of Linguistics*, 24, 393–431.

Kempson, R. (1995). Ellipsis in a labelled deduction system. *Bulletin of Interest Group in Pure and Applied Logic*, 3, 489–526.

Kempson, R. (1996). Semantics, pragmatics and interpretation. In Lappin (ed.), pp. 561–98.

Kempson, R. and Gabbay, D. (1998). Crossover: a unified view. *Journal of Linguistics*, 34, 73–124.

Kempson, R., Meyer-Viol, W., and Gabbay, D. (1997). On representationalism in semantics: a dynamic account of who. In P. Dekker, M. Stokhof and Y. Venema (eds), *The Proceedings of the 11th Amsterdam Colloquium* (pp. 193–9). Amsterdam: University of Amsterdam.

Kempson, R., Meyer-Viol, W., and Gabbay, D. (1999a). VP ellipsis: towards a dynamic structural account. In S. Lappin and E. Benmamoun (eds), *Fragments: Studies in Ellipsis and Gapping* (pp. 227–90). Oxford: Oxford University Press.

Kempson, R., Meyer-Viol, W., and Gabbay, D. (1999b). Interpretation as labeled deduction: who, a case study. In R. Borsley and I. Roberts (eds), *Syntactic Categories*. New York: Academic Press.

Kempson, R., Meyer-Viol, W., and Gabbay, D. (In preparation). *Dynamic Syntax: The Deductive Flow of Natural Language*. Oxford: Blackwell.

Kenstowicz, M. and Kisseberth, C. (1979). *Generative Phonology: Description and Theory*. New York: Academic Press.

Kent, R. D. and Read, C. (1992). *The Acoustic Analysis of Speech.* San Diego: Singular Publishing Group.

Kertesz, A. (1979). *Aphasia and Associated Disorders: Taxonomy, Localization and Recovery.* New York: Grune and Stratton.

Kertesz, A., Harlock, W., and Coates, R. (1979). Computer tomographic localization, lesion size, and prognosis in aphasia and nonverbal impairment. *Brain and Language,* 8, 34–50.

Kertesz, A., Sheppard, A., and MacKenzie, R. (1982). Localization in transcortical sensory aphasia. *Archives of Neurology,* 39, 475–8.

Khanna, A. L., Verma, M. K., Agnihotri, R. K., and Sinha, S. K. (1998). *Adult ESOL Learners in Britain.* Clevedon: Multilingual Matters.

Kibrik, A. A. (1991). Maintenance of reference in sentence and discourse. In W. P. Lehmann and H.-J. J. Hewitt (eds), *Language Typology* (pp. 57–84). Amsterdam and Philadelphia: John Benjamins.

Kibrik, A. E. (1979). Canonical ergativity and Daghestan languages. In F. Plank (ed.), *Ergativity* (pp. 61–78). London: Academic Press.

Kibrik, A. E. (1985). Toward a typology of ergativity. In J. Nichols and A. Woodbury (eds), *Grammar Inside and Outside the Clause* (pp. 268–323). Cambridge: Cambridge University Press.

Kilborn, K. and Cooreman, A. (1987). Sentence interpretation strategies in adult Dutch–English bilinguals. *Applied Psycholinguistics,* 8, 415–31.

Kim, C. W. (1980). On the origin and structure of the Korean script. Inaugural lecture as Chair of Linguistics, University of Illinois, Urbana-Champaign. In his *Sojourns in Language,* Vol. 2. *Collected Papers* (pp. 721–34). Seoul: Tower Press, 1988.

Kim-Renaud, Y.-K. (ed.) (1997). *The Korean Alphabet.* Honolulu: University of Hawaii Press.

King, R. (1969). *Historical Linguistics and Generative Grammar.* Englewood Cliffs, NJ: Prentice-Hall.

Kinsbourne, M. (1971). The minor cerebral hemisphere as a source of aphasic speech. *Archives of Neurology,* 25, 302–6.

Kiparsky, P. (1968). Linguistic universals and linguistic change. In E. Bach and R. T. Harms (eds), *Universals in Linguistic Theory* (pp. 171–202). New York: Holt, Rinehart, and Winston.

Kiparsky, P. (1970). Metrics and morphophonemics in the Kalevala. In D. C. Freeman (ed.), *Linguistics and Literary Style* (pp. 165–81). New York: Holt, Rinehart, and Winston.

Kiparsky, P. (1971). Historical linguistics. In W. O. Dingwall (ed.), *A Survey of Linguistic Science* (pp. 576–649). College Park: University of Maryland Press.

Kiparsky, P. (1972). Metrics and morphophonemics in the Rigveda. In M. Brame (ed.), *Contributions to Generative Phonology* (pp. 171–200). Austin: University of Texas Press.

Kiparsky, P. (1977). The rhythmic structure of English verse. *Linguistic Inquiry,* 8, 189–247.

Kiparsky, P. and Youmans, G. (eds) (1989). *Phonetics and Phonology,* Vol. 1. *Rhythm and Meter.* San Diego: Academic Press.

Kirsner, K. (1986). Lexical function: is a bilingual account necessary? In Vaid (ed.).

Klar, K., O'Hehir, B., and Sweetser, E. (1984). Welsh poetics in the Indo-European tradition: the case of the Book of Aneirin. *Studia Celtica,* 18, 30–51.

Klavans, J. (1997). Computational linguistics. In W. O'Grady, M. Dobrovolsky, and M. Aronoff (eds), *Contemporary Linguistics* (ch. 17, pp. 627–65). New York: St Martin's Press.

Klein, W. and Perdue, C. (1992). *Utterance Structure: Developing Grammars Again*. Amsterdam: John Benjamins.

Klein, W. and Perdue, C. (1997). The basic variety (or: couldn't natural languages be much simpler?). *Second Language Research*, 13:4, 301–47.

Klima, E. (1964). Relatedness between grammatical systems. *Language*, 40, 1–20.

Klima, E. (1965). Studies in diachronic transformational syntax. Ph.D. dissertation, Harvard University.

Klima, E. and Bellugi, U. (1979). *The Signs of Language*. Cambridge, MA: Harvard University Press.

Klima, E. and Bellugi, U. (1982). The acquisition of three morphological systems in American Sign Language. *Papers and Reports on Child Language Development*, 21, 1–35.

Kloss, H. (1966). Types of multilingual communities. *Sociological Inquiry*, 36, 2.

Kluender, R. and Kutas, M. (1993a). Bridging the gap: evidence from ERPs on the processing of unbounded dependencies. *Journal of Cognitive Neuroscience*, 5, 196–214.

Kluender, R. and Kutas, M. (1993b). Subjacency as a processing phenomenon. *Language and Cognitive Processes*, 8, 573–633.

Knopman, D. S., Selnes, O. A., Niccum, K., and Rubens, A. B. (1984). Recovery of naming in aphasia: relationships among fluency, comprehension, and CT findings. *Neurology*, 34:11, 1461–70.

Knopman, D. S., Selnes, A., Niccum, N., Rubens, A. B., Yock, D., and Larson, D. (1983). A longitudinal study of speech fluency in aphasia: CT correlates of recovery and persistent nonfluency. *Neurology*, 33:9, 1170–8.

Koehn, E. H. (1976). The historical tense in Apalai narrative. *International Journal of American Linguistics*, 42:3, 243–52.

Konig, E. and Van der Auwera, J. (eds) (1994). *The Germanic Languages*. London: Routledge.

Koopman, H. (1982). Control from Comp and comparative syntax. *Linguistic Review*, 2, 365–81.

Kopitar, J. (1829). Albanische, walachische und bulgarische Sprache. *Jahrbucher der Literatur*, 46, 59–106.

Koskenniemi, K. (1983). Two-level morphology: a general computational model for word-form recognition and production. Ph.D. thesis, University of Helsinki.

Kramer, J. (1994). Lëtzebuergesch – eine Nationalsprache ohne Norm. In I. Fodor and C. Hagége (eds), *Language Reform, History and Future*, Vol. 6 (pp. 391–405). Hamburg: Buske.

Krashen, S. (1985). *The Input Hypothesis: Issues and Implications*. New York: Longman.

Krashen, S. (1994). The Input Hypothesis and its rivals. In N. Ellis (ed.), *Implicit and Explicit Learning of Languages* (pp. 45–78). London: Academic Press.

Krashen, S. and Terrell, T. D. (1988). *The Natural Approach: Language Acquisition in the Classroom*. Hemel Hempstead: Prentice-Hall.

Krashen, S., Scarcella, R., and Long, M. (eds) (1982). *Child–Adult Differences in Second Language Acquisition*. Rowley, MA: Newbury House.

Kraus, C. J. (1787). Rezension des Allgemeinen vergleichenden Worterbuches von Pallas. *Allgemeinen Literatur-Zeitung*, nos 235–7. [English translation, 1985: *Historiographia Linguistica*, 11, 229–60.]

Kroll, J. F. (1993). Accessing conceptual representation for words in a second language. In Schreuder and Weltens (eds).

Kuno, S. (1972a). Functional sentence perspective: a case study from Japanese and English. *Linguistic Inquiry*, 3, 269–320.

Kuno, S. (1972b). Pronominalization, reflexivization, and direct discourse. *Linguistic Inquiry*, 3, 161–96.

Kuno, S. (1973). *The Structure of the Japanese Language*. Cambridge, MA: MIT Press.

Kuno, S. (1975). Three perspectives in the functional approach to syntax. *CLS Parasession on Functionalism*, 276–336. Chicago: University of Chicago.

Kuno, S. (1987). *Functional Syntax: Anaphora, Discourse, and Empathy*. Chicago: University of Chicago Press.

Kurylowicz, J. (1947). La nature des procès dites analogiques. *Acta Linguistica*, 5, 15–37.

Kuter, L. (1989). Breton v. French: language and the opposition of political, economic, social, and cultural values. In Dorian (ed.), pp. 75–89.

Labov, W. (1963). The social motivation of sound change. *Word*, 19, 273–309.

Labov, W. (1966). *The Social Stratification of English in New York City*. Washington, DC: Center for Applied Linguistics.

Labov, W. (1972a). *Language in the Inner City: Studies in the Black English Vernacular*. Philadelphia: University of Pennsylvania Press.

Labov, W. (1972b). *Sociolinguistic Patterns*. Philadelphia: University of Pennsylvania Press.

Labov, W. (1972c). The study of language in its social context. In P. P. Giglioli (ed.), *Language and Social Context* (pp. 283–308). Harmondsworth: Penguin.

Labov, W. (1972d). The transformation of experience in narrative syntax. In W. Labov, *Language in the Inner City* (pp. 354–96).

Labov, W. (1982). Building on empirical foundations. In W. Lehmann and Y. Malkiel (eds), *Perspectives on Historical Linguistics* (pp. 17–82). Current Issues in Linguistic Theory, 24. Amsterdam: John Benjamins.

Labov, W. (1988). The judicial testing of linguistic theory. In D. Tannen (ed.), *Linguistics in Context: Connecting Observation and Understanding* (pp. 159–82). Norwood, NJ: Ablex.

Labov, W. (1989). The child as linguistic historian. *Language Variation and Change*, 1, 85–94.

Labov, W. (1990). The interaction of sex and social class in the course of linguistic change. *Language Variation and Change*, 2, 205–54.

Labov, W. (1994). *Principles of Linguistic Change: Internal Factors*. Oxford: Blackwell.

Labov, W. (1997). Some further steps in narrative analysis. In *Oral Versions of Personal Experience: Three Decades of Narrative Analysis*. A special issue of the *Journal of Narrative and Life History*, Vol. 7, ed. M. G. W. Bamberg. New York: Erlbaum.

Labov, W. and Waletzky, J. (1967). Narrative analysis: oral versions of personal experience. In J. Helm (ed.), *Essays on the Verbal and Visual Arts. Proceedings of the 1966 Annual Spring Meeting of the American Ethnological Society* (pp. 12–44). Seattle: University of Washington Press.

Ladd, D. R. (1996). *Intonational Phonology*. Cambridge: Cambridge University Press.

Ladefoged, P. (1971). *Preliminaries to Linguistic Phonetics*. Chicago: University of Chicago Press.

Ladefoged, P. (1993). *A Course in Phonetics*, 3rd edn. New York: Harcourt Brace Jovanovich.

Ladefoged, P. (1997). Linguistic phonetic descriptions. In W. J. Hardcastle and J. Laver (eds), *The Handbook of Phonetic Sciences* (pp. 589–618). Oxford: Blackwell.

Ladefoged, P. and Maddieson, I. (1996). *The Sounds of the World's Languages*. Oxford: Blackwell.

Lado, R. (1957). *Linguistics across Cultures*. Ann Arbor: University of Michigan Press.

Laferriere, M. (1979). Ethnicity in phonological variation and change. *Language*, 55, 603–17.

Laka, I. (1992). Ergatives for unergatives. UCLA Colloquium.

Lakoff, G. and Johnson, M. (1980). *Metaphors We Live By*. Chicago: Chicago University Press.

Lakoff, G. and Turner, M. (1989). *More than Cool Reason. A Field Guide to Poetic Metaphor*. Chicago: Chicago University Press.

Lakoff, R. (1989). The limits of politeness: therapeutic and courtroom discourse. *Multilingua*, 8, 101–30.

Lakoff, R. (1990). *Talking Power: The Politics of Language*. New York: Basic Books.

Lakshmanan, U. (1991). Morphological uniformity and null subjects in child second language acquisition. In L. Eubank (ed.), *Point Counterpoint: Universal Grammar in the Second Language* (pp. 389–410). Amsterdam: John Benjamins.

Lambert, L. and Carberry, S. (1991). A tripartite plan-based model of dialogue. *Proceedings of the 29th Annual Meeting of the Association for Computational Linguistics* (pp. 45–74). Berkeley, CA: Association for Computational Linguistics.

Lambert, W. E. (1990). Persistent issues in bilingualism. In B. Harley, P. Allen, J. Cummins, and M. Swain (eds), *The Development of Second Language Proficiency* (pp. 201–20). Cambridge: Cambridge University Press.

Lambrecht, K. (1994). *Information Structure and Sentence Form*. Cambridge: Cambridge University Press.

Lane, H. (1984). *When the Mind Hears: A History of the Deaf*. New York: Random House.

Lappin, S. (1982). On the pragmatics of mood. *Linguistics and Philosophy*, 4, 559–78.

Lappin, S. (1989). Donkey pronouns unbound. *Theoretical Linguistics*, 15, 263–86.

Lappin, S. (1991). Concepts of logical form in linguistics and philosophy. In Kasher (ed.), pp. 300–33.

Lappin, S. (1996a). The interpretation of ellipsis. In S. Lappin (ed.), pp. 145–76.

Lappin, S. (1996b). Generalized quantifiers, exception phrases, and logicality. *Journal of Semantics*, 13, 197–220.

Lappin, S. (1998). Semantic types for natural language. Inaugural lecture, SOAS, University of London.

Lappin, S. (ed.) (1996). *The Handbook of Contemporary Semantic Theory*. Oxford: Blackwell.

Lappin, S. and Benmamoun, E. (eds) (1999). *Fragments: Studies in Ellipsis and Gapping*. Oxford: Oxford University Press.

Lappin, S. and Francez, N. (1994). E-type pronouns, I-sums, and donkey anaphora. *Linguistics and Philosophy*, 17, 391–428.

Larsen-Freeman, D. and Long, M. (1991). *An Introduction to Second Language Acquisition Research*. London and New York: Longman.

Larson, R. and Segal, G. (1995). *Knowledge of Meaning*. Cambridge, MA: MIT Press.

Lascarides, A. and Asher, N. (1993). Temporal interpretation, discourse relations, and commonsense entailment. *Linguistics and Philosophy*, 16, 437–93.

Lashley, K. S. (1929). *Brain Mechanisms and Intelligence*. Chicago: University of Chicago Press.

Lashley, K. S. (1950). In search of the engram. *Symposium of the Society for Experimental Biology*, 4, 454–82.

Lasnik, H. (1989). *Essays on Anaphora*. Dordrecht: Kluwer.

Lasnik, H. and Stowell, T. (1991). Weakest crossover. *Linguistic Inquiry*, 22, 687–720.

Laver, J. (1980). *The Phonetic Description of Voice Quality*. Cambridge: Cambridge University Press.

Laver, J. (1991). *The Gift of Speech: Papers in the Analysis of Speech and Voice.* Edinburgh: Edinburgh University Press.

Laver, J. (1994a). *Principles of Phonetics.* Cambridge: Cambridge University Press.

Laver, J. (1994b). Speech. In R. E. Asher. and J. M. Y. Simpson (eds), *Encyclopedia of Language and Linguistics,* Vol. 8 (pp. 4101–9). Oxford: Pergamon.

Laver, J. (1994c). Speech technology: an overview. In R. E. Asher and J. M. Y. Simpson (eds), *Encyclopedia of Language and Linguistics,* Vol. 8 (pp. 4274–89). Oxford: Pergamon.

Le Page, R. B. and Tabouret-Keller, A. (1985). *Acts of Identity: Creole-based Approaches to Language and Ethnicity.* Cambridge: Cambridge University Press.

Lecours, A.-R. and Joanette, Y. (1984). François Moutier or "From folds to folds." *Brain Cognition,* 3, 198–230.

Lee, C. D. (1993). *Signifying as a Scaffold for Literary Interpretation: The Pedagogical Implications of an African American Discourse Genre.* Urbana, IL: National Council of Teachers of English.

Lee, F. A. (1999). Antisymmetry and the syntax of San Lucas Quiavini Zapotec. Ph.D. dissertation, UCLA.

Lemke, J. (1990). *Talking Science: Language, Learning and Values.* Norwood, NJ: Ablex.

Lemke, J. (1995). *Textual Politics: Discourse and Social Dynamics.* London: Taylor and Francis.

Lenneberg, E. H. (1960). Language, evolution, and purposive behavior. In S. Diamond (ed.), *Culture in History: Essays in Honor of Paul Radin* (pp. 869–93). New York: Columbia University Press.

Lenneberg, E. H. (1967). *Biological Foundations of Language.* New York: Wiley.

Leopold, W. (1947). *Speech Development of a Bilingual Child: A Linguist's Record,* Vol. 2: *Sound Learning in the First Two Years.* Evanston, IL: Northwestern University Press.

Levelt, W. J. M. (1989). *Speaking: From Intention to Articulation.* Cambridge, MA: MIT Press.

Levi, J. N. (1994). *Language and Law: A Bibliographic Guide to Social Science Research in the U.S.A.* Chicago: American Bar Association.

Levine, D. N. and Sweet, E. (1982). The neuropathological basis of Broca's aphasia and its implications for the cerebral control of speech. In D. Caplan, J. C. Marshall, and A. Arbib (eds), *Neural Models of Language Processes* (pp. 29–326). New York: Academic Press.

Levinson, S. (forthcoming). *Generalized Conversational Implicature.* Cambridge: Cambridge University Press.

Levinson, S. (1983). *Pragmatics.* Cambridge: Cambridge University Press.

Levinson, S. (1987). Minimization and conversational inference. In J. Vershueren and M. Bertuccelli-Papi (eds), *The Pragmatic Perspective* (pp. 61–129). Amsterdam: John Benjamins.

Levinson, S. (1996). Three levels of meaning. In F. Palmer (ed.), *Grammar and Meaning* (pp. 90–115). Cambridge: Cambridge University Press.

Lewis, D. (1972). General semantics. In G. Harman and D. Davidson (eds), *Semantics of Natural Language* (pp. 169–218). Dordrecht: Reidel.

Lewis, M. (1993). *The Lexical Approach: The State of ELT and a Way Forward.* Hove: Language Teaching Publications.

Lhuyd, E. (1707). Archaeologia Britannica. Archaeologia Britannica, giving some account additional to what has been hitherto publish'd, of the languages, histories and customs of the original inhabitants of Great Britain: from collections and observations in travels through Wales, Cornwall, Bas-Bretagne, Ireland and Scotland.

Oxford: Printed at the Theater for the Author. [Rpr. 1969 (*English Linguistics 1500–1800*, no. 136, a collection of facsimile reprints selected and edited by R. C. Alston) Menston, England: Scolar Press.]

Li, C. N. and Thompson, S. (1976). Subject and topic: a new typology of language. In C. N. Li (ed.), *Subject and Topic* (pp. 457–89). New York: Academic Press.

Li, P. and MacWhinney, B. (1996). Cryptotype, overgeneralization, and competition: a connectionist model of the learning of English reversive prefixes. *Connection Science*, 8, 3–30.

Liberman, A. M., Cooper, F. S., Shankweiler, D. S., and Studdert-Kennedy, M. (1967). Perception of the speech code. *Psychological Review*, 74, 431–61.

Liberman, I. Y. and Liberman, A. M. (1992). Whole language versus code emphasis: underlying assumptions and their implications for reading instruction. In P. B. Gough, L. C. Ehri, and R. Treiman (eds), *Reading Acquisition* (pp. 343–66). Hillsdale, NJ: Erlbaum.

Liceras, J. M. (1989). On some properties of the "pro-drop" parameter: looking for missing subjects in non-native Spanish. In S. Gass and J. Schachter (eds), *Linguistic Perspectives on Second Language Acquisition* (pp. 109–33). Cambridge: Cambridge University Press.

Lichtheim, L. (1885). Brain: on aphasia. *Abstracts of British and Foreign Journals*, 433–84.

Liddell, S. K. (1980). *American Sign Language Syntax*. The Hague: Mouton.

Lieber, R. (1992). *Deconstructing Morphology*. Chicago: University of Chicago Press.

Lieberman, P. (1984). *The Biology and Evolution of Language*. Cambridge, MA: Harvard University Press.

Lieberman, P. and Crelin, E. S. (1971). On the speech of Neanderthal Man. *Linguistic Inquiry*, 11, 203–22.

Lieberson, S., Dalto, G., and Johnston, E. (1975). The course of mother tongue diversity in nations. *American Journal of Sociology*, 81, 34–61.

Lightbown, P. (1987). Classroom language as input to second language acquisition. In C. W. Pfaff (ed.), *First and Second Language Acquisition Processes*. Rowley, MA: Newbury House.

Lillo-Martin, D. (1997). The modular effects of sign language acquisition. In M. Marschark, P. Siple, D. Lillo-Martin, R. Campbell, and V. Everhart (eds), *Relations of Language and Thought: The View from Sign Language and Deaf Children* (pp. 62–109). New York: Oxford University Press.

Lillo-Martin, D. (1999). Modality effects and modularity in language acquisition: the acquisition of American Sign Language. In T. K. Bhatia and W. C. Ritchie (eds), *Handbook of Language Acquisition* (pp. 531–67). San Diego: Academic Press.

Lindau, M., Norlin, K., and Svantesson, J. (1990). Cross-linguistic differences in diphthongs, *Journal of the International Phonetic Association*, 20, 10–14.

Lindblom, B. (1983). Economy of speech gestures. In P. F. MacNeilage (ed.), *The Production of Speech* (pp. 217–46). New York: Springer-Verlag.

Lindblom, B. (1986). Phonetic universals in vowel systems. In J. J. Ohala. and J. J. Jaeger (eds), *Experimental Phonology* (pp. 13–44). Orlando, FL: Academic Press.

Lindblom, B. and Maddieson, I. (1988). Phonetic universals in consonant systems. In L. M. Hyman and C. N. Li (eds), *Language, Speech and Mind: Studies in Honor of Victoria A. Fromkin* (pp. 62–80). New York: Routledge.

Linebarger, M. C. (1990). Neuropsychology of sentence parsing. In A. Caramazza (ed.), *Cognitive Neuropsychology and Neurolinguistics: Advances in Models of Cognitive Function and Impairment* (pp. 55–122). Hillsdale, NJ: Erlbaum.

Linebarger, M. C., Schwartz, M. F., and Saffran, E. M. (1983). Sensitivity to grammatical structure in so-called agrammatic aphasics. *Cognition*, 13, 361–92.

Litman, D. and Allen, J. (1987). A plan recognition model for subdialogues in conversation. *Cognitive Science*, 11, 163–200.

Lloyd, P. M. (1987). *From Latin to Spanish*, Vol. 1: *Historical Phonology and Morphology of the Spanish Language*. *Memoirs of the American Philosophical Society*, 173. Philadelphia: American Philosophical Society.

LoCastro, V. (1987). Aizuchi: a Japanese conversational routine. In L. E. Smith (ed.), *Discourse across Cultures* (pp. 101–13). New York: Prentice-Hall.

Locke, J. (1690). *Essay Concerning Human Understanding*. London: Basset.

Long, M. (1981). Input, interaction and second language acquisition. In H. Winitz (ed.), *Native Language and Foreign Language Acquisition* (pp. 259–78). Annals of the New York Academy of Sciences, 379.

Loprieno, A. (1995). *Ancient Egyptian*. Cambridge: Cambridge University Press.

Lorber, J. and Farrell, S. A. (eds) (1991). *The Social Construction of Gender*. London: Sage.

Lottner, C. (1862). Ausnahmen der ersten Lautverschiebung. *Zeitschrift fur vergleichende Sprachforschung*, 11, 161–205. [Tr. in W. Lehmann (ed.), *A Reader in 19th Century Historical Indo-European Linguistics*, Bloomington: Indiana University Press.]

Lucy, J. A. (1992). *Language Diversity and Thought: A Reformulation of the Linguistic Relativity Hypothesis*. Cambridge and New York: Cambridge University Press.

Ludtke, H. (1985). Diachronic irreversibility in word-formation and semantics. In J. Fisiak (ed.), *Historical Semantics: Historical Word-formation* (pp. 355–66). Berlin: Mouton.

Luria, A. R. (1970). *Traumatic Aphasia*. The Hague: Mouton.

Luria, A. R. (1973). *The Working Brain*. New York: Basic Books.

Lyons, J. (1963). *Structural Semantics*. Cambridge: Cambridge University Press.

MacAulay, D. (ed.) (1993). *Celtic Languages*. Cambridge: Cambridge University Press.

Macaulay, R. K. S. (1976). Social class and language in Glasgow. *Language in Society*, 5, 173–88.

Mackenzie Beck, J. (1997). Organic variation of the vocal apparatus. In W. J. Hardcastle and J. Laver (eds), *The Handbook of Phonetic Sciences* (pp. 256–97). Oxford: Blackwell.

Mackin, R. (1978). On collocations: words shall be known by the company they keep. In P. Strevens (ed.), *In Honour of A. S. Hornby* (pp. 149–65). Oxford: Oxford University Press.

MacNeilage, P. (1998). The "frame / content" theory of evolution of speech production. *Behavioral and Brain Sciences*, 21, 499–546.

MacWhinney, B. (1987). Applying the Competition Model to bilingualism. *Applied Psycholinguistics*, 8, 315–27.

MacWhinney, B. L., Leinbach, L., Taraban, R., and McDonald, J. L. (1989). Language learning: cues or rules? *Journal of Memory and Language*, 28, 255–77.

Maddieson, I. (1984). *Patterns of Sounds*. Cambridge: Cambridge University Press.

Major, R. (1990). L2 acquisition, L1 loss and the Critical Period Hypothesis. In J. Leather, and A. James (eds), *New Sounds 1990*. Amsterdam: University of Amsterdam.

Major, R. (1994). Current trends in interlanguage phonology. In M. Yavas (ed.), *First and Second Language Phonology* (pp. 14–25). San Diego: Singular.

Makino, T. (1993). *Perspectives on Second Language Acquisition*. Tokyo: Yumi Press.

Malone, J. L. (1982). Generative phonology and Turkish rhyme. *Linguistic Inquiry*, 13:3, 550–3.

Malone, J. L. (1988). On the global-phonological nature of classical Irish alliteration. *General Linguistics*, 28:2, 91–103.

Mann, W. C. and Thompson, S. (1987). *Rhetorical Structure Theory: A Theory of Text Organization*. ISI Reprint Series 87–190. Information Sciences Institute, University of Southern California, Marina del Rey.

Marcus, M., Santorini, B., and Marcinkiewicz, M. A. (1993). Building a large annotated corpus of English: the Penn Treebank. *Computational Linguistics*, 19:2, 313–30.

Marie, P. (1906). Revision de la question de l'aphasie: la troisième circonvolution frontale gauche ne joue aucun role special dans la fonction du langage. *Semaine Medicale*, 26, 241–7.

Martin, J. R. (1989). *Factual Writing: Exploring and Challenging Social Reality*. Oxford: Oxford University Press.

Martin, J. R. (1990). Literacy in science: learning to handle text as technology. In F. Christie (ed.), *Literacy for a Changing World* (pp. 79–117). Melbourne: Australian Council for Educational Research.

Martin, J. R. (1991). Critical literacy: the role of a functional model of language, *Australian Journal of Reading*, 14, 117–32.

Martin, J. R. (1992). *English Text: System and Structure*. Philadelphia: John Benjamins.

Martin, R. and Ramoni, C. (1994). Verbal working memory and stative processing: a multiple components view. *Neuropsychology*, 8, 506–23.

Martin, R., Wetzel, W. F., Blossom-Stach, C., and Feher, E. (1989). Syntactic loss versus processing deficit: an assessment of two theories of agrammatism and syntactic comprehension deficits. *Cognition*, 32, 157–91.

Masdeu, J. C., Schoene, W. C., and Funkenstein, H. (1978). Aphasia following infarction of the left supplementary motor area: a clinicopathological study. *Neurology*, 28, 220–3.

Masica, C. P. (1991). *The Indo-Aryan Languages*. Cambridge: Cambridge University Press.

Mathesius, V. (1928). On linguistic characterology with illustrations from modern English. *Actes du Premier Congres International de Linguistes a la Haye* (pp. 56–63). [Repr. in J. Vachek (ed.) (1964), pp. 59–67.]

Mathesius, V. (1929). Functional linguistics. In Vachek (ed.) (1983), pp. 121–42.

Mathesius, V. (1975). On the information bearing structure of the sentence. In S. Kuno (ed.), *Harvard Studies in Syntax and Semantics* (pp. 467–80). Cambridge, MA: Harvard University Press.

Mattern, N. (1974). Anticipation in German-English simultaneous interpreting. Unpubl. M.A. thesis, Saarbrucken.

May, R. (1991). Syntax, semantics, and logical form. In Kasher (ed.), pp. 334–59.

Mazzocchi, F. and Vignola, L. A. (1980). Localization of lesions in aphasia: clinical-CT scan correlations in stroke patients. *Cortex*, 15, 627–54.

McAlpin, D. W. (1981). *Proto-Elamo-Dravidian: The Evidence and its Implications*. Philadelphia: American Philosophical Society.

McCarthy, J. (1982). *Formal Problems in Semitic Phonology and Morphology*. New York: Garland Press.

McCarthy, J. (1988). Feature geometry and dependency: a review. *Phonetica*, 43, 84–108.

McCarthy, J. and Prince, A. (1993). Prosodic morphology 1: constraint interaction and satisfaction. MS, University of Massachusetts, Amherst and Rutgers University.

McCarthy, J. and Prince, A. (1998). Prosodic morphology. In Spencer and Zwicky (eds) (pp. 283–305).

McCarthy, M. J. (1984). A new look at vocabulary in EFL. *Applied Linguistics*, 5, 12–22.

McCarthy, R. A. and Warrington, E. K. (1984). A two-route model of speech production: evidence from aphasia. *Brain*, 107, 463–85.

McClelland, J. L. and Rumelhart, D. E. (1986). Amnesia and distributed memory. In J. L. McClelland and D. E. Rumelhart (eds), *Parallel Distributed Processing* (pp. 503–28). Cambridge, MA: MIT Press.

McCloskey, J. (1979). *Transformational Syntax and Model Theoretic Semantics*. Dordrecht: Reidel.

McDonough, S. (1995). *Strategy and Skill in Learning a Foreign Language*. London: Edward Arnold.

McGlone, J. (1980). Sex differences in human brain asymmetry: a critical survey. *Behavioral and Brain Sciences*, 3, 215–63.

McGuinness, D. (1997). *Why Our Children Can't Read: And What We Can Do about It*. New York: Free Press.

McKeown, K. R. (1985). *Text Generation: Using Discourse Strategies and Focus Constraints to Generate Natural Language Text*. Cambridge: Cambridge University Press.

McKinnon, R. and Osterhout, L. (1996). Constraints on movement phenomena in sentence processing: evidence from event-related brain potentials. *Language and Cognitive Processes*, 11:5, 495–523.

McLaughlin, B. (1987). *Theories of Second-language Learning*. London: Edward Arnold.

McMenamin, G. R. (1993). *Forensic Stylistics*. Amsterdam: Elsevier.

McTear, M. and Conti-Ramsden, G. (1992). *Pragmatic Disability in Children*. London: Whurr.

Mehan, H. (1979). *Learning Lessons: Social Organization in the Classroom*. Cambridge, MA: Harvard University Press.

Meier, R. P. (1991). Language acquisition by deaf children. *American Scientist*, 9, 60–70.

Meier, R. P. and Newport, E. (1990). Out of the hands of babes: on a possible sign advantage in language acquisition. *Language*, 66, 1–23.

Meillet, A. (1912). L'évolution des formes grammaticales. *Scientia*, 12:26, Milan. [Repr. 1951, in *Linguistique historique et linguistique générale*, pp. 130–48. Paris: Klincksieck.]

Meisel, J. M. (1990). Early differentiation of languages in bilingual children. In K. Hyltenstam and L. K. Obler (eds), *Bilingualism across the Lifespan* (pp. 13–40). Cambridge: Cambridge University Press.

Meisel, J. M. and Muller, N. (1992). Finiteness and verb placement in early child grammars. In J. M. Meisel (ed.), *The Acquisition of Verb Placement* (pp. 109–38). Dordrecht: Kluwer.

Meisel, J. M., Clahsen, H., and Pienemann, M. (1981). On determining developmental stages in natural second language acquisition. *Studies in Second Language Acquisition*, 3:2, 109–35.

Melchert, H. C. (1991). Death and the Hittite King. In *Perspectives on Indo-European Language, Culture and Religion: Studies in Honor of Edgar C. Polome*, Vol. 1 (pp. 182–8). *Journal of Indo-European Studies*, Monograph 7. McLean, VA: Institute for the Study of Man.

Melvold, J. and Pesetsky, D. (1995). Reading is not like speaking, *The Boston Globe*, Oct. 29 (Learning Section).

Menn, L. and Stoel-Gammon, C. (1995). Phonological development. In P. Fletcher and B. MacWhinney (eds), *The Handbook of Child Language* (pp. 335–60). Oxford: Blackwell.

Merriman, W. (1999). Competition, attention, and young children's lexical processing. In B. MacWhinney (ed.), *The Emergence of Language* (pp. 331–58). Hillsdale, NJ: Erlbaum.

Metcalf, G. J. (1974). The Indo-European hypothesis in the sixteenth and seventeenth centuries. In D. Hymes (ed.), *Studies in the History of Linguistics: Traditions and Paradigms* (pp. 233–57). Bloomington: Indiana University Press.

Metter, E. J., Kempler, D., Jackson, C. A., Hanson, W. R., Riege, W. H., Camras, L. R., Mazziotta, J. C., and Phelps, M. E. (1987). Cerebellar glucose metabolism and chronic aphasia. *Neurology*, 37, 1599–1606.

Metter, E., Riege, W., Hanson, W., Jackson, C., Kempler, D., and VanLancker, D. (1983). Comparison of metabolic rates, language and memory, and subcortical aphasias. *Brain and Language*, 19, 33–47.

Metter, E., Riege, W., Hanson, W., Jackson, C., Kempler, D., and VanLancker, D. (1988). Subcortical structures in aphasia: an analysis based on (F-18)-fluorodeoxyglucose positron emission tomography and computed tomography. *Archives of Neurology*, 45, 1229–34.

Miceli, G., Silveri, M. C., Romani, C., and Caramazza, A. (1989). Variation in the pattern of omissions and substitutions of grammatical morphemes in the spontaneous speech of so-called agrammatic patients. *Brain and Language*, 36, 447–92.

Miceli, G., Silveri, M., Villa, G., and Caramazza, A. (1984). On the basis for the agrammatic's difficulty in producing main verbs. *Cortex*, 20, 207–20.

Michaels, S. (1981). "Sharing time": children's narrative styles and differential access to literacy. *Language in Society*, 10, 423–42.

Milan, C. (1989). Falsche Freunde. Ein besonderes Problem der kontrastiven Lexikologie (Deutsch–Italienisch). *Sprachwissenschaft*, 14, 384–404.

Milberg, W. and Blumstein, S. E. (1981). Lexical decision and aphasia: evidence for semantic processing. *Brain and Language*, 14, 371–85.

Miller, C. and Swift, K. (1976). *Words and Women*. Garden City, NY: Anchor Press.

Miller, G. A. and Johnson-Laird, P. N. (1976). *Language and Perception*. Cambridge, MA: Harvard University Press.

Miller, J. (1989). *Womanwords*. London: Longman.

Miller, L. S. (1995). *An American Imperative: Accelerating Minority Educational Advancement*. New Haven, CT: Yale University Press.

Milner, B. (1974). Hemispheric specialization: its scope and limits. In F. O. Schwartz and F. G. Warden (eds), *The Neurosciences: Third Study Program* (pp. 75–89). Cambridge, MA: MIT Press.

Milner, B., Branch, C., and Rasmussen, T. (1964). Observations on cerebral dominance. In A. de Reuck and M. O'Connor (eds), *Disorders of Language* (pp. 200–14). London: J. and A. Churchill Ltd.

Milroy, J. (1992). *Linguistic Variation and Change*. Oxford: Blackwell.

Milroy, L. (1987). *Language and Social Networks*, 2nd edn. Oxford: Blackwell.

Milroy, L. and Margrain, S. (1980). Vernacular language loyalty and social network. *Language in Society*, 9:1, 43–70.

Milroy, L. and Milroy, J. (1992). Social network and social class: toward an integrated sociolinguistic model. *Language in Society*, 26, 1–26.

Milroy, L. and Milroy, J. (1997). Varieties and variation. In F. Coulmas (ed.), *The Handbook of Sociolinguistics* (pp. 47–64). Oxford: Blackwell.

Milroy, L. and Muyskens, P. (eds) (1995). *One Speaker, Two Languages*. Cambridge: Cambridge University Press.

Mithen, S. (1996). *The Prehistory of the Mind: A Search for the Origins of Art, Religion and Science*. London: Thames and Hudson.

Mithun, M. (1984). The evolution of noun incorporation. *Language*, 60, 847–94.

Mithun, M. (1999). *The Languages of Native North America*. Cambridge: Cambridge University Press.

Moats, L. C. (1994). The missing foundation in teacher education: knowledge of the structure of spoken and written language. *Annals of Dyslexia*, 44, 81–102.

Mohr, J., Watters, W., and Duncan, G. (1975). Thalamic hemorrhage and aphasia. *Brain and Language*, 2, 3–17.

Mohr, J., Pessin, M., Finkelstein, S., Finkelstein, H., Duncan, G., and Davis, K. (1978). Broca aphasia: pathologic and clinical. *Neurology*, 26, 311–24.

Mohri, M. and Sproat, R. (1996). An efficient compiler for weighted rewrite rules. In *34th Annual Meeting of the Association for Computational Linguistics* (pp. 231–8). Morristown, NJ: Association for Computational Linguistics.

Molloy, R., Brownell, H. H., and Gardner, H. (1990). Discourse comprehension by right hemisphere stroke patients: deficits of prediction and revision. In Y. Joanette and H. H. Brownell (eds), *Discourse Ability and Brain Damage: Theoretical and Empirical Perspectives* (pp. 113–30). New York: Springer-Verlag.

Montague, R. (1974). The proper treatment of quantification in ordinary English. In R. Montague, *Formal Philosophy*, ed. R. Thomason (pp. 247–70). New Haven, CT: Yale University Press.

Moortgat, M. (1988). *Categorial Investigations*. Dordrecht: Foris.

Morais, J., Bertelson, P., Cary, L., and Alegria, J. (1986). Literacy training and speech segmentation. *Cognition*, 24, 45–64.

Morais, J., Cary, L., Alegria, J., and Bertelson, P. (1979). Does awareness of speech as a sequence of phones arise spontaneously? *Cognition*, 7, 323–31.

Morgan, J. (1986). *From Simple Input to Complex Grammar*. Cambridge, MA: MIT Press.

Morrill, G. (1994). *Type-logical Grammar*. Dordrecht: Kluwer.

Mountford, J. (1990). Language and writing-systems. In N. E. Collinge (ed.), *An Encyclopaedia of Language* (pp. 701–39). London: Routledge.

Moutier, F. (1908). *L'Aphasie de Broca*. Paris: Steinheil.

Moyle, R. M. (1986). *Alyawarra Music: Songs and Society in a Central Australian Community*. Canberra: Australian Institute of Aboriginal Studies.

Mühlhäusler, P. (1986). *Pidgin and Creole Linguistics*. Oxford: Blackwell.

Muller, J.-C. (1986) [1786]. Early stages of language comparison from Sassetti to Sir William Jones (1786). *Kratylos*, 31, 1–31.

Munro, P. (1988). Diminutive syntax. In W. Miller (ed.), *A Festschrift for Mary R. Haas* (pp. 539–56). The Hague: Mouton.

Munro, P. (1996). Making a Zapotec dictionary. *Dictionaries*, 17, 131–55.

Munro, P. (1997). The Garifuna gender system. In J. H. Hill, P. J. Mistry, and L. Campbell (eds), *The Life of Languages: Papers in Honor of William Bright* (pp. 443–61). The Hague: Mouton.

Munro, P. (1998). Chickasaw expressive "say" constructions. In Hinton and Munro (eds), pp. 180–6.

Munte, T. F., Heinze, H. J., and Mangun, G. R. (1993). Dissociation of brain activity related to syntactic and semantic aspects of language. *Journal of Cognitive Neuroscience*, 5, 335–44.

Muravyova, I. A. (1998). Chukchee (Paleo-Siberian). In Spencer and Zwicky (eds), pp. 521–38.

Murtha, S., Chertkow, H., Beauregard, M., Dixon, R., and Evans, A. (in press). Anticipation causes increased blood flow to the anterior cingulate cortex. *Human Brain Mapping*.

Muysken, P. (1995). Codeswitching and grammatical theory. In Milroy and Muysken (eds), pp. 177–98.

Myers, G. (1990). *Writing Biology: Texts in the Social Construction of Scientific Knowledge*. Madison: University of Wisconsin Press.

Myers-Scotton, C. (1993a). *Duelling Languages: Grammatical Structure in Codeswitching*. Oxford: Oxford University Press.

Myers-Scotton, C. (1993b). *Social Motivations for Codeswitching: Evidence from Africa*. Oxford: Oxford University Press.

Naeser, M. A. and Hayward, R. W. (1979). Lesion localization in aphasia with cranial computed tomography and the Boston Diagnostic Aphasia Exam. *Neurology*, 28, 545–51.

Naeser, M. A., Hayward, R. W., Laughlin, S. A., and Zatz, L. M. (1981a). Quantitative CT scan studies in aphasia, 1. Infarct size and CT numbers. *Brain and Language*, 12, 140–64.

Naeser, M. A., Hayward, R. W., Laughlin, S. A., Becker, J. M. T., Jernigan, T. L., and Zatz, L. M. (1981b). Quantitative CT scan studies in aphasia, 2. Comparison of the right and left hemispheres. *Brain and Language*, 12, 165–89.

Naeser, M. A., Alexander, M. P., Helm-Estabrooks, N., Levine, H. L., Laughlin, S. A., and Geschwind, N. (1982). Aphasia with predominantly subcortical lesion sites: description of three capsular/putaminal aphasia syndromes. *Archives of Neurology*, 39, 2–14.

Nagy, N. and Reynolds, W. (1997). Optimality theory and variable word-final deletion in faetar. *Language Variation and Change*, 9:1, 37–55.

Naiman, N., Fröhlich, M., Stern, H., and Todesco, A. (1995). *The Good Language Learner*. Clevedon: Multilingual Matters.

Nakanishi, A. (1980). *Writing Systems of the World: Alphabets, Syllabaries, Pictograms*. Rutland, VT: Tuttle.

Nation, I. S. P. (1990). *Teaching and Learning Vocabulary*. Boston, MA: Heinle and Heinle.

Naveh, J. (1987). *Early History of the Alphabet*, 2nd edn. Jerusalem: Magnes.

Neale, S. (1990). *Descriptions*. Cambridge, MA: MIT Press.

Neale, S. (1996). Paul Grice and the philosophy of language. *Linguistics and Philosophy*, 19, 509–59.

Neilson, J. M. (1936). *Agnosia, Apraxia, Aphasia*. New York: Holber.

Nelde, P. H. (ed.) (1989). *Urban Language Conflict: Urbane Sprachkonflikte*. Bonn: Dummler.

Nelde, P. H., Wölk, W., and Stary, Z. (eds) (1995). *Contact Linguistics: An Interdisciplinary Handbook of Contemporary Research*. Berlin and New York: Gruyter.

Nemser, W. (1971). Approximative systems of foreign language learners. *International Review of Applied Linguistics*, 9, 115–24.

Nerbonne, J. (1996). Computational semantics. In Lappin (ed.), pp. 461–84.

Nettle, D. (1999). *Linguistic Diversity*. Oxford: Oxford University Press.

Neufeld, G. (1977). Language learning ability in adults: a study on the acquisition of prosodic and articulatory features. *Working Papers on Bilingualism*, 12, 45–60.

Neville, H., Nicol, J. L., Barss, A., Forster, K. L., and Garrett, M. F. (1991). Syntactically based sentence processing classes: evidence from event-related brain potentials. *Journal of Cognitive-Neuroscience*, 3, 151–65.

Newmeyer, F. J. (1986). *Linguistic Theory in America*. Orlando, FL: Academic Press.

Newmeyer, F. J. (1991). Functional explanation in linguistics and the origins of language. *Language and Communication*, 11, 3–28.

Newmeyer, F. J. (1998). *Language Form and Language Function*. Cambridge, MA: MIT Press.

Newport, E. L. (1976). Motherese: the speech of mothers to young children. In N. Castellan, D. Pisoni, and G. Potts (eds), *Cognitive Theory*, Vol. 2. Hillsdale, NJ: Erlbaum.

Newport, E. L. (1981). Constraints on structure: evidence from American Sign Language and language learning. In W. A. Collins (ed.), *Aspects of the Development of Competence. Minnesota Symposium on Child Psychology*, Vol. 14 (pp. 93–124). Hillsdale, NJ: Erlbaum.

Newport, E. L. (1990). Maturational constraints on language learning. *Cognitive Science*, 14, 11–28.

Newport, E. L. and Meier, R. P. (1985). The Acquisition of American Sign Language. In D. Slobin (ed.), *The Cross-Linguistic Study of Language Acquisition*, Vol. 1 (pp. 881–938). Hillsdale, NJ: Erlbaum.

Nichols, J. (1984). Functional theories of grammar. *Annual Review of Anthropology*, 13, 97–117.

Nichols, J. (1992). *Linguistic Diversity in Space and Time*. Chicago: University of Chicago Press.

Nichols, J. (2000). *Diversity and Stability in Language*. In Joseph and Janda (eds).

Nihalani, P. (1975). Velopharyngeal opening in the formation of voiced stops in Sindhi. *Journal of the International Phonetic Association*, 32, 89–102.

Nikolayev, S. L. and Starostin, S. A. (1994). *A North Caucasian Etymological Dictionary*. Moscow: Asterisk.

Noble, W. and Davidson, I. (1996). *Human Evolution, Language and Mind: A Psychological and Archaeological Inquiry*. Cambridge: Cambridge University Press.

Noel, G., Collard, M., Dupont, H., and Huvelle, R. (1977). Nouvelles possibilités de correlations anatomo-cliniques en aphasiologie grace a la tomodensitometrie cérébrale. *Acta Neurologica Belgica*, 77, 351–62.

Nolan, F. (1983). *The Phonetic Bases of Speaker Recognition*. Cambridge: Cambridge University Press.

Norde, M. (1999). Deflexion as a counterdirectional factor in grammatical change. In a special issue of *Language Sciences*, ed. L. Campbell.

Norman, J. (1988). *Chinese*. Cambridge: Cambridge University Press.

O'Barr, W. (1982). *Linguistic Evidence: Language, Power and Strategy in the Courtroom*. New York: Academic Press.

Ochs, E. (1988). *Culture and Language Development*. Cambridge: Cambridge University Press.

Ochs, E. (1993). Constructing social identity: a language socialization perspective. *Research on Language and Social Interaction*, 26:3, 287–306.

Ochs, E. and Schieffelin, B. (1989). Language has a heart. *Text*, 9:1, 7–25.

Ochs, E., Schegloff, E. A., and Thompson, S. (eds) (1996). *Interaction and Grammar*. Cambridge: Cambridge University Press.

O'Connor, M. (1983). Writing systems, native speaker analyses, and the earliest stages of Northwest Semitic orthography. In C. L. Meyers and M. O'Connor (eds), *The Word of the Lord Shall Go Forth: Essays in Honor of David Noel Freedman in Celebration of His Sixtieth Birthday* (pp. 439–65). Winona Lake, IN: Eisenbrauns.

O'Donnell, K. (1990). Difference and dominance: how labor and management talk conflict. In A. Grimshaw (ed.), *Conflict Talk* (pp. 210–40). Cambridge: Cambridge University Press.

O'Grady, W., Dobrovolsky, M., and Aronoff, M. (eds) (1997). *Contemporary Linguistics*, 3rd edn. New York: St Martin's Press.

Ohala, J. (ed.) (1989). *On the Quantal Nature of Speech*. Theme issue of *Journal of Phonetics*, 17.

Ohala, J. J. (1980). The acoustic origin of the smile. *Journal of the Acoustical Society of America*, 68, S33.

Ohala, J. J. (1993). The phonetics of sound change. In C. Jones (ed.), *Historical Linguistics: Problems and Perspectives* (pp. 237–78). New York: Longman.

Ohala, J. J. (1994). The frequency code underlies the sound-symbolic use of voice pitch. In L. Hinton, J. Nichols, and J. J. Ohala (eds), *Sound Symbolism* (pp. 325–47). Cambridge: Cambridge University Press.

Ohala, J. J. (2000). Phonetics and historical phonology. In Joseph and Janda (eds).

Oksaar, E. (1970). Zum Spracherwerb des Kindes in Zweisprachiger Umgebung. *Folia Linguistica*, 4, 330–58.

Olsen, T. S., Bruhn, P., and Oberg, R. (1986). Cortical hypertension as a possible cause of subcortical aphasia. *Brain*, 109, 393–410.

Olson, R. K. (1994). Language deficits in "specific" reading disability. In M. A. Gernsbacher (ed.), *Handbook of Psycholinguistics* (pp. 895–916). San Diego: Academic Press.

O'Malley, J. and Chamot, A. (1989). *Learning Strategies in Second Language Acquisition*. Cambridge: Cambridge University Press.

Osterhout, L. and Holcomb, P. (1992). Event-related brain potentials elicited by syntactic anomaly. *Journal of Memory and Language*, 31, 785–806.

Osterhout, L. and Holcomb, P. (1993). Event-related potentials and syntactic anomaly: evidence of anomaly detection during the perception of continuous speech. *Language and Cognitive Processes*, 8, 413–37.

Osthoff, H. and Brugmann, K. (1878). *Morphologische Untersuchungen auf dem Gebiete der indogermanischen Sprachen*. Leipzig: S. Hirzel.

Otsu, Y. and Naoi, K. (1986). Structure-dependency in L2 acquisition. Paper presented at JACET. Cited in White 1989.

Ovenden, D., Corbet, G., and Arnold, N. (1979). *Collins Handguide to the Wild Animals of Britain and Europe*. London: Collins.

Owens, J. (1988). The foundations of grammar: an introduction to medieval Arabic grammatical theory. *Studies in the History of the Language Sciences*, 45. Amsterdam: John Benjamins.

Owens, R. (ed.) (1996). *The Translator's Handbook*, 3rd edn. London: Aslib.

Oyama, S. (1976). A sensitive period in the acquisition of a non-native phonological system. *Journal of Psycholinguistic Research*, 5, 261–85.

Ozog, A. C. K. (1987). The syntax of the mixed language of Malay. *RELC Journal*, 18, 72–90.

Paap, K. R., Noel, R. W., and Johansen, L. S. (1992). Dual-route models of print to sound: red herrings and real horses. In R. Frost and L. Katz (eds), *Orthography, Phonology, Morphology, and Meaning* (pp. 293–318). New York: Elsevier.

Padden, C. A. (1988). *Interaction of Morphology and Syntax in American Sign Language*. New York: Garland.

Page, N. (1986). *A Conrad Companion*. Basingstoke: Macmillan.

Pahl, R. E. (1989). Is the emperor naked? Some questions on the adequacy of sociological theory in urban and regional research. *International Journal of Urban and Regional Research*, 13:4, 709–20.

Paivio, A. (1971). *Imagery and Verbal Processes*, London: Holt, Rinehart, and Winston.

Paivio, A. and Desrochers, A. (1979). Effects of an imagery mnemonic on second language recall. *Canadian Journal of Psychology*, 33, 17–28.

Panagos, J. M. and Prelock, P. A. (1982). Phonological constraints on the sentence production of language-disordered children. *Journal of Speech and Hearing Research*, 25, 171–6.

Paradis, J. and Genesee, F. (1996). Syntactic acquisition in bilingual children: autonomous or independent? *Studies in Second Language Acquisition*, 18, 1–25.

Parkinson, S. (1988). Portuguese. In M. Harris and N. Vincent (eds), *The Romance Languages* (pp. 131–69). London: Croom Helm.

Parsons, J. T. (1952). *The Social System*. London: Tavistock Press.

Patkowski, M. (1980). The sensitive period for the acquisition of syntax in a second language. *Language Learning*, 30, 449–72.

Patterson, K., Seidenberg, M. S., and McClelland, J. L. (1989). Connections and disconnections: acquired dyslexia in a computational model of reading processes. In R. Morris (ed.), *Parallel Distributed Processing: Implications for Psychology and Neurobiology* (pp. 131–81). New York: Oxford University Press.

Paul, H. (1920) [1880]. *Prinzipien der Sprachgeschichte*, 5th edn. Tübingen: Max Niemeyer.

Pawley, A. K. (1998). The trans New Guinea phylum hypothesis: a reassessment. In J. Miedema, C. Ode, and R. A. C. Dam (eds), *Perspectives on the Bird's Head of Irian Jaya, Indonesia* (pp. 655–90). Amsterdam: Rodopi.

Pawley, A. (1966). The structure of Kalam: a grammar of a New Guinea Highlands language. Ph.D. dissertation, University of Auckland.

Pearson, B. A. (1988). Power and politeness in conversation: encoding of face-threatening acts at church business meetings. *Anthropological Linguistics*, 30, 68–93.

Pedersen, H. (1962) [1931]. *The Discovery of Language: Linguistic Science in the Nineteenth Century*. Bloomington: Indiana University Press.

Penny, R. (1991). *A History of the Spanish Language*. Cambridge: Cambridge University Press.

Peperkamp, S. and Mehler, J. (1999). Signed and spoken language: a unique underlying system? *Language and Speech*, 42, 333–46.

Perani, D., Vallar, G., Cappa, S., Messa, C., and Fazio, F. (1987). Aphasia and neglect after cortical stroke: a clinical / cerebral study. *Brain*, 110, 1211–29.

Percival, W. K. (1982/6). Renaissance linguistics: the old and the new. In T. Bynon and F. R. Palmer (eds), *Studies in the History of Western Linguistics, in Honour of R. H. Robins* (pp. 56–68). Cambridge: Cambridge University Press.

Pereira, F. (1990). Categorial semantics and scoping. *Computational Linguistics*, 16, 1–10.

Pereira, F. and Pollack, M. (1991). Incremental interpretation. *Artificial Intelligence*, 50, 37–82.

Perfetti, C. (1997). Sentences, individual differences, and multiple texts: three issues in text comprehension. *Discourse Processes*, 23, 337–55.

Perfetti, C., Goldman, S. R., and Hogaboam, T. W. (1979). Reading skill and the identification of words in discourse context. *Memory and Cognition*, 7, 273–82.

Perkell, J. S. and Klatt, D. H. (1986). *Invariance and Variability in Speech Processes*. Hillsdale, NJ: Erlbaum.

Perkins, D. (1992). *Smart Schools: From Training Memories to Educating Minds*. New York: Free Press.

Perkins, M. and Howard, S. (eds) (1995). *Case Studies in Clinical Linguistics*. London: Whurr.

Perkins, R. D. (1989). Statistical techniques for determining language sample size. *Studies in Language*, 13, 293–315.

Perry, J. (1979). The problem of the essential indexical. *Nous*, 13, 93–21.

Perry, J. (1993). *The Problem of the Essential Indexical and Other Essays*. Oxford: Oxford University Press.

Petitto, L. A. (1987). On the autonomy of language and gesture: evidence from the acquisition of personal pronouns in American Sign Language. *Cognition*, 27, 1–52.

Philippaki-Warburton, I. (1994). The subjunctive mood and the syntactic status of the particle na in modern Greek. *Folia Linguistica*, 28, 297–328.

Phillips, S. U. (1985). Strategies for clarification in judges' use of language: from the written to spoken. *Discourse Processes*, 8, 421–36.

Pica, T., Young, R., and Doughty, C. (1987). The impact of interaction on comprehension. *TESOL Quarterly*, 21, 737–58.

Pick, A. (1973). *Aphasia*. Springfield, IL: Thomas.

Pienemann, M. (1993). The teachability hypothesis. MS, Language Acquisition Research Centre, Sydney.

Pienemann, M. and Johnston, M. (1987). Factors influencing the development of language proficiency. In D. Nunan (ed.), *Applying Second Language Acquisition Research* (pp. 45–141). National Curriculum Resource Centre, Adult Migrant Education Program, Adelaide.

Pinker, S. (1994). *The Language Instinct: How the Mind Creates Language*. New York: HarperCollins.

Pinker, S. and Bloom, P. (1990). Natural language and natural selection [with peer commentary]. *Behavioral and Brain Sciences*, 13, 707–84.

Pittam, J. (1994). *Voice in Social Interaction: An Interdisciplinary Approach*. Thousand Oaks, CA: Sage.

Plaut, D. C., McClelland, J. L., Seidenberg, M. S., and Patterson, K. E. (1996). Understanding normal and impaired word reading: computational principles in quasi-regular domains. *Psychological Review*, 103, 56–115.

Poizner, H., Klima, E., and Bellugi, U. (1987). *What the Hands Reveal about the Brain*. Cambridge, MA: MIT Press.

Pollack, M. E. (1986). A model of plan inference that distinguishes between the beliefs of actors and observers. *Proceedings of the 24th Annual Meeting of the Association for Computational Linguistics* (pp. 207–14). Berkeley, CA: Association for Computational Linguistics.

Pollack, M. E. (1990). Plans as complex mental attitudes. In P. R. Cohen, J. Morgan, and M. E. Pollack (eds), *Intentions in Communication* (pp. 77–104). Cambridge, MA: MIT Press.

Pollard, C. and Sag, I. A. (1994). *Head-driven Phrase Structure Grammar*. Chicago: University of Chicago Press.

Pope, M. (1975). *The Story of Archaeological Decipherment: From Egyptian Hieroglyphs to Linear B*. New York: Scribner's.

Poplack, S. (1980). Sometimes I'll start a sentence in English y termino en espanol. *Linguistics*, 18, 581–616.

Poser, W. J. (1990). Evidence for foot structure in Japanese. *Language*, 66:1, 78–105.

Posner, M. I., Inhoff, A. W., Friedrich, F. I., and Cohen, A. (1987). Isolating attentional systems: a cognitive-anatomical analysis. *Psychobiology*, 15:2, 107–21.

Posner, M. L., Peterson, S. E., Fox, P. T., and Raichle, M. E. (1988). Localization of cognitive operations in the human brain. *Science*, 240, 1627–31.

Posner, R. (1996). *Romance Languages*. Cambridge: Cambridge University Press.

Postal, P. (1964). Underlying and superficial linguistic structure. *Harvard Educational Review*, 34, 246–66.

Postal, P. (1993). Remarks on weak crossover. *Linguistic Inquiry*, 24, 539–56.

Potter, B. (1997). Who/indefiniteness and the structure of the clause in western Apache. Ph.D. dissertation, UCLA.

Poulisse, N. (1990). *The Use of Compensatory Strategies by Dutch Learners of English*. Berlin: Mouton.

Poulisse, N. (1996). Strategies. In P. Jordens and J. Lalleman (eds), *Investigating Second Language Acquisition*. Berlin: Mouton.

Prakash, P., Rekha, D., Nigam, R., and Karanth, P. (1993). Phonological awareness, orthography, and literacy. In R. J. Scholes (ed.), *Literacy and Language Analysis* (pp. 55–70). Hillsdale, NJ: Erlbaum.

Premack, D. (1976). *Intelligence in Ape and Man*. Hillsdale, NJ: Erlbaum.

Preminger, A. and Brogan, T. V. F. (eds) (1993). *The New Princeton Encyclopedia of Poetry and Poetics*. Princeton: Princeton University Press.

Prince, A. (1989). Metrical forms. In P. Kiparsky and G. Youmans (eds), *Phonetics and Phonology*, Vol. 1. *Rhythm and Meter* (pp. 45–80). San Diego: Academic Press.

Prince, A. and Smolensky, P. (1993). Optimality theory: constraint interaction and satisfaction. MS, University of Massachusetts, Amherst, and Rutgers University.

Prince, E. (1981a). Topicalization, focus-movement, and Yiddish-movement: a pragmatic differentiation. *BLS*, 7, 249–64.

Prince, E. (1981b). Toward a taxonomy of given-new information. In P. Cole (ed.), *Radical Pragmatics* (pp. 223–55). New York: Academic Press.

Pullum, G. and Ladusaw, W. (1996). *Phonetic Symbol Guide*, 2nd edn. Chicago: University of Chicago Press.

Pulvermuller, F. and Schumann, J. (1994). Neurobiological mechanisms of language acquisition. *Language Learning*, 44, 681–734.

Putz, M. (ed.) (1995). *Discrimination through Language in Africa?* Berlin and New York: Gruyter.

Quine, W. V. (1960). *Word and Object*. Cambridge, MA: MIT Press.

Radcliffe-Brown, A. R. (1940). On social structure. *Journal of the Royal Anthropological Institute*, 70, 1–12.

Radford, A. (1990). *Syntactic Theory and the Acquisition of English Syntax*. Oxford: Blackwell.

Ramshaw, L. A. (1991). A three-level model for plan exploration. *Proceedings of the 29th Annual Meeting of the Association for Computational Linguistics* (pp. 36–46). Berkeley, CA: Association for Computational Linguistics.

Rask, R. K. (1818). Undersögelse om det gamle Nordiske eller Islandiske Sprogs Orindelse. Copenhagen: Gyldendal. [English translation by Niels Ege, *Investigations of the Origin of the Old Norse or Icelandic Language*. Copenhagen: The Linguistic Circle of Copenhagen, 1993.]

Rayner, K. and Pollatsek, A. (1989). *The Psychology of Reading*. Englewood Cliffs, NJ: Prentice-Hall.

Read, C. (1986). *Children's Creative Spelling*. London: Routledge and Kegan Paul.

Regan, V. (1998). *Contemporary Approaches to Second Language Acquisition in a Social Context*. Dublin: University College Dublin Press.

Reinhart, T. (1983). *Anaphora and Semantic Interpretation*. Chicago: University of Chicago Press.

Reuchlin, J. (1506). *De rudimentis Hebraicis libri tres*. Pforzheim: Thomas Anselm. [Repr. 1974, Hildesheim: Georg Olms.]

Reyle, U. (1993). Dealing with ambiguities by underspecification: construction, representation and deduction. *Journal of Semantics*, 10, 123–79.

Rickford, J. (1986). The need for new approaches to social class analysis in sociolinguistics. *Language and Communication*, 6, 215–21.

Riddoch, M. J. and Humphreys, G. W. (1987). Visual object processing in optic aphasia: a case of semantic access agnosia. *Cognitive Neuropsychology*, 4:2, 131–85.

Rijkhoff, J., Bakker, D., Hengeveld, K., and Kahrel, P. (1993). A method of language sampling. *Studies in Language*, 17, 169–203.

Robins, R. H. (1990). *A Short History of Linguistics*, 3rd edn. London: Longman.

Rogoff, B. and Toma, C. (1997). Shared thinking: cultural and institutional variations. *Discourse Processes*, 23, 471–97.

Romaine, S. (1985). Variable rules, O.K.? Or can there be sociolinguistic grammars? *Language and Communication*, 5, 53–67.

Romaine, S. (1988). *Pidgin and Creole Languages*. London: Longman.

Romaine, S. (1994a). *Bilingualism*. Oxford: Blackwell.

Romaine, S. (1994b). *Language in Society*. New York: Oxford University Press.

Romaine, S. (1995). *Bilingualism*, 2nd edn. Oxford: Blackwell.

Romaine, S. (ed.) (1991). *Language in Australia*. Cambridge: Cambridge University Press.

Roman, M., Brownell, H. H., Potter, H. H., Seibold, M. S., and Gardner, H. (1987). Script knowledge in right hemisphere-damaged and in normal elderly adults. *Brain and Language*, 31, 151–70.

Rosler, F., Putz, P., Friederici, A., and Hahne, A. (1993). Event-related potentials while encountering semantic and syntactic constraint violations. *Journal of Cognitive Neuroscience*, 5, 345–62.

Ross, J. (1967). *Constraints on Variables in Syntax*. Cambridge, MA: MIT Press.

Rubin, D. C. (1995). *Memory in Oral Traditions: The Cognitive Psychology of Epic, Ballads, and Counting-out Rhymes*. Oxford: Oxford University Press.

Ruhlen, M. (1987). *A Guide to the World's Languages*, Vol. 1. *Classification*. Stanford: Stanford University Press.

Ruhlen, M. (1994a). *On the Origin of Languages: Studies in Linguistic Taxonomy*. Stanford: Stanford University Press.

Ruhlen, M. (1994b). *The Origin of Language: Tracing the Evolution of the Mother Tongue*. New York: Wiley.

Russell, W. R. and Esper, M. L. E. (1961). *Traumatic Aphasia*. London: Oxford University Press.

Russom, G. (1987). *Old English Meter and Linguistic Theory*. Cambridge: Cambridge University Press.

Sacks, H. (1984). On doing "being ordinary." In J. M. Atkinson and J. Heritage (eds), *Structures of Social Action: Studies in Conversation Analysis* (pp. 413–29). Cambridge: Cambridge University Press.

Sacks, H. (1992). *Lectures on Conversation*, Vols 1 and 2. Ed. G. Jefferson, with an intro. by E. A. Schegloff. Oxford: Blackwell.

Sacks, H., Schegloff, E. A., and Jefferson, G. (1974). A simplest systematics for the organization of turn-taking for conversation. *Language*, 50, 696–735.

Saffran, L., Aslin, R., and Newport, E. (1996). Statistical learning by 8-month-old infants. *Science*, 274, 1926–8.

Sag, I. A. and Wasow, T. (1999). *Syntactic Theory: A Formal Introduction*. Stanford: CSLI.

Sajnovics, J. (1770). *Demonstratio idiorna Ungarorum et Lapponum idem esse*. Copenhagen: Typis Collegi Societatis Iesu. [2nd edn, Trnava (Tyrnau), Hungary, 1770; photolithic reproduction, Bloomington: Indiana University; The Hague: Mouton, 1968.]

Salmons, J. C. and Joseph, B. D. (1998). Introduction. In J. C. Salmons and B. D. Joseph (eds), *Nostratic: Sifting the Evidence. Current Issues in Linguistic Theory*, 142 (pp. 1–9). Amsterdam: John Benjamins.

Sampson, G. (1985). *Writing Systems*. London: Hutchinson; Stanford, CA: Stanford University Press. [Corrected pbk. reprint, London, 1987.]

Sampson, G. (1995). *English for the Computer*. Oxford: Oxford University Press.

Sanctius (Brocensis), Franciscus [Francisco Sanchez (de las Brozas)]. (1587). *Minerva seu de causis linguae latinae*. Salamanca: Ioannes and Andreas Renaut fratres.

Sanders, R. E. (1994). A neo-rhetorical perspective: the enactment of role-identities as interactive and strategic. In S. J. Sigman (ed.), *The Consequentiality of Communication* (pp. 67–120). Hillsdale, NJ: Erlbaum.

Sandler, W. (1993). Sign language and modularity. *Lingua*, 89:4, 315–51.

Sandler, W. (1994). One phonology or two? Sign language and phonological theory. *GLOT International Journal of Linguistics*, 3–8.

Sandler, W. (1999). Prosody in two natural modalities. *Language and Speech*, 42, 127–42.

Sandler, W. and Lillo-Martin, D. (forthcoming). *Sign Language and Language Universals*. Cambridge: Cambridge University Press.

Sands, B. (1998). *Eastern and Southern African Khoisan: Evaluating Claims of Distant Linguistic Relationship*. Cologne: Koppe.

Sankoff, G. (1980). Language use in multilingual societies: some alternate approaches. In G. Sankoff, *The Social Life of Language* (pp. 29–46). Philadelphia: University of Pennsylvania Press.

Sapir, E. (1921). *Language*. New York: Harcourt, Brace, and Co.

Sapir, E. (1930–1). The Southern Paiute language. *Proceedings of the American Academy of Arts and Sciences*, 65.

Sapir, E. (1949). The psychological reality of phonemes. In D. G. Mandelbaum (ed.), *Selected Writings of Edward Sapir in Language, Culture, and Personality* (pp. 46–60). [Originally published in French as La Realité psychologique des phonemes, *Journal de Psychologie Normale et Pathologique*, 30 (1933): 247–65.]

Sartori, G. and Job, R. (1988). The oyster with four legs: a neuropsychological study on the interaction of visual and semantic information. *Cognitive Neuropsychology*, 5, 105–32.

Saussure, F. de (1959) [1916]. *Course in General Linguistics*. New York: McGraw-Hill.

Savage-Rumbaugh, E. S., Murphy, J., Sevcik, R. A., Brakke, K. E., Williams, S. L., and Rumbaugh, D. M. (1993). Language comprehension in ape and child. *Monographs of the Society for Research in Child Development*, serial no. 233, vol. 58, nos 3–4.

Savage-Rumbaugh, E. S. and Lewin, R. (1994). *Kanzi: The Ape at the Brink of the Human Mind*. New York: Wiley.

Savitch, W. J., Bach, E., Marsh, W., and Safran-Naveh, G. (1987). *The Formal Complexity of Natural Language*. Dordrecht: Reidel.

Savory, T. H. (1968). *The Art of Translation*. London: Cape.

Schachter, J. (1988). Second language acquisition and its relationship to Universal Grammar. *Applied Linguistics*, 9:3, 219–35.

Schank, R. C. and Abelson, R. P. (1977). *Scripts, Plans, Goals and Understanding: An Inquiry into Human Knowledge Structure*. Hillsdale, NJ: Erlbaum.

Schegloff, E. A. (1979). The relevance of repair to a syntax-for-conversation. In T. Givón (ed.), *Syntax and Semantics*, Vol. 12. *Discourse and Syntax* (pp. 261–86). New York: Academic Press.

Schegloff, E. A. (1996). Turn organization: one intersection of grammar and interaction. In E. Ochs, E. A. Schegloff, and S. A. Thompson (eds), *Interaction and Grammar* (pp. 52–133). Cambridge: Cambridge University Press.

Schegloff, E. A. and Sacks, H. (1973). Opening up closings. *Semiotica*, 8, 289–327.

Schegloff, E. A., Jefferson, G., and Sacks, H. (1977). The preference for self-correction in the organization of repair in conversation. *Language*, 53, 361–82.

Schieffelin, B. (1990). *The Give and Take of Everyday Life*. New York: Cambridge University Press.

Schiffrin, D. (1993). *Approaches to Discourse*. Oxford: Blackwell.

Schlegel, K. W. F. von. (1808). *Ueber die Sprache und Weisheit der Indier*. Heidelberg: Mohr und Zimmer.

Schleicher, A. (1861–2). *Compendium der vergleichenden Grammatik der indogerm schen Sprachen*, 2 vols. Weimar: Hermann Bhlau.

Schmandt-Besserat, D. (1992). *Before Writing*, 2 vols. Austin: University of Texas Press.

Schmidt, J. (1872). *Die Verwandtschaftsverhältnisse der indogermanischen Sprachen*. Weiman.

Schmidt, R. (1990). The role of consciousness in second language learning. *Applied Linguistics*, 11, 129–58.

Schnitzer, M. L. and Krasinski, E. (1997). The development of segmental phonological production in a bilingual child. *Journal of Child Language*, 21, 585–622.

Schourup, L. (1982/1985). *Common Discourse Particles in English Conversation: Outstanding Dissertations in Linguistics*. New York: Garland. [Revised version of 1982 Ohio State University Ph.D. dissertation.]

Schreuder, R. and Weltens, B. (eds) (1993). *The Bilingual Lexicon*. Amsterdam: John Benjamins.

Schuell, H. (1957). *Minnesota Test for the Differential Diagnosis of Aphasia*. Minneapolis: University of Minnesota Press.

Schuh, R. G. (1989). Towards a metrical analysis of Hausa verse prosody: Mutadaarik. In I. Haik and L. Tuller (eds), *Current Approaches to African Linguistics*, 6 (pp. 161–75). Dordrecht: Foris.

Schütz, A. (1965). *Phenomenology of the Social World*. Evanston, IL: Northwestern University Press.

Schwartz, B. and Sprouse, R. (1996). L2 cognitive states and the full transfer / full access model. *Second Language Research*, 12:1, 40–72.

Schwartz, M. (1984). What the classical aphasia categories can't do for us, and why. *Brain and Language*, 21, 1–8.

Schwartz, M. F., Linebarger, M. C., and Saffran, E. M. (1985). The status of the syntactic deficit theory of agrammatism. In M.-L. Kean (ed.), *Agrammatism* (pp. 83–124). New York: Academic Press.

Schwartz, M. F., Marin, O., and Saffran, E. M. (1979). Dissociations of language function in dementia: a case study. *Brain and Language*, 7, 277–306.

Schwartz, M., Saffran, E., and Marin, O. (1980). The word order problem in agrammatism 1: comprehension. *Brain and Language*, 10, 249–62.

Scollon, R. and Scollon, S. (1981). *Narrative, Literacy and Face in Interethnic Communication*. Norwood, NJ: Ablex.

Searle, D. and Wilson, D. (1981). On Grice's theory of conversation. In P. Werth (ed.), *Conversation and Discourse* (pp. 155–78). London: Croom Helm.

Searle, J. R. (1985). *Expression and Meaning: Studies in the Theory of Speech Acts.* Cambridge: Cambridge University Press.

Searle, J. (1969). *Speech Acts: An Essay in the Philosophy of Language.* Cambridge: Cambridge University Press.

Searle, J. (1975). Indirect speech acts. In P. Cole and J. L. Morgan (eds), *Syntax and Semantics,* Vol. 3. *Speech Acts* (pp. 58–92). New York: Academic Press.

Searle, J. (1979). *Expression and Meaning: Studies in the Theory of Speech Acts.* Cambridge: Cambridge University Press.

Searle, J. (1983). *Intentionality.* Cambridge: Cambridge University Press.

Searle, J. (1995). *The Construction of Social Reality.* London: Penguin.

Sebeok, T. (ed.) (1960). *Style in Language.* Cambridge, MA: MIT Press.

Sebeok, T. A., Hayes, A. S., and Bateson, M. C. (eds) (1964). *Approaches to Semiotics.* The Hague: Mouton.

Seidenberg, M. S. and McClelland, J. L. (1989). A distributed, developmental model of word recognition and naming. *Psychological Review,* 96, 523–68.

Seiles, O. A., Knopman, D. S., Niccum, N., Rubens, A. B., and Larson, D. (1983). Computed tomographic scan correlates of auditory comprehension deficits in aphasia: a prospective recovery study. *Annals of Neurology,* 13, 558–66.

Selinker, L. (1972). Interlanguage. *International Review of Applied Linguistics,* 10, 209–31.

Selinker, L. (1992). *Rediscovering Interlanguage.* London: Longman.

Selnes, O. A., Niccum, W., Knopman, D., and Rubens, A. B. (1984). Recovery of single word comprehension: CT scan correlates. *Brain and Language,* 21, 72–84.

Senghas, A. (1995). The development of Nicaraguan Sign Language via the language acquisition process. In D. MacLaughlin and S. McEwen (eds), *Proceedings of the 19th Annual Boston University Conference on Language Development.*

Senner, W. T. (ed.) (1989). *The Origins of Writing.* Lincoln: University of Nebraska Press.

Sgall, P., Hajicova, E., and Panevova, J. (1986). In J. L. Mey (ed.), *The Meaning of the Sentence in its Semantic and Pragmatic Aspects.* Dordrecht and Boston: Reidel.

Shallice, T. (1988a). *From Neuropsychology to Mental Structure.* Cambridge: Cambridge University Press.

Shallice, T. (1988b). Specialization within the semantic system. *Cognitive Neuropsychology,* 5, 133–42.

Shapiro, M. C. and Schiffman, H. F. (1981). *Language and Society in South Asia.* Delhi, Varanasi, Patna: Motilal Banarsidass.

Sharwood-Smith, M. (1993). Input enhancement in instructed SLA. *Studies in Second Language Acquisition,* 15, 165–79.

Sher, G. (1991). *The Bounds of Logic.* Cambridge, MA: MIT Press.

Sher, G. (1996). Semantics and logic. In Lappin (ed.), pp. 511–37.

Shibatani, M. (1990). *The Languages of Japan.* Cambridge: Cambridge University Press.

Shoaf, R. A. (ed.) (1989). *Geoffrey Chaucer: Troilus and Criseyde.* East Lansing, MI: Colleagues Press.

Shotter, J. (1993). *Conversational Realities: Constructing Life through Language.* London: Sage.

Shuken, C. (1979). Aspiration in Scottish Gaelic stop consonants. In H. Hollien and P. Hollien (eds), *Current Issues in the Phonetic Sciences,* Vol. 1 (pp. 451–8). Amsterdam: John Benjamins.

Shuken, C. (1984). [ʔ], [h] and parametric phonetics. In J. A. Higgs and R. Thelwell (eds), *Topics in Linguistic Phonetics in Honour of E. T. Uldall.* Occasional Papers in Linguistics and Language Learning, no. 9. Dept of Linguistics, New University of Ulster.

Shuy, R. (1987). Practice into theory versus theory into practice. In O. Tomić and R. Shuy (eds), *The Relation of Theoretical and Applied Linguistics* (pp. 99–113). New York and London: Plenum.

Shuy, R. W. (1990). Warning labels: language, law and comprehensibility. *American Speech*, 65, 291–303.

Shuy, R. W. (1993). *Language Crimes*. Oxford: Blackwell.

Shuy, R. W. (1998). *The Language of Confession, Interrogation and Deception*. Thousand Oaks, CA: Sage.

Silva-Corvalán, C. (ed.) (1995). *Spanish in Four Continents: Studies in Language Contact and Bilingualism*. Washington, DC: Georgetown University Press.

Silveri, M. C. and Gainotti, G. B. (1988). Interaction between vision and language in category specific semantic impairment for living things. *Cognitive Neuropsychology*, 5, 677–709.

Silverstein, M. (1976). Shifters, linguistic categories and cultural descriptions. In K. Basso and H. Shelby (eds), *Meaning in Anthropology* (pp. 11–56). Albuquerque: University of New Mexico Press.

Silverstein, M. (1977). Cultural prerequisites to grammatical analysis. In M. Saville-Troike (ed.), *Linguistics and Anthropology* (pp. 139–51). Washington, DC: Georgetown University Press.

Silverstein, M. (1987). The three faces of "function": preliminaries to a psychology of language. In M. Hickman (ed.), *Social and Functional Approaches to Language and Thought* (pp. 17–38). Orlando, FL: Academic Press.

Simmons, D. (1958). Cultural functions of the Efik tone riddle. *Journal of American Folklore*, 71, 123–38.

Singleton, D. (1989). *Language Acquisition: The Age Factor*. Clevedon: Multilingual Matters.

Singleton, D. (1995). A critical look at the Critical Period Hypothesis in second language acquisition research. In Singleton and Lengyel (eds), pp. 1–29.

Singleton, D. and Lengyel, Z. (eds) (1995). *The Age Factor in Second Language Acquisition: A Critical Look at the Critical Period Hypothesis*. Clevedon: Multilingual Matters.

Skehan, P. (1989). *Individual Differences in Second-Language Learning*. London: Edward Arnold.

Skinner, B. F. (1957). *Verbal Behavior*. New York: Appleton-Century-Crofts.

Skjaervø, P. O. (1995). Aramaic in Iran. *Aram*, 7, 283–318.

Skorik, P. J. (1977). *A Grammar of Chukchee*, Vol. 2 [In Russian]. Leningrad: Nauka.

Slaughter, H. B. and Watson-Gegeo, K. (1988). *Evaluation Report for the first year of the Hawaiian Language Immersion Program: A Report to the Planning and Evaluation Branch*. Department of Education, State of Hawaii.

Slavoff, G. R. and Johnson, J. S. (1996). The effects of age on the rate of learning a second language. *Studies in Second Language Acquisition*, 17:4, 16.

Smith, E. E. and Medin, D. L. (1981). *Categories and Concepts*. Cambridge, MA: Harvard University Press.

Smith, F. (1971). *Understanding Reading: A Psycholinguistic Analysis of Reading and Learning to Read*. New York: Holt, Rinehart, and Winston.

Smith, N. (1989). *The Twitter Machine*. Oxford: Blackwell.

Smitherman, G. (1977). *Talkin and Testifin: The Language of Black America*. Boston: Houghton Mifflin.

Snodgrass, J. G. (1984). Concepts and their surface representations. *Journal of Verbal Learning and Verbal Behavior*, 23, 3–22.

Snow, C. and Hoefnagel-Höhle, M. (1978). The critical age for language acquisition: evidence from second language learning. *Child Development*, 49:1, 114–28.

Snow, D. (1996). A linguistic account of developmental, semantic-pragmatic disorder: evidence from a case study. *Clinical Linguistics and Phonetics*, 10, 281–98.

Snow, M. M. (1998). Trends and issues in content-based instruction. *Annual Review of Applied Linguistics*, 18, 243–67.

Sofer, M. (ed.) (1997). *The Translator's Handbook*. Rockville, MD: Schreiber Publishing.

Sohn, H. (1999). *Korean*. Cambridge: Cambridge University Press.

Solan, L. M. (1993). *The Language of Judges*. Chicago: University of Chicago Press.

Sommer, V. (1992). *Der Lob der Luge*. Munich: Beck.

Spencer, A. (1991). *Morphological Theory*. Oxford: Blackwell.

Spencer, A. (1998). Morphophonological operations. In Spencer and Zwicky (eds) (pp. 123–43).

Spencer, A. and Zwicky, A. (eds) (1999). *Handbook of Morphology*. Oxford: Blackwell.

Sperber, D. (1975). *Rethinking Symbolism*. Cambridge: Cambridge University Press.

Sperber, D. and Wilson, D. (1981). On Grice's theory of conversation. In P. Werth (ed.), *Conversation and Discourse* (pp. 155–78). London: Croom Helm.

Sperber, D. and Wilson, D. (1982). Mutual knowledge and reference in theories of comprehension. In N. Smith (ed.), *Mutual Knowledge* (pp. 61–121). Oxford: Blackwell.

Sperber, D. and Wilson, D. (1992). On verbal irony. *Lingua*, 87, 53–76.

Sperber, D. and Wilson, D. (1995). *Relevance: Communication and Cognition*, 2nd edn. Oxford: Blackwell.

Sperber, D. and Wilson, D. (1997). The mapping between mental and public lexicon. *UCL Working Papers in Linguistics*, 9, 107–25.

Spieler, D. H. and Balota, D. A. (1997). Bringing computational models of word naming down to the item level. *Psychological Science*, 8, 411–16.

Spolsky, B. and Cooper, R. L. (1991). *The Languages of Jerusalem*. Oxford: Oxford University Press.

Sproat, R. (1992). *Morphology and Computation*. Cambridge, MA: MIT Press.

Sridhar, K. K. and Sridhar, S. N. (1986). Bridging the paradigm gap: second language acquisition theory and indigenised varieties of English. *World Englishes*, 5:1, 3–14.

Sridhar, S. N. (1993). What are applied linguistics? *International Journal of Applied Linguistics*, 3, 3–16.

Staal, J. F. (1974). The origin and development of linguistics in India. In D. Hymes (ed.), *Studies in the History of Linguistics: Traditions and Paradigms* (pp. 63–74). Bloomington: Indiana University Press.

Stabler, E. (1992). *The Logical Approach to Syntax*. Cambridge, MA: MIT Press.

Stankievicz, E. (1972). *A Baudouin de Courtenay Anthology*. Bloomington: Indiana University Press.

Stanovich, K. E. (1992). Speculations on the causes and consequences of individual differences in early reading acquisition. In P. B. Gough, L. C. Ehri, and R. Treiman (eds), *Reading Acquisition* (pp. 307–42). Hillsdale, NJ: Erlbaum.

Stanovich, K. E. (1993). Does reading make you smarter? Literacy and the development of verbal intelligence. In H. W. Reese (ed.), *Advances in Child Development and Behavior* (pp. 133–80). San Diego: Academic Press.

Steedman, M. (1996). *Surface Structure and Interpretation*. Cambridge, MA: MIT Press.

Steels, L. (1997). The synthetic modeling of language origins. *Evolution of Communication*, 1, 1–34.

Steever, S. B. (ed.) (1998). *The Dravidian Languages*. London: Routledge.

Stevens, K. N. (1972). The quantal nature of speech: evidence from articulatory-acoustic data. In E. E. David and P. B. Denes (eds), *Human Communication: A Unified View* (pp. 51–6). New York: McGraw-Hill.

Stevens, K. N. (1998). *Acoustic Phonetics*. Cambridge, MA: MIT Press.

Stocker-Edel, A. (1977). The responses of Wellingtonians to a foreigner's English. *Archivum Linguisticum*, 8, 13–27.

Stokoe, William C. (1960). *Sign Language Structure*. Silver Spring, MD: Linstok Press.

Strawson, P. (1952). *Introduction to Logical Theory*. London: Methuen.

Street, B. V. and Besnier, N. (1994). Aspects of literacy. In T. Ingold (ed.), *Companion Encyclopedia of Anthropology* (pp. 527–62). London: Routledge.

Stromswold, K., Caplan, D., Alpert, N., and Rauch, S. (1996). Localization of syntactic comprehension by positron emission tomography. *Brain and Language*, 52, 452–73.

Stubbs, M. (1976). *Language, Schools and Classrooms*. London: Methuen.

Stuckey, S. (1987). *Slave Culture: Nationalist Theory and the Foundations of Black America*. New York: Oxford University Press.

Stump, G. T. (1993). On rules of referral. *Language*, 69, 449–79.

Stygal, G. (1994). *Trial Language: Differential Discourse Processing and Discursive Formation*. Amsterdam: John Benjamins.

Suarez, J. A. (1983). *The Mesoamerican Indian Languages*. Cambridge: Cambridge University Press.

Subirana, A. (1964). The relationship between handedness and language function. *International Journal of Neurology*, 4, 215–34.

Supalla, E. (1986). The classifier system in American Sign Language. In C. Craig (ed.), *Noun Classes and Categorization* (pp. 181–214). Philadelphia: John Benjamins.

Supalla, E. and Webb, R. (1995). The grammar of international sign: a new look at pidgin languages. In K. Emmorey and J. Reilly (eds), *Language, Gesture, and Space*. Hillsdale, NJ: Erlbaum.

Supalla, S. J. (1990). Manually coded English: the modality question in sign language development. In P. Siple and S. D. Fischer (eds), *Theoretical Issues in Sign Language Research*, Vol. 2. *Psychology* (pp. 333–52). International Conference on Theoretical Issues in Sign Language Research. Chicago: University of Chicago Press.

Swain, M. (1986). Communicative competence: some roles of comprehensible input and comprehensible output in its development. In J. Cummins and M. Swain (eds), *Bilingualism in Education*. New York: Longman.

Swain, M. and Wesche, M. (1975). Linguistic interaction: case study of a bilingual child. *Language Sciences*, 37, 17–22.

Swales, J. M. (1990). *Genre Analysis: English in Academic and Research Settings*. Cambridge: Cambridge University Press.

Swinney, D. and Zurif, E. (1995). Syntactic processing in aphasia. *Brain and Language*, 50, 225–39.

Swinney, D., Zurif, E., and Nicol, J. (1989). The effects of focal brain damage on sentence processing: an examination of the neurological organization of a mental module. *Journal of Cognitive Neuroscience*, 1, 25–37.

Szij, E. (1981). *A Coursebook of Hungarian* [in Russian]. Budapest: Tankonyvkiado.

Taeschner, T. (1983). *The Sun Is Feminine*. Berlin: Springer.

Tannen, D. (1990). *You Just Don't Understand: Women and Men in Conversation*. New York: William Morrow.

Tannen, D. (1993). *Gender and Conversational Interaction*. Oxford: Oxford University Press.

Tarlinskaja, M. (1989). General and particular aspects of meter: literatures, epochs, poets. In P. Kiparsky and G. Youmans (eds), *Phonetics and Phonology*, Vol. 1. *Rhythm and Meter* (pp. 121–54). San Diego: Academic Press.

Tarone, E. E. (1980). Communication strategies, foreigner talk, and repair in interlanguage. *Language Learning*, 30:2, 417–31.

Tarone, E. E., Gass, S. M., and Cohen, A. D. (eds) (1994). *Research Methodology in Second Language Acquisition*. Hillsdale, NJ: Erlbaum.

Tarski, A. (1933). The concept of truth in formalized languages. In A. Tarski (1983), pp. 152–278.

Tarski, A. (1983). *Logic, Semantics and Mathematics*, 2nd edn. Tr. J. H. Woodger, ed. J. Corcoran. Indianapolis: Hackett.

Taylor, I. (1883). *The Alphabet: An Account of the Origin and Development of Letters*, 2 vols. London: Kegan, Paul, Trench.

Tene, D. (1995). Hebrew linguistic tradition. In E. F. K. Koerner and R. E. Asher (eds), *Concise History of the Language Sciences: From the Sumerians to the Cognitivists* (pp. 21–8). Oxford: Pergamon.

Teodorsson, S.-T. (1979). Phonological variation in classical Attic and the development of Koine. *Glotta*, 57, 61–75.

Terrace, H. S. (1979). *Nim*. New York: Knopf.

Thody, P. and Evans, H. (1985). *Faux Amis and Key Words: A Dictionary Guide to French Language, Culture and Society through Lookalikes and Confusables*. London: Athlone Press.

Thomas, G. (1991). *Linguistic Purism*. London and New York: Longman.

Thomason, S. G. (2000). Contact as a source of language change. In Joseph and Janda (eds).

Thomason, S. G. and Kaufman, T. (1988). *Language Contact, Creolization, and Genetic Linguistics*. Berkeley: University of California Press.

Thompson, G. (1996). *Introducing Functional Grammar*. London: Edward Arnold.

Thompson, H. (1977). The lack of subordination in American Sign Language. In L. Friedman (ed.), *On the Other Hand: New Perspectives on American Sign Language* (pp. 181–95). New York: Academic Press.

Tollefson, J. W. (1993). Language policy and power: Yugoslavia, the Philippines, and Southeast Asian refugees in the United States. *International Journal of the Sociology of Language*, 103, 73–95.

Toncheva, E. (1988). Errors in the use of articles in the interlanguage of Bulgarian learners of English. In A. Danchev (ed.), *Error Analysis: Bulgarian Learners of English* (pp. 127–9). Sofia: Narodna.

Tosi, O. (1979). *Voice Identification: Theory and Legal Applications*. Baltimore: University Park Press.

Towell, R. and Hawkins, R. (1994). *Approaches to Second Language Acquisition*. Clevedon: Multilingual Matters.

Trager, G. L. (1974). Writing and writing systems. In T. A. Sebeok (ed.), *Current Trends in Linguistics*, Vol. 12. *Linguistics and Adjacent Arts and Sciences* (pp. 373–496). The Hague: Mouton.

Trahey, M. and White, L. (1993). Positive evidence and pre-emption in the second language classroom. *Studies in Second Language Acquisition*, 15, 181–204.

Tramo, M. J., Baynes, K., and Volpe, B. T. (1988). Impaired syntactic comprehension and production in Broca's aphasia: CT lesion localization and recovery patterns. *Neurology*, 38, 95–8.

Trask, R. L. (1996). *Historical Linguistics*. London: Arnold.

Traugott, E. C. and Bernd, H. (1991). Introduction. In E. C. Traugott and B. Heine (eds), *Approaches to Grammaticalization* (pp. 1–14). Typological Studies in Language, 19. Amsterdam: John Benjamins.

Treiman, R. (1993). *Beginning to Spell: A Study of First-grade Children*. New York: Oxford University Press.

Treiman, R. (1998). Why spelling? The benefits of incorporating spelling into beginning reading instruction. In J. Metsala and L. C. Ehri (eds), *Word Recognition in Beginning Literacy* (pp. 289–313). Hillsdale, NJ: Erlbaum.

Treiman, R., Mullennix, J., Bijeljac-Babic, R., and Richmond-Welty, E. D. (1995). The special role of rimes in the description, use, and acquisition of English orthography. *Journal of Experimental Psychology: General*, 124, 107–36.

Treiman, R., Zukowski, A., and Richmond-Welty, E. D. (1995). What happened to the "n" of sink? Children's spellings of final consonant clusters. *Cognition*, 5:5, 1–38.

Trinkaus, E. and Shipman, P. (1993). *The Neandertals: Changing the Image of Mankind*. New York: Knopf.

Trubetzkoy, N. (1969) [1939]. *Grundzuge der Phonologie*. Prague [*Principles of Phonology*. Tr. C. A. M. Baltaxe. Berkeley: University of California Press.]

Trudgill, P. (1974). *The Social Differentiation of English in Norwich*. Cambridge: Cambridge University Press.

Trudgill, P. (ed.) (1978). *Sociolinguistic Patterns of British English*. London: Edward Arnold.

Tulving, E. (1972). Episodic and semantic memory. In E. Tulving and W. Donaldson (eds), *Organization of Memory* (pp. 381–403). New York: Academic Press.

Tulving, E. (1983). *Elements of Episodic Memory*. Oxford: Oxford University Press.

Tyler, L. (1985). Real-time comprehension processes in agrammatism: a case study. *Brain and Language*, 26, 259–75.

Tzoukermann, E. and Liberman, M. (1990). A finite-state morphological processor for Spanish. In *COLING-90*, 3 (pp. 277–86). International Conference on Computational Linguistics.

Vachek, J. (ed.) (1964). *A Prague School Reader in Linguistics*. Bloomington and London: Indiana University Press.

Vachek, J. (ed.) (1983). *Praguiana*. Amsterdam and Philadelphia: John Benjamins.

Vaid, J. (ed.) (1986). *Language Processing in Bilinguals: Psycholinguistic and Neurolinguistic Perspectives*. Hillsdale, NJ: Erlbaum.

Vainikka, A. and Young-Scholten, M. (1991). Verb raising in second language acquisition: the early stages. *Theories des Lexikons*, 4, Dusseldorf University.

Validuvi, E. (1992). *The Informational Component*. New York: Garland.

van Benthem, J. (1986). *Essays in Logical Semantics*. Dordrecht: Reidel.

van Benthem, J. and ter Meulen, A. (eds) (1997). *Handbook of Logic and Language*. Amsterdam: Elsevier.

Van Dijk, T. (1991). *Racism and the Press*. London: Routledge.

van Dijk, T. (ed.) (1997). *Discourse Studies*, 2 vols. London: Sage.

van Dijk, T. and Kintsch, W. (1983). *Strategies for Discourse Comprehension*. New York: Academic Press.

van Driem, G. (1997). Sino-Bodic. *Bulletin of the School of Oriental and African Studies*, 60, 455–88.

Van Orden, G. C. (1987). A ROWS is a ROSE: spelling, sound, and reading. *Memory and Cognition*, 15, 181–98.

Van Valin, R. D., Jr (1987). Aspects of the interaction of syntax and pragmatics: discourse coreference mechanisms and the typology of grammatical systems. In J. Verschueren and M. Bertuccelli-Papi (eds), *The Pragmatic Perspective: Selected Papers from the 1985 International Pragmatics Conference* (pp. 513–31). Amsterdam and Philadelphia: John Benjamins.

Van Valin, R. D., Jr (1991). Functionalist linguistic theory and language acquisition. *First Language*, 11, 7–40.

Van Valin, R. D., Jr (1993). A synopsis of role and reference grammar. In R. D. Van Valin, Jr (ed.), *Advances in Role and Reference Grammar* (pp. 1–164). Amsterdam and Philadelphia: John Benjamins.

Van Valin, R. D., Jr (1994). Extraction restrictions, competing theories and the argument from the poverty of the stimulus. In S. Lima, R. L. Corrigan, and G. K. Iverson (eds), *The Reality of Linguistic Rules* (pp. 243–59). Amsterdam and Philadelphia: John Benjamins.

Van Valin, R. D., Jr (1995). Toward a functionalist account of so-called extraction constraints. In E. Devriendt, L. Goosens and J. von der Auwera (eds), *Complex Structures: A Functionalist Perspective* (pp. 29–60). Berlin: Mouton.

Van Valin, R. D., Jr (1996). Role and reference grammar. In K. Brown and J. Miller (eds), *The Concise Encyclopedia of Syntactic Theories* (pp. 281–94). Oxford: Pergamon.

Van Valin, R. D., Jr (1998). The acquisition of WH-questions and the mechanisms of language acquisition. In M. Tomasello (ed.), *The New Psychology of Language: Cognitive and Functional Approaches to Language Structure* (pp. 221–49). Hillsdale, NJ: Erlbaum.

Van Valin, R. D., Jr and LaPolla, R. J. (1997). *Syntax: Structure, Meaning and Function.* Cambridge: Cambridge University Press.

Velázquez-Castillo, M. (1995). Noun incorporation and object placement in discourse: the case of Guaraní. In P. Downing and M. Noonan (eds), *Word Order in Discourse* (pp. 555–80). Amsterdam: John Benjamins.

Vellutino, F. R. (1987). Dyslexia. *Scientific American*, 256, 34–41.

Verner, K. (1877). *Eine Ausnahme der ersten Lautverschiebung. Zeitschrift fur vergleichende Sprachforschung*, 23, 97–130. Tr. in W. Lehmann (ed.), *A Reader in 19th Century Historical Indo-European Linguistics*. Bloomington: Indiana University Press.

Versteegh, K. (1997). *The Arabic Language.* New York: Columbia University Press.

Volterra, V. and Taeschner, R. (1978). The acquisition and development of language by bilingual children. *Journal of Child Language*, 5, 311–26.

Voorhoeve, C. L. (1977). Ta-poman: metaphorical use of words and poetic vocabulary in Asmat songs. In *Pacific Linguistics*, Vol. C (pp. 19–38).

Vygotsky, L. S. (1987). *The Collected Works of L. S. Vygotsky*, Vol. 1. *Problems of General Psychology. Including the Volume Thinking and Speech.* Ed. R. W. Rieber and A. S. Carton. New York: Plenum.

Walker, R. (1975). Conversational implicatures. In S. Blackburn (ed.), *Meaning, Reference and Necessity* (pp. 133–81). Cambridge: Cambridge University Press.

Wallace, W. D. (1986). The admissibility of expert testimony on the discourse analysis of recorded conversations. *University of Florida Law Review*, 38, 69–115.

Wanner, E. and Maratsos, M. (1978). An ATN approach to comprehension. In M. Halle, G. Miller, and J. Bresnan (eds), *Linguistic Theory and Psychological Reality* (pp. 119–61). Cambridge, MA: MIT Press.

Wardhaugh, R. (1983). *Language and Nationhood: The Canadian Experience.* Vancouver: New Star Books.

Wardhaugh, R. (1992). *An Introduction to Sociolinguistics.* Oxford: Blackwell.

Warrington, E. K. (1975). The selective impairment of semantic memory. *Quarterly Journal of Experimental Psychology*, 27, 635–57.

Warrington, E. K. (1981a). Concrete word dyslexia. *British Journal of Psychology*, 72, 175–96.

Warrington, E. K. (1981b). Neuropsychological studies of verbal semantic systems. *Philosophical Transactions of the Royal Society of London*, B295, 411–23.

Warrington, E. K. (1987). Localization of lesions associated with impairments of semantic memory. Presentation at the European Cognitive Neuropsychology Society, Bressanone, Italy.

Warrington, E. K. and McCarthy, R. (1983). Category specific access dysphasia. *Brain*, 106, 859–78.

Warrington, E. K. and McCarthy, R. (1987). Categories of knowledge: further fractionation and an attempted integration. *Brain*, 110, 1273–96.

Warrington, E. K. and Shallice, T. (1979). Semantic access dyslexia. *Brain*, 102, 43–63.

Warrington, E. K. and Shallice, T. (1984). Category specific semantic impairments. *Brain*, 107, 829–53.

Waters, G. S., Caplan, D., and Hildebrandt, N. (1991). On the structure of verbal short-term memory and its functional role in sentence comprehension: evidence from neuropsychology. *Cognitive Neuropsychology*, 8:2, 81–126.

Watkins, C. W. (1962). *Indo-European Origins of the Celtic Verb*. Dublin: Institute for Advanced Studies.

Watson, I. (1991). Phonological processing in two languages. In E. Bialystok (ed.), *Language Processes in Bilingual Children* (pp. 25–48). Cambridge: Cambridge University Press.

Watts, R. J., Ide, S., and Ehlich, K. (eds) (1992). *Politeness in Language: Studies in Its History, Theory and Practice*. Berlin: de Gruyter.

Waugh, L. and Halle, M. (eds) (1984). *Roman Jakobson 1896–1982: Russian and Slavic Grammar*. Berlin: Gruyter.

Webster, A. (1988). The prevalence of speech and language difficulties in childhood: some brief research notes. *Child Language Teaching and Therapy*, 4, 85–91.

Weinreich, U. (1968). *Languages in Contact*. The Hague: Mouton. [1st edn 1953. New York: Linguistic Circle of New York, Publication no. 2.]

Weinreich, U., Labov, W., and Herzog, M. I. (1968). Empirical foundations for a theory of language change. In W. Lehmann and Y. Malkiel (eds), *Directions for Historical Linguistics* (pp. 95–195). Austin: University of Texas Press.

Weinstein, B. (1983). *The Civic Tongue: Political Consequences of Language Choices*. New York: Longman.

Weisenberg, T. and McBride, K. (1935). *Aphasia*. New York: Commonwealth Fund.

Werker, J. F. (1995). Exploring developmental changes in cross-language speech perception. In L. Gleitman and M. Liberman (eds.), *An Invitation to Cognitive Science: Language*, Vol. 1 (pp. 87–106). Cambridge, MA: MIT Press.

Wernicke, C. (1974) [1872]. The aphasic symptom complex: a psychological study on a neurological basis. *Boston Studies in the Philosophy of Science*, 4, 34–97.

Westerhål, D. (1989). Quantifiers in formal and natural languages. In D. Gabbay and F. Guenther (eds), *Handbook of Philosophical Logic*, Vol. 4 (pp. 1–131). Dordrecht: Reidel.

Westermann, D. and Ward, I. C. (1933). *Practical Phonetics for Students of African Languages*. London: Oxford University Press.

Whalen, M. R. and Zimmerman, D. H. (1990). Describing trouble: practical epistemology in citizen calls to the police. *Language in Society*, 19, 465–92.

White, L. (1989). *Universal Grammar and Second Language Acquisition*. Amsterdam: John Benjamins.

White, L. (1986). Implications of parametric variation for adult second language acquisition: an investigation of the pro-drop parameter. In V. J. Cook (ed.), *Experimental Approaches to Second Language Acquisition* (pp. 55–72). Oxford: Pergamon.

White, L. (1991). The verb-movement parameter in second language acquisition. *Language Acquisition*, 1, 337–60.

White, L. and Genesee, F. (1996). How native is near-native? The issue of ultimate attainment in adult second language acquisition. *Second Language Research*, 17, 1.

Widdowson, H. G. (1998). Retuning, calling the tune, and paying the piper: a reaction to Rampton. *International Journal of Applied Linguistics*, 8, 131–40.

Wieden, W. and Nemser, W. (1991). *The Pronunciation of English in Austria*. Tübingen: Gunter Narr.

Wierzbicka, A. (1992). *Semantics, Culture and Cognition*. Oxford: Oxford University Press.

Wilbur, R. B. (1987). *American Sign Language: Linguistic and Applied Dimensions*. Boston: Little Brown.

Williams, F. (1974). The identification of linguistic attitudes. *International Journal of the Sociology of Language*, 3, 21–32.

Williams, G. (1966). *Adaptation and Natural Selection: A Critique of Some Current Evolutionary Thought*. Princeton: Princeton University Press.

Williams, G. (1992a). *Natural Selection: Domains, Levels and Challenges*. New York: Oxford University Press.

Williams, G. (1992b). *Sociolinguistics: A Sociological Critique*. London: Routledge.

Williams, L. (1977). The perception of consonant voicing by Spanish English bilinguals. *Perception and Psychophysics*, 21:4, 289–97.

Williamson, K. (1969). Igbo. In E. Dunstan (ed.), *Twelve Nigerian Languages: A Handbook on Their Sound Systems for Teachers of English* (pp. 85–96). London: Longmans Green.

Wilson, D. (1995). Is there a maxim of truthfulness? *UCL Working Papers in Linguistics*, 7, 197–214.

Wilson, D. and Sperber, D. (1988a). Mood and the analysis of nondeclarative sentences. In J. Dancy, J. Moravcsik, and C. Taylor (eds), *Human Agency: Language, Duty and Value* (pp. 77–101). Stanford: Stanford University Press.

Wilson, D. and Sperber, D. (1988b). Representation and relevance. In R. Kempson (ed.), *Mental Representation. The Interface between Language and Reality* (pp. 133–53). Cambridge: Cambridge University Press.

Wilson, D. and Sperber, D. (1993). Linguistic form and relevance. *Lingua*, 90, 1–25.

Wilss, W. (1978). Syntactic anticipation in German-English simultaneous interpreting. In D. Gerver and H. W. Sinaiko (eds), *Language Interpretation and Communication*. NATO Conference Series 3: Human Factors 6 (pp. 343–52). New York and London: Plenum Press.

Winteler, J. (1876). *Die Kerenzer mundart des Kantons Glarus in ihrem Grundzugen dargestellt*. Leipzig and Heidelberg.

Winters, M. (1995). The nature of the so-called analogical processes [A translation of Kurylowicz 1947.] *Diachronica: International Journal for Historical Linguistics*, 12:1, 13–45.

Wode, H. (1981). *Learning a Second Language*. Tübingen: Narr.

Wolfe Quintero, K. (1992). Learnability and the acquisition of extraction in relative clauses and wh-questions. *Studies in Second Language Acquisition*, 14:1, 39–71.

Wolfram, W. and Schilling-Estes, E. (1995). Moribund dialects and the endangerment canon: the case of the Ocracoke Brogue. *Language*, 71, 696–722.

Wood, C. (1982). Implications of simulated lesion experiments for the interpretation of lesions in real nervous systems. In D. Caplan, J. C. Marshall, and M. A. Arbib (eds), *Neural Models of Language Processes* (pp. 511–29). New York: Academic Press.

Woodard, R. D. (1996). Writing systems. In *The Atlas of Languages: The Origin and Development of Languages throughout the World* (pp. 162–209). London: Quarto; New York: Facts on File.

Woodbury, A. C. (1987). Rhetorical structure in a Central Alaskan Yupik Eskimo traditional narrative. In J. Sherzer and A. C. Woodbury (eds), *Native American Discourse: Poetics and Rhetoric* (pp. 176–239). Cambridge: Cambridge University Press.

Woodward, A. L., Markman, E. M., and Fitzsimmons, C. M. (1994). Rapid word learning in 13- and 18-month-olds. *Developmental Psychology*, 30, 553–66.

Wunderlich, D. (1996). Minimalist morphology: the role of paradigms. In G. Booij and J. van Marle (eds), *Yearbook of Morphology 1995* (pp. 93–114). Dordrecht: Kluwer.

Wundt, W. M. (1900). *Volkerpsychologie II: Die Sprache*. Leipzig: Engelmann.

Wurm, S. A. (1982). *Papuan Languages of Oceania*. Tübingen: Narr.

Yamamoto, A. Y. (1995). Our roles as linguist and anthropologist in the Native American community and their efforts in maintaining and perpetuating their ancestral languages. *Languages of the World and Linguistic News Lines*, 9, 3–18.

Yarnell, P. R., Monroe, M. A., and Sobel, L. (1976). Aphasia outcome in stroke: a clinical and neuroradiological correlation. *Stroke*, 7, 516–22.

Young, R. and He, A. W. (eds) (1998). *Talking and Testing: Discourse Approaches to the Assessment of Oral Language Proficiency*. Amsterdam: John Benjamins.

Younger, D. H. (1967). Recognition and parsing of context-free languages in time N^3. *Information and Control*, 10, 189–208.

Zadrozny, W. (1994). From compositional to systematic semantics. *Linguistics and Philosophy*, 17, 329–42.

Zaenen, A. (1983). On syntactic binding. *Linguistic Inquiry*, 14, 469–504.

Zeps, V. J. (1963). The meter of the so-called trochaic Latvian folk songs. *International Journal of Slavic Linguistics and Poetics*, 7, 123–8.

Zingeser, L. B., and Berndt, R. S. (1988). Grammatical class and context effects in a case of pure anomia: implications for models of lexical processing. *Cognitive Neuropsychology*, 4, 473–516.

Zurif, E. B. (1982). The use of data from aphasia in constructing a performance model of language. In D. Caplan, J. C. Marshall, and M. A. Arbib (eds), *Neural Models of Language Processes* (pp. 203–7). New York: Academic Press.

Zurif, E., Swinney, D., Prather, P., Solomon, J., and Bushell, C. (1993). An on-line analysis of syntactic processing in Broca's and Wernicke's aphasia. *Brain and Language*, 45, 448–64.

Index

elicitation, in fieldwork 132, 133, 577
ellipsis 415–16, 426n
  vehicle change 426n
Ellis, R. 488
elsewhere condition 230
embedded clauses 287–8, 301
  in sign languages 535–6, 560
embedding problem 108, 109–10, 120, 125
Emmerik, Wim 548–9
emotion, role of language in construction of 440
Empty Category Principle (ECP) 502
empty morphemes 357
enculturation 648, 651–2
endangered languages 104, 137, 141, 145, 645
endecasillabo 451
Enga 30
English 21, 109, 517, 518, 522, 698, 700
  changes in 105–7, 111, 113
  compared with Mohawk 285–94
  denominal verbs 233
  iambic pentameter 450–1, 452, 453, 455
  in India 706
  in Ireland 528
  irregular verb forms 225–6
  plural marker 202–3
  sound inventory of 183
  spelling 182, 666–7
  word order 342, 362, 364
  as a world language 530, 531, 710
  see also American English, Early Modern English, Middle English, Old English
Englishization 707, 708
enjambement 451
entities 375
epiglottal 167
epigraphy 76
episodes
  boundaries in narrative 460–1
  in discourse 435
episodic culture 10
epistemology, role of language in construction of 440
Epstein, S. D. 502, 510
equal bilingualism 704
equal multilingualism 704

equipollent antonyms 252, 253, 254
equivalence sets 456
ergative case 217, 340, 352–3
ergativity 147
Error Analysis 489
errors
  in child language 478–81, 640, 671
  in child sign language 551–2
ESF (European Science Foundation) project 491–2
Eskimo 38, 219
Eskimo-Aleut 25, 40, 177
Esperanto 562n
Estonian 22
Estrangelo 47, 48
Ethiopian Semitic subgroup 33, 365
Ethiopic
  abugida 57–8 table 3.11, 67, 72, 73, 74
  Classical 74
ethnic/cultural identities, constructed by language use 439
ethnicity 531, 569, 574
  and national languages 704
ethnography of speaking 431–2, 677
ethnolinguistics 431–2
ethnomethodology 576
ethnomusicology 454
ethnopragmatics 431–2
Etruscan 25, 54, 69
etymology 82, 86, 94
  development of 86–7
Eurasia, languages of northern 24–5
Eurasiatic 25, 40
Europe, languages of 20–5
European Union 531
EUROSLA (European Second Language Association) 488
evaluation problem 108, 110, 112–13, 120
Evans, Howard 699–700
Evans, James 63, 392n
event related potentials (ERPs) 558, 582, 605–6
evidentials 459
evolution
  "brain-first" view of 5
  and modality 562n
evolution of language 1, 2, 11, 65–6, 93–4
Ewe 35

Printed and bound in the UK by
CPI Antony Rowe, Eastbourne